The Presence of Others

Voices and Images That Call for Response

FOURTH EDITION

The Presence of Others

Voices and Images That Call for Response

ANDREA A. LUNSFORD
Stanford University

JOHN J. RUSZKIEWICZ
The University of Texas at Austin

BEDFORD/ST. MARTIN'S
Boston ◆ New York

For Bedford/St. Martin's

Developmental Editor: Mikola De Roo
Production Editor: Sarah Ludwig
Production Supervisor: Yexenia (Jessie) Markland
Marketing Manager: Brian Wheel
Art Director: Lucy Krikorian
Text and Cover Design: Anna George
Copy Editor: Judith Green Voss
Photo Research: Joan Scafarello
Composition: Pine Tree Composition
Printing and Binding: R.R. Donnelley & Sons Company

President: Joan E. Feinberg
Editorial Director: Denise B. Wydra
Editor in Chief: Nancy Perry
Director of Marketing: Karen Melton Soeltz
Director of Editing, Design, and Production: Marcia Cohen
Managing Editor: Erica T. Appel

Library of Congress Control Number: 2003107895

Manufactured in the United States of America.

9 8 7 6 5 4
f e d c b a

For information, write: Bedford/St. Martin's, 75 Arlington Street, Boston, MA 02116 (617-399-4000)

ISBN: 0-312-40434-4

Acknowledgments

Acknowledgments and copyrights appear at the back of the book on pages 797–800, which constitute an extension of the copyright page.

Preface

"For excellence," writes philosopher Hannah Arendt, "the presence of others is always required." Not genius, she tells us, not divine inspiration, not even good old-fashioned hard work, but *others.* In choosing a title for this text, we thought of Arendt's statement, because this book aims to lead students toward excellence in reading and writing, toward excellence in thinking through difficult ideas and topics, and toward excellence in articulating their own positions on issues and providing good reasons for supporting those positions, always in relation to other people's thoughts, words, and images.

Given these aims, we have been delighted at the response from those using the first three editions of *The Presence of Others:* teachers and students report that they have indeed been spurred to react to the many perspectives presented in the text, saying "yes" to some, and "no" or even "maybe" to others. They have been moved to think hard about these differing viewpoints and about their own positions. Equally important, they tell us that the multiple—and often competing—voices and views in this text call out for response, leading from reading and thinking to writing and often back again.

Two of the voices calling out for response in this book belong to us, the editors, Andrea Lunsford and John Ruszkiewicz. Longtime friends, we take very different views on most issues, and we make many of those views and opinions known in *The Presence of Others.* But disagreement, conflict, and agonism are not guiding principles of this book. It is not a tennis match of ideas, one that will yield winners and losers. Rather, we are interested in how we all come to know and to take positions on various issues, how we can nurture productive exchanges of ideas. These are the kinds of open discussions the readings from *The Presence of Others* have generated in our own classes.

So we invite readers to join the conversation yet again: to question, challenge, and delight in many points of view, including our own. For this fourth edition, we've tried our best to provide a balanced set of readings that represent widely varying opinions on the ideas and topics that shape our times—ranging from education to ethics, from science and technology to the world of work. Many of these provocative readings will likely surprise anyone who believes that attitudes can be predicted by labels as equivocal as "liberal" or "conservative"—just as we have been surprised by the complex positions students have taken in our classes.

The Presence of Others thus aims to open and sustain animated conversation among the seventy-seven readings, the editors and students whose commentaries accompany the readings, and the teachers and students who we hope will put forth their own ideas and responses. To encourage this engagement, we offer a variety of pedagogical features.

NOTABLE FEATURES

A *balance of viewpoints* gives every student ideas to support and to dispute. Readings represent many genres as well—short stories, speeches, sermons, prayers, poems, personal memoirs, satires, mission statements, Web pages, photographs, and advertisements, as well as essays and articles—and they take a wide range of varying and sometimes opposing perspectives. In Chapter 9 on work, for instance, Eric Schlosser and Dagoberto Gilb rub conversational shoulders with Benjamin Franklin, bell hooks, and Naomi Barko. Cross-references throughout lead readers back and forth among the readings, drawing them deeper into the discussion.

The *editorial apparatus* encourages students to join the conversation as well. Each chapter opens with a visual text and a series of *brief quotations* from the readings, giving a glimpse of what's to come. *Headnotes* to each reading provide background information and offer some explanation for our editorial choices. Because these introductions often offer our own strong opinions about the selection, each one is signed with our respective initials. The selections are followed by sequences of *questions* that ask students to challenge the text (and sometimes the headnote), to make connections with other readings, and to join the conversation by writing. One or more of the questions in each reading is designed for group work, which we hope will encourage further dialogue and make the presence of others evident right there in the classroom. A *list of other readings and Web resources* concludes each chapter.

An *annotated reading* in each chapter includes commentary by the editors and student commentators, demonstrating how to ask critical questions and read with a critical eye.

A strong emphasis on reading images and visual rhetoric throughout *The Presence of Others* helps students to consider how images achieve their power and how written and visual texts work together. The visual text that opens each thematic chapter—a photo, a magazine illustration, a brochure—is accompanied by questions to help students read images critically. In addition, at least one selection in each chapter includes its original illustration(s), enabling students to consider how written and visual texts work together. The fourth edition includes over forty visual texts, some in full color, for students to respond to and analyze, including photographs, Web sites, advertisements, magazine covers, cartoons, posters, TV screen shots, paintings, and logos.

Chapters 1 and 2 provide strategies on *reading and thinking critically* and on moving *from reading to writing.* In addition, *guidelines for writing a critical response essay* and *a sample student essay* appear in Chapter 2, showing students how they might respond in writing to what they have read.

Readings from online sources and *material on the challenges of reading and writing online* in the introductory chapters guide students in thinking critically about how texts and rhetorical strategies differ between online and print media.

A companion Web site, **<bedfordstmartins.com/presenceofothers>,** offers students the best and most current Internet links for further research. Bedford/St. Martin's TopLinks—a topical links database accessible through the site—guides students to the best links with the most useful information on the ideas presented in *The Presence of Others.*

The accompanying *Guide for Teachers,* written by Dr. Melissa Goldthwaite and revised for the fourth edition by Dr. Sharan Daniel, provides detailed advice for teaching this book, including commentary on each selection, sequenced reading and writing assignments, and a selection of essays and articles regarding current controversies over the college curriculum.

NEW TO THIS EDITION

- **The thirty-seven fresh, new readings** generally offer a more pragmatic, diverse collection of views and authors on the thought-provoking topics that shape our world. Among the authors and topics newly represented are George W. Bush and Molly Ivins on stem-cell research; Sarah Vowell on democracy and media responsibility; David Brooks on the myth of a "common America"; Jimmy Carter and Elie Wiesel on what makes a just war.
- **The introductory chapters on reading, thinking critically, and writing have been thoroughly revised and updated** to give students more advice on reading visual and online texts critically; identifying their audiences; drafting, getting and giving feedback, revising, and editing; adding visuals to their own writing; and taking the best possible advantage of their computers or word processors.
- **A new chapter on American cultural myths** (Chapter 7, "American Cultural Myths: The Good, the Bad, and the Ugly") presents texts and images that offer a range of perspectives on some of the beliefs, attitudes, and myths that dominate U.S. culture. The readings address such questions as what it means to be an American, what constitutes patriotism in modern-day America, and how the media shape and often manipulate the public perception of American values.
- **Expanded coverage of visuals throughout the book, with more than thirty visual images new to this edition:**

- **Visuals are now included in the two introductory chapters on reading, thinking critically, and writing.** These images have been added to illustrate visually the authors' points about critical reading and writing, and to show how visuals can function within written texts and interact with them.
- **A new full-color photo essay, "American Myths and Images—From the Covers of *Time*," appears in Chapter 7, "American Cultural Myths: The Good, the Bad, and the Ugly."** Each of these color images is a full cover from *Time* magazine that visually represents a different American cultural myth. Each image is followed by several questions that ask students to examine, evaluate, and even challenge the image and the American myth it depicts.

ACKNOWLEDGMENTS

This anthology has changed considerably in the nine years since we first began exploring its possibilities, primarily because of the presence of many, many others whose perspectives and voices echo in these pages. Of great importance have been the extensive support and ongoing spirited conversation we have received from the Bedford/St. Martin's staff, and particularly from editor Mika De Roo, whose expert guidance and incisive evidence we deeply appreciate. We also thank managing editor Erica Appel and project editor Sarah Ludwig, who managed this complex project with aplomb, and designer Anna George, whose visual literacy knows no bounds. For this edition, we are especially grateful for the insights and extensive legwork of photo researcher Joan Scafarello and art director Lucy Krikorian. Thanks also to new media editors Harriet Wald and Coleen O'Hanley for their work on *The Presence of Others* Web site.

In addition to these friends at Bedford/St. Martin's, we are indebted to many colleagues: first and especially to Sharan Daniel of Stanford University, who assisted in searching for the best possible readings, in writing the accompanying apparatus, and in updating and revising the *Guide for Teachers* for the fourth edition. We also owe sincere thanks to Melissa Goldthwaite of Saint Joseph's University, who prepared earlier editions of the *Guide for Teachers*. This manual we believe to be thoroughly informed by contemporary writing and reading theories as well as by Melissa's practical experience from having taught the materials in the text.

We are particularly grateful to the students who agreed to add their voices to this text: Heather Ricker, Jennifer Smith, and Teresa Essman from The Ohio State University, Joshua G. Rushing from the University of Texas, and Beatrice Kim from Stanford University. And we salute as well the many other students who have taught us over the years how to be better classroom colleagues. In many subtle ways, their voices are everywhere present in this text.

Finally, we have been instructed and guided by extraordinarily astute reviewers, with whom we have been in conversation throughout this project. We thank Alan Bart Cameron, Bronx Community College of The City University of New York; Deborah Coxwell-Teague, Florida State University; Stacy M. Clanton, Southern Arkansas University; Kevin Davis, East Central University; Chidsey Dickson, Christopher Newport University; Michelle Dowd, Chaffey College; Mary Ann Duncan Simmons, University of North Carolina–Wilmington; Mara Fagin, Modesto Junior College; Philip Gaines, Montana State University; Susan Gerson, Fairleigh Dickinson University; Gary R. Hafer, Lycoming College; Tracy Hudson, Winthrop University; Mary G. Jackson, St. Mary's University; Mary Kasimer, St. Cloud Technical College; Dennis Keen, Spokane Community College; Leonard King Vandegrift IV, California State Polytechnic–Pomona; Marsha B. Kruger, University of Nebraska–Omaha; Theresa Madden, Howard Community College; Renee H. Major, Louisiana State University; Bobby L. Matthews, Louisiana State University; Mary McAleer Balkun, Seton Hall University; Linda F. Mercer, University of Cincinnati; Daniel Melzer, Florida State University; Marisa Anne Pagnattaro, University of Georgia; Kris Peleg, Century College; Melissa Scully, St. Mary's University; Shelina Shariff, Northern Kentucky University; Melissa Simko Sanders, University of Cincinnati; Tracey Teets Schwarze, Christopher Newport University; Lisa Wilde, Howard Community College; and John M. Yozzo, East Central University.

Andrea A. Lunsford
John J. Ruszkiewicz

Contents

JOHN HENRY NEWMAN *The Idea of a University* 52

"If then a practical end must be assigned to a University course, I say it is that of training good members of society."

VISUALS: *Mission Statements from The University of Minnesota; Morehouse College; The Evergreen State College; California State University, Monterey Bay; and Thomas Aquinas College* ***[Web site screen shots]*** 57

"Our graduates will have an understanding of interdependence and global competence, distinctive technical and educational skills, the experience and abilities to contribute to California's high-quality workforce, the critical thinking abilities to be productive citizens, and the social responsibility and skills to be community builders."

JON SPAYDE *Learning in the Key of Life* 64

"The American tradition, in learning as well as jazz and activism, is improvisatory. There are as many ways to become an educated American as there are Americans." ***[illustrated]***

ADRIENNE RICH *What Does a Woman Need to Know?* 71

"What does a woman need to know to become a self-conscious, self-defining human being?"

SHELBY STEELE *The Recoloring of Campus Life* 78

"What has emerged on campus in recent years . . . is a *politics of difference,* a troubling, volatile politics in which each group justifies itself, its sense of worth and its pursuit of power, through difference alone." ***[annotated and with readers' response]***

JENNIFER L. CROISSANT *Can This Campus Be Bought?* 99

"Science, or knowledge production more generally, has always had deep connections to the general political economy of its time, ... Thus, we cannot argue for some untainted "ivory tower" or "golden age" of institutional independence. We need instead to articulate the values and goals that should direct a wide range of commercial ventures on campus."

MIKE ROSE *Lives on the Boundary* 109

"If the canon itself is the answer to our educational inequities, why has it historically invited few and denied many?"

MICHAEL SOKOLOVE *Football Is a Sucker's Game* 124

"Football is the S.U.V. of the college campus: aggressively big, resource-guzzling, lots and lots of fun and potentially destructive of everything around it."

PART THREE WHO WE ARE

PART FOUR HOW WE LIVE

I liked everything about money except the prospect of buckling down and making it." ***[illustrated]***

EDWARD TENNER *Body Smarts* *767*

"Today's advanced cyborg technology is a harbinger of neither a utopian nor an apocalyptic future."

BELL HOOKS *Work Makes Life Sweet* *774*

". . . southern black work traditions taught us the importance of working with integrity irrespective of the task."

DAGOBERTO GILB *Work Union* *783*

"It is human to work, to bend and trip, to lift and pull. It's never about getting tired or dirty. There is nothing wrong with sweat and toil. It is only about conditions and decent wages that there can come complaint."

ERIC SCHLOSSER From *Behind the Counter* *787*

"Fast food kitchens often seem like a scene from *Bugsy Malone,* a film in which all the actors are children pretending to be adults. No other industry in the United States has a workforce so dominated by adolescents."

MARGE PIERCY *To Be of Use* *793*

"The work of the world is common as mud."

Acknowledgments 797

Index 801

Profiles of the Editors and Student Commentators

Throughout *The Presence of Others,* you will read the comments of the editors who chose the selections and wrote the introductions. You will also meet four student editors — two from The Ohio State University, one from The University of Texas at Austin, and one from Stanford University — and learn their opinions. To give perspective to their sometimes strong, sometimes controversial remarks, we include the following brief self-portraits of Andrea A. Lunsford (A.L.), John J. Ruszkiewicz (J.R.), Teresa Essman (T.E.), Joshua G. Rushing (J.G.R.), Heather Ricker (H.R.), and Beatrice Kim (B.K.). Use these biographies to help you read particular introductions, commentaries, or afterwords with more awareness of the editors' experiences, sensitivities, and blind spots. Think, too, about how your own ideas and beliefs have been shaped by your upbringing, communities, and education.

Andrea Abernethy Lunsford I was born in Oklahoma and have lived in Maryland, Florida, Texas, Washington, Ohio, British Columbia, and California. Yet when I think of "home" I think of the soft rolling foothills of the Smoky Mountains in eastern Tennessee. The hills there are full of Cunninghams, and my granny, Rosa Mae Iowa Brewer Cunningham, and her husband, William Franklin, seemed to know all of them. Like many people in this region, my mother's folks claimed Scottish descent. Indeed, when I later traveled to Scotland, I discovered that many of the songs we sang on my grandparents' big porch were Scottish.

The only one of her large family to enjoy postsecondary education, my Mama graduated with training in teaching and in French from Maryville College in Tennessee. An uncle helped pay her way to school, and it was on a visit to see him that she met my father, another Scottish descendant, Gordon Grady Abernethy. His college education cut short by World War II, Dad gave up his goal of following his father into dentistry and instead took examinations to become a certified public accountant. In hard times, he and my mother left Oklahoma and settled near her family, where Dad got a job with a defense contractor at Oak Ridge. Mama taught briefly and then stayed home with me and, later, with my two sisters and brother. I played in a special playhouse I built in the woods, spent weekends with my grandparents and dozens of Cunningham cousins, and alternated attending my grandparents' Baptist church (where they baptized my cousins by plunging them into a river) and my parents' Presbyterian church, where baptisms seemed like a snap. On occasional Sundays, I got to visit a sister church whose congregation was black, where the music was mesmerizing, and where I first began to recognize this country's legacy of segregation and racism. My family, I learned, was proud to have fought for the North, although supporting the Union's cause did not exempt them—or me—from that legacy.

We read a lot in Sunday School and at Summer Bible School, and at home as well. There I had the luxury of receiving books as gifts, especially from my father's sister, and of being read to often: *Gulliver's Travels* as it appeared in *The Book of Knowledge* (our family's one encyclopedia), "Joseph and His Coat of Many Colors" from Hurlbut's *Stories of the Bible,* Tigger and Roo and Christopher Robin from A. A. Milne, and poems from *A Child's Garden of Verses* are among my earliest memories of texts that grew, over the years, into an animated chorus of voices I still carry with me. Later, I read all of the Nancy Drew, Hardy Boys, and Cherry Ames Senior Nurse series, to be regularly punished for reading in school when I should have been doing something else. Like many young women, I was often "lost in a book," living in a world of heroines and heroes and happy endings. Only slowly and painfully did I come to question the master plot most of these stories reproduced, to realize that endings are never altogether happy and that the roles I play in my own story have been in some important senses scripted by systems beyond my control.

My father wanted me to begin secretarial work after high school, but when I won a small scholarship and got a student job, he and my mother agreed to help me attend our state school, the University of Florida. I graduated with honors but was encouraged by my (male) advisor not to pursue graduate school but rather to "go home and have babies." Instead, I became a teacher, a reasonable job for a woman to aspire to in 1965. Probably no memory from these college years is more vivid to me than the assassination of President John F. Kennedy, though I have many rival memories—police mowing down demonstrators with rushing water from fire hoses (and worse); the Selma bombings; Rosa Parks defying orders to sit in the back of the bus; the violent attempts to block James Meredith's enrollment at the University of Mississippi; Martin Luther King Jr. on the steps of the Lincoln Memorial. These images come together for me in the nightmare series of assassinations: John Kennedy, Malcolm X, Martin Luther King Jr., Robert Kennedy. Like so many others of my generation, these life-changing events intensified my engagement with civil rights, feminism, and activism for social justice, commitments I took with me when, after seven years of teaching, I gathered my courage to apply to graduate school and pursue a Ph.D. The events of the 1960s also helped reaffirm my commitment to a career in education and led me to the concerns that have occupied me ever since: What can I know and learn from and through my relationships with others? What are the rights—and responsibilities—of teaching? What is the connection between teaching and learning? What does it mean to be fully literate in an information age?

I pursued these questions in graduate school at Ohio State and beyond, all the while trying to live through two marriages and the loss of my granny; of both my parents; of my brother, Gordon Abernethy; of a much-loved aunt, Elizabeth McKinsey; and, most recently, of my sister Kerry Abernethy. Such experiences have led me to think hard not only about the burdens and hard sorrows every human life entails but also about the privileges my status as a white, relatively middle-class woman has afforded me. These privileges are considerable, and I do not wish to forget them. In addition, I have enjoyed the support of a vital network of women friends and colleagues. Thanks in large measure to them, I am now a professor in a large research university, can savor the time I can spend with those I love (especially Lisa Ede, my sisters Ellen and Liz, and their children), and am somewhat able to indulge my desire to experience as much of the world as possible. I even have season tickets to basketball and football games (no mean feat these days). These relationships—and my very special relationship with my students—have added to the chorus of animated voices I carry with me always.

These and other formative relationships and experiences have helped me learn a lesson that informs my teaching, my life, and my work on this book: that where you stand influences in great measure what you can see. My college advisor, standing as he did in an all-white male professoriate, couldn't quite "see" a young woman joining this elite group, even as a student. My parents, standing as they did in a lower-middle-class, single-income family with vivid memories of the depression, couldn't easily "see" beyond the desire for their oldest daughter to get a good, steady job as soon as possible. And I, standing where *I* do now, am not able to "see" through my students' eyes, to experience the world as they experience it.

Keeping this point in mind leads me to two acts that are by now habitual: examining where I stand, with all that implies about inevitable partial vision and perspective; and asking myself where others stand as well. So I came to this textbook project with John, my friend of almost thirty years now, with at least one specific agenda item: to look as carefully and respectfully as I could at his perspective, at where he stands, and to do the same thing for myself and for every voice included in this text. Such acts are necessary, I believe, before I can say that my opinions are fully considered. My view will always be heavily informed by where I stand. But insofar as I am able to entertain other points of view, I have a chance to understand my own better and to broaden my point of view as well.

John J. Ruszkiewicz My grandparents never spoke much about their reasons for emigrating from eastern Europe early in the twentieth century; their grounds for starting new lives in the United States must have seemed self-evident. Like the immigrants welcomed by Emma Lazarus's poem "The New Colossus," included in this anthology, they abandoned those "old countries" willingly. They rarely talked to me about the places they left behind because there were few fond memories. So I'm a second-generation American with roots in, but no strong ties to, Slovakia, Poland, and Ukraine.

My father and mother were both born in rural Pennsylvania, my dad with five brothers and sisters, my mom with seven—eight if you count the infant boy who died of measles. Both my grandfathers mined coal in western Pennsylvania, as did several uncles—a difficult and dangerous living. After World War II, my parents moved to Cleveland, where jobs were more plentiful, and my father began a thirty-year stretch on the loading dock at Carling's Brewery. I did my share of manual labor, too, for a short time working in a tool-and-die factory, even paying dues to the Teamsters.

But my blue-collar stints were merely summer jobs between college semesters. Education would be my generation's ticket to the American dream. My parents never allowed my brother (who became a physician) or me to think we had any choice but college. We attended parochial schools, where headstrong nuns and priests introduced us to learning, personal responsibility, and culture. (By eighth grade, students at St. Benedict's elementary school could sing three high Masses and two Requiems, one of those services in Gregorian chant. We knew what most of the Latin words meant, too.) As grade-schoolers, we had homework—hours of it—every night. High school was the same, only tougher. I didn't have a free period in high school until the semester I graduated—and I'm still grateful for that rigor.

The ethnic neighborhood in Cleveland where I grew up in the 1950s is now considered inner-city. It was very much *in the city* when I lived there too, but a nine- or ten-year-old could safely trudge to church alone at 6:00 A.M. to serve Mass or ride the rapid transit downtown to see a baseball game. I did so, often. In the long, hot summer of 1966, however, Cleveland erupted in racial riots. From my front porch, I could see fires burning.

Politically, I come from a family of Democrats—my gregarious mother, far more interested in people than issues, was a party worker in Cleveland's 29th Ward. One of my first political memories is watching John F. Kennedy parade down Euclid Avenue in 1960 during his presidential campaign. But frankly, I was more interested in the new Chrysler convertible ferrying the portly governor of Ohio. I have retained my fondness for old Chryslers—and just about anything with four wheels.

The first president I voted for was George McGovern, but what could you expect from a kid who spent high school listening to Bob Dylan and who went to college in the sixties? Nevertheless, it was during an antiwar rally at St. Vincent College in Latrobe, Pennsylvania, that my drift to the political right began. I had read enough about the history of Vietnam to know that the communist Viet Cong were no angels, but the people at that demonstration spoke as if they were. A professor of physics delivered an impassioned anti-American speech filled with what I knew to be falsehoods, but no one seemed to care. That moment resonates, even after all these years.

Despite the activist times, my college days remained focused on academic subjects—philosophy, history, literature, and cinema. St. Vincent's was small enough to nurture easy commerce among disciplines, so I knew faculty from every field, and my roommates were all science majors with views of the world different from my own. Debate was intense, frequent, and good-natured. Emotionally I leaned left, but intellectually I found, time and again, that conservative writers described the world more accurately for me. I think they still do.

National politics didn't matter much in graduate school at Ohio State in the mid 1970s—though I was the only Ph.D. candidate in English who would admit to voting for Gerald Ford. My interests then were mainly *Beowulf*, Shakespeare, and rhetoric. I met my coeditor, Andrea Lunsford, during our first term at Ohio State in an Old English class; we graduated on the same day five years later. She inspired me to think seriously about teaching as well as scholarship, and I remain in her debt for that insight.

Today, I consider myself an academic and political conservative. Where I work, that makes me a member of the counterculture, a role I now frankly enjoy. Unfortunately, there still aren't many conservatives among humanities professors in American universities. That's a shame because the academy would be a richer place were it more genuinely diverse. On the other hand, given the country's drift to the right since the events of 9/11, we probably need a more progressive academy to maintain some balance.

Like any good conservative, I prefer to keep my life simple—I could be content with a good truck, a sensible dog, and a capable racquetball partner. But for the past twenty-five years, I've been teaching at the University of Texas at Austin, where life is rarely dull or simple. If in the past I've been embroiled in controversies over political correctness, today my campus concerns are chiefly administrative as the Division of Rhetoric and Composition, where I work, looks for opportunities to make writing a greater part of students' lives.

It's about classroom matters that my coeditor Andrea and I are most likely to agree—since our political stands differ by about 180 degrees. So when I first proposed an anthology for writing classes that would broaden the range of readings available to students and make the political persuasion of the editors a part of the package, Andrea agreed to the project. She said it embodied the feminist concept of "situated knowledge." Well, sure, if that makes her happy. I'm no theorist. I'm just glad to have the ongoing privilege and pleasure of working with my good friend and political *other.*

Teresa Essman Born and raised in central Ohio, I am a country girl through and through. I hate shoes, love fresh vegetables, and live for the smell of autumn when my family presses and cans fresh apple cider.

My family has had an enormous impact on who I have become. My parents encouraged me to form my own opinions, rarely pushing their own views on me. Perhaps it is because of this upbringing that I have little patience with people who cling self-righteously to ideas but are unable to back them up. One of my pet peeves has always been people who believe in something simply because they think they should, or because their parents believed it.

My family has had an indirect influence on me, as well. As the youngest of four kids and one of seventeen grandchildren on my mom's side, I have had ample opportunities to watch people. You can learn a great deal about how you want to run your own life that way. Don't get me wrong; I don't imply passivity. I like to watch how people live and then decide if those are things I want to do. The misfortunes and triumphs of others can be learning tools, if you choose to pay attention.

In my four years at Ohio State, I learned two very important things: never stop questioning, and never give up on yourself. I firmly believe I can never stop learning because there will always be people who know more than I do about an issue or hold a perspective I have yet to consider. By questioning those people, I can only broaden my views and understanding.

I am currently studying to become a physical therapist, a career path that marks a great achievement for me. At Ohio State, admission into the physical therapy program is intensely competitive. I made it past the first cuts the first year I applied but was turned down for admission. I was crushed because for years I had been determined I was going to become a pediatric physical therapist. I was bombarded with pamphlets from well-meaning people about finding another course for my life, changing my major, and moving on. I just couldn't do it; I knew I could not be as happy in another profession, so I steeled myself, buckled down for another year, and reapplied. Happily, I received notice of my admission. (Later I found out that less than 15 percent of the applicants had been offered positions that year.) Now, in the first two years of professional training, I couldn't be happier with my decision not to give up on my dream. My father told me that if I wanted it badly enough, I would get in. Well, Daddy, I wanted it. So there!

After graduation, I would like to travel to another country, possibly Honduras, and work in the orphanages there for a year or so. So many of the children there are physically handicapped and just left in cribs because the facilities don't have the funding to care for them properly. I would like to change that somehow. Ultimately, I want to have my own pediatric physical therapy practice in the United States, incorporating the use of animals in therapy. I plan to have a few llamas (another one of my life passions) from my llama ranch included, along with dogs and miniature horses. All of this may sound a bit strange, but I can think of no better way to combine my love of kids, animals, and the country.

Joshua G. Rushing Although I was made in Japan (conceived on a parental vacation), I cannot claim to be anything other than a pure Texan—as well as a father, husband, former college student, and full-time Marine. During my time in the corps, almost a decade now, I have been fortunate to be granted extended visits to exotic locations such as Europe, the Middle East, and the Arctic Circle. In addition to getting to see the world outside the United States, I have enjoyed my long stay in coastal North Carolina, where I was stationed for almost four years, and my time in New Orleans and Los Angeles. But no matter where I am, in my soul a neon Lone Star perpetually flashes to the rhythm of a Willie Nelson tune.

That I refer to my "soul" seems strange, considering my pragmatic agnosticism. Having previously staked claims on both sides of the divine fence (for which I wish there were a saddle), I have been forced between a rock (the lack of empirical evidence for the existence of God, hence the need for faith) and a hard place (the same void of conclusive proof that there is not a God, hence the same need for faith).

I tend to be no more polar in politics than I am in religion. My centrist beliefs might make it seem as though I lead a fairly dull life when it comes to opinions, but, on the contrary, I have found that practicing the fine and delicate art of fence-riding allows me to take sides in more arguments than William F. Buckley Jr. My niche affords me the freedom to play the incessant devil's advocate. One would be hard pressed to find an issue on which I could not disagree with people — no matter what side of the argument they're on. Having said that, I must admit that the inevitable responsibilities of life have been swaying me from my well-worn tracks down the middle. As I grow older, my political views are starting to lean to the right — a predictable trend that, in my experience, affects most people.

Glancing to the future, I still wonder what I will be after my stint in the Marines. I have no clue and, truthfully, not even a desire for a particular profession. I have always been envious of peers who have known since they were four that they wanted to be doctors and at my age are now graduating from medical school. My strongest hopes are to be a good father and husband; besides that I think I will abide by the old Scottish proverb: "Be happy while you're living for you're a long while dead."

Heather Ricker As someone who delayed declaring a major in English as long as I could as an undergraduate, I'm the kind of person who thinks over most decisions a long time. When I come across new ideas, I let them percolate in my head, asking myself questions before coming to a conclusion. My academic interests hover around the humanities, fueled by the fascination with literature I've had since I first felt the thrill of entering the fictional worlds of Laura Ingalls Wilder and Cam Jansen. Music is another of my passions: I love to listen to Sarah Brightman sing in the *Phantom,* to Louis Armstrong's version of *What a Wonderful World,* and to hundreds of other great musicians. To relax or just for fun, I also enjoy playing the piano and skiing and swimming. As a little girl, I plastered my bedroom walls and ceiling with maps; I still have an endless fascination with other cultures and have the traveling bug.

Nevertheless, there's no place like home. As I've grown up, this phrase has taken on more meaning for me. Like many other American families, my family made a big move in the middle of my childhood. It took us from the front range of the Rocky Mountains, which I tenaciously loved with my ten-year-old heart, to the heart of the Midwest. This unknown, not very exciting place had little to recommend itself. Coming from the diversity of Denver, I considered myself a city girl and therefore an expert judge of the merits of city life. This move also took me away from one set of grandparents.

But this loss was balanced by being closer to the other side of the family, who live on the East Coast. From then on, our family summer vacations alternated between one side of the family and the country and the other. The relationships I developed with grandparents, aunts, uncles, and cousins by these visits, phone calls, and letters reinforced my identity and definition of home. I learned about who they were, unconsciously knowing this was a part of me. Now I realize how much their ideas and values have affected me. I'm glad to have these reference points as I sort out life's challenges; my knowledge of my relatives' experience gives me a starting point from which to explore other viewpoints. The ideas that have influenced me include the political liberalism, Catholicism, and working-class values of my Irish grandparents as well as the feminism and nontraditional religious views held by my other grandparents. My parents have influenced me by their own search for spiritual truth, which has introduced me to the teachings of various churches. A strong faith in God and family is important to me and influences the way I look at life and issues. Nevertheless, my own views in many specific areas are not yet set. I want to be able to adapt my views when there are good arguments for doing so.

Beatrice Kim "I am a Korean with a southern accent. At least that's what my friends from Washington would say. Of course, my friends in the Rio Grande Valley would argue that I am a Korean who speaks Spanish with a *gringo* accent. And my family would argue that I am a Korean who speaks Korean with an American accent. So I am a Korean southerner with a southern accent for English, a *gringo* accent for Spanish, and an American accent for Korean. I suppose I'm just a person who talks funny."

The preceding paragraph was the opening to my Stanford application essay. I began with this paragraph because it demonstrates the gift I've received from living in so many diverse cultural places. I was born in Michigan, lived in Mississippi when the miscegenation laws were still in effect, spent my elementary years in Walla Walla, Washington, where the population was 99.9 percent white, lived in McAllen, Texas, where the population was 70 percent Mexican, and now I find myself in Stanford, California, a beautiful concoction of browns, yellows, whites, blacks, and everything in between.

Growing up throughout the United States, I have experienced prejudice as a member of both a minority race and a minority gender. As a youngster, I heard the constant singsong taunts of children singing, "My mom is Chinese, my dad is Japanese . . ." with the corresponding hand movements of stretching the eyelids up and down. And because I grew up in a traditional Korean family, ruled by the patriarchic customs of Asian culture, my "role" as a woman has been pressed upon me time and time again. "Girls don't do that" is a directive that I have been subjected to not only from my family but also from close friends who unknowingly conform to society's "laws" of gender bias. All of us, I believe—men as well as women—are hurt by such limiting ideas.

Still, the wonderful friends of different ethnicities and genders that I encounter every day have helped me put my negative experiences in perspective and have reenforced my faith in people. Because of my experiences both old and new, I feel that I will always be sincerely empathetic to the cause of spreading knowledge and encouraging tolerance in others.

As I wrap up my undergraduate college career—I am currently a junior with a Communication major and a Creative Writing minor—I am uncertain of what life after college holds for me. But I am sure of one thing: my strong love for God, family, and friends and my diverse experiences from my past and at Stanford will carry me through.

On Reading and Thinking Critically

1

Introduction

THIS IS A BOOK for and about reading. Its pages contain voices joined in conversation and debate over issues important to all of us: What, how, and under what circumstances should we learn and become educated? Who are we as individuals and as members of various groups and cultures? What do we believe and why? How do the media try to influence us? Why and how do we work? In the conversations surrounding these and other issues, the editors of this book have joined the dialogue; you will find our reasons for choosing particular selections and our thoughts about these selections running throughout this text. The primary aim of the book, however, is to invite *you* to join this conversation, to add your voice to the discussion in these pages. Doing so invites you to assume the perspective of a *critical reader.*

• • •

WHAT IS CRITICAL READING?

If you've been wondering what critical reading is, you're already demonstrating one of the hallmarks of a critical reader: an inquisitive attitude, one that probes for definitions, explanations, assumptions, and proofs. Perhaps we can further clarify what we mean by critical reading by focusing on two everyday uses of the word *critical.* In its most common usage, *critical* means acting like a critic, as in "many voters have been highly critical of current American foreign policy," or "some members of the African American community have been critical of what they see as Terry McMillan's negative treatment of men in her novels." In this sense of the word, *critical* suggests that you have explored an issue and are ready to evaluate it, to see whether and how it meets your standards.

But *critical* is also used to denote something of special importance, as in "critical care unit" or "a critical point in negotiations." In this sense of the word, *critical* suggests that you attach importance to what you are examining and to your own critical responses to it. For the purposes of this book, then, **critical readers are those who bring all their powers to bear on understanding, analyzing, and evaluating some important question, issue, or perspective contained in a text**. That "text" will usually take the form of words on a page or screen, but it might also involve other media—images, photographs, film clips, audio clips—all working together to make a point. So, whether reading a book, digesting an online editorial, or viewing a documentary, critical readers do not accept things blindly or at face value. Instead, they examine texts and issues from many perspectives, saying both *yes* and *no* to them until they are ready to take their own stances.

Saying *Yes, No,* and *Maybe*

The chapters of this book will offer you many chances to practice saying *yes* and *no*—and sometimes *maybe*—to ideas. For example, as you examine the selections in Chapter 3, Education, you will encounter widely varying perspectives on higher education and many different questions about its nature and purpose. As you read Adrienne Rich's "What Does a Woman Need to Know?" Rich's arguments may at first seem perfectly reasonable, and you may say *yes* to her ideas. But then you may begin to wonder about them and find yourself thinking, *maybe*, or perhaps even *no*, especially when you realize that her essay was written decades ago. Are Rich's ideas about education appropriate today, and do they respond to the problems women need to confront? Are the charges she brings both fair and accurate? All of these acts—saying *yes, maybe*, and/or *no*—are necessary for critical reading, for the kind of reading that is open to new ideas but that insists on thinking them through from every perspective.

Critical reading is not a skill limited to college English classes. It is what you do when you understand the terms of a contract you are about to sign, decide which of several automobile financing plans will work best for you, master the material necessary to do well on an important examination, evaluate the arguments for or against a political proposal or candidate, or compare doctors' opinions about whether you should undergo surgery. It is the kind of reading Mortimer Adler is talking about when he says, "When [people] are in love and are reading a love letter, they read for all they are worth. They read every word three ways; they read between the lines and in the margins; they read the whole in terms of the parts, and each part in terms of the whole."

WHY BECOME A CRITICAL READER?

Given our definition of critical reading, the answer to this question is probably already obvious to you. Critical readers are the players in this world. They find themselves "in on" the conversation surrounding any issue. They are the people others turn to for advice or counsel because they resist ready-made or hand-me-down opinions whenever they can. Much in our society makes such critical reading difficult; we are, after all, inundated with canned opinions and images on television and in other mass media as well as in religious, political, and even educational institutions (see Figure 1.1). In fact, so many forces are trying to make up our minds for us that many people question whether we control language at all, rather than the other way around.

You can probably think of many instances in which language seems to be "in control." When you go to a movie, for instance, you notice how commercials entice you to buy grotesquely overpriced popcorn and soda. Or you may be aware that educational labels like *honors* or *remedial* have dramatically affected your life. Many studies suggest that we tend to live up (or down) to such labels—for better or worse. This fact of modern life led one

Figure 1.1. A parody advertisement. Taken from *Adbusters* <http://adbusters.org>, this ad uses a sheep image to suggest the media's manipulation of public opinion.

language theorist to say that the words we try to control are already "half-way in someone else's mouth," meaning that the expressions we use are already so weighed down with societal meanings that it is hard not to accept those meanings. That is, it's hard for any one person to resist the lure of advertising or to reject the power of educational or social labels.

To some extent, this theory rings true: we do not absolutely control the language we use or read. But to accept such a position totally is to give up on trying to make your voice heard or to bring about any change. Why become a critical reader, then? To resist being controlled by other people's language, to exert some control of your own, to test your wits, to define your own perspective on any issue, to contribute to the thoughts and actions related to those issues. **You become a critical reader, in short, to get involved in the conversation and to make your voice count.**

ARE YOU A CRITICAL READER?

Our guess is that you are already a critical reader when you need to be. You may want to take stock of your general reading habits, however, by answering the following questions. As a rule, when you are reading important material, do you:

1. Read carefully, either with or without skimming first?
2. "Talk back" to what you are reading, noting what does or doesn't make sense, what seems right or wrong?
3. Ask questions as you read?
4. Take notes in the margins or on a separate sheet of paper?
5. Ask yourself why the writer takes the position he or she does?
6. Think about the writer's perspective—what his or her interests are in writing the piece?
7. Ask what larger social, economic, political, or other conditions may have influenced the creation of the piece of writing?
8. Consider what in your experience and background leads you to agree with or like, or to disagree with or dislike, the piece of writing?
9. Imagine other ways of looking at the subjects or ideas presented?
10. Summarize the gist of what you have read?
11. Compare what you're reading with other things you have read about the subject?

Do You Read Online Materials Critically?

Being a strong critical reader is increasingly important in a time when information is traded with such immense speed and quantity via electronic networks. The Internet and the Web connect us in new ways while digital technologies allow us to store greater and greater quantities of information. Things you read online one day may change dramatically—or disappear—the next day. The film you watched in the theater may make a different statement when you see the director's cut on DVD and read about the new version on a Web log. In addition, since just about anyone can create a Web site or contribute to an online discussion without the scrutiny of an editor or a publisher, you need to be especially critical when reading electronic materials. When you are reading online, do you:

1. Check to find out who is responsible for a document, a posting, or a Web site or log? Is it, for example, a commercial site whose main goal is to sell, rather than to evaluate, a particular product?
2. Check to see when the item was put on the Net, or when it was last updated?
3. Ask what the item's "credentials" are? Is it, for example, a research report that carries the authority of a respected group such as the Linguistics Society of America or the Association of Consulting Engineers?
4. Check any links to see what they might reveal about the credibility and trustworthiness of the item?
5. Consider how the use of graphics, color, visual images, and so on affect the message of the item?

Examining Your Reading Habits If you answered *yes* to most of the questions in the two preceding lists, you are already reading with a critical eye, and you will understand what we mean when we say reading is a partnership: the text in front of you has words and images set down, but you are the one who realizes the ideas in those words and images, tests them against what you know, and puts them to use in your life.

Take five or ten minutes to write or draw a description of yourself as a reader. How do you usually approach a text that you want or need to understand? Do you usually practice critical reading habits? Why, or why not? Bring your description to class for discussion. Compare your description with those of two or three other students in your class, noting the ways in which your reading strategies are similar and/or different.

HOW CAN YOU BECOME A MORE CRITICAL READER?

If you have compared the way you read to how your friends and classmates do it, you have probably noticed some differences. Indeed, habits of reading vary widely, and even highly skilled readers differ in their approaches. Moreover, what works for your friends or expert readers may not work for you. That's because your reading strategies are connected to who you are—to your gender, age, cultural background, life experiences, prior reading experiences, even your eyesight. In addition, you probably read differently depending on your purpose and situation: you might just skim the ingredients listed on a food package to check that the food doesn't contain too much fat, whereas you might linger over the directions for operating a digital camera to make sure that you don't make a mistake.

Thus, part of your job as a critical reader is to appreciate your own preferred strategies. You need to recognize the strengths and weaknesses of your reading strategies and to build on your strengths. To help you, we can offer some general guidelines. You can experiment with them to develop a personal blueprint for effective critical reading. We hope that these guidelines will help you when you tackle difficult reading material or material for which you have almost no background. In the annotated essays in Chapters 3 through 9 of this book, you will find examples of most of these guidelines, written in the margins as our responses to those essays.

Previewing

- Determine your purpose for reading. Is it to gather information for a writing assignment? To determine whether a source will be useful for a research project? To study for an examination? To prepare for class discussion? To determine your own stance toward a topic—and what in your experience and background leads you to take that stance?
- Consider the title and subtitle, if there is one. What do they tell you about what is to come? If you are reading online, what does the home page or site tell you about its content or links?
- Think about what you already know about the subject. What opinions do you hold on this subject? What assumptions do you bring to the subject? If you find yourself reacting very favorably or unfavorably to the subject, ask where that reaction is coming from: what has influenced you to respond in that way?
- What major topics do you anticipate? What do you hope to learn? What other things about this topic have you read?
- What do you know about the author(s)? What expertise does he or she have in the subject? What particular perspective on the subject might he or she hold? If an author isn't identified, why is that? Does the piece represent the opinion or work of a group or institution? What can you discover about that group or institution?
- What does the headnote or opening of the reading tell you?
- Look at how the text is structured. Are there subdivisions? Read over any headings. Skim the opening sentences of each paragraph. For a Web site, check to see if there is a site map, or explore the architecture of the site: does it offer a sequence of pages, a hierarchy of materials, or a ring of connected items?

- Decide what you think the main point or theme of the text will be. Does the material lead to one specific point or encourage you to construct your own meanings?
- Check to see if the conclusion contains a summary of the main point or a statement of its significance—or look for an abstract of the text that gives a comparable synopsis. Previewing either of these elements can help you read more efficiently and critically.

Annotating

- Read carefully, marking places that are confusing or that you want to reread.
- Identify key points or arguments, important terms, recurring images, and interesting ideas, either by underlining them in the text or by making notes in the margin.
- Note any statements you question or disagree with and any counterevidence or counterarguments that occur to you.
- Note any sources used in the text.

Summarizing

- Summarize the main points. Do they match your expectations? Why, or why not?
- Jot down any points you want to remember, questions you want to raise, and ideas for how you may use this material.

Analyzing

- Identify evidence that supports the main argument or illustrates the main point. Is it sufficient to convince you? Is there any evidence that seems to contradict the author's point?
- Identify the writer's underlying assumptions about the subject, where he or she is "coming from" on this issue.
- Ask what may have led the author to this position.
- Consider how the writer's stance affects his or her presentation of the material or argument.
- Describe the writer's tone. Is it cautious? Angry? Insulting? Serious or amusing? How is the tone created, and what effects does it strive to achieve?

- Question the sources used. Ask yourself whether each source is relevant to the topic, whether it is timely, whether it carries sufficient expertise, and whether its perspective or position on the subject is different from yours or from others' you know and respect. If so, why?
- Think of other points of view on this topic, perhaps from other things you have read or seen. Is the author's perspective the most persuasive? Why, or why not?
- Examine the way the writer presents information or data. Read any accompanying tables and charts carefully. Look at any photographs or drawings that are part of the text. How do these visual elements expand or illuminate the points the writer seeks to make?

Rereading

- Reread quickly to be sure you have understood the reading.
- Identify the author's purpose(s). Were those purposes accomplished?
- Determine whether the questions you had during the first reading have been answered.

Responding

- What one question would you like to ask the writer? How do you think the writer might respond?
- Think about the reading as a whole. What did you like best about it? What puzzled or irritated you? What caused you to like or dislike the piece? Were your expectations met? If not, why not? What more would you like to know about the subject? Remember to explore the reasons for your reaction to the reading: what influences may have led to that response?
- Note what you have learned about effective writing from this reading.
- If you keep a reading log, record these notes there. (For sample reading log entries, see the Afterwords on pp. 95 and 219.)

Examining Your Critical Literacy To practice reading a text critically, turn to one of the texts in this book that is *not* annotated and analyze the piece using the guidelines for thinking and reading critically. For an example of one student's critical response to a reading, see pp. 44–46.

HOW CAN YOU READ VISUAL TEXTS CRITICALLY?

Today, images crowd in from all directions, not only from television, video, film, and the Web, but from traditional print texts as well—from the graphs and charts in a financial report to the daily newspaper to the textbook you hold in your hand. And as we have indicated throughout this chapter, far from being mere decoration, these images carry part or most of the message readers are intended to receive. As a result, critical readers pay very careful attention to the visuals in any text they read, understanding that these have a significant impact on how readers interpret and respond to those texts. If a picture *is* sometimes worth a thousand words, it pays to spend some time thinking about what makes that picture so valuable.

Some visual texts in and of themselves embody ideas or arguments. Consider the now-famous electoral map from the U.S. presidential election of 2000; it showed a nation sharply divided both politically and geographically (see Figure 1.2). Studying the map, you could make many deductions about political and social trends in the country. And that, in fact, is what David Brooks does in "One Nation, Slightly Divisible," an essay we have included in this anthology because it is an extended critical reading of a visual text. Still, it is important to remember that the electoral map itself was not created to embody any particular political or social trends. It simply reported the outcome of an election.

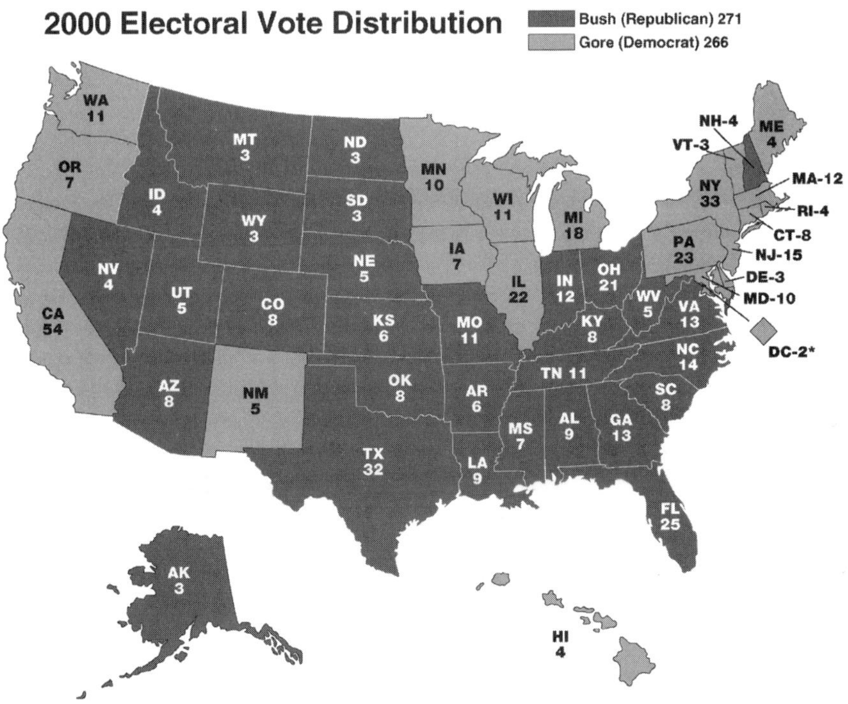

Figure 1.2. Electoral map of the 2000 presidential election. In this map, taken from the Federal Election Commission's Web site <http://www.fec.gov/>, states Al Gore won are in gray, and states George W. Bush won are in black.

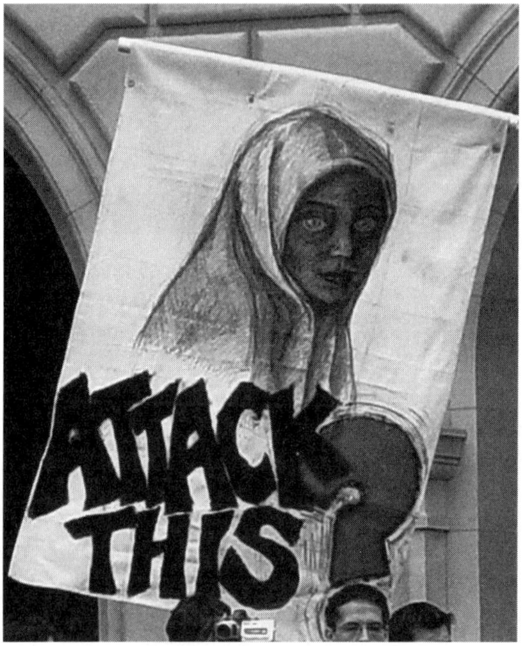

Figure 1.3. An antiwar poster. Students used this poster to protest the war against Iraq in spring 2003.

Figure 1.4. An anti-SUV parking sign. Source: *Stay Free!* Magazine Web site <http://stayfreemagazine.org/suv/>.

My other car got squished by an SUV.
www.suvlove.com

Figure 1.5. A pro-SUV bumper sticker.

Other images, however, are more deliberately crafted to influence you. Such images demand especially careful and critical reading so that you can appreciate both the arguments they offer and how such arguments are made. Just as important, you have to understand the context in which images operate, asking the same questions about authors, audience, and purpose that you would raise for a written piece. Consider, for example, the different analytical techniques you would have to use with Figure 1.3, a poster carried by university students during an antiwar rally in spring 2003, and Figures 1.4 and 1.5, an anti-SUV parking sign and a pro-SUV bumper sticker, respectively. All three images make relatively simple points about complex issues, yet the images have substance too.

The following questions can help you shape your critical reading of similar visual texts—whether they stand on their own, as in a photograph or painting, or are combined with print—beginning with those you find throughout this book. To get started, take a close look at the front cover to see what it may tell you about the content of this book, the goals of the editors, and the overall message it sends. You will see only a few words on this cover: the title, subtitle, names of editors, and notice of "Fourth Edition." What effect do size and placement have on the meaning and emphasis these words convey? Note also the background of the cover and its use of color. What does the color add or suggest? Take a close look at the images on the cover: how many can you identify? The following questions will help you read the visuals in this text, and those all around you, with a critical eye.

For Charts, Graphs, and Tables

1. What information does the chart, graph, or table convey?
2. Does it present numbers or statistics? How does the visual representation affect your understanding of the information? Does it emphasize or downplay, or even exaggerate or understate, anything?

3. Does it illustrate a trend or change? If so, does it emphasize the change fairly or not?
4. Does it highlight anything (a particular year? a topic?) to attract your attention?

For Photographs, Drawings, and Advertisements

1. Why was the visual created? What does its main meaning or message seem to be? How does the visual make you notice and perhaps remember this message?
2. What in the visual is your eye drawn to, and why?
3. What is in the foreground? In the background? What is in focus or out of focus? Is the most important part of the visual blended into the rest, or is it contrasted somehow? What details are included or emphasized? What is omitted or de-emphasized, and why?
4. What is placed high in the visual? What is placed low? To the left? To the right?
5. How are light and color used? How do they affect your reading of the visual?
6. Is anything in the visual repeated, intensified, or exaggerated? Look for anything that is made to seem "supernormal" or idealized (by airbrushing or computer manipulation, for example). What effect does the exaggeration or repetition have on you as a reader?
7. Is anything downplayed? Ambiguous? Confusing or distracting? If so, what effect does this have on your reading of the visual? Does any ambiguity call on you as a reader to fill in some gaps? If so, to what effect?
8. What values or ideals does the visual convey or allude to? Family values? The good life? Harmony? Success? Beauty? Power? Pleasure? Sex appeal? Youth? Wisdom? Adventure? Is the visual text reinforcing or questioning these values? How does it do so?
9. Does the visual include imagery or people that carry very positive—or very negative—associations? If so, how do such images or people affect your response? (Think of ads that use celebrities to make readers notice—and buy!—the product.)
10. Does the visual use humor? If so, how does the humor affect your reaction?
11. How does the visual relate to any written text that accompanies it? Do the two reinforce each other, or does one undermine the other?

HOW CAN YOU READ ONLINE TEXTS CRITICALLY?

As we have already indicated more generally, the texts you encounter online, especially pages on the Web, require new reading skills because they combine many different elements—including headlines, printed words, static images, moving images, sounds, and even film clips. Chances are you quickly picked up the skills for navigating these electronic texts and thus barely realized how many new conventions you were absorbing, from scrolling pages (rather than turning them) to clicking items to move to new places or to open email messages. But you need to do more than just explore online texts; you need to appreciate how they work to attract and direct your attention.

In many cases, the visual and, to a lesser extent, aural items on a Web page are designed to encourage you to select specific menus or links. But commercial pages usually offer many more options than you need just to keep you browsing and looking. More and more, Web pages are also interrupted by pop-up advertisements designed to get you to move to more sites. The visual clutter of many commercial pages, especially those for some Web search engines (Google is a welcome exception), may even surprise you. The box for typing in a search term is often obscured by blinking images and clusters of links, all competing for your attention and, often, your money.

So you have to learn to filter out the clutter on electronic pages and evaluate their overall design to determine what information is being offered to you and in what order. The way that information is presented usually tells you what the site designers or sponsors value. They may use colors or images to highlight ideas they want you to encounter and bury less important material deep in a site or omit it entirely.

You should be especially careful with online texts that fail to identify themselves clearly. Look for information about identity, authorship, sponsorship, and currency. If an online text resists even your basic attempts to read it critically, you should perhaps move on to another. There are likely to be dozens of additional choices, whatever subject you are exploring.

1. How does the online text combine visual and written material? Which dominates, and to what effect?
2. What perspective is represented in text? What group or individual is responsible for the information provided? What is the credibility or reputation of the author or sponsor? Is the text sponsored by or linked to a commercial enterprise? For Web sites, be sure to check out the domain name: *.com* indicates a commercial site; *.edu* indicates a site sponsored by an educational institution; *.org* indicates a nonprofit organization; and *.gov* indicates a government site. Is there an email address you can use to contact those responsible for the text?

3. Does the text include links to other online texts? If so, what do the links tell you about the credibility and usefulness of the text you are reading? Following the links will also give you a sense of context for the growing number of Web logs on the Net.
4. How current is the text? When was it last updated? These days, some sites are updated almost minute by minute. Others contain dated (and hence, inaccurate) information.
5. How easy is it to find information in this text? Does it have a search function and/or a site map that will help you read it?
6. What about this text makes it worth bookmarking (or not)?

WHAT DOES READING HAVE TO DO WITH WRITING?

In one sense, critical reading *is* writing. That is, as you read carefully, asking questions and talking back to a text, you inevitably create your own version of the text. Even if that interpretation is not written down on paper, it is "written" in your mind, composed and put into words you can understand and remember. And if you add some of your own ideas—or those you and classmates develop together—to what you read, you can build a new work altogether, one you might later write down.

As our society uses electronic texts more often, reading and writing will almost certainly become even more intertwined. The "reader" of interactive fiction or a hypertext, for instance, may write part of the text. Those on electronic bulletin boards or Web logs may write their own ideas and responses into what they are reading on the screen, something first written by another reader.

But critical reading is also closely related to your own writing because it enables you to assess what you have written, to say *yes* and *no* and *maybe* to your own ideas—to evaluate the logic of your prose, the effectiveness of your word choices, the degree to which you have gotten your points across. In short, you can apply these same reading strategies to your own writing, to see your own words with a critical eye. Thus, reading critically and writing effectively become reciprocal activities, strengthening each other as you learn to use language more powerfully.

Because we are convinced that reading and writing are closely related, we want this text to offer you many opportunities for moving back and forth from reading to writing to reading. We will, in fact, invite you to experiment with a number of kinds of writing as you read your way into the conversations taking place in the chapters that follow. We turn now, therefore, to Chapter 2, From Reading to Writing, for an overview of the writing practices this book invites you to experience.

From Reading to Writing 2

Introduction

NO ONE CAN PREDICT how you will respond to what you read, but the act of reading does often lead to action. Maybe reading a pamphlet handed to you on campus will convince you to vote for a student government candidate. Or a slick brochure arriving in the mail could lead you to buy apartment insurance—or to complain about false advertising to a state regulatory agency. Gaudy graphics on a Web page might entice you to click for more information, or maybe all that design clutter offends you so much that you remove the annoying site from your "favorites" list. A dull book could make you reconsider your major; a great book might change your life.

One action that reading often provokes is writing, which can preserve and extend your ideas. When you write about what you have read, you enter a conversation someone else has started, contribute your own ideas to it, and invite still others to join you. Sometimes these conversations will be simple and immediate, as when you respond quickly to email or IM requests from people you know well. At other times, your reading and writing will bridge wider gaps, perhaps even between different cultures or eras, and then you'll need to respond much more deliberately. In figure 2.1, a woman holds a writing instrument in one hand and a book in the other, speaking across the centuries about the importance of literacy in Roman culture.

WRITING TO LEARN

Most classes in college will require some written work. Although these tasks may seem too routine to think of as actual "writing," don't underestimate them. Writing of almost any kind can fix ideas in your mind and stimulate your thinking. Following are some types of college writing that may help you learn better: class notes, lab notes, reading notes and annotations, listserv messages, comments on other students' writing, research log entries, abstracts of articles, summaries, outlines,

Figure 2.1. Sappho. Source: a fresco from Herculaneum, Alinari/Art Resource, NY.

annotated bibliographies, essay examinations, and class presentations. Consider such writing assignments as opportunities to learn.

LEARNING TO WRITE EFFECTIVELY

In many of your college courses, instructors will ask you to prepare formal essays or other extended pieces of writing related to what you read, hear, or learn. The following guidelines are designed to help you respond effectively to such assignments.

Considering the Assignment

Find out as much as you can about an assignment before starting to write.

- Analyze a writing project carefully. Look for key words in the assignment, such as *analyze, summarize, compare, contrast, illustrate, argue, defend, refute, persuade, respond,* and so on.
- If you don't understand an assignment, ask your instructor for clarification.
- Pay attention to limits on length and time. The length of an assignment will surely influence the focus and thesis of any essay. In general, the shorter the piece, the narrower its focus will need to be.
- Note whether you are asked to use a particular format (a lab report, for example, or a memo) and whether you are expected to include any visuals in your writing.
- Plan your time to allow for all necessary reading, thinking, drafting, and editing.

Considering Purpose and Audience

Beyond what the assignment itself dictates, consider the larger purpose of the writing. In all your school writing, one purpose will be to demonstrate that you have done a fine job of responding to the assignment, but beyond that very large-scale purpose lie additional purposes. An assignment that asks you to prepare a report suggests that your purpose will be to inform, while an assignment that asks you to prepare an editorial column will call for a clear argumentative position. How will your writing accomplish your purposes successfully? Your responses to that question will help determine the form, organization, tone, style, and length of your writing. Here are some other questions to help you think about purpose:

- Does the assignment itself specify a purpose?
- What does your instructor expect you to do in this assignment? What do you need to do to meet those expectations?
- How do you want readers to react to your writing? Do you want them to be entertained? Should they learn something? Should they be moved to action?
- Where might you like to have this piece read? Will it appear in print or online?

Consider also who will read your piece. The primary audience for your college writing may be instructors, but *they* may have in mind some other specific audience—your classmates, for example, or the general public. Following are some questions that can help identify key characteristics of your audience:

- Do your readers belong to some identifiable group: college students, Democrats, women, parents, sociologists?
- What is your relationship to your readers? Is it friend to friend? Employee to employer? Citizen to community? Some other relationship?
- How would you characterize your readers? What assumptions can you legitimately make about your audience members? What values and principles do you hold in common with them? What differences are there between you? What attitudes might disturb or offend them?
- Are your readers likely to know more or less than you do about your subject? What background information do you need to provide?
- What languages and varieties of English do your audience members know and use? What special language, if any, might they expect you to use?
- Are your readers likely to be engaged by your subject, or do you have to win their attention?
- Are your readers likely to be favorable, neutral, or hostile to your positions?
- Should you use simple, general language, or technical language?
- Should you use images or other forms of illustration? Would adding sound and/or video clips be appropriate to your purpose and readers?
- Are you addressing more than one audience? If so, do any of the audiences seem incompatible?
- Is your writing going online, where it can be read by the general public? Remember that the Internet now allows you to reach countless readers, so you need to take special care to examine how—and if—such distant readers will understand your arguments, references, allusions, and so on.

Generating Ideas and Making Plans

You don't need to know what you are going to say before you begin writing. Even so, all writers must start somewhere. You may find the following techniques helpful in discovering ideas:

- Take a quick written inventory of everything you know about your subject, followed by a list of what you think you'll need to research.
- Read any assigned material carefully, annotating key information, summarizing main points, and noting connections among readings.
- Try specific techniques for developing ideas, such as freewriting, brainstorming, or journal writing. (Consult a writing handbook for more about these techniques.)

- Get more information—from your library's databases, from the Web, from professional organizations, from friends or instructors, and so on.
- Do field research. Conduct a survey or some interviews—or carry out a detailed and careful observation of some phenomenon.
- Get involved in discussions about your subject. Talk to people. Listen to their ideas and opinions. Read a newsgroup or join a listserv.
- Draw on your personal experiences, especially when dealing with social, cultural, and political issues. *Your* experience counts.

Once you have ideas, sketch out a plan—a scheme to make a project manageable. Here are some ways of working out a plan:

- Fix on a tentative thesis statement, claim, or main point you want to prove, defend, or illustrate. Think of it as a commitment to your readers.
- Prepare a scratch outline by listing the major ideas you want to cover and then arranging them in an order that makes sense to you. If you have access to brainstorming software, take advantage of it: a program like Inspiration, for example, makes creating an idea map very easy—and the program will turn your idea map into a formal outline with one keystroke.
- Construct a formal outline if you find such devices useful.
- Try a "zero draft"—a quick, discardable version of an essay to help you focus on the major issues.

DRAFTING

Drafting is the point in the writing process when you commit your words and thoughts to the page or screen. The cold swimming hole approach works best for some writers: just plunge in and start writing. After all, you can't do much as a writer until you produce some words. In case you don't much like cold water, however, here's some other advice for getting started on a first draft:

- Make a commitment to begin writing. Sometimes just getting started is the hardest part of writing, so setting a date and time for beginning can be important.
- Control your expectations. No one expects a first draft to be perfect. In fact, no one expects a final draft to be the last word on any subject. So take it easy.
- Skip the introduction if you find yourself stuck on the opening sentences. Start somewhere else, perhaps with an idea you are especially eager to develop. Then write another portion of the essay, and then another. You can put all the parts together later.

- If you are working on a computer, set up a folder or file for your essay, choosing a clear and relevant file name, and save your document often.
- Have all your information close at hand and arranged according to when you will need it.
- Set some reasonable goals, especially for longer projects. Commit yourself to writing for at least thirty minutes, or until you have at least one or two pages, before getting up from your desk.
- Stop writing at a place where you know exactly what should come next. That way, beginning again will be easier. Reward yourself when you meet your goal.
- Try a quick draft: sketch out the full essay without stopping.

Getting—and Giving—Feedback

Seek responses from other readers. Within whatever guidelines your instructor establishes, ask classmates, friends, or any potential readers to read and react to your drafts. Here are some guidelines for your readers to use in reviewing your draft:

- Begin by describing what you think the draft is saying. That description might prove enlightening to the author. Go on to paraphrase the thesis as a promise: *In this paper, the writer promises to* ___________. Then see whether the draft fulfills that promise.
- Decide whether the draft carries out the assignment and, if not, what the writer can do to better fulfill it.
- List the major points in order. Then decide which points, if any, need to be explained more or less fully. Should any be eliminated? Are any confusing or boring? How well are the major points supported by evidence, examples, details, and so on?
- Consider how visuals—photographs, charts, graphs, maps, screen shots, and so on—are used to support the major ideas. How well are visuals integrated into the text? Are they introduced, commented on, and clearly labeled?
- Point out any word, phrase, or sentence that is confusing or unclear.
- Describe what is most memorable in the draft.
- List the strengths of the draft. How can they be enhanced?
- List the weaknesses. How might they be eliminated or minimized?
- Suggest specific revisions. What more do you as a reader want or need to know? Which other arguments or ideas should be considered?

Revising

Respond to comments on a first draft by looking at the entire assignment anew. Reshape the essay as much as necessary to serve your purpose, your subject matter, and your readers. Here are some specific suggestions for revising:

- To gain perspective, put a printed draft aside for a day or two.
- Be as tough minded as you can about the condition of a draft. Discard whole paragraphs or pages when they simply don't work. Don't just tinker or look for the easiest way of salvaging weak material. You may need a new thesis or a completely different structure.
- Consider very carefully any responses you've received—but don't overreact to criticism.
- Consider alternative plans for organization. Be flexible.
- Consider the overall strategy of the essay. Might a different point of view or tone make it more effective?
- Review your thesis or main idea. Is the thesis fully explained and supported?
- Reconsider whether you know enough about your subject to write about it with authority. If not, go back to your sources or do more reading.
- Pay attention to transitions. You can help your readers with a few careful phrases that point to where you're going—or where you've been.
- Pay attention to visual details—to any images you are using and the design of the text. Test them with readers to make sure they are appropriate and effective.

Editing

Once you've revised your draft, it's time to edit your work by paying close attention to the structure of paragraphs, the shape of sentences, the choice of words, the presentation of visuals, and the conventions of punctuation and mechanics.

- Reconsider openings and closings. In academic writing, introductions should capture the reader's attention and identify key points, while conclusions should summarize ideas and draw implications.
- Read your draft aloud, paying attention to the length, variety, rhythm, and coherence of sentences.

- Look for wordiness. Stylistically, nothing hurts an essay more than empty phrases.
- Take advantage of your word processor. In addition to making sure you've run the spell check at least twice, consider searching for words you often confuse: *their* for *there,* for example. Then use the search function in your program to find all instances of such words, and double-check to make sure that each usage is correct.
- Consider your vocabulary for appropriateness. Is it appropriate to use contractions or slang or dialect? Do any technical terms need defining?
- Check any documentation of sources for the correct form. Reconsider also the way you incorporate sources—do you quote, paraphrase, and summarize appropriately? Do you weave quotations smoothly into your own text? Do your Web links make sense?
- Check for problems of grammar and usage, particularly for any types of errors that have caused you problems in the past.
- For detailed examples and answers to questions of grammar, usage, and style, check a handbook.
- Find a suitable title. For most academic work, titles should provide clear descriptions of the contents. Titles are also important for online documents.

Preparing the Final Version

Now is the time to assemble and check your final version.

- Review the assignment to be sure you have met all requirements of form. Does your instructor want a title page? An outline? A Works Cited page?
- Be sure your name appears in the proper place(s).
- Paginate and clip printed pages together. (Do not staple them.)
- Proofread one last time for typographical errors, spelling errors, and other slips. If you have a spell checker, run it for a final check.
- Make sure the final version is presented professionally, whether a printed text or an electronic document.

AN ALPHABETICAL CATALOG OF THE WRITING ASSIGNMENTS IN THIS BOOK

Throughout *The Presence of Others* we invite you to respond to the readings we've selected, to join in conversation with all the people who've collaborated to write this book—writers, editors, reviewers, and students. Following is an alphabetical catalog of guidelines to the writing assignments you may be asked to do as you use this book. As you read and use these guidelines, remember that a *text* can be an article, a visual, a Web site—anything that you "read."

Analyzing

Analytical writing puts ideas under scrutiny. To analyze a text—whether a print, visual, or electronic one—question the validity of arguments, the accuracy of facts, the logical relationship of ideas, the fairness of conclusions, and the assumptions underlying them. Here are some suggestions for analyzing a text:

- To begin, identify exactly what you want to analyze, from a paragraph to a full work.
- Note any preconceptions or assumptions you bring to the topic of your analysis. Think about how they may affect your analysis.
- Mark the text and any visuals you are analyzing thoroughly. Annotate in the margins, highlight key quotations, and circle terms or features you think are especially important.
- Divide the text into its main ideas, and look at each one carefully. What support and details exist for each idea?
- Look for connections between and among ideas. Are these connections clear and logical to you? Do you see the point of intriguing juxtapositions of ideas or visuals?
- Try to think of opposing points of view or alternative perspectives on the topic. Does the writer consider them fairly?

For an example of analysis, see the essay by Adrienne Rich (p. 71).

Writing a Rhetorical Analysis In its simplest form, a rhetorical analysis explores two basic questions: What is the writer's purpose? How is that purpose presented to an intended audience? Answers to these important questions help readers appreciate the options that writers face and the possible reasons behind particular choices of language, image, genre, and so on. A rhetorical analysis does not focus on what a text means but rather looks at the particular strategies a writer uses to get across that meaning and gauges their success. A rhetorical analysis can also consider how a writer's cultural, economic, social, or political contexts affect the reading and writing of the text. Here are tips for examining a text rhetorically:

- Try to define the major purpose of the text, but understand that it may be composed for more than one reason. Identify these multiple purposes when you can, pointing out in your analysis where they may conflict. When possible, show where such conflicts may have affected the writer's choice of arguments, evidence, vocabulary, examples, visual elements, and so on.

- Try to identify a primary audience and describe its expectations. What do members of the primary audience know about the subject, and what do they need to know? How does the text address their expectations or needs?
- Identify any secondary audiences. How do their needs differ from those of the primary audience?
- Explore the author's attitude toward the topic or issue—is it favorable or unfavorable? Mocking or satirical? Judgmental or neutral? What is the author's stake in the subject?
- Explore the relationship of the author to the audience. Does he or she maintain a position of distance and authority or seek to "come close to" readers?
- Explain how the text uses rhetorical strategies, including choice of evidence and detail, the author's tone and voice, the vocabulary choices, and the kinds of sentences.

For an example of a rhetorical analysis, see the essay by David Brooks (p. 581).

Writing a Critical Analysis A critical analysis may examine many of the same issues as those in a rhetorical analysis. But a critical analysis usually makes more value judgments about the integrity of a text—its power and its reach.

A critical analysis looks carefully at the logic of a text, identifying its claims and assessing the premises and evidence that support those claims. Critical analysis seeks to answer questions such as these: Does the author make a coherent claim? Are the assumptions behind the claim defensible? Are the connections among assumptions, claims, and evidence logical? Is the evidence presented sufficient and reliable? Is the text fair, or is the author biased in a way that undermines the credibility of the piece?

A critical analysis also looks at the *success* of a text—at how persuasive it is, how well it makes emotional or ethical appeals, how successfully it moves or delights readers. Here are some tips for examining a text critically:

- Understand the intended audience(s) and purpose(s). Consider the work's historical, social, and political contexts in some detail.
- Identify the claims, both stated and implied.
- Identify the premises behind the claims, and determine how those assumptions would be received by the intended reader(s).

- Examine the evidence for each claim. What are the sources of information? Study any statistics and how they are used. Consider the sources and reliability of polls and surveys.
- Explore the logic of the argument. Does the writer use any logical fallacies? Consider, too, the rhetorical force of the evidence. Is it sufficient? Overwhelming?
- Consider the way the writer presents himself or herself. Does the author make a persuasive, appealing case? Is he or she appropriately engaged in or deliberately removed from the text?
- If visuals are included, do they fairly and appropriately support the author's points?
- Consider the way the text makes its overall appeal. Is the format appropriate to its audience? Is it appropriately serious? Humorous? Academic? Colloquial?

For an example of critical analysis, see the essay by Michael Pollan (p. 222).

Arguing

Among a writer's toughest jobs is making a persuasive argument, one that moves readers to reaffirm a commitment—or to consider changing their minds or taking action. Almost all the readings and visuals in this book contain arguments. As you work at reading these texts, you may want to construct arguments of your own. Here are some suggestions for writing an effective academic argument:

- Develop a clear, carefully limited thesis to defend. This thesis will often evolve gradually as you learn about your subject.
- Find some good reasons for your audience to agree with the thesis. Support all statements with specific and appropriate evidence, including visuals if appropriate.
- Show that any evidence you have gathered is fair, appropriate, and accurate; that your various arguments support one another; and that they outweigh possible counterarguments.
- When building an argument from something you've read:
    - ▸ Regard the text and everything connected with it as potential evidence. This would include the language and style of the writer, his or her background and reputation, the time and place of publication, the reputation of the publisher, visuals that accompany the written text, and so on.
    - ▸ When appropriate, quote from a piece of evidence carefully to demonstrate the points you are making. Bring the writer's voice into the conversation, but don't let his or her words be a substitute for what you have to say.

- Appeal to the readers you are trying to convince by connecting your argument to subjects they are likely to know and care about. An effective argument stimulates thinking and conversation. It doesn't close off discussion or create enemies.

For examples of effective arguments, see the essays by J. Michael Bishop (p. 280) and Barbara Dafoe Whitehead (p. 667).

Brainstorming

Brainstorming is an activity that can jump-start your thinking. It consists simply of putting down ideas—about a reading, a writing topic, a problem to solve, whatever—just as they come to mind. Although you can certainly brainstorm alone, it often works better in a group because you can bounce your ideas off other people. If you are working with a group, assign one person to jot down notes.

You can brainstorm either as you read or immediately afterward. Here are some specific tips for brainstorming:

- List your thoughts as they occur. Put down whatever comes to mind; let your ideas flow. Prune and reorder ideas *later.*
- Don't judge the quality of your brainstorming prematurely. Record your intuitions. Give yourself slack to explore ideas—even silly or outlandish ones.
- Once you've written all your thoughts down, look for connections among them. What conclusions can you draw about your position on the subject by looking at these connections?

Comparing and Contrasting

Strictly speaking, when you compare things, you are looking for similarities; when you contrast them, you are pointing out differences. Here are some suggestions for comparing and contrasting:

- Break your subject into parts or aspects that can be studied profitably. As the old saying goes, you don't want to compare apples and oranges.
- Pursue your comparison or contrast analysis systematically, point by point, using visuals as well as words if they are appropriate. Group the comparisons or contrasts purposefully so that they make or support a point about your subject.
- Use appropriate transitional words and phrases. Readers can easily get lost if you jump from one point of comparison or contrast to another without providing the necessary bridges.

- Be fair. Even when you are inclined to favor one side over another, be sure to consider the other side fairly.

The selections by Shelby Steele (p. 78) and Ron Suskind (p. 634) provide examples of comparing and contrasting.

Defining

When asked to define a word or concept in a paragraph, you're usually expected to write an extended explanation of the term, accompanied by illustrations and examples. Terms can also be defined through descriptions of their components, descriptions of processes (how something works), or any appropriate combination of these methods. Here are some suggestions for defining:

- To define a term, place it within a larger category and then list features or characteristics that distinguish it from other items in that category: "A skyscraper is a building of unusual height."
- Then expand the simple definition by providing additional distinguishing details: "A skyscraper is a building of unusual height, most often supported by a steel skeleton and having many stories. The earliest skyscrapers appeared in American cities, especially Chicago and New York, late in the nineteenth century. The height of buildings was confined at first by construction techniques that required massive masonry walls and by the limits of elevator technology. The invention of steel skeletons that supported both floors and walls and the development of high-speed elevators made much taller buildings possible. Among the most famous skyscrapers are the Empire State Building in New York and the Sears Tower in Chicago."
- In most cases, try to keep the tone of a formal definition factual and impersonal. An extended definition, however, can be composed in many different registers, from the serious to the satiric.

Differences over definitions often give rise to the disagreements that people have about important political and social issues. Therefore, always be sensitive to the key words in a text. Quite often, while you and other readers agree on the core meanings of such important terms (their denotations), you may not share the feelings, images, and associations that these words evoke (their connotations). For examples of definition, see the essays by Peter J. Gomes (p. 242) and Dave Barry (p. 402).

Describing

A description provides a snapshot of something—explaining what it looks like at a particular moment. You can describe things through words or visuals.

- Consider your perspective on the item you want to describe. From what angle are you observing it? Share this point of view with readers.
- Spend some quiet time observing what you plan to describe very carefully.
- Record the most distinctive features and details, those that will enable readers to visualize what you are describing. In most types of writing, your goal is to convey an accurate *impression* of what you have seen, be it person, thing, or even idea.
- Written descriptions depend heavily on modifiers—words that convey concrete, sensory details by specifying shape, size, color, smell, and so on. Modifiers should be chosen very deliberately—and used sparingly.

For an effective example of description, see the selection by Terry Tempest Williams (p. 655).

Writing a Dialogue

A dialogue is a conversation between two or more people—as in an interview, where ideas and opinions are exchanged, or in fiction or nonfiction writing, where a conversation is reproduced or imagined. To write such a conversation, you need to know something about the way the participants think, how they view the world, even the way they speak. Writing a fictional dialogue thus requires—and allows—imaginative role playing. Here are some suggestions for creating one:

- Try to put yourself within the minds of the characters, and consider how they might respond to each other. Look closely at the typical attitudes, interests, habits, and expressions used by your characters. Try to reproduce them.
- It's not enough just to have characters "talk"; you have to decide on a subject for them to talk about. The liveliest dialogues usually feature some exchange of ideas or opinions.
- Set the dialogue in a particular place and time.
- A dialogue can be a stimulating way to respond to a reading. Imagine a dialogue among yourself and some friends on the reading—or place yourself in conversation with the writer. What would you like to say to Jessica Cohen (p. 191) or Mary Shelley (p. 274)? What might they say to you?

Evaluating

Writing an evaluation involves making and justifying judgments. First, you need to determine the appropriate criteria for the evaluation. Obviously, you wouldn't use the same standards in evaluating an elementary school play that you would in reviewing one produced by the Yale Repertory Theater. In most reviews, it is best to take a clear position. Don't make your evaluation so subtle that no one can tell what your stance is. Here are some suggestions for writing an evaluation:

- Determine the appropriate criteria for the evaluation. Sometimes these standards will be obvious or given. In other cases, you will have to establish and define them. Readers will want to know why you are applying certain measures so that they can determine whether to trust your opinions.
- Measure your subject according to these standards.
- Base your evaluation on clear and sufficient evidence. A good evaluation is based on tangible facts and compelling arguments.
- Let readers see how you arrived at your judgment. For example, if you are raising doubts about the competence of an author, make clear what led you to that conclusion. If you are evaluating something visual, include illustrations if possible.
- Arrange your arguments in logical order—perhaps in order of increasing importance. Sometimes you can bolster your argument by comparing and contrasting your subject with objects or ideas already familiar to your readers.

For an example of evaluation, see the selection by Todd Oppenheimer (p. 298).

Exploring

The point of exploratory writing is to examine subjects imaginatively, so such pieces are often more tentative than reports or more purely argumentative writing. Exploratory essays allow you to take risks, to jump into controversies too complex to be resolved easily. So when you want to explore an issue in writing, try to go beyond predictable and safe positions. Following are some strategies for doing so:

- Read a series of provocative articles from various perspectives. Talk with friends or classmates. Reach for dialogue, discussion, and debate.
- Be prepared for multiple drafts. Your best ideas are likely to emerge during the composing process.
- Be open to alternative views and voices, especially those that are heard less frequently. Bring other writers into the discussion.
- As the essay evolves, show it to interested readers and ask for their frank responses. Incorporate questions, debates, or other material into

the discussion. Dialogue can be a particularly stimulating technique for exploration.

- Don't expect to wrap up this kind of writing with a neat bow. Be prepared for gaps and gaffes. Exploratory writing often produces more questions than answers.

For examples of exploratory writing, see the essays by Wendy Shalit (p. 251), Andrew Sullivan (p. 380), and Zora Neale Hurston (p. 414).

Freewriting

Freewriting is a technique for generating ideas. When you freewrite about something, you follow ideas to see where they lead. Freewriting in response to an essay might be prompted by particular words, phrases, passages, or images that you have highlighted while reading. It can also be useful for exploring connections between two or three different selections. Here are some specific tips for freewriting:

- One way to get started is by answering a question—for instance, "What does this topic make me think of?" or "When I think of this topic, what do I feel?"
- Write nonstop for a fixed period of time—five or ten minutes, perhaps. Don't stop during that time; the point is to generate as much material as you can.
- If you can't think of anything to write, put down a nonsense phrase or repeat a key word just to keep your pen or cursor moving.
- Don't stop to question or correct your work while freewriting. Forget about style and correctness. Get the intellectual juices flowing.
- After freewriting, read the words you have produced to recover the ideas you may have generated. If you have come up with observations worthy of more exploration, make those ideas the focus of more freewriting.

Interviewing

We routinely ask people questions to satisfy our curiosity, but to turn a conversation with an interesting and knowledgeable person into a useful interview, you need to do your homework. The first step is to decide who you wish to interview—and you don't have to limit yourself to experts. Friends and classmates have knowledge and opinions you might tap by interviewing them. Think of an interview as a high-powered conversation, a new way to learn. Here are some suggestions for arranging, conducting, and recording an interview:

- Determine the purpose of your interview, and make sure it relates closely to your topic.
- Call or write ahead for an appointment, and specify how long the interview will take. If you want to tape-record the session, ask for permission to do so.
- Prepare your questions in advance, perhaps brainstorming a preliminary list, then augmenting it with who-what-where-when-why-how items. Arrange your queries in a sensible order, perhaps beginning with more factual questions and then moving to more complex questions of opinion.
- Prepare some open-ended questions—the kind that can't be answered in a word or phrase. Give yourself leeway to take the conversation down any paths that open up spontaneously.
- Try out your questions on one or two people to make sure they are clear and understandable. If not, revise.
- Get any equipment you need ready beforehand—from your pen to your tape recorder, laptop, and so on—and make sure the recording device you plan to use is working properly before you begin the interview.
- Be on time!
- Record your subject's responses carefully, later double-checking with him or her any direct quotations you might want to use. Even if you are taping, take notes.
- Record time, date, place, and other pertinent information about the conversation for your records.
- After an interview, summarize the information briefly in your own words.
- Remember to follow up with a thank-you note or email.

Writing a Letter to the Editor

A familiar kind of persuasive writing is the letter to the editor, in which writers explain why they agree or disagree with something they've read. Such letters are typically composed in response to positions taken by newspapers, magazines, or journals. In most cases, letters to the editor are spirited arguments, somewhat personal, and carefully targeted.

Letters to the editor follow the conventions of business letters and should be dated and signed. Here are some suggestions for writing one:

- Think about who reads the periodical to which the letter will be sent. Because such a letter is intended for publication, it is usually written more to win the support of other readers than to influence editors or publishers.

- Identify your target article within the first line or two. Let readers know exactly what piece provoked your ire or admiration.
- Make your case quickly. Since space for letters is very limited in most publications, expect to make only one or two points. Execute them powerfully and memorably, using the best examples and reasons you can.
- When appropriate, use irony, satire, or humor.

Narrating

Whereas descriptions usually refer to stationary things, narratives depict motion, whether it be the action of a single person or the unfurling of a complex historical event, such as a war or social movement. When you narrate, you usually tell a story of some kind. But a narrative may also explain *how something occurred* (analyzing a process) or *why something happened* (tracing cause and effect). Here are some suggestions for narrating:

- Place the events you are discussing in a meaningful order, usually chronological—first this happened, then this, then this, and so on.
- Provide necessary background information by answering the questions who, what, where, when, why, and how the events occurred.
- Most narratives call for some description. Flesh out any characters and describe any scenic details necessary to the narrative. Consider using appropriate images.
- Use transitional phrases (*then, next, on the following day*) or series (*in the spring, during the summer, later in the year*) to keep the sequence of the narrative clear. Remember, however, that the sequence doesn't always have to be chronological (you've certainly seen flashbacks in movies).

For examples of narration, see the selections by Mary Shelley (p. 274) and Maxine Hong Kingston (p. 391).

Writing to an Online Forum or Listserv

In some courses, you may be expected to write about a topic or reading in an online forum or on a listserv. In a topic forum, you typically respond to a prompt on a Web page and read what your classmates have to say there; postings to and from a listserv are exchanged as email messages. Whichever technology is used, electronic discussions provide instantaneous communication and rapid response—which are both their strength and their weakness.

But you can learn to write effectively in these environments with just a little practice.

- If you are the first to post a response to a prompt from an instructor or classmate, address the question directly and thoughtfully; you may be setting the tone for an entire discussion.
- When you join a discussion already in progress, get a feel for the conversation before posting a message. Pay attention to both the content and the tone of the forum. Let your message suggest that you have given due consideration to the thoughts of others who have already contributed to the discussion. Avoid the temptation to fire off just a few quick words in response to a classmate's posting. No one wants to open a message that says simply *You're wrong!* or *I agree.*
- Be sure your message places your ideas in context. Quite often, you'll be responding to a specific question or to messages others have already sent. So sometimes it helps to repeat portions of previous messages in your posting, but don't copy long strings of text. Such repetition may clutter your own message and even make it hard to find.
- Consider how the title of your posting might convey both your context and your point. In most forums, the responses to an original posting will be linked by the familiar abbreviation *Re,* which means "with reference to." You can keep a string of responses going, but vary the title of your message slightly to indicate your own slant.

  Newman's THE IDEA OF A UNIVERSITY
  Re: Newman's THE IDEA OF A UNIVERSITY—Still relevant?
  Re: Newman's THE IDEA OF A UNIVERSITY—Who cares?
  Re: Newman's THE IDEA OF A UNIVERSITY—I care.
  Re: Newman's THE IDEA OF A UNIVERSITY—Kagan cares too.

- Remember to consider differences your group may have, not only in terms of computer compatibility but also in terms of accessibility. Will everyone in your group be able to read what you have posted with ease?
- Edit your posting before you send it. Online communications tend to be less formal than other kinds of writing. But show respect for your classmates by editing messages before you send them into the public square. Remember that you won't be able to recall or correct your blunders once you send a posting electronically.

Parodying

Your appreciation of a written work can't be tested better than by parody. A *parody* is an imitation of an author, a work, or an attitude written with a humorous and sometimes critical edge. Parody succeeds when readers recognize both your target and your criticism; they should laugh at the wit in your mimicking something they too have experienced.

When you write a parody, you are in certain ways collaborating with other writers. You will necessarily learn much about the way they think and use language. Here are some suggestions for writing a parody:

- Choose a distinctive idea or work to parody. The more recognizable an attitude or famous a work is, the easier it will be to poke fun at. But even the most vapid work can be mocked for its dullness.
- Look for familiar subjects, motifs, images, or opinions, and distort them enough to be funny but not so much that the original idea becomes unrecognizable.
- When parodying a well-known work or writer, try shifting from a serious theme to a frivolous one; for example, imagine a pompous opera critic reviewing Eminem's latest video or a dour news commentator interviewing the ghost of Elvis.
- Pinpoint the habits of language ordinarily used to discuss your subject—typical sentence openers, preferred jargon, distinctive patterns of repetition, favorite sentence patterns, unusual punctuation. Then exaggerate those habits.
- Don't make your parody too long. Parody is a form of wit, and brevity is its soul.
- Above all, have fun. When a parody ceases being funny, it becomes simply tedious imitation.

For an example of parody, see the article from *The Onion,* "New National Parks Website Makes National Parks Obsolete" (p. 366).

Writing a Position Paper

A position paper is a short (often one-page or one-screen) argument that can sometimes be exploratory. In it, you will usually present a thesis—a statement that needs to be proved or defended. But such a paper is often assigned to jump-start discussions or to get various points of view on the table, so feel free to take risks and examine new approaches. A position paper need not have the gloss of a polished argument, and its language can be livelier than that of more formal academic arguments. It should stimulate your readers—often your classmates—to respond actively to your ideas. Here are some suggestions for writing a position paper:

- Begin by taking a stand on a subject. Find a statement you can defend reasonably well.
- Support your thesis with various kinds of evidence—arguments, examples, statistics, illustrations, expert opinions, and so on.

- If the position paper is very brief, suggest the direction a fuller argument might take.
- Write an open-ended conclusion, qualifying your original thesis or pointing to avenues for further study.

For an example of a position paper, see the selection by Ward Churchill (p. 536).

Proposing Solutions

Proposals identify a problem and suggest action that will remedy the problem. You need to convince readers first that a problem exists and is serious, then that your solution is a feasible remedy. Often you will try as well to inspire your readers to take some action.

- To demonstrate that the problem exists, give examples and cite evidence such as statistics or the testimony of experts. Use photographs or other visuals if appropriate.
- Consider your audience. Are readers likely to be aware of the problem? Try to connect the problem to concerns they might have.
- To convince readers to accept your solution, you need to show that it is feasible—and that it is better than other solutions that might reasonably be proposed. Again, visuals may help here.

For an example of an essay that proposes a solution, see the selection by Adrienne Rich (p. 71).

Keeping a Reading Log

Many writers use reading logs to record their feelings and detailed impressions about what they're reading and thinking. Your instructor may ask you to keep one and turn it in as part of your work for a course. You may decide to keep such a log in a notebook or on your computer. For a computer reading log, make sure to set up a special folder or file for it, label it clearly, and then save each entry with an identifiable title. Here are some suggestions for keeping a reading log:

- If you want to remember what you've read, take time to summarize the text or list its main ideas. You may want to keep a double-entry log—one set of pages reserved for summaries, paraphrases, and quotations, and another set of pages reserved for your reactions and responses to what you are reading.

- Write out your immediate reactions to the text. These may include memorable lines; things that made you angry, sad, puzzled, or delighted; or things that you want to know more about. Later, in a more extended comment, summarize your thoughts about the text. Reflect on what in the piece and in your experience may have shaped your reactions.
- Make some notes about the author's perspective, where he or she seems to be coming from, noting places in the text that provide clues to the perspective.
- Write in an informal, exploratory style, almost as if you were talking to yourself.
- Date your entries and be sure to identify the text.
- Look at your commentary in the context of your notes on other readings. Do you see any useful or interesting connections?

For examples of writing that is similar to reading log entries, see the editors' responses to Anthony Brandt's essay (p. 213).

Reporting

Doing a report is one of the most common academic assignments. Reports are explanations that transfer information from writers to readers. That information may come directly from the writers' minds or from other sources of information—from traditional libraries to field research to computer networks.

- Focus a report on a thesis, a clear statement of purpose. The thesis is the main point or controlling idea of a piece of writing. A thesis statement makes a promise to readers, telling them what to expect, and it limits the subject matter and scope of your report.
- Acknowledge any sources you use.
- Define any terms your readers are unlikely to know.
- Arrange information according to a plan your readers can easily follow. For example, a report on the major events of the Cold War could follow a chronological organization: first, second, third. A report on the Cold War policies of Joseph Stalin and Harry Truman might use a structure comparing and contrasting the two leaders.
- Use visuals if they will help readers follow your points.
- Conclude by summarizing your work and exploring its implications.
- Give the report a concise, factual, and descriptive title.

For an example of a report, see the selection by Mark Clayton (p. 207).

WORKING WITH SOURCES

Much of your college writing will involve the use of source materials. Following are guidelines for evaluating, quoting, paraphrasing, and summarizing sources.

Evaluating Sources

Not all sources are equally authoritative or useful. Here are some general tips for evaluating sources; consult your instructor, librarian, or writing handbook for further advice.

- Note whether a source is a primary or secondary one.
- Learn the differences between scholarly and trade books, and choose sources appropriate to your work. The claims in scholarly books are systematically documented and carefully reviewed; trade books may be just as factual and reliable, but they typically lack formal documentation.
- Understand the differences between scholarly journals and popular magazines. Both may serve your research needs, but in different ways. Journals written for specialists will often be highly technical and, consequently, difficult for people outside a profession to read; popular magazines serve wider audiences and present more accessible—if less authoritative—information.
- Take advantage of the databases that are available through your library. Most college libraries pay for subscriptions to the most reliable and credible databases, such as LexisNexis, thus giving you free access to them.
- Understand the limits of commercial online sources. Web sites, for example, vary enormously in quality, from those carefully maintained by institutions and professional organizations to playful home pages posted by individuals. Be especially careful with sites associated with familiar figures or institutions but not actually maintained or authorized by them.

Quoting

Quoting involves noting a source's *exact words.* In working with the selections in this book, you will have many opportunities to use direct quotation. Many of the headnotes that introduce each reading show examples of direct quotation.

- Copy quotations *carefully,* with punctuation, capitalization, and spelling exactly as in the original.
- Use ellipses to indicate any omitted words.

- Bracket any words you need to add to the quotation.
- Enclose the quotation in quotation marks.

Paraphrasing

A paraphrase accurately states all the relevant information from a passage *in your own words and phrasing,* without any additional comment or elaboration. Use paraphrases when you want to cite ideas from a source but have no need to quote exact words.

- Include the main points and some important details from the original, in the same order in which they are presented in the source.
- Use your own words and sentence structures. If you want to include especially memorable language from the original, enclose it in quotation marks.
- Leave out your own comments and reactions.
- Recheck the paraphrase against the original to be sure that the words and structures are your own and that they express the author's meaning accurately.

Summarizing

A summary concisely restates key ideas *in your own words.* Sometimes you may need to summarize something in a sentence or two: "In *The Culture of Disbelief,* Stephen L. Carter argues that American culture pressures people with strong religious beliefs not to act on their principles." Often a more detailed synopsis is necessary. Preparing such a summary takes some planning. Here are some suggestions:

- Outline the text you are summarizing. Identify its main points, subpoints, and key bits of supporting evidence.
- Flesh out the outline with necessary details, taking care to show the connections between key ideas.
- Check that your concise version of a longer work can stand on its own. Remember that your readers may not have access to the original piece, so all references need to be clear.
- Double-check against the piece you are summarizing to make sure the wording in your summary is your own.

For an example of summary, see portions of Barbara Dafoe Whitehead's essay (p. 667).

Deciding Whether to Quote, Paraphrase, or Summarize

- *Quote*

  Wording that expresses a point so perfectly that you cannot improve or shorten it without weakening the meaning you need

  Authors' opinions you wish to emphasize

  Respected authorities whose opinions support your own ideas

  Authors whose opinions challenge or vary from others in the field
- *Paraphrase*

  Passages that you do not wish to quote but whose details you wish to note *fully*
- *Summarize*

  Long passages whose *main points* you wish to record *selectively*

Integrating Sources into Your Writing

Integrate quotations, paraphrases, and summaries into your own writing carefully, often by using a signal phrase such as *he said* or *she remarks*. Choose the verbs you use to introduce source material carefully; be sure they express your thoughts accurately. Notice, for instance, the difference between saying someone "said," "claimed," or "asserted."

In the following sentence, "As Richard deCordova notes in a memorable phrase, the studios wanted to convince millions of moviegoers that 'the real hero behaved just like the reel hero'" (Gallager, 2), the signal verb *notes* makes it clear that the quotation is by deCordova and that the author agrees with it: If the author had wanted to indicate that deCordova's point is more open to disagreement or that other authorities might disagree with it, she would have chosen a different verb such as *claims* or *asserts*. For effective integration of sources, see the many quotations in Robert D. King's essay (p. 428).

Integrating Visuals into Your Writing

Remember that any visuals you use need to be as carefully integrated into your text as quotations, paraphrases, or summaries. In addition, make sure that you introduce each visual and comment on it in some way. Finally, label (as figures or tables) and number (Figure 1, Figure 2, and so on) all visuals, provide a caption that includes the source information, and cite the source in your list of works cited. (See, for example, **Figures 2.2 and 2.3,** which are numbered and have captions with source information.) Even if you create a visual (such as a bar graph) by using information from a source (such as the Gallup Poll), you must cite that source. If you use a photograph you took yourself, cite that as well.

Acknowledging Sources

When quoting, paraphrasing, or summarizing sources in formal essays, reports, or research projects, be sure to acknowledge all sources according to the conventions required by your field or instructor. In this time of instant access to information on the Internet and the Web, it is especially important to avoid cutting and pasting anything from an online source into your own text without full citation.

Plagiarism, using the words of others without citation, has been much in the news in the last few years, with at least two distinguished historians accused of using the work of others without acknowledgment and online companies such as <turnitin.com> springing up to try to ferret out cheaters. So it's well worth taking extra care to make sure you have not been careless or sloppy in your use of sources.

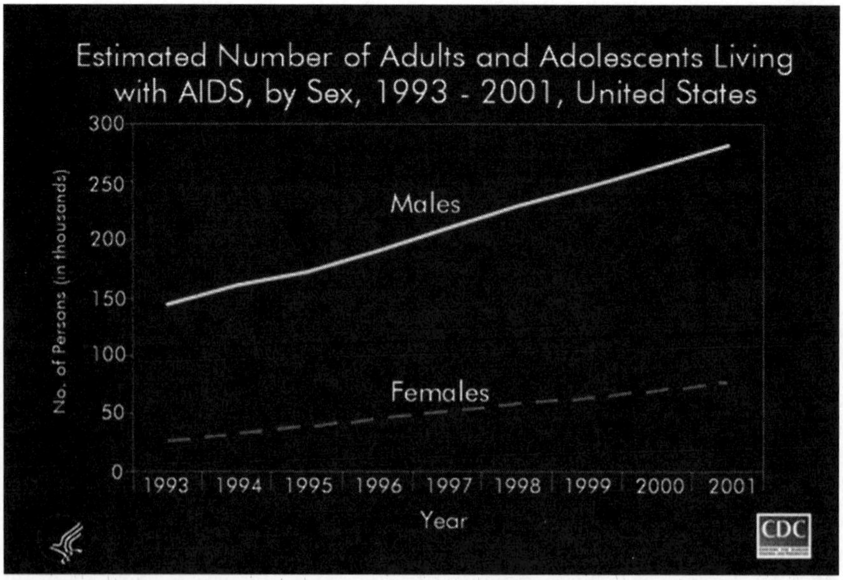

Figure 2.2. Estimated U.S. AIDS Cases by Sex, 1993–2001. Source: Centers for Disease Control and Prevention (CDC).

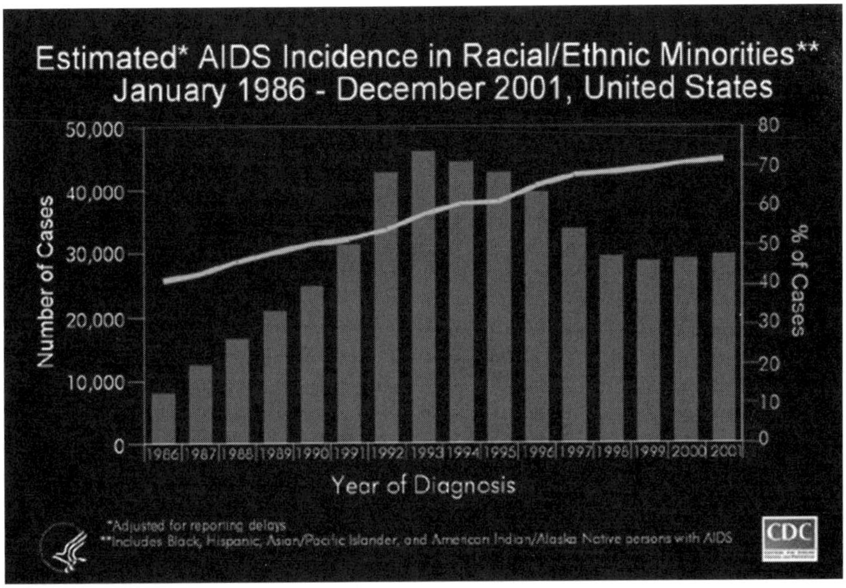

Figure 2.3. Estimated U.S. AIDS Incidence in Racial/Ethnic Minorities, 1986–2001. Source: CDC.

WORKING WITH OTHERS

The title for this book recalls a remark by philosopher Hannah Arendt that "for excellence, the presence of others is always required." Nowhere is Arendt's observation more accurate than in the college community. Your college coursework will call on you to read, write, and research a vast amount of material. But you will not—or need not—do all that reading, writing, and researching alone. Instead, you can be part of a broad conversation that includes all the texts you read; all the writing you produce; all the discussions you have with teachers, friends, family members, and classmates; all the observations and interviews you conduct. Throughout this book, we draw on Arendt's concept—from our title to the way we group readings in conversation with one another to the many assignments that ask you to work with others.

Collaboration can play an important part in all the writing you do, first if you talk with others about your topic and your plans for approaching it, then if you seek responses to your draft and gather suggestions for improving it. In much the same way, reading can be done "with others"—first by entering into mental conversation with the author and with the social and historical forces at work shaping the author's text, then by comparing your understanding of the text with that of other readers and using points of agreement or disagreement as the basis for further analysis.

As you read this book, the most immediate and valuable of your collaborators may be your classmates. Indeed, you can learn a great deal by listening carefully both to them and to your instructor. You can profit even more by talking over issues with them, by comparing notes and ideas with them, and by using them as a first and very important audience for your writing. They will inevitably offer you new perspectives, new ways of seeing and knowing.

- Once you establish a group, consider trading phone numbers, email addresses, and schedules, and set a time to meet.
- Set an agenda for each meeting. If you intend to study or compare certain readings, be sure everyone knows in advance and brings the essay or book to the meeting. Perhaps begin by brainstorming major questions group members have about the reading.
- Use the group to work through difficult readings. If a reading is especially long, have each member take one section to explain and "teach" to the others.
- If the group corresponds via email, be sure to create a mailbox for the project where you can collect and keep all relevant correspondence.
- If you need to prepare something as a group, decide on a fair and effective means of dividing the task. Assign each group member specific duties. Arrange for a time to meet when those individual duties will have been accomplished. At the meeting, work to review the various parts and put them together.
- If a project involves a group presentation or report, figure out what each member will contribute. Plan all the work that is to be done, and schedule any necessary meetings. For the presentation, make sure every group member is involved in some way. Decide on any visual aids or handouts in advance, and prepare them carefully. Finally, *practice the presentation.* Everyone will benefit from a dress rehearsal. If it's possible to get someone to videotape the rehearsal, do so; you'll learn a great deal from watching yourself do an actual presentation.
- Most important, listen to every member of the group carefully and respectfully; everyone's ideas must be taken into consideration. If conflict arises—and in any lively and healthy collaboration, it will—explore all areas of the conflict openly and fairly before seeking a resolution.
- At each meeting, take time to assess the effectiveness of the group. Consider these questions: What has the group accomplished so far? How has the group been most helpful? How has it been least helpful? What have you personally contributed? What has each of the others contributed? How can all members make the group more effective?

A SAMPLE CRITICAL RESPONSE ESSAY

We have outlined in this chapter some of the ways you may be asked to respond to selected readings in your writing classes. A type of response you are most likely to be asked to do is a critical response essay (guidelines for writing a critical analysis begin on p. 24). Read the following critical response essay by Jennifer E. Smith to see how one student responds to the selection in this book by J. Michael Bishop, "Enemies of Promise" (p. 280).

JENNIFER E. SMITH
Questioning the Promises of Science

Jennifer E. Smith wrote "Questioning the Promises of Science" when she was a first-year student at The Ohio State University. Her instructor had asked the class to choose one essay from the chapter on science and technology in this text and respond critically to it. Smith chose the piece by J. Michael Bishop, "Enemies of Promise."

It is overwhelming to think of the number of questions that science seeks to answer. Science tries to explain how every aspect of the universe works; it is indeed a broad topic. For this reason, as J. Michael Bishop concludes in his essay "Enemies of Promise," educating the public about the advancements, or even general knowledge, of science is difficult. Thus, Bishop points out, the scientific ignorance of the public leads to a fear of science: "[r]esistance to science is born of fear." Though Bishop, on behalf of the scientific community, takes responsibility for neglecting public scientific education, he seems to accuse all those who question science of suffering from ignorance. Though I agree with Bishop's point about the lack of education in the sciences, I disagree with his approach. Bishop does not prove his point well in "Enemies of Promise"; he does not offer sufficient counterarguments to his postmodern detractors, nor does he offer any solutions to the problems with education, which he claims are the cause of postmodern critiques.

Bishop begins "Enemies of Promise" by marveling over the "fruits of scientific inquiry" and questioning why "science today is increasingly mistrusted and under attack." Throughout the essay, Bishop seems too proud of the scientific field to admit that current scientific methods are less than perfect. Even in the age of computer technology, scientists, *humans,* still perform the research. When humans are involved, there will always be some degree of bias; business and politics will have their influence. Though these biases may be minimal and are usually unintended, they still exist; science is not immune to human nature. Bishop does not recognize this and angrily dismisses the postmodern view, which calls science on its biases, as "arrant nonsense." The postmodern view may be an exaggerated response to the frustration associated with the politics of science, but these critics do raise some valid points and should not be dismissed. It is ironic that the scientific community, which was born out of questioning that which was assumed to be known, is now angered when its own knowledge is questioned. Bishop shows this anger throughout the essay when he responds to his critics. He refers to postmodernism as "either a strategy for advancement in parochial precincts . . . or a display of ignorance." Instead of debating Václav Havel's remarks on science, Bishop accuses him of using "angry words" whose "precise meaning is elusive." Bishop also refers to all questioners of science as a "chorus of criticism and doubt."

While his easy dismissal of some critics is troubling, Bishop does offer a good response to the criticisms of Brown and Lamm. Brown is frustrated by the "'knowledge paradox,'" which Bishop paraphrases as "an expansion of fundamental knowledge accompanied by an increase in social problems." Lamm no longer believes "that biomedical research contributes to the improvement of human health" because of the lack of access in the United States to these health care advancements as well as the abundance of social diseases in today's society. Bishop points out that Brown and Lamm are placing blame on science for "the failures of individuals or society to use the knowledge that science has provided." He also notes that critics often expect too much, too soon, from science and fail to realize that scientific study is dependent on feasibility and that results are often unpredictable.

Bishop continues "Enemies of Promise" by noting the stereotypes that the public has about scientists themselves and how these stereotypes contribute to the general mistrust of science. According to him, the public has "exaggerated expectations about what science can accomplish" because of the rapid successes of science in the past. Bishop then attacks the 1992 film *Lorenzo's Oil,* equating it with some sort of anti-science propaganda. The movie does portray scientists according to common stereotypes; as Bishop points out, it shows them as "insensitive, close-minded, and self-serving." However, Bishop does little to disprove this stereotype; in fact, throughout the essay he shows signs of possessing all of these characteristics. He is obviously close-minded in response to his critics, especially postmodernists. He seems insensitive in his discussion of the true life story behind *Lorenzo's Oil* and in the way he discusses other people's scientific ignorance. Though Bishop is not obviously "self-serving," he does seem overly proud of his role as a scientist and of the role of science in general. Describing our age as one "of scientific triumph," he sees science as "one of the great, ennobling tasks of humankind" and biomedical research as "one of the great triumphs of human endeavor."

Bishop begins his conclusion to "Enemies of Promise" well with his discussion of the difficulties in educating people about science. He admits how far behind the United States is in the process and notes that most scientists specialize and are often ignorant about fields of science outside their own. Bishop correctly places blame for this lack of education with the scientific community. However, as soon as he notes this problem, instead of offering a solution, he returns to praising science with flowery language: "We of science have begun the quest well, by building a method of ever-increasing power, a method that can illuminate all that is in the natural world." The concluding paragraph is consistent with the rest of the essay in that it focuses too much on building up science as the quintessence of human reason rather than addressing the real problems of educating others about science.

Bishop's pride seems to have prevented him from providing a proper focus in his essay. For his argument to be a convincing one, the focus should have been directed toward the education problem. Bishop concludes that those who question science do so out of ignorance, yet he offers no suggestions for how to diminish this ignorance. Instead, the whole essay seems to focus on asserting how great science is, not with evidence but with catchy phrases. As a result, this essay seems to support the stereotypes that the public has about scientists and their egocentricity.

Chicago

Football 2002

We found this brochure online, under the University of Chicago home page, by following links to *Art, Culture, and Athletics;* then to the *Athletic Department;* then to *Football;* and then to *Prospective Student Athletes.* Look carefully at the cover of this brochure, reproduced on the preceding page, and note the position of the various elements, the foreground and background, and the action conveyed. ■ What in the picture first draws your eye, and what message does that central image send—to both you and to prospective student athletes? ■ What effect does the university seal and the name *Chicago* have on this image? ■ If the primary audience for this brochure is prospective football players at the University of Chicago, who might the secondary audiences be? ■ What message about the University of Chicago is this brochure intended to send?

3

Education: The Idea of a University

If then a practical end must be assigned to a University course, I say it is that of training good members of society.

JOHN HENRY NEWMAN, *The Idea of a University*

Our graduates will have an understanding of interdependence and global competence, distinctive technical and educational skills, the experience and abilities to contribute to California's high-quality workforce, the critical thinking abilities to be productive citizens, and the social responsibility and skills to be community builders.

CALIFORNIA STATE UNIVERSITY, MONTEREY BAY, *Our Vision Statement*

The American tradition, in learning as well as jazz and activism, is improvisatory. There are as many ways to become an educated American as there are Americans.

JON SPAYDE, *Learning in the Key of Life*

What does a woman need to know to become a self-conscious, self-defining human being?

ADRIENNE RICH, *What Does a Woman Need to Know?*

What has emerged on campus in recent years . . . is a *politics of difference,* a troubling, volatile politics in which each group justifies itself, its sense of worth and its pursuit of power, through difference alone.

SHELBY STEELE, *The Recoloring of Campus Life*

Science, or knowledge production more generally, has always had deep connections to the general political economy of its time. . . . Thus, we cannot argue for some untainted "ivory tower" or "golden age" of institutional independence. We need instead to articulate the values and goals that should direct a wide range of commercial ventures on campus.

JENNIFER L. CROISSANT, *Can This Campus Be Bought?*

If the canon itself is the answer to our educational inequities, why has it historically invited few and denied many?

MIKE ROSE, *Lives on the Boundary*

Football is the S.U.V. of the college campus: aggressively big, resource-guzzling, lots and lots of fun and potentially destructive of everything around it.

MICHAEL SOKOLOVE, *Football Is a Sucker's Game*

The greatest shortcoming, I believe, of most attempts at liberal education today, with their individualized, unfocused, scattered curricula, and ill-defined purpose, is their failure to enhance the students' understanding of their status as free citizens of a free society and the responsibilities it entails.

DONALD KAGAN, *What Is a Liberal Education?*

We real cool. We / Left school. GWENDOLYN BROOKS, *We Real Cool*

Introduction

YOU MAY BE SURPRISED to learn that until fairly recently in the United States most people either did not have the resources to attend college or were excluded from the majority of colleges for other reasons (such as race or gender). Today, however, nearly half of all high school graduates extend their education at a two-year or four-year college or university. And many older individuals who had never pursued higher education or had left college for some reason are now returning to the classroom. More and more people are attending college these days—but what kind of education are they receiving?

In fact, questions about the purpose of education have been under scrutiny at least since Socrates was put on trial in 399 B.C. on charges of corrupting the youth of Athens by his teaching of philosophy. But no one seems to agree these days in the United States, any more than in ancient Greece, about what the role of higher education should be. Who should be encouraged to attend colleges and universities—and who should not be? Should education be a mechanism for advancing the welfare of the nation—augmenting its productivity, management skills, and technology and preserving the quality of its workforce? Should it be an instrument of social change—teaching ideas of social justice, adjusting to new demographics in the population it serves, and providing the rationale for radical reforms of the economic order? Should it exist primarily to stimulate the intellect and the imagination of students? Or should schooling serve other or multiple purposes?

In this chapter, we have selected readings that bring different perspectives—and offer very different answers—to these central questions about the purposes of higher education. We hope these readings will lead you to consider such questions yourself, to think hard and long about what higher education is for and what it *should* be for in the future. Before you begin reading, however, you may want to think over some of the issues raised in this chapter. Here are some questions to get you started thinking:

- What are your reasons for coming to college? Do you think your reasons correspond to your college's or university's goals for its students?
- In what ways was your decision to attend college shaped or influenced by factors outside your control?
- What should be the goals of higher education? If you were president of your college or university, what would you list as the school's aims? What would be your top priorities?

• • •

JOHN HENRY NEWMAN
The Idea of a University

JOHN HENRY NEWMAN's The Idea of a University *is among the most famous attempts to define a liberal arts education. Originally written in 1852 in response to a papal proposal for a Roman Catholic university in Ireland,* The Idea of a University *served as an intellectual manifesto for Catholics, who had long been an oppressed minority in the British Isles. Full emancipation occurred for them only in 1829; prior to that date, Catholics had been denied political rights in England and Ireland as well as admission to the great British universities, Oxford and Cambridge.*

Newman (1801–90), a well-known Anglican priest who had converted to the Roman church, wrote The Idea of a University *to explore what a Catholic university would be like—how it might merge religious and secular concerns. He was also responding to a world growing ever more secular in its interests, more scientific in its methods, more utilitarian in its philosophy. Revolutions in technology and industrial organization seemed to be reshaping every human endeavor, including the university.*

Newman had reservations about these changes, many of which we take for granted today, such as the division of universities into various "schools" (arts, sciences, professional schools), the selection by students of their own programs of study, and the establishment of areas of specialization (what we would call majors*). His aim in this essay is to defend the value of learning for its own sake.*

The Idea of a University *is an example of deliberative rhetoric: Newman is both recommending and defending the proposal for a Catholic university. He faces both an entrenched Anglican tradition and a scholarly community leaning in the direction of what is today called* secular humanism. *The following excerpts from this book-length work do not focus on religious issues, however. Instead, they explain several of Newman's goals for the liberal arts university.* —J.R.

DISCOURSE V
KNOWLEDGE ITS OWN END

1

I have said that all branches of knowledge are connected together, because the subject-matter of knowledge is intimately united in itself, as being the acts and the work of the Creator. Hence it is that the Sciences, into which our knowledge may be said to be cast, have multiplied bearings one on another, and an internal sympathy, and admit, or rather demand, comparison and adjustment. They complete, correct, balance each other. This consideration, if well-founded, must be taken into account, not only as regards the attainment of truth, which is their common end, but as regards the influence which they exercise upon those whose education consists in the study of them. I have said already, that to give undue prominence to one is to be unjust to another; to neglect or supersede these is to divert those from their proper object. It is to unsettle the boundary lines between science and science, to disturb their action, to destroy the harmony which binds them together. Such a proceeding will have a corresponding effect when introduced into a place of education. There is no science but tells a different tale, when viewed as a portion of a whole, from what it is likely to suggest when taken by itself, without the safeguard, as I may call it, of others.

Let me make use of an illustration. In the combination of colors, very different effects are produced by a difference in their selection and juxtaposition; red, green, and white, change their shades, according to the contrast to which they are submitted. And, in like manner, the drift and meaning of a branch of knowledge varies with the company in which it is introduced to the student. If his reading is confined simply to one subject, however such division of labor may favor the advancement of a particular pursuit, a point into which I do not here enter, certainly it has a tendency to contract his mind. If it is incorporated with others, it depends on those others as to the kind of influence which it exerts upon him. Thus the Classics, which in England are the means of refining the taste, have in France subserved the spread of revolutionary and deistical doctrines. In Metaphysics, again, *Butler's Analogy of Religion** which has had so much to do with the conversion to the Catholic faith of members of the University of Oxford, appeared to Pitt* and others, who had received a different training, to operate only in the direction of infidelity. And so again, Watson, Bishop of Llandaff,* as I think he tells us in the narrative of his life, felt the science of Mathematics to indispose the mind to religious belief, while others see in its investigations the best parallel, and thereby defense, of the Christian Mysteries. In like manner, I suppose, Arcesilas* would not have handled logic as Aristotle, nor Aristotle have criticized poets as Plato; yet reasoning and poetry are subject to scientific rules.

It is a great point then to enlarge the range of studies which a University professes, even for the sake of the students; and, though they cannot pursue every subject which is open to them, they will be the gainers by living among those and under those who represent the whole circle. This I conceive to be the advantage of a seat of universal learning, considered as a place of education. An assemblage of learned men, zealous for their own sciences, and rivals

---

Butler's Analogy of Religion: a defense of Christian revelation (1736) by Joseph Butler (1692–1752)

Pitt: William Pitt (1708–78), British parliamentarian and orator

Watson, Bishop of Llandaff: Richard Watson (1737–1816), a professor of chemistry and divinity

Arcesilas: Greek philosopher (c. 316–241 B.C.) who advocated rational skepticism

of each other, are brought, by familiar intercourse and for the sake of intellectual peace, to adjust together the claims and relations of their respective subjects of investigation. They learn to respect, to consult, to aid each other. Thus is created a pure and clear atmosphere of thought, which the student also breathes, though in his own case he only pursues a few sciences out of the multitude. He profits by an intellectual tradition, which is independent of particular teachers, which guides him in his choice of subjects, and duly interprets for him those which he chooses. He apprehends the great outlines of knowledge, the principles on which it rests, the scale of its parts, its lights and its shades, its great points and its little, as he otherwise cannot apprehend them. Hence it is that his education is called "Liberal." A habit of mind is formed which lasts through life, of which the attributes are, freedom, equitableness, calmness, moderation, and wisdom; or what in a former Discourse I have ventured to call a philosophical habit. This then I would assign as the special fruit of the education furnished at a University, as contrasted with other places of teaching or modes of teaching. This is the main purpose of a University in its treatment of its students.

And now the question is asked me, What is the *use* of it? and my answer will constitute the main subject of the Discourses which are to follow.

• • •

Discourse VII
Knowledge Viewed in Relation to Professional Skill

10

But I must bring these extracts to an end. Today I have confined myself to saying that that training of the intellect, which is best for the individual himself, best enables him to discharge his duties to society. The Philosopher, indeed, and the man of the world differ in their very notion, but the methods, by which they are respectively formed, are pretty much the same. The Philosopher has the same command of matters of thought, which the true citizen and gentleman has of matters of business and conduct. If then a practical end must be assigned to a University course, I say it is that of training good members of society. Its art is the art of social life, and its end is fitness for the world. It neither confines its views to particular professions on the one hand, nor creates heroes or inspires genius on the other. Works indeed of genius fall under no art; heroic minds come under no rule; a University is not a birthplace of poets or of immortal authors, of founders of schools, leaders of colonies, or conquerors of nations. It does not promise a generation of Aristotles or Newtons, of Napoleons or Washingtons, of Raphaels or Shakespeares, though such miracles of nature it has before now contained within its precincts. Nor is it content on the other hand with forming the critic or the experimentalist, the economist or the engineer, though such too it includes within its scope. But a University training is the great ordinary means to a great but ordinary end; it aims at raising the intellectual tone of society, at cultivating the public mind, at purifying the national taste, at supplying true principles to popular enthusiasm and fixed aims to popular aspiration, at giving enlargement and sobriety to the ideas of the age, at facilitating the exercise of political power, and refining the intercourse of private life. It is the education which gives a man a clear conscious view of his own opinions and judgments, a truth in developing them, an eloquence in expressing them, and a force in urging them. It teaches him to see things as they are, to go right to the point, to disentangle a skein of thought, to detect what is sophistical, and to discard what is irrelevant. It prepares him to fill any post with credit, and to master any subject with facility. It shows him how to accommodate himself to others, how to throw himself into their state of mind, how to bring before them his own, how to influence them, how to come to an understanding with them, how to bear with them. He is at home in any society, he has common ground with every class; he knows when to speak and when to be silent; he is able to converse, he is able to listen; he can ask a question pertinently, and gain a lesson seasonably, when he has nothing to impart himself; he is ever ready, yet never in the way; he is a pleasant companion, and a comrade you can depend upon; he knows when to be serious and when to trifle, and he has a sure tact which enables him to trifle with gracefulness and to be serious with effect. He has the repose of a mind which lives in itself, while it lives in the world, and which has resources for its happiness at home when it cannot go abroad. He has a gift which serves him in public, and supports him in retirement, without which good fortune is but vulgar, and with which failure and disappointment have a charm. The art which tends to make a man all this, is in the object which it pursues as useful as the art of wealth or the art of health, though it is less susceptible of method, and less tangible, less certain, less complete in its result.

QUESTIONING THE TEXT

1. Examine the goals Newman explicitly provides for the university in the passage from Discourse VII. Do these goals still seem relevant today? Why, or why not? If you keep a reading log, answer this question there.
2. As you reread Newman's essay, record your reactions to his style in the margins. Does it feel stuffy or solemn? Does it move you or impress you? When you are finished, draw some conclusions from your comments.

3. The introduction emphasizes that Newman's *The Idea of a University* was written in response to changes occurring in the United Kingdom in the nineteenth century. Do any of these changes seem relevant to events in the United States in the twenty-first century?

MAKING CONNECTIONS

4. Would Mike Rose or the students he describes in "Lives on the Boundary" (p. 109) fit into the university Newman describes? Write a two- to three-page essay exploring this issue.
5. Donald Kagan (p. 141) describes Newman as struggling against current opinion from secular and religious quarters in his own time (the mid-nineteenth century). He also outlines some of the challenges posed to Newman's ideas by later thinkers. Discuss the similarities and differences in Newman's and Kagan's ideas of knowledge pursued for its own sake. In what ways do you think discussion of liberal education has changed and in what ways has it remained the same since Newman's era?

JOINING THE CONVERSATION

6. Can Newman's concept of *liberal arts* survive in our world today? Does it deserve to? Why, or why not? Write a position paper on this subject.
7. For a national newsmagazine, write an evaluation of American higher education as you imagine Newman might regard it if he were living today. What might he admire? What would he criticize?
8. With a group of classmates, discuss the usefulness of the education you have had in high school and college. Which courses of study seem to have the most direct application to daily life? Which, if any, seem designed primarily as learning for its own sake?

THE UNIVERSITY OF MINNESOTA; MOREHOUSE COLLEGE; THE EVERGREEN STATE COLLEGE; CALIFORNIA STATE UNIVERSITY, MONTEREY BAY; and THOMAS AQUINAS COLLEGE

Mission Statements

If John Henry Newman had been able to build a Web site for his ideal university, what might it have looked like, and how would it have represented his goals for the institution? These are questions we had in mind as we set out to browse contemporary college and university Web sites, much as you may have done as you began thinking about which schools you might prefer or be able to attend. Of special interest to us are the ways in which various institutions describe their goals within the confines of a computer screen, where space is limited and readers are often impatient. So we decided to take a closer look at these representations, and to choose several for you to examine in the context of this chapter's discussion of education.

The five statements we have chosen represent different kinds of schools in different areas of the country. The University of Minnesota, in Minneapolis, is one of the country's largest research universities; it has extensive undergraduate and graduate curricula. In contrast, California State University, Monterey Bay, is a relatively new and as yet small school that focuses primarily on undergraduates. Morehouse College (in Atlanta, Georgia), The Evergreen State College (in Olympia, Washington), and Thomas Aquinas College (in Santa Paula, California) are all liberal arts colleges. Morehouse is one of the country's most distinguished historically black colleges and admits only male students; Evergreen State, a coeducational school, is equally well known for its emphasis on experimentation and innovation. And Thomas Aquinas is distinctive in its own way, with a curriculum focused on the Great Books and a religious (Roman Catholic) orientation.

You may want to visit the Web sites of these five schools to discover more about their campuses, students, faculty, and staff. Or you may decide to visit your own campus Web site, seeking out its statement of mission, vision, or belief in order to compare it to the ones offered here. If you do visit, be sure to note the use of color and visual images, which often carry a good part of the messages the schools wish to convey. Which school's mission most appeals to your own goals and values? —A.L. and J.R.

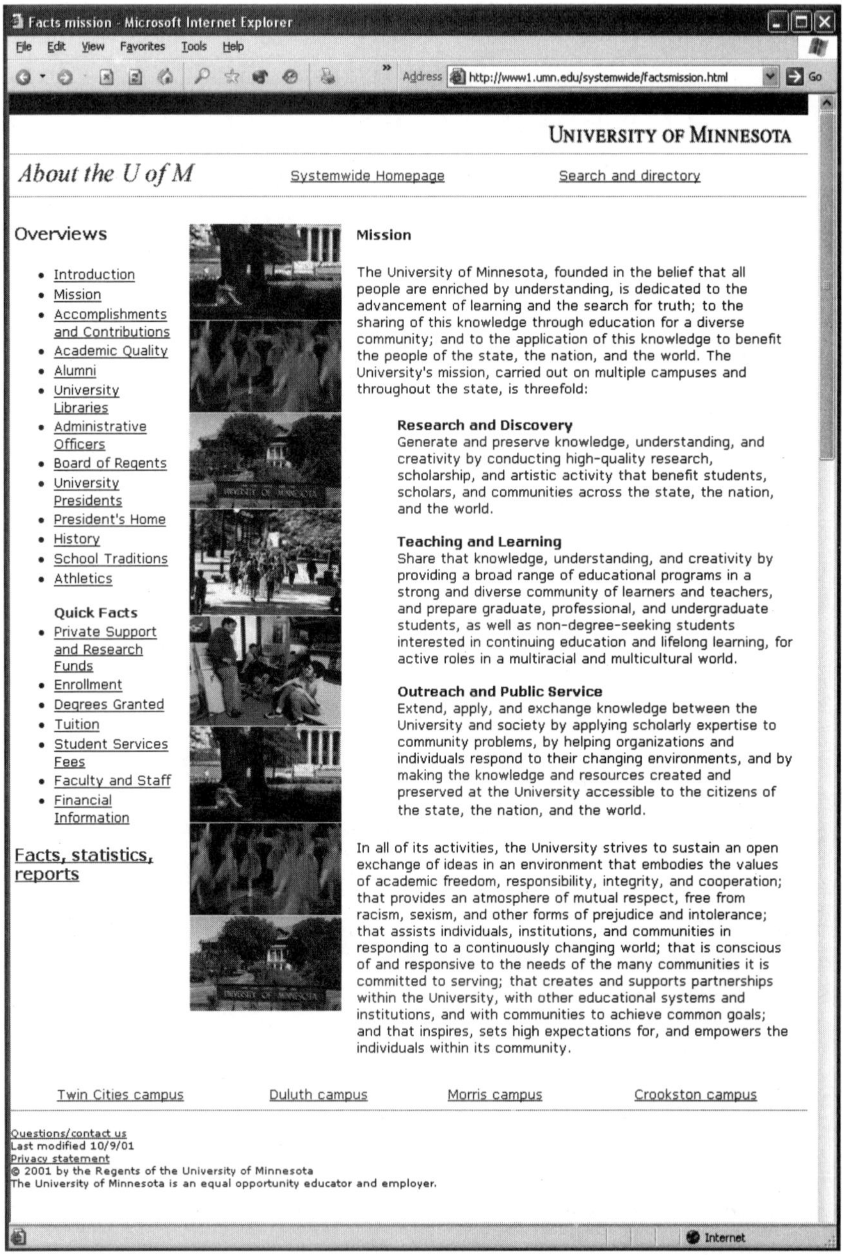

Facts mission - Microsoft Internet Explorer

File Edit View Favorites Tools Help

Address http://www1.umn.edu/systemwide/factsmission.html Go

UNIVERSITY OF MINNESOTA

About the U of M Systemwide Homepage Search and directory

Overviews

- Introduction
- Mission
- Accomplishments and Contributions
- Academic Quality
- Alumni
- University Libraries
- Administrative Officers
- Board of Regents
- University Presidents
- President's Home
- History
- School Traditions
- Athletics

Quick Facts

- Private Support and Research Funds
- Enrollment
- Degrees Granted
- Tuition
- Student Services Fees
- Faculty and Staff
- Financial Information

Facts, statistics, reports

Mission

The University of Minnesota, founded in the belief that all people are enriched by understanding, is dedicated to the advancement of learning and the search for truth; to the sharing of this knowledge through education for a diverse community; and to the application of this knowledge to benefit the people of the state, the nation, and the world. The University's mission, carried out on multiple campuses and throughout the state, is threefold:

Research and Discovery
Generate and preserve knowledge, understanding, and creativity by conducting high-quality research, scholarship, and artistic activity that benefit students, scholars, and communities across the state, the nation, and the world.

Teaching and Learning
Share that knowledge, understanding, and creativity by providing a broad range of educational programs in a strong and diverse community of learners and teachers, and prepare graduate, professional, and undergraduate students, as well as non-degree-seeking students interested in continuing education and lifelong learning, for active roles in a multiracial and multicultural world.

Outreach and Public Service
Extend, apply, and exchange knowledge between the University and society by applying scholarly expertise to community problems, by helping organizations and individuals respond to their changing environments, and by making the knowledge and resources created and preserved at the University accessible to the citizens of the state, the nation, and the world.

In all of its activities, the University strives to sustain an open exchange of ideas in an environment that embodies the values of academic freedom, responsibility, integrity, and cooperation; that provides an atmosphere of mutual respect, free from racism, sexism, and other forms of prejudice and intolerance; that assists individuals, institutions, and communities in responding to a continuously changing world; that is conscious of and responsive to the needs of the many communities it is committed to serving; that creates and supports partnerships within the University, with other educational systems and institutions, and with communities to achieve common goals; and that inspires, sets high expectations for, and empowers the individuals within its community.

Twin Cities campus Duluth campus Morris campus Crookston campus

Questions/contact us
Last modified 10/9/01
Privacy statement
© 2001 by the Regents of the University of Minnesota
The University of Minnesota is an equal opportunity educator and employer.

Internet

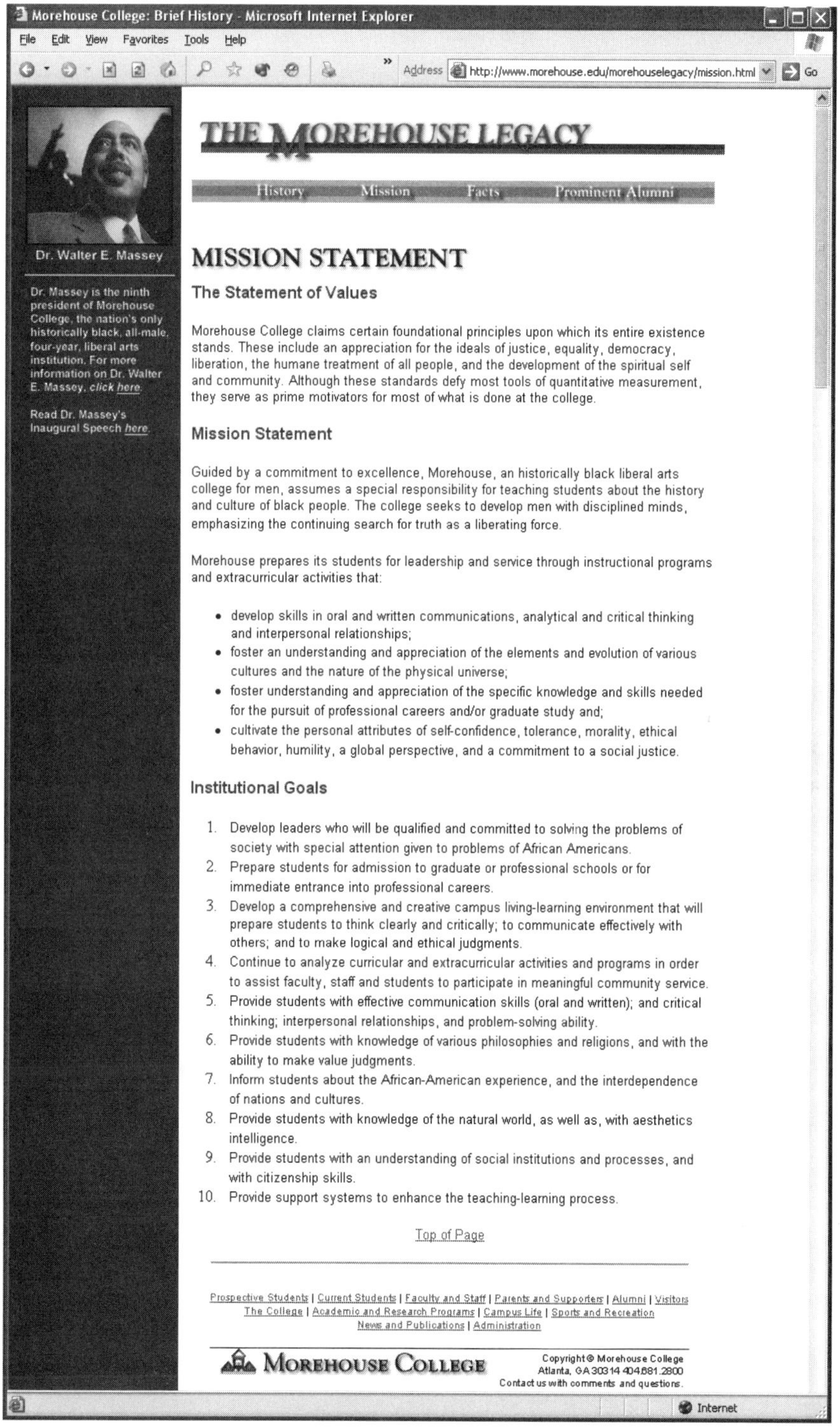

Morehouse College: Brief History - Microsoft Internet Explorer

File Edit View Favorites Tools Help

Address http://www.morehouse.edu/morehouselegacy/mission.html Go

THE MOREHOUSE LEGACY

History Mission Facts Prominent Alumni

Dr. Walter E. Massey

Dr. Massey is the ninth president of Morehouse College, the nation's only historically black, all-male, four-year, liberal arts institution. For more information on Dr. Walter E. Massey, *click here*.

Read Dr. Massey's Inaugural Speech *here*.

MISSION STATEMENT

The Statement of Values

Morehouse College claims certain foundational principles upon which its entire existence stands. These include an appreciation for the ideals of justice, equality, democracy, liberation, the humane treatment of all people, and the development of the spiritual self and community. Although these standards defy most tools of quantitative measurement, they serve as prime motivators for most of what is done at the college.

Mission Statement

Guided by a commitment to excellence, Morehouse, an historically black liberal arts college for men, assumes a special responsibility for teaching students about the history and culture of black people. The college seeks to develop men with disciplined minds, emphasizing the continuing search for truth as a liberating force.

Morehouse prepares its students for leadership and service through instructional programs and extracurricular activities that:

- develop skills in oral and written communications, analytical and critical thinking and interpersonal relationships;
- foster an understanding and appreciation of the elements and evolution of various cultures and the nature of the physical universe;
- foster understanding and appreciation of the specific knowledge and skills needed for the pursuit of professional careers and/or graduate study and;
- cultivate the personal attributes of self-confidence, tolerance, morality, ethical behavior, humility, a global perspective, and a commitment to a social justice.

Institutional Goals

1. Develop leaders who will be qualified and committed to solving the problems of society with special attention given to problems of African Americans.
2. Prepare students for admission to graduate or professional schools or for immediate entrance into professional careers.
3. Develop a comprehensive and creative campus living-learning environment that will prepare students to think clearly and critically; to communicate effectively with others; and to make logical and ethical judgments.
4. Continue to analyze curricular and extracurricular activities and programs in order to assist faculty, staff and students to participate in meaningful community service.
5. Provide students with effective communication skills (oral and written); and critical thinking; interpersonal relationships, and problem-solving ability.
6. Provide students with knowledge of various philosophies and religions, and with the ability to make value judgments.
7. Inform students about the African-American experience, and the interdependence of nations and cultures.
8. Provide students with knowledge of the natural world, as well as, with aesthetics intelligence.
9. Provide students with an understanding of social institutions and processes, and with citizenship skills.
10. Provide support systems to enhance the teaching-learning process.

Top of Page

Prospective Students | Current Students | Faculty and Staff | Parents and Supporters | Alumni | Visitors
The College | Academic and Research Programs | Campus Life | Sports and Recreation
News and Publications | Administration

MOREHOUSE COLLEGE

Copyright © Morehouse College
Atlanta, GA 30314 404.681.2800
Contact us with comments and questions.

Internet

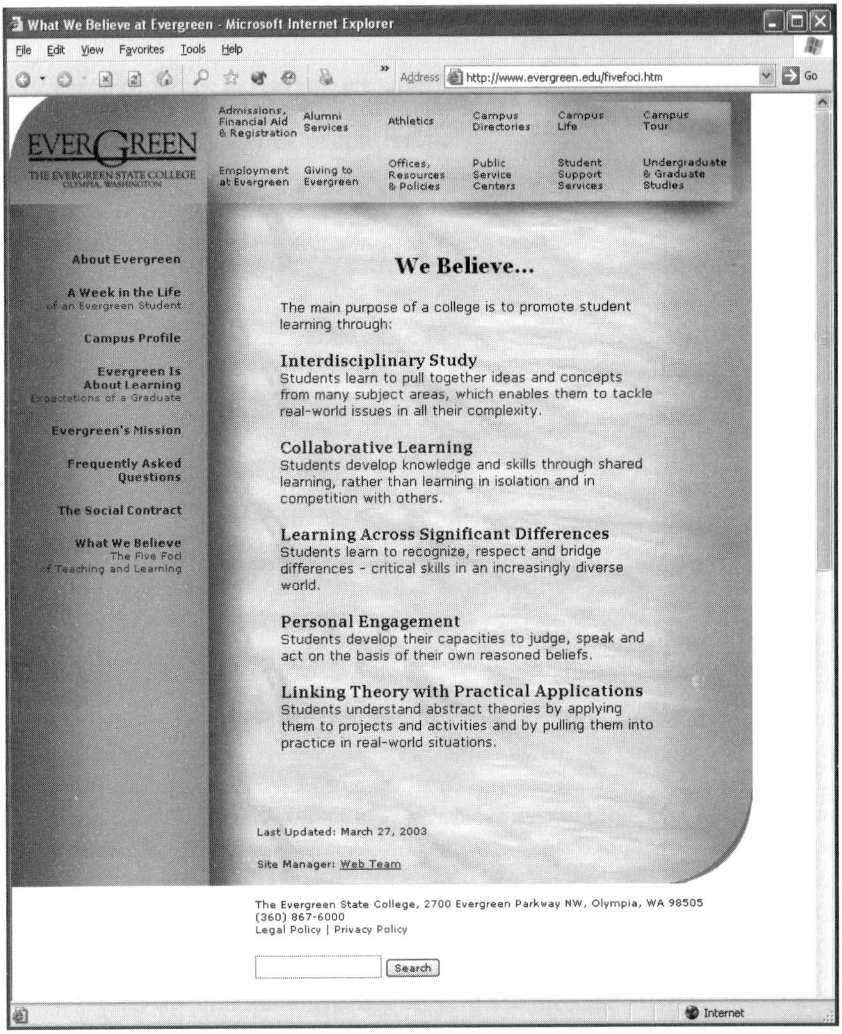
What We Believe at Evergreen - Microsoft Internet Explorer
File Edit View Favorites Tools Help
Address http://www.evergreen.edu/fivefoci.htm
Go
Admissions, Financial Aid & Registration
Alumni Services
Athletics
Campus Directories
Campus Life
Campus Tour
EVERGREEN
THE EVERGREEN STATE COLLEGE
OLYMPIA, WASHINGTON
Employment at Evergreen
Giving to Evergreen
Offices, Resources & Policies
Public Service Centers
Student Support Services
Undergraduate & Graduate Studies
About Evergreen
A Week in the Life of an Evergreen Student
Campus Profile
Evergreen Is About Learning
Expectations of a Graduate
Evergreen's Mission
Frequently Asked Questions
The Social Contract
What We Believe
The Five Foci of Teaching and Learning
We Believe...
The main purpose of a college is to promote student learning through:
Interdisciplinary Study
Students learn to pull together ideas and concepts from many subject areas, which enables them to tackle real-world issues in all their complexity.
Collaborative Learning
Students develop knowledge and skills through shared learning, rather than learning in isolation and in competition with others.
Learning Across Significant Differences
Students learn to recognize, respect and bridge differences - critical skills in an increasingly diverse world.
Personal Engagement
Students develop their capacities to judge, speak and act on the basis of their own reasoned beliefs.
Linking Theory with Practical Applications
Students understand abstract theories by applying them to projects and activities and by pulling them into practice in real-world situations.
Last Updated: March 27, 2003
Site Manager: Web Team
The Evergreen State College, 2700 Evergreen Parkway NW, Olympia, WA 98505
(360) 867-6000
Legal Policy | Privacy Policy
Search
Internet

The CSUMB Vision

CALIFORNIA STATE UNIVERSITY
Monterey Bay

LINKS TO:
What's New • Events
General Information • News
Academics • Library
Employment Opportunities
Around the Bay
The CSUMB Vision
Site Map

Our Vision Statement

Our Mission

Faces of CSUMB

Join Us! Jobs @ CSUMB

Our Vision Statement

California State University, Monterey Bay (CSUMB) is envisioned as a comprehensive state university which values service through high quality education. The campus will be distinctive in serving the diverse people of California, especially the working class and historically undereducated and low-income populations. It will feature an enriched living and learning environment and year-round operation. The identity of the university will be framed by substantive commitment to multilingual, multicultural, gender-equitable learning. The university will be a collaborative, intellectual community distinguished by partnerships with existing institutions both public and private, cooperative agreements which enable students, faculty, and staff to cross institutional boundaries for innovative instruction, broadly defined scholarly and creative activity, and coordinated community service.

The university will invest in preparation for the future through integrated and experimental use of technologies as resources to people, catalysts for learning, and providers of increased access and enriched quality learning. The curriculum of CSUMB will be student and society centered and of sufficient breadth and depth to meet statewide and regional needs, specifically those involving both inner-city and isolated rural populations, and needs relevant to communities in the immediate Tri-County region (Monterey, Santa Cruz, and San Benito). The programs of instruction will strive for distinction, building on regional assets in developing specialty clusters in such areas as: the sciences (marine, atmospheric, and environmental); visual and performing arts and related humanities; languages, cultures, and international studies; education; business; studies of human behavior, information, and communication, within broad curricular areas; and professional study.

The university will develop a culture of innovation in its overall conceptual design and organization, and will utilize new and varied pedagogical and instructional approaches including distance learning. Institutional programs will value and cultivate creative and productive talents of students, faculty, and staff, and seek ways to contribute to the economy of the state, the wellbeing of our communities, and the quality of life and development of its students, faculty, and service areas.

The education programs at CSUMB will:

- Integrate the sciences, the arts and humanities, liberal studies, and professional training;

- Integrate modern learning technology and pedagogy to create liberal education adequate for the contemporary world;

- Integrate work and learning, service and reflection;

- Recognize the importance of global interdependence;

- Invest in languages and cross-cultural competence;

- Emphasize those topics most central to the local area's economy and ecology, and California's long-term needs;

- Offer a multicultural, gender-equitable, intergenerational, and accessible residential learning environment.

The university will provide a new model of organizing, managing, and financing higher education:

- The university will be integrated with other institutions, essentially collaborative in its orientation, and active in seeking partnerships across institutional boundaries. It will develop and implement various arrangements for sharing courses, curriculum, faculty, students, and facilities with other institutions.

- The organizational structure of the university will reflect a belief in the importance of each administrative staff and faculty member, working to integrate the university community across "staff" and "faculty" lines.

- The financial aid system will emphasize a fundamental commitment to equity and access.

- The budget and financial systems, including student fees, will provide for efficient and effective operation of the university.

- University governance will be exercised with a substantial amount of autonomy and independence within a very broad CSU systemwide policy context.

- Accountability will emphasize careful evaluation and assessment of results and outcomes.

Our vision of the goals of California State University, Monterey Bay includes: a model pluralistic academic community where all learn and teach one another in an atmosphere of mutual respect and pursuit of excellence; a faculty and staff motivated to excel in their respective fields as well as to contribute to the broadly defined university environment. Our graduates will have an understanding of interdependence and global competence, distinctive technical and educational skills, the experience and abilities to contribute to California's high quality work force, the critical thinking abilities to be productive citizens, and the social responsibility and skills to be community builders. CSUMB will dynamically link the past, present, and future by responding to historical and changing conditions, experimenting with strategies which increase access, improve quality, and lower costs through education in a distinctive CSU environment. University students and personnel will attempt analytically and creatively to meet critical state and regional needs, and to provide California with responsible and creative leadership for the global 21st century.

–September 27, 1994

Our Mission Statement

From the Campus Strategic Planning Committee:

"To build a multicultural learning community founded on academic excellence from which all partners in the educational process emerge prepared to contribute productively, responsibly, and ethically to California and the global community."

Last updated 31 JUL 2001 by: webfolk

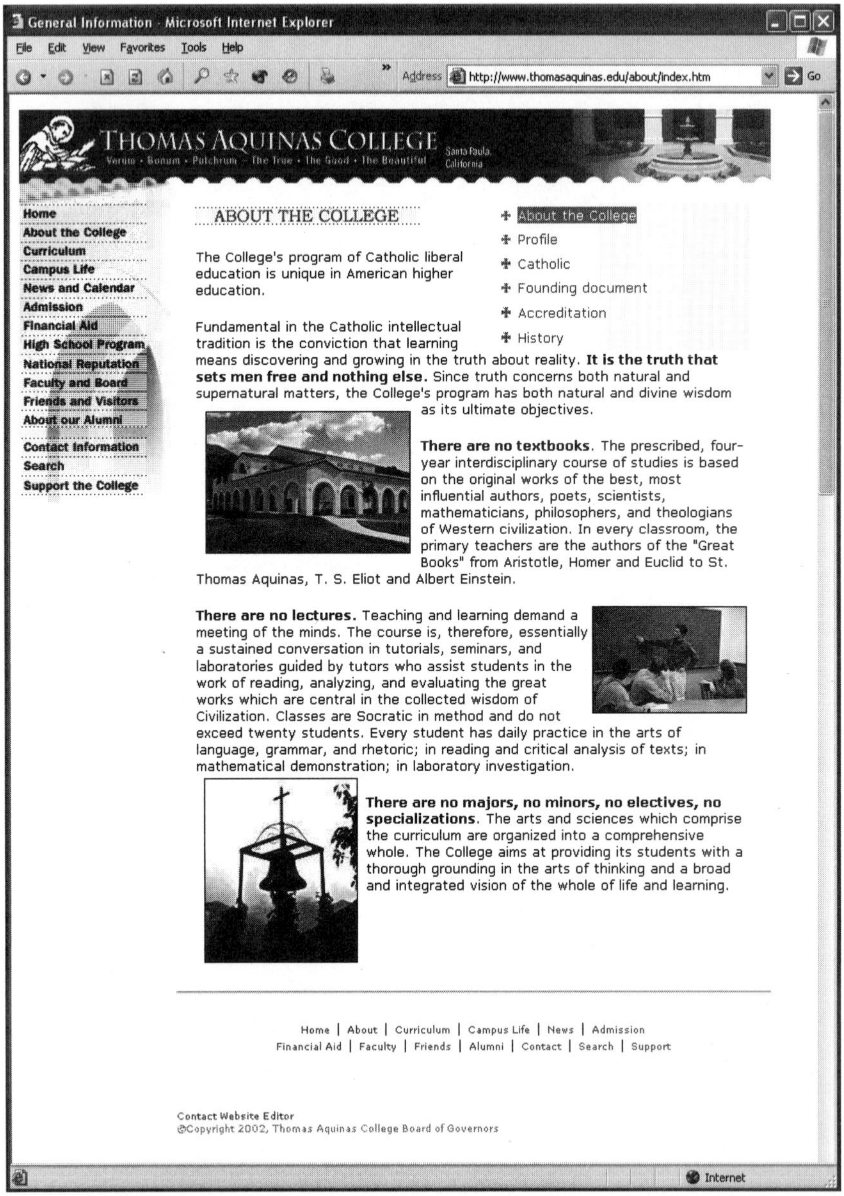
General Information - Microsoft Internet Explorer

File Edit View Favorites Tools Help

Address http://www.thomasaquinas.edu/about/index.htm Go

THOMAS AQUINAS COLLEGE Santa Paula, California

Verum · Bonum · Pulchrum · The True · The Good · The Beautiful

Home
About the College
Curriculum
Campus Life
News and Calendar
Admission
Financial Aid
High School Program
National Reputation
Faculty and Board
Friends and Visitors
About our Alumni
Contact Information
Search
Support the College

ABOUT THE COLLEGE

- About the College
- Profile
- Catholic
- Founding document
- Accreditation
- History

The College's program of Catholic liberal education is unique in American higher education.

Fundamental in the Catholic intellectual tradition is the conviction that learning means discovering and growing in the truth about reality. **It is the truth that sets men free and nothing else.** Since truth concerns both natural and supernatural matters, the College's program has both natural and divine wisdom as its ultimate objectives.

There are no textbooks. The prescribed, four-year interdisciplinary course of studies is based on the original works of the best, most influential authors, poets, scientists, mathematicians, philosophers, and theologians of Western civilization. In every classroom, the primary teachers are the authors of the "Great Books" from Aristotle, Homer and Euclid to St. Thomas Aquinas, T. S. Eliot and Albert Einstein.

There are no lectures. Teaching and learning demand a meeting of the minds. The course is, therefore, essentially a sustained conversation in tutorials, seminars, and laboratories guided by tutors who assist students in the work of reading, analyzing, and evaluating the great works which are central in the collected wisdom of Civilization. Classes are Socratic in method and do not exceed twenty students. Every student has daily practice in the arts of language, grammar, and rhetoric; in reading and critical analysis of texts; in mathematical demonstration; in laboratory investigation.

There are no majors, no minors, no electives, no specializations. The arts and sciences which comprise the curriculum are organized into a comprehensive whole. The College aims at providing its students with a thorough grounding in the arts of thinking and a broad and integrated vision of the whole of life and learning.

Home | About | Curriculum | Campus Life | News | Admission
Financial Aid | Faculty | Friends | Alumni | Contact | Search | Support

Contact Website Editor
©Copyright 2002, Thomas Aquinas College Board of Governors

Internet

QUESTIONING THE TEXT

1. Four of the five statements use different terms to describe what we had been thinking of as *goals statements:* two use the word *mission,* while the others refer to *beliefs* or *vision.* Three head their pages with a noun or noun phrase—"Mission," "Mission Statement," "Our Vision Statement"—while one leads off with a noun-verb combination—"We Believe" and another with a prepositional phrase, "About the College." Think carefully about these differing terms and phrases, and spend five or ten minutes brainstorming with your classmates about the effect these choices have on readers. What differing messages do they send?
2. Examine the format and organizing principles of each mission statement. Include all aspects of the Web page in your analysis, including any use of columns, varying fonts or type sizes, illustrations, headings, buttons, and so on. Which statement do you find most effective in terms of organization, and why?
3. Are any aspects of college life as you know it absent from these mission statements? Identify some of those components and then, in a group, discuss possible explanations for the omissions.

MAKING CONNECTIONS

4. Choose another reading from this chapter and use it as the basis for inferring a "mission statement" that the author might write for his or her ideal university. Which one of the mission statements reproduced here would this inferred statement most resemble, and why?
5. In "What Is a Liberal Education?" (p. 141) Donald Kagan criticizes "most attempts at liberal education today," characterizing the curricula as "individualized, unfocused, [and] scattered" (paragraph 19). How might he react to the mission statements presented here? Does his critical characterization seem to apply to any of these colleges or universities? Why, or why not?

JOINING THE CONVERSATION

6. Working with two classmates, draft a mission statement that you think reflects the goals of your college or university. You may need to gather some data from the college catalog, student newspaper, Web site, and so on to complete this assignment.
7. Write a parody of a college mission statement. Use the parody as a way to explore problems in education today rather than just to poke fun at an institution.

JON SPAYDE
Learning in the Key of Life

"THE WHOLE WORLD'S A CLASSROOM," says Jon Spayde, a concept he much prefers to narrower definitions of education that limit it to what takes place in school, where it is too often equated with technical competence or "training for competitiveness." Noting that training *is often a code word for the education of poor Americans, Spayde rejects these narrow utilitarian goals in favor of enriched study of the humanities* in the context of everyday life. *This "in-the-streets definition of education" assumes that learning takes place across the span of a lifetime, not just in sixteen years of formal schooling, and that what is being learned takes root and is nurtured through connections we make in "the real world." A truly good education, Spayde argues, may well be one "carpentered out of the best combination we can make of school, salon, reading, online exploration, walking the streets, hiking in the woods, museums, poetry classes at the Y, and friendship. . . ."*

Spayde's definition of education is perhaps particularly appealing at a time when change is so swift that the shelf life of technical knowledge is six months (at best). In addition, his definition appeals to my own sense that much of our most important and lasting education has always taken place outside of—or on the periphery of—school. In this brief essay, however, Spayde is short on specifics. Although he offers several examples of "in-the-streets education," he hasn't the time or space to set forth any concrete proposals for change. As a result, I would like to hear much more about how ordinary citizens and students might take up this new definition of education in their own lives. If you would like to hear more, check out other work by Spayde, well-known interviewer, editor, and longtime contributor to the Utne Reader *(where this essay first appeared in May–June 1998).* —A.L.

What does it mean—and more important, what *should* it mean—to be educated?

This is a surprisingly tricky and two-sided question. Masquerading as simple problem-solving, it raises a whole laundry list of philosophical conundrums: What sort of society do we want? What is the nature of humankind? How do we learn best? And—most challenging of all—what is the Good? Talking about the meaning of education inevitably leads to the question of what a culture considers most important.

Yikes! No wonder answers don't come easily in 1998, in a multiethnic, corporation-heavy democracy that dominates the globe without having much of a sense of its own soul. For our policyheads, education equals something called "training for competitiveness" (which often boils down to the mantra

Left to right from top: Lao Tzu Toni Morrison Black Elk Anaïs Nin Henry David Thoreau Orson Welles Thelonious Monk Groucho Marx Leo Tolstoy Miles Davis Jane Austen Johann Sebastian Bach Billie Holiday Jalal ad-Din ar-Rumi Bart Simpson Gabriel Garcia Marquez Mohandas Gandhi Simone de Beauvoir

of "more computers, more computers"). For multiculturalists of various stripes, education has become a battle line where they must duke it out regularly with incensed neo-traditionalists. Organized religion and the various "alternative spiritualities"—from 12-step groups to Buddhism, American style—contribute their own kinds of education.

Given all these pushes and pulls, is it any wonder that many of us are beginning to feel that we didn't get the whole story in school, that our educations didn't prepare us for the world we're living in today?

We didn't; we couldn't have. So what do we do about it? 5

The first thing, I firmly believe, is to take a deep, calm breath. After all, we're not the first American generation to have doubts about these matters. One of the great ages of American intellectual achievement, the period just before the Civil War, was ruled by educational misfits. Henry David Thoreau was fond of saying, "I am self-educated; that is, I attended Harvard College," and indeed Harvard in the early 19th century excelled mainly in the extent and violence of its food fights.

Don't get me wrong: Formal education is serious stuff. There is no divide in American life that hurts more than the one between those we consider well educated and those who are poorly or inadequately schooled. Talking about education is usually the closest we get to talking about class; and no wonder—education, like class, is about power. Not just the power that Harvard- and Stanford-trained elites have to dictate our workweeks, plan our communities, and fiddle with world financial markets, but the extra power that a grad school dropout who, let's say, embraces voluntary simplicity and makes $14,000 a year, has over a high school dropout single mom pulling down $18,000. That kind of power has everything to do with attitude and access: an attitude of empowerment, even entitlement, and access to tools, people, and ideas that make living—at any income level—easier, and its crises easier to bear.

That's something Earl Shorris understands. A novelist and journalist, Shorris started an Ivy League–level adult education course in humanities for low-income New Yorkers at the Roberto Clemente Family Guidance Center on the Lower East Side, which he described in his book *New American Blues* (Norton, 1997). On the first day of class, Shorris said this to the students, who were Asians, whites, blacks, and Hispanics at or near the poverty line: "You've been cheated. Rich people learn the humanities; you didn't. The humanities are a foundation for getting along in the world, for thinking, for learning to reflect on the world instead of just reacting to whatever force is turned against you. . . . Do all rich people, or people who are in the middle, know the humanities? Not a chance. But some do. And it helps. It helps to live better and enjoy life more. Will the humanities make you rich? Absolutely. But not in terms of money. In terms of life." And the Clemente course graduates did get rich in this way. Most of them went on to further higher education, and even the hard-luck Abel Lomas (not his real name), who got mixed up in a drug bust after he graduated, dumbfounded the classics-innocent prosecutor with arguments drawn from Plato and Sophocles.

By deliberately refusing to define poor Americans as nothing more than economic units whose best hope is "training" at fly-by-night computer schools, Shorris reminds us all that genuine education is a discourse—a dialogue—carried on within the context of the society around us, as well as with the mighty dead. School helps, but it's just the beginning of the engagement between ideas and reality—as Abel Lomas can attest.

Shorris' radical idea—more controversial even than expecting working-class students to tackle a serious college curriculum—was to emphasize the humanities, those subtle subjects that infuse our minds with great, gushing ideas but also equip us to think and to argue. As more and more colleges, goaded by demands for "global competitiveness" from government officials and business leaders, turn themselves into glorified trade schools churning out graduates with highly specialized skills but little intellectual breadth, you might think humanities would go the way of the horse and buggy. 10

"It's an enormous error to believe that technology can somehow be the content of education," says John Ralston Saul, a Canadian historian and critic with years of experience in the business world. "We insist that everyone has to learn computer technology, but when printing came in with Gutenberg and changed the production and distribution of knowledge profoundly, nobody said that everyone should learn to be a printer. Technical training is training in what is sure to be obsolete soon anyway; it's self-defeating, and it won't get you through the next 60 years of your life." Training, says Saul, is simply "learning to fit in as a passive member of a structure. And that's the worst thing for an uncertain, changing time."

Oberlin College environmental studies professor David Orr poses an even fiercer challenge to the argument that education in the 21st century should focus primarily on high-tech training. In a recent article in the British magazine *Resurgence* (No. 179), he defines something he calls "slow knowledge": It is knowledge "shaped and calibrated to fit a particular ecological and cultural context," he writes, distinguishing it from the "fast knowledge" that zips through the terminals of the information society. "It does not imply lethargy, but rather thoroughness and patience. The aim of slow knowledge is resilience, harmony, and the preservation of long-standing patterns that give our lives aesthetic, spiritual, and social meaning." Orr says that we are focusing far too much of our energy and resources on fast knowledge, ignoring all the richness and meaning slow knowledge adds to our lives. Indeed, slow knowledge is what's needed to save the planet from ecological disaster and other threats posed by technological, millennial society.

"Culturally, we just are slow learners, no matter how fast individuals can process raw data," he says. "There's a long time gap between original insights and the cultural practices that come from them. You can figure out what you *can* do pretty quickly, but the ethical understanding of what you *ought* to do comes very slowly."

Miles Harvey, a Chicago journalist who assembled a list of environmental classics for *Outside* magazine (May 1996), reminds us that much of the divisiveness in contemporary debates on education boils down to a time issue. "The canon makers say you've only got so much time, so you have to choose between, say, Shakespeare and Toni Morrison, on the assumption that you can't get to both," he says. "Well, it is hard. The level of creativity and intellectual activity in this country would jump up if we had a four-day work-week."

But suppose we redefined this issue from the very beginning. Suppose we abandoned the notion that learning is a time-consuming and obligatory filling of our heads, and replaced it with the idea, courtesy of Goethe, that "people cannot learn what they do not love"—the idea of learning as an encounter infused with eros. We always find time for what we truly love, one way or another. Suppose further that love, being an inclusive spirit, refused to choose between Shakespeare and Toni Morrison (or Tony Bennett, for that matter), and we located our bliss in the unstable relationship between the two, rattling from book to book, looking for connections and grandly unconcerned about whether we've read "enough," as long as we read what we read with love.

And we wouldn't just read. We would reflect deeply on the relationship between our everyday lives and big philosophical questions—for, as Nietzsche memorably said, "Metaphysics are in the street." The Argentine novelist Ernesto Sabato glosses him this way: "[By metaphysics Nietzsche means] those final problems of the human condition: death, loneliness, the meaning of existence, the desire for power, hope, and despair." The whole world's a classroom, and to really make it one, the first thing is to believe it is. We need to take seriously the proposition that reflection and knowledge born out of contact with the real world, an education carpentered out of the best combination we can make of school, salon, reading, online exploration, walking the streets, hiking in the woods, museums, poetry classes at the Y, and friendship, may be the best education of all—not a makeshift substitute that must apologize for itself in the shadow of academe.

One of the things I like about this in-the-streets definition of education is how classical it is. In what's still one of the best concise summaries of classical education, Elizabeth Sutton Lawrence notes in *The Growth of Modern Education* (1971), that ancient Greek education "came largely from firsthand experience, in the marketplace, in the Assembly, in the theater, and in the religious celebration; through what the Greek youth saw and heard." Socrates met and challenged his adult "pupils" in the street, at dinner parties, after festivals, not at some Athenian Princeton.

Educational reactionaries want to convince us that the Western classical tradition is a carefully honed reading list. But as the dynamic classicist and philosopher Martha Nussbaum, who teaches at the University of Chicago Law School, insists, "The very idea that we should have a list of Great Books would have horrified the ancients. If you take to heart what the classical philosophers had to say, you'll never turn them into monuments. Their goal was to enliven the mind, and they knew that to enliven the mind you need to be very alert to what is in the world around you."

To really believe this casts a new light, to say the least, on the question of what the content of our learning ought to be. In her latest book, *Cultivating Humanity: A Classical Defense of Reform in Liberal Education* (Harvard University Press, 1997), Nussbaum argues compellingly that study of the non-Western world, of women's issues, of alternative sexuality, and of minority cultures is completely in line with classical principles, in particular the Stoic ideal of the "world citizen" with a cultivated ability to put her- or himself into the minds and lives of the members of divergent groups and cultures.

And New York jazz and rock writer Gene Santoro—trained in the 20
classics and Dante studies—points out there's nothing frivolous about paying attention to popular culture: "Popular culture, and particularly popular music, is the place where the dominant culture is most heavily affected by marginal cultures. Jazz, for example, became wide enough to take in much of the range of American reality, from the African American experience to the European classical tradition to the Latin and Caribbean spirit. It's the artistic version of the American social experience, and if you care about this culture, you'll look at it." And, he adds in a Socratic vein, "Jazz can help you think. It's both disciplined and unpredictable. It gives you tradition but doesn't let you settle into preconceived notions."

Colin Greer—co-editor of *The Call to Character* and *The Plain Truth of Things,* progressive responses to William Bennett's *Book of Virtues*—suggests further ways to make the most of the relationship between books and what's going on in the streets. "You could study the moments of major change in the world," he proposes. "The end of slavery. The early struggle against child labor. Woman suffrage. The organization of labor. People have forgotten what it really took to accomplish these things: What pragmatic things were done and how people learned to be generous and decent to their opponents. It's important to know the real story of how change works, and recognize that to fall short of your highest goals is OK as long as you stick to the struggle."

You get the idea. The American tradition, in learning as well as jazz and activism, is improvisatory. There are as many ways to become an educated American as there are Americans. To fall short of your highest goals—mastering that imaginary "complete" reading list, say—is OK as long as you stick to the struggle. And the joy.

QUESTIONING THE TEXT

1. Spayde opens his essay with a question: "What does it mean—and more important, what *should* it mean—to be educated?" After reading the essay carefully with this question in mind, identify the answers

Spayde provides. Do his answers fulfill the implicit promise he makes in the opening—to tell readers what it means to be educated? Why, or why not?

2. Look carefully at the illustration that accompanies this essay (you might review the discussion of reading visual texts on p. 8 before doing so). In what ways does this illustration add evidence or proof for the argument Spayde is making?
3. Spayde uses first-person plural forms (especially *we* and *our*) often in his essay. Why do you think Spayde made this choice? What is its effect on you as a reader? Are you included in this *we*—and why, or why not?

MAKING CONNECTIONS

4. Which of the writers in this chapter would be most likely to approve of what Spayde calls "in-the-streets education?" Choose one writer who would likely *not* approve of Spayde's definition of education, and write a one-page criticism of Spayde from that writer's point of view.
5. Look back at the five college mission statements (pp. 58–62). Which mission fits best with the kind of education Spayde advocates? Which fits least well—and why?

JOINING THE CONVERSATION

6. Working with two classmates, come up with a name for a hypothetical college that will promote Spayde's vision of education. Then create a home page for that college.
7. Working on your own or with a classmate, try writing your own extended definition of what it means to be educated. (For guidelines on writing definitions, see p. 27.)

ADRIENNE RICH

What Does a Woman Need to Know?

ADRIENNE RICH (b. 1929) has been a writer and a teacher all her life. Winner of the Yale Series of Younger Poets Award in 1951 for her first volume of poems, A Change of World, *of the National Book Award for Poetry in 1974 (for* Diving into the Wreck*), and of numerous other awards, she has also written novels, plays, essays, and speeches, including the one you are about to read.*

If John Henry Newman describes the university as "an assemblage of learned men," Rich looks at college from a slightly different perspective, noting the "changing landscape of knowledge itself" and asking "what does a woman need to know?" to negotiate such a landscape. Rich's question is particularly appropriate in context, for she delivered this speech as a commencement address to the graduates of a women's college, Smith, in 1979. Speaking directly to her audience, Rich pulls no punches; she is not sanguine about the state of women's education. In fact, she finds that "there is no women's college today which is providing young women with the education they need for survival as whole persons in a world which denies women wholeness." In the face of what she sees as a fact of life in the academy, Rich argues that women should gain all the knowledge they can from their university educations and from the professions they enter. But they should also realize that what they most need to know will have to be self-taught.

Rich challenges women students to take control of their own learning experience, to find out what they need to know, and to take responsibility for seeing that they learn it. Although she does not say so directly, the substance and site of this commencement address suggest an implicit argument for attending same-sex institutions, a topic of considerable interest to the first-year college students I am teaching, more than two decades after Rich's address. I chose this speech not only because it raises the issue of all-female or all-male schools, however, but because I wish I had heard such a commencement address when I graduated from college. In the thirty-something years since my graduation day, I have come to recognize how much my own career has been influenced by the kinds of schools I attended, by the kinds of teachers I had (no women in my college experience!), and by the kinds of models I emulated (all of them male/masculine). While I still value some of those teachers and models, Rich suggests that I might profit from asking what they did not *teach me—and how I might have taught myself better.*

—A.L.

I have been very much moved that you, the class of 1979, chose me for your commencement speaker. It is important to me to be here, in part because Smith is one of the original colleges for women, but also because she has chosen to continue identifying herself as a women's college. We are at a point in history where this fact has enormous potential, even if that potential is as yet unrealized.

The possibilities for the future education of women that haunt these buildings and grounds are enormous, when we think of what an independent women's college might be: a college dedicated both to teaching women what women need to know and, by the same token, to changing the landscape of knowledge itself. The germ of those possibilities lies symbolically in The Sophia Smith Collection, an archive much in need of expansion and increase, but which by its very existence makes the statement that women's lives and work are valued here and that our foresisters, buried and diminished in male-centered scholarship, are a living presence, necessary and precious to us.

Suppose we were to ask ourselves simply: What does a woman need to know to become a self-conscious, self-defining human being? Doesn't she need a knowledge of her own history, of her much-politicized female body, of the creative genius of women of the past—the skills and crafts and techniques and visions possessed by women in other times and cultures, and how they have been rendered anonymous, censored, interrupted, devalued? Doesn't she, as one of that majority who are still denied equal rights as citizens, enslaved as sexual prey, unpaid or underpaid as workers, withheld from her own power—doesn't she need an analysis of her condition, a knowledge of the women thinkers of the past who have reflected on it, a knowledge, too, of women's world-wide individual rebellions and organized movements against economic and social injustice, and how these have been fragmented and silenced?

Doesn't she need to know how seemingly natural states of being, like heterosexuality, like motherhood, have been enforced and institutionalized to deprive her of power? Without such education, women have lived and continue to live in ignorance of our collective context, vulnerable to the projections of men's fantasies about us as they appear in art, in literature, in the sciences, in the media, in the so-called humanistic studies. I suggest that not anatomy, but enforced ignorance, has been a crucial key to our powerlessness.

There is—and I say this with sorrow—there is no women's college today which is providing young women with the education they need for survival as whole persons in a world which denies women wholeness—that knowledge which, in the words of Coleridge, "returns again as power." The existence of Women's Studies courses offers at least some kind of life line. But even Women's Studies can amount simply to compensatory history; too often they fail to challenge the intellectual and political structures that must be challenged if women as a group are ever to come into collective, nonexclusionary freedom. The belief that established science and scholarship—which have so relentlessly excluded women from their making—are "objective" and "value-free" and that feminist studies are "unscholarly," "biased," and "ideological" dies hard. Yet the fact is that all science, and all scholarship, and all art are ideological; there is no neutrality in culture. And the ideology of the education you have just spent four years acquiring in a women's college has been largely, if not entirely, the ideology of white male supremacy, a construct of male subjectivity. The silences, the empty spaces, the language itself, with its excision of the female, the methods of discourse tell us as much as the content, once we learn to watch for what is left out, to listen for the unspoken, to study the patterns of established science and scholarship with an outsider's eye. One of the dangers of a privileged education for women is that we may lose the eye of the outsider and come to believe that those patterns hold for humanity, for the universal, and that they include us.

And so I want to talk today about privilege and about tokenism and 5
about power. Everything I can say to you on this subject comes hard-won, from the lips of a woman privileged by class and skin color, a father's favorite daughter, educated at Radcliffe, which was then casually referred to as the Harvard "Annex." Much of the first four decades of my life was spent in a continuous tension between the world the Fathers taught me to see, and had rewarded me for seeing, and the flashes of insight that came through the eye of the outsider. Gradually those flashes of insight, which at times could seem like brushes with madness, began to demand that I struggle to connect them with each other, to insist that I take them seriously. It was only when I could finally affirm the outsider's eye as the source of a legitimate and coherent vision, that I began to be able to do the work I truly wanted to do, live the kind of life I truly wanted to live, instead of carrying out the assignments I had been given as a privileged woman and a token.

For women, all privilege is relative. Some of you were not born with class or skin-color privilege; but you all have the privilege of education, even if it is an education which has largely denied you knowledge of yourselves as women. You have, to begin with, the privilege of literacy; and it is well for us to remember that, in an age of increasing illiteracy, 60 percent of the world's illiterates are women. Between 1960 and 1970, the number of illiterate men in the world rose by 8 million, while the number of illiterate women rose by 40 million.[1] And the number of illiterate women is increasing. Beyond literacy, you have the privilege of training and tools which can allow you to go beyond the content of your education and re-educate yourselves—to debrief yourselves, we might call it, of the false messages of your education in this culture, the messages telling you that women have not really cared about power or learning or creative opportunities because of a psychobiological need to serve men and produce children; that only a few atypical women have been exceptions to this rule; the messages telling you that woman's experience is neither normative nor central to human experience. You have the training and the tools to do independent research, to evaluate data, to criticize, and to express in language and visual forms what you discover. This is a privilege, yes, but only if you do not give up in exchange for it the deep knowledge of the unprivileged, the knowledge that, as a woman, you have historically been viewed and still are viewed as existing, not in your own right, but in the service of men. And only if you refuse to give up your capacity to think as a woman, even though in the graduate schools and

[1]United Nations, Department of International Economic and Social Affairs, Statistical Office, *1977 Compendium of Social Statistics* (New York: United Nations, 1980).

professions to which many of you will be going you will be praised and rewarded for "thinking like a man."

The word *power* is highly charged for women. It has been long associated for us with the use of force, with rape, with the stockpiling of weapons, with the ruthless accrual of wealth and the hoarding of resources, with the power that acts only in its own interest, despising and exploiting the powerless—including women and children. The effects of this kind of power are all around us, even literally in the water we drink and the air we breathe, in the form of carcinogens and radioactive wastes. But for a long time now, feminists have been talking about redefining power, about that meaning of power which returns to the root—*posse, potere, pouvoir:* to be able, to have the potential, to possess and use one's energy of creation—*transforming power.* An early objection to feminism—in both the nineteenth and twentieth centuries—was that it would make women behave like men—ruthlessly, exploitatively, oppressively. In fact, radical feminism looks to a transformation of human relationships and structures in which power, instead of a thing to be hoarded by a few, would be released to and from within the many, shared in the form of knowledge, expertise, decision making, access to tools, as well as in the basic forms of food and shelter and health care and literacy. Feminists—and many nonfeminists—are, and rightly so, still concerned with what power would mean in such a society, and with the relative differences in power among and between women here and now.

Which brings me to a third meaning of power where women are concerned: the false power which masculine society offers to a few women, on condition that they use it to maintain things as they are, and that they essentially "think like men." This is the meaning of female tokenism: that power withheld from the vast majority of women is offered to a few, so that it appears that any "truly qualified" woman can gain access to leadership, recognition, and reward; hence, that justice based on merit actually prevails. The token woman is encouraged to see herself as different from most other women, as exceptionally talented and deserving, and to separate herself from the wider female condition; and she is perceived by "ordinary" women as separate also, perhaps even as stronger than themselves.

Because you are, within the limits of all women's ultimate outsiderhood, a privileged group of women, it is extremely important for your future sanity that you understand the way tokenism functions. Its most immediate contradiction is that, while it seems to offer the individual token woman a means to realize her creativity, to influence the course of events, it also, by exacting of her certain kinds of behavior and style, acts to blur her outsider's eye, which could be her real source of power and vision. Losing her outsider's vision, she loses the insight which both binds her to other women and affirms her in herself. Tokenism essentially demands that the token deny her identification with women as a group, especially with women less privileged than she: if she is a lesbian, that she deny her relationships with individual women; that she perpetuate rules and structures and criteria and methodologies which have functioned to exclude women; that she renounce or leave undeveloped the critical perspective of her female consciousness. Women unlike herself—poor women, women of color, waitresses, secretaries, housewives in the supermarket, prostitutes, old women—become invisible to her; they may represent too acutely what she has escaped or wished to flee.

President Conway tells me that ever-increasing numbers of you are 10
going on from Smith to medical and law schools. The news, on the face of it, is good: that, thanks to the feminist struggle of the past decade, more doors into these two powerful professions are open to women. I would like to believe that any profession would be better for having more women practicing it, and that any woman practicing law or medicine would use her knowledge and skill to work to transform the realm of health care and the interpretations of the law, to make them responsive to the needs of all those—women, people of color, children, the aged, the dispossessed—for whom they function today as repressive controls. I would like to believe this, but it will not happen even if 50 percent of the members of these professions are women, unless those women refuse to be made into token insiders, unless they zealously preserve the outsider's view and the outsider's consciousness.

For no woman is really an insider in the institutions fathered by masculine consciousness. When we allow ourselves to believe we are, we lose touch with parts of ourselves defined as unacceptable by that consciousness; with the vital toughness and visionary strength of the angry grandmothers, the shamanesses, the fierce marketwomen of the Ibo Women's War, the marriage-resisting women silkworkers of prerevolutionary China, the millions of widows, midwives, and women healers tortured and burned as witches for three centuries in Europe, the Beguines of the twelfth century, who formed independent women's orders outside the domination of the Church, the women of the Paris Commune who marched on Versailles, the uneducated housewives of the Women's Cooperative Guild in England who memorized poetry over the washtub and organized against their oppression as mothers, the women thinkers discredited as "strident," "shrill," "crazy," or "deviant" whose courage to be heretical, to speak their truths, we so badly need to draw upon in our own lives. I believe that every woman's soul is haunted by the spirits of earlier women who fought for their unmet needs and those of their children and their tribes and their peoples, who refused to accept the prescriptions of a male church and state, who took risks and resisted, as women today—like Inez Garcia, Yvonne Wanrow, Joan Little, Cassandra Peten—are fighting their rapists and batterers. Those spirits dwell in us, trying to speak to us. But we can choose to be deaf; and tokenism, the myth of the "special" woman, the unmothered Athena sprung from her father's brow, can deafen us to their voices.

In this decade now ending, as more women are entering the professions (though still suffering sexual harassment in the workplace, though still, if they have children, carrying two full-time jobs, though still vastly outnumbered by men in upper-level and decision-making jobs), we need most profoundly to remember that early insight of the feminist movements as it evolved in the late sixties: *that no woman is liberated until we all are liberated.* The media flood us with messages to the contrary, telling us that we live in an era when "alternate life styles" are freely accepted, when "marriage contracts" and "the new intimacy" are revolutionizing heterosexual relationships, that shared parenting and the "new fatherhood" will change the world. And we live in a society leeched upon by the "personal growth" and "human potential" industry, by the delusion that individual self-fulfillment can be found in thirteen weeks or a weekend, that the alienation and injustice experienced by women, by Black and Third World people, by the poor, in a world ruled by white males, in a society which fails to meet the most basic needs and which is slowly poisoning itself, can be mitigated or dispersed by Transcendental Meditation. Perhaps the most succinct expression of this message I have seen is the appearance of a magazine for women called *Self.* The insistence of the feminist movement, that each woman's selfhood is precious, that the feminine ethic of self-denial and self-sacrifice must give way to a true woman identification, which would affirm our connectedness with all women, is perverted into a commercially profitable and politically debilitating narcissism. It is important for each of you, toward whom many of these messages are especially directed, to discriminate clearly between "liberated life style" and feminist struggle, and to make a conscious choice.

It's a cliché of commencement speeches that the speaker ends with a peroration telling the new graduates that however badly past generations have behaved, their generation must save the world. I would rather say to you, women of the class of 1979: Try to be worthy of your foresisters, learn from your history, look for inspiration to your ancestresses. If this history has been poorly taught to you, if you do not know it, then use your educational privilege to learn it. Learn how some women of privilege have compromised the greater liberation of women, how others have risked their privileges to further it; learn how brilliant and successful women have failed to create a more just and caring society, precisely because they have tried to do so on terms that the powerful men around them would accept and tolerate. Learn to be worthy of the women of every class, culture, and historical age who did otherwise, who spoke boldly when women were jeered and physically harassed for speaking in public, who—like Anne Hutchinson, Mary Wollstonecraft, the Grimké sisters, Abby Kelley, Ida B. Wells-Barnett, Susan B. Anthony, Lillian Smith, Fannie Lou Hamer—broke taboos, who resisted slavery—their own and other people's. To become a token woman—whether you win the Nobel prize or merely get tenure at the cost of denying your sisters—is to become something less than a man indeed, since men are loyal at least to their own world view, their laws of brotherhood and male self-interest. I am not suggesting that you imitate male loyalties; with the philosopher Mary Daly, I believe that the bonding of women must be utterly different and for an utterly different end: not the misering of resources and power, but the release, in each other, of the yet unexplored resources and transformative power of women, so long despised, confined, and wasted. Get all the knowledge and skill you can in whatever professions you enter; but remember that most of your education must be self-education, in learning the things women need to know and in calling up the voices we need to hear within ourselves.

QUESTIONING THE TEXT

1. Rich says that the term *power* is "highly charged for women," and she uses it in several different senses in this essay. Look carefully at these different meanings of *power.* Which meaning fits best with your own understanding—and would you agree that *power* is "highly charged for women"?
2. Rich lists three broad areas of knowledge that, she argues, women most need. What reasons and evidence does she offer to explain why women need such knowledge?
3. How does A.L.'s reference to her own school experience affect your reading of Rich's essay, if at all? Why do you think A.L. included this information in the introduction?

MAKING CONNECTIONS

4. Do you agree with Rich that women's educational needs are different from men's? Why, or why not? In "The Idea of a University" (p. 52), John Henry Newman seems to suggest that all students have the same basic needs. How might Rich respond to him on this point?
5. Donald Kagan's "What Is a Liberal Education?" (p. 141) criticizes colleges for failing to provide students with the kind of education they need to be effective citizens. How does his perspective differ from that of Rich? Would the two authors agree on any aspects of a good education? Write a one-page dialogue between the two authors on the subject of what a university should teach its students.

JOINING THE CONVERSATION

6. What, if any, changes has your school made in the last twenty-five years or so to accommodate the needs and interests of women students? Consider such factors as increased hiring of women faculty, the opening of a women's student center or a women's studies program or department, speakers on women's issues, improvements in campus safety. Write a brief editorial intended for your campus newspaper in which you reflect on the extent to which your school is "user-friendly" for women and whether women at your school can learn what they most "need to know."
7. Try your own hand at writing a brief essay answering the question "What does a woman [or man] need to know?" You may want to compare your essay with those of other classmates, noting points of agreement and disagreement—particularly among women and men.

SHELBY STEELE
The Recoloring of Campus Life

Shelby Steele's book on race relations in the United States, The Content of Our Character *(1990), takes its title from Martin Luther King Jr.'s "I Have a Dream" speech, delivered at a civil rights demonstration in Washington, D.C., in 1963. In that address, King called for the eradication of racial prejudices: "I have a dream my four little children will one day live in a nation where they will not be judged by the color of their skin but by the content of their character." More than a generation later, Steele (b. 1946) poses the painful question of whether the civil rights establishment has abandoned King's dream. Has the goal of desegregation, he asks, been supplanted by ethnic and racial separation? Has the ideal of equal opportunity been tainted by quotas?*

The lengthy chapter of the book reprinted here examines the sensitive subject of race relations on campus frankly and openly. Steele, a research fellow at the conservative Hoover Institution at Stanford University, is a controversial figure, a black man whose views, like those of Supreme Court Justice Clarence Thomas, affirmative action opponent Ward Connerly, and economist Thomas Sowell, challenge the agenda of many civil rights organizations. Steele confronts the anxieties of both blacks and whites with uncommon directness. Because of the national discomfort we feel in talking about race and racism, some people regard views like Steele's as politically "incorrect." Judge for yourself whether he is raising issues that ought not to be matters of debate. —J.R.

The U.S. has about 3,000 colleges and universities. Do 80 incidents a year—most involving ethnic "insensitivity"—really constitute an increase in racial tensions? Was there a time when such incidents were fewer? —J.R.

What is this institute—and what is its agenda? —A.L.

In the past few years, we have witnessed what the National Institute Against Prejudice and Violence calls a "proliferation" of racial incidents on college campuses around the country. Incidents of on-campus "intergroup conflict" have occurred at more than 160 colleges in the last two years, according to the institute. The nature of these incidents has ranged from open racial violence—most notoriously, the October 1986 beating of a black student at the University of Massachusetts at Amherst after an argument about the World Series turned into a racial bashing, with a crowd of up to three thousand whites chasing twenty blacks—to the harassment of minority students and acts of racial or ethnic insensitivity, with by far the greatest number of episodes falling in the last two categories. At Yale last year, a swastika and the words "white power" were painted on the university's Afro-American cultural center. Racist jokes

Are such anonymous acts the result of true hatred for other races, or are they simply immature behavior? —T.E.

These examples make me think of racist acts on my own campus—but also of attempts to counter those acts with acts of respect and generosity for all people. —A.L.

were aired not long ago on a campus radio station at the University of Michigan. And at the University of Wisconsin at Madison, members of the Zeta Beta Tau fraternity held a mock slave auction in which pledges painted their faces black and wore Afro wigs. Two weeks after the president of Stanford University informed the incoming freshman class last fall that "bigotry is out, and I mean it," two freshmen defaced a poster of Beethoven—gave the image thick lips—and hung it on a black student's door.

Why do racial incidents proliferate on campuses usually regarded as "progressive"—Stanford, Berkeley, Wisconsin, U Mass? —J.R.

In response, black students around the country have rediscovered the militant protest strategies of the sixties. At the University of Massachusetts at Amherst, Williams College, Penn State University, University of California–Berkeley, UCLA, Stanford University, and countless other campuses, black students have sat in, marched, and rallied. But much of what they were marching and rallying about seemed less a response to specific racial incidents than a call for broader action on the part of the colleges and universities they were attending. Black students have demanded everything from more black faculty members and new courses on racism to the addition of "ethnic" foods in the cafeteria. There is the sense in these demands that racism runs deep. Is the campus becoming the battleground for a renewed war between the races? I don't think so, not really. But if it is not a war, the problem of campus racism does represent a new and surprising hardening of racial lines within the most traditionally liberal and tolerant of America's institutions—its universities.

Are they implying whites and blacks teach differently based on skin color? Isn't this racism, too? —T.E.

Is he suggesting that racism doesn't run deep? If so, I'll need a lot of evidence to be convinced. —A.L.

As a black who has spent his entire adult life on predominantly white campuses, I found it hard to believe that the problem of campus racism was as dramatic as some of the incidents seemed to make it. The incidents I read or heard about often seemed prankish and adolescent, though not necessarily harmless. There is a meanness in them but not much menace; no one is proposing to reinstitute Jim Crow on campus. On the California campus where I now teach, there have been few signs of racial tension.

Interesting that he presents his own perspective ("not much menace") as the only one. Other African Americans may not have this perspective. —A.L.

Steele must never have been the target of any of these types of racist acts. He would view them more harshly if he had. —T.E.

And, of course, universities are not where racial problems tend to arise. When I went to college in the mid-sixties, colleges were oases of calm and understanding in a racially tense society; campus life—with its traditions of tolerance and fairness, its very distance from the "real" world—imposed a degree of broad-mindedness on even the most provincial students. If I met whites who were not anxious to be friends with blacks, most were at least vaguely friendly to the cause of our freedom. In any case, there was no guerrilla activity against our presence, no "mine field of racism" (as one black student at Berkeley recently put it to me) to negotiate. I wouldn't say that the phrase "campus racism" is a contradiction in terms, but until recently it certainly seemed an incongruence.

I was in college at this same time, and this does not describe my experience on a very racist and often hostile campus. —A.L.

But a greater incongruence is the generational timing of this new problem on the campuses. Today's undergraduates were born after the passage of the 1964 Civil Rights Act. They grew up in an age when racial equality was for the first time enforceable by law. This too was a time when blacks suddenly appeared on television, as mayors of big cities, as icons of popular culture, as teachers, and in some cases even as neighbors. Today's black and white college students, veterans of "Sesame Street" and often of integrated grammar and high schools, have had more opportunities to know each other than any previous generation in American history. Not enough opportunities, perhaps, but enough to make the notion of racial tension on campus something of a mystery, at least to me.

He's now assuming *it's a "new" problem, but he hasn't proven it.* —A.L.

To look at this mystery, I left my own campus with its burden of familiarity and talked with black and white students at California schools where racial incidents had occurred: Stanford, UCLA, and Berkeley. I spoke with black and white students—not with Asians and Hispanics—because, as always, blacks and whites represent the deepest lines of division, and because I hesitate to wander onto the complex territory of other minority groups. A phrase by William H. Gass—"the hidden internality of things"—describes, with maybe a little too much grandeur, what I hoped to find. But it is what I wanted to find, for this is the kind of problem that makes a black person nervous, which

I don't follow him here. What does he mean by "hidden internality"? —A.L.

is not to say that it doesn't unnerve whites as well. Once every six months or so someone yells "nigger" at me from a passing car. I don't like to think that these solo artists might soon make up a chorus, or worse, that this chorus might one day soon sing to me from the paths of my own campus.

I have long believed that the trouble between the races is seldom what it appears to be. It was not hard to see after my first talks with students that racial tension on campus is a problem that misrepresents itself. It has the same look, the archetypal pattern, of America's timeless racial conflict—white racism and black protest. And I think part of our concern over it comes from the fact that it has the feel of a relapse, illness gone and come again. But if we are seeing the same symptoms, I don't believe we are dealing with the same illness. For one thing, I think racial tension on campus is more the result of racial equality than inequality.

Maybe this is what he means—the old appearance/reality binary. —A.L.

Has racism ever really "gone"? —T.E.

Is this the main point he is arguing? —A.L.

How to live with racial difference has been America's profound social problem. For the first hundred years or so following emancipation it was controlled by a legally sanctioned inequality that kept the races from each other. No longer is this the case. On campuses today, as throughout society, blacks enjoy equality under the law—a profound social advancement. No student may be kept out of a class or a dormitory or an extracurricular activity because of his or her race. But there is a paradox here: on a campus where members of all races are gathered, mixed together in the classroom as well as socially, differences are more exposed than ever. And this is where the trouble starts. For members of each race—young adults coming into their own, often away from home for the first time—bring to this site of freedom, exploration, and (now, today) equality, very deep fears, anxieties, inchoate feelings of racial shame, anger, and guilt. These feelings could lie dormant in the home, in familiar neighborhoods, in simpler days of childhood. But the college campus, with its structures of interaction and adult-level competition—the big exam, the dorm, the mixer—is another matter. I think campus racism is born of the rub between racial difference and a setting, the campus itself, devoted to interaction and

He's right: higher education challenges the comfortable assumptions most students bring to campus. —J.R.

I've never experienced such feelings where race is concerned, and I come from a predominantly white community. —T.E.

equality. On our campuses, such concentrated micro-societies, all that remains unresolved between blacks and whites, all the old wounds and shames that have never been addressed, present themselves for attention—and present our youth with pressures they cannot always handle.

I have mentioned one paradox: racial fears and anxieties among blacks and whites, bubbling up in an era of racial equality under the law, in settings that are among the freest and fairest in society. But there is another, related paradox, stemming from the notion of—and practice of—affirmative action. Under the provisions of the Equal Employment Opportunity Act of 1972, all state governments and institutions (including universities) were forced to initiate plans to increase the proportion of minority and women employees and, in the case of universities, of students too. Affirmative action plans that establish racial quotas were ruled unconstitutional more than ten years ago in *University of California* v. *Bakke,* but such plans are still thought by some to secretly exist, and lawsuits having to do with alleged quotas are still very much with us. But quotas are only the most controversial aspect of affirmative action; the principle of affirmative action is reflected in various university programs aimed at redressing and overcoming past patterns of discrimination. Of course, to be conscious of past patterns of discrimination—the fact, say, that public schools in the black inner cities are more crowded and employ fewer top-notch teachers than a white suburban public school, and that this is a factor in student performance—is only reasonable. But in doing this we also call attention quite obviously to difference: in the case of blacks and whites, racial difference. What has emerged on campus in recent years—as a result of the new equality and of affirmative action and, in a sense, as a result of progress—is a *politics of difference,* a troubling, volatile politics in which each group justifies itself, its sense of worth and its pursuit of power, through difference alone.

This idealistic view of a university as "free and fair" would be contested by many. —A.L.

The beneficiaries of affirmative action are usually middle-class students—not poor minority youth from inner cities. Do middle-class whites resent that fact? —J.R.

Identity politics (I get my identity solely and only through one characteristic, such as race) to me is different from politics of difference, which seeks to honor differences among all people while not ignoring commonalities. —A.L.

In this context, racial, ethnic, and gender differences become forms of sovereignty, campuses become balkanized, and each group fights with whatever means are available. No doubt there are many factors that have contributed to the rise of racial tension on campus: What has been the role of fraternities, which have returned to campus with their inclusions and exclusions? What role has the heightened notion of college as some first step to personal, financial success played in increasing competition, and thus tension? But mostly, what I sense is that in interactive settings, fighting the fights of "difference," old ghosts are stirred and haunt again. Black and white Americans simply have the power to make each other feel shame and guilt. In most situations, we may be able to deny these feelings, keep them at bay. But these feelings are likely to surface on college campuses, where young people are groping for identity and power, and where difference is made to matter so greatly. In a way, racial tension on campus in the eighties might have been inevitable.

Black shame and white guilt? Steele's analysis looks simplistic. Can he sustain it? —J.R.

Steele implies that college students are shallow, that they would immediately focus on race if any problem arose. This is not my experience. —T.E.

I would like, first, to discuss black students, their anxieties and vulnerabilities. The accusation black Americans have always lived with is that they are inferior—inferior simply because they are black. And this accusation has been too uniform, too ingrained in cultural imagery, too enforced by law, custom, and every form of power not to have left a mark. Black inferiority was a precept accepted by the founders of this nation; it was a principle of social organization that relegated blacks to the sidelines of American life. So when young black students find themselves on white campuses surrounded by those who have historically claimed superiority, they are also surrounded by the myth of their inferiority.

Of course, it is true that many young people come to college with some anxiety about not being good enough. But only blacks come wearing a color that is still, in the minds of some, a sign of inferiority. Poles, Jews, Hispanics, and other groups also endure degrading stereotypes. But two things make the myth of black inferiority a far heavier burden—the broadness of its scope and its incarnation in color. There are not only more stereotypes of blacks than of other groups, but these stereotypes are also more dehumanizing, more focused on the most despised human traits: stupidity, laziness, sexual immorality, dirtiness, and so on. In America's racial and ethnic hierarchy,

When he uses "of course" I always wonder whether I'll agree with what comes next! —A.L.

blacks have clearly been relegated to the lowest level—have been burdened with an ambiguous, animalistic humanity. Moreover, this is made unavoidable for blacks by sheer visibility of black skin, a skin that evokes the myth of inferiority on sight. Today this myth is sadly reinforced for many black students by affirmative action programs, under which blacks may often enter college with lower test scores and high school grade point averages than whites. "They see me as an affirmative action case," one black student told me at UCLA. This reinforces the myth of inferiority by implying that blacks are not good enough to make it into college on their own.

I have often wondered if any blacks felt affirmative action projects were just racist and belittling. —T.E.

Test scores reflect biased test designs, and grades can too. I don't buy this argument. —A.L.

So when a black student enters college, the myth of inferiority compounds the normal anxiousness over whether he or she will be good enough. This anxiety is not only personal but also racial. The families of these students will have pounded into them the fact that blacks are not inferior. And probably more than anything it is this pounding that finally leaves the mark. If I am not inferior, why the need to say so?

This myth of inferiority constitutes a very sharp and ongoing anxiety for young blacks, the nature of which is very precise: it is the terror that somehow, through one's actions or by virtue of some "proof" (a poor grade, a flubbed response in class), one's fear of inferiority—inculcated in ways large and small by society—will be confirmed as real. On a university campus where intelligence itself is the ultimate measure, this anxiety is bound to be triggered.

A black student I met at UCLA was disturbed a little when I asked him if he ever felt vulnerable—anxious about "black inferiority"—as a black student. But after a long pause, he finally said, "I think I do." The example he gave was of a large lecture class he'd taken with over three hundred students. Fifty or so black students sat in the back of the lecture hall and "acted out every stereotype in the book." They were loud, ate food, came in late—and generally got lower grades than whites in the class. "I knew I would be seen like them, and I didn't like it. I never sat by them." Seen like what, I asked, though we both knew the answer. "As lazy, ignorant, and stupid," he said sadly.

Or smart but bored? —A.L.

Steele makes a convincing distinction here. Growing up, I heard Polish jokes and slurs, but not often enough to think that society really believed the stereotype. That makes a difference. —J.R.

Had the group at the back been white fraternity brothers, they would not have been seen as dumb whites, of course. And a frat brother who worried about his grades would not worry that he [had] been seen "like them." The terror in this situation for the black student I spoke with was that his own deeply buried anxiety would be given credence, that the myth would be verified, and that he would feel shame and humiliation not because of who he was but simply because he was black. In this lecture hall his race, quite apart from his performance, might subject him to four unendurable feelings—diminishment, accountability to the preconceptions of whites, a powerlessness to change those preconceptions, and finally, shame. These are the feelings that make up his racial anxiety, and that of all blacks on any campus. On a white campus a black is never far from these feelings, and even his unconscious knowledge that he is subject to them can undermine his self-esteem. There are blacks on any campus who are not up to doing good college-level work. Certain black students may not be happy or motivated or in the appropriate field of study—*just like whites.* (Let us not forget that many white students get poor grades, fail, drop out.) Moreover, many more blacks than whites are not quite prepared for college, may have to catch up, owing to factors beyond their control: poor previous schooling, for example. But the white who has to catch up will not be anxious that his being behind is a matter of his whiteness, of his being racially inferior. The black student may well have such a fear.

I don't buy this—the fraternity stereotype is quite strong, too. Why wouldn't a frat brother be disturbed? —T.E.

I'm irritated by his continued attempts to speak for all African Americans. —A.L.

Do Asian American students feel similarly pressured by a stereotype that marks them all as diligent, hard-working, and extraordinarily smart? —J.R.

This, I believe, is one reason why black colleges in America turn out 37 percent of all black college graduates though they enroll only 16 percent of black college students. Without whites around on campus, the myth of inferiority is in abeyance and, along with it, a great reservoir of culturally imposed self-doubt. On black campuses, feelings of inferiority are personal; on campuses with a white majority, a black's problems have a way of becoming a "black" problem.

Going to an all-black college doesn't shut out the rest of the world. I don't buy this. —T.E.

But this feeling of vulnerability a black may feel, in itself, is not as serious a problem as what he or she does with it. To admit that one is made anxious in integrated situations about the myth of racial inferiority is difficult for young blacks. It seems like admitting that one is racially inferior. And so, most often, the student will deny harboring the feelings. This is where some of the pangs of racial tension begin, because denial always involves distortion.

Do all *blacks feel this way? Steele is generalizing.* —T.E.

In order to deny a problem we must tell ourselves that the problem is something different from what it really is. A black student at Berkeley told me that he felt defensive every time he walked into a classroom of white faces. When I asked why, he said, "Because I know they're all racists. They think blacks are stupid." Of course it may be true that some whites feel this way, but the singular focus on white racism allows this student to obscure his own underlying racial anxiety. He can now say that his problem—facing a classroom of white faces, *fearing* that they think he is dumb—is entirely the result of certifiable white racism and has nothing to do with his own anxieties, or even that this particular academic subject may not be his best. Now all the terror of his anxiety, its powerful energy, is devoted to simply *seeing* racism. Whatever evidence of racism he finds—and looking this hard, he will no doubt find some—can be brought in to buttress his distorted view of the problem while his actual deep-seated anxiety goes unseen.

This helps explain the dilemma of many black students on mainly white campuses. —J.R.

This seems a kind of false either/or argument to me. Either the problem is all *external (white racists) or* all *internal (deep-seated anxieties).* —A.L.

Denial, and the distortion that results, places the problem *outside* the self and in the world. It is not that I have any inferiority anxiety because of my race; it is that I am going to school with people who don't like blacks. This is the shift in thinking that allows black students to reenact the protest pattern of the sixties. *Denied racial anxiety–distortion–reenactment* is the process by which feelings of inferiority are transformed into an exaggerated white menace—which is then protested against with the techniques of the past. Under the sway of this process, black students believe that history is repeating itself, that it's just like the sixties, or fifties. In fact, it is not-yet-healed wounds from the past, rather than the inequality that created the wounds, that is the real problem.

Obsessive attention to race can breed racist feelings. That's one reason I'm uneasy with multicultural curriculums that emphasize difference. —J.R.

This process generated an unconscious need to exaggerate the level of racism on campus—to make it a matter of the system, not just a handful of students. Racism is the avenue away from the true inner anxiety. How many students demonstrating for black theme dorms—demonstrating in the style of the sixties, when the battle was to win for blacks a place on campus—might be better off spending their time reading and studying? Black students have the highest dropout rate and the lowest grade point average of any group in American universities. This need not be so. And it is not the result of not having black theme dorms.

People said the same thing to the '60s civil rights protesters. —A.L.

It was my very good fortune to go to college in 1964, when the question of black "inferiority" was openly talked about among blacks. The summer before I left for college, I heard Martin Luther King speak in Chicago, and he laid it on the line for black students everywhere: "When you are behind in a footrace, the only way to get ahead is to run faster than the man in front of you. So when your white roommate says he's tired and goes to sleep, you stay up and burn the midnight oil." His statement that we were "behind in a footrace" acknowledged that, because of history, of few opportunities, of racism, we were, in a sense, "inferior." But this had to do with what had been done to our parents and their parents, not with inherent inferiority. And because it was acknowledged, it was presented to us as a challenge rather than a mark of shame.

Of the eighteen black students (in a student body of one thousand) who were on campus in my freshman year, all graduated, though a number of us were not from the middle class. At the university where I currently teach, the dropout rate for black students is 72 percent, despite the presence of several academic support programs, a counseling center with black counselors, an Afro-American studies department, black faculty, administrators, and staff, a general education curriculum that emphasizes "cultural pluralism," an Educational Opportunities Program, a mentor program, a black faculty and staff association, and an administration and faculty that often announce the need to do more for black students.

At my university, these programs are less prominent. At Stanford, only 3 percent of the faculty are African American. —A.L.

It may be unfair to compare my generation with the current one. Parents do this compulsively and to little end but self-congratulation. But I don't congratulate my generation. I think we were advantaged. We came along at a time when racial integration was held in high esteem. And integration was a very challenging social concept for both blacks and whites. We were remaking ourselves—that's what one did at college—and making history. We had something to prove. This was a profound advantage; it gave us clarity and a challenge. Achievement in the American mainstream was the goal of integration, and the best thing about this challenge was its secondary message—that we *could* achieve.

Integration *is a goal rarely mentioned in campus discussions of racial problems these days.* —J.R.

Is "achievement in the American mainstream" another way of saying "being like white people"? —A.L.

There is much irony in the fact that black power would come along in the late sixties and change all this. Black power was a movement of uplift and pride, and yet it also delivered the weight of pride—a weight that would burden black students from then on. Black power "nationalized" the black identity, made blackness itself an object of celebration, an allegiance. But if it transformed a mark of shame into a mark of pride, it also, in the name of pride, required the denial of racial anxiety. Without a frank account of one's anxieties, there is no clear direction, no concrete challenge. Black students today do not get as clear a message from their racial identity as my generation got. They are not filled with the same urgency to prove themselves because black pride has said, *You're already proven, already equal, as good as anybody.*

This may be true, but it's another one of those either/or arguments I'm always leery of. —A.L.

The "black identity" shaped by black power most forcefully contributes to racial tensions on campuses by basing entitlement more on race than on constitutional rights and standards of merit. With integration, black entitlement derived from constitutional principles of fairness. Black power changed this by skewing the formula from rights to color—if you were black, you were entitled. Thus the United Coalition Against Racism (UCAR) at the University of Michigan could "demand" two years ago that all black professors be given immediate tenure, that there [be] a special pay incentive for black professors, and that money be provided for an all-black student union. In this formula, black becomes the very color of entitlement, an extra right in itself, and a very dangerous grandiosity is promoted in which blackness amounts to specialness.

I agree. It's just as racist (and negative) to have all-black unions as it is to have all-white ones. —T.E.

Race is, by any standard, an unprincipled source of power. And on campuses the use of racial power by one group makes racial, ethnic, or gender difference a currency of power for all groups. When I make my *difference* into power, other groups must seize upon their difference to contain my power and maintain their position relative to me. Very quickly a kind of politics of difference emerges in which racial, ethnic, and gender groups are forced to assert their entitlement and vie for power based on the single quality that makes them different from one another.

I agree. Balkanization can present a danger, but that doesn't *mean we should reject difference.* —A.L.

On many campuses today academic departments and programs are established on the basis of difference—black studies, women's studies, Asian studies, and so on—despite the fact that there is nothing in these "difference" departments that cannot be studied within traditional academic disciplines. If their rationale is truly past exclusion from the mainstream curriculum, shouldn't the goal now be complete inclusion rather than separateness? I think this logic is overlooked because those groups are too interested in the power their difference can bring, and they insist on separate departments and programs as tribute to that power.

This politics of difference makes everyone on campus a member of a minority group. It also makes racial tension inevitable. To highlight one's difference as a source of advantage is also, indirectly, to inspire the enemies of that difference. When blackness (and femaleness) become power, then white maleness is also sanctioned as power. A white male student I spoke with at Stanford said, "One of my friends said the other day that we should get together and start up a white student union and come up with a list of demands."

Quite true—but does one lead to the other? —T.E.

It is certainly true that white maleness has long been an unfair source of power. But the sin of white male power is precisely its use of race and gender as a source of entitlement. When minorities and women use their race, ethnicity, and gender in the same way, they not only commit the same sin but also, indirectly, sanction the very form of power that oppressed them in the first place. The politics of difference is based on a tit-for-tat sort of logic in which every victory only calls one's enemies to arms.

This elevation of difference undermines the communal impulse by making each group foreign and inaccessible to others. When difference is celebrated rather than remarked, people must think in terms of difference, they must find meaning in difference, and this meaning comes from an endless process of contrasting one's group with other groups. Blacks use whites to define themselves as different, women use men, Hispanics use whites and blacks, and on it goes. And in the process each group mythologizes and mystifies its difference, puts it beyond the full comprehension of outsiders. Difference becomes inaccessible preciousness toward which outsiders are expected to be simply and uncomprehendingly reverential. But beware: in this world, even the insulated world of the college campus, preciousness is a balloon asking for a needle. At Smith College graffiti appears: "Niggers, spics, and chinks. Quit complaining or get out."

Another either/or. I don't accept the notion that we must honor only one or the other—difference or community. —A.L.

I think that those who run our colleges and universities are every bit as responsible for the politics of difference as are minority students. To correct the exclusions once caused by race and gender, universities—under the banner of affirmative action—have relied too heavily on race and gender as criteria. So rather than break the link between difference and power, they have reinforced it. On most campuses today, a well-to-do black student with two professional parents is qualified by his race for scholarship monies that are not available to a lower-middle-class white student. A white female with a private school education and every form of cultural advantage comes under the affirmative action umbrella. This kind of inequity is an invitation to backlash.

These generalizations simply are not true. Affirmative action at my school does nothing *to advantage the students described here.* —A.L.

What universities are quite rightly trying to do is compensate people for past discrimination and the deprivations that followed from it. But race and gender alone offer only the grossest measure of this. And the failure of universities has been their backing away from the challenge of identifying principles of fairness and merit that make finer and more equitable distinctions. The real challenge is not simply to include a certain number of blacks, but to end discrimination against all blacks and to offer special help to those with talent who have also been economically deprived.

I agree. —A.L.

With regard to black students, affirmative action has led universities to correlate color with poverty and disadvantage in so absolute a way as to encourage the politics of difference. But why have they gone along with this? My belief is that it is due to the specific form of racial anxiety to which whites are most subject.

I agree. These special funds make me uncomfortable. —T.E.

Most of the white students I talked with spoke as if from under a faint cloud of accusation. There was always a ring of defensiveness in their complaints about blacks. A white student I spoke to at UCLA told me: "Most white students on this campus think the black student leadership here is made up of oversensitive crybabies who spend all their time looking for things to kick up a ruckus about." A white student at Stanford said, "Blacks do nothing but complain and ask for sympathy when everyone really knows that they don't do well because they don't try. If they worked harder, they could do as well as everyone else."

That these students felt accused was most obvious in their compulsion to assure me that they were not racist. Oblique versions of some-of-my-best-friends-are stories came ritualistically before or after critiques of black students. Some said flatly, "I am not a racist, but . . ." Of course, we all deny being racist, but we only do this compulsively, I think, when we are working against an accusation of bias. I think it was the color of my skin itself that accused them.

This was the meta-message that surrounded these conversations like an aura, and it is, I believe, the core of white American racial anxiety. My skin not only accused them; it judged them. And this judgment was a sad gift of history that brought them to account whether they deserved such accountability or not. It said that wherever and whenever blacks

Too bad Steele deliberately avoided talking with Hispanic and Asian minorities. Their perspectives on the matter of "guilt" would have enriched the discussion here. —J.R.

were concerned, they had reason to feel guilt. And whether it was earned or unearned, I think it was guilt that set off the compulsion in these students to disclaim. I believe it is true that, in America, black people make white people feel guilty.

Guilt is the essence of white anxiety just as inferiority is the essence of black anxiety. And the terror that it carries for whites is the terror of discovering that one has reason to feel guilt where blacks are concerned—not so much because of what blacks might think but because of what guilt can say about oneself. If the darkest fear of blacks is inferiority, the darkest fear of whites is that their better lot in life is at least partially the result of their capacity for evil—their capacity to dehumanize an entire people for their own benefit and then to be indifferent to the devastation their dehumanization has wrought on successive generations of their victims. This is the terror that whites are vulnerable to regarding blacks. And the mere fact of being white is sufficient to feel it, since even whites with hearts clean of racism benefit from being white—benefit at the expense of blacks. This is a conditional guilt having nothing to do with individual intentions or actions. And it makes for a very powerful anxiety because it threatens whites with a view of themselves as inhuman, just as inferiority threatens blacks with a similar view of themselves. At the dark core of both anxieties is a suspicion of incomplete humanity.

So, the white students I met were not just meeting me; they were also meeting the possibility of their own inhumanity. And this, I think, is what explains how some young white college students in the late eighties could so frankly take part in racially insensitive and outright racist acts. They were expected to be cleaner of racism than any previous generation—they were born into the Great Society. But this expectation overlooks the fact that, for them, color is still an accusation and judgment. In black faces there is a discomforting reflection of white collective shame. Blacks remind them that their racial innocence is questionable, that they are the beneficiaries of past and present racism, and the sins of the father may well have been visited on the children.

Steele overgeneralizes. All whites are not racists. —T.E.

And yet young whites tell themselves that they had nothing to do with the oppression of black people. They have a stronger belief in their racial innocence than any previous generation of whites and a natural hostility toward anyone who would challenge that innocence. So (with a great deal of individual variation) they can end up in the paradoxical position of being hostile to blacks as a way of defending their own racial innocence.

I think this is what the young white editors of the *Dartmouth Review* were doing when they harassed black music professor William Cole. Weren't they saying, in effect, I am so free of racial guilt that I can afford to attack blacks ruthlessly and still be racially innocent? The ruthlessness of these attacks was a form of denial, a badge of innocence. The more they were charged with racism, the more ugly and confrontational their harassment became (an escalation unexplained even by the serious charges against Professor Cole). Racism became a means of rejecting racial guilt, a way of showing that they were not, ultimately, racists.

The politics of difference sets up a struggle for innocence among all groups. When difference is the currency of power, each group must fight for the innocence that entitles it to power. To gain this innocence, blacks sting whites with guilt, remind them of their racial past, accuse them of new and more subtle forms of racism. One way whites retrieve their innocence is to discredit blacks and deny their difficulties, for in this denial is the denial of their own guilt. To blacks this denial looks like racism, a racism that feeds black innocence and encourages them to throw more guilt at whites. And so the cycle continues. The politics of difference leads each group to pick at the vulnerabilities of the other.

Steele is lumping all administrators together; this makes me skeptical of the following argument. —T.E.

Men and women who run universities—whites, mostly—participate in the politics of difference because they handle their guilt differently than do many of their students. They don't deny it, but still they don't want to *feel* it. And to avoid this feeling of guilt they have tended to go along with whatever blacks put on the table rather than work with them to assess their real needs. University administrators have too often been afraid of guilt and have relied on negotiation and capitulation more to appease their own guilt than to help blacks and other minorities. Administrators would never give white students a racial theme dorm where they could be "more comfortable with people of their own kind," yet more and more universities are doing this for black students, thus fostering a kind of voluntary segregation. To avoid the anxieties of integrated situations blacks ask for theme dorms; to avoid guilt, white administrators give theme dorms.

This is undoubtedly often true. —A.L.

When everyone is on the run from their anxieties about race, race relations on campus can be reduced to the negotiation of avoidances. A pattern of demand and concession develops in which both sides use the other to escape themselves. Black studies departments, black deans of student affairs, black counseling programs, Afro houses, black theme dorms, black homecoming dances and graduation ceremonies—black students and white administrators have slowly engineered a machinery of separatism that, in the name of sacred difference, redraws the ugly lines of segregation.

Black students have not sufficiently helped themselves, and universities, despite all their concessions, have not really done much for blacks. If both faced their anxieties, I think they would see the same thing: academic parity with all other groups should be the overriding mission of black students, and it should also be the first goal that universities have for their black students. Blacks can only *know* they are as good as others when they are, in fact, as good—when their grades are higher and their dropout rate lower. Nothing under the sun will substitute for this, and no amount of concessions will bring it about.

White professors who make comparable observations are sometimes charged with racism. What does such an accusation reveal about the advocates of a campus "politics of difference"? —J.R.

Universities can never be free of guilt until they truly help black students, which means leading and challenging them rather than negotiating and capitulating. It means inspiring them to achieve academic parity, nothing less, and helping them to see their own weaknesses as their greatest challenge. It also means dismantling the machinery of separatism, breaking the link between difference and power, and skewing the formula for entitlement away from race and gender and back to constitutional rights.

As for the young white students who have rediscovered swastikas and the word "nigger," I think that they suffer from an exaggerated sense of their own innocence, as if they were incapable of evil and beyond the reach of guilt. But it is also true that the politics of difference creates an environment that threatens their innocence and makes them defensive. White students are not invited to the negotiating table from which they see blacks and others walk away with concessions. The presumption is that they do not deserve to be there because they are white. So they can only be defensive, and the less mature among them will be aggressive. Guerrilla activity will ensue. Of course this is wrong, but it is also a reflection of an environment where difference carries power and where whites have the wrong "difference."

Not an exaggerated sense of their own importance and power? —A.L.

Basing affirmative action programs (if we must have them) on economic need, not race and gender, would do more to ease tensions on campus than most current solutions. —J.R

I think universities should emphasize commonality as a higher value than "diversity" and "pluralism"—buzzwords for the politics of difference. Difference that does not rest on a clearly delineated foundation of commonality is not only inaccessible to those who are not part of the ethnic or racial group, but also antagonistic to them. Difference can enrich only the common ground.

I want to value commonality and *diversity without establishing a hierarchy where one must always be on top.* —A.L.

Integration has become an abstract term today, having to do with little more than numbers and racial balances. But it once stood for a high and admirable set of values. It made difference second to commonality, and it asked members of all races to face whatever fears they inspired in each other. I doubt the word will have a new vogue, but the values, under whatever name, are worth working for.

Afterwords

The most striking line to me in this selection is Steele's almost casual observation that "every six months or so someone yells 'nigger' at me from a passing car." I admire the courageous way he reacts to such racist acts, refusing to dwell on the pain and insult he must certainly feel. Taking no pleasure in the convincing evidence he has that racism endures in the United States, Steele patiently searches for solutions to the problem, exempting no one from scrutiny, treating no one with contempt. That search is what "The Recoloring of Campus Life" is all about.

In the years since Steele wrote "The Recoloring of Campus Life," the racial issues he explores have been debated intensely in the United States—especially the fairness of affirmative action policies, which had been imposed chiefly by executive order and judicial fiat without the deliberative scrutiny of the legislative process. Despite demagoguery on both sides, the debate has at least made it possible to talk more openly about the enmities Steele records in his groundbreaking chapter. Such honesty will be required in order to open up American education to once-excluded groups without discriminating and segregating anew. The key to success may well be keeping bureaucrats and politicians, especially those in Washington, out of the loop when it comes to decisions about college admissions and enrollment. —J.R.

While I agree with many individual points Steele makes (all students should be challenged to achieve their full potential; commonalities among us are important and should be nurtured), I came away disappointed in this article for several reasons. First, Steele seems too glib in his dismissal of affirmative action, which for all its flaws helped him to achieve and to prosper. In addition, his tendency to locate the source of racial tension in individual anxieties—inferiority for African Americans, guilt for Caucasians—tends to put the blame for problems on campus on individuals or on "a handful of students." In doing so, Steele ignores the degree to which the system of higher education and much else in American society—with its hypercompetition, rank-ordering, and glorification of the kind of extreme individualism that breeds alienation—work to fuel racism that ends up harming all students. Finally, I find that Steele thinks, ironically, in black-and-white terms: either commonality or *difference; either affirmative action* or *equality for all; either black studies, women's studies, and so on* or *a fair and "common" core. My own experience tells me that such polarized thinking is usually oversimplified and that "both/and" is preferable to "either/or." I want to celebrate and value and understand differences among people* and *those common ties that bind us together. I want to know and appreciate what makes me unique, as well as what makes me like other folks, including Shelby Steele. The college campus, I believe, is just the place to enact such a "both/and" philosophy. That's why I like being there. And that's why I have a more hopeful reading of "the recoloring of campus life" than does Steele.* —A.L.

As a college student reading Steele's article, I believe that many of his points make sense. I agree that many affirmative action programs lead some whites to resent the extra aid given to black students. It is difficult to see someone who is not as qualified receive special benefits based on an externality, especially with financial aid, when money matters are often a determining factor in the ability to attend college. However, these special programs never led me to believe black students were unqualified or could not earn scholarships any other way.

Steele overgeneralizes. I do not like to be told, as a Caucasian student, the way in which my race affects how I view my African American classmates. I am sure that some students feel the way Steele believes I should, but to imply that all white students feel guilt seems ludicrous to me. I think, in most cases, generalizations are harmful to the proposed argument; they force readers like me to be skeptical of the arguments.

I personally feel very boxed in by Steele's argument. Blacks think one way, whites think another, according to him. We either have affirmative action or complete equality (if such a thing is possible). This mode of thinking bothers me because the world operates in such vast terms that gray areas are unavoidable. Such polar arguments make it seem as if all campuses are alive with inescapable racial tensions and that noticing differences brings out the racist in everyone. I disagree: college is a place of learning and discovery. It is possible to see differences in background (or color) and understand that those differences do not have to alienate us from others. All people possess qualities that are innately different from or the same as those of others. We can recognize and appreciate these differences without considering them obstacles to be overcome before any similarities can be discovered. —T.E.

QUESTIONING THE TEXT

1. "The Recoloring of Campus Life" contains a great number of cause-and-effect analyses. Identify one example of an effect that Steele traces to its root causes, and then write a paragraph assessing the persuasiveness of his reasoning.
2. Steele notes that about once every six months, someone yells a racial epithet at him from a passing car. Freewrite about such an incident, perhaps describing a similar experience and/or considering how it would feel to be a victim of one.
3. Look at the use of quotation marks in the annotations next to Steele's text. Which ones are used to mark direct quotations, and which ones are used for some other purpose? What other purposes do A.L., T.E., and J.R. have for placing certain words in quotes?

MAKING CONNECTIONS

4. Compare the perspectives on education and power offered by Steele and by Adrienne Rich in "What Does a Woman Need to Know?" (p. 71). How do their ideas about the power afforded by education — and its relation to the power derived from race or gender — differ? Do you find one author's argument about power and education more persuasive than the other? Why, or why not?
5. Would John Henry Newman's concept of the university, as described starting on p. 52, be able to accommodate the kinds of problems with "difference" that Steele describes? Explore the question in a brief essay.

JOINING THE CONVERSATION

6. Steele seems to blame affirmative action programs for many of the racial problems on campuses. Talk to officials on your campus or use the library to augment your understanding of such programs. How do they operate? What is their relationship to the sensitive issue of quotas? Bring your findings to class for discussion.
7. Steele inveighs against the establishment of black "theme" dorms. In a brief column such as might appear in a student newspaper, argue for or against the establishment of dormitories, student unions, or campus cultural programs designed to serve particular ethnic or racial groups.
8. Steele deliberately does not explore the status of other minorities on campus—notably Hispanic and Asian students. With a group of classmates, discuss the problems faced by these groups or others on your campus, such as women, homosexuals, older students, men, Christians, Jews, and so on. Then write a report applying what Steele observes about black-white relationships to the relationship between one of these groups and other students.

JENNIFER L. CROISSANT

Can This Campus Be Bought? Commercial Influence in Unfamiliar Places

Do you attend a Pepsi— or a Coca-Cola— school? What brand name supports your college's or university's athletic teams? What is the relationship between large corporations and your curriculum? Jennifer L. Croissant (b. 1965) asks these and other questions in the following article, which challenges readers to consider the degree to which higher education in America is being bought— and sold— by commercial interests.

Croissant, who is an associate professor in the Program on Culture, Science, Technology, and Society in the Department of Material Science and Engineering at the University of Arizona, has written extensively on social issues affecting science and technology and on science education. Editor of Degrees of Compromise: Industrial Interests and Academic Values *(2001), Croissant is also active in the Pole Pilots Track and Field Club.*

This essay originally appeared in Academe, *the journal of the American Association of University Professors. I chose it for inclusion because, as a college professor and researcher, I am increasingly concerned that the ideal of the university as a place devoted to free and open inquiry— without commercial constraints and the drive to make all knowledge a commodity— is in great danger today.* —A.L.

When Pepsi received the vending contract for the University of Arizona 1
in 1998, we soda consumers at the university expected a discount, given the likely volume of purchasing among the 35,000 people on our campus. Instead, we got a price increase, and decreased shelf and fountain space in campus stores and cafeterias for competing brands. At about the same time, our athletic department developed a contract with Nike for apparel and equipment to supply our sports teams.

An editorial in the school newspaper quipped that one of the things we promised the corporation was a tattoo across the foreheads of the incoming class. Protests against the deals ranged from placid discussions between a Students Against Sweatshops group and university president Peter Likins, to peaceful sit-ins on the lawn, to organized labor symposia and students chaining themselves to the doors of the administration building. Despite these protests, the contracts were signed. While we don't tattoo the first-year students, Nike apparel is ubiquitous, even to the extent of displacing prior contracts that varsity sports teams had had with other suppliers.

Image and Ethics

The effects of commercial activities on university campuses are garnering increased scrutiny from both scholars and activists. Much of the research in this area, including my own, has focused on the connections among commercial activities, values, and research. We need to think critically about the way our relationships with vendors and benefactors affect students and the university image. Students are developing their identities, and that includes brand and lifestyle identities as well as the disciplinary and occupational identities that are the focus of faculty work. The obvious sites for studying the influence of commerce on academic life—the tripartite tradition of teaching, research, and service—have been pretty thoroughly covered in research on higher education. Various scholars have noted that as the distinctions between categories such as research and service or contracts and gifts have blurred, ethical expectations and rules of conduct have also lost clarity.

But other important dimensions of university activities have largely been overlooked. Student life, philanthropy, and vendor relationships are also changing because of commercialization. These features of the university, while perhaps not of central concern to faculty, are important parts of the image of an academic institution, and they are visible to students, the community, businesses, and other institutions.

Universities and their commercial activities are also part of a larger system of connections and images that contribute to the legitimacy of academic institutions as producers of reliable knowledge and sites of independent discourse. When students protest subcontractor wages for service employees at Harvard, they are making a statement about the university's image and conduct.

Because of our increasing involvement with commercial activities, we need to make sure that the university does not betray its educational values and objectives. Commercial connections can help to establish an institution's relevance and, especially for public colleges and universities, a kind of accountability. Having industrial advisory committees, corporate "partners," new philanthropic ventures, vendor contracts, and fairs in the quadrangle allows a university to display an image of being connected and responsive to outside interests. But connection can also mean interference and loss of autonomy, an erosion of core academic values.

We come packaged at Arizona as part of the Pacific-10 Conference. The "Pac-10" provides a league for intercollegiate competition, as well as a reference group for comparison among many other parameters, such as library size, enrollment, and faculty salaries. The conference maintains a Web site, coordinates television revenues and scheduling, and provides for corporate sponsorship of its activities.

In the section of the conference Web site titled "corporate partner opportunities," potential partners are promised "one-stop shopping" for the attention of "260,000 students, 2 million alumni, and 42 million people living in Pac-10 states." In addition to the Internet exposure they receive on the conference Web site, corporate partners get to use conference logos for their own promotional activities, including hospitality gatherings at conference championships and advertising in conference publications and on sports television networks. Independently, the University of Arizona has its own stable of corporate partners, representing national as well as local firms. Some of the Arizona partners, such as Pepsi, are in competition with the Pac-10 partners, such as 7-Up.

Student Life in the Marketplace

So what do these matters have to do with faculty? Think in terms of freedom of expression. When Penn State established vendor relationships with Pepsi in the early 1990s, a policy memo was circulated, and reported in the school newspaper, prohibiting all university employees from advocating for, or otherwise representing, other beverage corporations. No such explicit policy exists at Arizona, but the disruption of coaches' prior relationships with team sponsors as a result of the umbrella Nike contract seems to point in that direction. The worst story I have heard about occurred in a high school, where a student who wore a Coca-Cola t-shirt during "Pepsi Day" was sent home.

10 The larger problem is that these commercial relationships seem so natural to us now that it is difficult even to articulate grounds for critical thinking about corporate ties. Does it really matter to the conduct of academic affairs that our public space, "the mall," is perpetually covered with touring sideshows from Ford, Esprit, and Pepsi, as well as from craft vendors and credit-card hawkers? Those worried about student credit-card debt have protested the latter, but no one is particularly concerned about the other displays, aside from the clutter they create.

Such displays, however, point to the more subtle and important side of packaging campuses to vendors and sponsors. We, as faculty, have been lamenting the students-as-consumers model, where customer satisfaction is all too frequently taken as a surrogate for learning. The conflation of student and consumer (and citizen and consumer) is really the most insidious part of corporate relationships on campus. For many students, to be a citizen is to be a consumer, and nothing more. Freedom means freedom to purchase.

Freedom of speech is elided by freedom of consumption, but no one seems to notice that the choices for consumption are extremely constrained. The most publicly visible activity near the "speaker's corner" set aside on the mall for public speaking is often the buying and selling of goods. Interesting civic activities, such as Holocaust memorial readings or rallies against relationship and sexual violence, are overwhelmed by inflatable climbing walls and Velcro-bungee games. Almost nowhere on campus, outside the academic classroom, seems exempt from commercial discourse (and classrooms, plastered in posters advertising cheap beer and Internet services, are not themselves totally exempt). This segregation makes classrooms and critiques of consumerism seem remote and irrelevant.

Philanthropy as Advertising

As student life becomes increasingly commercialized, so, too, does the pattern of outside gifts to the university. The distinction between philanthropy and advertising, or philanthropy and research contracts, seems to be eroding. Posthumous and anonymous gifts from benefactors to academic institutions have often been publicized, but the fanfare surrounding large donations and capital campaigns has reached new heights. The Gates Foundation Minority Fellowship Program, for example, spends more on advertising than on the scholarships themselves. Many named chairs are now tied specifically to corporations. Seymour Papert, for example, held the LEGO chair at the Massachusetts Institute of Technology, which upon his retirement was renamed the LEGO Papert Chair. References to the chair appear in LEGO press releases and on the corporation's Web site to emphasize the educational value of LEGO toys.

Corporations are not in the business of philanthropy for its own sake. Activities such as corporate-sponsored endowed chairs must produce economic benefits for their sponsors, even if the benefits are largely intangible. Philanthropy confers a kind of legitimacy on the donor, and it provides resources and the aura of being worthy of gifts to the recipient.

But even the traditional form of individual philanthropy should be examined for the multiple benefits and costs to the giving and the receiving parties. It has long been customary for alumni to support their majors and for business schools to be named in honor of wealthy alumni who give hefty gifts. Not too many of these alumni are, however, still alive, and also embroiled in legal conflict. But now we have the Eller School of Business and Public Administration at the University of Arizona, named for regional advertising executive Karl Eller, who made a substantial donation. The Eller Enterprises are wrangling with the city of Tucson and the county over billboard and lighting regulations meant to protect the skies from light pollution and the local population from billboard blight. To what extent should we be looking our gift horses in the mouths? Is Eller's philanthropy an attempt to garner public support and perhaps influence, indirectly, city council action on billboard regulations? Does the gift help to signal the legitimacy of Eller Enterprises?

A big "gift" with no strings attached is, in theory, significantly different from a research contract with explicit performance goals. But today's donor programs, many of which are sponsored by corporations rather than anonymous individuals, may challenge the gift-contract distinction. Unlike more traditional, individual philanthropic efforts that need not obey the calculus of profit, corporations do not just give money away.

Consequently, as relationships with corporate vendors and sponsors become increasingly important, we can expect subtle accommodations to the needs of industrial and commercial interests on campus. Explicit firings for critiques of corporate activities may not become widespread, but other forms of forced acquiescence in the status quo might be expected. Will departments or units heavily dependent on the largesse of one particular sponsor tolerate criticism of that sponsor by faculty members?

The example of the relationship between the Swiss-based corporation Novartis and the Department of Plant and Microbial Biology at the University of California, Berkeley, is apt here. The multimillion dollar grant from the corporation surely enables the department to pursue an expanded research program. But it also puts subtle constraints on the scope of its program, affecting the faculty's freedom to engage in other research relationships and students' ability to determine the direction of their research. The corporation's claim to the intellectual property rights to all research from the department also affects the choices made by it. Reward structures at research institutions generally favor those who bring in external funds in contracts and grants. Although censorship is far too strong a word for the constraints on imagination that can occur in conditions of resource dependency, we can expect some accommodations.

Vendor Relations

At the same time that the way corporations and universities handle gifts and contracts is changing, institutional support services and vendor relations are also being transformed. Although some faculty members are very much involved in helping to select software packages for students or in setting the parameters for hardware purchases for their units, most faculty are clueless about such processes. These decisions are frequently based on the expectations that future employers have for graduates: Can a future project manager use Excel? Can an engineering student solve modeling equations with Matlab? Do the architecture students know Autocad? Are your students facile in some discipline-specific modeling software? Where have all the Apples gone?

An interesting cycle seems to have emerged. Expectations regarding 20
new technologies are present either in fact, in the prospective workplaces of our students, or in the imaginations of vendors selling supplies to universities. Students are exposed to specific systems, and not necessarily informed of the

alternatives. They take their training to their future work sites, perhaps influencing purchasing decisions. The expectations are then presented back to the universities by alumni, employers, and vendors, requiring institutions to purchase and maintain new technology or expensive upgrades.

In the course of a project to upgrade its student information system, the University of Arizona somehow became an Oracle campus. At the same time that we are purchasing a system from this well-established software production firm that specializes in data management, Arizona's staff is contributing to its development. It is expected that modifications to the software made by Arizona employees will fall under complex intellectual property agreements.

One of the possible capabilities of the system is an online grading function that faculty will use to keep course records. At a nearby community college, a similar system has made interim reporting of grades a requirement. So far, faculty have not discussed how the system will affect intellectual property rights, institutional policy, or workload. We have not questioned whether we may have to submit interim grades or develop grading practices compatible with the computer system, nor have we considered that software produced at the university for this project may belong to Oracle.

In a separate venture, AOL and Cisco Systems have combined forces with the university's Center for Computing and Information Technology (CCIT). The CCIT is the nonacademic unit responsible for the university's computer infrastructure, e-mail system, and software and hardware licensing. Three local high schools purchase hardware (switching equipment and cabling) at a "substantial discount," which is partly underwritten by AOL. As noted in the campus computing newsletter, the schools also pay a "yearly $500 fee to CCIT . . . although expenses are much higher than that." CCIT staff get free training in Cisco products, and the successful high school students get a Cisco Certified Network Associate certificate.

Three features of this relationship bear critical attention. First, a fair amount of money is changing hands, back and forth among schools, vendors, and the computer center. It seems that university resources subsidize the program to some extent, which would be an unusual transfer of public resources to the private sector. Second, this venture resembles distance-education initiatives in that it is largely independent of oversight by regularly appointed faculty members. CCIT employees, some of whom have Ph.D.'s, all have staff rather than faculty appointments and teach courses outside any disciplinary curricula.

The third issue has to do with providing vendor-specific training. It is 25
hard to argue against the opportunities that Cisco training might offer the students, who come from some of the more disadvantaged high schools in the area (in a region with a lot of disadvantaged schools). Their Cisco certification can give them access to job opportunities in the telecommunications and information sector. Whether such employment is meant to be in lieu of, or a precursor to, a traditional university education is unclear. In addition, the

training is in a specific vendor's systems, rather than, say, in general principles of networking, which could provide wider employment horizons.

Consider that in other circumstances companies pay their employees to get advanced, firm-specific training. Under the Arizona-AOL-Cisco deal, the students are not compensated for learning a specific corporate system; instead, their schools (or the taxpayers, at least) pay for them to receive this training. In other words, a public institution is subsidizing training that corporations usually provide to their own workers. Even though this program is described as a "gift" from AOL, it seems to be a very expensive gift for the university to receive. Especially disturbing is the dearth of program oversight and the lack of much discussion about the partnership's effectiveness and legitimacy.

Legitimacy

The question of legitimacy is clearly at issue in any relationship between a commercial enterprise and the university. Science, or knowledge production more generally, has always had deep connections to the general political economy of its time, whether or not it has been tied to specific industries or corporations.

Thus we cannot argue for some untainted "ivory tower" or "golden age" of institutional independence. We need instead to articulate the values and goals that should direct a wide range of commercial ventures on campus.

What seem to be in tension are the values of connection and autonomy. Discourses about connection and accountability generally strengthen the power that the various constituencies of the university (the public, students, the administration, businesses, the state) have to intervene in university life. In these discourses, it is good to be connected to the outside world, to display multiple ties to multiple audiences, to exchange resources (both money and personnel), and to demonstrate relevance. The corporatization of university life brings a new model of connectedness and accountability to the forefront as a model of legitimacy. Connection and accountability become the markers of successful campus ventures, whether in research, teaching, or service.

Discourses about autonomy are usually based on disciplinary expertise. 30
Faculty, for example, use academic-freedom arguments to preserve our control over syllabi, although at Arizona we are now required to point out that "objectionable material" may be present in certain kinds of courses. Academic institutions have, until recently, based much of their institutional legitimacy in the discourse about autonomy.

What happens to core values such as objectivity or neutrality under conditions in which business connections measure legitimacy? Biotechnology companies, for example, need the autonomy of university-based research to help maintain at least the image of objectivity in analyzing new drugs for distribution to the public. Ties that are too close undermine the public's trust that the knowledge produced is unbiased and reliable. Ties that are too loose, such as unrestricted and anonymous philanthropy, provide too few of the benefits that corporations seek.

Some of the advantages for corporate sponsors are visible and measurable: the chance to direct research and solve specific technological or scientific problems. Such benefits often accrue in traditional corporate sponsorship of research. With the new relationships, however, some of the favorable effects are intangible and more difficult to quantify and critique. Corporations gain legitimacy, visibility, and access to markets. Universities get to seem "relevant" and connected, and they gain needed cash, perhaps at the expense of independence and autonomy.

At the same time that the development office at the University of Arizona cheers large donations, others get nervous that our public institution is intensifying a cycle of dependency on corporate finances. When the law school received the gift of a large endowment, state legislators got the idea that professional programs need not be funded by the state, because wealthy benefactors and eager students can foot the bills. The benefits that corporate "partners" provide in underwriting the athletic program, or that benefactors give to departments, come to be seen as replacements for base funding for routine operating expenses, increasing our dependency on and responsiveness to corporate connections. The point is not to make an argument for pure autonomy, expecting constituencies to hand us blank checks and trust that we will produce socially optimal knowledge and well-educated students. Too much administrative bloat, too many inefficiencies, and plenty of poor performance make it hard for people to see that as a likely outcome. But complete connection, especially through identification with corporate benefactors, erodes ideas about objectivity that are important to maintaining the legitimacy of universities as sites for unfettered, and reliable, inquiry. When it becomes clear that we are indeed "Nike-Pepsi U," it will be obvious, at least to me, that we have moved too far along the autonomy-connection continuum.

QUESTIONING THE TEXT

1. In paragraph 6, Croissant warns her colleagues in higher education, "[W]e need to make sure that the university does not betray its educational values and objectives" with its commercial associations. Addressing the areas of student life, philanthropy, and vendor relations, which she claims have been overlooked in recent critiques of campus-commercial relationships, Croissant argues that these facets of university activity have an indirect impact on education through the image they present to students and others. How does she make her argument in regard to each of these three areas? What kind of evidence does she pro-

vide to support her claim that commercial relationships can have an adverse impact on an academic institution?

2. This essay opens with two examples of commercial interests encroaching upon campus life. What is the point of each example? In what other ways might Croissant have introduced the conflicts that she addresses? How would different opening strategies change the essay?
3. Croissant refrains from drawing a distinct line on the "autonomy-connection continuum" that universities should not cross. Rather, she concludes, "When it becomes clear that we are indeed 'Nike-Pepsi U,' it will be obvious, at least to me, that we have [gone] too far. . . ." (paragraph 33). Try to develop a set of criteria by which to judge what actions by a university might constitute traveling "too far" on this continuum.

MAKING CONNECTIONS

4. Croissant identifies a "tension" between "the values of connection and autonomy," between an academic institution's need to represent its various "constituencies" (paragraph 29) and its need to pursue teaching and research free of distortion from outside influences. How do her concerns complicate the ideas of knowledge for its own sake espoused by John Henry Newman (p. 52) or Donald Kagan (p. 141)? How might Croissant agree or disagree with these authors' ideas of a university's connections to public or corporate life?
5. Croissant and Michael Sokolove (p. 124) both address the influences of nonacademic activity and commercial interests on higher education. How do their concerns differ, and how are they similar?

JOINING THE CONVERSATION

6. Croissant observes that commercial enterprises are crowding out the noncommercial exchange of ideas in central "mall" areas of many campuses. She asserts, "For many students, to be a citizen is to be a consumer, and nothing more. Freedom means freedom to purchase" (paragraph 11). Does your campus have a space dedicated to public debate? Is it also open to vendors? Do you think the marketplace of ideas on your campus is becoming too commercialized? Discuss this question with your classmates.
7. Take a tour of your campus, and note the names of buildings. For whom are the buildings named? Can you identify a connection between each building and its namesake? What do your answers suggest about commercial and philanthropic relationships at your school?

8. Croissant's concerns about the impact of commercial interests on education might also apply to other kinds of pursuits. Religious, civic, or athletic organizations, for example, can find themselves in comparable conflicts with commercial interests. Have you encountered similar conflicts in situations outside of academe? If so, how do they inform your understanding of the educational predicaments Croissant addresses?

MIKE ROSE
Lives on the Boundary

As a child, Mike Rose (b. 1944) never thought of going to college. The son of Italian immigrants, he was placed in the "vocational track" in school (through a clerical error, as it turns out) and, as he says, "lived down to expectations beautifully." He was one of those who might well have been excluded from the university. In his prize-winning volume Lives on the Boundary *(1989), Rose recalls those circumstances that opened up the university to him, and he argues forcefully that education in a democracy must be truly open to all, a theme he pursues in* Possible Lives *(1996).*

In the excerpt from Lives on the Boundary *that follows, Rose describes several students he has known, considering the ways in which the "idea of a university" either includes or excludes them. In an extended discussion of what he calls the "canonical curriculum," he concludes that "books* can *spark dreams," but "appeals to elevated texts can also divert attention from the conditions that keep a population from realizing its dreams."*

I wanted to include this passage from Rose's book because he explicitly addresses the many calls for a university curriculum based on "Great Books," books that by definition exclude the experiences of the students Rose describes. In addition, I chose this selection because Rose is a graceful prose stylist, a gifted scholar, and a much-valued friend.

A professor of education at UCLA, Rose is also a truly extraordinary teacher. His own story, and the stories of those students whose lives he has touched, attest to the transformational power of the kind of educational experience he advocates. To "have any prayer of success" at making such experiences possible, Rose says, "we'll need many . . . blessings." We'll also need many more teachers and writers like Mike Rose. —A.L.

I have a vivid memory of sitting on the edge of my bed—I was twelve or thirteen maybe—listening with unease to a minute or so of classical music. I don't know if I found it as I was turning the dial, searching for the Johnny Otis Show or the live broadcast from Scribner's Drive-In, or if the tuner had simply drifted into another station's signal. Whatever happened, the music caught me in a disturbing way, and I sat there, letting it play. It sounded like the music I heard in church, weighted, funereal. Eerie chords echoing from another world. I leaned over, my fingers on the tuner, and, in what I remember as almost a twitch, I turned the knob away from the melody of these strange instruments. My reaction to the other high culture I encountered—*The Iliad* and Shakespeare and some schoolbook poems by Longfellow and

Lowell—was similar, though less a visceral rejection and more a rejecting disinterest, a sense of irrelevance. The few Shakespearean scenes I did know—saw on television, or read or heard in grammar school—seemed snooty and put-on, kind of dumb. Not the way I wanted to talk. Not interesting to me.

There were few books in our house: a couple of thin stories read to me as a child in Pennsylvania (*The Little Boy Who Ran Away,* an *Uncle Remus* sampler), the *M* volume of the *World Book Encyclopedia* (which I found one day in the trash behind the secondhand store), and the Hollywood tabloids my mother would bring home from work. I started buying lots of Superman and Batman comic books because I loved the heroes' virtuous omnipotence—comic books, our teachers said, were bad for us—and, once I discovered them, I began checking out science fiction novels from my grammar school library. Other reading material appeared: the instructions to my chemistry set, which I half understood and only half followed, and, eventually, my astronomy books, which seemed to me to be magical rather than discursive texts. So it was that my early intrigue with literacy—my lifts and escapes with language and rhythm—came from comic books and science fiction, from the personal, nonscientific worlds I created with bits and pieces of laboratory and telescopic technology, came, as well, from the Italian stories I heard my uncles and parents tell. It came, too, from the music my radio brought me: music that wove in and out of my days, lyrics I'd repeat and repeat—"gone, gone, gone, jumpin' like a catfish on a pole"—wanting to catch that sound, seeking other emotional frontiers, other places to go. Like rocker Joe Ely, I picked up Chicago on my transistor radio.

Except for school exercises and occasional cards my mother made me write to my uncles and aunts, I wrote very little during my childhood; it wasn't until my last year in high school that Jack MacFarland* sparked an interest in writing. And though I developed into a good reader, I performed from moderately well to terribly on other sorts of school literacy tasks. From my reading I knew vocabulary words, and I did okay on spelling tests—though I never lasted all that long in spelling bees—but I got C's and D's on the ever-present requests to diagram sentences and label parts of speech. The more an assignment was related to real reading, the better I did; the more analytic, self-contained, and divorced from context, the lousier I performed. Today some teachers would say I was a concrete thinker. To be sure, the development of my ability to decode words and read sentences took place in school, but my orientation to reading—the way I conceived of it, my purpose for doing it—occurred within the tight and untraditional confines of my home. The quirks and textures of my immediate environment combined with my escapist fantasies to draw me to books. "It is what we are excited about that educates us," writes social historian Elizabeth Ewen. It is what taps our curiosity and dreams. Eventually, the books that

---

Jack MacFarland: a man whom Rose describes as "the teacher who saved [my] life"

seemed so distant, those Great Books, would work their way into my curiosity, would influence the way I framed problems and the way I wrote. But that would come much later—first with Jack MacFarland (mixed with his avant-garde countertradition), then with my teachers at Loyola and UCLA—an excitement and curiosity shaped by others and connected to others, a cultural and linguistic heritage received not from some pristine conduit, but exchanged through the heat of human relation.

A friend of mine recently suggested that education is one culture embracing another. It's interesting to think of the very different ways that metaphor plays out. Education can be a desperate, smothering embrace, an embrace that denies the needs of the other. But education can also be an encouraging, communal embrace—at its best an invitation, an opening. Several years ago, I was sitting in on a workshop conducted by the Brazilian educator Paulo Freire. It was the first hour or so and Freire, in his sophisticated, accented English, was establishing the theoretical base of his literacy pedagogy—heady stuff, a blend of Marxism, phenomenology, and European existentialism. I was two seats away from Freire; in front of me and next to him was a younger man, who, puzzled, finally interrupted the speaker to ask a question. Freire acknowledged the question and, as he began answering, he turned and quickly touched the man's forearm. Not patronizing, not mushy, a look and a tap as if to say: "You and me right now, let's go through this together." Embrace. With Jack MacFarland it was an embrace: no-nonsense and cerebral, but a relationship in which the terms of endearment were the image in a poem, a play's dialogue, the winding narrative journey of a novel.

5 More often than we admit, a failed education is social more than intellectual in origin. And the challenge that has always faced American education, that it has sometimes denied and sometimes doggedly pursued, is how to create both the social and cognitive means to enable a diverse citizenry to develop their ability. It is an astounding challenge: the complex and wrenching struggle to actualize the potential not only of the privileged but, too, of those who have lived here for a long time generating a culture outside the mainstream and those who, like my mother's parents and my father, immigrated with cultural traditions of their own. This painful but generative mix of language and story can result in clash and dislocation in our communities, but it also gives rise to new speech, new stories, and once we appreciate the richness of it, new invitations to literacy.

Pico Boulevard, named for the last Mexican governor of California, runs an immense stretch west to east: from the wealth of the Santa Monica beaches to blighted Central Avenue, deep in Los Angeles. Union Street is comparatively brief, running north to south, roughly from Adams to Temple, pretty bad off all the way. Union intersects Pico east of Vermont Avenue and too far to the southwest to be touched by the big-money development that is turning downtown Los Angeles into a whirring postmodernist dreamscape.

The Pico-Union District is very poor, some of its housing as unsafe as that on Skid Row, dilapidated, overcrowded, rat-infested. It used to be a working-class Mexican neighborhood, but for about ten years now it has become the concentrated locale of those fleeing the political and economic horror in Central America. Most come from El Salvador and Guatemala. One observer calls the area a gigantic refugee camp.

As you move concentrically outward from Pico-Union, you'll encounter a number of other immigrant communities: Little Tokyo and Chinatown to the northeast, Afro-Caribbean to the southwest, Koreatown to the west. Moving west, you'll find Thai and Vietnamese restaurants tucked here and there in storefronts. Filipinos, Southeast Asians, Armenians, and Iranians work in the gas stations, the shoe-repair stores, the minimarts. A lawnmower repair shop posts its sign in Korean, Spanish, and English. A Korean church announces "Jesus Loves You" in the same three languages. "The magnitude and diversity of immigration to Los Angeles since 1960," notes a report from UCLA's Graduate School of Architecture and Urban Planning, "is comparable only to the New York-bound wave of migrants around the turn of the century." It is not at all uncommon for English composition teachers at UCLA, Cal-State L.A., Long Beach State—the big urban universities and colleges—to have, in a class of twenty-five, students representing a dozen or more linguistic backgrounds: from Spanish and Cantonese and Farsi to Hindi, Portuguese, and Tagalog. Los Angeles, the new Ellis Island.

On a drive down the Santa Monica Freeway, you exit on Vermont and pass Rick's Mexican Cuisine, Hawaii Discount Furniture, The Restaurant Ecuatoriano, Froggy's Children's Wear, Seoul Autobody, and the Bar Omaha. Turn east on Pico, and as you approach Union, taking a side street here and there, you'll start seeing the murals: The Virgin of Guadalupe, Steve McQueen, a scene resembling Siqueiros's heroic workers, the Statue of Liberty, Garfield the Cat. Graffiti are everywhere. The dreaded Eighteenth Street gang—an established Mexican gang—has marked its turf in Arabic as well as Roman numerals. Newer gangs, a Salvadoran gang among them, are emerging by the violent logic of territory and migration; they have Xed out the Eighteenth Street *placas* and written their own threatening insignias in place. Statues of the Blessed Mother rest amid potted plants in overgrown front yards. There is a rich sweep of small commerce: restaurants, markets, bakeries, legal services ("Income Tax y Amnestia"), beauty salons ("Lolita's Magic Touch—Salon de Belleza—Unisex"). A Salvadoran restaurant sells teriyaki burgers. A "Discoteca Latina" advertises "great rap hits." A clothing store has a Dick Tracy sweatshirt on a half mannequin; a boy walks out wearing a blue t-shirt that announces "Life's a Beach." Culture in a Waring blender.

There are private telegram and postal services: messages sent straight to "domicilio a CentroAmerica." A video store advertises a comedy about immigration: *Ni de Aqui/Ni de Alla,* "Neither from Here nor from There." The poster displays a Central American Indian caught on a wild freeway ride: a

Mexican in a sombrero is pulling one of the Indian's pigtails, Uncle Sam pulls the other, a border guard looks on, ominously suspended in air. You see a lot of street vending, from oranges and melons to deco sunglasses: rhinestones and plastic swans and lenses shaped like a heart. Posters are slapped on posters: one has rows of faces of the disappeared. Santa Claus stands on a truck bumper and waves drivers into a ninety-nine cent outlet.

Families are out shopping, men loiter outside a cafe, a group of young girls 10
collectively count out their change. You notice, even in the kaleidoscope you pick out his figure, you notice a dark-skinned boy, perhaps Guatemalan, walking down Pico with a cape across his shoulders. His hair is piled in a four-inch rockabilly pompadour. He passes a dingy apartment building, a *pupuseria,* a body shop with no name, and turns into a storefront social services center. There is one other person in the sparse waiting room. She is thin, her gray hair pulled back in a tight bun, her black dress buttoned to her neck. She will tell you, if you ask her in Spanish, that she is waiting for her English class to begin. She might also tell you that the people here are helping her locate her son—lost in Salvadoran resettlement camps—and she thinks that if she can learn a little English, it will help her bring him to America.

The boy is here for different reasons. He has been causing trouble in school, and arrangements are being made for him to see a bilingual counselor. His name is Mario, and he immigrated with his older sister two years ago. His English is halting, unsure; he seems simultaneously rebellious and scared. His caseworker tells me that he still has flashbacks of Guatemalan terror: his older brother taken in the night by death squads, strangled, and hacked apart on the road by his house. Then she shows me his drawings, and our conversation stops. Crayon and pen on cheap paper; blue and orange cityscapes, eyes on billboards, in the windshields of cars, a severed hand at the bus stop. There are punks, beggars, piñatas walking the streets—upright cows and donkeys—skeletal homeboys, corseted girls carrying sharpened bones. "He will talk to you about these," the caseworker tells me. "They're scary, aren't they? The school doesn't know what the hell to do with him. I don't think he really knows what to do with all that's in him either."

In another part of the state, farther to the north, also rich in immigration, a teacher in a basic reading and writing program asks his students to interview one another and write a report, a capsule of a classmate's life. Caroline, a black woman in her late forties, chooses Thuy Anh, a Vietnamese woman many years her junior. Caroline asks only five questions—Thuy Anh's English is still difficult to understand—simple questions: What is your name? Where were you born? What is your education? Thuy Anh talks about her childhood in South Vietnam and her current plans in America. She is the oldest of nine children, and she received a very limited Vietnamese education, for she had to spend much of her childhood caring for her brothers and sisters. She married a serviceman, came to America, and now spends virtually all of her time pursuing a high school equivalency, struggling with textbook descriptions of the American political process, frantically trying to improve her computational skills. She is not doing very well at this. As one of her classmates observed, she might be trying too hard.

Caroline is supposed to take notes while Thuy Anh responds to her questions, and then use the notes to write her profile, maybe something like a reporter would do. But Caroline is moved to do something different. She's taken by Thuy Anh's account of watching over babies. "Mother's little helper," she thinks. And that stirs her, this woman who has never been a mother. Maybe, too, Thuy Anh's desire to do well in school, her driven eagerness, the desperation that occasionally flits across her face, maybe that moves Caroline as well. Over the next two days, Caroline strays from the assignment and writes a two-and-a-half page fiction that builds to a prose poem. She recasts Thuy Anh's childhood into an American television fantasy.

Thuy Anh is "Mother's little helper." Her five younger sisters "are happy and full of laughter . . . their little faces are bright with eyes sparkling." The little girls' names are "Hellen, Ellen, Lottie, Alice, and Olie"—American names—and they "cook and sew and make pretty doll dresses for their dolls to wear." Though the family is Buddhist, they exchange gifts at Christmas and "gather in the large living room to sing Christmas carols." Thuy Anh "went to school every day she could and studied very hard." One day, Thuy Anh was "asked to write a poem and to recite it to her classmates." And, here, Caroline embeds within her story a prose poem—which she attributes to Thuy Anh:

> My name is Thuy Anh I live near the Ocean. I see the waves boisterous and impudent bursting and splashing against the huge rocks. I see the white boats out on the blue sea. I see the fisher men rapped in heavy coats to keep their bodys warm while bringing in large fishes to sell to the merchants, Look! I see a larg white bird going on its merry way. Then I think of how great God is for he made this great sea for me to see and yet I stand on dry land and see the green and hillie side with flowers rising to the sky. How sweet and beautiful for God to have made Thuy Anh and the sea.

I interview Caroline. When she was a little girl in Arkansas, she "would 15
get off into a room by myself and read the Scripture." The "poems in King Solomon" were her favorites. She went to a segregated school and "used to write quite a bit" at home. But she "got away from it" and some years later dropped out of high school to come west to earn a living. She's worked in a convalescent hospital for twenty years, never married, wishes she had, comes, now, back to school and is finding again her love of words. "I get lost . . . I'm right in there with my writing, and I forget all my surroundings." She is classified as a basic student—no diploma, low-level employment, poor test scores—

had been taught by her grandmother that she would have to earn her living "by the sweat of my brow."

Her work in the writing course had been good up to the point of Thuy Anh's interview, better than that of many classmates, adequate, fairly free of error, pretty well organized. But the interview triggered a different level of performance. Caroline's early engagement with language reemerged in a lyrical burst: an evocation of an imagined childhood, a curious overlay of one culture's fantasy over another's harsh reality. Caroline's longing reshaped a Vietnamese girlhood, creating a life neither she nor Thuy Anh ever had, an intersection of biblical rhythms and *Father Knows Best.*

Over Chin's bent head arches a trellis packed tight with dried honeysuckle and chrysanthemum, sea moss, mushrooms, and ginseng. His elbow rests on the cash register—quiet now that the customers have left. He shifts on the stool, concentrating on the writing before him: "A young children," he scribbles, and pauses. "Young children," that doesn't sound good, he thinks. He crosses out "children" and sits back. A few seconds pass. He can't think of the right way to say it, so he writes "children" again and continues: "a young children with his grandma smail . . ." "Smail." He pulls a Chinese-English dictionary from under the counter.

In front of the counter and extending down the aisle are boxes of dried fish: shark fins, mackerel, pollock. They give off a musky smell. Behind Chin are rows of cans and jars: pickled garlic, pickled ginger, sesame paste. By the door, comic books and Chinese weeklies lean dog-eared out over the thin retaining wire of a dusty wooden display. Chin has found his word: It's not *smail,* it's *smile.* "A young children with his grandma smile. . . ." He reaches in the pocket of his jeans jacket, pulls out a piece of paper, and unfolds it. There's a word copied on it he has been wanting to use. A little bell over the door jingles. An old man comes in, and Chin moves his yellow pad aside.

Chin remembers his teacher in elementary school telling him that his writing was poor, that he didn't know many words. He went to middle school for a few years but quit before completing it. Very basic English—the ABCs and simple vocabulary—was, at one point, part of his curriculum, but he lived in a little farming community, so he figured he would never use it. He did, though, pick up some letters and a few words. He immigrated to America when he was seventeen, and for the two years since has been living with his uncle in Chinatown. His uncle signed him up for English classes at the community center. He didn't like them. He did, however, start hanging out in the recreation room, playing pool and watching TV. The English on TV intrigued him. And it was then that he turned to writing. He would "try to learn to speak something" by writing it down. That was about six months ago. Now he's enrolled in a community college literacy program and has been making strong progress. He is especially taken with one tutor, a woman in her mid-thirties who encourages him to write. So he writes for her. He writes stories about his childhood in China. He sneaks time when no one is in the store or when customers are poking around, writing because he likes to bring her things, writing, too, because "sometime I think writing make my English better."

The old man puts on the counter a box of tea guaranteed to help you 20
stop smoking. Chin rings it up and thanks him. The door jingles and Chin returns to his writing, copying the word from his folded piece of paper, a word he found in *People* magazine: "A young children with his grandma smile *gleefully.*"

Frank Marell, born Meraglio, my oldest uncle, learned his English as Chin is learning his. He came to America with his mother and three sisters in September 1921. They came to join my grandfather who had immigrated long before. They joined, as well, the millions of Italian peasants who had flowed through Customs with their cloth-and-paper suitcases, their strange gestural language, and their dark, empty pockets. Frank was about to turn eight when he immigrated, so he has faint memories of Calabria. They lived in a one-room stone house. In the winter, the family's scrawny milk cow was brought inside. By the door there was a small hole for a rifle barrel. Wolves came out of the hills. He remembers the frost and burrs stinging his feet as he foraged the countryside for berries and twigs and fresh grass for the cow. *Chi esce riesce,* the saying went—"he who leaves succeeds"—and so it was that my grandfather left when he did, eventually finding work amid the metal and steam of the Pennsylvania Railroad.

My uncle remembers someone giving him bread on the steamship. He remembers being very sick. Once in America, he and his family moved into the company housing projects across from the stockyard. The house was dirty and had gouges in the wood. Each morning his mother had to sweep the soot from in front of the door. He remembers rats. He slept huddled with his father and mother and sisters in the living room, for his parents had to rent out the other rooms in order to buy clothes and shoes and food. Frank never attended school in Italy. He was eight now and would enter school in America. America, where eugenicists were attesting, scientifically, to the feeblemindedness of his race, where the popular press ran articles about the immorality of these swarthy exotics. Frank would enter school here. In many ways, you could lay his life like a template over a current life in the Bronx, in Houston, in Pico-Union.

He remembers the embarrassment of not understanding the teacher, of not being able to read or write. Funny clothes, oversize shoes, his hair slicked down and parted in the middle. He would lean forward—his assigned seat, fortunately, was in the back—and ask other Italian kids, ones with some English, to tell him what for the love of God was going on. He had big, sad eyes, thick hands, skin dark enough to yield the nickname Blacky. Frank remembers other boys—Carmen Santino, a kid named Hump, Bruno Tucci—who couldn't catch on to this new language and quit coming to school.

Within six months of his arrival, Frank would be going after class to the back room of Pete Mastis's Dry Cleaners and Shoeshine Parlor. He cleaned and shined shoes, learned to operate a steam press, ran deliveries. He listened to the radio, trying to mimic the harsh complexities of English. He spread Pete Mastis's racing forms out before him, copying words onto the margins of newsprint. He tried talking to the people whose shoes he was shining, exchanging tentative English with the broken English of Germans and Poles and other Italians.

Eventually, Frank taught his mother to sign her name. By the time he was in his teens, he was reading flyers and announcements of sales and legal documents to her. He was also her scribe, doing whatever writing she needed to have done. Frank found himself immersed in the circumstance of literacy.

With the lives of Mario and Caroline and Chin and Frank Marell as a 25
backdrop, I want to consider a current, very powerful set of proposals about literacy and culture.

There is a strong impulse in American education—curious in a country with such an ornery streak of antitraditionalism—to define achievement and excellence in terms of the acquisition of a historically validated body of knowledge, an authoritative list of books and allusions, a canon. We seek a certification of our national intelligence, indeed, our national virtue, in how diligently our children can display this central corpus of information. This need for certification tends to emerge most dramatically in our educational policy debates during times of real or imagined threat: economic hard times, political crises, sudden increases in immigration. Now is such a time, and it is reflected in a number of influential books and commission reports. E. D. Hirsch* argues that a core national vocabulary, one oriented toward the English literate tradition—Alice in Wonderland to zeitgeist—will build a knowledge base that will foster the literacy of all Americans. Diane Ravitch* and Chester Finn* call for a return to a traditional historical and literary curriculum: the valorous historical figures and the classical literature of the once-elite course of study. Allan Bloom,* Secretary of Education William Bennett, Mortimer Adler* and the Paideia Group, and a number of others have affirmed, each in their very different ways, the necessity of the Great Books:

E. D. Hirsch: author of *Cultural Literacy: What Every American Needs to Know,* which argues for a standard national public school curriculum that would ensure that all Americans share a common cultural vocabulary

Diane Ravitch: author of *Developing National Standards in Education* and an Education Department official in the Reagan administration

Chester Finn: undersecretary of education in the Reagan administration

Allan Bloom: author of *The Closing of the American Mind* (1987)

Mortimer Adler: educator and philosopher, author of many books, including three volumes on the Paideia Proposal, an educational framework based on ancient Greek concepts

Plato and Aristotle and Sophocles, Dante and Shakespeare and Locke, Dickens and Mann and Faulkner. We can call this orientation to educational achievement the canonical orientation.

At times in our past, the call for a shoring up of or return to a canonical curriculum was explicitly elitist, was driven by a fear that the education of the select was being compromised. Today, though, the majority of the calls are provocatively framed in the language of democracy. They assail the mediocre and grinding curriculum frequently found in remedial and vocational education. They are disdainful of the patronizing perceptions of student ability that further restrict the already restricted academic life of disadvantaged youngsters. They point out that the canon—its language, conventions, and allusions—is central to the discourse of power, and to keep it from poor kids is to assure their disenfranchisement all the more. The books of the canon, claim the proposals, the Great Books, are a window onto a common core of experience and civic ideals. There is, then, a spiritual, civic, and cognitive heritage here, and *all* our children should receive it. If we are sincere in our desire to bring Mario, Chin, the younger versions of Caroline, current incarnations of Frank Marell, and so many others who populate this book—if we truly want to bring them into our society—then we should provide them with this stable and common core. This is a forceful call. It promises a still center in a turning world.

I see great value in being challenged to think of the curriculum of the many in the terms we have traditionally reserved for the few; it is refreshing to have common assumptions about the capacities of underprepared students so boldly challenged. Many of the people we have encountered in these pages have displayed the ability to engage books and ideas thought to be beyond their grasp. There were the veterans: Willie Oates* writing, in prison, ornate sentences drawn from *The Mill on the Floss.** Sergeant Gonzalez* coming to understand poetic ambiguity in "Butch Weldy."* There was the parole aide Olga who no longer felt walled off from *Macbeth.* There were the EOP* students at UCLA, like Lucia who unpackaged *The Myth of Mental Illness* once she had an orientation and overview. And there was Frank Marell who, later in his life, would be talking excitedly to his nephew about this guy Edgar Allan Poe. Too many people are kept from the books of the canon, the Great Books, because of misjudgments about their potential. Those books eventually proved important to me, and, as best I know how, I invite my students to engage them. But once we grant the desirability of equal curricular treatment and begin to consider what this equally distributed curriculum would contain, problems arise: If the canon itself is the answer to our educational inequities,

---

Willie Oates, Sergeant Gonzalez: students in a veterans' program that Rose worked in
The Mill on the Floss: a novel (1860) by George Eliot (1819–80)
"Butch Weldy": a poem in *Spoon River Anthology* (1915) by Edgar Lee Masters (1869–1950)
EOP: Equal Opportunity Program

why has it historically invited few and denied many? Would the canonical orientation provide adequate guidance as to how a democratic curriculum should be constructed and how it should be taught? Would it guide us in opening up to Olga that "fancy talk" that so alienated her?

Those who study the way literature becomes canonized, how linguistic creations are included or excluded from a tradition, claim that the canonical curriculum students would most likely receive would not, as is claimed, offer a common core of American experience. Caroline would not find her life represented in it, nor would Mario. The canon has tended to push to the margin much of the literature of our nation: from American Indian songs and chants to immigrant fiction to working-class narratives. The institutional messages that students receive in the books they're issued and the classes they take are powerful and, as I've witnessed since my Voc. Ed. days, quickly internalized. And to revise these messages and redress past wrongs would involve more than adding some new books to the existing canon—the very reasons for linguistic and cultural exclusion would have to become a focus of study in order to make the canon act as a democratizing force. Unless this happens, the democratic intent of the reformers will be undercut by the content of the curriculum they propose.

And if we move beyond content to consider basic assumptions about 30
teaching and learning, a further problem arises, one that involves the very nature of the canonical orientation itself. The canonical orientation encourages a narrowing of focus from learning to that which must be learned: It simplifies the dynamic tension between student and text and reduces the psychological and social dimensions of instruction. The student's personal history recedes as the what of the classroom is valorized over the how. Thus it is that the encounter of student and text is often portrayed by canonists as a transmission. Information, wisdom, virtue will pass from the book to the student if the student gives the book the time it merits, carefully traces its argument or narrative or lyrical progression. Intellectual, even spiritual, growth will *necessarily* result from an encounter with Roman mythology, *Othello,* and "I heard a Fly buzz—when I died—,"* with biographies and historical sagas and patriotic lore. Learning is stripped of confusion and discord. It is stripped, as well, of strong human connection. My own initiators to the canon—Jack MacFarland, Dr. Carothers, and the rest—knew there was more to their work than their mastery of a tradition. What mattered most, I see now, were the relationships they established with me, the guidance they provided when I felt inadequate or threatened. This mentoring was part of my entry into that solemn library of Western thought—and even with such support, there were still times of confusion, anger, and fear. It is telling, I think, that once that rich social network slid away, once I was in graduate school in intense,

"I heard a Fly buzz—when I died—": poem by Emily Dickinson (1830–86)

solitary encounter with that tradition, I abandoned it for other sources of nurturance and knowledge.

The model of learning implicit in the canonical orientation seems, at times, more religious than cognitive or social: Truth resides in the printed texts, and if they are presented by someone who knows them well and respects them, that truth will be revealed. Of all the advocates of the canon, Mortimer Adler has given most attention to pedagogy—and his Paideia books contain valuable discussions of instruction, coaching, and questioning. But even here, and this is doubly true in the other manifestos, there is little acknowledgement that the material in the canon can be not only difficult but foreign, alienating, overwhelming.

We need an orientation to instruction that provides guidance on how to determine and honor the beliefs and stories, enthusiasms, and apprehensions that students reveal. How to build on them, and when they clash with our curriculum—as I saw so often in the Tutorial Center at UCLA—when they clash, how to encourage a discussion that will lead to reflection on what students bring and what they're currently confronting. Canonical lists imply canonical answers, but the manifestos offer little discussion of what to do when students fail. If students have been exposed to at least some elements of the canon before—as many have—why didn't it take? If they're encountering it for the first time and they're lost, how can we determine where they're located—and what do we do then?

Each member of a teacher's class, poor *or* advantaged, gives rise to endless decisions, day-to-day determinations about a child's reading and writing: decisions on how to tap strength, plumb confusion, foster growth. The richer your conception of learning and your understanding of its social and psychological dimensions, the more insightful and effective your judgments will be. Consider the sources of literacy we saw among the children in El Monte: shopkeepers' signs, song lyrics, auto manuals, the conventions of the Western, family stories and tales, and more. Consider Chin's sources—television and *People* magazine—and Caroline's oddly generative mix of the Bible and an American media illusion. Then there's the jarring confluence of personal horror and pop cultural flotsam that surfaces in Mario's drawings, drawings that would be a rich, if volatile, point of departure for language instruction. How would these myriad sources and manifestations be perceived and evaluated if viewed within the framework of a canonical tradition, and what guidance would the tradition provide on how to understand and develop them? The great books and central texts of the canon could quickly become a benchmark against which the expressions of student literacy would be negatively measured, a limiting band of excellence that, ironically, could have a dispiriting effect on the very thing the current proposals intend: the fostering of mass literacy.

To understand the nature and development of literacy we need to consider the social context in which it occurs—the political, economic, and cultural forces that encourage or inhibit it. The canonical orientation discourages deep analysis of the way these forces may be affecting performance. The canonists ask that schools transmit a coherent traditional knowledge to an ever-changing, frequently uprooted community. This discordance between message and audience is seldom examined. Although a ghetto child can rise on the lilt of a Homeric line—books *can* spark dreams—appeals to elevated texts can also divert attention from the conditions that keep a population from realizing its dreams. The literacy curriculum is being asked to do what our politics and our economics have failed to do: diminish differences in achievement, narrow our gaps, bring us together. Instead of analysis of the complex web of causes of poor performance, we are offered a faith in the unifying power of a body of knowledge, whose infusion will bring the rich and the poor, the longtime disaffected and the uprooted newcomers into cultural unanimity. If this vision is democratic, it is simplistically so, reductive, not an invitation for people truly to engage each other at the point where cultures and classes intersect.

I worry about the effects a canonical approach to education could have on 35
cultural dialogue and transaction—on the involvement of an abandoned underclass and on the movement of immigrants like Mario and Chin into our nation. A canonical uniformity promotes rigor and quality control; it can also squelch new thinking, diffuse the generative tension between the old and the new. It is significant that the canonical orientation is voiced with most force during times of challenge and uncertainty, for it promises the authority of tradition, the seeming stability of the past. But the authority is fictive, gained from a misreading of American cultural history. No period of that history was harmoniously stable; the invocation of a golden age is a mythologizing act. Democratic culture is, by definition, vibrant and dynamic, discomforting and unpredictable. It gives rise to apprehension; freedom is not always calming. And, yes, it can yield fragmentation, though often as not the source of fragmentation is intolerant misunderstanding of diverse traditions rather than the desire of members of those traditions to remain hermetically separate. A truly democratic vision of knowledge and social structure would honor this complexity. The vision might not be soothing, but it would provide guidance as to how to live and teach in a country made up of many cultural traditions.

We are in the middle of an extraordinary social experiment: the attempt to provide education for all members of a vast pluralistic democracy. To have any prayer of success, we'll need many conceptual blessings: A philosophy of language and literacy that affirms the diverse sources of linguistic competence and deepens our understanding of the ways class and culture blind us to the richness of those sources. A perspective on failure that lays open the logic of error. An orientation toward the interaction of poverty and ability that undercuts simple polarities, that enables us to see simultaneously the constraints poverty places on the play of mind and the actual mind at play within those constraints. We'll need a pedagogy that encourages us to step back and consider the threat of the standard classroom and that shows us, having stepped back, how to step forward to invite a student across the boundaries of that powerful room. Finally, we'll need a revised store of images of educational excellence, ones closer to egalitarian ideals—ones that embody the reward and turmoil of education in a democracy, that celebrate the plural, messy human reality of it. At heart, we'll need a guiding set of principles that do not encourage us to retreat from, but move us closer to, an understanding of the rich mix of speech and ritual and story that is America.

QUESTIONING THE TEXT

1. What do you think Rose means when he says that "a failed education is social more than intellectual in origin" (paragraph 5)? Look back to A.L.'s profile on p. xxv. Does anything there suggest a time when her education failed for social—or intellectual—reasons? Describe a time when your education failed—or succeeded—largely because of social reasons. If you keep a reading log, record your answers there.
2. Rose quotes a friend who says that education can be thought of as "one culture embracing another" (paragraph 4). Give a few examples from his essay that illustrate this embrace, and then give an example from your own educational experience.
3. Why do you think Rose includes the stories of Mario, Caroline, Chin, and Frank Marell as a backdrop for his discussion about current concepts of literacy in America? What do their stories have in common? What kinds of students does he leave unmentioned?

MAKING CONNECTIONS

4. Imagine Rose responding to Donald Kagan's arguments (p. 141) about what a university should teach the students he's concerned with. What would Rose and Kagan agree on? Where would they disagree—and why?
5. Spend some time thinking about one of the students Rose describes. Then write a brief poem (using Gwendolyn Brooks as a model, perhaps; see p. 154) that characterizes that student's attitude toward school.

JOINING THE CONVERSATION

6. Try to remember a time when your relationship with someone (teacher, parent, coach, religious leader) made it easier (or harder) for you to learn what that person was trying to teach you. Write a brief description

of this event for your class, concluding by summarizing those things about the person that most *helped* (or *hindered*) your learning from him or her.

7. Rose remembers that his earliest interest in literacy came from "comic books and science fiction, from the personal, nonscientific worlds I created with bits and pieces of laboratory and telescopic technology, came, as well, from the Italian stories I heard my uncles and parents tell" (paragraph 2). Brainstorm with two or three other students about your earliest out-of-school experiences with reading and writing. How were they like or unlike your experiences of reading and writing in school?

MICHAEL SOKOLOVE
Football Is a Sucker's Game

During my thirty years in academe, I have always been at schools with massive athletic departments and football teams that play in prime time, first at The Ohio State University and then at the University of Texas at Austin. So I found Michael Sokolove's "Football Is a Sucker's Game"—a lengthy essay exploring the efforts of the University of South Florida to establish an NCAA Division I-A gridiron program—compelling reading.

It is possible, I think, to be a fan of college football and still have doubts about what football programs have become in the last few decades—grossly overfunded, overproduced commercial ventures wholly disconnected from the major and even peripheral purposes of a university. Sokolove shows how schools get sucked into spiraling commitments and expenditures when school administrators, looking for an easy way to get public attention for their institutions, decide to play with the big boys of the NCAA.

What he doesn't show is how such programs lose their hold on the very students the football teams are supposed to represent. These days, ordinary undergraduates at Division I-A schools may not be able to get—or afford—decent seats at a "big" game. They've been squeezed out by alumni or businesses whose handsome contributions buy them prime real estate in a stadium enlarged every decade to cover the salaries of coaches paid like Hollywood celebrities.

Moreover, chances are most students have never taken a class with a football player or studied in the same library with one. And don't even try to make the case that football builds character or school spirit or community. Too many recent post-game victory riots undermine any notion that football, as played in Division I at least, has much to do with our better angels.

Michael Sokolove is a journalist and a writer for the New York Times Magazine, *where the following essay first appeared (in December 2002). He is also the author of* Hustle: The Myth, Life, and Lies of Pete Rose *(1990).* —J.R.

The University of South Florida sprawls over nearly 1,500 acres in a once sparsely populated section of Tampa, close to where the city bleeds into unincorporated Hillsborough County. The campus is pancake flat and in desperate need of more trees and shade. Grass comes up in stubborn clumps through sandy soil. I can't say that I was shocked when I learned of a previous use of this parcel of land: a practice bombing range.

In many other ways, though, the University of South Florida is attractive—and useful. It has produced about 170,000 graduates in its four-decade history. It has a medical school and some well-regarded academic programs.

Current enrollment stands at 39,000, and students tend to be grounded and hard-working rather than rich and entitled. (A professor told me that one challenge of his job is teaching morning classes to students who may have worked the late shift at Chili's.) What U.S.F. does not have is any kind of national profile. It has no standing. No buzz. The latest edition of the Princeton Review's *Best 345 Colleges* does not rank it low on the list—it leaves it off entirely.

University officials want U.S.F. in the guidebooks. They want fewer commuters, more out-of-state students, more residence halls and more of a "traditional" campus feel, by which they mean a campus with a soul and some spirit. It is a big job, and the burden for getting it done has fallen, largely, to Jim Leavitt.

"Sit down," he says as I enter his office one morning this fall. It's clear to me that I'm not only supposed to sit, but to do so in silence. His office is a mess. Clothes are strewn everywhere. About 50 videotapes are scattered on the floor by his desk. Leavitt himself doesn't look so great, either. His brown hair is a tousled mop, a modified crewcut gone to seed. He gives the impression of being simultaneously weary and wired.

5 Leavitt continues at what he was doing before I arrived, drawing with a red pen on an unlined sheet of paper. At one point he reaches behind him on the floor for his Pepsi, which he drinks by the two-liter bottle. When he finally speaks again, his voice leaks out in the weak rasp of someone who does more yelling than sleeping. "I'm sorry," he says, "but I was in here late last night and I never even got to this. To be honest with you, there aren't enough hours in the day. But I've really got to get through it. It's important."

After several more minutes, when he is finally done, I walk around behind Leavitt to inspect his handiwork. On the white paper are a series of squiggles and arrows, 11 on each side of the page.

"What is it?" I inquire.

"A punt return," he says.

Football is the S.U.V. of the college campus: aggressively big, resource-guzzling, lots and lots of fun and potentially destructive of everything around it. Big-time teams award 85 scholarships and, with walk-ons, field rosters of 100 or more players. (National Football League teams make do with half that.) At the highest level, universities wage what has been called an "athletic arms race" to see who can build the most lavish facilities to attract the highest-quality players. Dollars are directed from general funds and wrestled from donors, and what does not go into cherry-wood lockers, plush carpets and million-dollar weight rooms ends up in the pockets of coaches, the most exalted of whom now make upward of $2 million a year.

10 The current college sports landscape is meaner than ever, more overtly commercial, more winner-take-all. And just as in the rest of the economy, the gap between rich and poor is widening. College sports now consists of a class of super-behemoths—perhaps a dozen or so athletic departments with

budgets of $40 million and up—and a much larger group of schools that face the choice of spending themselves into oblivion or being embarrassed on the field. (Which may happen in any case.) It is common for lesser college football teams to play at places like Tennessee or Michigan, where average attendance exceeds 100,000, in return for "guarantees" from the host school of as much as $500,000. They are paid, in other words, to take a beating.

Any thought of becoming one of the giants and sharing in the real money is in most cases a fantasy. Universities new to Division I-A football (in addition to U.S.F., the University of Connecticut and the University of Buffalo have just stepped up to the big time) know that the first level of competition is financial. It is a dangerous game. "The mantra of the need to 'spend money to make money' can be used to justify a great deal of spending, without leading an institution to any destination other than a deeper financial hole," write James Shulman and William Bowen in *The Game of Life: College Sports and Educational Values,* their 2001 examination of the finances of college athletics.

The current college bowl season began last week and ends Jan. 3 with the national championship game, the Fiesta Bowl. This year, the cartel of teams belonging to the Bowl Championship Series—members of the six most prominent conferences plus independent Notre Dame, a total of 63 teams—will split a guaranteed payoff of at least $120 million from the Fiesta, Orange, Sugar and Rose Bowls. Teams outside the B.C.S. are eligible to play in such low-wattage affairs as the Humanitarian Bowl, the Motor City Bowl and the Continental Tire Bowl. For the privilege, they will almost certainly lose money, because the bowl payouts will not even cover travel and other expenses.

"We are receiving letters and calls from conferences that want in," Mike Tranghese, coordinator of the five-year-old B.C.S., told me. "And we have formed a presidential oversight panel to form an answer." But letting more members in would mean splitting up the money more ways. I asked Tranghese if I was missing something in assuming the B.C.S. had no incentive to cut more schools in. "If you were missing something, I would let you know," he said. "The B.C.S. consists of the major teams as determined by the marketplace. Any other system is socialism. And if we're going to have socialism, then why don't we share our endowments?"

One reason B.C.S. members do not want to share is that college sports have become so immensely expensive that even some of the biggest of the big lose money. The University of Michigan, which averages more than 110,000 fans for home football games, lost an estimated $7 million on athletics over the course of two seasons, between 1998 and 2000. Ohio State had athletic revenues of $73 million in 1999–2000 and "barely managed to break even," according to the book *Unpaid Professionals: Commercialism and Conflict in Big-Time College Sports,* by Andrew Zimbalist, a Smith College economics professor. A state audit revealed that the University of Wisconsin lost $286,700 on its Rose Bowl appearance in 1998 because it took a small army, a traveling party of 832, to Pasadena.

The endemic criminal and ethical scandals of college sports are connected by a straight line to the money. Teams that do not win do not excite their boosters, fill up stadiums, appear on national TV or get into postseason play, thereby endangering the revenue stream that supports the immense infrastructure. It is the desperation for cash, every bit as much as the pursuit of victory, that causes university athletic departments to overlook all kinds of rule-breaking until it splatters out into the open. 15

One day this fall I opened my morning sports page and, in glancing at the college football briefs, took note that it was a particularly bad day for the Big Ten. The headlines were: "Spartan Tailback Dismissed"; "Iowa Player Arrested"; "Wisconsin Back Stabbed." The Michigan State Spartans dismissed two co-captains within 10 days: the starting quarterback, who checked into rehab for a substance-abuse problem, as well as the tailback, who was accused of drunken driving and eluding arrest by dragging a police officer with his car. The next day, the head coach, Bobby Williams, with his team's record at 3–6, was fired—and sent off with a $550,000 buyout.

At tiny Gardner-Webb University in Boiling Springs, N.C.—a Baptist institution in its first season of Division I basketball—the university president resigned in the fall after acknowledging that he ordered a change in the calculation of a star basketball player's grade-point average. At Florida State University, quarterback Adrian McPherson was suspended days before his arrest for supposedly stealing a blank check, then expressed shock at the discipline meted out by the normally lenient head coach, Bobby Bowden. (When a star player was accused of theft a few years back, Bowden said, "I'm praying for a misdemeanor.") The University of Alabama at Birmingham, which started football just over a decade ago, is playing this season under a cloud. The trustees of the Alabama higher-education system have given the university two years to reverse a $7.6 million budget deficit or face being shut down. In addition, pending civil suits charge that a 15-year-old girl who enrolled at U.A.B. was sexually assaulted, repeatedly, by a large number of football and basketball players, as well as by the person who performed as the school's mascot, a dragon.

The list goes on. Ohio State's thrilling 14–9 victory over Michigan on Nov. 23 occasioned a full-scale riot by inebriated Buckeye fans who burned cars, looted businesses and caused tens of thousands of dollars in damage before 250 police officers finally restored order at 5 A.M. These sorts of things have become the background music of college sports.

Being a striving team trying to keep up in a big-time conference can be a particular kind of debacle. Rutgers University, in this regard, is Exhibit A. It belongs to the Big East, a B.C.S. football conference that also boasts powerful basketball programs. Rutgers can't compete in either sport. Its cellar-dwelling teams draw poor crowds, and the athletic department ran a deficit of about $13 million last year.

A dissident group, the Rutgers 1,000, has waged a passionate campaign 20
to get Rutgers to leave the Big East and to de-emphasize athletics. This has led, indirectly, to yet an entirely new way of throwing money away on sports. The administration tried to block publication of a Rutgers 1,000 advertisement in an alumni magazine. Not only did Rutgers lose the ensuing court battle, but it also spent $375,000 fighting it, including court-ordered reimbursement of legal fees to the A.C.L.U., which took up the case of the Rutgers 1,000 as a free-speech issue.

"Schools get on a treadmill, and there's no getting off," says James Shulman, an author of *The Game of Life*. "They have to stay on; they have too much invested." The former Princeton basketball coach Pete Carill once said of the big-time programs: "If you want to get into the rat race, you've got to be a rat."

Another way to look at big-time college sports is as a sucker's game, one with many more losers than winners. Notre Dame, a great football team before it was a great university, is the prototype for all schools hoping to hitch a ride on the back of a popular sports team. Duke certainly has become more celebrated and academically selective in the years its basketball team has been a perennial Final Four participant. But Notre Dame and Duke are exceptions. For every Notre Dame and Duke, there are many more like Rutgers and U.A.B., schools that spend millions in a hopeless mission to reach the top.

The University of South Florida, nonetheless, wants in on the gamble and in on the perceived spoils. The new gospel there is that football is "the tip of the marketing sword." I heard the phrase from several administrators at U.S.F. Vicki Mitchell explained the concept to me. She had directed a highly successful university-wide fund-raising campaign, but in May, not long after the team jumped to Division I-A, she moved to the athletic department to raise money specifically for sports. Under Mitchell, the office devoted to sports fund-raising was ramped up from three staff members to eight, and in the first three months of this fiscal year she and her team brought in $1.6 million, just $200,000 less than the total raised in the previous 12 months. "The easiest way to build a U.S.F. brand is to build an athletic program that is known, and that means football," Mitchell said. "Maybe that's not what the university wants to be known for, but it's reality."

Nearly two decades ago, the exploits of the Boston College quarterback Doug Flutie and the success of the team were credited with increasing applications by 25 percent and transforming B.C. from a regional to a national university. The syndrome was even given a name: the Flutie effect. That's the kind of magic U.S.F. is trying to catch.

U.S.F. didn't play football at any level until 1997. Its founding presi- 25
dent, John Allen, who presided over the university from 1957 to 1970, was that rare thing in football-crazed Florida—a staunch opponent of the sport. In the 1980's, U.S.F. alumni and Tampa businessmen began pushing for foot-

ball, and the U.S.F. administration began lobbying a reluctant state Board of Regents for a team. In 1993, the outgoing president, Frank Borkowski, in his final weeks at U.S.F. and with the Regents' decision on football pending, hired Lee Roy Selmon—a former N.F.L. star and one of the most admired men in Tampa—to lead football fund-raising. That was the pivotal moment. "I was in a pretty tight box," recalls Borkowski, now chancellor at Appalachian State University. "The Regents did not want us to have a team." But to deny football would have been a slap to Selmon.

Jim Leavitt was hired in 1995, two years before the University of South Florida Bulls played their first game. From the start, the university intended to move quickly to the N.C.A.A.'s highest level and eventually challenge football factories like Florida State, the University of Florida and the University of Miami. By the time the current U.S.F. president, Judy Genshaft, arrived in 2000, the program was in full bloom. Genshaft's term has so far been marked by a thorny dispute spawned by her suspension of Sami Al-Arian, a tenured professor of computer science, over charges that he had ties to terrorism. Compared to the fallout from that, football has been pure pleasure.

Genshaft, who attends the team's games and keeps a jersey in her office with her name on the back, was an undergraduate at Wisconsin and a longtime administrator at Ohio State. "I know big sports," she says, "and I love big sports. It brings more visibility, more spirit, more community engagement. Even researchers coming to us from other big universities, they are expecting sports to be part of campus life."

The rationales put forth for big-time sports are not easily proved or disproved. One example is the assumption that successful teams spur giving to the general funds of universities. "The logic is reasonable enough," Zimbalist wrote in *Unpaid Professionals*. "A school goes to the Rose Bowl or to the Final Four. Alumni feel proud and open up their pocketbooks." But Zimbalist looked at the available evidence and concluded that winning teams, at best, shake loose dollars given specifically for sports. And only for a time; when on-field fortunes reverse, or a scandal occurs, the money often dries up.

Genshaft says that U.S.F. can play football at the highest level without financial or ethical ruin. "It's a risk and it is expensive," she says. "But we've decided that football is part of who we are and where we're going."

But others see disaster as the only possible result. At Rutgers, the sports 30
program has split the campus community and spawned an angry and unusually organized opposition. "The reality of sports at this level is it can't be done right," says William C. Dowling, an English professor and one of the leaders of the Rutgers 1,000. "It's not possible, anywhere, even at the so-called best places. Look at the differences in SAT levels."

One study showed the SAT scores of football players at Division I-A schools to be 271 points lower than incoming nonathletes. "You have kids brought to campus and maybe, maybe they could be real students if they studied 60 hours a week and did nothing else," Dowling says. "But everyone knows that's not happening. It's not their fault. They've been lied to in high school, all these African-American kids who get told that playing ball is their way up in society, even though it's never been that for any other ethnic group in America. It's dishonest. It's filthy."

When Vicki Mitchell pitches U.S.F. donors, however, she sells the program as if it were in a state of grace—unsullied by scandal, at least so far, and still operating with a degree of fiscal sanity. She begins by painting a picture of what life is like at the really big football powers. To secure a season ticket at one of those schools in a desirable part of the stadium, if that's even possible, can set a donor back tens of thousands of dollars. "I'll say to someone: 'You're a sports fan. You need to get on board, because everyone knows what it costs at those other places. Our aspirations are no less, but we're not there yet. We're young. We're fun. We're a growth stock. Get in now while it's still affordable.'"

I met head coach Jim Leavitt for the first time just a few days before the biggest home game in the history of University of South Florida football. The opponent, Southern Mississippi, was the strongest team ever to visit U.S.F. and a favorite to break its 15-game home winning streak. U.S.F. had lost an early-season road game at Oklahoma, then the second-ranked team in the nation, but outplayed the powerful Sooners for long stretches. Leavitt's team was surging in the national polls; the *New York Times* computer rankings would place it as high as 18th in the nation, ahead of such tradition-rich football powers as Tennessee, Florida State, Auburn, Clemson and Nebraska. These accomplishments, for a program playing just its sixth season, were nothing short of astounding.

As the showdown against Southern Mississippi loomed, two things obsessed Leavitt: winning the game, and money. "The kind of money we need is big, big money," he said to me not long after saying hello. He kept returning to the same point. "We have what we need for a beginning program, but we're not a beginning program anymore." Then: "I don't know what this program will look like in the future. It can be big. But you've got to have money. You've got to have facilities. If you don't, it ain't gonna happen."

Leavitt, 46, grew up in nearby St. Petersburg. He was a high-school sports star, a defensive back at the University of Missouri, then an assistant coach at several universities before he came home to be the first coach of U.S.F. football.

Leavitt has won praise not just for winning, but also for doing so on the cheap. He and his nine assistant coaches work out of a complex of four trailers, in front of which Leavitt erected a split-rail fence "to make it look like the Ponderosa." Leavitt proudly told me that the couch in his office, on which he sometimes lies down for the night, is a $700 vinyl number rather than one of those $5,000 leather cruise ships to be found in the offices of so many other coaches.

This era of frugality, though, has just ended. In early November, the university unveiled drawings for a long-hoped-for training and office complex that will be as big as a football field—104,000 square feet over two floors that will serve most of the university's men's and women's teams but will be dominated by football.

Leavitt views this as natural and right. He tells me about Oklahoma, coached by his close friend Bob Stoops, which already has "an outrageous setup, everything you can imagine," and has just raised yet another $100 million. "I imagine they'll tell you it's not for football only, and I would assume it's not," Leavitt says. "But I'm pretty sure football will get what it needs first. As it should, in my opinion."

Like many football coaches, Leavitt is no fan of Title IX regulations that mandate equal opportunity for female athletes. "Don't get me wrong," he says, "I am a big proponent of women's sports. I want us to be great at women's sports. But football should be separate from the Title IX thing, because nobody else operates like we do. We're revenue-producing."

To build the U.S.F. athletic complex will cost as much as $15 million. 40
To furnish it—starting with $425,000 in weight-training equipment, a $65,000 hydrotherapy tub, portable X-ray machines, satellite uplinks and downlinks, trophy cases for a U.S.F. sports hall of fame in the atrium entrance—will cost up to $5 million more.

Despite aggressive fund-raising, private pledges for this facility have reached only $5 million, so it will be built on borrowed money. The construction bond will be backed partly by the "athletic fee" charged to students, which for those who attend full time has reached $224 a year—a fairly substantial add-on to a tuition of only $2,159.

Mitchell says the university considers students "its biggest donor," and student leaders are, in fact, courted like boosters. In October, the student government president and vice president flew on a private jet with President Genshaft to the big game at Oklahoma.

U.S.F. calculates that the football team brings in, roughly, $4 million in revenue and spends about the same amount. But as in most athletic departments, the accounting makes no attempt to measure the true resources used.

One day, I stood in a humid basement room and watched the laundry—muddy Bulls jerseys and pants, T-shirts, sweat socks, wrist- and headbands, jockstraps—from 105 football players being cleaned. Several colossal washers and dryers were fed by three athletic-department employees. They perform this task early August through late November, six days a week, 10 hours a day.

None of this—the salaries, the utility costs, the $8,000 a year just in 45
laundry detergent—is charged against football. Nor is there any attempt to break out football's share of such costs as sports medicine, academic tutoring, strength and conditioning, insurance, field upkeep or the rest of its share of the more than $5 million in general expenses of the athletic department not assigned to a specific sport.

In the papers I was shown, I also could find no evidence that a $2 million fee to join Conference USA (which is not a B.C.S. conference) as a football-playing member in 2003 was accounted for in football's expense ledger. The money was borrowed from the university's general endowment, and the athletic department is paying the interest.

So when Jim Leavitt says that his football team is revenue-producing, that should not be understood as profit-generating. I would not pretend to know what football really costs at U.S.F., but it's clearly a lot more than $4 million, maybe even twice that. And another big bill is about to come due: Leavitt's next contract.

Just in case Judy Genshaft didn't know she had a hot coach on her hands who needed a big raise, she could have learned it from reading the local press. The articles began after the end of the 2001 season, when Leavitt entertained some job feelers. "U.S.F. Needs to Make Commitment to Leavitt," read a headline in the *Tampa Tribune*. "U.S.F. said it wanted to play in the big leagues and built an impressive foundation," the columnist Joe Henderson wrote. "Now it has to finish the job, or risk that Leavitt will listen the next time someone calls."

Columns like these are the essential component of setting the market for a coach and driving up his price. An echo chamber of sports journalists, boosters, alumni, fans and national sports pundits anoints the coach a civic treasure and then campaigns that this indispensable figure must be properly rewarded lest the community risk having him stolen away. This is how it happens everywhere.

As Leavitt's Bulls piled up victory after victory this season, it got ever noisier in the echo chamber. A story by the *Tampa Tribune's* U.S.F. beat man noted that Leavitt's $180,000 salary was way out of whack, that the average for Conference USA coaches was $410,000, that the coach at Houston—whose team Leavitt's slaughtered, 45–6!—could approach $1 million and that Leavitt was in fact one of the lowest-paid coaches in all of Division I-A.

A *St. Petersburg Times* columnist, Gary Shelton, celebrated Leavitt's single-mindedness—he has never purchased a CD, doesn't go to the movies, was barely aware of the Florida governor's race—and implied that the coach was too dedicated to the next game and next victory to properly focus on his own self-interest.

The drumbeat on Leavitt's behalf overlooked two things. One is that Leavitt's original contract runs through 2005, although that probably doesn't matter since college coaches are rarely held to the deals they sign. The other unaddressed question was more significant: how would U.S.F. square its big-time ambitions with its still small-time revenues?

For all the fevered energy and earnest expectations behind U.S.F. football, attendance at home games has long been stuck between 20,000 and 30,000. The team plays way across town, at the 65,000-seat Raymond James Stadium, home of the N.F.L.'s Tampa Bay Buccaneers. "We've flatlined," says Tom Veit, associate athletic director. "We had tire-kickers in the beginning, something like 50,000 at the first game in '97, and we need to bring them back in."

Students have not been dependable fans. About 3,500 live on campus; nearly 10,000 more live in off-campus garden apartments, most of which have swimming pools and frequent keg parties. Fifty-nine percent of U.S.F. students are female, so young men, the natural college football audience, may have a particular incentive not to stray too far from home. "If you want it to be," says the student government vice president, Dave Mincberg, "it's like spring break 24/7 around here."

One function that U.S.F. football does serve is as content, cheap pro- 55
gramming in the 500-channel universe. Under a contract with ESPN Plus, U.S.F. football (and basketball) games are constantly up on the satellite—along with dozens of other games to be pulled down by viewers with a dish and a college sports package. The ubiquity of these televised college games makes the dream of a marketing bonanza—Jim Leavitt's fightin' Bulls as the tip of the sword—all the more difficult to achieve. Instead of becoming a "brand" like the well-known sports schools, U.S.F. is more likely to blend in with its anonymous brethren in Sports Satellite World, the Northern Arizonas, Coastal Carolinas and Boise States.

But U.S.F. has set its course. It's on the treadmill. It plays Alabama next season, Penn State in 2005 and the University of Florida in 2008. It didn't schedule these games to be embarrassed. Rebuilding with a new coach would be difficult competitively and, even more so, commercially. "If we lose Jim Leavitt, from a marketing point of view, that's not a place I want to be," Veit says. "I don't want to be me at that point. He's a hometown guy. He wins. People like him."

When the local sportswriters ask Leavitt about his contract, he gives carefully bland responses. He doesn't have an agent, and it could be argued that with his fawning press, he hardly needs one. The articles clearly please him. One day he says to me: "The Tampa paper is going to have another piece coming up on my salary. But you know, I don't pay too much attention. I don't deserve anything. I'm just glad I have a job. I'm blessed.

"And I mean that. I have zero interest in leaving here. But then people say to me, 'What if you were offered $1 million to go somewhere else?' Well, then I'd probably leave. Let's be realistic."

I asked him what he thought his market value was, and he did not hesitate. "About $500,000 or $600,000," he said. "At least."

The biggest of the big-time college sporting events are intoxicating. 60
The swirl of colors, the marching bands, the deafening roars, the over-the-top political incorrectness—Florida State's Seminole mascot riding in on horseback; a Mississippi State coach some years back, on the eve of a game against the Texas Longhorns, castrating a bull. The whole thing is a little reminiscent of what I've heard some Catholic friends of mine say: even if you're a little ambivalent about the message, the pageantry will get you every time.

In college sports, the heady mix of anticipation, adrenaline, camaraderie and school pride is the gloss over the grubby reality. Pro sports operate within some financial parameters, governed by a profit motive. College sport, by contrast, is a mad cash scramble with squishy rules. Universities run from conference to conference, chasing richer TV deals; coaches from school to school, chasing cash. It's a game of mergers and acquisitions—of running out on your partners before they run out on you.

It's understandable why universities with hundreds of millions already invested in sports can't find a way out. Far less understandable is why a school like U.S.F. would, with eyes wide open, walk in. "I felt then and still feel that U.S.F. could be a model football program," says Frank Borkowski, the former president. "One with clear policies and rules, attractive to bright students, that would not go the way of so many programs—a corrupt way."

But the whole framework of college sports, with its out-of-control spending and lax academic and ethical standards, is rotten; it's difficult to be clean within it. The "student athletes," as the N.C.A.A. insists on calling them, feel the hypocrisy. When one is caught taking the wrong thing from the wrong person—not the usual perks but actual money—what ensues is a "Casablanca"-like overabundance of shock, then a bizarre penalty phase that almost always punishes everyone but the guilty parties. Thus, when the University of Michigan finally acknowledged this fall that some members of its famed "Fab Five" basketball teams of the early 1990's may have accepted payments from a booster, the university tried to get out in front of N.C.A.A. sanctions by disqualifying this year's team—whose players were about 8 years old in the Fab Five years—from participating in the 2003 N.C.A.A. tournament.

With the greater opportunities being afforded female athletes, it should be no surprise that an outsize sense of entitlement now extends to the women. Deborah Yow, the athletic director at the University of Maryland (and one of the few women leading a big athletic department), told me about a conversation she had with an athlete who had rejected Maryland.

"We just lost a great recruit in the sport of women's lacrosse, in which 65
we have won seven national championships," Yow said. "And one of the comments that the recruit made was that the school she had chosen over us had a beautiful new lacrosse stadium with a lovely locker room, and she even described the lockers in some detail. They were wood; that was the word she kept using. And, as she said, they all had that Nike gear hanging everywhere. And I've been to that facility. And I know that what she said was true."

In theory, Yow could have been pleased to be rejected by such a spoiled child. But she does not have that luxury. Instead, she felt relieved that a planned complex to be used by Maryland's women's lacrosse team would be the equal of this other palace. "We, as athletic directors, are interested in having the best possible facilities because we have noticed along the way that recruits are interested in this, that it does matter," she says.

College sport could not survive if it were viewed only as mass entertainment. On another level, it serves as a salvation story. The enterprise rests mostly on a narrative of young men pulled from hopeless situations, installed at universities, schooled in values by coaches and sent off into the world as productive citizens.

No one is better suited to tell the story than Lee Roy Selmon. The youngest of nine children in Eufala, Okla., he excelled in athletics and earned a football scholarship, as did two of his brothers, to the University of Oklahoma. Lee Roy Selmon became the first-ever draft pick of the new Tampa Bay Buccaneers, an N.F.L. Hall of Famer, then a Tampa banker. The Lee Roy Selmon Expressway is one of the city's major thoroughfares.

To Selmon, who became U.S.F.'s athletic director a year and a half ago, college sports is a giant scholarship program for needy children. Of football's 100-player rosters, he says, "The more people here, the more people getting an education, the better. It's about generations—about student athletes developing abilities, being citizens, having families and being able to nurture their children."

70 One evening, I visited with some U.S.F. football players at their mandatory study hall, which takes place inside a wide-open rectangular room as big as a good-size banquet hall. Their monitor, Vik Bhide, a trim engineering student, sat just inside the front door, paging through a book called "The Dimensions of Parking." The players clustered at round tables, reading textbooks or writing. Most had started their day very early and had already attended classes, lifted weights, endured a three-hour practice and gone to meetings in which they watched game film with coaches.

I took a walk through the room and peeked at the players' coursework. John Miller, a freshman offensive lineman, was studying vocabulary words from a textbook. On his list were "burgeoning," "inflection," "emanate," "insidious" and "obscenity." "It's a lot of hard words," he said. "But they're good for you."

Vince Brewer, a junior running back, was about to start an informative speech, which he thought he'd write on the subject of what causes a player to pass out during practice. "We get told a lot about dehydration, and the professor said to pick something you know a lot about." Chris Carothers, a massive offensive lineman, told me bluntly that he does not much like school, "but as a football player, it's something you've got to do."

In all of my interactions with U.S.F. football players, I was struck at how mannerly they were. Nearly all are from Florida, many from small towns, and in a classically Southern way, they are yes-sir, no-sir types. Maybe because U.S.F. has not yet reached its ambitions and neither the team nor its players are widely famous—not even on their own campus—there wasn't a lot of swagger.

"My mom and dad had me when they were in 11th grade," Marquel Blackwell, the Bulls' star quarterback, said. "I was raised, basically, by my two grandmothers. The main thing they taught me was how to respect other people."

75 Not a whole lot of trouble has attached to Jim Leavitt's boys in the six years of U.S.F. football, nothing of the sort that occurs at some places and serves to indict a whole program. There have been some scuffles, as well as a gunplay accident in which a player was wounded.

"We encourage the players to be as much a part of normal campus life as possible," said Phyllis LaBaw, the associate athletic director for academic support. But no one pretends that they really are much like the typical U.S.F. student.

Nearly 70 percent of the U.S.F. football team is black on a campus that is otherwise 70 percent white. (Only 11 percent of U.S.F. students are black; the rest of the minority population is Hispanic and Asian and Native American.) The football players tend to be poorer than other students and more in need of academic help.

To be a football player at U.S.F., or an athlete of any kind, is like taking your mother to school with you—or several mothers. Academic counselors meet with athletes at least weekly. They sometimes follow them right to the door of a classroom, which in the trade is known as "eyeballing" a player to class. Where a lot of players are grouped in one class, tutors sometimes sit in and take notes. Counselors communicate directly with professors. "We don't ever ask for favors," LaBaw said. "But professors do provide us with information, which is vital."

Football players who miss a class or a mandatory study session get "run" by coaches—meaning they must show up on the practice field at 6 A.M. to be put through a series of sprints by a coach who is not happy to be there at that hour. "It is very punitive," LaBaw said.

80 LaBaw's department employs four full-time counselors and about 40 tutors and has an annual budget of $400,000. The staff serves all 450 intercollegiate athletes at U.S.F., so the 105 football players are less than a quarter of the clients—but as is the case with so much else, football sucks up more resources than its raw numbers would indicate. "They need more help," LaBaw said of the footballers, "but what we're doing works. Last year our football players had a mean G.P.A. of 2.52, which if we were already in Conference USA would have been the best in the conference—including Army."

LaBaw is part den mother, part drill sergeant—loving and supportive or confrontational and blunt, depending on the needs of the moment. Under her desk, she keeps a big box; when the season began, it had 5,000 condoms in it, all different colors. She hands them out like lollipops along with however much sex education she can blurt out.

Her effort, while well intentioned, is a version of closing the barn door after the horses have run out. Of the 105 players on U.S.F.'s football team—most of them between 18 and 23 years old—about 30 are fathers and many have produced multiple children. "I would say there's a total of 60 children from this team, and that's a conservative estimate," said LaBaw. "It's amazing how quickly it occurs, usually in the first year. Or they come to school already fathers."

What this means is that the recipients of Lee Roy Selmon's scholarship program for needy young men are recreating the need that many of them came from—children living in poverty, without fathers at home. With their five hours per day of football-related activity on top of class and studying, the fathers have no time even to change a diaper, let alone work to financially support their children. Most of the children live with their mothers or aunts or grandmothers. Some who are nearby spend the day at the university's day-care center, yet another cost of college football since the service is offered virtually free to U.S.F. students.

In DeAndrew Rubin's portrait in the U.S.F. football media guide, it says that his father drowned when he was 11 months old. It adds, "Father had given him a teddy bear for his first Christmas in 1978, and he places it in his locker during every game."

Rubin, 24, has two children, 3 years old and 10 months, and is engaged 85
to their mother, his girlfriend since high school. They live just 30 minutes away in St. Petersburg. "I see them as often as I can, so if I would pass, they would remember me," he said. "I can't help that much financially, but emotionally I want to be there for them."

Unlike several other U.S.F. fathers who said they planned to make the N.F.L., Rubin is considered a prospect, although no sure thing. "It would be good for our situation," he said. "I don't want to have to work a 9-to-5; I guess nobody really does."

LaBaw spends a lot of time talking to the players. "Those who are fathers, there's a comfort aspect—having children is an opportunity to be surrounded by more love. Which is what they've always had, from grandmothers and aunts and cousins. But there is also this trophy aspect. It's let me show you the pictures, or the multiple pictures."

Football is at the center of Jim Leavitt's world, so he is not one to question the time or money devoted to it. He does not seem to have a great deal of interest in the nonfootball world. Leavitt makes appearances on campus and in the community, often related to fund-raising, but several people told me he can be brusque. If he says he has 20 minutes to give, then he's normally out the door in 20 minutes. There is always a practice to conduct or a football tape to be watched. He watches game tapes, and tapes of practices. "I sit and watch film all day long," he says. "I'm a recluse."

Because football is so central to him, he assumes his team's success is widely known and that it translates into other realms—he believes, without a doubt, in the concept of football as tip of the marketing sword. "We've had guys drafted into the N.F.L.," he says. "We have two guys with Super Bowl rings. How much does the university spend for that? What's it worth? That's worldwide publicity for the University of South Florida, right?"

I asked Leavitt if his long football hours left him much time with his 90
7-year-old daughter. "Quality time," he said, then repeated it as if trying to convince himself. "Quality time. It's got to be quality time."

There is one slice of humanity that Leavitt connects with—his players. "That's why I'm in this," he says. "The players. The relationships I have with those young men and the ability to make a difference in their lives. My mission is to help young people in every aspect of life. If I lose sight of that, I'll get out of coaching. The other reason I coach is for that moment when you are victorious. That's hard to create in any other part of life. You feel such contentment. That moment is so powerful." At halftime of U.S.F.'s season finale against Houston, Leavitt grew so agitated that he excitedly head-butted several of his helmeted players and came away bloody.

Beyond the field, Leavitt had reason to believe he had made a difference. His players respond to him as an authority figure and as a friend. They have absorbed his laser focus. They play football. They go to class and mandatory study hall. When the season is over, they lift weights and run. Marquel Blackwell, the quarterback, told me that more established programs like Florida and Nebraska showed interest in him but wanted to switch his position. Of Leavitt, he says: "He believed in me, and I believe in him back. I've given my heart to that man."

On the night of the big game, with U.S.F.'s home winning streak on the line against Southern Mississippi, President Genshaft played host to a couple of dozen guests in a luxury box at Raymond James Stadium—a crowd that included Florida's lieutenant governor and an assortment of local business types and politicos. Mike Griffin, the student government president, was in the box, too, wearing a "Bulls for Jeb" campaign button.

Because of Selmon's icon status, his box is the more coveted invitation, and Vicki Mitchell and her staff put together his list for maximum impact. They had targeted a wealthy U.S.F. graduate and Los Angeles lawyer as a potential big donor, but he had become critical of the athletic program on chat rooms devoted to U.S.F. sports. (Fund-raisers monitor such things.) Selmon called the lawyer during a trip to Los Angeles, just to warm him up, then invited him to fly in and sit in his box for the game. The lawyer accepted and showed up at the game with a friend who wore a muscle shirt. But both men fidgeted and looked impatient, then bolted at halftime.

The large-framed woman sitting in a corner of the box paid much more 95
interest and stayed to the end. Selmon spent time visiting with her, at one point positioning himself on one knee in the aisle next to her. She was another potentially deep-pocketed donor: Lucille Harrison, a Florida resident and Shaquille O'Neal's mother.

U.S.F. beat the odds. It preserved its home winning streak in a stirring game decided on the last play, a missed Southern Mississippi field-goal attempt. By season's end, Leavitt's long hours had paid off beyond what any football prognosticator could have predicted. The Bulls finished the season with a record of 9–2, including a dismantling of Bowling Green, then ranked 25th in the nation. A bid to a minor bowl, the money-losing kind, looked possible, but the bowls snubbed U.S.F. in favor of teams with lesser records but bigger names. Leavitt immediately surfaced as a possibility to fill open coaching jobs at marquee schools, including Alabama and Michigan State. The new program was at a crossroads. Was it going to ante up for its coach, and his assistants too, which could easily add an instant $500,000 or more to the annual football budget? Or would it start all over with someone new?

As the field goal flew wide in the Southern Miss game, one of Selmon's guests, an alum and successful stockbroker, jumped out of his seat, threw his arms around the U.S.F. athletic director and got right to the point. "We've got to keep this man!" he shouted, referring to Leavitt. "Let's raise this man some money and keep him here!"

On Dec. 12, the University of South Florida ripped up Jim Leavitt's contract and signed him to a new five-year deal that more than doubled his salary. If he keeps winning, he probably won't make it to the final year of this contract, either, when he's scheduled to make nearly $700,000. U.S.F. will have to pay more to keep him, or other programs will come looking to steal him away. That's how it is when you decide to play with the big boys. The bills just keep on getting bigger.

QUESTIONING THE TEXT

1. Is this article more about college football, big-time college sports in general, football at the University of South Florida, or another subject? Why do you think the editors included this article in a chapter on education?
2. As a feature article published in the *New York Times Magazine,* this piece is arguably of a different genre than the other prose selections in this chapter. As a journalist, Sokolove probably saw himself as writing a *report* on college football rather than making an *argument* about it. Do you think he does make an argument? Does the article have a thesis? If so, what is it, and how does Sokolove support it?
3. What does the opening description of the University of South Florida campus have to do with the rest of the article? What details in this description stand out, and how do they prepare you for information that follows? What other descriptive details does Sokolove provide throughout the article, and what points do they seem to make or emphasize?

MAKING CONNECTIONS

4. How do you think Adrienne Rich (p. 71) would react to this article? Would she agree or disagree with the perspective offered by Sokolove? Rich asserts, "[N]o woman is really an insider in the institutions fath-

ered by masculine consciousness. When we allow ourselves to believe we are, we lose touch with parts of ourselves defined as unacceptable by that consciousness. . . ." (paragraph 11). What evidence does Sokolove provide that would support or rebut this claim?

5. Sokolove quotes U.S.F. Athletic Director Lee Roy Selmon as saying, "The more people here [in the football program], the more people getting an education, the better. It's about generations—about student athletes developing abilities, becoming citizens, having families and being able to nurture their children" (paragraph 69). Does this view of a big-football program's role at a public university answer the criticisms raised by Sokolove elsewhere in the article? Do you think Mike Rose (p. 109) would agree with Selmon's claims about the educational opportunity that college football affords its players? Why, or why not?
6. Sokolove suggests that players on the team at a big-football school encounter a different educational experience than do other students at the same school. Do you think these players' college education might in any way qualify as "in-the-streets" learning, as described by Jon Spayde (p. 64)? How so, or how not?

JOINING THE CONVERSATION

7. How is the situation at your school similar to or different from the one described by Sokolove, or by J.R. in his introduction to the article? Does your school have a football program? J.R. asserts that at the big-football schools, "ordinary undergraduates" get "squeezed out" of the stands "by alumni or businesses whose handsome contributions buy them prime real estate in a stadium enlarged every decade to cover the salaries of coaches paid like Hollywood celebrities." Is this the case at your school? Can you imagine it happening? What do you think of this claim? Write your response individually, and then discuss the questions among athletes and nonathletes in your class.
8. Sokolove mentions the five hours that football consumes in each player's day at the University of South Florida. Freewrite about the kinds of activities that compete with your study time. Do the various demands on your time enable you to empathize with the football players' situations, or not? Explain.

DONALD KAGAN
What Is a Liberal Education?

*D*ONALD *K*AGAN'S *"What Is a Liberal Education?" explores the rationales that Western societies since the time of Aristotle have offered for the pursuit of higher learning. In this essay, originally published in* Reconstructing History, *edited by Elizabeth Fox-Genovese and Elizabeth Lasch-Quinn (1999), Kagan shows that education typically serves the interests and beliefs of an era. The Greeks and Romans (in the Republican period, at least) needed active and eloquent citizens; the city-states of the Renaissance required ambassadors, secretaries, and courtiers; at a later time, both the British and American systems of higher education hoped to produce either worldly gentlemen or unworldly scholars.*

Like any version of history, Kagan's survey of Western education represents only one possible version of a complicated story, but I believe it merits attention because it helps us understand what is happening in colleges and universities today. In other words, to appreciate the present, we need some sense of the past. The first half of Kagan's essay may demand the kind of line-by-line annotation that Mortimer Adler famously recommends in How to Read a Book, *but the reward will be a clearer sense of the range of options available to students and educators today. Kagan believes that the consequences of our choices may have a profound impact on our ability to preserve our democracy and our freedom.*

For more than a quarter century, Donald Kagan (b. 1932) has taught at Yale University, where he is Sterling Professor of Classics and History. His many books include a four-volume study of the Peloponnesian War as well as On the Origins of War and the Preservation of Peace *(1995) and* While America Sleeps *(2000).*

—J.R.

What is a liberal education and what is it for? In our time, in spite of the arguments over core curricula, canons, and multiculturalism, the real encounter is avoided and the questions ignored. From Cicero's *artes liberales* to the *trivium* and *quadrivium* of the medieval schoolmen, to the *studia humanitatis* of the Renaissance humanists, to Cardinal Newman's *Idea of a University*, to the attempts at common curricula in the first half of this century, to the chaotic cafeteria that passes for a curriculum in most American universities today, the concept has suffered from vagueness, confusion, and contradiction. From the beginning the champions of a liberal education have thought that it seeks at least four kinds of goals.

One was an end in itself, the achievement of that contemplative life that Aristotle thought was the greatest happiness; knowledge, and the acts of acquiring and considering it were the ends of this quest, and good in themselves. A second goal was to shape the character, the style, the taste of a person, to make him good himself and better able to fit well into the society of others like him. A third was to prepare him for a useful career in the world, one appropriate to his status as a free man. For Cicero and Quintillian this meant a career as an orator that would allow a man to protect his private interests and those of his friends in the law courts and to advance the public interest in the assemblies, senate, and magistracies. The fourth goal was to contribute to the educated citizen's freedom. The ancients thought that free citizens should be not ignorant and parochial but learned and cosmopolitan; they should not be ruled by others, but must take part in their own government; servants specialized in some specific and limited task, but free men must know something of everything and understand general principles without yielding to the narrowness of expertise. The Romans, in fact, claimed all these benefits as the products of a liberal education. To achieve their goal the recommended course of study was literature, history, philosophy, and rhetoric, gleaned from an informal canon of authors generally thought to provide the best examples in all respects.

It was once common to think of the medieval university as a place that focused on learning for its own sake. Recent studies, however, have made it clear that the medieval universities, whatever their commitment to learning for its own sake, were also institutions that trained their students for professional careers. Graduates in the liberal arts earned a license to teach others what they had learned and to make a living that way. Some studied the liberal arts to prepare for careers in medicine, theology, and law, and for important positions in church and state.

The seven liberal arts of the Middle Ages consisted of the *trivium* (grammar, rhetoric, and logic) and the *quadrivium* (arithmetic, geometry, astronomy, and music). The discovery and absorption of Aristotle's works in the twelfth century quickly led to the triumph of logic and dialectic over the other arts. They were the glamour subjects of the time, believed to be the best means for training and disciplining the mind and to provide the best tools for successful careers in both church and state. The dominant view of knowledge and truth was that they both already existed. They needed only to be learned, organized, and harmonized. There was nothing still to be discovered; knowledge and truth had only to be systematized and explained. The great summas of the twelfth century and after set out to do exactly that and, with their help, an ambitious scholar could hope to achieve some semblance of universal knowledge. They believed that this was good in itself, for to the medieval mind God was the source of all truth, and to comprehend truth was to come closer to divinity. Thus, there is something to the claim that scholars of the Middle Ages prized learning as something intrinsically good. But they also placed great value on the practical rewards of their liberal education, and rightly so, for their logical, dialectical, mathematical, and rhetorical studies were the best available training for the clerks, notaries, lawyers, canons, and managers so badly needed in the high Middle Ages. Missing from the list of benefits claimed for the liberal education was the training appropriate to the free gentlemen sought by the Romans, but this ideal of the classical world had no real place in medieval society.

That ancient goal of the liberal arts had great appeal, however, for the 5
humanists of the Renaissance. Typically citizens of the newly flourishing city-states of northern Italy, they made a conscious effort to return to the ideas and values of the classical age. As Christians they continued to study the church fathers but rejected the commentaries and summas of the medieval schoolmen and went directly to the sources themselves, applying the powerful new tools of philological analysis. Their greatest innovation and delight, however, was the study of classical texts by the pagan authors, whose focus on the secular world and elevation of the importance of mankind appealed to them. Their idea of a liberal education, the *studia humanitatis,* continued to include grammar and rhetoric from the old curriculum but added the study of a canon of classical poets, historians, and political and moral philosophers. They thought these studies delightful in themselves but also essential for achieving the goals of a liberal education: to become wise and to speak eloquently. The emphasis was on use and action: the beneficiary of a humanistic liberal education learned what was good so that he could practice virtue. The varied and demanding life of the Renaissance city-state led to a broad definition of the qualities needed for a successful and good life, one that increasingly resembled the ancient view.

Castiglione's *Book of the Courtier,* aimed at educated noblemen living in ducal courts, set forth the ideal of the well-rounded man who united in his person a knowledge of language, literature, and history with athletic, military, and musical skills, all framed by good manners and good moral character. These qualities were thought to be desirable in themselves, but they would also be most useful to a man making his way in the courts of Renaissance Italy. The civic humanists, chiefly citizens of the republic of Florence, applied the humanistic education in a way that suited their own experience. They wanted it to train good men for public service, for leadership in the cultural and political life of their city. Such humanists as Colluccio Salutati, Leonardo Bruni, and Poggio Bracciolini served as chancellors of Florence, defending it against aggression with the skills and abilities perfected by their training. They also found time to write histories of their city intended to celebrate its virtues and win for it the devotion of its citizens, a no less important contribution to its survival and flourishing.

For the Italian humanists, as for their classical predecessors, freedom still meant the ability to control one's own life, to dispose of one's own time, to put aside concern for gain and to devote oneself to the training of mind, body, and spirit for the sake of higher things. No more than the ancients did the humanists think that liberal education should be remote from the responsibilities and rewards of the secular life of mankind. Their study, to be sure, pursued a knowledge of virtue, but that knowledge was aimed at virtuous action in the public interest, and such action sought fame as its reward.

The idea of liberal education came to America by way of the English colleges and universities, where the approach of the Renaissance humanists gained favor only in the eighteenth century. In Georgian England, "Humane learning came specifically to mean the direct study of the most renowned classical texts, and especially those authors who were literary figures."[1] But the English version of a humanistic liberal education selected only some elements from the program of the Renaissance humanists and rejected the others. There was little interest in the hard training that turned philology into a keen and powerful tool for the critical examination of primary sources and the discovery of truth. Nor was liberal education meant as preparation for an active life of public service. It was the education of one of Castiglione's courtiers rather than one of the civic humanists' chancellors. The result was an education that suited English society in the eighteenth century, one where the landed aristocracy was still powerful and where connections and favor were very important. A liberal education was one suitable to a free man, who, it was assumed, was well born and rich enough to afford it. It was to be a training aimed at gaining command of arts that were "liberal," "such as fit for Gentlemen and Scholars," as a contemporary dictionary put it, and not those that were servile—"Mechanick Trades and Handicrafts" suited for "meaner People."[2] It was an education for gentlemen, meant not to prepare its recipients for a career or some specific function, but to produce a well-rounded man who would feel comfortable and be accepted in the best circles of society and get on in the world. It placed special emphasis on preparing young men to make the kind of educated conversation required in polite society.

The universities continued with the old Aristotelian curriculum centering on logic and religion. Their main contribution to the current idea of liberal education was to give their students the opportunity to make the right sort of friends, and "Friendship," as one schoolmaster put it, ". . . is known to heighten our joys, and to soften our cares," but, no less important, "by the attachments which it forms . . . is often the means of advancing a man's fortunes in this world."[3]

Such an education prized sociability. It took a dim view of solitary study 10
aimed at acquiring knowledge for its own sake, which was called pedantry, a terrible term of abuse at that time. Pedants were thought to be fussy, self-

---

[1]Sheldon Rothblatt, *Tradition and Change in English Liberal Education* (London: Faber and Faber, 1976), 43.

[2]Rothblatt, *Tradition and Change,* 25.

[3]Quoted in Rothblatt, *Tradition and Change,* 62.

absorbed, engaged in the study of knowledge that was useless. We find fathers writing to warn their sons at the university against the dangers of working too hard and becoming pedants, ruining their health, and damaging their social life. Education was meant to shape character and manners much more than intellect. The universities, with their cloistered atmosphere, were seen by some to be irrelevant, useless, and even damaging to the social goals and the economic advantages that English gentlemen sought for their sons in the age of Enlightenment.

The first decade of the nineteenth century brought a great change to English universities. The number of undergraduates entering the universities grew rapidly, with young scholars full of intellectual energy and boldness. If their energies were as untapped, their interests as undirected, their leisure as copious as in the past, who could tell what dangers might befall? The response of the university faculties was to revive a medieval device that had fallen into disuse—competitive examinations. These examinations had the desired effect, absorbing the time and energy of the undergraduates and turning their minds away from dangerous channels. For most students a liberal education came to mean the careful study of a limited list of Latin and Greek classics, with emphasis on mastery of the ancient languages, but it was now justified on a new basis, not the Humanism of the Renaissance: this kind of learning cultivated and strengthened the intellectual faculties. Commissions investigating Oxford and Cambridge in the 1850s concluded that, "It is the sole business of the University to train the powers of the mind."[4] This new definition, the limited curriculum, and the examination system that connected them soon came under attack from different directions. The growth of industry and democracy led some critics to demand a more practical education that would be "useful" in ways that the Oxbridge liberal education was not. It would train its students for particular vocations, on the one hand, and on the other, it would provide the expertise the new kind of leaders needed in the modern world. At the same time, very different critics complained that the old values of liberal education had been undermined by the sharply limited classical curriculum, the sentence-parsing and fact-cramming imposed by the examinations. Liberal education, they insisted, must not be narrow, pedantic, one-sided—in short, illiberal. It must be useful in more than a pragmatic sense; it must train the character and the whole man, not merely the mind. Still others argued that the restless, tumultuous, industrial society of the nineteenth century, increasingly lacking agreement on a common core of values, needed leaders trained in more than style and manners. Liberal education must become general education, including languages, modern as well as ancient, literature, history, and the natural sciences. In the words of one writer, "A man of the highest education ought to know something of everything, and every-

[4]Rothblatt, *Tradition and Change,* 130.

thing of something."[5] This was a call for a new "universal knowledge." Its advocates urged broadening the field of learning to include all that was known, and synthesizing and integrating the information collected by discovering the philosophical principles that underlay it all. As one Victorian put it, "The summit of a liberal education . . . is Philosophy—meaning by Philosophy the sustained effort . . . to frame a complete and reasoned synthesis of the facts of the universe."[6]

The new universal education remained intellectual and academic, not practical and professional. It was, therefore, attacked as useless, but its champions insisted that although it was not *merely* useful, it was useful nonetheless. Cardinal Newman was the most famous proponent of the new program, but he resisted the idea of usefulness entirely. "That alone is liberal knowledge," he said, "which stands on its own pretensions, which is independent of sequel, expects no complement, refuses to be informed (as it is called) by any end, or absorbed in any art, in order to present itself to our contemplations. The most ordinary pursuits have this specific character, if they are self-sufficient and complete; the highest lose it, when they minister to something beyond them."[7] Newman's intention was to resist the pressure on the secular side from those who wanted chiefly practical training and on the religious side from those Irish Catholics (for his remarks were prompted by the creation of a new Catholic university in Dublin) who wanted what amounted to a seminary. Newman was an intellectual, an academic, and an Aristotelian, and he defended the ancient idea of the value of learning and knowledge for their own sake at a time when the tide was running against it, as it usually does. The result was the same one that befell King Canute. In the last decades of the century, Newman's idea of knowledge for its own sake and the whole concept of universal knowledge for the purpose of philosophical understanding were swept away by a great educational tidal wave from across the channel, chiefly from Germany. Originality and discovery now became the prime values. The idea of the university as a museum, a repository of learning, gave way to the notion that it should be dynamic, a place where knowledge was discovered and generated. Scientific method and the new values were not confined to the natural sciences but were applied to the old humanistic studies, as well, with good results. The new methods and the new zeal for research invigorated the study of history, literature, and theology, and even the classics, symbol of the old order and chief target of reformers.

These gains, however, exacted a price. The new knowledge required specialization, hard, narrow training at the expense of broad, general educa-

---

[5]F. W. Farrar, *Essays on a Liberal Education* (London: MacMillan and Co., 1867), 87.

[6]Farrar, *Essays on a Liberal Education,* 140.

[7]Cardinal John Henry Newman, *On the Scope and Nature of University Education* (London: J. M. Dent & Sons, Ltd., 1915), 103.

tion for the purpose of philosophical understanding, at which the advocates of "universal knowledge" had aimed. Champions of the new order, therefore, changed the definition of liberal education. A famous Oxford classical philologist put it this way: "The essence of a liberal education is that it should stand in constant relation to the advance of knowledge. Research and discovery are the processes by which truth is directly acquired; education is the preparation of the mind for its reception, and the creation of a truth-loving habit."[8] He believed that knowledge obtained by rigorous research would produce truth and that only truth could lead to morality. Research, therefore, would provide a new basis for morality.

That required the application of scientific method to all subjects which, in turn, demanded specialization. Science and social science kept creating new fields and subfields, all of which had equal claim to attention and a place in a liberal education, since all employed the correct method and all claimed to produce new knowledge and truth. No one dared to rank subjects according to an idea of their intrinsic value or their usefulness. Practitioners in each field came to have more in common with their fellow investigators in other universities than with their colleagues in other fields at their own. Both they and their students became more professional in their allegiance and in their attitudes. The distinction between a liberal and a professional education became ever more vague, and some denied that there was any. Although these developments were well under way at the end of the last century [the nineteenth] they seem to me to be the forces that have shaped our own universities and remain influential today.

I have rehearsed this inadequate capsule history of the idea of a liberal 15
education, first, because such knowledge is good in itself, but also because I think it may be a useful basis for examining the status of liberal education today. When I ask which of these images of liberal education most resembles what passes by that name in American colleges today, I come to conclusions that surprise me. It seems to me that the education provided at a typical liberal arts college today comes closest to achieving the goals sought by English gentlemen in the eighteenth century. To be sure, success in that world did not require any particular set of studies or any specialization, for the graduates could look forward to a comfortable life supported by their landed estates. Otherwise, I am sure the training then would have contained some equivalent of our modern departmental major. In most other respects our curricula today, with their lack of any set of subjects studied in common, the lack of agreement on any particular method of training the mind, the lack of a culminating examination testing the acquisition of a body of knowledge, and the emphasis on well-roundedness, defined only as the opposite of narrowness and achieved by taking a few courses in some specified number of different fields—all these fit the eighteenth-century English model nicely.

---

[8]Henry Nettleship, quoted in Rothblatt, *Tradition and Change,* 169.

If we examine the full reality rather than only the formal curriculum, the similarities seem even greater. I submit that in America today the most important social distinction, one almost as significant as the old one between gentle and simple, is whether or not one has a college education. Within the favored group finer distinctions place a liberal education as opposed to a vocational or merely professional one at the top of the social pyramid. Graduates of the more prestigious liberal arts colleges are most likely to gain the best positions and to marry the most desired partners. The fact that each year there are at least seven applicants for every place in the freshman classes of such colleges at a cost of more than twenty-five thousand dollars each year for four years shows that this is widely understood. Apart from any preprofessional training they may obtain, successful applicants gain about the same advantages as those sought by young Englishmen from their less formal eighteenth-century education. They sharpen useful skills in writing and speaking, they pick up enough of subjects thought interesting in their circle and of the style of discussing them to permit agreeable and acceptable conversation. They learn the style and manners to make them comfortable in a similarly educated society. They learn and absorb the political attitudes favored by the group they are entering. They have excellent opportunities to make friends who may be advantageous to them in later life. The practical task of learning to make a living is largely left to professional schools and on-the-job training.

Other objectives, I think, are less well served. The search for general, universal knowledge and for the philosophical principles on which it may be based has long since been abandoned. It might be thought, at least, that those values produced by the study of the natural sciences, of research, and of scientific method flourish in today's version of liberal education; I mean the rigorous training of the mind, the inculcation of a "truth-loving habit," and the universal triumph of the scientific method. I don't think that such a goal for liberal education was ever adequate; nevertheless its achievement would be worth a good deal, but I do not think our modern versions of liberal education achieve even that. In liberal arts colleges today the study of mathematics and the natural sciences is separated from other studies in important ways. The hard sciences are committed to rigorous training of the mind in a single method, the scientific one. Teachers of science continue to believe in the cumulative and progressive character of knowledge and in the possibility of moving toward truth. Students who major in these subjects are likely to acquire the method and to share these beliefs. While teachers and students are interested in the practical uses of science, I think many of them come to value learning and knowledge as good in themselves, although their scope is often limited. These are all good reasons, apart from those of practical necessity, for encouraging the serious study of natural science for all students. Even so, only a minority of students in liberal arts colleges major in mathematics or natural science. In some places students who do not major in these subjects are required to study neither; in others there is a minimal requirement that rarely achieves the desired goals.

Nor do I think that most modern attempts at liberal education sufficiently encourage students to pursue learning and knowledge as a serious and valuable contribution to their own lives. The absence of a core of common studies limits the possibility of taking learning seriously and making it an important part of life. Students follow different paths, read different books, ask different questions. They have no common intellectual ground. The result is to impoverish conversation and the thought that can arise from it, acknowledged since the time of Socrates as perhaps the most potent form of education. Serious talk on serious subjects based on shared knowledge is difficult, since the knowledge that comes from learning is scattered and specialized and thus unavailable to serve as the substance of important discussions. Belief in the intrinsic value of learning is diminished, since what each student has learned in courses is peculiar to himself or herself and not truly available for critical discussion. It is merely "academic," confined to forgotten papers and examinations, playing no part in the serious consideration of real issues and problems. If there were a general agreement on a body of knowledge worth learning, one that all educated people could share, and one, therefore, that could readily serve as the basis for serious discussion of important questions and might, thereby, yield wisdom, there would be a far greater chance of success than there is today.

The greatest shortcoming, I believe, of most attempts at liberal education today, with their individualized, unfocused, scattered curricula, and ill-defined purpose, is their failure to enhance the students' understanding of their status as free citizens of a free society and the responsibilities it entails. To my mind, liberal education is inconceivable outside a free society. Every successful civilization must pass on its basic values to each generation; when it no longer does so its days are numbered. The danger is particularly great in a society such as our own, the freest the world has known, whose special character is to encourage doubt and questioning even of its own values and assumptions. Such questioning has always been and remains a distinctive, admirable, and salutary part of our education and way of life. So long as there was a shared belief in the personal and social morality taught by tradition, so long as there was a belief in the excellence of the tradition and institutions of the nation, and so long as these beliefs were communicated in the schools, such questioning was also safe. Our tradition of free critical inquiry counteracted the tendency for received moral and civic teachings to become ethnocentric complacency and intolerance and prevented patriotism from degenerating into arrogant chauvinism. When students came to college they found their values and prejudices challenged by the books they read, by their fellow students from other places and backgrounds, and by their teachers.

I suggest to you that the situation is far different today. Whatever the 20
formal religious attachments of our students may be, I find that a firm belief in traditional values is rare. Still rarer are an informed understanding of the traditions and institutions of our country and their roots in the more remote past and an appreciation of their special qualities and virtues. The admirable, even

the uniquely good elements are taken for granted as if they were universally available, had always existed, and required no special effort to preserve. All shortcomings, however, are quickly noticed and harshly condemned. Our society is judged not against the experience of human societies in other times and places, but against the Kingdom of Heaven. There is great danger in this, for our society, no less than others now and in the past, requires the allegiance and devotion of its citizens if it is to defend itself and progress toward a better life. In my experience, however, traditional beliefs have not been replaced by a new set of beliefs firmly set on different traditions. Instead, I find a cultural void, an ignorance of the past, a sense of rootlessness and aimlessness, as though not only the students but also the world were born yesterday, a feeling that the students are attached to the society in which they live only incidentally and accidentally. Having little or no sense of the human experience through the ages, of what has been tried, of what has succeeded and what has failed, of what is the price of cherishing some values as opposed to others or of how values relate to one another, they leap from acting as though anything were possible, without cost, to despairing that nothing is possible. They are inclined to see other people's values as mere prejudices, one no better than another, while viewing their own inclinations as entirely valid, for they see themselves as autonomous entities entitled to be free from interference by society and from obligation to it.

Because of the cultural vacuum in their earlier education and because of the informal but potent education they receive from the communications media, which both shape and reflect the larger society, today's liberal arts students come to college, it seems to me, bearing a relativism verging on nihilism, an individualism that is really isolation from community. Each one resembles, as Aristotle put it, a single checker apart from a game of checkers. The education they too often receive in college these days, it seems to me, is more likely to reinforce this condition than to change it. In this way, too, it fails in its liberating function, in its responsibility to shape free men and women. Earlier generations who came to college with traditional beliefs rooted in the past had them challenged by hard questioning and by the requirement to consider alternatives. They were thereby unnerved, and thereby liberated, by the need to make reasoned choices. The students of today and tomorrow deserve the same opportunity; they, too, must be liberated from the tyranny that comes from the accident of being born at a time when and in a place where a particular set of ideas is current. But that liberation can come only from a return to the belief that we may have something to learn from the past. The challenge to the relativism, nihilism, and privatism of the present can best be presented by a careful and respectful examination of earlier ideas; such ideas have not been rejected by the current generation but are merely unknown to them.

When today's students have been allowed to consider the alternatives they, too, can enjoy the freedom of making an informed and reasoned choice.

The liberal education needed for the students of today and tomorrow, I suggest, should require a common program of studies for all its students as part of the full curriculum. That would have many advantages, for it would create an intellectual communion among students and teachers that does not now exist. It would also affirm that some questions are of fundamental importance to everyone, regardless of his or her origins and plans, that we must all think about our beliefs, our responsibilities, and our relationships with one another and with the society in which we live. The program to meet these goals should include the study of mathematics and science, of literature, philosophy, and history (in which I include the history of the arts and sciences) from their beginnings. It would be a study that tries to meet the past on its own terms, examining it critically but also respectfully, always keeping alive the possibility that the past may contain wisdom that can be useful to us today. It would include moral and civic goals among its purposes, critically and seriously examining the beliefs discussed, private and public, personal and political. Such an education would show the modern student times and worlds where the common understanding was quite different from his and her own—where it was believed that human beings have a nature and capacities different from those of the other animals, that their nature is gregarious and can reach its highest perfection only by living a good life in a well ordered society. It would reveal that a good society requires citizens who understand and share its values and accept their own connection with it and dependence on it, that there must be mutual respect among citizens and their common effort both for their own flourishing and for its survival. Students enjoying such an education would encounter the idea that freedom is essential to the good and happy life of human beings but that freedom requires good laws and respect for them.

Aristotle rightly observed that in matters other than scientific, people learn best not by precept, but by example. Let me conclude, therefore, by making it clear that the colleges that claim to offer a liberal education today and tomorrow must make their commitment to freedom clear by their actions. To a university, even more than to other institutions in a free society, the right of free speech, the free exchange of ideas, the presentation of unpopular points of view, the freedom to move about and make use of the university's facilities without interference, are vital. Discussion, argument, and persuasion are the devices appropriate to the life of the mind, not suppression, obstruction, and intimidation. Yet for more than three decades, our colleges and universities have permitted speakers to be shouted down or prevented from speaking, buildings to be forcibly occupied and access to them denied, student newspapers to be seized and disposed of, speech codes that enforce approved opinions to be imposed, and various modes of intimidation to be employed with much success. Most of the time the perpetrators have gone unpunished in any significant way. Colleges and universities that permit such attacks on freedom and take no firm and effective action to deter and punish those who carry them out sabotage the most basic educational freedoms. To defend those freedoms is the first obligation of anyone who claims to engage in liberal education.

The history of the human race shows that liberty is a rare flower and that societies in which freedom has flourished have been few and short-lived. There is no reason to take freedom for granted, for it seems to require both good fortune and careful cultivation to have any chance at all. We seem to have lost sight of the most basic and noblest purpose of liberal learning: to pass on to each new generation the heritage of freedom and to provide each man and woman with the knowledge needed to understand, cherish, and protect it. If liberty is to survive we must demonstrate our commitment to it in both word and deed. Most important of all, we must provide our children with an education shaped by the purpose of creating citizens of a free society who will love liberty, who will understand the discipline and sacrifice needed to preserve it, and who will be eager to do so.

QUESTIONING THE TEXT

1. Kagan begins his essay with a brief history of Western liberal education, suggesting "it may be a useful basis for examining the status of liberal education today" (paragraph 15). Do you think the historical opening effectively serves this purpose? What other effects does this opening have on your reading of the essay?
2. To whom do you think Kagan is writing? How do his tone and diction suggest characteristics of the audience he envisions? Do you feel as if you are part of his intended audience? Why, or why not?

MAKING CONNECTIONS

3. Keeping in mind the four goals Kagan attributes to liberal education (paragraph 2), review the college mission statements presented earlier in this chapter (p. 57). Do these institutions seem to pursue goals similar to those Kagan lists, or do they depart from the liberal arts tradition that Kagan describes? How might you account for the similarities or differences between Kagan's characterization of that tradition and the statements presented by these colleges?
4. Kagan is identified as a professor of classics and history at Yale University. How do you think his academic discipline—the subjects he studies and the methods of inquiry used in those subjects—may affect his perspective on education? Consider whether the opinions expressed by other professors in this chapter—Adrienne Rich (p. 71), Shelby Steele (p. 78), Jennifer L. Croissant (p. 99), Mike Rose (p. 109)—may be similarly influenced by their academic specialties.

5. Imagine a conversation between Kagan and Adrienne Rich (p. 71). How might Rich respond to Kagan's claims about the value of a common curriculum for all students? How do you think Kagan would respond to Rich's assertions about what a "woman needs to know"?

JOINING THE CONVERSATION

6. Is there a common curriculum at your college or university? Is there one within the college or department in which you study? Are there any courses that all students must take? Write an essay to your school administrators in favor of or against common course requirements, using ideas from Kagan's essay and others in this chapter, such as those of Adrienne Rich (p. 71) or Mike Rose (p. 109).
7. Consider the first part of Kagan's essay, in which he describes the societies that fostered the liberal arts tradition. Write an exploratory essay on the extent to which you think liberal education, as described in this essay, "is inconceivable outside a free society," as Kagan claims in paragraph 19.

GWENDOLYN BROOKS
We Real Cool

*W*HEN *G*WENDOLYN *B*ROOKS *(b. 1917) was a little girl, her mother said, "You're going to be the first* lady *Paul Laurence Dunbar," a powerful and well-known black poet. Brooks met her mother's challenge and then some, becoming the first African American writer to win the Pulitzer Prize (for* Annie Allen *in 1950) and the first African American woman to be elected to the National Institute of Arts and Letters or to serve as Consultant in Poetry to the Library of Congress. A 1936 graduate of Chicago's Wilson Junior College, Brooks has received over seventy honorary degrees.*

In her most distinguished career, Brooks has drawn on the traditions of African American sermons and musical forms—especially the blues, jazz, and the spiritual—to explore the American condition and, in particular, the realities of African American life. Her brief poem "We Real Cool" depicts a group of young hookey players who have rejected—or been rejected by—their schools. This is the first poem by Brooks I ever read, and it inspired me to seek out her other poetry and prose and to be a lifelong fan of her work. It also made me think about what my life would have been like if I had "left school."

—A.L.

The Pool Players.
Seven at the Golden Shovel.

We real cool. We
Left school. We

Lurk late. We
Strike straight. We

Sing sin. We
Thin gin. We

Jazz June. We
Die soon.

IN RESPONSE

1. What message do you take away from Brooks's poem? In what ways does it speak personally to you? If you keep a reading log, answer this question there.
2. How do you think the students in the reading by Mike Rose (p. 109) might respond to the poem?
3. Brooks's poem was written in 1960, and it refers to and uses the style of an even earlier jazz tradition. Write your own contemporary version of "We Real Cool," calling on present-day styles of music and culture to do so.

OTHER READINGS

hooks, bell. "Eros, Eroticism, and the Pedagogical Process." *Teaching to Transgress: Education as the Practice of Freedom.* New York: Routledge, 1994. Stresses the centrality of the body and the importance of passion in teaching.

Kolodny, Annette. *Failing the Future: A Dean Looks at Higher Education in the Twenty-first Century.* Durham, NC: Duke UP, 1998. Explores the current problems in higher education and offers practical solutions and workable programs for change.

Kors, Alan Charles, and Harvey A. Silverglate. *The Shadow University: The Betrayal of Liberty on America's Campuses.* New York: Free, 1998. Argues that universities today oppose American traditions of freedom.

McNamara, Patrick H. "All Is Not Lost: Teaching Generation X." *Commonweal* 21 Apr. 1995. Reports that teaching the traditional Western canon works with students today.

Orenstein, Peggy. *School Girls: Young Women, Self-Esteem, and the Confidence Gap.* New York: Doubleday, 1994. Explores issues of self-esteem among female adolescents.

Pratt, Mary Louise. "Humanities for the Future: Reflections on the Western Culture Debate at Stanford." *South Atlantic Quarterly* 89.1 (Winter 1990): 7–25. On revising the Stanford humanities course to include more on cultural diversity.

Ravitch, Diane. *The Language Police: How Pressure Groups Restrict What Students Learn.* New York: Knopf, 2003. An analysis of the effects of the anti-bias and sensitivity guidelines in educational publishing on the textbooks used by today's students.

Rorty, Richard. "The Unpatriotic Academy." *New York Times* 13 Feb. 1994: E15. Urges leftist academics to consider the virtues of patriotism.

Rose, Mike. *Possible Lives: The Promise of Public Education in America.* New York: Houghton, 1995. Provides a richly detailed account of what goes on in good classrooms around the country.

Sowell, Thomas. *Inside American Education: The Decline, the Deception, the Dogmas.* New York: Free, 1993. Finds failure and corruption in the American educational establishment.

ELECTRONIC RESOURCES

http://www.clas.ufl.edu/CLAS/american-universities.html
Lists Web sites for many American colleges and universities.

http://chronicle.com
Outlines the content of current issues of a weekly newspaper covering higher education issues.

http://www.mcli.dist.maricopa.edu/cc/
Lists Web sites for many two-year schools.

Look carefully at the photograph on the preceding page, which shows Elizabeth Eckford, an African American teenager, on her way to enroll in (previously all-white) Central High School in Little Rock, Arkansas, on September 4, 1957. What first draws your attention to this photograph? ■ What story does the photo tell, both about each individual and about the group as a whole? ■ What dominant impression does it create? ■ What underlying and competing values seem to be at work in it?

Moralities: Most Sacred Values

4

I have tried to make clear that it is wrong to use immoral means to attain moral ends. But now I must affirm that it is just as wrong, or perhaps even more so, to use moral means to preserve immoral ends.

MARTIN LUTHER KING JR., *Letter from Birmingham Jail*

We, the People of the United States, who a little over two hundred years ago ordained and established the Constitution, have a serious problem: too many of us nowadays neither mean what we say nor say what we mean.

STEPHEN L. CARTER, *The Rules about the Rules*

All over the world most women who can't have children must simply accept the fact and adopt, or find other roles in society. But especially here in the United States wealth can enable such couples to have a child of their own and to determine how closely that child will resemble the one they might have had—or the one they dream of having.

JESSICA COHEN, *Grade A: The Market for a Yale Woman's Eggs*

One of the great mysteries of modern politics is which story lines get told and which get ignored.

SARAH VOWELL, *Democracy and Things Like That*

"Cheating *is* an answer. . . . It might not be a good answer, but none the less it is an answer."

MARK CLAYTON, *A Whole Lot of Cheatin' Going On*

Morality can survive without religion, it appears; children can be taught the importance of right versus wrong without benefit of religious training.

ANTHONY BRANDT, *Do Kids Need Religion?*

[M]orality is an artifact of human culture, devised to help us negotiate social relations. It's very good for that. But just as we recognize that nature doesn't provide an adequate guide for human social conduct, isn't it anthropocentric to assume that our moral system offers an adequate guide for nature?

MICHAEL POLLAN, *An Animal's Place*

We need passionate followers of an ideal of civic virtue, an ideal that does not conform, as St. Paul says in Romans 12:1&2, but is transformed by the renewing of one's mind and one's soul.

PETER J. GOMES, *Civic Virtue and the Character of Followership*

I don't want to have sex because "I guess" I want it. I want to wait for something more exciting than that, and modesty helps me understand why.

WENDY SHALIT, *The Future of Modesty*

For a war to be just, it . . . can be waged only as a last resort, with all nonviolent options exhausted. In the case of Iraq, it is obvious that clear alternatives to war exist.

JIMMY CARTER, *Just War—or a Just War?*

Though I oppose war, I am in favor of intervention when, as in this case because of Hussein's equivocations and procrastinations, no other option remains.

ELIE WIESEL, *Peace Isn't Possible in Evil's Face*

I had not yet done the things / that would need forgiving.

KATHLEEN NORRIS, *Little Girls in Church*

Introduction

GEORGE JOHNSON OPENS *Fire in the Mind* (1995), a book on the relationship of faith and science, by citing a Navajo creation story:

> When all the stars were ready to be placed in the sky First Woman said, "I will use these to write the laws that are to govern mankind for all time. These laws cannot be written on the water as that is always changing its form, nor can they be written in the sand as the wind would soon erase them, but if they are written in the stars they can be read and remembered forever."

The myth gives shape to the enduring human desire for a firm moral sense, a guide to right and wrong as immutable as the stars.

Just as persistent among nations and people is a fear of moral decline. The Hebrew prophets in biblical times regularly denounced the sins and abominations of the Israelites. The ancient Romans had Cato the Censor to deplore their precipitous retreat from virtue. Martin Luther protested the corruption he found in the Catholic Church of the Renaissance, and his twentieth-century American namesake, Martin Luther King Jr., challenged a nation to restore its sense of justice by ending racial discrimination. Of course, reading history this way leads one to suspect that nearly every age views itself as a period of decline in need of prophets to set things right.

Some Americans, too, wonder at the beginning of a new millennium whether their national culture can sink much lower than it already has—the news honeying in scandal, corruption, and hate crimes, while pop culture celebrates greed, conspicuous consumption, and promiscuous sex, while bingeing on so-called "reality TV." Consider the Enron and Arthur Anderson scandals, the dragging death of a black man in Texas, the murder of a gay college student in California, the hate crimes against Muslims following the September 11 attacks. To many, something seems rotten in the soul of the nation.

But is that perception accurate? And, if so, how does one restore the moral sense of a people grown too diverse and, perhaps, too worldly to look to the stars (or their equivalent) for guidance? Long-term trends are full of contradictions. There's been an increase in the rate of divorce and a surge in out-of-wedlock births, but a renewed concern for the institution of marriage and traditional families; a coarsening of social discourse, yet growing interest in manners and civility; an increase in juvenile violence, but an overall drop in crime; a steady number of abortions and a remarkably high rate of church going; a widening rift between rich and poor, yet dwindling support for welfare programs. Trends and numbers like these, of course, can support quite different moral interpretations—they can be read in varying ways. For instance, one writer may interpret the evident decline of the nuclear family in the United States as a threat to the country's moral core, while another regards it as welcome evidence that society is enlarging its moral vision to accept new kinds of families. To some, the steady abortion rate represents women having the freedom to exercise a moral choice; to others, it memorializes a new Holocaust.

So in thinking about behavior and choices, it seems we ought to think not of *morality* but *moralities*. To that end, in this chapter, we present authors locating their ethical assumptions in religion, philosophy, art, and even consumption. But this diversity of approach to questions of good and evil does not in itself necessarily signal the triumph of moral relativism—the belief that moral choices are made on the basis of individual or local, not universal, standards. The desire for surety transcends time and cultures, and the assertion that there is a universal moral sense continues to be heard. It is, in fact, one of the issues most under scrutiny and debate.

You might think that moral issues are too hypothetical to win your attention. But, as this chapter demonstrates, you face practical ethical choices almost every day in school, in the workplace, and in your personal life. Moreover, we probably need not fear for the health of our society as long as debates about moralities—the kind you and your classmates might have in a dorm room or classroom—remain robust and honorable. Following are some questions to keep the debate alive:

- Do you and your friends discuss moral issues? If so, what topics come up regularly or provoke the most discussion?
- What sorts of moral issues affect you most directly or often? When do you find yourself most conscious of making a moral choice?
- Do you believe people share a common moral sense or that morality is a matter of personal belief?
- What makes a particular belief "religious"? What do the terms *religion* and *God* mean to you? To people with views or religious convictions different than your own?
- How important is morality to your generation? Would you characterize yourself and your peers as more or less "moral" or "ethical" than generations before or after your own?

MARTIN LUTHER KING JR.

Letter from Birmingham Jail

THE REVEREND MARTIN LUTHER KING JR. (1929–68) is remembered today for many accomplishments: his leadership of the movement for civil rights for African Americans in the 1950s and 1960s; his advocacy of nonviolent resistance to oppressive systems; his Christian ministry; his powerful and moving sermons and speeches. In King, all these elements coalesced in a figure who won the Nobel Peace Prize, changed the face of American public life, and reframed the questions any society striving to enact truly democratic principles must face. When he was assassinated in Memphis on April 4, 1968, the world lost a major spokesperson for the values of equality, freedom, and social justice—for all.

King attended Morehouse College (see p. 59 for the current Morehouse mission statement) and later received his Ph.D. in theology from Boston University. But extensive education and high intelligence did not protect him from racist forces, which eventually led to his murder and which are still present in the United States more than thirty years after King's death. But in the face of such hostility, King's moral commitment never faltered. In March 1963, he led the March on Washington and delivered, at the foot of the Lincoln Memorial, one of his most memorable and moving speeches, "I Have a Dream," to some quarter of a million people, the largest protest demonstration in American history up to that time. The next month, King led a major protest against unfair hiring practices in Birmingham, Alabama, for which he was arrested and put in jail. While in prison, he wrote a long letter responding to local white religious leaders of several faiths, who had criticized his actions as "unwise" and "untimely." "Letter from Birmingham Jail," reprinted here in the revised version published in Why We Can't Wait *(1964), has emerged as a classic text on civil rights. In it, King clearly and forcefully articulates the moral principles on which his actions rest—and challenges not only the clergy of the time but all readers today to examine their own.* —A.L.

My Dear Fellow Clergymen:

While confined here in the Birmingham city jail, I came across your recent statement calling my present activities "unwise and untimely." Seldom do I pause to answer criticism of my work and ideas. If I sought to answer all the criticisms that cross my desk, my secretaries would have little time for anything other than such correspondence in the course of the day, and I would have no time for constructive work. But since I feel that you are men of genuine good will and that your criticisms are sincerely set forth, I want to try to answer your statement in what I hope will be patient and reasonable terms.

I think I should indicate why I am here in Birmingham, since you have been influenced by the view which argues against "outsiders coming in." I have the honor of serving as president of the Southern Christian Leadership Conference, an organization operating in every southern state, with headquarters in Atlanta, Georgia. We have some eighty-five affiliated organizations across the South, and one of them is the Alabama Christian Movement for Human Rights. Frequently we share staff, educational, and financial resources with our affiliates. Several months ago the affiliate here in Birmingham asked us to be on call to engage in a nonviolent direct-action program if such were deemed necessary. We readily consented, and when the hour came, we lived up to our promise. So I, along with several members of my staff, am here because I was invited here. I am here because I have organizational ties here.

But more basically, I am in Birmingham because injustice is here. Just as the prophets of the eighth century B.C. left their villages and carried their "thus saith the Lord" far beyond the boundaries of their home towns, and just as the Apostle Paul left his village of Tarsus and carried the gospel of Jesus Christ to the far corners of the Greco-Roman world, so am I compelled to carry the gospel of freedom beyond my own home town. Like Paul, I must constantly respond to the Macedonian call for aid.

Moreover, I am cognizant of the interrelatedness of all communities and states. I cannot sit idly by in Atlanta and not be concerned about what happens in Birmingham. Injustice anywhere is a threat to justice everywhere. We are caught in an inescapable network of mutuality, tied in a single garment of destiny. Whatever affects one directly, affects all indirectly. Never again can we afford to live with the narrow, provincial "outside agitator" idea. Anyone who lives inside the United States can never be considered an outsider anywhere within its bounds.

You deplore the demonstrations taking place in Birmingham. But your 5
statement, I am sorry to say, fails to express a similar concern for the conditions that brought about the demonstrations. I am sure that none of you would want to rest content with the superficial kind of social analysis that deals merely with effects and does not grapple with underlying causes. It is unfortunate that demonstrations are taking place in Birmingham, but it is even more unfortunate that the city's white power structure left the Negro community with no alternative.

In any nonviolent campaign there are four basic steps: collection of the facts to determine whether injustices exist; negotiation; self-purification; and direct action. We have gone through all these steps in Birmingham. There can be no gainsaying the fact that racial injustice engulfs this community. Birmingham is probably the most thoroughly segregated city in the United States. Its ugly record of brutality is widely known. Negroes have experienced grossly unjust treatment in the courts. There have been more unsolved bombings of Negro homes and churches in Birmingham than in any other city in the nation. These are the hard, brutal facts of the case. On the basis of these conditions, Negro leaders sought to negotiate with the city fathers. But the latter consistently refused to engage in good-faith negotiation.

Then, last September, came the opportunity to talk with leaders of Birmingham's economic community. In the course of the negotiations, certain promises were made by the merchants—for example, to remove the stores' humiliating racial signs. On the basis of these promises, the Reverend Fred Shuttlesworth and the leaders of the Alabama Christian Movement for Human Rights agreed to a moratorium on all demonstrations. As the weeks and months went by, we realized that we were the victims of a broken promise. A few signs, briefly removed, returned; the others remained.

As in so many past experiences, our hopes had been blasted, and the shadow of deep disappointment settled upon us. We had no alternative except to prepare for direct action, whereby we would present our very bodies as a means of laying our case before the conscience of the local and the national community. Mindful of the difficulties involved, we decided to undertake a process of self-purification. We began a series of workshops on nonviolence, and we repeatedly asked ourselves: "Are you able to accept blows without retaliating?" "Are you able to endure the ordeal of jail?" We decided to schedule our direct-action program for the Easter season, realizing that except for Christmas, this is the main shopping period of the year. Knowing that a strong economic-withdrawal program would be the by-product of direct action, we felt that this would be the best time to bring pressure to bear on the merchants for the needed change.

Then it occurred to us that Birmingham's mayoral election was coming up in March, and we speedily decided to postpone action until after election day. When we discovered that the Commissioner of Public Safety, Eugene "Bull" Connor, had piled up enough votes to be in the run-off, we decided again to postpone action until the day after the run-off so that the demonstrations could not be used to cloud the issues. Like many others, we wanted to see Mr. Connor defeated, and to this end we endured postponement after postponement. Having aided in this community need, we felt that our direct-action program could be delayed no longer.

You may well ask, "Why direct action? Why sit-ins, marches, and so 10
forth? Isn't negotiation a better path?" You are quite right in calling for negotiation. Indeed, this is the very purpose of direct action. Nonviolent direct action seeks to create such a crisis and foster such a tension that a community which has constantly refused to negotiate is forced to confront the issue. It seeks so to dramatize the issue that it can no longer be ignored. My citing the creation of tension as part of the work of the nonviolent-resister may sound rather shocking. But I must confess that I am not afraid of the word "tension." I have earnestly opposed violent tension, but there is a type of constructive, nonviolent tension which is necessary for growth. Just as Socrates felt that it was necessary to create a tension in the mind so that individuals

could rise from the bondage of myths and half-truths to the unfettered realm of creative analysis and objective appraisal, so must we see the need for nonviolent gadflies to create the kind of tension in society that will help men rise from the dark depths of prejudice and racism to the majestic heights of understanding and brotherhood.

The purpose of our direct-action program is to create a situation so crisis-packed that it will inevitably open the door to negotiation. I therefore concur with you in your call for negotiation. Too long has our beloved Southland been bogged down in a tragic effort to live in monologue rather than dialogue.

One of the basic points in your statement is that the action that I and my associates have taken in Birmingham is untimely. Some have asked: "Why didn't you give the new city administration time to act?" The only answer that I can give to this query is that the new Birmingham administration must be prodded about as much as the outgoing one, before it will act. We are sadly mistaken if we feel that the election of Albert Boutwell as mayor will bring the millennium to Birmingham. While Mr. Boutwell is a much more gentle person than Mr. Connor, they are both segregationists, dedicated to maintenance of the status quo. I have hoped that Mr. Boutwell will be reasonable enough to see the futility of massive resistance to desegregation. But he will not see this without pressure from devotees of civil rights. My friends, I must say to you that we have not made a single gain in civil rights without determined legal and nonviolent pressure. Lamentably, it is an historical fact that privileged groups seldom give up their privileges voluntarily. Individuals may see the moral light and voluntarily give up their unjust posture; but, as Reinhold Niebuhr has reminded us, groups tend to be more immoral than individuals.

We know through painful experience that freedom is never voluntarily given by the oppressor; it must be demanded by the oppressed. Frankly, I have yet to engage in a direct-action campaign that was "well timed" in the view of those who have not suffered unduly from the disease of segregation. For years now I have heard the word "Wait!" It rings in the ear of every Negro with piercing familiarity. This "Wait" has almost always meant "Never." We must come to see, with one of our distinguished jurists, that "justice too long delayed is justice denied."

We have waited for more than 340 years for our constitutional and God-given rights. The nations of Asia and Africa are moving with jetlike speed toward gaining political independence, but we still creep at horse-and-buggy pace toward gaining a cup of coffee at a lunch counter. Perhaps it is easy for those who have never felt the stinging darts of segregation to say, "Wait." But when you have seen vicious mobs lynch your mothers and fathers at will and drown your sisters and brothers at whim; when you have seen hate-filled policemen curse, kick, and even kill your black brothers and sisters; when you see the vast majority of your twenty million Negro brothers smothering in an airtight cage of poverty in the midst of an affluent society;

when you suddenly find your tongue twisted and your speech stammering as you seek to explain to your six-year-old daughter why she can't go to the public amusement park that has just been advertised on television, and see tears welling up in her eyes when she is told that Funtown is closed to colored children, and see ominous clouds of inferiority beginning to form in her little mental sky, and see her beginning to distort her personality by developing an unconscious bitterness toward white people; when you have to concoct an answer for a five-year-old son who is asking "Daddy, why do white people treat colored people so mean?"; when you take a cross-country drive and find it necessary to sleep night after night in the uncomfortable corners of your automobile because no motel will accept you; when you are humiliated day in and day out by nagging signs reading "white" and "colored"; when your first name becomes "nigger," your middle name becomes "boy" (however old you are) and your last name becomes "John," and your wife and mother are never given the respected title "Mrs."; when you are harried by day and haunted by night by the fact that you are a Negro, living constantly at tiptoe stance, never quite knowing what to expect next, and are plagued with inner fears and outer resentments; when you are forever fighting a degenerating sense of "nobodiness"—then you will understand why we find it difficult to wait. There comes a time when the cup of endurance runs over, and men are no longer willing to be plunged into the abyss of despair. I hope, sirs, you can understand our legitimate and unavoidable impatience.

You express a great deal of anxiety over our willingness to break laws. 15
This is certainly a legitimate concern. Since we so diligently urge people to obey the Supreme Court's decision of 1954 outlawing segregation in the public schools, at first glance it may seem rather paradoxical for us consciously to break laws. One may well ask: "How can you advocate breaking some laws and obeying others?" The answer lies in the fact that there are two types of laws: just and unjust. I would be the first to advocate obeying just laws. One has not only a legal but a moral responsibility to obey just laws. Conversely, one has a moral responsibility to disobey unjust laws. I would agree with St. Augustine that "an unjust law is no law at all."

Now, what is the difference between the two? How does one determine whether a law is just or unjust? A just law is a man-made code that squares with the moral law or the law of God. An unjust law is a code that is out of harmony with the moral law. To put it in the terms of St. Thomas Aquinas: An unjust law is a human law that is not rooted in eternal law and natural law. Any law that uplifts human personality is just. Any law that degrades human personality is unjust. All segregation statutes are unjust because segregation distorts the soul and damages the personality. It gives the segregator a false sense of superiority and the segregated a false sense of inferiority. Segregation, to use the terminology of the Jewish philosopher Martin Buber, substitutes an "I–it" relationship for an "I–thou" relationship and ends up relegating persons to the status of things. Hence segregation is not only politically, economically, and sociologically unsound, it is morally wrong and sinful. Paul Tillich has said that sin is separation. Is not segregation an existential expression of man's tragic separation, his awful estrangement, his terrible sinfulness? Thus it is that I can urge men to obey the 1954 decision of the Supreme Court, for it is morally right; and I can urge them to disobey segregation ordinances, for they are morally wrong.

Let us consider a more concrete example of just and unjust laws. An unjust law is a code that a numerical or power majority group compels a minority group to obey but does not make binding on itself. This is *difference* made legal. By the same token, a just law is a code that a majority compels a minority to follow and that it is willing to follow itself. This is *sameness* made legal.

Let me give another explanation. A law is unjust if it is inflicted on a minority that, as a result of being denied the right to vote, had no part in enacting or devising the law. Who can say that the legislature of Alabama which set up that state's segregation laws was democratically elected? Throughout Alabama all sorts of devious methods are used to prevent Negroes from becoming registered voters, and there are some counties in which, even though Negroes constitute a majority of the population, not a single Negro is registered. Can any law enacted under such circumstances be considered democratically structured?

Sometimes a law is just on its face and unjust in its application. For instance, I have been arrested on a charge of parading without a permit. Now, there is nothing wrong in having an ordinance which requires a permit for a parade. But such an ordinance becomes unjust when it is used to maintain segregation and to deny citizens the First-Amendment privilege of peaceful assembly and protest.

I hope you are able to see the distinction I am trying to point out. In no 20
sense do I advocate evading or defying the law, as would the rabid segregationist. That would lead to anarchy. One who breaks an unjust law must do so openly, lovingly, and with a willingness to accept the penalty. I submit that an individual who breaks a law that conscience tells him is unjust, and who willingly accepts the penalty of imprisonment in order to arouse the conscience of the community over its injustice, is in reality expressing the highest respect for law.

Of course, there is nothing new about this kind of civil disobedience. It was evidenced sublimely in the refusal of Shadrach, Meshach, and Abednego to obey the laws of Nebuchadnezzar,* on the ground that a higher moral law was at stake. It was practiced superbly by the early Christians, who were willing to face hungry lions and the excruciating pain of chopping blocks rather than

---

Shadrach, Meshach, and Abednego . . . Nebuchadnezzar: In the biblical Book of Daniel, the Babylonian king Nebuchadnezzar orders the three Israelites thrown into a fiery furnace for refusing to worship a golden idol, but they emerge unharmed.

submit to certain unjust laws of the Roman Empire. To a degree, academic freedom is a reality today because Socrates practiced civil disobedience. In our own nation, the Boston Tea Party represented a massive act of civil disobedience.

We should never forget that everything Adolf Hitler did in Germany was "legal" and everything the Hungarian freedom fighters* did in Hungary was "illegal." It was "illegal" to aid and comfort a Jew in Hitler's Germany. Even so, I am sure that, had I lived in Germany at the time, I would have aided and comforted my Jewish brothers. If today I lived in a Communist country where certain principles dear to the Christian faith are suppressed, I would openly advocate disobeying that country's anti-religious laws.

I must make two honest confessions to you, my Christian and Jewish brothers. First, I must confess that over the past few years I have been gravely disappointed with the white moderate. I have almost reached the regrettable conclusion that the Negro's great stumbling block in his stride toward freedom is not the White Citizen's Counciler* or the Ku Klux Klanner, but the white moderate, who is more devoted to "order" than to justice; who prefers a negative peace which is the absence of tension to a positive peace which is the presence of justice; who constantly says, "I agree with you in the goal you seek, but I cannot agree with your methods of direct action"; who paternalistically believes he can set the timetable for another man's freedom; who lives by a mythical concept of time and who constantly advises the Negro to wait for a "more convenient season." Shallow understanding from people of good will is more frustrating than absolute misunderstanding from people of ill will. Lukewarm acceptance is much more bewildering than outright rejection.

I had hoped that the white moderate would understand that law and order exist for the purpose of establishing justice and that when they fail in this purpose they become the dangerously structured dams that block the flow of social progress. I had hoped that the white moderate would understand that the present tension in the South is a necessary phase of the transition from an obnoxious negative peace, in which the Negro passively accepted his unjust plight, to a substantive and positive peace, in which all men will respect the dignity and worth of human personality. Actually, we who engage in nonviolent direct action are not the creators of tension. We merely bring to the surface the hidden tension that is already alive. We bring it out in the open, where it can be seen and dealt with. Like a boil that can never be cured so long as it is covered up but must be opened with all its ugliness to the natural medicines of air and light, injustice must be exposed, with all the tension its exposure creates, to the light of human conscience and the air of national opinion, before it can be cured.

Hungarian freedom fighters: In 1956, Hungarians revolted against the Marxist government imposed on them by the former Soviet Union.

White Citizen's Counciler: member of a group organized to resist the desegregation of schools ordered by the Supreme Court's *Brown v. Board of Education* decision

In your statement you assert that our actions, even though peaceful, 25
must be condemned because they precipitate violence. But is this a logical assertion? Isn't this like condemning a robbed man because his possession of money precipitated the evil act of robbery? Isn't this like condemning Socrates because his unswerving commitment to truth and his philosophical inquiries precipitated the act by the misguided populace in which they made him drink hemlock? Isn't this like condemning Jesus because his unique God-consciousness and never-ceasing devotion to God's will precipitated the evil act of crucifixion? We must come to see that, as the federal courts have consistently affirmed, it is wrong to urge an individual to cease his efforts to gain his basic constitutional rights because the quest may precipitate violence. Society must protect the robbed and punish the robber.

I had also hoped that the white moderate would reject the myth concerning time in relation to the struggle for freedom. I have just received a letter from a white brother in Texas. He writes: "All Christians know that the colored people will receive equal rights eventually, but it is possible that you are in too great a religious hurry. It has taken Christianity almost two thousand years to accomplish what it has. The teachings of Christ take time to come to earth." Such an attitude stems from a tragic misconception of time, from the strangely irrational notion that there is something in the very flow of time that will inevitably cure all ills. Actually, time itself is neutral; it can be used either destructively or constructively. More and more I feel that the people of ill will have used time much more effectively than have the people of good will. We will have to repent in this generation not merely for the hateful words and actions of the bad people, but for the appalling silence of the good people. Human progress never rolls in on wheels of inevitability; it comes through the tireless efforts of men willing to be co-workers with God, and without this hard work, time itself becomes an ally of the forces of social stagnation. We must use time creatively, in the knowledge that the time is always ripe to do right. Now is the time to make real the promise of democracy and transform our pending national elegy into a creative psalm of brotherhood. Now is the time to lift our national policy from the quicksand of racial injustice to the solid rock of human dignity.

You speak of our activity in Birmingham as extreme. At first I was rather disappointed that fellow clergymen would see my nonviolent efforts as those of an extremist. I began thinking about the fact that I stand in the middle of two opposing forces in the Negro community. One is a force of complacency, made up in part of Negroes who, as a result of long years of oppression, are so drained of self-respect and a sense of "somebodiness" that they have adjusted to segregation; and in part of a few middle-class Negroes who, because of a degree of academic and economic security and because in some ways they profit by segregation, have become insensitive to the problems of the masses. The other force is one of bitterness and hatred, and it comes perilously close to advocating violence. It is expressed in the various black nationalist groups that are springing up across the nation, the largest and best-known being Elijah Muhammad's Muslim movement. Nourished by the Negro's frustration over the continued existence of racial discrimination, this movement is made up of people who have lost faith in America, who have absolutely repudiated Christianity, and who have concluded that the white man is an incorrigible "devil."

I have tried to stand between these two forces, saying that we need emulate neither the "do-nothingism" of the complacent nor the hatred and despair of the black nationalist. For there is the more excellent way of love and nonviolent protest. I am grateful to God that, through the influence of the Negro church, the way of nonviolence became an integral part of our struggle.

If this philosophy had not emerged, by now many streets of the South would, I am convinced, be flowing with blood. And I am further convinced that if our white brothers dismiss as "rabblerousers" and "outside agitators" those of us who employ nonviolent direct action, and if they refuse to support our nonviolent efforts, millions of Negroes will, out of frustration and despair, seek solace and security in Black-nationalist ideologies—a development that would inevitably lead to a frightening racial nightmare.

Oppressed people cannot remain oppressed forever. The yearning for 30
freedom eventually manifests itself, and that is what has happened to the American Negro. Something within has reminded him of his birthright of freedom, and something without has reminded him that it can be gained. Consciously or unconsciously, he has been caught up by the *Zeitgeist,* and with his black brothers of Africa and his brown and yellow brothers of Asia, South America, and the Caribbean, the United States Negro is moving with a sense of great urgency toward the promised land of racial justice. If one recognizes this vital urge that has engulfed the Negro community, one should readily understand why public demonstrations are taking place. The Negro has spent many pent-up resentments and latent frustrations, and he must release them. So let him march; let him make prayer pilgrimages to the city hall; let him go on freedom rides—and try to understand why he must do so. If his repressed emotions are not released in nonviolent ways, they will seek expression through violence; this is not a threat but a fact of history. So I have not said to my people, "Get rid of your discontent." Rather, I have tried to say that this normal and healthy discontent can be channeled into the creative outlet of nonviolent direct action. And now this approach is being termed extremist.

But though I was initially disappointed at being categorized as an extremist, as I continued to think about the matter I gradually gained a measure of satisfaction from the label. Was not Jesus an extremist for love: "Love your enemies, bless them that curse you, do good to them that hate you, and pray for them which despitefully use you, and persecute you." Was not Amos an extremist for justice: "Let justice roll down like waters and righteousness like an everflowing stream." Was not Paul an extremist for the Christian gospel: "I bear in my body the marks of the Lord Jesus." Was not Martin Luther an extremist: "Here I stand; I cannot do otherwise, so help me God." And John Bunyan: "I will stay in jail to the end of my days before I make a butchery of my conscience." And Abraham Lincoln: "This nation cannot survive half slave and half free." And Thomas Jefferson: "We hold these truths to be self-evident, that all men are created equal. . . ." So the question is not whether we will be extremists, but what kind of extremists we will be. Will we be extremists for hate or for love? Will we be extremists for the preservation of injustice or for the extension of justice? In that dramatic scene on Calvary's hill three men were crucified. We must never forget that all three were crucified for the same crime—the crime of extremism. Two were extremists for immorality, and thus fell below their environment. The other, Jesus Christ, was an extremist for love, truth, and goodness, and thereby rose above his environment. Perhaps the South, the nation, and the world are in dire need of creative extremists.

I had hoped that the white moderate would see this need. Perhaps I was too optimistic; perhaps I expected too much. I suppose I should have realized that few members of the oppressor race can understand the deep groans and passionate yearnings of the oppressed race, and still fewer have the vision to see that injustice must be rooted out by strong, persistent, and determined action. I am thankful, however, that some of our white brothers in the South have grasped the meaning of this social revolution and committed themselves to it. They are still all too few in quantity, but they are big in quality. Some—such as Ralph McGill, Lillian Smith, Harry Golden, James McBridge Dabbs, Anne Braden, and Sarah Patton Boyle—have written about our struggle in eloquent and prophetic terms. Others have marched with us down nameless streets of the South. They have languished in filthy, roach-infested jails, suffering the abuse and brutality of policemen who view them as "dirty nigger-lovers." Unlike so many of their moderate brothers and sisters, they have recognized the urgency of the moment and sensed the need for powerful "action" antidotes to combat the disease of segregation.

Let me take note of my other major disappointment. I have been so greatly disappointed with the white church and its leadership. Of course, there are some notable exceptions. I am not unmindful of the fact that each of you has taken some significant stands on this issue. I commend you, Reverend Stallings, for your Christian stand on this past Sunday, in welcoming Negroes to your worship service on a nonsegregated basis. I commend the Catholic leaders of this state for integrating Spring Hill College several years ago.

But despite these notable exceptions, I must honestly reiterate that I have been disappointed with the church. I do not say this as one of those negative critics who can always find something wrong with the church. I say this as a minister of the gospel, who loves the church; who was nurtured in its bosom; who has been sustained by its spiritual blessings and who will remain true to it as long as the cord of life shall lengthen.

When I was suddenly catapulted into the leadership of the bus protest in 35
Montgomery, Alabama, a few years ago, I felt we would be supported by the white church. I felt that the white ministers, priests, and rabbis of the South would be among our strongest allies. Instead, some have been outright opponents, refusing to understand the freedom movement and misrepresenting its leaders; all too many others have been more cautious than courageous and have remained silent behind the anesthetizing security of stained glass windows.

In spite of my shattered dreams, I came to Birmingham with the hope that the white religious leadership of this community would see the justice of our cause and, with deep moral concern, would serve as the channel through which our just grievances could reach the power structure. I had hoped that each of you would understand. But again I have been disappointed.

I have heard numerous southern religious leaders admonish their worshipers to comply with a desegregation decision because it is the law, but I have longed to hear white ministers declare: "Follow this decree because integration is morally right and because the Negro is your brother." In the midst of blatant injustices inflicted upon the Negro, I have watched white churchmen stand on the sideline and mouth pious irrelevancies and sanctimonious trivialities. In the midst of a mighty struggle to rid our nation of racial and economic injustice I have heard many ministers say: "Those are social issues, with which the gospel has no real concern." And I have watched many churches commit themselves to a completely otherworldly religion which makes a strange, un-Biblical distinction between body and soul, between the sacred and the secular.

I have traveled the length and breadth of Alabama, Mississippi, and all the other southern states. On sweltering summer days and crisp autumn mornings I have looked at the South's beautiful churches with their lofty spires pointing heavenward. I have beheld the impressive outlines of her massive religious-education buildings. Over and over I have found myself asking: "What kind of people worship here? Who is their God? Where were their voices when the lips of Governor Barnett dripped with words of interposition and nullification? Where were they when Governor Wallace* gave a clarion call for defiance and hatred? Where were their voices of support when bruised and weary Negro men and women decided to rise from the dark dungeons of complacency to the bright hills of creative protest?"

Yes, these questions are still in my mind. In deep disappointment I have wept over the laxity of the church. But be assured that my tears have been tears of love. There can be no deep disappointment where there is not deep love. Yes, I love the church. How could I do otherwise? I am in the rather unique position of being the son, the grandson, and the great-grandson of preachers. Yes, I see

---

Governor Barnett . . . Governor Wallace: Ross Barnett and George Wallace were governors of Mississippi and Alabama, respectively, who resisted the racial integration of schools in their states.

the church as the body of Christ. But, oh! How we have blemished and scarred that body through social neglect and through fear of being nonconformists.

There was a time when the church was very powerful—in the time 40
when the early Christians rejoiced at being deemed worthy to suffer for what they believed. In those days the church was not merely a thermometer that recorded the ideas and principles of popular opinion; it was a thermostat that transformed the mores of society. Whenever the early Christians entered a town, the people in power became disturbed and immediately sought to convict the Christians for being "disturbers of the peace" and "outside agitators." But the Christians pressed on, in the conviction that they were "a colony of heaven," called to obey God rather than man. Small in number, they were big in commitment. They were too God-intoxicated to be "astronomically intimidated." By their effort and example they brought an end to such ancient evils as infanticide and gladiatorial contests.

Things are different now. So often the contemporary church is a weak, ineffectual voice with an uncertain sound. So often it is an archdefender of the status quo. Far from being disturbed by the presence of the church, the power structure of the average community is consoled by the church's silent—and often even vocal—sanction of things as they are.

But the judgment of God is upon the church as never before. If today's church does not recapture the sacrificial spirit of the early church, it will lose its authenticity, forfeit the loyalty of millions, and be dismissed as an irrelevant social club with no meaning for the twentieth century. Every day I meet young people whose disappointment with the church has turned into outright disgust.

Perhaps I have once again been too optimistic. Is organized religion too inextricably bound to the status quo to save our nation and the world? Perhaps I must turn my faith to the inner spiritual church, the church within the church, as the true *ekklesia** and the hope of the world. But again I am thankful to God that some noble souls from the ranks of organized religion have broken loose from the paralyzing chains of conformity and joined us as active partners in the struggle for freedom. They have left their secure congregations and walked the streets of Albany, Georgia, with us. They have gone down the highways of the South on tortuous rides for freedom. Yes, they have gone to jail with us. Some have been dismissed from their churches, have lost the support of their bishops and fellow ministers. But they have acted in the faith that right defeated is stronger than evil triumphant. Their witness has been the spiritual salt that has preserved the true meaning of the gospel in these troubled times. They have carved a tunnel of hope through the dark mountain of disappointment.

I hope the church as a whole will meet the challenge of this decisive hour. But even if the church does not come to the aid of justice, I have no despair about the future. I have no fear about the outcome of our struggle in

---

ekklesia: Greek word for the early Christian church

Birmingham, even if our motives are at present misunderstood. We will reach the goal of freedom in Birmingham and all over the nation, because the goal of America is freedom. Abused and scorned though we may be, our destiny is tied up with America's destiny. Before the pilgrims landed at Plymouth, we were here. Before the pen of Jefferson etched the majestic words of the Declaration of Independence across the pages of history, we were here. For more than two centuries our forebears labored in this country without wages; they made cotton king; they built the homes of their masters while suffering gross injustice and shameful humiliation—and yet out of a bottomless vitality they continued to thrive and develop. If the inexpressible cruelties of slavery could not stop us, the opposition we now face will surely fail. We will win our freedom because the sacred heritage of our nation and the eternal will of God are embodied in our echoing demands.

Before closing I feel impelled to mention one other point in your state- 45
ment that has troubled me profoundly. You warmly commended the Birmingham police force for keeping "order" and "preventing violence." I doubt that you would have so warmly commended the police force if you had seen its dogs sinking their teeth into unarmed, nonviolent Negroes. I doubt that you would so quickly commend the policemen if you were to observe their ugly and inhumane treatment of Negroes here in the city jail; if you were to watch them push and curse old Negro women and young Negro girls; if you were to see them slap and kick old Negro men and young boys; if you were to observe them, as they did on two occasions, refuse to give us food because we wanted to sing our grace together. I cannot join you in your praise of the Birmingham police department.

It is true that the police have exercised a degree of discipline in handling the demonstrators. In this sense they have conducted themselves rather "nonviolently" in public. But for what purpose? To preserve the evil system of segregation. Over the past few years I have consistently preached that nonviolence demands that the means we use must be as pure as the ends we seek. I have tried to make clear that it is wrong to use immoral means to attain moral ends. But now I must affirm that it is just as wrong, or perhaps even more so, to use moral means to preserve immoral ends. Perhaps Mr. Connor and his policemen have been rather nonviolent in public, as was Chief Pritchett in Albany, Georgia, but they have used the moral means of nonviolence to maintain the immoral end of racial injustice. As T. S. Eliot has said, "The last temptation is the greatest treason: To do the right deed for the wrong reason."

I wish you had commended the Negro sit-inners and demonstrators of Birmingham for their sublime courage, their willingness to suffer, and their amazing discipline in the midst of great provocation. One day the South will recognize its real heroes. They will be the James Merediths,* with the noble

James Merediths: The U.S. Supreme Court ordered the admission of James Meredith, a black student, to the segregated University of Mississippi in 1962 despite resistance from state officials.

sense of purpose that enables them to face jeering and hostile mobs, and with the agonizing loneliness that characterizes the life of the pioneer. They will be old, oppressed, battered Negro women, symbolized in a seventy-two-year-old woman in Montgomery, Alabama, who rose up with a sense of dignity and with her people decided not to ride segregated buses, and who responded with ungrammatical profundity to one who inquired about her weariness: "My feets is tired, but my soul is at rest." They will be the young high school and college students, the young ministers of the gospel and a host of their elders, courageously and nonviolently sitting in at lunch counters and willingly going to jail for conscience' sake. One day the South will know that when these disinherited children of God sat down at lunch counters, they were in reality standing up for what is best in the American dream and for the most sacred values in our Judaeo-Christian heritage, thereby bringing our nation back to those great wells of democracy which were dug deep by the founding fathers in their formulation of the Constitution and the Declaration of Independence.

Never before have I written so long a letter. I'm afraid it is much too long to take your precious time. I can assure you that it would have been much shorter if I had been writing from a comfortable desk, but what else can one do when he is alone in a narrow jail cell, other than write long letters, think long thoughts, and pray long prayers?

If I have said anything in this letter that overstates the truth and indicates an unreasonable impatience, I beg you to forgive me. If I have said anything that understates the truth and indicates my having a patience that allows me to settle for anything less than brotherhood, I beg God to forgive me.

I hope this letter finds you strong in the faith. I also hope that circum- 50
stances will soon make it possible for me to meet each of you, not as an integrationist or a civil-rights leader but as a fellow clergyman and a Christian brother. Let us all hope that the dark clouds of racial prejudice will soon pass away and the deep fog of misunderstanding will be lifted from our fear-drenched communities, and in some not too distant tomorrow the radiant stars of love and brotherhood will shine over our great nation with all their scintillating beauty.

Yours for the cause of Peace and Brotherhood,
MARTIN LUTHER KING JR.

QUESTIONING THE TEXT

1. King's letter is written to the white clergy of Birmingham, including those of Protestant, Catholic, and Jewish faiths. Look carefully at the sources King cites in his letter, and note which ones seem most likely to appeal to members of these religious groups.

2. In a number of places in his "Letter," King mentions or alludes to Socrates. Review an account of Socrates' life. What makes him a particularly appropriate and powerful example for King to use? Can you think of any risks King takes in relying on Socrates as a key figure in his argument?
3. Working with one or two classmates, identify all of the evidence King offers in his "Letter" to prove that racial injustice is immoral.
4. Is this piece of writing really a letter? What qualities and elements of it allow you to answer this question—one way or the other?

MAKING CONNECTIONS

5. King positions himself between the "'do-nothingism' of the complacent" and the "hatred and despair of the black nationalist" (paragraph 28). In "An Animal's Place," Michael Pollan (p. 222) similarly presents two stances toward nonhuman animals: "You [eat them and] look away—or you stop eating animals" (paragraph 32). He then asks, "And if you don't want to do either?" and proceeds to explore an answer. Each writer thus describes the parameters of current debate on his issue. How does this strategy influence your response to each writer and to his argument? In what kinds of rhetorical situations does this approach seem likely to work well?
6. In "The Rules about the Rules" (p. 179), Stephen L. Carter says that "[i]ntegrity . . . requires three steps: (1) *discerning* what is right and what is wrong; (2) *acting* on what you have discerned, even at personal cost; and (3) *saying openly* that you are acting on your understanding of right from wrong" (paragraph 15). Would King likely agree with Carter's description of these steps? What evidence of these three steps do you find in King's "Letter"?

JOINING THE CONVERSATION

7. Have you ever written a long letter to someone, a letter that was important to you and in which you tried hard to make a convincing case for something you believed or felt? If so, what were the features of that letter? How successful and effective was it? Take time to brainstorm about a letter you might write today. To whom would you address it? What would you argue for—or against? Where would you find support and evidence? What would be the most difficult part of writing the letter?
8. King uses a great many pronouns in his "Letter," including *you* to refer to the clergymen (there were no women clergy in Birmingham at the time) and *we* to refer to the nonviolent protesters in particular and the

larger African American community in general. Working with one or two classmates, look carefully at how King uses pronouns in the reading. Then write a brief report to your class describing King's use of pronouns and explaining what effect(s) they have on readers today—and what effect(s) they may have been intended to have on the clergymen to whom the letter was addressed.

STEPHEN L. CARTER
The Rules about the Rules

It is still too early to know the long-term consequences of the recent political and ethical scandals—one president accused of perjury and obstruction of justice in 1998; another accused of winning the 2000 election through the Supreme Court rather than the Electoral College; CEOs of major corporations such as Enron indicted and convicted in 2002; and in 2003 the prestigious New York Times *faced with the fact that one of its reporters had been fabricating and falsifying stories for years. If little else, we have learned that Shakespeare's clown Dogberry (borrowing from scripture) has spoken truthfully: "[t]hey that touch pitch will be defiled."*

Stephen L. Carter (b. 1954), William Cromwell Nelson Professor of Law at Yale, probably isn't surprised by any of these messes, since he has for some time been detecting a wavering in the nation's ethical compass. His response, a book-length meditation, Integrity *(1996), asks its readers to consider the slippage in ethics evident everywhere in our culture—in our legal system, media, sports, businesses, and marriages. He even devotes a section to academic letters of recommendation, arguing that teachers have debased this essential part of job and professional school applications because they are unwilling to deal with students honestly.*

Integrity *is not the first book in which Carter, playing the role of public intellectual, has helped to set the agenda for a serious national discussion of issues. Earlier,* Reflections of an Affirmative Action Baby *(1991) contributed to the continuing and uneasy debate over racial preferences in academia and the workplace. Even more influential was the award-winning* The Culture of Disbelief *(1993), which, contrary to much opinion, insists that people of faith have a right to exert their influence in politics. More recently, Carter has written* Civility *(1998), a call for a more decent and polite society, and* The Emperor of Ocean Park *(2002), his first novel.*

The selection that follows, "The Rules about the Rules," is the opening chapter of Integrity. *Omitted from the selection is a brief concluding section that summarizes the subsequent chapters of the book.* —J.R.

My first lesson in integrity came the hard way. It was 1960 or thereabouts and I was a first-grader at P.S. 129 in Harlem. The teacher had us all sitting in a circle, playing a game in which each child would take a turn donning a blindfold and then trying to identify objects by touch alone as she handed them to us. If you guessed right, you stayed in until the next round. If you guessed wrong, you were out. I survived almost to the end, amazing the entire class with my abilities. Then, to my dismay, the teacher realized what I had known, and relied upon, from the start: my blindfold was tied imperfectly and a sliver of bright reality leaked in from outside. By holding the unknown object in my lap instead of out in front of me, as most of the other children did, I could see at least a corner or a side and sometimes more—but always enough to figure out what it was. So my remarkable success was due only to my ability to break the rules.

Fortunately for my own moral development, I was caught. And as a result of being caught, I suffered, in front of my classmates, a humiliating reminder of right and wrong: I had cheated at the game. Cheating was wrong. It was that simple.

I do not remember many of the details of the "public" lecture that I received from my teacher. I do remember that I was made to feel terribly ashamed; and it is good that I was made to feel that way, for I had something to be ashamed of. The moral opprobrium that accompanied that shame was sufficiently intense that it has stayed with me ever since, which is exactly how shame is supposed to work. And as I grew older, whenever I was even tempted to cheat—at a game, on homework—I would remember my teacher's stern face and the humiliation of sitting before my classmates, revealed to the world as a cheater.

That was then, this is now. Browsing recently in my local bookstore, I came across a book that boldly proclaimed, on its cover, that it contained instructions on how to *cheat*—the very word occurred in the title—at a variety of video games. My instincts tell me that this cleverly chosen title is helping the book to sell very well. For it captures precisely what is wrong with America today: we care far more about winning than about playing by the rules.

Consider just a handful of examples, drawn from headlines of the mid- 5
1990s: the winner of the Miss Virginia pageant is stripped of her title after officials determine that her educational credentials are false; a television network is forced to apologize for using explosives to add a bit of verisimilitude to a tape purporting to show that a particular truck is unsafe; and the authors of a popular book on management are accused of using bulk purchases at key stores to manipulate the *New York Times* best-seller list. Go back a few more years and we can add in everything from a slew of Wall Street titans imprisoned for violating a bewildering variety of laws in their frantic effort to get ahead, to the women's Boston Marathon winner branded a cheater for spending part of the race on the subway. But cheating is evidently no big deal: some 70 percent of college students admit to having done it at least once.[1]

That, in a nutshell, is America's integrity dilemma: we are all full of fine talk about how desperately our society needs it, but, when push comes to shove, we would just as soon be on the winning side. A couple of years ago as I sat watching a televised football game with my children, trying to explain to them what was going on, I was struck by an event I had often noticed but on which I had never reflected. A player who failed to catch a ball thrown his way hit the

---

[1]On cheating by college students, see Karen Thomas, "Rise in Cheating Called Response to Fall in Values," *USA Today,* August 2, 1995, p. 1A. I do not know whether the irony of the headline was intentional.

ground, rolled over, and then jumped up, celebrating as though he had caught the pass after all. The referee was standing in a position that did not give him a good view of what had happened, was fooled by the player's pretense, and so moved the ball down the field. The player rushed back to the huddle so that his team could run another play before the officials had a chance to review the tape. (Until 1992, National Football League officials could watch a television replay and change their call, as long as the next play had not been run.) But viewers at home did have the benefit of the replay, and we saw what the referee missed: the ball lying on the ground instead of snug in the receiver's hands. The only comment from the broadcasters: "What a heads-up play!" Meaning: "Wow, what a great liar this kid is! Well done!"

Let's be very clear: that is exactly what they meant. The player set out to mislead the referee and succeeded; he helped his team to obtain an advantage in the game that it had not earned. It could not have been accidental. He knew he did not catch the ball. By jumping up and celebrating, he was trying to convey a false impression. He was trying to convince the officials that he had caught the ball. And the officials believed him. So, in any ordinary understanding of the word, he lied. And that, too, is what happens to integrity in American life: if we happen to do something wrong, we would just as soon have nobody point it out.

Now, suppose that the player had instead gone to the referee and said, "I'm sorry, sir, but I did not make the catch. Your call is wrong." Probably his coach and teammates and most of his team's fans would have been furious: he would not have been a good team player. The good team player lies to the referee, and does so in a manner that is at once blatant (because millions of viewers see it) and virtually impossible for the referee to detect. Having pulled off this trickery, the player is congratulated: he is told that he has made a heads-up play. Thus, the ethic of the game turns out to be an ethic that rewards cheating. (But I still love football.) Perhaps I should have been shocked. Yet, thinking through the implications of our celebration of a national sport that rewards cheating, I could not help but recognize that we as a nation too often lack integrity, which might be described, in a loose and colloquial way, as the courage of one's convictions. And although I do not want to claim any great burst of inspiration, it was at about that time that I decided to write this book.

Toward a Definition

We, the People of the United States, who a little over two hundred years ago ordained and established the Constitution, have a serious problem: too many of us nowadays neither mean what we say nor say what we mean. Moreover, we hardly expect anybody else to mean what they say either.

A couple of years ago I began a university commencement address by 10
telling the audience that I was going to talk about integrity. The crowd broke

into applause. Applause! Just because they had heard the word *integrity*—that's how starved for it they were. They had no idea how I was using the word, or what I was going to say about it, or, indeed, whether I was for it or against it. But they knew they liked the idea of simply talking about it. This celebration of integrity is intriguing: we seem to carry on a passionate love affair with a word that we scarcely pause to define.

The Supreme Court likes to use such phrases as the "Constitution's structural integrity" when it strikes down actions that violate the separation of powers in the federal government.[2] Critics demand a similar form of integrity when they argue that our age has seen the corruption of language or of particular religious traditions or of the moral sense generally. Indeed, when parents demand a form of education that will help their children grow into people of integrity, the cry carries a neo-romantic image of their children becoming adults who will remain uncorrupted by the forces (whatever they are) that seem to rob so many grown-ups of . . . well, of integrity.

Very well, let us consider this word *integrity*. Integrity is like the weather: everybody talks about it but nobody knows what to do about it. Integrity is that stuff we always say we want more of. Such leadership gurus as Warren Bennis insist that it is of first importance. We want our elected representatives to have it, and political challengers always insist that their opponents lack it. We want it in our spouses, our children, our friends. We want it in our schools and our houses of worship. And in our corporations and the products they manufacture: early in 1995, one automobile company widely advertised a new car as "the first concept car with integrity." And we want it in the federal government, too, where officials all too frequently find themselves under investigation by special prosecutors. So perhaps we should say that integrity is like *good* weather, because everybody is in favor of it.

Scarcely a politician kicks off a campaign without promising to bring it to government; a few years later, more often than is healthy for our democracy, the politician slinks cravenly from office, having been lambasted by the press for lacking that self-same integrity; and then the press, in turn, is skewered for holding public figures to a measure of integrity that its own reporters, editors, producers, and, most particularly, owners could not possibly meet. And for refusing to turn that critical eye inward, the press is mocked for—what else?—a lack of integrity.

Everybody agrees that the nation needs more of it. Some say we need to return to the good old days when we had a lot more of it. Others say we as a nation have never really had enough of it. And hardly any of us stop to explain exactly what we mean by it—or how we know it is even a good thing—or why everybody needs to have the same amount of it. Indeed, the only trouble with integrity is that everybody who uses the word seems to

---

[2]See, for example, *Ryder v. United States,* 115 S. Ct. 2031 (1995).

mean something slightly different. So in a book about integrity, the place to start is surely with a definition.

When I refer to integrity, I have something very simple and very specific in mind. Integrity, as I will use the term, requires three steps: (1) *discerning* what is right and what is wrong; (2) *acting* on what you have discerned, even at personal cost; and (3) *saying openly* that you are acting on your understanding of right from wrong.[3] The first criterion captures the idea of integrity as requiring a degree of moral reflectiveness. The second brings in the ideal of an integral person as steadfast, which includes the sense of keeping commitments. The third reminds us that a person of integrity is unashamed of doing the right. . . . I hope that even readers who quarrel with my selection of the term *integrity* to refer to the form of commitment that I describe will come away from the book understanding why the concept itself, whatever it may be called, is a vital one.

The word *integrity* comes from the same Latin root as *integer* and historically has been understood to carry much the same sense, the sense of *wholeness:* a person of integrity, like a whole number, is a whole person, a person somehow undivided. The word conveys not so much a single-mindedness as a completeness; not the frenzy of a fanatic who wants to remake all the world in a single mold but the serenity of a person who is confident in the knowledge that he or she is living rightly. The person of integrity need not be a Gandhi but also cannot be a person who blows up buildings to make a point. A person of integrity lurks somewhere inside each of us: a person we feel we can trust to do right, to play by the rules, to keep commitments. Perhaps it is because we all sense the capacity for integrity within ourselves that we are able to notice and admire it even in people with whom, on many issues, we sharply disagree.

Indeed, one reason to focus on integrity as perhaps the first among the virtues that make for good character is that it is in some sense prior to everything else: the rest of what we think matters very little if we lack essential integrity, the courage of our convictions, the willingness to act and speak in behalf of what we know to be right. In an era when the American people are crying out for open discussion of morality—of right and wrong—the ideal of integrity seems a good place to begin. No matter what our politics, no matter what causes we may support, would anybody really want to be led or followed or assisted by people who *lack* integrity? People whose words we could not trust, whose motives we didn't respect, who might at any moment toss aside everything we thought we had in common and march off in some other direction?

The answer, of course, is no: we would not want leaders of that kind, even though we too often get them. The question is not only what integrity

[3]In this I am influenced to some extent by the fine discussion of integrity in Martin Benjamin's book *Splitting the Difference: Compromise and Integrity in Ethics and Politics* (Lawrence: University Press of Kansas, 1990).

is and why it is valuable, but how we move our institutions, and our very lives, closer to exemplifying it. In raising this question, I do not put myself forward as an exemplar of integrity, but merely as one who in daily life goes through many of the struggles that I will describe in these pages. The reader will quickly discover that I frequently use the word *we* in my analysis. The reason is that I see the journey toward a greater understanding of the role of integrity in our public and private lives as one that the reader and I are making together.

Integrity and Religion

The concept we are calling *integrity* has had little attention from philosophers, but has long been a central concern to the religions. Integrity, after all, is a kind of wholeness, and most religions teach that God calls us to an undivided life in accordance with divine command. In Islam, this notion is captured in the understanding that all rules, legal or moral, are guided by the *sharia,* the divine path that God directs humans to walk. In Judaism, study of the Torah and Talmud reveals the rules under which God's people are expected to live. And Christians are called by the Gospel to be "pure in heart" (Matt. 5:8), which implies an undividedness in following God's rules.

Indeed, although its antecedents may be traced to Aristotle, the basic concept of integrity was introduced to the Western tradition through the struggle of Christianity to find a guide for the well-lived life. The wholeness that the Christian tradition identified as central to life with integrity was a wholeness in obedience to God, so that the well-lived life was a life that followed God's rules. Thomas Aquinas put it this way: "[T]he virtue of obedience is more praiseworthy than other moral virtues, seeing that by obedience a person gives up his own will for God's sake, and by other moral virtues something less."[4] John Wesley, in a famous sermon, was more explicit: "[T]he nature of the covenant of grace gives you no ground, no encouragement at all, to set aside any instance or degree of obedience."[5]

But obedience to what? Traditional religions teach that integrity is found in obedience to God. Moses Maimonides put the point most simply: "Everything that you do, do for the sake of God."[6] And a Professor W. S. Tyler, preaching a sermon at Amherst College in 1857, pointed the way to generalizing the concept beyond the religious sphere: "[I]ntegrity implies im-

---

[4]St. Thomas Aquinas, *The Summa Theologica,* tr. Father L. Shapcote, revised by Daniel L. Sullivan, 2d ed. (Chicago: Encyclopedia Britannica, 1990), 2a2ae, 104, 3.

[5]John Wesley, "On the Law Established Through Faith," in *The Works of the Rev. John Wesley,* vol. 8 (London: Thomas Cordeaux, 1811), p. 144.

[6]Quoted in Abraham Joshua Heschel, *Maimonides: A Biography,* tr. Joachim Neugroschel (New York: Image Books, 1991), p. 203. The German edition was published in 1935.

plicit obedience to the dictates of conscience—in other words, a heart and life habitually controlled by a sense of duty."[7]

But this is not a book about religion as such, still less about Christian doctrine. This book, rather, tries to honor our own national understanding of the word, in a tradition that is somewhat more secular but is, in its way, equally profound. My hope is to use traditional religious understandings to illuminate a concept that now has a distinct and honored place in the American ethical narrative, but to allow the narrative to tell its own story. So, although I have quoted Aquinas and will quote him again, this book is not about how Aquinas thought of integrity; it is about how we Americans think, or have thought, or should think, of it. Our demand for it illustrates that we think about it often, and a little desperately; my hope in this book is to demonstrate the value of the concept—to show *why* we think of the word with such affection—and then to examine the interplay of the integrity concept with a range of American problems and institutions.

In choosing integrity as my subject, I have tried to select an element of good character that is independent of the particular political views that one might hold; indeed, I would suspect that all of us, whatever our politics, would value, and perhaps demand, a degree of integrity in our associates, our government, and even our friends and families. So it is best that we try to reach some agreement on just what it is that we are valuing and demanding.

A good citizen, a person of integrity, I will refer to as one who leads an *integral life.* An integral life in turn requires all three steps of the definition, to which I will occasionally refer as the rules or criteria of integrity. Once this definition is understood, there are implications, from politics to marriage, from the way bosses write letters of recommendation to the way newspaper editors choose which stories to run. . . . I am, by training and persuasion, a lawyer, and so the reader should not be surprised to find many legal examples. . . ; indeed, there is even a bit of constitutional analysis. But if this is not a book about Christianity, still less is it a book about law, and certainly it is not a work of philosophy. It is, rather, a book about Americans and our society, about what we are, what we say we aspire to be, and how to bring the two closer to balance.

The Three Steps

25 Integrity, I should explain before proceeding, is not the same as honesty, although honesty obviously is a desirable element of good character as well. From our definition, it is clear that one cannot have integrity without also displaying a measure of honesty. But one can be honest without being

[7]W. S. Tyler, Integrity the Safeguard of Public and Private Life (Springfield: Samuel Bowles, 1857), p. 6.

integral, for integrity, as I define it, demands a difficult process of discerning one's deepest understanding of right and wrong, and then further requires action consistent with what one has learned. It is possible to be honest without ever taking a hard look inside one's soul, to say nothing of taking any action based on what one finds. For example, a woman who believes abortion is murder may state honestly that this is what she thinks, but she does not fulfill the integrity criteria unless she also works to change abortion law. A man who believes in our national obligation to aid the homeless cannot claim to be fulfilling the criteria unless he works to obtain the aid he believes is deserved—and perhaps provides some assistance personally.

All too many of us fall down on step 1: we do not take the time to discern right from wrong. Indeed, I suspect that few of us really know just what we believe—what we value—and, often, we do not really want to know. Discernment is hard work; it takes time and emotional energy. And it is so much easier to follow the crowd. We too often look the other way when we see wrongdoing around us, quite famously in the widely unwitnessed yet very unprivate murder of Kitty Genovese* thirty years ago. We refuse to think in terms of right and wrong when we elect or reject political candidates based on what they will do for our own pocketbooks. On the campuses, too many students and not a few professors find it easier to go along with the latest trends than to risk the opprobrium of others by registering an objection. Indeed, social psychologists say that this all too human phenomenon of refusing to think independently is what leads to mob violence. But a public-spirited citizen must do a bit of soul-searching—must decide what he or she most truly and deeply believes to be right and good—before it is possible to live with integrity.

The second step is also a tough one. It is far easier to know what one believes—to know, in effect, right from wrong—than it is to do something about it. For example, one may believe that the homeless deserve charity, but never dispense it; or one may think that they are bums who should not be given a dime, yet always dig into one's pockets when confronted. We Americans have a remarkable capacity to say one thing and do another, not always out of true hypocrisy but often out of a lack of self-assurance. We see this in our politics, where nobody wants to be the one to say that the retirees who receive Social Security payments are, for the most part, receiving not a return on an investment but direct subventions from the payments being made by today's workers toward their own retirements—which, if done by a private investment firm, would be an illegal pyramid scheme. The late legal scholar Robert Cover illustrated the point quite powerfully when he examined the puzzling question of how avowedly antislavery judges in the early nineteenth century could hand down obviously proslavery decisions.[8] Equally puzzling to

---

Kitty Genovese: In March 1964, Genovese was stabbed to death in a New York City neighborhood while thirty-eight residents looked on, failing to come to her assistance.

[8]See Robert Cover, *Justice Accused: Antislavery and the Judicial Process* (New Haven, CT: Yale University Press, 1975).

many political activists is their inability to recruit support from people they know to be committed to their causes, who frequently explain that they simply do not want to get involved.

But in order to live with integrity, it is sometimes necessary to take that difficult step—to get involved—to fight openly for what one believes to be true and right and good, even when there is risk to oneself. I would not go so far as to insist that morally committed citizens living integral lives must fight their way through life, strident activists in behalf of all their beliefs; but I worry deeply about the number of us who seem happy to drift through life, activists in behalf of none of our beliefs.

This leads to the third step, which seems deceptively simple, but is often the hardest of all: the person truly living an integral life must be willing to say that he or she is acting consistently with what he or she has decided is right. When the statements of a person of integrity are the result of discernment, of hard thought, we treat them as reliable, even when they are indicators of the future—"You've got the job" or "Till death do us part." But forthrightness also matters because people of integrity are willing to tell us *why* they are doing what they are doing. So it does not promote integrity for one to cheat on taxes out of greed but to claim to be doing it as a protest; indeed, it does not promote integrity to do it as a protest unless one says openly (including to the Internal Revenue Service) that that is what one is doing. It does not promote integrity to ignore or cover up wrongdoing by a co-worker or family member. And it does not promote integrity to claim to be doing the will of God when one is actually doing what one's political agenda demands.

This third step—saying publicly that we are doing what we think is 30
right, even when others disagree—is made particularly difficult by our national desire to conform. Most of us want to fit in, to be accepted, and admitting to (or proudly proclaiming) an unpopular belief is rarely the way to gain acceptance. But if moral dissenters are unwilling to follow the example of the civil rights movement and make a proud public show of their convictions, we as a nation will never have the opportunity to be inspired by their integrity to rethink our own ideas.

This last point bears emphasis. Integrity does not always require following the rules. Sometimes—as in the civil rights movement—integrity requires *breaking* the rules. But it also requires that one be open and public about both the fact of one's dissent and the reasons for it. . . . A person who lives an integral life may sometimes reach moral conclusions that differ from those of the majority; displaying those conclusions publicly is a crucial aspect of the wholeness in which integrity consists.

Instead of a nation of public dissenters, we have become a nation experienced in misdirection—in beguiling the audience into looking in one direction while we are busy somewhere else. The media culture unfortunately rewards this, not only because a misleading sound bite is more attractive (that is, marketable) than a principled argument, but also because the media seem far more interested in tracking down hypocrisy than in reporting episodes of integrity.

Indeed, to bring the matter full circle, the media will get a healthy share of blame in this book: blame for oversimplification and for interfering with, rather than enabling, the search for right and wrong that each of us must undertake in order to live a life of integrity. But only a share of the blame. If indeed we allow the distractions of living to prevent the discernment of right and wrong so necessary to living with integrity, we should blame neither the media nor the schools nor the government nor our employers, but only ourselves. As I will explain, we as a society can and should do far more to train our children—and ourselves!—in the difficult work of sorting right from wrong and then doing the right and despising the wrong. We can try to blame other forces that interfere; but in the end, when the children grow up, they must make right choices for themselves.

Corruption

If integrity has an opposite, perhaps it is corruption—the getting away with things we know to be wrong. We say that we are a nation that demands integrity, but are we really? We call ourselves a nation of laws, but millions of us cheat on our taxes. We seem not to believe in the integrity of our commitments, with half of marriages ending in divorce. We say we want integrity in our politics, and our politicians promise it endlessly. (Try searching the Nexis database for uses of the word *integrity* by politicians and commentators, and you will be inundated.) But we reward innuendo and smear and barefaced lies with our votes.

Corruption is corrosive. We believe we can do it just a little, but I wonder whether we can. Nearly all of us break small laws—I do it all the time—laws governing everything from the speed at which we may drive to when and how we may cross the street. Few of us will stop on the highway to retrieve the paper bag that the wind whips out the window of our moving car; we may not have thrown it out intentionally, but it still came from our car and it's still littering. These I shall refer to as acts of unintegrity, not an attractive neologism, but one way of avoiding the repeated use of the word *corruption,* which might be misleading. And one who engages in repeated acts of unintegrity may be said to be living an unintegral life.

Some of these acts of unintegrity can be cured by simple calls upon the virtue of consistency. It is both amusing and sad to hear liberals who have fought against the portrayal of vicious racial stereotypes in the media now saying that portrayals of sex and family life in the media affect nobody's behavior; it is just as amusing, and just as sad, to see conservatives bash the President of the United States for criticizing hateful speech on the nation's airwaves and then turn around and bash Hollywood for speech the right happens to hate.

But inconsistency is the easiest example of unintegrity to spot. There are harder examples—as we shall see, there may even be some cases in which a lack of integrity is unavoidable—and I shall deal with many of them. . . .

When I began working on this book, I shared the story about the cheating football player with a few of my colleagues over lunch in the wood-paneled faculty dining room at the Yale Law School. Like me, they are lawyers, so none could be too outraged: our task in life, after all, is sometimes to defend the indefensible. They offered a bewildering array of fascinating and sophisticated arguments on why the receiver who pretended to catch the ball was doing nothing wrong. One in particular stuck in my mind. "You don't know if he was breaking the rules," one of the best and brightest of my colleagues explained, "until you know what the rules are about following the rules."

On reflection, I think my colleague was exactly right. And that, maybe better than anything else, sums up what this book is about. What are our rules about when we follow the rules? What are our rules about when we break them? Until we can answer those two questions, we will not know how much integrity we really want in our public and private lives, to say nothing of how to get it. . . .

QUESTIONING THE TEXT

1. Carter opens "The Rules about the Rules" with an anecdote from his own life that relates to the principle of integrity. In what ways does this narrative set you up for the discussion that follows? Does it make you think about the author? Does it lead you to recall times when you have acted dishonestly yourself? What does it do to make the prospect of an entire book on the subject of integrity less daunting?
2. Carter observes that "integrity is like *good* weather, because everybody is in favor of it" (paragraph 12). For the next several days, make a record of all the times you encounter the term *integrity* and the contexts in which it appears. Then compare your findings with those of your classmates. From your informal research, what conclusions, if any, can you draw about current attitudes toward integrity? When and where does the term occur most often—or has *integrity* become a word rarely spoken and written now?

MAKING CONNECTIONS

3. In Mark Clayton's article on campus plagiarism, "A Whole Lot of Cheatin' Going On" (p. 207), one student playing devil's advocate asserts that "Cheating *is* an answer. . . . It might not be a good answer,

but none the less it is an answer" (paragraph 2). Can you imagine an act of scholastic dishonesty that meets Carter's three conditions for integrity (paragraph 15)? In a group, explore this possibility.

4. Use Carter's definition of integrity to assess the act of civil disobedience that Terry Tempest Williams describes in "The Clan of One-Breasted Women" (p. 655). Compare your conclusion with those of your classmates. Be prepared to describe the general conditions that might make acts of civil disobedience defensible.

JOINING THE CONVERSATION

5. Carter defines *integrity* (in paragraphs 25–32) by enumerating its three necessary characteristics. Try to define another moral abstraction (such as *loyalty, courage, modesty,* or *civility*) in approximately the same way, by first enumerating the steps or criteria that identify the term and then providing examples of the concept as you have defined it.
6. Most schools have documents defining *plagiarism, collusion, cheating,* and other acts of academic dishonesty. Review your institution's policies on scholastic integrity or its honor code—if it has one. Then discuss these policies with your classmates, either in face-to-face conversation or in an online forum or listserv. After the discussion, write a short essay about the integrity of academic work. Is cheating a major problem in your classes? Are there ever good reasons to cheat? Can plagiarism or collusion be defended or eliminated? Why, or why not?
7. Write a brief portrait of someone you know who might fairly be described as "a person of integrity." Use your portrait as an indirect way of defining or exploring the concept of integrity.

JESSICA COHEN
Grade A: The Market for a Yale Woman's Eggs

When I got my December 2002 copy of the Atlantic Monthly, *the title of this essay captured my attention. As a college teacher, I gravitate toward stories about higher education, though I can never remember reading one about marketing college women's eggs. As I read, I identified with the author: how utterly odd to be so actively recruited—almost wooed—and then rejected as not good enough for the apparently wealthy couple intent on buying an egg from just the right (meaning perfect) donor!*

Cohen is a recent graduate of Yale, where she majored in history. While at Yale she cofounded the all-female Sphincter Troupe, a group of women comedians who got together when they decided the comedy scene at Yale was a very restricted one. The essay that follows was first published in slightly different form in the Fall 2001 issue of a student publication, the New Journal; *it later won the* Atlantic Monthly's *student essay contest.*

Cohen's ambivalent feelings about the business of marketing children eventually led her to decide that "this process was something I didn't want to be a part of," even though the idea of receiving $25,000 for an egg was very attractive. Had you been in Cohen's position, what would you have decided—and why? —A.L.

Early in the spring of last year a classified ad ran for two weeks in the *Yale Daily News:* "EGG DONOR NEEDED." The couple that placed the ad was picky, and for that reason was offering $25,000 for an egg from the right donor.

As a child I had a book called *Where Did I Come From?* It offered a full biological explanation, in cartoons, to answer those awkward questions that curious tots ask. But the book is now out of date. Replacing it is, for example, *Mommy, Did I Grow in Your Tummy?: Where Some Babies Come From,* which explains the myriad ways that children of the twenty-first century may have entered their families, including egg donation, surrogacy, *in vitro* fertilization, and adoption. When conception doesn't occur in the natural way, it becomes very complicated. Once all possible parties have been accounted for—egg donor, sperm donor, surrogate mother, paying couple—as many as five people can be involved in conceiving and carrying a child. No wonder a new book is necessary.

The would-be parents' decision to advertise in the *News*—and to offer a five-figure compensation—immediately suggested that they were in the market for an egg of a certain rarefied type. Beyond their desire for an Ivy League donor, they wanted a young woman over five feet five, of Jewish heritage, athletic, with a minimum combined SAT score of 1500, and attractive.

I was curious—and I fit all the criteria except the SAT score. So I e-mailed Michelle and David (not their real names) and asked for more information about the process and how much the SAT minimum really meant to them. Then I waited for a reply.

Donating an egg is neither simple nor painless. Following an intensive screening and selection process the donor endures a few weeks of invasive medical procedures. First the donor and the woman who will carry the child must coordinate their menstrual cycles. Typically the donor and the recipient take birth-control pills, followed by shots of a synthetic hormone such as Lupron; the combination suppresses ovulation and puts their cycles in sync. After altering her cycle the donor must enhance her egg supply with fertility drugs in the same way an infertile woman does when trying to conceive. Shots of a fertility hormone are administered for seven to eleven days, to stimulate the production of an abnormally large number of egg-containing follicles. During this time the donor must have her blood tested every other day so that doctors can monitor her hormone levels, and she must come in for periodic ultrasounds. Thirty-six hours before retrieval day a shot of hCG, human chorionic gonadotropin, is administered to prepare the eggs for release, so that they will be ready for harvest.

The actual retrieval is done while the donor is under anesthesia. The 5
tool is a needle, and the product, on average, is ten to twenty eggs. Doctors take that many because "not all eggs will be good," according to Surrogate Mothers Online, an informational Web site designed and maintained by experienced egg donors and surrogate mothers. "Some will be immature and some overripe."

Lisa, one of the hosts on Surrogate Mothers Online and an experienced egg donor, described the process as a "rewarding" experience. When she explained that once in a while something can go wrong, I braced myself for the fine print. On very rare occasions, she wrote, hyperstimulation of the ovaries can occur, and the donor must be hospitalized until the ovaries return to normal. In even rarer cases the ovaries rupture, resulting in permanent infertility or possibly even death. "I must stress that this is very rare," Lisa assured prospective donors. "I had two very wonderful experiences. . . . The second [time] I stayed awake to help the doctor count how many eggs he retrieved."

David responded to my e-mail a few hours after I'd sent it. He told me nothing about himself, and only briefly alluded to the many questions I had asked about the egg-donation process. He spent the bulk of the e-mail describing a cartoon, and then requested photos of me. The cartoon was a scene with a "couple that is just getting married, he a nerd and she a beauty," he wrote. "They are kvelling about how wonderful their offspring will be with his brains and her looks." He went on to describe the punch line: the next panel showed a nerdy-looking baby thinking empty thoughts. The following paragraph was more direct. David let me know that he and his wife were flexible on most criteria but that Michelle was "a real Nazi" about "donor looks and donor health history."

This seemed to be a commentary of some sort on the couple's situation and how plans might go awry, but the message was impossible to pin down. I thanked him for the e-mail, asked where to send my pictures, and repeated my original questions about egg donation and their criteria.

In a subsequent e-mail David promised to return my photos, so I sent him dorm-room pictures, the kind that every college student has lying around. Now they assumed a new level of importance. I would soon learn what this anonymous couple, somewhere in the United States, thought about my genetic material as displayed in these photographs.

Infertility is not a modern problem, but it has created a modern indus- 10
try. Ten percent of American couples are infertile, and many seek treatment from the $2-billion-a-year infertility industry. The approximately 370 fertility clinics across the United States help prospective parents to sift through their options. I sympathize with women who cannot use their own eggs to have children. The discovery must be a sober awakening for those who have always dreamed of raising a family. When would-be parents face this problem, however, their options depend greatly on their income. All over the world most women who can't have children must simply accept the fact and adopt, or find other roles in society. But especially here in the United States wealth can enable such couples to have a child of their own and to determine how closely that child will resemble the one they might have had—or the one they dream of having.

The Web site of Egg Donation, Inc., a program based in California, contains a database listing approximately 300 potential donors. In order to access the list interested parties must call the company and request the user ID and the password for the month. Once I'd given the receptionist my name and address, she told me the password: "colorful." I hung up and entered the database. Potential parents can search for a variety of features, narrowing the pool as much as they like according to ethnic origin, religion of birth, state of residence, hair color, eye color, height, and weight. I typed in the physical and religious characteristics that Michelle and David were looking for and found four potential donors. None of them had a college degree.

The standard compensation for donating an egg to Egg Donation is $3,500 to $5,000, and additional funds are offered to donors who have advanced degrees or are of Asian, African-American, or Jewish descent. Couples searching for an egg at Egg Donation can be picky, but not as picky as couples advertising in the *Yale Daily News*. Should couples be able to pay a premium on an open market for their idea of the perfect egg? Maybe a modern-day Social Darwinist would say yes. Modern success is measured largely in financial terms, so why shouldn't the most successful couples, eager to pay more, have access to the most expensive eggs? Of course, as David illustrated in his first e-mail, input does not always translate perfectly into output—the donor's desirable characteristics may never actually be manifested in the child.

If couples choose not to find their eggs through an agency, they must do so independently. An Internet search turned up a few sites like Surrogate Mothers Online, where would-be donors and parents can post classified ads. More than 500 classifieds were posted on the site: a whole marketplace, an eBay for genetic material.

"Hi! My name is Kimberly," one of the ads read. "I am 24 years old, 5′11″ with blonde hair and green eyes. I previously donated eggs and the couple was blessed with BIG twin boys! The doctor told me I have perky ovaries! . . . The doctor told me I had the most perfect eggs he had ever seen." The Web site provided links to photographs of Kimberly and an e-mail address. Would-be parents on the site offered "competitive" rates, generally from $5,000 to $10,000 for donors who fit their specifications.

About a week after I sent my pictures to David and Michelle, I received 15
a third e-mail: "Got the pictures. You look perfect. I can't say this with any authority. That is my wife's department." I thought back to the first e-mail, where he'd written, "She's been known to disregard a young woman based on cheekbones, hair, nose, you name it." He then shifted the focus. "My department is the SAT scores. Can you tell me more about your academic performance? What are you taking at Yale? What high school did you attend?"

The whole thing seemed like a joke. I dutifully answered his questions, explaining that I was from a no-name high school in the Midwest, I couldn't do math or science, and my academic performance was, well, average; I couldn't help feeling a bit disconcerted by his particular interest in my SAT score.

Michelle and David now had my educational data as well as my photos. They were examining my credentials and trying to imagine their child. If I was accepted, a harvest of my eggs would be fertilized by the semen of the author of the disturbing e-mails I had received. A few embryos would be implanted; the remaining, if there were any, would be frozen; and then I would be out of the picture forever.

The modern embryo has been frozen, stolen, aborted, researched, and delivered weeks early, along with five or six instant siblings. The summer of 2001 was full of embryo news, and the first big story was President Bush's deliberation on stem-cell research. The embryos available for genetic research include those frozen by fertility clinics for later use by couples attempting *in vitro* fertilization.

Embryos took the spotlight again when Helen Beasley, a surrogate mother from Shrewsbury, England, decided to sue a San Francisco couple for parental rights to the twin fetuses she was carrying. The couple and Beasley had agreed that they would pay her $20,000 to carry one child created from a donated egg and the father's sperm. The agreement also called for selective reduction—the abortion of any additional embryos. Beasley claimed that there had been a verbal agreement that such reduction would occur by the twelfth week. The problem arose when Beasley, who had discovered she was carrying twins, was told to abort one, but the arrangements for the reduction weren't made until the thirteenth week. Fearing for her own health and objecting to the abortion of such a highly developed fetus, she refused. At that time she was suing for the right to put the babies up for adoption. She was also seeking the remainder of the financial compensation specified in the contract. The couple did not want the children, and yet had the rights to the genetic material; Beasley was simply a vessel. The case is only one of a multitude invited by modern fertility processes. On August 15, 2001, *The New York Times* reported that the New Jersey Supreme Court had upheld a woman's rights to the embryos that she and her ex-husband had created and frozen six years before. A strange case for child-custody lawyers.

Nearly ten years ago, at the University of California at Irvine's Center 20
for Reproductive Health, doctors took the leftover frozen embryos from previous clients and gave them without consent to other couples and to research centers. Discovery of the scam resulted in more than thirty prosecutions: a group of children had biological parents who hadn't consented to their existence and active parents who had been given stolen goods. Who can say whether throwing the embryos away would have been any better?

Even if Michelle and David liked my data, I knew I'd have a long way to go before becoming an actual donor. The application on Egg Donation's Web site is twelve pages long—longer than Yale's entrance application. The first two pages cover the basics: appearance, name, address, age, and other mundane details. After that I was asked if I'd ever filed for bankruptcy or ever had counseling, if I drank, what my goals in life were, what two of my favorite books were, what my paternal grandfather's height and weight were, what hobbies I had, what kind of relationship I would want to have with the parents and child, and so forth. A few fill-in-the-blanks were thrown in at the end: "I feel strongly about____. I am sorry I did not____. In ten years I want to be____." Not even my closest friends knew all these things about me. If Egg Donation, offering about a fifth what Michelle and David were offering, wanted all this information, what might Michelle and David want?

Michelle and David were certainly trying hard. On one classified-ad site I came across a request that was strangely familiar: "Loving family seeks exceptional egg donor with 1500 SAT, great looks, good family health history, Jewish heritage and athletic. Height 5′4″–5′9″, Age 18–29. We will pay EXTREMELY well and will take care of all expenses. Hope to hear from you." The e-mail address was David and Michelle's familiar AOL account. Theirs was the most demanding classified on the site, but also the only one that offered to pay "EXTREMELY well."

I kept dreaming about all the things I could do with $25,000. I had gone into the correspondence on a whim. But soon, despite David's casual tone and the optimistic attitude of all the classifieds and information I read, I realized that this process was something I didn't want to be a part of. I understand the desire for a child who will resemble and fit in with the family. But once a couple starts choosing a few characteristics, shooting for perfection is too easy—especially if they can afford it. The money might have changed my life for a while, but it would have led to the creation of a child encumbered with too many expectations.

After I'd brooded about these matters, I received the shortest e-mail of the correspondence. The verdict on my pictures was in: "I showed the pictures to [my wife] this AM. Personally, I think you look great. She said ho-hum."

David said he might reconsider, and that he was going to keep one of 25
my pictures. That was it. No good-bye, no thanks for my willingness to be, in effect, the biological mother of their child. I guess I didn't fit their design; my genes weren't the right material for their *chef d'oeuvre.* So I was rejected as a donor. I keep imagining the day when David and Michelle's child asks where he or she came from. David will describe how hard they both worked on the whole thing, how many pictures they looked at, and how much money they spent. The child will turn to them and say, "Ho-hum."

QUESTIONING THE TEXT

1. In this essay, Cohen recounts her experience as a respondent to an advertisement for an egg donor and also comments on that experience; the essay thus interweaves narrative and commentary. After you've read the essay once thoroughly, skim through it again and note which passages present the narrative of Cohen's encounter and which passages comment on her experience or related issues. How does the arrangement of narrative and commentary lead you toward particular judgments about Cohen's experience, the actions of David and Michelle, or issues related to egg donation? Consider the effects that a different arrangement of the passages might have on you as a reader.
2. A.L. says that in reading this piece she "identified with" Cohen. Did you? In what ways does Cohen get you to sympathize with her, even if you have not been in the position she describes? Are there points in the text where you feel less sympathetic toward her? If so, explain why.
3. How do you think Cohen felt about her experience? Does she reveal her emotions in this essay? If so, in what words or passages? Does her writing elicit an emotional response from you as you read? If so, where and how?

MAKING CONNECTIONS

4. Consider the moral dilemmas that Cohen raises in her essay. How would you compare her concerns to those raised by Mary Shelley in the selection from *Frankenstein* presented in Chapter 5 (p. 274)?
5. Do you think it took courage for Cohen to publish her account in a national magazine? Compare Cohen's situation to that of Wendy Shalit (p. 251), who published an article in a national magazine expressing her complaint against the coed bathrooms at her college. What advantages and disadvantages do you see in the kind of publicity these articles probably brought upon the two women? Consider how the consequences might have been different (or similar) for men writing on similar kinds of issues.

JOINING THE CONVERSATION

6. Imagine yourself as a prospective parent in a position similar to that of Michelle or David in this essay: You and your partner want to have a child but are biologically prevented from doing so. Given unlimited financial means, what options would you consider seriously? What options would you refuse to consider? Reconsider the options, assuming you have *limited* financial means. What factors enter into your decision, and how do you weigh the different considerations? Compose your thoughts in an essay responding to Cohen or to Michelle and David.
7. Cohen points out that egg donation "is neither simple nor painless." Consider other donor roles that require invasive surgeries, such as the donation of organs or bone marrow by living volunteers. How do those cases compare to the donation of an egg or of sperm? With a group of classmates, identify the different moral issues at stake in various types of human biological donor situations.
8. By Cohen's admission, the lure of $25,000 provided a strong enticement to respond to the advertisement requesting an egg donor. Have you ever been tempted by money to do something you might not otherwise consider? Conversely, have you ever donated time, services, money, or goods as a volunteer? With classmates, use your experiences to identify criteria you might use to judge whether a job, a risk, or a sacrifice of some kind is worth undertaking.

SARAH VOWELL
Democracy and Things Like That

As a student, I once sat in an auditorium and listened in awe as John F. Kennedy gave a speech. I remember the sound of his voice, the easiness of his laugh, the intense but relaxed way he spoke to a crowd of young people. The next day when I read reports of this event, I had a hard time even recognizing it: Kennedy was represented as aggressive, mean-spirited, too liberal and, well, too northeastern.

From that time on, I have been fascinated with media representations of political figures. In "Democracy and Things Like That," Sarah Vowell takes on this same issue, focusing extensively on a speech Al Gore gave to students at Concord High School during the 1999 presidential campaign season. The experience the students had with Gore—he was easygoing and friendly and knowledgeable, and he used a personal story to suggest that students can make a difference in this world—wasn't what turned up in the newspaper accounts. Rather, these accounts zeroed in on one line from Gore's speech, which the reporter had actually gotten wrong. In spite of the mistaken quotation, the story spread throughout the news media and into late-night talk shows. One student's response to this debacle gave Vowell the title of this essay: "You're focusing on one little itty-bitty microscopic thing," said this student, "that when misquoted can mean something completely different but when quoted correctly it means a great thing for democracy and things like that."

Sarah Vowell pursues the implications of this story, interviewing the teacher of the media literacy class whose students had heard Gore's speech and asking where responsibility lies in such cases; neither Vowell nor the teacher, Joanne McGlynn, come to a simple or pat answer to this question. What they do conclude is that students who examine media representations closely begin to be more critical in their thinking. As one student remarked toward the end of the media literacy course, "I can't even turn on the radio without thinking anymore." Surely that is as good an outcome as any teacher could wish.

I chose this essay, which is part of Vowell's book The Partly Cloudy Patriot *(2002), because of the great need we have for critical media literacy today and because I admire this young writer's style. Referred to by the* Los Angeles Times *as "a Madonna of Americana," Vowell's work, such as a documentary on the Trail of Tears, is often featured on National Public Radio's series* This American Life. *Of Cherokee ancestry, Vowell is also the author of* Radio On: A Listener's Diary *(1997) and* Take the Cannoli: Stories from the New World *(2000). Although she currently lives in New York City, Vowell says, "I've lived in so many places, I think of the whole country as my home."* —A.L.

It all started in 1999, when Joanne McGlynn's media literacy class at Concord High School in Concord, New Hampshire, invited all the presidential candidates to speak. Known to loiter in New Hampshire ceaselessly before the state's primary elections, a whopping 50 percent of the eight major candidates accepted: Alan Keyes, Orrin Hatch, Gary Bauer, and Al Gore. They were asked to speak on the subject of school violence, not just because of the murders at Columbine earlier that year but also because a Concord High student was killed at school a couple of years earlier.

Gore spoke to the student body on November 30, 1999. And, contrary to conventional wisdom regarding his charisma deficiency, he was a hit. Students Lucas Gallo, Ashley Pettengill, and Alyssa Spellman recall the event.

Lucas claims, "He wasn't as stiff as people say he was. He comes out, takes his jacket off. He walks around, talks to the audience."

Ashley remembers, "There was the question that said, 'What do you like to do for fun?' And he mentioned that he liked *The Simpsons*."

"He understood that we are people," Alyssa says. "We are kids but 5
we're not dumb. We understand what's going on, and he respected that."

Lucas laughs, admitting, "He was still Gore. But he wasn't quite as stiff. He didn't just get up and talk like the other candidates did. He was kind of a neat speaker to see."

While the students were impressed by Gore's easygoing manner—his form—Joanne McGlynn was pleased with his content, the way he talked about school violence. "He was very careful to describe the complicated nature of what might have caused what happened at Columbine," she recalls. "He didn't say, 'It is just because those two boys played video games.' He used a little analogy about when you catch a cold or when you don't. He said that some kids in this auditorium had the insulation of a loving family, of teachers who cared about them, of a supportive school system and said perhaps they were insulated from some of these outside forces. And, therefore, were immune from committing those kinds of acts."

Then, during the question and answer period, something happened that seemed unremarkable at the time. A boy stood up and asked a mundane question about how high school students could become more involved in politics.

"He answered in a lengthy response," McGlynn recalls. "He thought for a moment, paused, and said, 'I know there's a lot of cynicism in the country right now, especially among young people.' He said, 'I think it's caused by a number of things. Maybe we need campaign finance reform.' And he went on and talked about how he supported McCain-Feingold. He then said, 'But I think you kids should look in the mirror.'

"I think that leaders can make a difference," Gore told the student. 10
"But I think you also have to examine your own hearts. We are so privileged to live in this country. If that sounds corny to you, you should examine that attitude. Seriously. Think about South Africa. They just recently became a democracy. When they had their first election, you know what the

percentage turnout was? It was like 95 percent. People waited in lines to vote that were seven miles long. Here we have a constantly declining voter turnout. I think it's because a lot of people feel like they cannot make an individual difference. But you can."

McGlynn says, "So he challenged them to get involved, and then he said, 'Let me tell you a little story."

In the days that followed Gore's appearance, this little story was twisted, distorted and, ultimately, more fought over than a piece of Jerusalem real estate. And so I will quote his anecdote in its entirety:

> Let me tell you a quick story. Twenty years ago, I got a letter from a high school student in West Tennessee about how the water her family was drinking from a well tasted funny. She wrote me how her grandfather had a mysterious ailment that paralyzed part of his body, that she was convinced was related to the water. Then her father also became mysteriously ill. People thought she was imagining things. We investigated, and what we found was that one mile from her home a chemical company had dug a big trench and they were dumping millions of gallons of hazardous chemical waste into the ground. It had seeped down into the water table and contaminated her family's well and the wells of other families in that rural area. I called for a congressional investigation and a hearing. I looked around the country for other sites like that. I found a little place in upstate New York called Love Canal. I had the first hearing on that issue and Toone, Tennessee—that was the one you didn't hear of. But that was the one that started it all. We passed a major national law to clean up hazardous dump sites. And we had new efforts to stop the practices that ended up poisoning water around the country. We've still got work to do. But we made a huge difference. And it all happened because one high school student got involved.

The night after the speech, Joanne McGlynn's at home, and a friend calls her, asking if she's seen *The New York Times*. "He said, 'Did you notice the Love Canal comment?' And I said, 'I remember he told a story about Love Canal.' And he said, 'The *Times* says that Gore's taking credit for finding Love Canal.' And I thought, Uh-oh. I got a bit nervous. I thought, Is that the way this story is going to be covered?"

The New York Times article in question, by Katherine Seelye, ran on December 1, 1999. In a seventeen-paragraph piece about one day in the Gore campaign, four paragraphs are devoted to the Concord High appearance. Seelye quoted Gore, "'I found a little place in upstate New York called Love Canal. I had the first hearing on that issue and Toone, Tennessee,' he said. 'But I was the one that started it all.'" It is curious that *The Washington Post* made the exact same mistake. Also on December 1, the *Post* staff writer Ceci Connolly quoted, "'I was the one that started it all.'"

Alyssa recalls, "We came into class and Ms. McGlynn was like, 'You 15
guys are not going to believe this.' And she wrote the quote up on the board

and she said, 'Did he say this?' and we were like 'What? What?' 'Did he say this: I was the one that started it all.' Then we were like, No, he was talking about the girl. That event started it all. And then we looked at all the newspapers and we were like, Wow."

Ashley: "She then played us back the tape that our TV production class had made and the actual quote was 'that was the one that started it all,' referring to the city in Tennessee."

According to Alyssa, "We definitely said we have to do something about this. And we were definitely I think shocked that, that one little word, *one little word,* totally changed the context and totally changed what everyone thought about it."

After the *Times,* and the *Post,* the Love Canal mistake snowballed. *U.S. News & World Report* listed "I was the one that started it all" as one of its quotes of the week. There was the following little roundtable about Gore and Love Canal on ABC's *This Week with Sam Donaldson and Cokie Roberts,* among the two hosts, George Stephanopoulos and Bill Kristol.

"Gore again revealed his Pinocchio problem," quips Stephanopoulos. "He says he was the model for *Love Story,* created the Internet, and this time he sort of discovered Love Canal. It was a kind of exaggeration."

"He said," says Roberts, "that he discovered Love Canal when he had 20
hearings on it after people had been evacuated."

Kristol, reading from a paper that is presumably either the *Post* or the *Times,* says, "Yeah, 'I found a little place in upstate New York called Love Canal. I was the one that started it all.'"

Then *The Late Show with David Letterman* dreamed up a list of "The Top Ten Other Achievements Also Claimed by Al Gore." "Number 5," Letterman announces, "Pulled U.S. out of early '90s recession by personally buying 6,000 T-shirts.

NUMBER 4: Started CBS situation comedy with Juan Valdez titled "Juan for Al, Al for Juan."

NUMBER 3: Was inspiration for Ozzy Osbourne song "Crazy Train."

NUMBER 2: Came up with popular catchphrase "Don't go there, girlfriend."

And the number one other achievement claimed by Al Gore: Gave mankind fire!

Initially, the students at Concord High were upset about the misquote. But the more they thought about it, and the more they watched the misquote evolve, they were really flabbergasted by the misrepresentation of Gore's appearance at their school. Alyssa complains, "He was trying to say that kids can make a difference. He was trying to say what so many high school kids in this country don't believe."

Lucas understands that Gore was "running for president, so he has to be a bit selfish and kind of boost himself when he's speaking, but the message—

they totally missed the point of the entire story that he told. He was trying to make it a clear point for us that we need to get involved and that we should. And that we can do something to help. And the media didn't even mention the message he was trying to explain or anything."

Ashley thinks, "The actual quote itself was, I think, completely innocent. It wasn't a 'look how great I am, look what I did in Love Canal' it was a 'look how great you can be.' That's what his message was, and that's what the papers overlooked."

I played devil's advocate with Ashley, asking her, So what? The reporters got one word wrong but they got the gist of what Gore was saying right. What would she say to that?

She replied, "I would say, 'You're wrong.' You're focusing on one little itty-bitty microscopic thing that when misquoted can mean something completely different but when quoted correctly it means a great thing for democracy and things like that."

If I can come clean on whom I identify with the most in this story, it isn't the students or their teacher. I identify with *The New York Times* reporter Katherine Seelye, who misheard a word. *She* was the one that started it all. I am convinced that this woman, whose job it is to follow around a man with two jobs—running for president and being vice president—is beyond overworked. I know this partly because the first chance she got to return my phone call about all of this was at 1:15 in the morning. This poor reporter, this gatekeeper of democracy, was getting her first break in the day in the middle of the night. And, considering that I am a writer who has publicly misspelled names, confused Sinclair Lewis with Upton Sinclair, and gotten who knows how many things wrong over the years, I am one pot who should not be calling the Gray Lady black. Both *The New York Times* and *The Washington Post* did publish corrections. And this is what Seelye told me. About the students of Concord High, she said, "These kids are well-intentioned. They're paying attention. We did get one word wrong. But they are magnifying what happened. Gore did say, 'I found a little town in upstate New York called Love Canal.' He called the AP in Buffalo the next day and apologized for presuming to take credit for that."

The journalists were in fact correct when they said that Love Canal was already a front-page story, an official national emergency, months before Al Gore ever held hearings. But Gore never claimed to have been the one to have first brought Love Canal to national attention. He only claimed to have held the first congressional hearings on it, which he did, after receiving that letter from Toone in 1978.

In the end, it's possible that the main difference between the ways the reporters and the class heard Gore's speech is that the reporters were listening for some new sound bite from Gore they hadn't heard before, whereas the students were listening for Gore's thoughts on school violence, an issue that is of grave concern to them, an issue Gore actually addressed. Their teacher

Joanne McGlynn points out, "I think what shocks me though is that there seems, on some parts of the media that we've talked to, very little remorse. That surprises me. That it was just a word. I guess I have my own bias or perception as I look at the event. The week before Al Gore came, our entire school had to practice a lockdown procedure. And a lockdown procedure is something that I had never experienced except as a kid in Catholic school in Rhode Island in the early sixties. The nuns had us hiding under our desks or putting our heads down to protect us from nuclear fallout for when the Russians were going to bomb us. And in 1999 we were being asked to run through an event as though a sniper were out in the hallway. This came down as a recommendation from the state of New Hampshire, their safety planning group, and it just so happened that we had our first practice session the week before Al Gore came to Concord High School. So our principal came over the intercom and said, 'Teachers, please implement the lockdown procedure.' We knew ahead of time this was going to happen sometime during the next two days. I had to take my freshmen and move them away from the door, get them on the floor, turn their desks on their sides so they would be protected as much as they could be in case someone came into the room or attempted to come into the room with a gun. We had to be silent. I had to go out in the hallway and lock the door and grab any kid who might have been returning from the bathroom, hoping this kid was not the person we needed to worry about, grab that kid, pull him in, and ask my students to be quiet. I have to tell you, it was very unsettling. The thought that one of ours, one of our students could be out in the hallway trying to harm us—it's a very complicated emotional response. Many of us were very uncomfortable during the lockdown. But we couldn't show that to the kids, wanted to show the kids that they were safe and not to worry. So, I thought Gore did a good job talking about this issue. I thought this issue should be one of the prime ones in our presidential campaign, and I feared immediately when I heard Love Canal that, somehow, what had happened at Concord High would become a joke. And, in some ways, that is what happened."

On his talk show *Hardball,* Chris Matthews chuckled. "Let's talk about Al Gore and have some fun. We've gone from the serious part of the program, now here's the hilarious part. Al Gore keeps taking a little bit of truth and building it up into this epochal role in history."

Joanne sighs. "It just makes me sad that the wise-guy attitude seems to dominate the press right now. That's what I pick up on. Not to pick on Chris Matthews, but he spent two nights having a blast with this story about Love Canal. Getting a big chuckle out of 'Dan Quayle may not be able to spell *potato* but now Al Gore's going to claim he invented it.' Well, maybe where Chris works that seems like a funny thing to say, but where I work, it didn't seem that funny. Where I work, pretending to be hiding behind desks with kids, afraid that Klebold and Harris are outside my door, it didn't seem that funny. And I'm not saying our candidates should be untested, unquestioned, uncriticized. What I am saying, if that's all we do, and if all we do is make fun of them, then we're losing something too, I think."

Ashley tells me, "I feel like some reporters are just saying what [the candidates] did wrong." When I ask the sixteen-year-old what we lose when the press omits descriptions of how a candidate might actually make a good president, she answers, "I think we miss out on every reason to vote for them."

At Concord High School, a politician actually spoke inspiringly and connected with the audience. Which, to me, *is* news. But no reporter reported this. And in fact these kinds of moments are routinely overlooked by the press. They're barely part of our national political discourse. But why? For one thing, so much political speech is lies, spin, and misrepresentation, it's understandable that journalists report these inspiring moments skeptically, if at all. And, beyond that, the way most of the press works is pretty much as you suspect; representatives of the news media carry around story lines of the candidates in their heads, and reporters light up when reality randomly corroborates these pictures.

One of the great mysteries of modern politics is which story lines get told and which get ignored. And, in the primary season, that story line is still up for grabs. John McCain's story line—hero—threatened to become "hypocrite" in light of his helping a major donor with the FCC. Not long after George W. Bush flunked a foreign policy pop quiz, his name tag at the correspondents' dinner was destined to read, "Hello, my name is Dunderhead." Gore's story line—that he's a bore—is spiced up by this secondary story line: that he's a braggart, that he takes credit for ridiculous things, for inventing the Internet and for being the real-life Oliver of *Love Story*. So of course the Love Canal misunderstanding screamed to reporters because it brought this particular fuzzy snapshot of Gore into sharper focus.

It is telling that both the reporter for the *Times* and the one for the *Post* heard the exact same word incorrectly, almost as if that was what they wanted to hear. Joanne McGlynn says that this is a seductive impulse for both reporters and voters. She says, "This editor for *U.S. News & World Report* called and said that; this was after he admitted that he was sorry they had published a misquote. He told me a story about George Bush, Sr., running for president in 1992. And I remember the story myself that George Bush went into a supermarket and was stunned to find a scanner. I guess he was used to old cash registers and made a comment that showed he was surprised to see a scanner. What this gentleman from *U.S. News & World Report* told me was, actually, the pool reporter got that story wrong, that it was actually some kind of *new* scanner that Bush remarked on. But that comment then became the iconic moment for Bush being out of touch with Middle America. And that was it. I think that might have hurt Bush big time. Now, it turned out—if this man from *U.S. News & World Report* is right—not to be accurate. Now, if it wasn't accurate, was it not true? I mean, was Bush out of touch with Middle America? It's the same thing going back to Gore: Does Gore take credit? It makes me question. And I have to say, I am going to keep my eyes open in a way I hadn't before, particularly when things automatically fit my mind-set. I'm going to be a little careful. It didn't surprise me that maybe President Bush didn't know about a scanner. But if he did, it's too bad that got out there. It's not fair."

I looked at Joanne McGlynn's syllabus for her media studies course, the one she handed out at the beginning of the year, stating the goals of the class. By the end of the year, she hoped her students would be better able to challenge everything from novels to newscasts, that they would come to identify just who is telling a story and how that person's point of view affects the story being told. I'm going to go out on a limb here and say that this lesson has been learned. In fact, just recently, a student came up to McGlynn and told her something all teachers dream of hearing. The girl told the teacher that she was listening to the radio, singing along with her favorite song, and halfway through the sing-along she stopped and asked herself, "What am I singing? What do these words mean? What are they trying to tell me?" And then, this young citizen of the republic jokingly complained, "I can't even turn on the radio without thinking anymore."

QUESTIONING THE TEXT

1. A.L. says she chose this essay in part because she "admire[s] this young writer's style." Do you agree with A.L.? If so, what aspects of Vowell's writing style do you find admirable, and why? How are they effective? If not, what aspects don't you admire in Vowell's style? Why aren't they effective?
2. At least half of the text in this essay is comprised of quotations. What effects does Vowell achieve with her extensive use of other people's words? Could paraphrases or summaries of these quotations work just as well in some places? Why, or why not?

MAKING CONNECTIONS

3. Vowell suggests that the reporters at Concord High School heard what they expected to hear. "[T]he way most of the press works is pretty much as you suspect," she explains; "representatives of the news media carry around story lines of the candidates in their heads, and reporters light up when reality randomly corroborates these pictures" (paragraph 34). With your classmates, explore the ways in which these preconceived notions might resemble the prejudices confronted by Martin Luther King Jr. in his "Letter from Birmingham Jail" (p. 163). Explain, using examples from the texts.

4. Both Vowell and Wendy Shalit ("The Future of Modesty," p. 251) address instances of student participation in issues of public debate. Discuss with your classmates the differences you find in these situations. What can you learn from these essays about your potential as students to make a difference in matters of public concern?
5. Stephen L. Carter, in "The Rules about the Rules" (p. 179), says the media are partly to blame for the erosion of integrity value in American society. He faults the media for "oversimplification and for interfering with, rather than enabling, the search for right and wrong that each of us must undertake in order to live a life of integrity" (paragraph 33). Neither Carter nor Vowell comes down too hard on the media, though. Starting with the comments by these authors on media culpability, discuss further the ways in which journalists do or do not encourage moral behavior among their audiences.

JOINING THE CONVERSATION

6. In her headnote to Vowell's essay, A.L. recounts an experience much like that of the students at Concord High School, in which an event she witnessed was rendered almost unrecognizable to her in a news story about it. Have you ever been in a similar situation? Have you attended an event or participated in one—perhaps a school play, concert, or athletic event—that was covered by a newspaper? Was the report accurate, in your judgment? Try an experiment with some friends: Go to a public meeting or other event, and write a news report on what transpires. Be sure to include some direct quotations in your report. Compare reports. What differences do you find between your account and those of your friends? How do you explain those differences?
7. Vowell admits that in the story she presents, she identifies more closely with the *New York Times* reporter than with the teacher or the students. With whom do you identify most, and why?
8. Study the ways in which Vowell introduces quotations and integrates them into her argument. Use this technique to write a brief essay that creates a conversation in which you and at least two of the writers in this chapter discuss how or why one should defend one's moral principles—even if they are unpopular.

MARK CLAYTON
A Whole Lot of Cheatin' Going On

Have you ever cheated on a college paper or examination? If you have not, *studies suggest you are an exception — as many as 80 percent of students admit to at least one incident of scholastic dishonesty in their careers. As the director of a major university writing program, I've had to deal with many cases of plagiarism, and they are painful experiences for instructors and students alike. When faculty members discover that a student of theirs has copied or downloaded a paper, they typically feel betrayed and angry — as if they've been violated professionally. Students themselves are, for the most part, remorseful when confronted with evidence of their cheating. But a surprising number play the sullen and resentful victim, blaming their scholastic dishonesty on unreasonable instructors, demanding (and irrelevant) curricula, or work schedules they can't quite manage.*

Many students are also simply confused by the complexities of citing sources correctly or by the confusing status of source material in electronic formats. When material moves so effortlessly from screen to the page, it's hard to recall just who owns what material and harder still to enforce the intellectual property rights of authors.

Not surprisingly, scholastic integrity is a potent topic on many campuses. When my department hosted an online forum on the subject, we quickly got more than a hundred postings, mostly from students who condemned cheating. But you can read more about this forum and concerns about academic integrity on campuses nationwide in the following selection by Mark Clayton, originally published as a feature story in the Christian Science Monitor *(January 19, 1999). Clayton (b. 1957), higher education writer for the* Monitor *since 1997, said in an email conversation with me that he is surprised by how casual students are about plagiarism and how unaware they often are of the serious consequences of cheating. "It might sound corny," Clayton notes, "but those [students] I interviewed said parents and educators need to make greater efforts to make clear to students that dishonesty has a real price in the real world — just as honesty has long-term rewards. After that, it's up to students."* —J.R.

Sitting in the glow of his computer screen at 2 A.M. on Oct. 26, 1998, John Smolik, a University of Texas freshman, fires off an e-mail message to an online debate over academic cheating on the Austin campus.

Many of the 100-plus student messages argue that cheaters only hurt themselves. Not so says Mr. Smolik's missive, labeled "reality check!" "Cheating *is* an answer," he writes. "It might not be a good answer, but none the less it is an answer."

Actually, Smolik "disagrees with cheating" and was simply playing devil's advocate, he said in a recent interview. But he allows that his provocative message put forward a widely shared view. And researchers agree.

Across America, college students and college-bound high-schoolers appear to be cheating like there's no tomorrow, student surveys show.

The Center for Academic Integrity in Nashville studied 7,000 students on 26 small-to-medium-size college campuses in 1990, 1992, and 1995. Those studies found that nearly 80 percent admitted to cheating at least once.

"We've seen a dramatic increase in the more-explicit forms of test cheating" and illegitimate "collaboration," says Donald McCabe, associate provost at Rutgers University in Newark, who founded CAI and did its studies.

He and others blame poor role models and lack of parental guidance for the growing acceptance of cheating in colleges. Easy access to the Internet, with its vast and often hard-to-trace resources, is another factor.

Add to that a pervasive change in societal values, and students can easily be snared if they lack a strong moral compass—as well as a campus where peers and administrators take a firm stand against dishonesty.

"Nobody cheated [in the 1960s] because of the peer pressure and likelihood of being turned in," claims Johan Madson, associate provost for student affairs at Vanderbilt University in Nashville. "Students of this generation are reluctant to turn their classmates in. They feel everyone ought to have their own right to do their own thing."

The problem is hardly limited to college campuses. Critics also point to 10
widespread cheating in high school as a reason for colleges' current woes.

Who's Who among American High School Students, which lists 700,000 high-achieving students, surveyed these top performers last year and found that 80 percent said they had cheated during their academic careers. Joe Krouse, associate publisher of the listing, says it is "the highest level we've ever seen."

Mr. Krouse taps adult behavior as a factor. "Because adults and role models in society do it, some students may have used those examples to rationalize cheating," he says. In a survey conducted in 1997–98, he also found that 66 percent of the parents of these top students said cheating was "not a big deal."

Colleges Are Watching More Closely

Whatever the reason for cheating, its sheer volume is capturing the attention of more than a few schools. Most, chary of their images, downplay dishonesty, unwilling to air dirty laundry in public. Yet a few are confronting cheating by making it highly public—on campus, at least.

The University of Texas is the nation's largest university with about 50,000 students. It has roughly 180 academic-integrity cases pop up annually, says Kevin Price, assistant dean of students. The school is trying to raise the profile of integrity issues during orientation with skits, a 10-page handout on plagiarism, and a newsletter called the *Integrity Herald* for faculty.

Another sign of academic stirring: the Center for Academic Integrity, 15
founded in 1993, already has 175 member schools and is drafting a framework of principles that could be applied nationwide to lower student cheating.

Schools like Stanford University, Georgetown University, the University of Delaware, and a half-dozen others are also buffing up or introducing new honor codes.

But Mr. Madson at Vanderbilt University says what is most needed is for students themselves to take charge and reject the attitude that cheating can be justified.

Students say time and workload pressure are major factors spurring academic dishonesty, followed by parental pressure. "It's definitely what you get assigned—and how long you have to do it—that right there determines whether you're going to cheat," says Smolik, the University of Texas freshman.

Anne-Elyse Smith, another freshman at Texas, reasoned in an online debate that it may not be smart to cheat, but it could be educationally valuable.

"People should hold themselves accountable to a standard at which they 20
are comfortable, and get out of the education what they can," she wrote. "If that

involves looking at one answer on a quiz, I think the person is more likely to remember that one answer since they had to resort to cheating to obtain it."

A Little Imagination, a Lot of High Tech

Whether copying another student's homework, cheating on a test, or plagiarizing an essay, cheating is limited only by imagination—and technology. Some program their calculators with formulas, but rig them to show an empty memory if an instructor checks.

But what alarms some campus officials the most is the Internet's proven potential for explosive growth in negative areas such as pornography—and the possibility that plagiarism could be next. Web sites sporting names like "Cheater.com" and "School Sucks" offer tools for rampant plagiarism at the click of a mouse. "Download your workload" the latter site suggests, boasting more than 1 million term-paper downloads.

Such savvy borrowing may be lost on some educators, but others, like librarians, are catching up. "Students are finding it so easy to use these sources that they will dump them in the middle of the papers without any attribution," says John Ruszkiewicz, an English professor at Texas. "What they don't realize is how readily [professors] can tell the material isn't the student's and how easy it is for instructors to search this material on the Web."

Anthony Krier, a reference librarian at Franklin Pierce College Library in Rindge, N.H., is one such literary bloodhound. Last semester, he investigated nine cases of plagiarism, three of them involving the Internet. One student had downloaded and passed off as his own a morality essay, apparently unaware of the irony, Mr. Krier says.

Some colleges are fighting back with explicit warnings, more detailed 25
orientations, and classes on how to cite sources—and lawsuits. Boston University sued five online "term-paper mills" in 1997. The case was rejected by a federal judge last month. School officials vow to refile.

Last fall, the dean of the school's College of Communication, Brent Baker, wrote a letter to students urging them to protect their "good name" by reviewing carefully the school's code of conduct. To drive home the point, he attached a listing of 13 unnamed cases and the penalties—probation, suspension, and expulsion—meted out.

Likewise, the 152 reports of academic dishonesty for 1997–98 at the University of Southern California in Los Angeles "is higher than previous comparable years beginning in 1991," wrote Sandra Rhoten, assistant dean in the office of student conduct, in a letter in the campus newspaper describing violations and sanctions assessed.

"We had a full-blown, two-year campaign [starting in 1995] to educate people about the problem," Ms. Rhoten says in an interview. "Sometimes faculty feel alone in this. We're reassuring them that we take this seriously too."

The Expectation of Honesty

Being blunt is the idea. Talking about the expectation of honesty is constant. And along with explicit warning shots, freshmen at USC are getting more intensive and detailed training in what constitutes plagiarism and other forms of cheating, Rhoten says.

The school passes out brochures on plagiarism, has regular coverage in 30
the student paper on cheating cases, and has beefed up orientation courses with training to explain subtler issues like unauthorized collaboration—the largest area of student honor violation at USC and many other campuses, Mr. McCabe and others say.

For instance, Lucia Brawley, a senior majoring in English at Harvard University in Cambridge, Mass., does not believe cheating is a big problem at her school. But when asked about the collaboration issue, she is less sure.

"With people I know in the sciences, there's so much to do and so little time, they help each other," she says. "You go to a lecture today, I'll go next week. You do the reading this week, I'll do it next week. It's a gray area."

Ultimately, though, it is students who will have to uphold academic integrity themselves, many say.

The University of Virginia has a student-run honor code whose "single sanction" for violators is expulsion. It is one of the nation's strictest. Even after more than a century, it remains controversial on campus. Of 11 cheating cases last semester, five resulted in expulsion. But the code has also created an atmosphere of trust that means students can take unproctored exams. "Many of our alumni attribute their success in life to this school's honor code," says Cabell Vest, a graduate student who chairs UVA's honor council.

At Vanderbilt, which also has a strict code, 20 academic dishonesty cases 35
are under review, Madson says—triple the number a few years ago. But he is confident the school is creating an atmosphere less tolerant of cheating. "You just can't have an academic enterprise that isn't based on integrity and honesty," he says. "Nobody wants somebody building bridges to take shortcuts."

QUESTIONING THE TEXT

1. Clayton quotes a provost from Vanderbilt who asserts that "[n]obody cheated [in the 1960s] because of the peer pressure and likelihood of being turned in" (paragraph 9). Examine this statement in the context in which it is made, and then decide how you might go about testing its validity. What would you have to read and examine and who would you have to interview to confirm or refute its validity?
2. One student in the online debate asserts that "it may not be smart to cheat, but it could be educationally valuable." Examine the student's

full statement and its rationale (paragraphs 19–20). Then discuss the implications of the statement with your classmates, either in face-to-face conversation or in an online forum or listserv.

3. Examine the image that accompanies "A Whole Lot of Cheatin' Going On." What does it depict? How does it shape your perception of the essay? For instance, does it seem less serious than the subject warrants? Does it remind you of what it is like to take examinations?

MAKING CONNECTIONS

4. In "Democracy and Things Like That," Sarah Vowell (p. 198) presents a case in which journalists perpetuated a misquotation—by listening for and repeating what they wanted to hear, rather than what was said—and in the process, misrepresented an encounter between presidential candidate Al Gore and a group of high school students. What similarities and differences do you see between the journalists' wrongdoing and the students' cheating discussed by Clayton? Discuss this question with a group of classmates, and see if you can derive principles for the responsible use of sources by journalists and by student writers. Should different standards apply to each group? Why, or why not?
5. Read the college mission statements in Chapter 3 (p. 57), and imagine how you might present a school's position on cheating. Write a position statement for your institution on the issue of scholastic integrity. Imagine the statement as a Web page. What issues would you present? What visuals might you use? What links might you make?

JOINING THE CONVERSATION

6. Conduct a series of interviews on your campus to explore the issue of scholastic integrity within a small group you can readily identify—for instance, your fraternity or sorority, the Young Democrats, or the club volleyball team. Use Clayton's article to prepare a list of interview questions about plagiarism, cheating, and collusion at your institution; avoid questions that can be answered by a simple yes or no. Then write a brief report summarizing what you've discovered locally about scholastic integrity. Quote freely from your interviews, but be sure to protect the interviewees' anonymity.
7. Locate a copy of your institution's policies on cheating, plagiarism, and collusion. Then write a critical analysis of these statements. Are the statements clear? Are important terms carefully defined? Do the statements provide a convincing ethical rationale for the policies announced? Do the policies account for changes as a result of electronic technology?

ANTHONY BRANDT
Do Kids Need Religion?

ANTHONY BRANDT, a contributing editor at Parenting *magazine, focuses on the relationship of children to religious faith. Brandt speaks as a parent, one concerned about how best to help his children face the losses and traumas life always brings. In this essay, published in 1991 in the progressive* Utne Reader, *he describes himself as a "run-of-the-mill modern skeptic," without faith or belief, and asks us to consider the uses of religion in what he terms a largely secular society. Might religion serve as a unifying cultural force, even for people who don't "believe"? Even more important, Brandt asks, "What sort of meaning does a secular society offer a child?" These questions suggest that Brandt (b. 1936) is searching for a basis on which parents can make some very hard choices about how they will (and should) raise their children.*

I admire Brandt's straightforward approach here, his willingness to consider various options, and his refusal to argue that his *way to spirituality is the only or even the best way. In addition, I find that Brandt establishes some common ground for* all *people, regardless of differences in religious faith or creed, when he says, "The longing for meaning is something we all share."* —A.L.

This happened nearly 20 years ago, so I may not have all the details right. As I remember, my daughter was about 10 years old. She had spent the weekend with her grandparents, and while she was gone, a house down the road from ours burned to the ground. Three children died in the fire. One was a houseguest. The other two were my daughter's closest friends.

I know children who have experienced the death of a loved one "up close and personal." Our society holds death so much at arm's length and tries to deny it in so many ways that we don't in any way prepare children (or ourselves) for its reality. —A.L.

My wife went to see the bereaved parents. They were devout Catholics and they took their loss amazingly well. They talked to her about their two girls being angels in heaven now, and they really believed it. At the funeral, they were strong and brave, braver than many others there, including myself.

My tears were bitter. I didn't think their children were angels, I thought they were dead. I had little confidence in any sort of existence beyond that. I was not a devout Catholic or a devout anything. I was your run-of-the-mill modern skeptic who long before had stopped going to church, thought most religious doctrine absurd, and was resolved to live without the illusions of belief.

What does your run-of-the-mill modern skeptic tell his 10-year-old daughter when her closest friends have just died in a fire? My wife and I told her what had happened when she got home from her grandparents' house. I was crying and so was my wife, but my daughter just sat there, stunned, in shock. I wanted so much to console her, to find something to say that would explain, would justify these deaths and give them meaning. But I didn't think these deaths had any meaning. All I could come up with was something I didn't believe. "Maybe there is a heaven," I said, "and that's where they are." Yeah, maybe. And maybe not.

I'm old enough to know now that there's no living without illusions of some sort, that we all need to find or generate some kind of meaning for our lives if life is not to become unbearable. But what kind? It goes without saying that we are no longer a religious society in the conventional sense of the word. Religion no longer stands at the center of our culture as it did a hundred or so years ago. Rather, we are a thoroughly secularized society. The miracles we marvel at are the miracles of technology. For the answers to our questions about the meaning of things, we look not to the elders of a church, but to science.

Is Brandt saying that meaning is always in some sense an illusion? I wouldn't use the word illusion *here. A construct, perhaps, but not an illusion.* —A.L.

Doesn't Brandt underestimate the influence of religion in the USA here? —J.R.

An event like the cruel and pointless death of three little girls, however, presents a fundamental challenge. What sort of meaning does a secular society offer a child? What do parents with no religious beliefs do when their children start asking those difficult questions about where Grandpa has gone, Grandpa having just died, or why Jesus was crucified, and why people are so mean, and what will happen to them when they die?

It might, in fact, be harder *for a believer to explain to children why a benevolent God would allow such a tragedy to befall the faithful.* —J.G.R.

For some parents, to be sure, questions like these present no problem. Either they have religious beliefs and are confident they can transmit them to their kids, or they have no religious beliefs at all and see no reason to raise their children to have any. I asked one father what he had done about his kids' religious education and he said, "Nothing whatsoever." Well, I went on, how did he answer their questions about God and things like that? He didn't remember there being any. And even if there are questions, a parent can say, "Go ask your mother" or "I'm no expert on that" or simply "I don't know," and let it go at that. Western culture is so secularized that parents can evade or dismiss "religious" questions without feeling that they're merely getting themselves off the hook. No one is surprised anymore by this kind of religious indifference.

Surprised? No. But what are the consequences? —J.R.

For believers, too, the problem doesn't exist. Secure in their own faith, they can confidently answer the questions of a child.

How can he be so sure? Don't all people—believers or not—have doubts? —J.G.R.

Another mother and father, not so secure in their faith, say it was actually their children who brought them back to religion. They had both been raised Roman Catholic; each had children from a previous marriage; both had lapsed from the church. But they were sending their kids to a Protestant Sunday school. One night at dinner the oldest child said, "Don't you think we should pray for this food?" This was something of a shock. It was even more so when the child said, in prayer, "And thank you, God, for bringing our whole family together." The following Sunday the parents went to church. They have been actively involved (in a Protestant congregation) ever since. "Children come up with some really interesting questions," the mother told me, "and we still have to do a lot of explaining. But we have faith. We don't feel that we're alone with these questions."

This isn't at all clear to me. Faith in what? And what does this faith have to do with not "being alone" with these questions? —A.L.

For those of us without faith it's not so easy. Do we send our kids to Sunday school when we ourselves never go to church? Do we have them baptized even though we have no intention of raising them to be religious? I argued against having my son baptized. It's a meaningless ritual, I said. I didn't think he had been "born in sin," so why wash him free of it, even symbolically? Why bow to convention simply for convention's sake? I gave in, but only to keep peace in the family.

The author seems earnest. Why do I feel uneasy as a reader? —J.R.

For me religious education raised the issue of honesty. I thought it would be hypocritical to make my kids attend Sunday school when I not only didn't go to church but also didn't have any

Are there reasons for sending children to Sunday school that go beyond religious beliefs? —A.L.

religious beliefs. My parents had sent me to Sunday school when neither of them was in the least religious, and under the circumstances I came to think Sunday school was a joke. I learned a few Bible stories, but that was all. I believed I should spare my children that kind of charade. My wife took them to church from time to time, but only once or twice did they attend a Sunday school class.

I'm still wondering whether we did the right thing. In *Childhood and Society* the renowned psychoanalyst Erik Erikson makes the unsettling remark that "many are proud to be without religion whose children cannot afford their being without it." Children may not need a religious upbringing, but, says Erikson, they do need a sense of "basic trust," a feeling not only that their fundamental bodily needs will be met and that their parents love them and will take care of them, but also that they have not been abandoned to the empty haphazardness of existence.

Children can be taught moral values and courage without religion. —J.G.R.

I can't see offhand why religion is the only thing that could fulfill this need not to feel abandoned. —A.L.

Erikson relates this sense of trust to the psychosocial origins of religious life. "The parental faith which supports the trust emerging in the newborn," he writes, "has throughout history sought its institutional safeguard . . . in organized religion." The trust of the infant in the parents, in other words, finds its parallel—and takes its mature form—in the parents' trust in God. The implication is that if trust has no institutional reinforcement, it will tend to wither. Basic trust will become basic mistrust, and there will be more work for mental health experts such as Erikson.

The institutional form that trust has taken in America has historically remained within the Judeo-Christian tradition, and the decision to deny that tradition to a child ought at the very least to be well thought out. Children will become aware of the tradition with or without parental teaching; they'll bring it home from school or the playground, wanting to know why their friend Jimmy says they'll go to hell if they don't go to church, or why Alice is getting a beautiful white confirmation dress and they're not. A psychoanalyst, Ana-Marie Rizzuto, once pointed out that no matter what parents teach their children, "religious symbols and language are so widely present in this society that

Brandt equates religion with objects and symbols, not beliefs and moral choices. I'm disappointed that all he's worried about is that his children won't fit into a Judeo-Christian culture. —J.R.

virtually no child reaches school age without having constructed—with or without religious instruction—an image or images of God."

I broached the subject with one couple who have a three-year-old daughter. The father, Pete, was raised in a fundamentalist family and rebelled against it; religion holds a kind of perverse fascination for him, but he is not what you would call a believer. His wife, Valerie, has no religious beliefs to speak of. Yet they both want their daughter to go to Sunday school. "I don't want her to grow up in a religious vacuum," says Pete. He thinks that if they don't give her a religious background they will be depriving her of a choice later on. If she has the background, she can always reject it when she gets older, he says; if she doesn't, there will be nothing to reject but nothing to affirm, either. He doesn't think she would be likely to come to that crossroads on her own. Valerie agrees with this reasoning: "I want her to know the Bible stories, the mythology," she says. "It's a major part of our culture. And I want her to have a sense of mystery, of awe." A sense, says Pete, that in our society has largely been lost.

If this approach seems paradoxical coming from parents who are not themselves believers, it also makes a certain amount of sense. No matter what we believe in, our society's Judeo-Christian tradition retains a good deal of its power. I reject organized religion, yet I cannot listen to Mozart's *Requiem Mass* without being moved. Perhaps nonpracticing Jews feel the same when they hear Hebrew prayers sung. Much of Western culture springs from religious feeling; we are secular but our heritage is not, and there is no true identification with a culture without some feel for its past. To raise children in a culture without at least exposing them to its religious traditions, even if you yourself have abandoned the beliefs on which they are based, may be doing them a disservice. The children will be exposed to those traditions in any case, so why not give them some real instruction?

What he wants for his children is "religious appreciation," not religion. No hard choices here—religion as art. —J.R.

Why does religious instruction have to come from a church? —J.G.R.

There's a big difference between introducing children to the religious traditions of our culture (which are quite diverse) and training them into one set of religious beliefs as absolutely the truth and the one way. —A.L.

Pete and Valerie are not alone; among the nonbelieving parents I talked to, theirs was a common rationale for sending their children to Sunday school, and the most common solution to the problem. Several other parents, however, admitted to qualms. "Kids pick up on your real feelings about things pretty fast," one father said. "If you're making them do something you yourself don't believe in, they're going to figure it out." And a mother told me, "I think you can transmit values to your kids, but belief is different. Values—respect for other people, respect for life, not taking what doesn't belong to you, things like that—they're universal, they're everywhere. But belief is a special thing. You have to come to it on your own; nobody can impose it on you."

How typical of our times to regard "values" as universal and belief as contingent. We'd better hope there is no God! —J.R.

Too, it is impossible to predict with any confidence what effect a religious education will have on children. It can be more than a little uncomfortable when your children take religious teaching more seriously than you do. It is unsettling to think that they might need religion when you have decided you do not. Do kids in fact need religion? They need "basic trust," as Erikson says, but beyond that, nobody has conclusive answers. We used to think that without religious beliefs, social behavior would come unglued. "If God is dead," wrote Dostoyevski, "then everything is permitted." It hasn't happened.

Well, yes, or any other training, for that matter. Some of the most horrible characters in our history, for instance, were thoroughly trained in religious and/or other traditions. —A.L.

Wrong. What—besides racism and sexism—is regarded as sinful these days? Pornography? Idolatry? Abortion? Covetousness? —J.R.

Morality can survive without religion, it appears; children can be taught the importance of right versus wrong without benefit of religious training. Jean Piaget and Lawrence Kohlberg* have shown that moral understanding is acquired in stages, that it is a developmental process that unfolds, to some extent, as naturally as intelligence itself.

All of Brandt's sources are psychologists. What's his own background? —J.G.R.

My daughter, now age 27, who was exposed to little more than my own deep skepticism, is studying Buddhism. As I write, in fact, she is in Tibet, on a journey that I'm sure is at least partly spiritual. I have made spiritual journeys during my adult life, all of them outside the sphere of Christianity that I was raised in. I continue to distrust and dislike organized religion but find it hard, as I grow

---

Jean Piaget (1896–1980) *and Lawrence Kohlberg* (1927–87): psychologists who studied the mental and moral development of children and young adults

older, to live with only my vague faith that life must have some kind of meaning, even if I don't know what it is.

To believe is to be connected, and those of us who don't believe cannot help but miss the feelings that come with belonging to something larger than ourselves. I hope my children find a straighter road than I've found. "I very much wish I had had some religion, for my kids' sake," one father told me. "My son's into tarot cards now. There's not much comfort in tarot cards."

This is an interesting definition of belief— "to be connected." I'll have to think about this; I'm not sure I agree.
—A.L.

The longing for meaning is something we all share, parent and child alike. But it may be that this is an area where a parent can't help a child much. Meaning may be something all of us have to find in our own way. I don't know. I am loath to give advice. Robert Coles* quotes a black woman who worked as a servant for a wealthy white Southern family: "My momma told me: Remember that you're put here only for a few seconds of God's time, and he's testing you. He doesn't want answers, though. He wants you to know how to ask the right questions." Teaching our kids how to ask the right questions may be the best we can do.

This is a safe and predictable conclusion. No strong position is taken. I'm disappointed.
—J.R.

I end up wondering where Brandt stands on his original question. I'll need to reread this to decide whether his answer is yes, no, or maybe.
—A.L.

Afterwords

I agree that human beings seek meaning, that we yearn for meaning so strongly that we will make meaning(s) at all cost. Further, I consider this yearning to be a function related to our being inside a world of languages—which is why the philosopher Kenneth Burke defines people as "symbol-using, symbol-abusing animals." Language allows us to assign meaning, and if this capacity is by definition human, *then it makes perfect sense that we would need to assign meaning,* demand *to make meaning.*

That said, I'm willing to follow in Brandt's steps as he explores the central question of his essay, which I would rephrase as, "Will religion help kids make or find meaning?" Put this way, my answer would be conditional: organized religion can *help people make meaning, and it can do so largely by way of its own language, its symbolicity. But I'd also say that organized religion won't* automatically *help kids or anyone else find meaning.*

Robert Coles: an educational psychologist (b. 1929) whose work on the ethical life of children has been widely influential

Brandt claims not to have religion, but rather "spirituality." What seems to give meaning to him and his life is his connection to others, particularly his family, and his commitment to intellectual inquiry, to continued probing of important issues, including those of religion and meaning. In this regard, I am most sympathetic to him. I find meaning in my own life in relationship to someone else, either in person (as with my friends, my family, and especially my students) or in words (with persons I know only through books). Meaning, it strikes me, isn't ever in us or indeed in *any one thing; rather, meaning arises out of connections and relations. For me, these are the pathways to spirituality, ones I'd like to share with "kids" of all ages.* —A.L.

One reason I am not now particularly religious is that I am unmoved by "soft" notions of religion such as put forth by Brandt and to some extent by A.L. Raised in a strict Catholic tradition, I take little solace or intellectual satisfaction in faith represented chiefly as a quest for meaning or selfhood. Religion makes more sense to me if it also deals with timeless, if evolving, truths.

To offer religion to children as an alternative to harsh reality—as a way of explaining to a ten-year-old why her best friends died in a fire, to use Brandt's example—trivializes religion. That a nonbelieving parent like Brandt might expose his children to organized religion because he wants them to know the tradition behind Mozart's Requiem *is to treat faith with secular contempt, rendering it as worthless as sunshine patriotism. Religion is about hard choices, not easy ones; about truths, not feelings. Questions of faith compel individuals to face the abyss and to confront the responsibility we have for our own souls. Religion defines meaning not in terms of historical and cultural artifacts, but in terms of a higher power. At some point, this faith requires a difficult, uncompromising, and honest* credo.

I am not able to speak that word yet, but when and if I do, I don't expect my life to be any easier. —J.R.

As an agnostic parent, I looked forward to reading this piece. After reading it, I feel let down, mostly because it seems long on questions and short on answers.

I wanted guidance, but instead I got descriptions of wishy-washy parents relying on religious institutions they have no faith in to give their children moral security and structure. How hypocritical! I expected a spectrum of authoritative opinions, but Brandt relies solely on psychologists.

Because this issue is so critical to me, I may have wanted too much from Brandt. In raising my son, Luke, I can relate to some of Brandt's experiences. But I feel I might be setting Luke up for a spiritual fall if I were to raise him in a religion I have no faith in myself. He might ultimately lose faith in me as well as in religion. Apparently, what I want no writer can objectively give: answers to an eternal enigma. —J.G.R.

QUESTIONING THE TEXT

1. What would be the effect of changing Brandt's title question to "Do Kids Need Morality?" What evidence in the essay relates Brandt's discussion of religion to issues of morality?

2. What is Brandt's answer to his title question, "Do Kids Need Religion?" What in the essay most clearly tells you what the answer is? If you keep a reading log, answer these questions there.
3. Look at the questions A.L., J.R., and J.G.R. pose in their marginal commentary on this piece. Choose several of their questions and decide what functions each question serves. Can you see any differences in the kinds of questions each reader tends to ask?

MAKING CONNECTIONS

4. Judging from their selections in this chapter, what advice would Martin Luther King Jr. (p. 163) and Stephen L. Carter (p. 179) likely give Brandt about children and religion? Imagine that you are either King or Carter, and write a letter to Brandt offering such advice.
5. In what ways might Brandt's spiritual quest be compared to that depicted in Kathleen Norris's "Little Girls in Church" (p. 265)? How do Brandt and Norris differ in their relationship to belief or faith?
6. A.L. rephrases Brandt's question to read, "Will religion help kids make or find meaning?" (p. 219). This question suggests a more general one: to what extent does morality depend on religious belief? In most selections in this chapter on moralities, religion is mentioned in one way or another. Working with a classmate, pick two or more selections, and explore the relationships suggested between religion and morals. Then discuss how you might revise the selections to make the same arguments without using religious premises or allusions. Do you think the revised arguments would be as strong as the originals? Explain.

JOINING THE CONVERSATION

7. Like other authors in this chapter, Brandt seems to distinguish between *spirituality* (or *spiritual quest*) and *religion*. Try your hand at comparing and contrasting these terms in writing, and bring your definitions to class for discussion.
8. Working with two or three classmates, answer Brandt's question, "Do kids need religion?" Then together draw up a list of reasons, examples, or other evidence to support your answer. Finally, on your own, draft a one-page position paper beginning with either "Kids need religion" or "Kids don't need religion."

MICHAEL POLLAN
An Animal's Place

THROUGH THE FOUR EDITIONS OF THIS BOOK, I have been seeking essays that raise important issues compellingly. But none of my choices so far have been as powerful an example of good argument as Michael Pollan's "An Animal's Place." It brings to the public square the argument that the welfare of animals—a back-burner issue in many minds—requires immediate attention.

It's relatively easy to make a sentimental argument for the welfare of animals—to appeal, for example, to pet owners' devotion to their cats or dogs. The most famous probably occurs in Laurence Sterne's novel Tristram Shandy *(1759–67), when Uncle Toby spares the life of a fly:*

> *—Go—says he, one day at dinner, to an over-grown one which had buzz'd about his nose, and tormented him cruelly all dinner-time,—and which, after infinite attempts, he had caught at last, as it flew by him; . . . Go, says he, lifting up the sash, and opening his hand as he spoke, to let it escape;—go poor Devil, get thee gone, why should I hurt thee?—This world surely is wide enough to hold both thee and me.*

But it is another matter entirely to make people appreciate the disturbing moral costs involved in dining on hamburger, pork tenderloin, and chicken fajitas—or in enjoying the supple textures of leather coats, Gucci purses, or Ferragamo shoes.

Can we justify the uses we make of animals when the price they pay is lives of pointless suffering? That's the tough question Pollan poses in "An Animal's Place," understanding full well that a relatively small but active insurgency already says no *and that a largely indifferent public prefers its steaks marbled and rare.*

Pollan's essay, originally published in the New York Times Magazine *(November 10, 2002), embodies all the principles of a fair and principled rhetoric, grabbing both the mind and heart. From the very first paragraph, he conveys his own reservations about the concept of animal rights, assuring readers that he will deal with the subject fairly. Gradually, he unfolds the complexities of a substantial moral issue while avoiding sensationalism. Yet his sensible argument for change will, I think, move many readers (including habitual meat eaters) to ponder deeply what might be done to lessen the suffering of the animals we use for food and clothing. I suspect you will find "An Animal's Place" persuasive and powerful writing.*

Michael Pollan has written about environmentalism and nature for many years; his work has been published in the New York Times, Esquire, Vogue, House & Garden, *and* Harper's Magazine. *His most recent book is* The Botany of Desire: A Planet's-Eye View of the World *(2002).* —J.R.

The first time I opened Peter Singer's *Animal Liberation,* I was dining alone at the Palm, trying to enjoy a rib-eye steak cooked medium-rare. If this sounds like a good recipe for cognitive dissonance (if not indigestion), that was sort of the idea. Preposterous as it might seem to supporters of animal rights, what I was doing was tantamount to reading *Uncle Tom's Cabin* on a plantation in the Deep South in 1852.

Singer and the swelling ranks of his followers ask us to imagine a future in which people will look back on my meal, and this steakhouse, as relics of an equally backward age. Eating animals, wearing animals, experimenting on animals, killing animals for sport: all these practices, so resolutely normal to us, will be seen as the barbarities they are, and we will come to view "speciesism"—a neologism I had encountered before only in jokes—as a form of discrimination as indefensible as racism or anti-Semitism.

Even in 1975, when *Animal Liberation* was first published, Singer, an Australian philosopher now teaching at Princeton, was confident that he had the wind of history at his back. The recent civil rights past was prologue, as one liberation movement followed on the heels of another. Slowly but surely, the white man's circle of moral consideration was expanded to admit first blacks, then women, then homosexuals. In each case, a group once thought to be so different from the prevailing "we" as to be undeserving of civil rights was, after a struggle, admitted to the club. Now it was animals' turn.

That animal liberation is the logical next step in the forward march of moral progress is no longer the fringe idea it was back in 1975. A growing and increasingly influential movement of philosophers, ethicists, law professors and activists are convinced that the great moral struggle of our time will be for the rights of animals.

So far the movement has scored some of its biggest victories in Europe. 5
Earlier this year, Germany became the first nation to grant animals a constitutional right: the words "and animals" were added to a provision obliging the state to respect and protect the dignity of human beings. The farming of animals for fur was recently banned in England. In several European nations, sows may no longer be confined to crates nor laying hens to "battery cages"—stacked wired cages so small the birds cannot stretch their wings. The Swiss are amending their laws to change the status of animals from "things" to "beings."

Though animals are still very much "things" in the eyes of American law, change is in the air. Thirty-seven states have recently passed laws making some forms of animal cruelty a crime, 21 of them by ballot initiative. Following protests by activists, McDonald's and Burger King forced significant improvements in the way the U.S. meat industry slaughters animals. Agribusiness and the cosmetics and apparel industries are all struggling to defuse mounting public concerns over animal welfare.

Once thought of as a left-wing concern, the movement now cuts across ideological lines. Perhaps the most eloquent recent plea on behalf of animals, a new book called *Dominion,* was written by a former speechwriter for President Bush. And once outlandish ideas are finding their way into mainstream opinion. A recent Zogby poll found that 51 percent of Americans believe that primates are entitled to the same rights as human children.

What is going on here? A certain amount of cultural confusion, for one thing. For at the same time many people seem eager to extend the circle of our moral consideration to animals, in our factory farms and laboratories we are inflicting more suffering on more animals than at any time in history. One by one, science is dismantling our claims to uniqueness as a species, discovering that such things as culture, tool making, language and even possibly self-consciousness are not the exclusive domain of Homo sapiens. Yet most of the animals we kill lead lives organized very much in the spirit of Descartes, who famously claimed that animals were mere machines, incapable of thought or feeling. There's a schizoid quality to our relationship with animals, in which sentiment and brutality exist side by side. Half the dogs in America will receive Christmas presents this year, yet few of us pause to consider the miserable life of the pig—an animal easily as intelligent as a dog—that becomes the Christmas ham.

We tolerate this disconnect because the life of the pig has moved out of view. When's the last time you saw a pig? (Babe doesn't count.) Except for our pets, real animals—animals living and dying—no longer figure in our everyday lives. Meat comes from the grocery store, where it is cut and packaged to look as little like parts of animals as possible. The disappearance of animals from our lives has opened a space in which there's no reality check, either on the sentiment or the brutality. This is pretty much where we live now, with respect to animals, and it is a space in which the Peter Singers and Frank Perdues of the world can evidently thrive equally well.

Several years ago, the English critic John Berger wrote an essay, "Why 10
Look at Animals?" in which he suggested that the loss of everyday contact between ourselves and animals—and specifically the loss of eye contact—has left us deeply confused about the terms of our relationship to other species. That eye contact, always slightly uncanny, had provided a vivid daily reminder that animals were at once crucially like and unlike us; in their eyes we glimpsed something unmistakably familiar (pain, fear, tenderness) and something irretrievably alien. Upon this paradox people built a relationship in which they felt they could both honor and eat animals without looking away. But that accommodation has pretty much broken down; nowadays, it seems, we either look away or become vegetarians. For my own part, neither option seemed especially appetizing. Which might explain how I found myself reading *Animal Liberation* in a steakhouse.

This is not something I'd recommend if you're determined to continue eating meat. Combining rigorous philosophical argument with journalistic description, *Animal Liberation* is one of those rare books that demand that you either defend the way you live or change it. Because Singer is so skilled in argument, for many readers it is easier to change. His book has converted countless thousands to vegetarianism, and it didn't take long for me to see why: within a few pages, he had succeeded in throwing me on the defensive.

Singer's argument is disarmingly simple and, if you accept its premises, difficult to refute. Take the premise of equality, which most people readily accept. Yet what do we really mean by it? People are not, as a matter of fact, equal at all—some are smarter than others, better looking, more gifted. "Equality is a moral idea," Singer points out, "not an assertion of fact." The moral idea is that everyone's interests ought to receive equal consideration, regardless of "what abilities they may possess." Fair enough; many philosophers have gone this far. But fewer have taken the next logical step. "If possessing a higher degree of intelligence does not entitle one human to use another for his or her own ends, how can it entitle humans to exploit nonhumans for the same purpose?"

This is the nub of Singer's argument, and right around here I began scribbling objections in the margin. But humans differ from animals in morally significant ways. Yes they do, Singer acknowledges, which is why we shouldn't treat pigs and children alike. Equal consideration of interests is not the same as equal treatment, he points out: children have an interest in being educated; pigs, in rooting around in the dirt. But where their interests are the same, the principle of equality demands they receive the same consideration. And the one all-important interest that we share with pigs, as with all sentient creatures, is an interest in avoiding pain.

Here singer quotes a famous passage from Jeremy Bentham, the 18th-century utilitarian philosopher, that is the wellspring of the animal rights movement. Bentham was writing in 1789, soon after the French colonies freed black slaves, granting them fundamental rights. "The day may come," he speculates, "when the rest of the animal creation may acquire those rights." Bentham then asks what characteristic entitles any being to moral consideration. "Is it the faculty of reason or perhaps the faculty of discourse?" Obviously not, since "a full-grown horse or dog is beyond comparison a more rational, as well as a more conversable animal, than an infant." He concludes: "The question is not, Can they reason? nor, Can they talk? but, Can they suffer?"

Bentham here is playing a powerful card philosophers call the "argu- 15
ment from marginal cases," or A.M.C. for short. It goes like this: there are humans—infants, the severely retarded, the demented—whose mental function cannot match that of a chimpanzee. Even though these people cannot reciprocate our moral attentions, we nevertheless include them in the circle of our moral consideration. So on what basis do we exclude the chimpanzee?

Because he's a chimp, I furiously scribbled in the margin, and they're human! For Singer that's not good enough. To exclude the chimp from moral consideration simply because he's not human is no different from excluding the slave simply because he's not white. In the same way we'd call that exclusion racist, the animal rightist contends that it is speciesist to discriminate against the chimpanzee solely because he's not human.

But the differences between blacks and whites are trivial compared with the differences between my son and a chimp. Singer counters by asking us to imagine a hypothetical society, that discriminates against people on the basis of something nontrivial—say, intelligence. If that scheme offends our sense of equality, then why is the fact that animals lack certain human characteristics any more just as a basis for discrimination? Either we do not owe any justice to the severely retarded, he concludes, or we do owe it to animals with higher capabilities.

This is where I put down my fork. If I believe in equality, and equality is based on interests rather than characteristics, then either I have to take the interests of the steer I'm eating into account or concede that I am a speciesist. For the time being, I decided to plead guilty as charged. I finished my steak.

But Singer had planted a troubling notion, and in the days afterward, it grew and grew, watered by the other animal rights thinkers I began reading: the philosophers Tom Regan and James Rachels; the legal theorist Steven M. Wise; the writers Joy Williams and Matthew Scully. I didn't think I minded being a speciesist, but could it be, as several of these writers suggest, that we will someday come to regard speciesism as an evil comparable to racism? Will history someday judge us as harshly as it judges the Germans who went about their ordinary lives in the shadow of Treblinka? Precisely that question was recently posed by J. M. Coetzee, the South African novelist, in a lecture delivered at Princeton; he answered it in the affirmative. If animal rightists are right, "a crime of stupefying proportions" (in Coetzee's words) is going on all around us every day, just beneath our notice.

It's an idea almost impossible to entertain seriously, much less to accept, 20
and in the weeks following my restaurant face-off between Singer and the steak, I found myself marshaling whatever mental power I could muster to try to refute it. Yet Singer and his allies managed to trump almost all my objections.

My first line of defense was obvious. Animals kill one another all the time. Why treat animals more ethically than they treat one another? (Ben Franklin tried this one long before me: during a fishing trip, he wondered, "If you eat one another, I don't see why we may not eat you." He admits, however, that the rationale didn't occur to him until the fish were in the frying pan, smelling "admirably well." The advantage of being a "reasonable creature," Franklin remarks, is that you can find a reason for whatever you want to do.) To the "they do it, too" defense, the animal rightist has a devastating reply: do you really want to base your morality on the natural order? Murder and rape are natural, too. Besides, humans don't need to kill other creatures in order to survive; animals do. (Though if my cat, Otis, is any guide, animals sometimes kill for sheer pleasure.)

This suggests another defense. Wouldn't life in the wild be worse for these farm animals? "Defenders of slavery imposed on black Africans often made a similar point," Singer retorts. "The life of freedom is to be preferred."

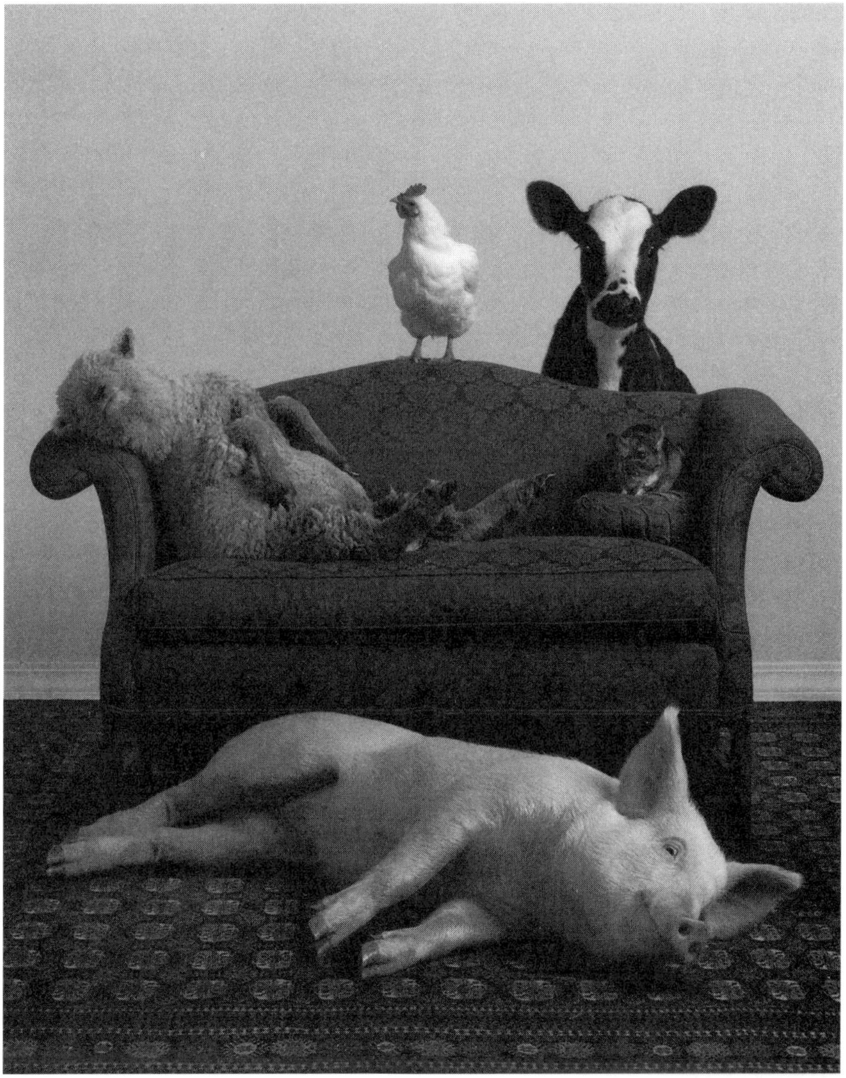

But domesticated animals can't survive in the wild; in fact, without us they wouldn't exist at all. Or as one 19th-century political philosopher put it, "The pig has a stronger interest than anyone in the demand for bacon. If all the world were Jewish, there would be no pigs at all." But it turns out that this would be fine by the animal rightists: for if pigs don't exist, they can't be wronged.

Animals on factory farms have never known any other life. Singer replies that "animals feel a need to exercise, stretch their limbs or wings, groom themselves and turn around, whether or not they have ever lived in conditions that permit this." The measure of their suffering is not their prior experiences but the unremitting daily frustration of their instincts.

O.K., the suffering of animals is a legitimate problem, but the world is 25
full of problems, and surely human problems must come first! Sounds good, and yet all the animal people are asking me to do is to stop eating meat and wearing animal furs and hides. There's no reason I can't devote myself to solving humankind's problems while being a vegetarian who wears synthetics.

But doesn't the fact that we could choose to forgo meat for moral reasons point to a crucial moral difference between animals and humans? As Kant pointed out, the human being is the only moral animal, the only one even capable of entertaining a concept of "rights." What's wrong with reserving moral consideration for those able to reciprocate it? Right here is where you run smack into the A.M.C.: the moral status of the retarded, the insane, the infant and the Alzheimer's patient. Such "marginal cases," in the detestable argot of modern moral philosophy, cannot participate in moral decision making any more than a monkey can, yet we nevertheless grant them rights.

That's right, I respond, for the simple reason that they're one of us. And all of us have been, and will probably once again be, marginal cases ourselves. What's more, these people have fathers and mothers, daughters and sons, which makes our interest in their welfare deeper than our interest in the welfare of even the most brilliant ape.

Alas, none of these arguments evade the charge of speciesism; the racist, too, claims that it's natural to give special consideration to one's own kind. A utilitarian like Singer would agree, however, that the feelings of relatives do count for something. Yet the principle of equal consideration of interests demands that, given the choice between performing a painful medical experiment on a severely retarded orphan and on a normal ape, we must sacrifice the child. Why? Because the ape has a greater capacity for pain.

Here in a nutshell is the problem with the A.M.C.: it can be used to help the animals, but just as often it winds up hurting the marginal cases. Giving up our speciesism will bring us to a moral cliff from which we may not be prepared to jump, even when logic is pushing us.

And yet this isn't the moral choice I am being asked to make. (Too bad; 30
it would be so much easier!) In everyday life, the choice is not between babies and chimps but between the pork and the tofu. Even if we reject the "hard utilitarianism" of a Peter Singer, there remains the question of whether we owe animals that can feel pain any moral consideration, and this seems impossible to deny. And if we do owe them moral consideration, how can we justify eating them?

This is why killing animals for meat (and clothing) poses the most difficult animal rights challenge. In the case of animal testing, all but the most radical animal rightists are willing to balance the human benefit against the cost to the animals. That's because the unique qualities of human consciousness carry weight in the utilitarian calculus: human pain counts for more than that of a mouse, since our pain is amplified by emotions like dread; similarly, our deaths are worse than an animal's because we understand what death is in a way they don't. So the argument over animal testing is really in the details: is this particular procedure or test really necessary to save human lives? (Very often it's not, in which case we probably shouldn't do it.) But if humans no longer need to eat meat or wear skins, then what exactly are we putting on the human side of the scale to outweigh the interests of the animal?

I suspect that this is finally why the animal people managed to throw me on the defensive. It's one thing to choose between the chimp and the retarded child or to accept the sacrifice of all those pigs surgeons practiced on to develop heart-bypass surgery. But what happens when the choice is between "a lifetime of suffering for a nonhuman animal and the gastronomic preference of a human being?" You look away—or you stop eating animals. And if you don't want to do either? Then you have to try to determine if the animals you're eating have really endured "a lifetime of suffering."

Whether our interest in eating animals outweighs their interest in not being eaten (assuming for the moment that is their interest) turns on the vexed question of animal suffering. Vexed, because it is impossible to know what really goes on in the mind of a cow or a pig or even an ape. Strictly speaking, this is true of other humans, too, but since humans are all basically wired the same way, we have excellent reason to assume that other people's experience of pain feels much like our own. Can we say that about animals? Yes and no.

I have yet to find anyone who still subscribes to Descartes's belief that animals cannot feel pain because they lack a soul. The general consensus among scientists and philosophers is that when it comes to pain, the higher animals are wired much like we are for the same evolutionary reasons, so we should take the writhings of the kicked dog at face value. Indeed, the very premise of a great deal of animal testing—the reason it has value—is that animals' experience of physical and even some psychological pain closely resembles our own. Otherwise, why would cosmetics testers drip chemicals into the eyes of rabbits to see if they sting? Why would researchers study head trauma by traumatizing chimpanzee heads? Why would psychologists attempt to induce depression and "learned helplessness" in dogs by exposing them to ceaseless random patterns of electrical shock?

That said, it can be argued that human pain differs from animal pain by 35
an order of magnitude. This qualitative difference is largely the result of our possession of language and, by virtue of language, an ability to have thoughts about thoughts and to imagine alternatives to our current reality. The philosopher Daniel C. Dennett suggests that we would do well to draw a distinction between pain, which a great many animals experience, and suffering, which depends on a degree of self-consciousness only a few animals appear to

command. Suffering in this view is not just lots of pain but pain intensified by human emotions like loss, sadness, worry, regret, self-pity, shame, humiliation and dread.

Consider castration. No one would deny the procedure is painful to animals, yet animals appear to get over it in a way humans do not. (Some rhesus monkeys competing for mates will bite off a rival's testicle; the very next day the victim may be observed mating, seemingly little the worse for wear.) Surely the suffering of a man able to comprehend the full implications of castration, to anticipate the event and contemplate its aftermath, represents an agony of another order.

By the same token, however, language and all that comes with it can also make certain kinds of pain more bearable. A trip to the dentist would be a torment for an ape that couldn't be made to understand the purpose and duration of the procedure.

As humans contemplating the pain and suffering of animals, we do need to guard against projecting on to them what the same experience would feel like to us. Watching a steer force-marched up the ramp to the kill-floor door, as I have done, I need to remind myself that this is not Sean Penn in *Dead Man Walking,* that in a bovine brain the concept of nonexistence is blissfully absent. "If we fail to find suffering in the animal lives we can see," Dennett writes in *Kinds of Minds,* "we can rest assured there is no invisible suffering somewhere in their brains. If we find suffering, we will recognize it without difficulty."

Which brings us—reluctantly, necessarily—to the American factory farm, the place where all such distinctions turn to dust. It's not easy to draw lines between pain and suffering in a modern egg or confinement hog operation. These are places where the subtleties of moral philosophy and animal cognition mean less than nothing, where everything we've learned about animals at least since Darwin has been simply . . . set aside. To visit a modern CAFO (Confined Animal Feeding Operation) is to enter a world that, for all its technological sophistication, is still designed according to Cartesian principles: animals are machines incapable of feeling pain. Since no thinking person can possibly believe this any more, industrial animal agriculture depends on a suspension of disbelief on the part of the people who operate it and a willingness to avert your eyes on the part of everyone else.

From everything I've read, egg and hog operations are the worst. Beef cattle in America at least still live outdoors, albeit standing ankle deep in their own waste eating a diet that makes them sick. And broiler chickens, although they do get their beaks snipped off with a hot knife to keep them from cannibalizing one another under the stress of their confinement, at least don't spend their eight-week lives in cages too small to ever stretch a wing. That fate is reserved for the American laying hen, who passes her brief span piled together with a half-dozen other hens in a wire cage whose floor a single page of this magazine could carpet. Every natural instinct of this animal is thwarted, leading to a range of behavioral "vices" that can include cannibalizing her cagemates and rubbing her body against the wire mesh until it is featherless and bleeding. Pain? Suffering? Madness? The operative suspension of disbelief depends on more neutral descriptors, like "vices" and "stress." Whatever you want to call what's going on in those cages, the 10 percent or so of hens that can't bear it and simply die is built into the cost of production. And when the output of the others begins to ebb, the hens will be "force-molted"—starved of food and water and light for several days in order to stimulate a final bout of egg laying before their life's work is done.

Simply reciting these facts, most of which are drawn from poultry-trade magazines, makes me sound like one of those animal people, doesn't it? I don't mean to, but this is what can happen when . . . you look. It certainly wasn't my intention to ruin anyone's breakfast. But now that I probably have spoiled the eggs, I do want to say one thing about the bacon, mention a single practice (by no means the worst) in modern hog production that points to the compound madness of an impeccable industrial logic.

Piglets in confinement operations are weaned from their mothers 10 days after birth (compared with 13 weeks in nature) because they gain weight faster on their hormone- and antibiotic-fortified feed. This premature weaning leaves the pigs with a lifelong craving to suck and chew, a desire they gratify in confinement by biting the tail of the animal in front of them. A normal pig would fight off his molester, but a demoralized pig has stopped caring. "Learned helplessness" is the psychological term, and it's not uncommon in confinement operations, where tens of thousands of hogs spend their entire lives ignorant of sunshine or earth or straw, crowded together beneath a metal roof upon metal slats suspended over a manure pit. So it's not surprising that an animal as sensitive and intelligent as a pig would get depressed, and a depressed pig will allow his tail to be chewed on to the point of infection. Sick pigs, being underperforming "production units," are clubbed to death on the spot. The U.S.D.A.'s recommended solution to the problem is called "tail docking." Using a pair of pliers (and no anesthetic), most but not all of the tail is snipped off. Why the little stump? Because the whole point of the exercise is not to remove the object of tail-biting so much as to render it more sensitive. Now, a bite on the tail is so painful that even the most demoralized pig will mount a struggle to avoid it.

Much of this description is drawn from *Dominion,* Matthew Scully's recent book in which he offers a harrowing description of a North Carolina hog operation. Scully, a Christian conservative, has no patience for lefty rights talk, arguing instead that while God did give man "dominion" over animals ("Every moving thing that liveth shall be meat for you"), he also admonished us to show them mercy. "We are called to treat them with kindness, not because they have rights or power or some claim to equality but . . . because they stand unequal and powerless before us."

Scully calls the contemporary factory farm "our own worst nightmare" and, to his credit, doesn't shrink from naming the root cause of this evil: unfettered capitalism. (Perhaps this explains why he resigned from the Bush administration just before his book's publication.) A tension has always existed between the capitalist imperative to maximize efficiency and the moral imperatives of religion or community, which have historically served as a counterweight to the moral blindness of the market. This is one of "the cultural contradictions of capitalism"—he tendency of the economic impulse to erode the moral underpinnings of society. Mercy toward animals is one such casualty.

More than any other institution, the American industrial animal farm offers a nightmarish glimpse of what capitalism can look like in the absence of moral or regulatory constraint. Here in these places life itself is redefined—as protein production—and with it suffering. That venerable word becomes "stress," an economic problem in search of a cost-effective solution, like tail-docking or beak-clipping or, in the industry's latest plan, by simply engineering the "stress gene" out of pigs and chickens. "Our own worst nightmare" such a place may well be; it is also real life for the billions of animals unlucky enough to have been born beneath these grim steel roofs, into the brief, pitiless life of a "production unit" in the days before the suffering gene was found.

Vegetarianism doesn't seem an unreasonable response to such an evil. Who would want to be made complicit in the agony of these animals by eating them? You want to throw something against the walls of those infernal sheds, whether it's the Bible, a new constitutional right or a whole platoon of animal rightists bent on breaking in and liberating the inmates. In the shadow of these factory farms, Coetzee's notion of a "stupefying crime" doesn't seem far-fetched at all.

But before you swear off meat entirely, let me describe a very different sort of animal farm. It is typical of nothing, and yet its very existence puts the whole moral question of animal agriculture in a different light. Polyface Farm occupies 550 acres of rolling grassland and forest in the Shenandoah Valley of Virginia. Here, Joel Salatin and his family raise six different food animals—cattle, pigs, chickens, rabbits, turkeys and sheep—in an intricate dance of symbiosis designed to allow each species, in Salatin's words, "to fully express its physiological distinctiveness."

What this means in practice is that Salatin's chickens live like chickens; his cows, like cows; pigs, pigs. As in nature, where birds tend to follow herbivores, once Salatin's cows have finished grazing a pasture, he moves them out and tows in his "eggmobile," a portable chicken coop that houses several hundred laying hens—roughly the natural size of a flock. The hens fan out over the pasture, eating the short grass and picking insect larvae out of the cowpats—all the while spreading the cow manure and eliminating the farm's parasite problem. A diet of grubs and grass makes for exceptionally tasty eggs and contented chickens, and their nitrogenous manure feeds the pasture. A few weeks later, the chickens move out, and the sheep come in, dining on the lush new growth, as well as on the weed species (nettles, nightshade) that the cattle and chickens won't touch.

Meanwhile, the pigs are in the barn turning the compost. All winter long, while the cattle were indoors, Salatin layered their manure with straw, wood chips—and corn. By March, this steaming compost layer cake stands three feet high, and the pigs, whose powerful snouts can sniff out and retrieve the fermented corn at the bottom, get to spend a few happy weeks rooting through the pile, aerating it as they work. All you can see of these pigs, intently nosing out the tasty alcoholic morsels, are their upturned pink hams and corkscrew tails churning the air. The finished compost will go to feed the grass; the grass, the cattle; the cattle, the chickens; and eventually all of these animals will feed us.

I thought a lot about vegetarianism and animal rights during the day I 50
spent on Joel Salatin's extraordinary farm. So much of what I'd read, so much of what I'd accepted, looked very different from here. To many animal rightists, even Polyface Farm is a death camp. But to look at these animals is to see this for the sentimental conceit it is. In the same way that we can probably recognize animal suffering when we see it, animal happiness is unmistakable, too, and here I was seeing it in abundance.

For any animal, happiness seems to consist in the opportunity to express its creaturely character—its essential pigness or wolfness or chickenness. Aristotle speaks of each creature's "characteristic form of life." For domesticated species, the good life, if we can call it that, cannot be achieved apart from humans—apart from our farms and, therefore, our meat eating. This, it seems to me, is where animal rightists betray a profound ignorance about the workings of nature. To think of domestication as a form of enslavement or even exploitation is to misconstrue the whole relationship, to project a human idea of power onto what is, in fact, an instance of mutualism between species. Domestication is an evolutionary, rather than a political, development. It is certainly not a regime humans imposed on animals some 10,000 years ago.

Rather, domestication happened when a small handful of especially opportunistic species discovered through Darwinian trial and error that they were more likely to survive and prosper in an alliance with humans than on their own. Humans provided the animals with food and protection, in exchange for which the animals provided the humans their milk and eggs and—yes—their flesh. Both parties were transformed by the relationship: animals grew tame and lost their ability to fend for themselves (evolution tends to edit out unneeded traits), and the humans gave up their hunter-gatherer ways for the settled life of agriculturists. (Humans changed biologically, too, evolving such new traits as a tolerance for lactose as adults.)

From the animals' point of view, the bargain with humanity has been a great success, at least until our own time. Cows, pigs, dogs, cats and chickens have thrived, while their wild ancestors have languished. (There are 10,000 wolves in North America, 50,000,000 dogs.) Nor does their loss of autonomy seem to trouble these creatures. It is wrong, the rightists say, to treat animals as "means" rather than "ends," yet the happiness of a working animal like the dog consists precisely in serving as a "means." Liberation is the last thing such a creature wants. To say of one of Joel Salatin's caged chickens that "the life of freedom is to be preferred" betrays an ignorance about chicken preferences—which on this farm are heavily focused on not getting their heads bitten off by weasels.

But haven't these chickens simply traded one predator for another—weasels for humans? True enough, and for the chickens this is probably not a bad deal. For brief as it is, the life expectancy of a farm animal would be considerably briefer in the world beyond the pasture fence or chicken coop. A sheep farmer told me that a bear will eat a lactating ewe alive, starting with her udders. "As a rule," he explained, "animals don't get 'good deaths' surrounded by their loved ones."

The very existence of predation—animals eating animals—is the cause of 55
much anguished hand-wringing in animal rights circles. "It must be admitted," Singer writes, "that the existence of carnivorous animals does pose one problem for the ethics of Animal Liberation, and that is whether we should do anything about it." Some animal rightists train their dogs and cats to become vegetarians. (Note: cats will require nutritional supplements to stay healthy.) Matthew Scully calls predation "the intrinsic evil in nature's design . . . among the hardest of all things to fathom." Really? A deep Puritan streak pervades animal rights activists, an abiding discomfort not only with our animality, but with the animals' animality too.

However it may appear to us, predation is not a matter of morality or politics; it, also, is a matter of symbiosis. Hard as the wolf may be on the deer he eats, the herd depends on him for its well-being; without predators to cull the herd, deer overrun their habitat and starve. In many places, human hunters have taken over the predator's ecological role. Chickens also depend for their continued well-being on their human predators—not individual chickens, but chickens as a species. The surest way to achieve the extinction of the chicken would be to grant chickens a "right to life."

Yet here's the rub: the animal rightist is not concerned with species, only individuals. Tom Regan, author of *The Case for Animal Rights,* bluntly asserts that because "species are not individuals . . . the rights view does not recognize the moral rights of species to anything, including survival." Singer concurs, insisting that only sentient individuals have interests. But surely a species can have interests—in its survival, say—just as a nation or community or a corporation can. The animal rights movement's exclusive concern with individual animals makes perfect sense given its roots in a culture of liberal individualism, but does it make any sense in nature?

In 1611 Juan da Goma (aka Juan the Disoriented) made accidental landfall on Wrightson Island, a six-square-mile rock in the Indian Ocean. The island's sole distinction is as the only known home of the Arcania tree and the bird that nests in it, the Wrightson giant sea sparrow. Da Goma and his crew stayed a week, much of that time spent in a failed bid to recapture the ship's escaped goat—who happened to be pregnant. Nearly four centuries later, Wrightson Island is home to 380 goats that have consumed virtually every scrap of vegetation in their reach. The youngest Arcania tree on the island is more than 300 years old, and only 52 sea sparrows remain. In the animal rights view, any one of those goats have at least as much right to life as the last Wrightson sparrow on earth, and the trees, because they are not sentient, warrant no moral consideration whatsoever. (In the mid-80's a British environmental group set out to shoot the goats, but was forced to cancel the expedition after the Mammal Liberation Front bombed its offices.)

The story of Wrightson Island (recounted by the biologist David Ehrenfeld in *Beginning Again*) suggests at the very least that a human morality based on individual rights makes for an awkward fit when applied to the natural world. This should come as no surprise: morality is an artifact of human culture, devised to help us negotiate social relations. It's very good for that. But just as we recognize that nature doesn't provide an adequate guide for human social conduct, isn't it anthropocentric to assume that our moral system offers an adequate guide for nature? We may require a different set of ethics to guide our dealings with the natural world, one as well suited to the particular needs of plants and animals and habitats (where sentience counts for little) as rights suit us humans today.

To contemplate such questions from the vantage of a farm is to appreci- 60
ate just how parochial and urban an ideology animals rights really is. It could thrive only in a world where people have lost contact with the natural world, where animals no longer pose a threat to us and human mastery of nature seems absolute. "In our normal life," Singer writes, "there is no serious clash of interests between human and nonhuman animals." Such a statement assumes a decidedly urbanized "normal life," one that certainly no farmer would recognize.

The farmer would point out that even vegans have a "serious clash of interests" with other animals. The grain that the vegan eats is harvested with a combine that shreds field mice, while the farmer's tractor crushes woodchucks in their burrows, and his pesticides drop songbirds from the sky. Steve Davis, an animal scientist at Oregon State University, has estimated that if America were to adopt a strictly vegetarian diet, the total number of animals killed every year would actually increase, as animal pasture gave way to row crops. Davis contends that if our goal is to kill as few animals as possible, then people should eat the largest possible animal that can live on the least intensively cultivated land: grass-fed beef for everybody. It would appear that killing animals is unavoidable no matter what we choose to eat.

When I talked to Joel Salatin about the vegetarian utopia, he pointed out that it would also condemn him and his neighbors to importing their food from distant places, since the Shenandoah Valley receives too little rainfall to grow many row crops. Much the same would hold true where I live, in New England. We get plenty of rain, but the hilliness of the land has dictated an agriculture based on animals since the time of the Pilgrims. The world is full of places where the best, if not the only, way to obtain food from the land is by grazing animals on it—especially ruminants, which alone can transform grass into protein and whose presence can actually improve the health of the land.

The vegetarian utopia would make us even more dependent than we already are on an industrialized national food chain. That food chain would in turn be even more dependent than it already is on fossil fuels and chemical fertilizer, since food would need to travel farther and manure would be in short supply. Indeed, it is doubtful that you can build a more sustainable agriculture without animals to cycle nutrients and support local food production. If our concern is for the health of nature—rather than, say, the internal consistency of our moral code or the condition of our souls—then eating animals may sometimes be the most ethical thing to do.

There is, too, the fact that we humans have been eating animals as long as we have lived on this earth. Humans may not need to eat meat in order to survive, yet doing so is part of our evolutionary heritage, reflected in the design of our teeth and the structure of our digestion. Eating meat helped make us what we are, in a social and biological sense. Under the pressure of the hunt, the human brain grew in size and complexity, and around the fire where the meat was cooked, human culture first flourished. Granting rights to animals may lift us up from the brutal world of predation, but it will entail the sacrifice of part of our identity—our own animality.

Surely this is one of the odder paradoxes of animal rights doctrine. It 65
asks us to recognize all that we share with animals and then demands that we act toward them in a most unanimalistic way. Whether or not this is a good idea, we should at least acknowledge that our desire to eat meat is not a trivial matter, no mere "gastronomic preference." We might as well call sex—also now technically unnecessary—a mere "recreational preference." Whatever else it is, our meat eating is something very deep indeed.

Are any of these good enough reasons to eat animals? I'm mindful of Ben Franklin's definition of the reasonable creature as one who can come up with reasons for whatever he wants to do. So I decided I would track down Peter Singer and ask him what he thought. In an e-mail message, I described Polyface and asked him about the implications for his position of the Good Farm—one where animals got to live according to their nature and to all appearances did not suffer.

"I agree with you that it is better for these animals to have lived and died than not to have lived at all," Singer wrote back. Since the utilitarian is concerned exclusively with the sum of happiness and suffering and the slaughter of an animal that doesn't comprehend that death need not involve suffering, the Good Farm adds to the total of animal happiness, provided you replace the slaughtered animal with a new one. However, he added, this line of thinking doesn't obviate the wrongness of killing an animal that "has a sense of its own existence over time and can have preferences for its own future." In other words, it's O.K. to eat the chicken, but he's not so sure about the pig. Yet, he wrote, "I would not be sufficiently confident of my arguments to condemn someone who purchased meat from one of these farms."

Singer went on to express serious doubts that such farms could be practical on a large scale, since the pressures of the marketplace will lead their owners to cut costs and corners at the expense of the animals. He suggested, too, that killing animals is not conducive to treating them with respect. Also, since humanely raised food will be more expensive, only the well-to-do can afford morally defensible animal protein. These are important considerations, but they don't alter my essential point: what's wrong with animal agriculture—with eating animals—is the practice, not the principle.

What this suggests to me is that people who care should be working not for animal rights but animal welfare—to ensure that farm animals don't suffer and that their deaths are swift and painless. In fact, the decent-life-merciful-death line is how Jeremy Bentham justified his own meat eating. Yes, the philosophical father of animal rights was himself a carnivore. In a passage rather less frequently quoted by animal rightists, Bentham defended eating animals on the grounds that "we are the better for it, and they are never the worse. . . . The death they suffer in our hands commonly is, and always may be, a speedier and, by that means, a less painful one than that which would await them in the inevitable course of nature."

My guess is that Bentham never looked too closely at what happens in a 70
slaughterhouse, but the argument suggests that, in theory at least, a utilitarian can justify the killing of humanely treated animals—for meat or, presumably, for clothing. (Though leather and fur pose distinct moral problems. Leather is a byproduct of raising domestic animals for food, which can be done humanely. However, furs are usually made from wild animals that die brutal deaths—usually in leg-hold traps—and since most fur species aren't domesticated, raising them on farms isn't necessarily more humane.) But whether the issue is food or fur or hunting, what should concern us is the suffering, not the killing. All of which I was feeling pretty good about—until I remembered that utilitarians can also justify killing retarded orphans. Killing just isn't the problem for them that it is for other people, including me.

During my visit to Polyface Farm, I asked Salatin where his animals were slaughtered. He does the chickens and rabbits right on the farm, and would do the cattle, pigs and sheep there too if only the U.S.D.A. would let him. Salatin showed me the open-air abattoir he built behind the farmhouse—a sort of outdoor kitchen on a concrete slab, with stainless-steel sinks, scalding tanks, a feather-plucking machine and metal cones to hold the birds upside down while they're being bled. Processing chickens is not a pleasant job, but Salatin insists on doing it himself because he's convinced he can do it more humanely and cleanly than any processing plant. He slaughters every other Saturday through the summer. Anyone's welcome to watch.

I asked Salatin how he could bring himself to kill a chicken.

"People have a soul; animals don't," he said. "It's a bedrock belief of mine." Salatin is a devout Christian. "Unlike us, animals are not created in God's image, so when they die, they just die."

The notion that only in modern times have people grown uneasy about killing animals is a flattering conceit. Taking a life is momentous, and people have been working to justify the slaughter of animals for thousands of years. Religion and especially ritual has played a crucial part in helping us reckon the moral costs. Native Americans and other hunter-gatherers would give thanks to their prey for giving up its life so the eater might live (sort of like saying grace). Many cultures have offered sacrificial animals to the gods, perhaps as a way to convince themselves that it was the gods' desires that demanded the slaughter, not their own. In ancient Greece, the priests responsible for the slaughter (priests!—now we entrust the job to minimum-wage workers) would sprinkle holy water on the sacrificial animal's brow. The beast would promptly shake its head, and this was taken as a sign of assent. Slaughter doesn't necessarily preclude respect. For all these people, it was the ceremony that allowed them to look, then to eat.

Apart from a few surviving religious practices, we no longer have any 75
rituals governing the slaughter or eating of animals, which perhaps helps to explain why we find ourselves where we do, feeling that our only choice is to either look away or give up meat. Frank Perdue is happy to serve the first customer; Peter Singer, the second.

Until my visit to Polyface Farm, I had assumed these were the only two options. But on Salatin's farm, the eye contact between people and animals whose loss John Berger mourned is still a fact of life—and of death, for neither the lives nor the deaths of these animals have been secreted behind steel walls. "Food with a face," Salatin likes to call what he's selling, a slogan that probably scares off some customers. People see very different things when they look into the eyes of a pig or a chicken or a steer—a being without a soul, a "subject of a life" entitled to rights, a link in a food chain, a vessel for pain and pleasure, a tasty lunch. But figuring out what we do think, and what we can eat, might begin with the looking.

We certainly won't philosophize our way to an answer. Salatin told me the story of a man who showed up at the farm one Saturday morning. When Salatin noticed a PETA bumper sticker on the man's car, he figured he was in for it. But the man had a different agenda. He explained that after 16 years as a vegetarian, he had decided that the only way he could ever eat meat again was if he killed the animal himself. He had come to look.

"Ten minutes later we were in the processing shed with a chicken," Salatin recalled. "He slit the bird's throat and watched it die. He saw that the animal did not look at him accusingly, didn't do a Disney double take. The animal had been treated with respect when it was alive, and he saw that it could also have a respectful death—that it wasn't being treated as a pile of protoplasm."

Salatin's open-air abattoir is a morally powerful idea. Someone slaughtering a chicken in a place where he can be watched is apt to do it scrupulously, with consideration for the animal as well as for the eater. This is going to sound quixotic, but maybe all we need to do to redeem industrial animal agriculture in this country is to pass a law requiring that the steel and concrete walls of the CAFO's and slaughterhouses be replaced with . . . glass. If there's any new "right" we need to establish, maybe it's this one: the right to look.

80 No doubt the sight of some of these places would turn many people into vegetarians. Many others would look elsewhere for their meat, to farmers like Salatin. There are more of them than I would have imagined. Despite the relentless consolidation of the American meat industry, there has been a revival of small farms where animals still live their "characteristic form of life." I'm thinking of the ranches where cattle still spend their lives on grass, the poultry farms where chickens still go outside and the hog farms where pigs live as they did 50 years ago—in contact with the sun, the earth and the gaze of a farmer.

For my own part, I've discovered that if you're willing to make the effort, it's entirely possible to limit the meat you eat to nonindustrial animals. I'm tempted to think that we need a new dietary category, to go with the vegan and lactovegetarian and piscatorian. I don't have a catchy name for it yet (humanocarnivore?), but this is the only sort of meat eating I feel comfortable with these days. I've become the sort of shopper who looks for labels indicating that his meat and eggs have been humanely grown (the American Humane Association's new "Free Farmed" label seems to be catching on), who visits the farms where his chicken and pork come from and who asks kinky-sounding questions about touring slaughterhouses. I've actually found a couple of small processing plants willing to let a customer onto the kill floor, including one, in Cannon Falls, Minn., with a glass abattoir.

The industrialization—and dehumanization—of American animal farming is a relatively new, evitable and local phenomenon: no other country raises and slaughters its food animals quite as intensively or as brutally as we do. Were the walls of our meat industry to become transparent, literally or even figuratively, we would not long continue to do it this way. Tail-docking and sow crates and back-clipping would disappear overnight, and the days of slaughtering 400 head of cattle an hour would come to an end. For who could stand the sight? Yes, meat would get more expensive. We'd probably eat less of it, too, but maybe when we did eat animals, we'd eat them with the consciousness, ceremony and respect they deserve.

QUESTIONING THE TEXT

1. In his introduction, J.R. praises this article as the most "powerful . . . example of good argument" that he has ever selected for this book. He gives several reasons for his assessment, stating that the article "embodies

all the principles of a fair and principled rhetoric, grabbing both the mind and heart" and that it "unfolds the complexities of a substantial moral issue while avoiding sensationalism." Working with a classmate, look for examples in Pollan's text that would support J.R.'s claims. Do you agree with J.R.'s assessment of the argument? Why, or why not?

2. What is Pollan's main claim? Where does he reveal this claim? Why do you think he chooses not to put this thesis in the opening paragraph?

MAKING CONNECTIONS

3. "More than any other institution, the American industrial animal farm offers a nightmarish glimpse of what capitalism can look like in the absence of moral or regulatory constraint," Pollan writes (paragraph 45). In "Grade A: The Market for a Yale Woman's Eggs" (p. 191), Jessica Cohen raises a similar issue when she asks, "Should couples be able to pay a premium on an open market for their idea of the perfect egg?" (paragraph 12). Compare the moral and economic concerns in these two arguments. Can you derive a principle that you think should guide human behavior in each of these cases?
4. Pollan suggests that "speciesism" may one day become a "form of discrimination as indefensible as racism or anti-Semitism" (paragraph 2). Use the arguments against racism presented in Martin Luther King Jr.'s "Letter from Birmingham Jail" (p. 163) to judge the validity of Pollan's analogy.
5. It seems that Pollan's main objection to the animal rights movement is that it is parochial, or narrow: it neglects species in its concentration on individuals (paragraphs 57–60). How does this argument compare to that of Peter J. Gomes in "Civic Virtue and the Character of Followership" (p. 242)? Do you think Gomes and Pollan would agree on certain moral principles of human behavior? Explain, using specific examples from each writer's argument.

JOINING THE CONVERSATION

6. Do you or does someone you know make a living from an animal farm, or from another related business that is implicated in the animal rights conflicts Pollan raises (for example, that of a butcher, grocer, restaurateur, or leather goods merchant)? Put yourself in the position of someone whose livelihood depends on the killing of animals, and write a letter to Pollan, responding to his concerns. Can you lend further support to his argument, or do you disagree with some of his points?

7. Pollan says that he tries to limit his consumption of meat to that produced on "nonindustrial" farms (paragraph 81). Use the Internet to research other consumer boycotts related to food production. Discuss with classmates whether you would be willing to support any of these movements.

PETER J. GOMES

Civic Virtue and the Character of Followership: A New Take on an Old Hope

As a very amateur photographer fond of western landscapes, I sometimes return from road trips with prints of canyons, cliffs, or rock formations that seem out of kilter—distorted and oddly incomprehensible—until I turn them 180 degrees and look at them the way I originally shot them. To some extent, that's what the Reverend Peter J. Gomes does in the following lecture on leadership. In a portion of the lecture not included here, he reviews an American political and social landscape that seems familiar and distorted all at the same time, a free nation in which prosperous and oddly contented people complain constantly about the quality of the nation's leaders. Deftly, then, Gomes rotates this portrait and asks his listeners to examine it again, from their point of view as citizens and followers. Can a nation have distinguished leaders, he wonders in the section reprinted here, if leaders do not have virtuous men and women to follow them? In other words, to understand leadership we must also appreciate what Gomes calls good "followership."

Aside from the intriguing issues Gomes raises and the historical perspectives he offers, I chose this selection because it captures a potent rhetorical moment. Gomes delivered "Civic Virtue and the Character of Followership" to a large and enthusiastic audience at the University of Texas on March 24, 1997, his artful phrases and sonorous voice providing a potent lesson in eloquence. Portions of the speech reproduced here in printed form retain some of the oral features that made his performance so memorable. But they only hint at the brightness of the occasion.

Gomes (b. 1942) is Plummer Professor of Christian Morals and Pusey Minister in the Memorial Church at Harvard University. One of America's most distinguished preachers, he is the author of The Good Life: Truths That Last in Times of Need *(2002).* —J.R.

. . .

. . . Those of us who have had to read, and then subsequently have had to teach, the history of the Romans and the Greeks, understand that the greatness of those cultures was never the great leader, it was always the good people, and it is that inversion, or reversion, that has produced much of the dilemma of our modern secular industrialized west. What we have lost, in my opinion, is not a succession of able leaders in church or state or in the civic body, in the sense of a legitimate peoplehood, not just an aggregate population but the sense of an identity and an obligation as people. We have lost, or at least have mislaid, the concept of civic virtue. This is not just shorthand, this notion of civic virtue, again an appeal to conservative culture and family values, this is not an attempt to elect again Bill Bennett* as our philosopher king, but it is an attempt to address the need for a recovery of a sensibility, a sense of what it means to share and to serve in a state which is not driven by our own immediate interests. That is perhaps one of the most radical statements that a speaker would be permitted to get away with today before a reasonably comprehending audience.

A citizen is one who belongs and who has obligations: those are the two fundamental pillars upon which the notion of belonging to the *civitas,* the people or the city, is based, the notion of belonging, of having an identity of which one is proud and by which one is defined, and having an obligation to share and to serve in behalf of that greater good. The purpose of such an aggregation of citizens is not rights but obligations, and consists not first in self but first in duty. Now these are stern, old-fashioned, and strangely foreign words to us because for at least a hundred years and maybe a hundred more years than that, we have been taught by precept and example exactly the opposite, and I would be the last person to deny that I have benefited from parts of that agenda. I have enjoyed the benefits of living in a state which takes care of and is concerned for and is passionate about the individual, which allows individual rights and individual merits to determine the cultural marketplace of ideas, and which is concerned at great cost to protect the individual over against an overweening or an imperious or an indifferent state. We are in this country remarkably free from the tyranny of majoritarian rule, though that is always present in the process by which we do our business. I, and all of you, have taken the benefit of all of that, but we have reached the point, I think, where it is important to say well and good, but not enough. There must be more to this, and in part that more is the return to something which we may once have understood but from which we have long departed.

The Roman understood that to be a citizen of the republic or of the empire was to belong to something that was great and good that exceeded the individual compass of his own experience or his own needs, or his own opportunities. Citizenship in that sense was the highest right to which an individual could aspire, to be a part of such a community. It was in 1986, for example, that somebody struggled greatly with trying to achieve the kind of culture in which citizenship could be affirmed in this way. I quote from Václav Havel: "Without free, self-respecting and autonomous citizens, there can be no free and independent nations. Without internal peace, that is, peace among citizens and between citizens and the state, there can be no guarantee of external peace." That is an attempt to define the relationship of the individual to the whole, the private agenda to the public weal.

Bill Bennett: William J. Bennett, former U.S. drug czar and secretary of education. Author of *The Book of Virtues:A Treasury of Great Moral Stories* (1993).

It was the American judge at the Nuremberg Trials and a justice of the Supreme Court, Judge Robert Jackson, who wrote in 1950, "It is not the function of our government to keep the citizen from falling into error, it is the function of the citizen to keep the government from falling into error."

It would be no less robust an American than Theodore Roosevelt, who in 1902 would say that "The first requirement of a good citizen in this republic of ours is that he shall be able to pull his weight."

Now, these are invocations of relationships as well as of obligations and responsibilities, but the best of these senses of citizenship is contained not in the words of a philosopher or a politician or a theorist of government, but rather in the Nebraska-bred and Plains-fed poet and writer, Willa Cather, who defined happiness in this way: "That is happiness; to be dissolved into something complete and great." Let me repeat that: "That is happiness; to be dissolved into something complete and great." Now we would not necessarily look to that phrase to define the essence or the nature of citizenship and followership, but I suggest that that may very well be an exercise not in English literature but in civics. Modernity, contemporary American culture, would in that definition of Willa Cather, emphasize happiness: "That is happiness . . ." for everybody, even those who can hardly read or write, knows that we are guaranteed the right to the pursuit of happiness. All other obligations fall into disrepair by comparison to our pursuit of happiness, and that is the resonant word: I have a right to be happy, I have a desire to be happy, I have a constitutional liberty to be happy, and I will be as happy as I can be no matter how miserable it makes me or anybody else.

We focus on the word happiness, but those of you who know how to parse a sentence, those of you who know the functions of punctuation, should know when you see "That is happiness;" (semi-colon), that behind the semi-colon is what it is all about, that that is where the expectation is to be fulfilled. So, when she says "That is happiness;" (semi-colon), she then says "to be dissolved into something complete and great." That is what it is about, and strange and foreign is the notion to be dissolved into something complete and great. The notion to be dissolved is offensive to many of us, it means is all of me not to be preserved intact? You mean I'm going to be submerged into something other than myself, my solo apparition is not going to maintain its autonomy and its integrity? To be dissolved? I'm not sure I like that, and to be dissolved into something complete and great? Does that imply that I myself am not complete unless I am dissolved into something? Does it imply that there is something greater than I am, and that without being dissolved into it I will not know what happiness is? Well, the simple answer to that is yes! That is exactly what it means. It means that to be a part of that which is larger, greater, more whole, more complete than I am, is the source of ultimate joy and happiness and responsibility. To be lost into something larger than you are but that unites what you are with all of those other elements is an extraordinary experience.

I was driven around your enormous campus today, shown all of the great and the good landmarks, and of course the most powerful and domineering specter on your horizon is not your famous or infamous tower; oh, by no means, it is not that tower, it is your football stadium, where ritually you are all dissolved into something complete and great, and if you're sober enough to realize what's happening, it's happiness, and you know what it's like. There is no such thing as a solitary autonomous football fan, for either you are with that mindless, screaming, soulless horde, or you're doing other things elsewhere, but you're not up there reading Plato or playing your flute or saying your prayers, you're dissolved into something complete and great. Now all analogies are untidy, all metaphors are a little messy, that's why we have so many of them, and I won't stake my entire reputation on the analogy of the UT [University of Texas] football stadium to the idea of civic virtue, but you get the idea. You can figure it out for yourselves, and go home and speculate on it if you will. That is what it's about, but we, I think, have this inner longing, this deep-seated longing for this great leader on this white horse, at least we think that's what we want. Every November we hear about how bleak the choices are, how few white horses and how far too many potentially inadequate horsemen and women there are to ride them, but I don't think that's the real longing. That is the sort of thing you tell to the pollsters, and we all know that we don't tell the truth in that setting, we tell the truth to God but we lie to the pollsters.

I think that this basic longing we have is not for this Anthony Lewis–like leader.* I think the civil yearning, groaning, is for something worth believing in, something worthy of our loyalty and passion, something that suggests that to follow is as honorable as to lead, and in fact, that is what I mean by "followership," the notion that the loyalty to an idea and not to an individual, to a passion and not to a program, to a vision and not to an entitlement, is the entity to which we give our ultimate loyalty. We are led by that conviction, by that consensus; and the articulation of that conviction, that sensitivity, that sense of place and person, is what I call "followership," being led by that which is greater than any of us or any of our needs or our ambitions.

Now, because I am both an academic and a clergyman, I have examples 10
to offer to you, historical examples which you can examine at your leisure in the university library with your professors, or elsewhere. They are well known; I didn't make any of them up, they may be strange to some of you but that's your problem; you haven't read widely or deeply enough, and I hope that by the time this term is over you will correct that for your sake as well as for that of the republic. I have three examples of citizenship that I want to talk about as exemplifying this followership.

Anthony Lewis–like leader: In a portion of the lecture not reprinted here, Gomes discusses an article in which *New York Times* columnist Anthony Lewis calls for "a leader who can lift our aspirations."

Citizenship, in the first case, for Jesus and for St. Paul, was the kingdom of heaven for those two great figures of the world, and in the kingdom of heaven where all of us are meant to be followers there is not a great deal of talk about leadership. There is not a great deal of talk about leadership in the Bible; there is a lot of talk about it in the church, but one must never confuse the church with the Bible. There is not a great deal of talk about leadership in the Bible but there is tremendous talk about followership in the Bible, and to follow Jesus and to follow Paul and to follow God is to enter the kingdom of heaven where the ordinary rules of engagement don't take place anymore, they do not apply. The Beatitudes* tell you that the ordinary convictions about how society is to be organized no longer work. In this world the meek do not inherit the earth. As we say in Cambridge, the meek do not inherit the earth, the meek go to Yale, and you will have your own version of that here I am sure, but in the kingdom of heaven the meek inherit the earth because the ordinary rules of engagement are suspended. Those who mourn are blessed, they are not overwhelmed by their sorrow, and the notion of leadership is overcome by the notion of fellowership, reunion, community, as opposed to the led and the leader. That is one model of leadership. When Paul says "Our citizenship is in heaven," which he does in the epistles, he is saying that the standard for our civic virtue is derived from that heavenly model as opposed to this old broken down earthly one.

Well, Jesus and Paul may be a little much for you; this is, after all, a state university and we perhaps shouldn't be too evangelical under these auspices, so let me take you a few years down the road to St. Augustine. Now, nobody can argue with St. Augustine, a dead white male indeed, but even that does not disqualify him from being taken seriously. In probably the greatest book in the west apart from the Bible, *The City of God,* Augustine talks about the notion of citizenship, of belonging to something that overwhelms and transcends the particularities of our mundane earthly existence; and to be a citizen of the city of God while living on earth is to anticipate bliss, and joy, and to have an identity which is formed both by that to which we belong and that to which we aspire. So, Augustine manages this double hat-trick, that is to say, we celebrate that to which we aspire and we make it happen by the nature of that to which we belong here and now, so that we're not overwhelmed, daunted, or intimidated by this fallen world because we are, in his delicious phrase, a "colony of heaven"; we are an outpost of an external overwhelming force into which ultimately we are to be dissolved.

Now, perhaps that is a little medieval and esoteric and foreign, for after all Augustine was an African and spoke Latin, so if we want to bring this a little closer to home, well, we come to Massachusetts where all good things in

Beatitudes: the blessings offered by Jesus in the Sermon on the Mount, such as "Blessed are the poor in spirit, for theirs is the kingdom of heaven," from the biblical New Testament (Matt. 5:3–12)

the new world began, of course, and we look first at the landing in 1620 in my native town of Plymouth, of the Pilgrims, those people who landed on or near or under or around Plymouth Rock, that disappointing stone that you've all visited and wondered whether this is it. Well it *is* it, but there's more to it than that, and the more to it I'm about to tell you. They produced a remarkable document called the Mayflower Compact, in which they defined themselves, aboard the *Mayflower* in November 1620, as a civil body politic. Now there's a great deal of romantic nonsense about the Mayflower Compact, and you may have learned about it in high school. Undo it, let me put you straight, I, as president of the Pilgrim Society. The civil body politic of which they were speaking was not some pure abstraction either from the Bible or from Plato, or even from Machiavelli or Thomas More, of whom they would have disapproved. It was an attempt, an expedient, to provide for the necessary ordering of society by a group of willful and ignorant and unruly people who needed wise restraints in order to make them free, and the best way that that freedom could be defined, protected, and derived was by the submission of those freedoms in a larger body, the civil body politic. That is the phrase which they extorted from each other and which is at the heart of the Mayflower Compact.

Now, a more famous iteration of this occurs ten years later in Boston Harbor, when Governor Winthrop lands with his Puritans aboard the ship *Arbella,* and in perhaps the most evocative words with which the new settlements in the new world were introduced, Winthrop preaches a sermon aboard the ship, reminding these vain and varied and aggressive Englishmen that the eyes of the world were to be upon them as they started up this new Puritan colony. They were not fleeing in exile and huddled masses yearning to be free, they were going to be an exemplary community to which the world would look. In order to ensure that the world would find them, Winthrop preached them a sermon entitled "A New Modell of Christian Charity," in which he preached the gospel of Christian community which has essentially at its heart charity and submission. He used as one of his texts that marvelous passage from the Sermon on the Mount, that wonderful figure, "We shall be as a city set on a hill," which has become one of the touchstone phrases of our civilized life. So familiar has it become that when it was used in Ronald Reagan's first campaign, people thanked Peggy Noonan* for writing it, thinking that such a clever word-mistress as she was would come up with such an evocative and effective metaphor for the American republic. It took a few people to remind other people, particularly Peggy Noonan, that she didn't make it up, that actually Jesus had said it some time ago, or whoever the Jesus Seminar says said it, and that it was a phrase of some great antiquity but of current power as well.

Peggy Noonan (b. 1950): speechwriter for Ronald Reagan and the first George Bush

So, this notion of a city set on a hill is a city not of rampant individual- 15
ists out trying to make as much of the real estate deal as they can of that city set on a hill, but is actually a city of people who submit themselves to each other and to the common good, out of charity, which is equally translated as love. Submission and love, those are not two words that you hear when you associate the notion of leadership, but they are words that you hear at the heart of the notion of followership. So, the kingdom of heaven, the city of God, the city set on a hill—these are extraordinary, demanding illustrations of what it is I think we desperately yearn for, deserve, and desire; and what is common to them all is the sense of being dissolved into something that is complete and great and that aspires to live up to its highest ideals even when it falls short of those ideals.

What it takes to do that, to achieve that, is not a panoply of powerful leaders but an ever-increasing horde of faithful, articulate, inspired followers from whom, in the fullness of time, when and where and as necessary, appropriate leadership will come. The future health of the republic will not depend, in my opinion, on our ability to ferret out yet more leaders and to generate yet more heroic three-initialled figures to lead us across whatever bridges we happen to be stranded on in the middle. That is not where the future well-being of the republic is. It occurs to me that the future well-being of the republic is to generate an ever-succeeding succession of generations of young men and women like yourselves who are pleased, privileged, and honored to be part of something greater than yourselves, greater than your own ambition, and greater than your own achievement, who in submission and in love are prepared to be citizens of the city of God, members of the republic of virtue, citizens of this great republic of ours. The strength of a people consists not in the greatness of its leaders: that is the thesis I have been beating over and over again. The strength of a people consists in the quality of its followers, people who are led not by leaders but by visions, ideas, ideals, and passions. The great hope of a community, such as this university, is the great hope of the republic itself.

In a small parish church in the little village of Sandwich in Kent, England, in the diocese of Canterbury, there is on the wall an epitaph to a schoolmaster who was schoolmaster to a dear old friend of mine, now a retired bishop. He recalled sitting in the parish church during compulsory chapel as a young boy, when he read this epitaph to the former headmaster of the school, and I jotted it down when he told it to me some years ago: "As a follower he led, as a leader he served, and so he set the feet of many upon the path of life."

Those of us who teach, those of us who aspire to teach, and those of us who learn, and those of us who aspire to learn, could not ask for any better summation of our spot in the world than that. We need no new cadre of leaders—God spare us yet another crop—who will get our trains to run on time while balancing the budget, and at no extra cost to us. Spare us such leaders. We need passionate followers of an ideal of civic virtue, an ideal that does not conform, as St. Paul says in Romans 12:1&2, but is transformed by the renewing of one's mind and one's soul. If we address the question of what it means to follow and what is worth following, what it means to belong, and what it means to be submissive and loving for the larger and general good, and see that as an honorable and compelling and inescapable vocation for us all, leadership will take its place. It will follow from followership in a wonderful application of the biblical principle, when indeed the first will be last and the last will be first, and the first vocation for all of us ought to be as worthy followers of a worthy ideal. Thank you. . . .

QUESTIONING THE TEXT

1. What particular features in the language of Gomes's lecture indicate that it was originally delivered to a live audience? Highlight sentences, phrases, words, and any other items that look like a residue of a spoken, rather than a written, text.
2. Gomes makes quite a point (in paragraphs 6–7) about the semicolon in a sentence he quotes from author Willa Cather: "That is happiness; to be dissolved into something complete and great." Check a writing handbook to see what semicolons do (if you don't already know). Then, in a few sentences of your own, analyze Gomes's interpretation of Cather's claim.

MAKING CONNECTIONS

3. Like Martin Luther King Jr. in "Letter from Birmingham Jail" (p. 163), Gomes is an African American preacher addressing an audience that is predominantly (though not exclusively) white. In a group, explore the dynamics of this rhetorical situation. Consider, especially, how Gomes's reception today may be shaped by the historical influence of King as teacher and minister.
4. After you have thought about the way Gomes defines good "followership," read Marge Piercy's poem "To Be of Use" (p. 793). Do Gomes and Piercy describe the same thing? Compare and contrast their portraits of the people "who do what has to be done."

JOINING THE CONVERSATION

5. Gomes draws upon a variety of sources to argue that it is the responsibility of good citizens to keep the state from error—and not vice versa. Write a comparison or contrast essay that explores this notion, investi-

gating how a government or institution (perhaps even a college) tries to shape the behavior of its citizens. Conversely, you could consider how citizens (or students) might try to reshape the character and actions of a state or institution. This essay will be easier to write if you work with specific examples of policies, actions, protests, or political movements.

6. A crowd pulling together at a football game is Gomes's example of people ritually dissolving their individuality "into something complete and great" (paragraph 8). Write an essay arguing whether a football crowd is or is not an appropriate analogy for a society that is coming together to achieve a greater good than an individual acting alone might produce.
7. Write an essay evaluating Gomes's conclusion: "The strength of a people consists in the quality of its followers, people who are led not by leaders but by visions, ideas, ideals, and passions" (paragraph 16). Judge it according to your own experiences as well as by evidence of history as you know it.

WENDY SHALIT
The Future of Modesty

*E*ARLY IN A BOOK-LENGTH STUDY *of sexual modesty, perhaps the first such volume ever written by a woman, author Wendy Shalit (b. 1975) introduces readers to* modestyniks*— Orthodox Jewish women who ascribe to a traditional code of behavior that forbids touching between the sexes before marriage. Such behavior seems so odd that many people assume that* modestyniks *must be* abuseniks; *that is, women who are reacting to some previous sexual trauma by repressing sexual desire. Yet, contrary to all expectations, Shalit observes that* modestyniks *seem remarkably well adjusted, even "twinkling," in comparison to most young women living supposedly less repressive lifestyles. So why is modesty so often reduced to a pathology? Shalit concludes that modesty has been misunderstood by our culture, which confuses modesty with prudery. In contrast, she argues that modesty is both natural and erotic. She decides to explore the virtue of modesty in more depth, looking at it historically, culturally, even personally. Some of the conclusions she reaches appear in "The Future of Modesty," a section from her book* A Return to Modesty: Discovering the Lost Virtue *(1999).*

Shalit's study grew out of an article she had written while a student at Williams College to protest unisex bathrooms in her dormitory. She found herself unwilling to accept either the facilities shared with men or the assumptions about sex and sexuality that made coed bathrooms possible. Her willingness to challenge the ideology prevailing at her college led to the discovery that many others shared her belief that both women and men have much to gain from appreciating privacy and the power of mystery in sex.

Shalit graduated from Williams in 1997 with a degree in philosophy. Her writings have appeared in Commentary, Reader's Digest, *and the* Wall Street Journal.

—J.R.

Every day, it seems, another girl is assaulted in school. The day after a 15-year-old girl was sexually assaulted at her Queens high school, *The New York Post* reported: "A teacher at Martin Luther King Jr. High School assigned an explicit sex poem titled *Climaxin'* to his class full of 15-year-olds." It is, needless to say, rather hard to prosecute boys who assault girls when their teachers are doing more or less the same thing to them in the classroom.

Anne Roiphe writes in her latest book, *Fruitful,* that "in the nineteen fifties . . . I was not afraid of being raped; I was afraid of being talked about." She and other women of her generation rejected the culture which valued modesty, because they didn't want to be talked about. A culture which values modesty, after all, had its disadvantages. Obviously you can't praise dressing modestly without, implicitly, condemning immodesty. And one must grant that being talked about *is* unpleasant. It can feel oppressive.

But what is the alternative? We who have grown up in a culture of immodesty tend to find rape much worse than being talked about. You can fear being talked about and still feel safe, whereas if you fear rape and stalking, cannot safely walk in the street alone, cannot be a 9-year-old girl in school without being sodomized, you cannot feel safe. A culture which valued modesty surely had its drawbacks, but now that we have experimented with its opposite, we who have had our sex education in kindergarten and were assigned poems about orgasms instead of Shakespeare in school, we who have watched in horror as our perpetrators of sexual assault get younger and younger—well, we take a different view of things.

Still, even if we could agree it is desirable to return to a culture of modesty, would it even be possible? Don't notions of modesty and shame differ between cultures? Which style would we opt for? In eighteenth-century France, deep décolletage was allowed, but it was considered indecent to reveal the point of the shoulder. The Indian woman is also reticent about revealing her shoulders, but then the Chinese woman is shy about showing her foot, and the Muslim woman, her face. And there is always Stendhal's native woman of Madagascar to reckon with, the one who exposes all the things we cover up here, but would "rather die of shame than expose her arms." What is one to make of her?

Stendhal concludes that therefore sexual modesty must be mostly 5
taught, a product of culture, but is this the only conclusion one could reach about the woman from Madagascar? To me the salient detail is not that she covers up a different part of her body, but that even in Madagascar there is something a woman would "rather die" than reveal. As Kurt Riezler pointed out in 1943, we could not trace, discern, and compare the different manifestations of shame were a fundamentally similar, even universal, attitude to shame not presupposed:

> Anthropologists, in comparing cultures, find different tribes ashamed of different things. Obviously they could not make such comparisons unless they had a certain knowledge of an attitude called shame as distinct from the contents of shame, the *pudenda*. . . . Habits are products of yesterday's conditions. But how is it that each of the different stories has a chapter about shame?

Perhaps the same is true of modesty—another universal instinct hidden within us, suppressed sometimes, but always ready to show its face if we would only allow it. Frances Benton concluded as much in 1956 when she remarked that modesty was a relative, but nonetheless universal, virtue:

> Specific rules about modesty change with the styles. Our Victorian ancestors, for instance, would judge us utterly depraved for wearing the modern bathing suit. Real modesty, however, is a constant and desirable quality. It is based not on fashion but on appropriateness. A woman boarding a subway in shorts at the rush hour is immodest not because the shorts are in themselves indecent, but because they are worn in the

wrong place at the wrong time. A well-mannered and self-respecting woman avoids clothes or behavior that are inappropriate or conspicuous.

Of course to us, that shorts rule seems as quaint as Victorian bathing attire did to Frances Benton. And yet, this may be precisely why modesty is ripe for a return these days. There is simply nowhere else to go in the direction of immodesty, only back.

Though no one wants to be accused of being "prudish," or "reactionary," or—worst of all—"not comfortable with her body," at the same time there is an emerging consensus that things have gone too far.

This is why a counterrevolution may be just around the corner.

10 When I returned to college after publishing an anti-coed bathroom article, I was positively overwhelmed with letters and e-mail messages from female students. Each began a different way—some serious ("I had to share a bathroom with four football players my sophomore year, and it was the most horrible year of my life"), others gleeful ("Dear Sister Chastity: *I can't stand it either!*"). But all eventually got to the same point, which was, I thought *I* was the only one who couldn't stand these bathrooms. One female student confessed that her doctor said she had contracted a urinary infection because she wasn't going to the bathroom enough. "I'm simply too embarrassed," she confided.

Even one girl who *liked* the coed bathrooms wrote me a gushing letter about my "bravery" for "speaking out," as if I had written an anti-Castro screed in Cuba, instead of just a piece about toilets in a free country. To appreciate how much these letters amazed me, one must understand that when I wrote this article I was absolutely sure that I was the only one who was uncomfortable with our coed bathrooms. Our college administration never requires our bathrooms to be coed—students are simply assigned to rooms their freshman year, boys and girls on the same floor, and then they all vote on whether it's "okay" for the floor bathrooms to be coed. Since the procedure was so democratic, and the votes in all the other freshman dorms always went the same way, I naturally assumed that the other students must like the idea of coed bathrooms. But as soon as I spoke up and started to receive these strange letters, each reporting the same "eerie" feeling, it became clear to me that in fact many college students were like me, uncomfortable with not having privacy, but not wanting to seem "uncool" by objecting. Students from various other colleges also wrote to tell me that this was happening all over the country, and wasn't it ridiculous? A few years later, *The New York Times* reported on the "open living arrangements that have been the vogue on campuses for years." Even secular Yale students weren't terribly pleased with today's dormitory arrangements: "Some quietly confessed that the permissiveness of residence life sometimes made them uncomfortable." Soon after, a *New York Times Magazine* profile found that to one young woman, "those same dormitories represent immorality itself, an arena of coed bathrooms, safe-sex manuals and free condoms, a threat to her very soul."

At my own college, the administration ended up changing its policy:

> A Triumph for Modesty: Some incoming freshmen will have to deal with fewer awkward moments than their predecessors, as the College is planning to renovate the Fayerweather and East College dorms this summer, providing a second bathroom for each entry (read: one for each sex). . . . It appears that Wendy Shalit '97, whose article in *Reader's Digest* condemning the bathroom situation garnered Williams dubious distinction in the national spotlight, will finally be avenged.
>
> — *Williams Free Press,* May 19, 1998

The grownups may be afraid to admit it, but clearly the children are rebelling. College students are refusing to live in coed dormitories, and the newest locker room trend among grade and high school students is refusing to shower after gym class. As Dirk Johnson explains in his "Students Still Sweat, They Just Don't Shower" report: "Students across the United States have abandoned school showers, and their attitudes seem to be much the same whether they live in inner-city high-rises, on suburban cul-de-sacs or in far-flung little towns in cornfield country." As he continues:

> Modesty among young people today seems, in some ways, out of step in a culture that sells and celebrates the uncovered body in advertisements, on television and in movies. But some health and physical education experts contend that many students withdraw precisely because of the overload of erotic images . . . the reasons seem as varied as insecurities about body image [to] heightened sexual awareness.

Or, to put it differently, in a different age, when young students were not endlessly bombarded with sexual images, showering could be innocent, a simple matter of proper hygiene. But now that everything has been sexualized, even the most harmless sphere becomes poisoned.

We all want to be cool, to pretend not to care, but our discomfort with 15
immodesty keeps cropping up. In one episode of *Beverly Hills 90210,* America's most popular, and surely most immodest, teen TV drama, aspiring actress "Brenda" accepts a role that requires her to take off her clothes. When the critical moment arrives, though, she can't bring herself to strip. By the end, she muses, "On second thought, maybe masks aren't so bad after all."

Many young women today are having related "second thoughts." *Seventeen* magazine reports that teens are now demanding workshops on manners, of all things. As Alix Strauss explains, "Today's kids want to return to an era of courteousness. Plus, this is about more than just manners. It deals with improving your self-image and self-esteem."

Adults would be mistaken, though, if they thought this return to dignity and propriety is just for show. Today's young women aren't just learning their social graces, but changing their fundamental attitude about sex. For example, in a marked departure from their usual of-course-you-should-sleep-with-everyone pabulum, a 1997 issue of *Glamour* ran an article called "Casual Sex: Why Confident Women Are Saying No." The article explained the role played by oxytocin, the hormone produced during both sex and childbirth which many researchers suspect may be responsible for the bonding response in women. Biologically-based differences between the sexes? Yes. Essentialist? Yes.

Yet later on in the year, all three letters published in response to this piece were positive. Each woman sounded relieved to learn that there was nothing wrong with her for being emotionally attached to her sexual partners. "K.C." from Atlanta wrote that she felt as if the article "was written about me! I am involved in a relationship of sorts with a wonderful guy. From the beginning we established that for us, sex was that and nothing more—no strings attached. Now I am starting to get emotionally involved with him, whether I want to or not. *Glamour* readers, the phrase *casual sex* is the world's biggest oxymoron!" Another woman, Drew Pinkney in Detroit, said she found the article "fascinating. . . . Could this explain why we so often feel irrational attachments for lovers we barely know? Perhaps for women, casual, merely physical sex just isn't in our nature." These kinds of thoughts would have been unheard of in a women's magazine ten years ago.

Clearly modern woman still longs for courtship and romance to satisfy her erotic imagination, but she can only dream inside the world of romance novels and nineteenth-century period dramas. Why? Because outside of fantasy land, the fundamental prerequisite for courtship, a social sanction for modesty, has been denied her.

Thus, the most compelling rationale for a return to modesty is our dis- 20
covery that our culture of immodesty isn't, finally, as sexy as we thought it was going to be. In an article entitled "Modesty Belles: Cover-all Glamour Dives into the Lead," the *Sunday Mirror* reports that "SIZZLING swimwear gets a girl noticed, but it's not always the most revealing style that sends temperatures soaring."

> We put eight of this year's hottest looks to the test and came up with some surprising results. It seems modesty now rules the waves. Today's beach belle prefers a style which leaves more than a little to the imagination. . . . Even the men on our panel of six judges chose a glamorous Forties-styles one-piece over a skimpy string bikini.

But is our current interest in modesty and codes of conduct just a craze, or will today's young women succeed in changing the cultural climate? I think we may succeed, because there is enough dissatisfaction with the current state of affairs, as well as a recognition that the revolution our parents engineered hasn't worked. The most common complaint I hear from women my age is that there is no longer any "dating scene." Young people go out in packs, they drink, they "hook up," and the next day life returns to normal. I suppose you could find much depressing in this behavior—for starters, that there is not even a pretense of anticipation of a love that will last forever in the cold expression, "to hook up"—but there is also a lot about this behavior that should give us hope, and that is the fact that all of them have to drink to do it.

They aren't drinking wine to begin delightful conversation. They are drinking beer and hard liquor to get drunk—precisely to cut off delightful conversation and get "right to the point," as it were. That is the advertised purpose of most college parties, and this kind of drinking is really quite a stark admission: that in fact we realize we are not just like the lower animals, that our romantic longings and hopes should inform our most intimate actions, and that if the prevailing wisdom decrees "hook-ups" don't matter, that sex is "no big deal," then we must numb ourselves in order to go through with it. Thus we pay tribute to the importance of modesty by the very lengths to which we must go to stifle it.

Also, if our hook-ups didn't really matter, then why would we have our checkups? Why all this guerrilla etiquette gushing up from the quarters of the liberated? And why is the most pressing question in all the women's magazines still "how to overcome your hang-ups"?

These kinds of things give me hope that a restoration of a culture of modesty might not only be desirable, but possible. We're all modest already, deep down—because we're human—we just need to stop drinking so much, get off our Prozac, and come out of the closet about it. Like Modesty Anonymous. We would all admit that we are powerless over our embarrassment. That one blush was just never enough.

I'm not a happily married woman or spinster who now wants to spoil 25
your fun. I'm writing because I see so much unhappiness around me, so many women settling for less, because I don't want to settle for less and because I don't think you should have to, either. In 1997, *Marie Claire* tells us about "Daisy Starr's one-night stand." She "knew Joe a bit from going into the bar/cafe where he works . . . we got to his house, we watched cartoons. . . . When I went home with him that night, I hadn't planned on having sex, but I guess I wanted it."

I don't want to have sex because "I guess" I want it. I want to wait for something more exciting than that, and modesty helps me understand why.

It is possible for a young woman to hope for something more, many of us do, and we hereby enter a plea that society permit us to hope for something more. But consider yourself forewarned: If you refuse to be cured of your sensitivity or your womanhood, if you start defending your right to your illusions, be prepared for people to tell you that you are silly and childish. Be prepared for some to make fun of you directly, and for others to be more sophisticated about it and try to reduce your hopes to various psychological maladies.

Don't believe them for a second.

Because the question has been thoroughly examined, in all of its boring detail, the data calibrated and recalibrated, multiple regressions have been performed, and in fact, not all modestyniks are abuseniks. It's actually quite within her rights for a young woman to want to be a woman.

Our culture's message to young women is, It's a free society, dearie, just 30
one teensy footnote, by the way: *You'd better be having many hook-ups—or else! Shyness will not be tolerated! Hang-ups will not be tolerated! Rejection-sensitivity will not be tolerated! Go on Prozac! Lose your curves! Stop being a woman! Stop being a woman!*

But what would happen, I wonder, if women, instead of seeing their romantic hopes as "hang-ups" to get rid of, instead of being ashamed of themselves for being women, would start to be proud of their hesitation, their hopes, and their dignity? What would happen if they stopped listening to those who say womanhood is a drag, and began to see themselves as individuals with the power to turn society around?

Society might very well have to turn around.

QUESTIONING THE TEXT

1. If you have Internet access, use a search engine or an online book service (such as Amazon.com) to locate several reviews of Shalit's *A Return to Modesty*. Read the reviews, and briefly summarize for your classmates the reactions of readers to her argument.
2. Shalit addresses her readers very directly near the end of "The Future of Modesty": "I'm writing because I see so much unhappiness around me, so many women settling for less, because I don't want to settle for less and because I don't think you should have to, either" (paragraph 25). Analyze the entire selection carefully, and then write a brief evaluation of Shalit's ability to connect with her intended audience. Does she do an effective job? Why, or why not? If you have time, you might examine her entire book and extend your evaluation to include more evidence.
3. Shalit claims that younger people are rebelling against the sexual permissiveness they have grown up with. Examine the evidence she offers to support her thesis and, in a group, discuss other phenomena in society and popular culture that you see as either supporting or countervailing this trend.

MAKING CONNECTIONS

4. Shalit defends modesty against the pressure to be "cool." Stephen L. Carter (p. 179) similarly defends integrity against the pressure to "win." Discuss with classmates the ways in which these dilemmas differ and the ways in which they are similar.

JOINING THE CONVERSATION

5. Before she wrote against coed bathrooms in dormitories, Shalit assumed that most other students liked the idea. In taking the position she did, she knew that she risked looking "uncool." Have you had moral objections to a policy or administrative assumption at your school but been similarly hesitant to voice a complaint? If so, consider writing a response to that policy now, perhaps as a letter to the editor to a local or campus newspaper. Alternatively, write a narrative about your experiences dealing with a policy you regard as wrongheaded or even immoral.
6. The headnote to this selection briefly defines terms that Shalit uses in her book. Review the definition of *modestynik,* reread Shalit's essay, and then write an imaginary dialogue that might occur between a modestynik and a fan of *Cosmo* or *GQ* as they watch and evaluate a contemporary television drama or sitcom together (such as *Will and Grace, The West Wing,* or *Gilmore Girls*).
7. In an exploratory essay that draws on sources in addition to Shalit, examine the assumptions behind some aspect of the sexual behavior of your generation (whatever that generation might be). Decide how decisions about right/wrong, ethical/immoral issues are made—if they are. Look for phenomena in the surrounding culture (church, school, clubs, music, movies, advertisements) that send signals about appropriate choices. The essay need not be personal, but do focus on a particular aspect of the question, not on the entire issue of sexual mores.

JIMMY CARTER
Just War—or a Just War?

ON INAUGURATION DAY IN 1981, only moments after Ronald Reagan was sworn in as president, Iran released the fifty-two American hostages it had held for 444 days. Many at the time felt that this hostage crisis had cost Jimmy Carter (b. 1924) the presidency; certainly Reagan based a lot of his campaign on criticisms of Carter's handling of the situation, only to dispatch Carter to Germany to meet the hostages on their return. I was teaching at the University of British Columbia that year, and when I turned on my radio to hear the latest reports, I was startled to hear the voice of a friend—Doug Sager, who had been in graduate school with J.R. and me some five years earlier—reporting on the return of the hostages. Later, in a phone conversation, Doug told me how he had, quite by accident, turned out to be the only reporter/photographer on hand when the hostages touched down on their way to Germany. As a result, he got an exclusive, almost unheard of for a young stringer for the BBC.

I remember this event, and Carter's presidency, especially in regard to the brief editorial Jimmy Carter wrote to the New York Times *on March 9, 2003, just before President Bush's declaration on March 19 of the start of a war against Iraq. As he points out in the editorial, Jimmy Carter knows all about the frustration associated with international crises. He also knows what it means to be president of the United States as well as a deeply committed Christian. He brings all of this experience and authority to bear in words intended for the Bush administration, and his message is straightforward and simple. "For a war to be just," he says, "it must meet clearly defined criteria." As you will see, Carter sets forth four such criteria and concludes that none of them is met in the situation in Iraq. In the aftermath of the war, as no weapons of mass destruction have been found, many readers may want to consider Carter's argument.*

Carter, the thirty-ninth president of the United States, currently serves as chair of the Carter Center in Atlanta. Winner of the 2002 Nobel Peace Prize, he is working as hard as ever to discover peaceful ways to resolve world conflicts. —A.L.

Profound changes have been taking place in American foreign policy, reversing consistent bipartisan commitments that for more than two centuries have earned our nation greatness. These commitments have been predicated on basic religious principles, respect for international law, and alliances that resulted in wise decisions and mutual restraint. Our apparent determination to launch a war against Iraq, without international support, is a violation of these premises.

As a Christian and as a president who was severely provoked by international crises, I became thoroughly familiar with the principles of a just war, and it is clear that a substantially unilateral attack on Iraq does not meet these standards. This is an almost universal conviction of religious leaders, with the most notable exception of a few spokesmen of the Southern Baptist Convention who are greatly influenced by their commitment to Israel based on eschatological, or final days, theology.

For a war to be just, it must meet several clearly defined criteria.

The war can be waged only as a last resort, with all nonviolent options exhausted. In the case of Iraq, it is obvious that clear alternatives to war exist. These options—previously proposed by our own leaders and approved by the United Nations—were outlined again by the Security Council on Friday. But now, with our own national security not directly threatened and despite the overwhelming opposition of most people and governments in the world, the United States seems determined to carry out military and diplomatic action that is almost unprecedented in the history of civilized nations. The first stage of our widely publicized war plan is to launch 3,000 bombs and missiles on a relatively defenseless Iraqi population within the first few hours of an invasion, with the purpose of so damaging and demoralizing the people that they will change their obnoxious leader, who will most likely be hidden and safe during the bombardment.

The war's weapons must discriminate between combatants and non- 5
combatants. Extensive aerial bombardment, even with precise accuracy, inevitably results in "collateral damage." Gen. Tommy R. Franks, commander of American forces in the Persian Gulf, has expressed concern about many of the military targets being near hospitals, schools, mosques and private homes.

Its violence must be proportional to the injury we have suffered. Despite Saddam Hussein's other serious crimes, American efforts to tie Iraq to the 9/11 terrorist attacks have been unconvincing.

The attackers must have legitimate authority sanctioned by the society they profess to represent. The unanimous vote of approval in the Security Council to eliminate Iraq's weapons of mass destruction can still be honored, but our announced goals are now to achieve regime change and to establish a Pax Americana in the region, perhaps occupying the ethnically divided country for as long as a decade. For these objectives, we do not have international authority. Other members of the Security Council have so far resisted the enormous economic and political influence that is being exerted from Washington, and we are faced with the possibility of either a failure to get the necessary votes or else a veto from Russia, France and China. Although Turkey may still be enticed into helping us by enormous financial rewards and partial future control of the Kurds and oil in northern Iraq, its democratic Parliament has at least added its voice to the worldwide expressions of concern.

The peace it establishes must be a clear improvement over what exists. Although there are visions of peace and democracy in Iraq, it is quite possible that the aftermath of a military invasion will destabilize the region and prompt terrorists to further jeopardize our security at home. Also, by defying overwhelming world opposition, the United States will undermine the United Nations as a viable institution for world peace.

What about America's world standing if we don't go to war after such a great deployment of military forces in the region? The heartfelt sympathy and friendship offered to America after the 9/11 attacks, even from formerly antagonistic regimes, has been largely dissipated; increasingly unilateral and domineering policies have brought international trust in our country to its lowest level in memory. American stature will surely decline further if we launch a war in clear defiance of the United Nations. But to use the presence and threat of our military power to force Iraq's compliance with all United Nations resolutions—with war as a final option—will enhance our status as a champion of peace and justice.

QUESTIONING THE TEXT

1. In rhetoric, *ethos* refers to an appeal from the character of the writer or speaker—a statement that persuades you to believe the argument or take it seriously because the speaker seems credible or trustworthy. How does Carter use ethos in his effort to persuade readers that war in this case is not just? Do you find this ethical appeal effective? Why, or why not?
2. Given the constraints of the op-ed—a genre that is usually limited to 750 words or so—does Carter do a good job of supporting his contention that the situation in Iraq did not meet the criteria of a just war? How might he strengthen the argument, if he were allowed more space?
3. Does Carter address potential counterarguments to his position? What other potential arguments against his claims might he have addressed?

MAKING CONNECTIONS

4. Given the preceding explanation of ethos, compare the ethical appeals—appeals from ethos—of other writers in this chapter. How do these appeals contribute to their moral arguments?
5. Carter's op-ed and that of Elie Wiesel (p. 262) pose contrary opinions on the same issue. Which do you find more convincing, and why?

JOINING THE CONVERSATION

6. Write an op-ed of 700 to 800 words, presenting a third position on the question of whether the war with Iraq in March–April 2003 was justified.

ELIE WIESEL
Peace Isn't Possible in Evil's Face

*E*VEN THE WINNER OF A NOBEL PEACE PRIZE *like Elie Wiesel (b. 1928) can sometimes be an advocate for war when he believes the greater evil is to remain silent in the face of evil. Wiesel became an eyewitness to the most profound evil of the twentieth century when, in 1944 as an adolescent, he was deported to the Auschwitz concentration camp. There he saw men, women, and children slaughtered by a German Nazi regime committed to the extinction of Jews and other groups it considered inferior or threatening.*

Author of more than thirty books, including his most well-known autobiographical novel, Night *(1961), Wiesel has dedicated his life to making certain that the victims of the Holocaust will never be forgotten and that the lessons learned from that genocide will not be ignored by contemporary leaders. For his efforts, Wiesel, born in Romania but now an American citizen, won the Nobel Peace Prize in 1986. He chaired the commission that recommended the creation of a Holocaust Memorial Museum on the Mall in Washington, D.C. That museum opened in 1993.*

By virtue of his life and his work, Wiesel was uniquely positioned in spring 2003 to assess the righteousness of a looming American and British war to disarm the Iraqi regime of President Saddam Hussein. The following op-ed piece appeared in the Los Angeles times on March 11, 2003. In taking up the cause of the war, Wiesel found himself on the other side of the question from 2002 Nobel Peace Laureate and former President of the United States, Jimmy Carter. As you will see, Wiesel believes that "where evil is in control," we have an obligation to act. He, if anyone, should know precisely why. —J.R.

Under normal circumstances, I might have joined those peace marchers who, here and abroad, staged public demonstrations against an invasion of Iraq. After all, I have seen enough of the brutality, the ugliness, of war to oppose it heart and soul. Isn't war forever cruel, the ultimate form of violence? It inevitably generates not only loss of innocence but endless sorrow and mourning. How could one not reject it as an option?

And yet, this time I support President Bush's policy of intervention to eradicate international terrorism, which, most civilized nations agree, is the greatest threat facing us today. Bush has placed the Iraqi war into that context; Saddam Hussein is the ruthless leader of a rogue state to be disarmed by whatever means is necessary if he does not comply fully with the United Nations' mandates to disarm. If we fail to do this, we expose ourselves to terrifying consequences.

In other words: Though I oppose war, I am in favor of intervention when, as in this case because of Hussein's equivocations and procrastinations, no other option remains.

The recent past shows that only military intervention stopped bloodshed in the Balkans and destroyed the Taliban regime in Afghanistan. Moreover, had the international community intervened in Rwanda, more than 800,000 men, women and children would not have perished there.

Had Europe's great powers intervened against Adolf Hitler's aggressive 5
ambitions in 1938 instead of appeasing him in Munich, humanity would have been spared the unprecedented horrors of World War II.

Does this apply to the present situation in Iraq? It does. Hussein must be stopped and disarmed. Even our European allies who oppose us now agree in principle, though they insist on waiting.

But time always plays in dictators' favor. Having managed to hide his biological weapons, Hussein's goal is to be able to choose the time and the place for using them. Surely that is why he threw out the U.N. inspectors four years ago. If he now appears to offer episodic minor concessions, just as surely that is because American troops are massing at his borders.

In certain political circles, one hears demands for proof that Hussein is still in possession of forbidden weapons. Some European governments evidently do not believe Secretary of State Colin L. Powell's statement that Hussein has such weapons, but I do, and here is why:

Powell is a great soldier and one who does not like war. It was he who prevailed upon then-President Bush in 1991 not to enter Baghdad. It was he who advised the current president not to bypass the U.N. system. If he says that he has proof of Hussein's criminal disregard of the U.N. resolutions, I believe him. I believe that a man of his standing would not jeopardize his name, his career, his prestige, his past and his honor.

We have known for a long time that the Iraqi ruler is a mass murderer. 10
In the late 1980s, he ordered tens of thousands of his own citizens gassed to death. In 1990, he invaded Kuwait. After his defeat, he set its oil fields on fire, thus causing the worst ecological disaster in history. He also launched Scud missiles on Israel, which was not a participant in that war. He should have been indicted then for crimes against humanity. Serbia's Slobodan Milosevic was arrested and brought to trial for less.

Add to the evidence against him Hussein's conversation with CBS anchor Dan Rather. Listening to him declaring that Iraq was not defeated in 1991 made one wonder about his sanity; he appears to live a world of fantasy and hallucination.

The nightmarish question of what such a man might do with his arsenal of unconventional weaponry is why, more than ever, some of us believe in intervention. We must deal sooner rather than later with this madman whose possession of weapons of mass destruction threatens to provoke an ever-widening conflagration. What it comes down to is this: We have a moral obligation to intervene where evil is in control. Today, that place is Iraq.

QUESTIONING THE TEXT

1. Like Jimmy Carter ("Just War—or a Just War?" p. 259), Wiesel makes some appeals from ethos—references to his own credibility or trustworthiness—in his argument. J.R. alludes to these ethical appeals with the comment, "Wiesel believes that 'where evil is in control,' we have an obligation to act. He, if anyone, should know precisely why." Do you find Wiesel's appeals from ethos persuasive? Why, or why not?
2. Make a list of Wiesel's reasons for supporting war with Iraq, paraphrasing them. What are the bases of those reasons? Do they support Wiesel's claim that war fulfills a "moral obligation" to act against "evil"? Explain.

MAKING CONNECTIONS

3. Compare Wiesel's and Carter's respective arguments on the question of whether to wage war in the particular situation they address. On what points do they agree and disagree?
4. How does the issue of "just war" compare to other moral issues addressed in this chapter? With a group of classmates, see if you can agree upon a continuum of issues addressed, from least to most pressing. Upon what criteria will you base your judgments? If you have trouble coming to a consensus, what are the sticking points?

JOINING THE CONVERSATION

5. Have you ever faced a life-or-death question? Can you imagine one that you might face, personally or professionally, sometime in the future? Freewrite on the possibilities you envision, exploring ways in which issues raised by writers in this chapter might help you make a difficult decision that could have a great impact on your life or on the lives of others.

KATHLEEN NORRIS
Little Girls in Church

Kathleen Norris (b. 1947) has published many works since graduating from Bennington College in 1969. In addition to Little Girls in Church *(1995), from which the following poem is taken, Norris has published five poetry chapbooks and two other full-length books of poetry,* Falling Off *(1971) and* The Middle of the World *(1981). Although she lives in western South Dakota with her husband, the poet David Dwyer, she has written two compelling nonfiction books while living in monasteries, including* Dakota: A Spiritual Geography *(1993). In* Cloister Walk *(1996), a second book of nonfiction, she continues her exploration of spiritual places and spaces. Her favorite piece in this book, Norris says, is one that describes and reflects on the wide-ranging responses that Benedictine nuns gave to her question of why they do or do not wear habits. A more recent book is* Amazing Grace: A Vocabulary of Faith *(1998), a meditation on the language of Christian belief.*

Norris's poem "Little Girls in Church" also records a wide range of responses to the question of faith and its moral relationship to institutionalized religion. For me, the poem calls up the many Sundays I spent in my grandmother's Baptist church and in my parents' Presbyterian one, days that run together in my memory of Bible-school stories (I still vividly recall Joseph and his Coat of Many Colors), covered-dish suppers, prayer meetings, and songs—lots and lots of songs. I wonder what memories Norris's words may evoke for you.

—A.L.

I

I've made friends
with a five-year-old
Presbyterian. She tugs at her lace collar,
I sympathize. We're both bored.
I give her a pencil;
she draws the moon,
grass, stars, and
I name them for her,
printing in large letters.
The church bulletin
begins to fill.
Carefully, she prints her name
on it, *KATHY,* and hands it back.

Just last week,
in New York City, the Orthodox liturgy
was typically intimate,
casual. An old woman greeted the icons
one by one
and fell asleep
during the Great Litany.
People went in and out,
to smoke cigarettes and chat on the steps.

A girl with long brown braids
was led to the icons
by her mother. They kissed each one,
and the girl made a confession
to the youngest priest. I longed to hear it,
to know her name.

II

I worry for the girls.
I once had braids,
and wore lace that made me suffer.
I had not yet done the things
that would need forgiving.

Church was for singing, and so I sang.
I received a Bible, stars
for all the verses;
I turned and ran.

The music brought me back
from time to time,
singing hymns
in the great breathing body
of a congregation.
And once in Paris, as
I stepped into Notre Dame
to get out of the rain,
the organist began to play:
I stood rooted to the spot,
looked up, and believed.

It didn't last.
Dear girls, my friends,
may you find great love
within you, starlike
and wild, as wide as grass,
solemn as the moon.
I will pray for you, if I can.

IN RESPONSE

1. Norris's narrator talks about the songs and hymns of the church she attended. What songs or lullabies do you remember from your childhood? Choose one, and jot down what you remember of its words and what you liked (or disliked) about it. Bring your notes to class for discussion.
2. Think for a while about your own spiritual and/or religious beliefs—or about your secular beliefs. Then try your hand at writing a brief poem that would capture the essence of those beliefs. Bring your poem to class to share with others.
3. What in Norris's poem helps readers understand why she "worr[ies] for the girls"?

OTHER READINGS

Brilmayer, Lea. *American Hegemony: Political Morality in a One-Superpower World.* New Haven: Yale UP, 1994. Examines whether it is morally acceptable for the United States to dominate or police other countries.

Caputo, Philip. "Alone." *Men's Journal* Aug. 1998: 78–83. Argues that human civilization needs the moral centering provided by wilderness and solitude.

Friedman, Thomas L. *Longitudes and Attitudes: Exploring the World After September 11.* New York: Farrar Straus & Giroux, 2002. A collection of post-9/11 columns from the foreign affairs columnist of the *New York Times.*

Henry, Patrick, et al. "Symposium: Is Morality a Non-aim of Education?" *Philosophy and Literature* Apr. 1998: 136–99. Eight scholars respond to the claim that a university is not responsible for offering moral guidance to students.

Neuhaus, Richard John. "The Empty Creche." *National Review* 31 Dec. 1996: 29–31. Explores how removing Christian elements from the observance of Christmas undermines spiritual and moral values.

Norris, Kathleen. *Dakota: A Spiritual Geography.* New York: Ticknor, 1993. A memoir about place, morality, and spirituality.

Reeves, Richard. "I'm Sorry, Mr. President." *American Heritage* Dec. 1996: 53–55. A journalist apologizes for contributing to the corruption of public discourse.

Reid, Elwood. "My Body, My Weapon, My Shame." *GQ,* 1997: 360–367. A former football player recounts his experiences on the team at the University of Michigan.

Spencer, Colin. *Vegeterianism: A History.* New York: Four Walls Eight Windows, 2002. An in-depth account of vegetarianism from prehistory to the present.

ELECTRONIC RESOURCES

http://ispp.org/ISPP/bibliographies/genmorbibispp.html
Provides a bibliography for gender-related issues and moral reasoning.

http://www.indiana.edu/~wts/wts/plagiarism.html
Definitions, policies, and examples designed to help students understand the concept and consequences of plagiarism.

Look closely at the photograph of the AbioCor artificial heart on the preceding page. This artificial heart is currently in clinical trial stages and may be available to patients by mid-2004, pending FDA approval. How would you describe the presentation of the heart in the photograph? ■ Consider the way the heart is displayed as an object, the background and setting in which the heart is placed, the way it is framed as the photograph's subject. ■ How does this presentation affect your response to the image? ■ What does this image suggest about the relationships between humans and technologies? ■ What questions does it evoke for you?

5

Science and Technology: O Brave New World

Learn from me . . . how dangerous is the acquirement of knowledge, and how much happier that man is who believes his native town to be the world, than he who aspires to become greater than his nature will allow.

MARY SHELLEY, *Frankenstein*

Resistance to science is born of fear. Fear, in turn, is bred by ignorance. And it is ignorance that is our deepest malady. J. MICHAEL BISHOP, *Enemies of Promise*

Genetically engineered insects, fish and domesticated animals have also been introduced, like the sheep/goat hybrid "geep." JEREMY RIFKIN, *Biotech Century*

[T]he battle over computers . . . is not just the future versus the past, uncertainty versus nostalgia; it is about encouraging a fundamental shift in personal priorities—a minimizing of the real, physical world in favor of an unreal "virtual" world. TODD OPPENHEIMER, *The Computer Delusion*

The history of African-Americans since the discovery of the New World is the story of their encounter with technology, an encounter that has proved perhaps irremediably devastating to their hopes, dreams, and possibilities.

ANTHONY WALTON, *Technology Versus African-Americans*

Imagine the country we now inhabit—big, urban, prosperous—with one exception: the automobile has not been invented.

JAMES Q. WILSON, *Cars and Their Enemies*

That helpful House trio, Reps. Dick Armey, Tom DeLay and J. C. Watts, wrote Bush a letter calling stem-cell research "an industry of death." Funny, I've never heard any of them describe arms manufacturers that way.

MOLLY IVINS, *Bush's Brain Straddles the Fence Once Again*

The United States has a long and proud record of leading the world toward advances in science and medicine that improve human life. And the United States has a long and proud record of upholding the highest standards of ethics as we expand the limits of science and knowledge.

GEORGE W. BUSH, *Speech to the Nation on Stem Cell Research*

The old AI debates were about the technical abilities of machines. The new ones will be about the emotional vulnerabilities of people.

SHERRY TURKLE, *Cuddling Up to Cyborg Babies*

The economic advantage of massive, unregulated development of the parks was only one reason for the Website move. Safety was also a factor.

THE ONION, *New National Parks Website Makes National Parks Obsolete*

Introduction

TIME AND AGAIN in the twentieth century, we have found that scientists and engineers—like the hero of Mary Shelley's *Frankenstein* (1818)—have created technologies that drive our society to the limits of what it can grasp legally and ethically. Indeed, there seems to be no boundary to what the human imagination can first contemplate and then achieve. Scientists have already mapped out the genes that control life, performed surgery in the womb, extracted the secrets of the atom, and etched the pathways of human knowledge onto tiny silicon chips. Occasionally, experiments escape our control, and we watch them poison our landscapes or explode before our eyes. But the quest for knowledge continues.

Julius Caesar, a military genius and a shrewd politician, observed once that "it is better to have expanded the frontiers of the mind than to have pushed back the boundaries of the empire." As Caesar doubtless understood, the two achievements often amount to the same thing, the powers of mind enabling one people or nation to dominate others, to cast itself in the role of a god and its neighbors as servants or slaves.

This chapter is designed to explore the resonances of *Frankenstein,* the many questions it raises, and the ways it leads us to think about science, progress, and alienation. In our mythologies, ancient and modern, we show a fondness for rebels like Victor Frankenstein, who would steal the fire of the gods and, with their new knowledge, shake the foundations of empires. Yet we cannot entirely identify with such figures either. They remain a threat to us too, a reminder that humanity finally lacks the wisdom to play God.

Your own thinking about these issues may be stimulated by considering the following questions:

- Why do contemporary readers and moviegoers continue to find *Frankenstein* fascinating? What makes the intellectual dreamer or the rebel an attractive figure?

- Why does a society usually react with suspicion toward people who, like Victor Frankenstein's monster, seem different? How do we define the outsider? How does the outsider act as a result?
- How do we deal with new technologies or learn to assess the impact of older technologies we now take for granted?
- Does scientific or technological progress always entail some loss or disruptive change? You might want to discuss this issue with a group of classmates.

• • •

MARY SHELLEY
Frankenstein

*W*ITH FRANKENSTEIN, *Mary Shelley (1797–1851) created a myth as powerful, complex, and frightening as the monster in the novel itself. The book intrigues us today as a narrative with many dimensions and interpretations. It works as the story of a scientist whose ambitions exceed his understanding, as an account of a scientific project that begins with great promise but leads to disaster, as the lament of an alien creature spurned by his maker, as the tract of an outsider besieged by his sense of difference, as the protest of a rebel striking out against a conventional and restrictive society.*

The daughter of early feminist Mary Wollstonecraft and political theorist William Godwin, and the wife of Percy Bysshe Shelley, Mary Shelley began Frankenstein; or, The Modern Prometheus, *to use its full title, in the summer of 1816 after the poet Byron invited his friends at a lake resort in Switzerland to "each write a ghost story." The short piece she composed eventually grew through several revisions (1818, 1823, 1831) into the novel we know today.*

The protagonist of her work, Victor Frankenstein, is an ambitious young scholar who discovers how to bestow "animation upon lifeless matter." He uses this knowledge to assemble a grotesque manlike creature, and then, horrified by what he has done, abandons it the moment he brings it to life. The following selection from the novel is Victor's account of those events. —J.R.

I see by your eagerness, and the wonder and hope which your eyes express, my friend, that you expect to be informed of the secret with which I am acquainted; that cannot be: listen patiently until the end of my story, and you will easily perceive why I am reserved upon that subject. I will not lead you on, unguarded and ardent as I then was, to your destruction and infallible misery. Learn from me, if not by my precepts, at least by my example, how dangerous is the acquirement of knowledge, and how much happier that man is who believes his native town to be the world, than he who aspires to become greater than his nature will allow.

When I found so astonishing a power placed within my hands, I hesitated a long time concerning the manner in which I should employ it. Although I possessed the capacity of bestowing animation, yet to prepare a frame for the reception of it, with all its intricacies of fibers, muscles, and veins, still remained a work of inconceivable difficulty and labor. I doubted at first whether I should attempt the creation of a being like myself, or one of simpler organization; but my imagination was too much exalted by my first success to permit me to doubt of my ability to give life to an animal as complex and wonderful as man. The materials at present within my command hardly appeared adequate to so arduous an undertaking; but I doubted not that I should ultimately succeed. I prepared myself for a multitude of reverses; my operations might be incessantly baffled, and at last my work be imperfect: yet, when I considered the improvement which every day takes place in science and mechanics, I was encouraged to hope my present attempts would at least lay the foundations of future success. Nor could I consider the magnitude and complexity of my plan as any argument of its impracticability. It was with these feelings that I began the creation of a human being. As the minuteness of the parts formed a great hindrance to my speed, I resolved, contrary to my first intention, to make the being of a gigantic stature; that is to say, about eight feet in height, and proportionably large. After having formed this determination, and having spent some months in successfully collecting and arranging my materials, I began.

No one can conceive the variety of feelings which bore me onwards, like a hurricane, in the first enthusiasm of success. Life and death appeared to me ideal bounds, which I should first break through, and pour a torrent of light into our dark world. A new species would bless me as its creator and source; many happy and excellent natures would owe their being to me. No father could claim the gratitude of his child so completely as I should deserve theirs. Pursuing these reflections, I thought, that if I could bestow animation upon lifeless matter, I might in process of time (although I now found it impossible) renew life where death had apparently devoted the body to corruption.

These thoughts supported my spirits, while I pursued my undertaking with unremitting ardour. My cheek had grown pale with study, and my person had become emaciated with confinement. Sometimes, on the very brink of certainty, I failed; yet still I clung to the hope which the next day or the next hour might realize. One secret which I alone possessed was the hope to which I had dedicated myself; and the moon gazed on my midnight labors, while, with unrelaxed and breathless eagerness, I pursued nature to her hiding-places. Who shall conceive the horrors of my secret toil, as I dabbled among the unhallowed damps of the grave, or tortured the living animal to animate the lifeless clay? My limbs now tremble, and my eyes swim with the remembrance; but then a resistless, and almost frantic, impulse, urged me forward; I seemed to have lost all soul or sensation but for this one pursuit. It was indeed but a passing trance, that only made me feel with renewed acuteness so soon as, the unnatural stimulus ceasing to operate, I had returned to my old habits. I collected bones from charnel-houses; and disturbed, with profane fingers, the tremendous secrets of the human frame. In a solitary chamber, or rather cell, at the top of the house, and separated from all the other apartments by a gallery and staircase, I kept my workshop of filthy creation: my eye-balls were starting from their sockets in attending to the details of my employment. The dissecting room and the slaughter-house furnished many of my materials; and often did my human nature turn with loathing from my occupation, whilst, still urged on by an eagerness which perpetually increased, I brought my work near to a conclusion.

The summer months passed while I was thus engaged, heart and soul, in one pursuit. It was a most beautiful season; never did the fields bestow a more plentiful harvest, or the vines yield a more luxuriant vintage: but my eyes were insensible to the charms of nature. And the same feelings which made me neglect the scenes around me caused me also to forget those friends who were so many miles absent, and whom I had not seen for so long a time. I knew my silence disquieted them; and I well remembered the words of my father: "I know that while you are pleased with yourself, you will think of us with affection, and we shall hear regularly from you. You must pardon me if I regard any interruption in your correspondence as a proof that your other duties are equally neglected."

I knew well therefore what would be my father's feelings; but I could not tear my thoughts from my employment, loathsome in itself, but which had taken an irresistible hold of my imagination. I wished, as it were, to procrastinate all that related to my feelings of affection until the great object, which swallowed up every habit of my nature, should be completed.

I then thought that my father would be unjust if he ascribed my neglect to vice, or faultiness on my part; but I am now convinced that he was justified in conceiving that I should not be altogether free from blame. A human being in perfection ought always to preserve a calm and peaceful mind, and never to allow passion or a transitory desire to disturb his tranquility. I do not think that the pursuit of knowledge is an exception to this rule. If the study to which you apply yourself has a tendency to weaken your affections, and to destroy your taste for those simple pleasures in which no alloy can possibly mix, then that study is certainly unlawful, that is to say, not befitting the human mind. If this rule were always observed; if no man allowed any pursuit whatsoever to interfere with the tranquility of his domestic affections, Greece had not been enslaved; Caesar would have spared his country; America would have been discovered more gradually; and the empires of Mexico and Peru had not been destroyed.

But I forgot that I am moralizing in the most interesting part of my tale; and your looks remind me to proceed.

My father made no reproach in his letters, and only took notice of my silence by enquiring into my occupations more particularly than before. Winter, spring, and summer passed away during my labors; but I did not watch the blossom or the expanding leaves—sights which before always yielded me supreme delight—so deeply was I engrossed in my occupation. The leaves of that year had withered before my work drew near to a close; and now every day showed me more plainly how well I had succeeded. But my enthusiasm was checked by my anxiety, and I appeared rather like one doomed by slavery to toil in the mines, or any other unwholesome trade, than an artist occupied by his favorite employment. Every night I was oppressed by a slow fever, and I became nervous to a most painful degree; the fall of a leaf startled me, and I shunned my fellow-creatures as if I had been guilty of a crime. Sometimes I grew alarmed at the wreck I perceived that I had become; the energy of my purpose alone sustained me: my labors would soon end, and I believed that exercise and amusement would then drive away incipient disease; and I promised myself both of these when my creation should be complete.

It was on a dreary night of November, that I beheld the accomplishment of my toils. With an anxiety that almost amounted to agony, I collected the instruments of life around me, that I might infuse a spark of being into the lifeless thing that lay at my feet. It was already one in the morning; the rain pattered dismally against the panes, and my candle was nearly burnt out, when, by the glimmer of the half-extinguished light, I saw the dull yellow eye of the creature open; it breathed hard, and a convulsive motion agitated its limbs.

How can I describe my emotions at this catastrophe, or how delineate the wretch whom with such infinite pains and care I had endeavored to form? His limbs were in proportion, and I had selected his features as beautiful. Beautiful!—Great God! His yellow skin scarcely covered the work of muscles and arteries beneath; his hair was of lustrous black, and flowing; his teeth of a pearly whiteness; but these luxuriances only formed a more horrid contrast with his watery eyes, that seemed almost of the same color as the dun white sockets in which they were set, his shriveled complexion and straight black lips.

The different accidents of life are not so changeable as the feelings of human nature. I had worked hard for nearly two years, for the sole purpose of infusing life into an inanimate body. For this I had deprived myself of rest and health. I had desired it with an ardor that far exceeded moderation; but now that I had finished, the beauty of the dream vanished, and breathless horror and disgust filled my heart. Unable to endure the aspect of the being I had created, I rushed out of the room, and continued a long time traversing my bedchamber, unable to compose my mind to sleep. At length lassitude succeeded to the tumult I had before endured; and I threw myself on the bed in my clothes, endeavoring to seek a few moments of forgetfulness. But it was in vain; I slept, indeed, but I was disturbed by the wildest dreams. I thought I saw Elizabeth,* in the bloom of health, walking in the streets of Ingolstadt. Delighted and surprised, I embraced her; but as I imprinted the first kiss on her lips, they became livid with the hue of death; her features appeared to change, and I thought that I held the corpse of my dead mother in my arms; a shroud enveloped her form, and I saw the graveworms crawling in the folds of the flannel. I started from my sleep with horror; a cold dew covered my forehead, my teeth chattered, and every limb became convulsed; when, by the dim and yellow light of the moon, as it forced its way through the window shutters, I beheld the wretch—the miserable monster whom I had created. He held up the curtain of the bed; and his eyes, if eyes they may be called, were fixed on me. His jaws opened, and he

---

Elizabeth: adopted sister of Victor Frankenstein

muttered some inarticulate sounds, while a grin wrinkled his cheeks. He might have spoken, but I did not hear; one hand was stretched out, seemingly to detain me, but I escaped, and rushed down stairs. I took refuge in the courtyard belonging to the house which I inhabited; where I remained during the rest of the night, walking up and down in the greatest agitation, listening attentively, catching and fearing each sound as if it were to announce the approach of the demoniacal corpse to which I had so miserably given life.

Oh! no mortal could support the horror of that countenance. A mummy again endued with animation could not be so hideous as that wretch. I had gazed on him while unfinished; he was ugly then; but when those muscles and joints were rendered capable of motion, it became a thing such as even Dante* could not have conceived.

I passed the night wretchedly. Sometimes my pulse beat so quickly and hardly, that I felt the palpitation of every artery; at others I nearly sank to the ground through languor and extreme weakness. Mingled with this horror, I felt the bitterness of disappointment; dreams that had been my food and pleasant rest for so long a space were now become a hell to me; and the change was so rapid, the overthrow so complete!

15 Morning, dismal and wet, at length dawned, and discovered to my sleepless and aching eyes the church of Ingolstadt, its white steeple and clock, which indicated the sixth hour. The porter opened the gates of the court, which had that night been my asylum, and I issued into the streets, pacing them with quick steps, as if I sought to avoid the wretch whom I feared every turning of the street would present to my view. I did not dare return to the apartment which I inhabited, but felt impelled to hurry on, although drenched by the rain which poured from a black and comfortless sky.

QUESTIONING THE TEXT

1. How does Victor Frankenstein explain his drive to work hard to bring a nonliving entity to life? Annotate the margins of the *Frankenstein* selection to highlight places where Frankenstein explains his motives. Do you think any of these motives account for the continuing development of science and technology today? Explore this issue with classmates.
2. To create his monster, what does Victor Frankenstein have to do to himself and to other creatures? Have you ever been so single-minded in the pursuit of a goal or passion? Explain.
3. What precisely about the creature disappoints Frankenstein? In a group, discuss Frankenstein's rejection of his monster, exploring its meanings and implications.

Dante (1265–1321): Italian poet, author of *Divine Comedy*

4. J.R.'s introduction suggests that the Frankenstein story has become a modern myth. How many versions of Shelley's tale can you think of? List them.

MAKING CONNECTIONS

5. Victor Frankenstein warns that knowledge is dangerous: "how much happier that man is who believes his native town to be the world, than he who aspires to become greater than his nature will allow" (paragraph 1). Freewrite on this idea, taking into account the essay in this chapter by J. Michael Bishop (p. 280). Is it likely that men and women will ever live contentedly in their native towns? Why, or why not?
6. Can you think of ways in which the anthologized passage from the novel differs from film versions of the Frankenstein tale you may have seen? Brainstorm a list of differences and jot them down.

JOINING THE CONVERSATION

7. Write a parody of this selection from *Frankenstein*, perhaps detailing the creation and consequences of some similar but more recent "monster," understanding that term broadly or metaphorically. You might even read Dave Barry's "Guys vs. Men" (p. 402) in Chapter 6 for a perspective on the peculiarly male desire to build "neat stuff."
8. Working with a group, discuss the monster as a creature who is similar to but also different from a human being. Can you compare his situation to that of other individuals or groups considered "different" in society? Write a brief position paper about Frankenstein's monster as a symbol of what it means to be different. Is the comparison convincing? Why, or why not?
9. Some critics suggest that *Frankenstein* reflects an early view of industrialization as a monstrous creation out of control. Use the library to learn what changes the industrial revolution was imposing on the landscape of England during the nineteenth century. Try also to determine how favorably people regarded changes such as the building of factories, industrial plants, and railroads. This subject is complex enough to support a full-scale research paper. Give it a try.

J. MICHAEL BISHOP
Enemies of Promise

NOT LONG AGO I discovered that the on-board diagnostic system of my new vehicle will let me know via a "Check Engine" light when I haven't screwed the gas cap on tight enough to prevent fumes from polluting the atmosphere. The computer discovers the problem not by monitoring a crude switch on the gas cap itself but by checking the entire combustion process and searching for irregularities. Anomalies—even momentary ones—detected this way are stored in the computer's memory so a technician can fix them later. The technology in my car is almost as wondrous as that of the Internet, which enables me to converse with people anywhere in the world; or consider the science that produced an asthma medication that enables me to play racquetball without carrying an inhaler. As you might suspect, I'm not in the camp of those who denigrate science or criticize technological change.

I do understand the fears of the Luddites, who yearn for a world less chemically reprocessed and technologically demanding. But I also think that many who criticize science today have either short memories or little historical sense, which is why I wanted to share "Enemies of Promise" by J. Michael Bishop (b. 1936), a professor of microbiology and Chancellor at the University of California, San Francisco, and winner of the Nobel Prize. He warns that the misperceptions many people have about science could have serious consequences for all Americans. The piece is also a fine example of an expert writing clearly to an audience of nonspecialists—something scientists will have to do more often if faith in science is to be restored.

"Enemies of Promise" appeared originally in my favorite magazine, the Wilson Quarterly *(Summer 1995), a publication of the Woodrow Wilson International Center for Scholars.* —J.R.

We live in an age of scientific triumph. Science has solved many of nature's puzzles and greatly enlarged human knowledge. And the fruits of scientific inquiry have vastly improved human welfare. Yet despite these proud achievements, science today is increasingly mistrusted and under attack.

Some of the opposition to science comes from familiar sources, including religious zealots who relentlessly press for the mandatory teaching of creationism in the public schools. It is discouraging to think that more than a century after the publication of Charles Darwin's *Origin of Species* (1859), and seventy years after the Scopes trial dramatized the issue, the same battles must still be fought. But fight them we must.

Other antagonists of science are less familiar. Strange though it may seem, there is within academe a school of thought that considers science to be wholly fraudulent as a way of knowing. According to these "postmodernists," the supposedly objective truths of science are in reality all "socially constructed fictions," no more than "useful myths," and science itself is "politics by other means." Anyone with a working knowledge of science, anyone who looks at the natural world with an honest eye, should recognize all of this for what it is: arrant nonsense.

Science, of course, is not the exclusive source of knowledge about human existence. Literature, art, philosophy, history, and religion all have their insights to offer into the human condition. To deny that is scientism—the belief that the methods of the natural sciences are the only means of obtaining knowledge. And to the extent that scientists have at times indulged in that belief, they must shoulder some of the blame for the misapprehensions that some people have about science.

But science does have something inimitable to offer humankind: it is, in 5
the words of physician-author Lewis Thomas, "the best way to learn how the world works." A postmodernist poet of my acquaintance complains that it is in the nature of science to break things apart, thereby destroying the "mysterious whole." But we scientists take things apart in order to understand the whole, to solve the mystery—an enterprise that we regard as one of the great, ennobling tasks of humankind.

In the academic medical center where I work, the efficacy and benefits of science are a daily reality. So when I first encountered the postmodernist view of science some years ago, I dismissed it as either a strategy for advancement in parochial precincts of the academy or a display of ignorance. But now I am alarmed because the postmodernist cry has been joined, outside the academy, by other strong voices raised against science.

Consider these lines from Václav Havel, the widely admired Czech writer and statesman, who has vigorously expressed his disenchantment with the ethos of science: "Modern rationalism and modern science . . . now systematically leave [the natural world] behind, deny it, degrade and defame it—and, of course, at the same time, colonize it."

Those are angry words, even if their precise meaning is elusive. And anger is evident, too, in Havel's main conclusion: "This era [of science and rationalism] has reached the end of its potential, the point beyond which the abyss begins."

Even some influential men who know science well and who have been good friends to it in the past have joined in the chorus of criticism and doubt. Thanks in part to Havel's ruminations, Representative George E. Brown, Jr. (D.-Calif.), who was trained as a physicist, reports that his faith in science has been shaken. He complains of what he calls a "knowledge paradox": an expansion of fundamental knowledge accompanied by an increase in social problems. He implies that it shouldn't be that way, that as science progresses, the problems of society should diminish. And he suggests that Congress and the "consumers" of scientific research may have to take more of a hand in determining how science is conducted, in what research gets funded.

A similar critique has been made by former Colorado governor Richard Lamm. He claims no longer to believe that biomedical research contributes to the improvement of human health—a truly astonishing stance. To validate his skepticism, he presents the example of the University of Colorado Medical Center. It has done "little or nothing," he complains, about increasing primary care, expanding medical coverage to the uninsured, dealing with various addictions and dietary excesses, and controlling violence. As if biomedical research, or even academic medical centers, had either the resources or the capabilities to do what Lamm desires!

The source of these dissatisfactions appears to be an exaggerated view of what science can do. For example, agitation within Congress may induce the National Science Foundation to establish a center for research on violence, but only the naive would expect a quick fix for that momentous problem. Three-quarters of a century after the death of the great German sociologist Max Weber (1864–1920), the social and behavioral sciences have yet to produce an antidote for even one of the common social pathologies. The genesis of human behavior entails complexities that still lie beyond the grasp of human reason.

Critics such as Brown and Lamm blame science for what are actually the failures of individuals or society to use the knowledge that science has provided. The blame is misplaced. Science has produced the vaccines required to control many childhood infections in the United States, but our nation has failed to deploy properly those vaccines. Science has sounded the alarm about acid rain and its principal origins in automobile emissions, but our society has not found the political will to bridle the internal combustion engine. Science has documented the medical risks of addiction to tobacco, yet our federal government still spends large amounts of money subsidizing the tobacco industry.

These critics also fail to understand that success in science cannot be dictated. The progress of science is ultimately driven by feasibility. Science is the art of the possible, of the soluble, to recall a phrase from the late British immunologist and Nobel laureate Sir Peter Medawar. We seldom can force nature's hand; usually, she must tip it for us.

Nor is it possible, especially in the early stages of research, to anticipate what benefits are likely to result. My own experience is a case in point. In 1911, Peyton Rous at the Rockefeller Institute in New York City discovered a virus that causes cancer in chickens, a seemingly obscure observation. Yet 65 years later, that chicken virus was the vehicle by which Harold Varmus and I, and our colleagues, were able to uncover genes that are involved in the genesis of human cancer. The lesson of history is clear: the lines of inquiry that may prove most fruitful to science are generally unpredictable.

Biologist John Tyler Bonner has whimsically recalled an exchange he 15
had some decades ago with the National Science Foundation, which had given him a grant for a research project. "After the first year, I wrote that things had not worked out very well—had tried this, that, and the other thing, and nothing had really happened. [The foundation] wrote back, saying, 'Don't worry about it—that is the way research goes sometimes. Maybe next year you will have better luck.'" Alas, no scientist today would think of writing such a report, and no scientist today could imagine receiving such a reply.

The great successes of science have helped to create the exaggerated expectations about what science can accomplish. Why has malaria not been eradicated by now? Why is there still no cure for AIDS? Why is there not a more effective vaccine for influenza? When will there be a final remedy for the common cold? When will we be able to produce energy without waste? When will alchemy at last convert quartz to gold?

When scientists fail to meet unrealistic expectations, they are condemned by critics who do not recognize the limits of science. Thus, playwright and AIDS activist Larry Kramer bitterly complains that science has yet to produce a remedy for AIDS, placing much of the blame on the National Institutes of Health (NIH)—"a research system that by law demands compromise, rewards mediocrity and actually punishes initiative and originality."

I cannot imagine what law Kramer has in mind, and I cannot agree with his description of what the NIH expects from its sponsored research. I have assisted the NIH with peer review for more than twenty years. Its standards have always been the same: it seeks work of the highest originality and demands rigor as well. I, for one, have never knowingly punished initiative or originality, and I have never seen the agencies of the NIH do so. I realize with sorrow that Mr. Kramer is unlikely to believe me.

Biomedical research is one of the great triumphs of human endeavor. It has unearthed usable knowledge at a remarkable rate. It has brought us international leadership in the battle against disease and the search for understanding. I wonder how all this could have been accomplished if we scientists did business in the way that Kramer and critics like him claim that we do.

The bitter outcry from AIDS activists over the past decade was echoed 20
in the 1992 film *Lorenzo's Oil,* which portrays medical scientists as insensitive, close-minded, and self-serving, and dismisses controlled studies of potential remedies as a waste of precious time. The film is based on a true story, the case of Lorenzo Odone, a child who suffers from a rare hereditary disease that cripples many neurological functions and leads at an agonizing pace to death.

Offered no hope by conventional medical science, Lorenzo's desperate parents scoured the medical literature and turned up a possible remedy: the administration of two natural oils known as erucic and oleic acid. In the face of the skepticism of physicians and research specialists, Lorenzo was given the oils and, in the estimation of his parents, ceased to decline—perhaps even improved marginally. It was a courageous, determined, and even reasoned effort by the parents. (Mr. Odone has since received an honorary degree from at least one university.) Whether it was effective is another matter.

The movie portrays the treatment of Lorenzo as a success, with the heroic parents triumphant over the obstructionism of medical scientists. The film ends with a collage of parents testifying that the oils had been used successfully to treat Lorenzo's disease in their children. But it fails to present any of the parents who have tried the oils with bitter disappointment. And, of course, all of this is only anecdotal information. Properly controlled studies are still in progress. To date, they have not given much cause for hope.

Meanwhile, as if on cue, medical scientists have since succeeded in isolating the damaged gene responsible for the rare disease. Thus, the stage is set for the development of decisive clinical testing and effective therapy (although the latter may be long in coming).

If misapprehensions abound about what science can and cannot do, so do misplaced fears of its hazards. For more than five years now, my employer, the University of California, San Francisco, has waged a costly battle for the right to perform biomedical research in a residential area. For all intents and purposes, the university has lost. The opponents were our neighbors, who argued that we are dangerous beyond tolerance; that we exude toxic wastes, infectious pathogens, and radioactivity; that we put at risk the lives and limbs of all who come within reach—our own lives and limbs included, I suppose, a nuance that seems lost on the opposition. One agitated citizen suggested in a public forum that the manipulation of recombinant DNA at the university had engendered the AIDS virus; another declared on television her outrage that "those people are bringing DNA into my neighborhood."

Resistance to science is born of fear. Fear, in turn, is bred by ignorance. 25
And it is ignorance that is our deepest malady. The late literary critic Lionel Trilling described the difficulty well, in words that are even more apposite now than when he wrote them: "Science in our day lies beyond the intellectual grasp of most [people]. . . . This exclusion . . . from the mode of thought which is habitually said to be the characteristic achievement of the modern age . . . is a wound . . . to our intellectual self-esteem . . . a diminution of national possibility . . . a lessening of the social hope."

The mass ignorance of science confronts us daily. In recent international testing, U.S. high school students finished ninth in physics among the top twelve nations, eleventh in chemistry, and dead last in biology. Science is poorly taught in most of our elementary and secondary schools, when it is taught at all. Surveys of adult Americans indicate that only a minority accepts evolution as an explanation for the origin of the human species. Many do not even know that the Earth circles the Sun. In a recent committee hearing, a prominent member of Congress betrayed his ignorance of how the prostate gland differs from the testes.

Accountants, laborers, lawyers, poets, politicians, and even many physicians look upon science with bewilderment.

Do even we scientists understand one another? A few years ago, I read of a Russian satellite that gathers solar light to provide constant illumination of large areas of Siberia. "They are taking away the night," I thought. "They are taking away the last moments of mystery. Is nothing sacred?" But then I wondered what physicists must think of biologists' hopes to decipher the entire human genome and perhaps recraft it, ostensibly for the better.

Writing an article about cancer genes for *Scientific American* some years ago, I labored mightily to make the text universally accessible. I consulted students, journalists, laity of every stripe. When these consultants all had approved, I sent the manuscript to a solid-state physicist of considerable merit. A week later, the manuscript came back with this comment: "I have read your paper and shown it around the staff here. No one understands much of it. What exactly is a gene?"

Robert M. Hazen and James Trefil, authors of *The Sciences: An Integrated Approach* (1994), tell of twenty-three geophysicists who could not distinguish between DNA and RNA, and of a Nobel Prize–winning chemist who had never heard of plate tectonics. I have encountered biologists who thought string theory had something to do with pasta. We may be amused by these examples; we should also be troubled. If science is no longer a common culture, what can we rightfully expect of the laity by way of understanding?

Lionel Trilling knew where the problem lay in his time: "No successful 30
method of instruction has been found . . . which can give a comprehension of sciences . . . to those students who are not professionally committed to its mastery and especially endowed to achieve it." And there the problem lies today: perplexing to our educators, ignored by all but the most public-minded of scientists, bewildering and vaguely disquieting to the general public.

We scientists can no longer leave the problem to others. Indeed, it has always been ours to solve, and all of society is now paying for our neglect. As physicist and historian of science Gerald Holton has said, modern men and women "who do not know the basic facts that determine their very existence, functioning, and surroundings are living in a dream world . . . are, in a very real sense, not sane. We [scientists] . . . should do what we can, or we shall be pushed out of the common culture. The lab remains our workplace, but it must not become our hiding place."

The enterprise of science embodies a great adventure: the quest for understanding in a universe that the mathematician Freeman Dyson once characterized as "infinite in all directions, not only above us in the large but also below us in the small." We of science have begun the quest well, by building a method of ever-increasing power, a method that can illuminate all that is in the natural world. In consequence, we are admired but also feared, mistrusted, even despised. We offer hope for the future but also moral conflict and ambiguous choice. The price of science seems large, but to reject science is to deny the future.

QUESTIONING THE TEXT

1. Have you ever encountered the attitude toward science that Bishop describes as *postmodern?* If so, explain this notion of science as a set of "socially constructed fictions" (paragraph 3). Share your work with classmates, and explore the difference between science as a useful fiction and science as an ennobling fact.
2. Are there any words, concepts, or examples in "Enemies of Promise" that you don't understand? Based on Bishop's text, how would you characterize his intended readership?
3. What is J.R.'s attitude toward scientific progress as demonstrated in his introduction? How does the introduction influence your reading of Bishop's "Enemies of Promise"?

MAKING CONNECTIONS

4. On the Internet, explore a Usenet group or listserv that discusses scientific issues. Follow a discussion or controversy for several days, and then write a paragraph reporting on it.
5. Victor Frankenstein, in Mary Shelley's selection from *Frankenstein* (p. 274), describes this way his rejection of the monster that he had created: "I felt the bitterness of disappointment; dreams that had been my food and pleasant rest for so long a space were now become a hell to me; and the change was so rapid, the overthrow so complete!" (paragraph 14). Does the rejection of science in our time as described by Bishop reflect disappointment and bitterness that we have not created the technological Utopia that once seemed just over the horizon? Freewrite on this subject, and then write a position paper on this question: has science today become Dr. Frankenstein's monster?

JOINING THE CONVERSATION

6. Write a 200-word summary or abstract of "Enemies of Promise" for readers who might not have time to study the entire piece.
7. Choose an example of a scientific or technological change that has occurred in the last hundred years; read about it in the library, using at least three different sources, and then write an evaluation of that change.
8. Examine a technology that you believe has caused more problems than it has solved, and write an essay in which you propose a solution to at least one of those problems. Trace the cause of the problem in the technology—is it a problem in the science, in social attitudes, in politics, or something else?

JEREMY RIFKIN

Biotech Century: Playing Ecological Roulette with Mother Nature's Designs

JEREMY RIFKIN (b. 1945) is well known as a social activist. Organizer of the 1968 March on the Pentagon, Rifkin helped draw public attention to alleged U.S. war crimes in Vietnam. By the late 1970s, he was focusing his efforts on biotechnology, concentrating, for example, on the dangers of genetic engineering in the beef industry and in many everyday food substances. As president of the nonprofit Foundation on Economic Trends, Rifkin has gained a wide audience that includes both devoted admirers and scornful opponents: the National Milk Producers call him a "food terrorist," while reviewer and journalist Scott Landon concludes that he is a "fine synthesizer of cutting-edge issues." His most recent book is The Hydrogen Economy: The Creation of the World-Wide Energy Web and the Redistribution of Power on Earth *(2002).*

Rifkin himself does not take well to being labeled an antitechnology zealot, saying over and over again that he supports the use of biotechnology for making pharmaceuticals and for applying new knowledge of genetics to preventive medicine. How you respond to Rifkin's concerns in "Biotech Century" will probably be closely connected to your own value system as well as to the evidence provided for or against Rifkin's thesis.

The essay reprinted here, published in the May–June 1998 issue of E/The Environmental Magazine, *is adapted from Rifkin's book* The Biotech Century: Harnessing the Gene and Remaking the World *(1998). I chose this piece because Rifkin's trademark use of overstatement makes his claims very clear—and hard to ignore. In addition, while I am generally an advocate and admirer of science and scientific discovery, I have my own fears about human attempts to master—and effectively change—the natural world.* —A.L.

We're in the midst of a great historic transition into the Biotech Age. The ability to isolate, identify and recombine genes is making the gene pool available, for the first time, as the primary raw resource for future economic activity on Earth. After thousands of years of fusing, melting, soldering, forging and burning inanimate matter to create useful things, we are now splicing, recombining, inserting and stitching living material for our own economic interests. Lord Ritchie-Calder, the British science writer, cast the biological revolution in the proper historical perspective when he observed that "just as we have manipulated plastics and metals, we are now manufacturing living materials."

The Nobel Prize–winning chemist Robert F. Curl of Rice University spoke for many of his colleagues in science when he proclaimed that the 20th century was "the century of physics and chemistry. But it is clear that the next century will be the century of biology."

Global "life-science" companies promise an economic renaissance in the coming Biotech Century—they offer a door to a new era of history where the genetic blueprints of evolution itself become subject to human authorship. Critics worry that the reseeding of the Earth with a laboratory-conceived second Genesis could lead to a far different future—a biological Tower of Babel and the spread of chaos throughout the biological world, drowning out the ancient language of creation.

A Second Genesis

Human beings have been remaking the Earth for as long as we have had a history. Up to now, however, our ability to create our own second Genesis has been tempered by the restraints imposed by species boundaries. We have been forced to work narrowly, continually crossing close relatives in the plant or animal kingdoms to create new varieties, strains and breeds. Through a long, historical process of tinkering and trial and error, we have redrawn the biological map, creating new agricultural products, new sources of energy, more durable building materials, and life-saving pharmaceuticals. Still, in all this time, nature dictated the terms of engagement.

But the new technologies of the Genetic Age allow scientists, corpora- 5
tions and governments to manipulate the natural world at the most fundamental level—the genetic one. Imagine the wholesale transfer of genes between totally unrelated species and across all biological boundaries—plant, animal and human—creating thousands of novel life forms in a brief moment of evolutionary time. Then, with clonal propagation, mass-producing countless replicas of these new creations, releasing them into the biosphere to propagate, mutate, proliferate and migrate. This is, in fact, the radical scientific and commercial experiment now underway.

Global Powers at Play

Typical of new biotech trends is the bold decision by the Monsanto Corporation, long a world leader in chemical products, to sell off its entire chemical division in 1997 and anchor its research, development and marketing in biotech-based technologies and products. Global conglomerates are rapidly buying up biotech start-up companies, seed companies, agribusiness and agrochemical concerns, pharmaceutical, medical and health businesses, and food and drink companies, creating giant life-science complexes from which to fashion a bio-industrial world. The concentration of power is impressive. The top 10 agrochemical companies control 81 percent of the \$29 billion per year global agrochemical market. Ten life-science companies control 37 percent of the $15 billion per year global seed market. Meanwhile, pharmaceutical companies spent more than $3.5 billion in 1995 buying up biotech firms. Novartis, a giant new firm resulting from the $27 billion merger of Sandoz and Ciba-Geigy, is now the world's largest agrochemical company, the second-largest seed company and the second-largest pharmaceutical company.

Global life-science companies are expected to introduce thousands of new genetically engineered organisms into the environment in the coming century. In just the past 18 months, genetically engineered corn, soy and cotton have been planted over millions of acres of U.S. farmland. Genetically engineered insects, fish and domesticated animals have also been introduced, like the sheep/goat hybrid "geep."

Virtually every genetically engineered organism released into the environment poses a potential threat to the ecosystem. To appreciate why this is so, we need to understand why the pollution generated by genetically modified organisms is so different from the pollution resulting from the release of petrochemical products into the environment.

Because they are alive, genetically engineered organisms are inherently more unpredictable than petrochemicals in the way they interact with other living things in the environment. Consequently, it is much more difficult to assess all of the potential impacts that a genetically engineered organism might have on the Earth's ecosystems.

Genetically engineered products also reproduce. They grow and they 10
migrate. Unlike petrochemical products, it is difficult to constrain them within a given geographical locale. Finally, once released, it is virtually impossible to recall genetically engineered organisms back to the laboratory, especially those organisms that are microscopic in nature.

The risks in releasing novel, genetically engineered organisms into the biosphere are similar to those we've encountered in introducing exotic organisms into the North American habitat. Over the past several hundred years, thousands of non-native organisms have been brought to America from other regions of the world. While many of these creatures have adapted to the North American ecosystems without severe dislocations, a small percentage of them have run wild, wreaking havoc on the flora and fauna of the continent. Gypsy moth, Kudzu vine, Dutch elm disease, chestnut blight, starlings and Mediterranean fruit flies come easily to mind.

Whenever a genetically engineered organism is released, there is always a small chance that it, too, will run amok because, like nonindigenous species, it has been artificially introduced into a complex environment that has developed a web of highly integrated relationships over long periods of evolutionary history. Each new synthetic introduction is tantamount to playing ecological roulette. That is, while there is only a small chance of it triggering an environmental explosion, if it does, the consequences could be significant and irreversible.

SPREADING GENETIC POLLUTION

Nowhere are the alarm bells going off faster than in agricultural biotechnology. The life-science companies are introducing biotech crops containing newly discovered genetic traits from other plants, viruses, bacteria and animals. The new genetically engineered crops are designed to perform in ways that have eluded scientists working with classical breeding techniques. Many of the new gene-spliced crops emanating from laboratories seem more like creations from the world of science fiction. Scientists have inserted "antifreeze" protein genes from flounder into the genetic code of tomatoes to protect the fruit from frost damage. Chicken genes have been inserted into

potatoes to increase disease resistance. Fire-fly genes have been injected into the biological code of corn plants. Chinese hamster genes have been inserted into the genome of tobacco plants to increase sterol production.

Ecologists are unsure of the impacts of bypassing natural species boundaries by introducing genes into crops from wholly unrelated plant and animal species. The fact is, there is no precedent in history for this kind of "shotgun" experimentation. For more than 10,000 years, classical breeding techniques have been limited to the transference of genes between closely related plants or animals that can sexually interbreed, limiting the number of possible genetic combinations. Natural evolution appears to be similarly circumscribed. By contrast, the new gene-splicing technologies allow us to bypass all previous biological boundaries in nature, creating life forms that have never before existed. For example, consider the ambitious plans to engineer transgenic plants to serve as pharmaceutical factories for the production of chemicals and drugs. Foraging animals, seed-eating birds and soil insects will be exposed to a range of genetically engineered drugs, vaccines, industrial enzymes, plastics and hundreds of other foreign substances for the first time, with untold consequences. The notion of large numbers of species consuming plants and plant debris containing a wide assortment of chemicals that they would normally never be exposed to is an unsettling prospect.

Much of the current effort in agricultural biotechnology is centered on the 15
creation of herbicide-tolerant, pest-resistant and virus-resistant plants. Herbicide-tolerant crops are a favorite of companies like Monsanto and Novartis that are anxious to corner the lucrative worldwide market for their herbicide products. More than 600 million pounds of poisonous herbicides are dumped on U.S. farm land each year, most sprayed on corn, cotton and soybean crops. Chemical companies gross more than $4 billion per year in U.S. herbicide sales alone.

To increase their share of the growing global market for herbicides, life-science companies have created transgenic crops that tolerate their own herbicides (see "Say It Ain't Soy," *In Brief* March/April, 1997). The idea is to sell farmers patented seeds that are resistant to a particular brand of herbicide in the hope of increasing a company's share of both the seed and herbicide markets. Monsanto's new "Roundup Ready" patented seeds, for example, are resistant to its best-selling chemical herbicide, Roundup.

The chemical companies hope to convince farmers that the new herbicide-tolerant crops will allow for a more efficient eradication of weeds. Farmers will be able to spray at any time during the growing season, killing weeds without killing their crops. Critics warn that with new herbicide-tolerant crops planted in the fields, farmers are likely to use even greater quantities of herbicides to control weeds, as there will be less fear of damaging their crops in the process of spraying. The increased use of herbicides, in turn, raises the possibility of weeds developing resistance, forcing an even greater use of herbicides to control the more resistant strains.

The potential deleterious impacts on soil fertility, water quality and beneficial insects that result from the increased use of poisonous herbicides, like Monsanto's Roundup, are a disquieting reminder of the escalating environmental bill that is likely to accompany the introduction of herbicide-tolerant crops.

The new pest-resistant transgenic crops pose similar environmental problems. Life-science companies are readying transgenic crops that produce insecticide in every cell of each plant. Several crops, including Ciba Geigy's pest-resistant "maximizer corn" and Rohm and Haas's pest-resistant tobacco are already available on the commercial market. A growing body of scientific evidence points to the likelihood of creating "super bugs" resistant to the effects of the new pesticide-producing genetic crops.

The new generation of virus-resistant transgenic crops pose the equally 20
dangerous possibility of creating new viruses that have never before existed in

nature. Concerns are surfacing among scientists and in scientific literature over the possibility that the protein genes could recombine with genes in related viruses that find their way naturally into the transgenic plant, creating a recombinant virus with novel features.

A growing number of ecologists warn that the biggest danger might lie in what is called "gene flow"—the transfer of genes from altered crops to weedy relatives by way of cross-pollination. Researchers are concerned that manufactured genes for herbicide tolerance, and pest and viral resistance might escape and, through cross pollination, insert themselves into the genetic makeup of weedy relatives, creating weeds that are resistant to herbicides, pests and viruses. Fears over the possibility of transgenic genes jumping to wild weedy relatives heightened in 1996 when a Danish research team, working under the auspices of Denmark's Environmental Science and Technology Department, observed the transfer of just such a gene—something critics of deliberate-release experiments have warned of for years and biotech companies have dismissed as a remote or nonexistent possibility.

Transnational life-science companies project that within 10 to 15 years, all of the major crops grown in the world will be genetically engineered to include herbicide-, pest-, virus-, bacteria-, fungus- and stress-resistant genes. Millions of acres of agricultural land and commercial forest will be transformed in the most daring experiment ever undertaken to remake the biological world. Proponents of the new science, armed with powerful gene-splicing tools and precious little data on potential impacts, are charging into this new world of agricultural biotechnology, giddy over the potential benefits and confident that the risks are minimum or non-existent. They may be right. But, what if they are wrong?

Insuring Disaster

The insurance industry quietly let it be known several years ago that it would not insure the release of genetically engineered organisms into the environment against the possibility of catastrophic environmental damage, because the industry lacks a risk-assessment science—a predictive ecology—with which to judge the risk of any given introduction. In short, the insurance industry clearly understands the Kafka-esque implications of a government regime claiming to regulate a technology in the absence of clear scientific knowledge.

Increasingly nervous over the insurance question, one of the biotech trade associations attempted early on to raise an insurance pool among its member organizations, but gave up when it failed to raise sufficient funds to make the pool operable. Some observers worried, at the time, and continue to worry—albeit privately—over what might happen to the biotech industry if a large-scale commercial release of a genetically altered organism were to result in a catastrophic environmental event. For example, the introduction and spread of a new weed or pest comparable to Kudzu vine, Dutch elm disease or gypsy moth, might inflict costly damage to flora and fauna over extended ranges.

Corporate assurances aside, one or more significant environmental mishaps 25
are an inevitability in the years ahead. When that happens, every nation is going to be forced to address the issue of liability. Farmers, landowners, consumers and the public at large are going to demand to know how it could have happened and who is liable for the damages inflicted. When the day arrives—and it's likely to come sooner rather than later—"genetic pollution" will take its place alongside petrochemical and nuclear pollution as a grave threat to the Earth's already beleaguered environment.

Allergic to Technology?

The introduction of new genetically engineered organisms also raises a number of serious human health issues that have yet to be resolved. Health professionals and consumer organizations are most concerned about the potential allergenic effects of genetically engineered foods. The Food and Drug Administration (FDA) announced in 1992 that special labeling for genetically engineered foods would not be required, touching off protest among food professionals, including the nation's leading chefs and many wholesalers and retailers.

With two percent of adults and eight percent of children having allergic responses to commonly eaten foods, consumer advocates argue that all gene-spliced foods need to be properly labeled so that consumers can avoid health risks. Their concerns were heightened in 1996 when *The New England Journal of Medicine* published a study showing genetically engineered soybeans containing a gene from a Brazil nut could create an allergic reaction in people who were allergic to the nuts. The test result was unwelcome news for Pioneer Hi-Bred International, the Iowa-based seed company that hoped to market the new genetically engineered soy. Though the FDA said it would label any genetically engineered foods containing genes from common allergenic organisms, the agency fell well short of requiring across-the-board labeling, leaving *The New England Journal of Medicine* editors to ask what protection consumers would have against genes from organisms that have never before been part of the human diet and that might be potential allergens. Concerned over the agency's seeming disregard for human health, the *Journal* editors concluded that FDA policy "would appear to favor industry over consumer protection."

Depleting the Gene Pool

Ironically, all of the many efforts to reseed the biosphere with a laboratory-conceived second Genesis may eventually come to naught because of a massive catch-22 that lies at the heart of the new technology revolution.

On the one hand, the success of the biotech revolution is wholly dependent on access to a rich reservoir of genes to create new characteristics and properties in crops and animals grown for food, fiber and energy, and products used for pharmaceutical and medical purposes. Genes containing beneficial traits that can be manipulated, transformed and inserted into organisms destined for the commercial market come from either the wild or from traditional crops and animal breeds. Notwithstanding its awesome ability to transform nature into commercially marketable commodities, the biotech industry still remains utterly dependent upon nature's seed stock—germplasm—for its raw resources. At present, it is impossible to create a "useful" new gene in the laboratory. In this sense, biotechnology remains an extractive industry. It can rearrange genetic material, but cannot create it. On the other hand, the very practice of biotechnology—including cloning, tissue culturing and gene splicing—is likely to result in increasing genetic uniformity, a narrowing of the gene pool, and loss of the very genetic diversity that is so essential to guaranteeing the success of the biotech industry in the future.

In his book *The Last Harvest,* Paul Raeburn, the science editor for *Business Week,* penetrates to the heart of the problem. He writes, "Scientists can accomplish remarkable feats in manipulating molecules and cells, but they are utterly incapable of re-creating even the simplest forms of life in test tubes. Germplasm provides our lifeline into the future. No breakthrough in fundamental research can compensate for the loss of the genetic material crop breeders depend upon."

Agricultural biotechnology greatly increases the uniformity of agricul- 30
tural practices, as did the Green Revolution when it was introduced more than 30 years ago. Like its predecessor, the goal is to create superior varieties that can be planted as monocultures in agricultural regions all over the world. A handful of life-science companies are staking out the new biotech turf, each aggressively marketing their own patented brands of "super seeds"—and soon "super" farm animals as well. The new transgenic crops and animals are designed to grow faster, produce greater yields, and withstand more varied environmental and weather-related stresses. Their cost effectiveness, in the short run, is likely to guarantee them a robust market. In an industry where profit margins are notoriously low, farmers will likely jump at the opportunity of saving a few dollars per acre and a few cents per pound by shifting quickly to the new transgenic crops and animals.

However, the switch to a handful of patented transgenic seeds and livestock animals will likely further erode the genetic pool as farmers abandon the growing of traditional varieties and breeds in favor of the commercially more competitive patented products. By focusing on short-term market priorities, the biotech industry threatens to destroy the very genetic heirlooms that might one day be worth their weight in gold as a line of defense against new resistant diseases or superbugs.

Most molecular biologists and the biotechnology industry at large have all but dismissed the growing criticism of ecologists, whose recent studies suggest that the biotech revolution will likely be accompanied by the proliferation and spread of genetic pollution and the wholesale loss of genetic diversity. Nonetheless, the uncontrollable spread of super weeds, the buildup of resistant strains of bacteria and new super insects, the creation of novel viruses, the destabilization of whole ecosystems, the genetic contamination of food, and the steady depletion of the gene pool are no longer minor considerations, the mere grumbling of a few disgruntled critics. To ignore the warnings is to place the biosphere and civilization in harm's way in the coming years. Pestilence, famine, and the spread of new kinds of diseases throughout the world might yet turn out to be the final act in the script being prepared for the biotech century.

QUESTIONING THE TEXT

1. Rifkin uses an analogy to help support his argument: "The risks in releasing novel, genetically engineered organisms into the biosphere are similar to those we've encountered in introducing exotic organisms into the North American habitat" (paragraph 11). He goes on to mention some "severe dislocations" that have resulted—Dutch elm disease, for example. Working with two classmates, explore Rifkin's analogy, beginning perhaps by brainstorming about movies or TV shows you have seen that illustrate the analogy—*28 Days Later,* for instance. Then try to think of counterexamples to Rifkin's argument, genetically altered things that have been introduced but that have not been disastrous (such as disease-resistant corn). Prepare a brief report for your class that either supports or challenges Rifkin's analogical argument.
2. Reread Rifkin's essay, noting his use of metaphors ("synthetic introduction is . . . ecological roulette"; a "biological Tower of Babel") and similes ("new gene-spliced crops . . . [are] like creations from the world of science fiction"). Then write a critical response to Rifkin's essay based on your understanding of how he uses metaphors, similes, and other figures of speech to help make his case.
3. Look carefully at the illustrations by Tadeusz Majewski that accompany this essay. Working with a classmate, determine what the illustrations add to Rifkin's argument, what they might distract from, or what they might emphasize, downplay, and so on. Summarize the thesis of Rifkin's argument, and then write a one- or two-page report that explains to your class how the illustrations work in relation to the thesis.

MAKING CONNECTIONS

4. Rifkin has a number of worries similar to those of Victor Frankenstein. If Mary Shelley were writing *Frankenstein* (p. 274) in the twenty-first century, what might be the characteristics of the "monster" the doctor

wishes to create? Where would the major pitfalls lie in accomplishing his goals? Make a list of characteristics and pitfalls, and bring it to class for discussion.

JOINING THE CONVERSATION

5. Try your hand at writing a letter of response to Rifkin. In it, make sure that you demonstrate your understanding of his argument; then give your response to that argument, and conclude with a series of questions about the "Biotech Century" you would most like to have answered. Bring your letter to class for discussion.
6. Working with two classmates, do some research on the claims Rifkin makes in his essay. One person might interview a senior professor in biology or biotechnology; one might search the Web for the latest research on genetic engineering in agriculture; another might seek out reviews of Rifkin's book and track down the reviews of several proponents and critics. After gathering as much material as you can, meet to share information and to decide what conclusions you can draw from it. Then prepare a 15- to 20-minute presentation for your class on "Rifkin's Claims: An Expanded View."

TODD OPPENHEIMER
The Computer Delusion

In "The Computer Delusion," Todd Oppenheimer, the 1998 San Francisco Schools' Volunteer of the Year and winner of many awards for investigative reporting, argues that the tremendous emphasis on computers and technology in elementary and secondary schools, and especially in the lower grades, can actually decrease the effectiveness of learning and teaching. Yet local, state, and national governments are pouring funds into more and more technology for schools, often, Oppenheimer thinks, to the detriment of other programs. Students, teachers, parents, and policy makers must confront these issues immediately, he argues, and to help with that endeavor he looks closely at five claims that underlie the move to computerize U.S. schools.

Oppenheimer's critique, "The Computer Delusion," published in the July 1997 issue of the Atlantic Monthly, *is anchored in his own experience. As associate editor at* Newsweek Interactive, *Oppenheimer has spent a great deal of time in cyberspace, exploring the uses of chat rooms and bulletin boards, initiating and conducting online discussion forums, and preparing numerous reports on experiments with new media. So although I have been a strong advocate of technology in the classroom, and especially in the writing classroom, reading Oppenheimer's essay gave me pause. Perhaps on these issues I am moving closer to Sherry Turkle, whom Oppenheimer quotes: "[t]he possibilities of using this thing [computer technology] poorly so outweigh the chance of using it well, it makes people like us, who are fundamentally optimistic about computers, very reticent."*

In addition to my own concerns about how best to use technology in education, I chose this essay partly because I am drawn to Oppenheimer's sense that we—people like you and me—must take responsibility for how technology will be used, both in and out of schools. In an online article in the Columbia Journalism Review, *Oppenheimer concludes by saying, "It's my hope that the news gurus of tomorrow will be those who can redefine responsibility—ours and that of our readers." Given the demand for instant gratification of what Oppenheimer calls "always-restless" cybercitizens, who disappear at a click if they aren't being entertained, this is a very tall order. Oppenheimer continues to pursue his critique of technology in the schools in his most recent work,* The Flickering Mind: The Technology Crisis in Our Schools, and How Learning Can Be Saved *(2003).* —A.L.

In 1922 Thomas Edison predicted that "the motion picture is destined to revolutionize our educational system and . . . in a few years it will supplant largely, if not entirely, the use of textbooks." Twenty-three years later, in 1945, William Levenson, the director of the Cleveland public schools' radio station, claimed that "the time may come when a portable radio receiver will be as common in the classroom as is the blackboard." Forty years after that the noted psychologist B. F. Skinner, referring to the first days of his "teaching machines," in the late 1950s and early 1960s, wrote, "I was soon saying that, with the help of teaching machines and programmed instruction, students could learn twice as much in the same time and with the same effort as in a standard classroom." Ten years after Skinner's recollections were published, President Bill Clinton campaigned for "a bridge to the twenty-first century . . . where computers are as much a part of the classroom as blackboards." Clinton was not alone in his enthusiasm for a program estimated to cost somewhere between $40 billion and $100 billion over the next five years. Speaker of the House Newt Gingrich, talking about computers to the Republican National Committee early this year, said, "We could do so much to make education available twenty-four hours a day, seven days a week, that people could literally have a whole different attitude toward learning."

I began teaching in the mid-1960s and remember all the talk of the "smart" teaching machines. In fact, I helped design an individually paced program in English—though I didn't like it much and didn't think it taught students very well. —A.L.

A good point; availability of technology without proper motivation is not sufficient to create a learning environment. —H.R.

If history really is repeating itself, the schools are in serious trouble. In *Teachers and Machines: The Classroom Use of Technology Since 1920* (1986), Larry Cuban, a professor of education at Stanford University and a former school superintendent, observed that as successive rounds of new technology failed their promoters' expectations, a pattern emerged. The cycle began with big promises backed by the technology developers' research. In the classroom, however, teachers never really embraced the new tools, and no significant academic improvement occurred. This provoked consistent responses: the problem was money, spokespeople argued, or teacher resistance, or the paralyzing school bureaucracy. Meanwhile, few people questioned the technology advocates' claims. As results continued to lag, the blame was finally laid on the machines. Soon schools were sold on the next generation of technology, and the lucrative cycle started all over again.

I remember "telecourses" from the late 1950s. They were awful stuff—we laughed at them more than we learned from them. —J.R.

But their reasons for not doing so get glossed over. I know of many classrooms right now, for instance, where new computers sit in unopened cartons, not because the teachers haven't embraced them but because the teachers' rooms are not wired properly for them. —A.L.

Today's technology evangels argue that we've learned our lesson from past mistakes. As in each previous round, they say that when our new hot

It seems to me that the role of business in education needs to be scrutinized. What are the dynamics of power between educators and businesses? —H.R.

technology—the computer—is compared with yesterday's, today's is better. "It can do the same things, plus," Richard Riley, the U.S. Secretary of Education, told me this spring.

How much better is it, really?

The promoters of computers in schools again offer prodigious research showing improved academic achievement after using their technology. The research has again come under occasional attack, but this time quite a number of teachers seem to be backing classroom technology. In a poll taken early last year U.S. teachers ranked computer skills and media technology as more "essential" than the study of European history, biology, chemistry, and physics; than dealing with social problems such as drugs and family breakdown; than learning practical job skills; and than reading modern American writers such as Steinbeck and Hemingway or classic ones such as Plato and Shakespeare.

What kind of a poll? What teachers were consulted, and how many? I'm suspicious of this "finding." —A.L.

In keeping with these views New Jersey cut state aid to a number of school districts this past year and then spent $10 million on classroom computers. In Union City, California, a single school district is spending $27 million to buy new gear for a mere eleven schools. The Kittridge Street Elementary School, in Los Angeles, killed its music program last year to hire a technology coordinator; in Mansfield, Massachusetts, administrators dropped proposed teaching positions in art, music, and physical education, and then spent $333,000 on computers; in one Virginia school the art room was turned into a computer laboratory. (Ironically, a half dozen preliminary studies recently suggested that music and art classes may build the physical size of a child's brain, and its powers for subjects such as language, math, science, and engineering—in one case far more than computer work did.) Meanwhile, months after a New Technology High School opened in Napa, California, where computers sit on every student's desk and all academic classes use computers, some students were complaining of headaches, sore eyes, and wrist pain.

What is the payoff or trade-off when music classes are cut to fund classroom computers? I want to compare what skills are being represented developmentally by each program. —H.R.

He's right about the costs. Maintaining the computers for our writing programs costs more than $250,000 a year. —J.R.

Throughout the country, as spending on technology increases, school book purchases are stagnant. Shop classes, with their tradition of

Maybe lowering book purchases by itself is not a totally

negative result. I can't help thinking of the money I waste buying books that are ordered by my professors and then scarcely incorporated into the class or not at all. Having certain online references could relieve space limitations as well as conserve funds. —H.R.

teaching children building skills with wood and metal, have been almost entirely replaced by new "technology education programs." In San Francisco only one public school still offers a full shop program—the lone vocational high school. "We get kids who don't know the difference between a screwdriver and a ball peen hammer," James Dahlman, the school's vocational-department chair, told me recently. "How are they going to make a career choice? Administrators are stuck in this mindset that all kids will go to a four-year college and become a doctor or a lawyer, and that's not true. I know some who went to college, graduated, and then had to go back to technical school to get a job." Last year the school superintendent in Great Neck, Long Island, proposed replacing elementary school shop classes with computer classes and training the shop teachers as computer coaches. Rather than being greeted with enthusiasm, the proposal provoked a backlash.

I'd count shop as a "technology program" too—why should the definition of technology *be limited to computers?* —A.L.

Aren't students increasingly able to gain computer-related skills at home? —H.R.

Interestingly, shop classes and field trips are two programs that the National Information Infrastructure Advisory Council, the Clinton Administration's technology task force, suggests reducing in order to shift resources into computers. But are these results what technology promoters really intend? "You need to apply common sense," Esther Dyson, the president of EDventure Holdings and one of the task force's leading school advocates, told me recently. "Shop with a good teacher probably is worth more than computers with a lousy teacher. But if it's a poor program, this may provide a good excuse for cutting it. There will be a lot of trials and errors with this. And I don't know how to prevent those errors."

The need for good teachers, not just high-tech equipment, is right on. All the students I've talked with agree that the teacher makes the difference. —H.R.

The issue, perhaps, is the magnitude of the errors. Alan Lesgold, a professor of psychology and the associate director of the Learning Research and Development Center at the University of Pittsburgh, calls the computer an "amplifier," because it encourages both enlightened study practices and thoughtless ones. There's a real risk, though, that the thoughtless practices will dominate, slowly dumbing down huge numbers of tomorrow's adults. As Sherry Turkle, a professor of the sociology of science at the

The powerful nature of the medium as well as the capacity for errors make for an effective argument for being cautious about children's exposure to computers. —H.R.

Massachusetts Institute of Technology and a longtime observer of children's use of computers, told me, "The possibilities of using this thing poorly so outweigh the chance of using it well, it makes people like us, who are fundamentally optimistic about computers, very reticent."

Turkle's comment hits home: one can be enthusiastic about computers but still question their place in education. —J.R.

Perhaps the best way to separate fact from fantasy is to take supporters' claims about computerized learning one by one and compare them with the evidence in the academic literature and in the everyday experiences I have observed or heard about in a variety of classrooms.

Five main arguments underlie the campaign to computerize our nation's schools.

I appreciate the focus that these five points bring to the article, but I wonder about who the "supporters" are who set forth these arguments: what primary sources is Oppenheimer drawing on in summarizing these points? —A.L.

- Computers improve both teaching practices and student achievement.
- Computer literacy should be taught as early as possible; otherwise students will be left behind.
- To make tomorrow's work force competitive in an increasingly high-tech world, learning computer skills must be a priority.
- Technology programs leverage support from the business community—badly needed today because schools are increasingly starved for funds.
- Work with computers—particularly using the Internet—brings students valuable connections with teachers, other schools and students, and a wide network of professionals around the globe. These connections spice the school day with a sense of real-world relevance, and broaden the educational community.

What makes someone "computer literate"? How long should this process take? —H.R.

"The Filmstrips of the 1990s"

Clinton's vision of computerized classrooms arose partly out of the findings of the presidential task force—thirty-six leaders from industry, education, and several interest groups who have guided the Administration's push to get computers into the schools. The report of the task force, "Connecting

K–12 Schools to the Information Superhighway" (produced by the consulting firm McKinsey & Co.), begins by citing numerous studies that have apparently proved that computers enhance student achievement significantly. One "meta-analysis" (a study that reviews other studies—in this case 130 of them) reported that computers had improved performance in "a wide range of subjects, including language arts, math, social studies and science." Another found improved organization and focus in students' writing. A third cited twice the normal gains in math skills. Several schools boasted of greatly improved attendance.

Everything depends on how one defines "improved performance" here—and I cannot believe that computers alone improve performance in, for example, writing. —A.L.

Unfortunately, many of these studies are more anecdotal than conclusive. Some, including a giant, oft-cited meta-analysis of 254 studies, lack the necessary scientific controls to make solid conclusions possible. The circumstances are artificial and not easily repeated, results aren't statistically reliable, or, most frequently, the studies did not control for other influences, such as differences between teaching methods. This last factor is critical, because computerized learning inevitably forces teachers to adjust their style—only sometimes for the better. Some studies were industry-funded, and thus tended to publicize mostly positive findings. "The research is set up in a way to find benefits that aren't really there," Edward Miller, a former editor of the *Harvard Education Letter,* says. "Most knowledgeable people agree that most of the research isn't valid. It's so flawed it shouldn't even be called research. Essentially, it's just worthless." Once the faulty studies are weeded out, Miller says, the ones that remain "are inconclusive"—that is, they show no significant change in either direction. Even Esther Dyson admits the studies are undependable. "I don't think those studies amount to much either way," she says. "In this area there is little proof."

Why are solid conclusions so elusive? Look at Apple Computer's "Classrooms of Tomorrow," perhaps the most widely studied effort to teach using computer technology. In the early 1980s Apple shrewdly realized that donating computers to schools might help not only students but also company sales, as Apple's ubiquity in classrooms turned legions of families into Apple loyalists. Last year, after the *San Jose Mercury News* (published in Apple's Silicon Valley home) ran a series questioning the effectiveness of computers in schools, the paper printed an opinion-page response from Terry Crane, an Apple vice-president. "Instead of isolating students," Crane wrote, "technology actually encouraged them to collaborate more than in traditional classrooms. Students also learned to explore and represent information dynamically and creatively, communicate effectively about complex processes, become independent learners and self-starters and become more socially aware and confident."

In my own classrooms, the use of technology has indeed fostered a collaborative environment. Even the ability to set up virtual "meetings" has been a tremendous help to students and teachers. —A.L.

Crane didn't mention that after a decade of effort and the donation of equipment worth more than $25 million to thirteen schools, there is scant evidence of greater student achievement. To be fair, educators on both sides of the computer debate acknowledge that today's tests of student achievement are shockingly crude. They're especially weak in measuring intangibles such as enthusiasm and self-motivation, which do seem evident in Apple's classrooms and other computer-rich schools. In any event, what is fun and what is educational may frequently be at odds. "Computers in classrooms are the filmstrips of the 1990s," Clifford Stoll, the author of *Silicon Snake Oil: Second Thoughts on the Information Highway* (1995), told *The New York Times* last year, recalling his own school days in the 1960s. "We loved them because we didn't have to think for an hour, teachers loved them because they didn't have to teach, and parents loved them because it showed their schools were high-tech. But no learning happened."

I think Stoll way overstates the case! I've always remembered Aristotle's injunction that learning is life's greatest pleasure. So while I take the point here—learning and fun may sometimes be at odds—I believe as well that they do not have to be at odds, and that technology in the classroom doesn't have to be just about "fun." —A.L.

Stoll somewhat overstates the case—obviously, benefits can come from strengthening a student's motivation. Still, Apple's computers may bear less responsibility for that change than Crane suggests. In the beginning, when Apple did little more than dump computers in classrooms and homes, this produced no real results, according to Jane David, a consultant Apple hired to study its classroom initiative. Apple quickly learned that teachers needed to change their classroom approach to what is commonly called "project-oriented learning." This is an increasingly popular teaching method, in which students learn through doing and teachers act as facilitators or partners rather than as didacts. (Teachers sometimes refer to this approach, which arrived in classrooms before computers did, as being "the guide on the side instead of the sage on the stage.") But what the students learned "had less to do with the computer and more to do with the teaching," David concluded. "If you took the computers out, there would still be good teaching there." This story is heard in school after school, including two impoverished schools—Clear View Elementary School, in southern California, and the Christopher Columbus middle school, in New Jersey—that the Clinton Administration has loudly celebrated for turning themselves around with computers. At Christopher Columbus, in fact, students' test scores rose before computers arrived, not afterward, because of relatively basic changes: longer class periods, new books, after-school programs, and greater emphasis on student projects and collaboration.

During recent visits to some San Francisco-area schools I could see what it takes for students to use computers properly, and why most don't.

Interesting. Does Oppenheimer make this sentence into a separate paragraph to give it special emphasis? To build the credibility of his firsthand experience? —A.L.

On a bluff south of downtown San Francisco, in the middle of one of the city's lower-income neighborhoods, Claudia Schaffner, a tenth-grader, tapped away at a multimedia machine in a computer lab at Thurgood Marshall Academic High School, one of half a dozen special technology schools in the city. Schaffner was using a physics program to simulate the trajectory of a marble on a small roller coaster. "It helps to visualize it first, like 'A is for Apple' with kindergartners," Schaffner told me, while mousing up and down the virtual roller coaster. "I can see how the numbers go into action." This was lunch hour, and the students' excitement about what they can do in this lab was palpable. Schaffner could barely tear herself away. "I need to go eat some food," she finally said, returning within minutes to eat a rice dish at the keyboard.

Why are computers so addictive? I know people who became "glued" to the computer even after short periods of time. This doesn't seem healthy to me. —H.R.

Schaffner's teacher is Dennis Frezzo, an electrical-engineering graduate from the University of California at Berkeley. Despite his considerable knowledge of computer programming, Frezzo tries to keep classwork focused on physical projects. For a mere $8,000, for example, several teachers put together a multifaceted robotics lab, consisting of an advanced lego engineering kit and twenty-four old 386-generation computers. Frezzo's students used these materials to build a tiny electric car, whose motion was to be triggered by a light sensor. When the light sensor didn't work, the students figured out why. "That's a real problem—what you'd encounter in the real world," Frezzo told me. "I prefer they get stuck on small real-world problems instead of big fake problems"—like the simulated natural disasters that fill one popular educational game. "It's sort of the Zen approach to education," Frezzo said. "It's not the big problems. Isaac Newton already solved those. What come up in life are the little ones."

Technical glitches occur in college classrooms, too, after diverting attention from course work to technology. —J.R.

It's one thing to confront technology's complexity at a high school—especially one that's blessed with four different computer labs and some highly skilled teachers like Frezzo, who know enough, as he put it, "to keep computers in their place." It's quite another to grapple with a high-tech future in the lower grades, especially at everyday schools that lack special funding or technical support. As evidence, when *U.S. News & World Report* published a cover story last fall on schools that make computers work, five of the six were high schools—among them Thurgood Marshall. Although the sixth was an elementary school, the featured program involved children with disabilities—the one group that does show consistent benefits from computerized instruction.

So "what it takes for students to use computers properly" is money and a really expert teacher who can "keep computers in their place." Now I expect we're going to hear why most schools don't meet these standards. —A.L.

Artificial Experience

Consider the scene at one elementary school, Sanchez, which sits on the edge of San Francisco's Latino community. For several years Sanchez, like many other schools, has made do with a roomful of basic Apple IIes. Last year, curious about what computers could do for youngsters, a local entrepreneur donated twenty costly Power Macintoshes—three for each of five classrooms, and one for each of the five lucky teachers to take home. The teachers who got the new machines were delighted. "It's the best thing we've ever done," Adela Najarro, a third-grade bilingual teacher, told me. She mentioned one boy, perhaps with a learning disability, who had started to hate school. Once he had a computer to play with, she said, "his whole attitude changed." Najarro is now a true believer, even when it comes to children without disabilities. "Every single child," she said, "will do more work for you and do better work with a computer. Just because it's on a monitor, kids pay more attention. There's this magic to the screen."

So I got a surprise here—Oppenheimer is still concentrating on schools where computers "work." —A.L.

Scary? What exactly is the screen's magic, and does it make students think or merely amuse them? —J.R.

Down the hall from Najarro's classroom her colleague Rose Marie Ortiz had a more troubled relationship with computers. On the morning I visited, Ortiz took her bilingual special-education class of second-, third-, and fourth-graders into the lab filled with the old Apple IIes. The students look forward to this weekly expedition so much that Ortiz gets exceptional behavior from them all morning. Out of date though these machines are, they do offer a range of exercises, in subjects such as science, math, reading, social studies, and problem solving. But owing to this group's learning problems and limited English skills, math drills were all that Ortiz could give them. Nonetheless, within minutes the kids were excitedly navigating their way around screens depicting floating airplanes and trucks carrying varying numbers of eggs. As the children struggled, many resorted to counting in whatever way they knew how. Some squinted at the screen, painstakingly moving their fingers from one tiny egg symbol to the next. "*Tres, cuatro, cinco, seis* . . . ," one little girl said loudly, trying to hear herself above her counting neighbors. Another girl kept a piece of paper handy, on which she marked a line for each egg. Several others resorted to the slow but tried and true—their fingers. Some just guessed. Once the children arrived at answers, they frantically typed them onto the screen, hoping it would advance to something fun, the way

Ironically, here's a school setting where technology would seem to hold out enormous potential to help students and teachers. What's gone wrong? —A.L.

Nintendos, Game Boys, and video-arcade games do. Sometimes their answers were right, and the screen did advance; sometimes they weren't; but the children were rarely discouraged. As schoolwork goes, this was a blast.

"It's highly motivating for them," Ortiz said as she rushed from machine to machine, attending not to math questions but to computer glitches. Those she couldn't fix she simply abandoned. "I don't know how practical it is. You see," she said, pointing to a girl counting on her fingers, "these kids still need the hands-on"—meaning the opportunity to manipulate physical objects such as beans or colored blocks. The value of hands-on learning, child-development experts believe, is that it deeply imprints knowledge into a young child's brain, by transmitting the lessons of experience through a variety of sensory pathways. "Curiously enough," the educational psychologist Jane Healy wrote in *Endangered Minds: Why Children Don't Think and What We Can Do about It* (1990), "visual stimulation is probably not the main access route to nonverbal reasoning. Body movements, the ability to touch, feel, manipulate, and build sensory awareness of relationships in the physical world, are its main foundations." The problem, Healy wrote, is that "in schools, traditionally, the senses have had little status after kindergarten."

Even more experienced users now probably expect a visual or aural payoff for their computer work. Have we been programmed to expect stimulation from the screen? —J.R.

Ortiz believes that the computer-lab time, brief as it is, dilutes her students' attention to language. "These kids are all language-delayed," she said. Though only modest sums had so far been spent at her school, Ortiz and other local teachers felt that the push was on for technology over other scholastic priorities. The year before, Sanchez had let its librarian go, to be replaced by a part-timer.

Here is the Western emphasis on rationality and the mind—as opposed to the rest of the body—and I believe that our educational system has been skewed strongly away from sensation as it relates to knowing and learning. I'd like to read Healy's book. —A.L.

When Ortiz finally got the students rounded up and out the door, the kids were still worked up. "They're never this wired after reading group," she said. "They're usually just exhausted, because I've been reading with them, making them write and talk." Back in homeroom Ortiz showed off the students' monthly handwritten writing samples. "Now, could you do that on the computer?" she asked. "No, because we'd be hung up on finding the keys." So why does Ortiz bother taking her students to the computer lab at all? "I guess I come in here for the computer literacy. If everyone else is getting it, I feel these kids should get it too."

Some computerized elementary school programs have avoided these pitfalls, but the record subject by subject is mixed at best. Take writing, where by all accounts and by my own observations the computer does encourage practice—changes are easier to make on a keyboard than with an eraser, and the lettering looks better. Diligent students use these conveniences to improve their writing, but the less committed frequently get seduced by electronic opportunities to make a school paper look snazzy. (The easy "cut and paste" function in today's word-processing programs, for example, is apparently encouraging many students to cobble together research materials without thinking them through.) Reading programs get particularly bad reviews. One small but carefully controlled study went so far as to claim that Reader Rabbit, a reading program now used in more than 100,000 schools, caused students to suffer a 50 percent drop in creativity. (Apparently, after forty-nine students used the program for seven months, they were no longer able to answer open-ended questions and showed a markedly diminished ability to brainstorm with fluency and originality.) What about hard sciences, which seem so well suited to computer study? Logo, the high-profile programming language refined by Seymour Papert and widely used in middle and high schools, fostered huge hopes of expanding children's cognitive skills. As students directed the computer to build things, such as geometric shapes, Papert believed, they would learn "procedural thinking," similar to the way a computer processes information. According to a number of studies, however, Logo has generally failed to deliver on its promises. Judah Schwartz, a professor of education at Harvard and a co-director of the school's Educational Technology Center, told me that a few newer applications, when used properly, can dramatically expand children's math and science thinking by giving them new tools to "make and

In papers where I have done major revising by the cut-and-paste method, I've found that I finish them without having a clear recollection of the flow of my arguments. —H.R.

I want to say "Yes, but . . ." to Oppenheimer's remarks about computers and writing. I think he understates the benefits of computers in writing classes. —J.R.

Despite the improvements, I'm skeptical of educational software programs. When I used them in junior high, I learned less about the subject being presented than about the computer functions themselves. —H.R.

explore conjectures." Still, Schwartz acknowledges that perhaps "ninety-nine percent" of the educational programs are "terrible, really terrible."

In the hard sciences, do computers make what is genuinely complex look appealingly simple? —J.R.

Even in success stories important caveats continually pop up. The best educational software is usually complex—most suited to older students and sophisticated teachers. In other cases the schools have been blessed with abundance—fancy equipment, generous financial support, or extra teachers—that is difficult if not impossible to duplicate in the average school. Even if it could be duplicated, the literature suggests, many teachers would still struggle with technology. Computers suffer frequent breakdowns; when they do work, their seductive images often distract students from the lessons at hand—which many teachers say makes it difficult to build meaningful rapport with their students.

With such a discouraging record of student and teacher performance with computers, why has the Clinton Administration focused so narrowly on the hopeful side of the story? Part of the answer may lie in the makeup of the Administration's technology task force. Judging from accounts of the task force's deliberations, all thirty-six members are unequivocal technology advocates. Two thirds of them work in the high-tech and entertainment industries. The effect of the group's tilt can be seen in its report. Its introduction adopts the authoritative posture of impartial fact-finder, stating that "this report does not attempt to lay out a national blueprint, nor does it recommend specific public policy goals." But it comes pretty close. Each chapter describes various strategies for getting computers into classrooms, and the introduction acknowledges that "this report does not evaluate the relative merits of competing demands on educational funding (e.g., more computers versus smaller class sizes)."

The Clinton administration's ties to Hollywood were well known, and many of the advisors were strongly connected to related high-tech firms—thus the particular view of computers as necessary and good for education. —A.L.

When I spoke with Esther Dyson and other task-force members about what discussion the group had had about the potential downside of computerized education, they said there hadn't been any. And when I asked Linda Roberts, Clinton's lead technology adviser in the Department of Education, whether the task force was influenced

How can we raise both sides of the issue for debate where it will count? —H.R.

I've followed Dyson's work for years now, and I am extremely surprised at her answer. —A.L.

Oppenheimer here asks just the right questions for his critical analysis. —J.R.

by any self-interest, she said no, quite the opposite: the group's charter actually gave its members license to help the technology industry directly, but they concentrated on schools because that's where they saw the greatest need.

That sense of need seems to have been spreading outside Washington. Last summer a California task force urged the state to spend $11 billion on computers in California schools, which have struggled for years under funding cuts that have driven academic achievement down to among the lowest levels in the nation. This task force, composed of forty-six teachers, parents, technology experts, and business executives, concluded, "More than any other single measure, computers and network technologies, properly implemented, offer the greatest potential to right what's wrong with our public schools." Other options mentioned in the group's report—reducing class size, improving teachers' salaries and facilities, expanding hours of instruction—were considered less important than putting kids in front of computers.

"Hypertext Minds"

I worry that devoting too many hours to any *medium puts kids at risk in some way. If Howard Gardner is right in his claim that all people have multiple intelligences—not simply one IQ—then we have to allow children time to develop these multiple intelligences, and doing so will mean widely varying activities.* —A.L.

Today's parents, knowing firsthand how families were burned by television's false promises, may want some objective advice about the age at which their children should become computer literate. Although there are no real guidelines, computer boosters send continual messages that if children don't begin early, they'll be left behind. Linda Roberts thinks that there's no particular minimum age—and no maximum number of hours that children should spend at a terminal. Are there examples of excess? "I haven't seen it yet," Roberts told me with a laugh. In schools throughout the country administrators and teachers demonstrate the same excitement, boasting about the wondrous things that children of five or six can do on computers: drawing, typing, playing with elementary science simulations and other programs called "educational games."

Will schools have to worry about teaching these basic skills to children? Within a few years, might not computers—in one form or another—be as common as TVs? —J.R.

The schools' enthusiasm for these activities is not universally shared by specialists in childhood development. The doubters' greatest concern is for the very young—preschool through third grade, when a child is most impressionable. Their apprehension involves two main issues.

First, they consider it important to give children a broad base—emotionally, intellectually, and in the five senses—before introducing something as technical and one-dimensional as a computer. Second, they believe that the human and physical world holds greater learning potential.

The importance of a broad base for a child may be most apparent when it's missing. In *Endangered Minds,* Jane Healy wrote of an English teacher who could readily tell which of her students' essays were conceived on a computer. "They don't link ideas," the teacher says. "They just write one thing, and then they write another one, and they don't seem to see or develop the relationships between them." The problem, Healy argued, is that the pizzazz of computerized schoolwork may hide these analytical gaps, which "won't become apparent until [the student] can't organize herself around a homework assignment or a job that requires initiative. More commonplace activities, such as figuring out how to nail two boards together, organizing a game . . . may actually form a better basis for real-world intelligence."

False causality? I encountered the problem Healey describes in student papers long before computers were available. —J.R.

Others believe they have seen computer games expand children's imaginations. High-tech children "think differently from the rest of us," William D. Winn, the director of the Learning Center at the University of Washington's Human Interface Technology Laboratory, told *Business Week* in a recent cover story on the benefits of computer games. "They develop hypertext minds. They leap around. It's as though their cognitive strategies were parallel, not sequential." Healy argues the opposite. She and other psychologists think that the computer screen flattens information into narrow, sequential data. This kind of material, they believe, exercises mostly one half of the brain—the left hemisphere, where primarily sequential thinking occurs. The "right brain" meanwhile gets short shrift—yet this is the hemisphere that works on different kinds of information simultaneously. It shapes our multi-faceted impressions, and serves as the engine of creative analysis.

Opinions diverge in part because research on the brain is still so sketchy, and computers are so new, that the effect of computers on the brain remains a great mystery. "I don't think we know anything about it," Harry Chugani, a pediatric neurobiologist at Wayne State University, told me. This very ignorance makes skeptics wary. "Nobody knows how kids' internal wiring works," Clifford Stoll wrote in *Silicon Snake Oil,* "but anyone who's directed away from social interactions has a head start on turning out weird. . . . No computer can teach what a walk through a pine forest feels like. Sensation has no substitute."

I often think that if I were beginning my studies all over again, I would focus on neuroscience. Especially in the last few years, a number of excellent books about how the brain/mind works and develops have appeared, and I read all of them with great interest! —A.L.

This points to the conservative developmentalists' second concern: the danger that even if hours in front of the screen are limited, unabashed enthusiasm for the computer sends the wrong message: that the mediated world is more significant than the real one. "It's like TV commercials," Barbara Scales, the head teacher at the Child Study Center at the University of California at Berkeley, told me. "Kids get so hyped up, it can change their expectations about stimulation, versus what they generate themselves." In *Silicon Snake Oil,* Michael Fellows, a computer scientist at the University of Victoria, in British Columbia, was even blunter. "Most schools would probably be better off if they threw their computers into the Dumpster."

Many college students seem to have a healthy skepticism about computers. Few students get hooked. —J.R.

Faced with such sharply contrasting viewpoints, which are based on such uncertain ground, how is a responsible policymaker to proceed? "A prudent society controls its own infatuation with 'progress' when planning for its young," Healy argued in *Endangered Minds.*

> Unproven technologies . . . may offer lively visions, but they can also be detrimental to the development of the young plastic brain. The cerebral cortex is a wondrously well-buffered mechanism that can withstand a good bit of well-intentioned bungling. Yet there is a point at which fundamental neural substrates for reasoning may be jeopardized for

children who lack proper physical, intellectual, or emotional nurturance. Childhood—and the brain—have their own imperatives. In development, missed opportunities may be difficult to recapture.

The problem is that technology leaders rarely include these or other warnings in their recommendations. When I asked Dyson why the Clinton task force proceeded with such fervor, despite the classroom computer's shortcomings, she said, "It's so clear the world is changing."

Must computer training come early? Computers and software are getting easier to operate, not harder. Can't we afford to introduce children to computers when they are ready? —J.R.

Real Job Training

In the past decade, according to the presidential task force's report, the number of jobs requiring computer skills has increased from 25 percent of all jobs in 1983 to 47 percent in 1993. By 2000, the report estimates, 60 percent of the nation's jobs will demand these skills—and pay an average of 10 to 15 percent more than jobs involving no computer work. Although projections of this sort are far from reliable, it's a safe bet that computer skills will be needed for a growing proportion of tomorrow's work force. But what priority should these skills be given among other studies?

When will this trend plateau? Oppenheimer implies that schools are overpreparing for this trend. —H.R.

In fact, over 50 percent of all jobs are now classified as "information" jobs. But simple knowledge of technical aspects of computers does not prepare people to do well at such jobs. —A.L.

Listen to Tom Henning, a physics teacher at Thurgood Marshall, the San Francisco technology high school. Henning has a graduate degree in engineering, and helped to found a Silicon Valley company that manufactures electronic navigation equipment. "My bias is the physical reality," Henning told me, as we sat outside a shop where he was helping students to rebuild an old motorcycle. "I'm no technophobe. I can program computers." What worries Henning is that computers at best engage only two senses, hearing and sight—and only two-dimensional sight at that. "Even if they're doing three-dimensional computer modeling, that's still a two-D replica of a three-D world. If you took a kid who grew up on Nintendo, he's not going to have the necessary skills. He needs to have done it first with Tinkertoys or clay, or carved it out of balsa wood." As David Elkind, a professor of child development at Tufts University, puts it, "A dean of the University of Iowa's school of engineering used to say the best engineers were the farm boys," because they knew how machinery really worked.

Surely many employers will disagree, and welcome the commercially applicable computer skills that today's high-tech training can bring them. What's striking is how easy it is to find other employers who share Henning's and Elkind's concerns.

Kris Meisling, a senior geological-research adviser for Mobil Oil, told me that "people who use computers a lot slowly grow rusty in their ability to think." Meisling's group creates charts and maps—some computerized, some not—to plot where to drill for oil. In large one-dimensional analyses, such as sorting volumes of seismic data, the computer saves vast amounts of time, sometimes making previously impossible tasks easy. This lures people in his field, Meisling believes, into using computers as much as possible. But when geologists turn to computers for "interpretive" projects, he finds, they often miss information, and their oversights are further obscured by the computer's captivating automatic design functions. This is why Meisling still works regularly with a pencil and paper—tools that, ironically, he considers more interactive than the computer, because they force him to think implications through.

"You can't simultaneously get an overview and detail with a computer," he says. "It's linear. It gives you tunnel vision. What computers can do well is what can be calculated over and over. What they can't do is innovation. If you think of some new way to do or look at things and the software can't do it, you're stuck. So a lot of people think 'Well, I guess it's a dumb idea, or it's unnecessary.'"

High-tech firms here in Austin once snapped up graduate students in English who could program or create Web pages—the companies seemed to value literacy as much as technological skills. —J.R.

I have heard similar warnings from people in other businesses, including high-tech enterprises. A spokeswoman for Hewlett-Packard, the giant California computer-products company, told me the company rarely hires people who are predominantly computer experts, favoring instead those who have a talent for teamwork and are flexible

I have heard precisely the same stories from friends in Silicon Valley high-tech firms. —A.L.

and innovative. Hewlett-Packard is such a believer in hands-on experience that since 1992 it has spent $2.6 million helping forty-five school districts build math and science skills the old-fashioned way—using real materials, such as dirt, seeds, water, glass vials, and magnets. Much the same perspective came from several recruiters in film and computer-game animation. In work by artists who have spent a lot of time on computers "you'll see a stiffness or a flatness, a lack of richness and depth," Karen Chelini, the director of human resources for LucasArts Entertainment, George Lucas's interactive-games maker, told me recently. "With traditional art training, you train the eye to pay attention to body movement. You learn attitude, feeling, expression. The ones who are good are those who as kids couldn't be without their sketchbook."

Many jobs obviously will demand basic computer skills if not sophisticated knowledge. But that doesn't mean that the parents or the teachers of young students need to panic. Joseph Weizenbaum, a professor emeritus of computer science at MIT, told the *San Jose Mercury News* that even at his technology-heavy institution new students can learn all the computer skills they need "in a summer." This seems to hold in the business world, too. Patrick MacLeamy, an executive vice-president of Hellmuth Obata & Kassabaum, the country's largest architecture firm, recently gave me numerous examples to illustrate that computers pose no threat to his company's creative work. Although architecture professors are divided on the value of computerized design tools, in MacLeamy's opinion they generally enhance the process. But he still considers "knowledge of the hands" to be valuable—today's architects just have to develop it in other ways. (His firm's answer is through building models.) Nonetheless, as positive as MacLeamy is about computers, he has found the company's two-week computer training to be sufficient. In fact, when he's hiring, computer skills don't enter into his list of priorities. He looks for a strong character; an ability to speak, write, and comprehend; and a rich education in the history of architecture.

Two weeks! This figure surprises me; I wonder how much data MacLeamy has to back it up. —A.L.

The Schools That Business Built

Newspaper financial sections carry almost daily pronouncements from the computer industry and other businesses about their high-tech hopes for America's schoolchildren. Many of these are joined to philanthropic commitments to helping schools make curriculum changes. This sometimes gets businesspeople involved in schools, where they've begun to understand and work with the many daunting problems that are unrelated to technology. But if business gains too much influence over the curriculum, the schools can become a kind of corporate training center—largely at taxpayer expense.

For more than a decade scholars and government commissions have criticized the increasing professionalization of the college years—frowning at the way traditional liberal arts are being edged out by hot topics of the moment or strictly business-oriented studies. The schools' real job, the technology critic Neil Postman argued in his book *The End of Education* (1995), is to focus on "how to make a life, which is quite different from how to make a living." Some see the arrival of boxes of computer hardware and software in the schools as taking the commercial trend one step further, down into high school and elementary grades. "Should you be choosing a career in kindergarten?" asks Helen Sloss Luey, a social worker and a former president of San Francisco's Parent Teacher Association. "People need to be trained to learn and change, while education seems to be getting more specific."

I agree with Postman's general point, but I do not think that these two goals—making a life and making a living—need to be seen as antithetical. Can't one "make" both, and do a good job at each? —A.L.

Indeed it does. The New Technology High School in Napa (the school where a computer sits on every student's desk) was started by the school district and a consortium of more than forty businesses. "We want to be the school that business built," Robert Nolan, a founder of the school, told me last fall. "We wanted to create an environment that mimicked what exists in the high-tech business world." Increasingly, Nolan explained, business leaders want to hire people specifically trained in the skill they need. One of Nolan's partners, Ted Fujimoto, of the Landmark Consulting Group, told me that instead of just asking the business community for financial support, the school will now undertake a trade: in return for donating funds, businesses can specify what kinds of employees they want—"a two-way street." Sometimes the traffic is a bit heavy in one direction. In January, *The New York Times* published a lengthy education supplement describing numerous examples of how business is increasingly dominating school software and other curriculum materials, and not always toward purely educational goals.

People who like the idea that their taxes go to computer training might be surprised at what a poor investment it can be. Larry Cuban, the Stanford education professor, writes that changes in the classroom for which business lobbies rarely hold long-term value. Rather, they're often guided by labor-market needs that turn out to be transitory; when the economy shifts, workers are left unprepared for new jobs. In the economy as a whole, according to a recent story in *The New York Times,* performance trends in our schools have shown virtually no link to the rises and falls in the nation's measures of productivity and growth. This is one reason that school traditionalists push for broad liberal-arts curricula, which they feel develop students' values and intellect, instead of focusing on today's idea about what tomorrow's jobs will be.

I wish Oppenheimer would be more specific about those narrow technological skills businesses want students to develop. —J.R.

High-tech proponents argue that the best education software does develop flexible business intellects. In the *Business Week* story on computer games, for example, academics and professionals expressed amazement at the speed, savvy, and facility that young computer jocks sometimes demonstrate. Several pointed in particular to computer simulations, which some business leaders believe are becoming increasingly important in fields ranging from engineering, manufacturing, and troubleshooting to the tracking of economic activity and geopolitical risk. The best of these simulations may be valuable, albeit for strengthening one form of thinking. But the average simulation program may be of questionable relevance.

This reminds me of my cousin who graduated with a humanities degree and quickly acquired the skills to land a job as a computer troubleshooter. —H.R.

Sherry Turkle, the sociology professor at MIT, has studied youngsters using computers for more than twenty years. In her book *Life on the Screen: Identity in the Age of the Internet* (1995) she described a disturbing experience with a simulation game called SimLife. After she sat down with a thirteen-year-old named Tim, she was stunned at the way

> Tim can keep playing even when he has no idea what is driving events. For example, when his sea urchins become extinct, I ask him why.
>
> TIM: "I don't know, it's just something that happens."
>
> ST: "Do you know how to find out why it happened?"
>
> TIM: "No."
>
> ST: "Do you mind that you can't tell why?"
>
> TIM: "No. I don't let things like that bother me. It's not what's important."

Anecdotes like this lead some educators to worry that as children concentrate on how to manipulate software instead of on the subject at hand, learning can diminish rather than grow. Simulations, for example, are built on hidden assumptions, many of which are oversimplified if not highly questionable. All too often, Turkle wrote recently in *The American Prospect,* "experiences with simulations do not open up questions but close them down." Turkle's concern is that software of this sort fosters passivity, ultimately dulling people's sense of what they can change in the world. There's a tendency, Turkle told me, "to take things at 'interface' value." Indeed, after mastering SimCity, a popular game about urban planning, a tenth-grade girl boasted to Turkle that she'd learned the following rule: "Raising taxes always leads to riots."

Oppenheimer draws quite an inference from the single example he presents. I am not convinced. —J.R.

This is one of the most worrisome claims in Oppenheimer's article. I hope Turkle, whose research in this area is generally very well respected, will turn her attention to studying whether this claim holds up. —A.L.

The business community also offers tangible financial support, usually by donating equipment. Welcome as this is, it can foster a high-tech habit. Once a school's computer system is set up, the companies often drop their support. This saddles the school with heavy long-term responsibilities: maintenance of the computer network and the need for constant software upgrades and constant teacher training—the full burden of which can cost far more than the initial hardware and software combined. Schools must then look for handouts from other companies, enter the grant-seeking game, or delicately go begging in their own communities. "We can go to the well only so often," Toni-Sue Passantino, the principal of the Bayside Middle School, in San Mateo, California, told me recently. Last year Bayside let a group of seventh- and eighth-graders spend eighteen months and countless hours creating a rudimentary virtual-reality program, with the support of several high-tech firms. The companies' support ended after that period, however—creating a financial speed bump of a kind that the Rand Corporation noted in a report to the Clinton Administration as a common obstacle.

School administrators may be outwardly excited about computerized instruction, but they're also shrewdly aware of these financial challenges. In March of last year, for instance, when California launched its highly promoted "Net-Day '96" (a campaign to wire 12,000 California schools to the Internet in one day), school participation was far below expectations, even in technology-conscious San Francisco. In the city papers school officials wondered how they were supposed to support an Internet program when they didn't even have the money to repair crumbling buildings, install electrical outlets, and hire the dozens of new teachers recently required so as to reduce class size.

One way around the donation maze is to simplify: use inexpensive, basic software and hardware, much of which is available through recycling programs. Such frugality can offer real value in the elementary grades, especially since basic word-processing tools are most helpful to children just learning to write. Yet schools, like the rest of us, can't resist the latest toys. "A lot of people will spend all their money on fancy new equipment that can do great things, and sometimes it just gets used for typing classes," Ray Porter, a computer resource teacher for the San Francisco schools, told me

This solution has not proved viable: the equipment available through "recycling" is too outdated to allow students to create the kind of projects they need to succeed in their classes.
—A.L.

recently. "Parents, school boards, and the reporters want to see only razzle-dazzle state-of-the-art."

INTERNET ISOLATION

It is hard to visit a high-tech school without being led by a teacher into a room where students are communicating with people hundreds or thousands of miles away—over the Internet or sometimes through video-conferencing systems (two-way TV sets that broadcast live from each room). Video conferences, although fun, are an expensive way to create classroom thrills. But the Internet, when used carefully, offers exciting academic prospects—most dependably, once again, for older students. In one case schools in different states have tracked bird migrations and then posted their findings on the World Wide Web, using it as their own national notebook. In San Francisco eighth-grade economics students have e-mailed Chinese and Japanese businessmen to fulfill an assignment on what it would take to build an industrial plant overseas. Schools frequently use the Web to publish student writing. While thousands of self-published materials like these have turned the Web into a worldwide vanity press, the network sometimes gives young writers their first real audience.

This assessment of the Internet seems balanced—both good and bad are acknowledged. —J.R.

The free nature of Internet information also means that students are confronted with chaos, and real dangers. "The Net's beauty is that it's uncontrolled," Stephen Kerr, a professor at the College of Education at the University of Washington and the editor of *Technology in the Future of Schooling* (1996), told me. "It's information by anyone, for anyone. There's racist stuff, bigoted, hate-group stuff, filled with paranoia; bomb recipes; how to engage in various kinds of crimes, electronic and otherwise; scams and swindles. It's all there. It's all available." Older students may be sophisticated enough to separate the Net's good food from its poisons, but even the savvy can be misled. On almost any subject the Net offers a plethora of seemingly sound "research." But under close inspection much of it

Students in one of my classes identified a number of racist sites, analyzed the rhetorical strategies used by the sites, and wrote compelling counterarguments to them. —A.L.

proves to be ill informed, or just superficial. "That's the antithesis of what classroom kids should be exposed to," Kerr said.

This makes traditionalists emphasize the enduring value of printed books, vetted as most are by editing. In many schools, however, libraries are fairly limited. I now volunteer at a San Francisco high school where the library shelves are so bare that I can see how the Internet's ever-growing number of research documents, with all their shortcomings, can sometimes be a blessing.

The replacement of print books by cyber versions strikes me as impractical and unhealthy. —H.R.

Even computer enthusiasts give the Net tepid reviews. "Most of the content on the Net is total garbage," Esther Dyson acknowledges. "But if you find one good thing you can use it a million times." Kerr believes that Dyson is being unrealistic. "If you find a useful site one day, it may not be there the next day, or the information is different. Teachers are being asked to jump in and figure out if what they find on the Net is worthwhile. They don't have the skill or time to do that." Especially when students rely on the Internet's much-vaunted search software. Although these tools deliver hundreds or thousands of sources within seconds, students may not realize that search engines, and the Net itself, miss important information all the time.

Of course, neither students nor instructors need to come to the Internet without guidance. And learning to find information is a vital skill. —J.R.

The old axiom "garbage in, garbage out" may count double online: we all need to remember this and to think critically about the information we find online. —A.L.

"We need *less* surfing in the schools, not more," David Gelernter, a professor of computer science at Yale, wrote last year in *The Weekly Standard*. "Couldn't we teach them to use what they've got before favoring them with three orders of magnitude *more?*" In my conversations with Larry Cuban, of Stanford, he argued, "Schooling is not about information. It's getting kids to think about information. It's about understanding and knowledge and wisdom."

It may be that youngsters' growing fascination with the Internet and other ways to use computers will distract from yet another of Clinton's education priorities: to build up the reading skills of American children. Sherry Dingman, an assistant professor of psychology at Marist College, in Poughkeepsie, New York, who is optimistic about many computer applications, believes that if children start using computers before they have a broad foundation in reading from books, they will be cheated out of opportunities to develop imagination. "If we think we're going to take kids who haven't been read to, and fix it by sitting them in front of a computer, we're fooling ourselves," Dingman told me not long ago. This doesn't mean that teachers or parents should resort to books on CD-ROM, which Dingman considers "a great waste of time," stuffing children's minds with "canned" images instead of stimulating youngsters to create their own. "Computers are lollipops that rot your teeth" is how Marilyn Darch, an English teacher at Poly High School, in Long Beach, California, put it in *Silicon Snake Oil*. "The kids love them. But once they get hooked. . . . It makes reading a book seem tedious. Books don't have sound effects, and their brains have to do all the work."

Computer advocates like to point out that the Internet allows for all kinds of intellectual challenges—especially when students use E-mail, or post notes in "newsgroup" discussions, to correspond with accomplished experts. Such experts, however, aren't consistently available. When they are, online "conversations" generally take place when correspondents are sitting alone, and the dialogue lacks the unpredictability and richness that occur in face-to-face discussions. In fact, when youngsters are put into groups for the "collaborative" learning that computer defenders celebrate, realistically only one child sits at the keyboard at a time. (During my school visits children tended to get quite possessive about the mouse and the keyboard, resulting in frustration and noisy disputes more often than collaboration.) In combination these constraints lead to yet another of the childhood developmentalists' concerns—that computers encourage social isolation.

Just a Glamorous Tool

It would be easy to characterize the battle over computers as merely another chapter in the world's oldest story: humanity's natural resistance to change.

But that does an injustice to the forces at work in this transformation. This is not just the future versus the past, uncertainty versus nostalgia; it is about encouraging a fundamental shift in personal priorities—a minimizing of the real, physical world in favor of an unreal "virtual" world. It is about teaching youngsters that exploring what's on a two-dimensional screen is more important than playing with real objects, or sitting down to an attentive conversation with a friend, a parent, or a teacher. By extension, it means downplaying the importance of conversation, of careful listening, and of expressing oneself in person with acuity and individuality. In the process, it may also limit the development of children's imaginations.

I am most alarmed about this possibility. However, part of me wonders whether the "virtual" world isn't also real—and we just can't quite see it that way yet. —A.L.

Some either/or thinking going on here? —J.R.

Oppenheimer's definition of "reality" is vague and unconvincing. He doesn't address the issue that written texts have a similar distance from the "real" world. —H.R.

Perhaps this is why Steven Jobs, one of the founders of Apple Computer and a man who claims to have "spearheaded giving away more computer equipment to schools than anybody else on the planet," has come to a grim conclusion: "What's wrong with education cannot be fixed with technology," he told *Wired* magazine last year. "No amount of technology will make a dent. . . . You're not going to solve the problems by putting all knowledge onto CD-ROMS. We can put a Web site in every school—none of this is bad. It's bad only if it lulls us into thinking we're doing something to solve the problem with education." Jane David, the consultant to Apple, concurs, with a commonly heard caveat. "There are real dangers," she told me, "in looking to technology to be the savior of education. But it won't survive without the technology."

Arguments like David's remind Clifford Stoll of yesteryear's promises about television. He wrote in *Silicon Snake Oil,*

> "Sesame Street" . . . has been around for twenty years. Indeed, its idea of making learning relevant to all was as widely promoted in the seventies as the Internet is today.
>
> So where's that demographic wave of creative and brilliant students now entering college? Did kids really need to learn how to watch television? Did we inflate their expectations that learning would always be colorful and fun?

Computer enthusiasts insist that the computer's "interactivity" and multimedia features make this machine far superior to television. Nonetheless, Stoll wrote,

> I see a parallel between the goals of "Sesame Street" and those of children's computing. Both are pervasive, expensive and encourage children to sit still. Both display animated cartoons, gaudy numbers and weird, random noises. . . . Both give the sensation that by merely watching a screen, you can acquire information without work and without discipline.

As the technology critic Neil Postman put it to a Harvard electronic-media conference, "I thought that television would be the last great technology that people would go into with their eyes closed. Now you have the computer."

The lengthy essay ends with some specific proposals—all of which seem reasonable, given the evidence presented. —J.R.

The solution is not to ban computers from classrooms altogether. But it may be to ban federal spending on what is fast becoming an overheated campaign. After all, the private sector, with its constant supply of used computers and the computer industry's vigorous competition for new customers, seems well equipped to handle the situation. In fact, if schools can impose some limits—on technology donors and on themselves—rather than indulging in a consumer frenzy, most will probably find themselves with more electronic gear than they need. That could free the billions that Clinton wants to devote to technology and make it available for impoverished fundamentals: teaching solid skills in reading, thinking, listening, and talking; organizing inventive field trips and other rich hands-on experiences; and, of course, building up the nation's core of knowledgeable, inspiring teachers. These notions are considerably less glamorous than computers are, but their worth is firmly proved through a long history.

Is banning funding too extreme a reaction? Is this the only way to protect against the "dangers" of computers? What about school districts that don't have the necessary resources? —H.R.

Last fall, after the school administrators in Mansfield, Massachusetts, had eliminated proposed art, music, and physical-education positions in favor of buying computers, Michael Bellino, an electrical engineer at Boston University's Center for Space Physics, appeared before the Massachusetts Board of Education to protest. "The purpose of the schools [is] to, as one teacher argues, 'Teach carpentry, not hammer,'" he testified. "We need to teach the whys and ways of the world. Tools come and tools go. Teaching our children tools limits their knowledge to these tools and hence limits their futures."

Afterwords

As I read Oppenheimer's essay, I kept thinking back to 1983, the year I got my first real computer. As I recall, it was about twice the size of the one I now have on my desk, and about four or five times the size of my little laptop. And I struggled to memorize complicated codes, to figure out how to configure the right printer, and to remember which key to hit to center text and carry out other word-processing functions. I signed up for a word-processing class, but quickly withdrew in favor of trial and error—and the help of friends. Will I ever get the hang of this thing?

More than twenty years later, I find I have internalized a great deal of information about how to use the computer to my advantage, especially in communicating with people around the world, in searching for esoteric—and sometimes everyday—information, and in producing documents from short speeches to entire books. But I am still learning and experimenting with how best to use technology in my classrooms. While I routinely set up closed listservs for my classes and make materials available on the Web, I certainly have not perfected these strategies. Fortunately for me, the students in my classes are usually willing and able to help with the logistical problems we face, and they routinely have the best ideas about how to integrate technology into our courses. What I hope to do more of is team-teaching via technology.

Oppenheimer has given me a lot to think about in his warnings about computer "delusions." As a result, I will be particularly cautious in my use of technology in my classrooms. But I am certainly not ready to give up on its effectiveness. —A.L.

For the past ten years, I've taught all of my courses in a networked computer classroom. I often joke that I'm never more than five minutes away from throwing out the d—n machines and going back to paper and blackboards. That's because the technology never quite works as advertised: a printer goes offline; the browser software freezes on screen; the word processor formats a list the way it *wants to; and nobody remembers the passwords to the online forums.*

Yet I also know that I now take for granted much of what computers do for me. I correspond daily with a dozen people or more via email, can locate almost any information I need on the Web, expect flawless and immediate copies of everything I write, and depend on the word processor to catch my more egregious spelling and grammar errors. My class presentations now routinely rely on PowerPoint and an LCD projector, and I deliver my policy statements, syllabi, and assignments via course Web sites. I realize that I am hooked. The computer has become a permanent and necessary part of my pro-

fessional world. But it is only a tool. It hasn't made me smarter—just quicker, more productive, and, frankly, more frazzled.

So Oppenheimer's piece makes sense to me. He's not a Luddite who fears electronic technology, but an advocate for education. I think he overstates his case near the end of the essay, and he may underestimate the contributions computers can make to education. But learning is rarely easy, and students will be hurt if their machines make it seem so. —J.R.

Overall, I found this article interesting and often compelling. The craze for computer technology in schools is convincingly shown to be more extreme than prudence warrants. The arguments Oppenheimer makes about why the role of computers in classrooms should change seem to be arranged logically. He covers and anticipates in his article many of the questions that occurred to me.

I would have appreciated a clearer comparison between the skills developed in children by computer work and those skills developed by other areas of education. If this information was not yet available in 1997, when Oppenheimer was writing, a summary of what was being done—and by whom—to research these issues would have been particularly interesting to me. His conclusion struck me at first as an overreaction. In thinking it over, however, I've decided that his suggestion about controlling the influence government money has over educational practices might have some merit.

— H.R.

QUESTIONING THE TEXT

1. The five claims Oppenheimer explores are listed near the beginning of the essay (p. 302). Working with a classmate, review these five claims carefully. Then work together to create an outline of the rest of Oppenheimer's essay, labeling the parts of the essay that address each of the claims he considers. Which claims get most—or least—attention? Why might Oppenheimer have chosen to focus on some more sharply than others?
2. List the sources Oppenheimer refers to in his essay, including the writers and the titles of their works, if given. What do these sources seem to have in common? Why do you think Oppenheimer chose each one?

MAKING CONNECTIONS

3. Oppenheimer cites Sherry Turkle's work to help make the point that an overemphasis on technology in education can hinder rather than help students. Read Turkle's essay in this chapter, "Cuddling Up to Cyborg

Babies" (p. 359), and consider how you might use it to expand Oppenheimer's discussion. Does Turkle provide evidence in support of some of Oppenheimer's claims or evidence that would argue against some of them? Give some examples to back up your answer.

4. Might J. Michael Bishop (p. 280) label Oppenheimer an "enemy of promise"? Why, or why not?

JOINING THE CONVERSATION

5. You may or may not be among those who remember using computers from your earliest years. In either case, reflect for a while on the technologies you encountered during your early years in school. Did you encounter reading machines? Television and video? Overhead projectors? Computers? What else? Share your memories with two classmates, and brainstorm together for technologies you may have forgotten. Finally, write a letter to Oppenheimer in which you use your own school experience to support or challenge his argument.
6. Oppenheimer characterizes the "battle over computers" as being "about encouraging a fundamental shift in personal priorities—a minimizing of the real, physical world in favor of an unreal 'virtual' world" (pp. 323–324). Spend some time talking with two classmates about this statement, about what you think it means, and about what evidence you can see around you that relates to it. Then work independently on several freewriting "loops" in response to the statement. Start by writing for 10 to 15 minutes (without stopping) about whatever comes into your mind when you read the statement. Identify the most interesting sentence or idea in what you have written, and use it as the beginning of another "loop"; again, write for 10 to 15 minutes. (You may want to carry out several additional loops.) Finally, go over all your materials, and prepare a one-page critical response to Oppenheimer's statement.

ANTHONY WALTON
Technology Versus African Americans

ANTHONY WALTON is the author of Mississippi: An American Journey *(1996), in which he weaves lyrics, poems, excerpts from other writers, and photographs into a mosaic of his own family's history as plantation slaves in Mississippi and reflects on his own upbringing in a fairly affluent suburb of Chicago. In this and other works, Walton laments the "historical amnesia" characteristic of the United States, in which we consistently forget, or repress, a past that included slavery, lynchings, and other great injustices. Reading and research for* Mississippi *led Walton to examine the interactions of technology and African Americans, and what he found disturbed him: many important technological advancements, such as the cotton gin, had actually served to worsen the lives of African Americans.*

Walton (b. 1965) pursues this idea in "Technology Versus African Americans," which appeared in the January 1999 issue of the Atlantic Monthly. *Considering the large-sailed ships that allowed for the opening and flourishing of the slave trade, Walton concludes that "the slave wars and trade were only the first of many encounters with Western technology to prove disastrous for people of African descent." Walton sees the effects of this discriminatory relationship still at work today, as very few African Americans enter high-tech fields. (He notes that while African Americans comprise over 13 percent of the population, they earn a "shockingly low 1.8 percent of the Ph.D.s conferred in computer science.") In short, for a complex set of historical, social, and economic reasons, Walton argues, young African Americans do not seek out the technological/scientific professions.*

When I was in college in the early 1960s, professional possibilities seemed fairly narrow to me, though I didn't remark on it then. I could imagine myself as a secretary, a nurse, a teacher, perhaps a social worker — all jobs deemed appropriate for women at the time. I count myself enormously lucky to have chosen teaching, which has challenged and sustained my dreams and goals throughout my career. Others, of course, were not so lucky. And what of today? What professional possibilities seem open and beckoning to you? More important, what effect do such factors as gender, race, and class continue to exert on these possibilities? — A.L.

A friend of mine owns a one-man computer firm specializing in the design and construction of Internet Web sites—those commercial, entertainment, and informational junctions in cyberspace that can be visited from personal computers around the world. From time to time he contracts for more work than he can handle, and then he posts an electronic want ad stating the number of lines of computer code to be written, the requisite computer language, the specific functions of the program being built, and the pay he's offering per line.

This ad is often answered by programmers from, as might be expected, Silicon Valley towns like San Jose and Palo Alto, or from Austin, Texas, or Cambridge, Massachusetts. The respondent might be someone recently laid off from Digital, a hacking grad student at Northwestern, or a precocious thirteen-year-old who learned the C++ language as an extra-credit project in middle school. The work is sent out over the Internet, and sent back ready to be incorporated into my friend's project. These programmers, whoever they are and wherever they're from, have proved reliable and punctual; their transactions, miraculous to the uninitiated, are so commonplace in the digital kingdom as to go unremarked.

Shortly after my friend began hiring extra help, he started getting responses from programmers in India. The Indians, often from the subcontinent's technological center of Bangalore, were savvy, literate, and, best of all, both fast and cheap—a contractor's dream. Accordingly, he has parceled out more and more programming to them and less and less to Americans. Not so patriotic, but isn't that what GATT and NAFTA are all about?

Stories like this are usually presented as cautionary tales about the loss of American jobs to the hungry masses of the Third World. But there is another troubling aspect to this story, one that loomed larger for me as I learned about what my friend did in his business and *how* he did it. Why weren't more African Americans involved in these developments, this business revolution? The activity was so clean, so sophisticated, and so lucrative; not least of all, it was the future.

I was reminded of the computer journalist Robert X. Cringely's docu- 5
mentary film *Triumph of the Nerds* (1996), about the creation of the current cyber-elite. Cringely spent time with young people at swap meets, watching them become entranced with electronics and the technological future, building their own machines and dreaming of starting the next Apple. There were no blacks in sight. Young black Americans, who could have been cashing in on the bonanza that was then buzzing through cyberspace, *didn't appear to be aware of it.* What kind of job could be more appropriate for a technologically literate inner-city youth than to perform this kind of service? Conceivably, it could be done without any capital outlay: one could surf the Net at school or the library, get the assignment and specs, and send the finished work back. Democratic guerrilla capitalism. A good job at a good wage, as the presidential hopeful Michael Dukakis[*] used to say.

There are high school kids working part time utilizing high-tech skills and college kids who are dropping out of school to work in the industry, if not starting their own companies. And as for the kids at Cringely's swap meet, it's not *likely* that any of them will start the next big thing, but it is at least possible. Apple, Hewlett Packard, and Oracle were all started with almost no capital by folks fooling around in their garages.

Michael Dukakis (b. 1933): 1988 Democratic presidential candidate

Where are the armies of ghetto youths ready to meet the innovation and programming needs of an exponentially expanding electronic frontier and get rich in the process, in what is perhaps the last gold rush in American history?

The history of African Americans during the past 400 years is traditionally narrated as an ongoing struggle against oppression and indifference on the part of the American mainstream, a struggle charted as an upward arc progressing toward ever more justice and opportunity. This description is accurate, but there is another, equally true way of narrating that history, and its implications are as frightening for the country as a whole as they are for blacks as a group. The history of African Americans since the discovery of the New World is the story of their encounter with technology, an encounter that has proved perhaps irremediably devastating to their hopes, dreams, and possibilities.

From the caravels, compasses, navigational techniques, and firearms of the first Portuguese explorers who reached the coast of West Africa in the 1440s to the never-ending expansion of microchip computing power and its implications for our society, the black community has had one negative encounter after another with the technological innovations of the mainstream. Within American history this aspect of blacks' experience is unique. One might argue that the disadvantageous situation of blacks vis-à-vis technology has as much to do with issues of class and wealth as it does with race, but such a critique verges on the disingenuous. As a group, blacks still lag well behind whites economically, and they have often suffered from the uses of technology in ways that other groups have not. In fact, they were often intentionally singled out to suffer. Poor whites, non-black Hispanics, and Asians were not dragged from their native lands to work as slaves and then buffeted for hundreds of years by the vagaries of technology and an economy they did not control. The historical experience of each ethnic group is unique and composed of its own problems and opportunities (or lack thereof).

What is intriguing, and deeply disturbing, is that blacks have participated as equals in the technological world only as consumers, otherwise existing on the margins of the ethos that defines the nation, underrepresented as designers, innovators, and implementers of our systems and machines. As a group, they have suffered from something that can loosely be called technological illiteracy. Though this has not been the point of technological innovation, it has undeniably been its fallout. It is important that we understand and come to terms with this *now;* there are technological developments in the making that could permanently affect the destiny of black Americans, as Americans and as global citizens. The dark possibility presented by the end of highly paid low-skilled labor, ever more powerful information machines, and global capitalism renders current policy disagreements over welfare, affirmative action, integration versus separatism, and the like trivial by comparison.

These issues, in my view, go to the very marrow of black experience in North America. They may also become a matter of survival for blacks as a group and for the nation as a whole, since those two fates are inextricably connected. As the world gets faster and more information-centered, it also gets meaner: disparities of wealth and power strengthen; opportunities change and often fade away. How can black Americans achieve the promise of America when that promise is largely predicated on the sector of the country's economy (and history) that has proved most costly to them—when the disturbing outcome of their almost 500 years of encountering Western technology and its practitioners is that many regard them as at best the stepchild of the American experiment?

Europeans had prowled the Mediterranean for 2,000 years, sailing from Greece to Rome, from Rome to Egypt, from Spain to Morocco, and on hundreds of other routes, before any systematic sailing craft or technique was developed. In the 1400s the Portuguese prince who came to be known as Henry the Navigator (1394–1460) dispatched a series of voyages to make maps and chart data; by the mid-1440s the Portuguese, in search of new, unexploited trade routes, had reached Cape Verde and the Senegal River.

As they worked their way down the northwestern African coast, the Portuguese came up against what seemed at first an insurmountable problem: strong winds and currents from the north meant that a ship returning to Lisbon would have to travel long distances against the wind. Enter the caravel, with its three masts and large sails—a perfectly designed solution to the problem, and the machine that allowed Portugal to rule the waves from West Africa to India for a hundred years.

The Atlantic slave trade was one of the industries that emerged from this new capability. Western technology was involved with the rise of black slavery in other ways as well: Arab and African slave traders exchanged their human chattels for textiles, metals, and firearms, all products of Western technological wizardry, and those same slavers used guns, vastly superior to African weapons of the time, in wars of conquest against those tribes whose members they wished to capture.

15 The slave wars and trade were only the first of many encounters with Western technology to prove disastrous for people of African descent. In the United States, as in South America and the Caribbean, the slaves were themselves the technology that allowed Europeans to master the wilderness. Then, in 1793, as the efficiency of the slave economy on cotton plantations (where slaves cost more to maintain than they could generate in profits) was being questioned in some quarters, Eli Whitney, of Connecticut, invented a simple gin that allowed harvested cotton to be picked clean of seeds—an essential step before milling—on a far greater scale than had previously been possible.

Suddenly rendered cost-efficient, cotton farming became a way to get rich quick. Thousands of black Africans were imported to do the work; in Mississippi alone the number of slaves increased from 498 in 1784 to 195,211 by 1840. Here were the roots of the millions of African Americans who would come to populate the industrial Midwest, from Kansas City to Chicago to Pittsburgh to Buffalo. Those blacks, in the great migrations following the world wars, would compose the urban proletariat that is both pouring forth black success stories and struggling with social pathologies so difficult as to seem unsolvable.

The largest northward migration of blacks took place during and after the Second World War. This exodus was largely a result of the invention of the mechanical cotton picker, which enabled three or four workers to perform a task that on some farms had required hundreds if not thousands of hands. Displaced by machinery and no longer needed in the underdeveloped American South, where they had been brought solely to do this kind of work, they went north to the industrial cities, where they encountered another kind of technology—the great factories of mass production. It was a violent shift for many whose families had known only agriculture for hundreds of years. And the Irish, Slavic, German, and Italian immigrants who were already there, felt they'd done their time, and were ready to move up resented the new competition that drove down wages. Many of the most vicious and enduring stereotypes about blacks were born of this resentment.

When those northern factories began closing and moving offshore, owing to the information and communications revolutions of the 1970s, 1980s, and 1990s, blacks were left behind in the inner cities of the Rust Belt, suffering from the metamorphosis of our society into a series of suburban megalopolises. Improvements in communications and transportation have struck the further blow of rendering the city irrelevant as a business and economic center, allowing mainstream money to be pulled out. The resulting isolation and deprivation, most eloquently outlined in the theories of the Harvard sociologist William Julius Wilson, account for the desolate urban landscapes we now see in parts of Detroit, Chicago, and Gary, Indiana.

Technology in and of itself is not at fault; it's much too simple to say that gunpowder or agricultural machinery or fiber optics has been the enemy of an entire group of people. A certain machine is put to work in a certain way—the purpose for which it was designed. The people who design the machines are not intent on unleashing chaos; they are usually trying to accomplish a task more quickly, cleanly, or cheaply, following the imperative of innovation and efficiency that has ruled Western civilization since the Renaissance.

Yet another aspect of technology's great cost to blacks should be con- 20
sidered: while the Gilded Age roared through the last part of the nineteenth century and Carnegie, Rockefeller, Vanderbilt, and others made the first great American fortunes as they wired, tracked, and fueled the new industrial society, blacks were mired in Reconstruction and its successor, Jim Crow. This circumscription limited their life prospects and, worse, those of their descendants. As the great American technopolis was built, with its avatars from Thomas Edison to Alfred P. Sloan to Bill Gates, blacks were locked out, politically and socially—and they have found it difficult to work their way in.

Blacks have traditionally been poorly educated—look at the crisis in urban public schools—and deprived of the sorts of opportunities that create the vision necessary for technological ambition. Black folkways in America, those unspoken, largely unconscious patterns of thought and belief about what is possible that guide aspiration and behavior, thus do not encompass physics and calculus. Becoming an engineer—unlike becoming a doctor or a lawyer or an insurance salesman—has not been seen as a way up in the segregated black community. These folkways developed in response to very real historical conditions, to the limited and at best ambivalent interactions between blacks and technology in this country. Folkways, the "consciousness of the race," change at a slower pace than societal conditions do—and so a working strategy can turn into a crippling blindness and self-limitation.

Some blacks—like my father, who worked for nearly fifty years in a factory that, ironically, recently moved from Illinois to the low-wage Mississippi he left as a boy—have been able to operate within these narrow parameters, to accept slow and steady progress while positioning their children to jump into the mainstream. But blacks are also Americans, and as such are subject not only to notions of a steady rise but also to the restless ambition that seems a peculiarly American disease. Not channeled to follow the largely technological possibilities for success in this society, black folkways have instead embraced the sort of magical thinking that is encouraged by the media and corporations whose sole interest in blacks is as consumers.

You, too, can be Michael Jordan or Coolio—just buy the shoes, just have the right look. No need to study, no need to work, the powers that be are against you anyway. Young blacks believe that they have a better chance of becoming Jordan, a combination of genes, will, talent, and family that happens every hundred years, than of becoming Steve Jobs, the builder of two billion-dollar corporations, the first one started with his best friend while tinkering in his garage. They also don't dream of becoming programmers at Cisco Systems, a low-profile computer giant that hires 5,000 new workers a year and scours the globe to find them. Blacks make up 13 percent of the population in this country, yet in 1995 they earned a shockingly low 1.8 percent of the Ph.D.s conferred in computer science, 2.1 percent of those in engineering, 1.5 percent in the physical sciences, and 0.6 percent in mathematics. As I lamented earlier, the very opportunities that would allow young blacks to vault over decades of injury and neglect into the modern world go unclaimed—even unseen.

Mastery of technology is second only to money as the true measure of accomplishment in this country, and it is very likely that by tolerating this underrepresentation in the technological realm, and by not questioning and examining the folkways that have encouraged it, blacks are allowing themselves to be kept out of the mainstream once again. This time, however, they will be excluded from the greatest cash engine of the twenty-first century. Inner-city blacks in particular are in danger, as "clean communities"—such as Du Page County, outside Chicago, and the beautiful suburbs that ring the decay of Hartford, glittering cybercities on the hill, the latest manifestation of the American Dream—shed the past and learn to exist without contemplating or encountering the tragedy of the inner city.

But all dreams end, and when we wake, we must face reality. Despite 25
these trends, and the dangers they imply, not all is lost. What might be accomplished by an education system that truly tried to educate *everyone* to excellence, not just the children of elites and of the suburbs? Why not a technological Marshall Plan for the nation's schools? Even in this time of fiscal constriction and resistance to public expenditure—at least, any expenditure that does not directly benefit those doing the spending—such a plan is feasible. What if *uber*technocrats like Bill Gates and Larry Ellison (the billionaire CEO of Oracle) used their philanthropic millions to fund basic math and science education in elementary schools, to equip the future, instead of giving away merchandise that essentially serves to expand their customer base? That would be a gift worthy of their accomplishments, and one of true historical weight in the life of the nation.

And blacks must change as well. The ways that served their ancestors through captivity and coming to freedom have begun to lose their utility. If blacks are to survive as full participants in this society, they have to understand *and apply* what works *now*. Otherwise they will be unable to cross the next technological threshold that emerges in human civilization. Blacks have to imagine ways to encourage young people into the technological mainstream, because that looks like the future. In fact, it always has been the future, and blacks, playing catch-up yet again, must reach for it to ensure themselves a place at the American table.

QUESTIONING THE TEXT

1. Write a 250-word summary of Walton's essay. What is his thesis, and how does he support it? How does he organize his argument?
2. In paragraph 20, Walton mentions several figures in American technological development: [Andrew] Carnegie, [John D.] Rockefeller, [Cornelius] Vanderbilt, Thomas Edison, Alfred P. Sloan, and Bill Gates. Using your dictionary's biographical section, an encyclopedia, or another reference to identify those figures unfamiliar to you, consider why Walton might have chosen to mention these particular men. For Walton's purposes, what is significant about each man and his role in U.S. history?
3. Walton claims a special significance for the relationship of African Americans to technology. He writes: "Poor whites, non-black Hispanics, and Asians were not dragged from their native lands to work as slaves and then buffeted for hundreds of years by the vagaries of technology and an economy they did not control. The historical experience of each ethnic group is unique and composed of its own problems and opportunities (or lack thereof)" (paragraph 9). Consider the experiences other groups of Americans may have had with technology over the years; how do issues of race, ethnicity, class, or gender affect others' access to the fruits of technological progress? You might use your exploration to launch a research and writing project that delves into the relationship of women, Hispanics, or Native Americans, for example, to technology. Or you might study the history of Chinese Americans to investigate how their experiences with the U.S. economy differed from those of African Americans.

MAKING CONNECTIONS

4. Three of the essay titles in this chapter allude to antagonistic relationships. Walton's title does so with the word *versus,* and those of J. Michael Bishop (p. 280) and James Q. Wilson (p. 338) do so with the mention of the word *enemies*. What effects do these titles have on your reading of the essays? Are the essays as conflict oriented as their titles make them sound?
5. Consider the extent to which the detrimental effects of technology on African Americans, as described by Walton, resemble the unforeseen

consequences of Victor Frankenstein's experiment in the excerpt from Mary Shelley's *Frankenstein* (p. 274) or the effects for which scientists receive undue blame, according to J. Michael Bishop in "Enemies of Promise" (p. 280). What significant similarities or differences do you find in the unintended effects of progress addressed in each piece of writing? Your observations might serve as the basis for a research-based essay.

6. After reading Todd Oppenheimer's "The Computer Delusion" (p. 298), do you think that some of the problems Walton describes might be addressed by increasing attention to technology in U.S. education? Why, or why not? Write a brief essay explaining your position.

JOINING THE CONVERSATION

7. Walton notes that "folkways, . . . those unspoken, largely unconscious patterns of thought and belief about what is possible that guide aspiration and behavior" (paragraph 21) often prevent blacks in America from considering careers in technology. Think about folkways that might influence your aspirations, and consider the question that A.L. poses at the end of her introduction to this piece: "What professional possibilities seem open and beckoning to you? More important, what effect do such factors as gender, race, and class continue to exert on these possibilities?" Discuss this question with classmates to compare your insights and experiences.
8. "Mastery of technology is second only to money as the true measure of accomplishment in this country," Walton claims (paragraph 24). Do you agree or disagree? Write a brief essay or letter to the editor elaborating on or refuting Walton's assertion, using evidence from your own experience or research to support your claim.
9. Walton says that African American youth "believe that they have a better chance of becoming [Michael] Jordan . . . than of becoming Steve Jobs" (paragraph 23). He suggests that "to survive as full participants in this society," African Americans need to seek technological opportunities and "imagine ways to encourage young people into the technological mainstream" (paragraph 26). Has anyone ever told you that your dreams were impractical, that your real passions in life were unlikely to support you in the future? How did you deal with this dilemma? Did you compromise? What are the pros and cons of pursuing what seems an obvious path toward success, as Walton seems to advocate? Freewrite on these questions, and then discuss your thoughts with classmates.

JAMES Q. WILSON
Cars and Their Enemies

*M*ENTION THE WORD technology *and most people today think of silicon chips, DVD systems, high-definition TVs, and cellular phones—not the vehicles they drive. Yet even the highest-tech computers haven't had the impact on our lives (at least, not yet) of gasoline-powered motor vehicles, a form of technology now a century old. From sea to sea, the American landscape has been bulldozed and paved to serve our national desire to move at will from one place to another. Fast cars and burly trucks have shaped our national character, changing how we live, where we live, how we court, and maybe even how we think.*

Yet the car represents a technological direction by no means inevitable. James Q. Wilson opens "Cars and Their Enemies" by suggesting how deep and determined opposition to this technology would be if it had been invented today rather than at the end of the nineteenth century. But Wilson rejects any notion of the car as a Frankenstein monster, describing it instead as a rational choice, one that makes the lives of most people freer and more pleasurable. In defending this claim, he challenges the growing number of academic and social critics made uneasy by the prospect of more and more Americans driving alone to work in 5,000-pound Suburbans and even bigger Excursions, wasting fuel, clogging streets, and avoiding public transportation.

Wilson (b. 1931), a professor emeritus at UCLA and recipient of the Presidential Medal of Freedom (2003), is one of America's most respected social critics and conservative thinkers, writing widely on crime, ethics, and character. Among his recent books are The Moral Sense *(1993),* Moral Judgment *(1997), and* The Marriage Problem *(2002). "Cars and Their Enemies" originally appeared in the July 1997 volume of* Commentary, *a journal of neoconservative opinion.* —J.R.

Imagine the country we now inhabit—big, urban, prosperous—with one exception: the automobile has not been invented. We have trains and bicycles, and some kind of self-powered buses and trucks, but no private cars driven by their owners for business or pleasure. Of late, let us suppose, someone has come forward with the idea of creating the personal automobile. Consider how we would react to such news.

Libertarians might support the idea, but hardly anyone else. Engineers would point out that such cars, if produced in any significant number, would zip along roads just a few feet—perhaps even a few inches—from one another; the chance of accidents would not simply be high, it would be certain. Public-health specialists would estimate that many of these accidents would lead to serious injuries and deaths. No one could say in advance how common they would be, but the best experts might guess that the number of people killed by cars would easily exceed the number killed by murderers. Psychologists would point out that if any young person were allowed to operate a car, the death rate would be even higher, as youngsters—those between the ages of sixteen and twenty-four—are much more likely than older persons to be impulsive risk-takers who find pleasure in reckless bravado. Educators would explain that, though they might try by training to reduce this youthful death rate, they could not be optimistic they would succeed.

Environmentalists would react in horror to the idea of automobiles powered by the internal combustion engine, apparently the most inexpensive method. Such devices, because they burn fuel incompletely, would eject large amounts of unpleasant gases into the air, such as carbon monoxide, nitrogen oxide, and sulfur dioxide. Other organic compounds, as well as clouds of particles, would also enter the atmosphere to produce unknown but probably harmful effects. Joining in this objection would be people who would not want their view spoiled by the creation of a network of roads.

Big-city mayors would add their own objections, though these would reflect their self-interest as much as their wisdom. If people could drive anywhere from anywhere, they would be able to live wherever they wished. This would produce a vast exodus from the large cities, led in all likelihood by the most prosperous—and thus the most tax-productive—citizens. Behind would remain people who, being poorer, were less mobile. Money would depart but problems remain.

5 Governors, pressed to keep taxes down and still fund costly health, welfare, educational, and criminal-justice programs, would wonder who would pay for the vast networks of roads that would be needed to carry automobiles. Their skepticism would be reinforced by the worries of police officials fearful of motorized thieves evading apprehension, and by the opposition of railroad executives foreseeing the collapse of their passenger business as people abandoned trains for cars.

Energy experts would react in horror at the prospect of supplying the gasoline stations and the vast quantities of petroleum necessary to fuel automobiles which, unlike buses and trucks, would be stored at home and not at a central depot and would burn much more fuel per person carried than some of their mass-transit alternatives.

In short, the automobile, the device on which most Americans rely for not only transportation but mobility, privacy, and fun would not exist if it had to be created today. Of course, the car does exist, and has powerfully affected the living, working, and social spaces of America. But the argument against it persists. That argument dominates the thinking of academic experts on urban transportation and much of city planning. It can be found in countless books complaining of dreary suburban architecture, endless trips to and from work, the social isolation produced by solo auto trips, and the harmful effects of the car on air quality, noise levels, petroleum consumption, and road congestion.

In her recent book, *Asphalt Nation: How the Automobile Took Over America and How We Can Take It Back,* Jane Holtz Kay, the architecture critic for the *Nation,* assails the car unmercifully. It has, she writes "strangled" our lives and landscape, imposing on us "the costs of sprawl, of pollution, of congestion, of commuting." For this damage to be undone, the massively subsidized automobile will have to be sharply curtailed, by investing heavily in public transportation and imposing European-like taxes on gasoline. (According to Kay, if we cut highway spending by a mere $10 million, we could buy bicycles for all 93,000 residents of Eugene, Oregon, over the age of eleven.) What is more, people ought to live in cities with high population densities, since "for mass transit," as Kay notes, "you need mass." Housing should be built within a short walk of the corner store, and industries moved back downtown.

In Kay's book, hostility to the car is linked inextricably to hostility to the low-density suburb. Her view is by no means one that is confined to the political Left. Thus, Karl Zinsmeister, a conservative, has argued in the *American Enterprise* that we have become "slaves to our cars" and that, by using them to live in suburbs, we have created "inhospitable places for individualism and community life." Suburbs, says Zinsmeister, encourage "rootlessness," and are the enemy of the "traditional neighborhood" with its "easy daily interactions."

The same theme has been taken up by Mark Gauvreau Judge in the 10
Weekly Standard. Emerging from his home after a heavy snowfall, Judge, realizing that the nearest tavern was four miles away, concluded that he had to leave the suburbs. He repeats Zinsmeister's global complaint. Suburbanization, he writes, has fed, and sometimes caused,

> hurried life, the disappearance of family time, the weakening of generational links, our ignorance of history, our lack of local ties, an exaggerated focus on money, the anonymity of community life, the rise of radical feminism, the decline of civic action, the tyrannical dominance of TV and pop culture over leisure time.

Wow.

These people must live in or near very odd suburbs. The one in which I lived while my children were growing up, and the different ones in which my married daughter and married son now live, are not inhospitable, rootless, isolated, untraditional, or lacking in daily interactions. The towns are small. Life is organized around the family, for which there is a lot of time. Money goes farther for us than for Manhattanites struggling to get their children into the nursery school with the best link to Harvard. Television is less important than in big cities, where the streets are far less safe and TV becomes a major indoor activity. In most cases you can walk to a store. You know your neighbors. There is a Memorial Day parade. People care passionately and argue intensely about school policies and land-use controls. Of course, these are only my personal experiences—but unlike the critics, I find it hard to convert personal beliefs into cosmic generalizations.

Now I live in a suburb more remote from a big city than the one where my children were raised. Because population density is much lower, my wife and I walk less and drive more. But as I write this, my wife is at a neighborhood meeting where she will be joined by a travel agent, a retired firefighter, a hospital manager, and two housewives who are trying to decide how best to get the city to fix up a road intersection, prevent a nearby land development, and induce our neighbors to prepare for the fire season. On the way back, she will stop at the neighborhood mail station where she may talk to other friends, and then go on to the market where she will deal with people she has known for many years. She will do so by car.

And so back to our theme. Despite the criticisms of Kay and others, the use of the automobile has grown. In 1960, one-fifth of all households owned no car and only one-fifth owned two; by 1990, only one-tenth owned no car and over one-third owned two. In 1969, 80 percent of all urban trips involved a car and only one-twentieth involved public transport; by 1990, car use had risen to 84 percent and public transit had fallen to less than 3 percent. In 1990, three-fourths or more of the trips to and from work in nineteen out of our twenty largest metropolitan areas were by a single person in an automobile. The exception was the New York metropolitan region, but even there—with an elaborate mass-transit system and a residential concentration high enough to make it possible for some people to walk to work—solo car use made up over half of all trips to work.

Some critics explain this American fascination with the car as the unhappy consequence of public policies that make auto use more attractive than the alternatives. To Jane Holtz Kay, if only we taxed gasoline at a high enough rate to repay society for the social costs of automobiles, if only we had an elaborate mass-transit system that linked our cities, if only we placed major restraints on building suburbs on open land, if only we placed heavy restrictions on downtown parking, then things would be better.

Would they? Charles Lave, an economist at the University of California 15
at Irvine, has pointed out that most of Western Europe has long had just these sorts of anti-auto policies in effect. The result? Between 1965 and 1987, the growth in the number of autos per capita has been three times faster in Western Europe than in the United States. Part of the reason for the discrepancy is that the American auto market is approaching saturation: we now have roughly one car in existence for every person of driving age. But if this fact helps explain why the car market here is not growing rapidly, it does not explain the growth in Europe, which is the real story. Despite policies that penalize car use, make travel very expensive, and restrict parking spaces, Europeans, once they can afford to do so, buy cars, and drive them; according to

Lave, the average European car is driven about two-thirds as many miles per year as the average American car. One result is obvious: the heavily subsidized trains in Europe are losing business to cars, and governments there must pay an even larger share of the running cost to keep the trains moving.

In fact, the United States *has* tried to copy the European investment in mass transit. Relentlessly, transportation planners have struggled to find ways of getting people out of their cars and into buses, trains, and subways (and car pools). Relentlessly, and unsuccessfully. Despite spending about $100 billion, Washington has yet to figure out how to do it.

New subway systems have been built, such as the BART system in San Francisco and the Metro system in Washington, D.C. But BART, in the words of the transportation economist Charles L. Wright, "connects almost nothing to little else." The Metro is still growing, and provides a fine (albeit expensive) route for people moving about the city; but only 7 percent of all residential land area in Washington is within a mile of a Metro station, which means that people must either walk a long way to get to a stop or continue to travel by car. Between 1980 and 1990, while the Washington Metrorail system grew from 30 to 73 miles of line and opened an additional 30 stations, the number of people driving to work increased from 980,000 to 1,394,000, and the transit share of all commutes declined.

The European experience should explain why this is so: if people can afford it, they will want to purchase convenience, flexibility, and privacy. These facts are as close to a Law of Nature as one can get in the transportation business. When the industrial world became prosperous, people bought cars. It is unstoppable.

Suppose, however, that the anti-car writers were to win over the vastly more numerous pro-car drivers. Let us imagine what life would be like in a carless nation. People would have to live very close together so they could walk or, for healthy people living in sunny climes, bicycle to mass-transit stops. Living in close quarters would mean life as it is now lived in Manhattan. There would be few freestanding homes, many row houses, and lots of apartment buildings. There would be few private gardens except for flowerpots on balconies. The streets would be congested by pedestrians, trucks, and buses, as they were at the turn of the century before automobiles became common.

Moving about outside the larger cities would be difficult. People would 20
be able to take trains to distant sites, but when they arrived at some attractive locale it would turn out to be another city. They could visit the beach, but only (of necessity) crowded parts of it. They could go to a national park, but only the built-up section of it. They could see the countryside, but (mostly) through a train window. More isolated or remote locations would be accessible, but since public transit would provide the only way of getting there, the departures would be infrequent and the transfers frequent.

In other words, you could see the United States much as most Europeans saw their countryside before the automobile became an important means of locomotion. A train from London or Paris would take you to "the country" by way of a long journey through ugly industrial areas to those rural parts where either you had a home (and the means to ferry yourself to it) or there was a resort (that would be crowded enough to support a nearby train stop).

All this is a way of saying that the debate between car defenders and car haters is a debate between private benefits and public goods. List the characteristics of travel that impose few costs on society and, in general, walking, cycling, and some forms of public transit will be seen to be superior. Non-car methods generate less pollution, use energy a bit more efficiently, produce less noise, and (with some exceptions) are safer. But list the characteristics of travel that are desired by individuals, and (with some exceptions) the car is clearly superior. The automobile is more flexible, more punctual, supplies greater comfort, provides for carrying more parcels, creates more privacy, enables one to select fellow passengers, and, for distances over a mile or more, requires less travel time.

As a practical matter, of course, the debate between those who value private benefits and those who insist on their social costs is no real debate at all, since people select modes of travel based on individual, not social, preferences. That is why in almost every country in the world, the automobile has triumphed, and much of public policy has been devoted to the somewhat inconsistent task of subsidizing individual choices while attempting to reduce the costs attached to them. In the case of the automobile, governments have attempted to reduce exhaust pollution, make roadways safer, and restrict use (by tolls, speed bumps, pedestrian-only streets, and parking restrictions) in neighborhoods that attach a high value to pedestrian passage. Yet none of these efforts can alter the central fact that people have found cars to be the best means for getting about.

Take traffic congestion. Television loves to focus on grim scenes of gridlocked highways and angry motorists, but in fact people still get to work faster by car than by public transit. And the reason is not that car drivers live close to work and transit users travel a greater distance. According to the best estimates, cars outperform public transit in getting people quickly from their front doors to their work places. This fact is sometimes lost on car critics. Kay, for example, writes that "the same number of people who spend an hour driving sixteen lanes of highway can travel on a two-track train line." Wrong. Train travel is efficient *over a fixed, permanent route,* but people have to find some way to get to where the train starts and get to their final destination after the train stops. The *full* cost of moving people from home to work and back to the home is lower for cars than for trains. Moreover, cars are not subject to union strikes. The Long Island railroad or the bus system may shut down when workers walk off the job; cars do not.

The transportation argument rarely seems to take cognizance of the su- 25
periority of cars with respect to individual wants. Whenever there is a discussion about how best to move people about, mass-transit supporters typically overestimate, usually by a wide margin, how many people will leave their cars and happily hop onto trains or buses. According to one study, by Don Pickerell, the vast majority of American rail-transportation proposals greatly exaggerate the number of riders to be attracted; the actual ridership turns out to be about a third of the predicted level. For this reason, urban public transport almost never recovers from the fare box more than a fraction of the actual cost of moving people. Osaka, Japan, seems to be the only large city in the world that gets back from passengers what it spends; in Atlanta, Detroit, and Houston, public transit gets from passengers no more than a third of their cost.

So the real debate ought not be one between car enthusiasts and mass-transit advocates, but about ways of moderating the inevitable use of cars in order to minimize their deleterious effects.

One such discussion has already had substantial effects. Auto-exhaust pollution has been dramatically reduced in this country by redesigning engines, changing fuels (largely by removing lead), and imposing inspection requirements.

Since the mid-1960s, auto emissions have been reduced by about 95 percent. Just since 1982, ten years after the Clean Air Act was passed, carbon-monoxide levels have fallen by 40 percent and nitrogen-oxide levels by 25 percent. I live in the Los Angeles area and know from personal experience how irritating smog was in the 1950's. I also know that smog has decreased dramatically for most (but not all) of the region. The number of "smog alert" days called by the South Coast Air Quality Management District (AQMD) declined from 121 in the mid-1970's to seven in 1996. AQMD now predicts that by the year 2000 the number may fall to zero.

Nationally, very little of this improvement has come about from moving people from solo cars into car pools or onto mass transit. What experts call "Transportation Control Measures" (TCM's)—the combined effect of mass transit, car pools, telecommuting, and the like—have produced small reductions in smog levels. Transit expansion has decreased carbon monoxide by six-tenths of 1 percent and car pools by another seven-tenths of 1 percent. Adding BART to San Francisco has had only trivial effects on pollution. The Environmental Protection Agency (in the Clinton administration) has issued a report that puts it bluntly: "Efforts to reduce emissions through traditional TCM's have not generated significant air-quality benefits." The methods that *have* reduced pollution significantly are based on markets, not capital investments, and include smog fees, congestion pricing, gas taxes, and higher parking charges.

There is still more pollution to eliminate, but the anti-car enthusiasts 30
rarely approach the task rationally. General Motors now leases electric cars,

but they are very expensive and require frequent recharging from scarce power outlets. The electric car is an impressive engineering achievement, but not if you want to travel very far.

We could pass laws that would drive down even further the pollution output of cars, but this would impose huge costs on manufacturers and buyers without addressing the real source of auto pollution—a small percentage of older or modified cars that generate huge amounts of exhaust. Devices now exist for measuring the pollution of cars as they move on highways and then ticketing the offenders, but only recently has there been a large-scale trial of this method, and the results are not yet in. The method has the virtue of targeting enforcement on real culprits, but the defect (for car critics) of not requiring a "tough new law" aimed at every auto owner.

As for traffic congestion, that has indeed become worse—because highway construction has not kept pace with the growth of automobile use. But it is not as bad as some imagine—the average commuting time was the same in 1990 as in 1980—and it is not bad where it is often assumed to be bad. A road is officially called "congested" if its traffic volume exceeds 80 percent of its designed capacity. By this measure, the most congested highways are in and around Washington, D.C., and San Francisco. But if you drive these roads during rush hour, as I have, you will acquire a very different sense of things. The highways into Washington and San Francisco do produce blockages, usually at familiar intersections, bridges, or merges. They rarely last very long and, on most days, one can plan around them.

Indeed, the fact and consequences of auto congestion are greatly exaggerated in most large cities. During rush hour, I have driven into and out of Dallas, Kansas City, Phoenix, St. Louis, and San Diego without much more than an occasional slowdown. Moreover, despite the massive reliance on cars and a short-term decline in the economic vitality of their downtown areas, most of these cities have restored their central areas. Kansas City is bleak in the old downtown, but the shopping area (built 75 years ago!) called Country Club Plaza is filled with people, stores, and restaurants. San Diego and San Francisco have lively downtowns. Los Angeles even managed to acquire a downtown (actually, several downtowns) after it grew up without much of one—and this in a city allegedly "built around the car." Phoenix is restoring its downtown and San Diego never really lost its center.

Real congestion, by contrast, is found in New York City, Chicago, and Boston, where almost any movement on any downtown street is extremely difficult. From the moment you enter a car or taxi, you are in a traffic jam. Getting to the airport by car from Manhattan or Boston is vastly more difficult than getting there from San Francisco, Los Angeles, or Washington.

But the lesson in this should be disturbing to car critics: *car travel is most* 35
congested in cities that have the oldest and most highly developed rail-based transit systems. One reason is historical: having subways from their early days, these

cities built up to high levels of residential and commercial concentration. A car added to this mix has to navigate through streets surrounded by high office buildings and tall apartment towers. When many people in those buildings take cars or taxis, the congestion can be phenomenal.

But there is another reason as well. Even where rail transportation exists, people will not use it enough to relieve congestion. There is, for example, an excellent rail line from O'Hare Airport to downtown Chicago, and some people use it. But it has done little or nothing to alleviate congestion on the parallel highway. People do not like dragging suitcases on and off trains. And the train does not stop where people want to go—namely, where they live. It stops at busy street corners, sometimes in dangerous neighborhoods. If you take the train, you still must shift to a car at the end, and finding one is not always easy. This is why taking a car from the Los Angeles airport, though it will place you in a few pockets of congestion, gets you to your home faster (and with all of your belongings) than taking a train and taxi a comparable distance from O'Hare.

A great deal can still be done to moderate the social costs of automobile traffic. More toll roads can be built with variable rates that will allow people to drive—at different prices, depending on the level of congestion—to and from cities. Bridges into cities can charge tolls to ensure that only highly motivated people consume scarce downtown road space. (A friend of mine, a distinguished economist, was once asked, in derision, whether he would buy the Brooklyn Bridge. "I would if I could charge tolls on it," he replied.) Cars can be banned from streets that are capable of being pedestrian malls—though there are not many such places. (A number of such malls were created for the purpose of keeping people downtown who did not want to be downtown, and were doomed to failure from the start.)

Other measures are also possible. More bicycle pathways can be created, though these are rarely alternatives to auto transportation; some people do ride a bike to work, but few do so often. Street patterns in residential areas can be arranged to minimize the amount of through road traffic they must endure. Gasoline taxes can be set high enough to recover more of the social costs of operating automobiles. (This will not happen in a society as democratic as ours, but it is a good idea, and maybe someday a crisis will create an opportunity.)

Portland, Oregon, has become well-known among American cities for having adopted a law—the Urban Growth Boundary—that denies people the right to build almost any new structure in a green belt starting about twenty minutes from downtown. This means that new subdivisions to which one must travel by car cannot be created outside the line. The nice result is that outside the city, you can drive through unspoiled farm land.

The mayor and downtown business leaders like what they have created. 40
So do environmentalists, social-service organizations, and many ordinary

citizens. The policy, described in a recent issue of *Governing* magazine, is called the New Urbanism, and has attracted interest from all over the country. But the policy also has its costs. As the city's population grows, more people must be squeezed into less space. Housing density is up. Before the Urban Growth Boundary, the average Portland house was built on a lot about 13,000 feet square and row houses made up only 3 percent of all dwelling units. Now, the average lot size has fallen to 8,700 square feet and row houses make up 12 percent of the total. And housing prices are also up. Six years ago, Portland was the nation's 55th most affordable city; today, it is the 165th.

As density goes up in Portland, so will the problems associated with density, such as crime. Reserving land out of a city for scenic value is an important goal, but it must be balanced with supplying affordable housing. Portland will work out the balance, once people begin to yearn for lower density.

But even if we do all the things that can be done to limit the social costs of cars, the campaign against them will not stop. It will not stop because so many of the critics dislike everything the car stands for and everything that society constructs to serve the needs of its occupants.

Cars are about privacy; critics say privacy is bad and prefer group effort. (Of course, one rarely meets these critics in groups. They seem to be too busy rushing about being critics.) Cars are about autonomy; critics say that the pursuit of autonomy destroys community. (Actually, cars allow people to select the kind of community in which they want to live.) Cars are about speed; critics abhor the fatalities they think speed causes. (In fact, auto fatalities have been declining for decades, including after the 55-mile-per-hour national speed limit was repealed. Charles Lave suggests that this is because higher speed limits reduce the variance among cars in their rates of travel, thereby producing less passing and overtaking, two dangerous highway maneuvers.) Cars are about the joyous sensation of driving on beautiful country roads; critics take their joy from politics. (A great failing of the intellectual life of this country is that so much of it is centered in Manhattan, where one finds the highest concentration of nondrivers in the country.) Cars make possible Wal-Mart, Home Depot, the Price Club, and other ways of allowing people to shop for rock-bottom prices; critics want people to spend their time gathering food at downtown shops (and paying the much higher prices that small stores occupying expensive land must charge). Cars make California possible; critics loathe California. (But they loathe it for the wrong reason. The state is not the car capital of the nation; 36 states have more cars per capita, and their residents drive more miles.)

Life in California would be very difficult without cars. This is not because the commute to work is so long; in Los Angeles, according to Charles Lave, the average trip to work in 1994 was 26 minutes, five minutes *shorter* than in New York City. Rather, a carless state could not be enjoyed. You could not see the vast areas of farm land, the huge tracts of empty mountains and deserts, the miles of deserted beaches and forests.

No one who visits Los Angeles or San Francisco can imagine how 45
much of California is, in effect, empty, unsettled. It is an empire of lightly used roads, splendid vistas, and small towns, intersected by a highway system that, should you be busy or foolish enough to use it, will speed you from San Francisco to Los Angeles or San Diego. Off the interstate, it is a kaleidoscope of charming places to be alone.

Getting there in order to be alone is best done in one of the remarkably engineered, breathtakingly fast, modern cars that give to the driver the deepest sense of what the road can offer: the beauty of its views, the excitement of command, the passion of engagement.

I know the way. If you are a friend, you need only ask.

QUESTIONING THE TEXT

1. Review "Cars and Their Enemies," looking for places where Wilson characterizes the critics of automobiles. What terms or names does he give to these critics? Where do they live, and in Wilson's opinion, how do they typically behave? How does Wilson's treatment of "car haters" enhance or detract from his argument?
2. Does "Cars and Their Enemies" have a thesis you could state in one sentence? Reread the essay carefully, highlighting sentences you think make major points or summarize Wilson's thinking. Then review these major claims, and write a summary of Wilson's case in favor of the automobile.
3. Wilson, a sociologist by profession, uses both statistics and personal experiences to make his argument. Evaluate his use of these different kinds of evidence. Where does he cite statistics? Where does he rely on personal experience? How do you react to the highly personal last paragraph of the piece: "I know the way. If you are a friend, you need only ask"?

MAKING CONNECTIONS

4. Wilson opens by asking readers to envision a world without cars, and he proposes that very few people would support the introduction of such technology now. Using a similar imaginative notion, consider the discussions of computer technology in other essays in this chapter. Try thinking about the world before computers, for example, after reading Sherry Turkle's "Cuddling Up to Cyborg Babies" (p. 359) or Todd Oppenheimer's "The Computer Delusion" (p. 298). If we had the opportunity to introduce computers now, would we do so? Can you imagine a future time at which one might be able to reasonably argue,

as Wilson does about automobiles, that hardly anyone would support the introduction of computer technology? To bring about such misgivings toward computers what kinds of things would have to happen? Does Turkle's or Oppenheimer's essay suggest any likely possibilities? Explain.

5. Like Anthony Walton in "Technology Versus African Americans" (p. 329), Wilson uses historical data to support his claims, citing, for example, the growth in numbers of automobiles in the United States from 1965 to 1987. Compare these authors' use of history in their respective essays. Do such techniques as the presentation of historical narrative or the use of statistics increase these authors' credibility? Which historical claims do you find most and least compelling? Why?

JOINING THE CONVERSATION

6. Write an editorial for your campus newspaper in response to Wilson's piece, examining the issue of local transportation or, perhaps, traffic and parking at your school. In your argument, you need not simply agree or disagree with Wilson—just begin with his reflection on the automobile in American culture. Consider other possibilities for addressing the issue.
7. Write a brief essay exploring whether another older technology (besides the gasoline-powered car) might or might not be built if it were invented today rather than in the past. Use the first seven paragraphs of "Cars and Their Enemies" as a model for your piece.
8. Use both research materials and personal experience to write an essay on "_______ and Their Enemies," filling in the blank with a subject you can explore in depth. Present both your point of view on the topic and the ideas of those with whom you might disagree. Review Wilson's piece for ideas about organization and tone.

MOLLY IVINS
Bush's Brain Straddles the Fence Once Again

An editorialist's job is to serve up opinions, and Molly Ivins (b. 1944), whose widely syndicated column appears in the Fort Worth Star–Telegraph *as well as 113 other newspapers, takes to this job with special gusto. Since the highly contentious presidential election of 2000, Ivins has had a field day writing presidential and administration critiques, from broad lampoons and parodies to searching analyses.*

Some six months after the inauguration, during August 2001, I remember watching Bush on TV as he delivered what to me was a confusing speech on stem cell research. "What is he really saying," I remember asking myself, and to that question I added, "I wonder what Molly Ivins will make of this?" As it turns out, Ivins had already made her views on the Bush administration's policy on stem cell research crystal clear: "Bush's Brain Straddles Fence Once Again" appeared on July 18, 2001, a few weeks before Bush gave his speech to the nation. In this column, Ivins upholds the need for caution in heading down a slippery slope to "heaven knows what Frankenstein experiments." But she expresses confidence in society's ability to draw "distinctions on all kinds of slippery slopes," including this one. For Ivins, using stem cell research to work toward cures for diseases such as Alzheimer's need not lead to a Frankensteinian future.

At my university, which has a new Institute for Cancer/Stem Cell Biology and Medicine, students debate stem cell research and other scientific issues with vigor. They are especially thoughtful about the ethical implications of some genetic research and tough-minded in their examination of all sides of these issues. I chose this brief column because it is one I might well introduce to a class, challenging all of us to analyze the arguments Ivins makes and then doing some additional research of our own on this controversial issue. I am also a fan of Ivins's brand of humor, which I think of as wit with attitude. Keep an eye out and you'll see her work not only in newspapers but in journals such as Harper's, *the* Atlantic Monthly, Esquire, Mother Jones, *and many other progressive publications.* — A.L.

The Bush administration may be fixing to fish or cut bait on the stem cell research issue, except it appears it will actually try to straddle the issue. Good luck to them.

Those who believe life begins the instant an egg is fertilized by a sperm hold a theological position not subject to compromise. The pro-life movement initially opposed fetal-cell research because it thought it would somehow legitimize abortion, or allow women having abortions to think at least some good would come of it. Actually, stem cell research is done on left-over embryos in petri dishes that went unused during fertilization treatments, so we're not even talking about the possibility of a human life. Do you know anyone with Alzheimer's, Parkinson's, diabetes or a spinal cord injury? Stem cell research presents a real chance to find a cure for those conditions.

Biologically speaking, an embryo is not a person. About 25 percent of embryos never make their way through a woman's plumbing in time to attach themselves to the womb wall—they are washed out with the menstrual flood. We do not mourn them as dead people. Natalie Angier, in her book *Woman, an Intimate Geography,* says, "We all know about the high rate of miscarriages during the first trimester of pregnancy, and we have all heard that the majority of those miscarriages are blessed expulsions, eliminating embryos with chromosomes too distorted for being." Speaking of all the bad sperm and all the bad eggs the body rids itself of naturally through a process called apoptosis, Angier observes, "In that sense, we are good eggs, every one of us."

The theory that stem cell research is the beginning of the infamous slippery slope toward heaven knows what Frankenstein experiments in the future is genuinely worth considering. The more we mess with nature, the more we seem to learn about how ignorant we are. Nevertheless, the law draws distinctions on all kinds of slippery slopes: The difference between misdemeanor theft and felony theft is one penny. You can drink legally when you are 21 years old, but not when you are 20 years and 364 days old. In nine states, you can be executed if your IQ is 70, but not if it's 69. A woman can get an abortion in the first trimester for almost any reason, but must show serious threat to her life or health by the third trimester. These are all artificial distinctions. But society is capable of drawing them.

The depressing part of the Bush administration's lengthy indecision over 5
what is a no-brainer to those without the theological commitment to the fertilized-egg-as-human-being position is the political motive. It has been widely reported that Karl Rove, a.k.a., "Bush's brain," wants to outlaw stem cell research as part of his grand strategy to win Catholic voters over to the Republican Party permanently. This doesn't do anything to help those with Alzheimer's, but it would help the Republicans. That's some morality.

But Rove's political calculations appear to be off again: Polls show about 70 percent of all Catholics favor stem cell research. That helpful House trio, Reps. Dick Armey, Tom DeLay and J. C. Watts, wrote Bush a letter calling stem cell research "an industry of death." Funny, I've never heard any of them describe arms manufacturers that way.

As we inch into new areas of research that raise all kinds of bioethical questions, I often think we are lucky to be able to debate them openly and vigorously, for we sense the new and the strange, and are wary. It is the old wrongs that are harder to come to grips with.

As Tom Paine once wrote, "A long habit of not thinking a thing wrong gives it a superficial appearance of being right, and raises, at first, a formidable outcry in defense of custom."

QUESTIONING THE TEXT

1. Can you tell from reading Ivins's column what event prompted her to write this commentary? Is the impetus for her column explicit or implicit? Explain.
2. Summarize Ivins's argument. What is her main claim? How does she support it?
3. How would you describe Ivins's tone? How does she convey that tone? What effects do you think the tone is likely to have on her audience? How does the genre —that of a syndicated opinion column—influence the tone or other aspects of style available to Ivins as a writer?
4. What is the meaning of the quotation by Tom Paine at the end of the essay? Why do you think Ivins chooses to leave her readers with Paine's words rather than her own?

MAKING CONNECTIONS

5. As A.L. points out in her introduction, Ivins alludes in this essay to Frankenstein and to the rhetorical fallacy of a slippery slope. Read the selection from Mary Shelley's *Frankenstein* presented in this chapter (p. 274), and review as well the characteristics of a slippery-slope argument. Then discuss in class how these allusions serve Ivins's critique. Do you find the allusions effective?

JOINING THE CONVERSATION

6. In her opening sentence, Ivins criticizes the Bush administration for "straddl[ing] the issue" of stem cell research, whereas J.R., in his introduction to Bush's "Speech to the Nation on Stem Cell Research" (p. 353), praises the president for "split[ting] the difference between two incompatible positions." What do you think of Ivins's charge? Write an op-ed or letter to the editor presenting your informed opinion on Bush's attempt to negotiate the conflicting positions on this issue.
7. In paragraph 4, Ivins points out several matters of policy that hinge on "artificial distinctions." She cites these examples as evidence that "society is capable of drawing" such boundaries, to prevent sliding down a problematic slippery slope. Do some research into one of the areas she mentions—or another one in which a seemingly arbitrary distinction has been drawn—and write an essay defending or criticizing the wisdom of that distinction.

PRESIDENT GEORGE W. BUSH
Speech to the Nation on Stem Cell Research

Myopic media pundits, anticipating President George Bush's decision on whether to permit human stem cell research in federally supported laboratories, suggested in August 2001 that his upcoming speech could be a turning point for his administration and perhaps the most important address he would deliver while in office. Terrorist attacks in New York City and Washington, D.C., a month later would so alter the political landscape in the United States that the stem cell decision has since been largely forgotten, except perhaps by scientists and medical researchers living with its policy implications.

Molly Ivins aside, Bush's address on August 9, 2001, was reasonably well received by the public and media at the time, praised in particular for the clarity with which it spelled out the ethical dilemmas both scientists and politicians face when dealing with life-and-death issues. Are embryos that provide the stem cells potential human beings, or are they cellular material with the potential to benefit sufferers of Parkinson's disease, diabetes, heart disease, and other life-threatening conditions? In direct, everyday language that is the hallmark of his political rhetoric, Bush ultimately splits the difference between two incompatible positions, allowing research to continue on stem cells already harvested but not permitting the development of new stem cell lines.

Naturally, as the president foresaw, controversy continues today not only over stem cell research but human cloning. Scientists still fear that progress in reparative medicine in the United States will fall behind that of other countries where stem cell work is less restricted. But as I write this introduction, the European Parliament's Committee for the Environment and Public Health has just announced support for a ban on stem cell research.

I met George W. Bush (b. 1946) during his first year as Texas's chief executive, when the board of directors of the Texas Union hung his portrait in its Governor's Room as part of a long-standing tradition. Recent governors had ignored the ceremony, but Bush strolled in right on time, accompanied by a single security guard. With fewer than a dozen people in attendance, I soon had an opportunity to chat with him one-on-one, mostly about his father and his commitment to higher education. I was impressed by his command of the issue and remember his final remarks, spoken almost too deliberately for the event: "I just want you to know that I will never let you down. I will never let you down." I have thought about those words a lot, especially since 9/11.

—J.R.

Good evening. I appreciate you giving me a few minutes of your time tonight so I can discuss with you a complex and difficult issue, an issue that is one of the most profound of our time.

The issue of research involving stem cells derived from human embryos is increasingly the subject of a national debate and dinner table discussions. The issue is confronted every day in laboratories as scientists ponder the ethical ramifications of their work. It is agonized over by parents and many couples as they try to have children, or to save children already born.

The issue is debated within the church, with people of different faiths, even many of the same faith coming to different conclusions. Many people are finding that the more they know about stem cell research, the less certain they are about the right ethical and moral conclusions.

My administration must decide whether to allow federal funds, your tax dollars, to be used for scientific research on stem cells derived from human embryos. A large number of these embryos already exist. They are the product of a process called in vitro fertilization, which helps so many couples conceive children. When doctors match sperm and egg to create life outside the womb, they usually produce more embryos than are planted in the mother. Once a couple successfully has children, or if they are unsuccessful, the additional embryos remain frozen in laboratories.

5 Some will not survive during long storage; others are destroyed. A number have been donated to science and used to create privately funded stem cell lines. And a few have been implanted in an adoptive mother and born, and are today healthy children.

Based on preliminary work that has been privately funded, scientists believe further research using stem cells offers great promise that could help improve the lives of those who suffer from many terrible diseases—from juvenile diabetes to Alzheimer's, from Parkinson's to spinal cord injuries. And while scientists admit they are not yet certain, they believe stem cells derived from embryos have unique potential.

You should also know that stem cells can be derived from sources other than embryos—from adult cells, from umbilical cords that are discarded after babies are born, from human placenta. And many scientists feel research on these types of stem cells is also promising. Many patients suffering from a range of diseases are already being helped with treatments developed from adult stem cells.

However, most scientists, at least today, believe that research on embryonic stem cells offers the most promise because these cells have the potential to develop in all of the tissues in the body.

Scientists further believe that rapid progress in this research will come only with federal funds. Federal dollars help attract the best and brightest scientists. They ensure new discoveries are widely shared at the largest number of research facilities and that the research is directed toward the greatest public good.

10 The United States has a long and proud record of leading the world toward advances in science and medicine that improve human life. And the United States has a long and proud record of upholding the highest standards

of ethics as we expand the limits of science and knowledge. Research on embryonic stem cells raises profound ethical questions, because extracting the stem cell destroys the embryo, and thus destroys its potential for life. Like a snowflake, each of these embryos is unique, with the unique genetic potential of an individual human being.

As I thought through this issue, I kept returning to two fundamental questions: First, are these frozen embryos human life, and therefore, something precious to be protected? And second, if they're going to be destroyed anyway, shouldn't they be used for a greater good, for research that has the potential to save and improve other lives?

I've asked those questions and others of scientists, scholars, bioethicists, religious leaders, doctors, researchers, members of Congress, my Cabinet, and my friends. I have read heartfelt letters from many Americans. I have given this issue a great deal of thought, prayer and considerable reflection. And I have found widespread disagreement.

On the first issue, are these embryos human life—well, one researcher told me he believes this five-day-old cluster of cells is not an embryo, not yet an individual, but a pre-embryo. He argued that it has the potential for life, but it is not a life because it cannot develop on its own.

An ethicist dismissed that as a callous attempt at rationalization. Make no mistake, he told me, that cluster of cells is the same way you and I, and all the rest of us, started our lives. One goes with a heavy heart if we use these, he said, because we are dealing with the seeds of the next generation.

And to the other crucial question, if these are going to be destroyed 15
anyway, why not use them for good purpose—I also found different answers. Many argue these embryos are byproducts of a process that helps create life, and we should allow couples to donate them to science so they can be used for good purpose instead of wasting their potential. Others will argue there's no such thing as excess life, and the fact that a living being is going to die does not justify experimenting on it or exploiting it as a natural resource.

At its core, this issue forces us to confront fundamental questions about the beginnings of life and the ends of science. It lies at a difficult moral intersection, juxtaposing the need to protect life in all its phases with the prospect of saving and improving life in all its stages.

As the discoveries of modern science create tremendous hope, they also lay vast ethical mine fields. As the genius of science extends the horizons of what we can do, we increasingly confront complex questions about what we should do. We have arrived at that brave new world that seemed so distant in 1932, when Aldous Huxley wrote about human beings created in test tubes in what he called a "hatchery."

In recent weeks, we learned that scientists have created human embryos in test tubes solely to experiment on them. This is deeply troubling, and a warning sign that should prompt all of us to think through these issues very carefully.

Embryonic stem cell research is at the leading edge of a series of moral hazards. The initial stem cell researcher was at first reluctant to begin his research, fearing it might be used for human cloning. Scientists have already cloned a sheep. Researchers are telling us the next step could be to clone human beings to create individual designer stem cells, essentially to grow another you, to be available in case you need another heart or lung or liver.

I strongly oppose human cloning, as do most Americans. We recoil at 20
the idea of growing human beings for spare body parts, or creating life for our convenience. And while we must devote enormous energy to conquering disease, it is equally important that we pay attention to the moral concerns raised by the new frontier of human embryo stem cell research. Even the most noble ends do not justify any means.

My position on these issues is shaped by deeply held beliefs. I'm a strong supporter of science and technology, and believe they have the potential for incredible good—to improve lives, to save life, to conquer disease. Research offers hope that millions of our loved ones may be cured of a disease and rid of their suffering. I have friends whose children suffer from juvenile diabetes. Nancy Reagan has written me about President Reagan's struggle with Alzheimer's. My own family has confronted the tragedy of childhood leukemia. And, like all Americans, I have great hope for cures.

I also believe human life is a sacred gift from our Creator. I worry about a culture that devalues life, and believe as your President I have an important obligation to foster and encourage respect for life in America and throughout the world. And while we're all hopeful about the potential of this research, no one can be certain that the science will live up to the hope it has generated.

Eight years ago, scientists believed fetal tissue research offered great hope for cures and treatments—yet, the progress to date has not lived up to its initial expectations. Embryonic stem cell research offers both great promise and great peril. So I have decided we must proceed with great care.

As a result of private research, more than 60 genetically diverse stem cell lines already exist. They were created from embryos that have already been destroyed, and they have the ability to regenerate themselves indefinitely, creating ongoing opportunities for research. I have concluded that we should allow federal funds to be used for research on these existing stem cell lines, where the life and death decision has already been made.

Leading scientists tell me research on these 60 lines has great promise 25
that could lead to breakthrough therapies and cures. This allows us to explore the promise and potential of stem cell research without crossing a fundamental moral line, by providing taxpayer funding that would sanction or encourage further destruction of human embryos that have at least the potential for life.

I also believe that great scientific progress can be made through aggressive federal funding of research on umbilical cord, placenta, adult and animal stem cells which do not involve the same moral dilemma. This year, your government will spend $250 million on this important research.

I will also name a President's council to monitor stem cell research, to recommend appropriate guidelines and regulations, and to consider all of the medical and ethical ramifications of biomedical innovation. This council will consist of leading scientists, doctors, ethicists, lawyers, theologians and others, and will be chaired by Dr. Leon Kass, a leading biomedical ethicist from the University of Chicago.

This council will keep us apprised of new developments and give our nation a forum to continue to discuss and evaluate these important issues. As we go forward, I hope we will always be guided by both intellect and heart, by both our capabilities and our conscience.

I have made this decision with great care, and I pray it is the right one.

Thank you for listening. Good night, and God bless America. 30

QUESTIONING THE TEXT

1. Consider the arrangement of Bush's argument. At what point in the speech does he announce his position explicitly? How does he prepare the audience for that announcement? What claims does he present in support of his position? Why do you think he chose to organize his speech in this way?
2. In paragraph 11, Bush identifies two "fundamental questions" that proved crucial to his decision on this issue. How might he have arrived at these questions? What other questions might be considered fundamental to the issue of the government's policy toward stem cell research? How does the identification of key questions affect the debate on this issue and its possible outcomes?
3. How would you describe the tone of this speech? What words and phrases contribute to this tone?
4. The text of a speech differs in significant ways from a printed text intended for silent reading. For one thing, transitions from one idea to another need to be much clearer in a speech because listeners cannot go back and reread what they missed. Does Bush do a good job of maintaining clarity and coherence in this spoken message? Try editing his speech as an essay to be published in print. What would you change, and why?

MAKING CONNECTIONS

5. "Embryonic stem cell research is at the leading edge of a series of moral hazards," Bush warns (paragraph 19). Discuss this concern in comparison with those raised in Mary Shelley's *Frankenstein* (p. 274) and Jeremy

Rifkin's "Biotech Century" (p. 287). How does your reading of Shelley's and Rifkin's pieces inform your thoughts on the issues Bush discusses in his speech?

6. Molly Ivins's column, "Bush's Brain Straddles the Fence Once Again" (p. 350), was published before the president gave this speech. Whether Bush had her comments in mind is impossible to know, but his speech could be read as answering some of her points. Do you think Bush's speech adequately addresses her concerns? Why, or why not?

JOINING THE CONVERSATION

7. Write an essay responding to the president's policy announcement on stem cell research. Whether you agree with the president and choose to elaborate on his argument, or you disagree in some respect, support your claim with research. Be sure to use proper academic documentation to cite the sources of your evidence.
8. In her introduction to Molly Ivins's column on the Bush administration's stem cell research policy (p. 350), A.L. relates that she found the president's speech, which she viewed on television, "confusing." Do you agree? Why, or why not? You might look up the speech in the White House archives at <www.whitehouse.gov> and try listening to it or watching it online, to see how the medium (audio, audiovisual, or print) affects your comprehension of Bush's argument. Discuss your response(s) to the speech with your classmates.

SHERRY TURKLE
Cuddling Up to Cyborg Babies

I SHOULD HAVE KNOWN I WAS IN OVER MY HEAD when I heard my eleven-year-old nephew summon me to his computer monitor: "Burp into the microphone, Aunt Andrea, and then laugh really loud." I failed the burp test, but my laugh was acceptable, and Logan soon had attached the sound to a snake he had drawn, which was moving back and forth across the screen. After importing a picture of himself feigning shock and horror into this scene, Logan replayed it a couple of times, satisfied with his artwork. When I remarked that he'd made the snake look "almost real," however, Logan shot me a mildly withering look and said, "No way, Aunt A."

That was about a year ago, and I wonder if Logan has acquired any new robotic or otherwise virtual toys and, if so, how he describes his relationship to them. Sherry Turkle's research suggests that children are coming to new understandings of such relationships as well as about the concept of "aliveness." As one child in her study puts it, robotic pets and their kin are, at the very least, "sort of alive." Turkle makes clear that children can describe in quite sophisticated terms what being "sort of alive" entails.

Turkle's current research builds on earlier work, most notably The Second Self: Computers and the Human Spirit *(1984) and* Life on the Screen: Identity in the Age of the Internet *(1995), as she continues to ask how machines are affecting our cognitive and emotional lives. Turkle's latest book, tentatively titled* Simulation and Its Discontents, *will continue her analysis of technological-human interaction and the ethical, psychological, and intellectual implications these interactions hold for us.*

Sherry Turkle (b. 1948) is the Abby Rockefeller Mauzé Professor of Science, Technology, and Society at MIT, where she directs the MIT Initiative on Technology and Self. "Cuddling Up to Cyborg Babies" first appeared in the September 2000 edition of the UNESCO Courier. *I chose it because I find Turkle's work readily accessible and intellectually challenging, and because she consistently asks us to think hard about our relationships, including those with machines, from computers to digital dolls. As one who has never had the time or patience for a real dog or cat, maybe I'll check out one of these new virtual pets myself.* —A.L.

Children have always used their toys and playthings to create models for understanding their world. Fifty years ago, the genius of Swiss psychologist Jean Piaget showed it is the business of childhood to take objects and use how they "work" to construct theories of space, time, number, causality, life and mind. At that time, a child's world was full of things that could be understood in simple, mechanical ways. A bicycle could be understood in terms of its pedals and gears, a windup car in terms of its clockwork springs. Children were able to take electronic devices such as basic radios and (with some difficulty) bring them into this "mechanical" system of understanding.

Revisiting Merlin

But in the early 1980s, a first generation of computer toys changed the traditional story. When children removed the back of their computer toys to "see" how they worked, they found a chip, a battery, and some wires. Sensing that trying to understand these objects "physically" would lead to a dead end, children tried to use a "psychological" kind of understanding. They asked themselves if the games were conscious, if they had feelings and even if they knew how to "cheat." Earlier objects encouraged children to think in terms of a distinction between the world of psychology and the world of machines, but the computer did not. Its "opacity" encouraged children to see computational objects as psychological machines.

Among the first generation of computational objects was Merlin, which challenged children to games of tic-tac-toe. For children who had only played games with human opponents, reaction to this object was intense. For example, while Merlin followed an optimal strategy for winning tic-tac-toe most of the time, it was programmed to make a slip every once in a while. So when children discovered strategies that allowed them to win and then tried these strategies a second time, they usually would not work. The machine gave the impression of not being "dumb enough" to let down its defenses twice. Robert, seven, playing with his friends on the beach, watched his friend Craig perform the "winning trick," but when he tried it, Merlin did not slip up and the game ended in a draw.

Robert, confused and frustrated, threw Merlin into the sand and said, "Cheater. I hope your brains break." He was overheard by Craig and Greg, aged six and eight, who salvaged the by-now very sandy toy and took it upon themselves to set Robert straight. "Merlin doesn't know if it cheats," says Craig. "It doesn't know if you break it, Robert. It's not alive." Greg adds, "It's smart enough to make the right kinds of noises. But it doesn't really know if it loses. And when it cheats it don't even know it's cheating." Jenny, six, interrupts with disdain: "Greg, to cheat you have to know you are cheating. Knowing is part of cheating."

In the early 1980s such scenes were not unusual. Confronted with ob- 5
jects that spoke, strategized and "won," children were led to argue the moral and metaphysical status of machines on the basis of their psychologies: did the machines know what they were doing? Despite Jenny's objections that "knowing is part of cheating," children did come to see computational objects as exhibiting a kind of knowing. By doing so, they recast the Piagetian framework in which a definition of life centered around "moving of one's own accord."

Observing children in the world of the "traditional"—that is non-computational—objects, Piaget found that at first they considered everything that moved to be alive. Then only things that moved without an outside push or pull. Gradually, children refined the notion to mean "life motions," namely only those things that breathed and grew were taken to be alive.

Motion Gives Way to Emotion

Children broke with this orderly categorization by making distinctions about "machines that think." Their discussions about the computer's aliveness came to center on what the children perceived as the computer's psychological rather than physical properties. To put it simply, motion gave way to emotion and physics gave way to psychology as criteria for aliveness.

In the 1980s, the computational objects that evoked "artificial life" (the "Sim" series, for example, assigns the task of creating a functioning ecosystem or city) strained that order to the breaking point, Children still tried to impose strategies and categories, but they did so in the manner of theoretical bricoleurs, or tinkerers, making do with whatever materials were at hand and with any theory that fit a prevailing circumstance. When children confronted these new objects and tried to construct a theory about what is alive, we were able to see them cycling through theories of "aliveness."

"Sort of Alive" Robots

An eleven-year-old named Holly watched a group of robots with "on-board" computational intelligence navigate a maze. As the robots used different strategies to reach their goal, Holly commented on their "personalities" and "cuteness." She finally came to speculate on the robots' "aliveness" and blurted out an unexpected formulation: "It's like Pinocchio [the story of a puppet brought to life]. First Pinocchio was just a puppet. He was not alive at all. Then he was an alive puppet. Then he was an alive boy. A real boy. But he was alive even before he was a real boy. So I think the robots are like that. They are alive like Pinocchio but not like real boys." She cleared her throat and summed up: "They are sort of alive."

Robbie, a ten-year-old who has been given a modem for her birthday, 10
put the emphasis on mobility when she considered whether the creatures she has evolved while creating a virtual ecosystem through the game SimLife were alive. "I think they are a little alive in the game, but you cannot save your game [when you turn it off], so that all the creatures you have evolved go away. But if they could figure out how to get rid of that part of the program so that you would have to save the game and if your modem were on,

then they [the creatures] could get out of your computer and go to America Online [an Internet Service Provider]."

The resurfacing of motion (Piaget's *classical criterion for how a child decides* whether a "traditional" object is alive) is now bound up with notions of a presumed psychology: children are most likely to assume that the creatures in Sim games have a desire to "get out" of the system and evolve in a wider computational world.

Through the 1990s, children still spoke easily about factors which encouraged them to see the "stuff" of computers as the same "stuff" of which life is made. I observed a group of seven-year-olds playing with a set of plastic transformer toys that can take the shape of armored tanks, robots, or people. The transformers can also be put into intermediate states so that a "robot" arm can protrude from a human form or a human leg from a mechanical tank. Two of the children are playing with the toys, mixing human and machine parts. A third child insists that this is not right. The toys, he says, should not be placed in hybrid states. "You should play them as all tank or all people." An eight-year-old girl comforts the now upset third child. "It's okay to play them when they are in-between. It's all the same stuff," she said, "just yucky computer 'cy-dough-plasm.' "

This comment reflects a cyborg consciousness among today's children: a tendency to see computer systems as "sort of" alive, to fluidly cycle through various explanatory concepts, and to willingly transgress boundaries.

Feelings for Furby

Most recently, the transgressions have involved relationships with "virtual pets" and digital dolls (the first and most popular of these were Tamagotchis and Furbies) which raise new questions about the boundaries of what children consider as life. What these objects have that earlier computational objects did not is that they ask the child for nurturance. They ask the child to assess the object's "state of mind" in order to develop a successful relationship with the object. For example, in order to grow and be healthy; Tamagotchis (imaginary creatures "housed" in small screened devices) need to be fed, cleaned and amused. Going a step further, the furry electronic pets called Furbies simulate learning and loving. They are cuddly; they speak and play games with the child. Furbies add the dimensions of human-like conversation and tender companionship to the mix of what children can anticipate from computational objects. In my research on children and Furbies, I have found that when children play with these new objects they want to know their "state," not to get something "right," but to make the Furbies happy. Children want to understand Furby language, not to "win" in a game over the Furbies, but to have a feeling of mutual recognition. They do not ask how the objects "work," they take the affectively charged toys "at interface value."

In my previous research on children and computer toys, children de- 15
scribed the life-like status of machines in terms of their cognitive capacities (the toys could "know" things, "solve" puzzles). In my more recent studies, children describe the new toys, Furbies, as "sort of alive," which reflects their emotional attachments to the toys and their fantasies that the Furby might be emotionally attached to them. When asked whether the Furbies are alive, children tend not to speak about what the toy can do and focus instead on their feelings for the "pet" and how it might feel about them.

Emotional Vulnerability

"Well, the Furby is alive for a Furby," says Ron, six. "And you know, something this smart should have arms. It might want to pick up something or hug me." Katherine, age five, asks: "Is it alive? Well, I love it. It's more alive than a Tamagotchi because it sleeps with me. It likes to sleep with me." Jen, age nine, focuses not on what the object offers her, but what she can do for it. "I really like to take care of it. So, I guess it is alive, but it doesn't need to really eat, so it is as alive as you can be if you don't eat. A Furby is like an owl. But it is more alive than an owl because it knows more and you can talk to it. But it needs batteries so it is not an animal. It's not like an animal kind of alive."

Today's children are learning to distinguish between an "animal kind of alive" and a "Furby kind of alive." The category of "sort of alive" becomes increasingly used. Perceived intelligence or "knowing" is another key distinction.

Over the past five decades, research in artificial intelligence has not even come close to creating a machine as intelligent as a person. But it has succeeded in contributing to a certain deflation of our language in terms of how we use the word intelligence. It is now commonplace to talk about intelligent machines when we really are talking about machines that play chess or assess mortgage applications. These feats are wondrous, but intelligence used to mean a great deal more than that. We now face the prospect of a similar deflation of language in talking about affect and emotion. Children talk about an "animal kind of alive" and a "Furby kind of alive." Will they also talk about a "people kind of love" and a "computer kind of love"?

These questions bring us to a different world from the old "AI [artificial intelligence] debates" of the 1960s to 1980s in which researchers argued about whether machines could be "really" intelligent. The old debate was essentialist. The new objects sidestep such arguments about what is inherent in them and play instead on what they evoke in us: when we are asked to care for an object, when this cared-for object thrives and offers us its attention and concern, we experience it as intelligent, but more important, we feel a connection to it. The old AI debates were about the technical abilities of machines. The new ones will be about the emotional vulnerabilities of people.

QUESTIONING THE TEXT

1. What is Turkle's purpose in this article? How does she achieve it? What organizational strategy does she use in presenting her ideas?
2. In introducing this piece, A.L. tells an anecdote about her nephew's creation of a computer image. Throughout her article, Turkle similarly provides anecdotes about children playing with various types of toys. Turkle, however, does not reveal the sources of her anecdotes; she does not identify the children as relatives or even as people she observed personally. Where do you think her knowledge of these scenes comes from? Does it matter? Do you trust her experience, regardless of this lack of information about her sources? Why, or why not?

MAKING CONNECTIONS

3. Given Turkle's claims about the changes in children's interactions with toys and what she calls the "cyborg consciousness" of today's children (paragraph 13), what do you think about the issues raised in Todd Oppenheimer's "The Computer Delusion" (p. 298)? Does the historical perspective offered by Turkle give you further insight into the role that technology ought to play in children's education? Explain.
4. Compare the "aliveness" that children ascribe to toys such as the Furby and the "animation" that Victor Frankenstein bestowed on his creation in Mary Shelley's *Frankenstein* (p. 274). How do the potential problems associated with computerized toys compare to the problems Shelley poses in her novel? Are moral issues at stake in children's play with artificial pets?

JOINING THE CONVERSATION

5. Do you play computer games? Do you see any potential moral difficulties with any of those games? Freewrite to explore the broader ramifications of computer play. Then compose an argument outlining guidelines for parents or policy makers who are facing the question of how or whether to limit teenagers' recreational use of computers.
6. Where do you place yourself in Turkle's history? What were your favorite toys as a child? Did you play with any of those she describes? Did

you play with low-tech toys, such as stuffed animals, cards, or board games, either instead of or in addition to more high-tech toys? How do you think the playthings of your childhood might have shaped your attitudes toward other people, toward machines, toward the idea of "intelligence"? Discuss these questions with classmates.

THE ONION

New National Parks Web Site Makes National Parks Obsolete

DRIVING NORTH ON HIGHWAY 64 out of Williams, Arizona, heading for the Grand Canyon, you'll eventually reach the tiny settlement of Tusayan just before the south entrance to the national park. Like many tourist towns, Tusayan has a general store, a steak house, lots of hotels, a McDonald's, and, oh yes, an IMAX Theater. There, on a screen seven stories high and 82 feet wide, you can watch vivid images of the greatest natural wonder in the continental United States.

Or you could drive a few miles down the road and experience the canyon itself.

This juxtaposition between virtual reality and reality itself has always struck me as ironic and funny—though I did, in fact, take in the IMAX film during one of my four trips to the Grand Canyon. And the film, with its stomach-roiling aerial shots and thundering Dolby sound, did offer me perspectives on Colorado's famous canyon that I had never experienced on foot or from the air. (I took a helicopter tour once, too.)

After a century of films and two full generations of TV watching, we've become a culture that too often seems to prefer on-screen experiences to life itself. Concoct the most artificial human situations you can imagine, offer unusually attractive people an incentive to participate, set a film crew to work, and you've got something now called "reality TV." It's about as genuine as Martin Sheen playing the President of the United States.

So The Onion *isn't far off the mark in parodying the authority we give to virtual experiences by asking us to believe, for a comic moment, that the National Park Service intends to replace the Grand Canyon and all the rest of our national treasures with a Web site. But in this April 30, 1997 piece, there's a serious point as well. Our fascination with online and Web experiences has turned us inward in ways that we haven't yet fully fathomed. If the Web has created some worthwhile virtual communities, as it doubtless has, the Internet has also isolated us from some more direct human experiences. Two years ago, I stopped using a real-time classroom chat program to foster class discussion when a student asked me rather pointedly why, instead of sending email to the fellow sitting next to him, he couldn't just talk to him. There was no sensible response to that criticism.*

The Onion, *as most college students know, is one of the premier forums for biting political and cultural humor in the United States. It is available in both printed and online versions. You should buy the printed version, but you can see the virtual* Onion *at <theonion.com>.*

—J.R.

WASHINGTON, DC—In an effort to make America's natural wonders available to all citizens, the Department of the Interior announced Monday the creation of a $2 million National Parks Web site.

The new Web site clears the way for the wholesale development of the parks: Next Monday, bulldozers will begin leveling more than 100,000 square miles of pristine, federally protected national parkland, finally making it available for industrial use.

Jack Holm, designer of the Web site, believes nature lovers will find it superior to the real parks in every way. "You will experience the same grand mountains, lush grass and wide variety of fauna, without ever leaving your home," he said. "And when you spot an animal on your cyber-tour, like a majestic elk, you can click on the elk and access information about its habitat and diet. Elks in the wild do not offer this option."

The Web site, located at www.natparks.gov, will feature 72 pixels-per-inch photos of parks and "hyper text" on the parks' histories and wildlife. It will also offer camping options, with which visitors can set up a "virtual campsite" inside a national park and watch a quick-time movie of the setting sun while RealAudio playback of crickets and coyotes runs at 44.1 kilohertz.

"We digitally enhanced actual recordings of coyotes from Arizona's 5
Saguaro National Park," Holm said. "It should sound better than the real thing."

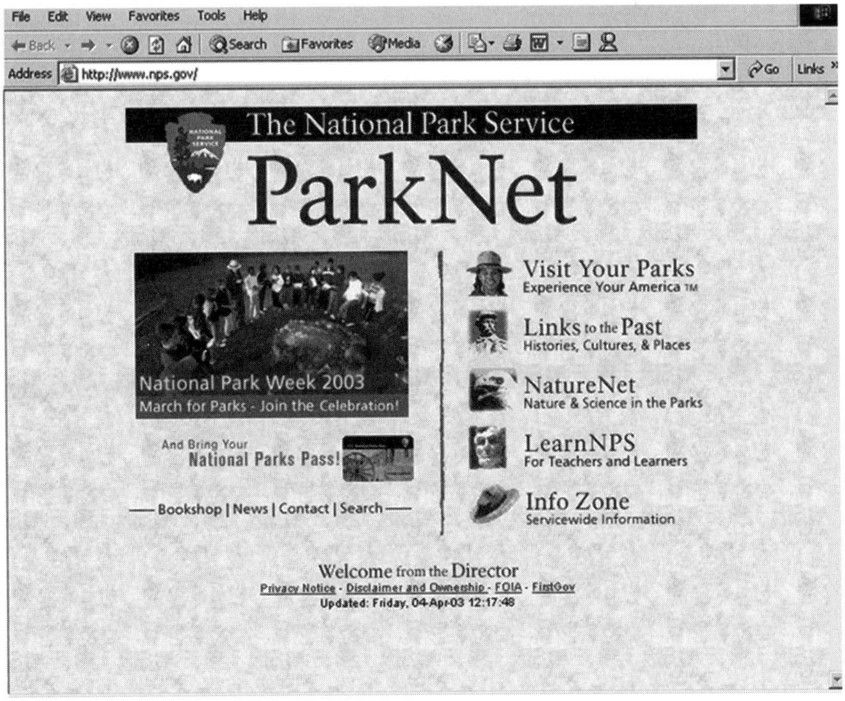

According to National Parks Destruction Chief Lew Hoffson, countless grizzlies, moose and bison will be incinerated when the 750,000-acre Yellowstone National Park is slash-burned to make room for what he says will be the nation's largest factory outlet mall.

"Yellowstone, like the other national parks, has proven to be a huge financial burden to taxpayers, costing more than $200 million a year to maintain," Hoffson said. "The new Yellowstone Factory Shoppes, on the other hand, are privately funded and should be immensely profitable right from the word go. It just makes sense."

The economic advantage of massive, unregulated development of the parks was only one reason for the Web site move. Safety was also a factor.

"Every year, between 30 to 40 national parks visitors are killed in accidents, ranging from animal attacks to falls off cliffs," Holm said. "The Web site will be far safer, with the greatest danger posed to visitors being possible neck and back strain from prolonged sitting at the computer station." To avoid such discomfort when visiting the new cyber-parks, Holm strongly advised taking a "stretch break" every 15 to 20 minutes.

Yet another advantage of Web-based camping will be the chance for 10
visitors to enjoy interacting with talking, anthropomorphic wildlife, such as PC Puffin, a friendly, wise-cracking aquatic cartoon bird who gives visitors tours of Alaska's Denali National Park. "Non-cyber-parks do not feature puffin-led tours, for in real life animals do not talk," Holm said.

U.S. Parks Department officials said the department is also planning an endangered-species Web site, enabling people to observe and study rare species on their computers. Once the Web site is up and running, the actual endangered animals will either be allowed to die out naturally in captivity or be killed off wholesale by poachers.

U.S. Sen. Spencer Abraham (R-MI), who sponsored the legislation, said that he and his family are planning a trip to the National Parks Web site this July. "We've never been to Yellowstone," he said, "and I understand we'll be able to download a sound effect of hot, splashing water digitally recorded right at Old Faithful. We're very excited."

QUESTIONING THE TEXT

1. *The Onion*, a parody of a newspaper, is sometimes mistaken by readers as the real thing. What makes this piece on national parks seem like a real news article? How does the piece mimic journalistic conventions? What gives it away as a spoof?
2. Parody often provides satirical criticism of political events or actions. Did this piece serve that function at the time when it first appeared? To find out, use the Internet to search your library's databases of articles in popular periodicals or the archives of newspaper Web sites; look for

articles on the national parks, technology, or environmental policies that may have been in the news shortly before this *Onion* piece appeared. Do some fact-checking to see if the people mentioned in the *Onion* article (Jack Holm, Lew Hoffson, U.S. Sen. Spencer Abraham) are real or fictional. What purpose do these figures serve in this parody?

3. Consider the publication in which this article first appeared. Who publishes *The Onion,* and for what purposes? How long has it been in operation? Who funds it? How much of this background information does *The Onion* itself provide in its paper or online publication, and how reliable is that information?

MAKING CONNECTIONS

4. In his introduction to this piece, J.R. tells of a real-time classroom chat program he stopped using because he saw no reason that students shouldn't simply talk face-to-face in the classroom. As J.R.'s anecdote suggests, the *Onion* article raises some issues similar to those addressed in Todd Oppenheimer's "The Computer Delusion" (p. 298). Using these two articles and your own experience or research, formulate a response to those who argue that the use of technology in education threatens to replace other valuable experiences in human learning. Try to expand on the examples in these articles or add new ones of your own to help identify some of technology's uses and limitations in education.

5. Consider this piece alongside "Cars and Their Enemies" (p. 338), in which James Q. Wilson claims that cars, decried by some critics as the scourge of contemporary society, make it possible for people to travel to the natural attractions of the American countryside. On what points do you think Wilson and the authors of the *Onion* article would agree? On what points might they diverge? What evidence from these articles supports your speculation? To help support his argument, Wilson creates a fanciful hypothetical situation—he asks readers to imagine that the car has not yet been invented. The *Onion* article itself is a fanciful invention. What do you make of the similarities and differences in the approaches used in these two pieces? To what extent do you find each piece of writing effective, and why?

JOINING THE CONVERSATION

6. Working with two classmates, write your own parody of a news story or other type of public or professional discourse. You might mimic a public statement or proclamation by a university president, for example,

or a letter of application for a job or internship, a personal statement for a college or professional school application, or a letter of acceptance or rejection. Be sure to attend to the conventions of the genre. Share your parody with classmates to see how well you succeeded with the humor and criticism you set out to achieve.

7. Evaluate the Web site of a national park. Does the Web site resemble the exaggerated depiction in *The Onion?* Does the site give you detailed information on the park's plant and animal life, as *The Onion* article suggests? What purposes do you think the Web site fulfills? What purposes should it fulfill? Does it make you more or less likely to visit the park than you might otherwise have been?

OTHER READINGS

Aveni, Anthony. "Time's Empire." *Wilson Quarterly* Summer 1998: 44–57. Traces the history of "time" as a concept and a technology.

Bolter, Jay David, and Richard Grusin. *Remediation: Understanding New Media.* Cambridge, MA: MIT P, 1999. Offers a new way to consider how new media borrow from and remake other media.

Bringsford, Selmer, "Chess Is Too Easy." *Technology Review* Mar.–Apr. 1998: 23–29. Explores the meaning of artificial intelligence.

Florman, Samuel C. *Blaming Technology: The Irrational Search for Scapegoats.* New York: St. Martin's, 1981. Argues for not turning away from technological change.

Haraway, Donna J. *Modest_Witness@Second_Millennium.FemaleMan©_Meets_OncoMouse™.* New York: Routledge, 1997. Explores contemporary technoscience and argues that we are all cyborgs.

Harding, Sandra. *Is Science Multicultural? Postcolonialisms, Feminisms, and Epistemologies.* Bloomington: Indiana UP, 1998. Explores what practitioners of European and American feminist and postcolonial science and technology studies can learn from each other.

Hines, Alicia Headlam, Alondra Nelson, and Thuy Linh N. Tu, eds. *Technicolor: Race, Technology, and Everyday Life.* New York: NYU P, 2001. A collection of case studies that document the history of technological innovation by people of color.

Johnson, George. *Fire in the Mind: Science, Faith, and the Search for Order.* New York: Knopf, 1995. Focuses on Los Alamos to explore the human drive for order as expressed in different cultural traditions.

Kolko, Beth E., Lisa Nakamura, and Gilbert B. Rodman, eds. *Race in Cyberspace.* New York: Routledge, 2000. An essay collection focusing on the effects of cyberspace on racial politics and identity.

Stoll, Clifford. *Silicon Snake Oil: Second Thoughts on the Information Highway.* New York: Doubleday, 1995. Warns that the Internet may not live up to its vaunted potential.

Ullman, Ellen. *Close to the Machine: Technophilia and Its Discontents.* San Francisco: City Lights, 1997. Uses her own experiences as a long-time computer programmer and techno-buff to question whether networking can allow for the kind of intimacy humans long for.

ELECTRONIC RESOURCES

http://www.nasa.gov
Gateway to a complex site on NASA's diverse missions.

http://www.pbs.org/wgbh/aso
Companion site to the PBS series *A Science Odyssey: 100 Years of Discovery.*

http://www.wired.com/news
Wired magazine's up-to-date news on subjects related to computers and electronic technology.

The photograph on the preceding page comes from a book called *Crowns: Portraits of Black Women in Church Hats,* by Michael Cunningham and Craig Marberry. Look carefully at this photograph, and spend some time jotting down the elements of self-expression you see at work here. ■ According to an anonymous source quoted on the inside flap of the book's cover, "A woman's hat speaks long before its wearer utters a word." If this statement is true, what does the hat in this picture say? ■ What do you make of the fact that we can't see the woman's face, yet we can see her hands very clearly? ■ How does the composition of the photograph affect your understanding of and response to it? ■ How are elements of your own clothing tied to or reflective of your identity?

Identities: The One in Many/The Many in One

6

If the first woman God ever made was strong enough to turn the world upside down all alone, these women together ought to be able to turn it back. . . .

SOJOURNER TRUTH, *Ain't I a Woman?*

Growing up homosexual was to grow up normally but displaced; to experience romantic love, but with the wrong person; to entertain grand ambitions, but of the unacceptable sort; to seek a gradual self-awakening, but in secret, not in public.

ANDREW SULLIVAN, *What Are Homosexuals For?*

She obeyed him; she always did as she was told.

MAXINE HONG KINGSTON, *No Name Woman*

. . . if God did not want us to make gender-based generalizations, She would not have given us genders.

DAVE BARRY, *Guys vs. Men*

I remember the very day that I became colored.

ZORA NEALE HURSTON, *How It Feels to Be Colored Me*

Years ago I learned that pain and wheelchair fatigue—*sitting,* and worrying about what can go wrong because I can't stand or walk—take most of my energy; I cannot live as normals do, and I must try to do only what is essential each day.

ANDRE DUBUS, *Witness*

I suggest that we relax and luxuriate in our linguistic richness and our traditional tolerance of language differences.

ROBERT D. KING, *Should English Be the Law?*

For many years, a towering old billboard over the expressway downtown proudly declared Grand Rapids "An All-American City." For me, that all-American designation meant all-white.

BICH MINH NGUYEN, *The Good Immigrant Student*

The reptilian instinct for survival does not just involve crime fears. . . . It also shows up in the extent to which people are willing to put other drivers at risk in order to diminish the odds that they will be injured themselves in a crash.

KEITH BRADSHER, *Reptile Dreams*

The Tribes see women variously, but they do not question the power of femininity. Sometimes they see women as fearful, sometimes peaceful, sometimes omnipotent and omniscient, but they never portray women as mindless, helpless, simple, or oppressed. PAULA GUNN ALLEN, *Where I Come From Is Like This*

If a multiracial category is included further down the road, . . . we may wish to add one more category, that of "multi-ethnic" origin, one which most Americans might wish to check. Then we would live to recognize the full importance of my favorite African American saying: We came in many ships but we now ride in the same boat. AMITAI ETZIONI, *The Monochrome Society*

The attitudes and actions which the Muslim totalitarians call Islam are unrecognizable to me. The institutions which nurtured my Muslim identity taught me something very different. Simply, that Islam is about the oneness of God, the unity of humankind and the responsibility of humans to realize the original intention of the Creator in his creation.

EBOO PATEL, *On Nurturing a Modern Muslim Identity*

I guess being colored doesn't make me not like
the same things other folks like who are other races.
So will my page be colored that I write?
Being me, it will not be white. LANGSTON HUGHES, *Theme for English B*

Introduction

"AND WHO ARE YOU?" a talkative snail asks Alice, the heroine of *Alice in Wonderland*, who replies, "I—I hardly know, sir, just at present—at least I know who I was when I got up this morning, but I think I must have been changed several times since then." Little wonder that Marshall McLuhan concludes his *The Medium Is the Massage* with this exchange, since in that book he argues that "electronic technology . . . is forcing us to reconsider and reevaluate practically every thought, every action, and every institution formerly taken for granted. Everything is changing—you, your family, your neighborhood, your education, your job, your government, your relation to 'the others.' And they're changing dramatically." Most of all, McLuhan insists, our ideas about who we are—our very identities—are changing.

What may be surprising to you is that McLuhan wrote those words in 1967 (or perhaps earlier since the book was published that year), over three decades before you take them up in this text. And those thirty years have seen many of McLuhan's claims borne out, particularly in the threat of electronic surveillance and a concomitant loss of privacy. Would McLuhan be surprised by the kinds of "identity theft" taking place today—such as online trickery or in warring countries, where people evicted from their homes for political and religious reasons are often stripped of all papers and thus left with no official identity? We don't think so.

But have our very ideas of identity changed? Many believe that they have—or that they are doing so right now. The view of self as autonomous, coherent, and unifying, a view associated with both eighteenth-century rationalism and Romanticism, for example, has been challenged on many fronts. In place of this singular, solitary self (celebrated in dramatic and unforgettable terms in Walt Whitman's "Song of Myself" and many other works of literature), multiple alternatives have emerged: a socially constructed self that grows up through a series of negotiations with others and with the environment; a self fashioned by forces beyond the control of the individual; and, most recently, a "virtual" self or selves that may (or may not) coalesce into one individual. In turn, these theoretical debates have left many wondering just how identity *is* constituted.

The selections in this chapter all circle around questions of identity formation. Is it related primarily to a genetic base? To gender, sexuality, and religion? To nation-state and politics? To race and ethnicity? To marketing? To language—or to any number of other crucially important sources of influence in individuals' lives, such as work, physical abilities, and so on? Looking back over our own lives, we can see ways in which our sense of identity has shifted over the decades; we can identify as well periods of tension in terms of identity, particularly during moments of great change or loss. Yet on most days, we'd probably respond to the question "Who are you?" not as Alice did but with the simple statement of our names. What's in a name? And what's in an identity?

We believe you have already thought quite a lot about these issues. To add to that thinking, consider the following questions:

- What things in your surroundings do you most closely identify with—family, friends, church, team, some other group—and why?
- Can you recall a time when someone identified you in some way that seemed completely surprising or foreign to you? If so, describe that time.
- How would you define your identity? Where do your identifying characteristics or features come from? How many "selves" can you identify in yourself?

• • •

SOJOURNER TRUTH
Ain't I a Woman?

*S*OJOURNER *T*RUTH *(1797–1883) took her name from mystical visions that urged her, after her escape from slavery, to sojourn and speak the truth. Although she never learned to write on paper, the words of her speeches often wrote on her listeners' souls. The following speech was written down by Elizabeth Cady Stanton (whose account differs from other renditions of the famous speech), an early proponent of women's rights, and printed in* The History of Woman Suffrage. *Truth delivered it at the Women's Rights Convention in Akron, Ohio, in 1851. On that occasion she spoke to an almost all-white audience, since African Americans were, ironically, not welcome at such events. In "Ain't I a Woman?" Truth claims her identity as a woman—and as equal to men. In doing so, she speaks not just for women but for many who are oppressed, combining her devotion to abolitionism and to women's suffrage. With vigor and humor, she argues for basic human rights as one feature of identity among "all God's children."*

This brief speech always reminds me of the power of the spoken word—and of the difference one voice can sometimes make. I love Truth's use of some of the colloquialisms I grew up with (like "out of kilter"), her familiar references to those in her audience as "honey" and "children," and other aspects of her speaking style that help me feel as though she is right here in front of me talking. I chose this speech for these reasons and because Truth counters perfectly all those voices down through the ages that have dismissed people such as her as "just" women. To hear her rebuttal, and to get at some of this speech's rhythmic power, try reading it aloud. —A.L.

Well, children, where there is so much racket there must be something out of kilter. I think that 'twixt the negroes of the South and the women of the North, all talking about rights, the white men will be in a fix pretty soon. But what's all this here talking about?

That man over there says that women need to be helped into carriages, and lifted over ditches, and to have the best place everywhere. Nobody ever helps me into carriages, or over mud-puddles, or gives me any best place! And ain't I a woman? Look at me! Look at my arm! I have ploughed and planted, and gathered into barns, and no man could head me! And ain't I a woman? I could work as much and eat as much as a man—when I could get it—and bear the lash as well! And ain't I a woman? I have borne thirteen children, and seen them most all sold off to slavery, and when I cried out with my mother's grief, none but Jesus heard me! And ain't I a woman?

Then they talk about this thing in the head; what's this they call it? [Intellect, someone whispers.] That's it, honey. What's that got to do with women's rights or negro's rights? If my cup won't hold but a pint, and yours holds a quart, wouldn't you be mean not to let me have my little half-measure full?

Then that little man in black there, he says women can't have as much rights as men, 'cause Christ wasn't a woman! Where did your Christ come from? Where did your Christ come from? From God and a woman! Man had nothing to do with Him.

If the first woman God ever made was strong enough to turn the world 5
upside down all alone, these women together ought to be able to turn it back, and get it right side up again! And now they is asking to do it, the men better let them.

Obliged to you for hearing me, and now old Sojourner ain't got nothing more to say.

QUESTIONING THE TEXT

1. Truth punctuates her speech with a rhetorical question—"And ain't I a woman?" What effect does the repetition of this question have on you as a reader? What answer does Truth invoke?
2. A.L.'s introduction reveals that she is a fan of Sojourner Truth. What criticisms *could* A.L. have leveled at Truth's argument?

MAKING CONNECTIONS

3. How might Sojourner Truth respond to Dave Barry's "Guys vs. Men" (p. 402)? Read that selection. Then, using Truth's humorous and conversational tone, write a brief speech in which she responds to "Guys vs. Men."
4. Several other selections in this chapter deal with the ways in which part of one's identity brings forth discrimination, bias, oppression. Choose one of these other selections, and read it carefully after rereading Truth's speech. What arguments can you find in common between Truth and the other author you chose? What differences in evidence and in argumentative strategy do you detect?

JOINING THE CONVERSATION

5. List as many reasons as you can to support the belief that men and women should or should not have the same rights and responsibilities. Explain from your own experiences *why* you believe as you do.
6. Try your hand at writing your own manifesto of identity, using a repeated question (such as "And ain't I a ________?") to organize your brief piece of writing.

ANDREW SULLIVAN
What Are Homosexuals For?

ANDREW SULLIVAN'S argument in favor of "normalizing" homosexual identity in America—understood as legalizing same-sex marriage and permitting gay men and women to serve in the military—speaks quietly and eloquently to the entire political spectrum. In Virtually Normal *(1995), Sullivan (b. 1963), former editor of the political journal the* New Republic *and homosexual himself, systematically examines arguments on all sides of a thorny issue to hammer out a compromise "politics of homosexuality." He places himself squarely in the middle, clearing ground for tolerance by seeming tolerant himself, acknowledging, for example, that conservative critics of homosexuality may be expressing "sincerely held moral beliefs." Yet he also bravely questions those who might be logical allies. About the radical activities of ACT UP, for example, Sullivan observes: "A politics which seeks only to show and not to persuade will only be as successful as its latest theatrical escapade, and will be as susceptible to the fashion of audiences as any other fad."*

Reviewed favorably in many periodicals, Virtually Normal *caused a minor ripple when it debuted, Sullivan himself playing the TV talk show circuit. But a book so sober and rational can change public opinion only one reader at a time. The more immediate accomplishment of* Virtually Normal *may have been to set a standard for civil argument at precisely the moment when America's public square had become a tough, bellicose place. This selection is from the epilogue of* Virtually Normal, *a personal part of Sullivan's book, and one that conveys the honesty and lucidity that make the entire work worth reading.* —J.R.

> Reason has so many shapes we don't know what to seize hold of; experience has just as many. What we infer from the similarity of events is uncertain, because they are always dissimilar: there is no quality so universal here as difference.
>
> —MICHEL DE MONTAIGNE

The discovery of one's homosexuality is for many people the same experience as acting upon it. For me, alas, this was not the case. Maybe, in some respects, this was intellectually salutary: I was able, from an early age, to distinguish, as my Church taught, the condition of homosexuality from its practice. But in life, nothing is as easily distinguished. Even disavowing homosexuality is a response to it; and the response slowly, subtly alters who you are. The sublimation of sexual longing can create a particular form of alienated person: a more ferocious perfectionist, a cranky individual, an extremely brittle emotionalist, an ideological fanatic. This may lead to some brilliant lives: witty, urbane, subtle, passionate. But it also leads to some devastating loneliness. The abandonment of intimacy and the rejection of one's emotional core are, I have come to believe, alloyed evils. All too often, they preserve the persona at the expense of the person.

I remember a man, a university figure, who knew everyone in a distant avuncular fashion. I suppose we all understood that somewhere he was a homosexual; he had few women friends, and no emotional or sexual life to speak of. He lived in a carefully constructed world of university gossip, intellectual argument, and intense, platonic relationships with proteges and students. He was immensely fat. One day, he told me, in his mid-forties, he woke up in a room at the Harvard Club in New York and couldn't move. He stayed there immobile for the morning and much of the afternoon. He realized at that moment that there was no honesty at the core of his life, and no love at its center. The recognition of this emptiness literally paralyzed him. He was the lucky one. He set about re-ordering his life; in his late middle age, he began to have adolescent affairs; he declared his sexuality loudly and somewhat crudely to anyone who could hear; he unloaded himself to his friends and loved ones. In one of those ultimately unintelligible tragedies, he died of a swift and deadly cancer three years later. But at his funeral, I couldn't help but reflect that he had at least tasted a few years of life. He had regained himself before he lost himself forever.

Others never experience such dreadful epiphanies. There was a time when I felt that the closeted homosexual was a useful social creature, and possibly happier than those immersed in what sometimes seems like a merciless and shallow subculture. But the etiolation of the heart which this self-abnegation requires is enormous. For many of us, a shared love is elusive anyway, a goal we rarely achieve and, when we do, find extremely hard to maintain. But to make the lack of such an achievement a condition of one's existence is to remove from a human life much that might propel it forward. Which is why I cannot forget the image of that man in a bed. He could not move. For him, there was no forward, no future to move into.

This is how the world can seem to many adolescent homosexuals; and I was no exception. Heterosexual marriage is perceived as the primary emotional goal for your peers; and yet you know this cannot be your fate. It terrifies and alarms you. While its form comforts, its content appalls. It requires a systematic dishonesty; and this dishonesty either is programmed into your soul and so warps your integrity, or is rejected in favor of—what? You scan your mind for an alternative. You dream grandiose dreams, construct a fantasy of a future, pour your energies into some massive distraction, pursue a consuming career to cover up the lie at the center of your existence. You are caught between escape and the constant daily wrench of self-denial. It is a vise from which many teenagers and young adults never emerge.

I was lucky. I found an escape, an escape into a world of ideas, into a 5
career, and into another country. America provided an excuse for a new beginning, as it had done for millions of immigrants before me. I often wonder, had I stayed in the place which reminded me so much of where I was from, whether I would have found a way to construct a measurably honest life. I don't know. But I do know that in this as well I was not alone. So many homosexuals find it essential to move away from where they are before they can regain themselves. Go to any major city and you'll find thousands of exiles from the heartland, making long-distance phone calls which echo with the same euphemisms of adolescence, the same awkward pauses, the same banal banter. These city limits are the equivalent of the adolescent's bedroom door: a barrier where two lives can be maintained with some hope of success and a minimal amount of mutual embarrassment.

It was in the safety of this exile that I could come home. I remember my first kiss with another man, the first embrace, the first love affair. Many metaphors have been used to describe this delayed homecoming—I was twenty-three—but to me, it was like being in a black-and-white movie that suddenly converted to color. The richness of experience seemed possible for the first time; the abstractions of dogma, of morality, of society, dissolved into the sheer, mysterious pleasure of being human. Perhaps this is a homosexual privilege: for many heterosexuals, the pleasures of intimacy and sexuality are stumbled upon gradually when young; for many homosexuals, the entire experience can come at once, when an adult, eclipsing everything, humiliating the developed person's sense of equilibrium, infantilizing and liberating at the same time. Sometimes I wonder whether some homosexuals' addiction to constant romance, to the thrill of the new lover, to the revelation of a new and obliviating desire, is in fact an attempt to relive this experience, again and again.

What followed over the years was not without its stupidity, excess, and hurt. But it was far realler than anything I had experienced before. I was never really "in the closet" in this sense. Until my early twenties, I was essentially heterosexual in public disclosure and emotionless in private life. Within a year, I was both privately and publicly someone who attempted little disguise of his emotional orientation. In this, I was convinced I was entering finally into normal life. I was the equal of heterosexuals, deserving of exactly the same respect, attempting to construct in the necessarily contrived world of the gay subculture the mirror image of the happy heterosexuality I imagined around me. Like many in my generation, I flattered myself that this was a first: a form of pioneering equality, an insistence on one's interchangeability with the dominant culture, on one's radical similarity with the heterosexual majority.

And in a fundamental sense, as I have tried to explain, this was true. The homosexual's emotional longings, his development, his dreams are human phenomena. They are, I think, instantly recognizable to any heterosexual, in their form if not their content. The humanity of homosexuals is clear everywhere. Perhaps nothing has illustrated this more clearly than the AIDS epidemic. Gay people have to confront grief and shock and mortality like anybody else. They die like all people die.

Except, of course, that they don't. Homosexuals in contemporary America tend to die young; they sometimes die estranged from their families; they die among friends who have become their new families; they die surrounded by young death, and by the arch symbols of cultural otherness. Growing up homosexual was to grow up normally but displaced; to experience romantic love, but with the wrong person; to entertain grand ambitions, but of the unacceptable sort; to seek a gradual self-awakening, but in secret, not in public.

But to live as an adult homosexual is to experience something else 10
again. By the simple fact of one's increasing cultural separation, the human personality begins to develop differently. As an adolescent and child, you are surrounded by the majority culture: so your concerns and habits and thoughts become embedded in the familiar and communicable. But slowly, and gradually, in adulthood, your friends and acquaintances become increasingly gay or lesbian. Lesbian women can find themselves slowly distanced from the company of men; gay men can find themselves slowly disentangled from women. One day, I glanced at my log of telephone calls: the ratio of men to women, once roughly even, had become six-to-one male. The women I knew and cared about had dwindled to a small but intimate group of confidantes and friends, women who were able to share my homosexual life and understand it. The straight men, too, had fallen in number. And both these groups tended to come from people I had met *before* I had fully developed an openly gay life.

These trends reinforced each other. Of course, like most gay people, I worked in a largely heterosexual environment and still maintained close links with my heterosexual family. But the environmental incentives upon me were clearly in another direction. I naturally gravitated toward people who were similar. Especially in your twenties, when romantic entanglement assumes a dominant role in life, you naturally socialize with prospective partners. Before you know where you are, certain patterns develop. Familiarity breeds familiarity; and, by no conscious process, your inculturation is subtly and powerfully different than that of your heterosexual peers.

In the world of emotional and sexual life, there were no clear patterns to follow: homosexual culture offered a gamut of possibilities, from anonymous sex to bourgeois coupling. But its ease with sexual activity, its male facility with sexual candor, its surprising lack of formal, moral stricture—all these made my life subtly and slowly more different than my straight male (let alone my straight female) peers'. In my late twenties, the difference became particularly acute. My heterosexual male friends became married; soon, my straight peers were having children. Weddings, babies, career couples, engagements: the calendar began to become crowded with the clatter of heterosexual bonding. And yet in my gay life, something somewhat different was occurring.

I remember vividly one Labor Day weekend. I had two engagements to attend. The first was a gay friend's thirtieth birthday party. It was held in the Deep South, in his family's seaside home. He had told his family he was gay the previous winter; he had told them he had AIDS that Memorial Day. His best friends had come to meet the family for the first time—two straight women, his boyfriend, his ex-boyfriend, and me. That year, we had all been through the trauma of his illness, and he was visibly thinner now than he had been even a month before. Although we attended to the typical family functions—dinners, beach trips, photo ops—there was a strained air of irony and sadness about the place. How could we explain what it was like to live in one's twenties and thirties with such a short horizon, to face mortality and sickness and death, to attend funerals when others were attending weddings? And yet, somehow the communication was possible. He was their son, after all. And after they had acclimatized to our mutual affection, and humor, and occasional diffidence, there was something of an understanding. His father took me aside toward the end of the trip to thank me for taking care of his son. I found it hard to speak any words of reply.

I flew directly from that event to another family gathering of another thirty-year-old friend of mine. This one was heterosexual; and he and his fiancee were getting married surrounded by a bevy of beaming acquaintances and family. In the Jewish ceremony, there was an unspoken, comforting rhythm of rebirth and life. The event was not untouched by tragedy: my friend's father had died earlier that year. But the wedding was almost an instinctive response to that sadness, a reaffirmation that the cycles and structures that had made sense of most of the lives there would be making sense of another two in the years ahead. I did not begrudge it at all; it is hard not to be moved by the sight of a new life beginning. But I could not help also feeling deeply, powerfully estranged.

AIDS has intensified a difference that I think is inherent between ho- 15
mosexual and heterosexual adults. The latter group is committed to the procreation of a new generation. The former simply isn't. Yes, there are major qualifications to this—gay men and lesbians are often biological fathers and mothers—but no two lesbians and no two homosexual men can be parents in the way that a heterosexual man and a heterosexual woman with a biological son or daughter can be. And yes, many heterosexuals neither marry nor have children and many have adopted children. But in general, the difference holds. The timeless, necessary, procreative unity of a man and a woman is inherently denied homosexuals; and the way in which fatherhood transforms heterosexual men, and motherhood transforms heterosexual women, and parenthood transforms their relationship, is far less common among homosexuals than among heterosexuals.

AIDS has only added a bitter twist to this state of affairs. My straight peers in their early thirties are engaged in the business of births; I am largely engaged in the business of deaths. Both experiences alter people profoundly. The very patterns of life of mothers and fathers with young children are vastly different than those who have none; and the perspectives of those who have stared death in the face in their twenties are bound to be different than those who have stared into cribs. Last year, I saw my first nephew come into the world, the first new life in my life to whom I felt physically, emotionally connected. I wondered which was the deeper feeling: the sense of excruciating pain seeing a member of my acquired family die, or the excruciating joy of seeing a member of my given family born. I am at a loss to decide; but I am not at a loss to know that they are different experiences: equally human, but radically different.

In a society more and more aware of its manifold cultures and subcultures, we have been educated to be familiar and comfortable with what has been called "diversity": the diversity of perspective, culture, meaning. And this diversity is usually associated with what are described as cultural constructs: race, gender, sexuality, and so on. But as the obsession with diversity intensifies, the possibility of real difference alarms and terrifies all the more. The notion of collective characteristics—of attributes more associated with blacks than with whites, with Asians than with Latinos, with gay men than with straight men, with men than with women—has become anathema. They are marginalized as "stereotypes." The acceptance of diversity has come to mean the acceptance of the essential sameness of all types of people, and the danger of generalizing among them at all. In fact, it has become virtually a definition of "racist" to make any substantive generalizations about a particular ethnicity, and a definition of "homophobic" to make any generalizations about homosexuals.

What follows, then, is likely to be understood as "homophobic." But I think it's true that certain necessary features of homosexual life lead to certain unavoidable features of homosexual character. This is not to say that they define any random homosexual: they do not. As with any group or way of life, there are many, many exceptions. Nor is it to say that they define the homosexual life: it should be clear by now that I believe the needs and feelings of homosexual children and adolescents are largely interchangeable with those of their heterosexual peers. But there are certain generalizations that can be made about adult homosexuals and lesbians that have the ring of truth.

Of course, in a culture where homosexuals remain hidden and wrapped in self-contempt, in which their emotional development is often stunted and late, in which the closet protects all sorts of self-destructive behavior that a more open society would not, it is still very hard to tell what is inherent in a homosexual life that makes it different, and what is simply imposed upon it. Nevertheless, it seems to me that even in the most tolerant societies, some of the differences that I have just described would inhere.

The experience of growing up profoundly different in emotional and 20
psychological makeup inevitably alters a person's self-perception, tends to make him or her more wary and distant, more attuned to appearance and its foibles, more self-conscious and perhaps more reflective. The presence of homosexuals in the arts, in literature, in architecture, in design, in fashion could be understood, as some have, as a simple response to oppression. Homosexuals have created safe professions within which to hide and protect each other. But why these professions? Maybe it's also that these are professions of appearance. Many homosexual children, feeling distant from their peers, become experts at trying to figure out how to disguise their inner feelings, to "pass." They notice the signs and signals of social interaction, because they do not come instinctively. They develop skills early on that help them notice the inflections of a voice, the quirks of a particular movement, and the ways in which meaning can be conveyed in code. They have an ear for irony and for double meanings. Sometimes, by virtue of having to suppress their natural emotions, they find formal outlets to express themselves: music, theater, art. And so their lives become set on a trajectory which reinforces these trends.

As a child, I remember, as I suppressed the natural emotions of an adolescent, how I naturally turned in on myself—writing, painting, and participating in amateur drama. Or I devised fantasies of future exploits—war leader, parliamentarian, famous actor—that could absorb those emotions that were being diverted from meeting other boys and developing natural emotional relationships with them. And I developed mannerisms, small ways in which I could express myself, tiny revolts of personal space—a speech affectation, a ridiculous piece of clothing—that were, in retrospect, attempts to communicate something in code which could not be communicated in language. In this homosexual archness there was, of course, much pain. And it came as no surprise that once I had become more open about my homosexuality, these mannerisms declined. Once I found the strength to be myself, I had no need to act myself. So my clothes became progressively more regular and slovenly; I lost interest in drama; my writing moved from fiction to journalism; my speech actually became less affected.

This, of course, is not a universal homosexual experience. Many homosexuals never become more open, and the skills required to survive the closet remain skills by which to earn a living. And many homosexuals, even once they no longer need those skills, retain them. My point is simply that the universal experience of self-conscious difference in childhood and adolescence—common, but not exclusive, to homosexuals—develops identifiable skills. They are the skills of mimesis; and one of the goods that homosexuals bring to society is undoubtedly a more highly developed sense of form, of style. Even in the most open of societies, I think, this will continue to be the case. It is not something genetically homosexual; it is something environmentally homosexual. And it begins young.

Closely connected to this is a sense of irony. Like Jews who have developed ways to resist, subvert, and adopt a majority culture, so homosexuals have found themselves ironizing their difference. Because, in many cases, they have survived acute periods of emotion, they are more likely to appreciate—even willfully celebrate—its more overwrought and melodramatic depictions. They have learned to see the funny side of etiolation. This, perhaps, is the true origin of camp. It is the ability to see agony and enjoy its form while ignoring its content, the ability to watch emotional trauma and not see its essence but its appearance. It is the aestheticization of pain.

This role in the aestheticization of the culture is perhaps enhanced by another unavoidable fact about most homosexuals and lesbians: their childlessness. This generates two related qualities: the relative freedom to procreate in a broader, structural sense, and to experiment with human relationships that can be instructive for the society as a whole.

The lack of children is something some homosexuals regard as a curse; 25
and it is the thing which many heterosexuals most pity (and some envy) about their homosexual acquaintances. But it is also an opportunity. Childless men and women have many things to offer a society. They can transfer their absent parental instincts into broader parental roles: they can be extraordinary teachers and mentors, nurses and doctors, priests, rabbis, and nuns; they can throw themselves into charity work, helping the needy and the lonely; they can care for the young who have been abandoned by others, through adoption. Or they can use all their spare time to forge an excellence in their field of work that is sometimes unavailable to the harried mother or burdened father. They can stay late in the office, be the most loyal staffer in an election campaign, work round the clock in a journalistic production, be the lawyer most able and willing to meet the emerging deadline.

One of their critical roles in society has also often been in the military. Here is an institution which requires dedication beyond the calling to the biological, nuclear family, that needs people prepared to give all their time to the common endeavor, that requires men and women able to subsume their personal needs into the formal demands of military discipline. Of all institutions in our society, the military is perhaps the most naturally homosexual, which is part of the reason, of course, why it is so hostile to their visible presence. The displacement of family affection onto a broader community also makes the homosexual an ideal person to devote him- or herself to a social institution: the university, the school, the little league, the Boy Scouts, the church, the sports team. Scratch most of these institutions and you'll find a homosexual or two sustaining many of its vital functions.

But the homosexual's contribution can be more than nourishing the society's aesthetic and institutional life. It has become a truism that in the field of emotional development, homosexuals have much to learn from the heterosexual culture. The values of commitment, of monogamy, of marriage, of stability are all posited as models for homosexual existence. And, indeed, of course, they are. Without an architectonic institution like that of marriage, it is difficult to create the conditions for nurturing such virtues, but that doesn't belie their importance.

It is also true, however, that homosexual relationships, even in their current, somewhat eclectic form, may contain features that could nourish the broader society as well. Precisely because there is no institutional model, gay relationships are often sustained more powerfully by genuine commitment. The mutual nurturing and sexual expressiveness of many lesbian relationships, the solidity and space of many adult gay male relationships, are qualities sometimes lacking in more rote, heterosexual couplings. Same-sex unions often incorporate the virtues of friendship more effectively than traditional marriages; and at times, among gay male relationships, the openness of the contract makes it more likely to survive than many heterosexual bonds. Some of this is unavailable to the male-female union: there is more likely to be greater understanding of the need for extramarital outlets between two men than between a man and a woman; and again, the lack of children gives gay couples greater freedom. Their failures entail fewer consequences for others. But something of the gay relationship's necessary honesty, its flexibility, and its equality could undoubtedly help strengthen and inform many heterosexual bonds.

In my own sometimes comic, sometimes passionate attempts to construct relationships, I learned something of the foibles of a simple heterosexual model. I saw how the network of gay friendships was often as good an emotional nourishment as a single relationship, that sexual candor was not always the same as sexual license, that the kind of supportive community that bolsters many gay relationships is something many isolated straight marriages could benefit from. I also learned how the subcultural fact of gay life rendered it remarkably democratic; in gay bars, there was far less socioeconomic stratification than in heterosexual bars. The shared experience of same-sex desire cut through class and race; it provided a humbling experience, which allowed many of us to risk our hearts and our friendships with people we otherwise might never have met. It loosened us up, and gave us a keener sense, perhaps, that people were often difficult to understand, let alone judge, from appearances. My heterosexual peers, through no fault of their own, were often denied these experiences. But they might gain from understanding them a little better, and not simply from a position of condescension.

As I've just argued, I believe strongly that marriage should be made 30
available to everyone, in a politics of strict public neutrality. But within this model, there is plenty of scope for cultural difference. There is something baleful about the attempt of some gay conservatives to educate homosexuals and lesbians into an uncritical acceptance of a stifling model of heterosexual normality. The truth is, homosexuals are not entirely normal; and to flatten their varied and complicated lives into a single, moralistic model is to miss what is essential and exhilarating about their otherness.

This need not mean, as some have historically claimed, that homosexuals have no stake in the sustenance of a society, but rather that their role is somewhat different; they may be involved in procreation in a less literal sense: in a society's cultural regeneration, its entrepreneurial or intellectual rejuvenation, its religious ministry, or its professional education. Unencumbered by children, they may be able to press the limits of the culture or the business infrastructure, or the boundaries of intellectual life, in a way that heterosexuals, by dint of a different type of calling, cannot. Of course, many heterosexuals perform similar roles; and many homosexuals prefer domesticity to public performance; but the inevitable way of life of the homosexual provides an opportunity that many intuitively seem to grasp and understand.

Or perhaps their role is to have no role at all. Perhaps it is the experience of rebellion that prompts homosexual culture to be peculiarly resistant to attempts to guide it to be useful or instructive or productive. Go to any march for gay rights and you will see the impossibility of organizing it into a coherent lobby: such attempts are always undermined by irony, or exhibitionism, or irresponsibility. It is as if homosexuals have learned something about life that makes them immune to the puritanical and flattening demands of modern politics. It is as if they have learned that life is fickle; that there are parts of it that cannot be understood, let alone solved; that some things lead nowhere and mean nothing; that the ultimate exercise of freedom is not a programmatic journey but a spontaneous one. Perhaps it requires seeing one's life as the end of a biological chain, or seeing one's deepest emotions as the object of detestation, that provides this insight. But the seeds of homosexual wisdom are the seeds of human wisdom. They contain the truth that order is in fact a euphemism for disorder; that problems are often more sanely enjoyed than solved; that there is reason in mystery; that there is beauty in the wild flowers that grow randomly among our wheat.

QUESTIONING THE TEXT

1. Sullivan begins by discussing how the cultural dominance of heterosexual marriage shapes the identity of young homosexuals. Consider the power of this social institution, whatever one's sexual orientation or expectations in life. What does it mean when our culture defines "normal" through the prism of heterosexual marriage? If you keep a reading log, answer this question there.
2. Sullivan presents the rituals and routines of heterosexual life through the eyes of a gay male who feels like an outsider. Describe an experience you have had as an outsider, looking in. Is this similar to the experience of women peering in at male institutions? Of men watching women socializing? Of poor looking at rich? Of the physically challenged considering the fully able? Of conservative students in liberal classrooms?

3. J.R.'s introduction to Sullivan's "What Are Homosexuals For?" praises the piece as an example of "civil argument." Do you find the essay as balanced and reasonable as the introduction promises? Use examples from the essay to support your answer.

MAKING CONNECTIONS

4. Maxine Hong Kingston's "No Name Woman" (p. 391) describes a woman whose life is destroyed because society cannot accept her out-of-wedlock pregnancy. Homosexuals, too, Sullivan argues, are culturally marginalized for their sexual behavior. In a group, discuss both the constraints society puts on sexuality and the reasons for them. Are there legitimate differences, for example, among *constraints, taboos,* and *prejudices*? Then write a short essay about one way society manages sexual behavior in your community—religious, social, or political.
5. Read Dave Barry's "Guys vs. Men" (p. 402) from the point of view that Sullivan offers. Does Barry's world of "guys" have room for homosexuals? Why, or why not? Write a paragraph or two on the subject.

JOINING THE CONVERSATION

6. Not many years ago, a common journal or essay assignment in college was to write about a first date or first love. With the selection by Sullivan in mind, write an essay exploring the appropriateness of such an assignment.
7. Sullivan argues that the way homosexuals are raised and the defenses they use to survive make them "more wary and distant, more attuned to appearance and its foibles, more self-conscious and perhaps more reflective" (paragraph 20). He also admits that such assertions come dangerously close to homophobic generalizations. Can people talk about the behavior of particular groups—whether gay men, lesbians, heterosexual women, or even "guys"—without engaging in harmful stereotypes? Explore this question by writing a dialogue between two people on different sides of this issue.

MAXINE HONG KINGSTON
No Name Woman

MAXINE HONG KINGSTON was born (in 1940) and raised in California, but her roots grow deep in Chinese soil and culture, as is evidenced in two highly acclaimed books, The Woman Warrior *(1970) and* China Men *(1980). (As this book goes to press, readers are awaiting the publication of Kingston's* The Fifth Book of Peace.*) In these and other works, Kingston explores the effects of Chinese legend and custom on her own identity as a woman and as a Chinese American. In "No Name Woman," an excerpt from* The Woman Warrior, *Kingston examines one identifying feature of most women—their ability to bear children—and she explores the consequences of that identifying mark.*

Many readers of this text may be able to identify a shadowy relative in their own past—an absent parent, a grandparent much discussed but seldom seen, a mysterious uncle or aunt or cousin—about whom older family members whispered. Few of us are likely to have written so powerfully about such a figure, however, or to have evoked in such a short space what it would be like to be "No Name Woman." I chose this selection precisely for its power. It has stayed vividly with me ever since I first read it—so vividly, in fact, that "No Name Woman" seems like someone I know personally. To me, she tells not only her own story but the story of all those whose lives are destroyed by narrow and rigid beliefs about what someone's identity must *be.* —A.L.

"You must not tell anyone," my mother said, "what I am about to tell you. In China your father had a sister who killed herself. She jumped into the family well. We say that your father has all brothers because it is as if she had never been born.

"In 1924 just a few days after our village celebrated seventeen hurry-up weddings—to make sure that every young man who went 'out on the road' would responsibly come home—your father and his brothers and your grandfather and his brothers and your aunt's new husband sailed for America, the Gold Mountain. It was your grandfather's last trip. Those lucky enough to get contracts waved good-bye from the decks. They fed and guarded the stowaways and helped them off in Cuba, New York, Bali, Hawaii. 'We'll meet in California next year,' they said. All of them sent money home.

"I remember looking at your aunt one day when she and I were dressing; I had not noticed before that she had such a protruding melon of a stomach. But I did not think, 'She's pregnant,' until she began to look like other pregnant women, her shirt pulling and the white tops of her black pants showing. She could not have been pregnant, you see, because her husband had been gone for years. No one said anything. We did not discuss it. In early summer she was ready to have the child, long after the time when it could have been possible.

"The village had also been counting. On the night the baby was to be born the villagers raided our house. Some were crying. Like a great saw, teeth strung with lights, files of people walked zigzag across our land, tearing the rice. Their lanterns doubled in the disturbed black water, which drained away through the broken bunds. As the villagers closed in, we could see that some of them, probably men and women we knew well, wore white masks. The people with long hair hung it over their faces. Women with short hair made it stand up on end. Some had tied white bands around their foreheads, arms, and legs.

"At first they threw mud and rocks at the house. Then they threw eggs 5
and began slaughtering our stock. We could hear the animals scream their deaths—the roosters, the pigs, a last great roar from the ox. Familiar wild heads flared in our night windows; the villagers encircled us. Some of the faces stopped to peer at us, their eyes rushing like searchlights. The hands flattened against the panes, framed heads, and left red prints.

"The villagers broke in the front and the back doors at the same time, even though we had not locked the doors against them. Their knives dripped with the blood of our animals. They smeared blood on the doors and walls. One woman swung a chicken, whose throat she had slit, splattering blood in red arcs about her. We stood together in the middle of our house, in the family hall with the pictures and tables of the ancestors around us, and looked straight ahead.

"At that time the house had only two wings. When the men came back, we would build two more to enclose our courtyard and a third one to begin a second courtyard. The villagers pushed through both wings, even your grandparents' rooms, to find your aunt's, which was also mine until the men returned. From this room a new wing for one of the younger families would grow. They ripped up her clothes and shoes and broke her combs, grinding them underfoot. They tore her work from the loom. They scattered the cooking fire and rolled the new weaving in it. We could hear them in the kitchen breaking our bowls and banging the pots. They overturned the great waist-high earthenware jugs; duck eggs, pickled fruits, vegetables burst out and mixed in acrid torrents. The old woman from the next field swept a broom through the air and loosed the spirits-of-the-broom over our heads. 'Pig.' 'Ghost.' 'Pig,' they sobbed and scolded while they ruined our house.

"When they left, they took sugar and oranges to bless themselves. They cut pieces from the dead animals. Some of them took bowls that were not broken and clothes that were not torn. Afterward we swept up the rice and sewed it back up into sacks. But the smells from the spilled preserves lasted. Your aunt gave birth in the pigsty that night. The next morning when I went up for the water, I found her and the baby plugging up the family well.

"Don't let your father know that I told you. He denies her. Now that you have started to menstruate, what happened to her could happen to you.

Don't humiliate us. You wouldn't like to be forgotten as if you had never been born. The villagers are watchful."

10 Whenever she had to warn us about life, my mother told stories that ran like this one, a story to grow up on. She tested our strength to establish realities. Those in the emigrant generations who could not reassert brute survival died young and far from home. Those of us in the first American generations have had to figure out how the invisible world the emigrants built around our childhoods fit in solid America.

The emigrants confused the gods by diverting their curses, misleading them with crooked streets and false names. They must try to confuse their offspring as well, who, I suppose, threaten them in similar ways—always trying to get things straight, always trying to name the unspeakable. The Chinese I know hide their names; sojourners take new names when their lives change and guard their real names with silence.

Chinese-Americans, when you try to understand what things in you are Chinese, how do you separate what is peculiar to childhood, to poverty, insanities, one family, your mother who marked your growing with stories, from what is Chinese? What is Chinese tradition and what is the movies?

If I want to learn what clothes my aunt wore, whether flashy or ordinary, I would have to begin, "Remember Father's drowned-in-the-well sister?" I cannot ask that. My mother has told me once and for all the useful parts. She will add nothing unless powered by Necessity, a riverbank that guides her life. She plants vegetable gardens rather than lawns; she carries the odd-shaped tomatoes home from the fields and eats food left for the gods.

Whenever we did frivolous things, we used up energy; we flew high kites. We children came up off the ground over the melting cones our parents brought home from work and the American movie on New Year's Day—*Oh, You Beautiful Doll* with Betty Grable one year, and *She Wore a Yellow Ribbon* with John Wayne another year. After the one carnival ride each, we paid in guilt; our tired father counted his change on the dark walk home.

15 Adultery is extravagance. Could people who hatch their own chicks and eat the embryos and the heads for delicacies and boil the feet in vinegar for party food, leaving only the gravel, eating even the gizzard lining—could such people engender a prodigal aunt? To be a woman, to have a daughter in starvation time was a waste enough. My aunt could not have been the lone romantic who gave up everything for sex. Women in the old China did not choose. Some man had commanded her to lie with him and be his secret evil. I wonder whether he masked himself when he joined the raid on her family.

Perhaps she encountered him in the fields or on the mountain where the daughters-in-law collected fuel. Or perhaps he first noticed her in the marketplace. He was not a stranger because the village housed no strangers. She had to have dealings with him other than sex. Perhaps he worked an adjoining field, or he sold her the cloth for the dress she sewed and wore. His demand must have surprised, then terrified her. She obeyed him; she always did as she was told.

When the family found a young man in the next village to be her husband, she stood tractably beside the best rooster, his proxy, and promised before they met that she would be his forever. She was lucky that he was her age and she would be the first wife, an advantage secure now. The night she first saw him, he had sex with her. Then he left for America. She had almost forgotten what he looked like. When she tried to envision him, she only saw the black and white face in the group photograph the men had taken before leaving.

The other man was not, after all, much different from her husband. They both gave orders: she followed. "If you tell your family, I'll beat you. I'll kill you. Be here again next week." No one talked sex, ever. And she might have separated the rapes from the rest of living if only she did not have to buy her oil from him or gather wood in the same forest. I want her fear to have lasted just as long as rape lasted so that the fear could have been contained. No drawn-out fear. But women at sex hazarded birth and hence lifetimes. The fear did not stop but permeated everywhere. She told the man, "I think I'm pregnant." He organized the raid against her.

On nights when my mother and father talked about their life back home, sometimes they mentioned an "outcast table" whose business they still seemed to be settling, their voices tight. In a commensal tradition, where food is precious, the powerful older people made wrongdoers eat alone. Instead of letting them start separate new lives like the Japanese, who could become samurais and geishas, the Chinese family, faces averted but eyes glowering sideways, hung on to the offenders and fed them leftovers. My aunt must have lived in the same house as my parents and eaten at an outcast table. My mother spoke about the raid as if she had seen it, when she and my aunt, a daughter-in-law to a different household, should not have been living together at all. Daughters-in-law lived with their husbands' parents, not their own; a synonym for marriage in Chinese is "taking a daughter-in-law." Her husband's parents could have sold her, mortgaged her, stoned her. But they had sent her back to her own mother and father, a mysterious act hinting at disgraces not told me. Perhaps they had thrown her out to deflect the avengers.

She was the only daughter; her four brothers went with her father, hus- 20
band, and uncles "out on the road" and for some years became western men. When the goods were divided among the family, three of the brothers took land, and the youngest, my father, chose an education. After my grandparents gave their daughter away to her husband's family, they had dispensed all the adventure and all the property. They expected her alone to keep the traditional ways, which her brothers, now among the barbarians, could fumble without detection. The heavy, deep-rooted women were to maintain the past against the flood, safe for returning. But the rare urge west had fixed upon our family, and so my aunt crossed boundaries not delineated in space.

The work of preservation demands that the feelings playing about in one's guts not be turned into action. Just watch their passing like cherry blossoms. But perhaps my aunt, my forerunner, caught in a slow life, let dreams grow and fade and after some months or years went toward what persisted. Fear at the enormities of the forbidden kept her desires delicate, wire and bone. She looked at a man because she liked the way the hair was tucked behind his ears, or she liked the question-mark line of a long torso curving at the shoulder and straight at the hip. For warm eyes or a soft voice or a slow walk—that's all—a few hairs, a line, a brightness, a sound, a pace, she gave up family. She offered us up for a charm that vanished with tiredness, a pigtail that didn't toss when the wind died. Why, the wrong lighting could erase the dearest thing about him.

It could very well have been, however, that my aunt did not take subtle enjoyment of her friend, but, a wild woman, kept rollicking company. Imagining her free with sex doesn't fit, though. I don't know any women like that, or men either. Unless I see her life branching into mine, she gives me no ancestral help.

To sustain her being in love, she often worked at herself in the mirror, guessing at the colors and shapes that would interest him, changing them frequently in order to hit on the right combination. She wanted him to look back.

On a farm near the sea, a woman who tended her appearance reaped a reputation for eccentricity. All the married women blunt-cut their hair in flaps about their ears or pulled it back in tight buns. No nonsense. Neither style blew easily into heart-catching tangles. And at their weddings they displayed themselves in their long hair for the last time. "It brushed the backs of my knees," my mother tells me. "It was braided, and even so, it brushed the backs of my knees."

At the mirror my aunt combed individuality into her bob. A bun could 25
have been contrived to escape into black streamers blowing in the wind or in quiet wisps about her face, but only the older women in our picture album wear buns. She brushed her hair back from her forehead, tucking the flaps behind her ears. She looped a piece of thread, knotted into a circle between her index fingers and thumbs, and ran the double strand across her forehead. When she closed her fingers as if she were making a pair of shadow geese bite, the string twisted together catching the little hairs. Then she pulled the thread away from her skin, ripping the hairs out neatly, her eyes watering from the needles of pain. Opening her fingers, she cleaned the thread, then rolled it along her hairline and the tops of her eyebrows. My mother did the same to me and my sisters and herself. I used to believe that the expression "caught by the short hairs" meant a captive held with a depilatory string. It especially hurt at the temples, but my mother said we were lucky we didn't have to have our feet bound when we were seven. Sisters used to sit on their beds and cry together, she said, as their mothers or their slave removed the bandages for a few minutes each night and let the blood gush back into their

veins. I hope that the man my aunt loved appreciated a smooth brow, that he wasn't just a tits-and-ass man.

Once my aunt found a freckle on her chin, at a spot that the almanac said predestined her for unhappiness. She dug it out with a hot needle and washed the wound with peroxide.

More attention to her looks than these pullings of hairs and pickings at spots would have caused gossip among the villagers. They owned work clothes and good clothes, and they wore good clothes for feasting the new seasons. But since a woman combing her hair hexes beginnings, my aunt rarely found an occasion to look her best. Women looked like great sea snails—the corded wood, babies, and laundry they carried were the whorls on their backs. The Chinese did not admire a bent back; goddesses and warriors stood straight. Still there must have been a marvelous freeing of beauty when a worker laid down her burden and stretched and arched.

Such commonplace loveliness, however, was not enough for my aunt. She dreamed of a lover for the fifteen days of New Year's, the time for families to exchange visits, money, and food. She plied her secret comb. And sure enough she cursed the year, the family, the village, and herself.

Even as her hair lured her imminent lover, many other men looked at her. Uncles, cousins, nephews, brothers would have looked, too, had they been home between journeys. Perhaps they had already been restraining their curiosity, and they left, fearful that their glances, like a field of nesting birds, might be startled and caught. Poverty hurt, and that was their first reason for leaving. But another, final reason for leaving the crowded house was the never-said.

She may have been unusually beloved, the precious only daughter, 30
spoiled and mirror-gazing because of the affection the family lavished on her. When her husband left, they welcomed the chance to take her back from the in-laws; she could live like the little daughter for just a while longer. There are stories that my grandfather was different from other people, "crazy ever since the little Jap bayoneted him in the head." He used to put his naked penis on the dinner table, laughing. And one day he brought home a baby girl, wrapped up inside his brown western-style greatcoat. He had traded one of his sons, probably my father, the youngest, for her. My grandmother made him trade back. When he finally got a daughter of his own, he doted on her. They must have all loved her, except perhaps my father, the only brother who never went back to China, having once been traded for a girl.

Brothers and sisters, newly men and women, had to efface their sexual color and present plain miens. Disturbing hair and eyes, a smile like no other, threatened the ideal of five generations living under one roof. To focus blurs, people shouted face to face and yelled from room to room. The immigrants I know have loud voices, unmodulated to American tones even after years away from the village where they called their friendships out across the fields. I have not been able to stop my mother's screams in public libraries or over telephones. Walking erect (knees straight, toes pointed forward, not pigeon-toed, which is Chinese-feminine) and speaking in an inaudible voice, I have tried to turn myself American-feminine. Chinese communication was loud, public. Only sick people had to whisper. But at the dinner table, where the family members came nearest one another, no one could talk, not the outcasts nor any eaters. Every word that falls from the mouth is a coin lost. Silently they gave and accepted food with both hands. A preoccupied child who took his bowl with one hand got a sideways glare. A complete moment of total attention is due everyone alike. Children and lovers have no singularity here, but my aunt used a secret voice, a separate attentiveness.

She kept the man's name to herself throughout her labor and dying; she did not accuse him that he be punished with her. To save her inseminator's name she gave silent birth.

He may have been somebody in her own household, but intercourse with a man outside the family would have been no less abhorrent. All the village were kinsmen, and the titles shouted in loud country voices never let kinship be forgotten. Any man within visiting distance would have been neutralized as a lover—"brother," "younger brother," "older brother"—115 relationship titles. Parents researched birth charts probably not so much to assure good fortune as to circumvent incest in a population that has but one hundred surnames. Everybody has eight million relatives. How useless then sexual mannerisms, how dangerous.

As if it came from an atavism deeper than fear, I used to add "brother" silently to boys' names. It hexed the boys, who would or would not ask me to dance, and made them less scary and as familiar and deserving of benevolence as girls.

But, of course, I hexed myself also—no dates. I should have stood up, 35
both arms waving, and shouted out across libraries, "Hey, you! Love me back." I had no idea, though, how to make attraction selective, how to control its direction and magnitude. If I made myself American-pretty so that the five or six Chinese boys in the class fell in love with me, everyone else—the Caucasian, Negro, and Japanese boys—would too. Sisterliness, dignified and honorable, made much more sense.

Attraction eludes control so stubbornly that whole societies designed to organize relationships among people cannot keep order, not even when they bind people to one another from childhood and raise them together. Among the very poor and the wealthy, brothers married their adopted sisters, like doves. Our family allowed some romance, paying adult brides' prices and providing dowries so that their sons and daughters could marry strangers. Marriage promises to turn strangers into friendly relatives—a nation of siblings.

In the village structure, spirits shimmered among the live creatures, balanced and held in equilibrium by time and land. But one human being flaring up into violence could open up a black hole, a maelstrom that pulled in the sky. The frightened villagers, who depended on one another to maintain the real, went to my aunt to show her a personal, physical representation of the break she made in the "roundness." Misallying couples snapped off the future, which was to be embodied in true offspring. The villagers punished her for acting as if she could have a private life, secret and apart from them.

If my aunt had betrayed the family at a time of large grain yields and peace, when many boys were born, and wings were being built on many houses, perhaps she might have escaped such severe punishment. But the men—hungry, greedy, tired of planting in dry soil, cuckolded—had been forced to leave the village in order to send food-money home. There were ghost plagues, bandit plagues, wars with the Japanese, floods. My Chinese brother and sister had died of an unknown sickness. Adultery, perhaps only a mistake during good times, became a crime when the village needed food.

The round moon cakes and round doorways, the round tables of graduated size that fit one roundness inside another, round windows and rice bowls—these talismans had lost their power to warn this family of the law: a family must be whole, faithfully keeping the descent line by having sons to feed the old and the dead who in turn look after the family. The villagers came to show my aunt and lover-in-hiding a broken house. The villagers were speeding up the circling of events because she was too shortsighted to see that her infidelity had already harmed the village, that waves of consequences would return unpredictably, sometimes in disguise, as now, to hurt her. This roundness had to be made coin-sized so that she would see its circumference: punish her at the birth of her baby. Awaken her to the inexorable. People who refused fatalism because they could invent small resources insisted on culpability. Deny accidents and wrest fault from the stars.

After the villagers left, their lanterns now scattering in various directions toward home, the family broke their silence and cursed her. "Aiaa, we're going to die. Death is coming. Death is coming. Look what you've done. You've killed us. Ghost! Dead Ghost! Ghost! You've never been born." She ran out into the fields, far enough from the house so that she could no longer hear their voices, and pressed herself against the earth, her own land no more. When she felt the birth coming, she thought that she had been hurt. Her body seized together. "They've hurt me too much," she thought. "This is gall, and it will kill me." With forehead and knees against the earth, her body convulsed and then relaxed. She turned on her back, lay on the ground. The black well of sky and stars went out and out forever; her body and her complexity seemed to disappear. She was one of the stars, a bright dot in blackness, without home, without a companion, in eternal cold and silence. An agoraphobia rose in her, speeding higher and higher, bigger and bigger; she would not be able to contain it; there would be no end to fear.

Flayed, unprotected against space, she felt pain return, focusing her body. This pain chilled her—a cold, steady kind of surface pain. Inside, spasmodically, the other pain, the pain of the child, heated her. For hours she lay on the ground, alternately body and space. Sometimes a vision of normal comfort obliterated reality: she saw the family in the evening gambling at the dinner table, the young people massaging their elders' backs. She saw them congratulating one another, high joy on the mornings the rice shoots came up. When these pictures burst, the stars drew yet further apart. Black space opened.

She got to her feet to fight better and remembered that old-fashioned women gave birth in their pigsties to fool the jealous, pain-dealing gods, who do not snatch piglets. Before the next spasms could stop her, she ran to the pigsty, each step a rushing out into emptiness. She climbed over the fence and knelt in the dirt. It was good to have a fence enclosing her, a tribal person alone.

Laboring, this woman who had carried her child as a foreign growth that sickened her every day, expelled it at last. She reached down to touch the hot, wet, moving mass, surely smaller than anything human, and could feel that it was human after all—fingers, toes, nails, nose. She pulled it up on to her belly, and it lay curled there, butt in the air, feet precisely tucked one under the other. She opened her loose shirt and buttoned the child inside. After resting, it squirmed and thrashed and she pushed it up to her breast. It turned its head this way and that until it found her nipple. There, it made little snuffling noises. She clenched her teeth at its preciousness, lovely as a young calf, a piglet, a little dog.

She may have gone to the pigsty as a last act of responsibility: she would protect this child as she had protected its father. It would look after her soul, leaving supplies on her grave. But how would this tiny child without family find her grave when there would be no marker for her anywhere, neither in the earth nor the family hall? No one would give her a family hall name. She had taken the child with her into the wastes. At its birth the two of them had felt the same raw pain of separation, a wound that only the family pressing tight could close. A child with no descent line would not soften her life but only trail after her, ghostlike, begging her to give it purpose. At dawn the villagers on their way to the fields would stand around the fence and look.

Full of milk, the little ghost slept. When it awoke, she hardened her 45
breasts against the milk that crying loosens. Toward morning she picked up the baby and walked to the well.

Carrying the baby to the well shows loving. Otherwise abandon it. Turn its face into the mud. Mothers who love their children take them along. It was probably a girl; there is some hope of forgiveness for boys.

"Don't tell anyone you had an aunt. Your father does not want to hear her name. She has never been born." I have believed that sex was unspeakable and words so strong and fathers so frail that "aunt" would do my father mysterious harm. I have thought that my family, having settled among immigrants who had also been their neighbors in the ancestral land, needed to clean their name, and a wrong word would incite the kinspeople even here. But there is more to this silence: they want me to participate in her punishment. And I have.

In the twenty years since I heard this story I have not asked for details nor said my aunt's name; I do not know it. People who comfort the dead can also chase after them to hurt them further—a reverse ancestor worship. The real punishment was not the raid swiftly inflicted by the villagers, but the family's deliberately forgetting her. Her betrayal so maddened them, they saw to it that she would suffer forever, even after death. Always hungry, always needing, she would have to beg food from other ghosts, snatch and steal it from those whose living descendants give them gifts. She would have to fight the ghosts massed at crossroads for the buns a few thoughtful citizens leave to decoy her away from village and home so that the ancestral spirits could feast unharassed. At peace, they could act like gods, not ghosts, their descent lines providing them with paper suits and dresses, spirit money, paper houses, paper automobiles, chicken, meat, and rice into eternity—essences delivered up in smoke and flames, steam and incense rising from each rice bowl. In an attempt to make the Chinese care for people outside the family, Chairman Mao encourages us now to give our paper replicas to the spirits of outstanding soldiers and workers, no matter whose ancestors they may be. My aunt remains forever hungry. Goods are not distributed evenly among the dead.

My aunt haunts me—her ghost drawn to me because now, after fifty years of neglect, I alone devote pages of paper to her, though not origamied into houses and clothes. I do not think she always means me well. I am telling on her, and she was a spite suicide, drowning herself in the drinking water. The Chinese are always very frightened of the drowned one, whose weeping ghost, wet hair hanging and skin bloated, waits silently by the water to pull down a substitute.

QUESTIONING THE TEXT

1. The narrator of "No Name Woman" tells several different versions of her aunt's life. Which do you find most likely to be accurate, and why?
2. What is the narrator's attitude toward the villagers? What in the text reveals her attitude—and how does it compare with your own attitude toward them?
3. A.L.'s introduction sympathizes with No Name Woman. If one of the villagers had written the introduction, how might it differ from A.L.'s?

MAKING CONNECTIONS

4. Andrew Sullivan's discussion in "What Are Homosexuals For?" (p. 380) is very different from Kingston's story of No Name Woman. But Sullivan does explore, sometimes implicitly, the reasons homosexuals might

choose to keep secrets as well as the complications if they choose to tell. After rereading these pieces, freewrite for 10 to 15 minutes on some secrets in our society that people are never supposed to tell.

JOINING THE CONVERSATION

5. Interview—or spend an hour or so talking with—one of your parents, grandparents, aunts, uncles, or another older person you know fairly well. Ask your interviewee to describe the attitudes that governed female sexual behavior—or female identity—in his or her day. How were "good girls" supposed to act? What counted as *bad* behavior—and what were the subtle or overt social punishments for that behavior? Write a brief report of your findings, comparing the older person's description of attitudes at an earlier time with those you hold today.
6. Try rewriting one of Kingston's versions of No Name Woman's story from the point of view of the man. How might he see things differently? After you have written this man's version, jot down a few things about him. What does he value? What does he think of women? What is his relationship to women? Finally, bring your version to class to compare with those of two classmates. After studying each version, work together to make a list of what the three versions have in common and a list of how they differ.

DAVE BARRY
Guys vs. Men

ONE OF THE FIRST WORDS I ever spoke was truck, *and about forty-five years later I finally bought one, a fully skid-plated 4 × 4 Yukon tall enough to scrape the garage roof and designed to roll me safely over the treacherous ravines and gullies between . . . home and work. Well, I'm man enough to admit that gas-guzzling Big Blue made as much sense as a drawbridge, and I eventually traded it in for a smaller, more environmentally friendly SUV. But the* guy *in me still yearns for tow hooks, a robust V-8, and a subwoofer that will pop rivets.*

If you don't understand what makes grown men covet "neat stuff" or ruin their knees to conquer at touch football, reading Dave Barry's "Guys vs. Men" may help a little. Barry (b. 1947) is, of course, a guy, and that fact helps him at least diagnose the problem of guyness—if it is one. Suffice to say that a lot of men will recognize themselves in the categories he describes. And some women may identify with the "stupid behavioral patterns" that mark men as guys. In fact, when I discussed Barry's essay in a writing class recently, the women insisted on a "guy" term of their own and came up with chick.

"Guys vs. Men" is the preface to Dave Barry's Complete Guide to Guys: A Fairly Short Book *(1995). Barry is a Pulitzer Prize–winning humorist who, early in his career, lectured to business audiences on effective writing. He has published more than a dozen books and collections of humor, including* Stay Fit and Healthy until You're Dead *(1985) and* Dave Barry Hits below the Beltway *(2001). Barry's syndicated column appears in more than 500 newspapers.* —J.R.

This is a book about guys. It's *not* a book about men. There are already way too many books about men, and most of them are *way* too serious.

Who might write "Chicks vs. Women"? Whoopi Goldberg? Serena Williams? Hillary Rodham Clinton? Maybe Mia Hamm? —A.L.

Men itself is a serious word, not to mention *manhood* and *manly*. Such words make being male sound like a very important activity, as opposed to what it primarily consists of, namely, possessing a set of minor and frequently unreliable organs.

Could a woman get away with such a trivialization of womanhood? The fact that a man can (and so successfully at that) is evidence in itself for Barry's argument. —J.G.R.

But men tend to attach great significance to Manhood. This results in certain characteristically masculine, by which I mean stupid, behavioral patterns that can produce unfortunate results such as violent crime, war, spitting, and ice hockey. These things have given males a bad name.[1] And the "Men's Movement," which is supposed to bring out the more positive aspects of Manliness, seems to be densely populated with loons and goobers.

So I'm saying that there's another way to look at males: not as aggressive macho dominators; not as sensitive, liberated, hugging drummers; but as *guys.*

And what, exactly, do I mean by "guys"? I don't know. I haven't thought that much about it. One of the major characteristics of guyhood is that we guys don't spend a lot of time pondering our deep innermost feelings. There is a serious question in my mind about whether guys actually *have* deep innermost feelings, unless you count, for example, loyalty to the Detroit Tigers, or fear of bridal showers.

But although I can't define exactly what it means to be a guy, I can describe certain guy characteristics, such as:

Guys Like Neat Stuff

By "neat," I mean "mechanical and unnecessarily complex." I'll give you an example. Right now I'm typing these words on an *extremely* powerful computer. It's the latest in a line of maybe ten computers I've owned, each one more powerful than the last. My computer is chock full of RAM and ROM and bytes and megahertzes and various other items that enable a computer to kick data-processing butt. It is probably capable of supervising the entire U.S. air-defense apparatus while simultaneously processing the tax return of every resident of Ohio. I use it mainly to write a newspaper column. This is an activity wherein I sit and stare at the screen for maybe ten minutes, then, using only my forefingers, slowly type something like:

He is counting on powerful stereotypes here, and with this one he seems right on target. Boys love toys, maybe? —A.L.

Aha! Barry's first slip—completely neglecting the computer's all-important functions of Solitaire and Hearts. How would we play these without a computer? —J.G.R.

Henry Kissinger looks like a big wart.*

I stare at this for another ten minutes, have an inspiration, then amplify the original thought as follows:

[1]Specifically, "asshole."

Henry Kissinger (b. 1923): foreign policy advisor to President Nixon and U.S. Secretary of State, 1973–77

Henry Kissinger looks like a big fat wart.

Then I stare at that for another ten minutes, pondering whether I should try to work in the concept of "hairy."

This is absurdly simple work for my computer. It sits there, humming impatiently, bored to death, passing the time between keystrokes via brain-teaser activities such as developing a Unified Field Theory of the universe and translating the complete works of Shakespeare into rap.[2]

How about dividing Shakespeare's characters into guys or men? Falstaff—now, there *was a guy.* —A.L.

Probably the most telltale line of this piece. —J.G.R.

In other words, this computer is absurdly overqualified to work for me, and yet soon, I guarantee, I will buy an *even more powerful* one. I won't be able to stop myself. I'm a guy.

Probably the ultimate example of the fundamental guy drive to have neat stuff is the Space Shuttle. Granted, the guys in charge of this program *claim* it has a Higher Scientific Purpose, namely to see how humans function in space. But of course we have known for years how humans function in space: They float around and say things like: "Looks real good, Houston!"

Less than amusing—especially in light of the space shuttle disasters. Is he implying that guys aren't interested in basic ethical questions like what results their gizmos have on people's lives? —A.L.

Little boys don't have to be taught to want toy cars or video games. —J.R.

No, the real reason for the existence of the Space Shuttle is that it is one humongous and spectacularly gizmo-intensive item of hardware. Guys can tinker with it practically forever, and occasionally even get it to work, and use it to place *other* complex mechanical items into orbit, where they almost immediately break, which provides a great excuse to send the Space Shuttle up *again*. It's Guy Heaven.

Other results of the guy need to have stuff are Star Wars, the recreational boating industry, monorails, nuclear weapons, and wristwatches that indicate the phase of the moon. I am not saying that women haven't been involved in the development or use of this stuff. I'm saying that, without guys, this stuff probably would not exist; just as, without women, virtually every piece of furniture in the world would still be in its original position. Guys

---

[2]To be or not? I got to *know*.
Might kill myself by the end of the *show*.

do not have a basic need to rearrange furniture. Whereas a woman who could cheerfully use the same computer for fifty-three years will rearrange her furniture on almost a weekly basis, sometimes in the dead of night. She'll be sound asleep in bed, and suddenly, at 2 A.M., she'll be awakened by the urgent thought: *The blue-green sofa needs to go perpendicular to the wall instead of parallel, and it needs to go there* RIGHT NOW. So she'll get up and move it, which of course necessitates moving other furniture, and soon she has rearranged her entire living room, shifting great big heavy pieces that ordinarily would require several burly men to lift, because there are few forces in Nature more powerful than a woman who needs to rearrange furniture. Every so often a guy will wake up to discover that, because of his wife's overnight efforts, he now lives in an entirely different house.

Another stereotype neatly deployed. And he counts on our not minding that he lumps all women into one category—it's part of what he has to do to make such portraits "funny." —A.L.

(I realize that I'm making gender-based generalizations here, but my feeling is that if God did not want us to make gender-based generalizations, She would not have given us genders.)

A tongue-in-cheek nod at the politically correct. Nice. —J.G.R.

Guys Like a Really Pointless Challenge

Not long ago I was sitting in my office at the *Miami Herald*'s Sunday magazine, *Tropic,* reading my fan mail,[3] when I heard several of my guy coworkers in the hallway talking about how fast they could run the forty-yard dash. These are guys in their thirties and forties who work in journalism, where the most demanding physical requirement is the ability to digest vending-machine food. In other words, these guys have absolutely no need to run the forty-yard dash.

But one of them, Mike Wilson, was writing a story about a star high-school football player who could run it in 4.38 seconds. Now if Mike had written a story about, say, a star high-school poet,

[3]Typical fan letter: "Who cuts your hair? Beavers?"

none of my guy coworkers would have suddenly decided to find out how well they could write sonnets. But when Mike turned in his story, they became *deeply* concerned about how fast they could run the forty-yard dash. They were so concerned that the magazine editor, Tom Shroder, decided that they should get a stopwatch and go out to a nearby park and find out. Which they did, a bunch of guys taking off their shoes and running around barefoot in a public park on company time.

OK. Now I know I am not and never can be a "guy." This is the last *thing I would do in response to a story about 40-yard dash times.* —A.L.

This is what I heard them talking about, out in the hall. I heard Tom, who was thirty-eight years old, saying that his time in the forty had been 5.75 seconds. And I thought to myself: This is ridiculous. These are middle-aged guys, supposedly adults, and they're out there *bragging* about their performance in this stupid juvenile footrace. Finally I couldn't stand it anymore.

"Hey!" I shouted. "*I* could beat 5.75 seconds."

So we went out to the park and measured off forty yards, and the guys told me that I had three chances to make my best time. On the first try my time was 5.78 seconds, just three-hundredths of a second slower than Tom's, even though, at forty-five, I was seven years older than he. So I just *knew* I'd beat him on the second attempt if I ran really, really hard, which I did for a solid ten yards, at which point my left hamstring muscle, which had not yet shifted into Spring Mode from Mail-Reading Mode, went, and I quote, "pop."

I may expire on the racquetball court some day. But I'll go happy—so long as I'm winning. —J.R.

Any guy who has ever competed in an "eat-til-you-puke" contest with 49-cent tacos can relate to this. —J.G.R.

I had to be helped off the field. I was in considerable pain, and I was obviously not going to be able to walk right for weeks. The other guys were very sympathetic, especially Tom, who took the time to call me at home, where I was sitting with an ice pack on my leg and twenty-three Advil in my bloodstream, so he could express his concern.

Who is it that proposed cutting out all *militaries the world over and resolving all foreign policy crises by sending out squads to play some game? I can just imagine Barry describing such scenes.* —A.L.

"Just remember," he said, "*you didn't beat my time.*"

Or "Last one to the moon has to eat the Berlin Wall." (It took them over 20 years to pay up for this one.) —J.G.R.

There are countless other examples of guys rising to meet pointless challenges. Virtually all sports fall into this category, as well as a large part of

U.S. foreign policy. ("I'll bet you can't capture Manuel Noriega!"* "Oh YEAH??")

GUYS DO NOT HAVE A RIGID AND WELL-DEFINED MORAL CODE

This is not the same as saying that guys are bad. Guys *are* capable of doing bad things, but this generally happens when they try to be Men and start becoming manly and aggressive and stupid. When they're being just plain guys, they aren't so much actively *evil* as they are *lost.* Because guys have never really grasped the Basic Human Moral Code, which I believe was invented by women millions of years ago when all the guys were out engaging in some other activity, such as seeing who could burp the loudest. When they came back, there were certain rules that they were expected to follow unless they wanted to get into Big Trouble, and they have been trying to follow these rules ever since, with extremely irregular results. Because guys have never *internalized* these rules. Guys are similar to my small auxiliary backup dog, Zippy, a guy dog[4] who has been told numerous times that he is *not* supposed to (1) get into the kitchen garbage or (2) poop on the floor. He knows that these are the rules, but he has never really understood *why,* and sometimes he gets to thinking: Sure, I am *ordinarily* not supposed to get into the garbage, but obviously this rule is not meant to apply when there are certain extenuating[5] circumstances, such as (1) somebody just threw away some perfectly good seven-week-old Kung Pao Chicken, and (2) I am home alone.

And so when the humans come home, the kitchen floor has been transformed into Garbage-Fest USA, and Zippy, who usually comes rushing

---

Manuel Noriega (b. 1934): Panamanian dictator removed from power by armed U.S. intervention in 1989

[4]I also have a female dog, Earnest, who *never* breaks the rules.

[5]I am taking some liberties here with Zippy's vocabulary. More likely, in his mind, he uses the term *mitigating.*

up, is off in a corner disguised in a wig and sunglasses, hoping to get into the Federal Bad Dog Relocation Program before the humans discover the scene of the crime.

When I yell at him, he frequently becomes so upset that he poops on the floor.

Guys do care about rules when it comes to their machines or games—the more complicated the better. Only guys could have invented f-stops or the infield fly rule. —J.R.

Morally, most guys are just like Zippy, only taller and usually less hairy. Guys are *aware* of the rules of moral behavior, but they have trouble keeping these rules in the forefronts of their minds at certain times, especially the present. This is especially true in the area of faithfulness to one's mate. I realize, of course, that there are countless examples of guys being faithful to their mates until they die, usually as a result of being eaten by their mates immediately following copulation. Guys outside of the spider community, however, do not have a terrific record of faithfulness.

I'm not saying guys are scum. I'm saying that many guys who consider themselves to be committed to their marriages will stray if they are confronted with overwhelming temptation, defined as "virtually any temptation."

Wonder if his wife read this? —J.G.R.

Well, that's a relief—considering that they will readily foul up their marriages. — A.L.

Okay, so maybe I *am* saying guys are scum. But they're not *mean-spirited* scum. And few of them—even when they are out of town on business trips, far from their wives, and have a clear-cut opportunity—will poop on the floor.

Guys Are Not Great at Communicating Their Intimate Feelings, Assuming They Have Any

This is an aspect of guyhood that is very frustrating to women. A guy will be reading the newspaper, and the phone will ring; he'll answer it, listen for ten minutes, hang up, and resume reading. Finally his wife will say: "Who was that?"

And he'll say: "Phil Wonkerman's mom."

(Phil is an old friend they haven't heard from in seventeen years.)

And the wife will say, "Well?"

And the guy will say, "Well what?"

And the wife will say, "What did she *say*?"

And the guy will say, "She said Phil is fine," making it clear by his tone of voice that, although he does not wish to be rude, he is trying to read the newspaper, and he happens to be right in the middle of an important panel of "Calvin and Hobbes."

But the wife, ignoring this, will say, "That's *all* she said?"

And she will not let up. She will continue to ask district-attorney-style questions, forcing the guy to recount the conversation until she's satisfied that she has the entire story, which is that Phil just got out of prison after serving a sentence for a murder he committed when he became a drug addict because of the guilt he felt when his wife died in a freak submarine accident while Phil was having an affair with a nun, but now he's all straightened out and has a good job as a trapeze artist and is almost through with the surgical part of his sex change and recently became happily engaged to marry a prominent member of the Grateful Dead, so in other words he is fine, which is *exactly* what the guy told her in the first place, but is that enough? No. She wants to hear *every single detail.*

Or let's say two couples get together after a long separation. The two women will have a conversation, lasting several days, during which they discuss virtually every significant event that has occurred in their lives and the lives of those they care about, sharing their innermost thoughts, analyzing and probing, inevitably coming to a deeper understanding of each other, and a strengthening of a cherished friendship. Whereas the guys will watch the play-offs.

This section on "communication," especially this *communication between men and women, is the subject of several books by Deborah Tannen, whose studies might suggest that Barry is not far off the mark here.* —A.L.

This is not to say the guys won't share their feelings. Sometimes they'll get quite emotional.

"That's not a FOUL??" they'll say.

Or: "YOU'RE TELLING ME THAT'S NOT A *FOUL*???"

I have a good friend, Gene, and one time, when he was going through a major medical development in his life, we spent a weekend together. During this time Gene and I talked a lot and enjoyed each other's company immensely, but—this is true—the most

Example Chart

Men	Guys
Vince Lombardi	Joe Namath
Oliver North	Gilligan
Hemingway	Gary Larson
Columbus	Whichever astronaut hit the first golf ball on the Moon
Superman	Bart Simpson
Doberman pinschers	Labrador retrievers
Abbott	Costello
Captain Ahab	Captain Kangaroo
Satan	Snidely Whiplash
The pope	Willard Scott
Germany	Italy
Geraldo	Katie Couric

intimate personal statement he made to me is that he has reached Level 24 of a video game called "Arkanoid." He had even seen the Evil Presence, although he refused to tell me what it looks like. We're very close, but there is a limit.

You may think that my friends and I are Neanderthals, and that a lot of guys are different. This is true. A lot of guys don't use words at *all*. They communicate entirely by nonverbal methods, such as sharing bait.

I am glad to say I know some men who really are *different, especially in the way they communicate their feelings.* —A.L.

Are you starting to see what I mean by "guyness"? I'm basically talking about the part of the male psyche that is less serious and/or aggressive than the Manly Manhood part, but still essentially very male. My feeling is that the world would be a much better[6] place if more males would stop trying so hard to be Men and instead settle for being Guys. Think of the historical problems that could have been avoided if

[6]As measured by total sales of [my] book.

more males had been able to keep their genderhood in its proper perspective, both in themselves and in others. ("Hey, Adolf, just because you happen to possess a set of minor and frequently unreliable organs, that is no reason to invade Poland.") And think how much happier women would be if, instead of endlessly fretting about what the males in their lives are thinking, they could relax, secure in the knowledge that the correct answer is: *very little.*

All kidding aside, I do think women need a better understanding of the way guys think, if that's the right verb for the process. —J.R.

C'mon, Dave . . . even you *had to do* some *thinking to come up with this book.* —A.L.

Yes, what we need, on the part of both genders, is more understanding of guyness. And that is why I wrote this book. I intend to explore in detail every major facet of guyhood, including the historical facet, the sociological facet, the physiological facet, the psychosexual facet, and the facet of how come guys spit so much. Every statement of fact you will read in this book is either based on actual laboratory tests, or else I made it up. But you can trust me. I'm a guy.

Stimulus-Response Comparison Chart: Women vs. Men vs. Guys

Stimulus	**Typical *Woman* Response**	**Typical *Man* Response**	**Typical *Guy* Response**
An untamed river in the wilderness.	Contemplate its beauty.	Build a dam.	See who can pee the farthest off the dam.
A child who is sent home from school for being disruptive in class.	Talk to the child in an effort to determine the cause.	Threaten to send the child to a military academy.	Teach the child how to make armpit farts.
Human mortality	Religious faith	The pyramids	Bungee-jumping

Afterwords

While reading "Guys vs. Men," most males and a great many women will likely discover a bit of the guy *within themselves. The kernels of truth residing within Barry's stereotypes are what make this essay funny and oddly provocative. When Barry observes that "Guys like neat stuff," he's acknowledging the inventiveness and curiosity that have driven human beings from chariots to Stealth bombers in a couple thousand years. We owe a debt to all the geeks and tinkerers who began a sentence "Wouldn't it be neat if . . . ?" and then followed through. Sometimes in their mania, guys land on the moon and sometimes they blow themselves up. I guess it's the responsibility of more proper "men" and "women" to make sure that the former happens more often than the latter.* —J.R.

What can I say? Some of my best friends are "guys"? I even know women who are "guys"? I wish I knew more real "guys"? Not likely. I admire Barry's way with words, and especially the way he can poke fun at himself. And I laughed out loud at some of the early parts of this essay. But in my serious moments, I worry about the need to "blow things up" and to outperform everyone at everything at every minute of the day and night. I worry about what the "culture of guyhood" has done (is doing?) to us all, and to men in particular. Squeezing infinitely varied males into the little square space allowed to "guys" can't be all that much fun. Can it? —A.L.

Dave Barry hits the nail on the head with this piece—or, to be more precise, the galvanized, flat-head 5-1/4" nail with a stainless steel, all-metal, lifetime-guaranteed hammer. Barry is right on with the simplicity of "guyness." Not even a man could complicate it, but for some reason I bet that women won't understand. —J.G.R.

QUESTIONING THE TEXT

1. Barry's humor obviously plays off of gross stereotypes about men. Underscore or annotate all the stereotypes you can find in the essay.
2. Barry employs a lengthy analogy featuring his dog Zippy to explore the moral behavior of guys (p. 407). In a group, discuss this analogy, focusing on the observations that seem especially apt.

MAKING CONNECTIONS

3. Pick any essay you have already read from this collection, and give it the Dave Barry treatment. That is, try your hand at making readers see the subject from a comic perspective. You might, for example, try writing a short article portraying the issues in James Q. Wilson's "Cars and Their

Enemies" (p. 338) as a battle between car nuts and tree-huggers. Or Wendy Shalit's concern over unisex bathrooms in "The Future of Modesty" (p. 251) may suggest other opportunities for humor. Be certain your comic piece makes a point.

4. Barry comically suggests that men love complicated gizmos that they can tinker with forever. Examine Barry's comic observations side by side with any of the readings in Chapter 5 on science and technology. Then, if you keep a reading log, write a serious response there to Barry's humorous observations. Is science a male obsession with how things work?

JOINING THE CONVERSATION

5. "Guys vs. Men" is almost a textbook exercise in writing an extended definition. Annotate the different techniques Barry uses to craft his definition (definition by contrast; class/characteristics; definition by example; negative definition). Then write a similar definitional piece—humorous if you like—contrasting two terms that might at first glance seem similar, such as chicks vs. women, cops vs. police officers, freshmen vs. first-year students.
6. Barry illustrates the competitiveness of men with a short anecdote about the forty-yard dash. Choose another stereotypical trait of either men or women (insensitivity, bad driving, excessive concern with appearance), and write an anecdote from your own experience that illustrates the trait. Try some of the techniques Barry uses to make his story funny: understatement, exaggeration, irony, self-deprecation, dialogue.

ZORA NEALE HURSTON
How It Feels to Be Colored Me

Zora Neale Hurston (1891–1960), born and raised in the first all-black town in the United States to be incorporated and self-governing (Eatonville, Florida), packed an astonishing number of careers and identities into her sixty-nine years. She was a "wardrobe girl" for traveling entertainers, a manicurist, an anthropologist and folklorist, a college professor, a drama coach, an editor, and—above all—a writer of great distinction. Author of numerous articles, essays, and stories as well as folklore collections, plays, and an autobiography, Hurston is today probably best known for her novels: Their Eyes Were Watching God *(1937),* Jonah's Gourd Vine *(1934), and* Moses, Man of the Mountain *(1939).*

Hurston studied anthropology at Barnard College, where she was the only African American student, and gained a strong reputation for her academic work on folklore. But by the 1930s, she was being criticized for what were said to be caricatures of blacks, especially in her "minstrel" novels. Her growing conservatism led to further attacks from writers such as Richard Wright, and by 1950, her reputation gone, she was working in Florida as a maid. Evicted from her home in 1956, she suffered a stroke in 1959 and died, penniless, the next year. In recent years, Alice Walker sought out her unmarked grave in Fort Pierce, Florida, and erected a marker in memory of Hurston and her work, which is, today, widely read and influential.

The essay that follows, published in World Tomorrow *(May 1928), challenges the notion that American identity is connected to freedom, the "home of the brave," and the "land of the free." Hurston is deeply aware of such ironies and of the bitter struggles obscured by the happy image of an American identity forged in the melting pot. But she is not cast down or resentful; she has no time to waste on negativity. I chose "How It Feels to Be Colored Me" for its irrepressible spirit in the face of what are clear inequalities in America, for its ironic self-representation, and for the sheer delight it gives me to think that Hurston's spirit has triumphed after all.*

— A.L.

I am colored but I offer nothing in the way of extenuating circumstances except the fact that I am the only Negro in the United States whose grandfather on the mother's side was *not* an Indian chief.

I remember the very day that I became colored. Up to my thirteenth year I lived in the little Negro town of Eatonville, Florida. It is exclusively a colored town. The only white people I knew passed through the town going to or coming from Orlando. The native whites rode dusty horses, the Northern tourists chugged down the sandy village road in automobiles. The town knew the Southerners and never stopped cane chewing* when they passed. But the Northerners were something else again. They were peered at cautiously from behind curtains by the timid. The more venturesome would come out on the porch to watch them go past and got just as much pleasure out of the tourists as the tourists got out of the village.

The front porch might seem a daring place for the rest of the town, but it was a gallery seat for me. My favorite place was atop the gate-post. Proscenium box for a born first-nighter. Not only did I enjoy the show, but I didn't mind the actors knowing that I liked it. I usually spoke to them in passing. I'd wave at them and when they returned my salute, I would say something like this: "Howdy-do-well-I-thank-you-where-you-goin'?" Usually automobile or the horse paused at this, and after a queer exchange of compliments, I would probably "go a piece of the way" with them, as we say in farthest Florida. If one of my family happened to come to the front in time to see me, of course negotiations would be rudely broken off. But even so, it is clear that I was the first "welcome-to-our-state" Floridian, and I hope the Miami Chamber of Commerce will please take notice.

During this period, white people differed from colored to me only in that they rode through town and never lived there. They liked to hear me "speak pieces" and sing and wanted to see me dance the parse-me-la, and gave me generously of their small silver for doing these things, which seemed strange to me for I wanted to do them so much that I needed bribing to stop. Only they didn't know it. The colored people gave no dimes. They deplored any joyful tendencies in me, but I was their Zora nevertheless. I belonged to them, to the nearby hotels, to the country—everybody's Zora.

But changes came in the family when I was thirteen, and I was sent to 5
school in Jacksonville. I left Eatonville, the town of the oleanders, as Zora. When I disembarked from the river-boat at Jacksonville, she was no more. It seemed that I had suffered a sea change. I was not Zora of Orange County any more. I was now a little colored girl. I found it out in certain ways. In my heart as well as in the mirror, I became a fast brown—warranted not to rub nor run.

But I am not tragically colored. There is no great sorrow dammed up in my soul, nor lurking behind my eyes. I do not mind at all. I do not belong to the sobbing school of Negrohood who hold that nature somehow has given them a lowdown dirty deal and whose feelings are all hurt about it. Even in the helter-skelter skirmish that is my life, I have seen that the world is to the strong* regardless of a little pigmentation more or less. No, I do not weep at the world—I am too busy sharpening my oyster knife.*

---

cane chewing: chewing sugar-cane stalks

the world is to the strong: an allusion to the biblical passage (in Ecclesiastes 9:11) that reads "The race is not to the swift, nor the battle to the strong"

sharpening my oyster knife: an allusion to the saying "The world is my oyster," which appears in Shakespeare's *The Merry Wives of Windsor*

Someone is always at my elbow reminding me that I am the granddaughter of slaves. It fails to register depression with me. Slavery is sixty years in the past. The operation was successful and the patient is doing well, thank you. The terrible struggle* that made me an American out of a potential slave said "On the line!" The Reconstruction said "Get set!"; and the generation before said "Go!" I am off to a flying start and I must not halt in the stretch to look behind and weep. Slavery is the price I paid for civilization, and the choice was not with me. It is a bully adventure and worth all that I have paid through my ancestors for it. No one on earth ever had a greater chance for glory. The world to be won and nothing to be lost. It is thrilling to think—to know that for any act of mine, I shall get twice as much praise or twice as much blame. It is quite exciting to hold the center of the national stage, with the spectators not knowing whether to laugh or to weep.

The position of my white neighbor is much more difficult. No brown specter pulls up a chair beside me when I sit down to eat. No dark ghost thrusts its leg against mine in bed. The game of keeping what one has is never so exciting as the game of getting.

I do not always feel colored. Even now I often achieve the unconscious Zora of Eatonville before the Hegira. I feel most colored when I am thrown against a sharp white background.

For instance at Barnard. "Beside the waters of the Hudson"* I feel my 10
race. Among the thousand white persons, I am a dark rock surged upon, and overswept, but through it all, I remain myself. When covered by the waters, I am; and the ebb but reveals me again.

Sometimes it is the other way around. A white person is set down in our midst, but the contrast is just as sharp for me. For instance, when I sit in the drafty basement that is The New World Cabaret with a white person, my color comes. We enter chatting about any little nothing that we have in common and are seated by the jazz waiters. In the abrupt way that jazz orchestras have, this one plunges into a number. It loses no time in circumlocutions, but gets right down to business. It constricts the thorax and splits the heart with its tempo and narcotic harmonies. This orchestra grows rambunctious, rears on its hind legs and attacks the tonal veil with primitive fury, rending it, clawing it until it breaks through to the jungle beyond. I follow those heathen—follow them exultingly. I dance wildly inside myself; I yell within, I whoop; I shake my assegai above my head, I hurl it true to the mark *yeeeeooww!* I am in the jungle and living in the jungle way. My face is painted red and yellow and

---

the terrible struggle: the Civil War

"Beside the waters of the Hudson": Barnard College is near the Hudson River in New York City. For another account of how it felt to be a black student at Columbia University in the early twentieth century, see the poem by Langston Hughes, "Theme for English B" (p. 507).

my body is painted blue. My pulse is throbbing like a war drum. I want to slaughter something—give pain, give death to what, I do not know. But the piece ends. The men of the orchestra wipe their lips and rest their fingers. I creep back slowly to the veneer we call civilization with the last tone and find the white friend sitting motionless in his seat, smoking calmly.

"Good music they have here," he remarks, drumming the table with his fingertips.

Music. The great blobs of purple and red emotion have not touched him. He has only heard what I felt. He is far away and I see him but dimly across the ocean and the continent that have fallen between us. He is so pale with his whiteness then and I am *so* colored.

At certain times I have no race, I am *me*. When I set my hat at a certain angle and saunter down Seventh Avenue, Harlem City, feeling as snooty as the lions in front of the Forty-Second Street Library,* for instance. So far as my feelings are concerned, Peggy Hopkins Joyce* on the Boule Mich* with her gorgeous raiment, stately carriage, knees knocking together in a most aristocratic manner, has nothing on me. The cosmic Zora emerges. I belong to no race nor time. I am the eternal feminine with its string of beads.

I have no separate feeling about being an American citizen and colored. 15
I am merely a fragment of the Great Soul that surges within the boundaries. My country, right or wrong.

Sometimes, I feel discriminated against, but it does not make me angry. It merely astonishes me. How *can* any deny themselves the pleasure of my company? It's beyond me.

But in the main, I feel like a brown bag of miscellany propped against a wall. Against a wall in company with other bags, white, red and yellow. Pour out the contents, and there is discovered a jumble of small things priceless and worthless. A first-water diamond, an empty spool, bits of broken glass, lengths of string, a key to a door long since crumbled away, a rusty knife-blade, old shoes saved for a road that never was and never will be, a nail bent under the weight of things too heavy for any nail, a dried flower or two still a little fragrant. In your hand is the brown bag. On the ground before you is the jumble it held—so much like the jumble in the bags, could they be emptied, that all might be dumped in a single heap and the bags refilled without altering the content of any greatly. A bit of colored glass more or less would not matter. Perhaps that is how the Great Stuffer of Bags filled them in the first place—who knows?

---

the lions in front of the Forty-Second Street Library: two statues of lions that stand in front of the main building of the New York Public Library, on Fifth Avenue at 42nd Street

Peggy Hopkins Joyce: a famous beauty who set fashions in the 1920s

the Boule Mich: the Boulevard Saint-Michel, a street in Paris

QUESTIONING THE TEXT

1. Color is a central theme in this brief essay. Jot down as many of the ways color appears as you can remember. Then go back and check the text. Complete your list, and compare it with the lists of others in your class. What are the different things color is attributed to?
2. In her introduction to this essay, A.L. makes absolutely clear how much she admires Hurston. How does her praise affect your evaluation of the essay?
3. Hurston exemplifies the *differences* among people in her vivid descriptions of her experience of jazz (paragraph 11). First, try to describe your experience with the kind of music that most engages and moves you. What do you find in common with or different from Hurston's experience? Does what you have discovered lead you to see "sharp" contrasts, as Hurston does, or commonalities? What do such contrasts and commonalities have to do with your race? With some other feature of your identity?

MAKING CONNECTIONS

4. Read Hurston's piece along with Langston Hughes's "Theme for English B" (p. 507). Do these writers hold different—or similar—views on commonalities among all people? Explain your answer in an informal statement (about a page or two) addressed to your class.
5. As the title of this essay suggests, Hurston shares her experiences with readers in order to capture what it feels like to be African American in the United States during the early part of the twentieth century. Bich Minh Nguyen, in "The Good Immigrant Student" (p. 441), and Paula Gunn Allen, in "Where I Come From Is Like This" (p. 458), also offer personal experiences, giving readers an idea of what it might feel like to be from a family of blended ethnicities and to grow up in a strange, often hostile, U.S. culture. Compare Hurston's essay to Nguyen's or Allen's. Which essay do you think best conveys "what it feels like" to be in the author's shoes (or skin)? What is it about the writing that enables you to empathize with the author? How does your own identity inform your response?

JOINING THE CONVERSATION

6. Hurston concludes with a simile about bags. First, consider what simile or metaphor you might use to describe your own race or ethnicity and its relationship to others. Begin perhaps by completing the sentence "But in the main, I feel like . . ." Then write an extended description of your simile or metaphor, and bring it to class for discussion.
7. Working with two or three classmates, draft a composite description of the metaphors you came up with. What do these metaphors have in common? How do they differ?

ANDRE DUBUS
Witness

ANDRE DUBUS (1937–99) was known to many as a "writer's writer." Author of eleven books and winner of numerous awards, including MacArthur and Guggenheim Fellowships and the runner-up Pulitzer Prize for 1992, Dubus has been described by reviewer Gary Kamiya as "one of the great psychological realists among contemporary writers of short fiction."

Dubus was also a powerful essayist. In "Witness," he takes readers with him on a typical Thursday—typical, that is, in the years since 1986, when he was hit by a car as he struggled to help two people whose car was disabled. That night, he lost most of his left leg; his right leg was shattered. On this particular Thursday, he spends time in his wheelchair and, while he waits to pick up his youngest daughters for dinner at his house, muses on pain and on the will to live. Read this essay, which originally appeared in the New Yorker *(July 21, 1997), and revisit the night of his accident, a night that led to an identity shift for Dubus, to bouts of depression, and to a long hiatus from writing. And join Dubus and his family on the day he decided to write this essay.*

In an interview with his hometown newspaper, Dubus recalled advice his daughter Nicole had given him: "keep writing essays about the wheelchair and let the wheelchair come into your stories and gradually it will leave." "Witness" is one of those essays, and I wanted to include it here because Dubus faces "sorrow and fear and rain" and still manages to make it through to the light. —A.L.

Thursday during the school year is a wheelchair day; they are all wheelchair days, but some more than others. On Thursdays I drive thirty minutes to Andover, the town where my daughters live. They are Cadence and Madeleine, fourteen and nine. I go to their school and park on the road that goes through the grounds and wait for their classes to end at three-twenty. My right leg hurts when I drive; it hurts when it is not at a ninety-degree angle, and most nights it hurts anyway. While driving I have to place my foot to the left of the brake pedal, and that angle makes my leg hurt sooner, and more. Often my back hurts. Years ago I learned that pain and wheelchair fatigue—*sitting,* and worrying about what can go wrong because I can't stand or walk—take most of my energy; I cannot live as normals do, and I must try to do only what is essential each day. So on Thursdays I neither write nor exercise. I make snacks for my daughters, wrap two ice packs around my leg, drive and wait, then take them to my house for dinner, then back to their house, and then I return to host a writers' workshop at my home. I like Thursdays.

I could leave my house at two-thirty or so, and my leg would not start hurting till after three, my back not till after four, or even later, or not at all. But I try to leave by one-thirty. I bring lunch and a book, and drive to the school. I park and eat a sandwich, drink water, and read. There is no telephone. I have a car phone, which I would not have as a biped. It is harmless. It can ring only when the ignition is on, and no one knows its number; I don't know its number. In the car, I read. The pain starts. At home the phone rings and rings, and when I am writing I don't answer; but when I am reading I feel that I should answer it. But even with the pain, there is peace in the car. The moral torque is that by the time the girls come out of school the pain is tiring me. I have to be wary of impatience and irritation. A few days ago I read that a samurai philosophy is to refrain until you can respond instead of reacting. I must work on that.

This fall, in 1996, there is another difficulty: the girls have a dog. And on Thursdays the dog is alone in the house and by late afternoon it needs to be walked, to relieve itself, be a leashed animal outdoors. So from school we drive to the house where the girls live with their mother, and they go inside. The house has front steps, so I have never been in it. I would need a man to get me inside, probably three—depending on the men—to go upstairs to the rooms where my daughters sleep. While I wait in the car, I cannot imagine what the girls are doing in the house whose walls and ceilings and furniture and rooms do not exist as images in my mind. Inside the girls are invisible and soundless; they do not come out with the dog. I admire what I call their anarchy. I cannot make them hurry, not even to a movie or a play, which I tell them will start whether or not we are there; they remain insouciant. I am flesh enclosing tension: we have never been late for a movie or a play. In the car, my leg and back do not admire the girls' anarchy. Patience is leaving, irritation arriving. I read. Then, to my right, I glimpse motion; I look and see the girls finally coming out of the house, the brown short-haired dog ahead of them. Cadence holds the taut leash. The dog is of medium size, younger, eager, wagging her tail, sniffing the air. They cross the street behind me, I watch them in the mirror, then they go through a tree line—again they are invisible—and into a large field. When they disappear I'm briefly frightened; someone could do something to them. I read, I smoke, sometimes I grunt or moan.

I want the girls to have a dog, and I want them to be happily walking the dog in the field. But I also want my leg to stop hurting. I want to be home with my leg on the wheelchair's leg rest. I want to be there eating dinner with my daughters.

A woman who was my Eucharistic minister, bringing me Communion 5
when I could not go to Mass for more than a year after I got hit, once said to me, "Don't think about what you want; think about what you need." What do I

need, sitting in this car? Courage? Patience? I can think only that I need the pain to leave me. My energy is flowing into it. And it is not bad pain. For bad pain there are good drugs. By now the ice packs are thawed. What I need, waiting for my girls, is for this part of the day to end. It does. After twenty-five minutes or so, they come through the tree line and cross the street and return the dog to their house. Time passes. Then they come out and get into the car and I drive to my home where a woman I pay is cooking dinner. It is five o'clock. The girls go to Cadence's room and shut the door and play classical music for the potted plants. They study, I answer phone messages, throw away mail, keep what I have to answer or pay. At five-thirty we eat.

On a Thursday in late October, I drove with my girls from the school to their house. The sky was blue, the air warm, and there were yellow and red autumn leaves; and at the girls' house, to relieve the pain in my leg, I got out of the car. I do this by lowering my wheelchair from a carrier that holds it on the roof. With Joan Didion's *The Last Thing He Wanted,* I got in my chair and went to the front of my car, using it as a shield against the very few moving cars on this street with houses and trees. My leg rested in front of me. Soon it would stop hurting. Two young boys wearing helmets were on skateboards in the road. My daughters have new neighbors across the street. Out of that house came a brown-haired woman in her thirties, carrying a very young boy. She looked at me, then called to the skateboarding boys, told them they could not play in the street. They stalled, pleaded, then skated to the sidewalk. She looked at me again. The boy in her arms wore glasses, and was squirming. The woman came to me, looking down now at my face. She said. "I've been wanting to talk to you for some time, I saw your accident."

"You did?"

"I was with my friend at the call box."

Ten years, three months, and one day before this lovely October afternoon, between midnight and one in the morning, on I-93 north of Boston, I saw a car stopped on the highway. It was a four-lane highway, and the car was in the third lane. There was another car in the breakdown lane, and two women were standing at an emergency call box. Now one of those two women was here, and I felt as I might if she had told me that long ago we were classmates. We introduced ourselves, shook hands. She said she had just moved to this street and had been talking to neighbors and had realized that I was the man she saw that night. She saw two men hit; the other one died within hours.

She said, "You're an author?" 10

"Yes."

The boy, not yet three, twisted in her arms, grunted, reached for my wheelchair. His thick glasses made his eyes seem large.

"You were hit by a silver—" She named a car I know nothing about, but not the right one.

I said, "It was a Honda Prelude."

"And it paralyzed you?"

"No. Only my leg's useless. I'm very lucky. I had three broken vertebrae in my back. But my spine was okay. My brain." I felt that I was reciting; as I spoke I was seeing her at the call box while I drove up to the driver's side of the car that had stopped, the last one I ever walked to. "Where were you coming from?" I asked.

"Joe's American Bar and Grill. My friend and I ate there, and had some drinks."

"The one at the mall?"

After we see a play, my girls and I eat at a seafood restaurant near Joe's at a mall; I was imagining us doing that, connecting places with this woman standing beside me.

"No. In Boston."

"Where were you going?"

"Andover. I haven't driven the same since that night."

"Neither have I."

The boy was strong and kept turning, lunging, reaching. She said, "I have to get his stroller."

She carried him across the street and into her house, and I sat among fallen leaves near the curb and looked up at yellow leaves and branches and the sky, and saw the woman and her friend at the restaurant, then at the call box. The two skateboarding boys were not ten years old; since that night she had borne three sons; and my daughter Madeleine had been born. The woman came out with her son strapped into a stroller and crossed the street. The boy reached for the leg rest of my chair. She said, "He goes to a special school. He sees a lot of kids in wheelchairs."

"What's wrong with him?"

"Probably autism. He's too young for the tests."

He was looking at a book with pictures. Then he started tearing it, its cover, too; he tore it in half, then into quarters. He was concentrating, grunting. I said, "He's very strong."

She smiled, and said. "They aren't supposed to be able to tear them."

"He's got a life in there."

"Oh, he does. It's me who's frustrated. Because I can't talk to him. And I know he's frustrated because he can't talk."

The girls came out with their dog and looked at me and the woman, and I said, "Have you met your neighbor?" They came to the sidewalk, and I said, "She was there the night I got hit."

Madeleine looked intently at her; Cadence's mouth opened, and in her cheeks color rose, and she said, "You *were?*"

I saw in her face something that was in my soul, though I did not know it yet; I felt only the curiosity you might feel on hearing an unusual sound in the dark outside your window; Cadence looked as though she had just heard something painful, but it had not yet fully struck her. I introduced the woman and her son to my girls, then they went off with their dog. I looked up at the woman, seeing her beside the highway watching me fly over the car, land on its trunk. My blood wanted to know; it rushed. She said, "The woman in the broken-down car was running around in the highway."

"She was standing in the speed lane. I was trying to get her off the road." The man who died was her brother.

For a moment I was there: a clear July night, no cars coming, everything I had to do seeming easy. I said, "I'm glad you had already called the state troopers. They saved my life. I might have bled to death."

"Someone else would have called."

"Maybe. But *after* I was hit."

The boy was trying to get out of his stroller; he reached for my leg rest, for a wheel of the chair, lunged and twisted in the straps.

"I have to take him in," she said.

I wanted to ask her what she saw, but I could not; it was like waiting to confess something, waiting for that moment, for the words to come. When I got hit, I did not lose consciousness, but have never remembered being hit, only flagging down a car for help, then lying on its trunk.

I watched her cross the street with her son and, at her stairs, lift him from the stroller and carry him inside. I began reading again. Soon a car turned the corner behind me and stopped at the woman's house; I watched a man go inside; he was not big, but his shoulders and chest were broad, and he walked with an energy that sometimes saddens me. When my daughters and their dog returned from the field, I moved to my car door, put the leg and arm rest into the back seat, and got in. Before I raised the wheelchair to its carrier, the man came out of the house, carrying his son, and walked to me. He reached over the wheelchair and we shook hands and exchanged names. His face did not have that serious look of some men, as though all play were gone from their lives, and there was only work, money, the future they may not be alive for. He was a man who could be joyful. I can now see his face more clearly than I see his wife's; when I try to remember her, I see her standing at the call box, a body whose face I could not see in the night.

"My wife said she talked to you."

"It's incredible. I've never met anyone who saw me get hit."

"She called me that night. What's it like for you, after ten years?"

"It's better. I'm used to some things. I still can't drive alone to Boston, at night on 93."

"Oh, that's a protective device."

"Really? You mean I don't have to think of myself as a wimp?"

"No, no. I believe everything we have is a gift."

We talked about his work, and his son, who was moving in his arms, and he said he'd like to have a beer with me sometime; he would get me up his steps. I told him I would like that. In his face were the sorrow and tenderness of love as he strongly held his writhing son, looking at the small face that seemed feral in its isolation. We shook hands and he went inside.

I started the car, picked up the switch that's attached to a wire on the floor, and pressed it, and the carrier on the roof lowered, two chains with an elongated hook, which I inserted into a slot under the chair's seat. I flicked the switch again, this time in the other direction, and the chains pulled the chair up. But when it reached the frame of the carrier, it stopped. The motor was silent. I released the switch, tried it again. It clicked. The chair did not move. I kept pushing the switch. Its click was disproportionately loud, a sound without promise; yet I kept doing it. The chair was too high for me to reach it and try to take it off the hook, and a thirty-inch metal frame was jutting out from my car.

This is why I have a car phone: for circumstances that require legs. My son-in-law, Tom, is a mechanic. I called him, thirty minutes away in southern New Hampshire. He said he would come. I was calm. I have never been calm when the wheelchair carrier fails, and usually I am not calm for hours after Tom has fixed it. But that day I was calm, maybe because I had started the day by going to Mass—this always helps—or maybe because my spirit was on the highway on the twenty-third of July in 1986.

I would not have the time to be rescued, then drive my daughters to my house for dinner at five-thirty. My daughters were still inside. When they came out, I told them, and we kissed goodbye, and they went back inside. I phoned the woman at my house, and said we would not need dinner. I read Didion. Tom came in his truck, looked under the hood, worked there for a while, then said it was fixed, for now, but he would have to get a part. My knowledge of things mechanical is very small: pens, manual typewriters, guns. I drove home, feeling that I was on the circumference of a broken circle whose separated ends were moving toward each other. Soon they would meet. Next time I saw her, I would ask everything.

Around seven-twenty, writers began arriving for the workshop, and some of us waited on the sundeck for those still on the road. I told them about the woman and said that next time I would ask her if she saw me get hit; when I heard myself say that, I was suddenly afraid of images I have been spared, and I said no, I would not ask her. We went to the living room, and I told the story again, to the people who had not been on the deck; this time, as I talked, curiosity and wonder left me, as though pushed out of my mouth by the dread rising from my stomach. I looked at the faces of the women and men sitting on the couch, the love seat, the window seat; we formed a rectangle. I was alone at one end. I felt faint, as if I had lost blood. I said, "I think I'll go into a little shock tonight, or tomorrow."

But I was calm that night, and Friday, and Saturday. On Sunday we had a family dinner with three of my grown children, their spouses, the older son's two small children, and Cadence and Madeleine. That morning the sky was blue, and I was on my bed, doing leg lifts. When I swung my leg and stump up for the fiftieth time, I began quietly to cry. Then I stopped. I made the bed, dressed, ate yogurt and strawberries, showered, dressed on my bed. The tears were gone and would not come back, but my soul was gray and cool, and pieces of it were tossed as by a breeze that had become a strong wind and could become a storm. I drove to the girls' house. They live on the corner of the street, and when I turned onto it I saw the woman in her yard. She was doing some kind of work, her back was to me, and I looked away from her, at the girls' house, and I phoned them to say I'm here.

At my house we cooked on the grill, and I sat on the deck, my face warmed by the sun, and talked with my children and enjoyed the afternoon. I looked up at my two sons and told them of suddenly crying while doing leg lifts, of being fragile now, and as I talked to them I made a decision I never make, a decision about writing, because my decisions usually gestate for months, often more than a year, before I try to write anything: I told them I would start writing this on Monday, because meeting the woman, shaking her hand, hearing her voice, seeing her sons, especially the youngest one, and shaking her husband's hand, hearing his witness—*She called me that night*—had so possessed me that I may as well plunge into it, write it, not to rid myself of it, because writing does not rid me of anything, but just to go there, to wherever the woman had taken me, to go there and find the music for it, and see if in that place there was any light.

Next day I woke to a wind that brought sorrow and fear and rain, while beyond the glass doors in front of my desk the sky was blue, and leaves were red and yellow, and I wrote. For ten days I woke and lived with this storm, and with the rain were demons that always come on a bad wind: loneliness, mortality, legs. Then it was gone, as any storm. They stop. The healing tincture of time, a surgeon told me in the hospital. On the eleventh day, I woke with a calm soul, and said a prayer of thanks. While I wrote this, the red and yellow leaves fell, then the brown ones, and the nights became colder, and some days, too, most of them now in late November, and I did not find the music. Everything I have written here seems flat: the horns dissonant, the drums lagging, the piano choppy. Today the light came; *I'm here.*

QUESTIONING THE TEXT

1. Why do you think the author chooses to call this essay "Witness"? How does the title affect your understanding of the essay? When formulating your answers, consider that the word *witness* can be used as a noun or verb.
2. This essay is self-reflexive; in other words, it can be read as the story of its own creation. Within that story is at least one other: the author's

account of the accident that changed his life profoundly. What effect do these and other aspects of the narrative structure (such as the heavy reliance on dialogue) have on your reading and understanding of the essay?

3. Dubus provides abundant description in this essay, engaging many senses. Choose several passages that you find particularly evocative. How does the description in these passages enhance your comprehension of Dubus's experiences and the meaning you think he intends to convey? Use your insights to write a three- to four-page analysis of Dubus's use of description in the essay.

4. In the last two paragraphs, Dubus comments on his writing of this essay. He describes writing as a means of revisiting an experience, of "find[ing] the music for it" and seeking "light" in the experience, if any is to be found. It is against this expectation of writing that Dubus assesses the essay. "I did not find the music," he writes. "Everything I have written here seems flat: the horns dissonant, the drums lagging, the piano choppy. Today the light came: *I'm here*." What do you make of this final comment? Why do you think Dubus chooses to end the essay this way? Discuss your thoughts with classmates.

MAKING CONNECTIONS

5. Dubus shares some thoughts about what it feels like to be an adult who is suddenly disabled by an accident. How does his experience compare to those of other writers, such as Zora Neale Hurston or Bich Minh Nguyen (see p. 414 and p. 441 for their respective essays), who, upon a life-changing event, found it necessary to adopt or adapt to new identities?

6. In their essays, Maxine Hong Kingston (p. 391) and Bich Minh Nguyen (p. 441) offer poignant glimpses into their relationships with their parents. Here we have a parent's perspective, in which Dubus provides glimpses into his relationships with his children. Reflect on what these essays reveal about the relationships between children and parents and about the challenges that developing and changing identities can pose to those relationships. Write two or three paragraphs, and share your reflections in a discussion with classmates.

JOINING THE CONVERSATION

7. How do you *feel* after reading Dubus's essay? Would you recommend it to someone else? Write a brief review of the essay for a teacher, and then write one for a peer—a classmate or a friend. What aspects of the

essay do you mention to your instructor but not to your peer, and vice versa?

8. In what ways can you relate to this essay? Have you struggled with a disability or dealt with some other experience presented in the essay? Write a brief reflection that you would be willing to share with your classmates, describing how Dubus's essay illuminates an experience of your own.

ROBERT D. KING

Should English Be the Law?

NO DOUBT ABOUT IT—our native tongue helps shape our personal identity, giving us not only words and literature in common with people who speak the same language but perhaps even habits of mind. And what is true for individuals may be the case for nations as well: their history and heritage are often embedded in their language. American English, for example, carries in its genes the Germanic tongue of the ancient peoples of Britain, including Angles, Saxons, and Jutes; the linguistic residue of Roman domination of Europe; the French idioms of a later band of Norman conquerors; the distinctive vocabulary of Africans brought to North America as slaves; and an infusion of terms from Native Americans and from Spanish-speaking peoples. English in general has long been especially receptive to words and expressions from other tongues. As a result, a dialect that originated with obscure tribes in a backwater of Europe has grown to become, arguably, the world's common language.

But some worry that English itself is now under assault on its turf in the United States. Despite genuine hostility to new groups of immigrants, from the Irish in the nineteenth century to the Vietnamese in the twentieth, Americans have eventually accepted wave after wave of opportunity seekers from all corners of the globe. And within a generation most immigrant families have assumed a distinctly American identity, with their children speaking English as glibly as youngsters whose ancestors booked passage on the Mayflower. *At least that's the melting-pot story many of us have lived and retold. But today, and not for the first time, some immigrants, especially from Mexico and Central America, seem reluctant to give up their native language and, with it, a portion of their culture and identity. This resistance has been strong enough to provoke a nativist response in the form of "English Only" legislation.*

But just how much of a country's identity is tied to its language? And is language diversity really a threat to national identity? These are some of the questions linguist Robert D. King examines in "Should English Be the Law?" an essay that appeared originally in the Atlantic Monthly *(April 1997). He puts the issue in historical and political perspective and comes up with surprising and, for many Americans, comforting answers.*

King (b. 1936) is Audre and Bernard Rapoport Chair of Jewish Studies at the University of Texas at Austin, where he also served as dean of Liberal Arts for almost a decade. Among his books is Nehru and the Language Politics of India *(1997).*

—J.R.

We have known race riots, draft riots, labor violence, secession, antiwar protests, and a whiskey rebellion, but one kind of trouble we've never had: a language riot. Language riot? It sounds like a joke. The very idea of

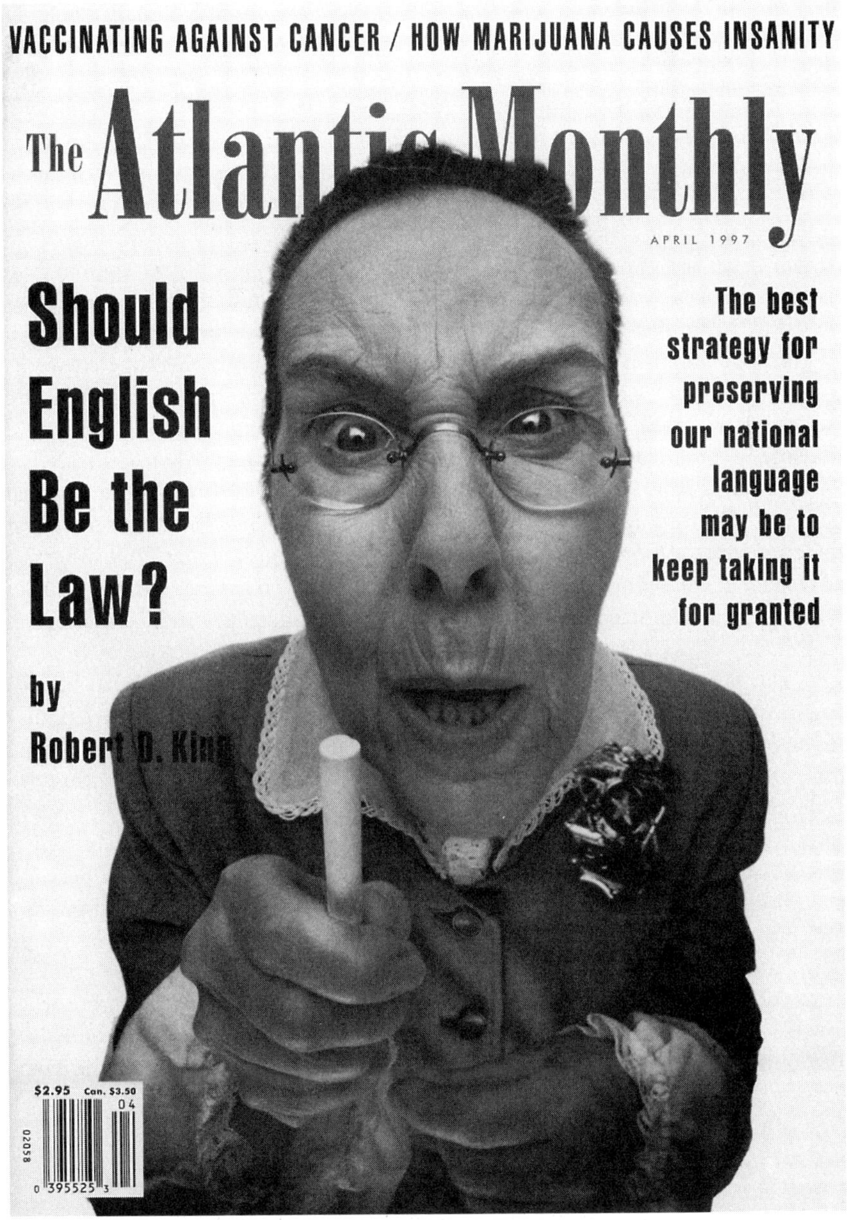
VACCINATING AGAINST CANCER / HOW MARIJUANA CAUSES INSANITY
The Atlantic Monthly
APRIL 1997
Should English Be the Law?
by Robert D. King
The best strategy for preserving our national language may be to keep taking it for granted
$2.95 Can. $3.50

language as a political force—as something that might threaten to split a country wide apart—is alien to our way of thinking and to our cultural traditions.

This may be changing. On August 1 of last year [1996] the U.S. House of Representatives approved a bill that would make English the official language of the United States. The vote was 259 to 169, with 223 Republicans and thirty-six Democrats voting in favor and eight Republicans, 160 Democrats, and one independent voting against. The debate was intense, acrid, and partisan. On March 25 of last year the Supreme Court agreed to review a case involving an Arizona law that would require public employees to conduct government business only in English. Arizona is one of several states that have passed "Official English" or "English Only" laws. The appeal to the Supreme Court followed a 6-to-5 ruling, in October of 1995, by a federal appeals court striking down the Arizona law. These events suggest how divisive a public issue language could become in America—even if it has until now scarcely been taken seriously.

Traditionally, the American way has been to make English the national language—but to do so quietly, locally, without fuss. The Constitution is silent on language: the Founding Fathers had no need to legislate that English be the official language of the country. It has always been taken for granted that English *is* the national language, and that one must learn English in order to make it in America.

To say that language has never been a major force in American history or politics, however, is not to say that politicians have always resisted linguistic jingoism. In 1753 Benjamin Franklin voiced his concern that German immigrants were not learning English: "Those [Germans] who come hither are generally the most ignorant Stupid Sort of their own Nation. . . . they will soon so out number us, that all the advantages we have will not, in My Opinion, be able to preserve our language, and even our government will become precarious." Theodore Roosevelt articulated the unspoken American linguistic-melting-pot theory when he boomed, "We have room for but one language here, and that is the English language, for we intend to see that the crucible turns our people out as Americans, of American nationality, and not as dwellers in a polyglot boarding house." And: "We must have but one flag. We must also have but one language. That must be the language of the Declaration of Independence, of Washington's Farewell address, of Lincoln's Gettysburg speech and second inaugural."

Official English

TR's linguistic tub-thumping long typified the tradition of American 5
politics. That tradition began to change in the wake of the anything-goes attitudes and the celebration of cultural differences arising in the 1960s. A 1975

amendment to the Voting Rights Act of 1965 mandated the "bilingual ballot" under certain circumstances, notably when the voters of selected language groups reached five percent or more in a voting district. Bilingual education became a byword of educational thinking during the 1960s. By the 1970s linguists had demonstrated convincingly—at least to other academics—that black English (today called African-American vernacular English or Ebonics) was not "bad" English but a different kind of authentic English with its own rules. Predictably, there have been scattered demands that black English be included in bilingual-education programs.

It was against this background that the movement to make English the official language of the country arose. In 1981 Senator S. I. Hayakawa, long a leading critic of bilingual education and bilingual ballots, introduced in the U.S. Senate a constitutional amendment that not only would have made English the official language but would have prohibited federal and state laws and regulations requiring the use of other languages. His English Language Amendment died in the Ninety-seventh Congress.

In 1983 the organization called U.S. English was founded by Hayakawa and John Tanton, a Michigan ophthalmologist. The primary purpose of the organization was to promote English as the official language of the United States. (The best background readings on America's "neolinguisticism" are the books *Hold Your Tongue,* by James Crawford, and *Language Loyalties,* edited by Crawford, both published in 1992.) Official English initiatives were passed by California in 1986, by Arkansas, Mississippi, North Carolina, North Dakota, and South Carolina in 1987, by Colorado, Florida, and Arizona in 1988, and by Alabama in 1990. The majorities voting for these initiatives were generally not insubstantial: California's, for example, passed by 73 percent.

It was probably inevitable that the Official English (or English Only—the two names are used almost interchangeably) movement would acquire a conservative, almost reactionary undertone in the 1990s. Official English is politically very incorrect. But its cofounder John Tanton brought with him strong liberal credentials. He had been active in the Sierra Club and Planned Parenthood, and in the 1970s served as the national president of Zero Population Growth. Early advisers of U.S. English resist ideological pigeonholing: they included Walter Annenberg, Jacques Barzun, Bruno Bettelheim, Alistair Cooke, Denton Cooley, Walter Cronkite, Angier Biddle Duke, George Gilder, Sidney Hook, Norman Podhoretz, Arnold Schwarzenegger, and Karl Shapiro. In 1987 U.S. English installed as its president Linda Chávez, a Hispanic who had been prominent in the Reagan Administration. A year later she resigned her position, citing "repugnant" and "anti-Hispanic" overtones in an internal memorandum written by Tanton. Tanton, too, resigned, and Walter Cronkite, describing the affair as "embarrassing," left the advisory board. One board member, Norman Cousins, defected in 1986, alluding to the "negative symbolic significance" of California's Official English initiative, Proposition 63.

The current chairman of the board and CEO of U.S. English is Mauro E. Mujica, who claims that the organization has 650,000 members.

The popular wisdom is that conservatives are pro and liberals are con. True, conservatives such as George Will and William F. Buckley Jr. have written columns supporting Official English. But would anyone characterize as conservatives the present and past U.S. English board members Alistair Cooke, Walter Cronkite, and Norman Cousins? One of the strongest opponents of bilingual education is the Mexican-American writer Richard Rodríguez, best known for his eloquent autobiography, *Hunger of Memory* (1982). There is a strain of American liberalism that defines itself in nostalgic devotion to the melting pot.

For several years relevant bills awaited consideration in the U.S. House 10
of Representatives. The Emerson Bill (H.R. 123), passed by the House last August, specifies English as the official language of government, and requires that the government "preserve and enhance" the official status of English. Exceptions are made for the teaching of foreign languages; for actions necessary for public health, international relations, foreign trade, and the protection of the rights of criminal defendants; and for the use of "terms of art" from languages other than English. It would, for example, stop the Internal Revenue Service from sending out income-tax forms and instructions in languages other than English, but it would not ban the use of foreign languages in census materials or documents dealing with national security. *"E Pluribus Unum"* can still appear on American money. U.S. English supports the bill.

What are the chances that some version of Official English will become federal law? Any language bill will face tough odds in the Senate, because some western senators have opposed English Only measures in the past for various reasons, among them a desire by Republicans not to alienate the growing number of Hispanic Republicans, most of whom are uncomfortable with mandated monolingualism. Texas Governor George W. Bush, too, has forthrightly said that he would oppose any English Only proposals in his state. Several of the Republican candidates for President in 1996 (an interesting exception is Phil Gramm) endorsed versions of Official English, as has Newt Gingrich. While governor of Arkansas, Bill Clinton signed into law an English Only bill. As President, he has described his earlier action as a mistake.

Many issues intersect in the controversy over Official English: immigration (above all), the rights of minorities (Spanish-speaking minorities in particular), the pros and cons of bilingual education, tolerance, how best to educate the children of immigrants, and the place of cultural diversity in school curricula and in the American society in general. The question that lies at the root of most of the uneasiness is this: Is America threatened by the preservation of languages other than English? Will America, if it continues on its traditional path of benign linguistic neglect, go the way of Belgium, Canada, and Sri Lanka—three countries among many whose unity is gravely imperiled by language and ethnic conflicts?

Language and Nationality

Language and nationalism were not always so intimately intertwined. Never in the heyday of rule by sovereign was it a condition of employment that the King be able to speak the language of his subjects. George I spoke no English and spent much of his time away from England, attempting to use the power of his kingship to shore up his German possessions. In the Middle Ages nationalism was not even part of the picture: one owed loyalty to a lord, a prince, a ruler, a family, a tribe, a church, a piece of land, but not to a nation and least of all to a nation as a language unit. The capital city of the Austrian Hapsburg empire was Vienna, its ruler a monarch with effective control of peoples of the most varied and incompatible ethnicities, and languages, throughout Central and Eastern Europe. The official language, and the lingua franca as well, was German. While it stood—and it stood for hundreds of years—the empire was an anachronistic relic of what for most of human history had been the normal relationship between country and language: none.

The marriage of language and nationalism goes back at least to Romanticism and specifically to Rousseau, who argued in his *Essay on the Origin of Languages* that language must develop before politics is possible and that language originally distinguished nations from one another. A little-remembered aim of the French Revolution—itself the legacy of Rousseau*—was to impose a national language on France, where regional languages such as Provençal, Breton, and Basque were still strong competitors against standard French, the French of the Ile de France. As late as 1789, when the Revolution began, half the population of the south of France, which spoke Provençal, did not understand French. A century earlier the playwright Racine* said that he had had to resort to Spanish and Italian to make himself understood in the southern French town of Uzès. After the Revolution nationhood itself became aligned with language.

In 1846 Jacob Grimm, one of the Brothers Grimm of fairy-tale fame but 15
better known in the linguistic establishment as a forerunner of modern comparative and historical linguists, said that "a nation is the totality of people who speak the same language." After midcentury, language was invoked more than any other single criterion to define nationality. Language as a political force helped to bring about the unification of Italy and of Germany and the secession

Rousseau: Jean-Jacques Rousseau (1712–78), French writer, political theorist, and philosopher

Racine: Jean-Baptiste Racine (1639–99), French dramatist and historiographer, author of *Andromaque* (1667) and *Phèdre* (1677)

of Norway from its union with Sweden in 1905. Arnold Toynbee* observed—unhappily—soon after the First World War that "the growing consciousness of Nationality had attached itself neither to traditional frontiers nor to new geographical associations but almost exclusively to mother tongues."

The crowning triumph of the new desideratum was the Treaty of Versailles, in 1919, when the allied victors of the First World War began redrawing the map of Central and Eastern Europe according to nationality as best they could. The magic word was "self-determination," and none of Woodrow Wilson's Fourteen Points* mentioned the word "language" at all. Self-determination was thought of as being related to "nationality," which today we would be more likely to call "ethnicity"; but language was simpler to identify than nationality or ethnicity. When it came to drawing the boundary lines of various countries—Czechoslovakia, Yugoslavia, Romania, Hungary, Albania, Bulgaria, Poland—it was principally language that guided the draftsman's hand. (The main exceptions were Alsace-Lorraine, South Tyrol, and the German-speaking parts of Bohemia and Moravia.) Almost by default language became the defining characteristic of nationality.

And so it remains today. In much of the world, ethnic unity and cultural identification are routinely defined by language. To be Arab is to speak Arabic. Bengali identity is based on language in spite of the division of Bengali-speakers between Hindu India and Muslim Bangladesh. When eastern Pakistan seceded from greater Pakistan in 1971, it named itself Bangladesh: *desa* means "country"; *bangla* means not the Bengali people or the Bengali territory but the Bengali language.

Scratch most nationalist movements and you find a linguistic grievance. The demands for independence of the Baltic states (Latvia, Lithuania, and Estonia) were intimately bound up with fears for the loss of their respective languages and cultures in a sea of Russianness. In Belgium the war between French and Flemish threatens an already weakly fused country. The present atmosphere of Belgium is dark and anxious, costive; the metaphor of divorce is a staple of private and public discourse. The lines of terrorism in Sri Lanka are drawn between Tamil Hindus and Sinhalese Buddhists—and also between the Tamil and Sinhalese languages. Worship of the French language fortifies the movement for an independent Quebec. Whether a united Canada will survive into the twenty-first century is a question too close to call. Much of the anxiety about language in the United States is probably fueled by the "Quebec problem": unlike Belgium, which is a small European country, or Sri Lanka, which is halfway around the world, Canada is our close neighbor.

Arnold Toynbee (1889–1975): English historian, author of the twelve-volume *A Study of History* (1934–61)

Fourteen Points: fourteen terms for peace outlined by U.S. president Woodrow Wilson on May 18, 1918, during World War I

Language is a convenient surrogate for nonlinguistic claims that are often awkward to articulate, for they amount to a demand for more political and economic power. Militant Sikhs in India call for a state of their own: Khalistan ("Land of the Pure" in Punjabi). They frequently couch this as a demand for a linguistic state, which has a certain simplicity about it, a clarity of motive—justice, even, because states in India are normally linguistic states. But the Sikh demands blend religion, economics, language, and retribution for sins both punished and unpunished in a country where old sins cast long shadows.

Language is an explosive issue in the countries of the former Soviet 20
Union. The language conflict in Estonia has been especially bitter. Ethnic Russians make up almost a third of Estonia's population, and most of them do not speak or read Estonian, although Russians have lived in Estonia for more than a generation. Estonia has passed legislation requiring knowledge of the Estonian language as a condition of citizenship. Nationalist groups in independent Lithuania sought restrictions on the use of Polish—again, old sins, long shadows.

In 1995 protests erupted in Moldova, formerly the Moldavian Soviet Socialist Republic, over language and the teaching of Moldovan history. Was Moldovan history a part of Romanian history or of Soviet history? Was Moldova's language Romanian? Moldovan—earlier called Moldavian—*is* Romanian, just as American English and British English are both English. But in the days of the Moldavian SSR, Moscow insisted that the two languages were different, and in a piece of linguistic nonsense required Moldavian to be writtin in the Cyrillic alphabet to strengthen the case that it was not Romanian.

The official language of Yugoslavia was Serbo-Croatian, which was never so much a language as a political accommodation. The Serbian and Croatian languages are mutually intelligible. Serbian is written in the Cyrillic alphabet, is identified with the Eastern Orthodox branch of the Catholic Church, and borrows its high-culture words from the east—from Russian and Old Church Slavic. Croatian is written in the Roman alphabet, is identified with Roman Catholicism, and borrows its high-culture words from the west—from German, for example, and Latin. One of the first things the newly autonomous Republic of Serbia did, in 1991, was to pass a law decreeing Serbian in the Cyrillic alphabet the official language of the country. With Croatia divorced from Serbia, the Croatian and Serbian languages are diverging more and more. Serbo-Croatian has now passed into history, a language-museum relic from the brief period when Serbs and Croats called themselves Yugoslavs and pretended to like each other.

Slovakia, relieved now of the need to accommodate to Czech cosmopolitan sensibilities, has passed a law making Slovak its official language. (Czech is to Slovak pretty much as Croatian is to Serbian.) Doctors in state hospitals must speak to patients in Slovak, even if another language would aid diagnosis and treatment. Some 600,000 Slovaks—more than 10 percent of the population—

are ethnically Hungarian. Even staff meetings in Hungarian-language schools must be in Slovak. (The government dropped a stipulation that church weddings be conducted in Slovak after heavy opposition from the Roman Catholic Church.) Language inspectors are told to weed out "all sins perpetrated on the regular Slovak language." Tensions between Slovaks and Hungarians, who had been getting along, have begun to arise.

The twentieth century is ending as it began—with trouble in the Balkans and with nationalist tensions flaring up in other parts of the globe. (Toward the end of his life Bismarck* predicted that "some damn fool thing in the Balkans" would ignite the next war.) Language isn't always part of the problem. But it usually is.

Unique Otherness

Is there no hope for language tolerance? Some countries manage to maintain their unity in the face of multilingualism. Examples are Finland, with a Swedish minority, and a number of African and Southeast Asian countries. Two others could not be more unlike as countries go: Switzerland and India.

German, French, Italian, and Romansh are the languages of Switzerland. The first three can be and are used for official purposes; all four are designated "national" languages. Switzerland is politically almost hyperstable. It has language problems (Romansh is losing ground), but they are not major, and they are never allowed to threaten national unity.

Contrary to public perception, India gets along pretty well with a host of different languages. The Indian constitution officially recognizes nineteen languages, English among them. Hindi is specified in the constitution as the national language of India, but that is a pious postcolonial fiction: outside the Hindi-speaking northern heartland of India, people don't want to learn it. English functions more nearly than Hindi as India's lingua franca.

From 1947, when India obtained its independence from the British, until the 1960s blood ran in the streets and people died because of language. Hindi absolutists wanted to force Hindi on the entire country, which would have split India between north and south and opened up other fracture lines as well. For as long as possible Jawaharlal Nehru, independent India's first Prime Minister, resisted nationalist demands to redraw the capricious state boundaries of British India according to language. By the time he capitulated, the country had gained a precious decade to prove its viability as a union.

Why is it that India preserves its unity with not just two languages to contend with, as Belgium, Canada, and Sri Lanka have, but nineteen? The answer is that India, like Switzerland, has a strong national identity. The two

---

Bismarck: Otto von Bismarck (1815–98), Prussian prime minister and chancellor of the German Empire

countries share something big and almost mystical that holds each together in a union transcending language. That something I call "unique otherness."

The Swiss have what the political scientist Karl Deutsch called "learned 30
habits, preferences, symbols, memories, and patterns of landholding": customs, cultural traditions, and political institutions that bind them closer to one another than to people of France, Germany, or Italy living just across the border and speaking the same language. There is Switzerland's traditional neutrality, its system of universal military training (the "citizen army"), its consensual allegiance to a strong Swiss franc—and fondue, yodeling, skiing, and mountains. Set against all this, the fact that Switzerland has four languages doesn't even approach the threshold of becoming a threat.

As for India, what Vincent Smith, in the *Oxford History of India,* calls its "deep underlying fundamental unity" resides in institutions and beliefs such as caste, cow worship, sacred places, and much more. Consider *dharma, karma,* and *maya,** the three root convictions of Hinduism; India's historical epics; Gandhi; *ahimsa* (nonviolence); vegetarianism; a distinctive cuisine and way of eating; marriage customs; a shared past; and what the Indologist Ainslie Embree calls "Brahmanical ideology." In other words, "We are Indian; we are different."

Belgium and Canada have never managed to forge a stable national identity; Czechoslovakia and Yugoslavia never did either. Unique otherness immunizes countries against linguistic destabilization. Even Switzerland and especially India have problems; in any country with as many different languages as India has, language will never *not* be a problem. However, it is one thing to have a major illness with a bleak prognosis; it is another to have a condition that is irritating and occasionally painful but not life-threatening.

History teaches a plain lesson about language and governments: there is almost nothing the government of a free country can do to change language usage and practice significantly, to force its citizens to use certain languages in preference to others, and to discourage people from speaking a language they wish to continue to speak. (The rebirth of Hebrew in Palestine and Israel's successful mandate that Hebrew be spoken and written by Israelis is a unique event in the annals of language history.) Quebec has since the 1970s passed an array of laws giving French a virtual monopoly in the province. One consequence—unintended, one wishes to believe—of these laws is that last year kosher products imported for Passover were kept off the shelves because the packages were not labeled in French. Wise governments keep their hands off language to the extent that it is politically possible to do so.

We like to believe that to pass a law is to change behavior; but passing laws about language, in a free society, almost never changes attitudes or

---

dharma, karma, and *maya:* In Hinduism, *dharma* is the moral and religious law; *karma* expresses the connection of past lives to future ones; *maya* describes the force that makes people believe that the phenomenal world is real.

behavior. Gaelic (Irish) is living out a slow, inexorable decline in Ireland despite enormous government support of every possible kind since Ireland gained its independence from Britain. The Welsh language, in contrast, is alive today in Wales in spite of heavy discrimination during its history. Three out of four people in the northern and western counties of Gwynedd and Dyfed speak Welsh.

I said earlier that language is a convenient surrogate for other national 35
problems. Official English obviously has a lot to do with concern about immigration, perhaps especially Hispanic immigration. America may be threatened by immigration; I don't know. But America is not threatened by language.

The usual arguments made by academics against Official English are commonsensical. Who needs a law when, according to the 1990 census, 94 percent of American residents speak English anyway? (Mauro E. Mujica, the chairman of U.S. English, cites a higher figure: 97 percent.) Not many of today's immigrants will see their first language survive into the second generation. This is in fact the common lament of first-generation immigrants: their children are not learning their language and are losing the culture of their parents. Spanish is hardly a threat to English, in spite of isolated (and easily visible) cases such as Miami, New York City, and pockets of the Southwest and southern California. The everyday language of south Texas is Spanish, and yet south Texas is not about to secede from America.

But empirical, calm arguments don't engage the real issue: language is a symbol, an icon. Nobody who favors a constitutional ban against flag burning will ever be persuaded by the argument that the flag is, after all, just a "piece of cloth." A draft card in the 1960s was never merely a piece of paper. Neither is a marriage license.

Language, as one linguist has said, is "not primarily a means of communication but a means of communion." Romanticism exalted language, made it mystical, sublime—a bond of national identity. At the same time, Romanticism created a monster: it made of language a means for destroying a country.

America has that unique otherness of which I spoke. In spite of all our racial divisions and economic unfairness, we have the frontier tradition, respect for the individual, and opportunity; we have our love affair with the automobile; we have in our history a civil war that freed the slaves and was fought with valor; and we have sports, hot dogs, hamburgers, and milk shakes—things big and small, noble and petty, important and trifling. "We are Americans; we are different."

If I'm wrong, then the great American experiment will fail—not be- 40
cause of language but because it no longer means anything to be an American; because we have forfeited that "willingness of the heart" that F. Scott Fitzgerald wrote was America; because we are no longer joined by Lincoln's "mystic chords of memory."

We are not even close to the danger point. I suggest that we relax and luxuriate in our linguistic richness and our traditional tolerance of language differences. Language does not threaten American unity. Benign neglect is a good policy for any country when it comes to language, and it's a good policy for America.

QUESTIONING THE TEXT

1. "Should English Be the Law?" is an argument—an essay that provides evidence in support of specific claims. What do you think are King's basic claims, and which pieces of evidence do you find either most convincing or most questionable? Offer your opinion in a brief critical analysis.
2. Near the end of his article (paragraph 40), King mentions Abraham Lincoln's phrase "mystic chords of memory," assuming that most of his readers will appreciate the allusion. Using the resources of your library reference room, track down the allusion if you do not recognize it, and then explore its aptness. In what context did Lincoln use that phrase? What do "mystic chords of memory" have to do with language and national identity?
3. "Should English Be the Law?" was published as a cover story in the April 1997 issue of the *Atlantic Monthly*. That cover, reproduced on p. 429, shows a stern schoolmarm wielding a piece of chalk. Working in a group, do a detailed analysis of this image, noting as many of its features as you can. Then, in a brief essay, explain whether you think the image fits King's article. If you could have commissioned cover art for King's piece, what might it have been?

MAKING CONNECTIONS

4. The problems of immigrants trying to learn English and adapt to American culture are discussed in the selection from Mike Rose's *Lives on the Boundary* (p. 109). Read the selection by Rose and then, in a short piece, describe whether King's analysis of the language problem in the United States confirms or contradicts Rose's observations. Don't hesitate to offer your own analysis.
5. In "Civic Virtue and the Character of Followership" (p. 242), Peter J. Gomes argues that the people of a nation should be linked by their shared visions, ideas, ideals, and passions. What relationships—if any—can you draw between Gomes's analysis of "good followership" and King's assertion that national unity depends on "unique otherness"

(paragraph 29)? Describe your reactions to these two authors in an exploratory essay.

JOINING THE CONVERSATION

6. King claims that a dispute over language often serves as a shorthand or surrogate for other national problems. For example, in some countries, conflicts over language are also about differences in religion or class status. In a small group, discuss some of the political and social issues that surround the "English Only" debate in the United States. Then write an argument on King's observation. Is the movement to make English the official language of the United States one issue or many?
7. King attempts briefly to describe the "unique otherness" of the American people, listing such traits as the frontier tradition, love of the automobile, a civil war, and even hot dogs. In an extended essay, explore the concept of "unique otherness" as King uses it in this selection—either by offering your own description of American otherness or by questioning the notion itself.

BICH MINH NGUYEN
The Good Immigrant Student

*W*HAT DOES IT MEAN TO ESTABLISH AN IDENTITY? *However else we might answer this question, much of this process gets shaped by a complex interaction among language, home, and school. Bich Minh Nguyen (b. 1974), whose first name is pronounced "Bit," reflects on these elements of identity formation as she describes growing up in Grand Rapids, Michigan, after immigrating from Vietnam with her father, sister, and grandmother in 1975, after the fall of Saigon. Unlike her sister Anh, who chose "rebellion rather than silence," Nguyen becomes the good immigrant student—shy, obedient, and quiet, always on time and always earning "the highest possible scores in every subject." But this identity, as hard earned as it was, did not reap the same rewards given liberally to the good* nonimmigrant *(in other words, white) students, nor did it lead to the invisibility Nguyen craved as a result of being treated, inevitably and continuously, as an outsider, a foreigner. Yet Nguyen perseveres, and in high school she begins to glimpse how it would feel to embody identity confidently, simply to be herself: "[T]here is a slipping between being good," she says, "and being unnoticed, and in that sliver of freedom I learned what it could feel like to walk in the world in plain, unself-conscious view."*

Nguyen obviously accomplished something else during her high school and college years: she established an identity as a writer. At the University of Michigan, where she received her MFA, Nguyen won major prizes for both essays and poetry; today she is a teacher at the University of North Carolina, Greensboro. She is coeditor of The Contemporary American Short Story: A Longman Anthology *(2003) and the forthcoming* I & Eye: Contemporary Creative Nonfiction *(2004). Her work has appeared in various books, including* Watermark: Vietnamese American Poetry and Prose *(1998),* Scribner's Best of the Fiction Workshops *(1999), and* Dream Me Home Safely: Writers on Growing up in America *(2003), as well as in* Gourmet *and the* Chicago Tribune.

The essay reprinted here first appeared in Tales Out of School: Contemporary Writers on Their Student Years *(2000). In it, she chronicles her Americanization, deciding that the cultures of early 1980s Grand Rapids simply did not allow her to engage in both assimilation and preservation of her Vietnamese heritage. Her account of her education also allows readers to explore with her the benefits and dangers of becoming the good immigrant student.*

I have been teaching for a long time, and I have loved almost every minute of it. Reading Bich Minh Nguyen's account leads me to look critically at my relationship with all students, particularly with students who have immigrated to the United States. I chose this essay because it speaks to the potential importance of student-teacher relationships in identity formation (on both sides) and because I aspire to be the kind of teacher Nguyen finds all too rare. —A.L.

My stepmother, Rosa, who began dating my father when I was three years old, says that my sister and I used to watch *Police Woman* and rapturously repeat everything Angie Dickinson said. But when the show was over Anh and I would resume our Vietnamese, whispering together, giggling in accents. Rosa worried about this. She had the idea that she could teach us English and we could teach her Vietnamese. She would make us lunch or give us baths, speaking slowly and asking us how to say *water,* or *rice,* or *house.*

After she and my father married, Rosa swept us out of our falling-down house and into middle-class suburban Grand Rapids, Michigan. Our neighborhood surrounded Ken-O-Sha Elementary School and Plaster Creek, and was only a short drive away from the original Meijer's Thrifty Acres. In the early 1980s, this neighborhood of mismatching street names—Poinsettia, Van Auken, Senora, Ravanna—was home to families of Dutch heritage, and everyone was Christian Reformed, and conservative Republican. Except us. Even if my father hadn't left his rusted-through silver Mustang, the first car he ever owned, to languish in the driveway for months we would have stuck out simply because we weren't white. There was my Latina stepmother and her daughter, Cristina, my father, sister, grandmother, and I, refugees from Saigon; and my half-brother born a year after we moved to the house on Ravanna Street.

Although my family lived two blocks from Ken-O-Sha, my stepmother enrolled me and Anh at Sherwood Elementary, a bus ride away, because Sherwood had a bilingual education program. Rosa, who had a master's in education and taught ESL and community ed in the public school system, was a big supporter of bilingual education. School mornings, Anh and I would be at the bus stop at the corner of our street quite early, hustled out of the house by our grandmother who constantly feared we would miss our chance. I went off to first grade, Anh to second. At ten o'clock, we crept out of our classes, drawing glances and whispers from the other students, and convened with a group of Vietnamese kids from other grades to learn English. The teachers were Mr. Ho, who wore a lot of short-sleeved button-down shirts in neutral hues, and Miss Huong, who favored a maroon blouse with puffy shoulders and slight ruffles at the high neck and wrists, paired with a tweed skirt that hung heavily to her ankles. They passed out photocopied booklets of Vietnamese phrases and their English translations, with themes such as "In the Grocery Store." They asked us to repeat slowly after them and took turns coming around to each of us, bending close to hear our pronunciations.

Anh and I exchanged a lot of worried glances, for we had a secret that we were quite embarrassed about: we already knew English. It was the Vietnamese part that gave us trouble. When Mr. Ho and Miss Huong gave instructions, or passed out homework assignments, they did so in Vietnamese. Anh and I received praise for our English, but were reprimanded for failing to complete our assignments and failing to pay attention. After a couple of weeks of this Anh announced to Rosa that we didn't need bilingual education.

Nonsense, she said. Our father just shrugged his shoulders. After that, Anh began skipping bilingual classes, urging me to do the same, and then we never went back. What was amazing was that no one, not Mrs. Eunice, my first grade teacher, or Mrs. Hankins, Anh's teacher, or even Mr. Ho or Miss Huong said anything directly to us about it. Or if they did, I have forgotten it entirely. Then one day my parents got a call from Miss Huong. When Rosa came to talk to me and Anh about it we were watching television the way kids do, sitting alarmingly close to the screen. Rosa confronted us with "Do you girls know English?" Then she suddenly said, "Do you know Vietnamese?" I can't remember what we replied to either question.

5 For many years, a towering old billboard over the expressway downtown proudly declared Grand Rapids "An All-American City." For me, that all-American designation meant all-white. I couldn't believe (and still don't) that they meant to include the growing Mexican-American population, or the sudden influx of Vietnamese refugees in 1975. I often thought it a rather mean-spirited prank of some administrator at the INS, deciding with a flourish of a signature to send a thousand refugees to Grand Rapids, a city that boasted having more churches per square mile than other city in the United States. Did that administrator know what Grand Rapids was like? That in school, everywhere I turned, and often when I closed my eyes, I saw blond blond blond? The point of bilingual education was assimilation. To my stepmother, the point was preservation: she didn't want English to take over wholly, pushing the Vietnamese out of our heads. She was too ambitious. Anh and I were Americanized as soon as we turned on the television. Today, bilingual education is supposed to have become both a method of assimilation and a method of preservation, an effort to prove that kids can have it both ways. They can supposedly keep English for school and their friends and keep another language for home and family.

In Grand Rapids, Michigan, in the 1980s, I found that an impossible task.

I transferred to Ken-O-Sha Elementary in time for third grade, after Rosa finally admitted that taking the bus all the way to Sherwood was pointless. I was glad to transfer, eager to be part of a class that wasn't, in my mind, tainted with the knowledge of my bilingual stigma. Third grade was led by Mrs. Alexander, an imperious, middle-aged woman of many plaid skirts held safe by giant gold safety pins. She had a habit of turning her wedding ring around and around her finger while she stood at the chalkboard. Mrs. Alexander had an intricate system of rewards for good grades and good behavior, denoted by colored star stickers on a piece of poster board that loomed over us all. One glance and you could see who was behind, who was striding ahead.

I was an insufferably good student, with perfect Palmer cursive and the highest possible scores in every subject. I had learned this trick at Sherwood. That the quieter you are, the shyer and sweeter and better-at-school you are, the more the teacher will let you alone. Mrs. Alexander should have let me alone. For, in addition to my excellent marks, I was nearly silent, deadly shy, and wholly obedient. My greatest fear was being called on, or in any way standing out more than I already did in the class that was, except for me and one black student, dough-white. I got good grades because I feared the authority of the teacher; I felt that getting in good with Mrs. Alexander would protect me, that she would protect me from the frightful rest of the world. But Mrs. Alexander was not agreeable to this notion. If it was my turn to read aloud during reading circle, she'd interrupt me to snap, "You're reading too fast" or demand, "What does that word mean?" Things she did not do to the other students. Anh, when I told her about this, suggested that perhaps Mrs. Alexander liked me and wanted to help me get smarter. But neither of us believed it. You know when a teacher likes you and when she doesn't.

Secretly, I admired and envied the rebellious kids, like Robbie Andrews who came to school looking bleary-eyed and pinched, like a hungover adult; Robbie and his ilk snapped back at teachers, were routinely sent to the principal's office, were even spanked a few times with the principal's infamous red paddle (apparently no one in Grand Rapids objected to corporal punishment). Those kids made noise, possessed something I thought was confidence, self-knowledge, allowing them to marvelously question everything ordered of them. They had the ability to challenge the given world.

Toward the middle of third grade Mrs. Alexander introduced a stuffed 10
lion to the pool of rewards: the best student of the week would earn the privilege of having the lion sit on his or her desk for the entire week. My quantity of gold stars was neck and neck with that of my two competitors, Brenda and Jennifer, both sweet-eyed blond girls with pastel-colored monogrammed sweaters and neatly tied Dock-Sides. My family did not have a lot of money and my stepmother had terrible taste. Thus I attended school in such ensembles as dark red parachute pants and a nubby pink sweater stitched with a picture of a unicorn rearing up. This only propelled me to try harder to be good, to make up for everything I felt was against me: my odd family, my race, my very face. And I craved that stuffed lion. Week after week, the lion perched on Brenda's desk or Jennifer's desk. Meanwhile, the class spelling bee approached. I didn't know I was such a good speller until I won it, earning a scalloped-edged certificate and a candy bar. That afternoon I started toward home, then remembered I'd forgotten my rain boots in my locker. I doubled back to school and overheard Mrs. Alexander in the classroom talking to another teacher. "Can you believe it?" Mrs. Alexander was saying. "A foreigner winning our spelling bee!"

I waited for the stuffed lion the rest of that year, with a kind of patience I have no patience for today. To no avail. In June, on the last day of school, Mrs. Alexander gave the stuffed lion to Brenda to keep forever.

The first time I had to read aloud something I had written—perhaps it was in fourth grade—I felt such terror, such a need not to have any attention upon me, that I convinced myself that I had become invisible, that the teacher could never call on me because she couldn't see me.

More than once, I was given the assignment of writing a report about my family history. I loathed this task, for I was dreadfully aware that my history could not be faked; it already showed on my face. When my turn came to read out loud the teacher had to ask me several times to speak louder. Some kids, a few of them older, in different classes, took to pressing back the corners of their eyes with the heels of their palms while they chanted, "Ching-chong, ching-chong!" during recess. (This continued until Anh, who was far tougher than me, threatened to beat them up.)

I have no way of telling what tortured me more: the actual snickers and remarks and watchfulness of my classmates, or my own imagination, conjuring disdain. My own sense of shame. At times I felt sickened by my obedience, my accumulation of gold stickers, my every effort to be invisible.

15 Yet Robbie Andrews must have felt the same kind of claustrophobia, trapped in his own reputation, in his ability to be otherwise. I learned in school that changing oneself is not easy, that the world makes up its mind quickly.

I've heard that Robbie dropped out of high school, got a girl pregnant, found himself in and out of first juvenile detention, then jail.

What comes out of difference? What constitutes difference? Such questions, academic and unanswered, popped up in every other course description in college. But the idea of difference is easy to come by, especially in school; it is shame, the permutations and inversions of difference and self-loathing, that we should be worrying about.

Imagined torment, imagined scorn. When what is imagined and what is desired turn on each other.

Some kids want to rebel; other kids want to disappear. I wanted to disappear. I was not brave enough to shrug my shoulders and flaunt my difference; because I could not disappear into the crowd, I wished to disappear entirely. Anyone might have mistaken this for passivity.

20 Once, at the end of my career at Sherwood Elementary, I disappeared on the bus home. Mine was usually the third stop, but that day the bus driver thought I wasn't there, and she sailed right by the corner of Ravanna and Senora. I said nothing. The bus wove its way downtown, and for the first time I got to see where other children lived, some of them in clean orderly neighborhoods, some near houses with sagging porches and boarded-up windows. All the while, the kid sitting across the aisle from me played the same cheerful song over and over on his portable boom box. *Pass the doochee from the left hand side, pass the doochee from the left hand side.* He and his brother turned out to be the last kids off the bus. Then the bus driver saw me through the rearview mirror. She walked back to where I was sitting and said, "How come you didn't get off at your stop?" I shook my head, don't know. She sighed and drove me home.

I was often doing that, shaking my head silently or staring up wordlessly. I realize that while I remember so much of what other people said when I was a child, I remember little of what I said. Probably because I didn't say much at all.

I recently came across in the stacks of the University of Michigan library *A Manual for Indochinese Refugee Education 1976–1977.* Some of it is silly, but much of it is a painstaking, fairly thoughtful effort to let school administrators and teachers know how to go about sensitively handling the influx of Vietnamese children in the public schools. Here is one of the most wonderful items of advice: "The Vietnamese child, even the older child, is also reported to be afraid of the dark, and more often than not, believes in ghosts. A teacher may have to be a little more solicitous of the child on gloomy, wintery days." Perhaps if Mrs. Alexander had read this, she would not have upbraided me so often for tracking mud into the classroom on rainy days. In third grade I was horrified and ashamed of my muddy shoes. I hung back, trying to duck behind this or that dark-haired boy. In spite of this, in spite of bilingual education, and shyness, and all that wordless shaking of my head, I was sent off every Monday to the Spectrum School for the Gifted and Talented. I still have no idea who selected me, who singled me out. Spectrum was (and still is) a public school program that invited students from every public elementary school to meet once a week and take specialized classes on topics such as the Middle Ages, Ellis Island, and fairy tales. Each student chose two classes, a major and minor, and for the rest of the semester worked toward final projects in both. I loved going to Spectrum. Not only did the range of students from other schools prove to be diverse, I found myself feeling more comfortable, mainly because Spectrum encouraged individual work. And the teachers seemed happy to be there. The best teacher at Spectrum was Mrs. King, whom every student adored. I still remember the soft gray sweaters she wore, her big wavy hair, her art-class handwriting, the way she'd often tell us to close our eyes when she read us a particular story or passage.

I believe that I figured out how to stop disappearing, how to talk and answer, even speak up, after several years in Spectrum. I was still deeply self-conscious, but I became able, sometimes, to maneuver around it.

Spectrum may have spoiled me a little, because it made me think about college and freedom, and thus made all the years in between disappointing and annoying.

In seventh grade I joined Anh and Cristina at the City School, a seventh 25
through twelfth grade public school in the Grand Rapids system that served as an early charter school; admission was by interview, and each grade had about fifty students. The City School had the advantage of being downtown, perched over old cobblestone roads, and close to the main public library. Art and music history were required. There were no sports teams. And volunteering was mandatory. But kids didn't tend to stay at City School; as they got

older they transferred to one of the big high schools nearby, perhaps wishing to play sports, perhaps wishing to get away from City's rather brutal academic system. Each half semester, after grades were doled out, giant dot-matrix printouts of everyone's GPAs were posted in the hallways.

I didn't stay at City, either. When my family moved to a different suburb, my stepmother promptly transferred me to Forest Hills Northern High School. Most of the students there came from upper-middle-class or very well-to-do families; the ones who didn't stood out sharply. The rich kids were the same as they were anywhere in America: they wore a lot of Esprit and Guess, drove nice cars, and ran student council, prom, and sports. These kids strutted down the hallways; the boys sat in a row on the long windowsill near a group of lockers, whistling or calling out to girls who walked by. Girls gathered in bathrooms with their Clinique lipsticks.

High school was the least interesting part of my education, but I did accomplish something: I learned to forget myself a little. I learned the sweetness of apathy. And through apathy, how to forget my skin and body for a minute or two, almost not caring what would happen if I walked into a room late and all heads swiveled toward me. I learned the pleasure that reveals itself in the loss, no matter how slight, of self-consciousness. These things occurred because I remained the good immigrant student, without raising my hand often or showing off what I knew. Doing work was rote, and I went along to get along. I've never gotten over the terror of being called on in class, or the dread in knowing that I'm expected to contribute to class discussion. But there is a slippage between being good and being unnoticed, and in that sliver of freedom I learned what it could feel like to walk in the world in plain, unself-conscious view.

I would like to make a broad, accurate statement about immigrant children in schools. I would like to speak for them (us). I hesitate; I cannot. My own sister, for instance, was never as shy as I was. Anh disliked school from the start, choosing rebellion rather than silence. It was a good arrangement: I wrote papers for her and she paid me in money or candy; she gave me rides to school if I promised not to tell anyone about her cigarettes. Still, I think of an Indian friend of mine who told of an elementary school experience in which a blond schoolchild told the teacher, "I can't sit by her. My mom said I can't sit by anyone who's brown." And another friend, whose family immigrated around the same time mine did, whose second grade teacher used her as a vocabulary example: "Children, this is what a *foreigner* is." And sometimes I fall into thinking that kids today have the advantage of so much more wisdom, that they are so much more socially and politically aware than anyone was when I was in school. But I am wrong, of course. I know not every kid is fortunate enough to have a teacher like Mrs. King, or a program like Spectrum, or even the benefit of a manual written by a group of concerned educators; I know that some kids want to disappear and disappear until they actually do. Sometimes I think I see them, in the blurry background of a magazine photo, or in a gaggle of kids following a teacher's aide across the street. The kids with heads bent down, holding themselves in such a way that they seem to be self-conscious even of how they breathe. Small, shy, quiet kids, such good, good kids, *immigrant, foreigner,* their eyes watchful and waiting for whatever judgment will occur. I reassure myself that they will grow up fine, they will be okay. Maybe I cross the same street, then another, glancing back once in a while to see where they are going.

QUESTIONING THE TEXT

1. This essay does not present an explicit thesis, per se. Rather, the author reveals meaning to her readers by relating her own experiences. If the author might be said to make a general statement about "the good immigrant student," what would it be? Try to come up with an implied thesis that the essay might support. What experiences does Nguyen present to back up that thesis?
2. Readers must take Nguyen's word for much of the information she presents here; it would be difficult, if not impossible, to verify many of her observations. How does this aspect of the essay affect your reading? Do you find Nguyen a credible source? Using examples from the text, explain how Nguyen establishes your trust or causes you to question her at specific points in your reading.

MAKING CONNECTIONS

3. Nguyen describes how her stepmother's efforts at providing her daughters a bilingual education failed to achieve the desired results. After reading about Nguyen's experience, consider Robert King's "Should English Be the Law?" (p. 428). Discuss with classmates the extent to which you think schools ought to provide bilingual education, and how they might best accommodate the needs of students like Bich Minh Nguyen and her sister Anh.
4. Like "The Good Immigrant Student," Maxine Hong Kingston's "No Name Woman" (p. 391) presents insights into the experience of one woman whose family emigrated to the United States. Although the experiences and insights offered in these essays are very different, each addresses a felt need to hide or deny a woman's existence. In what ways are these experiences of hiding similar? In what ways are they different? Could these impulses to hide apply as well to men? To women of other ethnicities or races? In what situations? Write down your thoughts on these questions, and then discuss your ideas with classmates.

JOINING THE CONVERSATION

5. Do you identify or sympathize with some of the experiences Nguyen describes in this essay? How does your identity—however you define it—affect your ability to understand the incidents and feelings she describes?
6. Think about your own experiences in elementary and secondary school. How did they shape your development into the person you are today? Write an essay that explores and illuminates ways in which your school years were formative for you.

KEITH BRADSHER
Reptile Dreams

*M*OST OF US WOULD PREFER TO BE KNOWN *for our accomplishments and our qualities as individuals. But advertisers and marketers prefer to think of us as creatures driven by desires that might be manipulated or exploited. Sometimes they have wanted us to think of ourselves as the Pepsi generation, and today they'd like us to identify with Calvin Klein, or Tommy Hilfiger, or one of thousands of other brand names or products. In short, advertisers and marketers want us to buy whatever they are selling, from tennis shoes to hamburgers to Subarus.*

There is, of course, a kind of logic to all of this. Birkenstocks and Fubu certainly are markers of identity—simple ways of saying with whom you stand. The same is often true of PC and Mac users and those who would buy only a Ford or only a Chevy or only a Fossil handbag: our purchases are intertwined with our identity. What drives us to link ourselves to a particular product? The following selection offers some possible answers.

Keith Bradsher (b. 1964) is the author of High and Mighty: The World's Most Dangerous Vehicles and How They Got That Way *(2002), from which this piece is taken. Here, he analyzes the theory that primal urges persuade more than a million people a year (myself included) to buy an SUV. Bradsher attributes this theory to Clotaire Rapaille, a Frenchman turned Detroit marketing expert. As you will see, Rapaille is convinced that people buy SUVs out of a primitive identification with lizards and snakes, resulting in a "desire for survival." Judge for yourself whether ad campaigns aimed at reptilian instincts are causing the popularity of overweight, gas-guzzling suburban warfare vehicles. Or do people just want to haul lumber and tow boats?*

Bradsher, a reporter and formerly Detroit bureau chief for the New York Times, *has been writing about SUVs since 1997. He has won the George Polk Award for his work and, at one time, drove a leased Chevy Lumina.* —J.R.

Automakers employ thousands of people to figure out which models will be popular next with American buyers, and thousands more to figure out how to promote their latest models. A French medical anthropologist by training, Clotaire Rapaille seems an unlikely person to have reshaped American automotive market research and marketing.

Tall and muscular at 60, with sandy blonde hair, Rapaille speaks with a strong French accent, having only moved to the United States at the age of 38. His background makes him an oddity in an industry dominated by the flat Midwestern accents of men (seldom women) who grew up in Midwestern cities like Cleveland, Toledo or Flint. Yet his psychological analysis of how sport utility vehicles appeal to people's most primitive instincts has helped to legitimize the cynical marketing of SUVs.

During the 1990s, Rapaille worked on more than 20 projects with David Bostwick, Chrysler's market research director; Francois Castaing, Chrysler's chief of vehicle engineering; and Bob Lutz. Castaing says that he and Lutz believed in gut instinct more than market research in designing new models, and that they showed prototypes to Rapaille only after the initial design work, so as to double-check that their instincts were right. But providing the reality check on possible future models is a considerable responsibility. Because Chrysler was the unquestioned design and marketing leader in Detroit during this period, Rapaille's work also influenced other automakers, with Ford and GM eventually retaining him for projects as well.

Clotaire Rapaille was born in Paris on August 10, 1941, less than two months after Hitler's troops occupied the city. His father was an army officer who had just been captured by the Germans and would spend the entire war in a forced labor camp; he would emerge from the camp a broken man. His mother, fearful of the dangers of occupied Paris, sent her baby son out of the city to be raised by his grandmother in Vallée de Chevreuse, a small town halfway between Paris and the Normandy coastline.

5 Rapaille's earliest memory is of playing outdoors under his grandmother's watchful eye when he was three, and unexpectedly seeing some German soldiers running away. "I said, 'How come the Germans are running away, the Germans never run away,' and then I saw a monster coming out of the forest, an American tank," he recalls. "A big American with a net on his helmet and flowers took me on the tank and gave me chocolates and gave me a ride."

That experience made an indelible impression. It convinced him at that early age that he wanted to become an American, because the French were losers in war while the Germans had been mean to everyone during the occupation.

Rapaille's parents and grandparents were nearly wiped out financially by the war, Rapaille put himself through college and graduate school in Paris by driving a beer delivery truck at night, then began consulting for Renault and Citroën, two big French automakers, in the early 1970s.

As he studied and then applied principles of psychological research, Rapaille became convinced that a person's first encounter with an object or idea shaped his or her emotional relationship with it for life. He would apply that conviction after moving in 1979 to America, where he became a prominent market researcher who specialized in psychoanalytic techniques.

Relying on the work of Carl Jung, the Swiss psychologist who founded analytic psychology, Rapaille divides people's reactions to a commercial product into three levels of brain activity. There is the cortex, for intellectual assessments of a product. There is the limbic, for emotional responses. And there is the reptilian, which he defines as reactions based on "survival and reproduction."

Rapaille focuses his attention on the deepest, most reptilian instincts 10
that people have about consumer products. He seeks to identify people's archetype of a product, the deepest emotional identity that the product holds for them based on their earliest encounter with it. His research has led him to some disturbing conclusions about how to sell sport utility vehicles, which he sees as the most reptilian vehicles of all because their imposing, even menacing appearance appeals to people's deep-seated desires for "survival and reproduction."

With the detachment of a foreigner, Rapaille sees Americans as increasingly fearful of crime. He acknowledges that this fear is irrational and completely ignores statistics showing that crime rates have declined considerably. He attributes the pervasive fear of crime mainly to violent television shows, violent video games and lurid discussions and images on the Internet, which make young and middle-aged Americans more focused on threats to their physical safety than they need to be. At the same time, he argues, the aging of the population means that there are more older Americans, who may pay less attention to violence in the media but are more cautious than young people about personal safety in general.

The fear is most intense among today's teenagers, Rapaille has found, attributing the trend to the addition of video games and increasingly menacing toy action figures on top of the steady diet of murders on television that baby boomers had. "There is so much emphasis on violence—the war is every day, everywhere," he said in an interview two weeks before the terrorist attacks of September 11, 2001. The response of teens, he added, is that "They want to give the message, 'I want to be able to destroy, I want to be able to fight back, don't mess with me.'" While teens do not buy many SUVs, youth culture nonetheless tends to shape the attitudes of broad segments of American society.

For Rapaille, the archetype of a sport utility vehicle reflects the reptilian desire for survival. People buy SUVs, he tells auto executives, because they are trying to look as menacing as possible to allay their fears of crime and other violence. The Jeep has always had this image around the world because of its heavy use in war movies and frequent appearances in newsreels from the 1940s and 1950s, and newer SUVs share the image. "I usually say, 'If you put a machine gun on the top of them, you will sell them better,'" he said. "Even going to the supermarket, you have to be ready to fight."

To reach such conclusions, Rapaille has run dozens of consumer focus groups, or "discoveries," as he prefers to call them. First, he asks a group of 30 people to sit in a windowless room and take turns speaking for an hour about their rational, reasoned responses to a vehicle. "They tell me things I don't really care about, and I don't listen," he said.

Then he tells the group to spend another hour pretending to be five- 15
year-old boys from another planet. He asks them to tell him little stories about the vehicle, to get at their emotional responses to the vehicle. But he later discards the notes on these stories as well.

What really interests him is the third stage of research. He asks the consumers to lie down on mats and he turns the lights way down in the room. Then he asks each consumer lying in the near darkness to tell him about his or her earliest associations with vehicles, in an attempt to get at their "reptilian" responses to various designs.

The answers in these consumer groups have persuaded Rapaille that American culture is becoming frighteningly atavistic and obsessed with crime. He cites as further proof the spread of gated communities and office buildings protected by private security guards, together with the tiny but growing market in the United States for luxury vehicles with bulletproof armor. "I think we're going back to medieval times, and you can see that in that we live in ghettos with gates and private armies," he said. "SUVs are exactly that, they are armored cars for the battlefield."

Even Rapaille says that a few of his ideas are too extreme to be practical. SUV buyers want to be able to take on street gangs with their vehicles and run them down, he said, while hastening that television commercials showing this would be inappropriate. He has unsuccessfully tried to persuade ad agency executives working for Chrysler to buy the television commercial rights to *Mad Max,* the 1979 film that launched Mel Gibson's career. The film shows heavily armed thugs in leather on motorcycles, driving around a post-Apocalyptic Australia and killing people so as to steal their gasoline. Rapaille wanted Chrysler to use computers to insert its SUVs into scenes from the movie, with the vehicle rescuing the hero or heroine from the clutches of one of the movie's nefarious villains in hockey masks. But the idea was dismissed as too controversial. And when I checked with someone in Hollywood, I learned that the rights to *Mad Max* are caught in a legal tangle that would make it nearly impossible to use the film for a commercial.

Yet the idea of being civil on the roads has disappeared and SUV design needs to reflect this, Rapaille says, "This is over, people don't care, and for some people, the message is it's *Mad Max* out there, it's a jungle out there and you're not going to kill me, if you attack me I will fight."

As a milder alternative, Rapaille admires SUV television ads like the one 20
that showed a Jeep climbing home over a pile of rocks at the bottom of a house's driveway. "Your house has become a castle," he said.

When Rapaille came to work for Chrysler, one of his first projects was to define what consumers really saw in the company's Jeeps. His cynical, even brutal view of the world fit perfectly with the "gut" of Bob Lutz, who oversaw Chrysler's light-truck operations in the United States upon his arrival from Ford in 1986. Lutz's corporate empire had grown a lot bigger in 1987, when Chrysler bought American Motors, including its profitable Jeep brand.

Lutz insisted on ever more powerful engines mounted in ever taller SUVs and pickup trucks with ever more menacing-looking front ends—an approach enthusiastically recommended by Rapaille. Lutz's instructions were consistent, said David C. McKinnon, Chrysler's director of vehicle exterior design: "Get them up in the air and make them husky." Lutz gave this advice even for two-wheel-drive versions of SUVs that were unlikely ever to go off-road and therefore did not need a lot of height and ground clearance, McKinnon said. Because Chrysler was Detroit's design leader during this period, and Lutz the most influential car guy in town, Lutz's decisions shaped the way SUVs were designed around the world.

The Jeep Grand Cherokee's debut at the Detroit auto show in 1992 was a vintage Lutz moment. With a large crowd of journalists gathered, he drove a Grand Cherokee up the steps of Detroit's convention center and smashed through a plate-glass window to enter the building. A special window had been installed in advance to make this a little less dangerous than it sounds. The television footage was nonetheless great, and established the Grand Cherokee's credentials as a rough-and-tough vehicle.

The Dodge Ram full-sized pickup truck came out two years later with a front end that was designed to look as big and menacing as a Mack truck; *USA Today* described it admiringly as the kind of vehicle that would make other motorists want to get out of your way.

In his book, *Guts,* Lutz wrote that the Ram's in-your-face styling was carefully chosen even though consumer focus groups showed that most Americans would loathe it. "A whopping 80 percent of the respondents disliked the bold new drop-fendered design. A lot even hated it!" he wrote. However, he explained, "the remaining 20 percent of the clinic participants were saying that they were truly, madly, deeply in love with the design! And since the old Ram had only about 4 percent of the market at the time, we figured, what the hell, even if only half of those positive respondents actually buy, we'll more than double our share! The result? Our share of the pickup market shot up to 20 percent on the radical new design, and Ford and Chevy owners gawked in envy!"

Ford and GM did not take the loss of sales lightly. They responded by making the Ford F-series pickups and the Chevrolet Silverado and GMC Sierra pickups more menacing, too. The Ford and GM pickups were then modified to make seven full-sized SUVs: the Ford Excursion, Ford Expedition, Lincoln Navigator, Chevrolet Tahoe. GMC Yukon, Chevrolet Suburban and GMC Yukon XL. Since all of these SUVs shared a lot of the same front-end parts with the pickup trucks on which they were based, the shift led by Dodge Ram toward more menacing front ends caused the entire full-sized SUV market to become more menacing. Close to 90 percent of the parts for a Ford Excursion are the same as for the Ford Super Duty pickup on which it is based, according to Ford. By turning the Ram into a brute, Lutz indirectly fed the highway arms race among SUVs.

When it comes to specific vehicles, the Dodge Durango comes closest to fitting Rapaille's Hobbesian view of life as being nasty, brutish and short. The Durango's front end is intended to resemble the face of a savage jungle cat, said Rapaille. The vertical bars across the grille represent teeth, and the vehicle has bulging fenders over the wheels that look like clenched muscles in a savage jaw.

"A strong animal has a big jaw, that's why we put big fenders." Rapaille says.

Minivans, by contrast, evoke feelings of being in the womb, and of caring for others, he says. Stand a minivan on its rear bumper and it has the silhouette of a pregnant woman in a floor-length dress. Not surprisingly, minivans are being crowded out of the market by SUVs. Rapaille even dislikes SUVs like the Mercedes M-Class that look a little like minivans.

Convertibles are suffering in the marketplace because women worry 30
that they might be assaulted by an intruder who climbs inside, Rapaille contends. "Women were telling me, if you drive a convertible with the top down, the message is 'Rape me.'"

The reptilian instinct for survival does not just involve crime fears, Rapaille says. It also shows up in the extent to which people are willing to put other drivers at risk in order to diminish the odds that they will be injured themselves in a crash. In other words, people in touch with their inner reptile are most likely to choose vehicles that look especially likely to demolish other people's cars in collisions.

"My theory is the reptilian always wins," he said. "The reptilian says, 'If there's a crash, I want the other guy to die.' Of course, I can't say that aloud."

But SUVs cannot just look macho and menacing on the outside, Rapaille believes. Inside, they must be as gentle, feminine and luxurious as possible. Rapaille's argument for this is based on the reptilian instinct for reproduction.

"Men are for outside and women are for inside, that's just life; to reproduce men have to take something outside and the women take something inside," Rapaille said. "The inside of an SUV should be the Ritz-Carlton, with a minibar. I'm going to be on the battlefield a long time, so on the outside I want to be menacing but inside I want to be warm, with food and hot coffee and communications."

Listen to other auto-market researchers try to define an SUV and you 35
often hear an almost literal echo of Rapaille's advice. "It's aggressive on the outside and it's the Ritz-Carlton on the inside, that's part of the formula," Chrysler's Bostwick said.

Rapaille's emphasis on reptilian instincts reflects not only his early encounter with the tank, he says, but also his subsequent, difficult upbringing. Rapaille says that his father never recovered from the psychological damage of his imprisonment, and his parents were divorced after the war. He was then sent off to a Jesuit school in Laval, France, and grew up there. "I had to stay there all year long because no one wanted to take care of me from my family, but I was alive, the reptilian was survival," he says.

Rapaille has loved automobiles since boyhood. But while he can now afford to buy an SUV, he doesn't own one. Instead, he owns a Rolls Royce and a Porsche 911. Sport utilities are too tall, he says, and he has a terror of rolling over. He likes the Rolls Royce but loves the Porsche, because it allows him to retain control of his destiny with its nimbleness, excellent brakes and tremendous stability. Compared to an SUV, he says, "A Porsche is safer." He may have emigrated to America, but in this respect he remains a European.

Rapaille's work helped automakers begin to understand who buys SUVs and why. But their research has gone far beyond archetypes. Lavishing huge sums, the auto industry has developed year by year an ever more detailed knowledge of what SUV buyers want, and then tapped into these desires with multibillion dollar advertising campaigns that are slick but extremely cynical.

QUESTIONING THE TEXT

1. In his opening paragraph, Bradsher announces, "Clotaire Rapaille seems an unlikely person to have reshaped American automotive market research and marketing." Although Bradsher creates doubt about Rapaille in the beginning of the essay, does he succeed in dispelling that doubt later on? Defend your answer with an analysis of the support provided in the essay, using examples from the text.
2. What feelings do you have toward Clotaire Rapaille as you read this essay? Do you like, dislike, respect, or admire him? How does Bradsher characterize Clotaire Rapaille? What words and phrases does he use to describe Rapaille? What anecdotes does he use to give a sense of what Rapaille is like?
3. How does Bradsher present Clotaire Rapaille's views in this essay? Does he present them uncritically, favorably, skeptically, or in some other fashion? Quote passages in the text to support your claims.
4. What does this essay say about the influence of gender on identity? What does it say about the identity of those who choose to drive SUVs? About those who make them?

MAKING CONNECTIONS

5. Compare the views of men and women presented in this essay with those presented in Dave Barry's "Guys vs. Men" (p. 402). What similarities and differences do you find in the perspectives of the two writers?

What limitations and strengths do you find in each of their arguments? Which essay is more convincing, and why?

6. Consider the extent to which Bradsher's essay captures a sense of American identity, and compare his observations with insights offered in other essays in this chapter, such as Maxine Hong Kingston's "No Name Woman" (p. 391), Bich Minh Nguyen's "The Good Immigrant Student" (p. 441), or Eboo Patel's "On Nurturing a Modern Muslim Identity" (p. 501). How do these essays characterize Americans? Evaluate one or more of these American character traits, and write an essay on why you find such characterizations accurate or inaccurate.

JOINING THE CONVERSATION

7. Think of your own car or a car you would choose to drive if money were no object. Describe the car in terms that convey its personality. Write an essay on what your car, or your ideal car, says about you. What does the car reveal about who you are and/or who you aspire to be?
8. Do you believe that Rapaille's concept of human psychological impulses toward cars is accurate? Use library resources to find research that would further support his claims or cast doubt on their validity. Write a newspaper op-ed or magazine guest column that presents your informed opinion on the automobile marketing practices described by Bradsher.

PAULA GUNN ALLEN
Where I Come From Is Like This

*W*HERE DID YOUR IDENTITY *as a woman or as a man come from? Can you remember your earliest encounter with traits that are traditionally considered feminine or masculine, especially as these traits were presented to you at home, at school, or in the media? Paula Gunn Allen (b. 1939) asks us to consider such questions and to examine not only how such identities are constructed but also what conflicting messages we receive about what it means to be a woman (or a man).*

In "Where I Come From Is Like This," Allen explores some of the deep contradictions between tribal Indian definitions of woman *and those of the industrial, non-Indian United States. In contrast to the vision of a woman she sees represented in the Anglo-European tradition—as "mindless, helpless, simple, or oppressed," Allen describes the strong, smart, competent women of her tribal tradition and experience. Faced with such highly incompatible definitions, Allen says, Indian women "must somehow harmonize and integrate both in their own lives."*

Born in New Mexico of Laguna Pueblo, Sioux, and Lebanese heritage, Allen has spent much of her life participating in and writing about the struggle to redefine Indian womanhood, a struggle she says she shares with her "non-Indian sisters." In her redefinition, Allen argues that tribal identity, with its connection to oral traditions, stories, and the land, must always be central. Memory, through which life-defining and affirming stories are shared across generations, is also key to her definition of womanhood. In the stories told her by her mother, grandmother, and great-grandmother lie the seeds of Allen's particular Indian womanhood, stories she will remember so that she can, in time, pass them to her own children and grandchildren.

As a little girl, I routinely wished I were a boy: boys, it seemed to me, got to do all the really cool stuff. Little around me in those formative years presented images of women that were independent, strong, or intellectual. Over the course of my life, I too have been participating in a redefinition of womanhood, and I am very glad to say that I grew to find strength and great pleasure in my identity as a woman. Like Paula Gunn Allen, I hope to remember this journey and to pass on these memories to my students, male and female alike. —A.L.

I

Modern American Indian women, like their non-Indian sisters, are deeply engaged in the struggle to redefine themselves. In their struggle they must reconcile traditional tribal definitions of women with industrial and postindustrial non-Indian definitions. Yet while these definitions seem to be more or less mutually exclusive, Indian women must somehow harmonize and integrate both in their own lives.

An American Indian woman is primarily defined by her tribal identity. In her eyes, her destiny is necessarily that of her people, and her sense of herself as a woman is first and foremost prescribed by her tribe. The definitions of woman's roles are as diverse as tribal cultures in the Americas. In some she is devalued, in others she wields considerable power. In some she is a familial/clan adjunct, in some she is as close to autonomous as her economic circumstances and psychological traits permit. But in no tribal definitions is she perceived in the same way as are women in western industrial and postindustrial cultures.

In the west, few images of women form part of the cultural mythos, and these are largely sexually charged. Among Christians, the madonna is the female prototype, and she is portrayed as essentially passive: her contribution is simply that of birthing. Little else is attributed to her and she certainly possesses few of the characteristics that are attributed to mythic figures among Indian tribes. This image is countered (rather than balanced) by the witch-goddess/whore characteristics designed to reinforce cultural beliefs about women, as well as western adversarial and dualistic perceptions of reality.

The tribes see women variously, but they do not question the power of femininity. Sometimes they see women as fearful, sometimes peaceful, sometimes omnipotent and omniscient, but they never portray women as mindless, helpless, simple, or oppressed. And while the women in a given tribe, clan, or band may be all these things, the individual woman is provided with a variety of images of women from the interconnected supernatural, natural, and social worlds she lives in.

As a half-breed American Indian woman, I cast about in my mind for 5
negative images of Indian women, and I find none that are directed to Indian women alone. The negative images I do have are of Indians in general and in fact are more often of males than of females. All these images come to me from non-Indian sources, and they are always balanced by a positive image. My ideas of womanhood, passed on largely by my mother and grandmothers, Laguna Pueblo women, are about practicality, strength, reasonableness, intelligence, wit, and competence. I also remember vividly the women who came to my father's store, the women who held me and sang to me, the women at Feast Day, at Grab Days,[1] the women in the kitchen of my Cubero home, the women I grew up with; none of them appeared weak or helpless, none of them presented herself tentatively. I remember a certain reserve on those lovely brown faces; I remember the direct gaze of eyes framed by bright-colored shawls draped over their heads and cascading down their backs. I remember the clean cotton dresses and carefully pressed hand-embroidered aprons they always wore; I remember laughter and good food, especially the sweet bread and the oven bread they gave us. Nowhere in my mind is there a

---

[1] *Grab Days:* Laguna ritnal in which women throw food and small items (like pieces of cloth) to those attending.

foolish woman, a dumb woman, a vain woman, or a plastic woman, though the Indian women I have known have shown a wide range of personal style and demeanor.

My memory includes the Navajo woman who was badly beaten by her Sioux husband; but I also remember that my grandmother abandoned her Sioux husband long ago. I recall the stories about the Laguna woman beaten regularly by her husband in the presence of her children so that the children would not believe in the strength and power of femininity. And I remember the women who drank, who got into fights with other women and with the men, and who often won those battles. I have memories of tired women, partying women, stubborn women, sullen women, amicable women, selfish women, shy women, and aggressive women. Most of all I remember the women who laugh and scold and sit uncomplaining in the long sun on feast days and who cook wonderful food on wood stoves, in beehive mud ovens, and over open fires outdoors.

Among the images of women that come to me from various tribes as well as my own are White Buffalo Woman, who came to the Lakota long ago and brought them the religion of the Sacred Pipe which they still practice; Tinotzin the goddess who came to Juan Diego to remind him that she still walked the hills of her people and sent him with her message, her demand, and her proof to the Catholic bishop in the city nearby. And from Laguna I take the images of Yellow Woman, Coyote Woman, Grandmother Spider (Spider Old Woman), who brought the light, who gave us weaving and medicine, who gave us life. Among the Keres she is known as Thought Woman who created us all and who keeps us in creation even now. I remember Iyatiku, Earth Woman, Corn Woman, who guides and counsels the people to peace and who welcomes us home when we cast off this coil of flesh as huskers cast off the leaves that wrap the corn. I remember Iyatiku's sister, Sun Woman, who held metals and cattle, pigs and sheep, highways and engines and so many things in her bundle, who went away to the east saying that one day she would return.

II

Since the coming of the Anglo-Europeans beginning in the fifteenth century, the fragile web of identity that long held tribal people secure has gradually been weakened and torn. But the oral tradition has prevented the complete destruction of the web, the ultimate disruption of tribal ways. The oral tradition is vital; it heals itself and the tribal web by adapting to the flow of the present while never relinquishing its connection to the past. Its adaptability has always been required, as many generations have experienced. Certainly the modern American Indian woman bears slight resemblance to her forebears—at least on superficial examination—but she is still a tribal woman in her deepest being. Her tribal sense of relationship to all that is continues to flourish. And though she is at times beset by her knowledge of the enormous gap between the life she lives and the life she was raised to live, and while she adapts her mind and being to the circumstances of her present life, she does so in tribal ways, mending the tears in the web of being from which she takes her existence as she goes.

My mother told me stories all the time, though I often did not recognize them as that. My mother told me stories about cooking and childbearing; she told me stories about menstruation and pregnancy; she told me stories about gods and heroes, about fairies and elves, about goddesses and spirits; she told me stories about the land and the sky, about cats and dogs, about snakes and spiders; she told me stories about climbing trees and exploring the mesas; she told me stories about going to dances and getting married; she told me stories about dressing and undressing, about sleeping and waking; she told me stories about herself, about her mother, about her grandmother. She told me stories about grieving and laughing, about thinking and doing; she told me stories about school and about people; about darning and mending; she told me stories about turquoise and about gold; she told me European stories and Laguna stories; she told me Catholic stories and Presbyterian stories; she told me city stories and country stories; she told me political stories and religious stories. She told me stories about living and stories about dying. And in all of those stories she told me who I was, who I was supposed to be, whom I came from, and who would follow me. In this way she taught me the meaning of the words she said, that all life is a circle and everything has a place within it. That's what she said and what she showed me in the things she did and the way she lives.

Of course, through my formal, white, Christian education, I discovered 10
that other people had stories of their own—about women, about Indians, about fact, about reality—and I was amazed by a number of startling suppositions that others made about tribal customs and beliefs. According to the un-Indian, non-Indian view, for instance, Indians barred menstruating women from ceremonies and indeed segregated them from the rest of the people, consigning them to some space specially designed for them. This showed that Indians considered menstruating women unclean and not fit to enjoy the company of decent (nonmenstruating) people, that is, men. I was surprised and confused to hear this because my mother had taught me that white people had strange attitudes toward menstruation: they thought something was bad about it, that it meant you were sick, cursed, sinful, and weak and that you had to be very careful during that time. She taught me that menstruation was a normal occurrence, that I could go swimming or hiking or whatever else I wanted to do during my period. She actively scorned women who took to their beds, who were incapacitated by cramps, who "got the blues."

As I struggled to reconcile these very contradictory interpretations of American Indians' traditional beliefs concerning menstruation, I realized that the menstrual taboos were about power, not about sin or filth. My conclusion was later borne out by some tribes' own explanations, which, as you may well imagine, came as quite a relief to me.

The truth of the matter as many Indians see it is that women who are at the peak of their fecundity are believed to possess power that throws male power totally out of kilter. They emit such force that, in their presence, any male-owned or -dominated ritual or sacred object cannot do its usual task. For instance, the Lakota say that a menstruating woman anywhere near a yuwipi man, who is a special sort of psychic, spirit-empowered healer, for a day or so before he is to do his ceremony will effectively disempower him. Conversely, among many if not most tribes, important ceremonies cannot be held without the presence of women. Sometimes the ritual woman who empowers the ceremony must be unmarried and virginal so that the power she channels is unalloyed, unweakened by sexual arousal and penetration by a male. Other ceremonies require tumescent women, others the presence of mature women who have borne children, and still others depend for empowerment on postmenopausal women. Women may be segregated from the company of the whole band or village on certain occasions, but on certain occasions men are also segregated. In short, each ritual depends on a certain balance of power, and the positions of women within the phases of womanhood are used by tribal people to empower certain rites. This does not derive from a male-dominant view; it is not a ritual observance imposed on women by men. It derives from a tribal view of reality that distinguishes tribal people from feudal and industrial people.

Among the tribes, the occult power of women, inextricably bound to our hormonal life, is thought to be very great; many hold that we possess innately the blood-given power to kill—with a glance, with a step, or with a judicious mixing of menstrual blood into somebody's soup. Medicine women among the Pomo of California cannot practice until they are sufficiently mature; when they are immature, their power is diffuse and is likely to interfere with their practice until time and experience have it under control. So women of the tribes are not especially inclined to see themselves as poor helpless victims of male domination. Even in those tribes where something akin to male domination was present, women are perceived as powerful, socially, physically, and metaphysically. In times past, as in times present, women carried enormous burdens with aplomb. We were far indeed from the "weaker sex," the designation that white aristocratic sisters unhappily earned for us all.

I remember my mother moving furniture all over the house when she wanted it changed. She didn't wait for my father to come home and help—she just went ahead and moved the piano, a huge upright from the old days, the couch, the refrigerator. Nobody had told her she was too weak to do such things. In imitation of her, I would delight in loading trucks at my father's store with cases of pop or fifty-pound sacks of flour. Even when I was quite small I could do it, and it gave me a belief in my own physical strength that advancing middle age can't quite erase. My mother used to tell me about the Acoma Pueblo women she had seen as a child carrying huge ollas (water pots) on their heads as they wound their way up the tortuous stairwell carved into the face of the "Sky City" mesa, a feat I tried to imitate with books and tin buckets. ("Sky City" is the term used by the Chamber of Commerce for the mother village of Acoma, which is situated atop a high sandstone table mountain.) I was never very successful, but even the attempt reminded me that I was supposed to be strong and balanced to be a proper girl.

Of course, my mother's Laguna people are Keres Indian, reputed to be 15
the last extreme mother-right people on earth. So it is no wonder that I got notably nonwhite notions about the natural strength and prowess of women. Indeed, it is only when I am trying to get non-Indian approval, recognition, or acknowledgement that my "weak sister" emotional and intellectual ploys get the better of my tribal woman's good sense. At such times I forget that I just moved the piano or just wrote a competent paper or just completed a financial transaction satisfactorily or have supported myself and my children for most of my adult life.

Nor is my contradictory behavior atypical. Most Indian women I know are in the same bicultural bind: we vacillate between being dependent and strong, self-reliant and powerless, strongly motivated and hopelessly insecure. We resolve the dilemma in various ways: some of us party all the time; some of us drink to excess; some of us travel and move around a lot; some of us land good jobs and then quit them; some of us engage in violent exchanges; some of us blow our brains out. We act in these destructive ways because we suffer from the societal conflicts caused by having to identify with two hopelessly opposed cultural definitions of women. Through this destructive dissonance we are unhappy prey to the self-disparagement common to, indeed demanded of, Indians living in the United States today. Our situation is caused by the exigencies of a history of invasion, conquest, and colonization whose searing marks are probably ineradicable. A popular bumper sticker on many Indian cars proclaims: "If You're Indian You're In," to which I always find myself adding under my breath, "Trouble."

III

No Indian can grow to any age without being informed that her people were "savages" who interfered with the march of progress pursued by respectable, loving, civilized white people. We are the villains of the scenario when we are mentioned at all. We are absent from much of white history except when we are calmly, rationally, succinctly, and systematically dehumanized. On the few occasions we are noticed in any way other than as howling, bloodthirsty beings, we are acclaimed for our noble quaintness. In this definition, we are exotic curios. Our ancient arts and customs are used to draw tourist money to state coffers, into the pocketbooks and bank accounts of scholars, and into support of the American-in-Disneyland promoters' dream.

As a Roman Catholic child I was treated to bloody tales of how the savage Indians martyred the hapless priests and missionaries who went among them in an attempt to lead them to the one true path. By the time I was through high school I had the idea that Indians were people who had benefitted mightily from the advanced knowledge and superior morality of the Anglo-Europeans. At least I had, perforce, that idea to lay beside the other one that derived from my daily experience of Indian life, an idea less dehumanizing and more accurate because it came from my mother and the other Indian people who raised me. That idea was that Indians are a people who don't tell lies, who care for their children and their old people. You never see an Indian orphan, they said. You always know when you're old that someone will take care of you—one of your children will. Then they'd list the old folks who were being taken care of by this child or that. No child is ever considered illegitimate among the Indians, they said. If a girl gets pregnant, the baby is still part of the family, and the mother is too. That's what they said, and they showed me real people who lived according to those principles.

Of course the ravages of colonization have taken their toll; there are orphans in Indian country now, and abandoned, brutalized old folks; there are even illegitimate children, though the very concept still strikes me as absurd. There are battered children and neglected children, and there are battered wives and women who have been raped by Indian men. Proximity to the "civilizing" effects of white Christians has not improved the moral quality of life in Indian country, though each group, Indian and white, explains the situation differently. Nor is there much yet in the oral tradition that can enable us to adapt to these inhuman changes. But a force is growing in that direction, and it is helping Indian women reclaim their lives. Their power, their sense of direction and of self will soon be visible. It is the force of the women who speak and work and write, and it is formidable.

20 Through all the centuries of war and death and cultural and psychic destruction have endured the women who raise the children and tend the fires, who pass along the tales and the traditions, who weep and bury the dead, who are the dead, and who never forget. There are always the women, who make pots and weave baskets, who fashion clothes and cheer their children on at powwow, who make fry bread and piki bread, and corn soup and chili stew, who dance and sing and remember and hold within their hearts the dream of their ancient peoples—that one day the woman who thinks will speak to us again, and everywhere there will be peace. Meanwhile we tell the stories and write the books and trade tales of anger and woe and stories of fun and scandal and laugh over all manner of things that happen every day. We watch and we wait.

My great-grandmother told my mother: never forget you are Indian. And my mother told me the same thing. This, then, is how I have gone about remembering, so that my children will remember too.

QUESTIONING THE TEXT

1. The author divides this essay into three sections headed with roman numerals. What distinguishes each section? Propose a descriptive heading for each section. Why do you think Allen divided the essay in this way?
2. Allen makes liberal use of lists in this essay. Some examples include lists of women she remembers (paragraph 6), traditional images of women in Native American lore (paragraph 7), characteristics associated with menstruating women (paragraphs 10 and 12), and the results of colonization (paragraph 19). Look at these lists and others throughout the essay, and assess their impact. What impressions do they create? How do they affect your overall reading of the essay? What purpose do the lists achieve for the author?

MAKING CONNECTIONS

3. After reading this essay and Amitai Etzioni's "The Monochrome Society" (p. 467), do you think Paula Gunn Allen would check Etzioni's proposed "multicultural" box on a survey if she had the option? Why, or why not? Use evidence from both essays to defend your answer.
4. Allen describes the powerful images of women maintained by the Laguna Pueblo and other tribes. Compare these images of women with those suggested by Clotaire Rapaille's psychological theory of gendered impulses, described in Keith Bradsher's "Reptile Dreams" (p. 450). Are the two visions of women's nature at odds with one another? Do you find one image more compelling than the other? Explore your thoughts in a brief essay.
5. According to Allen, "In the west, few images of women form part of the cultural mythos, and these are largely sexually charged" (paragraph 3). Do you think her assertion is true in the case of the American mythos? Peruse Chapter 7 of this book, American Cultural Myths: The Good, the Bad, and the Ugly (p. 511), and comment on whether the selections there uphold or challenge Allen's claim.

JOINING THE CONVERSATION

6. Allen describes a conflict between the images of women her mother conveyed to her through stories and those perpetuated in Western culture. In some ways, this conflict is similar to that described by Zora Neale Hurston (p. 414), who first encountered racism when she left her

African American hometown. Have you discovered a flattering or unflattering image of yourself, or some aspect of your identity, upon leaving home and encountering a new culture? What was the experience like? Write a memoir of a few pages, capturing your thoughts and feelings about a moment in which you realized a conflict between two perceptions of your identity.

AMITAI ETZIONI
The Monochrome Society

I CURRENTLY LIVE IN A REGION *demographically destined to become a so-called minority-majority state. And like Amitai Etzioni, author of "The Monochrome Society," I believe such a shift may make little difference politically or socially. That could be because I grew up in an area that would now be described as an ethnic enclave but was, in fact, a version of the majority-minority future—the east side of Cleveland, Ohio.*

In the part of the city I called home in the 1950s, white Anglo-Saxon Protestants were such a minority that their easy last names—Smith, Johnson, Jones—seemed unusual, lacking both the syllables and challenging consonant clusters commonly found along Buckeye Road. The people I knew were, for the most part, eastern European, with a smattering of Greeks, Jews, and Italians. An influx of Hungarian refugees to Cleveland following a failed 1956 uprising against a communist regime in the homeland only added to the character of the city (and the quality of the strudel!), where every block laid claim to its own churches, schools, and restaurants. The mix of ethnic groups, however, was not entirely harmonious, and real racism bubbled to the surface as more blacks from the South moved into the neighborhoods in search of better jobs and schools. Still, nobody I knew thought of himself or herself as any less American for the strong ethnic legacy that gave character to daily life. As young people, we did not envy the Anglos (their weddings were less fun than our funerals). Yet they had the neighborhoods, positions, and possessions we eventually aspired to, and they would provide patterns for the assimilation that followed.

In "The Monochrome Society," Etzioni examines the status of cultural identity in America today, finding the picture more complex than many might expect it to be. Indeed, in the course of his essay—supported by a huge number of surveys and polls worthy of careful scrutiny—he raises interesting questions about the usefulness of race and ethnicity as categories by which to characterize Americans. Etzioni (b.1929) is a distinguished sociologist and professor at the George Washington University perhaps best known as founder of the Communitarian Network, a movement intended to reform the political and moral character of the United States. He is the author of twenty books; his most recent work, The Monochrome Society *(2001), takes its title from the essay published here, a version of which first appeared in* The Public Interest *(fall 1999).*

—J.R.

Various demographers and other social scientists have been predicting for years that the end of the white majority in the United States is near, and that there will be a majority of minorities. A 1997 CNN special program was devoted to the forthcoming majority of people of color in America.[1] That same year, President Clinton called attention to this shift in an address at the University of California at San Diego on a renewed national dialogue about race relations.[2] His argument was that such a dialogue is especially needed as a preparation for the forthcoming end of the white majority, which will occur somewhere in the middle of this century. In his January 2000 State of the Union address, Clinton claimed that "within ten years there will be no majority race in our largest state, California. In a little more than fifty years, there will be no majority race in America. In a more interconnected world, this diversity can be our greatest strength."[3] White House staffer Sylvia Mathews provided the figures as 53% white and 47% a mixture of other ethnic groups by 2050.[4] Pointing to such figures, Clinton asked rhetorically if we should not act now to avoid America's division into "separate, unequal and isolated" camps.[5]

Some have reacted to the expected demise of the white majority with alarm or distress. Arthur M. Schlesinger, Jr., decries the "cult of ethnicity" that has undermined the concept of Americans as "one people."[6] He writes, "Watching ethnic conflict tear one nation after another apart, one cannot look with complacency at proposals to divide the United States into distinct and immutable ethnic and racial communities, each taught to cherish its own apartness from the rest."[7] He also criticizes diversity and multiculturalism, arguing that "the United States has to set a monocultural example in a world rent by savage ethnic conflict; the United States must demonstrate 'how a highly differentiated society holds itself together.'"[8] James Q. Wilson writes, "The third condition [for democracy] is *homogeneity* . . . as Daniel P. Moynihan has observed, the deepest and most pervasive source of human conflict is ethnic rivalry."[9]

Dale Maharidge, a professor and journalist who has conducted hundreds of interviews concerning race, class, and ethnicity in California, has written

---

[1]Cited in John Leo, "A Dubious 'Diversity' Report," *U.S. News & World Report,* 23 June 1997, 15.

[2]Speech by President Clinton Regarding Race Relations in America, The University of California at San Diego, *Federal News Service,* 14 June 1997, White House Briefing section.

[3]President Clinton's 2000 State of the Union Address, reprinted in *New York Times,* 28 January 2000, sec. A, p. 16.

[4]John F. Harris and John E. Yang, "Clinton Hopes to Prepare Nation for End of Clear White Majority," *Washington Post,* 14 June 1997, sec. A, p. 2.

[5]Speech by President Clinton Regarding Race Relations in America.

[6]Arthur M. Schlesinger, Jr., *The Disuniting of America* (New York: Norton, 1992), 15, 16.

[7]Ibid., 17–18.

[8]Ibid., 20. Cited in O. R. Dathorne, *In Europe's Image: The Need for American Multiculturalism* (Westport, Conn.: Bergin & Garvey, 1994), 113.

[9]Speech by James Q. Wilson on The History and Future of Democracy, Ronald Reagan Presidential Library, Simi Valley, Calif., 15 November 1999.

about the end of the white majority in America in his book, *The Coming White Minority: California's Eruptions and America's Future.* He reports that sometime between the date of his book's publication in 1996 and the year 2000, California's population will have become less than 50% white. He writes, "'Minorities' will be in the majority," a precursor to the 2050 state of racial composition nationwide, when "the nation will be almost half non-white."[10]

Maharidge comments that his interviews, observations, and research have shown that, especially in California,

> [W]hites are scared. The depth of white fear is underestimated and misunderstood by progressive thinkers and the media. Whites dread the unknown and not-so-distant tomorrow when a statistical turning point will be reached that could have very bad consequences for them. They fear the change that seems to be transforming their state into something different from the rest of the United States. They fear not only losing their jobs but also their culture. Some feel that California will become a version of South Africa, in which whites will lose power when minorities are the majority.[11]

Whites in California have demonstrated their fear of the "browning" of 5
America by forming residential " 'islands' that are surrounded by vast ethnic or transitional communities, as well as deserts, mountain wilderness, and the ocean," demonstrating, Maharidge predicts, "what the rest of America might become."[12] Whites and nonwhites alike also passed the anti-immigrant Proposition 187, which Maharidge links to these same fears about the end of the white majority. He warns, "California's electoral discord has emanated from whites. There is ample evidence that white tension could escalate. What will California be like in 2010, when nonwhites make up 60% of the population? . . . And how will California's actions influence the rest of the nation as non-Hispanic whites fall from 76% of the U.S. populace to just over half in 2050?"[13]

In contrast, John Isbister, a professor of economics at the University of California at Santa Cruz, asks us to ponder whether America is too white. He contends, "The decline in the white proportion is a healthy development for the country. . . . The principal case for a falling white proportion is simply this: it will be easier for us to transform a society of hostility and oppression

---

[10] Dale Maharidge, *The Coming White Minority: California's Eruptions and America's Future* (New York: Times Books/Random House, 1996), 1.

[11] Ibid., 11. For an additional telling study see Todd S. Purdum, "Shift in the Mix Alters the Face of California," *New York Times,* 4 July 2000, sec. A, p. 1.

[12] Ibid., 10.

[13] Ibid., 280–81.

into one of cooperation if we are dealing not with a majority versus several small minorities, but with groups of roughly equivalent size."[14]

One People

As I see it, both views—that of alarm and that which celebrates the ending of the white majority and the rise of a majority of minorities—are fundamentally wrong because these positions are implicitly and inadvertently racist: they assume that people's pigmentation, or, more generally, racial attributes, determine their visions, values, and votes.[15] Actually, I claim and will show that very often the opposite is true. The fact is that America is blessed with an economic and political system as well as culture and core values and much else that, while far from flawless, is embraced by most Americans of all races and ethnic groups. (To save breath, from here on, race is used to encompass ethnicity.) It is a grievous error to suggest that because American faces or skin tones may appear more diverse some fifty years from now, most Americans who hail from different social backgrounds will seek to follow a different agenda or hold a different creed than a white majority. While, of course, nobody can predict what people will believe or do fifty years hence, there is strong evidence that if they behave in any way that resembles current behavior of white, black, brown, yellow, red, or other Americans, they will share the same basic aspirations, core values, and mores. Moreover, current trends, during a period in which the nonwhite proportion of the population already has increased, further support the thesis that while the American society may well change, whites and nonwhites will largely change together.

A fair number of findings, we shall see shortly, support the thesis that American society is basically much more of one color—if one looks at conduct and beliefs rather than pigmentation and other such external, skin-deep indications.

---

[14]John Isbister, "Is America Too White?" in "*What, Then, Is the American, This New Man?*" Washington, D.C., Center for Immigration Studies Center, Paper 13, August 1998, 29.

[15]Donald Gabard and Terry Cooper problematize such determinism, specifically common understandings of race based on the existence of genetic differences among the races. They quote R. Cooper and R. David, who note, "No discrete package of gene differences has ever been described between two races, only relative frequencies of one or another trail," and, citing D. R. Williams, Gabard and Cooper write, "It is reported today that there are more genetic variations within the separate races than between them." Donald L. Gabard and Terry L. Cooper, "Race: Constructs and Dilemmas," *Administration & Society* 30, no. 4 (September 1998): 342. (Citing R. Cooper and R. David, "The Biological Concept of Race and its Application to Public Health and Epidemiology," *Journal of Health Politics, Policy and Law* 2 [1986]: 97–116 at p. 101 and D. R. Williams, "The Concept of Race in Health Services Research: 1966 to 1990," *Health Services Research* 29 (1994): 262–74.)

A word about the inadvertent racism involved in the opposite position. To argue that all or most members of a given social group behave the way some do is the definition of prejudice.[16] This holds true not merely when one argues that all (or most) Jews, blacks, or those belonging to any other social group have some unsavory qualities, but also when one argues that all (or most) of a given group are antiwhite, alienated, and so on because some (often actually a small minority) are.

10 One may argue that while of course there is no direct correlation between race and political conduct, social thinking, and the values to which one subscribes, there are strong correlations. But is this true? Even if one controls for class differences? Or, is race but one factor among many that affect behavior? And if this is the case, might it be that singling out this biological given and unyielding factor, rather than paying full attention to all the others, reflects a divisive political agenda rather than social fact? Above all, are there significant correlations between being nonwhite and most political, social, and ideological positions? I turn now to findings supporting the thesis that there are many more beliefs, dreams, and views that whites and nonwhites of all colors share than those that divide them.

Some findings out of many that could be cited illustrate this point: A 1992 survey found that most black and Hispanic Americans (86% and 85%, respectively) desired "fair treatment for all, without prejudice or discrimination."[17] One may expect that this value is of special concern to minorities, but white Americans who took part in this survey felt the same way. As a result, the proportion of all Americans who agreed with the quoted statement about the importance of fairness was close to the above figures, at 79%.[18]

A poll of New York residents showed that the vast majority of respondents considered teaching "the common heritage and values that we share as Americans" to be "very important."[19] One may expect this statement to reflect a white, majoritarian value. However, minorities endorsed this position more strongly than whites: 88% of Hispanics and 89% of blacks, compared to 70% of whites agreed.[20]

A nationwide poll found that equal proportions of blacks and whites, 93%, concurred that they would vote for a black presidential candidate.[21]

---

[16]See, for example, James M. Jones, *Prejudice and Racism* (Reading, Mass.: Addison-Wesley, 1972).

[17]*Democracy's Next Generation II: A Study of American Youth on Race* (Washington, D.C.: People for the American Way, 1992), 57–58.

[18]Ibid.

[19]*New York State United Teachers 1991 Education Opinion Survey: Final Report* (Albany, N.Y.: New York State United Teachers, 1991), sec. II, 5, 8.

[20]Ibid.

[21]Douglas Turner, "Amid the Black–White Divide, Convergence of Some Attitudes," *Buffalo News,* 11 June 1997, sec. A, p. 6.

Another national poll found that "over 80% of all respondents in every category—age, gender, race, location, education, and income—agreed" with the statement that freedom must be tempered by personal responsibility.[22]

Far from favoring placing stress on different heritages, approximately 85% of all parents; 83% of African American parents; 89% of Hispanic American parents; and 88% of foreign-born parents agreed with the statement, "To graduate from high school, students should be required to understand the common history and ideas that tie all Americans together."[23]

And far from stressing differences in the living conditions and economic 15
status of different groups, views about the nature of life in America are shared across racial lines. According to the National Opinion Research Center's (NORC) 1994 General Social Survey, 70% of blacks and 60% of whites agreed that "the way things are in America, people like me and my family have a good chance of improving our standard of living."[24] Likewise, 81% of blacks and 79% of whites reported to NORC that "the quality of life is better in America than in most other advanced industrial countries."[25] And, 84% of all parents surveyed—80% of foreign-born parents, 87% of Hispanic American parents, 73% of African American parents—agreed that "the U.S. is a unique country that stands for something special in the world."[26] Lawrence Otis Graham, an African American author, writing about African Americans, sums up the picture by stating, "Blacks, like any other group, want to share in the American dream."[27] The American dream, not some other or disparate one.

Close percentages of blacks (70%) and whites (65%), in a poll conducted in 1994, agreed that "the U.S. has made some or a lot of progress in easing black-white tensions in the past ten years."[28] In the same poll, 70% of whites and 65% of blacks said that "racial integration has been good for society."[29]

Sociologist Alan Wolfe finds in his middle-class morality project, which surveyed whites, blacks, Hispanics, Asians, Native Americans, and "others," that a striking majority of respondents disagreed or strongly disagreed with the

---

[22]Stephen Covey, "What Americans Agree On," *USA Weekend,* 6 July 1997, 4.

[23]*Public Agenda,* "A Lot to be Thankful For: What Parents Want Children to Learn about America," November 1998. Available at http://www.publicagenda.org/specials/thankful/thankful.htm. Accessed 7/14/00.

[24]Roper Center Data Review. Survey by the National Opinion Research Center–General Social Survey, 1994. Cited in "Thinking about Ethnicity," *Public Perspective* (February/March 1998): 59.

[25]Ibid., 58.

[26]*Public Agenda,* "A Lot to be Thankful For."

[27]Lawrence Otis Graham, cited in Frank Stasio, anchor, "Lawrence Otis Graham, author of *Our Kind of People,* Discusses the Elitism of Some Upper-Class African-Americans," *NPR Weekend Edition* (20 February 2000).

[28]Gerald F. Feib and Joe Davidson, "Shades of Gray: Whites, Blacks Agree on Problems; the Issue Is How to Solve Them," *Wall Street Journal,* 29 September 1994, sec. A, p. 6.

[29]Ibid.

statement, "There are times when loyalty to an ethnic group or to a race should be valued over loyalty to the country as a whole."[30]

Even in response to a deliberately loaded question, a 1997 poll showed that similarities between the races are much larger than differences. Asked, "Will race relations in this country ever get better?" 43% of blacks and 60% of whites replied in the affirmative.[31] (The pollsters tended to focus on the 17% who struck a different position rather than on the 43% who embraced the same one. The difference between 57% of blacks and 40% of whites who did not believe that race relations were going to get better was also 17%.)

While Americans hold widely ranging opinions on *what* should be done about various matters of social policy, people across racial and ethnic categories identify the same issues as important to them, and to the country. For instance in a 1996 survey, whites, African Americans, Latinos, and Asian Americans concurred that education was "the most important issue facing [their] community today."[32] Similarly, more than 80% of blacks, Latinos, and whites shared the belief that it was "'extremely important' to spend tax dollars on 'educational opportunities for children.'"[33] In another survey, 54% of blacks and 61% of whites ranked "increased economic opportunity" as the most important goal for blacks.[34] And 97% of blacks and 92% of whites rated violent crime a "very serious or most serious problem" in a 1994 poll.[35]

As we can see in Table 1, whites, African Americans, Latinos, and Asian 20
Americans agreed about areas of life that had gotten worse or harder for "people like [them]" between 1985 and 1995. Between 45% and 55% agreed that public schools had worsened; 50 to 60% agreed that getting a good job was more difficult; between 48% and 55% within each group agreed that finding "decent, affordable housing" was tougher, and between 34% and 48% found it more challenging "for families like [theirs] to stay together."[36]

---

[30]Alan Wolfe, *One Nation, After All: What Middle-Class Americans Really Think about God, Country, Family, Racism, Welfare, Immigration, Homosexuality, Work, the Right, the Left, and Each Other* (New York: Viking, 1998), 158.

[31]"Speaking Out: Teens and Adults See Different Worlds," *Time*/CNN poll from 23 September to 2 October 1997 by Yankelovich Partners, Inc. Cited in *Time,* 24 November 1997, 90. The poll cited compares the views of teens and adults; the percentages cited are the views of the adults only.

[32]U.S. Department of Justice, *Sourcebook of Criminal Justice Statistics 1996* (Washington, D.C.: U.S. Government Printing Office, 1997), 115. Cited in Jennifer Hochschild and Reuel R. Rogers, "Race Relations in a Diversifying Nation," forthcoming in *New Directions: African Americans in a Diversifying Nation,* ed. James Jackson (Washington, D.C.: National Policy Association).

[33]U.S. Department of Justice, *Sourcebook of Criminal Justice Statistics 1996,* 141.

[34]Feib and Davidson, "Shades of Gray," sec. A, p. 1.

[35]Ibid., sec. A, p. 6.

[36]Washington Post/Kaiser Family Foundation/Harvard School of Public Health Survey Project, *The Four Americas: Government and Social Policy Through the Eyes of America's Multi-racial and Multi-ethnic Society* (Washington, D.C.: Washington Post, 1995), 75–76. Cited in Hochschild and Rogers, "Race Relations in a Diversifying Nation."

Table 1 Are the Problems of People Like You Getting Worse?

"During the past ten years, has XXX gotten better, worse, or stayed the same (OR become easier or harder) for people like you (OR families like yours)?" (Numbers given are the percentage of people in each category saying "worse" or "harder.")

	Whites	*African Americans*	*Latinos*	*Asian Americans*
	N = 802	*N = 474*	*N = 252*	*N = 353*
Public schools	55	57	45	47
To get good jobs	56	60	50	56
To find decent, affordable housing	55	49	55	48
For families like yours to stay together	45	48	40	34
Health care	44	39	30	30

Source: Washington Post/Kaiser Family Foundation/Harvard School of Public Health Survey Project, 1995: 75–76. Reprinted with permission.

More specifically, the following percentages said that each area was "worse" or "harder"; public schools—whites 55%, African Americans 57%, Latinos 45%, Asian Americans 47%; getting good jobs—whites 56%, African Americans 60%, Latinos 50%, Asian Americans 56%; finding decent, affordable housing—whites 55%, African Americans 49%, Latinos 55%, Asian Americans 48%; for families like theirs to stay together—whites 45%, African Americans 48%, Latinos 40%, Asian Americans 34%.

Other problems that troubled America's communities highlighted points of convergence among the views of members of various racial and ethnic groups. "Between 80 and 90% of black, white, and 'other' Americans agreed that it was 'extremely important' to spend tax dollars on 'reducing crime' and 'reducing illegal drug use' among youth."[37] In addition, some shared public policy preferences emerged. Among whites, African Americans, Latinos, and Asian Americans surveyed by the *Washington Post*/Kaiser Family Foundation/Harvard School of Public Health Survey Project, between 75% and 82% of each group felt "strongly" that Congress should balance the budget. Between 30% and 41% were convinced that Congress should instate limited tax breaks for businesses; between 46% and 55% concurred that Congress should cut personal income taxes; between 53% and 59% agreed that Congress should reform Medicare (see Table 2).[38]

More specifically, the following percentages of each group felt "strongly" that Congress should take action on the following items: balance

[37]U.S. Department of Justice, *Sourcebook of Criminal Justice Statistics 1996,* 141–45.

[38]*Washington Post*/Kaiser Family Foundation/Harvard School of Public Health Survey Project, *The Four Americas,* 73–74.

Table 2 Policy Preferences for Congressional Action

"For each issue, please tell me if you think this is something Congress should do or should not do." (Numbers given are the percentage of people in each category saying "strongly feel Congress should do.")

	Whites	*African Americans*	*Latinos*	*Asian Americans*
	N = 802	*N = 474*	*N = 252*	*N = 353*
Limited tax breaks for businesses	39	41	41	30
Balance the budget	82	79	75	75
Cut personal income taxes	52	50	55	46
Reform the welfare system	83	73	81	68
Reform Medicare	53	58	59	58
Put more limits on abortion	35	32	50	24
Limit affirmative action	38	25	30	27

Source: Washington Post/Kaiser Family Foundation/Harvard School of Public Health Survey Project, 1995: 73–74. Reprinted with permission.

the budget—whites 82%, African Americans 79%, Latinos 75%, Asian Americans 75%; provide limited tax breaks for businesses—whites 39%, African Americans 41%, Latinos 41%, Asian Americans 30%; cut personal income taxes—whites 52%, African Americans 50%, Latinos 55%, Asian Americans 46%; reform Medicare—whites 53%, African Americans 58%, Latinos 59%, Asian Americans 58%. As well, 67% of all parents—68% of African American parents, 66% of Hispanic American parents, and 75% of foreign-born parents—told *Public Agenda* that the most important thing for public schools to do for new immigrant children was "to teach them English as quickly as possible, even if this means they fall behind in other subjects."[39]

More African Americans than whites or Hispanics thought that "the U.S. is the greatest country in the world, better than all others." However, the differences were small (African Americans 60%; whites 55%; Hispanic Americans 48%). The percentages were similarly close when respondents were asked to what extent they were proud to live under the American political system—76% of whites, 73% of African Americans, 71% of Hispanic Americans said they were proud.[40]

25 All this is not to suggest that there are no significant differences of opinion along social lines, especially when matters directly concern race relations. For instance, many whites and many blacks (although by no means all of either group) take rather different views of the guilt of O. J. Simpson. One

[39] *Public Agenda,* "A Lot to be Thankful For."

[40] For more complete details see "1996 Survey of American Political Culture," *Public Perspective* (February/March 1997): 6–7.

survey will stand for many with similar findings that could be cited: 62% of whites believed Simpson was guilty of the murders of which he was accused and acquitted, in contrast to 55% of African Americans who believed he was not guilty.[41]

Likewise, concerning affirmative action, 51% of blacks in a 1997 poll favored programs which "give preferential treatment to racial minorities," a much higher percentage than the 21% of whites who favored such programs.[42] And a very large difference appears when one examines voting patterns. For instance, in 1998, 55% of whites versus 11% of African Americans voted for Republican candidates for Congress.[43] And recent surveys have found several startling differences in the extent to which African Americans trust the government (Table 3).[44]

Still, if one considers attitudes toward the basic tenets of the American creed, the overwhelming majority of blacks are surprisingly accepting of them. A 1998 *Public Perspective* poll found that 54% of blacks and 66% of whites agreed with the statement, "In the United States today, anyone who works hard enough can make it economically." A 1994 national survey reported that 67% of blacks and 77% of whites agreed that "a basic American belief has been that if you work hard you can get ahead—reach your goals and get more," was still true. Most blacks (77%) said they preferred equality of opportunity to equality of results (compared to 89% of whites). When it came to "Do you see yourself as traditional or old-fashioned on things such as sex, morality, family life, and religion, or not?" the difference between blacks and whites was only 5%. When asked whether values in America were seriously declining, the difference was down to one percentage point.

A question from an extensive national survey conducted at the University of Virginia by James Davison Hunter and Carl Bowman asked: "How strong would you say the U.S. decline or improvement is in its moral and ethical standards?" Twenty-three percent of blacks and 33% of whites said there was a strong decline, while 40% of blacks and 38% of whites said there was a moderate decline, and 29% of blacks and 24% of whites said the standards were holding steady.[45] When asked "How strong would you say the U.S. decline or improvement is in the area of family life?" 18% of blacks and

---

[41] Jerelyn Eddings, "Black & White in America," *U.S. News & World Report,* 16 October 1995, 32.

[42] Survey by CBS News, *New York Times,* and *Public Agenda.* Available at http://www.publicagenda.org:80/issues/angles-graph.cfm7issue-type=race&id=202&graph=redflagsl.gif. Accessed 7/14/00.

[43] Survey by Voter News Service, November 1998. Cited in "The Shape of the American Electorate at Century's End," *Public Perspective* (December/January 1999): 69.

[44] Robert C. Smith and Richard Seltzer, *Contemporary Controversies and the American Racial Divide* (Lanham, Md.: Rowman & Littlefield, 2000), 86, 88, 121, 128.

[45] James Davison Hunter and Carl Bowman, *The State of Disunion: 1996 Survey of American Political Culture,* vol. 2, *Summary Tables* (Ivy, Va.: In Medias Res Educational Foundation, 1996), Table 4.E.

Table 3 Trusting the Government: Differences among African Americans and White Americans

Question	*African Americans (%)*	*Whites (%)*	*Difference (%)*
Some people say the CIA has been involved in importing cocaine for distribution in the black community. Do you think this is absolutely true, probably true, probably not true, or absolutely not true? (% responding true)	73	16	57
Some people say that HIV and AIDS are being used as part of a plot to deliberately kill African Americans. Do you think that this is absolutely true, probably true, probably not true, or absolutely not true? (% probably true and absolutely true)	62	21	41
Verdict [in the 1992 Rodney King trial] shows blacks cannot get justice in this country. (% agree)	81	27	54
Do you think blacks and other minorities receive same treatment as whites in the criminal justice system? (% no)	54	9	45

Source: Robert G. Smith and Richard Seltzer, *Contemporary Controversies and the American Radical Divide.* (Lanham, Md.: Rowman & Littlefield, 2000), 86, 88, 121, 128.

26% of whites said there was a strong decline, while 42% of blacks and 40% of whites saw a moderate decline, and 31% of blacks and 25% of whites said family life had held steady.[46] Roughly the same percentages of blacks and whites strongly advocated balancing the budget, cutting personal income taxes, reforming the welfare system, and reforming Medicare.[47] Percentages were also nearly even in responses to questions on abortion and marijuana.[48]

Hunter and Bowman found that "the majority of Americans do not . . . engage in identity politics—a politics that insists that opinion is mainly a function of racial, ethnic, or gender identity or identities rooted in sexual preference."[49] While there are some disagreements on specific issues and

[46]Hunter and Bowman, *The State of Disunion,* Table 4.C.

[47]*Washington Post*/Kaiser Family Foundation/Harvard School of Public Health Survey Project, *The Four Americas,* 73–74.

[48]Hunter and Bowman, *The State of Disunion,* Table 94, Table 93.I.

[49]James Davison Hunter and Carl Bowman, *The State of Disunion: 1996 Survey of American Political Culture,* vol. 1, *Summary Report* (Ivy, Va.: In Medias Res Educational Foundation, 1996), 34.

policies, this study found more similarities than discrepancies. Even when asked about such divisive issues as the direction of changes in race and ethnic relations, the similarities across lines were considerable. Thirty-two percent of blacks, 37% of Hispanics, and 40% of whites felt these relations were holding steady; 46%, 53%, and 44%, respectively, felt they had declined. (The remainder felt that they had improved.)[50] That is, on most issues, four out of five—or more—agreed with one another, while those who differed amounted to less than 20% of all Americans. There is no anti-anything majority here, nor is there likely to be one in the future.

Similarly, 81% of blacks, like 71% of all Americans, in a 1998 survey thought that blacks and whites "generally get along fairly well."[51] When asked in 1994, "When today's/your children reach your age, do you expect that race relations will have improved, will have worsened, or will be about the same as today?" a close 48% of blacks and 51% of whites concurred that relations would be better.[52] In 1998, the Gallup Organization found a similar position among whites and blacks (60% of whites and 54% of blacks agreed) that only a few white people dislike blacks. Only 5% of blacks and 2% of whites said that "almost all white people dislike blacks."[53]

Notably, nearly half of both blacks and whites want to set racial questions aside as much as possible. In a 1995 survey for *Newsweek,* Princeton Survey Research Associates found that 48% of blacks and 47% of whites agreed that the Census Bureau should stop collecting information on race and ethnicity "in an effort to move toward a more color-blind society—even if it becomes more difficult to measure progress on civil rights and poverty programs."[54]

As already suggested, many pollsters and those who write about their findings, tend to play up small differences and downplay large similarities. During my days at Columbia University's Bureau of Applied Social Research we were advised to use the "fully-only" writing device. Thus, we would write that fully, say 9% agreed with whatever we wanted to play up, while only 43% disagreed. It should hence be stressed that in most of the figures cited above the differences among the races are much smaller than the similarities. On most issues there are no findings that could be considered, even by a far-fetched interpretation, to show a "white" versus a "black" position, nor a

---

[50]Hunter and Bowman, *The State of Disunion,* vol. 2, Table 4J.

[51]Survey by Roper Starch Worldwide. Cited in "Thinking about Ethnicity," *Public Perspective* (February/March 1998): 58.

[52]Survey by Louis Harris and Associates, 26–29 October 1995. Cited in "Thinking about Ethnicity," *Public Perspective* (February/March 1998): 59.

[53]Thirty-one percent of blacks and 33% of whites stated that many whites "dislike blacks." Survey by the Gallup Organization, 5–7 October 1995. Cited in "Thinking about Ethnicity," *Public Perspective* (February/March 1998): 58.

[54]Survey by Princeton Survey Research Associates for *Newsweek,* 1–3 February 1995. Cited in "Rethinking Race," *Public Perspective* (June/July 1997): 41.

single position of any group of people of other colors. That is, none of these findings suggest—in fact, they directly contradict—that race determines a person's views, values, or votes.

Most interestingly, *differences among social groups that include both blacks and whites are often larger than differences among races.* For instance, sociologist Janet Saltzman Chafetz concludes her study of such differences with the statement that "in any dimension one wishes to examine—income, education, occupation, political and social attitudes, etc.—the range of difference within one race or gender group is almost as great as that between various groups."[55] A 1994 Kansas City study showed that "income differences between age groups in a given race are greater than income differences between entire races."[56] While much has been made of the digital divide, Alan Westin—the most systematic surveyor of this field—reports that differences in the use of computers and the Internet are larger between men and women than between the races.[57]

Rather little attention has been paid in this context to the fact that while African Americans are the least mainstreamed group, there is a growing black middle class, many members of which have adopted lifestyles and aspirations similar to those of other middle-class Americans—and which diverge from those of other black Americans. For instance, a 1998 *Wall Street Journal* public opinion poll showed differences within distinct classes of a single race to be greater than differences among those races, on several, albeit not on all, key issues. For instance, 82% of middle-class whites and 70% of non-middle-class whites reported satisfaction with their personal finances (a disparity of 12%), while 74% of middle-class blacks and 56% non-middle-class blacks reported such satisfaction (a difference of 18%). The differences of 12% and 18%, respectively, are higher than the differences in opinion between the races (8% difference between middle-class whites and blacks, and 14% difference between non-middle-class whites and blacks).[58] (William Julius Wilson is among the scholars who have pointed out the significance of class differences when studying racial differences.)

I am not suggesting that race makes no difference in a person's position, 35
feelings, or thinking. And one can find polls, especially in response to single questions, that show strong racial influence. However, race does not *determine* a person's response and often, on all important matters, Americans of different social backgrounds share many convictions, hopes, and goals, even in recent

---

[55]Janet Saltzman Chafetz, "Minorities, Gender, Mythologies, and Moderation." *Responsive Community* 4, no. 1 (Winter 1993/94): 41.

[56]E. Thomas McLanahan, "Do 'Disparities' Always Prove the Existence of Discrimination?" *Kansas City Star,* 25 October 1994, sec. B, p. 5.

[57]Alan Westin, personal communication, April 1998.

[58]John Simons, "Even Amid Boom Times, Some Insecurities Die Hard," *Wall Street Journal,* 10 December 1998, sec. A, p. 10.

years, as we see the beginning of the decline of the white majority. Moreover, each racial group is far from homogeneous in itself. Differences within each group abound, further contradicting any notion of a nonwhite united majority facing a unanimous white group, a view often promoted by champions of identity politics.

Race: A Social Construction

Many social scientists call into question the very category of race drawn on by those who foresee increasing racial diversity. Alain Corcos, author of several books on genetics, race, and racism, notes that "race is a slippery word," one that is understood in varying manners at various times, one without a single definition we may readily grasp. He writes, "Race is a slippery word because it is a biological term, but we use it every day as a social term. . . . Social, political, and religious views are added to what are seen as biological differences. . . . Race also has been equated with national origin, . . . with religion . . . with language."[59]

The diversity of characteristics by which race is and has been defined points to its unsatisfactory quality as a tool for categorizing human beings. Both anthropological and genetic definitions of race prove inadequate, because while each describes divisions among the human population, each fails to provide reliable criteria for making such divisions. As Corcos notes, they "are vague. They do not tell us how large divisions between populations must be in order to label them races, nor do they tell us how many there are."[60] Importantly, "These things are, of course, all matters of choice for the classifier."[61]

Considering the biology of race, Corcos notes that biological divisions do not hold up. "Geographical and social barriers have never been great enough to prevent members of one population from breeding with members of another. Therefore, any characteristic which may have arisen in one population at one time will be transferred later to other populations through mating."[62] Corcos further chronicles scientific and social scientific attempts to categorize humans into races by such sundry methods as craniology and evaluating skin coloring, nose size and shape, and other physical characteristics. Despite these efforts, "Scientists have been unable to classify humanity into races using physical characteristics such as skin color, shape of nose or hair,

---

[59]Alain Corcos, *The Myth of Human Races* (East Lansing, Mich.: Michigan State University Press, 1984), 10–11.

[60]Ibid., 12.

[61]Ibid.

[62]Ibid., 201.

eye color, brain size, etc. They also have been unable to use characteristics such as blood type or other genetic markers."[63]

Social anthropologist Audrey Smedley, professor at Virginia Commonwealth University, shares these observations. She admits there are apparent biophysical differences among humans, but reminds us that "race originated as the imposition of an arbitrary value system on the facts of biological (phenotypic) variations in the human species."[64] That is, she suggests race is imposed from *without,* not generated from within. Race "was the cultural invention of arbitrary meanings applied to what appeared to be natural divisions within the human species. The meanings had social value but no intrinsic relationship to the biological diversity itself."[65]

Racial categories are learned rather than innate. Like other cultural tra- 40
ditions such as food, clothing, and musical preferences, racial categories are passed from generation to generation. Psychological anthropologist Lawrence Hirschfeld finds "that children as young as three have a complex understanding of society's construction of racial categories. Children do not sort people into different races based only on physical differences. . . . Society's 'racial' assignments provide more of a signature of 'other' than do physical differences. For children, race does not define the person."[66]

To put these concepts in plainer language; at first it seems obvious that there are black, brown, yellow, and white people. But upon second thought, we realize that there are great differences within each group, even if we choose to focus on, for example, skin color rather than on, say, manners. And, these differences do not parallel one another. That is, persons with darker skin are not necessarily short (or tall), and so on. Race, which has been magnified in recent decades by identity politics, is but one imprecise social category, one that does not define human conduct any more than numerous other social attributes (especially income), and often to a much lesser extent.

Particularly telling is that many groups once considered separate races 100 years ago are no longer so viewed today. The classification changed in

[63]Ibid. See also Maurice Berger, *White Lies: Race and the Myths of Whiteness* (New York: Farrar, Straus, Giroux, 1999); Ian Haney-López, *White by Law: The Legal Construction of Race* (New York: New York University Press, 1996); Matthew Frye Jacobson, *Whiteness of a Different Color: European Immigrants and the Alchemy of Race* (Cambridge: Harvard University Press, 1998); Joe L. Kincheloe et al., eds., *White Reign: Deploying Whiteness in America* (New York: St. Martin's Press, 1998); Valerie Melissa Babb, *Whiteness Visible: The Meaning of Whiteness in American Literature and Culture* (New York: New York University Press, 1998); Grace Elizabeth Hale, *Making Whiteness: The Culture of Segregation in the South* (New York: Pantheon Books, 1998).

[64]Audrey Smedley, *Race in North America: Origin and Evolution of a Worldview* (Boulder, Colo.: Westview Press, 1993), 22.

[65]Ibid.

[66]Lawrence A. Hirschfeld, personal communication to Melvin D. Williams. Cited in Melvin D. Williams, *Race for Theory and the Biophobia Hypothesis: Humanics, Humanimals, and Macroanthropology* (Westport, Conn.: Praeger, 1998), 96–97.

law, public policy, the press, and in the public mind. Jewish, Slavic, Irish, Polish, and many other ethnic groups were considered races in 1910 in the United States. Matthew Frye Jacobson refers to the category of race as "fabricated" in his aptly titled book, *Whiteness of a Different Color: European Immigrants and the Alchemy of Race.*[67] A DNA study conducted by Howard University found that some 30% of all black males tested had some white DNA.[68]

Especially important for the future "monochrome-ness" of American society is the way Hispanic Americans come to view themselves and to be characterized by others. The special significance of this development, surprisingly infrequently discussed, is that Hispanics constitute the fastest-growing, major American social group due to high levels of immigration, high rates of childbirth, and because the group is gaining in political self-awareness and experience. Given that the number of African Americans is growing much more slowly (mainly because there is very little immigration from Africa), and that this group already has a relatively high level of political presence and hence less room to grow in this area, Hispanics are very likely to overtake African Americans in the next decade as the leading non-European group in American society.

As a result, in the next decades, we are quite likely to stop talking about a black and white society, one in which Hispanics are not mentioned at all or only as an afterthought, as countless books and essays did in the recent past, and instead focus on the relationship between European Americans and Hispanic Americans. The picture that is going to emerge from such a change in perspective will be deeply affected by the way Hispanics are depicted.

Some attempts have been made to define Hispanics as a separate race— 45
a brown one. If such a characterization had caught on, it would have increased divisiveness in America; fortunately, from the viewpoint of those who favor a monochrome society, most Americans and the media continue to view Hispanics as an ethnic group rather than a race.

Attempts to change the social construction of Hispanics, however, continue. Instead of simply treating them as one white group among others (groups that differ in their features, for instance, many immigrants from the Middle East are quite "dark," but are viewed as whites in contemporary America), continuous attempts are being made to classify Hispanics as something different—and to lump them with the nonwhite groups. Thus, recent press reports employed the category "non-Hispanic whites," who are projected to lose their majority in July 2001 in California, and in later years all over America.[69]

---

[67]Jacobsen, *Whiteness of a Different Color.* See also Oscar Handlin, *Race and Nationality in American Life* (Boston: Little, Brown, 1957), 150–53.

[68]Debra J. Dickerson, "Roots Come with Strings Attached," *Washington Post,* 7 May 2000, sec. B, pp. 1–2.

[69]Todd S. Purdum, "Shift in the Mix Alters the Face of California," *New York Times,* 4 July 2000, sec. A, p. 1.

There is of course no God-given or scientific reason to classify Hispanics as different from other white ethnic groups. Indeed, the category of "non-Hispanic whites" reflects a mixture of the ways statistics are kept (which themselves reflect normative and political pressures) and an ideological agenda, although those who use this term do not necessarily subscribe to it or are even aware of this agenda. (As Orlando Paterson says, "These are all basically political decisions, the census always just reflects changing attitudes.")[70]

The ways Hispanics come to see themselves in the near future is the single most important factor in determining to what extent America will continue to be a primarily monochrome society. If Hispanics view themselves largely as white, continue to share basic American values, and recognize that they are not all of one kind (just the way other white groups are not), America's diversity will not overwhelm its essential unity. If Hispanics view themselves as if they were a racial minority, of one kind, and increasingly ally themselves with those African Americans who seek social and normative separateness (which by itself is a declining number), maintaining a monochrome America will be seriously challenged.

"Asian Americans" and "Latinos"?

The very notion that there are social groups called "Asian Americans" or "Latinos" is largely a statistical artifact (reflecting the way social data are coded and reported), promoted by some ethnic leaders, and a shorthand the media find convenient. Most so-called Asian Americans do not see themselves, well, as Asian Americans, and many resent being labeled this way.[71] Many Japanese Americans do not feel a particular affinity to Filipino Americans, Pakistani Americans, or Korean Americans.[72] And the feeling is rather reciprocal. As Professor Paul Watanabe, from the University of Massachusetts, an expert on Asian Americans and himself an American of Japanese descent, puts it: "There's this concept that all Asians are alike, that they have the same history, the same language, the same background. Nothing could be more incorrect."[73]

William Westerman of the International Institute of New Jersey com- 50
plains about Americans who tend to ignore the cultural differences among

---

[70]Quoted in Steven A. Holmes, "The Politics of Race and the Census," *New York Times,* 19 March 2000, sec. 4, p. 3.

[71]See, for example, Eric Liu, *The Accidental Asian: Notes of a Native Speaker* (New York: Random House, 1998).

[72]Lena H. Sun, "Cultural Differences Set Asian Americans Apart: Where Latinos Have Common Threads, They Have None," *Washington Post,* 10 October 1995, sec. A, p. 8.

[73]Quoted in John Powers, "The Myth of the Model Minority," *Boston Globe Magazine,* 9 January 1994, 8.

Asian nations, which reflect thousands of years of tradition. He wonders how the citizens of the United States, Canada, and Mexico would feel if they were all treated as indistinguishable "North Americans."[74]

The same holds for the so-called Latinos, including three of my sons. Americans of Hispanic origin trace their origins to many different countries and cultures.[75] Eduardo Diaz, a social service administrator, puts it this way: "There is no place called Hispanica. I think it's degrading to be called something that doesn't exist. Even Latino is a misnomer. We don't speak Latin."[76] A Mexican American office worker remarked that when she is called Latina it makes her think "about some kind of island."[77] Many Americans from Central America think of themselves as "mestizo," a term that refers to a mixture of Central American Indian and European ancestry. Among those surveyed in the National Latino Political Survey in 1989, the greatest number of respondents chose to be labeled by their country of origin, as opposed to "pan-ethnic" terms such as "Hispanic" or "Latino."[78]

A recent extensive survey comparing Mexican, Puerto Rican, Cuban, and Central/South American attitudes and political behavior found numerous differences among these groups. Support for legal abortion ranged from 32% (Central/South Americans) to almost double that (60%, Puerto Ricans). In response to a question about party affiliation, the percentage of Hispanics identifying themselves as Republicans ranged from 12% (Central/South Americans) to 34% (Cubans).[79] Large differences were also found in the rate to which different Latino groups became United States citizens, which reflected differences in their feelings both about their country of origin and their willingness to become Americans. The percentages of those who had become citizens ranged from 53% (Cubans) to 26% (Central/South Americans).[80]

Another study found that:

> Just as majorities often disdain minorities, minorities often dislike one another, sometimes more harshly than majorities. For example, an early

---

[74]Daniel O'Donnell, "Standing on Ceremony," *Ashbury Park Press,* 1 September 1996, sec. D, p. 1.

[75]Rodolfo O. de la Garza, "Introduction," in *Ignored Voices: Public Opinion Polls and the Latino Community,* ed. Rodolfo O. de la Garza (Austin, Tex.: Center for Mexican American Studies, 1987), 4.

[76]Quoted in Ferdinand M. De Leon and Sally MacDonald, "Name Power—Taking Pride, and Control, in Defining Ourselves," *Seattle Times,* 28 June 1992, sec. A, p. 1.

[77]Ibid.

[78]Rodolfo O. de la Garza, "Researchers Must Heed New Realities When They Study Latinos in the U.S.," *Chronicle of Higher Education,* 2 June 1993, sec. B, p. 1.

[79]Survey by *Washington Post*/Kaiser Family Foundation/Harvard University, June 30–August 30, 1999 cited in *Public Perspective* 11, no. 2 (May/June 2000): 12–13.

[80]*Washington Post*/Kaiser Family Foundation/Harvard University National Survey on Latinos in America, June 30–August 30, 1999, Available at http://www.kff.org/content/2000/3023/LatinoFullTopline.Final.PDF. Accessed 7/14/00.

> 1990s Harris poll found that 46% of Hispanic Americans and 42% of African Americans agreed that Asians are "unscrupulous, crafty, and devious in business," whereas only 27% of whites thought so. Fully 68% of Asians and 49% of African Americans agreed that Hispanics tend "to have bigger families than they are able to support"—as did 50% of whites. Some 33% of Hispanics and 22% of Asians believed that African Americans, "Even if given a chance, aren't capable of getting ahead"—in contrast to 12% of whites. And "when it comes between choosing between people and money, Jews will choose money," thought 54% of African Americans, 43% of Hispanics and 35% of Asians, but only 12% of non-Jewish whites.[81]

The significance of these and other such data is that far from seeing a country divided into two or three hardened minority camps, we are witnessing an extension of a traditional American picture: Americans of different origins identifying with groups of other Americans from the same country, at least for a while, but not with any large or more lasting group.

Far from there being a new coalition of nonwhite minorities soon to 55
gain majority status (something President Clinton points to and Jesse Jackson dreams about as a rainbow, one that contains all colors but white), the groups differ greatly from each other—and within themselves.

To reiterate, on numerous issues, the differences among various minority groups are as big or bigger than those between these groups and "Anglo" Americans. For instance, while fewer Cuban Americans agree with the statement that U.S. citizens should be hired over noncitizens than Anglos (42% of Cubans compared to 51% of Anglos), other Hispanic groups agree more strongly than Anglos (55% of Puerto Ricans and 54% of Mexican Americans).[82] Quotas for jobs and college admissions are favored only by a minority of any of these four groups studied, but Cubans differ from Mexicans and Puerlo Ricans more (by 14%) than from Anglos (by 12%).[83]

The fact that various minorities do not share a uniform view, which could lead them to march lockstep with other minorities to a new America (as some on the left fantasize) is also reflected in elections. Cuban Americans tend to vote Republican, while other Americans of Hispanic origin are more likely to vote for Democratic candidates.[84] Amercians of Asian origin also cannot be counted on to vote one way or another. First-generation

---

[81]Philip Perlmutter, "From E Pluribus Unum to E Unum Pluribus," *American Outlook,* Summer 1999, 53–54.

[82]Rodolfo O. de la Garza, Louis DeSipio, F. Chris Garcia, and John Garcia, *Latino Voices: Mexican, Puerto Rican, and Cuban Perspectives on American Politics* (Boulder, Colo.: Westview Press, 1992), 102.

[83]Ibid., 110.

[84]de la Garza, "Researchers Must Heed New Realities When They Study Latinos in the U.S.," sec. B, pp. 1–3.

Vietnamese Americans tend to be strong anti-Communists and favor the Republican party, while older Japanese and Chinese Americans are more often Democrats, and Filipino Americans are more or less equally divided between the parties. (Of the Filipino Americans registered to vote, 40% list themselves as Democrats, 38% as Republicans, and 17% as independent.)[85]

The Lessons of "Nonwhite" States and Cities

Some social scientists argue that we can learn about the future, in which nonwhite majorities will prevail, by examining the states and cities in which minorities already comprise the majorities. For instance, Peter Morrison, former head of the Population Research Center at RAND, suggests that one can see the future in cities that have a majority composed of minorities.[86]

One clear way to examine the impact of the rise of nonwhite majorities is to study election results. They show, as did the survey data cited above, that people of a given racial background often do not vote for a candidate of their color—and above all, that nonwhite groups often do not jointly support any one candidate of any one color or racial background. Any suggestion that race or ethnicity determines for whom one casts one's vote is belied by the facts. For example, Peter Skerry notes that "when first elected to the San Antonio City Council in 1975, [the popular Henry] Cisneros was the candidate of the Anglo establishment and received a higher proportion of Anglo than Mexican votes cast."[87]

We often encounter the future first in California.[88] In a 1991 Los Ange- 60
les election for the California State Assembly, Korean American, Filipino American, and Japanese American groups each ran their own candidate, thus splitting the so called "Asian American" vote, not deterred by the fact that they thereby ensured the election of a white candidate.[89]

In some cities that contain nonwhite majorities, we find white, black, and Hispanic mayors alternating, despite only relatively small changes in the composition of the city population. For instance, in Los Angeles, which is roughly 64% nonwhite (specifically, nearly 40% Hispanic, 14% black, nearly

---

85Matt Miller, "Asian-Americans: A Political Enigma," *San Diego Union-Tribune,* 8 September 1996, sec. A, p. 1.

86Peter A. Morrison and William A. V. Clark, *Demographic Underpinnings of Political Empowerment in Multi-Minority Cities* (Santa Monica, Calif.: RAND, 1993), 3.

87Peter Skerry, *Mexican Americans: The Ambivalent Minority* (New York: Free Press, 1993), 34.

88Mirroring many counties in California, between 1992 and 1998, 43 U.S. counties became majority-minority. Overall, 225 counties in the country comprise nonwhite majorities. (Nancy Cleeland, "Beyond 2000: Orange County Diversity," *Los Angeles Times,* 28 September 1998, sec. A, p. 1.)

89Miller, "Asian-Americans."

10% Asian, and 0.5% American Indian according to the 1990 census),[90] Tom Bradley, an African American, served as mayor for 20 years, until 1993, when the citizens elected Richard Riordan, a white politician. New York City and San Francisco also have in recent years alternated between white and black mayors without witnessing any dramatic changes in the racial and ethnic backgrounds of those who inhabit those cities.

New York City, comprised of approximately 29% blacks, 24% Hispanics, and 7% Asians and Pacific Islanders (nearly 60% nonwhites),[91] elected the white Ed Koch, then chose the African American David Dinkins, followed by a white mayor, Rudolph Giuliani.[92] San Francisco, a city made up of roughly 55% minorities (approximately 11% black, 30% Asian, 14% Hispanic, and 0.5% American Indian),[93] was served by three white mayors from 1976 through 1995, but elected the African American Willie Brown in 1996. Dallas, which is about 30% black, 21% Hispanic, and 2% Asian, had no African American mayor until 1995.[94] Philadelphia, long served by white mayors, elected Wilson Goode to serve between 1984 and 1992 as the city's first African American mayor. Goode was followed by the white Edward Rendell in this city of nearly 40% blacks, 6% Hispanics, and 3% Asians. The fact that cities like Washington, D.C. (nearly 66% black)[95] and Detroit (nearly 76% black)[96] tend to elect black mayors is beside the point, because neither comprises a coalition of minorities but one minority, and the only one that usually envisions itself as a single group.

Additionally, Virginia, in which whites outnumber minorities significantly (1.5 million minorities and 4.8 million whites), has elected a black governor. L. Douglas Wilder served from 1989 to January 1994.[97] In the rural and conservative Second District of Georgia, a two-thirds white voter majority reelected Sanford D. Bishop, Jr., an African American Democrat, to serve as their representative.[98] The state of Washington, comprised of only 4.5%

---

[90]U.S. Bureau of the Census, *Statistical Abstract of the United States: 1995,* 115th ed. (Washington, D.C.: U.S. Government Printing Office, 1995), 45.

[91]Ibid.

[92]For an insightful analysis of politics, race, and ethnicity in New York City, see Jim Sleeper, *The Closest of Strangers: Liberalism and the Politics of Race in New York* (New York: W. W. Norton & Company, 1990).

[93]U.S. Bureau of the Census, *Statistical Abstract of the United States: 1995,* 46.

[94]Ibid., 44. Linda Kanamine, "Dallas Mayor: First for Texas," *USA Today,* 8 May 1995, sec. A, p. 3.

[95]U.S. Bureau of the Census, *Statistical Abstract of the United States: 1995,* 46.

[96]Ibid., 44.

[97]1992 data from Statistical Compendia Branch, Data User Services Division, Bureau of the Census, *1994 County & City Data Book* (Washington, D.C.: U.S. Government Printing Office, 1994), 2–3. Minorities in the *Data Book* are categorized as black, Hispanic, Asian, and Eskimo or Aleut.

[98]Kevin Sack, "In the Rural White South, Seeds of a Biracial Politics," *New York Times,* 30 December 1998, sec. A, p. 1.

Asian Americans, elected Gary Locke in 1996, putting in office the first Asian American governor in the mainland United States.[99] While one can find counter examples, the examples listed here indicate that the majority of minorities does not necessarily elect people of color, nor does the white majority necessarily elect white officials. Moreover, I expect more blurring in the future rather than less, given all the various vectors discussed in this analysis.

Intermarriage and the Rise of "Others"

Last but not least, the figures used by those who project a majority of minorities or the end of a white majority are misleading. These figures are based on a simplistic projection of past trends. How simplistic these projections often are can be quickly gleaned from the Census projection that the number of Native Americans will grow from 2,433,000 in 2000, or approximately 1% of the total population to 4,405,000, or approximately 1% of the total population by the year 2050, and to 6,442,000, or approximately 1% of the total population by the year 2100.[100] That is, 100 years and *no* change.

This tendency to depict the future as a continuation of the past is partic- 65
ularly misleading because it ignores the rapidly rising category of racially mixed Americans, the result of a rising number of cross-racial marriages and a rejection of monoracial categories by some others, especially Hispanic Americans.

One out of twelve marriages in 1995 (8.4%) were interracial/ethnic marriages. Intermarriage between Asian Americans and whites is particularly common; marriages between Hispanic Americans and whites are also rather frequent, while marriages between whites and blacks are the least common. In 1998, out-marriage by Hispanics of all generations totaled 16.7%, while non-Hispanic Asians out-married at a rate of 15% and non-Hispanic blacks out-married at a rate of 5%.[101]

Intermarriage between black and other Americans is less common, but also rising. "In 1990, 84% of all married black people over the age of 65 were

---

[99]Henry Weinstein, "Elections '96: 7 Democrats, 4 in GOP Win Governorships," *Los Angeles Times,* 6 November 1996, sec. A, p. 16.

[100]Population Projections Program, Population Division, U.S. Census Bureau, *Projections of the Total Resident Population by 5-Year Age Groups, Race, and Hispanic Origin with Special Age Categories: Middle Series, 1999 to 2000; Projections of the Total Resident Population by 5-Year Age Groups, Race, and Hispanic Origin with Special Age Categories: Middle Series, 2050 to 2070; Projections of the Total Resident Population by 5-Year Age Groups, Race, and Hispanic Origin with Special Age Categories: Middle Series, 2075 to 2100.* Available at http://www.census.gov/population/www/projections/natsum-T3.html. Accessed 7/5/00.

[101]Roberto Suro, "Mixed Doubles," *American Demographics,* November 1999: 58–59.

in both-black marriages, but only 53% of married blacks under 25 were," according to the Statistical Assessment Service.[102] And the Census Bureau finds that over the past 20 years, the number of marriages between blacks and whites has more than quadrupled, increasing from 65,000 in 1970 to 296,000 in 1994.[103] From 1960 to 1997, the percentage of all marriages that were interracial grew from 0.4% to 2.3%.[104] Similarly, researchers Douglas Besharov and Timothy Sullivan found that the number of black-white marriages constituted 1.7% of all marriages in 1960, but represented 6% of all marriages in 1990.[105] A study from the University of Michigan reports that in the 1940s about 2% of black men married white women, whereas by the 1980s about 8% did so. And while in the 1940s about 1% of married black women had married interracially, in the 1980s that figure had reached nearly 3%.[106] The number of intermarriages also increases with each subsequent generation living in the U.S. In the mid-1990s, slightly under 20% of first-generation Asian American women were intermarried, as opposed to slightly under 30% of the second generation and slightly over 40% of the third generation. Slightly under 10% of first-generation Hispanic women were intermarried, contrasting sharply with percentages in the mid-20s and mid-30s for second and third-generation women, respectively. Black intermarriage rates were much lower, even though there was an increase overall—no figures were over 5%.[107]

The trend toward intermarriage is strongest among the young; 30% of married Asian Americans have married outside the group, as have 16% of Hispanics and 11% of blacks in this age group.

> "This is the beginning point of a blending of the races," predicts William Frey, a sociologist at the State University of New York at Albany. It is likely "that in these households racial or ethnic attitudes will soften," he says in *American Demographics* (Nov. 1999), as families realize that they can embrace many cultures without losing any one facet of their identity.[108]

---

[102]Statistical Assessment Service, "Can Intermarriage Make You Smarter and Richer?" *Vital STATS,* August 1997. Available at http://www.stats.org/newsletters/9708/interrace2.htm. Accessed 7/3/00.

[103]Larry Bivins, "Experts: Increase in Mixed Marriages Gives Mixed Signals that Racism's on Rocks," *Detroit News,* 6 October 1996, sec. B, p. 5.

[104]U.S. Census Bureau data, cited in "Interracial Marriages: Percentage of All Marriages That Are Interracial, 1960–1997," *Public Agenda Online.* Available at http://www.publicagenda.org/issues/factfiles-detail.cfm?issue-type=family&list=17. Accessed 7/3/00.

[105]Ibid.

[106]Christopher Shea, "Intermarriage Rates Found to Be on the Rise," *Chronicle of Higher Education,* 2 May 1997, sec. A, p. 14.

[107]"The Melting Pot Survives," *The Economist,* 3 July 1999, 24.

[108]"Melting at Last," *The Wilson Quarterly* (Winter 2000): 11.

About half of third-generation Mexican Americans marry non-Hispanic whites; even higher numbers of Asian Americans do the same.[109] Gregory Rodriguez has provided figures on this phenomenon, as shown in Figure 1.[110]

Altogether, since 1970, the proportion of marriages among people of different racial or ethnic origin increased by 72%. The 1990 Census noted 1.5 million interracial marriages.[111] Some put the number of children of mixed-race parents at 3 million, not including Hispanic mestizos and black Americans who have European or Native American ancestry.[112]

Another indication of some blurring of the lines among the races in American society can be gleaned from the fact that in the 1990 Census, 4%, or 9.8 million Americans, chose to classify themselves as "others," i.e., not members of any particular racial group. In a Census 2000 practice run, this number had increased to 5.4% of the sample.[113] The increase from 4 to 5.4% may seem minor, but given the size of the population, many hundreds of thousands are involved.

Even if the trends already cited do not accelerate and continue only at the present pace, the figures for 2050 may read something like the following: 51% white; 14% multiracial; 35% minorities. Far from dividing the country still further, the rise of the "others" along with the fact that more and more Americans will be of mixed heritage, with divergent backgrounds, will serve to blur the racial lines. That is, while there may well be more Americans of non-European origin, a growing number of the American white majority will have a Hispanic daughter- or son-in-law, an Asian stepfather or stepmother, and a whole rainbow of cousins. If one must find a simple image for the future of America, Tiger Woods, or Hawaii, as I see it, seems more appropriate than a view of a country in which Louis Farrakhan and his followers and the Aryan Nation are threatening one another.

Regrettably, identity politics led the U.S. Census Bureau to drop the category of "other" from its 2000 Census. This in turn makes it more difficult for Americans of mixed background, or those who wish to forgo racial labels, to declare themselves as what I would like to call "All Americans."[114] Because the way the Census constructs its categories affects the way many others do—for instance, those overseeing admissions to colleges—the category of other or multiracial Americans may well not gain as fast as it would if the Census

[109] Linda Chavez, Response to "Is America Too White?" in *"What, Then, Is the American, This New Man?"*

[110] Gregory Rodriguez, *From Newcomers to Americans: The Successful Integration of Immigrants into American Society* (Washington, D.C.: National Immigration Forum, 1999).

[111] Anne-Marie O'Connor, "Race: Diversity at Work Has Role in Sharp Rise," *Los Angeles Times,* 27 April 1998, sec. A, p. 1.

[112] Michael Lind, "The Beige and the Black," *New York Times Magazine,* 16 August 1998, 38.

[113] John Fetto, "A Close Race," *American Demographics* (January 2000): 14.

[114] Amitai Etzioni, "New Issues: Rethinking Race," *Public Perspective* (June/July 1997): 39–41.

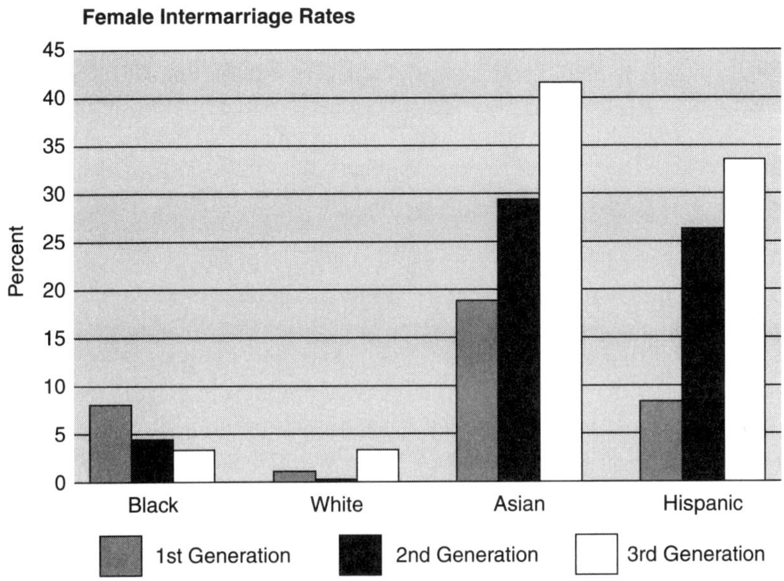

Figure 1. Female intermarriage rates. From: "Newcomers to America: The Successful Integration of Immigrants into American Society," National Immigration Forum, Washington, D.C., with permission.

followed its 1990 format. This in effect forces at least 10 million Americans into racial categories they seek to shed or modify, and makes American society seem more divided along racial lines than it actually is.

There are strong sociological reasons to argue that the U.S. Census reintroduce a nonracial category. (Others have suggested that this category be named "multiracial.") Inclusion of such a category would allow millions of Americans who are not, and do not see themselves as, members of any one race to be recognized as people with a blended heritage, reflecting the mixed heritage of America itself.

At issue is how we view ourselves as a nation. Are we going to continue 75
to be divided by race? Or will we welcome the blurring of the lines that divide the races?

The number of Americans who refused a monoracial category grew from about 2.5 million in 1970[115] to 9.8 million by 1990.[116] If the 2000

[115]U.S. Bureau of the Census, "Table 25: Population by Sex, Race, Residence, and Median Age: 1790 to 1973," *Statistical Abstract of the United States 1974,* 95th ed. (Washington, D.C.: U.S. Government Printing Office, 1974), 26.

[116]U.S. Census Bureau, "Quick Table P-IF: Age and Sex of Other Race Population: 1990," *U.S. Census Bureau American FactFinder Web Site.* Available at http://factfinder.census.gov/java-prod/dads.ui.pqr.PopQuickReportPage. Accessed 7/6/00.

Census had allowed, it is very likely that many more would have chosen the nonracial category. The main reason: rapidly increasing intermarriages.

The children of these couples are the main source of the continued increase in "multiracials." In addition, other Americans object to being racially categorized, or change their minds during their lifetime. The children of a couple I know—he black, she white—viewed themselves as white in primary school, black as adolescents, and now one passes as white and the other as black. What is gained by forcing such people to officially declare themselves one or the other?

The Census yielded to pressure from identity politics. It releases its data in two forms. One, a straightforward account; the other, "modified."[117] Here it reconfigured the statistics by re-boxing 9.8 million "other" Americans into monoracial categories!

Informal conversations with colleagues at the Census Bureau indicated that the Office of Management and Budget (which reviews all official questionnaires), yielded to pressure from several minority leaders. For instance, Ibrahim K. Sundiata from Brandeis University, who maintained that the "other" category reflects a drive to undermine black solidarity.[118]

Other African American leaders worried that the category of "other" would decrease the number of blacks in the nation's official statistics, and thus undermine the enforcement of antidiscrimination statutes and numerous social programs based on racial statistics. The NAACP and the Asian American Legal Defense and Education Fund, have disapproved of watering down nonwhite groups.[119]

As Gregory Rodriguez, a social researcher, states, "Some black groups, such as the NAACP and the Black Leadership Forum, a national coalition of the leaders of major civil rights organizations, are encouraging people to check just one box this year [2000]. The nuances and complexities of the multiracial future may be too threatening to the stark civil-rights era perspective forged in the segregationist past."[120]

Representative Carrie Meek (D-Fla.) explained: "The multiracial category would cloud the count of discrete minorities who are assigned to a lower track in public schools . . . kept out of certain occupations and whose progress toward seniority or promotion has been skewered."[121] Karen Narasaki, execu-

[117]U.S. Census Bureau, Population Division, Administrative Records and Methodology Research Branch, *Population of States by Modified Race and Hispanic Origin, April 1, 1990* (Washington, D.C.: U.S. Government Printing Office, 1998).

[118]Hannah Beech, "Don't You Dare List Them as 'Other,' " *U.S. News & World Report,* 8 April 1996, 56.

[119]Gregory Rodriguez, "Do the Multiracial Count?" *Salon,* 15 February 2000. Available at http://www.salon.com/news/feature/2000/02/15/census/index2.html. Accessed 7/3/00.

[120]Ibid.

[121]House Committee on Government Reform and Oversight, *Census 2000,* 106th Cong., 1st sess., April 23, 1997. Testimony of Bernard L. Ungar, Associate Director, Federal Management and Workforce Issues, General Government Division of United States, General Accounting Office.

tive director of the National Asian Pacific American Legal Consortium, said the civil rights groups "won less on the strength of our intellectual arguments, and more on our political strength, OMB backed down."[122]

Whatever the motives, the 2000 Census instead will allow Americans to mark as many racial categories as their hearts desire—as long as they define themselves racially. The battle is already on as to how the results will be counted. African and Asian American groups demand that anyone who marks their race in any combination be counted as fully theirs. The Census has not yet announced its pleasure.

Only if the Census Bureau were to release the information referring to blended Americans as "multiracial" (or "nonracial," best as "All American"), would it encourage the nation to view itself as less divided. There are several indications that the country is ready for widespread changes in our social categories and thinking. Georgia and Indiana have already required government agencies to use the multiracial category. In California there is an Association for MultiEthnic Americans,[123] and Ohio, Illinois, Georgia, Indiana, and Michigan have introduced legislation to create a multiracial category on college applications.[124]

The notion that everybody who has any features shared by many African 85
Americans and less common in other groups is black is particularly troubling, Colin Powell, of all people, articulated it when he objected to Tiger Woods considering himself All American, stating: "In America . . . when you look like me, you're black." Such views mirror the position of the American South (and South African apartheid) that everyone who has one drop of black blood, is all black. (Malcolm X quipped, "That must be *mighty* powerful blood.")[125] As Michael Lind says, "We're back to the one drop rule . . . I'm disgusted with the whole thing. This census should have been the first one not to identify people by race."[126] To reiterate, all concerned would be better off if we moved away from such rigid and immutable categorizations of people.

Further Moderation of Racial and Ethnic Leadership

Predicting the political attitudes of leaders is especially difficult, surely as compared to demographic trends. One reason is that these attitudes are affected by many considerations including the conditions of the economy and

---

[122]Quoted in Steven A. Holmes, "The Politics of Race and the Census."

[123]More information about the Association of MultiEthnic Americans is available at http://www.ameasite.org/. Accessed 7/3/00.

[124]Walter Lee Dozer, "Race: It's No Longer a Matter of Black and White," *Tampa Tribune,* 29 November 1995, sec. "Baylife," p. 1.

[125]Geneva Overholser, "Look at Tiger Woods and See the Face of America's Future," *International Herald Tribune,* 22 June 2000, 9.

[126]Quoted in Steven A. Holmes, "The Politics of Race and the Census." For much additional fine discussion see Peter Skerry, *Counting on the Census* (Washington, D.C.: Brookings Institution Press, 2000).

which party controls the White House and Congress. However, for the following reasons I expect a secular trend of continued moderation from minority leadership over the next decades. (There will of course be exceptions, but I am speaking of the general pattern.) The part of moderation I am focusing on here is the one relevant to the issue at hand; the move from separatism and identity politics to "normal" interest group politics, that implicitly accept the basic societal framework.

One of the main reasons is the relative decline of African Americans in the total demographic and political picture. The Census Bureau has projected that the African American population, which currently, in the year 2000, makes up approximately 13% of the total U.S. population, will grow to approximately 15% in 2050, where it will remain steady to 2100.[127] In contrast, the Hispanic population, which currently makes up approximately 12% of the total U.S. population, is projected to rise to approximately 24% of the total U.S. population in 2050 and approximately 33% in 2100.[128] The Hispanic population is going to grow more rapidly because there is every reason to expect much more immigration of Hispanic origin than from Africa. (One should also note that whatever immigration there is from the West Indies and Haiti, these immigrants do not necessarily see themselves as African American or even part of one black community.)

The relative increase of the role of Hispanics versus blacks is significant because so far "minorities" has been largely identified in people's minds with blacks. Indeed, very often reference to race relations still evokes the term black and white while other groups are not mentioned at all or only as a second thought. This will change in the future as Hispanics continue to grow in relative size as well as in political awareness and organization.

The difference is especially relevant because blacks have been much slower to intermarry and otherwise be absorbed into the American society than other minorities. And on average, their leadership has been less moderate and more given to identity politics than the leaders of other groups. However, black leadership recently has been becoming less confrontational. (Compare, for instance, the speeches of Reverend Al Sharpton and Louis Farrakhan in recent years to a decade earlier.) There are numerous reasons for this trend. Not least of them is the rapid increase in the proportion of blacks that are middle class who, on average, tend to be more moderate than other blacks. The black middle class has grown significantly since the advent of the civil

---

[127]Data extrapolated from figures in Population Projections Program, Population Division, Census Bureau, *Projections of the Total Resident Population by 5-Year Age Groups, Race, and Hispanic Origin with Special Age Categories: Middle Series, 2050 to 2070;* and Population Projections Program, Population Division, Census Bureau, *Projections of the Total Resident Population by 5-Year Age Groups, Race, and Hispanic Origin with Special Age Categories: Middle Series, 2075 to 2100.* Available at http://www.census.gov/population/www/projections/natsum-T3.html. Accessed 7/5/00.

[128]Ibid.

rights movement, and has "quadrupled since the '60s, doubling in the '80s alone."[129] In 1998, 40% of blacks defined themselves as middle class.[130] And, as Henry Louis Gates, Jr., states, "We don't have to pretend any longer that 35 million people can ever possibly be members of the same economic class. . . . Nor do they speak with one single voice, united behind one single leader. As each of us knows, we have never been members of one social or economic class and never will be."[131]

One may wonder whether Hispanic leadership in the future may be 90
driven to less moderate identity politics. This is of course hard to predict. However, one notes that there will be also a growing Hispanic middle class and there is no obvious reason to expect that their tendency to intermarry and move up the economic and social ladders will slow down significantly. In contrast, Asian American leaders have tended, on average, to be so local and conservative in their orientation that they may well move a bit toward identity politics. Such a move, however, would still leave them rather moderate by comparison to many earlier African American leaders.

All said and done, while identity politics may well not end, one can expect—with the dethroning and simultaneous moderation of large parts of the African American leadership of minorities—identity politics to subside to a considerable extent. This would be of considerable significance for the future of the monochrome society because it would serve to make it not merely a demographic trend and one evident among the members of various social groups, but also encompass the orientation of the leadership, which in turns affects the way we see ourselves and each other.

Another reason several African American leaders object to a multiracial category is that race data are used for the enforcement of civil rights legislation in employment, voting rights, housing and mortgage lending, health care services, and educational opportunities.[132] These leaders fear that the category could decrease the number of blacks in official statistics, and thus undermine efforts to enforce antidiscrimination statutes and undercut numerous social programs based on racial quotas.

What is a Race Anyhow?

One may wonder if the number of Americans involved is large enough to justify what at first seems like a tempest in a teapot. The underlying reason is that one tends to underestimate the number of Americans who might

---

[129] Salim Muwakkil, "Color Bind," *In These Times* 22, no. 8 (22 March 1998): 11.

[130] Abigail Thernstrom and Stephan Thernstrom, "Black Progress: How Far We've Come—and How Far We Have to Go," *The Brookings Review* 16, no. 2 (Spring 1998): 12.

[131] Henry Louis Gates, Jr., "The Two Nations of Black America," *The Brookings Review* 16, no. 2 (Spring 1998): 7.

[132] House Committee on Government Reform and Oversight, Testimony of Bernard L. Ungar. [See note 121 for full bibliographic information.]

qualify for the new category because one assumes that only those of a mixed racial heritage may fall into the All American box. Actually, there are considerable differences in color and other racial features within all racial groups, which makes the question of who is in versus out much more flexible than it often seems. For instance, many dark-skinned Hispanics who do not see themselves as black, and many light-skinned African Americans who do not wish to pass as white, would be free to choose the new category.

One should also note that those who study race professionally, especially physical and cultural anthropologists, strongly object to the concept of racial categorization. They point out that no single gene can be used to differentiate one race from another; moreover, indicators from blood types to texture of hair vary a great deal both among and within groups considered to be of one race. Indeed, the American Anthropological Association passed a resolution stating that "differentiating species into biologically defined 'race' has proven meaningless and unscientific."

The Merits of a New Category

Dropping the whole social construction of race does not seem in the 95
cards, even if the most far-reaching arguments against affirmative action and for a "color-blind" society win the day. However, there are strong sociological reasons to favor the inclusion of a multiracial category in the 2010 Census.

Introducing a multiracial category has the potential to soften racial lines that now divide America by rendering them more like economic differences and less like caste lines. Sociologists have long observed that a major reason the United States experiences relatively few confrontations along class lines is that Americans believe they can move from one economic stratum to another. (For instance, workers become forepersons, and forepersons become small business owners, who are considered middle class.) Moreover, there are not sharp class demarcation lines in this country as there are in England; in America many workers consider themselves middle class, dress up to go to work, and hide their tools and lunches in briefcases, while middle-class, super-liberal professors join labor unions. A major reason confrontations in America occur more often along racial lines is that color lines currently seem rigidly unchangeable.

If the new category is allowed, if more and more Americans choose this category in future decades, as there is every reason to expect given the high rates of intermarriage and a desire by millions of Americans to avoid being racially boxed in, the new Census category may go a long way in determining if America in the next century will be less caste-like and more class-like, a society in which differences are blurred.

Skeptics may suggest that how one marks a tiny box on the 2000 Census form is between one's self and the keepers of statistics. But, as this sociologist sees it, if the multiracial concept is allowed into the national statistics, it will also enter the social vocabulary. It will make American society less stratified along racial lines, less rigidly divided, and thus more communitarian.

The Ultimate Question

At stake is the question of what kind of America we envision for the longer run. Some see a complete blur of racial lines with Americans constituting some kind of new hybrid race. *Time* ran a cover story on the subject, led by a computer composite of a future American with some features of each race, a new, rather handsome breed (almond-shaped eyes, straight but dark hair, milk chocolate skin). This would take much more than a change in racial nomenclature, but it could serve as a step in that direction.

Others are keen to maintain strict racial lines and oppose intermarriage; 100
these same people often seek to maintain the races as separate "nations." (The term nation is significant because it indicates a high degree of tribalism.) In a world full of interracial strife, this attitude—however understandable its defensive nature in response to racial prejudice and discrimination—leaves at least this communitarian greatly troubled. The more communitarian view seems to be one in which those who seek to uphold their separate group identities will do so (hopefully viewing themselves and being viewed as subgroups of a more encompassing community rather than as separate nations), but those who seek to redefine themselves will be enabled to do so, leading to an ever larger group that is free from racial categorization.

If a multiracial category is included further down the road, maybe in the 2010 Census, we may wish to add one more category, that of "multi-ethnic" origin, one which most Americans might wish to check. Then we would live to recognize the full importance of my favorite African American saying: We came in many ships but we now ride in the same boat.

Multiculturalism or American Creed?

All this suggests that foreseeable changes in America's demography do not imply that the American creed is being or will be replaced by something called "multiculturalism."[133] Roberto Suro reminds us that we do not need to divest ourselves of plurality in order to achieve harmony. Suro writes,

---

[133]As Peter Skerry states, ". . . as an animating force in our communities and in our national life, assimilation is alive and well." Peter Skerry, "Do We Really Want Immigrants to Assimilate?" *Society* (March/April 2000): 69. See also, Peter D. Salins, *Assimilation, American Style* (New York: Basic Books, 1997); Charles Taylor, *Multiculturalism and the Politics of Recognition* (Princeton, N.J.: Princeton University Press, 1992); and Daniel Callahan, "Universalism and Particularism: Fighting to a Draw," *Hastings Center Report* 30, no. 1 (2000): 37–44.

> Americans have never thought of themselves as a single people as the Germans do. Although white, English-speaking Christians of European ancestry have set most of the norms for American society, there is still no sense of a *Volk* (a group that shares a common ancestry and culture and that embodies the national identity). Ideas, not biology, are what generate oneness and homogeneity in the United States, and so long as faith in those ideas has remained strong, the country has shown an extraordinary capacity to absorb people of many nationalities.[134]

The American creed always has had room for pluralism of subcultures, of people upholding some of the traditions and values of their countries of origin, from praying to playing in their own way. But American pluralism should be bound by a shared framework if America is to be spared the kind of ethnic tribalism of the type that—when driven to extremes—has torn apart countries as different as Yugoslavia and Rwanda, and has even reared its ugly head in well-established democracies such as Canada and the United Kingdom (where Scottish separatism is on the rise).

The social, cultural, and legal elements that constitute the framework that holds together the diverse mosaic are well known.[135] They include a commitment by all parties to the democratic way of life, to the Constitution and its Bill of Rights, and to mutual tolerance.[136] The mosaic is further fortified by a strong conviction that one's station in life is determined by hard work and saving, by taking responsibility for one's self and one's family. And, most Americans still share a strong sense that while we are different in some ways, in more ways we are joined by the shared responsibilities of providing a good society for our children and ourselves, one free of racial and ethnic strife, and providing the world with a model of a country whose economy and polity are thriving.

QUESTIONING THE TEXT

1. What is Etzioni's main thesis in this essay? What evidence does he present in support of that thesis, and how is that supporting evidence organized?

---

[134]Roberto Suro, *Strangers Among Us: How Latino Immigration is Transforming America* (New York: Alfred A. Knopf, 1998), 303–04.

[135]Peter I. Rose gives us an important understanding of cultural pluralism as first substantially presented by philosopher Horace Kallen in the early 1900s: "The basic premise was that there is strength in diversity, that being proud of one's past and appreciating where one came from complements rather than compromises membership in an ever more heterogeneous society. . . . Kallen saw the orchestra—that is, the society—as consisting of groups of instruments (nationalities) playing their separate parts while together making beautiful music resonant with harmony and good feeling." Peter I. Rose, *Tempest-Tost: Race, Immigration, and the Dilemmas of Diversity* (New York: Oxford University Press, 1997), 65.

[136]Etzioni, *The New Golden Rule,* 189–216.

2. After a first reading of the essay, do you have any strong responses to any particular part of it? After a second reading, do you feel differently? Discuss your reactions with classmates, and see if you can articulate reasons for your responses to the essay. Do your reactions have to do with the ideas or arguments, or with the tone or other stylistic features of the essay? Explain.
3. The argument in "The Monochrome Society" relies heavily on statistical evidence for support. Choose one or two supporting claims that Etzioni backs up with statistics—perhaps those claims that seem particularly intriguing or surprising—and examine the statistical evidence. Use the footnotes to find the sources of each piece of evidence, and look up the sources in the library. Then consider the following questions for each source: What study produced the data? Who performed the study? Are the researchers affiliated with a university, research institute, or other organization? How was the data obtained? Do the researchers explain the methodology they used? Given this information, do you think Etzioni uses the source fairly in making his claims? Does your analysis of Etzioni's statistical evidence in the instances you examined change your impression of his argument? Why, or why not?

MAKING CONNECTIONS

4. Compare Etzioni's vision of the "monochrome" or "multicultural" society with Zora Neale Hurston's depiction of life in her hometown of Eatonville, Florida, in "How It Feels to Be Colored Me" (p. 414). How does Etzioni's multicultural vision differ from or resemble the all-black town Hurston describes? What does this comparison suggest about the potential to achieve lasting racial harmony in the United States? What insight does it provide into the feasibility of Etzioni's views? Compose your answer as an argument that defends or opposes Etzioni's position.
5. Etzioni argues that race is a "social construction." Do other authors in this chapter, whether they address race directly or not, support this view? Choose an author who you think might also see race or ethnicity as a social construct, and describe how that author's opinion diverges from or parallels Etzioni's.

JOINING THE CONVERSATION

6. Etzioni speculates that if the U.S. Census and other demographic surveyors allowed a "multiracial" category, and if increasing numbers of Americans identified themselves with this category, the United States

would become "less caste-like and more class-like, a society in which differences are blurred" (paragraph 97). He presents this potential outcome as positive, in that "the United States experiences relatively few confrontations along class lines," which Americans often consider quite permeable (paragraph 96). Think about this proposition, and discuss with classmates the possible ramifications of the blurring of racial categories that Etzioni describes. Do you agree that it would be a good thing for race and ethnicity to become categories that are more like the economic class distinctions in the United States? Why, or why not?

7. Do some research into public debates about some aspect of affirmative action, such as discussions of affirmative action programs in college admissions or in the military. Write your own argument on the issue, using Etzioni's essay as a source. You might cite some of his claims in direct support of your own. Or, you might use his claims as potential counterarguments to your position, citing them and then refuting them.

EBOO PATEL
On Nurturing a Modern Muslim Identity

What does it mean to be a Muslim in the contemporary world? Some Westerners would probably try to ignore this question altogether, were it not for the unsettling politics of the Middle East. Even though large Muslim populations exist in many Western countries—including the United States—until recently, relatively few non-Muslims in our part of the world have taken the time to understand the Muslim heritage or the Islamic faith. Now, as Muslims in the Middle East rediscover the political leverage they once had on the world stage, the industrialized West is working to learn more about Muslim beliefs and practices.

One problem, of course, is that the practice of Islam is as conflicted as the practice of any other religion—Christianity included. Islam may seem like a cohesive and threatening religion to some Americans or Europeans, but in fact the two billion Muslims who follow it are from diverse communities wrestling with many philosophical and political choices.

Eboo Patel, a Rhodes Scholar at Oxford University, examines part of this conflict in his essay "On Nurturing a Modern Muslim Identity," published online by the journal Religious Education *and in print in* Crosscurrents *(Summer 2003). The essay, originally prepared for the Religious Education in a Global Society Conference organized by the Temple for Understanding in January 2002, draws a contrast between the fundamentalism of Al Qaida and the Taliban and more progressive forms of Islam. I won't pretend to know how accurately Patel describes the good works of the Aga Khan Development Network, but I am persuaded by Patel's insight that institutions are essential in shaping identities. If we want to raise children who think and act responsibly, we have to support schools, organizations, publications, and societies that embody the best of those traditions. That's as true for Muslims as for any other group or culture.*

A Muslim activist, Patel (b. 1976) is the founding director of the Chicago-based Interfaith Youth Core. He was recently recognized by the Utne Reader *as one of its "Young Visionaries" for his efforts to enhance interfaith cooperation. His personal heroes include Martin Luther King Jr., Catholic worker activist Dorothy Day, and the Dalai Lama.* —J.R.

A few days after the beginning of the bombing in Afghanistan, the Taliban organized a field trip for a handful of Western journalists to see the devastation. I was in Oxford at the time, and watched on Britain's Channel Four News as the convoy of white news correspondents passed a group of Afghan kids fixing a bicycle on the side of the road. One of the kids, who couldn't have been more than twelve, took a break from his work, stepped towards the convoy, flashed a menacing look and offered an insulting finger. Then he stepped back, smiled and waved.

With only this tidbit of evidence, we can extrapolate this story in several different directions. Perhaps this kid was frustrated by what he saw as yet another wave of foreign intruders in his land. Maybe he was just a scowly pre-adolescent.

I cannot help but think of him as an impressionable young Muslim. And as I watched him, I found myself wondering what he would consider an authentic Muslim identity as he grew up. Would he use his face to condemn other ways of being, believing and belonging, and his hands to attempt to destroy them? Or would his face be open to and welcoming of modern pluralism and his hands be able to contribute to it? The path he chooses has everything to do with the religious education he gets.

New York Times Foreign Affairs columnist Thomas Friedman recently has written that World War III will be fought against religious totalitarianism. Religious totalitarianism is not just the belief that one religion is right, but also that there is only one correct interpretation of that religion and everyone should practice it or else. Violence is only one arm of this system. Friedman argues that the real battleground is religious education, where the ideology of religious totalitarianism is fomented. Fifteen of the nineteen September 11 hijackers had Saudi passports. It's not too much of a stretch to think of them as products of an education system which wrapped an anti-modern ideology in Islamic rhetoric and injected it into impressionable young men.

For people who have been reading the media on the contemporary state 5
of the Muslim world, this will be a familiar story. The *New York Times,* the *International Herald Tribune,* the *New Yorker* and other publications which pride themselves on being in the know have pointed out the influence of religious totalitarians. In a recent *Sunday New York Times* in Winter 2001, a Malaysian lawyer and writer said: "The Saudis have used the prestige attendant on the fact that they are the guardians of the two holy centers, Mecca and Medina, and their enormous wealth, to propagate their own interpretation of the Koran. An underlying tenet of the Wahhabi* approach is this pan-Islamic sense that demands that converted people should be leached of their culture."

This is the same line that V. S. Naipaul* has been pushing for two decades: that Islam is a culture-crushing force. It will replace your language, your buildings, your clothes and your prayers. Furthermore, in its most militant and virulent form, Islam will take your sons and turn them into human bombs. And you should be thankful for it.

Is this true? Yes and no. First of all, Islam in and of itself does nothing. It is a word which stands for a deep and complex idea—submission to the will of God. People who call themselves Muslims seek to interpret this idea of

---

Wahhabi: a member of the Muslim puritan movement founded in the eighteenth century in central Arabia by Muhammad ibn Abd al-Wahhab and adopted by the Saudi family

V. S. Naipaul (b. 1932): Sir Vidiadhar Surajprasad, Trinidadian novelist of Indian descent

submission to the will of God in concrete ways in particular places and times. Muslims do things.

The problem is that we live in a time when the Muslim totalitarians are dominating. Why? Because they are building institutions that propagate their interpretation of Islam—just as the Christian totalitarians in America have powerful institutions; and the Jewish totalitarians in Israel have powerful institutions; and the Hindu totalitarians in India have powerful institutions.

What do I mean by institutions? Lobbying groups that pass policies, political organizations that get people elected, television and radio and magazines and publishing houses which articulate ideas, schools and universities, youth organizations and women's groups, bodies which raise and distribute money.

Al Qaida is a network of institutions: Schools and mosques which teach 10
eight year olds a certain ideology; organizations which lead them to Afghanistan; training camps which make them soldiers; manuals which offer advice on the prayers to whisper while engaging in violence. The religious identity—which is to say, the ways of being, believing, and belonging in relation with the transcendant—of too many young Muslims is being shaped by these institutions.

Perhaps the best way to understand the influence of institutions upon identity is to consider a food analogy. Many of my students come from small towns around the Midwest. Several became vegetarians when they moved to Chicago. When they return home, they find it difficult to refrain from eating meat. The reason is simple: In Chicago, the institutions of vegetarianism abound. There are several excellent vegetarian restaurants, many grocery stores have large sections of vegetarian items, vegetarian cookbooks are readily available in bookstores and communities of vegetarians are not hard to find. Such institutions are a rarity in Rantool and Kankakee, and therefore a vegetarian identity is difficult to maintain in those areas.

But as Susan Sontag said in her acceptance speech for the Jerusalem Prize, "Whatever is happening, there is always something else going on." We should rightfully be concerned about the influence the Muslim totalitarians are having upon Muslim religious identity, but we should also be aware of alternative efforts. I speak here of the progressive institution-building efforts of the Aga Khan Development Network, founded and led by Prince Karim al-Husseini Aga Khan IV. The Aga Khan is the spiritual leader of the world's 15 million Ismaili Muslims, a Shia community that believes that Allah provided the world the Prophet, the Qur'an and the continuous guidance of a living and present spiritual leader called the Imam. As an Ismaili, the Aga Khan is my spiritual leader. He is also recognized as one of the most significant Muslim leaders in the world. He and Prince Hassan of Jordan were the two Muslim representatives to the World Faiths Development Dialogue, a group founded by the President of the World Bank and the Archbishop of Canterbury. He has given commencement addresses at Brown University and MIT, and has been awarded honors from dozens of countries and universities around the world.

But the Aga Khan's most important legacy may be the thing he is known least for in the West: building institutions that will nurture a progressive Muslim identity. The programs of these institutions are focused on Central and South Asia, Africa and the Middle East. Though largely funded by the Aga Khan and the Ismaili community, the programs of the Aga Khan Development Network are nonsectarian.

In areas of Pakistan where militant madrassas* turned out the likes of the Taliban, Aga Khan schools give both boys and girls a broad and liberal education. They take pride in their Muslim heritage, learning that Muslims made significant advances in mathematics, optics, urban development, geography and navigation; that Islam inspired the poetry of Rumi and the science of Avicenna and the philosophy of al-Hallaj. They learn that Muslim states in the past such as the Fatimid Empire* protected minorities such as Christians and Jews, and that pluralism is one of the glorious creations of Allah. They learn that jihad means trying to be a better person, which means being more generous and honest and kind.

The Aga Khan University (AKU) is the most ambitious Ismaili educational project since the creation of Al-Azhar University in Fatimid, Cairo in the tenth century. AKU started with a medical school that focused on training nurses. Not only did this greatly improve the medical capacity in Pakistan, but it opened up unprecedented professional opportunities for Pakistani women. In addition to a medical school, Aga Khan University now has a school of education which trains teachers, again largely women. Two of my fellow doctoral students at the Oxford University Department of Educational Studies, Anjum and Razia, are faculty members in the School of Education at Aga Khan University. They were sponsored by AKU to get their doctorates at Oxford, and will return as senior faculty members. Both are women, both are Pakistani and Muslim, neither are Ismailis.

While Muslim totalitarians outlaw music and much poetry, the Aga Khan Trust for Culture (AKTC) recognizes the central role that culture plays in human and social development. In Fall 2000, the AKTC sponsored a performance of Tajiki musicians doing interpretations of Rumi's work in Paris. This performance took place during the same time that much of the world viewed Central Asia as a convenient place to put military bases rather than a land with a rich heritage inspired by Islam. And in contrast to the Muslim totalitarians who are funding architectural projects which impose Middle Eastern architectural forms on Asia and Africa, the Aga Khan Award for Architecture recognizes architects who use the Islamic heritage in creative ways to improve the built environment in a culturally appropriate and respectful manner.

---

madrassas: plural of madrassa (also madrasah), a Muslim institution of higher learning

the Fatimid Empire: an empire in North Africa and the Middle East from 909 to 1171. Fatimids took their name from Fatimah, daughter of Prophet Muhammad, whom they believed to be their ancestor

I think it was Edmund Burke who said that evil triumphs when good people do nothing. He could have added that the bad folks win when the good folks fail to build institutions which nurture their vision. The attitudes and actions which the Muslim totalitarians call Islam are unrecognizable to me. The institutions which nurtured my Muslim identity taught me something very different; simply, that Islam is about the oneness of God, the unity of humankind and the responsibility of humans to realize the original intention of the Creator in his creation.

Which vision of Islam will that Afghan kid that I saw on Britain's news be exposed to? Will he live in a neighborhood which allows women the opportunity to learn to read and write, or forces them into the shadows? Will the mosques he goes to have Muslim preachers that define jihad as a holy war against non-Muslims or as an internal struggle to realize his higher self? Will cultural organizations expose him to the great poets and architects and musicians whose art was inspired by Islam or will he understand Islam as a narrow and austere religion which eschews beauty? Will schools encourage him to apply Allah's greatest gift—a creative and independent mind—or will his teachers demand that he blindly follow their commands? Will he be surrounded by hospitals and relief organizations where he learns that the Muslim ethic is to heal and help or the guerrilla armies of warlords that teach brutality. Will his government seek to unite the tribes of Afghanistan and work together with the international community or pit Pashtun against Uzbek* and choose the path of isolation?

That twelve-year-old kid is powerful. All twelve-year-old kids are powerful. And, in the final analysis, all the work that we do is for them. The great Chicago poet Gwendolyn Brooks knew how powerful kids were. I will leave you with a few lines from her poem, "Boy Breaking Glass":

> I shall create!
> If not a note, a hole
> If not an overture, a desecration.

QUESTIONING THE TEXT

1. This essay is identified as being written for the Religious Education in a Global Society Conference organized by the Temple of Understanding in New York City in January 2002. Do you think the text was meant to be presented orally or in written form as you see it here? What evidence can you find in Patel's text to support your answer?

Pashtun: Pashto-speaking people of southeastern Afghanistan and northwestern Pakistan
Uzbek: Uzbek-speaking people of Central Asia (including Uzbekistan) and Afghanistan

2. Even if you did not have the contextual information provided in J.R.'s headnote to this piece, what can you glean about Patel's intended audience from the text itself? What events served as the impetus for this essay? What hints does the piece provide about the time in which Patel was writing?
3. Patel alludes to works by several other writers. Make a list of those writers, and briefly identify them, noting biographical information, titles and genres of some of their works, and issues or themes they most often address. Consult printed and online resources at your library to find information you don't already know about the authors. Why do you think Patel chooses to mention each author in his essay? Discuss your answers among classmates.

MAKING CONNECTIONS

4. In paragraphs 9 and 10, Patel provides a list of institutions he sees as contributing to religious identity by providing a religious education. He gives a definition of "religious identity" and then claims that, "the [religious identity] of too many young Muslims is being shaped by these institutions." Read another essay or two in this chapter—perhaps Bich Minh Nguyen's "The Good Immigrant Student" (p. 441) or Amitai Etzioni's "The Monochrome Society" (p. 467)—and consider Patel's claim in light of these other readings. Write an essay that supports or challenges the idea that identity is shaped by institutions, using evidence gathered from your readings.

JOINING THE CONVERSATION

5. Patel writes of the Afghan boy he saw on the television news: "The path he chooses has everything to do with the religious education he gets" (paragraph 3). Do you agree with this assessment? Do you think the same statement could be made about you? To what extent do you think your religious education (or the lack of one) has influenced or will influence the choices you make? Freewrite on these questions. You might also then use your ideas as the basis of a personal essay.
6. Consider Patel's use of the word *nurturing* in his title. What do you think he means by "nurturing" an "identity"? Can you envision nurturing an identity, for yourself or for a wider community? Are you interested in doing so? How would you approach such a task? Write a proposal that could serve as a personal resolution for your self-development or as a social or educational plan that you might present publicly as a newspaper op-ed or a letter to school or community leaders.

LANGSTON HUGHES
Theme for English B

As a young man in Joplin, Missouri, Langston Hughes (1902–67) worked as an assistant cook, a launderer, and a busboy—jobs similar to ones you may have held—before leaving to attend Columbia University in New York City. (He eventually graduated in 1929 from Lincoln University in Pennsylvania.) A prolific writer and part of the great artistic movement of the 1920s and 1930s known as the Harlem Renaissance, Hughes worked in many genres—novels, short stories, plays, essays, and poems. From his early collection of poems, The Weary Blues *(1926), to his posthumous volume of essays,* Black Misery *(1969), he explored numerous themes touching on the lives of African Americans, including that of higher education.*

The poem that follows, from 1926, describes one event in the speaker's college career and raises questions about relationships between instructors and students, between those "inside" the university and those "outside." It is one of my favorite poems, one of the few special ones I carry around with me and, in fact, now find that I know "by heart." With every new class I teach, I think of Hughes's "Theme for English B," for it speaks volumes to me about the necessity of respecting individual differences while at the same time valuing those bonds that link us to one another. —A.L.

The instructor said,

Go home and write
a page tonight.
And let that page come out of you —
Then, it will be true.

I wonder if it's that simple?
I am twenty-two, colored, born in Winston-Salem.
I went to school there, then Durham, then here
to this college on the hill above Harlem.
I am the only colored student in my class.
The steps from the hill lead down to Harlem,
through a park, then I cross St. Nicholas,
Eighth Avenue, Seventh, and I come to the Y,
the Harlem Branch Y, where I take the elevator
up to my room, sit down, and write this page:

It's not easy to know what is true for you or me
at twenty-two, my age. But I guess I'm what
I feel and see and hear. Harlem, I hear you:
hear you, hear me—we two—you, me talk on this page.
(I hear New York, too.) Me—who?
Well, I like to eat, sleep, drink, and be in love.
I like to work, read, learn, and understand life.
I like a pipe for a Christmas present,
or records—Bessie,* bop, or Bach.
I guess being colored doesn't make me not like
the same things other folks like who are other races.
So will my page be colored that I write?
Being me, it will not be white.
But it will be
a part of you, instructor.
You are white—
yet a part of me, as I am a part of you.
That's American.
Sometimes perhaps you don't want to be a part of me.
Nor do I often want to be a part of you.
But we are, that's true!
As I learn from you,
I guess you learn from me—
although you're older—and white—
and somewhat more free.

This is my page for English B.

IN RESPONSE

1. Near the end of the poem, the speaker says, addressing his instructor, "You are white— / yet a part of me, as I am a part of you. / That's American." What do you think Hughes means by "American"?
2. The speaker of this poem notes that given who he is, his theme will not be "white," but he goes on to say that it will still be "a part of you, instructor." What do you think he means? Can you describe a time when you've had a similar experience?
3. In "The Recoloring of Campus Life," Shelby Steele (p. 78) writes at length of the myth of inferiority among African American youths.

Bessie: Bessie Smith (1898?–1937), a famous blues singer

What, if any, evidence of a myth of inferiority do you find in Hughes's poem? How might Hughes respond to Steele's essay?

4. Would Hughes—or his teacher—likely be found in John Henry Newman's ideal university (p. 52)? Why, or why not?
5. Consider what effects your own gender, race, class, or family background has had on your success in school. Then write a brief (one- or two-page) essay explaining those effects.
6. Brainstorm with two or three classmates about whether it is important for students to identify with their teachers, to have a number of things in common with them. Come to an agreement among yourselves on how to answer this question, and then write one page explaining why you answered it as you did.

OTHER READINGS

Armstrong, Karen. *Islam: A Short History*. New York: Modern Library, 2000. A brief, thoughtful introduction to Islam that begins in the sixth century and ends with the present day and helps put Islamic fundamentalism into context.

Buckley, Christopher. "Tough Guys Don't Dance." *Backward and Upward: The New Conservative Writing*. Ed. David Brooks. New York: Vintage, 1996. 125–31. Ponders forms of macho posturing—real and fake.

Cruikshank, Margaret, ed. *The Lesbian Path: 37 Lesbian Writers Share Their Personal Experiences, Viewpoints, Traumas, and Joys*. Monterey: Angel, 1980. Personal narratives by gay women.

Heath, Shirley Brice, and Milbrey W. McLaughlin, eds. *Identity and Inner-City Youth: Beyond Ethnicity and Gender*. New York: Teachers College, 1993. Explores the reasons local clubs and youth groups help inner-city youth find and maintain self-esteem in ways schools often do not.

Kors, Alan Charles, and Harvey A. Silverglate. "Individual Identity: The Heart of Liberty." *The Shadow University: The Betrayal of Liberty on America's Campuses*. New York: Free, 1998. 187–209. Charges that American universities treat students not as individuals but as members of politicized groups.

Senna, Danzy. "The Mulatto Millennium." *Utne Reader* Sept.–Oct. 1998: 31–34. Considers the complexities of multiracial identity, arguing that categories (even the ones this author coins) don't always fit a person's identity.

Whitman, Walt. "Song of Myself." 1881. *Leaves of Grass*. Ed. Scully Bradley and Harold W. Blodgett. New York: Norton, 1973. A classic statement of American identity.

ELECTRONIC RESOURCES

http://www.identitytheft.org/
Offers information on restoring credit and on protecting identity, credit, and reputation.

http://memory.loc.gov
Gateway to a massive Library of Congress archive of photographs, manuscripts, and documents related to American history and identity.

http://www.nea.org/society/engonly.html (Search: English only.)
Web site of an organization that opposes "English only" legislation in the United States.

http://www.us-english.org/
Web site of an organization that favors "English only" legislation in the United States.

SUPPORTS

Look carefully at the photograph on the preceding page, which shows a rider in a rodeo barrel race. What part of the photo first captures your attention, and why? ■ What emotions does the photo evoke? ■ How does it do so? ■ Which images are in sharpest focus, and which are less distinct? ■ What elements of the barrel-racing scene were probably omitted in the framing or cropping of the photo? ■ How do the focus and framing contribute to the overall effect of the photo? ■ How does this image compare to your own idea of a cowboy? ■ What thoughts or questions does this photo inspire about myths of the American West?

7

American Cultural Myths: The Good, the Bad, and the Ugly

The history of the present King of Great Britain is a history of repeated injuries and usurpations, all having in direct object the establishment of an absolute Tyranny over these States. To prove this, let Facts be submitted to a candid world.

THOMAS JEFFERSON, *Declaration of Independence*

Fellow-citizens, pardon me, allow me to ask, why am I called upon to speak here to-day? What have I, or those I represent, to do with your national independence? Are the great principles of political freedom and of natural justice, embodied in that Declaration of Independence, extended to us? and am I, therefore, called upon to bring our humble offering to the national altar, and to confess the benefits and express devout gratitude for the blessings resulting from your independence to us?

FREDERICK DOUGLASS, *What to the Slave Is the Fourth of July?*

By 1900, the national project of "clearing" Native Americans from their land and replacing them with "superior" Anglo-American settlers was complete; the indigenous population had been reduced by as much as 98 percent while approximately 97.5 percent of their original territory had "passed" to the invaders.

WARD CHURCHILL, *Crimes against Humanity*

[I]t is certain that no culture can flourish without narratives of transcendent origin and power.

NEIL POSTMAN, *The Great Symbol Drain*

Dear America: . . . You have always wanted to be a city upon a hill, a light to all nations, and for a while you were. Give me your tired, your poor, you sang, and for a while you meant it.

MARGARET ATWOOD, *A Letter to America*

It is a myth that globalization involves the imposition of Americanized uniformity, rather than an explosion of cultural exchange.

PHILIPPE LEGRAIN, *Cultural Globalization Is Not Americanization*

When Blue America talks about social changes that convulsed society, it tends to mean the 1960s rise of the counterculture and feminism. When Red America talks about changes that convulsed society, it tends to mean World War II, which shook up old town establishments and led to a great surge of industry.

DAVID BROOKS, *One Nation, Slightly Divisible*

[O]ur flag is not just a logo for wars; it's the flag of American pacifists, too. It's the flag of all of us who love our country enough to do the hard work of living up to its highest ideals.

BARBARA KINGSOLVER, *And Our Flag Was Still There*

I am proud to have represented this program and humbled by the opportunities it has provided for me and for thousands of women since 1921. I will be even prouder when the Miss America Organization defines its mission and lives up to its potential.

KATE SHINDLE, *Miss America: More Than a Beauty Queen?*

You can't see the desert if you can't smell it. Dusty? Of course it's dusty—this is Utah! But it's good dust, good red Utahn dust, rich in iron, rich in irony.

EDWARD ABBEY, *Desert Solitaire*

"Give me your tired, your poor, / Your huddled masses yearning to breathe free, . . ."

EMMA LAZARUS, *The New Colossus*

stupid america, remember that chicanito / flunking math and english / he is the Picasso / of your western states

ABELARDO DELGADO, *Stupid America*

Introduction

IN A NEW YORK TIMES COLUMN (March 30, 2003) critical of how President Bush has betrayed the "foundational national myth" of the American cowboy, author Susan Faludi offers a succinct description of the role shared stories play in the culture of any country or people: "Mythologies," Faludi suggests, "are essential to defining who we are and, more importantly, who we want to be." One can hardly imagine a clearer way of explaining the concept: we tell stories to bind us to one another, reinterpreting and retelling the tales with each generation so that we eventually accumulate many versions of the same defining narratives.

This chapter explores only a few of the many myths that make up the American story. Of course, all people have such mythologies. For

Russians, the themes often focus on endurance and suffering, not surprising given the history and even geography of that sprawling country. For other ethnic groups, including both Jews and African Americans, the defining myths include tales of persecution and Diaspora.

American mythologies are particularly important now, with the United States assuming new roles on the world stage, because many of those tales reach well beyond the nation's borders. The American dream, interpreted in numerous ways, is becoming a part of the world's consciousness. In the past, people were drawn to the United States by promises of equality, opportunity, and freedom; they wanted to go to America to become American. Now the question may be to what extent an imperial America wants to extend—or even impose—its values beyond its continental limits.

We began our work on this chapter by brainstorming a list of national myths. Here are some of the myths we came up with:

- **Myth of the American frontier.** This myth is told through stories about extending control over nature, land, and people. The first frontiers were the Appalachians, later the vast American West, and finally the moon and outer space. (We seem not to have envisioned the depths of the ocean as a new frontier—yet.)
- **Myth of America as the land of opportunity.** Tales of immigrants coming to America for political and economic opportunity give life to this powerful story. However, this narrative has never accommodated the forced immigration of African slaves or the "assimilation" of Native Americans. And the myth is spoken differently along the southern borders of the United States.
- **Myth of America as the land of freedom and equality.** This is the great political myth—the story of the Revolution, the Declaration of Independence, the Civil War, and the civil rights movement—yet it consistently collides with the counterstory of American oppressions.
- **Myth of the American as a rugged individual.** Most Americans prefer to portray themselves as masters of their own destinies. Consequently, they are fond of political and economic success stories—from Edison the inventor to Amelia Earhart the aviator to the Jimmy Stewart character in *Mr. Smith Goes to Washington.*
- **Myth of America as the "city on a hill."** This is the narrative of American moral righteousness and superiority. It is both *The Scarlet Letter* and *To Kill a Mockingbird.* In a parodic way, it is also *The Simpsons.*
- **Myth of the American as a rebel.** Think of Captain Ahab and James Dean, Thoreau and Walt Whitman, Emily Dickinson and Madonna, the Roots and OutKast.

- **Myth of the open road.** The frontier becomes personal when Americans exercise their option to pack their bags and move on, to change their lives, to seek better (or more interesting) opportunities. You might think of *Moby Dick* as a road trip of a kind—or of Jack Kerouac's *On the Road* or Callie Kouhri's *Thelma and Louise.*

This list of myths is, of course, incomplete and always evolving. We encourage you to add to it and to embroider the items we have offered with details from your own experience. We hope, however, that these initial suggestions and the readings that follow will spark your interest in the cultural myths that either bind us together or heighten our sense of separation and difference. At the outset of this chapter, you may want to ponder these questions:

- How well have Americans lived up to the mythic visions of their founding documents—including the Declaration of Independence?
- In what ways do our national myths sometimes seem crafted to exclude certain "others"? Could these myths retain their power if they evolved to accommodate more people?
- How do other nations now regard American dreams and aspirations? Are we really the "city on a hill," or have we become a threatening cultural, economic, and military colossus?
- Do conflicting myths about equality and opportunity divide the American people along political lines? Or are American dreams and aspirations more widely shared than some believe?

THOMAS JEFFERSON
Declaration of Independence

WHAT CAN YOU SAY ABOUT THE Declaration of Independence (1776), the document that turned thirteen British colonies into what would become the United States of America? Surely it stands among the great political treatises of the Western world, as important as Plato's Republic, *the Magna Carta, and* the Declaration of the Rights of Man. *It was, in its time, as radical a political manifesto as could be imagined, and yet part of its greatness is that it obliged future generations to fulfill promises its signers could not meet.*

The Declaration of Independence probably could not be written today: it is too clear, too bold, too confident. Just imagine the resistance of politicians and various special interest groups to the notion of unalienable rights endowed by a Creator. And when was the last time you heard a bureaucrat in Washington musing on "the pursuit of happiness"? The Declaration is also probably too forthright for modern tastes about the rights of people to resist governments that fail them. Stylistically, it is way too economical as well. Imagine what a committee of government officials today would do with the task given to Thomas Jefferson (1743–1826), Benjamin Franklin, and John Adams. Why, the staff alone assigned to such a committee would probably outnumber some of the armies the Continental Congress mustered.

Certainly, Americans have not always lived up to the spirit of this splendid founding document. Still, I would argue that the Declaration of Independence is revered around the world in part because the nation it created has succeeded so well. Freedom and equality are mythic in the United States not only because of what the Declaration promised but what generations of Americans subsequently achieved in its name. The dustbin of history is doubtless heavy with political documents no less noble or idealistic than the Declaration of Independence. The French alone have shuffled through five republics, and the former Soviet Union had a real genius for publishing idealistic sentiments. But the Declaration endures, I think, because, in a splendid moment, perhaps blessed by that deity it does not name, it created both a dream and a people. —J.R.

In Congress, July 4, 1776.

The Unanimous Declaration of the Thirteen United States of America,

When in the Course of human events, it becomes necessary for one people to dissolve the political bands which have connected them with another, and to assume among the powers of the earth, the separate and equal station to which the Laws of Nature and of Nature's God entitle them, a decent respect to the opinions of mankind requires that they should declare the causes which impel them to the separation.

We hold these truths to be self-evident, that all men are created equal, that they are endowed by their Creator with certain unalienable Rights, that among these are Life, Liberty and the pursuit of Happiness.—That to secure these rights, Governments are instituted among Men, deriving their just powers from the consent of the governed,—That whenever any Form of Government becomes destructive of these ends, it is the Right of the People to alter or to abolish it, and to institute new Government, laying its foundation on such principles and organizing its powers in such form, as to them shall seem most likely to effect their Safety and Happiness. Prudence, indeed, will dictate that Governments long established should not be changed for light and transient causes; and accordingly all experience hath shewn, that mankind are more disposed to suffer, while evils are sufferable, than to right themselves by abolishing the forms to which they are accustomed. But when a long train of abuses and usurpations, pursuing invariably the same Object evinces a design to reduce them under absolute Despotism, it is their right, it is their duty, to throw off such Government, and to provide new Guards for their future security.—Such has been the patient sufferance of these Colonies; and such is now the necessity which constrains them to alter their former Systems of Government. The history of the present King of Great Britain is a history of repeated injuries and usurpations, all having in direct object the establishment of an absolute Tyranny over these States. To prove this, let Facts be submitted to a candid world.

He has refused his Assent to Laws, the most wholesome and necessary for the public good.

He has forbidden his Governors to pass Laws of immediate and pressing importance, unless suspended in their operation till his Assent should be obtained; and when so suspended, he has utterly neglected to attend to them.

He has refused to pass other Laws for the accommodation of large districts 5
of people, unless those people would relinquish the right of Representation in the Legislature, a right inestimable to them and formidable to tyrants only.

He has called together legislative bodies at places unusual, uncomfortable, and distant from the depository of their public Records, for the sole purpose of fatiguing them into compliance with his measures.

He has dissolved Representative Houses repeatedly, for opposing with manly firmness his invasions on the rights of the people.

He has refused for a long time, after such dissolutions, to cause others to be elected; whereby the Legislative powers, incapable of Annihilation, have returned to the People at large for their exercise; the State remaining in the mean time exposed to all the dangers of invasion from without, and convulsions within.

He has endeavoured to prevent the population of these States; for that purpose obstructing the Laws for Naturalization of Foreigners; refusing to pass others to encourage their migrations hither, and raising the conditions of new Appropriations of Lands.

He has obstructed the Administration of Justice, by refusing his Assent to Laws for establishing Judiciary powers.

He has made Judges dependent on his Will alone, for the tenure of their offices, and the amount and payment of their salaries.

He has erected a multitude of New Offices, and sent hither swarms of Officers to harrass our people, and eat out their substance.

He has kept among us, in times of peace, Standing Armies without the Consent of our legislatures.

He has affected to render the Military independent of and superior to the Civil power.

He has combined with others to subject us to a jurisdiction foreign to our constitution, and unacknowledged by our laws; giving his Assent to their Acts of pretended Legislation:

For Quartering large bodies of armed troops among us:

For protecting them, by a mock Trial, from punishment for any Murders which they should commit on the Inhabitants of these States:

For cutting off our Trade with all parts of the world:

For imposing Taxes on us without our Consent:

For depriving us in many cases, of the benefits of Trial by Jury:

For transporting us beyond Seas to be tried for pretended offences:

For abolishing the free System of English Laws in a neighbouring Province, establishing therein an Arbitrary government, and enlarging its Boundaries so as to render it at once an example and fit instrument for introducing the same absolute rule into these Colonies:

For taking away our Charters, abolishing our most valuable Laws, and altering fundamentally the Forms of our Governments:

For suspending our own Legislatures, and declaring themselves invested with power to legislate for us in all cases whatsoever.

He has abdicated Government here, by declaring us out of his Protection and waging War against us.

He has plundered our seas, ravaged our Coasts, burnt our towns, and destroyed the lives of our people.

He is at this time transporting large Armies of foreign Mercenaries to compleat the works of death, desolation and tyranny, already begun with circumstances of Cruelty & perfidy scarcely paralleled in the most barbarous ages, and totally unworthy the Head of a civilized nation.

He has constrained our fellow Citizens taken Captive on the high Seas to bear Arms against their Country, to become the executioners of their friends and Brethren, or to fall themselves by their Hands.

He has excited domestic insurrections amongst us, and has endeavoured to bring on the inhabitants of our frontiers, the merciless Indian Savages, whose known rule of warfare, is an undistinguished destruction of all ages, sexes and conditions.

In every stage of these Oppressions We have Petitioned for Redress in 30
the most humble terms: Our repeated Petitions have been answered only by repeated injury. A Prince whose character is thus marked by every act which may define a Tyrant, is unfit to be the ruler of a free people.

Nor have We been wanting in attentions to our Brittish brethren. We have warned them from time to time of attempts by their legislature to extend an unwarrantable jurisdiction over us. We have reminded them of the circumstances of our emigration and settlement here. We have appealed to their native justice and magnanimity, and we have conjured them by the ties of our common kindred to disavow these usurpations, which, would inevitably interrupt our connections and correspondence. They too have been deaf to the voice of justice and of consanguinity. We must, therefore, acquiesce in the necessity, which denounces our Separation, and hold them, as we hold the rest of mankind, Enemies in War, in Peace Friends.

We, therefore, the Representatives of the united States of America, in General Congress, Assembled, appealing to the Supreme Judge of the world for the rectitude of our intentions, do, in the Name, and by Authority of the good People of these Colonies, solemnly publish and declare, That these United Colonies are, and of Right ought to be Free and Independent States; that they are Absolved from all Allegiance to the British Crown, and that all political connection between them and the State of Great Britain, is and ought to be totally dissolved; and that as Free and Independent States, they have full Power to levy War, conclude Peace, contract Alliances, establish Commerce, and to do all other Acts and Things which Independent States may of right do. And for the support of this Declaration, with a firm reliance on the protection of divine Providence, we mutually pledge to each other our Lives, our Fortunes and our sacred Honor.

QUESTIONING THE TEXT

1. With a classmate, write a summary of the argument presented in the Declaration of Independence. Include in your summary a list of the main grievances, stated in language that is easily understandable to your classmates. What is the main claim used to justify the representatives' declaration of independence from Great Britain?
2. Who was the intended audience of the Declaration? Can you tell from the text itself? What rhetorical clues do you find that support your answer?

MAKING CONNECTIONS

3. Read Ward Churchill's "Crimes against Humanity" (p. 536), and then consider the following claim made against the King of England in the Declaration of Independence: "He has excited domestic insurrections

amongst us, and has endeavoured to bring on the inhabitants of our frontiers, the merciless Indian Savages, whose known rule of warfare, is an undistinguished destruction of all ages, sexes and conditions" (paragraph 29). Does Churchill's essay change your understanding of the Declaration and the assumptions made by its drafters? With the benefit of hindsight, reflect on what the Declaration of Independence meant to inhabitants of the thirteen new states, including those people who were not white male property owners. If you keep a writing log, record your thoughts there.

4. In "The Great Symbol Drain" (p. 545), Neil Postman claims that the narratives that once gave the United States a sense of shared meaning have lost their power to unite Americans, in part, because symbols such as the U.S. Constitution and the Statue of Liberty have become weak through overuse and trivialization. Although Postman doesn't mention the Declaration of Independence, he would probably include it among the eviscerated symbols that both contribute to and represent the lost American narrative, which some might call an American mythos. In preparation for class discussion, reread the Declaration of Independence, and try to infer from it a narrative of America's origins. In class, discuss whether Postman is right in claiming that such a narrative is no longer a powerful force of unity for Americans. Do you think that parts of the American mythos must be abandoned or revised? Can some of it be salvaged? Why, or why not?

JOINING THE CONVERSATION

5. Write an essay on "What the Declaration of Independence Really Says," for submission as an op-ed to your campus or local newspaper. Read through some of the other selections in this chapter for inspiration: you might take a critical or straightforward approach, and you might try a sarcastic, humorous, or solemn tone.
6. The Declaration of Independence has served as a model for many groups seeking justice over the years. One example is the 1848 "Declaration of Sentiments and Resolutions of the Seneca Falls Convention," written by Elizabeth Cady Stanton, which argues for women's rights. Do some research to investigate how later declarations used the original to make new arguments. Analyze the ways in which the later documents drew on the 1776 declaration to appeal to traditional American values for support of controversial positions. You might also consider whether and how the later documents may be read as revisions of the Declaration of Independence. Write an argument of 8 to 10 pages based on your research and analysis.

FREDERICK DOUGLASS
What to the Slave Is the Fourth of July?

As a kid, I looked forward to the Fourth of July: for me, it was all about fireworks and watermelon right from my Granny's spring house, and maybe a trip to Cade's Cove where we swam in the cool, clear waters. I was as unreflective about the meanings of this national day of celebration as anyone could possibly be. Consequently, just as I remember where I was when I learned that John F. Kennedy, Martin Luther King Jr., and Bobby Kennedy were assassinated, so too do I remember where I was and what I was doing when I first read Frederick Douglass. Since that first reading, I have turned to Douglass again and again, studying his messages and especially the way that he crafts them. And I have never thought of the Fourth of July in the same way: for me, the national holiday is a time for quiet reflection on where we as a country have been—and on where we must go.

Douglass (1817–95), born a slave in Maryland, escaped in 1838 and devoted himself to the abolitionist movement. Eventually, Douglass was forced to flee to England to escape being reenslaved; he returned in 1847 after paying his "owners" for his freedom. The publication of The Narrative of the Life of Frederick Douglass: An American Slave *(1845) brought Douglass international acclaim, and he went on to write many speeches and treatises, including* My Bondage and My Freedom *(1855) and* Life of Frederick Douglass *(1881). In addition, Douglass wrote for and published the important abolitionist newspaper* The North Star *as well as* Douglass' Monthly *and* New National Era. *During the Civil War, Douglass was a consultant to President Abraham Lincoln; he later served as U.S. ambassador to Haiti.*

In his writing—and in the speeches for which he was renowned—Douglass reveals his prodigious powers of persuasion, his thorough understanding of rhetorical principles and strategies, and his grasp of audience psychology. All these attributes are apparent in "What to the Slave Is the Fourth of July?" delivered at the invitation of the Rochester Ladies' Anti-Slavery Society in Rochester, New York on July 5, 1852. The excerpt that follows comprises roughly the first half of Douglass's speech and its closing. Reading this speech more than 150 years after its delivery will undoubtedly prompt you to ask, "What to me is the Fourth of July—and why?" —A.L.

Mr. President, Friends and Fellow Citizens: He who could address this audience without a quailing sensation, has stronger nerves than I have. I do not remember ever to have appeared as a speaker before any assembly more shrinkingly, nor with greater distrust of my ability, than I do this day. A feeling has crept over me, quite unfavorable to the exercise of my limited powers of speech. The task before me is one which requires much previous thought and study for its proper performance. I know that apologies of this sort are generally considered flat and unmeaning. I trust, however, that mine will not be so considered. Should I seem at ease, my appearance would much misrepresent me. The little experience I have had in addressing public meetings, in country school houses, avails me nothing on the present occasion.

The papers and placards say, that I am to deliver a 4th [of] July oration. This certainly sounds large, and out of the common way, for it is true that I have often had the privilege to speak in this beautiful Hall, and to address many who now honor me with their presence. But neither their familiar faces, nor the perfect gage I think I have of Corinthian Hall, seems to free me from embarrassment.

The fact is, ladies and gentlemen, the distance between this platform and the slave plantation, from which I escaped, is considerable—and the difficulties to be overcome in getting from the latter to the former, are by no means slight. That I am here to-day is, to me, a matter of astonishment as well as of gratitude. You will not, therefore, be surprised, if in what I have to say, I evince no elaborate preparation, nor grace my speech with any high sounding exordium. With little experience and with less learning, I have been able to throw my thoughts hastily and imperfectly together; and trusting to your patient and generous indulgence, I will proceed to lay them before you.

This, for the purpose of this celebration, is the 4th of July. It is the birthday of your National Independence, and of your political freedom. This, to you, is what the Passover was to the emancipated people of God. It carries your minds back to the day, and to the act of your great deliverance; and to the signs, and to the wonders, associated with that act, and that day. This celebration also marks the beginning of another year of your national life; and reminds you that the Republic of America is now 76 years old. I am glad, fellow-citizens, that your nation is so young. Seventy-six years, though a good old age for a man, is but a mere speck in the life of a nation. Three score years and ten is the allotted time for individual men; but nations number their years by thousands. According to this fact, you are, even now, only in the beginning of your national career, still lingering in the period of childhood. I repeat, I am glad this is so. There is hope in the thought, and hope is much needed, under the dark clouds which lower above the horizon. The eye of the reformer is met with angry flashes, portending disastrous times; but his heart may well beat lighter at the thought that America is young, and that she is still in the impressible stage of her existence. May he not hope that high lessons of wisdom, of justice and of truth, will yet give direction to her destiny? Were the nation older, the patriot's heart might be sadder, and the reformer's brow heavier. Its future might be shrouded in gloom, and the hope of its prophets go out in sorrow. There is consolation in the thought that America is young. Great streams are not easily turned from channels, worn deep in the course of ages. They may sometimes rise in quiet and stately majesty, and inundate the land, refreshing and fertilizing the earth with their mysterious properties. They may also rise in wrath and fury, and bear away, on their angry waves, the accumulated wealth of years of toil and hardship. They, however, gradually flow back to the same old channel, and flow on as serenely as ever. But, while the river may not be turned aside, it may dry up, and leave nothing behind but the withered branch, and the unsightly rock, to howl in the abyss-sweeping wind, the sad tale of departed glory. As with rivers so with nations.

Fellow-citizens, I shall not presume to dwell at length on the associa- 5
tions that cluster about this day. The simple story of it is that, 76 years ago, the people of this country were British subjects. The style and title of your "sovereign people" (in which you now glory) was not then born. You were under the British Crown. Your fathers esteemed the English Government as the home government; and England as the fatherland. This home government, you know, although a considerable distance from your home, did, in the exercise of its parental prerogatives, impose upon its colonial children, such restraints, burdens and limitations, as, in its mature judgement, it deemed wise, right and proper.

But, your fathers, who had not adopted the fashionable idea of this day, of the infallibility of government, and the absolute character of its acts, presumed to differ from the home government in respect to the wisdom and the justice of some of those burdens and restraints. They went so far in their excitement as to pronounce the measures of government unjust, unreasonable, and oppressive, and altogether such as ought not to be quietly submitted to. I scarcely need say, fellow-citizens, that my opinion of those measures fully accords with that of your fathers. Such a declaration of agreement on my part would not be worth much to anybody. It would, certainly, prove nothing, as to what part I might have taken, had I lived during the great controversy of 1776. To say now that America was right, and England wrong, is exceedingly easy. Everybody can say it; the dastard, not less than the noble brave, can flippantly discant on the tyranny of England towards the American Colonies. It is fashionable to do so; but there was a time when to pronounce against England, and in favor of the cause of the colonies, tried men's souls. They who did so were accounted in their day, plotters of mischief, agitators and rebels, dangerous men. To side with the right, against the wrong, with the weak against the strong, and with the oppressed against the oppressor! here lies the merit, and the one which, of all others, seems unfashionable in our day. The cause of liberty may be stabbed by the men who glory in the deeds of your fathers. But, to proceed.

Feeling themselves harshly and unjustly treated by the home government, your fathers, like men of honesty, and men of spirit, earnestly sought redress. They petitioned and remonstrated; they did so in a decorous, respectful, and loyal manner. Their conduct was wholly unexceptionable. This, however, did not answer the purpose. They saw themselves treated with sovereign indifference, coldness and scorn. Yet they persevered. They were not the men to look back.

As the sheet anchor takes a firmer hold, when the ship is tossed by the storm, so did the cause of your fathers grow stronger, as it breasted the chilling blasts of kingly displeasure. The greatest and best of British statesmen admitted its justice, and the loftiest eloquence of the British Senate came to its support. But, with that blindness which seems to be the unvarying characteristic of tyrants, since Pharaoh and his hosts were drowned in the Red Sea, the British Government persisted in the exactions complained of.

The madness of this course, we believe, is admitted now, even by England; but we fear the lesson is wholly lost on our present rulers.

Oppression makes a wise man mad. Your fathers were wise men, and if 10
they did not go mad, they became restive under this treatment. They felt themselves the victims of grievous wrongs, wholly incurable in their colonial capacity. With brave men there is always a remedy for oppression. Just here, the idea of a total separation of the colonies from the crown was born! It was a startling idea, much more so, than we, at this distance of time, regard it. The timid and the prudent (as has been intimated) of that day, were, of course, shocked and alarmed by it.

Such people lived then, had lived before, and will, probably, ever have a place on this planet; and their course, in respect to any great change (no matter how great the good to be attained, or the wrong to be redressed by it), may be calculated with as much precision as can be the course of the stars. They hate all changes, but silver, gold and copper change! Of this sort of change they are always strongly in favor.

These people were called tories in the days of your fathers; and the appellation, probably, conveyed the same idea that is meant by a more modern, though a somewhat less euphonious term, which we often find in our papers, applied to some of our old politicians.

Their opposition to the then dangerous thought was earnest and powerful; but, amid all their terror and affrighted vociferations against it, the alarming and revolutionary idea moved on, and the country with it.

On the 2d of July, 1776, the old Continental Congress, to the dismay of the lovers of ease, and the worshipers of property, clothed that dreadful idea with all the authority of national sanction. They did so in the form of a resolution; and as we seldom hit upon resolutions, drawn up in our day, whose transparency is at all equal to this, it may refresh your minds and help my story if I read it.

"Resolved, That these united colonies are, and of right, ought to be 15
free and Independent States; that they are absolved from all allegiance to the British Crown; and that all political connection between them and the State of Great Britain is, and ought to be, dissolved."

Citizens, your fathers made good that resolution. They succeeded; and to-day you reap the fruits of their success. The freedom gained is yours; and you, therefore, may properly celebrate this anniversary. The 4th of July is the first great fact in your nation's history—the very ring-bolt in the chain of your yet undeveloped destiny.

Pride and patriotism, not less than gratitude, prompt you to celebrate and to hold it in perpetual remembrance. I have said that the Declaration of Independence is the ring-bolt to the chain of your nation's destiny; so, indeed, I regard it. The principles contained in that instrument are saving principles. Stand by those principles, be true to them on all occasions, in all places, against all foes, and at whatever cost.

From the round top of your ship of state, dark and threatening clouds may be seen. Heavy billows, like mountains in the distance, disclose to the leeward huge forms of flinty rocks! That bolt drawn, that chain broken, and all is lost. Cling to this day—cling to it, and to its principles, with the grasp of a storm-tossed mariner to a spar at midnight.

The coming into being of a nation, in any circumstances, is an interesting event. But, besides general considerations, there were peculiar circumstances which make the advent of this republic an event of special attractiveness.

The whole scene, as I look back to it, was simple, dignified and sublime.

The population of the country, at the time, stood at the insignificant number of three millions. The country was poor in the munitions of war. The population was weak and scattered, and the country a wilderness unsubdued. There were then no means of concert and combination, such as exist now. Neither steam nor lightning had then been reduced to order and discipline. From the Potomac to the Delaware was a journey of many days. Under these, and innumerable other disadvantages, your fathers declared for liberty and independence and triumphed.

Fellow Citizens, I am not wanting in respect for the fathers of this republic. The signers of the Declaration of Independence were brave men. They were great men too—great enough to give fame to a great age. It does not often happen to a nation to raise, at one time, such a number of truly great men. The point from which I am compelled to view them is not, certainly, the most favorable; and yet I cannot contemplate their great deeds with less than admiration. They were statesmen, patriots and heroes, and for the good they did, and the principles they contended for, I will unite with you to honor their memory.

They loved their country better than their own private interests; and, though this is not the highest form of human excellence, all will concede that it is a rare virtue, and that when it is exhibited, it ought to command respect. He who will, intelligently, lay down his life for his country, is a man whom it is not in human nature to despise. Your fathers staked their lives, their fortunes, and their sacred honor, on the cause of their country. In their admiration of liberty, they lost sight of all other interests.

They were peace men; but they preferred revolution to peaceful submission to bondage. They were quiet men; but they did not shrink from agitating against oppression. They showed forbearance; but that they knew its limits.

They believed in order; but not in the order of tyranny. With them, nothing was "settled" that was not right. With them, justice, liberty and humanity were "final"; not slavery and oppression. You may well cherish the memory of such men. They were great in their day and generation. Their solid manhood stands out the more as we contrast it with these degenerate times.

How circumspect, exact and proportionate were all their movements! 25
How unlike the politicians of an hour! Their statesmanship looked beyond the passing moment, and stretched away in strength into the distant future. They seized upon eternal principles, and set a glorious example in their defence. Mark them!

Fully appreciating the hardship to be encountered, firmly believing in the right of their cause, honorably inviting the scrutiny of an on-looking world, reverently appealing to heaven to attest their sincerity, soundly comprehending the solemn responsibility they were about to assume, wisely measuring the terrible odds against them, your fathers, the fathers of this republic, did, most deliberately, under the inspiration of a glorious patriotism, and with a sublime faith in the great principles of justice and freedom, lay deep the corner-stone of the national superstructure, which has risen and still rises in grandeur around you.

Of this fundamental work, this day is the anniversary. Our eyes are met with demonstrations of joyous enthusiasm. Banners and pennants wave exultingly on the breeze. The din of business, too, is hushed. Even Mammon seems to have quitted his grasp on this day. The ear-piercing fife and the stirring drum unite their accents with the ascending peal of a thousand church bells. Prayers are made, hymns are sung, and sermons are preached in honor of this day; while the quick martial tramp of a great and multitudinous nation, echoed back by all the hills, valleys and mountains of a vast continent, bespeak the occasion one of thrilling and universal interests nation's jubilee.

Friends and citizens, I need not enter further into the causes which led to this anniversary. Many of you understand them better than I do. You could instruct me in regard to them. That is a branch of knowledge in which you feel, perhaps, a much deeper interest than your speaker. The causes which led to the separation of the colonies from the British crown have never lacked for a tongue. They have all been taught in your common schools, narrated at your firesides, unfolded from your pulpits, and thundered from your legislative halls, and are as familiar to you as household words. They form the staple of your national poetry and eloquence.

I remember, also, that, as a people, Americans are remarkably familiar with all facts which make in their own favor. This is esteemed by some as a national trait — perhaps a national weakness. It is a fact, that whatever makes for the wealth or for the reputation of Americans, and can be had cheap! will be found by Americans. I shall not be charged with slandering Americans, if I say I think the American side of any question may be safely left in American hands.

I leave, therefore, the great deeds of your fathers to other gentlemen 30
whose claim to have been regularly descended will be less likely to be disputed than mine!

The Present.

My business, if I have any here to-day, is with the present. The accepted time with God and his cause is the ever-living now.

> "Trust no future, however pleasant,
> Let the dead past bury its dead;
> Act, act in the living present,
> Heart within, and God overhead."

We have to do with the past only as we can make it useful to the present and to the future. To all inspiring motives, to noble deeds which can be gained from the past, we are welcome. But now is the time, the important time. Your fathers have lived, died, and have done their work, and have done much of it well. You live and must die, and you must do your work. You have no right to enjoy a child's share in the labor of your fathers, unless your children are to be blest by your labors. You have no right to wear out and waste the hard-earned fame of your fathers to cover your indolence. Sydney Smith* tells us that men seldom eulogize the wisdom and virtues of their fathers, but to excuse some folly or wickedness of their own. This truth is not a doubtful one. There are illustrations of it near and remote, ancient and modern. It was fashionable, hundreds of years ago, for the children of Jacob to boast, we have "Abraham to our father," when they had long lost Abraham's faith and spirit. That people contented themselves under the shadow of Abraham's great name, while they repudiated the deeds which made his name great. Need I remind you that a similar thing is being done all over this country to-day? Need I tell you that the Jews are not the only people who built the tombs of the prophets, and garnished the sepulchres of the righteous? Washington could not die till he had broken the chains of his slaves. Yet his monument is built up by the price of human blood, and the traders in the bodies and souls of men, shout—"We have Washington to our father." Alas! that it should be so; yet so it is.

> "The evil that men do, lives after them,
> The good is oft' interred with their bones."

Fellow-citizens, pardon me, allow me to ask, why am I called upon to 35
speak here to-day? What have I, or those I represent, to do with your national independence? Are the great principles of political freedom and of

---

Sydney Smith (1771–1845): English preacher and moral philosopher

natural justice, embodied in that Declaration of Independence, extended to us? and am I, therefore, called upon to bring our humble offering to the national altar, and to confess the benefits and express devout gratitude for the blessings resulting from your independence to us?

Would to God, both for your sakes and ours, that an affirmative answer could be truthfully returned to these questions! Then would my task be light, and my burden easy and delightful. For who is there so cold, that a nation's sympathy could not warm him? Who so obdurate and dead to the claims of gratitude, that would not thankfully acknowledge such priceless benefits? Who so stolid and selfish, that would not give his voice to swell the hallelujahs of a nation's jubilee, when the chains of servitude had been torn from his limbs? I am not that man. In a case like that, the dumb might eloquently speak, and the "lame man leap as an hart."

But, such is not the state of the case. I say it with a sad sense of the disparity between us. I am not included within the pale of this glorious anniversary! Your high independence only reveals the immeasurable distance between us. The blessings in which you, this day, rejoice, are not enjoyed in common. The rich inheritance of justice, liberty, prosperity and independence, bequeathed by your fathers, is shared by you, not by me. The sunlight that brought life and healing to you, has brought stripes and death to me. This Fourth [of] July is yours, not mine. You may rejoice, I must mourn. To drag a man in fetters into the grand illuminated temple of liberty, and call upon him to join you in joyous anthems, were inhuman mockery and sacrilegious irony. Do you mean, citizens, to mock me, by asking me to speak to-day? If so, there is a parallel to your conduct. And let me warn you that it is dangerous to copy the example of a nation whose crimes, lowering up to heaven, were thrown down by the breath of the Almighty, burying that nation in irrecoverable ruin! I can to-day take up the plaintive lament of a peeled and woe-smitten people!

"By the rivers of Babylon, there we sat down. Yea! we wept when we remembered Zion. We hanged our harps upon the willows in the midst thereof. For there, they that carried us away captive, required of us a song; and they who wasted us required of us mirth, saying, Sing us one of the songs of Zion. How can we sing the Lord's song in a strange land? If I forget thee, O Jerusalem, let my right hand forget her cunning. If I do not remember thee, let my tongue cleave to the roof of my mouth."

Fellow-citizens; above your national, tumultuous joy, I hear the mournful wail of millions! whose chains, heavy and grievous yesterday, are, to-day, rendered more intolerable by the jubilee shouts that reach them. If I do forget, if I do not faithfully remember those bleeding children of sorrow this day, "may my right hand forget her cunning, and may my tongue cleave to the roof of my mouth!" To forget them, to pass lightly over their wrongs, and to chime in with the popular theme, would be treason most scandalous and shocking, and would make me a reproach before God and the world. My subject, then fellow-citizens, is AMERICAN SLAVERY. I shall see, this day, and its popular characteristics, from the slave's point of view. Standing, there, identified with the American bondman, making his wrongs mine, I do not hesitate to declare, with all my soul, that the character and conduct of this nation never looked blacker to me than on this 4th of July! Whether we turn to the declarations of the past, or to the professions of the present, the conduct of the nation seems equally hideous and revolting. America is false to the past, false to the present, and solemnly binds herself to be false to the future. Standing with God and the crushed and bleeding slave on this occasion, I will, in the name of humanity which is outraged, in the name of liberty which is fettered, in the name of the constitution and the Bible, which are disregarded and trampled upon, dare to call in question and to denounce, with all the emphasis I can command, everything that serves to perpetuate slavery—the great sin and shame of America! "I will not equivocate; I will not excuse;" I will use the severest language I can command; and yet not one word shall escape me that any man, whose judgement is not blinded by prejudice, or who is not at heart a slaveholder, shall not confess to be right and just.

But I fancy I hear some one of my audience say, it is just in this circumstance that you and your brother abolitionists fail to make a favorable impression on the public mind. Would you argue more, and denounce less, would you persuade more, and rebuke less, your cause would be much more likely to succeed. But, I submit, where all is plain there is nothing to be argued. What point in the anti-slavery creed would you have me argue? On what branch of the subject do the people of this country need light? Must I undertake to prove that the slave is a man? That point is conceded already. Nobody doubts it. The slaveholders themselves acknowledge it in the enactment of laws for their government. They acknowledge it when they punish disobedience on the part of the slave. There are seventy-two crimes in the State of Virginia, which, if committed by a black man (no matter how ignorant he be), subject him to the punishment of death; while only two of the same crimes will subject a white man to the like punishment. What is this but the acknowledgement that the slave is a moral, intellectual and responsible being? The manhood of the slave is conceded. It is admitted in the fact that Southern statute books are covered with enactments forbidding, under severe fines and penalties, the teaching of the slave to read or to write. When you can point to any such laws, in reference to the beasts of the field, then I may consent to argue the manhood of the slave. When the dogs in your streets, when the fowls of the air, when the cattle on your hills, when the fish of the sea, and the reptiles that crawl, shall be unable to distinguish the slave from a brute, there will I argue with you that the slave is a man!

For the present, it is enough to affirm the equal manhood of the negro race. Is it not astonishing that, while we are ploughing, planting and reaping, using all kinds of mechanical tools, erecting houses, constructing bridges, building ships, working in metals of brass, iron, copper, silver and gold; that, while we are reading, writing and cyphering, acting as clerks, merchants and secretaries, having among us lawyers, doctors, ministers, poets, authors, editors, orators and teachers; that, while we are engaged in all manner of enterprises common to other men, digging gold in California, capturing the whale in the Pacific, feeding sheep and cattle on the hill-side, living, moving, acting, thinking, planning, living in families as husbands, wives and children, and, above all, confessing and worshipping the Christian's God, and looking hopefully for life and immortality beyond the grave, we are called upon to prove that we are men!

Would you have me argue that man is entitled to liberty? that he is the rightful owner of his own body? You have already declared it. Must I argue the wrongfulness of slavery? Is that a question for Republicans? Is it to be settled by the rules of logic and argumentation, as a matter beset with great difficulty, involving a doubtful application of the principle of justice, hard to be understood? How should I look to-day, in the presence of Americans, dividing, and subdividing a discourse, to show that men have a natural right to freedom? speaking of it relatively, and positively, negatively, and affirmatively. To do so, would be to make myself ridiculous, and lo offer an insult to your understanding. There is not a man beneath the canopy of heaven, that does not know that slavery is wrong for him.

What, am I to argue that it is wrong to make men brutes, to rob them of their liberty, to work them without wages, to keep them ignorant of their relations to their fellow men, to beat them with sticks, to flay their flesh with the lash, to load their limbs with irons, to hunt them with dogs, to sell them at auction, to sunder their families, to knock out their teeth, to burn their flesh, to starve them into obedience and submission to their masters? Must I argue that a system thus marked with blood, and stained with pollution, is wrong? No! I will not. I have better employments for my time and strength, than such arguments would imply.

What, then, remains to be argued? Is it that slavery is not divine; that God did not establish it; that our doctors of divinity are mistaken? There is blasphemy in the thought. That which is inhuman, cannot be divine! Who can reason on such a proposition? They that can, may; I cannot. The time for such argument is past.

At a time like this, scorching irony, not convincing argument, is 45
needed. O! had I the ability, and could I reach the nation's ear, I would, to-day, pour out a fiery stream of biting ridicule, blasting reproach, withering sarcasm, and stern rebuke. For it is not light that is needed, but fire; it is not the gentle shower, but thunder. We need the storm, the whirlwind, and the earthquake. The feeling of the nation must be quickened; the conscience of the nation must be roused; the propriety of the nation must be startled; the hypocrisy of the nation must be exposed; and its crimes against God and man must be proclaimed and denounced.

What, to the American slave, is your 4th of July? I answer: a day that reveals to him, more than all other days in the year, the gross injustice and cruelty to which he is the constant victim. To him, your celebration is a sham; your boasted liberty, an unholy license; your national greatness, swelling vanity; your sounds of rejoicing are empty and heartless; your denunciations of tyrants, brass fronted impudence; your shouts of liberty and equality, hollow mockery; your prayers and hymns, your sermons and thanksgivings, with all your religious parade, and solemnity, are, to him, mere bombast, fraud, deception, impiety, and hypocrisy—a thin veil to cover up crimes which would disgrace a nation of savages. There is not a nation on the earth guilty of practices, more shocking and bloody, than are the people of these United States, at this very hour.

Go where you may, search where you will, roam through all the monarchies and despotisms of the old world, travel through South America, search out every abuse, and when you have found the last, lay your facts by the side of the everyday practices of this nation, and you will say with me, that, for revolting barbarity and shameless hypocrisy, America reigns without a rival. . . .

Allow me to say, in conclusion, notwithstanding the dark picture I have 74 this day presented of the state of the nation, I do not despair of this country. There are forces in operation, which must inevitably work the downfall of slavery. "The arm of the Lord is not shortened," and the doom of slavery is certain. I, therefore, leave off where I began, with hope. While drawing encouragement from the Declaration of Independence, the great principles it contains, and the genius of American Institutions, my spirit is also cheered by the obvious tendencies of the age. Nations do not now stand in the same relation to each other that they did ages ago. No nation can now shut itself up from the surrounding world, and trot round in the same old path of its fathers without interference. The time was when such could be done. Long established customs of hurtful character could formerly fence themselves in, and do their evil work with social impunity. Knowledge was then confined and enjoyed by the privileged few, and the multitude walked on in mental darkness. But a change has now come over the affairs of mankind. Walled cities and empires have become unfashionable. The arm of commerce has borne away the gates of the strong city. Intelligence is penetrating the darkest corners of the globe. It makes its pathway over and under the sea, as well as on the earth. Wind, steam, and lightning are its chartered agents. Oceans no longer divide, but link nations together. From Boston to London is now a holiday excursion. Space is comparatively annihilated. Thoughts expressed on one side of the Atlantic are distinctly heard on the other. The far off and almost fabulous Pacific rolls in grandeur at our feet. The Celestial Empire, the mystery of ages, is being solved. The fiat of the Almighty, "Let there be Light," has not yet spent its force. No abuse, no outrage whether in taste, sport or avarice, can now hide itself from the all-pervading light. The iron shoe, and crippled foot of China must be seen, in contrast with nature. Africa must rise and put on her yet unwoven garment. "Ethiopia shall stretch out her hand unto

God." In the fervent aspirations of William Lloyd Garrison, I say, and let every heart join in saying it:

God speed the year of jubilee 75
The wide world o'er!
When from their galling chains set free,
Th' oppress'd shall vilely bend the knee,
And wear the yoke of tyranny
Like brutes no more.
That year will come, and freedom's reign,
To man his plundered rights again
Restore.

God speed the day when human blood
Shall cease to flow!
In every clime be understood,
The claims of human brotherhood,
And each return for evil, good,
Not blow for blow;
That day will come all feuds to end
And change into a faithful friend
Each foe.

God speed the hour, the glorious hour,
When none on earth
Shall exercise a lordly power,
Nor in a tyrant's presence cower;
But all to manhood's stature tower,
By equal birth!
THAT HOUR WILL COME, to each, to all,
And from his prison-house, the thrall
Go forth.

Until that year, day, hour, arrive,
With head, and heart, and hand I'll strive,
To break the rod, and rend the gyve,
The spoiler of his prey deprive—
So witness Heaven!
And never from my chosen post,
Whate'er the peril or the cost,
Be driven.

QUESTIONING THE TEXT

1. In her headnote, A.L. writes that Douglass presented this speech to the Rochester Ladies' Anti-Slavery Society in Rochester, New York. Even without knowing about this group, can you tell from Douglass's speech

whether the audience he addressed was primarily white or black? Does he seem to address only the members of the group that invited him to speak, or a broader audience? How can you tell?

2. Working with a classmate, identify passages in which Douglass appeals to values he assumes the audience shares with him. How does he make these appeals? What metaphors and images does he use? How does he draw upon values associated with the American fight for independence to argue for the abolition of slavery?
3. In class discussion, consider Douglass's effectiveness at addressing potential counterarguments. On what points does Douglass seem to anticipate objections from the audience? List as many of these objections as you can find. How does Douglass address them?

MAKING CONNECTIONS

4. In paragraphs 39 through 47 of this speech, Douglass acknowledges anger toward some members of his real audience, whereas Edward Abbey, in an excerpt from *Desert Solitaire* (p. 619), and Abelardo Delgado, in "Stupid America" (p. 625), both express anger at imagined audiences. How do these three writers differ in their approaches to expressing anger? What constraints does the rhetorical situation impose on each writer and his ability to express his emotions?
5. Working with one or two classmates, study the ways in which Douglass draws upon principles stated in the Declaration of Independence (p. 517) to make his argument. To which parts of the Declaration does he allude? What purposes do these allusions serve in Douglass's argument?
6. Douglass claims that "[his] spirit is . . . cheered by the obvious tendencies of the age" (paragraph 74), and he proceeds to describe a world that is continually shrinking. Consider his comments in relation to Philippe Legrain's arguments about globalization (p. 570). Do you think that Douglass would share Legrain's views of the current trends in cultural globalization? Why, or why not?

JOINING THE CONVERSATION

7. In her headnote, A.L. suggests asking yourself, "What to me is the Fourth of July—and why?" Write a speech or essay answering that question, or answer the same question about another national holiday. Think about how—or whether—you identify with the ideals represented by the holiday you choose to write on, and use vivid examples to convey your reasons.

8. Do some research into the occasion for Douglass's speech: find out about the origins and membership of the group he addressed, how his speech was received, what experience Douglass had as an orator before and after this occasion. Use your research in a speech or essay commemorating Douglass's address, for presentation at a campus event or publication in a campus or local newspaper. Choose an appropriate occasion to present your work: the Fourth of July, perhaps, a day during Black History Month, or even Labor Day, Martin Luther King's Birthday, or Memorial Day. Be sure to craft your opening to establish the relevance of your commemoration to the day on which you choose to present it.

WARD CHURCHILL

Crimes against Humanity

*W*ARD CHURCHILL *(b. 1947) is no stranger to controversy. A prolific writer and much-in-demand speaker, he has devoted most of his career to denouncing discrimination against and exploitation of Native American peoples. Churchill writes a regular column for the leftist* Z Magazine *(where the following article first appeared in March 1993) and is the author of numerous books, including* Fantasies of the Master Race *(1992);* Struggle for the Land *(1993);* From a Native Son *(1996);* Pacifism as Pathology *(1998), coauthored with Mike Ryan; and* Struggle for the Land: Native North American Resistance to Genocide, Ecocide, and Colonization *(2002).*

As these book titles suggest, Churchill, a professor of American Indian Studies at the University of Colorado, is a man with a mission. In "Crimes against Humanity," he brings satire—a serious, close-to-the-edge kind of satire—to that mission to highlight what he sees as major and ongoing offenses against Native Americans (from the derogatory use of Indian caricatures in team sports to the secret use of involuntary sterilization programs for Indian women).

I have long been interested in the effects of stereotypical labels and media images on people's sense of themselves, of who they are, of their identities. Churchill's essay is a hard one for me to read precisely because it makes these stereotypes visible to me in unusual and decidedly in-your-face ways. The very day I read this article, I noticed over a dozen unflattering images of Native Americans—in advertisements, on assorted food boxes in the supermarket, on billboards, seemingly everywhere I turned. Some I had noticed and been troubled by before—but not all. I wonder what your experience will be?

—A.L.

During the past couple of seasons, there has been an increasing wave of controversy regarding the names of professional sports teams like the Atlanta Braves, Cleveland Indians, Washington Redskins, and Kansas City Chiefs. The issue extends to the names of college teams like Florida State University Seminoles, University of Illinois Fighting Illini, and so on, right on down to high school outfits like the Lamar (Colorado) Savages. Also involved have been team adoption of mascots, replete with feathers, buckskins, beads, spears, and "warpaint" (some fans have opted to adorn themselves in the same fashion), and nifty little "pep" gestures like the "Indian Chant" and "Tomahawk Chop."

A substantial number of American Indians have protested that use of native names, images, and symbols as sports team mascots and the like is, by definition, a virulently racist practice. Given the historical relationship between Indians and non-Indians during what has been called the Conquest of America, American Indian Movement leader (and American Indian Anti-Defamation Council founder) Russell Means has compared the practice to contemporary Germans naming their soccer teams the "Jews," "Hebrews," and "Yids," while adorning their uniforms with grotesque caricatures of Jewish faces taken from the Nazis' anti-Semitic propaganda of the 1930s. Numerous demonstrations have occurred in conjunction with games—most notably during the November 15, 1992, matchup between the Chiefs and Redskins in Kansas City—by angry Indians and their supporters.

In response, a number of players—especially African Americans and other minority athletes—have been trotted out by professional team owners like Ted Turner, as well as university and public school officials, to announce that they mean not to insult but to honor native people. They have been joined by the television networks and most major newspapers, all of which have editorialized that Indian discomfort with the situation is "no big deal," insisting that the whole thing is just "good, clean fun." The country needs more such fun, they've argued, and "a few disgruntled Native Americans" have no right to undermine the nation's enjoyment of its leisure time by complaining. This is especially the case, some have argued, "in hard times like these." It has even been contended that Indian outrage at being systematically degraded—rather than the degradation itself—creates "a serious barrier to the sort of intergroup communication so necessary in a multicultural society such as ours."

Okay, let's communicate. We are frankly dubious that those advancing such positions really believe their own rhetoric, but, just for the sake of argument, let's accept the premise that they are sincere. If what they say is true, then isn't it time we spread such "inoffensiveness" and "good cheer" around among *all* groups so that *everybody* can participate *equally* in fostering the round of national laughs they call for? Sure it is—the country can't have too much fun or "intergroup involvement"—so the more, the merrier. Simple consistency demands that anyone who thinks the Tomahawk Chop is a swell pastime must be just as hearty in their endorsement of the following ideas—by the logic used to defend the defamation of American Indians—[and] should help us all really start yukking it up.

First, as a counterpart to the Redskins, we need an NFL team called 5
"Niggers" to honor Afro-Americans. Halftime festivities for fans might include a simulated stewing of the opposing coach in a large pot while players and cheerleaders dance around it, garbed in leopard skins and wearing fake bones in their noses. This concept obviously goes along with the kind of gaiety attending the Chop, but also with the actions of the Kansas City Chiefs, whose team members—prominently including black team members—lately appeared on a poster looking "fierce" and "savage" by way of wearing Indian regalia. Just a bit of harmless "morale boosting," says the Chiefs's front office. You bet.

So that the newly formed Niggers sports club won't end up too out of sync while expressing the "spirit" and "identity" of Afro-Americans in the above fashion, a baseball franchise—let's call this one the "Sambos"—should be formed. How about a basketball team called the "Spearchuckers"? A hockey team called the "Jungle Bunnies"? Maybe the "essence" of these teams could be depicted by images of tiny black faces adorned with huge pairs of lips. The players could appear on TV every week or so gnawing on chicken legs and spitting watermelon seeds at one another. Catchy, eh? Well, there's "nothing to be upset about," according to those who love wearing "war bonnets" to the Super Bowl or having "Chief Illiniwik" dance around the sports arenas of Urbana, Illinois.

And why stop there? There are plenty of other groups to include. "Hispanics"? They can be "represented" by the Galveston "Greasers" and San Diego "Spics," at least until the Wisconsin "Wetbacks" and Baltimore "Beaners" get off the ground. Asian Americans? How about the "Slopes," "Dinks," "Gooks," and "Zipperheads"? Owners of the latter teams might get their logo ideas from editorial page cartoons printed in the nation's newspapers during World War II: slant eyes, buck teeth, big glasses, but nothing racially insulting or derogatory, according to the editors and artists involved at the time. Indeed, this Second World War vintage stuff can be seen as just another barrel of laughs, at least by what current editors say are their "local standards" concerning American Indians.

Let's see. Who's been left out? Teams like the Kansas City "Kikes," Hanover "Honkies," San Leandro "Shylocks," Daytona "Dagos," and Pittsburgh "Polacks" will fill a certain social void among white folk. Have a religious belief? Let's all go for the gusto and gear up the Milwaukee "Mackerel Snappers" and Hollywood "Holy Rollers." The Fighting Irish of Notre Dame can be rechristened the "Drunken Irish" or "Papist Pigs." Issues of gender and sexual preference can be addressed through creation of teams like the St. Louis "Sluts," Boston "Bimbos," Detroit "Dykes," and the Fresno "Fags." How about the Gainesville "Gimps" and Richmond "Retards," so the physically and mentally impaired won't be excluded from our fun and games?

Now, don't go getting "overly sensitive" out there. None of this is demeaning or insulting, at least not when it's being done to Indians. Just ask the folks who are doing it, or their apologists like Andy Rooney in the national media. They'll tell you—as in fact they *have* been telling you—that there's been no harm done, regardless of what their victims think, feel, or say. The situation is exactly the same as when those with precisely the same mentality used to insist that Step 'n' Fetchit was okay, or Rochester on the *Jack Benny Show,* or Amos and Andy, Charlie Chan, the Frito Bandito, or any of the other cutesy symbols making up the lexicon of American racism. Have we communicated yet?

Let's get just a little bit real here. The notion of "fun" embodied in rit- 10
uals like the Tomahawk Chop must be understood for what it is. There's not a single non-Indian example used above which can be considered socially acceptable in even the most marginal sense. The reasons are obvious enough. So why is it different where American Indians are concerned? One can only

conclude that, in contrast to the other groups at issue, Indians are (falsely) perceived as being too few, and therefore too weak, to defend themselves effectively against racist and otherwise offensive behavior.

Fortunately, there are some glimmers of hope. A few teams and their fans have gotten the message and have responded appropriately. Stanford University, which opted to drop the name "Indians" from Stanford, has experienced no resulting drop-off in attendance. Meanwhile, the local newspaper in Portland, Oregon, recently decided its long-standing editorial policy prohibiting use of racial epithets should include derogatory team names. The Redskins, for instance, are now referred to as "the Washington team," and will continue to be described in this way until the franchise adopts an inoffensive moniker (newspaper sales in Portland have suffered no decline as a result).

Such examples are to be applauded and encouraged. They stand as figurative beacons in the night, proving beyond all doubt that it is quite possible to indulge in the pleasure of athletics without accepting blatant racism into the bargain.

Nuremberg Precedents

On October 16, 1946, a man named Julius Streicher mounted the steps of a gallows. Moments later he was dead, the sentence of an international tribunal composed of representatives of the United States, France, Great Britain, and the Soviet Union having been imposed. Streicher's body was then cremated, and—so horrendous were his crimes thought to have been—his ashes dumped into an unspecified German river so that "no one should ever know a particular place to go for reasons of mourning his memory."

Julius Streicher had been convicted at Nuremberg, Germany, of what were termed "crimes against humanity." The lead prosecutor in his case—Justice Robert Jackson of the United States Supreme Court—had not argued that the defendant had killed anyone, nor that he had personally committed any especially violent act. Nor was it contended that Streicher had held any particularly important position in the German government during the period in which the so-called Third Reich had exterminated some six million Jews, as well as several million Gypsies, Poles, Slavs, homosexuals, and other *untermenschen* ("subhumans").

The sole offense for which the accused was ordered put to death was in 15
having served as publisher/editor of a Bavarian tabloid entitled *Der Sturmer* during the early- to mid-1930s, years before the Nazi genocide actually began. In this capacity, he had penned a long series of virulently anti-Semitic editorials and "news" stories, usually accompanied by cartoons and other images graphically depicting Jews in extraordinarily derogatory fashion. This, the prosecution asserted, had done much to "dehumanize" the targets of his distortion in the mind of the German public. In turn, such dehumanization had

made it possible—or at least easier—for average Germans to later indulge in the outright liquidation of Jewish "vermin." The tribunal agreed, holding that Streicher was therefore complicit in genocide and deserving of death by hanging.

During his remarks to the Nuremberg tribunal, Justice Jackson observed that, in implementing its sentences, the participating powers were morally and legally binding themselves to adhere forever after to the same standards of conduct that were being applied to Streicher and the other Nazi leaders. In the alternative, he said, the victorious allies would have committed "pure murder" at Nuremberg—no different in substance from that carried out by those they presumed to judge—rather than establishing the "permanent benchmark for justice" which was intended.

Yet in the United States of Robert Jackson, the indigenous American Indian population had already been reduced, in a process which is ongoing to this day, from perhaps 12.5 million in the year 1500 to fewer than 250,000 by the beginning of the twentieth century. This was accomplished, according to official sources, "largely through the cruelty of [Euro-American] settlers," and an informal but clear governmental policy which had made it an articulated goal to "exterminate these red vermin," or at least whole segments of them.

Bounties had been placed on the scalps of Indians—any Indians—in places as diverse as Georgia, Kentucky, Texas, the Dakotas, Oregon, and California, and had been maintained until resident Indian populations were decimated or disappeared altogether. Entire peoples such as the Cherokee had been reduced to half their size through a policy of forced removal from their homelands east of the Mississippi River to what were then considered less preferable areas in the West.

Others, such as the Navajo, suffered the same fate while under military guard for years on end. The United States Army had also perpetrated a long series of wholesale massacres of Indians at places like Horseshoe Bend, Bear River, Sand Creek, the Washita River, the Marias River, Camp Robinson, and Wounded Knee.

Through it all, hundreds of popular novels—each competing with the 20
next to make Indians appear more grotesque, menacing, and inhuman—were sold in the tens of millions of copies in the United States. Plainly, the Euro-American public was being conditioned to see Indians in such a way as to allow their eradication to continue. And continue it did until the Manifest Destiny of the United States—a direct precursor to what Hitler would subsequently call *Lebensraumpolitik* ("the politics of living space")—was consummated.

By 1900, the national project of "clearing" Native Americans from their land and replacing them with "superior" Anglo-American settlers was complete; the indigenous population had been reduced by as much as 98 percent while approximately 97.5 percent of their original territory had "passed" to the invaders. The survivors had been concentrated, out of sight and mind of the public, on scattered "reservations," all of them under the self-assigned "plenary" (full) power of the federal government. There was, of course, no Nuremberg-style tribunal passing judgment on those who had fostered such circumstances in North America. No U.S. official or private citizen was ever imprisoned—never mind hanged—for implementing or propagandizing what had been done. Nor had the process of genocide afflicting Indians been completed. Instead, it merely changed form.

Between the 1880s and the 1980s, nearly half of all Native American children were coercively transferred from their own families, communities, and cultures to those of the conquering society. This was done through compulsory attendance at remote boarding schools, often hundreds of miles from their homes, where native children were kept for years on end while being systematically "deculturated" (indoctrinated to think and act in the manner of Euro-Americans rather than as Indians). It was also accomplished through a pervasive foster home and adoption program—including "blind" adoptions, where children would be permanently denied information as to who they were/are and where they'd come from—placing native youths in non-Indian homes.

The express purpose of all this was to facilitate a U.S. governmental policy to bring about the "assimilation" (dissolution) of indigenous societies. In other words, Indian cultures as such were to be caused to disappear. Such policy objectives are directly contrary to the United Nations 1948 Convention on Punishment and Prevention of the Crime of Genocide, an element of international law arising from the Nuremberg proceedings. The forced "transfer of the children" of a targeted "racial, ethnical, or religious group" is explicitly prohibited as a genocidal activity under the convention's second article.

Article II of the Genocide Convention also expressly prohibits involuntary sterilization as a means of "preventing births among" a targeted population. Yet, in 1975, it was conceded by the U.S. government that its Indian Health Service (IHS), then a subpart of the Bureau of Indian Affairs (BIA), was even then conducting a secret program of involuntary sterilization that had affected approximately 40 percent of all Indian women. The program was allegedly discontinued, and the IHS was transferred to the Public Health Service, but no one was punished. In 1990, it came out that the IHS was inoculating Inuit children in Alaska with hepatitis-B vaccine. The vaccine had already been banned by the World Health Organization as having a demonstrated correlation with the HIV syndrome, which is itself correlated to AIDS. As this is written, a "field test" of hepatitis-A vaccine, also HIV-correlated, is being conducted on Indian reservations in the northern plains region.

The Genocide Convention makes it a "crime against humanity" to 25
create conditions leading to the destruction of an identifiable human group, as such. Yet the BIA has utilized the government's plenary prerogatives to negotiate mineral leases "on behalf of" Indian peoples paying a fraction of standard royalty rates. The result has been "super profits" for a number of preferred U.S. corporations. Meanwhile, Indians, whose reservations ironically turned out to be in some of the most mineral-rich areas of North America, which

makes us the nominally wealthiest segment of the continent's population, live in dire poverty.

By the government's own data in the mid-1980s, Indians received the lowest annual and lifetime per capita incomes of any aggregate population group in the United States. Concomitantly, we suffer the highest rate of infant mortality, death by exposure and malnutrition, disease, and the like. Under such circumstances, alcoholism and other escapist forms of substance abuse are endemic to the Indian community, a situation which leads both to a general physical debilitation of the population and a catastrophic accident rate. Teen suicide among Indians is several times the national average.

The average life expectancy of a reservation-based Native American man is barely forty-five years; women can expect to live less than three years longer.

Such itemizations could be continued at great length, including matters like the radioactive contamination of large portions of contemporary Indian Country, the forced relocation of traditional Navajos, and so on. But the point should be made: genocide, as defined in international law, is a continuing fact of day-to-day life (and death) for North America's native peoples. Yet there has been—and is—only the barest flicker of public concern about, or even consciousness of, this reality. Absent any serious expression of public outrage, no one is punished and the process continues.

A salient reason for public acquiescence before the ongoing holocaust in Native North America has been a continuation of the popular legacy, often through more effective media. Since 1925, Hollywood has released more than two thousand films, many of them rerun frequently on television, portraying Indians as strange, perverted, ridiculous, and often dangerous things of the past. Moreover, we are habitually presented to mass audiences one-dimensionally, devoid of recognizable human motivations and emotions; Indians thus serve as props, little more. We have thus been thoroughly and systematically dehumanized.

30 Nor is this the extent of it. Everywhere, we are used as logos, as mascots, as jokes: Big Chief writing tablets, Red Man chewing tobacco, Winnebago campers, Navajo and Cherokee and Pontiac and Cadillac pickups and automobiles. There are the Cleveland Indians, the Kansas City Chiefs, the Atlanta Braves, and the Washington Redskins professional sports teams—not to mention those in thousands of colleges, high schools, and elementary schools across the country—each with their own degrading caricatures and parodies of Indians and/or things Indian. Pop fiction continues in the same vein, including an unending stream of New Age manuals purporting to expose the inner works of indigenous spirituality in everything from pseudophilosophical to do-it-yourself styles. Blond Yuppies from Beverly Hills amble about the country claiming to be reincarnated seventeenth-century Cheyenne Ushanians ready to perform previously secret ceremonies.

In effect, a concerted, sustained, and in some ways accelerating effort has gone into making Indians unreal. It is thus of obvious importance that the

PHOTO ESSAY:

American Myths and Images—from the Covers of *Time*

Recent events such as 9/11 and American interventions in Afghanistan and Iraq have led to wide-ranging reassessments of the role played by the United States on the world stage. Just as people from other nations have raised tough questions about the motives and ambitions of the world's only military superpower, Americans themselves have taken a new interest in their national values and symbols. In this photo essay (as well as in Chapter 7), we focus on some core American beliefs, attitudes, and myths to encourage just such an examination.

Each of the following images is a full cover from *Time*, a major news magazine published weekly in the United States since 1923. To make the cover of *Time* means something in American culture. Who or what appears within the famous red borders is often revealing of the national character.

You can extend your exploration of American myths and images by searching the *Time* covers archive yourself at <http://www.time.com/time/magazine/archives>.

HOLLYWOOD DREAMS: MARILYN MONROE, MAY 14, 1956

The celluloid dreams sold by Hollywood's filmmakers have reached around the world, showcasing glamour, excitement, wealth, and violence.

1. How well does the Marilyn Monroe on this *Time* cover match your own image of the star? How is Marilyn understood today?
2. What five Hollywood films would you select as most representative of American values, myths, or both?
3. How does Hollywood shape attitudes toward women and/or sexuality?

LAND OF EQUALITY: MARTIN LUTHER KING JR., FEBRUARY 18, 1957

While Martin Luther King Jr. symbolizes the American ideal of equality for all, the Montgomery bus boycott and many of his later campaigns helped reveal the flip side of that ideal, inequality.

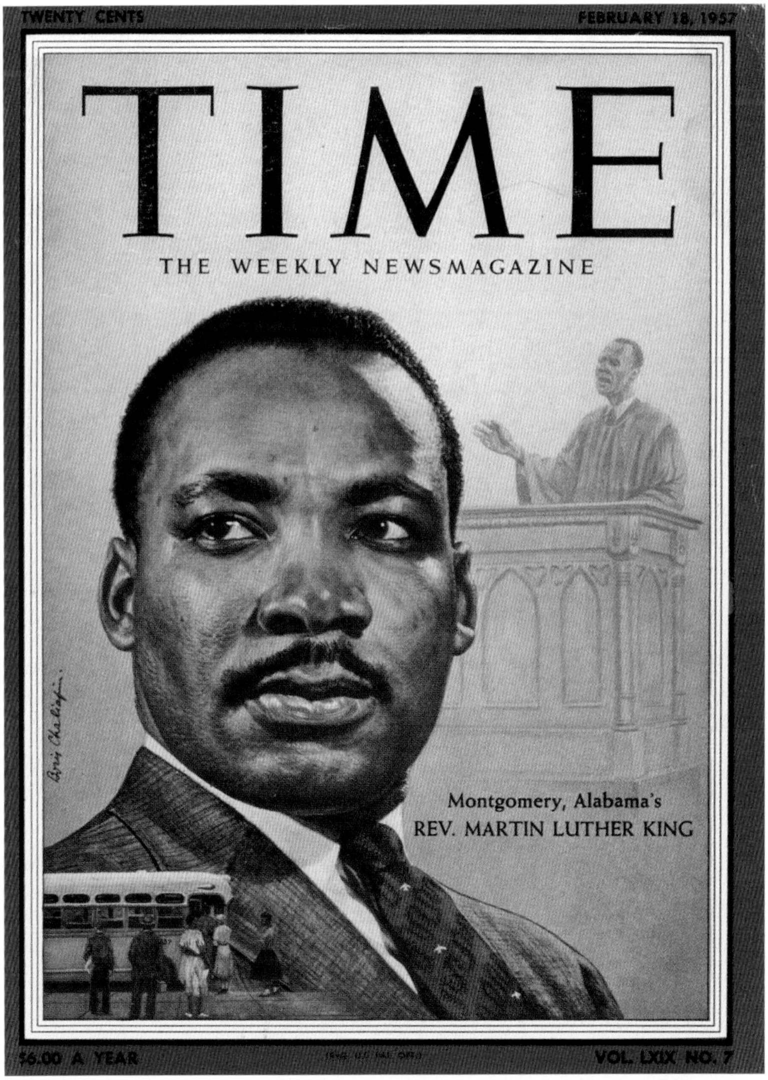

1. What do the different parts of this image (the central figure of King, the people and buses in the lower left, the African American man at the bar in the upper right) say about different aspects of America as the land of equality?
2. How does the use of color in this image work to reinforce values of equality?
3. What other images come to your mind when you think of the American goal of equality? Which of these is most positive? Which is the most negative?

AMERICAN FRONTIERS: MAN ON THE MOON, JULY 25, 1969

Frontiers have always driven Americans, from the time of the first contact (and ultimate devastation) of the Native Americans to the building of the railroad across the country, and more recently to the far reaches of space and the ocean.

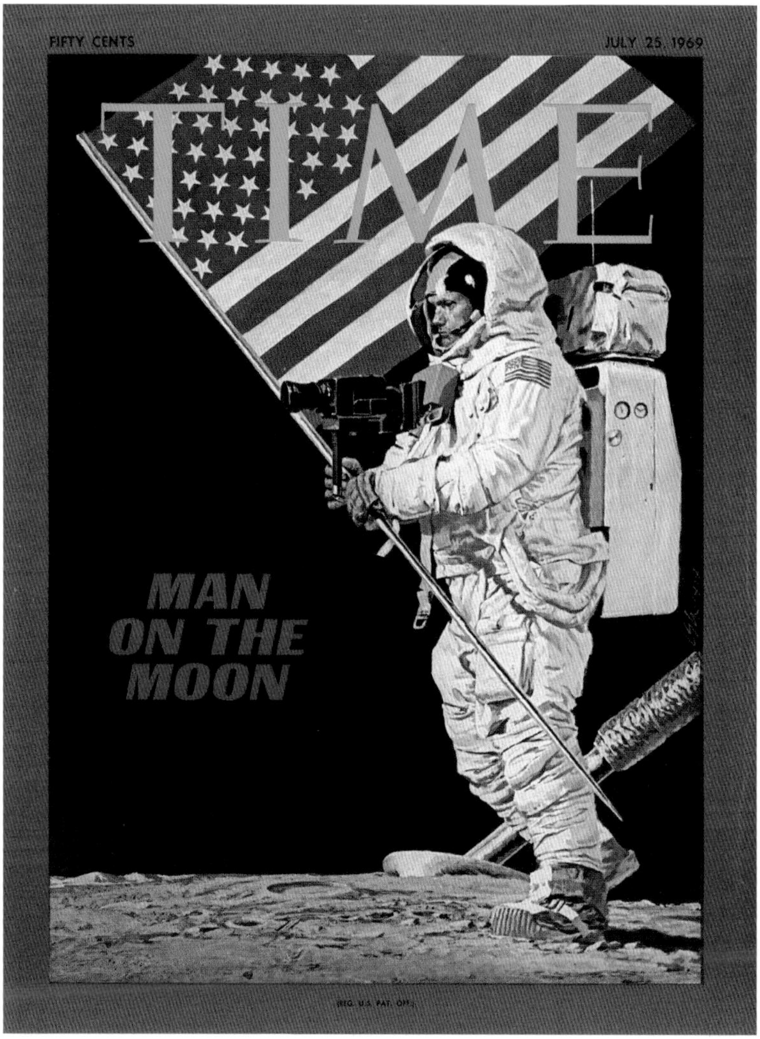

1. How does this image of Neil Armstrong planting the American flag on the moon accord with other images you have of American frontiers? Working with a classmate, make a brief list of songs (or films) that either celebrate or critique American frontier-seeking.
2. In addition to frontier-seeking, what other values does this *Time* cover represent?
3. How might this cover have been read by those living in other countries or cultures in 1969? What would this image have suggested to them about America and frontiers?

RUGGED INDIVIDUALISM: JOHN WAYNE, AUGUST 8, 1969

Many Americans prefer to think of themselves as people capable of making it on their own, tough as pioneers.

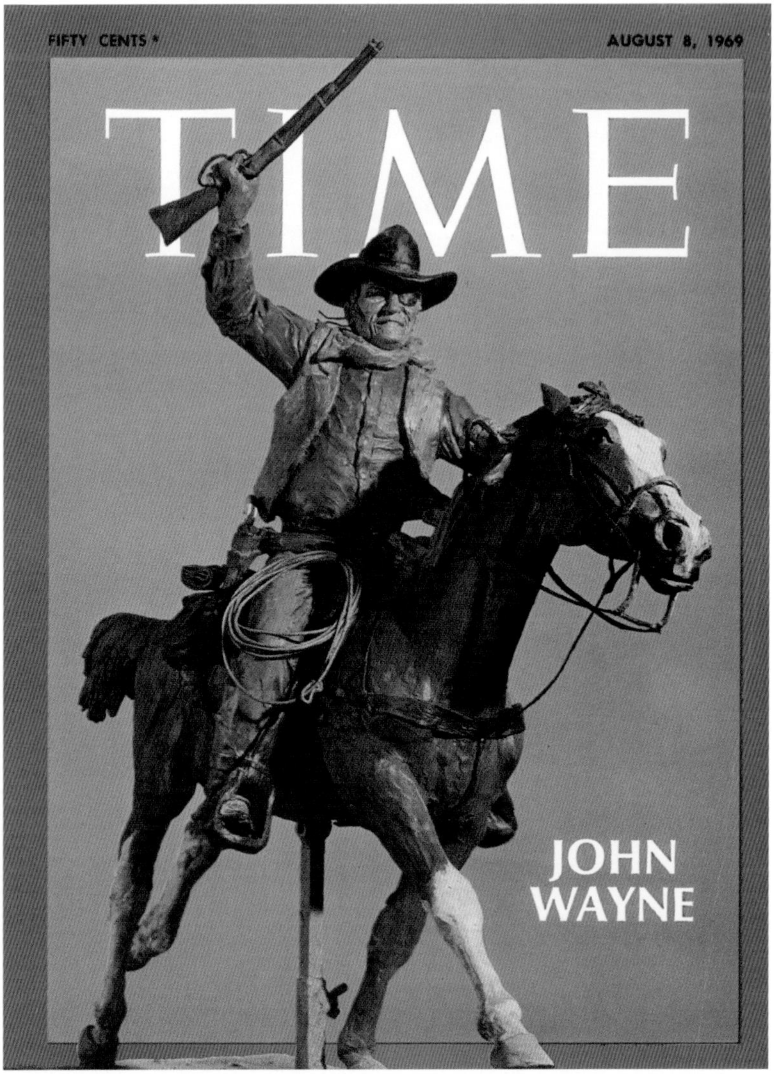

1. List the elements of the sculpture that mark John Wayne as a figure of myth, larger than life.
2. How might cowboy images of this sort be read into the American character by people from other cultures or countries?
3. Speculate on the reasons *Time* might have chosen to show Wayne in a sculpture representing his role in *True Grit* (1969) rather than in a still from the movie itself?

REBELS: PROTEST! MAY 18, 1970

The United States began in revolutionary protest against an established order, and Americans today still celebrate the rebel who sees the world differently.

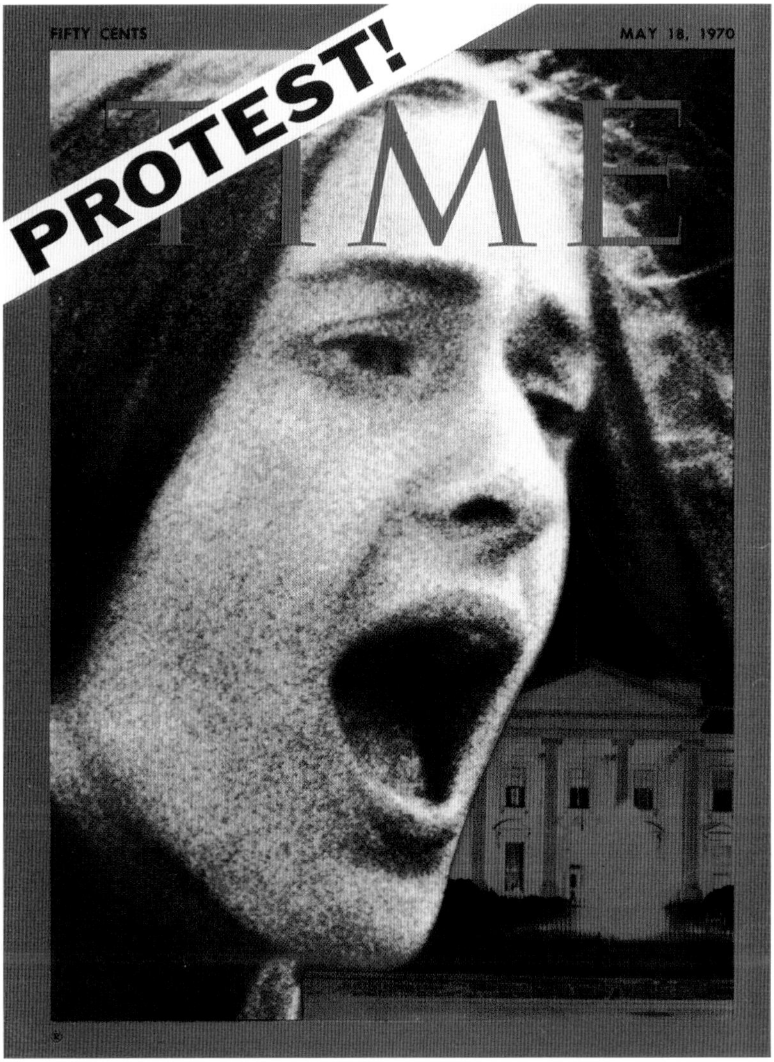

1. In a group, consider why protests so often involve college students. What subjects inspire protest today?
2. What messages does the *Time* cover convey, with its stark juxtaposition of a protestor and the White House? Study the visual elements carefully, and then research the history behind the cover. What was happening in May 1970?
3. Many iconic American rebels seem to be charismatic loners. Is there a contradiction in role between the rebel and the protestor? Make a list of contemporary rebels—for example, Bob Dylan, Camille Paglia, Ani DiFranco, and Mos Def—and discuss their influence.

LADY LIBERTY: HAIL, LIBERTY! JULY 14, 1986

"Give me your tired, your poor," words inscribed on the plaque at the base of Lady Liberty, have held out the ideal of liberty since the statue was given by France in celebration of the first U. S. centennial.

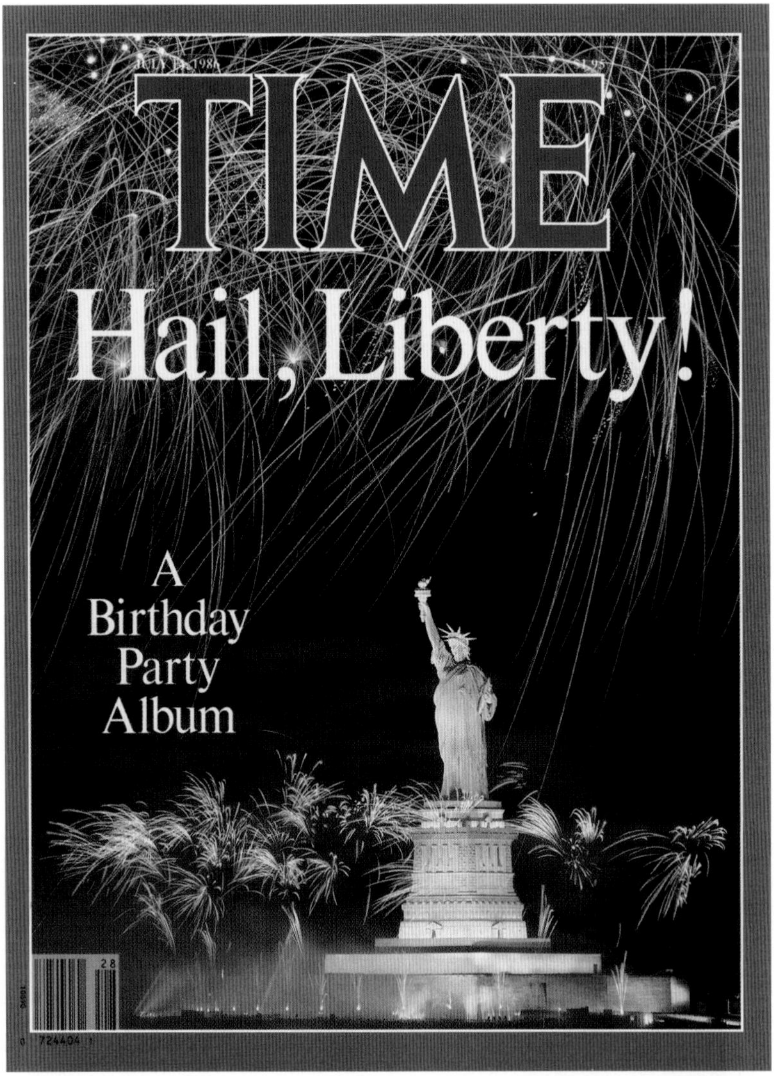

1. Why do you think *Time* may have decided to feature the Statue of Liberty on its cover for
   July 14, 1986—over a week after the July 4 "birthday"? Do a little research and see what you can find out.
2. What other icons represent liberty to you? List as many as you can, and then compare them for the ways in which they represent differing ideals.
3. What do the fireworks add to this image? Do they in any way comment on the ideals usually attributed to the Statue of Liberty?

RAGS TO RICHES: NAPSTER'S SHAWN FANNING, OCTOBER 2, 2000

When nineteen-year-old Shawn Fanning hit the jackpot with Napster, it seemed as if the myth of "little guy (or gal) makes good" was true.

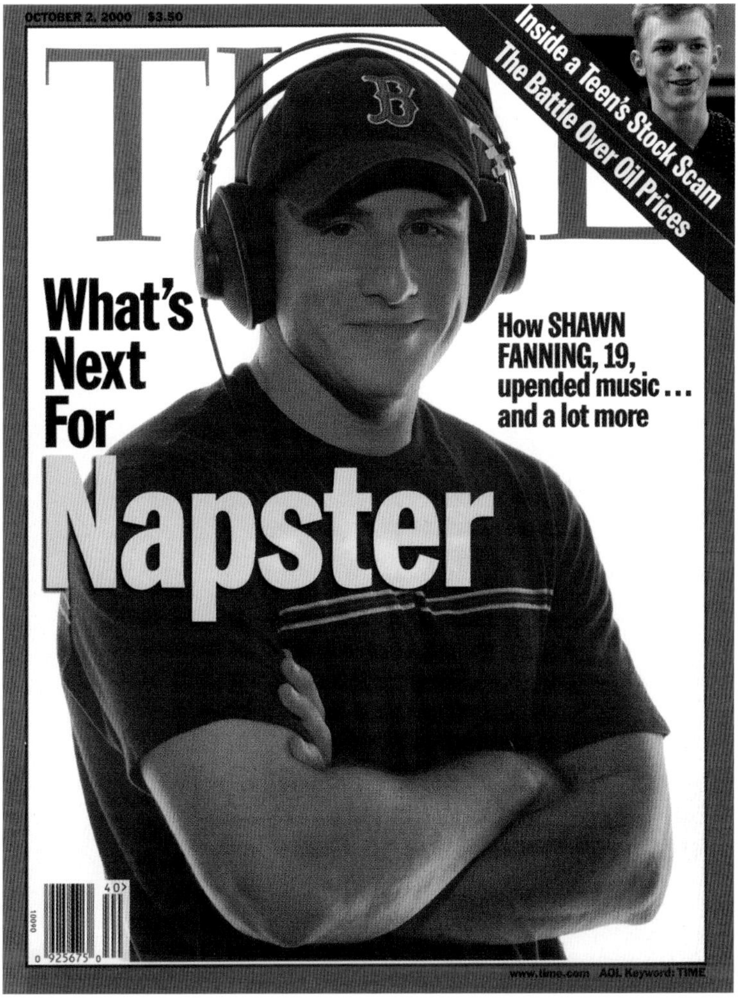

1. How does *Time's* representation of Fanning (the baseball cap, the headphones, the T-shirt, and so on) work to call up the "little guy makes good" myth?
2. Make a list of novels or films that have pursued this particular American myth. Share your list with others in your class and then, working together, consider which of your examples paints a rosy picture of the rags-to-riches myth and which ones present a darker view.
3. As you probably know, Napster started a war with the music industry over copyright protection, and that war is still raging. What is your opinion on this issue? In what ways might the "little guy makes good" myth, in general, raise questions of ethics?

TECHNOLOGY AS PROGRESS: SECRETS OF THE NEW MATRIX, MAY 12, 2003

Science and technology promise Americans and the world affluence and progress, though sometimes at a price.

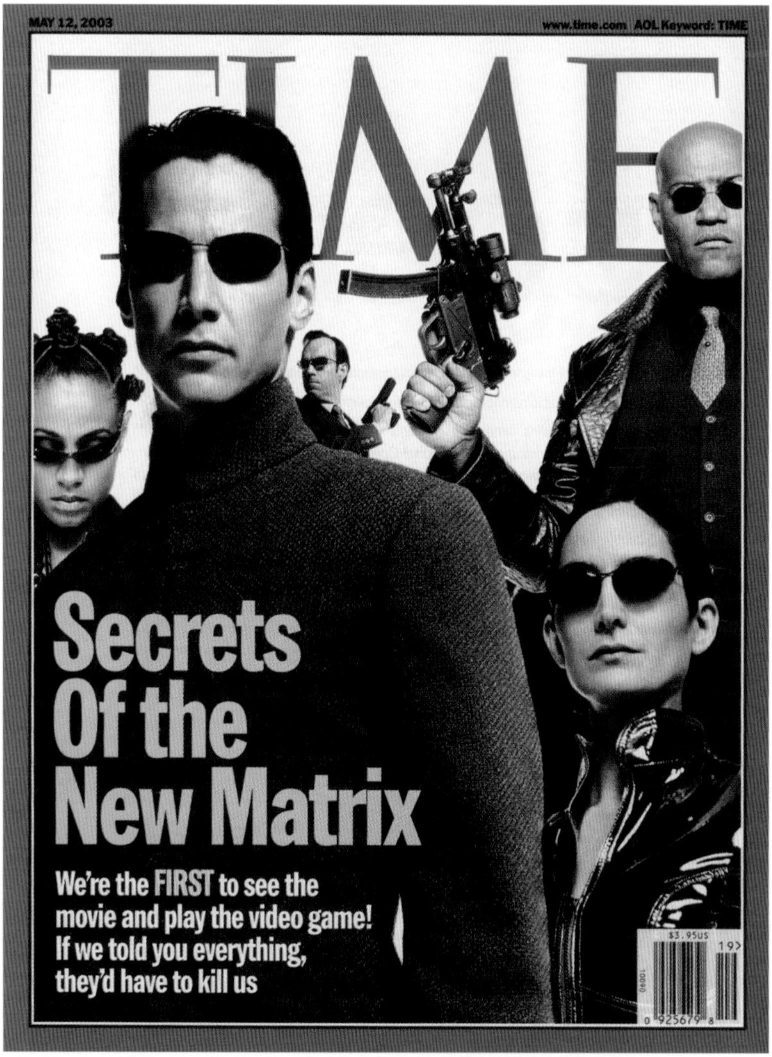

1. In what ways does *The Matrix* trilogy parody or debunk contemporary faith in progress? In what ways does American culture depend on this faith?

2. Identify some films that express a range of contrary attitudes toward science and technology? Consider examining films (and TV shows) from particular eras or decades.

3. Besides a faith in technology, what other American myths are embodied in this cover?

American public begin to think about the implications of such things the next time they witness a gaggle of face-painted and war-bonneted buffoons doing the Tomahawk Chop at a baseball or football game. It is necessary that they think about the implications of the grade-school teacher adorning a child in turkey feathers to commemorate Thanksgiving. Think about the significance of John Wayne or Charlton Heston killing a dozen "savages" with a single bullet the next time a western comes on TV. Think about why Land-o-Lakes finds it appropriate to market its butter with the stereotyped image of an "Indian princess" on the wrapper. Think about what it means when non-Indian academics profess—as they often do—to "know more about Indians than Indians do themselves." Think about the significance of charlatans like Carlos Castaneda and Jamake Highwater and Mary Summer Rain and Lynn Andrews churning out "Indian" bestsellers, one after the other, while Indians typically can't get into print.

Think about the real situation of American Indians. Think about Julius Streicher. Remember Justice Jackson's admonition. Understand that the treatment of Indians in American popular culture is not "cute" or "amusing" or just "good, clean fun."

Know that it causes real pain and real suffering to real people. Know that it threatens our very survival. And know that this is just as much a crime against humanity as anything the Nazis ever did. It is likely that the indigenous people of the United States will never demand that those guilty of such criminal activity be punished for their deeds. But the least we have the right to expect—indeed, to demand—is that such practices finally be brought to a halt.

QUESTIONING THE TEXT

1. Working with a classmate, look closely at Churchill's use of quotation marks in "Crimes against Humanity." What kinds of words and phrases does he enclose in quotation marks—and why? What effects—even subtle ones—do these marks have on your reading of the essay? Make notes on your findings and bring them to class for discussion.
2. Toward the end of the article, Churchill says "a concerted, sustained, and in some ways accelerating effort has gone into making Indians unreal" (paragraph 31). Make a list of the examples, statistics, and other types of evidence the writer uses to support this claim. Then write a brief summary of this evidence, and conclude with your observations on the potential consequences of making any group of people seem "unreal" to others.
3. Why do you think Churchill opens and closes this essay with a scathing discussion of the (mis)use of Native American names and images in big-league sports? In what ways does the opening discussion prepare you for Churchill's extended charge of "crimes against humanity"?

MAKING CONNECTIONS

4. Read Zora Neale Hurston's "How It Feels to Be Colored Me" (p. 414), and then compare the tone of that essay to the tone Churchill uses. How would you describe the tone of each piece, and in what ways do you find the tones particularly effective or ineffective? Write a paragraph or two in which you compare the tones and explain which you find most effective.
5. Paula Gunn Allen (p. 458) also addresses the effects of European-American conquest of Native American culture, arguing that tribal images of women in particular are valuable and need to be maintained. After rereading Allen's essay, think about how these two authors' comments on Native American history and culture affect your understanding of American myths, such as the myth of the American frontier or the myth of America as the land of opportunity. Does each essay challenge different aspects of American myth? Do the two essays combine to challenge some aspects of American myth? Use examples from the essays to support your answers.

JOINING THE CONVERSATION

6. Spend some time online, gathering the names of college teams in the state where you live or attend school. What categories do you find being used for such names, and what characteristics do they suggest? Might any of the names be considered offensive? Write a brief essay on your findings and bring it to class for discussion.
7. Working with two or three classmates, do some research on the native inhabitants in one of your home states or in the state you attend college. What is the native population of this state today, and what was it around 1500? What evidence marks the presence of native peoples—names of towns, rivers, mountains, reservations, company logos, sports teams, and so on? Did the native peoples of the state sign any treaties? If so, to what did they agree? As a group, analyze the information you have gathered, and prepare a 15-minute report for your class on "Native People of Our State—Then and Now."
8. Churchill demonstrates the power that labels can have in our society, saying that these labels cause "real pain and real suffering to real people" (paragraph 33). In a brief essay, reflect on the effects of labels that have been applied to you (by others or by yourself) and labels you have applied to others.

NEIL POSTMAN
The Great Symbol Drain

NEIL POSTMAN (b. 1931), a professor at New York University, is one of the most prolific writers on education, culture, and language in the United States. You can measure his intellectual range just by considering the titles of a few of his numerous books: Teaching as a Subversive Activity *(1969),* Teaching as a Conserving Activity *(1979),* Amusing Ourselves to Death: Public Discourse in the Age of Show Business *(1985),* The End of Education *(1995),* Building a Bridge to the Eighteenth Century: How the Past Can Improve Our Future *(1999). Concerned especially by the debased state of American popular culture, Postman believes that schools must deal more directly with the impact of technology on the process of learning.*

In "The Great Symbol Drain," a chapter from Technopoly: The Surrender of Culture to Technology *(1992), Postman asks readers to consider how technology and advertising are corroding the very images that bind us together and give coherence to our lives. It may help you in reading Postman's chapter to know that he defines* technopoly *as "the deification of technology, which means that the culture seeks its authorization in technology, finds its satisfactions in technology, and takes its orders from technology."*

—J.R.

It is possible that, some day soon, an advertising man who must create a television commercial for a new California Chardonnay will have the following inspiration: Jesus is standing alone in a desert oasis. A gentle breeze flutters the leaves of the stately palms behind him. Soft Mideastern music caresses the air. Jesus holds in his hand a bottle of wine at which he gazes adoringly. Turning toward the camera, he says, "When I transformed water into wine at Cana, *this* is what I had in mind. Try it today. You'll become a believer."

It's happened! An auto company used the Last Supper in an ad campaign in France, provoking outrage from church and clergy. —J.R.

I'm surprised that someone hasn't already made such a commercial. Anything—or anyone—can be used as a vehicle for advertising these days. —A.L.

If you think such a commercial is not possible in your lifetime, then consider this: As I write, there is an oft-seen commercial for Hebrew National frankfurters. It features a dapper-looking Uncle Sam in his traditional red, white, and blue outfit. While Uncle Sam assumes appropriate facial expressions, a voice-over describes the delicious and healthful frankfurters produced by Hebrew National. Toward the end of the commercial, the voice stresses that Hebrew National frankfurters surpass federal standards for such products. Why? Because, the voice says as the camera shifts our point of view upward toward heaven, "We have to answer to a Higher Authority."

Am I missing something here? Postman leaps from what is "incredible" in sentence 1 to what is "blasphemy" in sentence 2. I'll watch to see if he makes the connection clear. —A.L.

I will leave it to the reader to decide which is more incredible—Jesus being used to sell wine or God being used to sell frankfurters. Whichever you decide, you must keep in mind that neither the hypothetical commercial nor the real one is an example of blasphemy. They are much worse than that. Blasphemy is, after all, among the highest tributes that can be paid to the power of a symbol. The blasphemer takes symbols as seriously as the idolater, which is why the President of the United States (circa 1991) wishes to punish, through a constitutional amendment, desecrators of the American flag.

If there "can be no laws" against the ethical breach caused by trivialization, what alternatives remain? Educational ones? —H.R.

What we are talking about here is not blasphemy but trivialization, against which there can be no laws. In Technopoly,* the trivialization of significant cultural symbols is largely conducted by commercial enterprise. This occurs not because corporate America is greedy but because the adoration of technology pre-empts the adoration of anything else. Symbols that draw their meaning from traditional religious or national contexts must therefore be made impotent as quickly as possible—that is, drained of sacred or even serious connotations. The elevation of one god requires the demotion of another. "Thou shalt have no other gods before me" applies as well to a technological divinity as any other.

I don't see why "elevation of one" requires "demotion of another." Why can't both be elevated or demoted? —A.L.

I wonder whether the opposite is true in advertising: does a symbol actually gain its commercial power by being ubiquitous? Consider the Nike "swoosh," the golden arches, or the Ford blue oval. They seem almost like natural objects. —J.R.

There are two intertwined reasons that make it possible to trivialize traditional symbols. The first, as neatly expressed by the social critic Jay Rosen, is that, although symbols, especially images, are endlessly repeatable, they are not inexhaustible. Second, the more frequently a significant symbol is used, the less potent is its meaning. This is a point stressed in Daniel Boorstin's* classic book *The Image,* published thirty

If "symbols . . . are not inexhaustible," can new symbols be created? —H.R.

---

technopoly: Postman defines *technopoly* as "the deification of technology."

Daniel Boorstin (b. 1914): historian of the American experience and author of many works on history and culture, including *The Image: A Guide to Pseudo-events in America* (1971), *The Discoverers* (1983), and *The Seekers* (1998)

years ago.[1] In it, Boorstin describes the beginnings, in the mid-nineteenth century, of a "graphics revolution" that allowed the easy reproduction of visual images, thus providing the masses with continuous access to the symbols and icons of their culture. Through prints, lithographs, photographs, and, later, movies and television, religious and national symbols became commonplace, breeding indifference if not necessarily contempt. As if to answer those who believe that the emotional impact of a sacred image is always and ever the same, Boorstin reminds us that prior to the graphics revolution most people saw relatively few images. Paintings of Jesus or the Madonna, for example, would have been seen rarely outside churches. Paintings of great national leaders could be seen only in the homes of the wealthy or in government buildings. There were images to be seen in books, but books were expensive and spent most of their time on shelves. Images were not a conspicuous part of the environment, and their scarcity contributed toward their special power. When the scale of accessibility was altered, Boorstin argues, the experience of encountering an image necessarily changed; that is to say, it diminished in importance. One picture, we are told, is worth a thousand words. But a thousand pictures, especially if they are of the same object, may not be worth anything at all.

Not just accessibility to symbols but also the mentality of consumerism seem to be contributing to the demise of symbolic meaning. —H.R.

There may be a key difference between a picture as a work of art and an image as a cultural symbol: a work of art is powerful in itself, whereas an icon or symbol gains power from familiarity and repetition. —J.R.

What Boorstin and Rosen direct our attention to is a common enough pyschological principle. You may demonstrate this for yourself (if you have not at some time already done so) by saying any word, even a significant one, over and over again. Sooner than you expect, you will find that the word has been transformed into a meaningless sound, as repetition drains it of its symbolic value. Any male who has served in, let us say, the United States Army or spent time in a college dormitory has had this experience with what are called obscene words, especially the notorious four-letter word which I am loath to reproduce here. Words that you have been taught not

I tried doing just this—repeating the word mirror *over and over again—and the word took on wild and wonderful new meanings.* —A.L.

[1]Although in some ways Boorstin's book is dated, to him and his book go credit for calling early attention to the effects of an image society.

to use and that normally evoke an embarrassed or disconcerted response, when used too often, are stripped of their power to shock, to embarrass, to call attention to a special frame of mind. They become only sounds, not symbols.

Moreover, the journey to meaninglessness of symbols is a function not only of the frequency with which they are invoked but of the indiscriminate contexts in which they are used. An obscenity, for example, can do its work best when it is reserved for situations that call forth anger, disgust, or hatred. When it is used as an adjective for every third noun in a sentence, irrespective of the emotional context, it is deprived of its magical effects and, indeed, of its entire point. This is what happens when Abraham Lincoln's image, or George Washington's, is used to announce linen sales on Presidents' Day, or Martin Luther King's birthday celebration is taken as an occasion for furniture discounts. It is what happens when Uncle Sam, God, or Jesus is employed as an agent of the profane world for an essentially trivial purpose.

In Texas, the symbol of the Lone Star appears on everything from jars of salsa to plastic glasses. Yet it affirms a sense of place not as evident in other states where I have lived. The image still means something. —J.R.

An argument is sometimes made that the promiscuous use of sacred or serious symbols by corporate America is a form of healthy irreverence. Irreverence, after all, is an antidote to excessive or artificial piety, and is especially necessary when piety is used as a political weapon. One might say that irreverence, not blasphemy, is the ultimate answer to idolatry, which is why most cultures have established means by which irreverence may be expressed—in the theater, in jokes, in song, in political rhetoric, even in holidays. The Jews, for example, use Purim as one day of the year on which they may turn a laughing face on piety itself.

Here's "blasphemy" again, this time offered as a possible answer to "idolatry." It seems like the latter is a reference to something earlier in the article—but it really isn't. What is Postman doing with the word blasphemy*?* —A.L.

But there is nothing in the commercial exploitation of traditional symbols that suggests an excess of piety is itself a vice. Business is too serious a business for that, and in any case has no objection to piety, as long as it is directed toward the idea of consumption, which is never treated as a laughing matter. In using Uncle Sam or the flag or the American Eagle or images of presidents, in employing such names as Liberty Insurance, Freedom Transmission Repair, and Lincoln Savings and Loan, business does

Why is consumption such a dominant mentality? Once it takes hold of a society, can its influence be reversed? —H.R.

not offer us examples of irreverence. It is merely declaring the irrelevance, in Technopoly, of distinguishing between the sacred and the profane.

OK, I'm beginning to see a pattern in these pairs: blasphemy and idolatry; trivialization and elevation; sacred and profane. Postman is setting up a set of either-or *arguments; let's see where that takes him.* —A.L.

I am not here making a standard-brand critique of the excesses of capitalism. It is entirely possible to have a market economy that respects the seriousness of words and icons, and which disallows their use in trivial or silly contexts. In fact, during the period of greatest industrial growth in America—from roughly 1830 to the end of the nineteenth century—advertising did not play a major role in the economy, and such advertising as existed used straightforward language, without recourse to the exploitation of important cultural symbols. There was no such thing as an "advertising industry" until the early twentieth century, the ground being prepared for it by the Postal Act of March 3, 1879, which gave magazines low-cost mailing privileges. As a consequence, magazines emerged as the best available conduits for national advertising, and merchants used the opportunity to make the names of their companies important symbols of commercial excellence. When George Eastman invented the portable camera in 1888, he spent $25,000 advertising it in magazines. By 1895, "Kodak" and "camera" were synonymous, as to some extent they still are. Companies like Royal Baking Powder, Baker's Chocolate, Ivory Soap, and Gillette moved into a national market by advertising their products in magazines. Even magazines moved into a national market by advertising themselves in magazines, the most conspicuous example being *Ladies' Home Journal,* whose publisher, Cyrus H. K. Curtis, spent half a million dollars between 1883 and 1888 advertising his magazine in other magazines. By 1909, *Ladies' Home Journal* had a circulation of more than a million readers.

He seems to be implying that an economic condition—"low-cost mailing privileges"—provided the impetus for businesses to exploit symbols through advertising. —H.R.

Some products—such as Hershey's Chocolate—were not advertised at all until relatively recently. —J.R.

Curtis' enthusiasm for advertising notwithstanding, the most significant figure in mating advertising to the magazine was Frank Munsey, who upon his death in 1925 was eulogized by William Allen White* with the following words:

William Allen White (1868–1944): influential American journalist and longtime editor of the *Emporia* (Kansas) *Gazette*

"Frank Munsey contributed to the journalism of his day the talent of a meat packer, the morals of a money changer and the manners of an undertaker. He and his kind have about succeeded in transforming a once-noble profession into an 8% security. May he rest in trust." What was the sin of the malevolent Munsey? Simply, he made two discoveries. First, a large circulation could be achieved by selling a magazine for much less than it cost to produce it; second, huge profits could be made from the high volume of advertising that a large circulation would attract. In October 1893, Munsey took out an ad in the New York *Sun* announcing that *Munsey's Magazine* was cutting its price from 25 cents to 10 cents, and reducing a year's subscription from $3 to $1. The first 10-cent issue claimed a circulation of forty thousand; within four months, the circulation rose to two hundred thousand; two months later, it was five hundred thousand.

Munsey cannot, however, be blamed for another discovery, which for convenience's sake we may attribute to Procter and Gamble: that advertising is most effective when it is irrational. By irrational, I do not, of course, mean crazy. I mean that products could best be sold by exploiting the magical and even poetical powers of language and pictures. In 1892, Procter and Gamble invited the public to submit rhymes to advertise Ivory Soap. Four years later, H-O employed, for the first time, a picture of a baby in a high chair, the bowl of H-O cereal before him, his spoon in hand, his face ecstatic. By the turn of the century, advertisers no longer assumed that reason was the best instrument for the communication of commercial products and ideas. Advertising became one part depth psychology, one part aesthetic theory. In the process, a fundamental principle of capitalist ideology was rejected: namely, that the producer and consumer were engaged in a rational enterprise in which consumers made choices on the basis of a careful consideration of the quality of a product and their own self-interest. This, at least, is what Adam Smith had in mind. But today, the television commercial, for

Another binary pair: irrational and rational. I don't see these as opposites. Nor do I believe that people ever made decisions based solely on reason, as Postman suggests later in this paragraph. —A.L.

example, is rarely about the character of the products. It is about the character of the consumers of products. Images of movie stars and famous athletes, of serene lakes and macho fishing trips, of elegant dinners and romantic interludes, of happy families packing their station wagons for a picnic in the country—these tell nothing about the products being sold. But they tell everything about the fears, fancies, and dreams of those who might buy them. What the advertiser needs to know is not what is right about the product but what is wrong about the buyer. And so the balance of business expenditures shifts from product research to market research, which means orienting business away from making products of value and toward making consumers feel valuable. The business of business becomes pseudo-therapy; the consumer, a patient reassured by psychodramas.

The imagery is so obscure in some ads these days that I can't always figure out what's being sold. Or what is being sold is pure style—with no substance at all. —J.R.

This point, made repeatedly for at least the last twenty-five years, seems fairly accurate to me: advertisements are about the desires and fantasies of consumers. But it's not exactly new news! —A.L.

What this means is that somewhere near the core of Technopoly is a vast industry with license to use all available symbols to further the interests of commerce, by devouring the psyches of consumers. Although estimates vary, a conservative guess is that the average American will have seen close to two million television commercials by age sixty-five. If we add to this the number of radio commercials, newspaper and magazine ads, and billboards, the extent of symbol overload and therefore symbol drain is unprecedented in human history. Of course, not all the images and words used have been cannibalized from serious or sacred contexts, and one must admit that as things stand at the moment it is quite unthinkable for the image of Jesus to be used to sell wine. At least not a chardonnay. On the other hand, his birthday is used as an occasion for commerce to exhaust nearly the entire repertoire of Christian symbology. The constraints are so few that we may call this a form of cultural rape, sanctioned by an ideology that gives boundless supremacy to technological progress and is indifferent to the unraveling of tradition.

This claim—that our psyches are being not just manipulated but also devoured—sounds pretty scary and a bit extreme. —H.R.

Is Postman's irony directed at the advertising industry or consumers? Can trivialization be used to work against the industry, or does it only fuel it? —H.R.

I've been wondering when the title would come into play. Postman has been preparing readers for the concept he names in his title by giving lots of examples. Here, he pulls those examples together under the concept of "the great symbol drain." —A.L.

In putting it this way, I mean to say that mass advertising is not the cause of the great symbol drain. Such cultural abuse could not have occurred without technologies to make it possible and a world-view to make it desirable. In the institutional form it has taken in the United States, advertising is a symptom of a world-view that sees tradition as an obstacle to its claims. There can, of course, be no functioning sense of tradition without a measure of respect for symbols. Tradition is, in fact, nothing but the acknowledgment of the authority of symbols and the relevance of the narratives that gave birth to them. With the erosion of symbols there follows a loss of narrative, which is one of the most debilitating consequences of Technopoly's power.

I hope Postman explains this intriguing point more clearly. —H.R.

Yikes! Here, Postman makes an enormous leap—that the "draining" of symbols leads to the death of narratives, which are the key to tradition—and packs a huge argument into part of a paragraph. He'll have to offer a lot of evidence for me to accept this cause-effect leap. —A.L.

We may take as an example the field of education. In Technopoly, we improve the education of our youth by improving what are called "learning technologies." At the moment, it is considered necessary to introduce computers to the classroom, as it once was thought necessary to bring closed-circuit television and film to the classroom. To the question "Why should we do this?" the answer is: "To make learning more efficient and more interesting." Such an answer is considered entirely adequate, since in Technopoly efficiency and interest need no justification. It is, therefore, usually not noticed that this answer does not address the question "What is learning for?" "Efficiency and interest" is a technical answer, an answer about means, not ends; and it offers no pathway to a consideration of educational philosophy. Indeed, it blocks the way to such a consideration by beginning with the question of how we should proceed rather than with the question of why. It is probably not necessary to say that, by definition, there can be no education philosophy that does not address what learning is for. Confucius, Plato, Quintilian, Cicero, Comenius, Erasmus, Locke, Rousseau, Jefferson, Russell, Montessori, Whitehead, and Dewey—each believed that there was some transcendent political, spiritual, or social idea that must be advanced through education. Confucius advocated teaching "the Way" because in tradition he saw the best hope for social order. As our first systematic fascist, Plato wished education to produce philosopher kings. Cicero argued that education must free the student from the tyranny of the present. Jefferson

The answer Postman gives to his own question (why use technology in school?) is not the only possible reply. Other and better responses are available. —J.R.

This education example does not provide evidence for Postman's earlier claim; I'm disappointed. —A.L.

I see a common theme of freedom among the educational ideologies Postman mentions. How might the current emphasis on personal freedom relate to these earlier notions? To the erosion of symbols? —H.R.

thought the purpose of education is to teach the young how to protect their liberties. Rousseau wished education to free the young from the unnatural constraints of a wicked and arbitrary social order. And among John Dewey's aims was to help the student function without certainty in a world of constant change and puzzling ambiguities.

Only in knowing something of the reasons why they advocated education can we make sense of the means they suggest. But to understand their reasons we must also understand the narratives that governed their view of the world. By narrative, I mean a story of human history that gives meaning to the past, explains the present, and provides guidance for the future. It is a story whose principles help a culture to organize its institutions, to develop ideals, and to find authority for its actions. At the risk of repetition, I must point out again that the source of the world's greatest narratives has been religion, as found, for example, in Genesis or the Bhagavad-Gita or the Koran. There are those who believe—as did the great historian Arnold Toynbee—that without a comprehensive religious narrative at its center a culture must decline. Perhaps. There are, after all, other sources—mythology, politics, philosophy, and science, for example—but it is certain that no culture can flourish without narratives of transcendent origin and power.

Even when I agree with a writer, I get suspicious when I encounter any statement that claims "it is certain . . ." My instinctive reaction is to search for an exception or a qualifier to the statement. —J.R.

This does not mean that the mere existence of such a narrative ensures a culture's stability and strength. There are destructive narratives. A narrative provides meaning, not necessarily survival—as, for example, the story provided by Adolf Hitler to the German nation in the 1930s. Drawing on sources in Teutonic mythology and resurrecting ancient and primitive symbolism, Hitler wove a tale of Aryan supremacy that lifted German spirits, gave point to their labors, eased their distress, and provided explicit ideals. The story glorified the past, elucidated the present, and foretold the future, which was to last a thousand years. The Third Reich lasted exactly twelve years.

Many *narratives are and always have been destructive.* —A.L.

What happens when narratives abound but do not receive widespread respect? —H.R.

It is not to my point to dwell on the reasons why the story of Aryan supremacy could not endure. The point is that cultures must have narratives

Here, Postman links narrative with meaning, setting up yet another binary: either we have narrative, meaning, life, or *we have no narrative, no meaning, no life. I acknowledge the power of narratives to shape meaning and life, but I don't see the choice between narrative and nonnarrative as simply as Postman seems to.* —A.L.

and will find them where they will, even if they lead to catastrophe. The alternative is to live without meaning, the ultimate negation of life itself. It is also to the point to say that each narrative is given its form and its emotional texture through a cluster of symbols that call for respect and allegiance, even devotion. The United States Constitution, for example, is only in part a legal document, and, I should add, a small part. Democratic nations—England, for one—do not require a written constitution to ensure legal order and the protection of liberties. The importance of the American Constitution is largely in its function as a symbol of the story of our origins. It is our political equivalent of Genesis. To mock it, to ignore it, to circumvent it is to declare the irrelevance of the story of the United States as a moral light unto the world. In like fashion, the Statue of Liberty is the key symbol of the story of America as the natural home of the teeming masses, from anywhere, yearning to be free. There are, of course, several reasons why such stories lose their force. This book is, in fact, an attempt to describe one of them—i.e., how the growth of Technopoly has overwhelmed earlier, more meaningful stories. But in all cases, the trivialization of the symbols that express, support, and dramatize the story will accompany the decline. Symbol drain is both a symptom and a cause of a loss of narrative.

The symbolic power of the Constitution was never clearer than during the presidential impeachment hearing and trial in 1998–99. Both sides invoked it as the arbiter of truth and responsibility, of right and wrong. —J.R.

Is Postman saying there are no narratives in technopoly? It seems to me he has already demonstrated exactly the opposite. —A.L.

The educators I referred to above based their philosophies on narratives rich in symbols which they respected and which they understood to be integral to the stories they wanted education to reveal. It is, therefore, time to ask, What story does American education wish to tell now? In a growing Technopoly, what do we believe education is for? The answers are discouraging, and one of them can be inferred from any television commercial urging the young to stay in school. The commercial will either imply or state explicitly that education will help the persevering student to get a good job. And that's it. Well, not quite. There is also the idea that we educate ourselves to compete with the Japanese or the Germans in an economic struggle to be number one.

I agree with how Aristotle would answer this question about education: he said that learning is one of life's chief pleasures. —A.L.

As Postman notes, the fact that education leads to economic success is the sort of slick message TV ads can deliver in 30 seconds or less. More complex rationales for learning wouldn't fit the medium. —J.R.

Neither of these purposes is, to say the least, grand or inspiring. The story each suggests is that the United States is not a culture but merely an economy, which is the last refuge of an exhausted philosophy of education. This belief, I might add, is precisely reflected in the President's Commission Report, *A Nation at Risk,** where you will find a definitive expression of the idea that education is an instrument of economic policy and of very little else.

We may get a sense of the desperation of the educator's search for a more gripping story by using the "television commercial test." Try to imagine what sort of appeals might be effectively made on a TV commercial to persuade parents to support schools. (Let us, to be fair, sidestep appeals that might be made directly to students themselves, since the youth of any era are disinclined to think schooling a good idea, whatever the reasons advanced for it. See the "Seven Ages of Man"* passage in *As You Like It.*)

Can you imagine, for example, what such a commercial would be like if Jefferson or John Dewey prepared it? "Your children are citizens in a democratic society," the commercial might say. "Their education will teach them how to be valuable citizens by refining their capacity for reasoned thought and strengthening their will to protect their liberties. As for their jobs and professions, that will be considered only at a 'late and convenient hour'" (to quote John Stuart Mill,* who would be pleased to associate himself with Jefferson's or Dewey's purpose). Is there anyone today who would find this a compelling motivation? Some, perhaps, but hardly enough to use it as the basis of a national program. John Locke's* commercial would, I imagine, be

A Nation at Risk (1983): report of the National Commission on Excellence in Education that called for reform of education in the United States because of dropping scores on standardized tests

"Seven Ages of Man": from William Shakespeare's *As You Like It:* "the whining schoolboy, with his satchel / And shining morning face, creeping like snail / Unwillingly to school" (AYL 2.7)

John Stuart Mill (1806–73): English philosopher and advocate of Utilitarianism

John Locke (1632–1704): English philosopher and author of *An Essay Concerning Human Understanding* (1690)

even less appealing. "Your children must stay in school," he might say, "because there they will learn to make their bodies slaves of their minds. They will learn to control their impulses, and how to find satisfaction and even excitement in the life of the mind. Unless they accomplish this, they can be neither civilized nor literate." How many would applaud this mission? Indeed, whom could we use to speak such words—Barbara Bush?* Lee Iacocca?* Donald Trump?* Even the estimable Dr. Bill Cosby would hardly be convincing. The guffaws would resound from Maine to California.

In recent years, a valiant attempt has been made by some—for example, E. D. Hirsch, Jr.—to provide a comprehensive purpose to education. In his book *Cultural Literacy,* Hirsch defines literacy as the capacity to understand and use the words, dates, aphorisms, and names that form the basis of communication among the educated in our culture. Toward this end, he and some of his colleagues compiled a list that contains, according to them, the references essential to a culturally literate person in America. The first edition of the book (1987) included Norman Mailer but not Philip Roth, Bernard Malamud, Arthur Miller, or Tennessee Williams. It included Ginger Rogers but not Richard Rodgers, Carl Rogers, or Buck Rogers, let alone Fred Rogers. The second greatest home-run hitter of all time, Babe Ruth, was there, but not the greatest home-run hitter, Hank Aaron. The Marx Brothers were there, but not Orson Welles, Frank Capra, John Ford, or Steven Spielberg. Sarah Bernhardt was included, but not Leonard Bernstein. Rochester, New York, was on the list. Trenton, New Jersey, one of our most historic cities, was not. Hirsch included the Battle of the Bulge,* which pleased my brother, who fought in it in

Many have criticized the exclusivity and elitism of Hirsch's project, particularly this list of information deemed "essential" to one's "cultural literacy." —A.L.

Barbara Bush (b. 1925): much-respected wife of President George H. Bush

Lee Iacocca (b. 1924): flamboyant former auto executive and chair of Statue of Liberty–Ellis Island Centennial Commission

Donald Trump (b. 1946): renowned financier and billionaire real estate developer

Norman Mailer . . . Battle of the Bulge: Postman lists people, places, and things that literate Americans might be expected to recognize.

1944. But my uncle who died in the Battle of the Coral Sea, in 1942, might have been disappointed to find that it didn't make the list.

To fill in the gaps, Hirsch has had to enlarge his list, so that there now exists a *Cultural Literacy Encyclopedia.* We may be sure that Hirsch will continue to expand his list until he reaches a point where a one-sentence directive will be all he needs to publish: "See the *Encyclopedia Americana* and *Webster's Third International.*"

It is, of course, an expected outcome of any education that students become acquainted with the important references of their culture. Even Rousseau,* who would have asked his students to read only one book, *Robinson Crusoe* (so that they would learn how to survive in the wild),* would probably have expected them to "pick up" the names and sayings and dates that made up the content of the educated conversation of their time. Nonetheless, Hirsch's proposal is inadequate for two reasons that reflect the inadequacies of Technopoly. The first . . . is that the present condition of technology-generated information is so long, varied, and dynamic that it is not possible to organize it into a coherent educational program. How do you include in the curriculum Rochester, New York, or Sarah Bernhardt* or Babe Ruth? Or the Marx Brothers? Where does Ginger Rogers go? Does she get included in the syllabus under a unit titled "Fred Astaire's Dancing Partners"? (In which case, we must include Cyd Charisse and, if I am not mistaken, Winston Churchill's daughter, Sarah.) Hirsch's encyclopedic list is not a solution but a description of the problem of information glut. It is therefore essentially incoherent. But it also confuses a consequence of education with a purpose. Hirsch attempted to answer the question "What is

And the "information glut" has only gotten worse since Technopoly *was written. Thanks to the Internet, we now have access to more information than we can handle.* —J.R.

Rousseau: Jean-Jacques Rousseau (1712–78), French philosopher and thinker, author of *Emile; or, On Education* (1762)

Robinson Crusoe (1719–22): a novel about an island castaway by Daniel Defoe (1660–1731)

Rochester . . . Sarah Bernhardt: Postman offers more items from contemporary history and culture that educated people might be expected to know in Hirsch's view of education.

an educated person?" He left unanswered the question "What is an education for?" Young men, for example, will learn how to make lay-up shots when they play basketball. To be able to make them is part of the definition of what good players are. But they do not play basketball for that purpose. There is usually a broader, deeper, and more meaningful reason for wanting to play—to assert their manhood, to please their fathers, to be acceptable to their peers, even for the sheer aesthetic pleasure of the game itself. What you have to do to be a success must be addressed only after you have found a reason to be successful. In Technopoly, this is very hard to do, and Hirsch simply sidestepped the question.

Postman has raised this question several times. I wonder if he'll attempt to answer it. —A.L.

Not so Allan Bloom.* In his book *The Closing of the American Mind,* he confronts the question by making a serious complaint against the academy. His complaint is that most American professors have lost their nerve. They have become moral relativists, incapable of providing their students with a clear understanding of what is right thought and proper behavior. Moreover, they are also intellectual relativists, refusing to defend their own culture and no longer committed to preserving and transmitting the best that has been thought and said.

Hirsch and Bloom (and Matthew Arnold, who Postman alludes to with "the best that has been thought and said") sidestep the question: the best according to—and for—whom? —A.L.

Bloom's solution is that we go back to the basics of Western thought. He does not care if students know who Ginger Rogers and Groucho Marx* are. He wants us to teach our students what Plato, Aristotle, Cicero, Saint Augustine,* and other luminaries have had to say on the great ethical and epistemological questions. He believes that by acquainting themselves with great books our students will acquire a moral and intellectual foundation that will give meaning and texture to their lives. Though there is nothing especially original in this, Bloom is a serious education philosopher, which is to say, unlike Hirsch, he is a moralist who understands that Tech-

This suggestion is misleading—Great Books don't really give *meaning; they guide us to meaning.* —H.R.

Allan Bloom (1930–92): American educator and professor of philosophy and political science at the University of Chicago

Ginger Rogers and Groucho Marx: film stars

Plato . . . Augustine: major philosophers and thinkers

nopoly is a malevolent force requiring opposition. But he has not found many supporters.

Those who reject Bloom's idea have offered several arguments against it. The first is that such a purpose for education is elitist: the mass of students would not find the great story of Western civilization inspiring, are too deeply alienated from the past to find it so, and would therefore have difficulty connecting the "best that has been thought and said" to their own struggles to find meaning in their lives. A second argument, coming from what is called a "leftist" perspective, is even more discouraging. In a sense, it offers a definition of what is meant by elitism. It asserts that the "story of Western civilization" is a partial, biased, and even oppressive one. It is not the story of blacks, American Indians, Hispanics, women, homosexuals—of any people who are not white heterosexual males of Judeo-Christian heritage. This claim denies that there is or can be a national culture, a narrative of organizing power and inspiring symbols which all citizens can identify with and draw sustenance from. If this is true, it means nothing less than that our national symbols have been drained of their power to unite, and that education must become a tribal affair; that is, each subculture must find its own story and symbols, and use them as the moral basis of education.

Now I'm really getting tired of these pairs of supposed opposites: either we're all united under one "narrative of organizing power" or we're part of a "tribal affair," divided into many separate subcultures. I think there can be multiple narratives and that we, as citizens, can move among them. —A.L.

The tribalism Postman describes has become a driving force in American education as the nation's shared story and images have lost their resonance. Whether technology is the cause of these developments is another matter. —J.R.

Standing somewhat apart from these arguments are, of course, religious educators, such as those in Catholic schools, who strive to maintain another traditional view—that learning is done for the greater glory of God and, more particularly, to prepare the young to embrace intelligently and gracefully the moral directives of the church. Whether or not such a purpose can be achieved in Technopoly is questionable, as many religious educators will acknowledge.

I will reserve for the . . . final chapter [of *Technopoly*] my own view of the struggle to find a purpose for education. . . . But here it must be said that the struggle itself is a sign that our repertoire of significant national, religious, and mythological symbols has been seriously drained of its potency.

"We are living at a time," Irving Howe* has written, "when all the once regnant world systems that have sustained (also distorted) Western intellectual life, from theologies to ideologies, are taken to be in severe collapse. This leads to a mood of skepticism, an agnosticism of judgment, sometimes a world-weary nihilism in which even the most conventional minds begin to question both distinctions of value and the value of distinctions."[2]

Into this void comes the Technopoly story, with its emphasis on progress without limits, rights without responsibilities, and technology without cost. The Technopoly story is without a moral center. It puts in its place efficiency, interest, and economic advance. It promises heaven on earth through the conveniences of technological progress. It casts aside all traditional narratives and symbols that suggest stability and orderliness, and tells, instead, of a life of skills, technical expertise, and the ecstasy of consumption. Its purpose is to produce functionaries for an ongoing Technopoly. It answers Bloom by saying that the story of Western civilization is irrelevant; it answers the political left by saying there is indeed a common culture whose name is Technopoly and whose key symbol is now the computer, toward which there must be neither irreverence nor blasphemy. It even answers Hirsch by saying that there are items on his list that, if thought about too deeply and taken too seriously, will interfere with the progress of technology.

This is a very depressing scenario, and yet there are symbols here aplenty. I'm beginning to wonder if the "symbol drain" is as responsible for the rise of technopoly as Postman believes it to be. —A.L.

Does the image Postman draws of our times seem accurate? Technopoly does seem like an apt symbol at the beginning of a new millennium. —J.R.

I grant that it is somewhat unfair to expect educators, by themselves, to locate stories that would reaffirm our national culture. Such narratives must come to them, to some degree, from the political sphere. If our politics is symbolically impoverished, it is difficult to imagine how teachers can provide a weighty purpose to education. I am writing this chapter during the fourth week of the war against Iraq;* the rhetoric accompanying the onset

---

Irving Howe (1920–93): noted American literary critic and professor of English at Hunter College of the City University of New York

[2]*The New Republic,* February 18, 1991, p. 42.

war against Iraq: This Allied attack on Iraq began on January 16–17, 1991.

of the war is still fresh in mind. It began with the President's calling Americans to arms for the sake of their "life-style." This was followed by the Secretary of State's request that they fight to protect their jobs. Then came the appeal—at a late and convenient hour, as it were—to thwart the "naked aggression" of a little "Hitler." I do not say here that going to war was unjustified. My point is that, with the Cold War at an end, our political leaders now struggle, as never before, to find a vital narrative and accompanying symbols that would awaken a national spirit and a sense of resolve. The citizens themselves struggle as well. Having drained many of their traditional symbols of serious meaning, they resort, somewhat pitifully, to sporting yellow ribbons as a means of symbolizing their fealty to a cause. After the war, the yellow ribbons will fade from sight, but the question of who we are and what we represent will remain. Is it possible that the only symbol left to use will be an F-15 fighter plane guided by an advanced computer system?

Afterwords

The subtitle of Postman's book, The Surrender of Culture to Technology, *provides a key to my response to this reading. While I appreciate much of Postman's work and am grateful for his trenchant critiques of contemporary culture, I find myself resisting one major premise of "The Great Symbol Drain"—that technology is somehow outside of culture, or that technology is capable of usurping and transforming culture. Certainly, technologies have always played a role in constituting culture: think of the role of writing, one of the Western world's oldest technologies, in shaping recorded history, for example. But to see the influence as one-way seems overly simple to me. In addition, I am not a big fan of the type of* either-or *arguments that characterize much of Postman's piece (as I note in my annotations).*

With that said, and in spite of what I see as overgeneralization and extremism, I think Postman makes some very important points. He is right that symbols play a great role in our personal, social, and national lives. Images—like words—can trivialize, mock, or hurt us; or they can heal, uplift, and inspire us. So his warning to take symbols and images very seriously seems important to me. I also agree that the ground of a symbol can be shifted so as to change its meaning in significant ways. Literary theorist Joseph Bentley has called this move, in poetry and prose, "semantic gravitation"—the strategy of taking a word or phrase that has strong positive meanings and systematically associating it with highly negative connotations. That is precisely what Postman is complaining about in terms of a "symbol drain"—the trivialization and "blaspheming" of unifying national and cultural images. More specifically, he sees technopoly as in the business of using all symbols available to it to further commercial interests, "devouring the psyches of consumers." Postman may be right. But I hold out some faith in our ability to resist these commercial images, to read them critically, and to analyze the motives that lie behind their use. Certainly, students and teachers face a major challenge: to be critical of the ways in which technopoly seeks to manipulate our desires through symbols and stories, and, perhaps even more important, to create new stories that can enrich our lives beyond the realm of "skills, technical expertise, and the ecstasy of consumption." —A.L.

Postman has an eerie ability to forecast the future. Writing in 1985, in Amusing Ourselves to Death, *he warned that the trivializing effects of television and technology would eventually undermine serious political discourse in the United States. Almost twenty years later, we're living in the dark shadows of his prophecy—for the most part. More than ever, TV news has become a form of entertainment, especially on twenty-four-hour cable news networks like CNN and Fox. When the news is truly consequential, these media outlets do an adequate job. But more routinely when they turn their focus to political scandal, sensational crimes, or Hollywood gossip, they lose all perspective and standards in their frenetic competition for ratings.*

Yet some things have changed in ways Postman could not have predicted. As he was completing "The Great Symbol Drain" in 1992, he observed that political leaders, notably then-president George H. W. Bush, were struggling for words adequate to motivate Americans to support the first Persian Gulf War. Why? Because all the older symbols of national spirit had been drained of their power. Americans seemed to be fighting for oil to preserve a lavish lifestyle.

But the events of 9/11 in 2001 did do much to restore the American spirit (for a time, at least) and even to create new symbols and images. The World Trade Center towers, the Pentagon, and a field in western Pennsylvania have now joined Pearl Harbor as essential parts of the American story. So, in 2003, President George W. Bush had somewhat less trouble than his father in motivating the American people to support a second war with Iraq. This time, Americans were fighting terror.

So symbols can, it seems, sometimes recover their power in the "rockets' red glare"—that is, under genuine threats from potent enemies. But in a larger sense, Postman probably remains on target in warning that a blind faith in technology will not sustain us in the long run. It's ultimately an empty narrative—vacuous and morally bankrupt. Yet it may be precisely the story we revert to when our lives return to a kind of normalcy. —J.R.

I think part of the problem Postman calls "technopoly" is that people are searching for something to fill an emptiness left by the trivialization of ideologies. Technology and consumerism have shifted the focus from broad concepts of culture and society to those of the individual, creating an obsession with inner health and worth. It's discomforting to think what a mess this has made of our society. The question is not whether resistance is an option or a necessity—it is, of course, the latter—but how *to combat the influence of technopoly. I think Postman is right in saying that the burden of this problem cannot fall fully on educators, though they may play an important role in the struggle.*

Although I find this selection interesting and agree with much of what Postman says about the effects of symbols, overall I consider his argument too pessimistic. It seems to me that certain symbols are still held sacred by many people, myself included. —H.R.

QUESTIONING THE TEXT

1. Postman provides several examples of advertisements in which religious images and symbols have been trivialized. Working in a group, list additional examples of images or icons sacred to a particular religion or a people (for instance, to Native Americans) that have been abused in advertisements. Then, working independently, write an essay in which you examine your reaction to these commercials. Is the practice as harmful as Postman suggests on pp. 545–46, or do you have a different reaction to these advertising techniques?
2. Do images and words lose their power by repetition, as Postman claims? Conduct a survey of your campus environment. What dominant symbols are used by your college or university? By local organizations and the surrounding community? How often do you notice these images or symbols? In what circumstances do they have power, and when do they become like images of George Washington in advertisements for Presidents' Day sales? Report your findings in a short paper.

MAKING CONNECTIONS

3. Postman claims that technopoly has filled the void left by the abandoned narratives that once gave America meaning. Read David Brooks's "One Nation, Slightly Divisible" (p. 581), and consider the extent to which Postman's technopoly may account for the "common love for this nation" (paragraph 97) that Brooks describes toward the end of his essay. Do you think Brooks mistakes genuine unity for the false sense of shared meaning Postman ascribes to technopoly? Why, or why not?
4. According to Postman, cultures cannot survive without powerful narratives that explain their pasts and direct their futures. Is it possible that the great narrative for technopoly might be *Frankenstein?* Review that selection by Mary Shelley (p. 274), and consider how Dr. Frankenstein's monster functions as a symbol for cultures that rely (too?) heavily on technology and science. Discuss the issue with your classmates.

JOINING THE CONVERSATION

5. Working in a group, discuss the implications of Postman's claim "that advertising is most effective when it is irrational" (p. 550). Consider especially the roles images play in advertising: are images themselves irrational, or can they contribute to our deeper understanding of products or ideas? Using a carefully selected set of print or video advertisements as evidence, write an essay or create a Web site in response to Postman's statement.

6. The Constitution and the Statue of Liberty are, according to Postman, potent symbols of our shared national narrative. Write an essay in which you list and discuss other symbols or images that you believe are—or should be—a part of the story that gives meaning to the American experience.

MARGARET ATWOOD
A Letter to America

*A*s AMERICANS, *we surely have our myths of national identity—as the readings in this chapter demonstrate. But America—more specifically the United States—carries mythic status in many other places of the world as well. I first learned that lesson during the ten years I lived and taught in Vancouver, Canada, and I have been very grateful for the opportunity I had to see my home country through the eyes of others, whose vision was often clearer than mine. I learned this lesson again in the years that have elapsed since the September 11, 2001, terrorist bombings. Traveling in Europe and in Canada not long after those attacks, I read and heard what others sensed were America's strongest ideals: courage, endurance, hope. Still, in the aftermath of unsigned international treaties, a questionable war waged in Iraq, and other threatening actions, travel outside the United States is not always fun anymore: mythic images of America are overwhelmingly negative.*

In "A Letter to America" (first published on March 28, 2003 in the Globe and Mail*), Canadian novelist Margaret Atwood (b. 1939) catalogues the myths that were America to her, from the heroes of American literature to mythic outsiders like Marlon Brando in* On the Waterfront *to the "city on the hill, a light to all nations." Today, Atwood says, she is no longer sure what America stands for. The symbol of plenty, embodied by the Jolly Green Giant in Atwood's letter, can turn into a symbol of greed and destruction. The mythic ideal of generosity—a hand held out to all in need—can too easily turn into a King Midas complex. Atwood challenges Americans to read her letter and to reflect—and then to summon the great national "spirits of the past" to bring out the best, rather than the worst, in the national psyche.*

Atwood, a fellow of the Royal Society of Canada who has served as president of the Writers' Union of Canada, is the author of dozens of books, among them The Blind Assassin, *awarded the Booker Prize in 2000, and* Alias Grace, *which won the Giller Prize in 1996. Her latest work is* Oryx and Crake *(2003), a postapocalyptic tale set in a dry moonscape in the indeterminate future—which could, Atwood seems to be warning, be tomorrow.* —A.L.

Dear America: This is a difficult letter to write, because I'm no longer sure who you are.

Some of you may be having the same trouble. I thought I knew you: We'd become well acquainted over the past 55 years. You were the Mickey Mouse and Donald Duck comic books I read in the late 1940s. You were the radio shows—*Jack Benny, Our Miss Brooks.* You were the music I sang and danced to: the Andrews Sisters, Ella Fitzgerald, the Platters, Elvis. You were a ton of fun.

You wrote some of my favourite books. You created Huckleberry Finn, and Hawkeye, and Beth and Jo in *Little Women,* courageous in their different ways. Later, you were my beloved Thoreau, father of environmentalism, witness to individual conscience; and Walt Whitman, singer of the great Republic; and Emily Dickinson, keeper of the private soul. You were Hammett and Chandler, heroic walkers of mean streets; even later, you were the amazing trio, Hemingway, Fitzgerald, and Faulkner, who traced the dark labyrinths of your hidden heart. You were Sinclair Lewis and Arthur Miller, who, with their own American idealism, went after the sham in you, because they thought you could do better.

You were Marlon Brando in *On The Waterfront,* you were Humphrey Bogart in *Key Largo,* you were Lillian Gish in *Night of the Hunter.* You stood up for freedom, honesty and justice; you protected the innocent. I believed most of that. I think you did, too. It seemed true at the time.

You put God on the money, though, even then. You had a way of 5
thinking that the things of Caesar were the same as the things of God: that gave you self-confidence. You have always wanted to be a city upon a hill, a light to all nations, and for a while you were. Give me your tired, your poor, you sang, and for a while you meant it.

We've always been close, you and us. History, that old entangler, has twisted us together since the early 17th century. Some of us used to be you; some of us want to be you; some of you used to be us. You are not only our neighbours: In many cases—mine, for instance—you are also our blood relations, our colleagues, and our personal friends. But although we've had a ringside seat, we've never understood you completely, up here north of the 49th parallel.

We're like Romanized Gauls—look like Romans, dress like Romans, but aren't Romans—peering over the wall at the real Romans. What are they doing? Why? What are they doing now? (Why is the haruspex eyeballing the sheep's liver? Why is the soothsayer wholesaling the Bewares?)

Perhaps that's been my difficulty in writing you this letter: I'm not sure I know what's really going on. Anyway, you have a huge posse of experienced entrail-sifters who do nothing but analyze your every vein and lobe. What can I tell you about yourself that you don't already know?

This might be the reason for my hesitation: embarrassment, brought on by a becoming modesty. But it is more likely to be embarrassment of another sort. When my grandmother—from a New England background—was confronted with an unsavoury topic, she would change the subject and gaze out the window. And that is my own inclination: Mind your own business.

But I'll take the plunge, because your business is no longer merely your 10
business. To paraphrase Marley's Ghost, who figured it out too late, mankind

is your business. And vice versa: When the Jolly Green Giant goes on the rampage, many lesser plants and animals get trampled underfoot. As for us, you're our biggest trading partner: We know perfectly well that if you go down the plug-hole, we're going with you. We have every reason to wish you well.

I won't go into the reasons why I think your recent Iraqi adventures have been—taking the long view—an ill-advised tactical error. By the time you read this, Baghdad may or may not look like the craters of the Moon, and many more sheep entrails will have been examined. Let's talk, then, not about what you're doing to other people, but about what you're doing to yourselves.

You're gutting the Constitution. Already your home can be entered without your knowledge or permission, you can be snatched away and incarcerated without cause, your mail can be spied on, your private records searched. Why isn't this a recipe for widespread business theft, political intimidation, and fraud? I know you've been told all this is for your own safety and protection, but think about it for a minute. Anyway, when did you get so scared? You didn't used to be easily frightened.

You're running up a record level of debt. Keep spending at this rate and pretty soon you won't be able to afford any big military adventures. Either that or you'll go the way of the USSR: lots of tanks, but no air conditioning. That will make folks very cross. They'll be even crosser when they can't take a shower because your short-sighted bulldozing of environmental protections has dirtied most of the water and dried up the rest. Then things will get hot and dirty indeed.

You're torching the American economy. How soon before the answer to that will be, not to produce anything yourselves, but to grab stuff other people produce, at gunboat-diplomacy prices? Is the world going to consist of a few megarich King Midases, with the rest being serfs, both inside and outside your country? Will the biggest business sector in the United States be the prison system? Let's hope not.

If you proceed much further down the slippery slope, people around the world will stop admiring the good things about you. They'll decide that your city upon the hill is a slum and your democracy is a sham, and therefore you have no business trying to impose your sullied vision on them. They'll think you've abandoned the rule of law. They'll think you've fouled your own nest.

The British used to have a myth about King Arthur. He wasn't dead, but sleeping in a cave, it was said; in the country's hour of greatest peril, he would return. You, too, have great spirits of the past you may call upon: men and women of courage, of conscience, of prescience. Summon them now, to stand with you, to inspire you, to defend the best in you. You need them.

QUESTIONING THE TEXT

1. Atwood calls upon many literary and cultural figures to conjure an image of an America she says she once knew. With a classmate, find as many of these allusions as you can, and identify or describe them: where do they come from, and what do they mean? Next, consider what functions these allusions serve in the essay. What do they seem to contribute to Atwood's purpose? Do you agree that the allusions represent the ideals she associates with them? Could they be used in other ways?
2. This essay is written in the form of a letter. Think about how it compares to a letter to the editor, a genre described on p. 31. Discuss with your class how Atwood's choice of America as her addressee opens up possibilities and also imposes limitations on her message and her means of conveying it.
3. How would you describe Atwood's tone in this essay? Does it change in the course of her letter? Cite examples from the text to support your answers.

MAKING CONNECTIONS

4. Working with a classmate, try to revise Atwood's essay to include cultural references other than those she uses. For example, try alluding to the Declaration of Independence (p. 517) or to Frederick Douglass's "What to the Slave Is the Fourth of July?" (p. 522). Share your revisions with the whole class, and discuss how the revisions change the essay.
5. Read Emma Lazarus's "The New Colossus" (p. 622), and then reconsider Atwood's comment: "Give me your tired, your poor, you sang, and for a while you meant it" (paragraph 5). What period of American history might Atwood be thinking of when she says "for a while you meant it"? Do you think she is right that America has lost sight of the values reflected in these lines from Lazarus's poem? In considering these questions, you might consult other essays in this chapter, such as Frederick Douglass's "What to the Slave Is the Fourth of July?" (p. 522), Ward Churchill's "Crimes against Humanity" (p. 536), or Abelardo Delgado's "Stupid America" (p. 625). Use your answers to compose an essay that analyzes or responds to this criticism of Atwood's against the United States.

JOINING THE CONVERSATION

6. Compose a letter in which you comment on one or more of the issues Atwood raises. You might address your letter to Atwood; to the editor of the *Globe and Mail*, the Canadian newspaper that originally published

her essay; or to another country. When you're finished, think about how your letter compares to other pieces you have written for class. Did you use a different style or tone to appeal to your addressee?

7. List the ways in which Atwood accuses the United States of changing—or of forsaking its traditions—and consider whether some of these changes might be evidence of American myths. Share your speculations in class discussion. In your discussion, consider what makes for a national myth and how such a myth may differ from a tradition.

PHILIPPE LEGRAIN

Cultural Globalization Is Not Americanization

*P*RESIDENT *R*ONALD *R*EAGAN *was fond of representing his vision of America as a "shining city on a hill," borrowing the image from Governor John Winthrop of the Massachusetts Bay Colony. For many people, especially in the twentieth century when totalitarian regimes darkened the political landscape, the United States often seemed to be this mythic place. Immigrants by the millions, legal and illegal, swarmed across its borders to take refuge here and to build new lives.*

With the fall of the Soviet empire, however, the United States found itself in an entirely different role. Though U.S. international power and influence had been growing for more than a century—it had even toyed with European-style colonialism in the Philippines, Puerto Rico, and Cuba—not until after the Second World War did the nation become a permanent and deliberate player in international politics. The Cold War turned the United States into a superpower, and the subsequent implosion of international communism left America as an undisputed economic, cultural, and military colossus.

Now America's ideas, corporations, and aircraft carriers reach into all corners of the globe, threatening (in the views of some) to remake every nation in the American image. The code word for this process, welcomed in some quarters but feared in others, is globalization. *The shining city on a hill seems to have imperial ambitions.*

In fact, American power, both economic and military, is real. Whatever Margaret Atwood may think (see "A Letter to America," p. 565), the United States is managing its affairs much better than its European allies are managing theirs, spending proportionally less on guns now than at many times in the past. The United States is able to sustain seemingly massive deficits because of the sheer size of its economy, an engine still supporting much of the world economy, even in tough times.

Yet, as Philippe Legrain demonstrates in "Cultural Globalization Is Not Americanization," the world is a bigger and more interesting place than any *one nation, and much of the world's fear—or, in some quarters, envy—of American hegemony is misplaced. What has conquered the world, he argues, is not Mickey Mouse or Coca-Cola, but an attitude toward life that welcomes individual liberty, change, and diversity. As we learned on September 11, 2001, even such classic liberalism still has its enemies.*

Philippe Legrain has been an advisor to the World Trade Organization, a group often associated with globalization. He is also a writer for the Economist *and is the author of* Open World: The Truth about Globalization *(2002). The essay reprinted here first appeared in the* Chronicle of Higher Education *(May 9, 2003).*

—J.R.

"Listen man, I smoke, I snort . . . I've been begging on the street since I was just a baby. I've cleaned windshields at stoplights. I've polished shoes, I've robbed, I've killed. . . . I ain't no kid, no way. I'm a real man."

Such searing dialogue has helped make *City of God* a global hit. A chronicle of three decades of gang wars, it has proved compelling viewing for audiences worldwide. Critics compare it to Martin Scorsese's *Goodfellas.*

If you believe the cultural pessimists, Hollywood pap has driven out films like *Cidade de Deus,* as it is known in its home country. It is a Brazilian film, in Portuguese, by a little-known director, with a cast that includes no professional actors, let alone Hollywood stars. Its focus is not a person at all, but a drug-ridden, dirt-poor favela (slum) on the outskirts of Rio de Janeiro that feels as remote from the playground of the rich and famous as it does from God.

Yet *City of God* has not only made millions at the box office, it has also sparked a national debate in Brazil. It has raised awareness in the United States, Britain, and elsewhere of the terrible poverty and violence of the developing world. All that, and it makes you wince, weep, and, yes, laugh. Not bad for a film distributed by Miramax, which is owned by Disney, one of those big global companies that globaphobes compare to cultural vandals.

A lot of nonsense about the impact of globalization on culture passes for 5
conventional wisdom these days. Among the pro-globalizers, Thomas Friedman, columnist for the *New York Times* and author of *The Lexus and the Olive Tree* (Farrar, Straus & Giroux, 1999), believes that globalization is "globalizing American culture and American cultural icons." Among the antis, Naomi Klein, a Canadian journalist and author of *No Logo* (Picador, 2000), argues that "the buzzword in global marketing isn't selling America to the world, but bringing a kind of market masala to everyone in the world. . . . Despite the embrace of polyethnic imagery, market-driven globalization doesn't want diversity; quite the opposite. Its enemies are national habits, local brands and distinctive regional tastes."

Fears that globalization is imposing a deadening cultural uniformity are as ubiquitous as Coca-Cola, McDonald's, and Mickey Mouse. Europeans and Latin Americans, left-wingers and right, rich and poor—all of them dread that local cultures and national identities are dissolving into a crass all-American consumerism.

That cultural imperialism is said to impose American values as well as products, promote the commercial at the expense of the authentic, and substitute shallow gratification for deeper satisfaction.

City of God's success suggests otherwise. If critics of globalization were less obsessed with "Coca-colonization," they might notice a rich feast of cultural mixing that belies fears about Americanized uniformity. Algerians in Paris practice Thai boxing; Asian rappers in London snack on Turkish pizza; Salman Rushdie delights readers everywhere with his Anglo-Indian tales. Although—as with any change—there can be downsides to cultural globalization, this cross-fertilization is overwhelmingly a force for good.

The beauty of globalization is that it can free people from the tyranny of geography. Just because someone was born in France does not mean they can only aspire to speak French, eat French food, read French books, visit museums in France, and so on. A Frenchman—or an American, for that matter—can take holidays in Spain or Florida, eat sushi or spaghetti for dinner, drink Coke or Chilean wine, watch a Hollywood blockbuster or an Almodóvar,* listen to bhangra or rap, practice yoga or kickboxing, read *Elle* or the *Economist,* and have friends from around the world. That we are increasingly free to choose our cultural experiences enriches our lives immeasurably. We could not always enjoy the best the world has to offer.

Globalization not only increases individual freedom, but also revitalizes 10
cultures and cultural artifacts through foreign influences, technologies, and markets. Thriving cultures are not set in stone. They are forever changing from within and without. Each generation challenges the previous one; science and technology alter the way we see ourselves and the world; fashions come and go; experience and events influence our beliefs; outsiders affect us for good and ill.

Many of the best things come from cultures mixing: V. S. Naipaul's Anglo-Indo-Caribbean writing, Paul Gauguin painting in Polynesia, or the African rhythms in rock 'n' roll. Behold the great British curry. Admire the many-colored faces of France's World Cup-winning soccer team, the ferment of ideas that came from Eastern Europe's Jewish diaspora, and the cosmopolitan cities of London and New York. Western numbers are actually Arabic; zero comes most recently from India; Icelandic, French, and Sanskrit stem from a common root.

John Stuart Mill was right: "The economical benefits of commerce are surpassed in importance by those of its effects which are intellectual and moral. It is hardly possible to overrate the value, for the improvement of human beings, of things which bring them into contact with persons dissimilar to themselves, and with modes of thought and action unlike those with which they are familiar. . . . It is indispensable to be perpetually comparing [one's] own notions and customs with the experience and example of persons in different circumstances. . . . There is no nation which does not need to borrow from others."

It is a myth that globalization involves the imposition of Americanized uniformity, rather than an explosion of cultural exchange. For a start, many archetypal "American" products are not as all-American as they seem. Levi Strauss, a German immigrant, invented jeans by combining denim cloth (or "serge de Nîmes," because it was traditionally woven in the French town) with Genes, a style of trousers worn by Genoese sailors. So Levi's jeans are in fact an American twist on a European hybrid. Even quintessentially American

---

Almodóvar: Pedro Almodóvar (b. 1951), a Spanish film director exports are often tailored to local tastes. MTV in Asia promotes Thai pop stars and plays rock music sung in Mandarin. CNN en Español offers a Latin American take on world news. McDonald's sells beer in France, lamb in India, and chili in Mexico.

In some ways, America is an outlier, not a global leader. Most of the world has adopted the metric system born from the French Revolution; America persists with antiquated measurements inherited from its British-colonial past. Most developed countries have become intensely secular, but many Americans burn with fundamentalist fervor—like Muslims in the Middle East. Where else in the developed world could there be a serious debate about teaching kids Bible-inspired "creationism" instead of Darwinist evolution?

America's tastes in sports are often idiosyncratic, too. Baseball and 15
American football have not traveled well, although basketball has fared rather better. Many of the world's most popular sports, notably soccer, came by way of Britain. Asian martial arts—judo, karate, kickboxing—and pastimes like yoga have also swept the world.

People are not only guzzling hamburgers and Coke. Despite Coke's ambition of displacing water as the world's drink of choice, it accounts for less than 2 of the 64 fluid ounces that the typical person drinks a day. Britain's favorite takeaway is a curry, not a burger: Indian restaurants there outnumber McDonald's six to one. For all the concerns about American fast food trashing France's culinary traditions, France imported a mere $620 million in food from the United States in 2000, while exporting to America three times that. Nor is plonk from America's Gallo displacing Europe's finest: Italy and France together account for three-fifths of global wine exports, the United States for only a 20th. Worldwide, pizzas are more popular than burgers, Chinese restaurants seem to sprout up everywhere, and sushi is spreading fast. By far the biggest purveyor of alcoholic drinks is Britain's Diageo, which sells the world's best-selling whiskey (Johnnie Walker), gin (Gordon's), vodka (Smirnoff) and liqueur (Baileys).

In fashion, the ne plus ultra* is Italian or French. Trendy Americans wear Gucci, Armani, Versace, Chanel, and Hermès. On the high street and in the mall, Sweden's Hennes & Mauritz (H&M) and Spain's Zara vie with America's Gap to dress the global masses. Nike shoes are given a run for their money by Germany's Adidas, Britain's Reebok, and Italy's Fila.

In pop music, American crooners do not have the stage to themselves. The three artists who featured most widely in national Top Ten album charts in 2000 were America's Britney Spears, closely followed by Mexico's Carlos Santana and the British Beatles. Even tiny Iceland has produced a global star: Björk. Popular opera's biggest singers are Italy's Luciano Pavarotti, Spain's

---

ne plus ultra: the ultimate; the highest point

José Carreras, and the Spanish-Mexican Placido Domingo. Latin American salsa, Brazilian lambada, and African music have all carved out global niches for themselves. In most countries, local artists still top the charts. According to the IFPI, the record-industry bible, local acts accounted for 68 percent of music sales in 2000, up from 58 percent in 1991.

One of the most famous living writers is a Colombian, Gabriel García Márquez, author of *One Hundred Years of Solitude.* Paulo Coelho, another writer who has notched up tens of millions of global sales with *The Alchemist* and other books, is Brazilian. More than 200 million Harlequin romance novels, a Canadian export, were sold in 1990; they account for two-fifths of mass-market paperback sales in the United States. The biggest publisher in the English-speaking world is Germany's Bertelsmann, which gobbled up America's largest, Random House, in 1998.

Local fare glues more eyeballs to TV screens than American programs. 20
Although nearly three-quarters of television drama exported worldwide comes from the United States, most countries' favorite shows are homegrown.

Nor are Americans the only players in the global media industry. Of the seven market leaders that have their fingers in nearly every pie, four are American (AOL Time Warner, Disney, Viacom, and News Corporation), one is German (Bertelsmann), one is French (Vivendi), and one Japanese (Sony). What they distribute comes from all quarters: Bertelsmann publishes books by American writers; News Corporation broadcasts Asian news; Sony sells Brazilian music.

The evidence is overwhelming. Fears about an Americanized uniformity are over-blown: American cultural products are not uniquely dominant; local ones are alive and well.

With one big exception: cinema. True, India produces more films (855 in 2000) than Hollywood does (762), but they are largely for a domestic audience. Japan and Hong Kong also make lots of movies, but few are seen outside Asia. France and Britain have the occasional global hit, but are still basically local players. Not only does Hollywood dominate the global movie market, but it also swamps local products in most countries. American fare accounts for more than half the market in Japan and nearly two-thirds in Europe.

Yet Hollywood's hegemony is not as worrisome as people think. Note first that Hollywood is less American than it seems. Ever since Charlie Chaplin crossed over from Britain, foreigners have flocked to California to try to become global stars: Just look at Penelope Cruz, Catherine Zeta-Jones, and Ewan McGregor. Top directors are also often from outside America: Think of Ridley Scott or the late Stanley Kubrick. Some studios are foreign-owned: Japan's Sony owns Columbia Pictures, Vivendi Universal is French. Two of AOL Time Warner's biggest recent hit franchises, *Harry Potter* and *The Lord of the Rings,* are both based on British books, have largely British casts, and, in the case of *The Lord of the Rings,* a Kiwi director. To some extent, then, Hollywood is a global industry that just happens to be in America. Rather than exporting Americana, it serves up pap to appeal to a global audience.

Hollywood's dominance is in part due to economics: Movies cost a lot to 25
make and so need a big audience to be profitable; Hollywood has used America's huge and relatively uniform domestic market as a platform to expand overseas. So there could be a case for stuffing subsidies into a rival European film industry, just as Airbus was created to challenge Boeing's near-monopoly. But France has long pumped money into its domestic industry without persuading foreigners to flock to its films. As Tyler Cowen perceptively points out in his book *Creative Destruction: How Globalization Is Changing the World's Cultures* (Princeton University Press, 2002), "A vicious circle has been created: The more European producers fail in global markets, the more they rely on television revenue and subsidies. The more they rely on television and subsidies, the more they fail in global markets," because they serve domestic demand and the wishes of politicians and cinematic bureaucrats.

Another American export is also conquering the globe: English. Around 380 million people speak it as their first language and another 250 million or so as their second. A billion are learning it, about a third of the world's population are exposed to it, and by 2050, it is reckoned, half the world will be more or less proficient in it. A common global language would certainly be a big plus—for businessmen, scientists, and tourists—but a single one seems far less desirable. Language is often at the heart of national culture: The French would scarcely be French if they spoke English (although Belgian Walloons are not French even though they speak it). English may usurp other languages not because it is what people prefer to speak, but because, like Microsoft software, there are compelling advantages to using it if everyone else does.

But although many languages are becoming extinct, English is rarely to blame. People are learning English as well as—not instead of—their native tongue, and often many more languages besides. Some languages with few speakers, such as Icelandic, are thriving, despite Björk's choosing to sing in English. Where local languages are dying, it is typically national rivals that are stamping them out. French has all but eliminated Provençal, and German Swabian. So although, within the United States, English is displacing American Indian tongues, it is not doing away with Swahili or Norwegian.

Even though American consumer culture is widespread, its significance is often exaggerated. You can choose to drink Coke and eat at McDonald's without becoming American in any meaningful sense. One newspaper photo of Taliban fighters in Afghanistan showed them toting Kalashnikovs*—as

---

Kalashnikovs: Soviet assault rifles. Also known as AK47s, these rifles were developed in 1947 and named *Avtomat Kalashnikova* (AK) after their designer, Mikhail Timofeyevich Kalashnikov.

well as a sports bag with Nike's trademark swoosh. People's culture—in the sense of their shared ideas, beliefs, knowledge, inherited traditions, and art—may scarcely be eroded by mere commercial artifacts that, despite all the furious branding, embody at best flimsy values.

The really profound cultural changes have little to do with Coca-Cola. Western ideas about liberalism and science are taking root almost everywhere, while Europe and North America are becoming multicultural societies through immigration, mainly from developing countries. Technology is reshaping culture: Just think of the Internet. Individual choice is fragmenting the imposed uniformity of national cultures. New hybrid cultures are emerging, and regional ones reemerging. National identity is not disappearing, but the bonds of nationality are loosening.

As Tyler Cowen points out in his excellent book, cross-border cultural 30
exchange increases diversity within societies—but at the expense of making them more alike. People everywhere have more choice, but they often choose similar things. That worries cultural pessimists, even though the right to choose to be the same is an essential part of freedom.

Cross-cultural exchange can spread greater diversity as well as greater similarity: more gourmet restaurants as well as more McDonald's. And just as a big city can support a wider spread of restaurants than a small town, so a global market for cultural products allows a wider range of artists to thrive. For sure, if all the new customers are ignorant, a wider market may drive down the quality of cultural products: Think of tourist souvenirs. But as long as some customers are well informed (or have "good taste"), a general "dumbing down" is unlikely. Hobbyists, fans, artistic pride, and professional critics also help maintain (and raise) standards. Cowen concludes that the "basic trend is of increasing variety and diversity, at all levels of quality, high and low."

A bigger worry is that greater individual freedom may come at the expense of national identity. The French fret that if they all individually choose to watch Hollywood films they might unwittingly lose their collective Frenchness. Yet such fears are overdone. Natural cultures are much stronger than people seem to think. They can embrace some foreign influences and resist others. Foreign influences can rapidly become domesticated, changing national culture, but not destroying it. Germans once objected to soccer because it was deemed English; now their soccer team is emblematic of national pride. Amartya Sen, the Nobel prize-winning economist, is quite right when he says that "the culturally fearful often take a very fragile view of each culture and tend to underestimate our ability to learn from elsewhere without being overwhelmed by that experience."

Clearly, though, there is a limit to how many foreign influences a culture can absorb before being swamped. Even when a foreign influence is largely welcomed, it can be overwhelming. Traditional cultures in the developing world that have until now evolved (or failed to evolve) in isolation may be particularly vulnerable.

In *The Silent Takeover: Global Capitalism and the Death of Democracy* (Free Press, 2001), Noreena Hertz describes the supposed spiritual Eden that was the isolated kingdom of Bhutan in the Himalayas as being defiled by such awful imports as basketball and Spice Girls T-shirts. Anthony Giddens, the director of the London School of Economics and Political Science, has told how an anthropologist who visited a remote part of Cambodia was shocked and disappointed to find that her first night's entertainment was not traditional local pastimes but watching *Basic Instinct* on video.

Is that such a bad thing? It is odd, to put it mildly, that many on the left support multiculturalism in the West but advocate cultural purity in the developing world—an attitude they would be quick to tar as fascist if proposed for the United States or Britain. Hertz and the anthropologist in Cambodia appear to want people outside the industrialized West preserved in unchanging but supposedly pure poverty. Yet the Westerners who want this supposed paradise preserved in aspic rarely feel like settling there. Nor do most people in developing countries want to lead an "authentic" unspoiled life of isolated poverty.

In truth, cultural pessimists are typically not attached to diversity per se but to designated manifestations of diversity, determined by their preferences. "They often use diversity as a code word for a more particularist agenda, often of an anti-commercial or anti-American nature," Cowen argues. "They care more about the particular form that diversity takes in their favored culture, rather than about diversity more generally, freedom of choice, or a broad menu of quality options."

Cultural pessimists want to freeze things as they were. But if diversity at any point in time is desirable, why isn't diversity across time? Certainly, it is often a shame if ancient cultural traditions are lost. We should do our best to preserve them and keep them alive where possible. As Cowen points out, foreigners can often help, by providing the new customers and technologies that have enabled reggae music, Haitian art, and Persian carpet making, for instance, to thrive and reach new markets. But people cannot be made to live in a museum. We in the West are forever casting off old customs when we feel they are no longer relevant. Nobody argues that Americans should ban nightclubs to force people back to line dancing. People in poor countries have a right to change, too.

Moreover, some losses of diversity are a good thing. In 1850, some countries banned slavery, while others maintained it in various forms. Who laments that the world is now almost universally rid of it? More generally, Western ideas are reshaping the way people everywhere view themselves and the world. Like nationalism and socialism before it, liberalism—political ideas about individual liberty, the rule of law, democracy, and universal human rights, as well as economic ones about the importance of private property rights, markets, and consumer choice—is a European philosophy that has swept the world. Even people who resist liberal ideas, in the name of religion

(Islamic and Christian fundamentalists), group identity (communitarians), authoritarianism (advocates of "Asian values") or tradition (cultural conservatives), now define themselves partly by their opposition to them.

Faith in science and technology is even more widespread. Even those who hate the West make use of its technologies. Osama bin Laden plots terrorism on a cellphone and crashes planes into skyscrapers. Antiglobalization protesters organize by e-mail and over the Internet. José Bové manipulates 21st-century media in his bid to return French farming to the Middle Ages. China no longer turns its nose up at Western technology: It tries to beat the West at its own game.

True, many people reject Western culture. (Or, more accurately, "cul- 40
tures": Europeans and Americans disagree bitterly over the death penalty, for instance; they hardly see eye to eye over the role of the state, either.) Samuel Huntington, a professor of international politics at Harvard University, even predicts a "clash of civilizations" that will divide the 21st-century world. Yet Francis Fukuyama, a professor of international political economy at the Johns Hopkins University, is nearer the mark when he talks about the "end of history." Some cultures have local appeal, but only liberalism appeals everywhere (if not to all)—although radical environmentalism may one day challenge its hegemony. Islamic fundamentalism poses a threat to our lives but not to our beliefs. Unlike communism, it is not an alternative to liberal capitalism for Westerners or other non-Muslims.

Yet for all the spread of Western ideas to the developing world, globalization is not a one-way street. Although Europe's former colonial powers have left their stamp on much of the world, the recent flow of migration has been in the opposite direction. There are Algerian suburbs in Paris, but not French ones in Algiers; Pakistani parts of London, but not British ones of Lahore. Whereas Muslims are a growing minority in Europe, Christians are a disappearing one in the Middle East.

Foreigners are changing America even as they adopt its ways. A million or so immigrants arrive each year (700,000 legally, 300,000 illegally), most of them Latino or Asian. Since 1990, the number of foreign-born American residents has risen by 6 million to just over 25 million, the biggest immigration wave since the turn of the 20th century. English may be all-conquering outside America, but in some parts of the United States, it is now second to Spanish. Half of the 50 million new inhabitants expected in America in the next 25 years will be immigrants or the children of immigrants.

The upshot of all this change is that national cultures are fragmenting into a kaleidoscope of different ones. New hybrid cultures are emerging. In "Amexica" people speak Spanglish. Regional cultures are reviving. Repressed under Franco, Catalans, Basques, Gallegos, and others assert their identity in Spain. The Scots and Welsh break with British monoculture. Estonia is reborn from the Soviet Union. Voices that were silent dare to speak again.

Individuals are forming new communities, linked by shared interests and passions, that cut across national borders. Friendships with foreigners met on holiday. Scientists sharing ideas over the Internet. Environmentalists campaigning together using e-mail. House-music lovers swapping tracks online. Greater individualism does not spell the end of community. The new communities are simply chosen rather than coerced, unlike the older ones that communitarians hark back to.

Does that mean national identity is dead? Hardly. People who speak the 45
same language, were born and live near each other, face similar problems, have a common experience, and vote in the same elections still have plenty of things in common. For all our awareness of the world as a single place, we are not citizens of the world but citizens of a state. But if people now wear the bonds of nationality more loosely, is that such a bad thing? People may lament the passing of old ways. Indeed, many of the worries about globalization echo age-old fears about decline, a lost golden age, and so on. But by and large, people choose the new ways because they are more relevant to their current needs and offer new opportunities that the old ones did not.

The truth is that we increasingly define ourselves rather than let others define us. Being British or American does not define who you are: It is part of who you are. You can like foreign things and still have strong bonds to your fellow citizens. As Mario Vargas Llosa, the Peruvian author, has written: "Seeking to impose a cultural identity on a people is equivalent to locking them in a prison and denying them the most precious of liberties—that of choosing what, how, and who they want to be."

QUESTIONING THE TEXT

1. As Legrain indicates in his title, we should not be concerned that cultural globalization constitutes Americanization, but does he suggest that we should be concerned about globalization for other reasons? Find evidence in the text to support your answer.
2. Working with a classmate, summarize Legrain's thoughts on "diversity" and "globalization." How are these concepts related? What contradictions does he find in others' arguments about these ideas? Do you agree with his views on these concepts? Why, or why not?

MAKING CONNECTIONS

3. Legrain claims that "vot[ing] in the same elections" constitutes an aspect of national identity (paragraph 45). Do you think David Brooks, author of "One Nation, Slightly Divisible" (p. 581), would agree with Legrain

on this point? Why, or why not? Write a 3- to 4-page argument answering this question, drawing support from the two essays.

4. In paragraph 39, Legrain briefly remarks that "[f]aith in science and technology is even more widespread [than liberal democracy]." Given Legrain's other sentiments toward various manifestations of the spread of culture, how might he respond to Neil Postman's critique of technopoly in "The Great Symbol Drain" (p. 545)? Work with a classmate to answer this question, and share your answer with the class.

JOINING THE CONVERSATION

5. Think of an aspect of culture—perhaps a habit, tradition, food, or belief—that seems truly American to you, and do some research to discover its origins and history. Is this aspect of U.S. culture as American as you believed? Has it been imported into the United States from another country? Has it been transported out of the United States to other countries? Write an essay exploring the myth and truth surrounding the piece of American culture you've chosen to analyze.
6. Legrain claims that national identity still exists: "People who speak the same language, were born and live near each other, face similar problems, have a common experience, and vote in the same elections still have plenty of things in common" (paragraph 45). Pick one of these categories of identity, or another that you think of, and write an essay arguing that most (or many) Americans could be expected to identify with this aspect of experience. Support your argument with examples from your own experience, popular culture, readings in this chapter, or other sources you find.

DAVID BROOKS

One Nation, Slightly Divisible

*F*OLLOWING THE HARD-FOUGHT *American presidential contest of 2000, the electoral map that tallied the states going for Bush or Gore looked like a house divided. The coasts, both east and west, were awash in the blue of Democrat Gore, as were many Mid-Atlantic and Great Lakes states. Almost everything in between, with the exception of New Mexico, was red, indicating that these states had gone for Republican Bush. In the view of the pundits, Gore had won the urban enclaves and population centers—New York City, Chicago, Los Angeles, Atlanta—where the country's movers and shakers defined its policies and gave shape to its ideas; Bush had triumphed mainly in the sprawling heartland, that vast territory one flew over to get to other places. The map was certainly sobering in its suggestion that the United States had voted as two nations, a split made all the worse by the battle for Florida's decisive electoral votes.*

Of course, the United States has been divided regionally, culturally, and politically since its earliest days. At the time of the American Revolution, only a third of the colonists wanted independence from England. In the nineteenth century, the question of slavery pitted North against South. In the decades since the Civil War, America has seen fault lines emerge between immigrants and natives, men and women, haves and have-nots, even easterners and westerners.

Yet the red/blue dichotomy of the 2000 election seemed unusually ideological—a more abstract and fundamental quarrel of cultures and principles than had typically separated Americans one from another. Were the much ballyhooed "cultural wars" of the 1980s and 1990s—pitting secular, left-wing urban elites against conservative, religious zealots—just the harbinger of even more bruising class conflicts on the horizon? David Brooks sets out to answer that question in "One Nation, Slightly Divisible," an essay originally published in Atlantic Monthly *(December 2001). Brooks's piece is a comparison-contrast essay that treads slowly through two counties he chooses to represent the Red and Blue Americas. His observations are highly personal, and the validity of his conclusions rests, for the most part, on his ability to persuade readers that his observations are accurate. The story he tells is, to my mind, compelling, and his conclusion leads us to take another look at the 2000 election map. Indeed, the myth of an indivisible American nation may still be viable.*

David Brooks (b. 1961) is senior editor of the Weekly Standard, *a columnist for the* New York Times, *and a frequent contributor to* Newsweek *and* Atlantic Monthly. *He is the author of* Bobos in Paradise: The New Upper Class and How They Got There *(2001).* —J.R.

Sixty-five miles from where I am writing this sentence is a place with no Starbucks, no Pottery Barn, no Borders or Barnes & Noble. No blue *New*

York Times delivery bags dot the driveways on Sunday mornings. In this place people don't complain that Woody Allen isn't as funny as he used to be, because they never thought he was funny. In this place you can go to a year's worth of dinner parties without hearing anyone quote an aperçu he first heard on *Charlie Rose*. The people here don't buy those little rear-window stickers when they go to a summer-vacation spot so that they can drive around with "MV" decals the rest of the year; for the most part they don't even go to Martha's Vineyard.

The place I'm talking about goes by different names. Some call it America. Others call it Middle America. It has also come to be known as Red America, in reference to the maps that were produced on the night of the 2000 presidential election. People in Blue America, which is my part of America, tend to live around big cities on the coasts. People in Red America tend to live on farms or in small towns or small cities far away from the coasts. Things are different there.

Everything that people in my neighborhood do without motors, the people in Red America do with motors. We sail; they powerboat. We cross-country ski; they snowmobile. We hike; they drive ATVs. We have vineyard tours; they have tractor pulls. When it comes to yard work, they have rider mowers; we have illegal aliens.

Different sorts of institutions dominate life in these two places. In Red America churches are everywhere. In Blue America Thai restaurants are everywhere. In Red America they have QVC, the Pro Bowlers Tour, and hunting. In Blue America we have NPR, Doris Kearns Goodwin, and socially conscious investing. In Red America the Wal-Marts are massive, with parking lots the size of state parks. In Blue America the stores are small but the markups are big. You'll rarely see a Christmas store in Blue America, but in Red America, even in July, you'll come upon stores selling fake Christmas trees, wreath-decorated napkins, Rudolph the Red-Nosed Reindeer collectible thimbles and spoons, and little snow-covered villages.

We in the coastal metro Blue areas read more books and attend more 5
plays than the people in the Red heartland. We're more sophisticated and cosmopolitan—just ask us about our alumni trips to China or Provence, or our interest in Buddhism. But don't ask us, please, what life in Red America is like. We don't know. We don't know who Tim LaHaye and Jerry B. Jenkins are, even though the novels they have co-written have sold about 40 million copies over the past few years. We don't know what James Dobson says on his radio program, which is listened to by millions. We don't know about Reba or Travis. We don't know what happens in mega-churches on Wednesday evenings, and some of us couldn't tell you the difference between a fundamentalist and an evangelical, let alone describe what it means to be a Pentecostal. Very few of us know what goes on in Branson, Missouri, even though it has seven million visitors a year, or could name even five NASCAR drivers, although stock-car races are the best-attended sporting events in the country. We don't know how to shoot

or clean a rifle. We can't tell a military officer's rank by looking at his insignia. We don't know what soy beans look like when they're growing in a field.

All we know, or all we think we know, about Red America is that millions and millions of its people live quietly underneath flight patterns, many of them are racist and homophobic, and when you see them at highway rest stops, they're often really fat and their clothes are too tight.

And apparently we don't want to know any more than that. One can barely find any books at Amazon.com about what it is like to live in small-town America—or, at least, any books written by normal people who grew up in small towns, liked them, and stayed there. The few books that do exist were written either by people who left the heartland because they hated it (Bill Bryson's *The Lost Continent,* for example) or by urbanites who moved to Red America as part of some life-simplification plan (*Moving to a Small Town: A Guidebook for Moving from Urban to Rural America*; National Geographic's *Guide to Small Town Escapes*). Apparently no publishers or members of the Blue book-buying public are curious about Red America as seen through Red America's eyes.

Crossing the Meatloaf Line

Over the past several months, my interest piqued by those stark blocks of color on the election-night maps, I have every now and then left my home in Montgomery County, Maryland, and driven sixty-five miles northwest to Franklin County, in south-central Pennsylvania. Montgomery County is one of the steaming-hot centers of the great espresso machine that is Blue America. It is just over the border from northwestern Washington, D.C., and it is full of upper-middle-class towns inhabited by lawyers, doctors, stockbrokers, and establishment journalists like me—towns like Chevy Chase, Potomac, and Bethesda (where I live). Its central artery is a burgeoning high-tech corridor with a multitude of sparkling new office parks housing technology companies such as United Information Systems and Sybase, and pioneering biotech firms such as Celera Genomics and Human Genome Sciences. When I drive to Franklin County, I take Route 270. After about forty-five minutes I pass a Cracker Barrel—Red America condensed into chain-restaurant form. I've crossed the Meatloaf Line; from here on there will be a lot fewer sun-dried-tomato concoctions on restaurant menus and a lot more meatloaf platters.

Franklin County is Red America. It's a rural county, about twenty-five miles west of Gettysburg, and it includes the towns of Waynesboro, Chambersburg, and Mercersburg. It was originally settled by the Scotch-Irish, and has plenty of Brethren and Mennonites along with a fast-growing population of evangelicals. The joke that Pennsylvanians tell about their state is that it has Philadelphia on one end, Pittsburgh on the other, and Alabama in the middle.

Franklin County is in the Alabama part. It strikes me as I drive there that even though I am going north across the Mason-Dixon line, I feel as if I were going south. The local culture owes more to Nashville, Houston, and Daytona than to Washington, Philadelphia, or New York.

I shuttled back and forth between Franklin and Montgomery Countries 10
because the cultural differences between the two places are great, though the geographic distance is small. The two places are not perfect microcosms of Red and Blue America. The part of Montgomery County I am here describing is largely the Caucasian part. Moreover, Franklin County is in a Red part of a Blue state: overall, Pennsylvania went for Gore. And I went to Franklin County aware that there are tremendous differences within Red America, just as there are within Blue. Franklin County is quite different from, say, Scottsdale, Arizona, just as Bethesda is quite different from Oakland, California.

Nonetheless, the contrasts between the two counties leap out, and they are broadly suggestive of the sorts of contrasts that can be seen nationwide. When Blue America talks about social changes that convulsed society, it tends to mean the 1960s rise of the counterculture and feminism. When Red America talks about changes that convulsed society, it tends to mean World War II, which shook up old town establishments and led to a great surge of industry.

Red America makes social distinctions that Blue America doesn't. For example, in Franklin County there seems to be a distinction between those fiercely independent people who live in the hills and people who live in the valleys. I got a hint of the distinct and, to me, exotic hill culture when a hill dweller asked me why I thought hunting for squirrel and rabbit had gone out of fashion. I thought maybe it was just more fun to hunt something bigger. But he said, "McDonald's. It's cheaper to get a hamburger at McDonald's than to go out and get it yourself."

There also seems to be an important distinction between men who work outdoors and men who work indoors. The outdoor guys wear faded black T-shirts they once picked up at a Lynyrd Skynyrd concert and wrecked jeans that appear to be washed faithfully at least once a year. They've got wraparound NASCAR sunglasses, maybe a NAPA auto parts cap, and hair cut in a short wedge up front but flowing down over their shoulders in the back—a cut that is known as a mullet, which is sort of a cross between Van Halen's style and Kenny Rogers's, and is the ugliest hairdo since every hairdo in the seventies. The outdoor guys are heavily accessorized, and their accessories are meant to show how hard they work, so they will often have a gigantic wad of keys hanging from a belt loop, a tape measure strapped to the belt, a pocket knife on a string tucked into the front pants pocket, and a pager or a cell phone affixed to the hip, presumably in case some power lines go down somewhere and need emergency repair. Outdoor guys have a thing against sleeves. They work so hard that they've got to keep their arm muscles unencumbered and their armpit hair fully ventilated, so they either buy their shirts sleeveless or rip the sleeves off their T-shirts first thing, leaving bits of fringe hanging over their BAD TO THE BONE tattoos.

The guys who work indoors can't project this rugged proletarian image. It's simply not that romantic to be a bank-loan officer or a shift manager at the local distribution center. So the indoor guys adopt a look that a smart-ass, sneering Blue American might call Bible-academy casual—maybe Haggar slacks, which they bought at a dry-goods store best known for its appliance department, and a short-sleeved white Van Heusen shirt from the Bon-Ton. Their image projects not "I work hard" but "I'm a devoted family man." A lot of indoor guys have a sensitive New Age demeanor. When they talk about the days their kids were born, their eyes take on a soft Garth Brooks expression, and they tear up. They exaggerate how sinful they were before they were born again. On Saturdays they are patio masters, barbecuing on their gas grills in full Father's Day-apron regalia.

At first I thought the indoor guys were the faithful, reliable ones: the 15
ones who did well in school, whereas the outdoor guys were druggies. But after talking with several preachers in Franklin County, I learned that it's not that simple. Sometimes the guys who look like bikers are the most devoted community-service volunteers and church attendees.

The kinds of distinctions we make in Blue America are different. In my world the easiest way to categorize people is by headroom needs. People who went to business school or law school like a lot of headroom. They buy humongous sport-utility vehicles that practically have cathedral ceilings over the front seats. They live in homes the size of country clubs, with soaring entry atriums so high that they could practically fly a kite when they come through the front door. These big-headroom people tend to be predators: their jobs have them negotiating and competing all day. They spend small fortunes on dry cleaning. They grow animated when talking about how much they love their blackberries. They fill their enormous wall space with huge professional family portraits—Mom and Dad with their perfect kids (dressed in light-blue oxford shirts) laughing happily in an orchard somewhere.

Small-headroom people tend to have been liberal-arts majors, and they have liberal-arts jobs. They get passive-aggressive pleasure from demonstrating how modest and environmentally sensitive their living containers are. They hate people with SUVs, and feel virtuous driving around in their low-ceilinged little Hondas, which often display a RANDOM ACTS OF KINDNESS bumper sticker or one bearing an image of a fish with legs, along with the word "Darwin," just to show how intellectually superior to fundamentalist Christians they are.

Some of the biggest differences between Red and Blue America show up on statistical tables. Ethnic diversity is one. In Montgomery County 60 percent of the population is white, 15 percent is black, 12 percent is Hispanic, and 11 percent is Asian. In Franklin County 95 percent of the population is white. White people work the gas-station pumps and the 7-Eleven counters.

(This is something one doesn't often see in my part of the country.) Although the nation is growing more diverse, it's doing so only in certain spots. According to an analysis of the 2000 census by Bill Frey, a demographer at the Milken Institute, well over half the counties in America are still at least 85 percent white.

Another big thing is that, according to 1990 census data, in Franklin County only 12 percent of the adults have college degrees and only 69 percent have high school diplomas. In Montgomery County 50 percent of the adults have college degrees and 91 percent have high school diplomas. The education gap extends to the children. At Walt Whitman High School, a public school in Bethesda, the average SAT scores are 601 verbal and 622 math, whereas the national average is 506 verbal and 514 math. In Franklin County, where people are quite proud of their schools, the average SAT scores at, for example, the Waynesboro area high school are 495 verbal and 480 math. More and more kids in Franklin County are going on to college, but it is hard to believe that their prospects will be as bright as those of the kids in Montgomery County and the rest of upscale Blue America.

Because the information age rewards education with money, it's not 20
surprising that Montgomery County is much richer than Franklin County. According to some estimates, in Montgomery County 51 percent of households have annual incomes above $75,000, and the average household income is $100,365. In Franklin County only 16 percent of households have incomes above $75,000, and the average is $51,872.

A major employer in Montgomery County is the National Institutes of Health, which grows like a scientific boomtown in Bethesda. A major economic engine in Franklin County is the interstate highway Route 81. Trucking companies have gotten sick of fighting the congestion on Route 95, which runs up the Blue corridor along the northeast coast, so they move their stuff along 81, farther inland. Several new distribution centers have been built along 81 in Franklin County, and some of the workers who were laid off when their factories closed, several years ago, are now settling for $8.00 or $9.00 an hour loading boxes.

The two counties vote differently, of course—the differences, on a nationwide scale, were what led to those red-and-blue maps. Like upscale areas everywhere, from Silicon Valley to Chicago's North Shore to suburban Connecticut, Montgomery County supported the Democratic ticket in last year's presidential election, by a margin of 63 percent to 34 percent. Meanwhile, like almost all of rural America, Franklin County went Republican, by 67 percent to 30 percent.

However, other voting patterns sometimes obscure the Red-Blue cultural divide. For example, minority voters all over the country overwhelmingly supported the Democratic ticket last November. But—in many respects, at least—blacks and Hispanics in Red America are more traditionalist than blacks and Hispanics in Blue America, just as their white counterparts are. For example, the Pew Research Center for the People and the Press, in Washington, D.C., recently found that 45 percent of minority members in Red states agree with the statement "AIDS might be God's punishment for immoral sexual behavior," but only 31 percent of minority members in Blue states do. Similarly, 40 percent of minorities in Red states believe that school boards should have the right to fire homosexual teachers, but only 21 percent of minorities in Blue states do.

From Cracks to a Chasm?

These differences are so many and so stark that they lead to some pretty troubling questions: Are Americans any longer a common people? Do we have one national conversation and one national culture? Are we loyal to the same institutions and the same values? How do people on one side of the divide regard those on the other?

25 I went to Franklin County because I wanted to get a sense of how deep the divide really is, to see how people there live, and to gauge how different their lives are from those in my part of America. I spoke with ministers, journalists, teachers, community leaders, and pretty much anyone I ran across. I consulted with pollsters, demographers, and market-research firms.

Toward the end of my project the World Trade Center and the Pentagon were attacked. This put a new slant on my little investigation. In the days immediately following September 11 the evidence seemed clear that despite our differences, we are still a united people. American flags flew everywhere in Franklin County and in Montgomery County. Patriotism surged. Pollsters started to measure Americans' reactions to the events. Whatever questions they asked, the replies were near unanimous. Do you support a military response against terror? More than four fifths of Americans said yes. Do you support a military response even if it means thousands of U.S. casualties? More than three fifths said yes. There were no significant variations across geographic or demographic lines.

A sweeping feeling of solidarity was noticeable in every neighborhood, school, and workplace. Headlines blared, "A NATION UNITED" and "UNITED STATE." An attack had been made on the very epicenter of Blue America—downtown Manhattan. And in a flash all the jokes about and seeming hostility toward New Yorkers vanished, to be replaced by an outpouring of respect, support, and love. The old hostility came to seem merely a sort of sibling rivalry, which means nothing when the family itself is under threat.

But very soon there were hints that the solidarity was fraying. A few stray notes of dissent were sounded in the organs of Blue America. Susan Sontag wrote a sour piece in *The New Yorker* about how depressing it was to see what she considered to be a simplistically pro-American reaction to the attacks. At rallies on college campuses across the country speakers pointed out that America had been bombing other countries for years, and turnabout was fair play. On one NPR talk show I heard numerous callers express unease about what they saw as a crude us-versus-them mentality behind President Bush's rhetoric. Katha Pollitt wrote in *The Nation* that she would not permit her daughter to hang the American flag from the living-room window, because, she felt, it "stands for jingoism and vengeance and war." And there was evidence that among those with less-strident voices, too, differences were beginning to show. Polls revealed that people without a college education were far more confident than people with a college education that the military could defeat the terrorists. People in the South were far more eager than people in the rest of the country for an American counterattack to begin.

It started to seem likely that these cracks would widen once the American response got under way, when the focus would be not on firemen and rescue workers but on the Marines, the CIA, and the special-operations forces. If the war was protracted, the cracks could widen into a chasm, as they did during Vietnam. Red America, the home of patriotism and military service (there's a big military-recruitment center in downtown Chambersburg), would undoubtedly support the war effort, but would Blue America (there's a big gourmet dog bakery in downtown Bethesda) decide that a crude military response would only deepen animosities and make things worse?

So toward the end of my project I investigated Franklin County with a 30
heightened sense of gravity and with much more urgency. If America was not firmly united in the early days of the conflict, we would certainly not be united later, when the going got tough.

"The People Versus the Powerful"

There are a couple of long-standing theories about why America is divided. One of the main ones holds that the division is along class lines, between the haves and the have-nots. This theory is popular chiefly on the left, and can be found in the pages of *The American Prospect* and other liberal magazines; in news reports by liberal journalists such as Donald L. Barlett and James B. Steele, of *Time*; and in books such as *Middle Class Dreams* (1995), by the Clinton and Gore pollster Stanley Greenberg, and *America's Forgotten Majority: Why the White Working Class Still Matters* (2000), by the demographer Ruy Teixeira and the social scientist Joel Rogers.

According to this theory, during most of the twentieth century gaps in income between the rich and the poor in America gradually shrank. Then came the information age. The rich started getting spectacularly richer, the poor started getting poorer, and wages for the middle class stagnated, at best. Over the previous decade, these writers emphasized, remuneration for top-level executives had skyrocketed: now the average CEO made 116 times as much as the average rank-and-file worker. Assembly-line workers found themselves competing for jobs against Third World workers who earned less than a dollar an hour. Those who had once labored at well-paying blue-collar jobs were forced to settle for poorly paying service-economy jobs without benefits.

People with graduate degrees have done well over the past couple of decades: their real hourly wages climbed by 13 percent from 1979 to 1997, according to Teixeira and Rogers. But those with only some college education saw their wages fall by nine percent, while those with only high school diplomas saw their wages fall by 12 percent, and high school dropouts saw a stunning 26 percent decline in their pay.

Such trends have created a new working class, these writers argue—not a traditional factory-and-mill working class but a suburban and small-town working class, made up largely of service workers and low-level white-collar employees. Teixeira and Rogers estimate that the average household income for this group, which accounts for about 55 percent of American adults, is roughly $42,000. "It is not hard to imagine how [recent economic trends] must have felt to the forgotten majority man," they write.

> As at least part of America was becoming ever more affluent, an affluence that was well covered on television and in the evening news, he did not seem to be making much progress. What could he be doing wrong to be faring so poorly? Why couldn't he afford what others could? And why were they moving ahead while he was standing still?

Stanley Greenberg tailored Al Gore's presidential campaign to appeal to 35
such voters. Gore's most significant slogan was "The People Versus the Powerful," which was meant to rally members of the middle class who felt threatened by "powerful forces" beyond their control, such as HMOs, tobacco companies, big corporations, and globalization, and to channel their resentment against the upper class. Gore dressed down throughout his campaign in the hope that these middle-class workers would identify with him.

Driving from Bethesda to Franklin County, one can see that the theory of a divide between the classes has a certain plausibility. In Montgomery County we have Saks Fifth Avenue, Cartier, Anthropologie, Brooks Brothers. In Franklin County they have Dollar General and Value City, along with a plethora of secondhand stores. It's as if Franklin County has only forty-five coffee tables, which are sold again and again.

When the locals are asked about their economy, they tell a story very similar to the one that Greenberg, Teixeira, Rogers, and the rest of the wage-stagnation liberals recount. There used to be plenty of good factory jobs in Franklin County, and people could work at those factories for life. But some of the businesses, including the textile company J. Schoeneman, once Franklin County's largest manufacturer, have closed. Others have moved offshore. The remaining manufacturers, such as Grove Worldwide and JLG

Industries, which both make cranes and aerial platforms, have laid off workers. The local Army depot, Letterkenny, has radically shrunk its work force. The new jobs are in distribution centers or nursing homes. People tend to repeat the same phrase: "We've taken some hits."

And yet when they are asked about the broader theory, whether there is class conflict between the educated affluents and the stagnant middles, they stare blankly as if suddenly the interview were being conducted in Aramaic. I kept asking, Do you feel that the highly educated people around, say, New York and Washington are getting all the goodies? Do you think there is resentment toward all the latte sippers who shop at Nieman Marcus? Do you see a gulf between high-income people in the big cities and middle-income people here? I got only polite, fumbling answers as people tried to figure out what the hell I was talking about.

When I rephrased the question in more-general terms, as Do you believe the country is divided between the haves and the have-nots?, everyone responded decisively: yes. But as the conversation continued, it became clear that the people saying yes did not consider themselves to be among the have-nots. Even people with incomes well below the median thought of themselves as haves.

What I found was entirely consistent with the election returns from 40
November of last year. Gore's pitch failed miserably among the voters it was intended to target: nationally he lost among non-college-educated white voters by 17 points and among non-college-educated white men by 29 points. But it worked beautifully on the affluent, educated class: for example, Gore won among women with graduate degrees by 22 points. The lesson seems to be that if you run a campaign under the slogan "The People Versus the Powerful," you will not do well in the places where "the people" live, but you will do fantastically well in the places where "the powerful" live. This phenomenon mirrors, on a larger scale, one I noted a couple of years ago, when I traveled the country for a year talking about *Bobos in Paradise,* a book I had written on upscale America. The richer the community, the more likely I was to be asked about wage inequality. In middle-class communities the subject almost never came up.

Hanging around Franklin County, one begins to understand some of the reasons that people there don't spend much time worrying about economic class lines. The first and most obvious one is that although the incomes in Franklin County are lower than those in Montgomery County, living expenses are also lower—very much so. Driving from Montgomery County to Franklin County is like driving through an invisible deflation machine. Gas is thirty, forty, or even fifty cents a gallon cheaper in Franklin County. I parked at meters that accepted only pennies and nickels. When I got a parking ticket in Chambersburg, the fine was $3.00. At the department store in Greencastle there were racks and racks of blouses for $9.99.

The biggest difference is in real-estate prices. In Franklin County one can buy a nice four-bedroom split-level house with about 2,200 square feet of living space for $150,000 to $180,000. In Bethesda that same house would cost about $450,000. (According to the Coldwell Banker Real Estate Corporation, that house would sell for $784,000 in Greenwich, Connecticut; for $812,000 in Manhattan Beach, California; and for about $1.23 million in Palo Alto, California.)

Some of the people I met in Franklin County were just getting by. Some were in debt and couldn't afford to buy their kids the Christmas presents they wanted to. But I didn't find many who assessed their own place in society according to their income. Rather, the people I met commonly told me that although those in affluent places like Manhattan and Bethesda might make more money and have more-exciting jobs, they are the unlucky ones, because they don't get to live in Franklin County. They don't get to enjoy the beautiful green hillsides, the friendly people, the wonderful church groups and volunteer organizations. They may be nice people and all, but they are certainly not as happy as we are.

Another thing I found is that most people don't think sociologically. They don't compare themselves with faraway millionaires who appear on their TV screens. They compare themselves with their neighbors. "One of the challenges we face is that it is hard to get people to look beyond the four-state region," Lynne Woehrle, a sociologist at Wilson College, in Chambersburg, told me, referring to the cultural zone composed of the nearby rural areas in Pennsylvania, West Virginia, Maryland, and Virginia. Many of the people in Franklin County view the lifestyles of the upper class in California or Seattle much the way we in Blue America might view the lifestyle of someone in Eritrea or Mongolia—or, for that matter, Butte, Montana. Such ways of life are distant and basically irrelevant, except as a source of academic interest or titillation. One man in Mercersburg, Pennsylvania, told me about a friend who had recently bought a car. "He paid twenty-five thousand dollars for that car!" he exclaimed, his eyes wide with amazement. "He got it fully loaded." I didn't tell him that in Bethesda almost no one but a college kid pays as little as $25,000 for a car.

Franklin County is a world in which there is little obvious inequality, 45
and the standard of living is reasonably comfortable. Youth-soccer teams are able to raise money for a summer trip to England; the Lowe's hardware superstore carries Laura Ashley carpets; many people have pools, although they are almost always above ground; the planning commission has to cope with an increasing number of cars in the county every year, even though the population is growing only gradually. But the sort of high-end experiences that are everywhere in Montgomery County are entirely missing here.

On my journeys to Franklin County, I set a goal: I was going to spend $20 on a restaurant meal. But although I ordered the most expensive thing on the menu—steak au jus, "slippery beef pot pie," or whatever—I always failed. I began asking people to direct me to the most-expensive places in town. They would send me to Red Lobster or Applebee's. I'd go into a restaurant that looked from the outside as if it had some pretensions—may be a "Les Desserts" glass cooler for the key-lime pie and the tapioca pudding. I'd scan the menu and realize that I'd been beaten once again. I went through great vats of chipped beef and "seafood delight" trying to drop twenty dollars. I waded through enough surf-and-turfs and enough creamed corn to last a lifetime. I could not do it.

No wonder people in Franklin County have no class resentment or class consciousness; where they live, they can afford just about anything that is for sale. (In Montgomery County, however—and this is one of the most striking contrasts between the two counties—almost nobody can say that. In Blue America, unless you are very, very rich, there is always, all around you, stuff for sale that you cannot afford.) And if they sought to improve their situation, they would look only to themselves. If a person wants to make more money, the feeling goes, he or she had better work hard and think like an entrepreneur.

I could barely get fifteen minutes into an interview before the local work ethic came up. Karen Jewell, who helps to oversee the continuing-education program for the local Penn State branch campus, told me, "People are very vested in what they do. There's an awareness of where they fit in the organization. They feel empowered to be agents of change."

People do work extremely hard in Franklin County—even people in supposedly dead-end jobs. You can see it in little things, such as drugstore shelves. The drugstores in Bethesda look the way Rome must have looked after a visit from the Visigoths. But in Franklin County the boxes are in perfect little rows. Shelves are fully stocked, and cans are evenly spaced. The floors are less dusty than those in a microchip-processing plant. The nail clippers on a rack by the cash register are arranged with a precision that would put the Swiss to shame.

There are few unions in Franklin County. People abhor the thought of 50
depending on welfare; they consider themselves masters of their own economic fate. "People are really into the free market here," Bill Pukmel, formerly the editor of the weekly paper in Chambersburg, told me.

In sum, I found absolutely no evidence that a Stanley Greenberg-prompted Democratic Party (or a Pat Buchanan-led Republican Party) could mobilize white middle-class Americans on the basis of class consciousness. I found no evidence that economic differences explain much of anything about the divide between Red and Blue America.

Ted Hale, a Presbyterian minister in the western part of the county, spoke of the matter this way: "There's nowhere near as much resentment as you would expect. People have come to understand that they will struggle financially. It's part of their identity. But the economy is not their god. That's the thing some others don't understand. People value a sense of community far more than they do their portfolio." Hale, who worked at a church in East Hampton, New York, before coming to Franklin County, said that he saw a lot more economic resentment in New York.

Hale's observations are supported by nationwide polling data. Pew has conducted a broad survey of the differences between Red and Blue states. The survey found that views on economic issues do not explain the different voting habits in the two regions. There simply isn't much of the sort of economic dissatisfaction that could drive a class-based political movement. Eighty-five percent of Americans with an annual household income between $30,000 and $50,000 are satisfied with their housing. Nearly 70 percent are satisfied with the kind of car they can afford. Roughly two thirds are satisfied with their furniture and their ability to afford a night out. These levels of satisfaction are not very different from those found in upper-middle-class America.

The Pew researchers found this sort of trend in question after question. Part of the draft of their report is titled "Economic Divide Dissolves."

A Lot of Religion But Few Crusaders

This leaves us with the second major hypothesis about the nature of the 55
divide between Red and Blue America, which comes mainly from conservatives: America is divided between two moral systems. Red America is traditional, religious, self-disciplined, and patriotic. Blue America is modern, secular, self-expressive, and discomfited by blatant displays of patriotism. Proponents of this hypothesis in its most radical form contend that America is in the midst of a culture war, with two opposing armies fighting on behalf of their views. The historian Gertrude Himmelfarb offered a more moderate picture in *One Nation, Two Cultures* (1999), in which she argued that although America is not fatally split, it is deeply divided, between a heartland conservative population that adheres to a strict morality and a liberal population that lives by a loose one. The political journalist Michael Barone put it this way in a recent essay in *National Journal*: "The two Americas apparent in the 48 percent to 48 percent 2000 election are two nations of different faiths. One is observant, tradition-minded, moralistic. The other is unobservant, liberation-minded, relativistic."

The values-divide school has a fair bit of statistical evidence on its side. Whereas income is a poor predictor of voting patterns, church attendance—as Barone points out—is a pretty good one. Of those who attend religious services weekly (42 percent of the electorate), 59 percent voted for Bush, 39 percent for Gore. Of those who seldom or never attend religious services (another 42 percent), 56 percent voted for Gore, 39 percent for Bush.

The Pew data reveal significant divides on at least a few values issues. Take, for example, the statement "We will all be called before God on Judgment Day to answer for our sins." In Red states 70 percent of the people believe that statement. In Blue states only 50 percent do.

One can feel the religiosity in Franklin County after a single day's visit. It's on the bumper stickers: WARNING: IN CASE OF RAPTURE THIS VEHICLE WILL BE UNMANNED. REAL TRUCKERS TALK ABOUT JESUS ON CHANNEL 10. It's on the radio. The airwaves are filled not with the usual mixture of hit tunes but with evangelicals preaching the gospel. The book section of Wal-Mart features titles such as *The Beginner's Guide to Fasting, Deepen Your Conversation with God,* and *Are We Living in the End Times?* Some general stores carry the "Heroes of the Faith" series, which consists of small biographies of William Carey, George Müller, and other notable missionaries, ministers, and theologians—notable in Red America, that is, but largely unknown where I live.

Chambersburg and its vicinity have eighty-five churches and one synagogue. The Bethesda-Chevy Chase area, which has a vastly greater population, has forty-five churches and five synagogues. Professors at the local college in Chambersburg have learned not to schedule public lectures on Wednesday nights, because everybody is at prayer meetings.

Events that are part of daily life in Franklin County are unheard of in 60
most of Blue America. One United Brethren minister told me that he is asked to talk about morals in the public school as part of the health and sex-education curriculum, and nobody raises a fuss. A number of schools have a "Bible release program," whereby elementary school students are allowed to leave school for an hour a week to attend Bible-study meetings. At an elementary school in Waynesboro the Gideons used to distribute Bibles to any students who wanted them. (That ended after the village agnostic threatened to simultaneously distribute a booklet called *God Is Just Pretend.*)

There are healing ministries all throughout Franklin County, and even mainstream denominations have healing teams on hand after Sunday services. As in most places where evangelism is strong, the locals are fervently pro-Israel. Almost every minister I visited has mementos in his study from visits to Jerusalem. A few had lived in Israel for extended periods and spoke Hebrew. One delivered a tirade against CNN for its bias against the Jewish state. One or two pointed out (without quite bragging) that whereas some Jewish groups had canceled trips to Israel since the upsurge in intifada violence, evangelical groups were still going.

David Rawley, a United Brethren minister in Greencastle, spoke for many of the social conservatives I met when he said that looking at the mainstream Hollywood culture made him feel that he was "walking against the current." "The tremendous force of culture means we can either float or fight," Rawley said. "Should you drift or stand on a rock? I tell people there is a rock we can hang on—the word of God. That rock will never give way. That rock's never going to move." When I asked Rawley what he thought of big-city culture, he said, "The individual is swallowed up by the largeness of the city. I see a world that doesn't want to take responsibility for itself. They have the babies but they decide they're not going to be the daddies. I'd really have to cling to the rock if I lived there."

I met with Rawley at the height of the scandal involving Representative Gary Condit and the missing intern Chandra Levy. Levy's mother was quoted in *The Washington Times* as calling herself a "Heinz 57 mutt" when it came to religion. "All religions tie to similar beliefs," she said. "I believe in spirituality and God. I'm Jewish. I think we have a wonderful religion. I'm also Christian. I do believe in Jesus, too." The contrast between her New Age approach to spirituality and Rawley's Red America one could not have been greater.

Life is complicated, however. Yes, there are a lot of churches in Franklin County; there are also a lot of tattoo parlors. And despite all the churches and bumper stickers, Franklin County doesn't seem much different from anywhere else. People go to a few local bars to hang out after softball games. Teenagers drive recklessly along fast-food strips. Young women in halter tops sometimes prowl in the pool halls. The local college has a gay-and-lesbian group. One conservative clergyman I spoke with estimated that 10 percent of his congregants are gay. He believes that church is the place where one should be able to leave the controversy surrounding this sort of issue behind. Another described how his congregation united behind a young man who was dying of AIDS.

Sex seems to be on people's minds almost as much as it is anywhere 65
else. Conservative evangelical circles have their own sex manuals (Tim LaHaye wrote one of them before he moved on to the "Left Behind" series), which appear to have had some effect: according to a 1994 study conducted by researchers at the University of Chicago, conservative Protestant women have more orgasms than any other group.

Franklin County is probably a bit more wholesome than most suburbs in Blue America. (The notion that deviance and corruption lie underneath the seeming conformism of suburban middle-class life, popular in Hollywood and in creative-writing workshops, is largely nonsense.) But it has most of the problems that afflict other parts of the country: heroin addiction, teen pregnancy, and so on. Nobody I spoke to felt part of a pristine culture that is exempt from the problems of the big cities. There are even enough spectacular crimes in Franklin County to make a devoted *New York Post* reader happy. During one of my visits the front pages of the local papers were ablaze with the tale of a young woman arrested for assault and homicide after shooting her way through a Veterans of the Vietnam War post. It was reported that she had intended to rob the post for money to run away with her lesbian girlfriend.

If the problems are the same as in the rest of America, so are many of the solutions. Franklin County residents who find themselves in trouble go to their clergy first, but they are often referred to psychologists and therapists as part of their recovery process. Prozac is a part of life.

Almost nobody I spoke with understood, let alone embraced, the concept of a culture war. Few could see themselves as fighting such a war, in part because few have any idea where the boundary between the two sides lies.

People in Franklin County may have a clear sense of what constitutes good or evil (many people in Blue America have trouble with the very concept of evil), but they will say that good and evil are in all neighborhoods, as they are in all of us. People take the Scriptures seriously but have no interest in imposing them on others. One finds little crusader zeal in Franklin County. For one thing, people in small towns don't want to offend people whom they'll be encountering on the street for the next fifty years. Potentially controversial subjects are often played down. "We would never take a stance on gun control or abortion," Sue Hadden, the editor of the Waynesboro paper, told me. Whenever I asked what the local view of abortion was, I got the same response: "We don't talk about it much," or "We try to avoid that subject." Bill Pukmel, the former Chambersburg newspaper editor, says, "A majority would be opposed to abortion around here, but it wouldn't be a big majority." It would simply be uncivil to thrust such a raw disagreement in people's faces.

William Harter, a Presbyterian minister in Chambersburg, spans the divide between Red and Blue America. Harter was raised on a farm near Buffalo. He went to the prestigious Deerfield Academy, in Massachusetts, before getting a bachelor's degree in history from Williams College, a master's in education from Harvard, and, after serving for a while in the military, a Ph.D. in Judaism and Christian origins from the Union Theological Seminary, in Manhattan. He has lived in Chambersburg for the past twenty-four years, and he says that the range of opinion in Franklin County is much wider than it was in Cambridge or New York. "We're more authentically pluralistic here," he told me.

I found Harter and the other preachers in Franklin County especially 70
interesting to talk with. That was in part because the ones I met were fiercely intelligent and extremely well read, but also because I could see them wrestling with the problem of how to live according to the Scriptures while being inclusive and respectful of others' freedoms. For example, many of them struggle over whether it is right to marry a couple who are already living together. This would not be a consideration in most of Blue America.

"Some of the evangelicals won't marry [such couples]," Harter told me. "Others will insist that they live apart for six months before they'll marry them. But that's not the real world. These couples often don't understand the theological basis for not living together. Even if you don't condone their situations, you have to start where they are—help them have loyal marriages."

Divorce is tolerated much more than it used to be. And none of the ministers I spoke with said that they would condemn a parishioner who was having an affair. They would confront the parishioner, but with the goal of gently bringing that person back to Jesus Christ. "How could I love that person if I didn't?" Patrick Jones, of the United Brethren's King Street Church, in Chambersburg, asked. People in Franklin County are contemptuous of Bill

Clinton and his serial infidelities, but they are not necessarily fans of Kenneth Starr—at least not the Kenneth Starr the media portrayed. They don't like public scolds.

Roger Murray, a Pentecostal minister in Mercersburg, whose father was also a Pentecostal minister, exemplifies the way in which many church authorities are torn by the sometimes conflicting desires to uphold authority and respect personal freedom. "My father would preach about what you could do and what you couldn't do," Murray recalls. "He would preach about smoking, about TV, about ladies who dress provocatively, against divorce." As a boy, Murray used to go visit his uncle, and he would sit in another room when his uncle's family watched television. "I was sure they were going to hell," he told me. But now he would never dream of telling people how to live. For one thing, his congregants wouldn't defer. And he is in no rush to condemn others. "I don't think preaching against homosexuality is what you should do," he told me. "A positive message works better."

Like most of the people I met in Franklin County, Murray regards such culture warriors as Jerry Falwell and Pat Robertson as loose cannons, and televangelists as being far too interested in raising money. "I get pretty disgusted with Christian TV," he said. And that was before Falwell and Robertson made their notorious comments about the attacks of September 11 being a judgment from God. When I asked locals about those remarks, they answered with words like "disgusting," "horrendous," and "horrible." Almost no one in the county voted for Pat Buchanan; he was simply too contentious.

Certainly Red and Blue America disagree strongly on some issues, such 75
as homosexuality and abortion. But for the most part the disagreements are not large. For example, the Pew researchers asked Americans to respond to the statement "There are clear guidelines about what's good or evil that apply to everyone regardless of their situation." Forty-three percent of people in Blue states and 49 percent of people in Red states agreed. Forty-seven percent of Blue America and 55 percent of Red America agreed with the statement "I have old-fashioned values about family and marriage." Seventy percent of the people in Blue states and 77 percent of the people in Red states agreed that "too many children are being raised in day-care centers these days." These are small gaps. And, the Pew researchers found, there is no culture gap at all among suburban voters. In a Red state like Arizona suburban voters' opinions are not much different from those in a Blue state like Connecticut. The starkest differences that exist are between people in cities and people in rural areas, especially rural areas in the South.

The conservatism I found in Franklin County is not an ideological or a reactionary conservatism. It is a temperamental conservatism. People place tremendous value on being agreeable, civil, and kind. They are happy to sit quietly with one another. They are hesitant to stir one another's passions. They appreciate what they have. They value continuity and revere the past. They work hard to reinforce community bonds. Their newspapers are filled with items about fundraising drives, car washes, bake sales, penny-collection efforts, and auxiliary thrift shops. Their streets are lined with lodges: VFW, Rotarians, Elks, Moose. Luncheons go on everywhere. Retired federal employees will be holding their weekly luncheon at one restaurant, Harley riders at another. I became fascinated by a group called the Tuscarora Longbeards, a local chapter of something called the National Wild Turkey Federation. The Longbeards go around to schools distributing Wild About Turkey Education boxes, which contain posters, lesson plans, and CD-ROMs on turkey preservation.

These are the sorts of things that really mobilize people in Franklin County. Building community and preserving local ways are far more important to them than any culture war.

The Ego Curtain

The best explanation of the differences between people in Montgomery and Franklin Counties has to do with sensibility, not class or culture. If I had to describe the differences between the two sensibilities in a single phrase, it would be conception of the self. In Red America the self is small. People declare in a million ways, "I am normal. Nobody is better, nobody is worse. I am humble before God." In Blue America the self is more commonly large. People say in a million ways, "I am special. I have carved out my own unique way of life. I am independent. I make up my own mind."

In Red America there is very little one-upmanship. Nobody tries to be avant-garde in choosing a wardrobe. The chocolate-brown suits and baggy denim dresses hanging in local department stores aren't there by accident; people conspicuously want to be seen as not trying to dress to impress.

For a person in Blue America the blandness in Red America can be a 80
little oppressive. But it's hard not to be struck by the enormous social pressure not to put on airs. If a Franklin County resident drove up to church one day in a shiny new Lexus, he would face huge waves of disapproval. If one hired a nanny, people would wonder who died and made her queen.

In Franklin County people don't go looking for obscure beers to demonstrate their connoisseurship. They wear T-shirts and caps with big-brand names on them—Coke, McDonald's, Chevrolet. In Bethesda people prefer cognoscenti brands—the Black Dog restaurant, or the independent bookstore Politics and Prose. In Franklin County it would be an affront to the egalitarian ethos to put a Princeton sticker on the rear window of one's car. In Montgomery County some proud parents can barely see through their back windows for all the Ivy League stickers. People in Franklin County say they felt comfortable voting for Bush, because if he came to town he wouldn't act superior to anybody else; he could settle into a barber's chair and fit right in. They couldn't stand Al Gore, because they thought he'd always be trying to awe everyone with his accomplishments. People in Montgomery County tended to admire Gore's accomplishments. They were leery of Bush, because for most of his life he seemed not to have achieved anything.

I sometimes think that Franklin County takes its unpretentiousness a little too far. I wouldn't care to live there, because I'd find it too unchanging. I prefer the subtle and not-so-subtle status climbing on my side of the Ego Curtain—it's more entertaining. Still, I can't help respecting the genuine modesty of Franklin County people. It shows up strikingly in data collected by Mediamark Research. In survey after survey, residents of conservative Red America come across as humbler than residents of liberal Blue America. About half of those who describe themselves as "very conservative" agree with the statement "I have more ability than most people," but nearly two thirds of those who describe themselves as "very liberal" agree. Only 53 percent of conservatives agree with the statement "I consider myself an intellectual," but 75 percent of liberals do. Only 23 percent of conservatives agree with the statement "I must admit that I like to show off," whereas 43 percent of liberals do.

A Cafeteria Nation

These differences in sensibility don't in themselves mean that America has become a fundamentally divided nation. As the sociologist Seymour Martin Lipset pointed out in *The First New Nation* (1963), achievement and equality are the two rival themes running throughout American history. Most people, most places, and most epochs have tried to intertwine them in some way.

Moreover, after bouncing between Montgomery and Franklin Counties, I became convinced that a lot of our fear that America is split into rival camps arises from mistaken notions of how society is shaped. Some of us still carry the old Marxist categories in our heads. We think that society is like a layer cake, with the upper class on top. And, like Marx, we tend to assume that wherever there is class division there is conflict. Or else we have a sort of *Crossfire* model in our heads: where would people we meet sit if they were guests on that show?

But traveling back and forth between the two counties was not like 85
crossing from one rival camp to another. It was like crossing a high school cafeteria. Remember high school? There were nerds, jocks, punks, bikers, techies, druggies, God Squadders, drama geeks, poets, and Dungeons & Dragons weirdoes. All these cliques were part of the same school: they had different sensibilities; sometimes they knew very little about the people in the other cliques; but the jocks knew there would always be nerds, and the nerds knew there would always be jocks. That's just the way life is.

And that's the way America is. We are not a divided nation. We are a cafeteria nation. We form cliques (call them communities, or market segments, or whatever), and when they get too big, we form subcliques. Some people even get together in churches that are "nondenominational" or in political groups that are "independent." These are cliques built around the supposed rejection of cliques.

We live our lives by migrating through the many different cliques associated with the activities we enjoy and the goals we have set for ourselves. Our freedom comes in the interstices; we can choose which set of standards to live by, and when.

We should remember that there is generally some distance between cliques—a buffer zone that separates one set of aspirations from another. People who are happy within their cliques feel no great compulsion to go out and reform other cliques. The jocks don't try to change the nerds. David Rawley, the Greencastle minister who felt he was clinging to a rock, has been to New York City only once in his life. "I was happy to get back home," he told me. "It's a planet I'm a little scared of. I have no desire to go back."

What unites the two Americas, then, is our mutual commitment to this way of life—to the idea that a person is not bound by his class, or by the religion of his fathers, but is free to build a plurality of connections for himself. We are participants in the same striving process, the same experimental journey.

Never has this been more apparent than in the weeks following the 90
September 11 attacks. Before then Montgomery County people and Franklin County people gave little thought to one another: an attitude of benign neglect toward other parts of the country generally prevailed. But the events of that day generated what one of my lunch mates in Franklin County called a primal response. Our homeland was under attack. Suddenly there was a positive sense that we Americans are all bound together—a sense that, despite some little fissures here and there, has endured.

On September 11 people in Franklin County flocked to the institutions that are so strong there—the churches and the American Legion and the VFW posts. Houses of worship held spontaneous prayer services and large ecumenical services. In the weeks since, firemen, veterans, and Scouts have held rallies. There have been blood drives. Just about every service organization in the county—and there are apparently thousands—has mobilized to raise funds or ship teddy bears. The rescue squad and the Salvation Army branch went to New York to help.

Early every morning Ted Hale, the Presbyterian minister who once worked in East Hampton, goes to one of the local restaurants and sits as the regulars cycle through. One of the things that has struck him since the attacks is how little partisan feeling is left. "I expected to hear a certain amount of Clinton bashing, for creating the mess in which this could take place," he told me in October. "But there's been absolutely none of that." Instead Hale has been deluged with questions—about Islam, about why God restrains himself in the face of evil, about how people could commit such acts.

The area's churches have not been monolithic in their responses. Many of the most conservative churches—the Mennonites and the Brethren, for example—have pacifist traditions. Bill Harter, in contrast, told his congregation during a recent sermon that the pacifist course is not the right one. "We must face the fact that there is a power of evil loose in the universe, which is dedicated to attacking all that is good, all that comes from God," he said. This evil, Harter continued, has cloaked itself in a perverted form of one of the world's major faiths. Citing the Protestant theologian Reinhold Niebuhr, he reminded his congregants that there is no sinless way to defend ourselves against this hostile ideology. But defend we must. "We must humbly make our choice while recognizing that we must constantly turn to God for forgiveness," he told them.

The churches and synagogues in Bethesda, too, have been struggling. Over the Jewish High Holy Days, I heard of three synagogues in which the sermon was interrupted by a member of the congregation. In one instance the rabbi had said that it is always impossible to know where good and evil lie. A man rose up angrily to declare that in this case that sentiment was nonsense.

95 Most people in my part of Blue America know few who will be called on to fight in the war. In Franklin County military service is common. Many families have an enlisted son or daughter, and many more have a relative in the reserves or the National Guard. Franklin County is engaged in an urgent discussion, largely absent where I live, about how to fill in for the reservists called up for active duty.

Still, there's an attitude of determination in both places. If I had to boil down all the conversations I have had in Franklin and Montgomery Counties since September 11, the essence would be this: A horrible thing happened. We're going to deal with it. We're going to restore order. We got through Pearl Harbor. We're going to get through this. "There is no flaccidity," Harter observed, in words that apply to both communities.

If the September 11 attacks rallied people in both Red and Blue America, they also neutralized the political and cultural leaders who tend to exploit the differences between the two. Americans are in no mood for a class struggle or a culture war. The aftermath of the attacks has been a bit like a national Sabbath, taking us out of our usual pleasures and distractions and reminding us what is really important. Over time the shock will dissipate. But in important ways the psychological effects will linger, just as the effects of John F. Kennedy's assassination have lingered. The early evidence still holds: although there are some real differences between Red and Blue America, there is no fundamental conflict. There may be cracks, but there is no chasm. Rather, there is a common love for this nation—one nation in the end.

QUESTIONING THE TEXT

1. Whom do you envision as Brooks's primary audience? Do you think he writes mainly to people in Red or Blue America? What evidence in the essay supports your speculation about his audience?
2. With a classmate, locate and count the assertions Brooks makes about Red and Blue America. How many of each do you find? What do these numbers tell you about the focus of the essay? For each of the assertions, what kind of support does Brooks offer? Do you find his characterizations of Red and Blue America convincing? Why, or why not?
3. Reread Brooks's essay, tracing his reasoning from the images he presents of the divided America shown on the map of 2000 election results (see p. 9) to his conclusion that the United States is "one nation in the end" (paragraph 97). Does he persuade you that this conclusion is true? Write a response to his essay in which you support or challenge his view, providing reasons for your claims.

MAKING CONNECTIONS

4. Read the Declaration of Independence (p. 517), and consider the common principles and values espoused by the signers of that document. Compare those principles or values with the ones that Brooks identifies as uniting Americans today. What similarities and differences do you find? Use this comparison to discuss in class how you think American ideals may have changed, or how they may have endured, from 1776 until now.
5. Reconsider Brooks's descriptions of the differences between Blue and Red America in light of Ward Churchill's "Crimes against Humanity" (p. 536), which includes a criticism of the "national project of 'clearing' Native Americans from their land and replacing them with 'superior' Anglo-American settlers" (paragraph 21). In a group with two or three classmates, study the ways Brooks and Churchill discuss cultural conflicts within America. What terms do they use? How do they delineate differences? Does Churchill's essay give you a different perspective on the divisions that Brooks portrays? If so, how? Take notes on your group's discussion, and share your observations in discussion with the whole class.

JOINING THE CONVERSATION

6. Think of a cultural divide that you might examine in the way Brooks did. Is there a rival school or college, or a neighborhood that on the surface appears very different from your own, which you might visit for

a day and report on? Write an essay in which you illuminate the differences you perceive between the two cultures. Try to assess the extent to which these differences are sustained by myths—by beliefs passed on from one generation to another through narratives.

7. For class discussion, think about whether you identify with Brooks's characterizations of Blue or Red America—or Franklin or Montgomery counties. Do you see yourself on either side of the divide, or perhaps "span[ning] the divide" as Brooks describes William Harter (paragraph 69)? Jot down the ways in which you identify with some of his descriptions, or ways in which they seem foreign to you. Bring your notes, to share your response with classmates. Consider using your ideas as the basis for an op-ed for a newspaper or guest column for a magazine.

BARBARA KINGSOLVER
And Our Flag Was Still There

THE FLAG IS ONE OF THE OLDEST and most enduring elements of American mythology, a supreme symbol of patriotism. As Barbara Kingsolver (b. 1955) points out in the essay that follows, the flag and other American icons "grew out of war," a fact she alludes to in her title with its evocations of the "rockets' red glare" in the national anthem. For Kingsolver, this original association goes a long way toward explaining why, in the debate over what patriotic *should mean, those linking patriotism and war have a strong upper hand.*

In the aftermath of September 11, 2001, and the wars that followed, Kingsolver argues that it is time to "retire the rockets' red glare and the bloody bandage as obsolete symbols of Old Glory." Kingsolver knows such a goal is daunting, given the hate crimes and hate speech directed against many of those who stand up for peace rather than war or question the righteousness of making war. Yet this peaceful kind of patriotism has its place in America too, says Kingsolver: the flag belongs to all of us, she says, and she insists on waving it over "a few things I believe in," including our nation's commitment to protecting dissenting points of view.

Born and raised in Kentucky, Kingsolver graduated from DePauw University and later received a master of science degree from the University of Arizona. She worked at a number of professions, including x-ray technician and freelance journalist, before turning to fiction. Her novel The Bean Trees, *published in 1988, was followed by* Animal Dreams *(1990);* Pigs in Heaven *(1993);* The Poisonwood Bible *(1998), which was a finalist for the Pulitzer Prize for fiction; and* Prodigal Summer *(2000).*

Kingsolver says that reading Doris Lessing led her to "understand how a person could write about the problems of the world in a compelling and beautiful way. And it seemed to me that was the most important thing I could ever do. . . ." In her fiction and in her essays, including the one reprinted here, Kingsolver does write about the problems of our world, and she does so compellingly. As you read this essay, which comes from her recent collection Small Wonder *(2002), you may want to consider your own definitions of patriotism and the associations the American flag holds for you. How do they compare to those described in "And Our Flag Was Still There"?* —A.L.

My daughter came home from kindergarten and announced, "Tomorrow we all have to wear red, white, and blue."

"Why?" I asked, trying not to sound anxious.

"For all the people that died when the airplanes hit the buildings."

I said quietly, "Why not wear black, then? Why the colors of the flag, what does that mean?"

"It means we're a country. Just all people together." 5

I love my country dearly. Not long after the September 11 attacks, as I stood in a high school cafeteria listening to my older daughter and a hundred other teenagers in the orchestra play "Stars and Stripes Forever" on their earnest, vibrating strings, I burst into tears of simultaneous pride and grief. I love what we will do for one another in the name of inclusion and kindness. So I long to feel comforted and thrilled by the sight of Old Glory, as so many others seem to feel when our country plunges into war or dire straits. Symbols are many things to many people. In those raw months following the September 11 attacks, I saw my flag waved over used car and truck lots, designer-label clothing sales, and the funerals of genuine heroes. In my lifetime I have seen it waved over the sound of saber-rattling too many times for my comfort. When I heard about this kindergarten red-white-and-blue plan, my first impulse was to dread that my sweet child was being dragged to the newly patriotic cause of wreaking death in the wake of death. Nevertheless, any symbol conceived in liberty deserves the benefit of the doubt. We sent her to school in its colors because it felt to my daughter like some small thing she could do to help the people who were hurting. And because my wise husband put a hand on my arm and said, "You can't let hateful people steal the flag from us."

He didn't mean foreign terrorists, he meant certain Americans. Like the man in a city near us who went on a rampage, crying "I'm an American" as he shot at foreign-born neighbors, killing a gentle Sikh man in a turban and terrifying every brown-skinned person I know. Or the talk-radio hosts who viciously bullied members of Congress and anyone else for showing sensible skepticism during the mad rush toward war. After Representative Barbara Lee cast the House's only vote against handing over virtually unlimited war powers to a man whom fully half of us—let's be honest—didn't support a year before, so many red-blooded Americans threatened to kill her that she had to be assigned additional bodyguards.

While the anthrax threats in congressional and media offices were minute-by-minute breaking news, the letters of pseudo-patriotism carrying equally deadly threats to many other citizens did not get coverage. Hate radio reaches thousands of avid listeners, and fear stalked many families in the autumn and winter of our nation's discontent, when belonging to *any* minority—including the one arguing for peaceful and diplomatic solutions to violence—was enough to put one at risk. When fear rules the day, many minds are weak enough to crack the world into nothing but "me" and "evildoers," and as long as we're proudly killing unlike minds over there, they feel emboldened to do the same over here. For minds like that, the great attraction to patriotism is, as Aldous Huxley wrote, that "it fulfills our worst wishes. In the person of our nation we are able, vicariously, to bully and cheat. Bully and cheat, what's more, with a feeling that we are profoundly virtuous."

Such cowards have surely never arrived at a majority in this country, though their power has taken the helm in such dark moments as the McCarthy persecutions and the Japanese American internments. At such times, patriotism falls to whoever claims it loudest, and the rest of us are left struggling to find a definition in a clamor of reaction. In the days and months following September 11, some bully-patriots claiming to own my flag promoted a brand of nationalism that threatened freedom of speech and religion with death, as witnessed by the Sikhs and Muslims in my own community, and U.S. Representative Barbara Lee in hers. (Several of her colleagues confessed they wanted to vote the same way she did, but were frightened by the obvious threat from vigilante patriots.) Such men were infuriated by thoughtful hesitation, constructive criticism of our leaders, and pleas for peace. They ridiculed and despised people of foreign birth (one of our congressmen actually used the hideous term "rag heads") who've spent years becoming part of our culture and contributing their labor and talents to our economy. In one stunning statement uttered by a fundamentalist religious leader, this brand of patriotism specifically blamed homosexuals, feminists, and the American Civil Liberties Union for the horrors of September 11. In other words, these hoodlum-Americans were asking me to believe that their flag stood for intimidation, censorship, violence, bigotry, sexism, homophobia, and shoving the Constitution through a paper shredder? Well, *our* flag does not, and I'm determined that it never will. Outsiders can destroy airplanes and buildings, but only we the people have the power to demolish our own ideals.

It's a fact of our culture that the loudest mouths get the most airplay, 10
and the loudmouths are saying that in times of crisis it's treasonous to question our leaders. Nonsense. That kind of thinking allowed the seeds of a dangerous racism to grow into fascism during the international economic crisis of the 1930s. It is precisely in critical times that our leaders need *most* to be influenced by the moderating force of dissent. That is the basis of democracy, especially when national choices are difficult and carry grave consequences. The flag was never meant to be a stand-in for information and good judgment.

In the wake of the September 11 attacks, an amazing windfall befell our local flag-and-map store, which had heretofore been one of the sleepiest little independent businesses in the city. Suddenly it was swamped with unprecedented hordes of customers who came in to buy not maps, of course, but flags. After the stock quickly sold out, a cashier reported that customers came near to rioting as they stomped around empty-handed and the waiting list swelled to six hundred names. She said a few customers demanded to know why she personally wasn't in the back room sewing more Old Glories. Had I been in her position, I might have said, "Hey, friends and countrymen, wouldn't this be a great time to buy yourselves a map?" The sturdiest form of national pride is educated about the alternatives. And in fairness to my more polite compatriots, I was greatly heartened in that same season to see the country's best-seller lists suddenly swollen with books about Islam and relevant political history.

We're a much nobler country than our narrowest minds and loudest mouths suggest. I believe it is *my* patriotic duty to recapture my flag from the men who wave it in the name of jingoism and censorship. This is difficult, for many reasons. To begin with, when we civil libertarians on the one hand insist that every voice in the political spectrum must be heard, and the hard right on the other hand insists that our side should stuff a sock in it, the deck is stacked. And the next challenge is, I can never hope to match their nationalistic rightcousness. The last time I looked at a flag with an unambiguous thrill, I was thirteen. Right after that, Vietnam began teaching me lessons in ambiguity, and the lessons have kept coming. I've learned of things my government has done to the world that make me shudder: Covert assassinations of democratically elected leaders in Chile and the Congo; support of brutal dictators in dozens of nations because they smiled on our economic interests; training of torturers in a military camp in Georgia; secret support even of the rising Taliban in Afghanistan, until that business partnership came to a nasty end. In history books and numbers of our *Congressional Record* I've discovered many secrets that made me ashamed of how my country's proud ideology sometimes places last, after money for the win and power for the show. And yet, when I've dared to speak up about these skeletons in our closet, I've been further alienated from my flag by people who waved it at me, declaring I should love it or leave it. I always wonder, What makes them think that's their flag and not mine? Why are *they* the good Americans, and not me? I have never shrunk from sacrifice but have always faced it head on when I needed to, in order to defend the American ideals of freedom and human kindness.

I've been told the pacifists should get down on their knees and thank the men who gave their lives for our freedom, and I've thought about this, a lot. I believe absolutely that the American Revolution and the Civil War were ideological confrontations; if I had been born to a different time and gender with my present character otherwise intact, I might well have joined them, at least as a medic, or something. (Where I grew up, I'd likely have been conscripted into dying for the wrong side in the Civil War, but that's another story.) I wish I could claim to possess a nature I could honestly call pacifist, but I've had long friendships with genuine pacifists in the Quaker community and have seen in them a quality I lack. I can rarely summon the strength to pray for my enemies, as some do every day. On the rare occasions when my life has been put directly at risk by another, I've clawed like a lioness. My gut, if not my head, is a devotee of self-defense.

But my head is unconvinced by the sleight of hand and sloganeering that put the label "self-defense" on certain campaigns waged far from my bedroom window, against people who have no wish to come anywhere near it. It's extremely important to note that in my lifetime our multitude of wars in Central America and the Middle East have been not so much about the freedom of humans as about the freedom of financial markets. My spiritual faith does not allow me to accept equivalence of these two values; I wonder that anyone's does.

Our entry into wars most resembling self-defense, World War II and the 2001 Afghanistan campaign, both followed direct attacks on our country. The latter, at least, remains a far more convoluted entanglement than the headlines ever suggested. In the 1990s, most of us have now learned, the United States tacitly supported the viciously sexist, violent Taliban warlords—only to then bomb them out of power in 2001. I'm profoundly relieved to see any such violent men removed from command, of course. But I'm deeply uncomfortable, also, with the notion that two wrongs add up to one right, and I'm worried about the next turn of that logic. It is only prudent to ask questions, and only reasonable to discuss alternate, less violent ways to promote the general welfare. Americans who read and think have frequently seen how the much-touted "national interest" can differ drastically from their own.

And Americans who read and think are patriots of the first order—the kind who know enough to roll their eyes whenever anyone tries to claim sole custody of the flag and wield it as a blunt instrument. There are as many ways to love America as there are Americans, and our country needs us all. The rights and liberties described in our Constitution are guaranteed not just to those citizens who have the most money and power, but also to those who have the least, and yet it has taken hard struggle through every year of our history to hold our nation to that promise. Dissidents innocent of any crime greater than a belief in fair treatment of our poorest and ill-treated citizens have died right here on American soil for our freedom, as tragically as any soldier in any war: Karen Silkwood, Medgar Evars, Malcolm X, Denise McNair, Cynthia Wesley, Carole Robertson, Addie Mae Collins, Martin Luther King Jr., Albert Parsons, August Spies, Adolph Fisher, George Engel, Joe Hill, Nicola Sacco, Bartolomeo Vanzetti—the list of names stretches on endlessly and makes me tremble with gratitude. Any of us who steps up to the platform of American protest is standing on bloodstained and hallowed ground, and let no one ever dare call it un-American or uncourageous. While we peace lovers are down on our knees with gratitude, as requested, the warriors might do well to get down here with us and give thanks for Dr. King and Gandhi and a thousand other peacemakers who gave their lives to help lift humanity out of the trough of bare-toothed carnage. Where in the Bill of Rights is it written that the entitlement to bear arms—and use them—trumps any aspiration to peaceful solutions? I search my soul and find I cannot rejoice over killing, but that does not make me any less a citizen. When I look at the flag, why must I see it backlit with the rockets' red glare?

The first time I thought of it that way, I stumbled on a huge revelation. *This* is why the war supporters so easily gain the upper hand in the patriot game: Our nation was established with a fight for independence, so our iconography grew out of war. Anyone who is tempted to dismiss art as useless in matters of politics must agree that art is supremely powerful here, in connecting patriotism with war. Our national anthem celebrates it; our nationalist imagery memorializes it; our most familiar poetry of patriotism is inseparable from a battle cry. Our every military campaign is still launched with phrases about men dying for the freedoms we hold dear, even when this is impossible to square with reality. During the Gulf War [1990–91] I heard plenty of words about freedom's defense as our military rushed to the aid of Kuwait, a monarchy in which women enjoyed approximately the same rights as a nineteenth-century American slave. The values we fought for there are best understood by oil companies and the royalty of Saudi Arabia—the ones who asked us to do this work on the Iraq-Kuwaiti border, and with whom we remain friendly. (Not incidentally, we have never confronted the Saudis about women-hating Wahhabism and vast, unending support for schools of anti-American wrath.) After a swift and celebrated U.S. victory, a nation of Iraqi civilians was left with its hospitals, its water-delivery lines, and its food-production systems devastated, its capacity for reconstruction crushed by our ongoing economic sanctions, and its fate—at the time of this writing—still in the hands of one of the vilest dictators I've ever read about. There's the reality of war for you: Freedom often *loses.*

Stating these realities is not so poetic, granted, but it is absolutely a form of patriotism. Questioning our government's actions does not violate the principles of liberty, equality, and freedom of speech; it exercises them, and by exercise we grow stronger. I have read enough of Thomas Jefferson to feel sure he would back me up on this. Our founding fathers, those vocal critics of imperialism, were among the world's first leaders to understand that to a democratic people, freedom of speech and belief are not just nice luxuries, they're as necessary as breathing. The authors of our Constitution knew, from experience with King George and company, that governments don't remain benevolent to the interests of all, including their less powerful members, without constant vigilance and reasoned criticism. And so the founding fathers guaranteed the right of reasoned criticism in our citizenship contract—for *always.* No emergency shutdowns allowed. However desperate things may get, there are to be no historical moments when beliefs can be abridged, vegetarians required to praise meat, Christians forced to pray as Muslims, or vice versa. Angry critics have said to me in stressful periods, "Don't you understand it's *wartime?*" As if this were just such a historical moment of emergency shutdown. Yes, we all know it's wartime. It's easy to speak up for peace in peacetime—anybody can do that. Now is when it gets hard. But our flag is not just a logo for wars; it's the flag of American pacifists, too. It's the flag of all of us who love our country enough to do the hard work of living up to its highest ideals.

I have two American flags. Both were gifts. One was handmade out of colored paper by my younger child; it's a few stars shy of regulation but nonetheless cherished. Each has its place in my home, so I can look up from time to time and remember. That's *mine.* Maybe this is hard for some men to understand, but that emblem wasn't handed to me by soldiers on foreign soil; it wasn't *handed* to me by men at all—they withheld it from women for our nation's first century and a half. I would never have gained it if everyone's idea of patriotism had been simply to go along with the status quo. That flag protects and represents me only because of Ida B. Wells, Lucy Stone, Susan B. Anthony, and countless other women who risked everything so I could be a full citizen. Each of us who is female, or nonwhite, or without land, would have been guaranteed in 1776 the same voting rights as a horse. We owe a precious debt to courageous Americans before us who risked threats and public ridicule for an unpopular cause: ours. Now that flag is mine to carry on, promising me that I may, and that I must, continue believing in the dignity and sanctity of life, and stating that position in a public forum.

And so I would like to stand up for my flag and wave it over a few 20
things I believe in, including but not limited to the protection of dissenting points of view. After 225 years, I vote to retire the rockets' red glare and the bloody bandage as obsolete symbols of Old Glory. We desperately need a new iconography of patriotism. I propose that we rip strips of cloth from the uniforms of the unbelievably courageous firefighters who rescued the injured and panic-stricken from the World Trade Center on September 11, 2001, and remained at their posts until the buildings collapsed on them. Praise the red glare of candles held up in vigils everywhere as peace-loving people pray for the bereaved and plead for compassionate resolutions. Honor the blood donated to the Red Cross; respect the stars of all kinds who have used their influence to raise funds for humanitarian assistance; glory in the generous hands of schoolchildren collecting pennies, teddy bears, and anything else they think might help the kids who've lost their moms and dads. Let me sing praise to the ballot box and the jury box, and to the unyielding protest marches of my foremothers who fought for those rights so I could be fully human under our Constitution. What could be a more honorable symbol of American freedom than the suffragist's banner, the striker's picket, the abolitionist's drinking gourd, the placards of humane protest from every decade of our forward-marching history? Let me propose aloud that the dove is at least as honorable a creature as the carnivorous eagle. And give me liberty, now, with signs of life.

Shortly after the September attacks, my town became famous for a simple gesture in which some eight thousand people wearing red, white, or blue T-shirts assembled themselves in the shape of a flag on a baseball field and had their photograph taken from above. That picture soon began to turn up everywhere, but we saw it first on our newspaper's front page. Our family stood in silence for a minute looking at that stunningly beautiful photograph of a human flag, trying to know what to make of it. Then my teenager, who has a quick mind for numbers and a sensitive heart, did an interesting thing.

She laid her hand over part of the picture, leaving visible more or less five thousand people, and said, "In New York, that many might be dead." We stared at what that looked like—that many innocent souls, particolored and packed into a conjoined destiny—and shuddered at the one simple truth behind all the noise, which was that so many beloved, fragile lives were suddenly gone from us. That is my flag, and that's what it means: We're all just people, together.

QUESTIONING THE TEXT

1. Briefly summarize Kingsolver's argument. What is her main claim? How does she support that claim?
2. In personal anecdotes, Kingsolver provides glimpses into her life, describing scenes with her family and neighbors. She also alludes to a wide range of historical and political personages and events. With a classmate, examine some of these people and narratives, and discuss the rhetorical purposes you think they may serve in this essay. Which of the allusions and illustrations do you find most compelling, and why? Do you think the diverse range of characters and events that populate Kingsolver's essay help make it more persuasive? Why, or why not?
3. Kingsolver presents a list of people she describes as "[d]issidents innocent of any crime greater than a belief in fair treatment of our poorest and ill-treated citizens"—dissidents who "have died right here on American soil for our freedom" (paragraph 16). How many of the people on this list have you heard of? Divide up the list among classmates, and do some research on these individuals—where and when they lived, the causes they championed, how they died. Present your findings in class, and discuss why Kingsolver believes these people are worthy of admiration for their struggles. Do you agree with Kingsolver's judgment about them? Why, or why not?

MAKING CONNECTIONS

4. With a classmate, compare Kingsolver's essay to Frederick Douglass's speech, "What to the Slave Is the Fourth of July?" (p. 522). Both writers argue for their right to be included in national practices of patriotism. How do their arguments differ, and how are they similar? Share your observations in a discussion with the whole class.
5. Kingsolver criticizes the way the American flag has been deployed as a symbol of particularly militant or violent patriotism, but she expresses optimism that the flag can be rehabilitated to represent more peaceful

patriotic impulses as well. How does her criticism of this symbol differ from Neil Postman's criticism of the loss of meaning in national symbols and narratives, in "The Great Symbol Drain" (p. 545)? Do you think Postman would agree that symbols such as the U.S. flag could regain meaning? Working with a classmate, write a dialogue in which you imagine Postman and Kingsolver debating the potential for patriotic symbols to represent and convey unifying messages for Americans today.

JOINING THE CONVERSATION

6. As Kingsolver uses a line from the national anthem for the title of her essay, choose a line from a patriotic text—perhaps the Declaration of Independence (p. 517) or Emma Lazarus's "The New Colossus" (p. 622)—and imagine it as a title for a brief essay that you might publish online or in a periodical. In your essay, try to convey anew the significance of the line you've chosen as your title, illuminating its meaning for you and your readers, here and now.
7. As A.L. suggests in her headnote, consider your own definitions of *patriotism* and the associations the American flag holds for you. How do they compare to those described in "And Our Flag Was Still There"? Freewrite on this topic, and be prepared to share your thoughts in class discussion.

KATE SHINDLE
Miss America: More Than a Beauty Queen?

"THERE SHE IS . . . MISS AMERICA." That pageant theme song, crooned in 1955 (and long after) by host Bert Parks, calls up an American cultural myth of long standing. The Miss America Pageant, which grew out of a series of bathing beauty contests in Atlantic City, has been going strong, more or less, since 1921 when Margaret Gorman, crowned "the most beautiful bathing girl in America," soon became known as, simply, "Miss America."

From the beginning, Miss America seems to have been meant to represent the ideal of American womanhood. Indeed, the New York Times *remarked that Gorman was "the type of womanhood America needs; strong, red-blooded, able to shoulder the responsibilities of homemaking and motherhood. It is in her type that the hope of the country resides." Such a woman contrasted in many ways with the delicate Victorian ideal and fit better with the decade following the enfranchisement of women in the United States. But even as the pageant strove to represent its winners as those dedicated to the well-being of others and to good works, it was also often connected with good looks and more earthly pleasures.*

So will the real *Miss America please stand up? For Kate Shindle, 1998's Miss America, the scandals associated with the pageant are extremely frustrating because they detract attention from what Miss America should (and, at her best, does) stand for: supporting young women in their own educational and leadership pursuits. As an AIDS activist, Shindle raised millions for the cause during her year as Miss America and spent much of her time speaking out about AIDS and about HIV prevention.*

Since graduating from Northwestern, Shindle (b. 1977) has appeared in the Broadway production of Jekyll & Hyde *and the touring production of* Cabaret. *In 2002, she released a solo album,* Till Today, *part of the earnings of which she donates to the Elizabeth Glaser Pediatric AIDS Foundation.*

In the brief essay that follows, which originally appeared in Newsweek's *"My Turn" column (October 14, 2002), Shindle challenges the Miss America Organization to live up to its own ideals. In doing so, she asks us to rethink our myths of ideal American womanhood.*

—A.L.

For those of us who have walked down that Atlantic City runway with more than 700 rhinestones teetering on our heads, this time of year always evokes a little nostalgia. But for me, watching the new Miss America get crowned also brought feelings of frustration. Not only because the past 12 months have been a public-relations nightmare—two Miss North Carolinas?—but because organizers have spent so much time reacting to scandal that they've failed to take control of the Miss America image. It often seems that they can't even agree on what she stands for.

Figure 7.2 Margaret Gorman, the first Miss America, c. 1922. Source: Bettman/CORBIS

That's unfortunate, because Miss America contestants and the Miss America Organization have much to be proud of. The pageant is the nation's largest provider of women's scholarships, and encourages thousands of young women to take leadership roles in their communities. Each year, one individual is selected to travel 20,000 miles each month to advocate her chosen social cause.

As Miss America in 1998, I helped raise an estimated $20 million to $30 million for HIV/AIDS organizations worldwide, lobbied legislators for more funding and better health-education programs for those who were infected, and served as a moderator at the 12th World AIDS Conference in Geneva. The wholesome image that came with the job made it possible for me to talk about controversial issues—like condom availability and needle exchange—that would have been off-limits. It also allowed me to speak to thousands of

Figure 7.3 Kate Shindle, Miss America 1998

students across the country in schools that had never before opened their doors to an AIDS activist.

I thought my work on the front lines of a life-and-death issue made it clear that there is more to the Miss America program than swimsuits and evening gowns. I quickly realized that that wasn't the case. Though I was a dean's list student at Northwestern, suddenly people assumed I didn't have a brain. Administrators at one highly ranked university canceled an appearance, claiming that Miss America couldn't possibly have anything in common with their students. Another time, a representative of the group I had flown in to speak to picked me up at the airport, grabbed the heaviest of my three suitcases and said, "Is this the one that holds all the makeup?" I didn't bother to explain that it held my files on AIDS research.

Granted, the belief that beauty and brains are incompatible is an old 5
one, but organizers should do more throughout the year to counter the public's perception of Miss America as someone who does little more than turn up at boat shows. Last week the new Miss America, soon-to-be Harvard law student Erika Harold, took part in the World Health Organization's launch in Brussels of its world report on violence and health. This is a typical moment for Miss America, and about as far from a boat show as you can get.

Organizers also need to take a hard look at the program they broadcast each fall. In an era defined by cynicism, cultural institutions like Miss America practically beg to be mocked. I say, let everybody laugh. The show can't be all things to all people. Pageant officials should stop trying to make the competition culturally relevant with "Survivor"-like references about who's going to be "eliminated," and instead forge a clear identity and embrace it with no apologies. The contestants who go to Atlantic City each year are intelligent, capable women who have something to say. If organizers cut out the minefields—the trivia contests, the backstage dish sessions that threaten to make the contestants look bad—they'd have more time to say it. That would mean including more footage from the "personal interview" portion of the show, when contestants talk about their political views and platform issues.

I realize that none of these improvements will matter if nobody watches, and viewers aren't going to tune in just to hear contestants' political perspectives. Fair enough. But organizers should have enough respect for the contestants and the public to be honest about the competition. We're told it's about scholarship. We're told it's about leadership. If it's also about looks, then organizers should admit it, instead of capitalizing on the swimsuit competition while swearing that it is an insignificant part of the show.

Despite these problems, I am proud to have represented this program and humbled by the opportunities it has provided for me and for thousands of women since 1921. I will be even prouder when the Miss America Organization defines its mission and lives up to its potential.

QUESTIONING THE TEXT

1. What does Shindle see as the main problem(s) with the Miss America pageant? Who is at fault for the program's problems, according to this essay? Do you find Shindle's argument persuasive? Why, or why not? Support your answer with examples from the text.
2. What preconceptions did you have about Miss America before reading this essay? Does Shindle's description of her experience alter your perceptions of the Miss America role or the pageant's function? If so, how? If not, why?
3. In the headnote to this essay, A.L. suggests that in challenging the Miss America Organization to live up to its own ideals, Shindle is asking us to reconsider our myths of ideal American womanhood. Working with a classmate, see if you can find evidence in the essay of this broader purpose. Discuss whether or to what extent you agree with A.L.'s reading.

MAKING CONNECTIONS

4. With two or three classmates, find examples supporting Shindle's claim that "Miss America contestants and the Miss America Organization have

much to be proud of" (paragraph 2). What American ideals do you think these examples represent? As you read through some of the other selections in this chapter that address American ideals, which pieces do you think come closest to sharing Shindle's vision? (You might compare the values Shindle espouses to those expressed by Thomas Jefferson in the Declaration of Independence [p. 517], Frederick Douglass in "What to the Slave Is the Fourth of July?" [p. 522], or Emma Lazarus in "The New Colossus" [p. 622], for example.) Support your answer with examples from the texts.

5. Shindle and Edward Abbey, in his excerpt from *Desert Solitaire* (p. 619), both express frustration with others' failure to make the most of a valuable resource. For class discussion, be prepared to discuss how, and to what effect, each of these writers deals with this type of frustration. How do the sources of their frustration differ, and how do these differences affect your response to the texts? Are you more sympathetic to one cause than the other? If so, why? Which piece of writing do you find most compelling, and why?

JOINING THE CONVERSATION

6. Do some research into the Miss America Pageant, and write an essay that explores the pageant's relationship to myths of American womanhood. As the pageant has changed, have myths of womanhood changed as well? Has the pageant kept up with and reflected American ideals, as they are reflected in other cultural narratives? Has the pageant been at the forefront of change, providing new narratives of womanhood?
7. Why is there no Mr. America pageant quite analogous to the Miss America pageant? (There is a Mr. America body-building contest.) Discuss this question with a few classmates, and then write an essay responding to the question in a tone and style that you choose, for readers who might be interested in the insights you can offer on this topic. You might choose to address this question in a serious manner, perhaps using historical research, or you might choose a witty or sarcastic approach, for example.
8. Working with a small group of classmates, study Shindle's essay and others that have appeared in *Newsweek*'s "My Turn" feature. Analyze the genre of these essays: What topics are featured in the essays? Who are the writers, and what is their source of authority on the topics they address? How do they establish the relevance of their topics to the magazine's audience? What kinds of arguments are presented in the essays? What kind of evidence do the writers use to support their claims? Do

you have an experience that you might write about in a "My Turn" essay? Work with your group members to brainstorm the possibilities and draft outlines of your potential essays. Pursue your ideas in or out of class, sharing drafts with each other as you revise the essays for submission to the magazine.

EDWARD ABBEY
Desert Solitaire

I DON'T HAVE MUCH IN COMMON *with Edward Abbey (1927–89) politically, but I love the short passage reprinted here from* Desert Solitaire: A Season in the Wilderness *(1968), his autobiographical account of life as a ranger in the American southwest. I can still recall the first time I read it, the words resounding like an anthem in my mind. As you'll see, Abbey believes that we are losing our sense of wilderness—that essential component of the American experience—not only because we are destroying it but because we don't know how to experience it any more. And he doesn't mince words when describing both the problem and the solution.*

The frontier has long been part of American mythology, that hopeful sense of a horizon where we can find happiness and freedom. The quest has taken Americans first across the Appalachians (and, lest we forget, the Rio Grande) and later all the way to the moon. But much of the romance of the continent has been lost, and not exactly because we've run out of space. The sweeping vistas west of the Mississippi, for example, remain amazing and liberating, protected from abuse and overpopulation by their sheer ruggedness and sobering lack of water. Still, Abbey realized more than a generation ago what remains true today, that too many of us have willingly traded the grandeur and dangers of myths for the facsimiles offered by a theme-park culture.

I've made several trips to the national monument that is the subject of Abbey's manifesto—Arches National Park just outside Moab, Utah. It is still much the way he described it in the 1960s, a splendid track of desert where many of the remarkable stone formations can be viewed comfortably from a car. (Delicate Arch is one famous exception, requiring a notable hike.) The roads are still thick with sedans and trucks and clusters of harried tourists, many complaining about how difficult it is to find parking.

Nevertheless, the place has its secrets too. If you are willing to endure about ten miles of dirt road and then walk another two miles or so (round trip) of desert, you can have magnificent Tower Arch all to yourself, maybe eat lunch beneath it, enjoy the yucca and asters, and recall what this splendid continent is all about. Warning: you may get some red Utahn dust on your shoes. —J.R.

Ranger, where is Arches National Monument?
I don't know, mister. But I can tell you where it was.

Labor Day. Flux and influx, the final visitation of the season, they come in herds, like buffalo, down from The City. A veil of dust floats above the sneaky snaky old road from here to the highway, drifting gently downwind to settle upon the blades of the yucca, the mustard-yellow rabbitbrush, the petals of the asters and autumn sunflowers, the umbrella-shaped clumps of blooming wild buckwheat.

What can I tell them? Sealed in their metallic shells like molluscs on wheels, how can I pry the people free? The auto as tin can, the park ranger as opener. Look here, I want to say, for godsake folks get out of them there machines, take off those fucking sunglasses and unpeel both eyeballs, look around; throw away those goddamned idiotic cameras! For chrissake folks what is this life if full of care we have no time to stand and stare? eh? Take off your shoes for a while, unzip your fly, piss hearty, dig your toes in the hot sand, feel that raw and rugged earth, split a couple of big toenails, draw blood! Why not? Jesus Christ, lady, roll that window down! You can't see the desert if you can't smell it. Dusty? Of course it's dusty—this is Utah! But it's good dust, good red Utahn dust, rich in iron, rich in irony. Turn that motor off. Get out of that piece of iron and stretch your varicose veins, take off your brassiere and get some hot sun on your old wrinkled dugs! You sir, squinting at the map with your radiator boiling over and your fuel pump vapor-locked, crawl out of that shiny hunk of GM junk and take a walk—yes, leave the old lady and those squawling brats behind for a while, turn your back on them and take a long quiet walk straight into the canyons, get lost for a while, come back when you damn well feel like it, it'll do you and her and them a world of good. Give the kids a break too, let them out of the car, let them go scrambling over the rocks hunting for rattlesnakes and scorpions and anthills—yes sir, let them out, turn them loose; how dare you imprison little children in your goddamned upholstered horseless hearse? Yes sir, yes madam, I entreat you, get out of those motorized wheelchairs, get off your foam rubber backsides, stand up straight like men! like women! like human beings! and walk—walk—WALK upon our sweet and blessed land!

QUESTIONING THE TEXT

1. What is the main message Abbey, the park ranger, conveys in this excerpt? Try to restate the message in two ways—once dispassionately, and once capturing some of the emotion that Abbey displays toward his subject and his imaginary audience of park visitors. With classmates, discuss how Abbey's use of emotion influences the message. Does it merely intensify the message, or does it change the message in other ways?
2. Working with a classmate, study the metaphors and imagery Abbey uses in this excerpt. How do they affect your response to the text? Do you find some of the metaphors and images humorous? Do they cause you to empathize with the ranger or with the park visitors? Explain.
3. In class, discuss the effects of Abbey's diction. For example, consider whether or not his use of profanity is effective. What purpose does colloquial language, such as "them there machines," seem to serve?

MAKING CONNECTIONS

4. What attitudes or actions seem to be causing the ranger's frustration in this excerpt? As you read other selections in this chapter, what American myths do you find that might be connected to the attitudes that frustrate Abbey? Write an essay in which you explore the connections among an American myth, the misconceptions that myth encourages, and the frustrations that can arise from those misconceptions.
5. Read Abelardo Delgado's "Stupid America" (p. 625), and consider how he and Abbey use anger in these two pieces of writing. Do you find the expression of anger more effective in one piece than in the other? Do you find the use of anger effective at all? Why, or why not? Try using this technique in a short piece of creative writing.

JOINING THE CONVERSATION

6. Have you had an experience like that of the park ranger in this excerpt—one in which you became exasperated at the way others responded to something? Try freewriting about what you felt like saying to those people at the time, but couldn't. Consider revising your freewriting into a short essay or poem to read aloud in class.
7. With two or three classmates, do some research into the design and maintenance of public parks. What different approaches have people taken to address the dual challenges of preserving public lands while creating natural spaces for public enjoyment? Which approaches seem best to you, and why? Write an argument that presents and justifies the practices your group supports.

EMMA LAZARUS
The New Colossus

*W*HEN THE PEOPLE OF FRANCE *sent the Statue of Liberty to the United States as a gift of international friendship (the statue was presented, in France, on July 4, 1884, and was officially dedicated in 1886), it came without a pedestal to rest on. When essayist and poet Emma Lazarus (1849–87) heard of the art auction planned to raise funds for such a pedestal, she contributed a poem, "The New Colossus," (1883) which was later engraved on a plaque and attached to the pedestal. Most famous of the poem's lines are "Give me your tired, your poor, / Your huddled masses yearning to breathe free," to whom the statue "lift[s] my lamp beside the golden door" of America. These lines, and the statue to which they are attached, represent the myth of American freedom, democracy, and access.*

Yet the poem reveals tensions within this myth, beginning with the title, which calls for a new *colossus, one that would be unlike "the brazen giant of Greek fame." This new colossus, though, is also "mighty" and full of flame; she is one who is totally in command. So the new colossus perhaps has more in common with those gigantic ancient statues than might appear at first glance. Certainly the famed Statue of Liberty itself alludes to a number of other colossal figures. In particular, it is an echo of the Colossus of Rhodes, which stood over two thousand years ago at the entrance to the harbor on the island of Rhodes, located where the Mediterranean Sea meets the Aegean.*

As a counterpoint to this distinctly male figure, Lazarus evokes a woman, the "Mother of Exiles" who speaks, however, only through "silent lips." (See the Statue of Liberty Time *cover in the color photo essay.) What else might you say about these two images—the Colossus of Rhodes and the Statue of Liberty?* —A.L.

Not like the brazen giant of Greek fame,
With conquering limbs astride from land to land;
Here at our sea-washed, sunset gates shall stand
A mighty woman with a torch, whose flame
Is the imprisoned lightning, and her name
Mother of Exiles. From her beacon-hand
Glows world-wide welcome; her mild eyes command
The air-bridged harbor that twin cities frame.
"Keep, ancient lands, your storied pomp!" cries she
With silent lips. "Give me your tired, your poor,
Your huddled masses yearning to breathe free,
The wretched refuse of your teeming shore.
Send these, the homeless, tempest-tost to me,
I lift my lamp beside the golden door!"

Figure 7.4 The Colossus of Rhodes. The engraving is by Fischer Von Erlach (ca. 1721).

QUESTIONING THE TEXT

1. Reread A.L.'s headnote to this poem, and note the tensions she finds in the poem. List other tensions that you find in the poem, and note some thoughts on them in preparation for class discussion. Do you think they add to the poem's meaning? If so, how? Do you think they can, or should be, reconciled? Why, or why not? Which tensions do you think might have struck readers in Lazarus's day? Which ones do you think arise from current notions that may be at odds with those Lazarus is trying to present? Share your thoughts in discussion with classmates.
2. The headnote provides some context for this poem, noting that Lazarus contributed the poem to an art auction to help raise funds for a pedestal for the Statue of Liberty. Do further research into the history of the poem and its poet. What works made Lazarus famous enough to contribute her written art to this auction? How does "The New Colossus" compare to her other writings? Do you find it of similar quality? What did critics think at the time? Was it as highly acclaimed? Use your research as the basis of an essay illuminating the origin of this famous poem, or present a report to your classmates on what you discover.

MAKING CONNECTIONS

3. How might Ward Churchill (p. 536) or Abelardo Delgado (p. 625) respond to Lazarus's poem? Imagine you are one of these authors, and

write a letter to Lazarus critiquing or praising her poem and the images of America it presents.

JOINING THE CONVERSATION

4. What do you think Lazarus means by "the homeless, tempest-tost" in line 13? Did you initially think of a different—and probably today a more common—meaning of "the homeless" (in other words, people who live on the streets in this country)? In what other ways does the language of Lazarus's poem evoke images today that she might not have intended? Explore one or more of these images in an entry in your reading journal. Perhaps you could also use these thoughts in an essay on new layers of meaning that are now evoked by "The New Colossus" or the Statue of Liberty, the "Mother of Exiles."

ABELARDO DELGADO
Stupid America

In the brief poem that follows, Abelardo Delgado (b. 1931) challenges the stereotypes some people hold of Chicano/Chicanas, who are too often depicted in U.S. cultural mythos as threatening, unintelligent, or in some way unsavory. Such representations are not only stupid but ultimately destructive: unexamined preconceptions about others can, and often do, backfire on those who hold them. In addition, they blind those who hold such negative assumptions to potential beauty and creativity.

Born in Chihuahua, Mexico, Delgado—who now lives in Texas—is known as a leader of the Chicano/a movement of the 1970s. Author of Chicano: 25 Pieces of a Chicano Mind *(1969),* Bajo el Sol de Aztlán: Veinticinco Soles de Abelardo (Under the Sun of Aztlán: Twenty-Five Suns of Abelardo) *(1973), and* Letters to Louise *(1982), in which the following poem appears, Delgado has received the United Nations Colorado Human Rights Award for his work with migrant children (1995) and the El Sol Human Rights Award (1993).* —A.L.

Stupid American, see that chicano
with a big knife
in his steady hand
he doesn't want to knife you
he wants to sit on a bench
and carve christfigures
but you won't let him.
stupid america, hear that chicano
shouting curses on the street
he is a poet
without paper and pencil
and since he cannot write
he will explode.
stupid america, remember that chicanito
flunking math and english
he is the picasso
of your western states
but he will die
with one thousand masterpieces
hanging only from his mind.

IN RESPONSE

1. Whom does the speaker of this poem address? All Americans, or just some? If not all, then which ones? For class discussion, be prepared to support your answer with evidence from the text.
2. With classmates, discuss how the lack of capitalization and the omission of some punctuation affect your reading and interpretation of the poem. Do you think the poet's approaches to capitalization and punctuation are effective? Why, or why not?
3. Read one or two of the selections elsewhere in this book that present perspectives on ethnic and racial identities in the United States. You might, for example, choose Zora Neale Hurston's "How It Feels to Be Colored Me" (p. 414), Bich Minh Nguyen's "The Good Immigrant Student" (p. 441), Paula Gunn Allen's "Where I Come from Is Like This" (p. 458), or Michael Nava's "Gardenland, Sacramento, California" (p. 647). Write an essay in which you explore the ways Delgado's poem and these other pieces contribute to your understanding of what might be considered a common American experience or culture. Do you think a common American culture exists? If so, describe it in your essay, drawing from your readings. If not, explain why you find it impossible to locate such a common culture.
4. What might Delgado say in response to Emma Lazarus's poem, "The New Colossus" (p. 622)? Working with a classmate, compose a letter in which you present Delgado's response to Lazarus. You might read Margaret Atwood's "A Letter to America" (p. 565) for some ideas about how to compose such a hypothetical letter.
5. As A.L. notes, Delgado was a leader of the Chicano/a political movement of the 1970s. Do some research into the history of this movement, which informs the political context for Delgado's poetry. Write an 8- to 10-page essay that takes a few lines from Delgado's poetry as a point of departure, and explore an aspect of Chicano/a experience in the United States that Delgado and others strove to change. You might illuminate what life was like for a Chicano/a in a particular area of the United States in 1969, when this poem was written. Alternatively, you might try to capture some of the ways in which Chicano/a experience has changed since then.
6. Sometimes art serves activist purposes, as in the case of Delgado's poem. Think about how this poem might be read as an argument. Then find another, more recent example of politically motivated art to explore in a review essay. Analyze how your selected work of art argues for change, and critique its effectiveness. Consider submitting your review to a newspaper or magazine for publication.

OTHER READINGS

Berger, John. *Ways of Seeing*. New York: Viking, 1973. *A series of essays—some verbal, some purely pictorial—that explore multiple and contradictory ways of seeing images, often in terms of gender or sexuality. A classic text on this subject.*

Cunningham, Michael, Craig Marberry, and Maya Angelou. *Crowns: Portraits of Black Women in Church Hats*. New York: Doubleday, 2000. *An intriguing collection of photos that opens up a cultural tradition both endearing and significant.*

Faludi, Susan. "An American Myth Rides into the Sunset," *New York Times*, 30 Mar. 2003, Sec. 4:13. *The op-ed questions President's Bush's use of the cowboy image prior to the 2003 war with Iraq and briefly examines the role played by myths in American culture.*

Harwayne, Shelley, ed. *Messages to Ground Zero: Children Respond to September 11, 2001*. Portsmouth, NH: Heinemann, 2002. *The collection includes letters, poems, and pictures that offer the perspective of children—many of them from New York City—on core American themes and values in light of the terrorist bombings.*

Ravitch, Diane, ed. *The American Reader: Words That Moved a Nation*. 2nd ed. New York: Perennial, 2000. *An anthology of core documents relating to American history and culture.*

ELECTRONIC RESOURCES

http://www.time.com/time/magazine/archive/
A complete and searchable index of Time *magazine covers since 1923.*

http://memory.loc.gov/ammem/amhome.html
Homepage for "American Memory: Historical Collections for the National Digital Library." The site is maintained by the Library of Congress.

http://www.nmai.si.edu/index.asp
Homepage for the National Museum of the American Indian, opening on the Mall in Washington, D.C., in 2004.

Look carefully at the photograph on the preceding page of the “rock ’n’ roll family” of Ozzy and Sharon Osbourne featured on the reality television series, *The Osbournes*. What is the central focus of the photo? ■ What is in the background of the photo, and why? ■ What can you infer about the family from their body language, their expressions, and their dress? ■ What does the setting imply about this family? ■ How does this family portrait represent, or perhaps challenge, images of family life that are familiar to you? ■ What ideas about home does this picture evoke for you?

8

At Home: The Places I Come From

Well, college is supposed to be broadening, he muses, and there's no doubt he'll get broadened this year with a roommate like Cedric.

RON SUSKIND, *A Hope in the Unseen*

I remember early morning fogs in Georgia, not so dramatic as California ones, but magical too because out of the Southern fog of memory tramps my dark father, smiling and large, glowing with rootedness, and talking of hound dogs, biscuits and coons.

ALICE WALKER, *The Place Where I Was Born*

The best way to think of Gardenland is not as an American suburb at all, but rather as a Mexican village, transported perhaps from Guanajuato, where my grandmother's family originated, and set down lock, stock, and chicken coop in the middle of California.

MICHAEL NAVA, *Gardenland, Sacramento, California*

Most statistics tell us breast cancer is genetic, hereditary, with rising percentages attached to fatty diets, childlessness, or becoming pregnant after thirty. What they don't say is living in Utah may be the greatest hazard of all.

TERRY TEMPEST WILLIAMS, *The Clan of One-Breasted Women*

Just as no patient would have designed today's system of health care, so no child would have chosen today's culture of divorce.

BARBARA DAFOE WHITEHEAD, *The Making of a Divorce Culture*

In a 1990 *Newsweek* poll, 42 percent predicted that the family would be worse in ten years and exactly the same percentage predicted that it would be better.

STEPHANIE COONTZ, *The Way We Wish We Were*

The long-term-care facility . . . I work for is owned by a corporation that owns nursing homes throughout the country. Giving corporations like this control over the quality of medical care is handing over control to the fox.

JILL FRAWLEY, *Inside the Home*

Danger was everywhere and it was our father's lifelong duty to warn us.

DAVID SEDARIS, *Cyclops*

The garden is not a place to lose your cares; the garden is not a place of rest and repose. Even God did not find it so.

JAMAICA KINCAID, *Sowers and Reapers: The Unquiet World of a Flower Bed*

Grandpa's flowers are scattered
down the line of tombstones, decorating
the graves of his wife, his children

ED MADDEN, *Family Cemetery, near Hickory Ridge, Arkansas*

Introduction

CONSIDER FOR A MOMENT some well-known phrases that feature the word *home:* "home is where the heart is," for example, or "there's no place like home"; "home, sweet home"; "the home of the brave"; "you can't go home again." These phrases suggest that home is a place of comfort or solace, or at least "where the heart is." They capture what might be described as an American ideal of home: a place where you can be safe and secure and living among those who care unconditionally for you.

In one of the most famous opening passages in literature, however, Leo Tolstoy complicates such an ideal vision of home: "Happy families are all alike," he says, but "every unhappy family is unhappy in its own way" (*Anna Karenina*). Tolstoy's sentence suggests what most of us know already in our bones: homes can be sites not only of comfort and solace but of pain and bitter unhappiness as well. In addition, one person's happy home is another person's disaster; what may look like a peaceful, loving home from one perspective may look just the opposite from another.

As the selections in this chapter will illustrate, what is home to one person may well be a place that exists only in the imagination to another. And whatever your own individual experience has been, you have certainly had some experience with the concept of *home*. In fact, you have probably had multiple experiences with homes of various kinds, and some of these experiences may contradict or conflict with one another. This chapter may provide a timely opportunity, then, to consider the various places, people, or concepts you have known as home and to explore your own thinking about them.

Before you begin reading, you might want to consider these questions:

- What places could be categorized as home for you?
- What are some of the positive and/or negative qualities you associate with home?

- What kind of home would you most like to be part of? What problems might keep you from having the home and family you desire?
- How is home represented in the media? How is the word used in music and in the titles of films and TV and radio shows? You may want to brainstorm these questions with two or three classmates and bring your list to class for discussion.

• • •

RON SUSKIND

A Hope in the Unseen

*R*ON *S*USKIND'S A Hope in the Unseen: An American Odyssey from the Inner City to the Ivy League *(1998) tells the true story of Cedric Jennings, an African American youth from an inner-city school in Washington, D.C., who makes his way to an Ivy League college. His academic commitment and success mark him as an outsider at Frank W. Ballou Senior High, where he is taunted and ridiculed by classmates who don't understand his aspirations. While at Brown University, Cedric finds academic support, but he encounters prejudices of a different sort among much more privileged students to whom his race, poverty, and religious upbringing are a mystery.*

The differences between Cedric and his friends at Brown, particularly his roommate Rob, are not just metaphorical. To underscore the contrast between their worlds, I have juxtaposed two passages from A Hope in the Unseen *in the following selection: the first is from an early chapter describing Cedric at home in the Washington, D.C., apartment he shared with his mother, and the second is from a much later chapter introducing Cedric's college roommate. As you'll see, the two young men try to negotiate their differences, not entirely successfully, within a space familiar to many students across the country—a dormitory room.*

Suskind (b. 1959), a journalist currently writing for Esquire, *won a Pulitzer Prize in 1995 for two* Wall Street Journal *articles he wrote about Cedric Jennings's high school years.* A Hope in the Unseen *represents the continuation of that story, one that has inspired many readers. Describing the experience of writing about Cedric in a NEAToday online forum (November 11, 1998), Suskind observes that "[k]ids—all kids—are naturally hopeful and, like any living thing, they bend toward the light. A teacher who can see through the eyes of a student will find clues about where to shine that light." That sounds like good advice for everyone.*

Suskind is at present working on a book about a premodern people brought abruptly into the modern era. It is tentatively titled Island of the Resilient Heart. —J.R.

Apartment 307 on the third floor of the blond brick High View apartments at 1635 V Street, Southeast, is empty, dark, and warm at 6:04 P.M., when Cedric unlocks the door. There hasn't always been heat, with overdue bills and whatnot, and he always appreciates the warmth, especially after the long walk from the Anacostia bus and subway station in the icy dusk wind.

He slips out of his coat and backpack and goes from room to room turning on lights, something he's done since he was a small kid, coming home alone to apartments and tiptoeing, with a lump in his throat, to check if intruders were lurking inside closets and under beds.

It's not a very big place—two bedrooms, a small bathroom, a kitchenette, and an attached living and dining room—but it's one of the better apartments that he and his mother, Barbara, have lived in. He's even got his own bedroom in the far back corner.

He flips on the switch. It's like a bear's winter cave of strewn matter—a thick padding of clothes, magazines, rubber-soled shoes, books, loose papers, and more clothes.

Cedric turns on his beloved Sharp Trinitron, a 19-inch color TV that 5
his mother rented for him in ninth grade from a nearby Rent-a-Center (just paid off a month ago at an astonishing total price of nearly $1,500) and flops onto the bed. Like his proclivity for spying on street hustlers, the TV is a vital element of Cedric's secondhand life. He loves the tube, especially the racy, exhibitionist afternoon talk shows, which he watches for a few minutes tonight before turning to the local news—the lead story about a shooting not far from here—and then flipping to *The Flintstones,* a favorite.

He hears the thump of a door slamming.

"Lavar, you home?" comes the voice—calling him, as his mother always has, by his middle name—but he doesn't get up, figuring she'll wander back. In a moment, Barbara Jennings, hands on hips, is standing in the doorway.

In the sixteen and a half years since Cedric's birth, Barbara Jennings has been on a path of sacrifice and piety that has taken her far from the lighthearted haughtiness of her earlier self—the woman with a blonde wig, leather miniskirt, white knee-high boots, and a taste for malt liquor. Cedric has seen pictures of that skinny young thing, a striking girl with a quick smile who, as he has discerned from his mother's infrequent recollections, searched for love and found mostly trouble.

She stopped searching long ago. Barbara is a churchwoman now. On weekdays she works in a data input job at the Department of Agriculture, where she has been for almost eleven years, and splits the rest of her time between a church in a rough section of Washington north of the Capitol dome and this small, messy apartment.

Cedric looks her up and down and smiles thinly. Today, like most days, 10
she has opted for a black dress and sensible shoes, an outfit most appropriate to her general mood, needs, and heavier frame. But her features—her smallish nose and pretty, wide-set eyes—have held up well, even at forty-seven and without makeup.

"I thought you would have made dinner by now," she says, slipping a thin chain with her dangling Department of Agriculture photo ID from around her neck. "How long you been home?"

"Only a couple of minutes," Cedric says, turning back to the tube. "What we got to eat?"

"I don't know, whatever's in there," she says curtly before disappearing into her room to change out of her work clothes. Taking his cue, Cedric moves into the kitchen and begins breaking up ground beef into a frying pan. He pours in a can of navy beans, some oil, chopped onions, some pepper, salt, a little paprika, and other condiments. He does this without complaint or enthusiasm—it's what he does most nights—and soon there are two heaping plates of steaming hash.

"Hey, it's ready and all," he calls around a short breakwall behind the stove to Barbara, who's sitting in a bathrobe on the white living room couch watching TV.

Usually, he takes his plate to his room and she eats on the low, wide living room coffee table—each sitting in front of their own TV. Tonight, though, she clears away newspapers and unopened bills from the dining room table.

"I haven't talked to you in ages, it seems," she says softly as they sit down to eat.

"I've been around," he says, grateful for her attention. "Just been a lot going on—at school and whatever."

So it ends up being a night that they talk. It happens every couple of weeks. It's not needed more than that, Cedric figures. He knows that his mom wants to give him his space, now that he's sixteen and, by his reckoning, almost grown up, so she doesn't bother him in his room, where he spends most of his time. Maybe too much time, she tells him sometimes, but it's the only place he feels he has any privacy. After all, it's not as if he goes out late on weekend nights with friends, like most kids at school. Inside his room is the only place he can really relax.

He describes last week's assembly, about his not going, and she shakes her head dismissively. "What did I tell you? Before you know it, you'll be leaving them all behind. Just pay them no mind."

"Okay, okay," he says, "but what if I get rejected by MIT? That'd kill me." Barbara heeds this more carefully. It was she, after all, who found a description of the program in a scholarship book that someone gave to her at the office.

"You can't be worrying about MIT, Lavar. Just pray about it. If God has meant it to happen, it will." She looks up between bites and sees he's not convinced. "Look, your grades are perfect, your recommendations are good. What can they not like?"

"Yeah, I guess," he concedes.

"What's the point of getting down on yourself?" she says. "People will see that you're special."

He nods, letting her words sink in, and they eat for a while in silence—just the two of them, the way it has been for years. Barbara's two older girls, Cedric's half-sisters, are twenty-six and thirty-one and long gone, leaving mother and son to rely on each other in more ways than they can count.

Through years of ups and downs—times when he was certain that he was unworthy of success or love or any reasonable hope of getting something better—her faith in him has been his savior. It always amazes him. Having finished dinner quickly, he watches her clean her plate contentedly, and he shakes his head. She's just rock solid certain that he's going to MIT. Who knows, he wonders as he busses their plates and begins washing the dishes. Maybe she's right.

Both return to their customary evening routines—Barbara back to the couch and her sitcoms while Cedric dries and puts away the dishes and silverware. Quieter now, with the sink water not running, he hears what sound like pops from outside, almost certainly gunshots. He looks over at his mother sitting by the window but she doesn't react, so he begins wiping down the kitchen counters.

Gunshots are part of the background score here. Listen on most nights and a few pops are audible. The corner nearest the house—16th and V—is among the worst half-dozen or so spots in the city for crack cocaine dealing. The corner a block north—16th and U—is, of late, the very worst. There has been lots of shooting on both corners recently, but still they're open all night, and the traffic of buyers on 16th remains strong and steady in all weather.

Cedric knows that the surrounding mayhem is not something he and his mother need to talk much about. Still, it's always there, ionizing the air in the apartment, lending it some extra gravity, which, Cedric told his mother a couple of weeks ago, gives him "a little something to push against."

Cedric hangs up the wet dish towel on a drawer handle and strides toward the short hallway leading to his room. He glances quickly at Barbara as he passes and realizes that the TV is on but she's no longer watching it. Her eyes are on him.

He stops. "What you looking at?"

She pauses as though she's trying to remember something. "What did I once tell you?" she asks finally, in a tentative voice.

"Ma, what are you talking about, talking crazy?

"What did I once tell you, Lavar?"

"I don't know. You tell me lots of things."

She stands, tying her robe closed, and slowly points a finger at him, buying an extra moment to get the words from Scripture just so: "The race," she says with a satisfied smile, "goes not to the swift nor the strong, but he who endureth until the end."

Oh yes, that's a good one, Cedric agrees, and nods. Hasn't heard that one in a while. "Thank you, Jesus," he says to her with a wry smile as he makes his way toward the back bedroom. Stopping at the threshold, he turns and calls back: "But it wouldn't be so terrible to be all swift and strong—just once in a while—and let some other people do all the enduring."

Barbara, sunk back into the couch, can't help but laugh. . . .

• • •

Rob Burton opens the door, delighted to see that the room is empty. It's Saturday, early afternoon, and he's ready for a little down time. He played soccer for a while on the green near Andrews dorm in the late morning, and, with lunch now in his belly, he's feeling whipped. It was a late night of partying last night—drinking beer mostly, cruising around the campus, and then talking until all hours on the third floor with some of these new guys.

Flopping on his unmade bed, he remembers that one of them—a guy named Billy who got 5's, highest you can get, on all of his achievement tests—said he went to a private Catholic school in Baltimore.

Just like me, Rob thinks. Head propped on his pillow, he admires his corner lair. Got it just so. On the wall to his left are two glossy photos he tacked up yesterday. The nearest one is of him dancing, sweaty and close, with his girlfriend at his high school prom. He starred at the school, a private Catholic academy in Marblehead, his senior year—newspaper editor, varsity tennis and soccer player, second in the class. And a cute girlfriend, too. He broke it off with her this summer, and it's just as well, he realizes now, that he doesn't have an HTH (home town honey) like some of the guys. It would make things so complicated. He looks at the other photo, also a prom shot, of him and his best buddy in a drunken tuxedoed hug, and laughs. What a nut. Got to send him an e-mail later today, he thinks.

His mind wanders back to beloved Marblehead, a sumptuous seaside exurb of Boston where he could drink a bit, do some experimenting with his girlfriend in the back seat of his car, and then set off on his path to college and beyond. Rob's father is an obstetrician; his mother is a longtime emergency room doctor turned occupational physician. There was never any question about whether he would use his quick mind and good manners to excel. It was assumed in everything that cosseted him. His house is a stunning five-bedroom clapboard colonial, ten minutes from the blue Atlantic.

He misses it, but not terribly. He feels a sense of closure about it all after another excellent summer running a skiff at the Marblehead Yacht Club, hanging with his buddies, and going on a few trips with the folks. Sure, there was a sense that an era of his life was coming to an end. But it was time, no doubt, to take the next step.

He rolls onto his side, figuring he'll catch some sleep, and looks just to the left of his pillow at his favorite recent *Rolling Stone* cover—neatly taped up—a shot of Sting, all blond ease, gazing off remotely and effortlessly, very cool.

He lies there for a while, finds he doesn't really feel like napping, and sits up. Resting gently on top of his canvas bookbag, which is teetering on the edge of his desk right near the bed, is a letter home he started writing two days ago.

He snatches it, seeing if maybe he feels like finishing it.

> "Dear Mom and Dad,
>
> This is my first letter, one of many I can guarantee. It's August 31st, Thursday. I've been here approximately 24 hours and I'm beginning to slowly realize I'm here. I'm slowly touching down to earth.
>
> All is going well. After saying good-bye to Mom, I returned to my room to find Cedric and his mom unpacking. We are getting along well, although our tastes in music couldn't be more different. . . ."

Cedric. He pushes a pile of his sweaty clothes from this morning's soccer game away with his foot and puts the letter down on a cleared spot of floor. Well, college is supposed to be broadening, he muses, and there's no doubt he'll get broadened this year with a roommate like Cedric. But it'll work out. Casual and nonconfrontational, upbeat and accommodating, Rob can get along with anyone—it's a point of pride for him. If people are reasonable and open-minded, conflict always dissolves. Even if they just agree to disagree, at least they will have agreed on something. Not that he won't be challenged when it comes to Cedric. He's never really been close to a black guy, barely known any. The few encounters he's had were characterized by caution, by him feeling like he was walking on eggshells, not wanting to offend, inadvertently, with an inappropriate tone or casual remark. Last night with the guys, when all the talk shifted to roommates, Rob said to everyone it was going fine. There's a lot of interest in Cedric from the other kids, him being a black city kid and all. Everyone agreed that none of them had spent too much time with a person like that and, God knows, there aren't all that many of them here at Brown.

He looks across the room at the empty bed, at the hospital corners and fluffed pillows, everything in order, like a fortress. It seems like he and Cedric couldn't be more different, he thinks, looking at his mess of socks and papers and empty juice bottles. Different, it seems, in every way.

He grabs a pen, bent on finishing the letter. It's dated two days ago, he should get it done.

The door opens.

"Hey, Rob."

"Oh, hi, Cedric," Rob says, looking up from the notebook on his lap with the letter on top. "Where you been?"

"Lunch."

"Yeah, me too," Rob says, wondering if Cedric saw him there and thought that Rob might have snubbed him because they didn't sit together. "I didn't see you."

"Oh, no. I had to go to the corner and get a sandwich. I lost my temporary ID. I'm just living off this money my mom gave me. It's baaaaaad. I can't eat on my meal plan. It's like I don't exist." Rob commiserates and says he'll steal stuff for Cedric from the cafeteria if he wants.

Cedric putters around for a bit, hopping over to his chair and looking at some scheduling forms on his desk, while Rob turns back to the letter, not making much headway.

"Do you like mopping floors?" Cedric asks, after a bit.

"No, I don't *think* so," Rob says mawkishly, thinking it's some sort of joke.

"I just want to take a mop to it once a week, just to keep this place clean," Cedric says.

"Sure, you can do that if you want," Rob says, not thinking until a moment later that Cedric might have been hoping for more participation.

"You know, Rob, your feet smell bad."

"Oh come on, they do not."

"Do too! Man, walking around in your bare feet . . . that's disgusting."

Rob, accustomed to cut grass, thick pile carpets, and clean beach sand, has no idea what he's talking about. "Cedric, everyone walks barefoot."

"Maybe where you're from," Cedric says, raising his eyebrows. "Not 65
where I'm from."

Cedric sits on his bed and turns on the TV, flipping the channels, looking for something to watch. Rob doesn't watch much TV and told Cedric that the first day. Now, with the noise, he can't seem to concentrate on the letter.

Instead, he grabs a novel he's been reading over the summer and flops on his bed, trying to ignore the blare. After a while, he drops the book and decides to see whom he can find to hang out with up on the third floor. He'll let Cedric enjoy the company of his TV.

"I'm outta here," he says to no one in particular as the door slams. For the first time, he notices how nice his bare feet feel on the hallway carpet. . . .

QUESTIONING THE TEXT

1. In what ways does the matter of bare feet in the dorm room embody basic differences between the home environments Cedric and Rob have experienced? List some of those differences, and explore the implications of Cedric's complaint: "Rob, your feet smell bad" (paragraph 61).
2. Describing Cedric's apartment, Suskind notes that "[g]unshots are part of the background score here" (paragraph 27). Think about the noises at the place you currently think of as home. Would a stranger learn as much about your home from those sounds as readers discover about Cedric's life from the report of those gunshots? Why, or why not?
3. Television seems to play a major role in Cedric's life, both at his home and in his dormitory room. What comfort might TV offer a young man living in a hostile or an alien environment? Evaluate the part TV plays—if any—in your home life.

MAKING CONNECTIONS

4. Cedric's mother plays an important role in this piece, as does Michael Nava's grandmother in "Gardenland, Sacramento, California" (p. 647). Review both selections, and then describe the relationships these two young men have with their mother and grandmother, respectively. To what extent do the mother figures represent home?

5. Just for the fun of it, read Dave Barry's "Guys vs. Men" (p. 402). Then, using a humorous slant like Barry's, rewrite and expand the conversation between Cedric and Rob on the matter of smelly feet. Or write a new version of the scene, based on a roommate problem you have experienced.
6. According to Shelby Steele in "The Recoloring of Campus Life" (p. 78), "black people make white people feel guilty" (p. 92). Does Suskind's description of Rob support Steele's claim, or is the relationship between Rob and Cedric more complex? Discuss the issue both in class and in a position paper that explores relationships between different groups on your campus.

JOINING THE CONVERSATION

7. Can a dormitory really be a home? Write a brief argument of definition in which you explore and answer this question, drawing on your own experiences and the issues raised by *A Hope in the Unseen* or any other readings in this chapter.
8. Although Cedric is ultimately not admitted to the Massachusetts Institute of Technology (MIT), he receives a scholarship to Brown University, confirming his mother's faith in him. In an article brief enough to serve as an op-ed piece in your local newspaper, explore the roles that home and family play in directing the ambitions and hopes of young people.

ALICE WALKER
The Place Where I Was Born

ALICE WALKER (b. 1944), perhaps best known for her Pulitzer Prize-winning 1982 novel The Color Purple, *is a writer of distinction in many areas, including poetry and short stories as well as other novels* (The Third Life of Grange Copeland, *1970;* The Temple of My Familiar, *1989;* Possessing the Secret of Joy, *1992;* By the Light of My Father's Smile, *1998;* The Way Forward Is with a Broken Heart, *2000 and essays (*In Search of Our Mothers' Gardens, *1983;* The Same River Twice, *1996;* Anything We Love Can Be Saved: A Writer's Activism, *1997*). *After attending Spelman College and graduating from Sarah Lawrence in 1965, Walker moved to Mississippi and taught at Jackson State College while working as a civil rights activist during one of the most harrowing times in our nation's history. Her personal courage during those years is reflected in the actions of many of her fictional characters, as is her commitment to celebrating the lives and achievements of African American women.*

In the following brief prose poem (the opening of Walker's 1991 volume of poetry, Her Blue Body Everything We Knew*), Walker, one of eight children of Georgia sharecroppers Willie Lee and Minnie T. Walker, speaks evocatively of the "land of my birth," the "small rounded hills" and "big leaf poplar" and pines of middle Georgia that for her speak of home.*

I debated a long time with myself before choosing this selection, for I was tempted by many other pieces of Alice Walker's writing, particularly her powerful essay "Looking for Zora [Neale Hurston]," which describes another kind of homecoming. In the end, I was drawn to this less well-known piece, partly because it mixes the genres of poetry and prose, partly because I too grew up in the South and counted Brer Rabbit a friend, and partly because I hoped it would spark some very fond memories in you.
—A.L.

I am a displaced person. I sit here on a swing on the deck of my house in Northern California admiring how the fog has turned the valley below into a lake. For hours nothing will be visible below me except this large expanse of vapor; then slowly, as the sun rises and gains in intensity, the fog will start to curl up and begin its slow rolling drift toward the ocean. People here call it the dragon; and, indeed, a dragon is what it looks like, puffing and coiling, winged, flaring and in places thin and discreet, as it races before the sun, back to its ocean coast den. Mornings I sit here in awe and great peace. The mountains across the valley come and go in the mist; the redwoods and firs, oaks and giant bays appear as clumpish spires, enigmatic shapes of green, like the stone forests one sees in Chinese paintings of Guilin.*

It is incredibly beautiful where I live. Not fancy at all, or exclusive. But from where I sit on my deck I can look down on the backs of hawks, and the wide, satiny wings of turkey vultures glistening in the sun become my present connection to ancient Egyptian Africa. The pond is so still below me that the trees reflected in it seem, from this distance, to be painted in its depths.

All this: the beauty, the quiet, the cleanliness, the peace, is what I love. I realize how lucky I am to have found it here. And yet, there are days when my view of the mountains and redwoods makes me nostalgic for small rounded hills easily walked over, and for the look of big leaf poplar and the scent of pine.

I am nostalgic for the land of my birth, the land I left forever when I was thirteen—moving first to the town of Eatonton,* and then, at seventeen, to the city of Atlanta.

I cried one day as I talked to a friend about a tree I loved as a child. A tree that had sheltered my father on his long cold walk to school each morning: it was midway between his house and the school and because there was a large cavity in its trunk, a fire could be made inside it. During my childhood, in a tiny, overcrowded house in a tiny dell below it, I looked up at it frequently and felt reassured by its age, its generosity despite its years of brutalization (the fires, I knew, had to hurt), and its tall, old-growth pine nobility. When it was struck by lightning and killed, and then was cut down and made into firewood, I grieved as if it had been a person. Secretly. Because who among the members of my family would not have laughed at my grief?

I have felt entirely fortunate to have had this companion, and even today remember it with gratitude. But why the tears? my friend wanted to know. And it suddenly dawned on me that perhaps it *was* sad that it was a tree and not a member of my family to whom I was so emotionally close.

  O, landscape of my birth
because you were so good to me as I grew
I could not bear to lose you.
  O, landscape of my birth
because when I lost you, a part of my soul died.
  O, landscape of my birth
because to save myself I pretended it was *you*
who died.
  You that now did not exist
because I could not see you.

Guilin: a city in China (Kweilin or Kueilin) characterized by its mountains
Eatonton: the town in which Walker attended high school

But O, landscape of my birth
now I can confess how I have lied.
Now I can confess the sorrow
of my heart
as the tears flow
and I see again with memory's bright eye
my dearest companion cut down
and can bear to resee myself
so lonely and so small
there in the sunny meadows
and shaded woods
of childhood
where my crushed spirit
and stricken heart
ran in circles
looking for a friend.

Soon I will have known fifty summers.
Perhaps that is why
my heart
an imprisoned tree
so long clutched tight
inside its core
insists
on shedding
like iron leaves
the bars
from its cell.

You flow into me.
And like the Aborigine or Bushperson or Cherokee
who braves everything
to stumble home to die
no matter that cowboys
are herding cattle where the ancestors slept
I return to you, my earliest love.

Weeping in recognition at the first trees
I ever saw, the first hills I ever climbed and rested my
unbearable cares
upon, the first rivers I ever dreamed myself across,
the first pebbles I ever lifted up, warm from the sun, and put
into
my mouth.

O landscape of my birth
you have never been far from my heart.
It is *I* who have been far.
If you will take me back
Know that I
Am yours.

As a child I assumed I would always have the middle Georgia landscape to live in, as Brer Rabbit,* a native also, and relative, had his brier patch. It was not to be. The pain of racist oppression, and its consequence, economic impoverishment, drove me to the four corners of the earth in search of justice and peace, and work that affirmed my whole being. I have come to rest here, weary from travel, on a deck—not a Southern front porch—overlooking another world.

I am content; and yet, I wonder what my life would have been like if I had been able to stay home?

I remember early morning fogs in Georgia, not so dramatic as California ones, but magical too because out of the Southern fog of memory tramps my dark father, smiling and large, glowing with rootedness, and talking of hound dogs, biscuits and coons. And my equally rooted mother bustles around the corner of our house preparing to start a wash, the fire under the black wash pot extending a circle of warmth in which I, a grave-eyed child, stand. There is my sister Ruth, beautiful to me and dressed elegantly for high school in gray felt skirt and rhinestone brooch, hurrying up the road to catch the yellow school bus which glows like a large glow worm in the early morning fog.

QUESTIONING THE TEXT

1. Walker writes of a tree she "loved as a child." What about this tree is comforting and lovable—and sad? What in the natural world do you love most? Does this element "make up" for something else in any way? Explain.
2. Reread Walker's poem. What is the "lie" she has told? Discuss this question with one or two classmates.
3. Note the details of Walker's life that A.L. highlights in her introduction. Why do you think A.L. chooses these specifics? How does she want readers to view Walker?

Brer Rabbit: from African legend, a trickster figure popularized in the Uncle Remus stories by Joel Chandler Harris (1848–1908), also born in the country near Eatonton, Georgia

MAKING CONNECTIONS

4. Look carefully at the descriptions of home included in this essay and in those by Ron Suskind (p. 634) and Terry Tempest Williams (p. 655). In what ways do they reveal similar attitudes toward home, and in what ways do they differ? Which description of home is most compelling to you, and why? If you keep a reading log, answer these questions there. If not, respond in a paragraph for class discussion.
5. Which other writers in this chapter speak indirectly of "displaced persons"? How are their definitions of *displaced* similar or different? Try your hand at writing a definition of this term.

JOINING THE CONVERSATION

6. Working with two or three classmates, prepare an introduction to Alice Walker. Gather biographical information, and perhaps read two or three other works by Walker. You might watch *The Color Purple,* available on video, and check out Walker's writings about the making of that film. Pool your information, and select from it material for a 20-minute class presentation—"Introducing Alice Walker." (You may have gathered enough information for a more intensive research project on Walker. If so, talk with your instructor about pursuing such a project.)
7. Write your own brief essay titled "The Place Where I Was Born." If you wish, include a poem as Walker does in her essay.

MICHAEL NAVA
Gardenland, Sacramento, California

*"H*OME,*" THE OLD SAYING GOES, "is where the heart is." And where the heart is may not be a physical place at all but rather a mental place, an inner place of safety and security, a place like home. In the essay that follows, which was published in* Hometowns: Gay Men Write about Where They Belong *(1992), Michael Nava introduces us to his neighborhood, Gardenland, long-time home of his family and pretty much "a Mexican village, transported perhaps from Guanajuato, where my grandmother's family originated, and set down lock, stock, and chicken coop in the middle of California." As Nava (b. 1954) grows up, he realizes that he may be from Gardenland but he is not of Gardenland: his sexual and intellectual desires set him apart, leading him to run away "without leaving home." Yet Nava finds that his home community, paradoxically, served him well. I am drawn to Nava's essay for many reasons, but primarily, I think, because when I was a child I often found my home in books, as he did, and because I like to think that we can take our homes with us wherever we go.*

Nava, who has practiced law for a number of years, has published widely. His Henry Rios mystery series, which features a gay Hispanic lawyer and has won four Lambda Literary Awards, concluded in 2001 with Rag and Bone*—much to his fans' disappointment. Nava also publishes nonfiction; often cited is his* Created Equal: Why Gay Rights Matter to America *(1994). Today, he lives and practices law in San Francisco.* —A.L.

I grew up in a neighborhood of Sacramento called Gardenland, a poor community, almost entirely Mexican, where my maternal family, the Acunas, had lived since the 1920s. Sacramento's only distinction used to be that it was the state capital. Today, because it frequently appears on lists of the country's most livable cities, weary big-town urbanites have turned it into a boomtown rapidly becoming unlivable. But when I was a child, in the late fifties and early sixties, the only people who lived in Sacramento were the people who'd been born there.

Downtown the wide residential neighborhoods were lined with oaks shading turreted, run-down Victorian mansions, some partitioned into apartments, others still of a piece, but all of them exuding a shadowy small-town melancholy. The commercial district was block after block of shabby brick buildings housing small businesses. The city's skyline was dominated by the gold-domed capitol, a confectioner's spun-sugar dream of a building. It was set in a shady park whose grass seemed always to glisten magically, as if hidden under each blade of grass were an Easter egg.

Figure 8.2 Sacramento skyline and river

Sacramento's only other landmarks of note were its two rivers, the American and the Sacramento. They came together in muddy confluence beneath the slender iron joints of railroad bridges. Broad and shallow, the rivers passed as slowly as thought between the thick and tumble of their banks.

A system of levees fed into the rivers. One of these tributaries was called the Bannon Slough. Gardenland was a series of streets carved out of farmland backed up against the slough. It flowed south, curving east behind a street called Columbus Avenue, creating Gardenland's southern and eastern boundaries. The northern boundary was a street called El Camino. Beyond El Camino was middle-class tract housing. To the west, beyond Bowman Street, were fields and then another neighborhood that may just as well have existed on another planet for all I knew of it.

What I knew were the nine streets of Gardenland: Columbus, Jefferson, 5
Harding, Cleveland, El Camino, Peralta, Wilson, Haggin, and Bowman; an explorer, an odd lot of presidents, an unimaginative Spanish phrase, and three inexplicable proper names, one in Spanish, two in English. It was as if the streets had been named out of a haphazard perusal of a child's history text. There were two other significant facts about the streets in Gardenland; they all dead-ended into the levee and their names were not continued across El Camino Boulevard into the Anglo suburb, called Northgate. Gardenland's streets led, literally, nowhere.

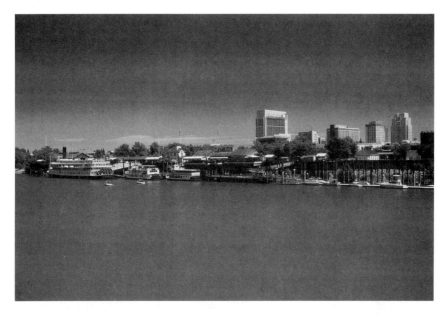

Unlike El Camino, where little square houses sat on little square lots, Gardenland had not been subdivided to maximum utility. Broad uncultivated fields stretched between and behind the ramshackle houses. Someone's "front yard" might consist of a quarter acre of tall grass and the remnants of an almond orchard. The fields were littered with abandoned farming implements and the foundations of long-gone houses. For a dreamy boy like me, these artifacts were magical. Finding my own world often harsh, I could imagine from these rusted pieces of metal and fragments of walls a world in which I would have been a prince.

But princes were hard to come by in Gardenland. Almost everyone was poor, and most residents continued to farm after a fashion, keeping vegetable gardens and flocks of chickens. There were neither sidewalks nor streetlights, and the roads, cheaply paved, were always crumbling and narrow as country lanes. At night, the streets and fields were lit by moonlight and the stars burned with millennial intensity above the low roofs of our houses.

The best way to think of Gardenland is not as an American suburb at all, but rather as a Mexican village, transported perhaps from Guanajuato, where my grandmother's family originated, and set down lock, stock, and chicken coop in the middle of California.

My cousin Josephine Robles had divided her tiny house in half and ran a beauty shop from one side. Above her porch was a wooden sign that said in big blue letters GARDENLAND and, in smaller print below, BEAUTY SALON. Over the years the weather took its toll and the bottom half faded completely, leaving only the word GARDENLAND in that celestial blue, like a road sign to a cut-rate Eden.

By the time I was born, in 1954, my family had lived in Gardenland for 10
at least twenty-five years. Virtually all I know of my grandfather's family, the Acunas, was that they were Yaqui Indians living in northern Mexico near the American border at Yuma, Arizona. My grandmother's family, the Trujillos, had come out of central Mexico in 1920, escaping the displacements caused by the Mexican Revolution of 1910. I have dim memories of my great-grandparents, Ygnacio and Phillipa Trujillo, doll-like, white-haired figures living in a big, dark two-story house in east Sacramento.

My grandparents settled on Haggin Avenue in a house they built themselves. My cousins, the Robles, lived two doors down. My family also eventually lived on Haggin Avenue, next door to my grandparents. Our house was the pastel plaster box that became standard suburban architecture in California in the fifties and sixties but it was the exception in Gardenland.

Most houses seemed to have begun as shacks to which rooms were added to accommodate expanding families. They were not built with privacy in mind but simply as shelter. We lived in a series of such houses until our final move to Haggin Avenue. In one of them, the living room was separated from the kitchen by the narrow rectangular bedroom in which my brothers and sisters and I slept. Adults were always walking through it while we were trying to sleep. This made for jittery children, but no one had patience for our complaints. It was enough that we had a place to live.

By the standards of these places, my grandparent's house was luxurious. It was a four-bedroom, L-shaped building that they had built themselves. My grandmother put up the original three rooms while my grandfather was in the navy during World War II. My aunt Socorro told me that my grandmother measured the rooms by having her children lie head to toe across a plot of ground. She bought the cement for the foundations, mixed and troweled it, and even installed pipes for plumbing. Later, when my grandfather returned, they added a series of long, narrow rooms paneled in slats of dark-stained pine, solid and thick walled.

Massive, dusty couches upholstered in a heavy maroon fabric, oversize beds soft as sponges, and a leather-topped dining room table furnished the house. Like the rusted combines in the field, these things seemed magical in their antiquity. I would slip into the house while my grandparents were both at work and wander through it, opening drawers and inspecting whatever presented itself to my attention. It was in this fashion that I opened a little-used closet and found it full of men's clothes that obviously were not my grandfather's. Later I learned that they had belonged to my uncle Raymond who had been killed in a car accident. In a subsequent exploration I found pictures of his funeral, including a picture taken of him in his casket, a smooth-faced, dark-skinned, pretty boy of fifteen.

Another time, I found a voluminous red petticoat in a cedar chest. 15
Without much hesitation, I put it on and went into my grandmother's bedroom where I took out her face powder and lipstick. I applied these in the careful manner of my grandmother, transforming myself in the dressing mirror beneath the grim gaze of a crucified Christ. Looking back, I don't think I was trying to transform myself into a girl, but only emulating the one adult in my family who loved me without condition. Because she was the soul of kindness, it never occurred to me, as a child, that my grandmother might be unhappy. Only looking back do I see it.

She and my grandfather slept in separate rooms at opposite ends of their house. In the evening, my grandfather would sit on a couch in front of the television quietly drinking himself into a stupor while my grandmother did needlework at the kitchen table. They barely spoke. I would sit with my grandmother, looking at pictures in the *Encyclopedia Americana,* comfortable with the silence, which, to her, must have been a deafening indictment of a failed marriage.

In my parents' house, the marriage of my mother and stepfather was as noisily unhappy as my grandparents' was quietly miserable. In each shabby house where we lived I would be awakened by their fights. I learned to turn myself into a stone, or become part of the bed or the walls so as to abate the terror I felt. No one ever spoke of it. There was only one house in which my family lived together peaceably but it only existed as a blueprint that had come somehow into my stepfather's possession.

In the evening, he would take it down from a shelf and unroll it on the kitchen table. Together we would study it, laying claim to rooms, planning alterations. At the time, we lived in a tiny one-bedroom cinder-block house. My brother and I slept on a bunk bed in an alcove off the kitchen. At night, I could hear mice scampering across the cement floor, terrifying me when I woke up having to pee and pick my way through the darkness to the bathroom.

When we finally moved from the cinder-block house, it was to another, bigger version of that house rather than to the dream house of the blueprint. One night, my mother's screaming woke me. I hurried into the bedroom she and my stepfather occupied and found him beating her. When I tried to stop him, he threw me across the room. The next morning my mother told me he was sorry, but it was too late. Where I lived no longer mattered to me because I learned to live completely within myself in rooms of rage and grief. Now I think these rooms were not so different from the rooms we all occupied, my unhappy family and I.

Although not literally cut off from the outside world, Gardenland was 20
little touched by it. We were tribal in our outlook and our practices. Anglos were generically called "paddies," whether or not they were Irish. All fair-skinned people were mysterious but also alike. Even TV, that great equalizer, only emphasized our isolation since we never saw anyone who looked remotely like us, or lived as we did, on any of the popular shows of the day. At school, the same homogeneity prevailed. Until I was nine I attended a neighborhood grade school where virtually every other child was like me, dark eyed and dark skinned, answering to names like Juarez, Delgadillo, Robles, Martinez. My own name, Michael Angel, was but an Anglicized version of Miguel Angel, a name I shared with at least three other of my classmates.

I had a remarkable amount of freedom as a child. As I said, we eventually lived on the same street as other members of my maternal family and I roamed their houses as unself-consciously as a Bedouin child might move among the tents of his people. I ate in whatever house I found myself at mealtime and the meals were the same in each of my relatives' houses—rice, beans, lettuce and tomato salad, stewed or fried meat, tortillas, salsa. My grandparents did not lock their doors at night—who did? what was there to steal?—so that I could slip into their house quietly and make my bed on their sofa when my parents were fighting.

But most of the time I spent outdoors, alone or with my friends. In spring, the field behind my house was overrun with thistles. We neighborhood kids put in long days cutting trails through them and hacking out clearings that became our forts. Tiring of the fields, we'd lurk in abandoned houses, empty barns, and chicken coops. When all other amusements failed, there was always Bannon Slough, a muddy brown creek that flowed between thickly wooded banks. It was too filthy to swim in. Instead, in the steep shadows of bridges and railroad trestles we taught each other how to smoke and to swear.

Just as often I would be off by myself. Early on, I looked for ways to escape my family. I found it in the stillness of the grass and the slap of the slough's brown water against the shore. There I discovered my own capacity for stillness. Lying on the slope of the levee, I could hear my own breath in the wind and feel my skin in the warm blades of grass that pressed against my neck. In those moments, Gardenland *was* Eden, and I felt the wonder and loneliness of the first being.

For, like Adam, I was lonely. Being everyone's child, I was no one's child. I could disappear in the morning and stay out until dusk and my absence went unnoticed. Children barely counted as humans in our tribe. We were more like livestock and our parents' main concern was that the head count at night matched the head count in the morning.

25 My loneliness became as much a part of me as my brown hair and the mole above my lip, something unremarkable. When I came out, I missed that sense of joining a community of others like me that so many of my friends describe. My habits of secrecy and loneliness were too deeply ingrained. I had become like my grandfather, who, in a rare moment of self-revelation, told me he was a "lone wolf"; the most unsociable of an unsociable tribe. Though I've changed as I've grown older, I still sometimes wonder if one reason I write is because I am filled with all the words I never spoke as a child.

Two things opened up for me the narrow passage through which I finally escaped Gardenland for good. The first was books. I learned to read early and, once started, could not get enough of books. In this affinity, I was neither encouraged nor discouraged by my family. Education beyond its most basic functions, learning how to read and write, to do sums, had absolutely no interest for them. My love of reading became simply another secret part of me.

There wasn't a library in Gardenland. Instead, a big white van pulled up to the corner of Wilson and El Camino, the city Bookmobile. Inside, patrons squeezed into a narrow passageway between tall shelves of books. The children's books occupied the bottom shelves. At the exit, a woman checked out books from a standing desk. The Bookmobile came once a week and I was a regular customer, always taking my limit of books.

Everything about the process pleased me. I was proud of my library card, a yellow piece of cardboard with my name typed on it, which I carried in a cowhide wallet that was otherwise empty. I liked taking books from the shelves, noting their heft and volume, the kind of type, whether they were illustrated, and I studied the record of their circulation, the checkout dates stamped in blue on stiff white cards in paper pockets on the inside covers. I loved the books as much as I loved reading. To me, they were organic things, as alive in their way as I was.

Like so many other bright children growing up in the inarticulate world of the poor, books fueled my imagination, answered my questions, led me to new ones, and helped me conceive of a world in which I would not feel so set apart. Yet I do not believe that my brains alone, even aided by my bookish fantasies, would have been enough to escape Gardenland. For this, I needed the kind of courage that arises out of desperation.

I found this courage in my homosexuality. Early on, I acquired a taste for 30
reading history, particularly ancient history. I suppose that pictures of ruined Greek cities reminded me of the crumbling, abandoned houses in the fields of Gardenland. But I was also fascinated by pictures of the nude male statues. There was something about the smooth, headless torsos, the irisless eyes of ephebes that made me stop my idle flipping through pages and touch the paper where these things were depicted. By the time I was twelve I understood that my fascination was rooted in my sexual nature. One day, walking to school, clutching my books to my chest, girl-style, I heard myself say, "I'm a queer."

It was absolutely clear to me that Gardenland could not accommodate this revelation. Gardenland provided the barest of existences for its people. What made it palatable was the knowledge that everyone was about the same, united in ethnicity and poverty and passivity. The only rituals were the rituals of family, and family was everything there. But I knew that I was not the same as everyone else. And I was certain that my family, already puzzled by my silent devotion to books, would reject me entirely if it became known exactly what thoughts occupied my silence.

Had I been a different child I would have run away from home. Instead, I ran away without leaving home. I escaped to books, to sexual fantasy, to painful, unrequited crushes on male classmates. No one ever knew. I turned myself into an outsider, someone at the margins of a community that was itself outcast. Paradoxically, by doing this, I learned the peasant virtues of my hometown, endurance and survival. As a member of yet another embattled community, those virtues I absorbed as a child continue to serve me.

QUESTIONING THE TEXT

1. What are some of Nava's assumptions about home in this essay? What assumptions about the idea of home, or about actual home life in America, does he call into question, and how does he do so?
2. This essay is full of vivid descriptions that convey a sense of what Nava's home was like in Gardenland. Read through the essay again, noting some of those descriptions. Which ones are most evocative for you? What emotions and thoughts do they evoke?

MAKING CONNECTIONS

3. Nava writes of ways in which he "escaped" home—both his family and Gardenland—without actually leaving. At the end of the essay, he reflects on how "those virtues I absorbed as a child continue to serve me." Alice Walker also writes of a home she fled, in "The Place Where I Was Born" (p. 642), and she, too, still feels a connection to her home. "I am content," she muses; "and yet, I wonder what my life would have been like if I had been able to stay home?" With a classmate, consider Nava's and Walker's complex relationships to their homes. Make a list of the ways in which these relationships are similar and different. Discuss the insights your comparison reveals about the idea of leaving home.
4. In writing of his parents and grandparents, Nava presents two images of marriage, one "noisily unhappy," the other "quietly miserable" (paragraph 17). Reflect on these descriptions of family life after reading Barbara Dafoe Whitehead's "The Making of a Divorce Culture" (p. 667). Do you imagine that the question of divorce would have arisen in Nava's family? Why, or why not? Do you think it would have been a reasonable consideration? What differences do you detect between your view of these marriages or home lives and Nava's view of them? What might account for those differences? Write a two-page response to these questions, and share your thoughts in class discussion.

JOINING THE CONVERSATION

5. Try your hand at writing a vivid description of your home, as Nava has done in this essay. Write an essay named after your hometown or neighborhood, showing readers what life is like there.
6. What aspects of your home seem to propel you away from it? What aspects beckon you to return? Discuss these questions with two or three classmates. What common experiences of home do you find within your small group, and what different ones?

TERRY TEMPEST WILLIAMS
The Clan of One-Breasted Women

It is currently a cliché to say that we live on a small planet—and perhaps a dying one as well. For all we hear of "Mother Earth," this parent of us all has not fared well at our hands. Witness the destruction of ancient forests; the death of rivers, lakes, even oceans; the filth of much city air; the disappearing species. The growing awareness of just how small and crowded—and necessary—the earth is may be at least partially responsible for an outpouring of work called "nature writing" or "environmental literature." Rachel Carson arguably sounded the alarm first, in the riveting opening of her 1963 classic explication of the effects of pesticides, Silent Spring. *Carson has now been joined by dozens of other distinguished writers, from Aldo Leopold to Barry Lopez and Leslie Marmon Silko—and Terry Tempest Williams.*

Terry Tempest Williams (b. 1955) was born, raised, and educated in Utah, earning her master's degree in environmental education at the University of Utah. Naturalist-in-residence at the Utah Museum of Natural History, Williams, as the following essay suggests, is also a powerful teller of stories in which she attempts to bring the earth to our attention and to convince us that "there is no separation between our bodies and the body of the earth." Her most recent work, a collection of poems, essays, and congressional testimony, is Red: Passion and Patience in the Desert *(2002).*

In "The Clan of One-Breasted Women," the epilogue of her 1991 book Refuge: An Unnatural History of Family and Place, *she explores the human connection to the earth in relation to the lives of women in her family who have died from or are living with cancer. If we poison Mother Earth, our home, she asks, will our own mothers (and we as well) not also be poisoned? This is a poignant question for me, since my mother and aunt also died of breast cancer. The latest figures from the National Institutes of Health, in fact, tell us that one in seven women in the United States today will contract such a cancer, and though medical researchers have identified some of the genetic bases of breast cancer, they have found no cure. These figures suggest that the issues Williams raises about the "home" represented by the earth and by our own bodies will touch every reader of this book, either directly or indirectly.*

—A.L.

The title fooled me. On my first reading some years ago, unaware of who Terry Tempest Williams was

I belong to a Clan of One-Breasted Women. My mother, my grandmothers, and six aunts have all had mastectomies. Seven are dead. The two who survive have just completed rounds of chemotherapy and radiation.

and perhaps influenced subtly by The Clan of the Cave Bear, *I did not take the title literally. The first page shocked me, then, into close attention. I am not from Utah, but my mother and aunt, now dead from breast cancer, belonged to this clan, as may I in my turn.* —A.L.

I've had my own problems: two biopsies for breast cancer and a small tumor between my ribs diagnosed as a "borderline malignancy."

This is my family history.

No, these are the women *of your family's history.* —J.G.R.

Most statistics tell us breast cancer is genetic, hereditary, with rising percentages attached to fatty diets, childlessness, or becoming pregnant after thirty. What they don't say is living in Utah may be the greatest hazard of all.

The issue of causality is raised powerfully here, making us wonder: what has changed to make Utah so dangerous? —J.R.

We are a Mormon family with roots in Utah since 1847. The "word of wisdom" in my family aligned us with good foods—no coffee, no tea, tobacco, or alcohol. For the most part, our women were finished having their babies by the time they were thirty. And only one faced breast cancer prior to 1960. Traditionally, as a group of people, Mormons have a low rate of cancer.

Williams is building her credibility, showing that her family's lifestyle did not include the typical cancer-causing agents. But she won't be able to rely on such arguments for long—I doubt they'd be accepted in a court of law. —A.L.

Is our family a cultural anomaly? The truth is, we didn't think about it. Those who did, usually the men, simply said, "bad genes." The women's attitude was stoic. Cancer was part of life. On February 16, 1971, the eve of my mother's surgery, I accidentally picked up the telephone and overheard her ask my grandmother what she could expect.

"Diane, it is one of the most spiritual experiences you will ever encounter."

I quietly put down the receiver.

Two days later, my father took my brothers and me to the hospital to visit her. She met us in the lobby in a wheelchair. No bandages were visible. I'll never forget her radiance, the way she held herself in a purple velvet robe, and how she gathered us around her.

"Children, I am fine. I want you to know I felt the arms of God around me."

Here is a dramatic juxtaposition of life and death. I wonder how she will weave these themes together in the rest of the essay—or if she will. —A.L.

We believed her. My father cried. Our mother, his wife, was thirty-eight years old.

A little over a year after Mother's death, Dad and I were having dinner together. He had just returned from St. George, where the Tempest Company was completing the gas lines that would service southern Utah. He spoke of his love for the country, the sandstoned landscape, bare-boned and beautiful. He had just finished hiking the Kolob trail in Zion National Park. We got caught up in reminiscing, recalling with fondness our walk up Angel's Landing on his fiftieth birthday and the years our family had vacationed there.

Over dessert, I shared a recurring dream of mine. I told my father that for years, as long as I could remember, I saw this flash of light in the night in the desert—that this image had so permeated my being that I could not venture south without seeing it again, on the horizon, illuminating buttes and mesas.

"You did see it," he said.

"Saw what?"

"The bomb. The cloud. We were driving home from Riverside, California. You were sitting on Diane's lap. She was pregnant. In fact, I remember the day, September 7, 1957. We had just gotten out of the Service. We were driving north, past Las Vegas. It was an hour or so before dawn, when this explosion went off. We not only heard it, but felt it. I thought the oil tanker in front of us had blown up. We pulled over and suddenly, rising from the desert floor, we saw it, clearly, this golden-stemmed cloud, the mushroom. The sky seemed to vibrate with an eerie pink glow. Within a few minutes, a light ash was raining on the car."

In my memory of the 1950s, the "mushroom cloud" blooms, a source of fear and pride. Like Plato's hemlock, "the bomb" was both poison and cure. —A.L.

I stared at my father.

"I thought you knew that," he said. "It was a common occurrence in the fifties."

The shift from the "light," the "golden-stemmed cloud," the "pink glow," and "light ash" to "contaminated" land and milk becomes explicitly a "deceit." —A.L.

It was at this moment that I realized the deceit I had been living under. Children growing up in the American Southwest, drinking contaminated milk from contaminated cows, even from the contaminated breasts of their mothers, my mother—members, years later, of the Clan of One-Breasted Women.

What does Williams mean by "deceit"? Could she, as late as the 1970s, have been unaware of nuclear testing that she claims, in the next paragraph, was a "well-known story"? —J.R.

It is a well-known story in the Desert West, "The Day We Bombed Utah," or more accurately, the years we bombed Utah: above ground atomic testing in Nevada took place from January 27, 1951, through July 11, 1962. Not only were the winds blowing north covering "low-use segments of the population" with fallout and leaving sheep dead in their tracks, but the climate was right. The United

States of the 1950s was red, white, and blue. The Korean War was raging. McCarthyism was rampant. Ike was it, and the cold war was hot. If you were against nuclear testing, you were for a communist regime.

Her characterization of the 1950s is grossly simplified, reducing a complex and difficult period to crude stereotypes. —J.R.

I do not recall questioning the need for nuclear testing until much later in the 1960s. Williams makes me want to study the times more carefully and see if any stories of "burns, blisters, and nausea" were being told. —A.L.

Much has been written about this "American nuclear tragedy." Public health was secondary to national security. The Atomic Energy Commissioner, Thomas Murray, said, "Gentlemen, we must not let anything interfere with this series of tests, nothing."

Again and again, the American public was told by its government, in spite of burns, blisters, and nausea, "It has been found that the tests may be conducted with adequate assurance of safety under conditions prevailing at the bombing reservations." Assuaging public fears was simply a matter of public relations. "Your best action," an Atomic Energy Commission booklet read, "is not to be worried about fallout." A news release typical of the times stated, "We find no basis for concluding that harm to any individual has resulted from radioactive fallout."

Her narrative here is inadequate too, using three quotations to speak for decades of controversy. —J.R.

On August 30, 1979, during Jimmy Carter's presidency, a suit was filed, *Irene Allen v. The United States of America.* Mrs. Allen's case was the first on an alphabetical list of twenty-four test cases, representative of nearly twelve hundred plaintiffs seeking compensation from the United States government for cancers caused by nuclear testing in Nevada.

Irene Allen lived in Hurricane, Utah. She was the mother of five children and had been widowed twice. Her first husband, with their two oldest boys, had watched the tests from the roof of the local high school. He died of leukemia in 1956. Her second husband died of pancreatic cancer in 1978.

In a town meeting conducted by Utah Senator Orrin Hatch, shortly before the suit was filed, Mrs. Allen said, "I am not blaming the government, I want you to know that, Senator Hatch. But I thought if my testimony could help in any way so this wouldn't happen again to any of the generations coming up after us . . . I am happy to be here this day to bear testimony of this."

The decision not to blame others seems an important part not only of Mormon culture as Williams presents it but of

God-fearing people. This is just one story in an anthology of thousands.

Williams's own strategy. She has testified before Congress on these issues; I'd like to read that testimony. —A.L.

On May 10, 1984, Judge Bruce S. Jenkins handed down his opinion. Ten of the plaintiffs were awarded damages. It was the first time a federal court had determined that nuclear tests had been the cause of cancers. For the remaining fourteen test cases, the proof of causation was not sufficient. In spite of the split decision, it was considered a landmark ruling. It was not to remain so for long.

In April 1987, the Tenth Circuit Court of Appeals overturned Judge Jenkins's ruling on the ground that the United States was protected from suit by the legal doctrine of sovereign immunity, a centuries-old idea from England in the days of absolute monarchs.

Her treatment of sovereign immunity—like her discussion of Cold War nuclear terror—seems dismissive. —J.R.

In January 1988, the Supreme Court refused to review the Appeals Court decision. To our court system it does not matter whether the United States government was irresponsible, whether it lied to its citizens, or even that citizens died from the fallout of nuclear testing. What matters is that our government is immune: "The King can do no wrong."

In Mormon culture, authority is respected, obedience is revered, and independent thinking is not. I was taught as a young girl not to "make waves" or "rock the boat."

"Just let it go," Mother would say. "You know how you feel, that's what counts."

For many years, I have done just that—listened, observed, and quietly formed my own opinions, in a culture that rarely asks questions because it has all the answers. But one by one, I have watched the women in my family die common, heroic deaths. We sat in waiting rooms hoping for good news, but always receiving the bad. I cared for them, bathed their scarred bodies, and kept their secrets. I watched beautiful women become bald as Cytoxan, cisplatin, and Adriamycin were injected into their veins. I held their foreheads as they vomited green-black bile, and I shot them with morphine when the pain became inhuman. In the end, I witnessed their last peaceful breaths, becoming a midwife to the rebirth of their souls.

This section is hardest for me to read. Her descriptions, vivid and hurtful as they are, pale in comparison with real-life experiences with these deaths. —A.L.

Although this evokes strong feelings in the reader, it seems a little too graphic. —J.G.R.

The price of obedience has become too high.

The fear and inability to question authority that ultimately killed rural communities in Utah during atmospheric testing of atomic weapons is the same fear I saw in my mother's body. Sheep. Dead sheep. The evidence is buried.

The paragraph would be more powerful without the phrase "But I can't prove they didn't." Citing evidence from her own experience might work better than raising the prickly matter of proving causality. —J.R.

I cannot prove that my mother, Diane Dixon Tempest, or my grandmothers, Lettie Romney Dixon and Kathryn Blackett Tempest, along with my aunts developed cancer from nuclear fallout in Utah. But I can't prove they didn't.

Exact causation is notoriously difficult to prove in almost any case. Perhaps our legal system needs to admit other kinds of proof? —A.L.

My father's memory was correct. The September blast we drove through in 1957 was part of Operation Plumbbob, one of the most intensive series of bomb tests to be initiated. The flash of light in the night in the desert, which I had always thought was a dream, developed into a family nightmare. It took fourteen years, from 1957 to 1971, for cancer to manifest in my mother—the same time Howard L. Andrews, an authority in radioactive fallout at the National Institutes of Health, says radiation cancer requires to become evident. The more I learn about what it means to be a "downwinder," the more questions I drown in.

What I do know, however, is that as a Mormon woman of the fifth generation of Latter-day Saints, I must question everything, even if it means losing my faith, even if it means becoming a member of a border tribe among my own people. Tolerating blind obedience in the name of patriotism or religion ultimately takes our lives.

As I recall from the 1950s, religious groups were often in the forefront of "Ban the Bomb" movements. —J.R.

Where do we draw the line? When can we feel civil disobedience is justified, even demanded? These are questions Williams—like Gandhi, Thoreau, and King—asks us to consider. —A.L.

When the Atomic Energy Commission described the country north of the Nevada Test Site as "virtually uninhabited desert terrain," my family and the birds at Great Salt Lake were some of the "virtual uninhabitants."

A second "dream" is introduced into the essay. Like the first dream, I wonder if this one is somehow related to a real event. —A.L.

One night, I dreamed women from all over the world circled a blazing fire in the desert. They spoke of change, how they hold the moon in their bellies and wax and wane with its phases. They mocked the presumption of even-tempered beings and made promises that they would never fear the witch inside themselves. The women danced wildly as sparks broke away from the flames and entered the night sky as stars.

And they sang a song given to them by Shoshone grandmothers:

Ah ne nah, nah	Consider the rabbits
nin nah nah—	How gently they walk on the earth—
ah ne nah, nah	Consider the rabbits
nin nah nah—	How gently they walk on the earth—
Nyaga mutzi	We remember them
oh ne nay—	We can walk gently also—
Nyaga mutzi	We remember them
oh ne nay—	We can walk gently also—

The little I know of Native American cultures suggests that the reverence for the earth that Williams draws on here is a powerful force. —A.L.

The women danced and drummed and sang for weeks, preparing themselves for what was to come. They would reclaim the desert for the sake of their children, for the sake of the land.

I read this section as a dream vision of the sort common among mystical poets imagining alternative worlds. —J.R

A few miles downwind from the fire circle, bombs were being tested. Rabbits felt the tremors. Their soft leather pads on paws and feet recognized the shaking sands, while the roots of mesquite and sage were smoldering. Rocks were hot from the inside out and dust devils hummed unnaturally. And each time there was another nuclear test, ravens watched the desert heave. Stretch marks appeared. The land was losing its muscle.

Here amid the images of death and destruction is an image of life—the "stretch marks" commonly experienced by women after giving birth. Williams seems to be returning to the earlier juxtaposition of life/death images. —A.L.

The women couldn't bear it any longer. They were mothers. They had suffered labor pains but always under the promise of birth. The red hot pains beneath the desert promised death only, as each bomb became a stillborn. A contract had been made and broken between human beings and the land. A new contract was being drawn by the women, who understood the fate of the earth as their own.

Under the cover of darkness, ten women slipped under a barbed-wire fence and entered the contaminated country. They were trespassing. They walked toward the town of Mercury, in moonlight, taking their cues from coyote, kit fox, antelope squirrel, and quail. They moved quietly and deliberately through the maze of Joshua trees. When a hint of daylight appeared they rested, drinking tea and sharing their rations of food. The women closed their eyes. The time had come to protest with the heart, that to deny one's genealogy with the earth was to commit treason against one's soul.

Are these the same Mormon women she said didn't drink tea at the beginning of this story? —J.G.R.

At dawn, the women draped themselves in mylar, wrapping long streamers of silver plastic around their arms to blow in the breeze. They wore clear masks, that became the faces of humanity. And when they arrived at the edge of Mercury, they carried all the butterflies of a summer day in their wombs. They paused to allow their courage to settle.

The town that forbids pregnant women and children to enter because of radiation risks was asleep. The women moved through the streets as winged messengers, twirling around each other in slow motion, peeking inside homes and watching the easy sleep of men and women. They were astonished by such stillness and periodically would utter a shrill note or low cry just to verify life.

The residents finally awoke to these strange apparitions. Some simply stared. Others called authorities, and in time, the women were apprehended by wary soldiers dressed in desert fatigues. They were taken to a white, square building on the other edge of Mercury. When asked who they were and why they were there, the women replied, "We are mothers and we have come to reclaim the desert for our children."

The soldiers arrested them. As the ten women were blindfolded and handcuffed, they began singing:

You can't forbid us everything
You can't forbid us to think—
You can't forbid our tears to flow
And you can't stop the songs that we sing.

The women continued to sing louder and louder, until they heard the voices of their sisters moving across the mesa:

It is unclear if this is still a dream or if it really happened. —J.G.R.

Ah ne nah, nah
nin nah nah—
Ah ne nah, nah
nin nah nah—

Nyaga mutzi
oh ne nay—
Nyaga mutzi
oh ne nay—

"Call for reinforcements," one soldier said.

"We have," interrupted one woman, "we have—and you have no idea of our numbers."

Williams exhibits the moral certitude common in the American tradition of civil disobedience, justifying crusades such as the civil rights and right-to-life movements. —J.R.

I crossed the line at the Nevada Test Site and was arrested with nine other Utahns for trespassing on military lands. They are still conducting nuclear tests in the desert. Ours was an act of civil disobedience. But as I walked toward the town of Mercury, it was more than a gesture of peace. It was a gesture on behalf of the Clan of One-Breasted Women.

So here is the actual equivalent of the dream, the point at which Williams answers her own questions about civil disobedience with personal action gesturing toward peace and "on behalf of the Clan of One-Breasted Women." —A.L.

As one officer cinched the handcuffs around my wrists, another frisked my body. She found a pen and a pad of paper tucked inside my left boot.

"And these?" she asked sternly.

Williams's pen and paper weapons—can they ever be a match for guns and bombs? In the past, they have proved more than equal. —A.L.

"Weapons," I replied.

Our eyes met. I smiled. She pulled the leg of my trousers back over my boot.

"Step forward, please," she said as she took my arm.

We were booked under an afternoon sun and bused to Tonopah, Nevada. It was a two-hour ride. This was familiar country. The Joshua trees standing their ground had been named by my ancestors, who believed they looked like prophets pointing west to the Promised Land. These were the same trees that bloomed each spring, flowers appearing like white flames in the Mojave. And I recalled a full moon in May, when Mother and I had walked among them, flushing out mourning doves and owls.

I'm surprised by the positive tone of the conclusion. It suggests that Williams hopes that the land will prevail, and that the "sweet smell of sage" can help women continue to bring forth life. —A.L.

The bus stopped short of town. We were released.

The officials thought it was a cruel joke to leave us stranded in the desert with no way to get home. What they didn't realize was that we were home, soul-centered and strong, women who recognized the sweet smell of sage as fuel for our spirits.

Afterwords

I take Terry Tempest Williams's piece to be operating on at least three levels. First, she is writing out her own grief at the pain and loss suffered by her mother, grandmothers, and six aunts, seven of whom had died of breast cancer at the time of this writing. Second, she is raising serious concerns about specific national policies that may well have left great parts of Utah and other western states toxic and extremely hazardous to human health. And third, she is offering an allegory about personal responsibility and civil disobedience, about the dual nature of scientific "advances," and about the need to protect and to celebrate the earth, our mutual home. Williams is not writing a traditional academic argument, in which she sets up building blocks of proof to support her. Instead, she is weaving several strands and stories here, trying to evoke not assent or capitulation but response—and responsibility—in her readers.

I agree with J.R. that citizens in a democracy will always have to face up to the hard decisions involved in "real-world struggles" such as the threat of the bomb. But I also believe that citizens need—and deserve—information about the hard choices leaders may be making. If we choose to trade a certain number of lives in order to deploy a weapon, let us at least know that we have made the choice. If we choose to damage the earth, and the earth's ability to regenerate itself, in order to pursue nuclear dominance, let us at least know what we are doing—and what the possible as well as the real consequences will be. Let us reject silence as well as the fear that too much knowing may cause in us. —A.L.

Certainly one appreciates the injury Terry Tempest Williams must feel at the unwillingness of the government to compensate Utah's civilian victims of nuclear testing. But I find her earth-mother visions off-putting and inappropriate. The Cold War that prompted the nuclear tests that likely destroyed much of her family was not a shaman's vision but a real-world struggle that ultimately liberated a quarter of the world's population. The threat of the bomb, the horrible power that Williams herself witnessed, tempered the ambitions of dictators cruel as Stalin and foolhardy as Mao—and probably spared us all a third world war. Home-front victims of this struggle, the members of Williams's family, obviously deserve remembrance, apology, and whatever compensation may give them slender comfort now. But I don't find any special wisdom in Terry Tempest Williams's essay—only a poetic but unfocused anger. —J.R.

Williams writes with a clear voice of her undeniable pain, suffering, and frustration. Her sincerity gives her story a tough edge. It is so honest that I am uncomfortable reading it.

I have one question, though: what about the men in her family? She never mentions any of the men getting cancer. Although she tells of her father witnessing a number of blasts, he is apparently alive. Are men immune from this radiation? No, since she gives an example of Irene Allen who lost two husbands to cancers supposedly from the effects of nuclear radiation. How can she be sure that the breast cancer is not heredi-

tary, if both Tempest men and women were equally exposed to the explosions but only the women have a history of cancer, and then of breast cancer only? I do not mean to suggest that her suffering could be any less than it is, but her perspective may be clouded by a severe personal bias. She may be giving the U.S. government a little too much blame and unlucky genes not enough. —J.G.R.

QUESTIONING THE TEXT

1. Williams says that she "cannot prove that my mother . . . or my grandmothers . . . along with my aunts developed cancer from nuclear fallout in Utah. But I can't prove they didn't" (p. 660). What strategies and pieces of evidence does Williams use to support her strong hunch that there is a relationship between the nuclear testing and the rate of cancer-related deaths?
2. Images of birth run alongside those of death in this essay. Reread the essay, highlighting all the images that have to do with birth. Then write an entry in your reading log (if you are keeping one) in which you reflect on how they add to the point Williams wants to make.
3. Why might Williams have decided to include her dream in this essay? How does it relate or speak to the section that immediately follows it?
4. What use does A.L. make of the metaphor "mother" in her introduction? How effective do you find the metaphor?

MAKING CONNECTIONS

5. Compare the role played by the earth in Williams's essay to its role in Ed Madden's "Family Cemetery, near Hickory Ridge, Arkansas" (p. 711). What does the natural world seem to signify for the family gathered for a funeral in Madden's poem? What has happened to the earth in Williams's piece? Reflect upon these differences in a paragraph or a reading log entry.
6. Both Williams and Barbara Dafoe Whitehead (p. 667) raise important questions about responsibility. What *is* a citizen's responsibility in the face of the kinds of urgent social and environmental problems they describe? Meet with two or three classmates to discuss how Whitehead and Williams might respond to this question. Then, working as a group or as individuals, write an essay about what a citizen's responsibility should be on a particular topic: nuclear testing and fallout, divorce, teen pregnancy, or any issue in which you feel citizens, yourself included, have much at stake.

JOINING THE CONVERSATION

7. Look into the environmental history of your city, region, or state, searching for issues of concern about the quality of water or air, for example. Then freewrite for half an hour or so about the issues that most concern you. What environmental hazards might you have encountered while you were growing up? Or was your region completely safe from contaminants? After you choose a topic and determine your stance on it, write a letter to the editor of your hometown newspaper raising the issues that concern you.
8. Williams describes a dream that in some ways turns out to be closely related to a real-life experience. How have your dreams been related to either predream or postdream real-life occurrences? In a brief essay, explore the relationships between "dream life" and "real life." If you keep a reading log, answer this question there.
9. Williams describes an act of civil disobedience in which she and other women took part. Spend some time thinking about your position on civil disobedience: when it is justified, when you would take such actions, when you would not take them, and so on. You might read about other acts of civil disobedience, such as those of Henry David Thoreau, Mahatma Gandhi, Martin Luther King Jr., or Rosa Parks. Then write a position paper explaining where you stand on the issue of civil disobedience and supporting your position with examples from your own, and others', experiences.

BARBARA DAFOE WHITEHEAD
The Making of a Divorce Culture

GROWING UP IN THE 1950S, I knew only one classmate whose parents were divorced. In my tight ethnic neighborhood, stable two-parent families were the rule, and divorce was something observed only occasionally on the silver screen. In fact, families breaking up seemed very much a Hollywood phenomenon. But Hollywood soon rubbed off on the rest of us.

Within a generation, we came to accept divorce as almost normal. But normal *here simply means that divorces now happen all the time, not that the pain of separation they cause has become easier to endure, especially for children. For me, that point was made most forcefully the first time I taught this "Home" chapter in an earlier edition of* The Presence of Others. *In class discussions, we explored all sorts of family concerns—from the changing role of fathers to conditions in nursing homes—but we had skirted one burning issue that emerged spontaneously as the theme of more than half the papers the unit produced. In draft after searing draft, my students detailed their personal and inevitably painful experiences with divorce. As we reviewed the drafts in subsequent class sessions, the writers often turned to each other for understanding and support as they recounted their feelings of hurt and betrayal. Clearly, for many students today, divorce has become a central event in their lives, shaping their views and attitudes toward family, commitment, and relationships with members of the opposite sex.*

Although it has become fashionable to talk about the normalcy of single parenthood and other nontraditional family arrangements, Barbara Dafoe Whitehead (b. 1944) argues that the willingness of American culture to accept divorce is genuinely new. A registered Democrat, Whitehead first came to public attention with an article she published in Atlantic Monthly *with the now-famous title "Dan Quayle Was Right" (April 1993). In the piece, Whitehead, wielding numerous studies and statistics, argues that then-vice president Quayle had correctly identified a major problem in American society when he attacked TV sitcom mom Murphy Brown for celebrating single parenthood. The argument of Whitehead's influential piece evolved into her* The Divorce Culture *(1997), a book-length study of the causes and consequences of soaring divorce rates in America. "The Making of a Divorce Culture" is the introduction to Whitehead's book. Married and the mother of three children, Whitehead has a Ph.D. from the University of Chicago. Her most recent book is* Why There Are No Good Men Left *(2002).*

—J.R.

Divorce is now part of everyday American life. It is embedded in our laws and institutions, our manners and mores, our movies and television shows, our novels and children's storybooks, and our closest and most important relationships. Indeed, divorce has become so pervasive that many people naturally assume it has seeped into the social and cultural mainstream over a long period of time. Yet this is not the case. Divorce has become an American way of life only as the result of recent and revolutionary change.

The entire history of American divorce can be divided into two periods, one evolutionary and the other revolutionary. For most of the nation's history, divorce was a rare occurrence and an insignificant feature of family and social relationships. In the first sixty years of the twentieth century, divorce became more common, but it was hardly commonplace. In 1960, the divorce rate stood at a still relatively modest level of nine per one thousand married couples. After 1960, however, the rate accelerated at a dazzling pace. It doubled in roughly a decade and continued its upward climb until the early 1980s, when it stabilized at the highest level among advanced Western societies. As a consequence of this sharp and sustained rise, divorce moved from the margins to the mainstream of American life in the space of three decades.

Ideas are important in revolutions, yet surprisingly little attention has been devoted to the ideas that gave impetus to the divorce revolution. Of the scores of books on divorce published in recent decades, most focus on its legal, demographic, economic, or (especially) psychological dimensions. Few, if any, deal fully with its intellectual origins. Yet trying to comprehend the divorce revolution and its consequences without some sense of its ideological origins, is like trying to understand the American Revolution without taking into account the thinking of John Locke, Thomas Jefferson, or Thomas Paine. This more recent revolution, like the revolution of our nation's founding, has its roots in a distinctive set of ideas and claims.

This book [*The Divorce Culture*] is about the ideas behind the divorce revolution and how these ideas have shaped a culture of divorce. The making of a divorce culture has involved three overlapping changes: first, the emergence and widespread diffusion of a historically new and distinctive set of ideas about divorce in the last third of the twentieth century; second, the migration of divorce from a minor place within a system governed by marriage to a freestanding place as a major institution governing family relationships; and third, a widespread shift in thinking about the obligations of marriage and parenthood.

Beginning in the late 1950s, Americans began to change their ideas 5
about the individual's obligations to family and society. Broadly described, this change was away from an ethic of obligation to others and toward an obligation to self. I do not mean that people suddenly abandoned all responsibilities to others, but rather that they became more acutely conscious of their responsibility to attend to their own individual needs and interests. At least as important as the moral obligation to look after others, the new thinking suggested, was the moral obligation to look after oneself.

This ethical shift had a profound impact on ideas about the nature and purpose of the family. In the American tradition, the marketplace and the public square have represented the realms of life devoted to the pursuit of individual interest, choice, and freedom, while the family has been the realm defined by voluntary commitment, duty, and self-sacrifice. With the greater emphasis on individual satisfaction in family relationships, however, family well-being became subject to a new metric. More than in the past, satisfaction in this sphere came to be based on subjective judgments about the content and quality of individual happiness rather than on such objective measures as level of income, material nurture and support, or boosting children onto a higher rung on the socioeconomic ladder. People began to judge the strength and "health" of family bonds according to their capacity to promote individual fulfillment and personal growth. As a result, the conception of the family's role and place in the society began to change. The family began to lose its separate place and distinctive identity as the realm of duty, service, and sacrifice. Once the domain of the obligated self, the family was increasingly viewed as yet another domain for the expression of the unfettered self.

These broad changes figured centrally in creating a new conception of divorce which gained influential adherents and spread broadly and swiftly throughout the society—a conception that represented a radical departure from earlier notions. Once regarded mainly as a social, legal, and family event in which there were other stakeholders, divorce now became an event closely linked to the pursuit of individual satisfactions, opportunities, and growth.

The new conception of divorce drew upon some of the oldest, and most resonant, themes in the American political tradition. The nation, after all, was founded as the result of a political divorce, and revolutionary thinkers explicitly adduced a parallel between the dissolution of marital bonds and the dissolution of political bonds. In political as well as marital relationships, they argued, bonds of obligation were established voluntarily on the basis of mutual affection and regard. Once such bonds turned cold and oppressive, peoples, like individuals, had the right to dissolve them and to form more perfect unions.

In the new conception of divorce, this strain of eighteenth-century political thought mingled with a strain of twentieth-century psychotherapeutic thought. Divorce was not only an individual right but also a psychological resource. The dissolution of marriage offered the chance to make oneself over from the inside out, to refurbish and express the inner self, and to acquire certain valuable psychological assets and competencies, such as initiative, assertiveness, and a stronger and better self-image.

10 The conception of divorce as both an individual right and an inner experience merged with and reinforced the new ethic of obligation to the self. In family relationships, one had an obligation to be attentive to one's own feelings and to work toward improving the quality of one's inner life. This ethical imperative completed the rationale for a sense of individual entitlement to divorce. Increasingly, mainstream America saw the legal dissolution of marriage as a matter of individual choice, in which there were no other stakeholders or larger social interests. This conception of divorce strongly argued for removing the social, legal, and moral impediments to the free exercise of the individual right to divorce.

Traditionally, one major impediment to divorce was the presence of children in the family. According to well-established popular belief, dependent children had a stake in their parents' marriage and suffered hardship as a result of the dissolution of the marriage. Because children were vulnerable and dependent, parents had a moral obligation to place their children's interests in the marital partnership above their own individual satisfactions. This notion was swiftly abandoned after the 1960s. Influential voices in the society, including child-welfare professionals, claimed that the happiness of individual parents, rather than an intact marriage, was the key determinant of children's family well-being. If divorce could make one or both parents happier, then it was likely to improve the well-being of children as well.

In the following decades, the new conception of divorce spread through the law, therapy, etiquette, the social sciences, popular advice literature, and religion. Concerns that had dominated earlier thinking on divorce were now dismissed as old-fashioned and excessively moralistic. Divorce would not harm children but would lead to greater happiness for children and their single parents. It would not damage the institution of marriage but would make possible better marriages and happier individuals. Divorce would not damage the social fabric by diminishing children's life chances but would strengthen the social fabric by improving the quality of affective bonds between parents and children, whatever form the structural arrangements of their families might happen to take.

As the sense of divorce as an individual freedom and entitlement grew, the sense of concern about divorce as a social problem diminished. Earlier in the century, each time the divorce rate increased sharply, it had inspired widespread public concern and debate about the harmful impact of divorce on families and the society. But in the last third of the century, as the divorce rate rose to once unthinkable levels, public anxiety about it all but vanished. At the very moment when divorce had its most profound impact on the society, weakening the institution of marriage, revolutionizing the structure of families and reorganizing parent-child relationships, it ceased to be a source of concern or debate.

The lack of attention to divorce became particularly striking after the 1980s, as a politically polarized debate over the state of the American family took shape. On one side, conservatives pointed to abortion, illegitimacy, and homosexuality as forces destroying the family. On the other, liberals cited domestic violence, economic insecurity, and inadequate public supports as the key problems afflicting the family. But politicians on both sides had almost nothing to say about divorce. Republicans did not want to alienate their upscale constituents or their libertarian wing, both of whom tended to favor easy divorce, nor did they want to call attention to the divorces among their own leadership. Democrats did not want to anger their large constituency among women who saw easy divorce as a hard-won freedom and prerogative, nor did they wish to seem unsympathetic to single mothers. Thus, except for bipartisan calls to get tougher with deadbeat dads, both Republicans and Democrats avoided the issue of divorce and its consequences as far too politically risky.

But the failure to address divorce carried a price. It allowed the middle 15
class to view family breakdown as a "them" problem rather than an "us" problem. Divorce was not like illegitimacy or welfare dependency, many claimed. It was a matter of individual choice, imposing few, if any, costs or consequences on others. Thus, mainstream America could cling to the comfortable illusion that the nation's family problems had to do with the behavior of unwed teenage mothers or poor women on welfare rather than with the instability of marriage and family life within its own ranks.

Nonetheless, after thirty years of persistently high levels of divorce, this illusion, though still politically attractive, is increasingly difficult to sustain in the face of a growing body of experience and evidence. To begin with, divorce has indeed hurt children. It has created economic insecurity and disadvantage for many children who would not otherwise be economically vulnerable. It has led to more fragile and unstable family households. It has caused a mass exodus of fathers from children's households and, all too often, from their lives. It has reduced the levels of parental time and money invested in children. In sum, it has changed the very nature of American childhood. Just as no patient would have designed today's system of health care, so no child would have chosen today's culture of divorce.

Divorce figures prominently in the altered economic fortunes of middle-class families. Although the economic crisis of the middle class is usually described as a problem caused by global economic changes, changing patterns in education and earnings, and ruthless corporate downsizing, it owes more to divorce than is commonly acknowledged. Indeed, recent data suggest that marriage may be a more important economic resource than a college degree. According to an analysis of 1994 income patterns, the median income of married-parent households whose heads have only a high school diploma is ten percent higher than the median income of college-educated single-parent households.[1] Parents who are college graduates *and* married form the new economic elite among families with children. Consequently, those who are concerned about what the downsizing of corporations is doing to workers should also be concerned about what the downsizing of families through divorce is doing to parents and children.

Widespread divorce depletes social capital as well. Scholars tell us that strong and durable family and social bonds generate certain "goods" and

---

[1]An analysis of income data provided by The Northeastern University Center for Labor Market Studies shows the following distribution by education and marital status:

Median Incomes for U.S. Families with Children, 1994

Education of Household Head	*Married Couple Families*	*Single Parent Families*
College Graduate	$71,263	$36,006
High School Graduate	$40,098	$14,698

Based on 1994 Current Population Statistics. Families with one or more children under 18. Age of household head: 22–62.

services, including money, mutual assistance, information, caregiving, protection, and sponsorship. Because such bonds endure over time, they accumulate and form a pool of social capital which can be drawn down upon, when needed, over the entire course of a life. An elderly couple, married for fifty years, is likely to enjoy a substantial body of social and emotional capital, generated through their long-lasting marriage, which they can draw upon in caring for each other and for themselves as they age. Similarly, children who grow up in stable, two-parent married households are the beneficiaries of the social and emotional capital accumulated over time as a result of an enduring marriage bond. As many parents know, children continue to depend on these resources well into young adulthood. But as family bonds become increasingly fragile and vulnerable to disruption, they become less permanent and thus less capable of generating such forms of help, financial resources, and mutual support. In short, divorce consumes social capital and weakens the social fabric. At the very time that sweeping socioeconomic changes are mandating greater investment of social capital in children, widespread divorce is reducing the pool of social capital. As the new economic and social conditions raise the hurdles of child-rearing higher, divorce digs potholes in the tracks.

It should be stressed that this book is not intended as a brief against divorce as such. We must assume that divorce is necessary as a remedy for irretrievably broken marriages, especially those that are marred by severe abuse such as chronic infidelity, drug addiction, or physical violence. Nor is its argument directed against those who are divorced. It assumes that divorce is difficult, painful, and often unwanted by at least one spouse, and that divorcing couples require compassion and support from family, friends, and their religious communities. Nor should this book be taken as an appeal for a return to an earlier era of American family life. The media routinely portray the debate over the family as one between nostalgists and realists, between those who want to turn back the clock to the fifties and those who want to march bravely and resolutely forward into the new century. But this is a lazy and misguided approach, driven more by the easy availability of archival photos and footage from 1950s television sitcoms than by careful consideration of the substance of competing arguments.

More fundamentally, this approach overlooks the key issue. And that 20
issue is not how today's families might stack up against those of an earlier era; indeed, no reliable empirical data for such a comparison exist. In an age of diverse family structures, the heart of the matter is what kinds of contemporary family arrangements have the greatest capacity to promote children's well-being, and how we can ensure that more children have the advantages of growing up in such families.

In the past year or so, there has been growing recognition of the personal and social costs of three decades of widespread divorce. A public debate has finally emerged. Within this debate, there are two separate and overlapping discussions.

The first centers on a set of specific proposals that are intended to lessen the harmful impact of divorce on children: a federal system of child-support collection, tougher child-support enforcement, mandatory counseling for divorcing parents, and reform of no-fault divorce laws in the states. What is striking about this discussion is its narrow focus on public policy, particularly on changes in the system of no-fault divorce. In this, as in so many other crucial discussions involving social and moral questions, the most vocal and visible participants come from the world of government policy, electoral politics, and issue advocacy. The media, which are tongue-tied unless they can speak in the language of left-right politics, reinforce this situation. And the public is offered needlessly polarized arguments that hang on a flat yes-or-no response to this or that individual policy measure. All too often, this discussion of divorce poses what *Washington Post* columnist E. J. Dionne aptly describes as false choices.

Notably missing is a serious consideration of the broader moral assumptions and empirical claims that define our divorce culture. Divorce touches on classic questions in American public philosophy—on the nature of our most important human and social bonds, the duties and obligations imposed by bonds we voluntarily elect, the "just causes" for the dissolution of those bonds, and the differences between obligations volunteered and those that must be coerced. Without consideration of such questions, the effort to change behavior by changing a few public policies is likely to founder.

The second and complementary discussion does try to place divorce within a larger philosophical framework. Its proponents have looked at the decline in the well-being of the nation's children as the occasion to call for a collective sense of commitment by all Americans to all of America's children. They pose the challenging question: "What are Americans willing to do 'for the sake of *all* children'?" But while this is surely an important question, it addresses only half of the problem of declining commitment. The other half has to do with how we answer the question: "What are individual parents obliged to do 'for the sake of their own children'?"

Renewing a *social* ethic of commitment to children is an urgent goal, but 25
it cannot be detached from the goal of strengthening the *individual* ethic of commitment to children. The state of one affects the standing of the other. A society that protects the rights of parents to easy, unilateral divorce, and flatly rejects the idea that parents should strive to preserve a marriage "for the sake of the children," faces a problem when it comes to the question of public sacrifice "for the sake of the children." To put it plainly, many of the ideas we have come to believe and vigorously defend about adult prerogatives and freedoms in family life are undermining the foundations of altruism and support for children.

With each passing year, the culture of divorce becomes more deeply entrenched. American children are routinely schooled in divorce. Mr. Rogers teaches toddlers about divorce. An entire children's literature is devoted to divorce. Family movies and videos for children feature divorced families. *Mrs. Doubtfire,* originally a children's book about divorce and then a hit movie, is aggressively marketed as a holiday video for kids. Of course, these books and movies are designed to help children deal with the social reality and psychological trauma of divorce. But they also carry an unmistakable message about the impermanence and unreliability of family bonds. Like romantic love, the children's storybooks say, family love comes and goes. Daddies disappear. Mommies find new boyfriends. Mommies' boyfriends leave. Grandparents go away. Even pets must be left behind.

More significantly, in a society where nearly half of all children are likely to experience parental divorce, family breakup becomes a defining event of American childhood itself. Many children today know nothing but divorce in their family lives. And although children from divorced families often say they want to avoid divorce if they marry, young adults whose parents divorced are more likely to get divorced themselves and to bear children outside of marriage than young adults from stable married-parent families.

Precisely because the culture of divorce has generational momentum, this book [*The Divorce Culture*] offers no easy optimism about the prospects for change. But neither does it counsel passive resignation or acceptance of the culture's relentless advance. What it does offer is a critique of the ideas behind current divorce trends. Its argument is directed against the ideas about divorce that have gained ascendancy, won our support, and lodged in our consciousness as "proven" and incontrovertible. It challenges the popular idea of divorce as an individual right and freedom to be exercised in the pursuit of individual goods and satisfactions, without due regard for other stakeholders in the marital partnership, especially children. This may be a fragile and inadequate response to a profoundly consequential set of changes, but it seeks the abandonment of ideas that have misled us and failed our children.

In a larger sense, this book is both an appreciation and a criticism of what is peculiarly American about divorce. Divorce has spread throughout advanced Western societies at roughly the same pace and over roughly the same period of time. Yet nowhere else has divorce been so deeply imbued with the larger themes of a nation's political traditions. Nowhere has divorce so fully reflected the spirit and susceptibilities of a people who share an extravagant faith in the power of the individual and in the power of positive thinking. Divorce in America is not unique, but what we have made of divorce is uniquely American. In exploring the cultural roots of divorce, therefore, we look at ourselves, at what is best and worst in our traditions, what is visionary and what is blind, and how the two are sometimes tragically commingled and confused.

QUESTIONING THE TEXT

1. Whitehead claims in the opening sentence that "[d]ivorce is now part of everyday American life." What evidence can you point to—from popular culture, American society, or your own experience—to support *or* refute that claim?

2. Arguing that the increasing divorce rate is due, in part, to a shift in the way marriage is viewed, Whitehead says Americans have moved from an ethic of obligation within families to an ethic of self-fulfillment. Working in a group, explore these abstractions and try to give them a more concrete shape. When does a family member act according to an ethic of obligation and when according to an ethic of self-fulfillment? How compatible are these different views of the family?

MAKING CONNECTIONS

3. Whitehead mentions a "goal of strengthening the *individual* ethic of commitment to children" (paragraph 25). In a brief essay, explore this notion more fully, using the selections by Ron Suskind (p. 634) and David Sedaris (p. 697) to furnish examples of such parental commitment. If appropriate, draw on examples from your own experience as well.
4. Read "The Rules about the Rules" (p. 179), from Stephen L. Carter's book *Integrity,* paying special attention to the three criteria Carter uses to define an act of integrity. Then write an essay in which you explore when and/or whether a divorce can fit that definition.

JOINING THE CONVERSATION

5. Whitehead disputes the popular argument that children are better off when divorce "make[s] one or both parents happier" (paragraph 11), suggesting that many contemporary problems can be traced to broken families. Write an essay exploring the consequences of divorce for children. For support, draw on library materials, your personal experience, and, possibly, firsthand information gathered through interviews.
6. Whitehead largely dismisses a series of public policy proposals "intended to lessen the harmful impact of divorce on children: a federal system of child-support collection, tougher child-support enforcement, mandatory counseling for divorcing parents, and reform of no-fault divorce laws in the states" (paragraph 22). Working in a group, discuss these and other options for making divorce less devastating for children, as well as ideas for making families more stable and successful. Then write a proposal paper on your own explaining one such idea. Your proposal need not endorse Whitehead's ideas about the causes or consequences of divorce.

STEPHANIE COONTZ
The Way We Wish We Were

*A*MERICANS PAY A HIGH PRICE *for their nostalgia about "traditional" families and homes, argues Stephanie Coontz in* The Way We Never Were: American Families and the Nostalgia Trap *(1992). In Coontz's view, as her title suggests, the good old days so many people long for never actually existed, and the futile effort to restore them keeps Americans from seeking realistic ways to enhance family life in the twenty-first century.*

In the following chapter from her book, Coontz (b. 1944), a professor of history and family studies at Evergreen State College in Washington, traces changes in American family life and values from colonial times to the present, in each case emphasizing the complexity of family relationships; the shifting influence of social, political, and economic changes on families; and the often careless use of statistical data to make shaky claims about families. The impact of Coontz's work has been substantial: she has served as a consultant for many government and community agencies interested in children and families. Her most recent books, The Way We Really Are: Coming to Terms with America's Changing Families *(1997) and* American Families: A Multicultural Reader *(1998), continue to provide rich and complex explorations of the meaning of family life in the United States.*

I chose this selection in part because recent discussions in my classes tend to support Coontz's claim that students' key images of the "traditional family" are often related to television representations of family life. In addition, I quite like the title of her chapter: "The Way We Wish We Were." Where home and family are concerned, my guess is that such wishes are widely divergent—and that they will be fascinating to discuss. —A.L.

When I begin teaching a course on family history, I often ask my students to write down ideas that spring to mind when they think of the "traditional family." Their lists always include several images. One is of extended families in which all members worked together, grandparents were an integral part of family life, children learned responsibility and the work ethic from their elders, and there were clear lines of authority based on respect for age. Another is of nuclear families in which nurturing mothers sheltered children from premature exposure to sex, financial worries, or other adult concerns, while fathers taught adolescents not to sacrifice their education by going to work too early. Still another image gives pride of place to the couple relationship. In traditional families, my students write—half derisively, half wistfully—men and women remained chaste until marriage, at which time they extricated themselves from competing obligations to kin and neighbors and committed themselves wholly to the marital relationship, experiencing an all-encompassing intimacy that our more crowded modern life seems to preclude. As one freshman wrote: "They truly respected the marriage vowels"; I assume she meant *I-O-U*.

Such visions of past family life exert a powerful emotional pull on most Americans, and with good reason, given the fragility of many modern commitments. The problem is not only that these visions bear a suspicious resemblance to reruns of old television series, but also that the scripts of different shows have been mixed up: June Cleaver suddenly has a Grandpa Walton dispensing advice in her kitchen; Donna Stone, vacuuming the living room in her inevitable pearls and high heels, is no longer married to a busy modern pediatrician but to a small-town sheriff who, like Andy Taylor* of *The Andy Griffith Show,* solves community problems through informal, old-fashioned common sense.

Like most visions of a "golden age," the "traditional family" my students describe evaporates on closer examination. It is an ahistorical amalgam of structures, values, and behaviors that never coexisted in the same time and place. The notion that traditional families fostered intense intimacy between husbands and wives while creating mothers who were totally available to their children, for example, is an idea that combines some characteristics of the white, middle-class family in the mid-nineteenth century and some of a rival family ideal first articulated in the 1920s. The first family revolved emotionally around the mother-child axis, leaving the husband-wife relationship stilted and formal. The second focused on an eroticized couple relationship, demanding that mothers curb emotional "overinvestment" in their children. The hybrid idea that a woman can be fully absorbed with her youngsters while simultaneously maintaining passionate sexual excitement with her husband was a 1950s invention that drove thousands of women to therapists, tranquilizers, or alcohol when they actually tried to live up to it.

Similarly, an extended family in which all members work together under the top-down authority of the household elder operates very differently from a nuclear family in which husband and wife are envisioned as friends who patiently devise ways to let the children learn by trial and error. Children who worked in family enterprises seldom had time for the extracurricular activities that Wally and the Beaver* recounted to their parents over the dinner table; often, they did not even go to school full-time. Mothers who did home production generally relegated child care to older children or servants; they did not suspend work to savor a baby's first steps or discuss with their husband how to facilitate a grade-schooler's "self-esteem." Such families emphasized formality, obedience to authority, and "the way it's always been" in their childrearing.

June Cleaver . . . Andy Taylor: Characters in various family-oriented television series. June Cleaver played a housewife in *Leave It to Beaver;* Donna Stone was a housewife in *The Donna Reed Show;* Andy Taylor was the sheriff of Mayberry in *The Andy Griffith Show.*

Wally and the Beaver: brothers in the television sitcom *Leave It to Beaver*

Nuclear families, by contrast, have tended to pride themselves on the 5
"modernity" of parent-child relations, diluting the authority of grandparents, denigrating "old-fashioned" ideas about childraising, and resisting the "interference" of relatives. It is difficult to imagine the Cleavers or the college-educated title figure of *Father Knows Best* letting grandparents, maiden aunts, or in-laws have a major voice in childrearing decisions. Indeed, the kind of family exemplified by the Cleavers . . . represented a conscious *rejection* of the Waltons' model.

The Elusive Traditional Family

Whenever people propose that we go back to the traditional family, I always suggest that they pick a ballpark date for the family they have in mind. Once pinned down, they are invariably unwilling to accept the package deal that comes with their chosen model. Some people, for example, admire the discipline of colonial families, which were certainly not much troubled by divorce or fragmenting individualism. But colonial families were hardly stable: High mortality rates meant that the average length of marriage was less than a dozen years. One-third to one-half of all children lost at least one parent before the age of twenty-one; in the South, more than half of all children aged thirteen or under had lost at least one parent.[1]

While there are a few modern Americans who would like to return to the strict patriarchal authority of colonial days, in which disobedience by women and children was considered a small form of treason, these individuals would doubtless be horrified by other aspects of colonial families, such as their failure to protect children from knowledge of sexuality. Eighteenth-century spelling and grammar books routinely used *fornication* as an example of a four-syllable word, and preachers detailed sexual offenses in astonishingly explicit terms. Sexual conversations between men and women, even in front of children, were remarkably frank. It is worth contrasting this colonial candor to the climate in 1991, when the Department of Health and Human Services was forced to cancel a proposed survey of teenagers' sexual practices after some groups charged that such knowledge might "inadvertently" encourage more sex.[2]

---

[1]Philip Greven, *Four Generations: Population, Land, and Family in Colonial Andover, Massachusetts* (Ithaca, N.Y.: Cornell University Press, 1970); Vivian Fox and Martin Quit, *Loving, Parenting, and Dying: The Family Cycle in England and America, Past and Present* (New York: Psychohistory Press, 1980), p. 401.

[2]John Demos, *A Little Commonwealth: Family Life in Plymouth Colony* (New York: Oxford University Press, 1970), p. 108; Mary Ryan, *Cradle of the Middle Class: The Family in Oneida County, New York, 1790–1865* (New York: Cambridge University Press, 1981), pp. 33, 38–39; Carroll Smith-Rosenberg, *Disorderly Conduct: Visions of Gender in Victorian America* (New York: Oxford University Press, 1985), p. 24.

Other people searching for an ideal traditional family might pick the more sentimental and gentle Victorian family, which arose in the 1830s and 1840s as household production gave way to wage work and professional occupations outside the home. A new division of labor by age and sex emerged among the middle class. Women's roles were redefined in terms of domesticity rather than production, men were labeled "breadwinners" (a masculine identity unheard of in colonial days), children were said to need time to play, and gentle maternal guidance supplanted the patriarchal authoritarianism of the past.

But the middle-class Victorian family depended for its existence on the multiplication of other families who were too poor and powerless to retreat into their own little oases and who therefore had to provision the oases of others. Childhood was prolonged for the nineteenth-century middle class only because it was drastically foreshortened for other sectors of the population. The spread of textile mills, for example, freed middle-class women from the most time-consuming of their former chores, making cloth. But the raw materials for these mills were produced by slave labor. Slave children were not exempt from field labor unless they were infants, and even then their mothers were not allowed time off to nurture them. Frederick Douglass* could not remember seeing his mother until he was seven.[3]

Domesticity was also not an option for the white families who worked 10
twelve hours a day in Northern factories and workshops transforming slave-picked cotton into ready-made clothing. By 1820, "half the workers in many factories were boys and girls who had not reached their eleventh birthday." Rhode Island investigators found "little half-clothed children" making their way to the textile mills before dawn. In 1845, shoemaking families and makers of artificial flowers worked fifteen to eighteen hours a day, according to the New York *Daily Tribune*.[4]

Within the home, prior to the diffusion of household technology at the end of the century, house cleaning and food preparation remained mammoth tasks. Middle-class women were able to shift more time into childrearing in this period only by hiring domestic help. Between 1800 and 1850, the proportion of servants to white households doubled, to about one in nine. Some servants were poverty-stricken mothers who had to board or bind out their own children. Employers found such workers tended to be "distracted," however; they usually preferred young girls. In his study of Buffalo, New

---

Frederick Douglass (1817–95): Son of a slave mother and white father, Douglass became an abolitionist leader and eloquent advocate for human rights.

[3]Frederick Douglass, *My Bondage and My Freedom* (New York: Dover, 1968), p. 48.

[4]David Roediger and Philip Foner, *Our Own Time: A History of American Labor and the Working Day* (London: Greenwood, 1989), p. 9; Norman Ware, *The Industrial Worker, 1840–1860* (New York: Quadrangle, 1964), p. 5; Barbara Wertheimer, *We Were There: The Story of Working Women in America* (New York: Pantheon, 1977), p. 91; Sean Wilentz, *Chants Democratic: New York City and the Rise of the Working Class, 1788–1850* (New York: Oxford University Press, 1984), p. 126.

York, in the 1850s, historian Lawrence Glasco found that Irish and German girls often went into service at the age of eleven or twelve.[5]

For every nineteenth-century middle-class family that protected its wife and child within the family circle, then, there was an Irish or a German girl scrubbing floors in that middle-class home, a Welsh boy mining coal to keep the home-baked goodies warm, a black girl doing the family laundry, a black mother and child picking cotton to be made into clothes for the family, and a Jewish or an Italian daughter in a sweatshop making "ladies" dresses or artificial flowers for the family to purchase.

Furthermore, people who lived in these periods were seldom as enamored of their family arrangements as modern nostalgia might suggest. Colonial Americans lamented "the great neglect in many parents and masters in training up their children" and expressed the "greatest trouble and grief about the rising generation." No sooner did Victorian middle-class families begin to withdraw their children from the work world than observers began to worry that children were becoming *too* sheltered. By 1851, the Reverend Horace Bushnell spoke for many in bemoaning the passing of the traditional days of household production, when the whole family was "harnessed, all together, into the producing process, young and old, male and female, from the boy who rode the plough-horse to the grandmother knitting under her spectacles."[6]

The late nineteenth century saw a modest but significant growth of extended families and a substantial increase in the number of families who were "harnessed" together in household production. Extended families have never been the norm in America; the highest figure for extended-family households ever recorded in American history is 20 percent. Contrary to the popular myth that industrialization destroyed "traditional" extended families, this high point occurred between 1850 and 1885, during the most intensive period of early industrialization. Many of these extended families, and most "producing" families of the time, depended on the labor of children; they were held together by dire necessity and sometimes by brute force.[7]

---

[5]Faye Dudden, *Serving Women: Household Service in Nineteenth-Century America* (Middletown, Conn.: Wesleyan University Press, 1983), p. 206; Susan Strasser, *Never Done: A History of American Housework* (New York: Pantheon, 1982); Lawrence Glasco, "The Life Cycles and Household Structure of American Ethnic Groups, in *A Heritage of Her Own: Toward a New Social History of American Women,* ed. Nancy Cott and Elizabeth Pleck (New York: Simon & Schuster, 1979), pp. 281, 285.

[6]Robert Bremmer et al., eds., *Children and Youth in America: A Documentary History* (Cambridge: Harvard University Press, 1970), vol. 1, p. 39; Barbara Cross, *Horace Bushnell: Minister to a Changing America* (Chicago: University of Chicago Press, 1958); Ann Douglas, *The Feminization of American Culture* (New York: Knopf, 1977), p. 52.

[7]Peter Laslett, "Characteristics of the Western Family Over Time," in *Family Life and Illicit Love in Earlier Generations,* ed. Peter Laslett (New York: Cambridge University Press, 1977); William Goode, *World Revolution and Family Patterns* (New York: Free Press, 1963); Michael Anderson, *Family Structure in Nineteenth-Century Lancashire* (Cambridge, England: Cambridge University Press, 1971); Tamara Hareven, ed., *Transitions: The Family and the Life Course in Historical*

There was a significant increase in child labor during the last third of the 15
nineteenth century. Some children worked at home in crowded tenement sweatshops that produced cigars or women's clothing. Reformer Helen Campbell found one house where "nearly thirty children of all ages and sizes, babies predominating, rolled in the tobacco which covered the floor and was piled in every direction."[8] Many producing households resembled the one described by Mary Van Kleeck of the Russell Sage Foundation in 1913:

> In a tenement on MacDougal Street lives a family of seven—grandmother, father, mother and four children aged four years, three years, two years and one month respectively. All excepting the father and the two babies make violets. The three year old girl picks apart the petals; her sister, aged four years, separates the stems, dipping an end of each into paste spread on a piece of board on the kitchen table; and the mother and grandmother slip the petals up the stems.[9]

Where children worked outside the home, conditions were no better. In 1900, 120,000 children worked in Pennsylvania mines and factories; most of them had started work by age eleven. In Scranton, a third of the girls between the ages of thirteen and sixteen worked in the silk mills in 1904. In New York, Boston, and Chicago, teenagers worked long hours in textile factories and frequently died in fires or industrial accidents. Children made up 23.7 percent of the 36,415 workers in southern textile mills around the turn of the century. When reformer Marie Van Vorse took a job at one in 1903, she found children as young as six or seven working twelve-hour shifts. At the end of the day, she reported: "They are usually beyond speech. They fall asleep at the tables, on the stairs; they are carried to bed and there laid down as they are, unwashed, undressed; and the inanimate bundles of rags so lie until the mill summons them with its imperious cry before sunrise."[10]

Perspective (New York: Academic Press, 1978); Tamara Hareven, "The Dynamics of Kin in an Industrial Community," in *Turning Points: Historical and Sociological Essays on the Family,* ed. John Demos and S. S. Boocock (Chicago: University of Chicago Press, 1978); Linda Gordon, *Heroes of Their Own Lives: The Politics and History of Family Violence, 1800–1960* (New York, Viking, 1988).

[8]Helen Campbell, *Prisoners of Poverty: Women Wage Workers, Their Trades and Their Lives* (Westport, Conn.: Greenwood Press, 1970), p. 206.

[9]Rosalyn Baxandall, Linda Gordon, and Susan Reverby, eds., *America's Working Women* (New York: Random House, 1976), p. 162.

[10]Rose Schneiderman, *All For One* (New York: P. S. Eriksson, 1967); John Bodnar, "Socialization and Adaptation: Immigrant Families in Scranton," in *Growing Up in America: Historical Experiences,* ed. Harvey Graff (Detroit: Wayne State Press, 1987), pp. 391–92; Robert and Helen Lynd, *Middletown: A Study in Modern American Culture* (New York: Harcourt Brace Jovanovich, 1956), p. 31; Barbara Wertheimer, *We Were There: The Story of Working Women in America* (New York: Pantheon, 1977), pp. 336–43; Francesco Cordasco, *Jacob Riis Revisited: Poverty and the Slum in Another Era* (Garden City, N.Y.: Doubleday, 1968); Campbell, *Prisoners of Poverty: Women Wage-Earners* (Boston: Arnoff, 1893); Lynn Weiner, *From Working Girl to Working Mother: The Female Labor Force in the United States, 1829–1980* (Chapel Hill: University of North Carolina Press, 1985), p. 92.

By the end of the nineteenth century, shocked by the conditions in urban tenements and by the sight of young children working full-time at home or earning money out on the streets, middle-class reformers put aside nostalgia for "harnessed" family production and elevated the antebellum model once more, blaming immigrants for introducing such "un-American" family values as child labor. Reformers advocated adoption of a "true American" family—a restricted, exclusive nuclear unit in which women and children were divorced from the world of work.

In the late 1920s and early 1930s, however, the wheel turned yet again, as social theorists noted the independence and isolation of the nuclear family with renewed anxiety. The influential Chicago School of sociology believed that immigration and urbanization had weakened the traditional family by destroying kinship and community networks. Although sociologists welcomed the increased democracy of "companionate marriage," they worried about the rootlessness of nuclear families and the breakdown of older solidarities. By the time of the Great Depression, some observers even saw a silver lining in economic hardship, since it revived the economic functions and social importance of kin and family ties. With housing starts down by more than 90 percent, approximately one-sixth of urban families had to "double up" in apartments. The incidence of three-generation households increased, while recreational interactions outside the home were cut back or confined to the kinship network. One newspaper opined: "Many a family that has lost its car has found its soul."[11]

Depression families evoke nostalgia in some contemporary observers, because they tended to create "dependability and domestic inclination" among girls and "maturity in the management of money" among boys. But, in many cases, such responsibility was inseparable from "a corrosive and disabling poverty that shattered the hopes and dreams of . . . young parents and twisted the lives of those who were 'stuck together' in it." Men withdrew from family life or turned violent; women exhausted themselves trying to "take up the slack" both financially and emotionally, or they belittled their husbands as failures; and children gave up their dreams of education to work at dead-end jobs.[12]

---

[11]For examples of the analysis of the Chicago School, see Ernest Burgess and Harvey Locke, *The Family: From Institution to Companionship* (New York: American Book Company, 1945); Ernest Mowrer, *The Family: Its Organization and Disorganization* (Chicago: University of Chicago Press, 1932); W. I. Thomas and F. Znaniecki, *The Polish Peasant in Europe and America,* 5 vols. (Boston: Dover Publications, 1918–20). On families in the Depression, see Steven Mintz and Susan Kellogg, *Domestic Revolutions: A Social History of American Family Life* (New York: Free Press, 1988), pp. 133–49, quote on p. 136.

[12]Glen Elder, Jr., *Children of the Great Depression: Social Change in Life Experience* (Chicago: University of Chicago Press, 1974), pp. 64–82; Lillian Rubin, *Worlds of Pain: Life in the Working-Class Family* (New York: Basic Books, 1976), p. 23; Edward Robb Ellis, *A Nation in Torment: The Great American Depression, 1929–1939* (New York: Coward McCann, 1970); Ruth Milkman, "Women's Work and the Economic Crisis," in *A Heritage of Her Own: Toward a New Social History of American Women,* ed. Nancy Cott and Elizabeth Pleck (New York: Simon & Schuster, 1979), pp. 507–41.

From the hardships of the Great Depression and the Second World War and the euphoria of the postwar economic recovery came a new kind of family ideal that still enters our homes in *Leave It to Beaver* and *Donna Reed* reruns. . . . [T]he 1950s were no more a "golden age" of the family than any other period in American history. . . . I will argue that our recurring search for a traditional family model denies the diversity of family life, both past and present, and leads to false generalizations about the past as well as wildly exaggerated claims about the present and the future. 20

The Complexities of Assessing Family Trends

If it is hard to find a satisfactory model of the traditional family, it is also hard to make global judgments about how families have changed and whether they are getting better or worse. Some generalizations about the past are pure myth. Whatever the merit of recurring complaints about the "rootlessness" of modern life, for instance, families are *not* more mobile and transient than they used to be. In most nineteenth-century cities, both large and small, more than 50 percent—and often up to 75 percent—of the residents in any given year were no longer there ten years later. People born in the twentieth century are much more likely to live near their birthplace than were people born in the nineteenth century.[13]

This is not to say, of course, that mobility did not have different effects then than it does now. In the nineteenth century, claims historian Thomas Bender, people moved from community to community, taking advantage . . . of nonfamilial networks and institutions that integrated them into new work and social relations. In the late twentieth century, people move from job to job, following a career path that shuffles them from one single-family home to another and does not link them to neighborly networks beyond the family. But this change is in our community ties, not in our family ones.[14]

A related myth is that modern Americans have lost touch with extended-kinship networks or have let parent-child bonds lapse. In fact, more Americans than ever before have grandparents alive, and there is good evidence that ties between grandparents and grandchildren have become stronger over the past fifty years. In the late 1970s, researchers returned to the

---

[13]Rudy Ray Seward, *The American Family: A Demographic History* (Beverly Hills: Sage, 1978); Kenneth Winkle, *The Politics of Community: Migration and Politics in Antebellum Ohio* (New York: Cambridge University Press, 1988); Michael Weber, *Social Change in an Industrial Town: Patterns of Progress in Warren, Pennsylvania, from the Civil War to World War I* (University Park: Pennsylvania State University Press, 1976), pp. 138–48; Stephen Thernstrom, *Poverty and Progress* (Cambridge: Harvard University Press, 1964).

[14]Thomas Bender, *Community and Social Change in America* (New Brunswick: Rutgers University Press, 1978).

"Middletown" studied by sociologists Robert and Helen Lynd in the 1920s and found that most people there maintained closer extended-family networks than in earlier times. There had been some decline in the family's control over the daily lives of youth, especially females, but "the expressive/emotional function of the family" was "more important for Middletown students of 1977 than it was in 1924." More recent research shows that visits with relatives did *not* decline between the 1950s and the late 1980s.[15]

Today 54 percent of adults see a parent, and 68 percent talk on the phone with a parent, at least once a week. Fully 90 percent of Americans describe their relationship with their mother as close, and 78 percent say their relationship with their grandparents is close. And for all the family disruption of divorce, most modern children live with at least *one* parent. As late as 1940, 10 percent of American children did not live with either parent, compared to only one in twenty-five today.[16]

What about the supposed eclipse of marriage? Neither the rising age of 25
those who marry nor the frequency of divorce necessarily means that marriage is becoming a less prominent institution than it was in earlier days. Ninety percent of men and women eventually marry, more than 70 percent of divorced men and women remarry, and fewer people remain single for their entire lives today than at the turn of the century. One author even suggests that the availability of divorce in the second half of the twentieth century has allowed some women to try marriage who would formerly have remained single all their lives. Others argue that the rate of hidden marital separation in the late nineteenth century was not much less than the rate of visible separation today.[17]

Studies of marital satisfaction reveal that more couples reported their marriages to be happy in the late 1970s than did so in 1957, while couples in their second marriages believe them to be much happier than their first ones. Some commentators conclude that marriage is becoming less permanent but more satisfying. Others wonder, however, whether there is a vicious circle in our country, where no one even tries to sustain a relationship. Between the late 1970s and late 1980s, moreover, reported marital happiness did decline

---

[15]Edward Kain, *The Myth of Family Decline: Understanding Families in a World of Rapid Social Change* (Lexington, Mass.: D. C. Heath, 1990), pp. 10, 37; Theodore Caplow, "The Sociological Myth of Family Decline," *The Tocqueville Review* 3 (1981): 366; Howard Bahr, "Changes in Family Life in Middletown, 1924–77," *Public Opinion Quarterly* 44 (1980): 51.

[16]*American Demographics,* February 1990; Dennis Orthner, "The Family in Transition," in *Rebuilding the Nest: A New Commitment to the American Family,* ed. David Blankenhorn, Steven Bayme, and Jean Bethke Elshtain (Milwaukee: Family Service America, 1990), pp. 95–97; Sar Levitan and Richard Belous, *What's Happening to the American Family?* (Baltimore: Johns Hopkins University Press, 1981), p. 63.

[17]Daniel Kallgren, "Women Out of Marriage: Work and Residence Patterns of Never Married American Women, 1900–1980" (Paper presented at Social Science History Association Conference, Minneapolis, Minn., October 1990), p. 8; Richard Sennett, *Families Against the City: Middle Class Homes in Industrial Chicago, 1872–1890* (Cambridge: Harvard University Press, 1984), pp. 114–15.

slightly in the United States. Some authors see this as reflecting our decreasing appreciation of marriage, although others suggest that it reflects unrealistically high expectations of love in a culture that denies people safe, culturally approved ways of getting used to marriage or cultivating other relationships to meet some of the needs that we currently load onto the couple alone.[18]

Part of the problem in making simple generalizations about what is happening to marriage is that there has been a polarization of experiences. Marriages are much more likely to be ended by divorce today, but marriages that do last are described by their participants as happier than those in the past and are far more likely to confer such happiness over many years. It is important to remember that the 50 percent divorce rate estimates are calculated in terms of a forty-year period and that many marriages in the past were terminated well before that date by the death of one partner. Historian Lawrence Stone suggests that divorce has become "a functional substitute for death" in the modern world. At the end of the 1970s, the rise in divorce rates seemed to overtake the fall in death rates, but the slight decline in divorce rates since then means that "a couple marrying today is more likely to celebrate a fortieth wedding anniversary than were couples around the turn of the century."[19]

A similar polarization allows some observers to argue that fathers are deserting their children, while others celebrate the new commitment of fathers to childrearing. Both viewpoints are right. Sociologist Frank Furstenberg comments on the emergence of a "good dad–bad dad complex": Many fathers spend more time with their children than ever before and feel more free to be affectionate with them; others, however, feel more free simply to walk out on their families. According to 1981 statistics, 42 percent of the children whose father had left the marriage had not seen him in the past year. Yet studies show steadily increasing involvement of fathers with their children as long as they are in the home.[20]

These kinds of ambiguities should make us leery of hard-and-fast pronouncements about what's happening to the American family. In many cases,

---

[18]Mary Jo Bane, *Here to Stay: American Families in the Twentieth Century* (New York: Basic Books, 1976); Stephen Nock, *Sociology of the Family* (Englewood Cliffs, N.J.: Prentice Hall, 1987); Kain, *Myth of Family Decline,* pp. 71, 74–75; Joseph Veroff, Elizabeth Douvan, and Richard Kulka, *The Inner American: A Self Portrait from 1957 to 1976* (New York: Basic Books, 1981); Norval Glenn, "The Recent Trend in Marital Success in the United States," *Journal of Marriage and the Family* 53 (1991); Tracy Cabot, *Marrying Later, Marrying Smarter* (New York: McGraw-Hill, 1990); Judith Brown, *Sanctions and Sanctuary: Cultural Perspectives on the Beating of Wives* (Boulder, Colo.: Westview Press, 1991); Maxine Baca Zinn and Stanley Eitzen, *Diversity in American Families* (New York: Harper & Row, 1987).

[19]Dorrian Apple Sweetser, "Broken Homes: Stable Risk, Changing Reason, Changing Forms," *Journal of Marriage and the Family* (August 1985); Lawrence Stone, "The Road to Polygamy," *New York Review of Books,* 2 March 1989, p. 13; Arlene Skolnick, *Embattled Paradise: The American Family in an Age of Uncertainty* (New York: Basic Books, 1991), p. 156.

[20]Frank Furstenberg, Jr., "Good Dads–Bad Dads: Two Faces of Fatherhood," in *The Changing American Family and Public Policy,* ed. Andrew Cherlin (Washington, D.C.: Urban Institute Press, 1988); Joseph Pleck, "The Contemporary Man," in *Handbook of Counseling and Psychotherapy,* ed. Murray Scher et al. (Beverly Hills: Sage, 1987).

we simply don't know precisely what our figures actually mean. For example, the proportion of youngsters receiving psychological assistance rose by 80 percent between 1981 and 1988. Does that mean they are getting more sick or receiving more help, or is it some complex combination of the two? Child abuse reports increased by 225 percent between 1976 and 1987. Does this represent an actual increase in rates of abuse or a heightened consciousness about the problem? During the same period, parents' self-reports about very severe violence toward their children declined 47 percent. Does this represent a real improvement in their behavior or a decreasing willingness to admit to such acts?[21]

Assessing the direction of family change is further complicated because many contemporary trends represent a reversal of developments that were themselves rather recent. The expectation that the family should be the main source of personal fulfillment, for example, was not traditional in the eighteenth and nineteenth centuries. . . . Prior to the 1900s, the family festivities that now fill us with such nostalgia for "the good old days" (and cause such heartbreak when they go poorly) were "relatively undeveloped." Civic festivals and Fourth of July parades were more important occasions for celebration and strong emotion than family holidays, such as Thanksgiving. Christmas "seems to have been more a time for attending parties and dances than for celebrating family solidarity." Only in the twentieth century did the family come to be the center of festive attention and emotional intensity.[22]

Today, such emotional investment in the family may be waning again. This could be interpreted as a reestablishment of balance between family life and other social ties; on the other hand, such a trend may have different results today than in earlier times, because in many cases the extrafamilial institutions and customs that used to socialize individuals and provide them with a range of emotional alternatives to family life no longer exist.

In other cases, close analysis of statistics showing a deterioration in family well-being supposedly caused by abandonment of tradition suggests a more complicated train of events. Children's health, for example, improved dramatically in the 1960s and 1970s, a period of extensive family transformation. It ceased to improve, and even slid backward, in the 1980s, when innovative social programs designed to relieve families of some "traditional" responsibilities were repealed. While infant mortality rates fell by 4.7 percent a year during the 1970s, the rate of decline decreased in the 1980s, and in both 1988 and 1989, infant mortality rates did not show a statistically significant decline.

---

[21]National Commission on Children, *Beyond Rhetoric: A New Agenda for Children and Families* (Washington, D.C.: GPO, 1991), p. 34; Richard Gelles and Jon Conte, "Domestic Violence and Sexual Abuse of Children," in *Contemporary Families: Looking Forward, Looking Back,* ed. Alan Booth (Minneapolis: National Council on Family Relations, 1991), p. 328.

[22]Arlene Skolnick, "The American Family: The Paradox of Perfection," *The Wilson Quarterly* (Summer 1980); Barbara Laslett, "Family Membership: Past and Present," *Social Problems* 25 (1978); Theodore Caplow et al., *Middletown Families: Fifty Years of Change and Continuity* (Minneapolis: University of Minnesota Press, 1982), p. 225.

Similarly, the proportion of low-birth-weight babies fell during the 1970s but stayed steady during the 1980s, and had even increased slightly as of 1988. Child poverty is lower today than it was in the "traditional" 1950s but much higher than it was in the nontraditional late 1960s.[23]

Wild Claims and Phony Forecasts

Lack of perspective on where families have come from and how their evolution connects to other social trends tends to encourage contradictory claims and wild exaggerations about where families are going. One category of generalizations seems to be a product of wishful thinking. As of 1988, nearly half of all families with children had both parents in the work force. The two-parent family in which only the father worked for wages represented just 25 percent of all families with children, down from 44 percent in 1975. For people overwhelmed by the difficulties of adjusting work and schools to the realities of working moms, it has been tempting to discern a "return to tradition" and hope the problems will go away. Thus in 1991, we saw a flurry of media reports that the number of women in the work force was headed down: "More Choose to Stay Home with Children" proclaimed the headlines; "More Women Opting for Chance to Watch Their Children Grow."[24]

The cause of all this commotion? The percentage of women aged twenty-five to thirty-four who were employed dropped from 74 percent to 72.8 percent between January 1990 and January 1991. However, there was an exactly equal decline in the percentage of men in the work force during the same period, and for both sexes the explanation was the same. "The dip is the recession," explained Judy Waldrop, research editor at *American Demographics* magazine, to anyone who bothered to listen. In fact, the proportion of *mothers* who worked increased slightly during the same period.[25]

This is not to say that parents, especially mothers, are happy with the 35
pressures of balancing work and family life. Poll after poll reveals that both men and women feel starved for time. The percentage of women who say they would prefer to stay home with their children if they could afford to do so rose from 33 percent in 1986 to 56 percent in 1990. Other polls show that even larger majorities of women would trade a day's pay for an extra day off. But, above all, what these polls reveal is women's growing dissatisfaction with

[23]*The State of America's Children, 1991* (Washington, D.C.: Children's Defense Fund, 1991), pp. 55–63; *Seattle Post-Intelligencer,* 19 April 1991; National Commission on Children, *Beyond Rhetoric,* p. 32; *Washington Post National Weekly Edition,* 13–19 May 1991; James Wetzel, *American Youth: A Statistical Snapshot* (Washington, D.C.: William T. Grant Foundation, August 1989), pp. 12–14.

[24]*USA Today,* 12 May 1991, p. 1A; Richard Morin, "Myth of the Drop Out Mom," *Washington Post,* 14 July 1991; Christine Reinhardt, "Trend Check," *Working Woman,* October 1991, p. 34; Howard Hayghe, "Family Members in the Work Force," *Monthly Labor Review* 113 (1990).

[25]Morin, "Myth of the Drop Out Mom"; Reinhardt, "Trend Check," p. 34.

the failure of employers, schools, and government to pioneer arrangements that make it possible to combine work and family life. They do not suggest that women are actually going to stop working, or that this would be women's preferred solution to their stresses. The polls did not ask, for example, how *long* women would like to take off work, and failed to take account of the large majority of mothers who report that they would miss their work if they did manage to take time off. Working mothers are here to stay, and we will not meet the challenge this poses for family life by inventing an imaginary trend to define the problem out of existence.

At another extreme is the kind of generalization that taps into our worst fears. One example of this is found in the almost daily reporting of cases of child molestation or kidnapping by sexual predators. The highlighting of such cases, drawn from every corner of the country, helps disguise how rare these cases actually are when compared to crimes committed within the family.

A well-publicized instance of the cataclysmic predictions that get made when family trends are taken out of historical context is the famous *Newsweek* contention that a single woman of forty has a better chance of being killed by a terrorist than of finding a husband. It is true that the proportion of never-married women under age forty has increased substantially since the 1950s, but it is also true that the proportion has *decreased* dramatically among women over that age. A woman over thirty-five has a *better* chance to marry today than she did in the 1950s. In the past twelve years, first-time marriages have increased almost 40 percent for women aged thirty-five to thirty-nine. A single woman aged forty to forty-four still has a 24 percent probability of marriage, while 15 percent of women in their late forties will marry. These figures would undoubtedly be higher if many women over forty did not simply pass up opportunities that a more desperate generation might have snatched.[26]

Yet another example of the exaggeration that pervades many analyses of modern families is the widely quoted contention that "parents today spend 40 percent less time with their children than did parents in 1965." Again, of course, part of the problem is where researchers are measuring from. A comparative study of Muncie, Indiana, for example, found that parents spent much more time with their children in the mid-1970s than did parents in the mid-1920s. But another problem is keeping the categories consistent. Trying to track down the source of the 40 percent decline figure, I called demographer John P. Robinson, whose studies on time formed the basis of this claim. Robinson's data, however, show that parents today spend about the same amount of time caring for children as they did in 1965. If the total amount of time devoted to children is less, he suggested, I might want to check how many fewer children

---

[26]"Too Late for Prince Charming," *Newsweek,* 2 June 1986, p. 55; John Modell, *Into One's Own: From Youth to Adulthood in the United States, 1920–1975* (Berkeley: University of California Press, 1989), p. 249; Barbara Lovenheim, *Beating the Marriage Odds: When You Are Smart, Single, and Over 35* (New York: William Morrow, 1990), pp. 26–27; *U.S. News & World Report,* 29 January 1990, p. 50; *New York Times,* 7 June 1991.

there are today. In 1970, the average family had 1.34 children under the age of eighteen; in 1990, the average family had only .96 children under age eighteen—a decrease of 28.4 percent. In other words, most of the decline in the total amount of time parents spend with children is because of the decline in the number of children they have to spend time with![27]

Now I am not trying to say that the residual amount of decrease is not serious, or that it may not become worse, given the trends in women's employment. Robinson's data show that working mothers spend substantially less time in primary child-care activities than do nonemployed mothers (though they also tend to have fewer children); more than 40 percent of working mothers report feeling "trapped" by their daily routines; many routinely sacrifice sleep in order to meet the demands of work and family. Even so, a majority believe they are *not* giving enough time to their children. It is also true that children may benefit merely from having their parents available, even though the parents may not be spending time with them.

But there is no reason to assume the worst. Americans have actually gained 40
free time since 1965, despite an increase in work hours, largely as a result of a decline in housework and an increasing tendency to fit some personal requirements and errands into the work day. And according to a recent Gallup poll, most modern mothers think they are doing a better job of communicating with their children (though a worse job of house cleaning) than did their own mothers and that they put a higher value on spending time with their family than did their mothers.[28]

Negotiating through the Extremes

Most people react to these conflicting claims and contradictory trends with understandable confusion. They know that family ties remain central to their own lives, but they are constantly hearing about people who seem to have *no* family feeling. Thus, at the same time as Americans report high levels of satisfaction with their *own* families, they express a pervasive fear that other people's families are falling apart. In a typical recent poll, for example, 71 percent of

---

[27]William Mattox, Jr., "The Parent Trap," *Policy Review* (Winter 1991): 6, 8; Sylvia Ann Hewlett, "Running Hard Just to Keep Up," *Time* (Fall 1990), and *When the Bough Breaks: The Cost of Neglecting Our Children* (New York: Basic Books, 1991), p. 73; Richard Whitmore, "Education Decline Linked with Erosion of Family," *The Olympian,* 1 October 1991; John Robinson, "Caring for Kids," *American Demographics,* July 1989, p. 52; "Household and Family Characteristics: March 1990 and 1989," *Current Population Reports,* series P-20, no. 447, table A-1. I am indebted to George Hough, Executive Policy Analyst, Office of Financial Management, Washington State, for finding these figures and helping me with the calculations.

[28]John Robinson, "Time for Work," *American Demographics,* April 1989, p. 68, and "Time's Up," *American Demographics,* July 1989, p. 34; Trish Hall, "Time on Your Hands? You May Have More Than You Think," *New York Times,* 3 July 1991, pp. C1, C7; Gannett News Service Wire Report, 27 August 1991.

respondents said they were "very satisfied" with their own family life, but more than half rated the overall quality of family life as negative: I'm okay; you're not."[29]

This seemingly schizophrenic approach does not reflect an essentially intolerant attitude. People worry about families, and to the extent that they associate modern social ills with changes in family life, they are ambivalent about innovations. Voters often defeat measures to grant unmarried couples, whether heterosexual or homosexual, the same rights as married ones. In polls, however, most Americans support tolerance for gay and lesbian relationships. Although two-thirds of respondents to one national poll said they wanted "more traditional standards of family life," the same percentage rejected the idea that "women should return to their traditional role." Still larger majorities support women's right to work, including their right to use child care, even when they worry about relying on day-care centers too much. In a 1990 *Newsweek* poll, 42 percent predicted that the family would be worse in ten years and exactly the same percentage predicted that it would be better. Although 87 percent of people polled in 1987 said they had "old-fashioned ideas about family and marriage," only 22 percent of the people polled in 1989 defined a family solely in terms of blood, marriage, or adoption. Seventy-four percent declared, instead, that family is any group whose members love and care for one another.[30]

These conflicted responses do not mean that people are hopelessly confused. Instead, they reflect people's gut-level understanding that the "crisis of the family" is more complex than is often asserted by political demagogues or others with an ax to grind. In popular commentary, the received wisdom is to "keep it simple." I know one television reporter who refuses to air an interview with anyone who uses the phrase "on the other hand." But my experience in discussing these issues with both the general public and specialists in the field is that people are hungry to get beyond oversimplifications. They don't want to be told that everything is fine in families or that if the economy improved and the government mandated parental leave, everything would be fine. But they don't believe that every hard-won victory for women's rights and personal liberty has been destructive of social bonds and that the only way to find a sense of community is to go back to some sketchily defined "traditional" family that clearly involves denying the validity of any alternative familial and personal choices.

Americans understand that along with welcome changes have come difficult new problems; uneasy with simplistic answers, they are willing to consider more nuanced analyses of family gains and losses during the past few decades. Indeed, argues political reporter E. J. Dionne, they are *desperate* to

---

[29]*New York Times,* 10 October 1989, p. A18.

[30]E. J. Dionne, Jr., *Why Americans Hate Politics* (New York: Simon & Schuster, 1991), pp. 110, 115, 325; *The Olympian,* 11 October 1989; *New York Times,* 10 October 1989; *Time,* 20 November 1989; *Seattle Post-Intelligencer,* 12 October 1990; Jerold Footlick, "What Happened to the Family?" *Newsweek Special Issue,* Winter/Spring 1990, p. 18.

engage in such analyses.[31] Few Americans are satisfied with liberal and feminist accounts that blame all modern family dilemmas on structural inequalities, ignoring the moral crisis of commitment and obligation in our society. Yet neither are they convinced that "in the final analysis," as David Blankenhorn of the Institute for American Values puts it, "the problem is not the system. The problem is us."[32]

Despite humane intentions, an overemphasis on personal responsibility 45
for strengthening family values encourages a way of thinking that leads to moralizing rather than mobilizing for concrete reforms. While values are important to Americans, most do not support the sort of scapegoating that occurs when all family problems are blamed on "bad values." Most of us are painfully aware that there is no clear way of separating "family values" from "the system." Our values may make a difference in the way we respond to the challenges posed by economic and political institutions, but those institutions also reinforce certain values and extinguish others. The problem is not to berate people for abandoning past family values, nor to exhort them to adopt better values in the future—the problem is to build the institutions and social support networks that allow people to act on their best values rather than on their worst ones. We need to get past abstract nostalgia for traditional family values and develop a clearer sense of how past families actually worked and what the different consequences of various family behaviors and values have been. Good history and responsible social policy should help people incorporate the full complexity and the tradeoffs of family change into their analyses and thus into action. Mythmaking does not accomplish this end.

QUESTIONING THE TEXT

1. Coontz is highly critical of some researchers' careless or deceptive use of statistics to make "wild claims and phony forecasts" about families. Look closely at the author's use of statistical evidence. Does Coontz use statistics in a fully explained and evenhanded way? Explain the reasons for your answer.
2. How might Coontz describe the way *she* wishes families were defined? Discuss this question with a classmate and then reread the selection, taking notes on the underlying assumptions Coontz makes about families—traditional or otherwise. Bring your notes to class for a discussion of "where the author is coming from" in this selection.
3. Working with a classmate, do some research into current statistics on birth rates, infant mortality rates, low-birth-weight babies, or child poverty. How do the current numbers compare to those Coontz cites?

---

[31]Dionne, *Why Americans Hate Politics.*

[32]David Blankenhorn, "Does Grandmother Know Best?" *Family Affairs* 3 (1990): 13, 16.

MAKING CONNECTIONS

4. Read Barbara Dafoe Whitehead's "The Making of a Divorce Culture" (p. 667), keeping Coontz's views on divorce in mind. Then write a two- to three-page essay comparing and contrasting the two writers' positions on divorce, and explaining which one you find more persuasive.
5. Compare Michael Nava's family, described in "Gardenland, Sacramento, California" (p. 647), with the "elusive traditional family" discussed by Coontz. In what ways does Nava's family resemble the traditional patriarchal family? What does Nava's essay contribute to your understanding of Coontz's argument? Does his depiction of family life help support some of her claims, or does it challenge her argument in some way? Explain.

JOINING THE CONVERSATION

6. Coontz says her students' visions of traditional family life "bear a suspicious resemblance to reruns of old television series" except that "the scripts of different shows have been mixed up" (paragraph 2). Working with a classmate, choose a television series, either current or rerun, that features a family/home, and watch and videotape as many episodes as you can within a week or so. Take notes during and after the episodes, jotting down the family members' characteristics, the roles they play, the values they represent, the kind of home they live in, and any other observations you make about the TV family. Compare your notes with your classmate's, noting any discrepancies and resolving them, if possible. Then, with your partner, prepare a 15-minute presentation (about six pages of double-spaced text with accompanying video clips) on "The American Family as Represented in [name of TV series]."
7. After freewriting or brainstorming about your own family experience, write a journal entry exploring how your experience matches up with or differs from any of the family paradigms Coontz describes. If you keep a reading log, write the entry there.
8. Imagine that you are asked to prepare a one- to two-page description of "a typical American family" to be placed in a time capsule marked for opening in 2150. Write the description; then ask several classmates to read and respond to it. With their feedback in mind, write a brief analysis of your description of the typical family, noting where you overgeneralize, leave out counterexamples, or use terms that may be unfamiliar to readers of the twenty-second century, for example. Bring your description and your analysis of it to class for discussion.

JILL FRAWLEY
Inside the Home

JILL FRAWLEY, a registered nurse and advocate for patients, left the employment of the nursing home she describes in this article. Originally published in the politically leftist Mother Jones *magazine in 1991, "Inside the Home" demonstrates in graphic detail why she left and, in so doing, exposes the "big lie" told by institutions such as the one she worked for: "long-term care facilities" owned by big corporations care little or nothing for the patients whose money supports them or for the employees who do their bidding.*

I chose this essay because—in spite of the designation "nursing home"—I had never considered the word home *to include such institutions. In fact, asked to list dozens of places that might count as "home," I would have failed to include facilities such as the one Frawley describes. And yet I have friends whose parents are even now in such homes. How, then, to explain my omission? Perhaps, I have reflected since reading Frawley's essay, because my silent neglect of such "homes" is part of the big lie she speaks of. Perhaps by ignoring them I bear some responsibility for the many nursing homes that are insufferable and insupportable.*

Perhaps I should think more carefully about what is and is not designated as a "home." And perhaps I should think more carefully when big corporations call themselves "families." Are they families I want to support or belong to? Are the homes they provide ones I'd want to inhabit? Now read "Inside the Home." —A.L.

I'm just one little nurse, in one little "care facility." Each shift I work, I carry in my soul a very big lie. I leave my job, and there aren't enough showers in the world to wash away my rage, my frustration, my impotence.

The long-term-care facility (nursing home) I work for is owned by a corporation that owns nursing homes throughout the country. Giving corporations like this control over the quality of medical care is handing over control to the fox. Every chicken in the coop knows there is no hope—only the ticking away of a life devoid of dignity or even minimal respect.

I watch the videos they show to new employees during "orientation." Smiling people spout corporate policy and speak of "guest relations." They tell us we are special; we are going to participate in a rewarding job. Elderly people in the video are dressed nicely; they are coherent and grateful for the help the staff member has time to give. We sign the attendance sheet: We saw it; now we know what "guest relations" means. It means to act in front of the families so that they think everything is okay.

The truth is ugly; I confess it in a burst of desperation. The elderly lie in feces and urine because there is only one aide for thirty patients. Eventually, they get changed abruptly—too fast, too harshly. They cry out in confused terror. Doors are closed to "protect their privacy"—but really so no one will see. The covers get flung back. It's evening bed check. The old person is shoved from one side of the bed to the other. He tries to protest; he thinks something bad is happening. Whip out the soiled underpad, wipe him, throw the covers over him . . . on to the next body.

No time for mouth care; sometimes no time for showers; never time to 5
hold someone's hand even for a moment. Aides feed the helpless two spoonfuls of pureed stuff, dripping down chins; no time to wait for them to swallow. It gets charted: "Resident didn't eat much tonight." She loses weight; she gets more frail as each day passes. The food is so bad I can't begin to describe it. The cook is young and doesn't care much; if I complain, he gets mad. One resident asks me for a cup of hot water so she can use the instant soup in her drawer. She can't eat the cold, badly cooked stuff that is on her tray. Slow starvation is hard to get used to.

Why is there only one aide on these halls night after night? Most employees don't stay. They can't stand being flung into jobs that are too hard, too horrid, for too little money. The ones that do stay have given up complaining. They shut their eyes and ears and do the best they can. They have children to support, no education, are caught by life in such a way that quitting would intensify their own suffering and not alleviate anyone else's.

We're always short-staffed. We know it's to save money. One tired aide does a double shift, straining to do a job it takes two people to do correctly. I guess when you make four dollars and something an hour, it takes working double shifts (that's sixteen hours) to make enough to live on. Tired people get impatient, make mistakes, take shortcuts. A nurse calls in sick. That means one nurse does three halls. One nurse to pass out medicines for eighty residents.

Patients are dropped or fall. My coworkers agree that it's a widespread practice to chart this to avoid problems. Every incident report I have ever seen states that the patient or resident was "found on the floor" or appeared to have bruises or skin tears of "unknown" origin. When there's no time to turn the bedridden every two hours, skin breaks down and ulcers develop. The elderly get skin tears and bruises because they are fragile, but also because there is no time to handle them gently. Again, we chart carefully so there is no blame. We let our old ones die for many reasons. Sometimes it is because of sickness; sometimes it is from neglect.

The admissions director is a nice lady. She lives uneasily with her task. She tells anxious families not to worry, that the facility will be like a second home to their relative. She tells them what they want to hear. The families go away determined to believe everything will be fine. Secretly, they are relieved that they won't have to deal with dementia, incontinence, or the total dependency of a senile elder.

The silence is ominous in the evening. Nothing to do; no place to go. 10
The residents sit and wait for death. The staff is ground down in despair and hopelessness. The guys at corporate headquarters must be patting each other on the back about the profits they're making.

It got bad at the place I work. Too many unhappy people; too much barely controlled anger always close to erupting. A corporate spokesperson was sent from headquarters to listen to grievances. He listened, this quiet, intelligent man who had been to our facility before. I asked some of my fellow workers why they weren't going to speak out. "It doesn't do any good," was the response. "He's been coming for three or four years. Nothing changes." I went; I spoke out; they were right. Nothing changes.

The elderly suffer quietly. They are afraid they will be punished if they speak up for themselves. Most of them can't speak for themselves. They just want to escape this hell. I do too. They need a place to stay; I need a job. We're trapped.

I am one little nurse, in one little care facility, living with this terrible secret. If they knew I was telling on them, I wouldn't have a job. What about my rent? What about my needs? But I need to tell. I confess to my participation in these crimes. I can't keep this secret any longer.

If you have an elderly relative in a facility:

1. Visit at odd hours.
2. Visit at mealtime.
3. Don't believe what the staff tells you.
4. Ask questions.
5. Don't worry if small items are missing. Petty theft is not serious. Abuse is.
6. Make sure your relative is clean.
7. Notice if your relative is losing weight.
8. Check your relative's skin for bruises.
9. Let "them" know you are watching.
10. Be polite to staff, but raise hell with the administrator or the director of nursing. Though they are just employees and will tell you what you want to hear, it's worth a try.
11. Contact local ombudsmen if you can't get results. If that doesn't work, contact the state regulatory agency.
12. Complain to headquarters or whoever owns the facility.
13. Don't allow yourself to be blackmailed by veiled threats of being forced to move your relative.
14. Don't give up; wear them down.

QUESTIONING THE TEXT

1. What does Frawley mean by the "big lie"? Write out a brief definition of this "big lie."

2. What is Frawley's attitude toward her employers? Toward her patients? Toward herself? Point to places in the essay that reveal these attitudes to you.
3. Look back at the questions A.L. poses at the end of her introduction to this reading. Are they rhetorical questions, or does she intend for you to answer them? How do you know?

MAKING CONNECTIONS

4. Review this chapter's essays, poems, and opening illustration (p. 629) and then list all the places in them that fall under the category *home*. What do all these places have in common? Try to write a definition of *home* that accommodates all these places.
5. Imagine a conversation among Frawley, Ron Suskind (p. 634), and Jamaica Kincaid (p. 703) on the definition of *home* and its importance. Write out a page or so of that conversation.

JOINING THE CONVERSATION

6. Think for a while about the work you now do or have done. What about that work made you feel good about what you were doing? Did anything about it seem like a "big lie"? What, if anything, filled you with frustration? Based on your exploration of these questions, write a brief position paper on "how I feel about the work I do (or have done)."
7. Working with several classmates, do some research on nursing homes in your area. How are they regulated? Who owns them? How much does it cost to stay in them? Who works there, and how are such people licensed or certified? Have each member of your group visit one nursing home, taking notes on the facility and its atmosphere and, if possible, talking with people who work there as well as with people who live there. Pool your notes, and then prepare a written or oral report for your class on whether your research does or does not support Frawley's picture of nursing homes.

DAVID SEDARIS
Cyclops

As we mention in the introduction to this chapter, the great Russian writer Leo Tolstoy opens his tragic novel Anna Karenina *with a famous sentence: "Happy families are all alike; every unhappy family is unhappy in its own way." He might have added a qualification: "There are no happy families."*

I'm not suggesting, of course, that home life is a perpetual sea of troubles. Still, I rather doubt that any family can totally escape the swells that give depth and character to human experience. Sometimes domestic problems are *Tolstoyan in scale, sufficient to break the heart and send pain rippling across whole generations. More often, however, family troubles seem more like acne—chronic and embarrassing, but ultimately survivable. They might even build character.*

David Sedaris (b. 1957) describes this off-the-rack sort of domestic strife particularly well in "Cyclops," a chapter from his autobiographical memoir Naked *(1997), where the facts of his adolescence in Raleigh, North Carolina, merge happily with fertile exaggerations, even fictions. It doesn't much matter: his tales of family life still have the ring of truth. For instance, in "Cyclops," you'll likely recognize the archetypal parent determined to scare the kids into responsible behavior. And you'll probably recall admonitions like these: Don't* ever *run with scissors; If you cross your eyes, they'll stay that way; If you lean back in that chair, you'll crack your head wide open! Most of us survive our dalliances with scissors and grow into adults capable of cutting paper without mishap. But not David Sedaris. And readers who need a good laugh can be grateful for his phobias.*

Named Time*'s Humorist of the Year in 2001, David Sedaris has been a contributor to National Public Radio's* Morning Edition *and is currently writing plays with his sister Amy. He is also the author of* Barrel Fever: Stories and Essays *(1994),* The SantaLand Diaries *and* Season's Greetings: Two Plays *(1998), and* Me Talk Pretty One Day *(2000).* —J.R.

When he was young my father shot out his best friend's eye with a BB gun. That is what he told us. "One foolish moment and, Jesus, if I could take it back, I would." He winced, shaking his fist as if it held a rattle. "It eats me alive," he said. "I mean to tell you that it absolutely tears me apart."

On one of our summer visits to his hometown, my father took us to meet this guy, a shoe salesman whose milky pupil hugged the corner of his mangled socket. I watched the two men shake hands and turned away, sickened and ashamed by what my father had done.

Our next-door neighbor received a BB gun for his twelfth birthday and accepted it as a personal challenge to stalk and maim any living creature:

sunbathing cats, sparrows, slugs, and squirrels—if it moved, he shot it. I thought this was an excellent idea, but every time I raised the gun to my shoulder, I saw my father's half-blind friend stumbling forth with an armload of Capezios. What would it be like to live with that sort of guilt? How could my father look himself in the mirror without throwing up?

While watching television one afternoon my sister Tiffany stabbed me in the eye with a freshly sharpened pencil. The blood was copious, and I rode to the hospital knowing that if I was blinded, my sister would be my slave for the rest of her life. Never for one moment would I let her forget what she'd done to me. There would be no swinging cocktail parties in her future, no poolside barbeques or episodes of carefree laughter, not one moment of joy—I would make sure of that. I'd planned my vengeance so thoroughly that I was almost disappointed when the doctor announced that this was nothing but a minor puncture wound, located not on but beneath the eye.

"Take a look at your brother's face," my father said, pointing to my 5
Band-Aid. "You could have blinded him for life! Your own brother, a Cyclops, is that what you want?" Tiffany's suffering eased my pain for an hour or two, but then I began to feel sorry for her. "Every time you reach for a pencil, I want you to think about what you've done to your brother," my father said. "I want you to get on your knees and beg him to forgive you."

There are only so many times a person can apologize before it becomes annoying. I lost interest long before the bandage was removed, but not my father. By the time he was finished, Tiffany couldn't lift a dull crayon without breaking into tears. Her pretty, suntanned face assumed the characteristics of a wrinkled, grease-stained bag. Six years old and the girl was broken.

Danger was everywhere and it was our father's lifelong duty to warn us. Attending the country club's Fourth of July celebration, we were told how one of his Navy buddies had been disfigured for life when a cherry bomb exploded in his lap. "Blew his balls right off the map," he said. "Take a second and imagine what that must have felt like!" Racing to the farthest edge of the golf course, I watched the remainder of the display with my hands between my legs.

Fireworks were hazardous, but thunderstorms were even worse. "I had a friend, used to be a very bright, good-looking guy. He was on top of the world until the day he got struck by lightning. It caught him right between the eyes while he was trout fishing and cooked his brain just like you'd roast a chicken. Now he's got a metal plate in his forehead and can't even chew his own food; everything has to be put in a blender and taken through a straw."

If the lightning was going to get me, it would have to penetrate walls. At the first hint of a storm I ran to the basement, crouching beneath a table and covering my head with a blanket. Those who watched from their front porches were fools. "The lightning can be attracted by a wedding ring or even the fillings in your teeth," my father said. "The moment you let down your guard is guaranteed to be the day it strikes."

In junior high I signed up for shop class, and our first assignment was to build a napkin holder. "You're not going to be using a table saw, are you?" my father asked. "I knew a guy, a kid about your size, who was using a table saw when the blade came loose, flew out of the machine, and sliced his face right in half." Using his index finger, my father drew an imaginary line from his forehead to his chin. "The guy survived, but nobody wanted anything to do with him. He turned into an alcoholic and wound up marrying a Chinese woman he'd ordered through a catalog. Think about it." I did. 10

My napkin holder was made from found boards and, once finished, weighed in at close to seven pounds. My bookshelves were even worse. "The problem with a hammer," I was told, "is that the head can fly off at any moment and, boy, let me tell you, you've never imagined pain like that."

After a while we began to wonder if my father had any friends who could still tie their own shoes or breathe without the aid of a respirator. With the exception of the shoe salesman, we'd never seen any of these people, only heard about them whenever one of us attempted to deep-fry chicken or operate the garbage disposal. "I've got a friend who buys a set of gloves and throws one of them away. He lost his right hand doing the exact same thing you're doing. He had his arm down the drain when the cat rubbed against the switch to the garbage disposal. Now he's wearing clip-on ties and having the restaurant waiters cut up his steak. Is that the kind of life you want for yourself?"

He allowed me to mow the lawn only because he was too cheap to pay a landscaper and didn't want to do it himself. "What happened," he said, "is that the guy slipped, probably on a pile of crap, and his leg got caught up in the blade. He found his foot, carried it to the hospital, but it was too late to sew it back on. Can you imagine that? The guy drove fifteen, twenty miles with his foot in his lap."

Regardless of the heat, I mowed the lawn wearing long pants, knee-high boots, a football helmet, and a pair of goggles. Before starting, I scouted the lawn for rocks and dog feces, slowly combing the area as if it were mined. Even then I pushed the mower haltingly, aways fearing that this next step might be my last.

Nothing bad ever happened, and within a few years I was mowing in shorts and sneakers, thinking of the supposed friend my father had used to illustrate his warning. I imagined this man jumping into his car and pressing on the accelerator with his bloody stump, a warm foot settled in his lap like a sleeping puppy. Why hadn't he just called an ambulance to come pick him up? How, in his shock, had he thought to search the weeds for his missing foot? It didn't add up. 15

I waited until my junior year of high school to sign up for driver's education. Before taking to the road, we sat in the darkened classroom, watching films that might have been written and directed by my father. *Don't do it,* I thought, watching the prom couple attempt to pass a lumbering dump truck.

Every excursion ended with the young driver wrapped around a telephone pole or burned beyond recognition, the camera focusing in on a bloody corsage littering the side of the highway.

I drove a car no faster than I pushed the lawn mower, and the instructor soon lost patience.

"That license is going to be your death warrant," my father said on the day I received my learner's permit. "You're going to get out there and kill someone, and the guilt is going to tear your heart out."

The thought of killing myself had slowed me down to five miles per hour. The thought of killing someone else stopped me completely.

My mother had picked me up from a play rehearsal one rainy night 20
when, cresting a hill, the car ran over something it shouldn't have. This was not a brick or a misplaced boot but some living creature that cried out when caught beneath the tire. "Shit," my mother whispered, tapping her forehead against the steering wheel. "Shit, shit shit." We covered our heads against the rain and searched the darkened street until we found an orange cat coughing up blood into the gutter.

"You killed me," the cat said, pointing at my mother with its flattened paw. "Here I had so much to live for, but now it's over, my whole life wiped out just like that." The cat wheezed rhythmically before closing its eyes and dying.

"Shit," my mother repeated. We walked door to door until finding the cat's owner, a kind and understanding woman whose young daughter shared none of her qualities. "You killed my cat," she screamed, sobbing into her mother's skirt. "You're mean and you're ugly and you killed my cat."

"She's at that age," the woman said, stroking the child's hair.

My mother felt bad enough without the lecture that awaited her at home. "That could have been a child!" my father shouted. "Think about that the next time you're tearing down the street searching for kicks." He made it sound as if my mother ran down cats for sport. "You think this is funny," he said, "but we'll see who's laughing when you're behind bars awaiting trial for manslaughter." I received a variation on the same speech after sideswiping a mailbox. Despite my mother's encouragement, I surrendered my permit and never drove again. My nerves just couldn't take it. It seemed much safer to hitchhike.

My father objected when I moved to Chicago, and waged a full-fledged 25
campaign of terror when I announced I would be moving to New York. "New York! Are you out of your mind? You might as well take a razor to your throat because, let me tell you something, those New Yorkers are going to eat you alive." He spoke of friends who had been robbed and bludgeoned by packs of roving gangs and sent me newspaper clippings detailing the tragic slayings of joggers and vacationing tourists. "This could be you!" he wrote in the margins.

I'd lived in New York for several years when, traveling upstate to attend a wedding, I stopped in my father's hometown. We hadn't visited since our grandmother moved in with us, and I felt my way around with a creepy familiarity. I found my father's old apartment, but his friend's shoe store had been converted into a pool hall. When I called to tell him about it, my father said, "What shoe store? What are you talking about?"

"The place where your friend worked," I said. "You remember, the guy whose eye you shot out."

"Frank?" he said. "I didn't shoot his eye out; the guy was born that way."

My father visits me now in New York. We'll walk through Washington Square, where he'll yell, "Get a look at the ugly mug on that one!" referring to a three-hundred-pound biker with grinning skulls tattooed like a choker around his neck. A young man in Central Park is photographing his girlfriend, and my father races to throw himself into the picture. "All right, sweetheart," he says, placing his arm around the startled victim, "it's time to get comfortable." I cower as he marches into posh grocery stores, demanding to speak to the manager. "Back home I can get this exact same cantaloupe for less than half this price," he says. The managers invariably suggest that he do just that. He screams at waiters and cuts in line at tony restaurants. "I have a friend," I tell him, "who lost his right arm snapping his fingers at a waiter."

"Oh, you kids," he says. "Not a one of you has got so much as a tea- 30
spoon of gumption. I don't know where you got it from, but in the end, it's going to kill you."

QUESTIONING THE TEXT

1. Note the various feelings you had while first reading this excerpt; identify where they occurred in your reading of the text. On a second or third reading, do you find you have different reactions to the events Sedaris describes? Why, or why not? At what point(s) do you find yourself smiling or laughing? Share your reactions to the essay in class discussion. Do some readers take the essay more seriously than others? Discuss the possible reasons for the different reactions your classmates recorded.
2. In his introduction, J.R. notes that this piece is a memoir excerpt in which "facts . . . merge happily with fertile exaggerations." Working with a classmate, see if you can agree upon which details are facts and which are probably exaggerations. Do you agree with J.R. that the two "merge happily"? Why, or why not?
3. Write a brief description of Sedaris's voice in this piece of writing. What tone does he achieve? What is his attitude toward the people he

writes about? Toward his readers? Cite passages in the text to support your claims.

MAKING CONNECTIONS

4. In this selection, Sedaris offers a glimpse of the relationships he and his siblings had at home with their father. Read the essays by Ron Suskind (p. 634) and Michael Nava (p. 647) in this chapter, and compare the parent-child relationships depicted in them. What do these relationships reveal about the idea of "home"? Do they suggest certain characteristics that make a home a healthy or nurturing place for children to grow and learn? Write out your answer, and bring it to class for discussion.
5. What do you think Stephanie Coontz, author of "The Way We Wish We Were." (p. 676), would make of this selection by Sedaris? Would she applaud it as a clear-eyed representation of life with his family? Would she see it as too incredible because of its exaggerations? After rereading Coontz's essay, write a brief review of Sedaris's "Cyclops" from what you consider Coontz's perspective.

JOINING THE CONVERSATION

6. Did a parent, other family member, or perhaps a favorite teacher make a lasting impression on you in his or her dogged effort to instill valuable life lessons? Try writing a caricature of that person, capturing the humor and poignancy of your relationship with that person and the effects those lessons had on you.
7. Would your siblings, friends, or parents recall scenes from your childhood or home the same way you do? To find out, write a paragraph describing a significant event in your life or a place in which you once lived, and ask someone who was there at the time to write about the same thing. Share your descriptions with each other, by email or by mail if necessary. Note the differences and talk together about them. Use this exercise as the basis for an essay on images of "home," the truth of experience, or the reliability of memory.

JAMAICA KINCAID
Sowers and Reapers: The Unquiet World of a Flower Bed

*W*HEN I FIRST READ *Jamaica Kincaid's essay, published in* The New Yorker *(January 22, 2001), it transported me almost immediately to my grandmother Cunningham's yard in Tennessee, with its huge and spreading weeping willow. As a child, I used to creep under the swinging branches, to the trunk, and sit there surrounded by green light and beauty, my own special garden. Now I wonder: Who planted that willow tree? Whose labor was expended—and at what cost? What I would give to ask my grandmother some questions, because she—as the last child born late in life to a Union soldier in the Civil War—would have undoubtedly had stories to tell. For me, however, this private garden invoked peace and solitude and harmony.*

But for Jamaica Kincaid (b. 1949), gardens are by no means peaceful; they are "unquiet" and "not a place to lose your cares; the garden is not a place of rest and repose." Her essay does much to illuminate this view, taking us to stark gardens next to nuclear power stations, to gardens memorializing the Holocaust, and to the gardens of Middleton Place and Monticello, where slaves made gardens—and what these gardens produced—possible. Thus the story she tells about gardens is a complex one that may not please everyone in her audience. What do you make of the gardens where you live? What histories can they tell about those who labored to create them?

I first encountered Kincaid in the pages of The New Yorker, *and I quickly sought out some of her other work. Born Elaine Potter Richardson in Antigua, Kincaid came to New York to study photography—and changed her name because members of her family objected to her writing. A number of her books explore homeland and family matters—including* At the Bottom of the River *(1983),* Annie John *(1985),* The Autobiography of My Mother *(1995),* My Brother *(1997),* A Small Place *(2000), and* Mr. Potter *(2002). In an interview with Marilyn Snell, Kincaid says that she always resists happy endings: "Americans like to be funny, they like to laugh and they like a happy ending—which accounts I think for the sorry state of American writing life." Read "Sowers and Reapers," and decide for yourself whether its ending is happy or not.*

—A.L.

Why must people insist that the garden is a place of rest and repose, a place to forget the cares of the world, a place in which to distance yourself from the painful responsibility that comes with being a human being?

The day after I spoke to a group of people at the Garden Conservancy's tenth-anniversary celebration, in Charleston, South Carolina, an American man named Frank Cabot, the chairman and founder of the organization and a very rich man, who has spent some of his money creating a spectacular garden in the surprisingly hospitable climate of eastern Canada, told me that he was sorry I had been invited, that he was utterly offended by what I had said and the occasion I had used to say it, for I had done something unforgivable—I had introduced race and politics into the garden.

There were three of us on a panel, and our topic was "My Favorite Garden." One of the speakers said that his favorite was Hidcote Manor, in England, created by an American Anglophile named Lawrence Johnston. (A very nice climbing yellow rose, which is sometimes available through the Wayside Gardens catalogue, is named after him.) There are at least a thousand gardens in every corner of the world, but especially in England, that should come before Hidcote as a choice for favorite garden. The garden of the film-maker Derek Jarman, who succumbed to AIDS in 1994, is a particularly good example. Dramatically set in the shadow of a nuclear-power station in Dungeness, Kent, surrounding a one-story house that has been painted black, this garden, when I saw it, was abloom with poppies in brilliant shades and with Crambe maritima (sea kale) and pathways lined with pebbles, the kind found at the seashore, and all sorts of worn-down objects that looked as if they were the remains of a long-ago shipwreck just found. When you see it for the first time, it so defies what you expect that this thought really will occur to you: Now, what is a garden? And, at the same time, you will be filled with pleasure and inspiration.

Another man spoke of a garden he was designing in Chicago which would include a re-creation of a quadripartite garden made by prisoners in Auschwitz. (This way of organizing a garden is quite common, and it has a history that begins with Genesis 2:10—"A river issues from Eden to water the garden, and it then divides and becomes four branches.") The garden in Auschwitz was created over many years and by many people, all of whom were facing death, and it gave me a sharp pang to realize that, while waiting to be brutally murdered, some people had made a garden.

I had prepared a talk in which I was going to say that my favorite gar- 5
den is the Garden of Eden, because every time I see a garden that I love it becomes my favorite garden until I see another garden that I love and completely forget the garden that so dominated my affections a short time before; and also because this garden, Eden, is described in the fewest words I have ever seen used to describe a garden, and yet how unforgettable and vivid the description remains: "And from the ground the Lord God caused to grow every tree that was pleasing to the sight and good for food, with the tree of life in the middle of the garden, and the tree of knowledge of good and bad."

But after that man spoke of the Holocaust garden, a nice speech on Eden was no longer possible.

I heard myself telling my audience that I had been surprised to see, on the way into my hotel, in the little park across the way, a statue of John Caldwell Calhoun, that inventor of the rhetoric of states' rights and the evil encoded in it, who was elected Vice-President of the United States twice. I remarked on how hard it must be for the black citizens of Charleston to pass each day by the statue of a man who hated them, cast in a heroic pose. And then I wondered if anyone in the audience had seen the Holocaust memorial right next to the statue of John Caldwell Calhoun: a strange cryptlike, criblike structure, another commemoration of some of the people who were murdered by the Germans. Then I said that John Caldwell Calhoun was not altogether so far removed from Adolf Hitler; that these two men seem to be more in the same universe than not.

It was all this and more that I said that made Frank Cabot angry at me, but not long after his outburst I joined a group of attendees to the conference who were going off to tour and have dinner at Middleton Place, the famous plantation. Middleton is a popular destination for Americans who are interested in gardens, garden history, or a whiff of the sweet stench that makes up so much of American history. It is, on the one hand, a series of beautiful rooms in the garden sense: there is a part for roses only, there is a part for azaleas, there is a part for camellias, and so on and so on. The most spectacular part of the garden is a grassy terrace made by human hands, and on the slope of the terrace are small and perfectly regular risings, so that when seen from below they look like stiff pleats in a skirt that has just been disturbed by a faint breeze. At the foot of the terrace are two small lakes that have been fashioned to look like a butterfly stilled by chloroform. It is all very beautiful, even slightly awesome; and then there is the awfulness, for those gardens and that terrace and those lakes were made by slaves. The water from the river adjacent to the plantation was channelled to flood the rice fields, and this was done by slaves, who had brought their rice-cultivation skills with them from Africa. For, as far as I know, there are no rice fields in England, Scotland, Ireland, or Wales. I was feeling quite sad about all this when I came upon a big rubble of bricks. It was all that remained of the main house on the plantation in the wake of the strategy, conceived by that ingenious pyromaniac and great general from the North, William Tecumseh Sherman, which had helped to bring the traitorous South to its knees. As I walked toward a tent to have a dinner of black-eyed peas and rice, ribs and chicken and sweet potatoes, a dinner that I think of as the cuisine of black people from the American South, and where I would hear the Lester Lanin orchestra accompany a white man imitating the voice of Louis Armstrong as he sang songs made famous by Louis Armstrong, I ran into Mr. Frank Cabot, and I kept from him a fact that I happen to know: Arthur Middleton, of Middleton plantation, was one of the signers of the Declaration of Independence.

Nowhere is the relationship between the world and the garden better documented than in Thomas Jefferson's "Garden and Farm Books," an obsessively detailed account of his domestic life. People like to say that Jefferson is an enigma, that he was a man of contradictions, as if those things could not be said of just about anybody. But you have only to read anything he wrote, and you will find the true man, Thomas Jefferson, who is always so unwittingly transparent, always most revealing when confident that he has covered his tracks. He tried to write an autobiography, but he stopped before he had written a hundred pages. In it he states that he was born, that his father's name was Peter, that he wrote the Declaration of Independence, that he went to France and witnessed the French Revolution. The whole thing reads as if it were composed by one of the many marble busts of him which decorate the vestibules of government buildings. The Jefferson to be found in the autobiography is the unwittingly transparent Jefferson. The Jefferson who is confident that he has covered his tracks is to be found in the "Garden and Farm Books." The first entry in the "Garden" book is so beautiful, and so simple a statement: "1766. Shadwell. Mar. 30. Purple hyacinth begins to bloom." It goes on: "Apr. 6. Narcissus and Puckoon open. [Apr.] 13. Puckoon flowers fallen. [Apr.] 16. a bluish colored, funnel-formed flower in low-grounds in bloom." (This must have been Mertensia virginica.) The entries continue in this way for years, until 1824: the peas are sown, the asparagus planted, the fruit trees planted, the vegetables reaped. Each entry reads as if it were a single line removed from a poem: something should come before, and something should come after. And what should come before and after is to be found in the "Farm" book, and it comes in the form of a list of names: Ursula, George, Jupiter, Davy, Minerva, Caesar, and Jamy; and the Hemings, Beverly, Betty, Peter, John, and Sally. (Why is it that people who readily agree that Jefferson owned Sally Hemings cannot believe that he slept with her?) It is they who sowed the peas, dug the trenches, and filled them with manure. It is they who planted and harvested the corn. And when Jefferson makes this entry in his "Garden" book, on April 8, 1794—"our first dish of Asparagus"—it is they who have made it possible for him to enjoy asparagus. None of these names appear in the "Garden" book; the garden is free of their presence, but they turn up in the "Farm" book, and in painful, but valuable-to-know, detail. Little Beverly Hemings, Jefferson's son by Sally, must have been a very small boy the year that he was allotted one and a half yards of wool. One year, John Hemings, Sally's uncle, received, along with Sally's mother, seven yards of linen, five yards of blue wool, and a pair of shoes. On and on it goes: the garden emerging from the farm, the garden unable to exist without the farm, the garden kept apart from the farm, race and politics kept out of the garden.

But, you know, the garden Jefferson made at Monticello is not really very 10
good. You don't see it and think, Now, there is something I would like to do. It is not beautiful in the way that the garden George Washington's slaves made at Mount Vernon is beautiful. (I owe this new appreciation of Mount Vernon to Mac Griswold and her excellent book *Washington's Gardens at Mount Vernon: Landscape of the Inner Man*.) There is hardly anything featured in the garden at Monticello that makes you want to rush home, subdue a few people, and re-

create it. And the reason might be that Jefferson was less interested in the garden than in the marvellous things grown there. Each year, I order packets of something he grew, Dolichos lablab, purple hyacinth beans, something no garden should be without. What is beautiful about Monticello is the views, whether you are looking out from the house or looking at it from far away. Jefferson did not so much make a garden as a landscape. The explanation for this may be very simple: his father was a surveyor. This might also explain why he is responsible for some of the great vistas we know—the American West.

Not long after I returned from Charleston, a small amount of money that I had not expected came my way. In my ongoing conversation with my garden, I had for a very long time wanted to build a wall to add to its shape and character. So I immediately called Ron Pembroke, the maker of the most excellent landscapes in the area where I live. My house is situated on a little rise, a knoll, and I find the way it looks from many angles in the general landscape to be very pleasing, and so I had firmly in mind just the kind of wall I wanted. But Ron Pembroke, after walking me up and down and back and forth with a measuring tape in his hand, and taking me in his truck to see the other walls he had built, convinced me that my design was really quite ugly and that his was beautiful and superior.

And so began the building of two hundred-foot-long walls, one above the other, separated by a terrace eight feet wide. One day, four men arrived in the yard, and they were accompanied by big pieces of machinery, including, of course, an earthmover. The men began to rearrange the slope that fell away from the house, and by the end of the day my nice house looked as if it were the only thing left standing after a particularly disastrous natural event. The construction of the walls went on. Day after day, four men, whose names were Jared Clawson, Dan, Tony, and John, came and dug trenches and pounded stakes into the ground after they had looked through a surveyor's instrument many times. One day, truckloads of coarsely pummelled gray stone were deposited in the driveway and carefully laid at the bottom of the trenches. Another day, truckloads of a beautiful gray, blue, yellowish, and glistening stone were delivered and left on the lawn. This stone came from a quarry in Goshen, Massachusetts, Ron Pembroke told me. It is the stone he prefers to use when he builds walls, and it is more expensive than other kinds of stone, but it does display his work to best advantage. My two walls, he said, would most likely require a hundred tons of stone.

The walls started to take shape, at first almost mysteriously. The four men began by placing stones atop one another, in a staggered arrangement, so that always one stone was resting on top of two. In the beginning, each stone they picked up seemed to be just the perfect one needed. But then things began to get more difficult. Sometimes a stone would be carried to the wall with great effort and, after being pounded into place, it would not look quite right to Tony and Dan and John and Jared Clawson.

And did I say that all this was being done in the autumn? I do not know if that is the ideal time to build a wall, but I was so happy to see my walls being made that I became very possessive of the time spent on them and wanted the four men to be building only my walls. I didn't begrudge them lunchtime or time taken to smoke a cigarette, but why did they have to stop working when the day was at an end, and why did the day have to come to an end, for that matter? How I loved to watch those men work, especially the man named Jared Clawson. It was he who built the stairs that made it possible to walk from the lower wall to the eight-foot-wide terrace, and then up to the level ground of a patio, which was made flush with the top of the upper wall. And the stairs were difficult to make, or so it seemed to me, for it took Jared Clawson ten days to make them.

One day, it was finished. The walls were built, and they looked fantastic. My friend Paige had given me twelve bottles of champagne, a present for my twentieth wedding anniversary. I loved the taste of this champagne so much that I gave a bottle to each of the men who had helped build my walls. How glad was my spirit when, at the end of all this, Ron Pembroke presented me with a bill, and I in turn gave him a check for the complete amount, and there was nothing between us but complete respect and admiration and no feeling of the injustice of it all, no disgust directed toward me and my nice house, beautifully set off by those dramatic walls, for he had his own house and his own wall and his own spouse and his own anniversary.

At the foot of the lower wall, I have planted five hundred daffodils, ranging in shade from bright yellow to creamy white. In the terrace separating the lower and the upper walls, I have planted two hundred Tulipa "Mrs. J. T. Scheepers," which is perhaps my favorite tulip in the world. In the four beds on either side of the patio, I have planted two hundred Tulipa "Blue Diamond," a hundred Tulipa "Angelique," and only fifty of Tulipa "Black Hero" because they were so expensive. Towering above these hundreds of bulbs, I planted the magnolias "Woodsman" and "Elizabeth" and "Miss Honeybee"; and then Magnolia zenii and Magnolia denudata. At the beginning of the woodland, which I can see from a certain angle if I am standing on the upper wall, I planted a hundred Fritillaria meleagris and fifty each of Galanthus elwesii and Galanthus nivalis.

Ron Pembroke refilled the trenches with a rich topsoil, a mixture of composted organic material and riverbank soil, but I did not see one earthworm wriggling around in it, and this made me worry, for I have such a reverence for earthworms, whose presence signifies that the soil is good. Their anxious, iridescent, wriggly form, when confronted with broad daylight, is very reassuring. We may be made from dust (the dust of the garden, I presume), but it is not to dust that we immediately return; first, we join the worms.

The garden is not a place to lose your cares; the garden is not a place of rest and repose. Even God did not find it so.

QUESTIONING THE TEXT

1. What argument does this essay make? Summarize it in a sentence or two. What evidence in the text supports your reading of the essay's argument? Explore these questions with one or two classmates, and then share your findings in class discussion.
2. How does Kincaid challenge the image of the garden as a "place of rest and repose, a place to forget the cares of the world"? Work with a classmate to list the ways in which she does so.
3. Before she delivered her talk to a garden conservancy audience, Kincaid says she intended to speak of the Garden of Eden as her "favorite garden" (paragraph 5). At the end of her essay, she alludes again to the Garden of Eden with the statement, "Even God did not find [the garden a place of rest]." What does the Garden of Eden suggest about the place of gardens in life? What other gardens does Kincaid describe? What purpose does each one seem to serve in the essay? Share your observations in class discussion.

MAKING CONNECTIONS

4. Kincaid conjures the common connection between gardens and memorials in her anecdote of "the little park" where she encountered a statue of John Caldwell Calhoun and a Holocaust memorial (paragraph 7). Her description of the latter as a "strange, cryptlike, criblike structure" is one of several arresting juxtapositions of pleasant and offensive images that contribute to her complicated portrayal of gardens in the essay. Compare Kincaid's essay to Ed Madden's poem, "Family Cemetery, near Hickory Ridge, Arkansas," at the end of this chapter (p. 711). What does each piece suggest about families, the lives they create for themselves, and the beauty they attempt to fashion in those lives? How does each author use imagery to evoke reflection on these topics? Note your responses in your reading log, if you keep one. You might also use your notes on these questions to begin writing an essay on gardens or memorials you have encountered.
5. In discussing Jefferson's gardens at Monticello and her own terraced garden, Kincaid presents two distinct models of labor. What does she imply about the work that goes into building people's homes and gardens? Relate her implicit comments about work to those in one of the selections in Chapter 9, such as "Work Makes Life Sweet" by bell hooks (p. 744) or "Behind the Counter" by Eric Schlosser (p. 789). Use these readings to help you think about the differences between hard

work that is well compensated and work that is exploitative. Talk over your responses with two classmates.

JOINING THE CONVERSATION

6. Write a personal history essay that explores the questions posed by A.L. in her introduction to "Sowers and Reapers": "What do you make of the gardens where you live? What histories can they tell about those who labored to create them?" Do research by interviewing family members and others who may have personal knowledge that could inform your essay. You could also consult library resources and local archives or historical societies.
7. Imagine that you were invited to speak, as Kincaid was, on your "favorite garden." What would you say? Compose a short speech on the topic to present before your class. Consider recording your speech for submission to a local radio program that accepts short oral essays.

ED MADDEN

Family Cemetery, near Hickory Ridge, Arkansas

WE FEEL THE TOUCH of our extended families at important moments of transition: birth, graduation, marriage, death. Anyone with a large clan knows, however, that such occasions can bring out the worst in people. Cousins grown a lanky foot taller in the last year may trade blows (or gossip) at a wedding; at a baptism, aunts from different sides of the family may quarrel over the choice of godparents; and otherwise dutiful children may spend a holiday reunion silently coveting Grandpa's power tools or Grandma's jewelry, wondering who will inherit these treasures someday.

Yet at such thresholds, we need our families too and look for support from the people who have known us from our birth, who share our rambling gait, conspicuous nose, and deepest memories.

In the following poem, Ed Madden writes about one such family time. Madden (b. 1963) is a poet and a professor at the University of South Carolina. He grew up on a rice and soybean farm in northeast Arkansas. His interests range from theology and feminist theory to pop culture and Elvis Presley, and his poems have appeared in College English, Christianity and Literature, *and elsewhere.* —J.R.

I

Redwing blackbirds shout
themselves hoarse from the oaks
of the cemetery. A crop-duster drones
above a nearby ricefield. The long

caravan of cars that left the church
is still arriving, the dust drifting
in waves that coat the dull green rows
of grain sorghum and soybeans, dust

still hanging in air hot
with the smell of Arkansas honeysuckle
and vetch and the sweet maroon
ferment of funeral roses.

II

I breathe deeply: the summer
grass rich at the verge of brown,
freshly mown, the musty, almost acrid
earth of this sandy hillside,

piled by the grave. These things
must be remembered, like the daffodils
in solemn yellow spurts that marked
my grandma's death, standing in silent

clusters of mourning at the cemetery,
dotting her yard like relatives, nodding,
touching, like cousins laughing, flaring
their bright lives against the grey spring wind.

III

Grandpa's flowers are scattered
down the line of tombstones, decorating
the graves of his wife, his children;
it seems the office of aunts to gather

the blooms, to drape these odd dots
and splashes, against brown earth, grey stone.
We the men, the sons and grandsons,
take the shovels in groups of three,

marking our ties with the thuds that fill
the grave: it is love, it is something
of God. And there must be a word
to fill the hole it creates.

IN RESPONSE

1. Read "Family Cemetery" alongside Alice Walker's piece (p. 642), and respond with a paragraph on your own definition of *family*. If you keep a reading log, write the paragraph there.

2. Examine the role that nature plays in "Family Cemetery." In a short analysis, explain your reaction to the sights, sounds, and smells in this poem.
3. In a group, share your experience of a family moment that you might turn into a poem.

OTHER READINGS

Ehrlich, Gretel. "Home Is How Many Places." *Islands, the Universe, Home.* New York: Viking, 1991. A mix of Chumash Indian history and personal narrative, this essay recounts the author's trip to the Santa Barbara Channel Islands.

Garr, Evan. "Is Going Home Possible?" *The American Enterprise* May/June 1998: 50–51. Defends "home-by-choice" mothers.

Hoagland, Edward. "A Peaceable Kingdom." *The Best American Essays 1998.* Eds. Cynthia Ozick and Robert Atwan. New York: Houghton, 1998. 157–62. Describes an idyllic country home.

Kidder, Tracy. *Home Town.* New York: Random, 1999. A portrait of life in Northampton, Massachusetts, at the end of the twentieth century.

Preston, John, ed. *Hometowns: Gay Men Write about Where They Belong.* New York: Dutton, 1992. A collection of essays by twenty-eight gay writers about their isolation during adolescence, their sense of home, and their need to belong.

Rushdie, Salman. *The Wizard of Oz.* London: BFI, 1992. An analysis of the classic film and a reflection on what it means to desire home.

Switzer, Ellen. *Anyplace but Here: Young, Alone, and Homeless.* Boston: Atheneum, 1992. A study based on numerous interviews with young people living on the streets.

Walker, Alice. "Home." *Anything We Love Can Be Saved.* New York: Random, 1997. 71–73. A short reflection that locates "home" for the author in the presence of family.

ELECTRONIC RESOURCES

http://www.outproud.org

The National Coalition for Gay, Lesbian, Bisexual & Transgender Youth provides coming-out stories, information about school safety, biographical profiles of role models, surveys, book reviews, and suggested readings.

http://www.salon1999.com/sneaks/sneakpeeks970108.html

Leora Tanenbaum reviews Barbara Dafoe Whitehead's *The Divorce Culture* and suggests additional material on the subject.

http://www.afa.net/

The American Family Association defends traditional family values, particularly against assaults in entertainment media.

http://www.fathers.com/

The National Center for Fathering offers fathers advice for improving their parenting skills.

Work sucks.
A comedy from Mike Judge, creator of 'Beavis and Butt-head' and co-creator of 'King of the Hill'
Office Space
TWENTIETH CENTURY FOX PRESENTS A MIKE JUDGE FILM "OFFICE SPACE"
RON LIVINGSTON JENNIFER ANISTON STEPHEN ROOT GARY COLE Music by JOHN FRIZZELL Film Editor DAVID RENNIE Production Designer EDWARD McAVOY Director of Photography TIM SUHRSTEDT, A.S.C.
R RESTRICTED
Executive Producer GUY RIEDEL Produced by MICHAEL ROTENBERG DANIEL RAPPAPORT Written for the Screen and Directed by MIKE JUDGE www.officeguy.com
FEBRUARY 19 ONLY IN THEATRES

Look carefully at the image on the preceding page of a promotional poster for the 1999 comedy film, *Office Space*. Does it make you laugh? ■ What elements in the poster contribute to its humor? ■ What other responses to the poster do you have? ■ How do the image and the text work together to achieve the poster's effects? ■ Why do you think the image of the man was placed on a plain white background? ■ What does this kind of background suggest about the worker's surroundings? ■ When you look at this picture, what familiar truths about work do you recognize?

9

Work: As Poor Richard Says . . .

We are taxed twice as much by our idleness, three times as much by our pride, and four times as much by our folly; and from these taxes the commissioners cannot ease or deliver us by allowing an abatement.

BENJAMIN FRANKLIN, *The Way to Wealth*

My first job was to jump off a burning ship into salt water with dangerous tides. I lived.

MERIDEL LESUEUR, *Women and Work*

[T]he biggest reason for the pay gap is not discrimination against individual women but rather discrimination against women's occupations. As the percentage of women in an occupation rises, wages tend to fall.

NAOMI BARKO, *The Other Gender Gap*

[I]nequality of *outcome* cannot be used as proof of inequality of *opportunity* unless the groups being compared are identical in all of their psychological traits, which is likely to be true only if we are blank slates. But the suggestion that the gender gap may arise, even in part, from differences between the sexes can be fightin' words.

STEVEN PINKER, *Gender*

I was materialistic to the core: I loved money; I loved the idea of money; I even liked novels about the rich and movies about how the poor became rich. I liked everything about money except the prospect of buckling down and making it.

ARTHUR KRYSTAL, *Who Speaks for the Lazy?*

Today's advanced cyborg technology is a harbinger of neither a utopian nor an apocalyptic future.

EDWARD TENNER, *Body Smarts*

[S]outhern black work traditions taught us the importance of working with integrity irrespective of the task.

BELL HOOKS, *Work Makes Life Sweet*

It is human to work, to bend and trip, to lift and pull. It's never about getting tired or dirty. There is nothing wrong with sweat and toil. It is only about conditions and decent wages that there can come complaint.

DAGOBERTO GILB, *Work Union*

Fast food kitchens often seem like a scene from *Bugsy Malone,* a film in which all the actors are children pretending to be adults. No other industry in the United States has a workforce so dominated by adolescents.

ERIC SCHLOSSER, *Behind the Counter*

The work of the world is common as mud. MARGE PIERCY, *To Be of Use*

Introduction

THE UNITED STATES OF AMERICA declared its independence from Great Britain in 1776, the same year that the Scottish philosopher Adam Smith (1723–90) published what would become the classic work on capitalism, *The Wealth of Nations.* The conjunction of events proved to be auspicious: nowhere on earth would the principles of free market capitalism be more enthusiastically applied than in the nation assembled from Britain's thirteen rebellious colonies. The revolutionaries in New York, Virginia, and Massachusetts fought not only for political liberty but also for the freedom to buy and sell in competitive world markets. At the time of the War of Independence, American entrepreneurs, schooled in the economic wisdom of Benjamin Franklin's Poor Richard, had already set into motion economic forces that would make the United States affluent and powerful.

The American Revolution also coincided with the dawn of the industrial revolution. Within a century after the shots fired at Lexington and Concord, powerful new machines capable of doing many times the work of manual laborers had transformed the economic structure of the nation. Processes as different as weaving, mining, and reaping would be successfully mechanized, reducing the cost of goods and making them available to more people. And the new industries would generate yet more capital, leading to still more entrepreneurship, investment, and development. It seemed that a formula for enduring prosperity had been discovered.

But the convergence of industrialism and capitalism also brought suffering. Human labor became a commodity measurable by the hour and subject to market forces. People looking for employment abandoned the countryside to crowd into urban slums with high crime and poor sanitation. Disease was rampant. Workers, many of them mere children, faced grueling days in dangerous factories and mines, earning meager wages that they then often had to spend in company stores. Mills and foundries brutalized the landscape, darkening the skies and fouling the rivers.

In England, conditions like these moved Karl Marx to write *Das Kapital* (vol. 1, 1867), in which he condemned laissez-faire capitalism, predicted its demise, and imagined a utopian socialist alternative: communism. For more than a century afterward, capitalists and communists struggled worldwide for economic and military supremacy—the United States and western Europe as the major proponents of free markets and entrepreneurship, and the Soviet Union, China, and eastern Europe as the advocates of socialism.

Socialism lost. Today, serious arguments for Marxist economics are still being made only perhaps in China, in Cuba, and in American universities. Overcoming industrialism's initial ills, capitalist countries offered their citizens vastly greater wealth and liberty than authoritarian Marxist regimes could. Labor unions and numerous reform movements in the West also helped quash monopolies and increase membership in the dominant middle class. Yet all is not perfect. Far from it.

In this chapter, we explore some of the economic problems and opportunities that Americans still face today—a subject both vast and complicated. Some of our selections examine the nature of American economic thinking; others look at the ways Americans actually work in or are excluded from the economic mainstream. At times, we can only point to areas for more reading and exploration. This is one chapter we know will raise many questions and provoke lengthy debates.

Following are some questions that you may want to think about as you read this chapter:

- How do Americans feel about work?
- Have the economic values of Americans changed? What major questions of economics divide people or political parties in the United States?
- What rights do workers have to a job? For what reasons may employers exclude someone from employment?
- Does the United States manage prosperity well?
- What is the mission of business?
- Do we put too much emphasis on work? Do Americans fear leisure?

• • •

BENJAMIN FRANKLIN
The Way to Wealth

*T*HE MAXIMS OR APHORISMS *that Benjamin Franklin (1704–90) recorded in* Poor Richard's Almanac *(first issue, 1733) have become part of American folk culture. Most Americans are introduced at a young age to Franklin's advice on waking early and hoarding change:*

> *Early to bed, and early to rise, makes a man healthy, wealthy, and wise.*
>
> *A penny saved is a penny earned.*

Because such adages are short and amusing, we're apt to dismiss them as childish stuff. Why, then, do they and many other sayings from Franklin's "The Way to Wealth" persist in our memories?

Perhaps common sense and thrift never go out of style. The adages Father Abraham doles out in the essay Franklin wrote to mark the twenty-fifth anniversary of Poor Richard's Almanac *still ring true to many readers eager to get ahead. To Franklin's credit, his advice was as stern and honest in 1758 as it is today: you get rich not by manipulating stock funds or light-footing your way through real estate deals but by working hard, spending little, saving a lot, and borrowing nothing.*

How deeply embedded in the American psyche are attitudes typified by Poor Richard's maxims? It is hard to say. Benjamin Franklin's fictional character reveals a disturbing mistrust of leisure. Serious writers have even described Franklin—an aggressive, hardheaded, and penurious genius—as the very embodiment of America's defining Protestant ethic. In some ways, perhaps old Ben still makes us feel guilty every time we reach for the MasterCard.

In "The Way to Wealth," Franklin's persona of Poor Richard is at an auction where he hears Father Abraham repeat the most famous maxims from Poor Richard's Almanac. *This framing device allows Richard (a.k.a. Franklin) to comment on his own wisdom without seeming to praise himself too much.* —J.R.

PREFACE TO POOR RICHARD IMPROVED

Courteous Reader,

I have heard that nothing gives an author so great pleasure, as to find his works respectfully quoted by other learned authors. This pleasure I have seldom enjoyed; for though I have been, if I may say it without vanity, an eminent author of almanacs annually now a full quarter of a century, my brother authors in the same way, for what reason I know not, have ever been very sparing in their applauses, and no other author has taken the least notice of me, so that did not my writings produce me some solid pudding, the great deficiency of praise would have quite discouraged me.

I concluded at length, that the people were the best judges of my merit; for they buy my works; and besides, in my rambles, where I am not personally known, I have frequently heard one or other of my adages repeated, with "as Poor Richard says" at the end on 't; this gave me some satisfaction, as it showed not only that my instructions were regarded, but discovered likewise some respect for my authority; and I own, that to encourage the practice of remembering and repeating those wise sentences, I have sometimes quoted myself with great gravity.

Judge, then, how much I must have been gratified by an incident I am going to relate to you. I stopped my horse lately where a great number of people were collected at a vendue* of merchant goods. The hour of sale not being come, they were conversing on the badness of the times and one of the company called to a plain clean old man, with white locks, "Pray, Father Abraham, what think you of the times? Won't these heavy taxes quite ruin the country? How shall we be ever able to pay them? What would you advise us to?" Father Abraham stood up, and replied, "If you'd have my advice, I'll give it you in short, for a *word to the wise is enough, and many words won't fill a bushel,* as Poor Richard says." They joined in desiring him to speak his mind, and gathering round him, he proceeded as follows:

"Friends," says he, "and neighbors, the taxes are indeed very heavy, and if those laid on by the government were the only ones we had to pay, we might more easily discharge them; but we have many others, and much more grievous to some of us. We are taxed twice as much by our idleness, three times as much by our pride, and four times as much by our folly; and from these taxes the commissioners cannot ease or deliver us by allowing an abatement. However, let us hearken to good advice, and something may be done for us; *God helps them that help themselves,* as Poor Richard says, in his Almanack of 1733.

"It would be thought a hard government that should tax its people one- 5
tenth part of their time, to be employed in its service. But idleness taxes many of us much more, if we reckon all that is spent in absolute sloth, or doing of nothing, with that which is spent in idle employments or amusements, that amount to nothing. Sloth, by bringing on diseases, absolutely shortens life. *Sloth, like rust, consumes faster than labor wears; while the used key is always bright,* as Poor Richard says. *But dost thou love life, then do not squander time, for that's the stuff life is made of,* as Poor Richard says. How much more than is necessary do we spend in sleep, forgetting that *the sleeping fox catches no poultry* and that *there will be sleeping enough in the grave,* as Poor Richard says.

"*If time be of all things the most precious, wasting time must be,* as Poor Richard says, *the greatest prodigality;* since, as he elsewhere tells us, *lost time is never found again; and what we call time enough, always proves little enough:* let us

vendue: a sale

then up and be doing, and doing to the purpose; so by diligence shall we do more with less perplexity. *Sloth makes all things difficult, but industry all easy,* as Poor Richard says; *and he that riseth late must trot all day, and shall scarce overtake his business at night;* while *laziness travels so slowly, that poverty soon overtakes him,* as we read in Poor Richard, who adds, *drive thy business, let not that drive thee,* and *early to bed, and early to rise, makes a man healthy, wealthy, and wise.*

"So what signifies wishing and hoping for better times. We may make these times better, if we bestir ourselves. *Industry need not wish,* as Poor Richard says, *and he that lives upon hope will die fasting. There are no gains without pains; then help hands, for I have no lands,* or if I have, they are smartly taxed. And, as Poor Richard likewise observes, *he that hath a trade hath an estate; and he that hath a calling, hath an office of profit and honor;* but then the trade must be worked at, and the calling well followed, or neither the estate nor the office will enable us to pay our taxes. If we are industrious, we shall never starve, for, as Poor Richard says, *at the workingman's house hunger looks in, but dares not enter.* Nor will the bailiff or the constable enter, for *industry pays debts, while despair increaseth them,* says Poor Richard. What though you have found no treasure, nor has any rich relation left you a legacy, *diligence is the mother of goodluck,* as Poor Richard says, and *God gives all things to industry. Then plow deep, while sluggards sleep, and you shall have corn to sell and to keep,* says Poor Dick. Work while it is called today, for you know not how much you may be hindered tomorrow, which makes Poor Richard say, *one today is worth two tomorrows,* and farther, *have you somewhat to do tomorrow, do it today.* If you were a servant, would you not be ashamed that a good master should catch you idle? Are you then your own master, *be ashamed to catch yourself idle,* as Poor Dick says. When there is so much to be done for yourself, your family, your country, and your gracious king, be up by peep of day; *let not the sun look down and say, inglorious here he lies.* Handle your tools without mittens; remember that *the cat in gloves catches no mice,* as Poor Richard says. 'Tis true there is much to be done, and perhaps you are weak-handed, but stick to it steadily; and you will see great effects, for *constant dropping wears away stones,* and *by diligence and patience the mouse ate in two the cable;* and *little strokes fell great oaks,* as Poor Richard says in his Almanack, the year I cannot just now remember.

"Methinks I hear some of you say, 'must a man afford himself no leisure?' I will tell thee, my friend, what Poor Richard says, *employ thy time well, if thou meanest to gain leisure; and, since thou art not sure of a minute, throw not away an hour.* Leisure is time for doing something useful; this leisure the diligent man will obtain, but the lazy man never; so that, as Poor Richard says *a life of leisure and a life of laziness are two things.* Do you imagine that sloth will afford you more comfort than labor? No, for as Poor Richard says, *trouble springs from idleness, and grievous toil from needless ease. Many without labor, would live by their wits only, but they break for want of stock.* Whereas industry gives comfort, and plenty, and respect: *fly pleasures, and they'll follow you. The diligent spinner has a large shift,** *and now I have a*

---

a large shift: change of clothing, wardrobe

sheep and a cow, everybody bids me good morrow; all which is well said by Poor Richard.

"But with our industry, we must likewise be steady, settled, and careful, and oversee our own affairs with our own eyes, and not trust too much to others; for, as Poor Richard says

I never saw an oft-removed tree,
Nor yet an oft-removed family,
That throve so well as those that settled be.

And again, *three removes* is as bad as a fire;* and again, *keep thy shop, and thy shop will keep thee;* and again, *if you would have your business done, go; if not, send.* And again,

He that by the plough would thrive,
Himself must either hold or drive.

And again, *the eye of a master will do more work than both his hands;* and again, *want of care does us more damage than want of knowledge;* and again, *not to oversee workmen is to leave them your purse open.* Trusting too much to others' care is the ruin of many; for, as the Almanack says, *in the affairs of this world, men are saved, not by faith, but by the want of it;* but a man's own care is profitable; for, saith Poor Dick, *learning is to the studious,* and *riches to the careful,* as well as *power to the bold,* and *heaven to the virtuous,* and farther, *if you would have a faithful servant, and one that you like, serve yourself.* And again, he adviseth to circumspection and care, even in the smallest matters, because sometimes *a little neglect may breed great mischief;* adding, *for want of a nail the shoe was lost; for want of a shoe the horse was lost; and for want of a horse the rider was lost, being overtaken and slain by the enemy; all for want of care about a horseshoe nail.*

"So much for industry, my friends, and attention to one's own business; 10
but to these we must add frugality, if we would make our industry more certainly successful. A man may, if he knows not how to save as he gets, keep his nose all his life to the grindstone, and die not worth a groat* at last. A *fat kitchen makes a lean will,* as Poor Richard says; and

Many estates are spent in the getting,
Since women for tea forsook spinning and knitting,
And men for punch forsook hewing and splitting.

If you would be wealthy, says he, in another Almanack, *think of saving as well as of getting: the Indies have not made Spain rich, because her outgoes are greater than her incomes.*

"Away then with your expensive follies, and you will not then have so much cause to complain of hard times, heavy taxes, and chargeable families; for, as Poor Dick says,

---

removes: moves
groat: a coin of small value

Women and wine, game and deceit,
Make the wealth small and the wants great.

And farther, *what maintains one vice would bring up two children.* You may think perhaps, that a little tea, or a little punch now and then, diet a little more costly, clothes a little finer, and a little entertainment now and then, can be no great matter; but remember what Poor Richard says, *many a little makes a mickle,** and farther, *Beware of little expenses; a small leak will sink a great ship;* and again, *who dainties love shall beggars prove;* and moreover, *fools make feasts, and wise men eat them.*

"Here you are all got together at this vendue of fineries and knicknacks. You call them goods; but if you do not take care, they will prove evils to some of you. You expect they will be sold cheap, and perhaps they may for less than they cost; but if you have no occasion for them, they must be dear to you. Remember what Poor Richard says; *buy what thou hast no need of, and ere long thou shalt sell thy necessaries.* And again, *at a great pennyworth pause a while:* he means, that perhaps the cheapness is apparent only, and not real; or the bargain, by straightening thee in thy business, may do thee more harm than good. For in another place he says, *many have been ruined by buying good pennyworths.* Again, Poor Richard says, *'tis foolish to lay out money in a purchase of repentance;* and yet this folly is practiced every day at vendues, for want of minding the Almanack. *Wise men,* as Poor Dick says, *learn by others' harms, fools scarcely by their own;* but *felix quem faciunt aliena pericula cautum.** Many a one, for the sake of finery on the back, have gone with a hungry belly, and half-starved their families. *Silks and satins, scarlet and velvets,* as Poor Richard says, *put out the kitchen fire.*

"These are not the necessaries of life; they can scarcely be called the conveniences; and yet only because they look pretty, how many want to have them! The artificial wants of mankind thus become more numerous than the natural; and, as Poor Dick says, *for one poor person, there are an hundred indigent.* By these, and other extravagancies, the genteel are reduced to poverty, and forced to borrow of those whom they formerly despised, but who through industry and frugality have maintained their standing; in which case it appears plainly, that *a plowman on his legs is higher than a gentleman on his knees,* as Poor Richard says. Perhaps they have had a small estate left them, which they knew not the getting of; they think, ''Tis day, and will never be night'; that a little to be spent out of so much is not worth minding; *a child and a fool,* as Poor Richard says, *imagine twenty shillings and twenty years can never be spent* but, *always taking out of the meal-tub, and never putting in, soon comes to the bottom;* as Poor Dick says, *when the well's dry, they know the worth of water.* But this they might have known before, if they had taken his advice; *if you would know*

---

mickle: a great deal
felix . . . cautum: the Latin version of the previous saying

the value of money, go and try to borrow some; for, he that goes a-borrowing goes a-sorrowing; and indeed so does he that lends to such people, when he goes to get it in again. Poor Dick farther advises, and says,

Fond pride of dress is sure a very curse;
E'er fancy you consult, consult your purse.

And again, *pride is as loud a beggar as want, and a great deal more saucy.* When you have bought one fine thing, you must buy ten more, that your appearance may be all of a piece; but Poor Dick says, *'tis easier to suppress the first desire, than to satisfy all that follow it.* And 'tis as truly folly for the poor to ape the rich, as for the frog to swell, in order to equal the ox.

Great estates may venture more,
But little boats should keep near shore.

'Tis, however, a folly soon punished; for *pride that dines on vanity sups on contempt,* as Poor Richard says. And in another place, *pride breakfasted with plenty, dined with poverty, and supped with infamy.* And after all, of what use is this pride of appearance, for which so much is risked, so much is suffered? It cannot promote health, or ease pain; it makes no increase of merit in the person, it creates envy, it hastens misfortune.

What is a butterfly? At best
He's but a caterpillar dressed
The gaudy fop's his picture just,

as Poor Richard says.

"But what madness must it be to run in debt for these superfluities! We are offered, by the terms of this vendue, *six months' credit;* and that perhaps has induced some of us to attend it, because we cannot spare the ready money, and hope now to be fine without it. But, ah, think what you do when you run in debt; you give to another power over your liberty. If you cannot pay at the time, you will be ashamed to see your creditor; you will be in fear when you speak to him; you will make poor pitiful sneaking excuses, and by degrees come to lose your veracity, and sink into base downright lying; for, as Poor Richard says, *the second vice is lying, the first is running in debt.* And again, to the same purpose, *lying rides upon debt's back.* Whereas a free-born Englishman ought not to be ashamed or afraid to see or speak to any man living. But poverty often deprives a man of all spirit and virtue: *'tis hard for an empty bag to stand upright,* as Poor Richard truly says.

"What would you think of that prince, or that government, who should 15
issue an edict forbidding you to dress like a gentleman or a gentlewoman, on pain of imprisonment or servitude? Would you not say, that you were free, have a right to dress as you please, and that such an edict would be a breach of your privileges, and such a government tyrannical? And yet you are about to put yourself under that tyranny, when you run in debt for such dress! Your

creditor has authority at his pleasure to deprive you of your liberty, by confining you in gaol* for life, or to sell you for a servant, if you should not be able to pay him! When you have got your bargain, you may, perhaps, think little of payment; but *creditors,* Poor Richard tells us, *have better memories than debtors;* and in another place says, *creditors are a superstitious sect, great observers of set days and times.* The day comes round before you are aware, and the demand is made before you are prepared to satisfy it, or if you bear your debt in mind, the term which at first seemed so long, will, as it lessens, appear extremely short. Time will seem to have added wings to his heels as well as shoulders. *Those have a short Lent,* said Poor Richard, *who owe money to be paid at Easter.* Then since, as he says, *The borrower is a slave to the lender, and the debtor to the creditor,* disdain the chain, preserve your freedom; and maintain your independency: be industrious and free; be frugal and free. At present, perhaps, you may think yourself in thriving circumstances, and that you can bear a little extravagance without injury; but,

> *For age and want, save while you may;*
> *No morning sun lasts a whole day,*

as Poor Richard says. Gain may be temporary and uncertain, but ever while you live, expense is constant and entire; and *'tis easier to build two chimneys than to keep one in fuel,* as Poor Richard says. So, *rather go to bed supperless than rise in debt.*

> *Get what you can, and what you get hold;*
> *'Tis the stone that will turn all your lead into gold,*

as Poor Richard says. And when you have got the philosopher's stone,* sure you will no longer complain of bad times, or the difficulty of paying taxes.

"This doctrine, my friends, is reason and wisdom; but after all, do not depend too much upon your own industry, and frugality, and prudence, though excellent things, for they may all be blasted without the blessing of heaven; and therefore, ask that blessing humbly, and be not uncharitable to those that at present seem to want it, but comfort and help them. Remember, Job* suffered, and was afterwards prosperous.

"And now to conclude, *experience keeps a dear school, but fools will learn in no other, and scarce in that;* for it is true, *we may give advice, but we cannot give conduct,* as Poor Richard says: however, remember this, *they that won't be counseled, can't be helped,* as Poor Richard says: and farther, that, *if you will not hear reason, she'll surely rap your knuckles.*"

---

gaol: jail
philosopher's stone: an alchemical object capable of turning crude metals into gold
Job: a figure in the Old Testament sorely tested by God

Thus the old gentleman ended his harangue. The people heard it, and approved the doctrine, and immediately practiced the contrary, just as if it had been a common sermon; for the vendue opened, and they began to buy extravagantly, notwithstanding his cautions and their own fear of taxes. I found the good man had thoroughly studied my almanacs, and digested all I had dropped on these topics during the course of five and twenty years. The frequent mention he made of me must have tired any one else, but my vanity was wonderfully delighted with it, though I was conscious that not a tenth part of the wisdom was my own, which he ascribed to me, but rather the gleanings I had made of the sense of all ages and nations. However, I resolved to be the better for the echo of it; and though I had at first determined to buy stuff for a new coat, I went away resolved to wear my old one a little longer. Reader, if thou wilt do the same, thy profit will be as great as mine. I am, as ever, thine to serve thee,

Richard Saunders
July 7, 1757

QUESTIONING THE TEXT

1. Which of the aphorisms Franklin repeats would you regard as outdated today? Why? Explain in a paragraph.
2. Based on this selection, what role do you think Franklin expects government to play in the lives of people? Explain.
3. Do you disagree with any assumptions or assertions in J.R.'s introduction? If so, which ones and why?

MAKING CONNECTIONS

4. Read Dagoberto Gilb's "Work Union" (p. 783), and annotate it from Poor Richard's point of view. What insights, if any, does Poor Richard's perspective bring to this contemporary piece?
5. Think about Poor Richard's aphorisms as you read Marge Piercy's "To Be of Use" (p. 793). How do the two perspectives differ? How are they similar? What does this comparison imply about the view of usefulness offered by Piercy?

JOINING THE CONVERSATION

6. Have American values strayed from the path charted by Franklin's Poor Richard, or are Americans still influenced by the attitudes toward get-

ting and spending described here? Write a short dialogue between Poor Richard and a contemporary figure — Peter J. Gomes (p. 242), Jeremy Rifkin (p. 287), or Bill Gates, for example.

7. What is Poor Richard's attitude toward debt? Would such an attitude today hurt or help the U.S. economy? Explain your answer in a short letter to the editor that quotes Poor Richard at least once.
8. Could a family or individual today live normally and comfortably according to Franklin's philosophy? What problems might arise? In an essay, describe what a life lived according to Poor Richard's advice might be like.
9. Try your hand at writing a few aphorisms that Poor Richard might recommend to Americans today, and bring them in to class for discussion.

MERIDEL LESUEUR
Women and Work

MERIDEL LESUEUR (1900–96) wrote all her life in the service of those too-often-invisible Americans who do the work of our world. LeSueur—a writer who held many other jobs, including actress, stuntwoman, and labor organizer—was a fascinating figure. From her earliest essays in the 1920s, her writings offer an unromanticized and vivid picture of twentieth-century work and workers (especially women), and she was well known as an author during the 1930s and 1940s. Her association with labor organizations and with communism, however, brought down the wrath of Senator Joseph McCarthy and his cohorts. Blacklisted in the 1950s, LeSueur had great difficulty publishing her work during the next thirty years, although the last two decades of her life were kinder to her. LeSueur reported doing the "best writing" of her life at ninety-four and rejoiced at the new audience she found among the American Indian, Chicano/a, and women's movements.

LeSueur's books and essays speak to all people who know what it is to work, and especially to those who do the work of writing. In the brief autobiographical essay that follows, she reflects on what work meant in her life, on the work she was allowed (and not allowed) to do, and on the 140 notebooks of writing she accumulated over the years—one hard-working woman's "letter to the world." I chose this selection because LeSueur's work and life demonstrate how one can live through the worst deprivations, the worst economic depressions, and still find meaningful work. I also chose this piece because it's inspirational to see someone writing and thinking and publishing right to the end of a long and truly remarkable life. "Women and Work" originally appeared in a 1994 collection of essays by the same title edited by Maureen R. Michelson.

—A.L.

When I was 10 years old in 1910 I knew my two brothers could be anything they wanted. I knew I could be a wife and mother, a teacher, a nurse or a whore. And without an education, I could not be a nurse or teacher and we were very poor. Women could be china painters, quiltmakers, embroiderers. They often wrote secretly. Even read certain books secretly. My mother tried to go to college and women could not take math or history, only the domestic sciences.

I began to write down what I heard, sitting under the quilting frames. I tried to listen to these imprisoned and silenced women. I had a passion to be witness and recorder of the hidden, submerged, and silent women. I did not want to be a writer; I did not know a woman writer; I did not read a woman writer. It was a thick, heavy silence and I began to take down what I heard.

My Gramma hated my writing. "We have tried to hide what has happened to us," she said, "and now you are going to tell it." "I am. I am going to tell it," I cried, and I began a long howl and cry that finally found its voice in the women's movement, as it is called. A book I wrote in 1930, cruelly criticized by male editors, was not published until 1975. My audience was women, who now wanted to talk, bear witness.

I made my living working in factories, writing for the labor movement. A good thing for a writer to keep close to life, to the happening, and I have lived in the most brutal century of two world wars, millions killed and exploited, and now the atom bomb and the global struggle.

I went to the International Women's Conference in Nairobi at 85 years 5
old to see the thousands of women now bearing their own witness and I read my poem *Solidarity,* which I wrote for the Vietnamese Women's Union, and it was translated at once into Swahili as I read it. A great climax to my life. I believe this is the most enlightened moment I have seen in history and rooted in my life's passion to bear witness to the common struggle, the heroic people rising out of the violence, all becoming visible and alive.

My struggle was never alone, always with others. This makes my life bright with comradeship, marches with banners, tribal courage, and warmth. Remember, I didn't vote 'til I was 19 in 1919. Women only came into the offices after the first World War. Every young man I knew in high school never returned. The fathers and husbands had been killed. A terrible reaction set in after that bloody war to consolidate patriarchal money and power. The twenties were a terrible sinking into the Depression.

My mother, wanting to be an actress, sent me to dramatic school. I tried to fulfill her desires. The theater then was developing actresses who exploited the sexist feminine, and males who had to be John Waynes. The plays were also made for this image of sexism. Coming from the prairies, I played *Lady Windermere's Fan* by Oscar Wilde, learning to walk and use a fan and speak British. I didn't cotton to that at all. I went to Hollywood where again, your career was based on sexism, the female stereotypes. You had to go every morning to the hiring hall and show your legs and teeth and get a job for the day signing a contract that if you were killed or injured the company would not be responsible. Many extras were killed. You were a dime a dozen and the studios were flooded with the beautiful prairie girls from the Midwest. It was a meat market and developed one of the greatest prostitute rings in Los Angeles, San Francisco, Seattle, and Las Vegas.

My first job was to jump off a burning ship into salt water with dangerous tides. I lived. You could make $25 a day, an enormous sum, and I could save it and hole in and write for a few months. So I began to write about the open market on women; cheap labor of women, oppression and silencing and bartering of women. Also, fighting in the unions and housing. In the Depression, women were not on any list. There were no soup kitchens for women.

Also, there was the danger of sterilization. Groups of women were netted and taken to women's prisons and might be sterilized by morning. There was a theory that the only solution to the Depression was sterilization of the workers. It began to be known Hitler had the same idea.

In desperation, I think, I boldly had two children at the beginning of the Depression. You couldn't get any other kind of life, and you might give birth to friends and allies. I had two girls, who all my life, have been just that.

10 I became a correspondent from the Middle West, reporting on the farmers' struggles, the third party, all that was happening. I wrote for several national magazines and began to have stories in *American Mercury,* and university quarterlies, and writings about my children were sold to the women's magazines. So I began to make a modest living at writing, which was wonderful. I became known as a witness, as I wanted to be. I became well known for two pieces: *Corn Village,* about the small town; and, I *Was Marching,* about the '34 teamsters' strike.

I feel we must be deeply rooted in the tribal family and in the social community. This is becoming a strong and beautiful force now in our societies. Women speaking out boldly, going to jail for peace and sanctuary, defending the children against hunger. We still get half of what men get. But as I saw in Nairobi the struggle of women is now global. My Gramma and mother are not any more silenced and alone. Writing has become with women not a concealment, but an illumination. We are not alone. The hundreds of women writers now who speak for us to a large audience.

This makes me write more than I ever did. I have 140 notebooks, my letter to the world, published some day for a new woman I dreamed of. I have 24 great grandchildren who have freedoms I could only dream of. One granddaughter is raising five children herself. Another has two sons. They are not alone; that's the point. They live in collectives and work in social fields with women and children. They have an independence I never had, a boldness and a communal life and support.

I am writing as I never wrote before. I have three books, besides my notebooks, to "finish." I call it getting in my crop before the frost! It is my best writing, I believe . . . I have learned to bear witness with love and compassion and warm readers to whom I am truthful. And they return my witness, so women rise from the darkness singing together, not the small and tortured chorus of my grandmothers, but millions becoming visible and singing.

QUESTIONING THE TEXT

1. LeSueur speaks of "female stereotypes." Reread her essay, highlighting every example of such stereotypes. How much evidence does LeSueur marshal to illustrate these stereotypes? Discuss these examples.

2. LeSueur calls Hollywood and the film industry a "meat market" (paragraph 7). What evidence does she give to support this analogy? Does the analogy still hold today? What evidence can you offer to support or refute it?

MAKING CONNECTIONS

3. Look through all the selections in this chapter, and decide which writer LeSueur has the most in common with as well as which writer she would probably disagree with most strongly. In an entry in your journal or reading log, explore these similarities and differences, and weigh in with your own ideas as well. Which of these writers do you have most in common with, and why?
4. Review Benjamin Franklin's "The Way to Wealth" (p. 720), and then try writing a few Poor Richard–like maxims as LeSueur might pen them. Bring the maxims to class for discussion.

JOINING THE CONVERSATION

5. Working with two or three classmates, draw up some questions you would like to ask people who are now in their eighties or nineties about their experiences with work. Start with your own grandparents or great-grandparents, or those of your friends. If possible, find three or four additional men and women to interview, perhaps through the American Association of Retired Persons or an assisted-living group in your community. Together, write a brief report for your class on your interviewees' experiences with work.
6. Spend some time thinking about the kind of work you most want to do. Then write an exploration of your knowledge and feelings about such work, including an examination of both positive and negative points. If you keep a reading log, explore this issue there.

NAOMI BARKO

The Other Gender Gap: Why Women Still Fail to Receive Comparable Wages for Comparable Work

*A*MONG PROPOSALS AIMED AT THE WORKPLACE, *few have raised the tempers of more folks than "comparable worth," which proposes that people who have "comparable skills, education, and experience be paid comparable amounts." Sounds simple, right? But the struggles and fights that have grown up around this concept are anything but simple. Into this fray comes freelance journalist Naomi Barko, who argues that "the other gender gap" is all about inequality of pay, and she uses several vivid and dramatic examples to support the efficacy of "comparable worth." Others were quick to respond: reviewing Barko's work, conservative American Enterprise Institute fellow Diana Furchgott-Roth attacks Barko and her argument, countering that "Comparable-worth systems are wreaking havoc in Canada, which has had some forms of comparable worth since the Canadian Human Rights Act was passed in the mid 1970s."*

When so much heat and light surround an issue, we can be pretty sure it is worth considering carefully. You may want, in fact, to do some research in your own community: How do pay scales compare for men and women? Can you detect evidence of a gender gap in pay? What other inequalities may be at work? Where I teach, students have been very active in monitoring pay issues for campus workers—and very successful in helping bring about change. In fact, students have been at the forefront of those responsible for increasing wages on my campus—for all workers. What's going on with such issues where you go to school? Barko's essay originally appeared in The American Prospect, *June 19–July 3, 2000.* —A.L.

Hazel Dews is slightly embarrassed when you ask about her salary. She pauses and then confesses that after twenty-five years cleaning the Russell Senate Office Building in Washington five nights a week, she makes barely $22,000 a year. That's not what really bothers her, though. What irks her is that men who do the same job earn $30,000.

The men, she explains, are called "laborers." They can progress five grades. The women, however, are called "custodial workers," which means they can only advance two grades. "But," she protests, "they scrub with a mop and bucket. We scrub with a mop and bucket. They vacuum. We vacuum. They push a trash truck. We push a trash truck. The only thing they do that we don't is run a scrub machine. But that's on wheels, so we could do it too."

Thirty-seven years after the Equal Pay Act of 1963, American women working full time still earn an average of 74 cents for each dollar earned by men, according to a new report published jointly by the AFL-CIO and the Institute for Women's Policy Research (IWPR) in Washington, D.C. This affects all economic classes, but its impact is strongest on lower-income workers: If men and women were paid equally, more than 50 percent of low-income households across the country—dual-earner as well as single-mother—would rise above the poverty line.

New figures challenge the long-heard arguments that women's lower pay results from fewer years in the workforce or time out for childbearing and rearing. The Women's Bureau of the Department of Labor cites a study by the president's Council of Economic Advisers showing that even in light of the vicissitudes of motherhood, 43 percent of the wage gap remains "unexplained," evidently due in large part to discrimination.

The Overview of Salary Surveys, published in 1999 by the National 5
Committee on Pay Equity (NCPE)—a coalition of thirty women's, civil rights, and religious groups—summarized twenty-three surveys of specific salary titles conducted by professional associations and trade magazines. It reported that, for instance, among women engineers—where the salary gap averages 26 percent—women with the same qualifications continue to earn less than men even after they've been in the field for many years (20.4 percent less among women with a B.S. degree and twenty to twenty-four years of experience; 19.2 percent less among women with an M.S. degree and twenty to twenty-four years experience). Yet another study found that women physicians earned less than men in forty-four of forty-five specialties, including obstetrics-gynecology (14 percent less) and pediatrics (15.8 percent less), with lower compensation only partly explainable by hours worked or time spent in the field. And a 1999 report by the American Association of University Professors found that though women had grown from 23 to 34 percent of faculty since 1975, the salary gap had actually widened in that time period.

But the biggest reason for the pay gap is not discrimination against individual women but rather discrimination against women's occupations. As the percentage of women in an occupation rises, wages tend to fall. More than 55 percent of employed women work in traditional "women's jobs"—librarians, clerical workers, nurses, teachers, and child-care workers. If these women are compared not to male workers but to women with similar education and experience in more gender-balanced occupations, they would earn about 18 percent—or $3,446—more per year, according to the IWPR. (The 8.5 percent of men in these jobs earn an average of $6,259 less per year than men of comparable backgrounds working in "men's" fields.)

Why are "women's jobs" less lucrative? Is a truck driver—who earns an average annual wage of $25,030—really 45 percent more valuable than a child-care worker who may have a four-year degree in early childhood education? Is a beginning engineer really worth between 30 and 70 percent more than a beginning teacher? Rarely, in the almost daily reports of teacher shortages, is it mentioned that the market alone cannot account for the striking disparity between teachers' and other professionals' salaries. No one ever suggests that it might have something to do with the fact that 75 percent of elementary and secondary schoolteachers are women.

In response to these disparities, women are beginning to mobilize. Three years ago, for example, Hazel Dews and 300 of her fellow women custodians joined the American Federation of State, County and Municipal Employees (AFSCME), which, after several futile attempts to negotiate, is now suing Dews's employer, the Architect of the Capitol, for equal pay. Since 1997, as women's membership in the labor movement has mushroomed to 40 percent, the AFL-CIO has conducted two surveys to discover the chief concerns of both union and nonunion working women. "And the runaway answer was equal pay," reports Karen Nussbaum, the director of the AFL-CIO's working women's department. Ninety-four percent of women in both surveys said equal pay was a top concern, and one-third—one-half of African-American women—said they did not have equal pay in their own jobs.

In 1999, calling pay equity a "family issue," the labor movement helped launch equal-pay bills in both houses of Congress and twenty-seven state legislatures. Also last year, as Dews and her co-workers were demonstrating at the Capitol, the Eastman Kodak Company was agreeing to pay $13 million in present and retroactive wages to employees underpaid on the basis of either race or gender. The Massachusetts Institute of Technology, after protests by women faculty, made an unprecedented admission that it had discriminated against women "in salaries, space, awards, resources and response to outside offers."

Moreover, since 1997, the Office of Federal Contract Compliance Pro- 10
grams (OFCCP) has collected $10 million in equal-pay settlements from such corporations as Texaco, US Airways, Pepsi-Cola, the computer manufacturer Gateway, and health insurer Highmark, Inc. At the same time, two major national chains, Home Depot and Publix Supermarkets, agreed to pay more than $80 million each to settle lawsuits based on sex discrimination.

Recently, advocates have arrived at what they believe to be an effective means of generating pay equity—the concept of "comparable worth," which, as the name suggests, requires two people with comparable skills, education, and experience to be paid comparable amounts, even when they're working at two very different jobs. The Xerox Corporation, for example, uses comparable-worth analysis, weighing such factors as education, experience, skill, responsibility, decision making, and discomfort or danger in working conditions, to set salary levels within the country. During the 1980s, some twenty state governments studied the comparable worth of their own employees and made adjustments totaling almost $750 million in increased pay to women. Minnesota, the leader in the field, has made pay-equity adjustments in 1,544 counties and localities.

Perhaps the most dramatic argument for comparable worth, however, was made by a man. In the class-action suit *AFSCME v. Washington State* in 1982, one of the nine named plaintiffs was Milt Tedrow, a licensed practical nurse at Eastern State Hospital in Spokane. Approaching retirement and realizing that his "woman's" job wouldn't give him much of a pension, Tedrow switched to carpentry at the same hospital. To qualify as an LPN, he had needed at least four years of experience, four quarters of schooling, and a license. As a carpenter, he was self-taught, had no paid work experience, and had no need of a license. And yet, when he transferred from the top of the LPN wage scale to the bottom of the carpenter's, his salary jumped more than $200 a month—from $1,614 to $1,826. Why, Tedrow wondered at the time, does the state resent "paying people decently who are taking care of people's bodies, when they'd pay a lot for someone fixing cars or plumbing"?

Since then, the courts have ruled that evidence of unfair salaries is not enough to prove violation of the Equal Pay Act. Plaintiffs must prove that employers intentionally discriminated by lowering women's wages in comparison to men's. But some unions have prevailed on comparable-worth questions by way of negotiations.

For example, Service Employees International Union Local 715, in Santa Clara County, just south of San Francisco, won nearly $30 million for 4,500 county employees, from secretaries to mental-health counselors. A study of some 150 job titles, performed by a consulting firm chosen jointly by the county and the union, showed that underpayment was common in job classes with more than 50 percent minorities, such as licensed vocational nurses and beginning social workers, and that 70 percent of such positions were filled by women. "We worked for at least three years to bring our male members along on this," says Kristy Sermersheim, Local 715's executive secretary. "When the county argued that in order to raise women's wages they'd have to lower men's, we refused to even discuss it. We kept regular pay negotiations completely separate."

15 Another key to the local's success was the staunch support of allies among local women's groups. "We had fifty-four women's community groups on our side," reports Sermersheim. "The National Organization for Women, the American Association of University Women, the League of Women Voters, the Silicon Valley women engineers. . . ." On the day the county board of supervisors voted on whether to proceed with the study, the local delivered 1,000 pink balloons—symbolizing the pink-collar ghetto—to workplaces around the city. "We had balloons everywhere," recalls Sermersheim. "We had Unitarian women out there singing 'Union Maid.'"

It is this kind of coalition that pay-equity advocates are counting on to push through the equal-pay bills now before state legislatures. Many of the new bills, unlike those passed in the 1980s, would extend comparable worth to private as well as public employees and would specifically extend benefits to minorities. Most are based on the Fair Pay Act designed in consultation with the NCPE—and introduced in Congress in 1999 by two Democrats, Senator Tom Harkin of Iowa and Representative Eleanor Holmes Norton of the District of Columbia. (A more modest Paycheck Fairness Act, backed by the Clinton administration, would toughen the Equal Pay Act of 1963 by removing present caps on damages and making it easier to bring class-action suits.)

So far, the new state bills have met with only modest success. The New Jersey and New Mexico legislatures have voted to study pay equity in both public and private employment, and Vermont's legislature voted to study just state employment. In Maine, where the new welfare laws gave rise to a commission to study poverty among working parents, it was discovered that the state already had a 1965 law on the books that mandated equal pay for both public and private employees and that specifically mentioned comparable worth. The state is now studying ways to put the law into effect.

Efforts like these have raised opposition from business and conservative groups. Economist Diana Furchgott-Roth, a resident fellow at the American Enterprise Institute who recently represented business at an NCPE forum, supports "equal pay for equal work" but claims that comparable worth causes labor shortages because men refuse to take jobs where their wages will be tied to women's. "How can a government bureaucrat calculate if a secretary is worth the same as a truck driver, or a nurse as an oil driller?"

In Ontario, Canada, where the practice of comparable worth is more common, day-care centers are actually closing down because parents can't afford to pay for the higher salaries, says Furchgott-Roth. But these charges turn out to be only partially true. Child-care centers in Ontario were threatened when a Progressive Conservative government succeeded the liberal New Democrats and slashed funding. But the centers have not closed down. After a court challenge and an enormous public outcry, the provincial government is still subsidizing pay equity for child-care workers (who, even with subsidies, earn an average of only $16,000 a year).

State employment officials in Minnesota and Wisconsin, two states with 20
comparable-worth laws, say that any labor shortages have far more to do with the tight labor market than with comparable worth. "There's a lot of flexibility in the law," says Faith Zwemke, Minnesota's pay-equity coordinator. "For information technology people, for instance, we can give them signing bonuses and let them advance faster within the parameters of the policy."

Some male workers inevitably do resent women getting increases. "But many men can see pay equity as a family issue," says Karen Nussbaum of the AFL-CIO. A recent poll by Democratic pollster Celinda Lake showed that six out of ten voters, both men and women, said equal pay was good for families.

Pay-equity advocates had better be patient and persistent. The market has been biased against women at least since it was written in the Old Testament that when a vow offering is made to God, it should be based on the value of the person, and "[if] a male, from the age of twenty years up to the age of sixty years, your assessment shall be fifty silver shekels . . . and if it is a female, your assessment shall be thirty shekels." At this rate, winning equal pay may take a long time.

QUESTIONING THE TEXT

1. Briefly summarize the problem Barko poses in this essay and the solution she recommends. Do you think she adequately argues for each? Is her description of the problem convincing? Do you find the solution feasible? Be prepared to discuss these questions in class, using examples from the text to support your answers.
2. Throughout this essay, Barko cites studies and statistics to support her claims. Working with a group of classmates, examine those pieces of evidence to see if they hold up under close scrutiny. What questions do the figures Barko uses raise? Do you need more information to assess how Barko has used statistical evidence? Use library or internet resources to search for the sources of studies she cites. Who did the research, under what auspices, and using what methods?

MAKING CONNECTIONS

3. According to one study, Barko writes, "even in light of the vicissitudes of motherhood, 43 percent of the wage gap remains 'unexplained,' evidently due in large part to discrimination" (paragraph 4). That last explanatory phrase—"evidently due in large part to discrimination"—is one that Steven Pinker challenges in the excerpt from the "Gender" chapter in his book *The Blank Slate*. Read Pinker's excerpt (p. 740), and note the ways in which he refutes the argument Barko makes here. How might Barko respond? Discuss the two authors' views in class, being careful to assess their claims using the evidence they offer. Can your class come to a consensus on the value of using "comparable-worth" assessments to achieve pay equity?
4. Meridel LeSueur draws from her experience in writing about "Women and Work" (p. 729). How does her essay inform your thoughts on the issues raised by Barko in this essay and by Steven Pinker in the excerpt from "Gender" (p. 740)?

JOINING THE CONVERSATION

5. A.L. remarks in her headnote to this essay that the amount of controversy surrounding the issue of pay equity between men and women suggests it is "worth considering carefully." Following her cue, work

with a team of classmates to investigate how fairly men and women are paid for comparable work in your own community—perhaps in your town or county, or on your campus. You might choose a particular institution or profession and compare wage and salary scales among men and women. Search Internet databases for articles on the topic, and look for other sources in the library. You might also then conduct interviews with workers in the fields you have chosen to study. Your research findings could serve as the basis for an article that you might submit to a local newspaper or magazine, offer to a labor organization, or publish on a class Web site.

6. Barko identifies Hazel Dews, whose experience opens this essay, as one of three hundred women who took union action to press their suit for comparable pay. Do you know someone who has participated in a similar labor action, or are you familiar with one through the news? Find out the details of the protest, including the outcome. Was the issue fairly resolved, or is it ongoing? Does the case serve as a good or bad example of labor or management actions? Write an op-ed piece that presents your opinion on the case and the issues it illuminates; depending on the circumstances and what you wish to say, you might make an argument of value, or you might propose an action or policy. Consider submitting your article to a newspaper for publication.

STEVEN PINKER
Gender

In the past several decades, few statistics have wielded more political power than the familiar comparison of male and female earnings in the United States. Here's Betty Friedan's version, as relayed by Steven Pinker: "women still earn no more than 72 cents for every dollar that men earn."

This kind of comparison works because it distills a complex mixture of political, cultural, and social relationships into a single malt of economic disparity. As long as the gap between male and female wages persists, the struggle for gender equity must continue.

Convincing as the argument seems, however, it has its critics, Steven Pinker (b. 1954) among them. Pinker, an evolutionary psychologist at the Massachusetts Institute of Technology and the author of several best-selling books on language, risks the ire of some fellow scientists and most feminist activists to suggest that the wage disparity may be due, in part, to biological differences between men and women. He dares to suggest that no amount of social engineering is going to convince large numbers of women to become engineers or mathematicians, nor are men ever likely to flock into developmental psycholinguistics or teaching.

This controversial thesis is just part of more sweeping claims Pinker asserts for the biological basis of human nature throughout The Blank Slate *(2002), the book from which our selection on "gender" is taken. In it, Pinker challenges the notion that society alone shapes human character and behavior, arguing instead that a preponderance of scientific evidence now suggests that biology and evolution play a substantial part in determining who we are and what we choose to do. There is, Pinker believes, a human nature that exists prior to culture, prior to nurture. Few theses in the intellectual world provoke more combustive reactions or have deeper implications than this one.*

Whether you agree with Pinker or not, this selection will give you some sense of him as a thinker and writer. Pinker also writes with great verve and erudition on language and cognition in such books as The Language Instinct *(1994),* How the Mind Works *(1997), and* Words and Rules *(1999).* —J.R.

By now many people are happy to say what was unsayable in polite company a few years ago: that males and females do not have interchangeable minds. Even the comic pages have commented on the shift in the debate, as we see in this dialogue be-

I know enough about Pinker's work to predict that he will be making an argument for genetic causes of difference: let's see where this leads. —A.L.

*The original notes accompanying this excerpt required cross-referencing with the bibliography at the end of Pinker's book. We have therefore reformatted the notes to include the most complete publication data. —EDS.

This cartoon is one of several Pinker reprints in his 400+-page book, usually to show that an issue he is raising actually resonates with the public. —J.R.

Is this supposed to be funny?? —A.L.

tween the free-associating, junkfood-loving Zippy and the cartoonist's alter ego Griffy:

But among many professional women the existence of sex differences is still a source of discomfort. As one colleague said to me, "Look, I know that males and females are not identical. I see it in my kids, I see it in myself, I know about the research. I can't explain it, but when I read claims about sex differences, *steam comes out of my ears.*" The most likely cause of her disquiet is captured in a recent editorial by Betty Friedan, the cofounder of the National Organization for Women and the author of the 1963 book *The Feminine Mystique:*

> Though the women's movement has begun to achieve equality for women on many economic and political measures, the victory remains incomplete. To take two of the simplest and most obvious indicators: women still earn no more than 72 cents for every dollar that men earn, and we are nowhere near equality in numbers at the very top of decision making in business, government, or the professions.[1]

Like Friedan, many people believe that the gender gap in wages and a "glass ceiling" that keeps women from rising to the uppermost levels of power are the two main injustices facing women in the West today. In his 1999 State of the Union ad-

There's an awkward transition at this point from the biological claim that men and women are wired differently to the political claim that they should be paid comparably. —J.R.

Friedan also mentions how educated women felt restless in their homes, taking care of children and feeding husbands. They wanted to explore their interests in the work field. This is important to keep in mind later in Pinker's argument. —B.K.

Of course women feel uncomfortable: those "sex differences" are always equated to "men are superior" and "women are inferior." —B.K.

Well, the *most likely cause of disquiet has got to be the long history of inequity based on gender.* —A.L.

[1]B. Friedan, "The Future of Feminism," *Free Inquiry*, Summer 1999.

dress, Bill Clinton said, "We can be proud of this progress, but 75 cents on the dollar is still only three-quarters of the way there, and Americans can't be satisfied until we're all the way there." The gender gap and the glass ceiling have inspired lawsuits against companies that have too few women, in the top positions, pressure on the government to regulate all salaries so men and women are paid according to the "comparable worth" of their jobs, and aggressive measures to change girls' attitudes to the professions, such as the annual Take Our Daughters to Work Day.

Scientists and engineers face the issue in the form of the "leaky pipeline." Though women make up almost 60 percent of university students and about half of the students majoring in many fields of science, the proportion advancing to the next career stage diminishes as they go from being undergraduates to graduate students to postdoctoral fellows to junior professors to tenured professors. Women make up less than 20 percent of the workforce in science, engineering, and technology development, and only 9 percent of the workforce in engineering.[2] Readers of the flagship journals *Science* and *Nature* have seen two decades of headlines such as "Diversity: Easier Said Than Done" and "Efforts to Boost Diversity Face Persistent Problems."[3] A typical story, commenting on the many national commissions set up to investigate the problem, said, "These activities are meant to continue chipping away at a problem that, experts say, begins with negative messages in elementary school, continues through undergraduate and graduate programs that erect barriers—financial, academic, and

Why is that? —B.K.

My own school encourages women (now a majority on campus) to become engineers and scientists but supports no programs to move more men into fields in which they are underrepresented, such as English or education. —J.R.

"Leaky pipeline" is a new metaphor for me, though its connotations are as odd as the one I am more familiar with: that few women make it into good positions in certain scientific fields because the "pool is too shallow." Both metaphors carry powerful and largely unexamined assumptions. —A.L.

[2]"Land of Plenty: Diversity as America's Competitive Edge in Science, Engineering, and Technology," Report of the Congressional Commission on the Advancement of Women and Minorities in Science, Engineering, and Technology Development, September 2000.

[3]J. Alper, "The Pipeline Is Leaking Women All the Way Along," *Science, 260,* April 16, 1993; J. Mervis, "Efforts to boost diversity face persistent problems," *Science, 284,* June 11, 1999; J. Mervis, "Diversity: Easier said than Done," *Science, 289,* March 16, 2000; J. Mervis, "NSF searches for right way to help women," *Science, 289,* July 21, 2000; J. Mervis, "Gender Equity: NSF Program Targets Institutional Change," *Science, 291,* July 21, 2001.

cultural—to all but the best candidates, and persists into the workplace.[4] A meeting in 2001 of the presidents of nine elite American universities called for "significant changes," such as setting aside grants and fellowships for women faculty, giving them the best parking spaces on campus, and ensuring that the percentage of women faculty equals the percentage of women students.[5]

Whoa. The president of my university attended this meeting: I've never heard anything at all about giving women the best parking spaces. What's the effect of Pinker's adding this detail? —A.L.

How would giving women "the best parking spaces" fill the gender gap? Preferential treatment such as this, along with the concept of "ladies first" or opening doors for women, is another form of sexism that makes the gap larger. —B.K.

But there is something odd in these stories about negative messages, hidden barriers, and gender prejudices. The way of science is to lay out every hypothesis that could account for a phenomenon and to eliminate all but the correct one. Scientists prize the ability to think up alternative explanations, and proponents of a hypothesis are expected to refute even the unlikely ones, Nonetheless, discussions of the leaky pipeline in science rarely even *mention* an alternative to the theory of barriers and bias. One of the rare exceptions was a sidebar to a 2000 story in *Science,* which quoted from a presentation at the National Academy of Engineering by the social scientist Patti Hausman:

> The question of why more women don't choose careers in engineering has a rather obvious answer: Because they don't want to. Wherever you go, you will find females far less likely than males to see what is so fascinating about ohms, carburetors, or quarks. Reinventing the curriculum will not make me more interested in learning how my dishwasher works.[6]

But this begs the question of why *women don't want to choose some careers.* —A.L.

An eminent woman engineer in the audience immediately denounced her analysis as "pseudoscience." But Linda Gottfredson, an expert in the literature on vocational preferences, pointed out that Hausman had the data on her side: "On average, women are more interested in dealing with people and men with things," Vocational tests also show that boys are more interested in "realistic,"

[4] J. Mervis, "Efforts to Boost Diversity," p. 1757.

[5] P. Healy, "Faculty Shortage: Women in Sciences," *Boston Globe,* January 31, 2001.

[6] C. Holden, "Parity as a Goal Sparks Bitter Battle," *Science, 289,* July 21, 2000, p. 380.

"theoretical," and "investigative" pursuits, and girls more interested in "artistic" and "social" pursuits.

Hausman and Gottfredson are lonely voices, because the gender gap is almost always analyzed in the following way. Any imbalance between men and women in their occupations or earnings is direct proof of gender bias—if not in the form of overt discrimination, then in the form of discouraging messages and hidden barriers. The possibility that men and women might differ from each other in ways that affect what jobs they hold or how much they get paid may never be mentioned in public, because it will set back the cause of equity in the workplace and harm the interests of women. It is this conviction that led Friedan and Clinton, for example, to say that we will not have attained gender equity until earnings and representation in the professions are identical for men and women. In a 1998 television interview, Gloria Steinem and the congresswoman Bella Abzug called the very idea of sex differences "poppycock" and "anti-American crazy thinking," and when Abzug was asked whether gender equality meant equal numbers in every field, she replied, "Fifty-fifty—absolutely."[7] This analysis of the gender gap has also become the official position of universities. That the presidents of the nation's elite universities are happy to accuse their colleagues of shameful prejudice without even considering alternative explanations (whether or not they would end up accepting them) shows how deeply rooted the taboo is.

Pinker is overstating here; most arguments for gender equity I am familiar with do not make such direct causal claims. Pinker is carefully choosing sources that hold the extreme view he wants to pit his argument against. —A.L.

Most societies and institutions have many "official stories" like that on the gender gap that can't be challenged easily. But falsehoods erode over time. As John Adams put it, "Facts are stubborn things." —J.R.

It is clear Pinker does not agree with Abzug's "fifty-fifty" argument. I'm interested to see his argument against it. —B.K.

The problem with this analysis is that inequality of *outcome* cannot be used as proof of inequality of *opportunity* unless the groups being compared are identical in all of their psychological traits, which is likely to be true only if we are blank slates. But the suggestion that the gender gap may arise, even in part, from differences between the sexes can be fightin' words. Anyone bringing it up is certain to be accused of "wanting to keep women in their

So here's the blank slate argument I've been expecting. Pinker is well known for taking the "nature" side in the old debate between "nature" and "nurture." —A.L.

[7]Quoted in C. Young, *Ceasefire! Why Women and Men Must Join Forces to Achieve True Equality* (New York: Free Press, 1999), pp. 22, 34–35.

place" or "justifying the status quo." This makes about as much sense as saying that a scientist who studies why women live longer than men "wants old men to die." And far from being a ploy by self-serving men, analyses exposing the flaws of the glass-ceiling theory have largely come from women, including Hausman, Gottfredson, Judith Kleinfeld, Karen Lehrman, Cathy Young, and Camille Benbow, the economists Jennifer Roback, Felice Schwartz, Diana Furchtgott-Roth, and Christine Stolba, the legal scholar Jennifer Braceras, and, more guardedly, the economist Claudia Goldin and the legal scholar Susan Estrich.[8]

A neat rhetorical touch here. Pinker bolsters his credibility on this touchy issue of gender by appealing to experts who are women. —J.R.

I believe these writers have given us a better understanding of the gender gap than the standard one, for a number of reasons. Their analysis is not afraid of the possibility that the sexes might differ, and therefore does not force us to choose between scientific findings on human nature and the fair treatment of women. If offers a more sophisticated understanding of the causes of the gender gap, one that is consistent with our best social science. It takes a more respectful view of women and their choices. And ultimately it promises more humane and effective remedies for gender inequities in the workplace.

At last, a more nuanced analysis: of course we don't have to choose between "human nature" and the "fair treatment of women." —A.L.

Before presenting the new analysis of the gender gap from equity feminists, let me reiterate three points that are not in dispute. First, discouraging

[8]S. Estrich, *Sex and Power* (New York: Riverhead Press, 2000); D. Furchtgott-Roth and C. Stolba, *Women's Figures: An Illustrated Guide to the Economic Progress of Women in America* (Washington, D.C.: American Enterprise Institute Press, 1999); C. Goldin, *Understanding the Gender Gap: An Economic History of American Workers* (New York: Oxford University Press, 1990); L. S. Gottfredson, "Reconsidering Fairness: A Matter of Social and Ethical Priorities, *Journal of Vocational Behavior, 29*, 1988, pp. 379–410; P. Hausman, *On the Rarity of Mathematically and Mechanically Gifted Females* (Santa Barbara, CA: The Fielding Institute, 1999); J. Kleinfeld, *MIT Tarnishes Its Reputation with Gender Junk Science*, Special Report (Arlington, VA: Independent Women's Forum, 1999), www.uaf.edu/northern/mitstudy; K. Lehrman, *The Lipstick Proviso: Women, Sex, and Power in the Real World* (New York: Doubleday, 1997); D. Lubinski and C. Benbow, "Gender Differences in Abilities and Preferences Among the Gifted: Implications for the Math-science Pipeline, *Current Directions in Psychological Science, 1*, 1992, pp. 61–66; J. Roback, "Beyond Equality," *Georgetown Law Journal, 82*, 1993, pp. 121–133; F. N. Schwartz, *Breaking with Tradition: Women and Work, the New Facts of Life* (New York: Warner Books, 1992); Young, *Ceasefire*!

Another skillful, if conventional, rhetorical move: Pinker qualifies his argument about gender difference to reduce any suspicion that he opposes equal opportunity for women. I doubt that it's enough, however, to satisfy those who prefer the "official position." —J.R.

So Pinker recognizes the factuality of inequity and discrimination based on gender. I'm still not ready to accept his claim that inequity in wages is based on genetic difference, however. —A.L.

women from pursuing their ambitions, and discriminating against them on the basis of their sex, are injustices that should be stopped wherever they are discovered.

Second, there is no doubt that women faced widespread discrimination in the past and continue to face it in some sectors today. This cannot be proven by showing that men earn more than women or that the sex ratio departs from fifty-fifty, but it can be proven in other ways. Experimenters can send out fake résumés or grant proposals that are identical in all ways except the sex of the applicant and see whether they are treated differently. Economists can do a regression analysis that takes measures of people's qualifications and interests and determines whether the men and the women earn different amounts, or are promoted at different rates, *when their qualifications and interests are statistically held constant.* The point that differences in outcome don't show discrimination unless one has equated for other relevant traits is elementary social science (not to mention common sense), and is accepted by all economists when they analyze data sets looking for evidence of wage discrimination.[9]

Third, there is no question of whether women are "qualified" to be scientists, CEOs, leaders of nations, or elite professionals of any other kind. That was decisively answered years ago: some are and some aren't, just as some men are qualified and some aren't. The only question is whether the proportions of qualified men and women must be identical.

As in many other topics related to human nature, people's unwillingness to think in statistical terms has led to pointless false dichotomies. Here is how to think about gender distributions in the professions without having to choose between the extremes of "women are unqualified" and "fifty-fifty absolutely," or between "there is no discrimination" and "there is nothing but discrimination."

Although I can appreciate Pinker's disclaimer, it doesn't do anything to obliterate present discriminations. —B.K.

Yes, we all agree discrimination exists. However, I feel all this argument does is set us up for a solution that Pinker is not giving. —B.K.

Pinker has himself set up a dichotomy between claims for the influence of "human nature" and the concept of a blank slate. I agree that such dichotomies are almost always destructive, so why does he keep referring to them? —A.L.

[9] K. Browne, *Divided Labors: An Evolutionary View of Women at Work* (London: Weidenfeld and Nicholson, 1998); Furchtgott-Roth and Stolba; Goldin.

In a free and unprejudiced labor market, people will be hired and paid according to the match between their traits and the demands of the job. A given job requires some mixture of cognitive talents (such as mathematical or linguistic skill), personality traits (such as risk taking or cooperation), and tolerance of lifestyle demands (rigid schedules, relocations, updating job skills). And it offers some mixture of personal rewards: people, gadgets, ideas, the outdoors, pride in workmanship. The salary is influenced, among other things, by supply and demand: how many people want the job, how many can do it, and how many the employer can pay to do it. Readily filled jobs may pay less; difficult-to-fill jobs may pay more.

People vary in the traits relevant to employment. Most people can think logically, work with people, tolerate conflict or unpleasant surroundings, and so on, but not to an identical extent; everyone has a unique profile of strengths and tastes. Given all the evidence for sex differences (some biological, some cultural, some both), the statistical distributions for men and women in these strengths and tastes are unlikely to be identical. If one now matches the distribution of traits for men and for women with the distribution of the demands of the jobs in the economy, the chance that the proportion of men and of women in each profession will be identical, or that the mean salary of men and of women will be identical, is very close to zero—even if there were no barriers or discrimination.

This paragraph is crucial to Pinker's argument. It presents the logical and material facts weighing against the political claim that a wage gap between men and women must be due to prejudice. —J.R.

None of this implies that women will end up with the short end of the stick. It depends on the menu of opportunities that a given society makes available. If there are more high-paying jobs that call for typical male strengths (say, willingness to put oneself in physical danger, or an interest in machines), men may do better on average; if there are more that call for typical female strengths (say, a proficiency with language, or an interest in people), women may do better on average. In either case, members of both sexes will be found in both kinds of jobs, just in different numbers. That is why some relatively prestigious professions are dominated by

But in the past and now, women have *ended up with the "short end of the stick."* —B.K.

Unfortunately, jobs that call for "typical male strengths" are almost always more valued—and better paid—than those that call for typical female attributes. —A.L.

women. An example is my own field, the study of language development in children, in which women outnumber men by a large margin.[10] In her book *The First Sex: The Natural Talents of Women and How They Are Changing the World*, the anthropologist Helen Fisher speculates that the culture of business in our knowledge-driven, globalized economy will soon favor women. Women are more articulate and cooperative, are not as obsessed with rank, and are better able to negotiate win-win outcomes. The workplaces of the new century, she predicts, will increasingly demand these talents, and women may surpass men in status and earnings.

In today's world, of course, the gap favors men. Some of the gap is caused by discrimination. Employers may underestimate the skills of women, or assume that an all-male workplace is more efficient, or worry that their male employees will resent female supervisors, or fear resistance from prejudiced customers and clients. But the evidence suggests that not *all* sex differences in the professions are caused by these barriers.[11] It is unlikely, for example, that among academics the mathematicians are unusually biased against women, the developmental psycholinguists are unusually biased against men, and the evolutionary psychologists are unusually free of bias.

In a few professions, differences in ability may play some role. The fact that more men than women have exceptional abilities in mathematical reasoning and in mentally manipulating 3-D objects is enough to explain a departure from a fifty-fifty sex ratio among engineers, physicists, organic chemists, and professors in some branches of mathematics (though of course it does not mean that the proportion of women should be anywhere near zero).

[10]In a random sample of 100 members of the International Association for the Study of Child Language, I counted 75 women and 25 men. The Stanford Child Language Research Forum lists 18 past keynote speakers on its web site (csli.stanford.edu/~clrf/history.html): 15 women and 3 men.

[11]Browne; Furchtgott-Roth and Stolba; Goldin; Gottfredson; Kleinfeld; Roback; Young, *Ceasefire!*

Even though the kids were nurtured in an "encouraging" environment and born during the feminist movement, the possibility that the differences in their preferences could be attributed to society, dictating what boys and girls should like, is neglected. —B.K.

In most professions, average differences in ability are irrelevant, but average differences in *preferences* may set the sexes on different paths. The most dramatic example comes from an analysis by David Lubinski and Camille Benbow of a sample of mathematically precocious seventh-graders selected in a nationwide talent search.[12] The teenagers were born during the second wave of feminism, were encouraged by their parents to develop their talents (all were sent to summer programs in math and science), and were fully aware of their ability to achieve. But the gifted girls told the researchers that they were more interested in people, "social values," and humanitarian and altruistic goals, whereas the gifted boys said they were more interested in things, "theoretical values," and abstract intellectual inquiry. In college, the young women chose a broad range of courses in the humanities, arts, and sciences, whereas the boys were geeks who stuck to math and science. And sure enough, fewer than 1 percent of the young women pursued doctorates in math, physical sciences, or engineering, whereas 8 percent of the young men did. The women went into medicine, law, the humanities, and biology instead.

It seems to me that math, physical sciences, and engineering could be seen—and taught—as having a great deal to contribute to people, "social values," and "humanitarian goals." If Pinker is right, making such changes would have no effect because women are genetically predisposed to be uninterested in these fields. Hmmmm . . . —A.L.

This asymmetry is writ large in massive surveys of job-related values and career choices, another kind of study in which men and women actually say what they want rather than having activists speak for them.[13] On average, men's self-esteem is more highly tied to their status, salary, and wealth, and so is their attractiveness as a sexual partner and marriage partner, as revealed in studies of what people look for in the opposite sex.[14] Not surprisingly, men say they are more keen to work longer hours and to sacrifice other parts of their

These differences in natural inclinations and abilities still do not explain the inequality in pay and treatment between the sexes for the same duties and jobs. —B.K.

[12]Lubinski and Benbow.

[13]See Browne and the references in note 8.

[14]D. M. Buss, "Mate preference mechanisms: Consequences for partner choice and intrasexual competition," in J. Barkow, L. Cosmides, and J. Tooby, eds., *The Adapted Mind: Evolutionary Psychology and the Generation of Culture* (New York: Oxford University Press, 1992); B. J. Ellis, "The evolution of sexual attraction: Evaluative mechanisms in women," in Barkow, Cosmides, and Tooby, eds.

Pinker is cataloguing differences associated with men; I assume he will soon do the same for women. He is clearly setting up his readers to accept the genetic differences argument.
—A.L.

lives—to live in a less attractive city, or to leave friends and family when they relocate—in order to climb the corporate ladder or achieve notoriety in their fields. Men, on average, are also more willing to undergo physical discomfort and danger, and thus are more likely to be found in grungy but relatively lucrative jobs such as repairing factory equipment, working on oil rigs, and jackhammering sludge from the inside of oil tanks. Women, on average, are more likely to choose administrative support jobs that offer lower pay in air-conditioned offices. Men are greater risk takers, and that is reflected in their career paths even when qualifications are held constant. Men prefer to work for corporations, women for government agencies and nonprofit organizations. Male doctors are more likely to specialize and to open up private practices; female doctors are more likely to be general practitioners on salary in hospitals and clinics. Men are more likely to be managers in factories, women more likely to be managers in human resources or corporate communications.

Mothers are more attached to their children, on average, than are fathers. That is true in societies all over the world and probably has been true of our lineage since the first mammals evolved some two hundred million years ago. As Susan Estrich puts it, "Waiting for the connection between gender and parenting to be broken is waiting for Godot." This does not mean that women in any society have ever been uninterested in work; among hunter-gatherers, women do most of the gathering and some of the hunting, especially when it involves nets rather than rocks and spears.[15] Nor does it mean that men in any society are indifferent to their children; male parental investment is a conspicuous and zoologically unusual feature of *Homo sapiens*. But it does mean that the biologically ubiquitous tradeoff between investing in a child and working to stay healthy (ultimately to beget or in-

[15]S. B. Hrdy, *Mother Nature: A History of Mothers, Infants, and Natural Selection* (New York: Pantheon Books, 1999).

vest in other children) may be balanced at different points by males and females. Not only are women the sex who nurse, but women are more attentive to their babies' well-being and, in surveys, place a higher value on spending time with their children.[16]

So even if both sexes value work and both sexes value children, the different weightings may lead women, more often than men, to make career choices that allow them to spend more time with their children—shorter or more flexible hours, fewer relocations, skills that don't become obsolete as quickly—in exchange for lower wages or prestige. As the economist Jennifer Roback points out, "Once we observe that people sacrifice money income for other pleasurable things we can infer next to nothing by comparing the income of one person with another's.[17] The economist Gary Becker has shown that marriage can magnify the effects of sex differences, even if they are small to begin with, because of what economists call the law of comparative advantage. In couples where the husband can earn a bit more than the wife, but the wife is a somewhat better parent than the husband, they might rationally decide they are both better off if she works less than he does.[18]

For these reasons, many women argue that careers should not be adversely affected by these decisions, as is clearly the case today. —A.L.

To repeat: none of this means that sex discrimination has vanished, or that it is justified when it occurs. The point is only that gender gaps *by themselves* say nothing about discrimination unless the slates of men and women are blank, which they are not. The only way to establish discrimination is to compare their jobs or wages when choices and qualifications are equalized. And in fact a recent study of data from the National Longitudinal Survey of Youth found that childless women between the ages of twenty-seven and thirty-three earn 98 cents to men's dollar.[19] Even to people who are

So gender gaps are related to discrimination only if minds are blank slates? Has Pinker supported this claim adequately? —A.L.

[16]Browne; Hrdy.

[17]Roback.

[18]G. S. Becker, *A Treatise on the Family,* enlarged ed. (Cambridge, MA: Harvard University Press, 1991).

[19]Furchtgott-Roth and Stolba.

cynical about the motivations of American employers, this should come as no shock. In a cutthroat market, any company stupid enough to overlook qualified women or to overpay unqualified men would be driven out of business by a more meritocratic competitor.

And yet these businesses do *exist and* do *thrive.* —B.K.

Another claim I'm suspicious of, especially since companies "stupid enough to overlook qualified women" are well documented. —A.L.

Now, there is nothing in science or social science that would rule out policies implementing a fifty-fifty distribution of wages and jobs between the sexes, if a democracy decided that this was an inherently worthy goal. What the findings do say is that such policies will come with costs as well as benefits. The obvious benefit of equality-of-outcome policies is that they might neutralize the remaining discrimination against women. But if men and women are not interchangeable, the costs have to be considered as well.

Some costs would be borne by men or by both sexes. The two most obvious are the possibility of reverse discrimination against men and of a false presumption of sexism among the men and women who make decisions about hiring and salary today. Another cost borne by both sexes is the inefficiency that could result if employment decisions were based on factors other than the best match between the demands of a job and the traits of the person.

This assumes that employers only look for compatibility between the person and the demands of the job without factoring in other variables, which I believe is currently untrue. —B.K.

But many of the costs of equality-of-outcome policies would be borne by *women.* Many women scientists are opposed to hard gender preferences in science, such as designated faculty positions for women, or the policy (advocated by one activist) in which federal research grants would be awarded in exact proportion to the number of men and women who apply for them. The problem with these well-meaning policies is that they can plant seeds of doubt in people's minds about the excellence of the beneficiaries. As the astronomer Lynne Hillenbrand said, "If you're given an opportunity for the reason of being female, it doesn't do anyone any favors; it makes people question why you're there."[20]

Again, this seems like a pretty big overstatement and another dichotomy set up: either give grants equally or don't give them at all. As for casting doubt on those chosen under a system of gender equality, who gains most by casting such doubt? —A.L.

This argument brings up the issue of affirmative action—an issue that could get complicated and messy. Although I feel Pinker's brief overview of this subject increases his readability, I feel he glosses over the important arguments for these policies and oversimplifies the issue altogether. —B.K.

Certainly there *are* institutional barriers to the advancement of women. People are mammals, and

[20]Quoted in C. Young, "Sex and Science," *Salon*, April 12, 2001.

we should think through the ethical implications of the fact that it is women who bear, nurse, and disproportionately raise children. One ought not to assume that the default human being is a man and that children are an indulgence or an accident that strikes a deviant subset. Sex differences therefore can be used to justify, rather than endanger, woman-friendly policies such as parental leave, subsidized childcare, flexible hours, and stoppages of the tenure clock or the elimination of tenure altogether (a possibility recently broached by the biologist and Princeton University president Shirley Tilghman).

I want to count the number of times Pinker has said "of course," thus suggesting that "of course" readers agree with him. —A.L.

Of course, there is no such thing as a free lunch, and these policies are also decisions—perhaps justifiable ones—to penalize men and women who are childless, have grown children, or choose to stay at home with their children. But even when it comes to weighing these tradeoffs, thinking about human nature can raise deep new questions that could ultimately improve the lot of working women. Which of the onerous job demands that deter women really contribute to economic efficiency, and which are obstacle courses in which men compete for alpha status? In reasoning about fairness in the workplace, should we consider people as isolated individuals, or should we consider them as members of families who probably will have children at some point in their lives and who probably will care for aging parents at some point in their lives? If we trade off some economic efficiency for more pleasant working conditions in all jobs, might there be a net increase in happiness? I don't have answers, but the questions are well worth asking.

There is one more reason that acknowledging sex differences can be more humane than denying them. It is men and women, not the male gender and the female gender, who prosper or suffer, and those men and women are endowed with brains—perhaps not identical brains—that give them values and an ability to make choices. Those choices should be respected. A regular feature of the lifestyle pages is the story about women who are made to feel ashamed about staying at home with their children. As they always say, "I thought feminism was supposed to be

Indeed, feminism is *about choice!* —A.L.

about choices." The same should apply to women who do choose to work but also to trade off some income in order to "have a life" (and, of course, to men who make that choice). It is not obviously progressive to insist that equal numbers of men and women work eighty-hour weeks in a corporate law firm or leave their families for months at a time do dodge steel pipes on a frigid oil platform. And it is grotesque to demand (as advocates of gender parity did in the pages of *Science*) that more young women "be conditioned to choose engineering," as if they were rats in a Skinner box.[21]

No one *should have to "work 80-hour weeks . . . or leave their families." Here's where choice is really important.* —A.L.

Gottfredson points out, "If you insist on using gender parity as your measure of social justice, it means you will have to keep many men and women out of the work they like best and push them into work they don't like."[22] She is echoed by Kleinfeld on the leaky pipeline in science: "We should not be sending [gifted] women the messages that they are less worthy human beings, less valuable to our civilization, lazy or low in status, if they choose to be teachers rather than mathematicians, journalists rather than physicists, lawyers rather than engineers.[23] These are not hypothetical worries: a recent survey by the National Science Foundation found that many more women than men say they majored in science, mathematics, or engineering under pressure from teachers or family members rather than to pursue their own aspirations—and that many eventually switched out for that reason.[24] I will give the final word to Margaret Mead, who, despite being wrong in her early career about the malleability of gender, was surely right when she said, "If we are to achieve a richer culture, rich in contrasting values, we must recognize the whole gamut of human potentialities, and so weave a less arbitrary social fabric, one in which each diverse human gift will find a fitting place."

If we shouldn't send such messages, then let's pay *teachers as much as other professionals.* —A.L.

Everyone I know would agree with Mead. So where does this leave Pinker and his argument? I accept many of his premises, but I still don't get the connection he is trying to make among gender, genes, and pay. —A.L.

---

[21]Quoted in Holden.

[22]Quoted in Holden.

[23]Kleinfeld.

[24]National Science Foundation, *Women, Minorities, and Persons with Disabilities in Science and Engineering: 1998,* www.nsf.gov/sbe/srs/nsf99338.

Afterwords

Last year, students in a first-year writing class on "Writing Experience: the Rhetoric of Experiment" read—and became intrigued by—the work of MIT evolutionary psychologist Steven Pinker. As the class drew to a close, the students decided to follow up on their interest by inviting Pinker to address undergraduate students at Stanford the next fall. Indeed, the students went on to make the invitation, raise the funds for Pinker's very hefty fee, and make all the arrangements for his visit. The night of the lecture, Pinker spoke to an over-flow crowd in one auditorium while, across campus, another speaker offered a vehement rebuttal to Pinker's work.

This class project graphically demonstrated to the students involved how contentious and long-standing the debate over nature vs. nurture has been. Like most teachers, I have had occasion to think about this debate a good bit, and to mull over the consequences of accepting one side of this debate as right. What seems pretty clear to me, at this point, is that neither side is "right": surely humans are deeply influenced by both biology and culture/society.

That being the case, it's especially interesting to me to see Pinker trying to tiptoe cautiously among the minefields in this debate, attempting to avoid the biggest drawbacks to the "nature" argument while still rejecting the claims for "nurture." While most of Pinker's writing seems, to me, to move too far toward the "human nature" extreme, arguing that our brains are structured in ways that shape all human experience, in the excerpt reprinted here, he is careful to qualify his more extreme claims and to consider counterarguments attentively. He would probably have gotten a very good grade from my students' first-year writing class! —A.L.

The Blank Slate, *the book from which this selection comes, brings to public attention an argument that has tied scientists, academics, and intellectuals up in knots since John Locke introduced the phrase* blank slate *in the seventeenth century. Are human beings the product of their biological heritage or are they born as blank slates, with the societies into which they are born determining most aspects of their lives? Put more succinctly, are people the products of "nature" or "nurture"? In* The Blank Slate, *Steven Pinker argues that what has been the prevailing theory among intellectuals, social scientists, and philosophers—that culture determines just about every aspect of human behavior—is crumbling as scientists reveal how much of our behavior, even our propensity for language, is inscribed in our genes.*

The notion that biology may trump—though certainly not replace—society in determining human behavior is controversial for good reasons. In the past, categories such as "race", "gender," "intelligence," and even "blood" have been used to discriminate against, control, and even destroy whole groups of people. Many fear that a claim that we "are born that way" is an invitation to declare some groups inherently better than others. Consequently, the opposition to Pinker as an advocate of the existence of a "human nature" has been intense, and the criticism of The Blank Slate *has been wide ranging.*

What I find most fascinating about the small slice of the book we include here is the way Pinker presents his arguments rhetorically. He doubtless knew when he chose the subject that writing on human nature put him in dangerous territory with some audiences. So he writes with great care, using devices such as concession and qualification to make room for his more controversial statements. Above all, he wants to seem reasonable, not shrill or cantankerous, a person of both intellect and sensitivity. Toward this end, he fills his essay on gender with the voices of authoritative women who share or support his views. It's a remarkably shrewd piece of writing. —J.R.

Pinker's style of writing is simple and easy to understand; he makes even his most difficult arguments accessible to the audience. However, there were many times I felt he was being sly with his arguments: inserting of course, obviously, certainly, *and so forth to make the reader accept his argument as a given. And I don't blame him. The stance he takes on biological determinism is controversial and, more importantly, unpopular.*

Although I believe he puts too much emphasis on biological factors, his consideration for opposing arguments and his implementation of quotations from women scholars made his argument easier to take. I can appreciate his view because his arguments are not one-sided but rather presented with both sides in mind, which makes skeptics like me more ready to recognize the value of his argument. —B.K.

QUESTIONING THE TEXT

1. Summarize Pinker's argument in a few sentences. What is his main claim? How does he support this claim?
2. Working with a classmate, examine the sources Pinker cites and the evidence he gathers from them. What information about these sources does Pinker provide in the essay? What useful information about the sources do you find missing? Do some library research to discover details about his sources and the organizations he cites that will help you determine whether you agree with his claims.
3. Pinker makes a crucial claim on p. 751: "[N]one of this means that sex discrimination has vanished, or that it is justified when it occurs. The point is only that gender gaps *by themselves* say nothing about discrimination unless the slates of men and women are blank, which they are not." Discuss with one or two classmates the effects of Pinker's style in this passage. What words and phrases does Pinker use to qualify his claim? How does he use sentence structure to emphasize certain elements in relationship to others? What are the effects of the words he has chosen? (How might synonyms for some words change his meaning, even slightly?) How do these stylistic choices affect your reading of this claim, and of Pinker's argument overall? Are you inclined to agree or disagree with him? Explain why.

MAKING CONNECTIONS

4. Consider Pinker's claims in light of those made by Naomi Barko in "The Other Gender Gap" (p. 733). Can the two arguments be reconciled in any way? In other words, can you agree with Barko and with Pinker on some points? Try doing so in a pair of one- or two-page essays—one presenting Barko's viewpoint and the other presenting Pinker's. Make each essay as convincing as possible; your readers should not be able to tell which argument really reflects your own opinion.
5. How might Pinker's arguments be extended to apply to race, ethnicity, sexual orientation, or other aspects of identity that have led to discrimination in employment and other arenas? Read one or two of the essays in Chapter 6 of this book in considering this question, and share your thoughts in class discussion. How does this discussion affect your view of Pinker's argument?

JOINING THE CONVERSATION

6. What subjects or careers were you most interested in as a child? Later in life? What subjects or careers were you encouraged to pursue? Do you think your gender played a role in the future your parents, teachers, friends—even you yourself—envisioned for you? Freewrite on these questions, and then share some of your thoughts with classmates. How do your experiences compare?
7. Have you ever found yourself in a situation that defied traditional expectations for your gender? How does this experience affect your response to Pinker's argument? Use your personal insight to write a short essay in the form of a letter to Pinker, responding to this excerpt on gender.

ARTHUR KRYSTAL

Who Speaks for the Lazy?

Arthur Krystal (b. 1947) takes on the task of answering his title question by drawing on his own intimate experience with a lifetime of laziness. But laziness, under Krystal's somewhat doleful gaze, is far from simple, having philosophical, psychological, even possible genetic underpinnings. In addition, as a subject, laziness can be the cause of work—as in Krystal's writing of this essay, which appeared in The New Yorker *(April 26, 1999) and no doubt landed the author a substantial fee.*

In a world seemingly run by workaholics who "relax" after hours by throwing themselves relentlessly into the secondary work of keeping fit (how many miles did you run today?), with the workweek getting longer instead of shorter, with the trend toward combining work with everything, including school, perhaps we need a little sympathy for laziness, for the sheer "disinclination to work." I might as well admit, however, that I read Krystal's essay with some mix of amusement and horror. I can't imagine anything more boring than experiencing the vegetative state Krystal describes as ultimate laziness: when "prying the cap off a Schlitz" is seen as "a good day's work." But my old-fashioned Protestant work ethic is showing. What's your own laziness quotient? Read Krystal's essay to see how you stack up among the truly imaginative lords of laziness. In fact, Krystal, who has written for the Times Literary Supplement, Harpers, *and the* New York Times Book Review *as well as serving as editor for* A Company of Readers: Uncollected Writings of W. H. Auden, Jacques Barzun, and Lionel Trilling *(2001), appears to be anything but lazy himself.* —A.L.

For a white American male, in good health and in possession of an advanced degree from an Ivy League school, I have, over the past twenty-five years, made a ridiculously small amount of money. And when I say small I mean *small.* Until five years ago, my best year netted me a little more than sixteen thousand dollars, and most years my annual income after taxes fluctuated between eight and ten thousand. Really. Being a writer only partially explains this woeful fiscal history. The real question is not so much how I've managed to survive but why I have accepted living in humble circumstances when my tastes are anything but. It's a question that friends, for whom my way of life has often been a subject of rueful and hilarious conversation, have speculated on. Here are some of the answers they've come up with: came of age in the sixties; never came of age; has an aversion to authority; has a structural anomaly of the brain; lost his mother when he was ten; was an only child; was an only child of parents who survived the war in Europe; read too many books at too early an age; found a really cheap, rent-stabilized apartment; is generally a moody, shiftless, self-absorbed individual.

The author relished everything about money except working for it.

Not making a lot of money says something about a man in a society where financial success is equated with acumen, resourcefulness, and social standing. Aside from those who enter professions in which money is not the main consideration—teaching, say, or diplomacy, or documentary filmmaking—the nonmoneyed are thought to lack the confidence or wherewithal to make the big bucks. There is an assumption that a feeling of ineligibility keeps us from realizing the earning potential both in ourselves and in the marketplace. It is, of course, just this entrepreneurial inner child that self-help books mean to awaken. True or not, success American-style is seen to be a matter of gumption, of get-up-and-go: economic hardship isn't about race or class, it's about character. Want money? Follow the appropriate twelve-step program, demonstrate the requisite stick-to-itiveness, and—badda badda bing—you're rolling in it.

Although it would be nice to say that the absence of a portfolio in my case suggested a well-developed ego, an indifference to the world's approval, I'm afraid that emotional immaturity as well as financial shortsightedness are nearer the mark. When I was in my twenties, it didn't matter that other men my age earned eighty grand a year while I survived on eight. I was healthy, strong, O.K.-looking, with a good head of hair (never discount male vanity as consolation for practically anything). There'd be time, I thought, to remedy matters. And let's be clear: I did not disdain the dollar. I was no ascetic, and my spiritual itch was more than satisfied by reading Hermann Hesse.* In truth, I was materialistic to the core: I loved money; I loved the idea of money; I even liked novels about the rich and movies about how the poor became rich. I liked everything about money except the prospect of buckling down and making it.

My father used to say that I became a writer so that I wouldn't have to work. Most writers will snort at this: what is writing *but* work? He had a point, though. The thought of being bound and defined by work that didn't interest me sent shivers down my spine. The solution was a string of part-time jobs that I could blow off whenever I wanted to—until I made it as a writer. Between 1971 and 1981, I drove a cab, hefted sacks of grain in an animal-feed warehouse, served time as a night watchman in a run-down hotel, lifted boxes on and off a conveyor belt, tutored philosophy, worked construction, loaded and unloaded trucks for UPS, and hauled freight along the Louisville-Cincinnati-Lexington triangle. None of these jobs paid more than four dollars an hour, and until 1992 I had no bank account: no checking, no savings. Also no car, no credit cards, no cashmere socks. Sometimes I moved from one city to another simply because I had a chance to house-sit or because a friend offered to put me up. I don't defend, and I most certainly don't recommend, this way of life. It may, in fact, no longer be feasible, given today's success-oriented ethos and the way prices have risen. In the mid-seventies, a quart of milk cost thirty cents in Boston; a carton of cigarettes, two dollars in South Carolina; filet mignon, four dollars a pound in Kentucky. One of the best Chambertins I ever drank set me back seventeen dollars in New Jersey.

5 Looking back, my peripatetic, hand-to-mouth existence puzzles more than it embarrasses me. Why did I settle for so little when I wanted so much more? And yet at the time it seemed like the life I should lead. Not because I wanted to be a writer (it wasn't as if the words to "Vissi d'arte"* filled my head) but because I saw myself—and this is where it does get a little embarrassing—in the light of books I had read as a teen-ager. I was great for poets and poetry

---

Hermann Hesse (1877–1962): German novelist

"Vissi d'arte": "I live for art," the beginning of an aria from the opera *Tosca,* by Giacomo Puccini (1858–1924)

and for whatever seemed fantastic, romantic, and tragic in books. I didn't exactly identify with Marlowe, Coleridge, Byron, Keats, Poe, Baudelaire, Rimbaud, and Pushkin,* but their examples did make me feel that hewing to the straight and narrow would somehow be disloyal to their own fervid imaginings.

One of the dangers of reading the right books at the wrong age is the tendency to confuse the creator with the creation. Since Des Esseintes, Pechorin, Stavrogin, Julien Sorel, Maldoror, and the Corsair* could have been given shape only by men very much like themselves, I decided around the age of fourteen to become a blasé voluptuary, a weary adventurer who travelled the world over, conquering women and boredom. This foolishness didn't last long, but for a time words and expressions like "anomie," "ennui," "spleen," "melancholy," and "alienated consciousness" made it difficult for me to think practically about the future.

But to say that I avoided long-term employment merely out of some misguided application of literature to life (where Emma Bovary* sought liaisons, I sought leisure) would be preposterous. I never wanted to work. Even as a kid, I thought working for money, whether I needed it or not, was a bad trade-off. In 1960, planted in front of an old RCA console, I warmed to the ersatz beatnik Maynard G. Krebs, on "The Many Loves of Dobie Gillis," who on hearing the word "work" would involuntarily yelp "Work!" as if an angry bee had suddenly dived into view. I didn't want to be Maynard G. Krebs, but then I didn't want to be much of anything. That annoying question kids have to contend with—"What do you want to be when you grow up?"—left me stupefied.

Not that I didn't have ambition. I had plans: I was going to write big, fat novels and make potloads of money. But what good is ambition without energy? It's nothing more than daydreaming. Novels demand drive and Trollope-like commitment.* Naturally, I wasn't up to it, although I did manage to become a regular contributor to various publications. Yet even as a recognized member of a guild I was a spectacular non-go-getter. You would not have seen my shining face at conferences, panel discussions, readings, parties, or wherever else editors, agents, and publishers showed up. Networking and self-promotion, the hallmarks of literary aspirants, demand hustle, and hustling, among other things, means moving briskly. I stayed home. I wrote about books, literary trends, academic criticism. And though I occasionally took on an assignment to write about boxing or business (experience obvi-

---

Marlowe . . . Pushkin: major writers and poets

Des Esseintes . . . the Corsair: heroic, defiant, or decadent characters in literary works

Emma Bovary: Heroine of *Madame Bovary,* novel by Gustave Flaubert (1821–80). Influenced by her reading of romantic novels, she pursues adulterous love affairs to disastrous effect.

Trollope-like commitment: Anthony Trollope (1815–82), an English novelist, was known to compose regularly 1,000 words per hour.

ously not required), my earnings pretty much stayed on an even keel. I wrote book reviews for the *money*.

Some men are born lazy, some acquire laziness, some have laziness thrust upon them. But, however gained, laziness remains ill-gotten. Because we make a virtue of what is necessary, the precept of work is like a commandment sans stone tablet. It's man's nature to work; without work, people tend to wilt. On the other hand, some people droop by design. Look at small children: not all are animated tykes scampering about the playground; there are always one or two likely to sit by themselves, ruminating on the fact that they have ten fingers and toes instead of nine or eleven. They are the suspect ones, the nascent lazy, and, left to their own devices, will probably not metamorphose into the movers and shakers of their generation.

Although laziness in its simplest terms is the disinclination to work, the condition is not reducible to a simple formula. For most of recorded history, laziness was thought to arise from the natural confluence of mind and body. The lazy suffered from melancholia, or an excess of black bile (carried by the blood to the brain), which in extreme cases kept them from finding solace in spiritual devotion. Those in whom the spirit failed to move or to be moved were afflicted with acedia—a condition that the early Church fathers felt deserved a measure of compassion, along with the usual tsk-tsking. But as the world grew older, and time got tangled up with the idea of progress, work, or busyness, rather than piety, took on antonymic meaning where laziness was concerned. By the late Middle Ages, acedia had come to include the notion of worldly sloth. And who was responsible for sloth? You were. Sloth didn't just slide into the world along with your squalling body; you had to seek it out and embrace it. 10

As a secular sin, laziness reached its apogee during the Industrial Revolution, when any sign of malingering was seen as a threat to the capitalist order. If you didn't work, you didn't produce, and if you didn't produce you were a parasite; you were, my friend, subversive. Don't get me wrong: I'm not defending the lazy. All I'm saying is that the subject makes people take extreme views. When Boswell suggested that "we grow weary when idle," the otherwise sensible Dr. Johnson* remonstrated, "That is, sir, because others being busy, we want company; but if we were idle, there would be no growing weary; we should all entertain one another." Is he kidding? The man obviously never hung out with the deadbeat crowd I used to know, for whom prying the cap off a Schlitz was a good day's work. Most people disdain the lazy not only because they serve no useful purpose but because their own metabolisms and circadian rhythms seem to recognize those whose own systems are out of sinc. The lazy are different from you and me. I mean, of course, just you.

Boswell . . . Dr. Johnson: Essayist James Boswell (1740–95) was the biographer of English man of letters Samuel Johnson (1709–84).

Medically, however, I'm fine. Two blood tests, years apart, revealed no bacterial parasites or high concentrations of viral antibodies, or any other noxious agents that could account for my usual indolence. No toxins in the air, no food groups, no glowing chunks of kryptonite rob me of my powers. Nor, when I look around, can I lay the blame on the sixties, or on my being an only child, or on my retreating into books at a tender age, or, for that matter, on family history. Although the early death of a parent so constricts the heart that it can never regain its original shape, plenty of children suffer loss and sadness and go on to lead busy, productive lives.

Sometimes the only good explanation for the arc life takes is that a person has only so much spring in his step, that one is born to travel only so far. And, while most of us want to get to the top, not all of us are willing to make the climb. My father wasn't entirely mistaken in claiming that I turned to writing in order to avoid work. Let's face it, some boys and girls become writers because the only workplace they're willing to visit is the one inside their heads. And even then it's a tough commute, since the same urge that leads them to write may also keep them from doing their work. That general discontent with the world which is at the bottom of all writing tends to pull writers down, deplete them of initiative, and make them wonder if it's worth doing at all. This applies as well to writers who churn out prose at a ferocious clip as it does to those of us who, like Bartleby,* prefer not to. The trick is to turn that urge to one's advantage. "I write of melancholy, by being busy to avoid melancholy," wrote the industrious Robert Burton.*

Likewise, writers who know themselves to be lazy conscientiously and routinely meet their inertia head-on. Profound laziness is not so much about doing nothing as it is about the strain of doing practically *anything*. Lazy people can accomplish things, thank you very much. We have our paroxysms of activity, the occasional eruptions of busyness and bursts of productivity. Walter Benjamin,* for instance, acknowledged that he had entered "the world under the sign of Saturn—the star of the slowest revolution, the planet of detours and delays," yet the man's formidable essays didn't, as they say, write themselves. Our first essayist, Montaigne,* also professed to have a wide streak of laziness, and Cyril Connolly,* whose journal *Horizon* helped keep English letters afloat during the Second World War, gloated, "Others merely live; I vegetate."

15 But vegetation among writers and thinkers takes peculiar forms. Someone who sits and conjures up names and explanations for characters or subatomic particles cannot be said to be doing nothing. A world of difference

---

Bartleby: the lead character in Herman Melville's short story "Bartleby the Scrivener" (1856), famous for his repeated remark, "I would prefer not to"

Robert Burton (1577–1640): author of *The Anatomy of Melancholy* (1621)

Walter Benjamin (1892–1940): influential German critic and essayist

Montaigne: Michel Eyquem, Seigneur de Montaigne (1533–92); French writer, author of *Essais* (first edition 1580)

Cyril Connolly (1903–74): English critic and editor

exists between a valetudinarian fused to his bed and Max Beerbohm,* who never voluntarily went out for a walk, because "it stops the brain." Still, the standard, hackneyed conception of laziness prevails. "Doomed as I was to a life of perpetual idleness, I did absolutely nothing," says the landscape painter in Chekhov's story* "The House with an Attic." "I spent hours looking out of the window at the sky, the birds, the avenues, read everything that was brought to me from the post, and slept. Sometimes I left the house and went for walks till late at night." Yes, yes, we've heard all this before. Don't be fooled: there's no uniformity about the lazy. Energetic people may all be alike, but the lazy cruise along at their own varying rates of speed. Some bite the bullet and go off to jobs; some stay home while their more energetic spouses tackle the workaday world; some really do watch the grass grow, or, its millennial equivalent, daytime television.

There is something preëmptive about laziness, something that smacks of a decision to refuse all offers even before they're put on the table. The lazy don't come to the table. And I think there is a philosophical component in this resistance. At bottom, laziness is negation, turning one's back on what others neutrally, cheerfully, or resignedly go to meet. The truly lazy—the ones who cannot bring themselves to greet and meet, to scheme and struggle, to interact on a daily basis with others—are, in effect, refusing to affix their signatures to the social contract. Given that success hinges on understanding, using, and occasionally subverting the social contract, the lazy don't stand a chance.

The secret to failure is far more elusive than the secret to success. Lagging behind when one could have advanced isn't just about laziness; it's about all the things that psychoanalysis takes a rather serious view of—the absence of love, coping with anger, rationalizing failure, the reluctance to supersede or replace one's father. Heavy stuff, and perhaps true, but the acknowledgment of which never put a dime in my pocket. Laziness just is. It's like being freckled or color-blind. Indeed, when the world was younger, intelligent people believed they had no choice in the matter of who was naughty or nice, passive or active. Hippocrates' theory of "temperament," which anchored Western medicine for two millennia, put some muscle behind varieties of human behavior. Well, not muscle exactly—more like four cardinal humors, whose relative proportion in the blood determined personality and moods. The Church fathers were on the right track; only the messenger and the manner of delivery were wrong. It's not black bile that causes Oblomov-like symptoms* but a certain kind of electro-chemical activity in the left

---

Max Beerbohm (1872–1956): English essayist and parodist

Chekhov's story: Anton Chekhov (1860–1904), Russian writer

Oblomov-like symptoms: Oblomov, a passive Russian noble described in a novel of the same name by Ivan Goncharov (1812–91), spent most of his time in bed.

frontal lobe of the brain, or whatever. The point is, everyone enters the world predisposed physiologically to think and feel in certain ways.

Happenstance also has its place; I don't deny that. But do any two people react identically to the same stimuli? The event that jump-starts one person's psyche does not necessarily have the same effect on another's. It's one thing to concede that certain tendencies can be reinforced or weakened by experience; it is quite another to think that some event during my formative years, which might have occurred but didn't, would have had me sharing a bucket of KFC with Bill Gates, or loping down a runway in Milan wearing a spiffy outfit by Valentino. In short, there's no contradiction in thinking that temperament defines you and thinking that you're still in charge of your life: temperament is the gas, but you've got a foot on the pedal.

Because of some elusive sequence of recombinant DNA and early experiences, I always knew I'd write things. I also knew I was an incurable lazybones. This accounts, in my case, for the odd tension between writing and laziness which Samuel Beckett describes to a T: "There is nothing to express, nothing with which to express, nothing from which to express, no power to express, no desire to express, together with the obligation to express." As a solid constituent of the couchant class, I can say that the obligation to express does not weigh heavily. Still, I have my moments—moments when I feel like addressing the fading shimmer of my own skin. I want answers. Or, more precisely, one big answer. In a sense, life is like an examination that has only one question—the one that asks why you're taking the exam in the first place. Having been instructed to "fill in the blank" (an aptly phrased command), you ponder, and then wonder if perhaps the truest answer is no answer at all. But in the end, because there is, after all, plenty of time to reflect and you do want to leave the room, you hunker down and fill in the blank. My own response is hardly profound or incisive: I'm taking the exam because I like writing sentences, and because—well, what else do I have to do?

As for the laziness that moves with me wherever I go, I have finally 20
found a way to make it "work" for me. Lassitude, aloofness, low-grade depression, coupled with a healthy respect for money, have gradually steered me to the obvious vocation. Yes, dear reader, I have become a screenwriter.

QUESTIONING THE TEXT

1. How does Krystal define *laziness*? By his own definition, is he truly lazy? Gather evidence from the essay to support your answers to these questions.
2. The illustration that accompanies this essay (p. 759) carries a reference to the author and to one of the points he makes. What other captions could effectively go with this illustration? Create several possible appropriate captions, and bring them to class for discussion.

3. Krystal ends his essay by revealing how he has finally made laziness "work" for him: he has "become a screenwriter." Is Krystal being ironic or satiric here? Reread the essay with this question in mind, and then write a one-paragraph explanation or elaboration of this final paragraph, exploring (in humorous terms if you want) what Krystal's meaning may be.

MAKING CONNECTIONS

4. Both Krystal and bell hooks (p. 774) talk about the way in which success in work has been measured in terms of the amount of money earned. In what ways are their attitudes toward this traditional linking of success with money similar? In what ways do their attitudes differ? Which view seems most persuasive to you, and why?
5. Imagine a brief correspondence between Benjamin Franklin (p. 720) and Arthur Krystal, in which Krystal offers advice on how to avoid work and Franklin counters with advice on how to cure laziness. Write a rough draft of their exchange. Then, after reading the exchange aloud to two or three classmates and getting feedback, revise the exchange. Finally, write a paragraph or two explaining which side of the conversation you find most effective—and why.

JOINING THE CONVERSATION

6. Write an extended definition of *laziness,* including a well-developed analogy and one or two metaphors. You may want to review the guidelines for writing definitions on p. xx. Bring the definition to class for discussion and reading aloud.
7. Use the resources of your library and the Internet to explore the literary and political concept of *Oblomovism,* briefly alluded to by Krystal (paragraph 17). Keywords for your search might include *Oblomov, Ivan Goncharov,* and the term *superfluous man.* Are there any contemporary equivalents of Oblomovism you can identify—the couch potato or the slacker, for example? Give examples of these types, and then write a short essay discussing how indolent people are portrayed today in literature, film, or popular culture.

EDWARD TENNER
Body Smarts

To be perfectly honest, "Body Smarts," an essay by Edward Tenner (b. 1944), adapted from his book Our Own Devices: The Past and Future of Body Technology *(2003), might seem more appropriate for the chapter on science and technology. The essay explores how people interact physically with all the gadgets and mechanisms, electronic and otherwise, that are increasingly a part of their lives. As you read the piece, however, you'll appreciate how often this synergy between flesh and fabrication is really about the work we do.*

Tenner is obviously on to something. If you use a PDA, consider how it acts as an extension of both your hand and your head. It organizes the people you know and manages the appointments you must keep. Sitting on its cradle or nestled in your pocket, it becomes like a new organ, beeping and buzzing when your life needs attention.

But the body/technology relationship works in both directions. As a consequence, the humble and much-neglected thumb, Tenner argues, is becoming the digit of choice today because of new technologies that favor it. I cannot dial my cell phone with my thumb, but apparently a whole generation of kids brought up on electronic games prefers this technique. And these speed dialers are traveling (or perhaps restoring) brain/hand pathways that may open up yet other human possibilities. Clearly, we don't just work with objects; we incorporate them into our lives at the deepest levels.

Tenner is also the author of Why Things Bite Back: Technology and the Revenge of Unintended Consequences *(1996). "Body Smarts" appeared originally in the spring 2003 issue of the* Wilson Quarterly. —J.R.

For more than 50 years, enthusiasts have proclaimed the coming of a new age of technologically augmented humanity, a somewhat unsettling era of bar-coded convicts and chip-implanted children. But technology has been reshaping the body since the very dawn of civilization. The feet of shod people, for example, are physiologically different from those of people who have always walked barefoot. Technologies as various as the thong sandal and the computer mouse have affected how we use our bodies—the *techniques* we employ in our everyday lives—and this coevolution of technology and the body has not always followed the course engineers and other designers imagined. The question now is whether mind, body, and machine will fuse in some radical new way over the next generation.

The enthusiasts themselves are far from agreement on the mechanism that might achieve such a fusion. For some, the new intimacy between humans and machines will simply involve more portable and powerful versions of devices we already take with us—computers, for example, that might be carried as we now carry cell phones and personal digital assistants (PDAs), to be viewed through special eyeglass displays. Spectacles might also transmit the emotional states of their wearers, so that a speaker, for example, could detect an audience's interest or boredom. There are already sneakers that can transmit or record information on a runner's performance, and civilian motorcycle helmets with intercoms and navigational aids built in.

Other enthusiasts scorn mere wearability. They're having sensors and transmitters surgically implanted in their bodies—as, for example, some deaf individuals have been fitted with cochlear implants that restore hearing. The cyborg, or human machine, is an especially powerful and persistent notion, perhaps because it seems a logical next step from technological symbiosis. (Politically, the cyborg idea—which for a few enthusiasts is a movement—spans a continuum from Paul Verhoeven's original *Robocop* film in 1987 to the work of cultural scholars such as Donna Haraway and Chris Hables Gray, who see the connection between human and machine as an emancipatory strategy against rigid economic and gender roles.)

But is the body really becoming more mechanized? Is the interaction of technology and human behavior all that new and frightening? Despite the legend, George Washington never wore wooden teeth, but his last pair of dentures, made of gold plates inset with hippopotamus teeth, human teeth, and elephant and hippo ivory, and hinged with a gold spring, were as good as the craftsmen of his time could produce. Still, he suffered great discomfort, and ate and spoke with difficulty (perhaps the enforced reserve enhanced his dignity). At any rate, if the nation's first president was a cyborg, it's not surprising that one in 10 Americans had some nondental implant—from pacemakers to artificial joints—by 2002. Nor was Washington an isolated case: Benjamin Franklin's bifocals and Thomas Jefferson's semireclining work chair were giant steps in human-mechanical hybridization. One might even say that John F. Kennedy was continuing the cyborg tradition when he became one of the first politicians to adopt the robotic signature machine, a giant and distinctively American step in the cloning of gesture.

The many amputations wounded soldiers suffered during the U.S. Civil 5
War led to the creation of an innovative artificial-limb industry. Today, responsive advanced prosthetics, wheelchairs, vision implants, and other assistive devices exceed the 19th century's wildest dreams. (There has even been litigation in the United States over whether a teenage swimmer with an artificial leg was unfairly barred from wearing a flipper on it.) But the first choice of medicine is still the conservation of natural materials and abilities. Thus, the trend in eye care has been from spectacles to contact lenses to laser surgery, and dentistry has moved steadily from dentures to prophylaxis and the conservation of endangered natural teeth. Some dental researchers believe that adults may be able to grow replacement teeth naturally. Other forms of regenera-

tion, including the recovery of function by paraplegics and quadriplegics, may follow.

The body remains surprisingly and reassuringly conservative, and humanity has stayed steadfastly loyal to objects that connect us with our environment. The traditional zori design—the sandal with a v-shaped thong separating the big toe from the others—is still used for some of the most stylish sandals. Athletic shoes with the most technically advanced uppers and soles still use a system of lacing at least 200 years old. For all their additional adjustments, most advanced new office chairs still rely on the 100-year-old principle of a spring-mounted lumbar support, and recliners still place the body in the same contours that library chairs did in the 19th century; according to industry sources, interest is fading in data ports built into recliners and in other technological enhancements. The QWERTY arrangement of the keyboard has resisted all reform, and alternatives to the flat conventional keyboard are expensive niche products, partly because, in the absence of discomfort, so few users are willing to learn new typing techniques. A century after the piano began to lose prestige and markets, it remains the master instrument, with a familiar keyboard.

Computers now allow the production of advanced progressive eyeglasses without the visible seam of bifocals, but wearers still hold them on their heads with the folding temples introduced in the 18th century. The latest NATO helmet still reflects the outlines of the medieval sallet. But then, our skills—like our foot bones, vertebrae, fingers, eyes, and ears—have not changed much. Even the automatic transmissions in our cars rely on a familiar tactile principle, a knob or handle and lever; the seemingly more efficient push-button shifter was largely abandoned after the Edsel. And the 21st century's automobiles are still directed and controlled by wheels and pedals—familiar from early modern sailing ships and wagons—rather than by the alternative interfaces that appear in patents and experimental cars. Meanwhile, many technological professionals study body techniques that need few or no external devices: yoga, martial arts, and the Alexander technique (a series of practices developed by a 19th-century Australian actor to promote more natural posture, motion, and speech).

Even Steve Mann, the Christopher Columbus of wearable computing, has misgivings about integrating himself with today's "smart" technology. Mann, who holds a Ph.D. in computer science from the Massachusetts Institute of Technology, was photographed as early as 1980 wearing a helmet equipped with a video camera and a rabbit-ears antenna. But in his book *Cyborg* (2001), he acknowledges being "increasingly uncomfortable with the idea of a cyborg future," where privacy is sacrificed for pleasure and convenience to a degree he compares to drug addiction.

Today's advanced cyborg technology is a harbinger of neither a utopian nor an apocalyptic future. Virtual reality helmets, often featured in scare scenarios of the future, are still not playthings; they're professional tools demanding rigorous training in physical and mental techniques if wearers are to avoid disorientation and lapses in judgment. At the other extreme of complexity, the miniature keyboards of cell phones and other devices are exerting a surprising influence at the level of everyday life. They're shifting the balance of power of the human hand from the index finger to the thumb. C. P. E. Bach elevated the role of the thumb in musical keyboarding 250 years ago, but touch-typing pioneers of the 20th century rediscovered the fourth and fifth fingers and banished the thumb to space bar duty. Now the thumb is enjoying a renaissance. It has returned to computing with the introduction of pen- and pencil-like devices such as the styluses used with PDAs. The latest computer mouse, developed by the Swedish physician and ergonomist Johan Ullman, is gripped and moved around the desk with a pen-shaped stick that uses the precision muscles of the thumb and fingers and doesn't twist the hand and tire the forearm. Even thumb-dependent pencils are resurgent, their unit sales having increased by more than 50 percent in the United States in the 1990s.

The biggest surprise is the thumb's role in electronics. In Japan today, so 10
many new data-entry devices rely on it that young people are called *oyayubi sedai*, the Thumb Generation. In Asia and Europe, users have turned technology on its head: Instead of using the voice recognition features of their phones, they're sending short text messages to friends, thumbs jumping around their cellular keyboards in a telegraphic imitation of casual speech. By spring 2002, there were more than 1.4 billion of these transmissions each month in the United Kingdom alone.

One British researcher, Sadie Plant, has found that thumbs all around the world are becoming stronger and more skillful. Some young Japanese are now even pointing and ringing doorbells with them. As Plant told *The Wall Street Journal*, "The relationship between technology and the users of technology is mutual. We are changing each other." Always attuned to social nuance, the "Style" section of *The Washington Post* also noted the ascent of the formerly humble digit. The major laboratories did not predestine the thumb to be the successor to the index finger, though they did help make the change possible; its full capacities were discovered through collaborative experimentation by users, designers, and manufacturers. The ascendancy of the thumb is an expression of the intimate relationship between head and hand described by the neurologist and hand injury specialist Frank Wilson, who speaks of the "24-karat thumb" in his book *The Hand* (1998): "The brain keeps giving the hand new things to do and new ways of doing what it already knows how to do. In turn, the hand affords the brain new ways of approaching old tasks and the possibility of understanding and mastering new tasks."

But change is not without cost. We learn new body skills to the neglect of others, and humanity has been losing not only languages but body techniques. Scores of resting positions known to anthropologists are being replaced by a single style of sitting. Countless variations of the infant-feeding bottle compete with the emotional and physiological rewards of nursing. The reclining chair, originally sold partly as a health device, has become an emblem of sedentary living. The piano's advanced development in the late 19th century prepared the way for the player piano, and ultimately for recorded music. Typewriter and computer keyboards eliminated much of the grind of learning penmanship, along with the pleasure of a personal hand (today's children may still grumble, but rarely must they learn the full, demanding systems of the 19th-century master penmen). The helmet wards off danger even as it encourages overconfident wearers to engage in new and dangerous activities. All these devices augment our powers, but in doing so they also gain a power over us.

The challenge within advanced industrial societies is to cope with a degree of standardization that threatens to choke off both new technologies and new techniques. We need a return to the collaboration between user and maker that marked so many of the great technological innovations, whether the shaping of the classic American fire helmet or the development of the touch method by expert typists and typing teachers. Research in even the most advanced technical processes confirms the importance of users. In the 1980s, for example, the economist Eric von Hippel studied change in high-technology industries such as those that manufacture scientific instruments, semiconductors, and printed circuit boards. Von Hippel found that up to 77 percent of the innovations in the industries were initiated by users. He therefore recommended that manufacturers identify and work with a vanguard of "lead users"—as was done in the past, for example, when 19th-century musicians worked with piano manufacturers, or when the typewriter entrepreneur James Densmore tested his ideas with the court reporter James O. Clephane in developing the QWERTY layout, an efficient arrangement for the four-finger typing technique that prevailed until the victory of the touch method in the 1890s. Today's cognitive psychologists of work are rejecting the older model of a single best set of procedures and learning from the experience of workers and rank-and-file operators how equipment and systems can be modified to promote greater safety and productivity. As one psychologist, Kim J. Vicente, has written, "Workers finish the design."

Design should be user friendly, of course, but it should also be user challenging. The piano keyboard is rightly celebrated as an interface that's at once manageable for the novice and inexhaustible for the expert. Information interfaces should similarly invite the beginner even as they offer the experienced user an opportunity to develop new techniques; they should not attempt to anticipate a user's every desire or need. The practice of participatory design, introduced in the 1970s by the mathematician and computer scientist Kristen Nygaard, began with Norwegian workers who wanted a say in the development of technology in their industries and was ultimately embraced by corporations worldwide.

15 The keyboard that's negotiated with a thumb is a threat to handwriting traditions, whether Asian or Western, and that's regrettable. But adapting to its use is a mark of human resourcefulness and ingenuity. The thumb, a proletarian digit ennobled in the digital age, is an apt symbol for a new technological optimism based on the self-reliance of users. The index finger—locating regulations and warnings in texts, wagging and lecturing in person—signifies authority, the rules. The thumb, by contrast, connotes the practical knowledge men and women have worked out for themselves, the "rules of thumb." It represents tacit knowledge, too, the skills we can't always explain, as with a "green thumb." And when extended during the almost lost art of hitchhiking, the thumb displays the right attitude toward the future: open and collaborative, but with a firm sense of direction.

QUESTIONING THE TEXT

1. Tenner occasionally italicizes the word *technique*, when he uses it near *technology*, a word with which it shares an etymological root. Summarize the relationship between technique and technology that you think Tenner is trying to illuminate in this essay.
2. With a classmate, list the pros and cons of technological development that Tenner raises in this essay. Use these lists to consider how you feel about what Tenner calls "the new intimacy between humans and machines" (paragraph 2). Record your response in your reading log, if you keep one.

MAKING CONNECTIONS

3. Tenner warns that technological change "is not without cost. We learn new body skills to the neglect of others, and humanity has been losing not only languages but body techniques" (paragraph 12). Consider Dagoberto Gilb's "Work Union" (p. 783) in light of this statement. Do Gilb's observations have to do with obsolete "body skills," or are other factors involved?
4. Read Eric Schlosser's excerpt, "Behind the Counter" (p. 787), and think about mechanization the fast food industry has introduced in the interest of standardization. How does this example of technology inform your understanding of Tenner's argument? Does it challenge or support some of Tenner's claims? Does it influence your thoughts about the pros and cons of technological advancement? Explain.

JOINING THE CONVERSATION

5. Tenner attempts to calm fears of rampant, dehumanizing technology in his essay, noting for example that "[v]irtual reality helmets, often featured in scare scenarios of the future, are still not playthings" (paragraph 9). With a classmate, find examples of such "scare scenarios" in popular culture—movies, television, science fiction, or other sources—and refute them using Tenner's reasoning and similar types of evidence.
6. For fun, try the reverse of the exercise in number 5. Working from examples of existing technology, use slippery-slope reasoning (one small choice leading to greater and greater consequences) to predict the most preposterous scary outcomes you can think of. Then share your fanciful predictions with classmates, and see if anyone detects a glimmer of possibility in them.

BELL HOOKS
Work Makes Life Sweet

*D*O PEOPLE WORK TO LIVE OR LIVE TO WORK*—or some combination of the two? In "Work Makes Life Sweet," from* Sisters of the Yam: Black Women and Self-Recovery *(1993), bell hooks (b. 1952) takes a look at the working traditions of African American women, noting that "[t]he vast majority of black women in the United States know in girlhood that [they] will be workers." She also considers the different circumstances that allow work to be "sweet" or that ensure that it will be sour—alienating and unsatisfying. In sum, she says the majority of black women she has talked with do not enjoy their work—and she goes on to offer reasons for such dissatisfaction as well as a way to "unlearn" conventional thinking about work so that it will once again have the capacity to make life sweet.*

For hooks, the work of writing seems sweet indeed, as evidenced by her publication of seventeen books in less than twenty years. Yet she often remarks on the ways in which her need to work for a living—accompanied by fears of poverty or joblessness—have interfered with her ability to live for the work of her writing. And for this work she is often criticized—for writing without extensive footnotes and bibliography, for not being "intellectual" enough, for writing about the same subjects (especially the intersection of class, race, and gender), even for writing too much. To these criticisms, hooks generally turns a deaf ear, saying "I'm playful, anybody who hangs with me knows that, but I am also a dead-serious intellectual woman who is on the job." To these criticisms, hooks also offers an outpouring of work: her most recent books include We Real Cool: Men, Masculinity, and Love *(2003);* A Woman's Mourning Song *(2004); and* Rock My Soul: Black People and Self-Esteem *(2004).*

In her Remembered Rapture: The Writer at Work *(1999), hooks offers recent ideas on the work of writing and on her passion for that work. What work, I wonder, do you have a passion for? In what ways does that work make your life sweet?*

—A.L.

"Work makes life sweet!" I often heard this phrase growing up, mainly from old black folks who did not have jobs in the traditional sense of the word. They were usually self-employed, living off the land, selling fishing worms, picking up an odd job here and there. They were people who had a passion for work. They took pride in a job done well. My Aunt Margaret took in ironing. Folks brought her clothes from miles around because she was such an expert. That was in the days when using starch was common and she knew how to do an excellent job. Watching her iron with skill and grace was like watching a ballerina dance. Like all the other black girls raised in the fifties that I knew, it was clear to me that I would be a working woman. Even though our mother stayed home, raising her seven children, we saw her constantly at work, washing, ironing, cleaning, and cooking (she is an incredible cook). And she never allowed her six girls to imagine we would not be working women. No, she let us know that we would work and be proud to work.

The vast majority of black women in the United States know in girlhood that we will be workers. Despite sexist and racist stereotypes about black women living off welfare, most black women who receive welfare have been in the workforce. In *Hard Times Cotton Mill Girls,** one can read about black women who went to work in the cotton mills, usually leaving farm labor or domestic service. Katie Geneva Cannon* remembers: "It was always assumed that we would work. Work was a given in life, almost like breathing and sleeping. I'm always surprised when I hear people talking about somebody taking care of them, because we always knew that we were going to work." Like older generations of southern black women, we were taught not only that we would be workers, but that there was no "shame" in doing any honest job. The black women around us who worked as maids, who stripped tobacco when it was the season, were accorded dignity and respect. We learned in our black churches and in our schools that it "was not what you did, but how you did it" that mattered.

A philosophy of work that emphasizes commitment to any task was useful to black people living in a racist society that for so many years made only certain jobs (usually service work or other labor deemed "undesirable") available to us. Just as many Buddhist traditions teach that any task becomes sacred when we do it mindfully and with care, southern black work traditions taught us the importance of working with integrity irrespective of the task. Yet these attitudes towards work did not blind anyone to the reality that racism made it difficult to work for white people. It took "gumption" to work with integrity in settings where white folks were disrespectful and downright hateful. And it was obvious to me as a child that the black people who were saying "work makes life sweet" were the folks who did not work for whites, who did what they wanted to do. For example, those who sold fishing worms were usually folks who loved to fish. Clearly there was a meaningful connection between positive thinking about work and those who did the work that they had chosen.

Most of us did not enter the workforce thinking of work in terms of finding a "calling" or a vocation. Instead, we thought of work as a way to make money. Many of us started our work lives early and we worked to acquire money to buy necessities. Some of us worked to buy school books or needed or desired clothing. Despite the emphasis on "right livelihood" that was present in our life growing up, my sisters and I were more inclined to think of work in relation to doing what you needed to do to get money to

---

Hard Times Cotton Mill Girls: an oral history of life in southern textile mills, compiled by Victoria Byerly (b. 1949), a former mill worker

Katie Geneva Cannon: The first black woman ordained a Presbyterian minister. She worked with Victoria Byerly, author of *Hard Times Cotton Mill Girls.*

buy what you wanted. In general, we have had unsatisfying work lives. Ironically, Mama entered the paid workforce very late, after we were all raised, working for the school system and at times in domestic service, yet there are ways in which she has found work outside the home more rewarding than any of her children. The black women I talked with about work tended to see jobs primarily as a means to an end, as a way to make money to provide for material needs. Since so many working black women often have dependents, whether children or other relatives, they enter the workforce with the realistic conviction that they need to make money for survival purposes. This attitude coupled with the reality of a job market that remains deeply shaped by racism and sexism means that as black women we often end up working jobs that we do not like. Many of us feel that we do not have a lot of options. Of the women I interviewed, the ones who saw themselves as having options tended to have the highest levels of education. Yet nearly all the black women I spoke with agreed that they would always choose to work, even if they did not need to. It was only a very few young black females, teenagers and folks in their early twenties, who talked with me about fantasy lives where they would be taken care of by someone else.

5 Speaking with young black women who rely on welfare benefits to survive economically, I found that overall they wanted to work. However, they are acutely aware of the difference between a job and a fulfilling vocation. Most of them felt that it would not be a sign of progress for them to "get off welfare" and work low-paying jobs, in situations that could be stressful or dehumanizing. Individuals receiving welfare who are trying to develop skills, to attend school or college, often find that they are treated with much greater hostility by social-service workers than if they were just sitting at home watching television. One woman seeking assistance was told by an angry white woman worker, "welfare is not going to pay for you to get your B.A." This young woman had been making many personal sacrifices to try and develop skills and educational resources that would enable her to be gainfully employed and she was constantly disappointed by the level of resentment toward her whenever she needed to deal with social services.

Through the years, in my own working life, I have noticed that many black women do not like or enjoy their work. The vast majority of women I talked to . . . agreed that they were not satisfied with their working lives even though they see themselves as performing well on the job. That is why I talk so much about work-related stress in [*Remembered Rapture*]. It is practically impossible to maintain a spirit of emotional well-being if one is daily doing work that is unsatisfying, that causes intense stress, and that gives little satisfaction. Again and again, I found that many black women I interviewed had far superior skills than the jobs they were performing called for but were held back because of their "lack of education," or in some cases, "necessary experience." This routinely prevented them from moving upward. While they performed their jobs well, they felt added tension generated in the work environment by supervisors who often saw them as "too uppity" or by their own struggle to maintain interest in their assigned tasks. One white-woman administrator shared that the clearly overly skilled black woman who works as an administrative assistant in her office was resented by white male "bosses" who felt that she did not have the proper attitude of a "subordinate." When I spoke to this woman she acknowledged not liking her job, stating that her lack of education and the urgent need to raise children and send them to college had prevented her from working towards a chosen career. She holds to the dream that she will return to school and someday gain the necessary education that will give her access to the career she desires and deserves. Work is so often a source of pain and frustration.

Learning how to think about work and our job choices from the standpoint of "right livelihood" enhances black female well-being. Our self-recovery is fundamentally linked to experiencing that quality of "work that makes life sweet." In one of my favorite self-help books, Marsha Sinetar's *Do What You Love, the Money Will Follow,* the author defines right livelihood as a concept initially coming from the teachings of Buddha which emphasized "work consciously chosen, done with full awareness and care, and leading to enlightenment." This is an attitude toward work that our society does not promote, and it especially does not encourage black females to think of work in this way. As Sinetar notes:

> Right Livelihood, in both its ancient and its contemporary sense, embodies self-expression, commitment, mindfulness, and conscious choice. Finding and doing work of this sort is predicated upon high self-esteem and self-trust, since only those who like themselves, who subjectively feel they are trustworthy and deserving dare to choose on behalf of what is right and true for them. When the powerful quality of conscious choice is present in our work, we can be enormously productive. When we consciously choose to do work we enjoy, not only can we get things done, we can get them done well and be intrinsically rewarded for our effort.

Black women need to learn about "right livelihood." Even though I had been raised in a world where elderly black people had this wisdom, I was more socialized by the get-ahead generation that felt how much money you were making was more important than what you did to make that money. We have difficult choices ahead.

As black females collectively develop greater self-esteem, a greater sense of entitlement, we will learn from one another's example how to practice right livelihood. Of the black women I interviewed the individuals who enjoyed their work the most felt they were realizing a particular vocation or calling. C.J. (now almost forty) recalls that generations of her family were college-educated. She was taught to choose work that would be linked with the political desire to enhance the overall well-being of black people. C.J. says, "I went to college with a mission and a passion to have my work be about African-Americans. The spirit of mission came to me from my family, who taught us that you don't just work to get money, you work to create meaning for yourself and other people." With this philosophy as a guiding standpoint, she has always had a satisfying work life.

When one of my sisters, a welfare recipient, decided to return to college, I encouraged her to try and recall her childhood vocational dreams and to allow herself adult dreams, so that she would not be pushed into preparing for a job that holds no interest for her. Many of us must work hard to unlearn the socialization that teaches us that we should just be lucky to get any old job. We can begin to think about our work lives in terms of vocation and calling. One black woman I interviewed, who has worked as a housewife for many years, began to experience agoraphobia. Struggling to regain her emotional well-being, she saw a therapist, against the will of her family. In this therapeutic setting, she received affirmation for her desire to finish her undergraduate degree and continue in a graduate program. She found that finishing a master's and becoming a college teacher gave her enormous satisfaction. Yet this achievement was not fully appreciated by her husband. A worker in a factory, whose job is long and tedious, he was jealous of her newfound excitement about work. Since her work brings her in touch with the public, it yields rewards unlike any he can hope to receive from his job. Although she has encouraged him to go back to school (one of his unfulfilled goals), he is reluctant. Despite these relational tensions, she has found that "loving" her work has helped her attend to and transform previous feelings of low self-esteem.

A few of the black women I interviewed claimed to be doing work 10
they liked but complained bitterly about their jobs, particularly where they must make decisions that affect the work lives of other people. One woman had been involved in a decision-making process that required her to take a stance that would leave another person jobless. Though many of her peers were proud of the way she handled this difficult decision, her response was to feel "victimized." Indeed, she kept referring to herself as "battered." This response troubled me for it seemed to bespeak a contradiction many women experience in positions of power. Though we may like the status of a power position and wielding power, we may still want to see ourselves as "victims" in the process, especially if we must act in ways that "good girls, dutiful daughters" have been taught are "bad."

I suggested to the women I interviewed that they had chosen particular careers that involved "playing hard ball" yet they seemed to be undermining the value of their choices and the excellence of their work by complaining that they had to get their hands dirty and suffer some bruises. I shared with them my sense that if you choose to play hardball then you should be prepared for the bruises and not be devastated when they occur. In some ways it seemed to me these black women wanted to be "equals" in a man's world while they simultaneously wanted to be treated like fragile "ladies." Had they been able to assume full responsibility for their career choices, they would have enjoyed their work more and been able to reward themselves for jobs well done. In some cases it seemed that the individuals were addicted to being martyrs. They wanted to control everything, to be the person "in power" but also resented the position. These individuals, like those I describe in the chapter on stress, seemed not to know when to set boundaries or that work duties could be shared. They frequently over-extended themselves. When we over-extend ourselves in work settings, pushing ourselves to the breaking point, we rarely feel positive about tasks even if we are performing them well.

Since many people rely on powerful black women in jobs (unwittingly turning us into "mammies" who will bear all the burdens—and there are certainly those among us who take pride in this role), we can easily become tragically over-extended. I noticed that a number of us (myself included) talk about starting off in careers that we really "loved" but over-working to the point of "burn-out" so that the pleasure we initially found dissipated. I remember finding a self-help book that listed twelve symptoms of "burn-out," encouraging readers to go down the list and check those that described their experience. At the end, it said, "If you checked three or more of these boxes, chances are you are probably suffering from burn-out." I found I had checked all twelve! That let me know it was time for a change. Yet changing was not easy. When you do something and you do it well, it is hard to take a break, or to confront the reality that I had to face, which was that I really didn't want to be doing the job I was doing even though I did it well. In retrospect it occurred to me that it takes a lot more energy to do a job well when you really do not want to be doing it. This work is often more tiring. And maybe that extra energy would be better spent in the search for one's true vocation or calling.

In my case, I have always wanted to be a writer. And even though I have become just that and I love this work, my obsessive fears about "not being poor" have made it difficult for me to take time away from my other career, teaching and lecturing, to "just write." Susan Jeffers' book, *Feel the Fear and Do It Anyway,* has helped me to finally reach the point in my life where I can take time to "just write." Like many black women who do not come from privileged class backgrounds, who do not have family we can rely on to help if the financial going gets rough (we in fact are usually the people who are relied on), it feels very frightening to think about letting go of financial security, even for a short time, to do work one loves but may not pay the bills. In my case, even though I had worked with a self-created financial program aimed at bringing me to a point in life when I could focus solely on writing, I still found it hard to take time away. It was then that I had to tap into my deep fears of ending up poor and counter them with messages that affirm my ability to take care of myself economically irrespective of the circumstance. These fears are not irrational (though certainly mine were a bit extreme). In the last few years, I have witnessed several family members go from working as professionals to unemployment and various degrees of homelessness. Their experiences highlighted the reality that it is risky to be without secure employment and yet they also indicated that one could survive, even start all over again if need be.

My sister V. quit a job that allowed her to use excellent skills because she had major conflicts with her immediate supervisor. She quit because the level of on-the-job stress had become hazardous to her mental well-being. She quit confident that she would find a job in a few months. When that did not happen, she was stunned. It had not occurred to her that she would find it practically impossible to find work in the area she most wanted to live in. Confronting racism, sexism, and a host of other unclear responses, months passed and she has not found another job. It has changed her whole life. While material survival has been difficult, she is learning more about what really matters to her in life. She is learning about "right livelihood." The grace and skill with which she has confronted her circumstance has been a wonderful example for me. With therapy, with the help of friends and loved ones, she is discovering the work she would really like to do and no longer feels the need to have a high-paying, high-status job. And she has learned more about what it means to take risks.

In *Do What You Love, the Money Will Follow,* Sinetar cautions those of 15
us who have not been risk-takers to go slowly, to practice, to begin by taking small risks, and to plan carefully. Because I have planned carefully, I am able to finally take a year's leave from my teaching job without pay. During this time, I want to see if I enjoy working solely as a writer and if I can support myself. I want to see if (like those old-time black folks I talk about at the start of the essay) doing solely the work I feel most "called" to do will enhance my joy in living. For the past few months, I have been "just writing" and indeed, so far, I feel it is "work that makes life sweet."

The historical legacy of black women shows that we have worked hard, long, and well, yet rarely been paid what we deserve. We rarely get the recognition we deserve. However, even in the midst of domination, individual black women have found their calling, and do the work they are best suited for. Onnie Lee Logan, the Alabama midwife who tells her story in *Motherwit,* never went to high school or college, never made a lot of money in her working life, but listened to her inner voice and found her calling. Logan shares:

> I let God work the plan on my life and I am satisfied at what has happened to me in my life. The sun wasn't shinin' every time and moon wasn't either. I was in the snow and the rain at night by my lonely self. . . . There had been many dreary nights but I didn't look at em as dreary nights. I had my mind on where I was going and what I was going for.
>
> Whatever I've done, I've done as well as I could and beyond. . . . I'm satisfied at what has happened in my life. Perfectly satisfied at what my life has done for me. I was a good midwife. One of the best as they say. This book was the last thing I had planned to do until God said well

> done. I consider myself—in fact if I leave tomorrow—I've lived my life and I've lived it well.

The life stories of black women like Onnie Logan remind us that "right livelihood" can be found irrespective of our class position, or the level of our education.

To know the work we are "called" to do in this world, we must know ourselves. The practice of "right livelihood" invites us to become more fully aware of our reality, of the labor we do and of the way we do it. Now that I have chosen my writing more fully than at any other moment of my life, the work itself feels more joyous. I feel my whole being affirmed in the act of writing. As black women unlearn the conventional thinking about work—which views money and/or status as more important than the work we do or the way we feel about that work—we will find our way back to those moments celebrated by our ancestors, when work was a passion. We will know again that "work makes life sweet."

QUESTIONING THE TEXT

1. hooks takes the term "right livelihood" (paragraph 17) from Marsha Sinetar's *Do What You Love, the Money Will Follow.* Look at the way hooks defines this term and at the passages she quotes from Sinetar's book. Then list the people mentioned in hooks's essay who successfully practice "right livelihood." What do they have in common?
2. According to hooks, under what circumstances can "work make life sweet"? Do you accept the conditions she offers? Might there be other circumstances in which work could make someone's life sweet? After thinking carefully about your responses to these questions, write a paragraph arguing for or against hooks's claims.

MAKING CONNECTIONS

3. Read hooks's essay alongside the selection by Dagoberto Gilb (p. 783). Then, working with a classmate, consider how hooks might respond to Gilb's views on work. Write up a dialogue between Gilb and hooks on the value of work and what work situations merit complaint.
4. Consider how hooks might respond to Schlosser's piece, which discusses how adolescents, recent immigrants, the elderly, and the disabled serve as the primary work force for the fast food industry (p. 789). Imagine you are hooks, and write a response to Schlosser's "Behind the Counter."

JOINING THE CONVERSATION

5. In paragraph 6, hooks claims "[i]t is practically impossible to maintain a spirit of emotional well-being if one is daily doing work that is unsatisfying. . . ." Does this statement reflect your firsthand experience of work? Write a journal entry describing your work experience and explaining why it does or does not support hooks's claim. If you keep a reading log, write the entry there.
6. Imagine that you are applying for the job of your dreams, one that would indeed make your life sweet. Write a job announcement or advertisement for the position, and bring it to class for discussion. Be prepared to explain your reasons for wanting this job as well as the ways you are—and are not—currently prepared for it.
7. Working with one or two classmates, discuss this slight revision of hooks's title: "Schoolwork Makes Life Sweet." Decide what conditions would need to exist for this statement to be accurate. Then, working together, write up a catalog description of the kind of schoolwork guaranteed to make life sweet. You may decide to take a humorous approach to this topic.

DAGOBERTO GILB
Work Union

*F*ROM THE TIME I WAS ABOUT ELEVEN YEARS OLD, *I picked up some extra money with babysitting gigs, but my first* real *job was at the soda fountain in our local drugstore. I wore a big apron (no gloves or hairnets then) and took orders and filled them—mostly for milk shakes, ice cream sodas, and sweetish concoctions like Cherry Cokes and Brown Cows. Sometimes I got tips, and these I coveted for weeks, deciding what I would treat myself to (usually a record with the latest hits). I held this job throughout high school, and every summer during college I returned home to similar jobs, though I eventually graduated to waiting tables at a full-blown restaurant. At the time, I felt fortunate to have this work and the money it brought in; looking back, I still feel lucky: throughout my life I have always had work to do and, almost always, work I believed in. The benefit of hindsight also tells me that my jobs have brought me into contact with many other people—and that's one of the things I value most about the work experiences I have had.*

In the very brief essay that follows, Dagoberto Gilb (b. 1950) criticizes those that look upon some work as good and other work as somehow beneath them, arguing that "there is only good in work." Gilb speaks from experience. He's worked at many jobs, from construction worker to high-rise carpenter to teacher and writer. In this last role, Gilb has been highly successful, winning awards for his collection of short stories, The Magic of Blood *(1993) and for his novel,* The Last Known Residence of Mickey Acuña *(1994). "Work Union" appears in a collection of Gilb's essays,* Gritos, *published in 2003. His current work is teaching creative writing at Southwest Texas State University. As you read Gilb's essay, think about your own current work—and the value you place on it. Does your system of value for work match that of society in general?*

— A.L.

From the richest high school to the poorest high school in America, students are being told that employment in the computer industry is nothing less than salvation from the indignities of the jobs those others have to do to survive. If you don't learn your computer skills well, if by some chance you're bored sitting in front of that screen, day after day under buzzing fluorescents, pecking at a vanilla keyboard, clicking a mouse, it's your problem, and there will be no excuse for your fate in this new economy: you will be doomed to menial, manual labor. That dirty, anybody-can-do-that work. Poor income, low prestige. Pues, así va la vida, compa, that's life if you don't get your stuff right.

But if every young person did learn software programming or Web-page design, if everybody was taught to be so good at these and the rest, there simply wouldn't be enough of those jobs to go around, and the current high income associated with that employment would, as we know, fall dramatically. What is being taught is not only these skills but a justification for keeping an imbalance of power between the new high-tech workers and jobs that will always be necessary—building the offices, highways, bridges where those others do their business through modems and cell phones.

There was a time when work, a man who worked, a man who worked hard, who sweated, got dirty, even, who built things with tools in his hands, was looked upon with respect and honor. And it was the union that made for more personal dignity and real wages.

Not everybody wants to sit at a desk for a living. So many of us come from cultures where it is expected that we will move our bodies in the wind and sun, at dawn and into dusk. Many of us have been taught by family that physical work feels good and is good—when the day is over, we know what we did because we see it, we feel the efforts in our feet and hands and bones, and when we go home, when the wife puts food on the table and the family sits down and eats, there is unmistakable pride that all of it is because we have done our job.

It is human to work, to bend and grip, to lift and pull. It's never about 5
getting tired or dirty. There is nothing wrong with sweat and toil. It is only about conditions and decent wages that there can come complaint. This is what so many people don't understand, especially those who sit in chairs in offices. They see us tired, they see us worried. They say, Well, if you don't like your situation, why don't you get a better job? Because it isn't the job, the kind of work. The job is good. Being a carpenter, an electrician, a plumber, a ironworker, a laborer, those are all good. What isn't good is to be earning a living that can't bring in enough money to raise a healthy family, buy a home, go to a dentist and doctor, and be around comfortably for grandchildren.

A writer from Detroit who worked years for the Fisher Body Plant in Flint, Michigan, has recently been profiled in the newspapers because he won a prize for his writing. In the exultation of winning, he has been quoted often about those years he worked on the assembly line, saying, "I can't stress to you enough how much I hated it." This writer, he is certainly a good man, but like so many, he simply forgot what a joy employment is, what a job means to people and their families. There is only good in work, and the very best people are those who work hard.

QUESTIONING THE TEXT

1. To whom do you think Gilb is writing? Can you infer anything about the audience he envisions? What clues about the potential audience do you find in the text?

2. Gilb claims that those who promote computer industry work are also advancing "a justification for keeping an imbalance of power between the new high-tech workers and jobs that will always be necessary — building the offices, highways, bridges where those others do their business through modems and cell phones" (paragraph 2). With a classmate, elaborate on this claim to explain Gilb's reasoning. What support does he provide for this claim? What unstated assumptions does the claim rely on? After explicating this claim, decide whether you agree with it, and note your reasons.

MAKING CONNECTIONS

3. Read Naomi Barko's "The Other Gender Gap" (p. 733), and consider the assumptions Gilb makes about work in this essay as he conjures images of men working in traditionally male jobs. In class discussion, consider how Gilb might respond to Barko's claim that women's work is devalued, often because "women's occupations" suffer from discrimination. Do you think Gilb contributes to that discrimination with descriptions like those offered in paragraphs 3 and 4, or do you think he would readily include descriptions of nurses, teachers, and day-care workers in his lists of honorable, hard jobs? What evidence in his essay supports your answer?
4. Compare Gilb's argument with that of bell hooks in "Work Makes Life Sweet" (p. 774) or that of Marge Piercy in "To Be of Use" (p. 793). On what points do the authors agree, and on what points do they differ? Which argument do you find most convincing, and why?
5. Gilb writes that "it isn't the job, the kind of work" that deserves complaint. "There is nothing wrong with sweat and toil. It is only about conditions and decent wages that there can come complaint. . . . What isn't good is to be earning a living that can't bring in enough money to raise a healthy family, buy a home, go to a dentist and doctor, and be around comfortably for grandchildren" (paragraph 5). Given these sentiments, what position do you think Gilb would take on the issue of "comparable worth" debated by Naomi Barko and Steven Pinker in this chapter?

JOINING THE CONVERSATION

6. "Work Union" can be read as an argument of praise or blame because Gilb praises "those who work hard" and blames those who overlook the value of physical labor. Write your own short argument of praise or

blame about a type of work you have done or a type of work you have been taught to respect. You might take a serious tone, as Gilb does here, or you might try writing a humorous or satirical piece. Think of your essay as a piece that you might share with others, perhaps on your Web site or as an op-ed for a campus or local newspaper.

7. With a group of classmates, list the jobs you have performed, and state how you feel about them. Having read Gilb's essay, does anyone in your group admit to feeling differently about those jobs now? Do you think Gilb would impart greater dignity to some of your more "menial" work than you do? What issues related to "conditions and decent wages" might you complain about now?

ERIC SCHLOSSER
Behind the Counter

I'M JUST OLD ENOUGH TO REMEMBER the first fast food restaurants appearing, bright and clean, at suburban crossroads in the 1950s—as well as the aptly named greasy spoons they replaced. We've since romanticized the latter, forgetting how dreadful the food in mom-and-pop operations could be and how unreliable the service usually was. You'd sit at a table waiting and waiting for a greasy lump of meatloaf served by a waitstaff who expected tips but did little to earn them. In contrast, McDonald's and its imitators were the epitome of efficiency—cheery places that served up burgers and fries better than mom made (the fries especially) and did so almost faster than a customer could pay for them. It didn't take long for clever marketing to drill the virtues of fast food into the public mind.

Nevertheless, after reading Eric Schlosser's sobering critique of the fast food industry, Fast Food Nation *(2001), you might never look at a Big Mac or Whopper the same way again. In this exposé, Schlosser asks his readers to ponder the real costs behind the relatively inexpensive burgers and fries Americans and, increasingly, the rest of the world devour in huge quantities every day. Pressure from the fast food companies to keep costs down, he argues, has lowered standards throughout the meatpacking and poultry industries and endangered or exploited workers at every level of production, from the farmers who raise chickens to the kids who peddle the patties.*

In "Behind the Counter," the excerpt from Fast Food Nation *reprinted here, Schlosser explains why the majority of workers at fast food chains are low-paid, inexperienced teenagers. The food production systems developed by McDonald's and its competitors require no special skills or dedication, just an ability to assemble, rather than cook, food items. As a result, the workers need minimal training, and they are all easily replaceable. In short, if you don't want the job, somebody else does.*

This is not to deny that young people laboring at a Wendy's or Burger King don't profit from their time behind the counter or gain some important work experience (though Schlosser has his doubts about the value of this training). Still, it's not surprising either that the employees processing your order usually aren't quite as bright-eyed as their TV-commercial counterparts. Maybe special orders do *upset them?*

Eric Schlosser is an investigative journalist and critic of corporate capitalism. A correspondent for the Atlantic, *he has written about agriculture, prisons, pornography, and, most recently in* Reefer Madness *(2003), about the American underground economy.*

—J.R.

Every Saturday Elisa Zamot gets up at 5:15 in the morning. It's a struggle, and her head feels groggy as she steps into the shower. Her little sisters, Cookie and Sabrina, are fast asleep in their beds. By 5:30, Elisa's showered, done her hair, and put on her McDonald's uniform. She's sixteen, bright-eyed and olive-skinned, pretty and petite, ready for another day of work. Elisa's mother usually drives her the half-mile or so to the restaurant, but sometimes Elisa walks, leaving home before the sun rises. Her family's modest townhouse sits beside a busy highway on the south side of Colorado Springs, in a largely poor and working-class neighborhood. Throughout the day, sounds of traffic fill the house, the steady whoosh of passing cars. But when Elisa heads for work, the streets are quiet, the sky's still dark, and the lights are out in the small houses and rental apartments along the road.

When Elisa arrives at McDonald's, the manager unlocks the door and lets her in. Sometimes the husband-and-wife cleaning crew are just finishing up. More often, it's just Elisa and the manager in the restaurant, surrounded by an empty parking lot. For the next hour or so, the two of them get everything ready. They turn on the ovens and grills. They go downstairs into the basement and get food and supplies for the morning shift. They get the paper cups, wrappers, cardboard containers, and packets of condiments. They step into the big freezer and get the frozen bacon, the frozen pancakes, and the frozen cinnamon rolls. They get the frozen hash browns, the frozen biscuits, the frozen McMuffins. They get the cartons of scrambled egg mix and orange juice mix. They bring the food upstairs and start preparing it before any customers appear, thawing some things in the microwave and cooking other things on the grill. They put the cooked food in special cabinets to keep it warm.

The restaurant opens for business at seven o'clock, and for the next hour or so, Elisa and the manager hold down the fort, handling all the orders. As the place starts to get busy, other employees arrive. Elisa works behind the counter. She takes orders and hands food to customers from breakfast through lunch. When she finally walks home, after seven hours of standing at a cash register, her feet hurt. She's wiped out. She comes through the front door, flops onto the living room couch, and turns on the TV. And the next morning she gets up at 5:15 again and starts the same routine.

Up and down Academy Boulevard, along South Nevada, Circle Drive, and Woodman Road, teenagers like Elisa run the fast food restaurants of Colorado Springs. Fast food kitchens often seem like a scene from *Bugsy Malone,* a film in which all the actors are children pretending to be adults. No other industry in the United States has a workforce so dominated by adolescents. About two-thirds of the nation's fast food workers are under the age of twenty. Teenagers open the fast food outlets in the morning, close them at night, and keep them going at all hours in between. Even the managers and assistant managers are sometimes in their late teens. Unlike Olympic gymnastics—an activity in which teenagers consistently perform at a higher level than adults—there's nothing about the work in a fast food kitchen that requires young employees. Instead of relying upon a small, stable, well-paid,

and well-trained workforce, the fast food industry seeks out part-time, un- 5
skilled workers who are willing to accept low pay. Teenagers have been the perfect candidates for these jobs, not only because they are less expensive to hire than adults, but also because their youthful inexperience makes them easier to control.

The labor practices of the fast food industry have their origins in the assembly line systems adopted by American manufacturers in the early twentieth century. Business historian Alfred D. Chandler has argued that a high rate of "throughput" was the most important aspect of these mass production systems. A factory's throughput is the speed and volume of its flow—a much more crucial measurement, according to Chandler, than the number of workers it employs or the value of its machinery. With innovative technology and the proper organization, a small number of workers can produce an enormous amount of goods cheaply. Throughput is all about increasing the speed of assembly, about doing things faster in order to make more.

Although the McDonald brothers had never encountered the term "throughput" or studied "scientific management," they instinctively grasped the underlying principles and applied them in the Speedee Service System. The restaurant operating scheme they developed has been widely adopted and refined over the past half century. The ethos of the assembly line remains at its core. The fast food industry's obsession with throughput has altered the way millions of Americans work, turned commercial kitchens into small factories, and changed familiar foods into commodities that are manufactured.

At Burger King restaurants, frozen hamburger patties are placed on a conveyer belt and emerge from a broiler ninety seconds later fully cooked. The ovens at Pizza Hut and at Domino's also use conveyer belts to ensure standardized cooking times. The ovens at McDonald's look like commercial laundry presses, with big steel hoods that swing down and grill hamburgers on both sides at once. The burgers, chicken, french fries, and buns are all frozen when they arrive at a McDonald's. The shakes and sodas begin as syrup. At Taco Bell restaurants the food is "assembled," not prepared. The guacamole isn't made by workers in the kitchen; it's made at a factory in Michoacán, Mexico, then frozen and shipped north. The chain's taco meat arrives frozen and precooked in vacuum-sealed plastic bags. The beans are dehydrated and look like brownish corn flakes. The cooking process is fairly simple. "Everything's add water," a Taco Bell employee told me. "Just add hot water."

Although Richard and Mac McDonald introduced the division of labor to the restaurant business, it was a McDonald's executive named Fred Turner who created a production system of unusual thoroughness and attention to detail. In 1958, Turner put together an operations and training manual for the company that was seventy-five pages long, specifying how almost everything should be done. Hamburgers were always to be placed on the grill in six neat rows; french fries had to be exactly 0.28 inches thick. The McDonald's operations manual today has ten times the number of pages and weighs about four pounds. Known within the company as "the Bible," it contains precise instructions on how various appliances should be used, how each item on the menu should look, and how employees should greet customers. Operators who disobey these rules can lose their franchises. Cooking instructions are not only printed in the manual, they are often designed into the machines. A McDonald's kitchen is full of buzzers and flashing lights that tell employees what to do.

At the front counter, computerized cash registers issue their own commands. Once an order has been placed, buttons light up and suggest other menu items that can be added. Workers at the counter are told to increase the size of an order by recommending special promotions, pushing dessert, pointing out the financial logic behind the purchase of a larger drink. While doing so, they are instructed to be upbeat and friendly. "Smile with a greeting and make a positive first impression," a Burger King training manual suggests. "Show them you are GLAD TO SEE THEM. Include eye contact with the cheerful greeting."

The strict regimentation at fast food restaurants creates standardized 10
products. It increases the throughput. And it gives fast food companies an enormous amount of power over their employees. "When management determines exactly how every task is to be done . . . and can impose its own rules about pace, output, quality, and technique," the sociologist Robin Leidner has noted, "[it] makes workers increasingly interchangeable." The management no longer depends upon the talents or skills of its workers—those things are built into the operating system and machines. Jobs that have been "de-skilled" can be filled cheaply. The need to retain any individual worker is greatly reduced by the ease with which he or she can be replaced.

Teenagers have long provided the fast food industry with the bulk of its workforce. The industry's rapid growth coincided with the baby-boom expansion of that age group. Teenagers were in many ways the ideal candidates for these low-paying jobs. Since most teenagers still lived at home, they could afford to work for wages too low to support an adult, and until recently, their limited skills attracted few other employers. A job at a fast food restaurant became an American rite of passage, a first job soon left behind for better things. The flexible terms of employment in the fast food industry also attracted housewives who needed extra income. As the number of baby-boom teenagers declined, the fast food chains began to hire other marginalized workers: recent immigrants, the elderly, and the handicapped.

English is now the second language of at least one-sixth of the nation's restaurant workers, and about one-third of that group speaks no English at all. The proportion of fast food workers who cannot speak English is even higher. Many know only the names of the items on the menu; they speak "McDonald's English."

The fast food industry now employs some of the most disadvantaged members of American society. It often teaches basic job skills—such as getting to work on time—to people who can barely read, whose lives have been chaotic or shut off from the mainstream. Many individual franchisees are genuinely concerned about the well-being of their workers. But the stance of the fast food industry on issues involving employee training, the minimum wage, labor unions, and overtime pay strongly suggests that its motives in hiring the young, the poor, and the handicapped are hardly altruistic.

QUESTIONING THE TEXT

1. This excerpt may not explicitly state the argument of the chapter of which it is a part, but it does create some impressions about fast food work. How would you summarize the messages Schlosser presents here about the fast food industry and teenagers' roles in it?
2. This selection begins and ends with images of employees in fast food chains. With a classmate, list the other aspects of the fast food industry illuminated in this excerpt. Then consider how Schlosser achieves transitions between these different aspects. What words and phrases does he use to signal the changes in topic? Do you find the transitions smooth or not? Do you and your classmate agree on this aspect of Schlosser's writing style? Explain.
3. Given the last line of this excerpt, what issue(s) do you think the next section of the chapter will address? Does the ending of this section make you want to read on? Why, or why not?

MAKING CONNECTIONS

4. Compare the work described in Schlosser's excerpt with that of "Work Union" by Dagoberto Gilb (p. 783). Would it be possible to write of fast food work in the way that Gilb writes of carpentry, plumbing, or ironwork? Why, or why not? Defend your position in a class discussion.
5. In "Work Makes Life Sweet" (p. 774), bell hooks asserts, "A philosophy of work that emphasizes commitment to any task was useful to black people living in a racist society that for so many years made only certain jobs . . . available to us" (paragraph 3). How does her argument inform your reading of Schlosser's piece, which points out that fast food chains often hire "marginalized workers: recent immigrants, the elderly, and the handicapped" (paragraph 11), in addition to teenagers. Use these two essays to consider how a job in the fast food industry might have a different meaning for a teenager than it does for one of these "marginalized" workers.

JOINING THE CONVERSATION

6. Have you ever worked in a fast food restaurant? Does your experience match Schlosser's description? Use your experience to write an essay responding to Schlosser's representation of the fast food industry's practices in this excerpt. If you haven't worked in such a restaurant, you might write from your experience as a fast food customer; comment on the insights Schlosser's writing provides into your experience "in front of the counter."
7. Write a brief essay about the job in which you learned "basic job skills — such as getting to work on time," which Schlosser mentions in his last paragraph. Try to capture what you learned from this job. Would you go back to that type of work? Under what circumstances might you consider doing so? In class, share your essays by reading them aloud. As you listen to others' experiences, what similarities emerge? What insights do your essays contribute to those provided in Schlosser's excerpt?

MARGE PIERCY
To Be of Use

*M*ARGE PIERCY *(b. 1936) is remarkable by any standard: she is the author of over two dozen books of poetry (including* The Moon Is Always Female *[1980] and* Mars and Her Children *[1992]) and fiction (including* Going Down Fast *[1969],* Woman on the Edge of Time *[1976],* Fly Away Home *[1984], and* He, She, and It *[1991]); a political activist (she helped organize Students for a Democratic Society in the 1960s); an ardent feminist; and a constant social critic. Piercy writes with passion and power that are hard to ignore. Often, her passion for justice and equity as well as for what she calls "work that is real" is born of hard experience. The child of often poor and working-class parents, Piercy (who is white and Jewish) grew up in a predominantly African American section of Detroit, where she learned firsthand about what she calls "the indifference of the rich, racism . . . the working-class pitted against itself." The first member of her family to attend college, she won a scholarship and graduated from the University of Michigan; she has contributed her prolific collection of manuscripts to its graduate library. Her latest books include* The Third Child: A Novel *(2003) and* Colors Passing Through Us: Poems *(2003).*

Many of Piercy's poems get their power from a kind of pent-up rage that explodes on the page in front of her readers. In fact, I first got to know her work through just such poems, a number of which (like "Barbie Doll," which appeared in the first edition of this book) haunt me still. But Piercy can be hopeful, even celebratory, as well. And in the following poem from To Be of Use *(1973), she is both, defining in vivid images and rhythmic cadences "work that is real." This is one of only four poems I carry with me always.*

—A.L.

The people I love the best
jump into work head first
without dallying in the shallows
and swim off with sure strokes almost out of sight.
They seem to become natives of that element,
the black sleek heads of seals
bouncing like half-submerged balls.

I love people who harness themselves, an ox to a heavy cart,
who pull like water buffalo, with massive patience,
who strain in the mud and the muck to move things forward,
who do what has to be done, again and again.

I want to be with people who submerge
in the task, who go into the fields to harvest

and work in a row and pass the bags along,
who stand in the line and haul in their places,
who are not parlor generals and field deserters
but move in a common rhythm
when the food must come in or the fire be put out.

The work of the world is common as mud.
Botched, it smears the hands, crumbles to dust.
But the thing worth doing well done
has a shape that satisfies, clean and evident.
Greek amphoras for wine or oil,
Hopi vases that held corn, are put in museums
but you know they were made to be used.
The pitcher cries for water to carry
and a person for work that is real.

IN RESPONSE

1. Piercy says work that is worth doing "has a shape that satisfies, clean and evident" (line 22). Think for a while about examples you could give of such work. Reflect on them and on your relationship to and feelings about them in a journal entry. If you keep a reading log, record your responses there.
2. Try your hand at adding a stanza to this poem, after the second stanza. Begin with the words "I love people who . . . ." Bring your stanza to class to share with others.
3. Which writers in this chapter might Piercy see as doing "work that is real"? In a brief exploratory essay, give reasons for your choices.

OTHER READINGS

Baida, Peter. *Poor Richard's Legacy: American Business Values from Benjamin Franklin to Donald Trump.* New York: Morrow, 1990. Examines the history of American attitudes toward enterprise and labor.

Bridges, William. *Job Shift: How to Prosper in a Workplace without Jobs.* Reading, MA: Addison, 1994. Argues that although "good, steady jobs" are declining, people can rethink work. Includes a career guide for the twenty-first century.

Friedman, Milton. *Capitalism and Freedom.* Chicago: U of Chicago P, 1962 (with Rose D. Friedman). Classic defense of free enterprise.

Hochschild, Arlie. *The Second Shift: Working Parents and the Revolution at Home.* New York: Viking, 1989. Case studies that reveal the difficulties of balancing work inside and outside the home.

Michelson, Maureen R., ed. *Women and Work: In Their Own Words.* Troutdale, OR: NewSage, 1994. Includes short autobiographical stories by working women and essays on women's work in the 1990s.

Richmond, Lewis. *Work as a Spiritual Practice: A Practical Buddhist Approach to Inner Growth and Satisfaction on the Job.* New York: Broadway, 1999. Suggestions for becoming more aware, awake, and engaged in one's work life.

Shields, Cydney, and Leslie C. Shields. *Work, Sister, Work: How Black Women Can Get Ahead in Today's Business Environment.* New York: Simon, 1994. A guide, especially for African American women, for attaining career goals and navigating corporate culture.

Snyder, Gary. "On the Path, Off the Trail." *The Practice of the Wild.* San Francisco: North Point, 1990. Uses paths and trails as metaphors for work, claiming that skills and work are reflections of the order found in nature.

ELECTRONIC RESOURCES

http://www.cei.org/
Site of the Competitive Enterprise Institute, which champions free enterprise and opposes government regulation of businesses and workplaces.

http://www.psy.pdx.edu/PsiCafe/Areas/Developmental/BioBasisDev/
Provides information on the role of nature on development.

http://www.dol.gov
Provides information about the Department of Labor.

http://www.ivillage.com/work/
Provides links to resources for working women.

Acknowledgments

Edward Abbey. "Episodes and Visions." From *Desert Solitaire: A Season in the Wilderness.* Copyright © 1968 by Edward Abbey. Renewed 1996 by Clarke Abbey. Reprinted with the permission of Don Congdon Associates, Inc.

Paula Gunn Allen. "Where I come from is Like This." From *The Sacred Hoop: Recovering the Feminie in American Indian Traditions.* Copyright © 1986 by Paula Gunn Allen. Reprinted with the permission of Beacon Press, Boston.

Margaret Atwood. "Letter to America." From *The Globe and Mail* (Canada, March 28, 2003). Also published in *The Nation,* April 14, 2003. Copyright © 2003 by Margaret Atwood. Reprinted with the permission of the author.

Naomi Barko. "The Other Gender Gap: Why Women Still Fail to Receive Comparable Wages for Comparable Work." From *Making Work Pay: America After Welfare,* edited by Robert Kuttner. Originally published in *The American Prospect* 11, no. 15 (June 19-July 3, 2000). Copyright © 2000 by The American Prospect. Reprinted with the permission of the publishers.

Dave Barry. "Guys vs. Men" from *Dave Barry's Complete Guide to Guys.* Copyright © 1995 by Dave Barry. Reprinted with the permission of Random House, Inc.

J. Michael Bishop. "Enemies of Promise." From *The Wilson Quarterly* (Summer 1995). Copyright © 1995 by J. Michael Bishop. Reprinted by permission of the author.

Keith Bradsher. "Reptile Dreams." From *High and Mighty: SUVs—the World's Most Dangerous Vehicles and How They Got That Way.* Copyright © 2002 by Keith Bradsher. Reprinted with the permission of Public Affairs.

Anthony Brandt. "Do Kids Need Religion?" From *Parenting* (December 1987). Copyright © 1987 by Anthony Brandt. Reprinted by permission of the author.

David Brooks. "One Nation, Slightly Divisible." From *The Atlantic Monthly,* December 2001. Copyright © 2001 by David Brooks. Reprinted by permission of the author.

Gwendolyn Brooks. "We Real Cool" from *Blacks* by Gwendolyn Brooks. Copyright © 1991 by Gwendolyn Brooks. 3 lines from "Boy Breaking Glass." Reprinted with the permission of Brooks Permissions.

Jimmy Carter. "Just War—or a Just War?" From *The New York Times,* March 9, 2003. Copyright © 2003 by The New York Times Company. Reprinted with permission.

Stephen L. Carter. "The Rules about Rules" from *Integrity* by Stephen L. Carter. Copyright © 1996 by Stephen L. Carter. Reprinted by permission of Basic Books, a member of Perseus Books L.L.C. via Copyright Clearance Center.

Ward Churchill. "Crimes Against Humanity." From *Z Magazine,* March 1993. Copyright © 1993 by Ward Churchill. Reprinted by permission of the author.

Mark Clayton. "A Whole Lot of Cheatin' Going On." Copyright © 1999 The Christian Science Publishing Society. Reproduced with permission. All rights reserved.

Jessica Cohen. "Grade A: The Market for a Yale Woman's Eggs." From *The Atlantic Monthly,* December 2002, p. 74. Copyright © 2002 by Jessica Cohen. Rerpinted with permission of the author.

Stephanie Coontz. "The Way We Wish We Never Were" from *The Way We Never Were* by Stephanie Coontz. © 1992 by Stephanie Coontz. Reprinted by permission of Basic Books, a member of Perseus Books, L.L.C. via Copyright Clearance Center.

Jennifer L. Croissant. "Can the Campus Be Bought? Commercial Influence in Unfamiliar Places." From *Academe* (September-October 2001). www.aaup.org.

Abelardo "Lalo" Delgado. "Stupid America." From *Chicano: 25 Pieces of a Chicano Mind.* Copyright © 1969 by Abelardo "Lalo" Delgado. Reprinted with the permission of the author.

Andre Dubus. "Witness." From *Meditations from a Movable Choir.* Copyright © 1998 by Andre Dubus. Reprinted with the permission of Alfred A. Knopf, a division of Random House, Inc.

Amitai Etzioni. Excerpt from *The Monochrome Society.* Copyright © 2001 by Amitai Etzioni. Reprinted with the permission of Princeton University Press.

Jill Frawley. "Inside the Home." From *Mother Jones* (1991). Copyright © 1991 by Foundation for National Progress. Reprinted with the permission of *Mother Jones.*

Dagoberto Gilb. "Work Union." From *Gritos.* Copyright © 2003 by Dagoberto Gilb. Reprinted with the permission of Witherspoon Associates.

Reverend Peter J. Gomes. "Civic Virtue and the Character of Followership: A New Take on an Old Hope." The Reverend Professor Peter J. Gomes, *Plummer Professor of Christian Morals and Pusey Minister in The Memorial Church, Harvard University,* is Preacher to Harvard University. All rights reserved.

Bill Griffith. *Zippy* cartoon. Copyright © Bill Griffith. Reprinted with special permission of King Features Syndicate.

bell hooks. "Work Makes Life Sweet" from *Sisters of the Yam,* pp. 41-52. Copyright © 1993 by bell hooks. "Keeping Close to Home, Class and Education" from *Talking Back,* pp. 73-83. Copyright © 1989 by bell hooks. Reprinted by permission of South End Press.

Langston Hughes. "Theme for English B" from *The Collected Poems of Langston Hughes,* edited by Arnold Rampersad and David Roessel. Copyright © 1994 by The Estate of Langston Hughes. Reprinted with the permission of Alfred A. Knopf, a division of Random House, Inc.

Zora Neale Hurtson. "How It Feels to Be Colored Me" from *The World Tomorrow* 11 (May 1928). Copyright © 1929 by Zora Neale Hurston. Renewed © 1956 by John C. Hurston. Later published in *I Love Myself When I'm Laughing,* edited by Alice Walker. New York Feminist Press (1973). Reprinted with the permission of Lucy C. Hurston.

Molly Ivins. "Bush's Brain Straddles the Fence Once Again." From *Louisville Eccentric Observer,* July 18, 2001. Copyright © 2001 by Molly Ivins. Reprinted with the permission of the author.

Donald Kagan. "What is a Liberal Education?" From *Reconstructing History: The Emergence of the New Historical Society* edited by Elizabeth Fox-Genovese and Elisabeth Lasch-Quinn. Copyright © 1999 by Routledge. Reprinted with the permission of Routledge/Taylor & Francis Books, Inc.

Jamaica Kincaid. "Sowers and Reapers: The Unquiet World of a Flower Bed." From *The New Yorker,* January 22, 2001. Copyright © 2001 by Jamaica Kincaid. Reprinted with the permission of The Wylie Agency, Inc.

Martin Luther King, Jr. "Letter from Birmingham Jail." Copyright © 1963 by Martin Luther King, Jr. Copyright renewed 1991 by Coretta Scott King. Reprinted by arrangement with The Heirs to the Estate of Martin Luther King, Jr., c/o Writers House, Inc. as agent for the proprietor.

Robert D. King. "Should English Be the Law?" © 1997 Robert D. King. First published in *The Atlantic Monthly,* April 1997. Reprinted by permission of the author.

Barbara Kingsolver. "And Our Flag Was Still There." From *Small Wonder.* Copyright © 2002 by Barbara Kingsolver. Reprinted with the permissions of HarperCollins Publishers, Inc.

Maxine Hong Kingston. "No Name Woman" from *The Woman Warrior* by Maxine Hong Kingston. Copyright © 1975 by Maxine Hong Kingston. Reprinted with the permission of Alfred A. Knopf, a division of Random House, Inc.

Arthur Krystal. "Who Speaks for the Lazy?" From *The New Yorker,* April 26 & May 3, 1999. Copyright © 1999 by Arthur Krystal. Reprinted with the permission of the author.

Philippe Legrain. "Cultural Globalization is not Americanization." From *The Chronicle of Higher Education,* May 9, 2003. Copyright © 2003 by Philippe Legrain. Reprinted with the permission of the author.

Meridel Lesuer. Excerpt from *Women and Work: In Their Own Words* by Maureen R. Michelson, ed. Copyright © 1994 by Maureen R. Michelson. Reprinted with permission of New Sage Press.

Ed Madden. "Family Cemetery, near Hickory Ridge, Arkansas." Reprinted with permission of the author.

Michael Nava. "Gardenland, Sacramento, California." From *Hometown: Gay Men Write About Where They Belong,* edited by John Preston. Copyright © 1991 by Michael Nava. Reprinted with the permission of the author and the Charlotte Sheedy Literary Agency.

"New National Parks Website Makes National Parks Obsolete." From *The Onion,* April 30, 1997. Copyright © 1997 by Onion, Inc. Reprinted with permission.

Bich Minh Nguyen. "The Good Immigrant Student." From *Tales Out of School*, edited by Susan Shreve and Porter Shreve. Copyright © 2000 by Bich Minh Nguyen. Reprinted with the permission of the author.

Kathleen Norris. Excerpt from *Little Girls in Church* by Kathleen Norris. Copyright © 1995 by Kathleen Norris. Reprinted with the permission of the University of Pittsburgh Press.

Todd Oppenheimer. "The Computer Delusion." Originally published in *The Atlantic Monthly*, July 1997, pp. 42-62. Copyright © 1997 by Todd Oppenheimer. Reprinted with the permission of Dunham Literary Agency as agents for the author.

Eboo Patel. "On Nurturing a Modern Muslim Identity: The Institutions of the Aga Khan Development Network." Updated version from *Crosscurrents*, Summer 2003, Vol. 53, No. 2. Copyright © 2003. Reprinted by permission of the author.

Marge Piercy. "To Be of Use." From *Circles on the Water* by Marge Piercy. Copyright © 1982 by Marge Piercy. Reprinted with the permission of Alfred A. Knopf, Inc.

Steven Pinker. Excerpt from "Gender" in *The Black Slate: The Modern Denial of Human Nature*. Copyright © 2002 by Steven Pinker. Reprinted with the permission of Viking Penguin, a division of Penguin Group (USA) Inc.

Michael Pollan. "An Animal's Place." From *The New York Times Magazine*, November 19, 2002. P. 58. Copyright © 2002 by Michael Pollan. Reprinted with the permission of International Creative Management, Inc.

Neil Postman. "The Great Symbol Drain" from *Technopoly* by Neil Postman. Copyright © 1993 by Neil Postman. Reprinted with permission of Alfred A. Knopf, a division of Random House, Inc.

Adrienne Rich. "What Does a Woman Need to Know?" From *Blood, Bread, and Poetry: Selected Prose 1979-1985* by Adrianne Rich. Copyright © 1986 by Adrianne Rich. Reprinted by permission of the author and W.W. Norton & Company, Inc.

Jeremy Rifkin. "A Biotech Century: Playing Ecological Roulette with Mother Nature's Designs." Adapted from *Biotech Century: Harnessing the Gene and Remaking the World* by Jeremy Rifkin. Copyright © 1998 by Jeremy Rifkin. Reprinted with the permission of the author, President of the Foundation on Economic Trends, Washington, D.C.

Mike Rose. "Lives on the Boundary" from "Crossing Boundaries" in *Lives on the Boundary: The Struggles and Achievements of America's Underprepared* by Mike Rose. Copyright © 1989 by Mike Rose. Reprinted with the permission of The Free Press, a Division of Simon & Schuster Adult Publishing Group.

Eric Schlosser. Excerpt from "Behind the Counter" in *Fast Food Nation*. Copyright © 2001 by Eric Schlosser. Reprinted with the permission of Houghton Mifflin Company. All rights reserved.

David Sedaris. "Cyclops." From *Naked*. Copyright © 1997 by David Sedaris. Reprinted with the permission of Little, Brown and Company (Inc.).

Wendy Shalit. Abridgment of Chapter 12, "Beyond Maturity," pp. 231-38 in *A Return to Modesty: Discovering the Lost Virtue* by Wendy Shalit. Copyright © 1999 by Wendy Shalit. Reprinted by permission of the author and The Free Press, a Division of Simon & Schuster Adult Publishing Group.

Kate Shindle. "Miss America: More Than a Beauty Queen?" From *Newsweek*, October 14, 2002. Copyright © 2002 by Newsweek, Inc. Reprinted with permission. All rights reserved.

Michael Sokolove. "Football is a Sucker's Game." From *The New York Times Magazine*, December 22, 2002. Copyright © 2002 by The New York Times Company. Reprinted with permission.

Jon Spayde. "Learning in the Key of Life" from *Utne Reader*, May/June 1998. Reprinted With the permission of Joe Spayde..

Shelby Steele. "The Recoloring of Campus Life" from *The Content of Our Character* by Shelby Steele. Copyright © 1990 by Shelby Steele. Reprinted by permission of St. Martin's Press, L.L.C.

Andrew Sullivan. "What Are Homosexuals For?" From *Virtually Normal: An Argument about Homosexuality* by Andrew Sullivan. Copyright © 1995 by Andrew Sullivan. Reprinted with the permission of Alfred A. Knopf, a division of Random House, Inc.

Ron Suskind. Excerpt from *A Hope in the Unseen* by Ron Suskind. Copyright © 1998 by Ron Suskind. Used by permission of Broadway Books, a division of Random House, Inc.

Edward Tenner. "Body Smarts." From *Our Own Devices: The Past and Future of Body Technology*. Copyright © 2003 by Edward Tenner. Reprinted with the permission of Alfred A. Knopf, a division of Random House, Inc.

Sherry Turkle. "Cuddling Up to Cyborg Babies." From *The UNESCO Courier*. Copyright © 2000 by Sherry Turkle. Reprinted with the permission of the author.

Sarah Vowell. "Democracy and Things Like That." From *The Partly Cloudy Patriot*. Copyright © 2002 by Sarah Vowell. Reprinted with the permission of the Simon & Schuster Adult Publishing Group.

Alice Walker. "The Place Where I Was Born." From *Her Blue Body: Everything We Know, Earthling Poems 1965-1990.* Copyright © 1991 by Alice Walker. Reprinted with the permission of Harcourt, Inc.

Anthony Walton. "Technology Versus African-Americans." From *The Atlantic Monthly* 283, No. 1 (January 1999). Copyright © 1999 by The Atlantic Monthly Company. Reprinted with permission.

Barbara Dafoe Whitehead. "The Making of a Divorce Culture" from *The Divorce Culture* by Barbara Dafoe Whitehead. Copyright © 1996 by Barbara Dafoe Whitehead. Reprinted by permission of Alfred A. Knopf, a division of Random House, Inc.

Eli Wiesel. "Peace Isn't Possible in Evil's Face." From *The Los Angeles Times*, March 11, 2003. Copyright © 2003 by Elirion Associates. Reprinted with the permission of Georges Borchardt, Inc., for the author.

Terry Tempest Williams. "The Clan of One-Breasted Women" from *Refuge: An Unnatural History of Family and Place* by Terry Tempest Williams. Originally published in *Northern Lights*, January 1990. Copyright © 1990 by Terry Tempest Williams. Reprinted by permission of Pantheon Books, a division of Random House, Inc.

James Q. Wilson. "Cars and Their Enemies." Reprinted from *Commentary*, July 1997, by permission of the author.

Figure: "Female Intermarriage Rates." Adapted from *From Newcomers to New Americans: The Successful Integration of Immigrants into American Society* by Gregory Rodriguez. (Washington: National Immigration Forum, July 1999). Reprinted by permission.

Cover Photo Acknowledgments

Peter Gomes: Photograph by Stu Rosner/Copyright 2003; *bell hooks:* Rose Hartman/Globe Photos; *Maxine Hong Kingston:* Tony Barboza/Ken Barboza Associates; *David Sedaris:* Photograph by Hugh Hamrick. Reprinted by permission of Hugh Hamrick and David Sedaris © 1997 by Hugh Hamrick; *Wendy Shalit:* © Susan Shacter/Corbis Outline; *Andrew Sullivan:* reproduced by permission; *Sarah Vowell:* Author photograph by Bennett Miller; *Elie Wiesel:* Jean Pierre Muller/AFP/Getty Images. Used with permission of Georges Borchardt, Inc.

Picture Credits

Chapter 1: 3, Image courtesy of www.adbusters.org. **9,** Federal Election Commission. **10,** (Top) Used with permission. (Bottom) © *Stay Free* magazine, 2000/www.stayfreemagazine.org). **11,** www.suvlove.com. **16,** Alinari/Art Resource/NY. **Chapter 3: 47,** Photograph by John Booz/courtesy University of Chicago. **59,** © 2003 Regents of the University of Minnesota. Reprinted with permission. **59,** Morehouse College. **60,** The Evergreen State College. **61,** California State University, Monterey Bay (CSUMB). **62,** Thomas Aquinas College, Santa Paula, California. **65,** Illustration by Anthony Karlic © 1998. **Chapter 4: 157,** © Bettmann/CORBIS. **208,** Illustration by Joe Rocco. **227,** "Animal Husbandry," **203** photomontage © William Wegman. **Chapter 5: 269,** © Reuters NewMedia Inc./CORBIS. **290–291,** Illustration by Tad Majewski/Three in a Box. **331,** Illustration by and © 2003 David Plunkert. **367,** National Park Service. **Chapter 6: 373,** Used with permission of Michael Cunningham. **429,** Photograph © Mel Lindstrom. Used with permission of Mel Lindstrom and *The Atlantic Monthly.* **Chapter 7: 511,** © Kevin Fleming/CORBIS. **614,** © Bettmann/CORBIS. **615,** Photograph by Jessica Wynne. **623,** © Historical Picture Archive/CORBIS. **Chapter 8: 629,** MTV Networks/courtesy Everett Collection. **648,** © PictureNet/CORBIS. **Chapter 9: 715,** "Office Space" © 1999 Twentieth Century Fox. All rights reserved. **741,** ZIPPY cartoon. Copyright Bill Griffith. Reprinted with special permission of King Features Syndicate. **759,** Illustration by Peter Till.

Picture Insert, 1–8 (all): Time, Inc./Time Life Pictures/Getty Images.

Index

A Guide for Teachers

FOURTH EDITION

The Presence of Others

voices and images that call for response

Andrea A. Lunsford
John J. Ruszkiewicz

Melissa A. Goldthwaite
Sharan Daniel

A Guide for Teachers

To Accompany

The Presence of Others

Voices and Images That Call for Response

Fourth Edition

A GUIDE FOR TEACHERS

Fourth Edition

Melissa A. Goldthwaite
Saint Joseph's University

Sharan Daniel
Stanford University

To Accompany

THE PRESENCE OF OTHERS

Voices and Images That Call for Response

Fourth Edition

Andrea A. Lunsford
John J. Ruszkiewicz

Bedford/St. Martin's
Boston ♦ New York

Manufactured in the United States of America.

8 7 6 5 4
f e d c b a

For information, write: Bedford/St. Martin's, 75 Arlington Street, Boston, MA 02116 (617-399-4000)

ISBN: 0-312-409443

Acknowledgments

Gerald Graff. "What Has Literary Theory Wrought?" Adapted from *The Chronicle of Higher Education* and *Beyond the Culture Wars: How Teaching the Conflicts Can Revitalize American Education.* Copyright © 1992. Reprinted by permission of the author and W.W. Norton, Inc.

Maxine Hairston. "Diversity, Ideology and Teaching Writing." From *College Composition and Communication*, May 1992. Copyright © 1992 by the National Council of Teachers of English. Reprinted with permission.

Susan C. Jarratt. "Rhetorical Power: What Really Happens in Politicized Classrooms." From the *Association of Departments of English Bulletin* 102 (Fall 1992). Copyright © 1992. Reprinted by permission of the Modern Language Association.

Preface

Teaching *The Presence of Others*

The Presence of Others is a college-level textbook designed for use in writing courses that emphasize the interrelatedness of reading and writing. Based on the principle that all language is social and that all reading and writing are done in a social context—in the presence of other readers, writers, and texts—this book is organized into chapters that present extended conversations about a wide variety of subjects that we hope will prove engaging to you and your students as you bring your voices into these conversations. The conversations this text presents are not unlike the "parlor conversations" Kenneth Burke discusses in *Philosophy of Literary Form*: "When you arrive, others have long preceded you and they are engaged in a heated discussion. . . . You listen for a while, until you decide that you have caught the tenor of the argument; then you put in your oar." These are the types of discussions we hope you and your students will engage in throughout the term.

Planning a Course

The Presence of Others provides many more opportunities for reading and writing than students could take advantage of in a semester or even a yearlong writing course. As a result, you will have the opportunity to choose which chapters or readings to focus on. Because the idea of an extended conversation is fundamental to this book, the **Making Connections** study questions that follow each selection as well as the commentary on the readings that is provided in this teacher's guide highlight links among readings within and across chapters. As you decide which readings to include in your syllabus, you may want to preview the Making Connections questions and the commentary in this guide to help you choose selections that are related in interesting ways and that illustrate a range of positions on a particular subject.

In addition to thinking about the relationships among groups of readings, you should consider the relationships among the chapters you choose to focus on or the subjects you choose to address, perhaps organizing your course around an overarching question that will initiate and sustain the conversation that you want your students and the voices in *The Presence of Others* to carry on throughout the term. Here are some questions you may want to consider:

How do individuals represent themselves and others?
This question encourages students to think about the ways in which particular writers (including student writers) represent themselves and others in their writing. You could organize your syllabus by chapter, asking students to think about how people represent themselves in terms of their education, morality, identity, home, or work. As an alternative, you could use selections from various chapters, asking students to consider how race, class, gender, sexual preference, ability, and age affect the ways particular people represent themselves and others.

What is knowledge, and what does it mean to know?
This question can prove an important one for students just beginning a college education. By using selections from **Chapter 3, Education**; **Chapter 4, Moralities**; and **Chapter 5, Science and Technology**, you can invite students to investigate their relationships to various kinds of knowledge as well as the sometimes conflict-ridden relationships among these sources of knowledge.

America: the one or the many?
This question would work well as the organizing principle for a course that focuses on diversity in American culture. In pursuing this question, it might be useful to start—or end—with **Chapter 3, Education**, which gives students a taste of the debate over how to make education more multicultural. As such, it invites students to reflect on the nature and purpose of the course you are teaching. Other chapters you might want to include are **Chapter 6, Identities**, and perhaps **Chapter 7, American Cultural Myths**.

What does popular culture mean?
A course organized around this question would critically analyze subjects not usually thought of as scholarly or academic. You might initiate this conversation with **Chapter 3, Education**, which discusses, implicitly and explicitly, what American education ought to be about. Students could then consult several serious inquiry selections from **Chapter 7, American Cultural Myths** and **Chapter 8, At Home**; and perhaps some selections from **Chapter 4, Moralities**. Whatever individual chapters or readings you decide to assign, we recommend that you begin the course by asking students to read **Chapter 1, On Reading and Thinking Critically**, and **Chapter 2, From Reading to Writing**. These chapters describe the kind of reading and writing that *The Presence of Others* asks students to do—reading and writing that are acts of meaning-making. These chapters can also provide you and your students with a common language for talking about reading and writing processes and with opportunities for self-reflection about those processes.

Special Features

Each chapter of readings (Chapters 3–9) includes special features designed to promote conversation among the readings as well as among the students who join in that conversation. In addition, these features aim to make explicit that the reading and writing that people do are products of their sometimes unique, sometimes socially shared positions. As you plan your course, you might want to think about how to use these special features to enhance students' understanding of not only the readings and the subjects they deal with, but also the acts of reading and writing.

Visual Texts

Each readings chapter includes at least two visual texts that can each be analyzed and studied in a variety of ways: in terms of who or what is represented (and how), what values are expressed, what effects the image has on viewers, how the composition conveys the purpose of the image, and how the visual text relates to the written texts in the chapter. Each chapter opens with a visual text that is accompanied by a series of questions intended to guide students' response to the image. Some readings also include visuals, and in each of these cases a study question takes the image as its focus. Within **Chapter 7, American Cultural Myths**, there is also a special insert, "Images That Call for Response," which includes six color images and questions about them. All of these visual texts and accompanying questions can be used as prompts for in-class writing exercises or response pieces. In addition, you might want to ask such questions as: What associations do students have with the image? What emotions does it evoke? You could instead ask students to write a short story, poem, or narrative essay in response to a visual text. Guidelines for reading visual texts are provided in **Chapter 1, On Reading and Thinking Critically** (pp. 11–12).

Introductory Questions

Each readings chapter begins with a brief introduction to the subject at hand, followed by general questions that invite students to explore the positions they already hold on the issue. You might want to ask students to write informally in response to these questions and to discuss their responses in small groups or as a whole class *before* they read the selections in the chapter. By discussing the introductory questions, you and your class can begin a conversation that the readings will then contribute to—rather than the other way around. Answering these questions and exploring their initial positions on an issue can also help students gain insight into their responses to the readings and give them an opportunity to reflect on how the readings may have led them to change their positions.

Opening Quotations

Each readings chapter opens with a series of quotations, one from each writer represented in the chapter. Asking students to respond to these quotations gives them another vehicle for exploring what they know about a subject before they read the selections. For example, you might have students read the quotations as snippets of a conversation that they have the opportunity to get in on and then write a reading log entry or in-class response in which they describe or anticipate (based on the quotations) some of the important issues that will be addressed in the chapter's selections. You might also ask students what they can guess about each author and reading based on the quotation.

Initial Readings

For each readings chapter, one selection was chosen to serve as the initial reading—the conversation starter, so to speak. In some cases, such as John Henry Newman's "The Idea of a University" **(Chapter 3)** and Mary Shelley's "Frankenstein" **(Chapter 5)**, the initial reading is a well-known or canonical text to which the other readings in the chapter respond. In other cases, the initial reading raises interesting questions that the other readings address more indirectly. In either case, it is useful for students to recognize that the conversations in each chapter have been constructed by the editors of this book and to realize that an important critical reading skill is the ability to see—and to create—connections among seemingly disparate ideas.

A Range of Views

In selecting the readings for Chapters 3–9, the editors' first goal was to create an interesting conversation, and that meant presenting as many different points of view in as many different voices and discourse forms as possible. Although it may be tempting to ask students to read only those selections that you like and agree with (criteria that are often related), we encourage you to give students—and yourself—the opportunity to hear and to respond to even those voices that make you shake with anger or annoyance. If your classroom is like most, the text that you like least or find the least persuasive will be the one some students like most—and vice versa. Differences in response—and reasons for those differences—can provoke important self-reflection and inspire productive class discussion.

Opportunities for Questioning the Text, Making Connections, and Joining the Conversation

Following each reading are study questions that invite students to do various kinds of response writing. In **Questioning the Text**, students are often asked to do a close analysis of some aspect of the reading—to define key terms or analyze the author's tone, for instance. Students are also often asked in these questions to describe their initial reaction to the selection or the issue it addresses. The **Making Connections** questions help students create links among various selections in the chapter, including the initial reading, readings that offer a sharply contrasting point of view, and readings that seem on the surface to share that selection's point of view. The final set of questions, **Joining the Conversation**, invites students to articulate their own position on or ideas about issues raised in the piece, often giving suggestions for doing additional research (library research, interviews, surveys, observation). Many of these writing assignments encourage students to work together in small groups and to present their findings to the class, thereby emphasizing the importance of conversation in the making of knowledge and the collective nature of most intellectual inquiry.

Editors' Profiles, Annotations, and Responses

Each of the readings chapters includes one annotated selection. The editors' profiles and their annotations of and responses to the reading can serve as models for how students might articulate their own responses to readings—and their reasons for responding as they do. Because the editors often take different positions on issues and have markedly different responses to the reading, students can see that there is not just one correct interpretation of a text or one acceptable position on an issue. You might wish to begin the course by writing your own profile and asking students to do the same; such profiles can be read aloud in class early in the term as an introduction and a reminder that all voices (teacher, student, editor, author) are important. Many of the study questions invite students to write responses similar in form to the editors' annotations and afterwords (and to keep track of those responses throughout the course by putting them in a reading journal). If you will be asking students to do this kind of writing, you might want to begin each chapter by assigning the annotated selection and asking students to respond to the annotations and editors' responses as well as to the reading, perhaps referring back to the editors' profiles for some explanation of why they respond as they do. Although some students may read this material carefully without explicit instructions to do so, other students will skim it or ignore it completely without instruction to do otherwise.

Other Readings and Electronic Resources

Each readings chapter ends with lists of **Other Readings** and **Electronic Resources** related to the chapter topic. These books, articles, and Web sites can be valuable resources for students who wish to research the topic further; they also serve as reminders that there are other voices in the conversation.

Sequenced Writing Assignments

This *Guide for Teachers* includes a group of sequenced writing assignments for each readings chapter. These assignments ask students to pursue a sustained line of inquiry over a series of related writing assignments. They usually call for a personal response to the texts, a critical analysis of the texts, and an articulation of the student's position on the issue (in light of the student's experience, reading, and critical analysis).

Contents

A Guide for Teachers

To Accompany

The Presence of Others

Voices and Images That Call for Response

Fourth Edition

Part One How We Learn

3 ■ Education: The Idea of a University (p. 49)

Chapter 3 gives students a taste of the ongoing and frequently heated debate over what and who higher education is for. Consequently, it is a good chapter to cover at the beginning of the course because the selections invite students to join a conversation about issues that are immediately relevant to them and that they may already have thought about. To give students the sense that they are familiar with the conversation in this chapter, you might ask them to explore in writing their views on higher education before they read (and find themselves influenced by) the selections. You might also ask students to talk in small groups about their responses to the questions at the end of the introduction to this chapter and to consider the ways in which (and perhaps the reasons why) their responses differ.

As you plan your discussion of this chapter, you might want to keep in mind some of the following questions raised by the selections:

- Should colleges and universities serve to pass on to students the great traditions and values of Western culture? (Newman, Rose, Kagan)
- Do colleges and universities need to change in order to accommodate students who were once excluded from the university? ("Mission Statements," Rich, Steele, Rose, Brooks, Hart)
- Should colleges and universities emphasize a unified view of culture and the commonalties among people, or should they emphasize people's differences? (Newman, Rich, Steele, Rose)
- What is (or should be) the relationship between university and society? (Newman, "Mission Statements," Spayde, Rich, Croissant, Rose, Sokolove, Steele)
- What is (or should be) the relationship between teachers and students in the classroom? ("Mission Statements," Rose, Kagan, Brooks)
- In what ways is knowledge acquired, passed on, or made in the university? Are some ways better than others? (Newman, "Mission Statements," Spayde, Rich, Rose, Kagan)

JOHN HENRY NEWMAN The Idea of a University (p. 52)

John Henry Newman argues passionately for what might now be called a traditional liberal arts education, one that teaches students to see humanity, culture, and the natural world as an intimately related and coherent whole. Newman also emphasizes the value of knowledge for its own sake and argues that universities are responsible for raising the intellectual tone of society. No matter what type of college students attend, though, they may have trouble getting beyond the difficulty of Newman's style to a consideration of his ideas.

Questions 1 and **3** ask students to deal with the difficulty of Newman's text by thinking about the contemporary relevance of his ideas. **Question 2** asks students to write explicitly about their experience of reading Newman, and thus gives them a place to talk about what they might have found boring or difficult about the text. All of these questions give students practice in being self-reflective about their reading. These questions also introduce students to the idea that readers construct meaning from texts, in part, by considering the relevance of the text to their own experience.

The relevance of Newman and the difficulty of reading his work are good topics for a small group or class discussion that could lead students to see that their attitude toward Newman's text is a product of their history of reading, their attitude toward education, their personal experience, and so on. By discussing these issues with others, students can see that their experience of reading and interpreting Newman's essay might be different from that of their teacher or peers and that the classroom itself can be seen as a site of conversation about particular texts and our reading of them.

Questions 4 and **5** ask students to reconsider Newman's idea of a university in light of two contemporary accounts of what a college education should be like. Although it may be fairly easy for students to see the similarities between Newman's and Donald Kagan's idea of a university, they should be encouraged to consider how any criticisms they had of Newman (for example, that his idea of a university may not be relevant to contemporary education) may also be true of Kagan. Similarly, if students find Kagan's idea of a university persuasive, you might ask them to reconsider any criticisms they had of Newman—are his ideas really as out-of-date as they might have seemed at first?

Students might be tempted to oversimplify Mike Rose's text by noting only the ways in which the diversity of the students he describes would make it difficult for them to fit into a university that emphasizes a unified view of culture and the benefits of knowledge for its own sake. You might ask them to consider whether some of the specific students Rose describes (or marginalized or disadvantaged students in general) could benefit from an education that aims to train people to be good members of society and to raise the intellectual tone of society. Either of these questions could be used as the basis of a more formal writing assignment.

Questions 6 and **7** invite students to use Newman's ideas as a means of evaluating the state of higher education today. To do so, students will need to draw on both their understanding of Newman's ideas of higher education and their own ideas about what higher education should be. Students could base their analysis of higher education on a variety of sources—their own and others' educational experiences (the kind of material that **Question 8** might elicit), their own college or university (based on a close reading of their college catalog or their college's core requirements), a survey of recent news stories and magazine and journal articles, or other readings in this chapter. Given that these questions ask students to take a position on a broad issue, you might ask students to write on one of these questions only after they have read several of the readings in the chapter.

Mission Statements from The University of Minnesota; Morehouse College; The Evergreen State College; California State University, Monterey Bay; and Thomas Aquinas College (p. 57)

These short mission statements give students a taste of the ways colleges and universities represent their differing values and goals. If students have access to computers in the classroom or at home, it might be helpful for them to visit the college Web sites in order to analyze whether the stated mission of each school is (or is not) reflected by the other online information. Whether assigned as homework or undertaken as an in-class activity, this assignment will provide students with an opportunity to do some Internet research.

Questions 1–3 help students hone their online analytical skills by asking them to be attentive to what is present and absent in each mission statement—and to be aware of the effects of both textual and visual components. **Question 1** points to the terms and phrases the selected schools use to define their values and goals: "mission," "vision," "we believe." While the question asks students to consider the differing messages these words send, you could also bring up the similarities between the words. For instance, these words all have religious associations. **Question 2** leads students to evaluate the format, organization, and visual aspects of the Web pages. For this question, it is beneficial—though not essential—to view the page online, since such interaction helps students see how the layout can affect readability and navigation. This question also might lead to a discussion of how colors and illustrations affect reading practices. While **Questions 1** and **2** ask students to be attentive to what is present in the mission statements, **Question 3** encourages them to consider what aspects of their experience are absent from the statements and to discuss explanations for the omissions. What does it mean, for instance, that the statements do not explicitly mention social opportunities or possible living arrangements for students? Are these aspects of the college experience not applicable to a school's educational mission? Should they be? Where might a prospective student look to find such information?

Questions 4 and **5** give students the chance to consider the educational values other authors in the chapter hold and how those values might be translated into a college mission statement. **Question 4** can be approached in at least two ways. First, you can have your students actually write a mission statement from the imagined perspective of one of the authors in the chapter, using the format and organization of one mission statement as a guide. For example, what would Rich's "We Believe" list look like? What would be the three bold headings for Spayde's "Mission"? How would Thomas define his own "Vision Statement"? Second, you can have students do a close reading of the mission statements to determine which authors in the chapter would best share the goals presented in those statements. For example, The Evergreen State College presents a goal of collaborative, active, connected learning. Which authors in the chapter would be expected to share these educational values? **Question 5** also encourages students to put the authors and the mission statements in dialogue—in this case, by using Kagan as an example.

Question 6 asks students to draft a mission statement that reflects the goals of the school they attend. Since most mission statements are probably not singly authored or written independently, this question might make a good group assignment, one that emphasizes the ways that goals are often established collaboratively. After students have crafted their own mission statement, they can look at the one the school has already established and see how it is similar to or different from their own. What might account for the differences? As a way of exploring educational problems, **Question 7** gives students the opportunity to write a parody. Guidelines on parodying are provided in **Chapter 2, From Reading to Writing** (p. 16).

JON SPAYDE Learning in the Key of Life (p. 64)

Unlike most of the other essays in this chapter, Jon Spayde's essay is not focused primarily on college and university learning. It is, however, concerned with one of the central questions of this chapter: What does it mean to be educated? As is evidenced by the college mission statements, the answer to this question depends on what one values. **Question 5** points students back to the mission statements and asks which mission fits best with Spayde's educational ideals—and which one fits least well. What kind of college would promote Spayde's vision? If there isn't one that already fits, students can create a hypothetical new college and make a mission statement or home page for it (**Question 6**).

Spayde sees education as a dialogue "carried on within the context of the society around us, as well as with the mighty dead." He argues that formal schooling is only the beginning of learning—not the end, nor necessarily the primary means. **Question 1** asks students to identify the other answers Spayde gives to his guiding question and to judge whether Spayde's answers are sufficient. An extension of this question would be to ask students to write their own answers to the question of what it means to be educated (**Question 7**). Part of coming up with their own answers will probably involve determining what other people's answers are and have been. **Question 4** asks students to think about which writer in this chapter would not approve of Spayde's definition of education and to write a critique from that writer's point of view. Such a critique could take one of many forms: a newspaper editorial, an imagined dialogue, a parody, or even a bulleted list with explanations of differing viewpoints.

Question 2 points students to the illustrations—a series of overlapping heads, representing figures from Jane Austen to Bart Simpson. It asks whether these illustrations are effective in adding evidence to Spayde's argument. The illustrations appear inclusive; many different figures are represented (for another discussion of inclusivity, refer to **Question 3**). However, it may be interesting to ask students why only heads are included in the illustrations. Do Spayde's ideals for education take more than heads into account?

ADRIENNE RICH What Does a Woman Need to Know? (p. 71)

Although more contemporary than the Newman selection, Adrienne Rich's 1979 commencement address may also seem out-of-date to students—or, conversely, they may find her too radical to be relevant. Many students respond negatively to feminist texts, and those students are likely to reject Rich's suggestions for what a woman needs to know. It may be helpful to spend some time discussing what the word *feminist* means to students and how Rich's text fits or doesn't fit the associations they have with feminism. In addition, you may wish to spend some class time discussing the commencement address genre and Rich's audience (graduates of a women's college). How might the genre and audience account for the content and tone of Rich's speech?

Question 1 asks students to consider the term *power* and the ways it is used in Rich's speech. This question also asks students to compare Rich's understandings of power with their own understandings. The associations students have with the word *power*—negative or positive—are likely to affect their response to Rich. **Question 2** asks students to identify the reasons and evidence Rich uses in arguing what women need to know. Before answering **Question 2**, students should list the three broad areas of knowledge Rich calls for; then they can identify her reasons and evidence. You may also wish to have small or large group discussions about whether students find Rich's reasons and support effective. Are the types of support Rich uses persuasive to students? Why, or why not? What others types of support could she have used?

The **Making Connections** questions ask students to put Rich into dialogue with John Henry Newman and Donald Kagan. Although **Question 4** does not explicitly ask students to write a dialogue between Rich and Newman, that would be one way to get students to "respond" to Newman. (It would also be a good way to see how students interpret Rich and Newman as "characters," and would provide the basis for a discussion of the ethos or persona that writers create.) Another possibility would be to ask students to write a letter from Rich to Newman in which she responds to his understanding of students' basic needs.

Question 5 does ask students to write a dialogue between Rich and Kagan on "what kind of education students need to be effective citizens." While students are given the topic for writing, you may ask them to choose a specific place to set the dialogue—in a coffee shop, at a university or political debate, in Kagan's office, in Rich's living room. In class, you could discuss how the place affects the conversation. What might these people say to one another in a private setting that they wouldn't say in a public forum?

In responding to **Question 6**, students will need to employ research techniques. They may need to work in groups or as a class to think of all the ways in which they can investigate how their university has changed to accommodate women. Since students new to the university will not have their own experience to draw on, they may need to interview women faculty members, read old campus newspapers or yearbooks, consider changes in curriculum by reading several years of sample syllabi, and so on. Students may also wish to consider whether different departments have accommodated women in different ways. Do some departments accommodate women better than others? Because of the demands of this kind of research, students may benefit from doing this project collaboratively. Since the second part of **Question 6** asks students to write an editorial for the campus newspaper, they may also want to bring in sample editorials from that paper so that, as a class, you can discuss the genre of editorial writing.

Question 7 will help students consider the types of knowledge they find important for women and men. It also encourages them to compare their essays and think about points of agreement and disagreement. You may want to encourage students to also include *why* they believe men and women need to know certain things.

SHELBY STEELE The Recoloring of Campus Life (p. 78)

If this reading is the first annotated essay your students will be confronting, prior to assigning it you will need to think about how you want them to use the annotations and the reading responses. You may also want to use Shelby Steele's text and various editorial commentary on it as the basis of a discussion on the positioned nature of reading and writing. In particular, students could consider how Steele positions himself in this essay (for example, as a black man who every six months or so experiences a racial slur) and how his position affects them as readers (**Question 3**). Students might also compare the effect of Steele's positioning with that of Jon Spayde, Adrienne Rich (**Question 4**), or Mike Rose, all of whom bring their personal experiences to bear on the subject of education, or they might compare the effect of Steele's text to readings whose authors do not talk about their personal experiences.

One of the reasons many readers find Steele's text persuasive is that he rejects the idea of entitlement programs as a means of redressing the wrongs done to African Americans in this country, even though he continues to experience some of these wrongs—like hearing "nigger" being yelled from a passing car. **Question 2** asks students to write about such an incident and to imagine how such an incident would make them feel. If a student hasn't been a victim of a racial slur, he or she may consider times when insults are the result of other kinds of hate (sexism, classism, homophobia) or reflect on what it means never to have been the victim of these kinds of hate. It is also possible to extend the question and to ask students to write about an incident in which they uttered a racial slur or were in the company of someone who did.

Another reason students may find Steele's text persuasive is that he offers what seem to be clear and reasonable explanations for some of the more troubling manifestations of racism in the United States. By asking students to trace one of these cause-and-effect analyses (**Question 1**), such as the argument that a politics of difference causes increased racial tension on campuses, you will give them an opportunity to better assess what makes Steele's argument persuasive—or not persuasive—for them as readers. Students thus get practice in responding not just to the substance of Steele's argument but also to the argumentative strategies he employs.

Like Newman and Kagan, Steele advocates an education that stresses the unity of culture and the commonalties among students rather than their differences. **Question 5** asks students to consider how well Newman's concept of the university would work given the problems with "differences" that Steele describes. Is Newman's concept of the university a viable solution to the problem of difference?

Question 4 asks students to compare Steele's idea of education, with its emphasis on commonality, with that of Adrienne Rich, who argues that women need an education distinct from that of men. The question asks students more specifically to compare these authors' perspectives on the power of education and the power of race or gender. In thinking about the latter, it might help students to consider how Steele and Rich see race and gender, respectively, as shaping students' sense of belonging in college, or their attitudes and beliefs about their potential to succeed academically. As students address the final part of the question—which author's argument they find more persuasive—you might ask them to think about how differences in tone and language affect their responses, and how those stylistic differences might be related to audience. Although Steele's text is from a book that might be said to address African Americans, his ideas have been enormously popular with conservative whites as well. Rich's text, on the other hand, is a commencement address at a women's college, and yet it has become a well-read text among feminists, achieving a following that extends far beyond the attendees of that 1979 commencement ceremony.

Questions 6–8 give students opportunities to articulate their positions on some of the issues raised by Steele. Although many students have strong opinions about affirmative action, few have actually researched how specific affirmative action programs work; **Question 6** gives them a chance to do so. Similarly, **Question 7** gives students the chance to express their opinion about what may be a hot debate on campus—the establishment of special dorms or cultural centers for specific groups. **Question 8** asks students to consider whether Steele's analysis of black/white relationships is true of other groups on campus. Again, this is a good opportunity for students to explore their thinking about current campus issues and to consider the similarities (and differences) among categories of difference, such as race, gender, sexual orientation, and religion.

JENNIFER L. CROISSANT Can This Campus Be Bought? Commercial Influence in Unfamiliar Places (p. 99)

Jennifer L. Croissant's is the first of two essays in this chapter that address the effects of nonacademic factors or programs on a university education. The other is Michael Sokolove's "Football Is a Sucker's Game," p. 124, which **Question 5** asks students to compare and contrast with Croissant's essay in terms of concerns about influences on education. Croissant presents a clear-eyed, practical perspective on commercial elements in higher education, asserting that they are unavoidable and that educators must thus take thoughtful care in reckoning with them. At the same time, she refrains from offering educators specific steps to take in judging commercial effects or what to do about them. **Questions 1–3** aim at helping students recognize the ways in which Croissant clarifies the problems posed to educators by commercialism, and the ways in which she leaves room for educators to figure out how to address those problems at their institutions. **Question 3** offers students a chance to supply some of the specifics Croissant has omitted, asking them to come up with criteria by which to judge what actions go too far toward creating a "Nike-Pepsi U."

In addition to comparing Croissant's essay to Sokolove's (**Question 5**), students are asked in **Question 4** to consider her views alongside those of John Henry Newman (p. 49) or Donald Kagan (p. 141). Croissant, Newman, and Kagan offer responses to various encroachments of secular or extra-academic concerns on traditional ideals of education. In doing so, each author makes assumptions about the relationship between the university and society, or the university and its "constituencies." You might frame this comparison by discussing how each author negotiates the tension between a university's obligation to serve as a standard-bearer (to tell people what they need) and its obligation to respond to the demands of the people it aims to serve (to ask people what they need).

Questions 6–8 ask students to consider the ramifications of Croissant's argument for their own campus or community. Students could prepare answers to **Questions 6** and **7** for homework and then discuss in class the extent to which they think their campus is influenced by commercial interests. **Question 8** may be especially pertinent to students who participate in cocurricular organizations or civic groups, as it extends the consideration of commercial effects to nonacademic arenas.

MIKE ROSE Lives on the Boundary (p. 109)

Like Adrienne Rich, Mike Rose is especially concerned with how to make the university more accessible to those students who were once excluded from it. The students who most interest Rose are those who are often thought of as "not college material" and labeled "remedial" or "underprepared," such as immigrants, the poor, high school dropouts, and adults returning to school after years of work or child-rearing. (**Questions 3** and **5** ask students to focus on individuals whom Rose describes.) Students are likely to have mixed reactions to the Rose selection, depending on their background and educational experience. For example, students from privileged backgrounds may feel that students like those Rose describes don't belong in college, while students who share characteristics of Rose's students may be made uncomfortably self-conscious by his essay.

Although it is important to talk about what higher education has to offer to all students, including those who are underprepared, it might be beneficial to take up Rose's assertion that successful (and failed) educational experiences are more social than intellectual in nature. Is such a statement true of all students or more true of those who are intimidated by school? **Questions 1, 2**, and **6** ask students to think about their own experience in working toward an answer to this question. Rich and Jon Spayde also emphasize the importance of social and material conditions for learning, while Newman and Donald Kagan describe education primarily in terms of books, academic subjects, and intellectual questions (**Question 4**).

Questions 2 and **7** ask students to think about the relationship between home culture and school culture as illustrated both by Rose's text and by their own experience. (The essay by hooks also explores the complex relationship between home and school.) By asking students to work together, **Question 7** gives them the opportunity to consider how differences in their own and their classmates' early literacy experiences may have affected their interest in reading and writing in school. From a consideration of these differences, students may be better prepared to consider the differences of Rose's students.

MICHAEL SOKOLOVE Football Is a Sucker's Game (p. 124)

In this *New York Times Magazine* article, Michael Sokolove criticizes the role that football plays at many American universities. He argues that while Notre Dame and Duke serve as prominent examples of universities whose strong football programs have enhanced their academic reputations, for other universities, football becomes a vast resource-consuming maw with little apparent return on the investment. He posits that football—and "big-time college sports" in general—can be viewed "as a sucker's game, one with many more losers than winners" (paragraph 22). Yet Sokolove upholds the journalist's value of balancing different perspectives, treating the example of the University of South Florida sympathetically as he describes its entrance into college football's Division I-A. This evenhanded approach may obscure Sokolove's argument for some readers, especially if they are not used to thinking of journalism—even feature stories like this one— not just as reporting, but possibly as arguing as well. **Questions 1–3** aim to help students read the article critically, with **Question 2** raising the issue of genre and **Question 3** encouraging them to examine the use of facts or description in furthering the article's argument.

The next three questions address Sokolove's article as a commentary on educational values espoused in other chapter selections. **Question 4** asks students to consider the place of big football or other sports programs in higher education from the feminist perspective offered by Adrienne Rich (p. 71). They may find evidence in Sokolove's article that would support Rich's views, or they may find that Sokolove offers some evidence to refute her claims. One of the most compelling arguments in support of big sports programs like football is the opportunity it affords underprivileged students to attend college and escape poverty. Sokolove presents this argument in the story of Lee Roy Selmon, beginning in paragraph 68. **Question 5** asks students to consider how Mike Rose, whose "Lives on the Boundary" (p. 109) is also very much concerned with broadening educational opportunities, might respond to this argument for big college football programs. **Question 6** gives students an opportunity to consider the extent to which football may be viewed as providing a different, nontraditional kind of education— another facet of the opportunity issue Sokolove raises in his interview with Selmon.

Questions 7 and **8** ask students to think about how the conflicts between sports and other university programs may affect them, whether they are athletes or not. In freewriting on competing demands on their time (**Question 8**), for example, students may find they can empathize with some of the pressures faced by players on high-profile sports teams. You might ask them to think about how the demands of work or cocurricular commitments come to compete with academics in a setting in which education is the ostensible goal. Even the seemingly straightforward answers to this question (such as "Without the job, I couldn't afford to stay in school") can illuminate the complex nature of a college education and all that it entails.

DONALD KAGAN What Is a Liberal Education? (p. 141)

Donald Kagan surveys concepts of liberal education from ancient Greece into the nineteenth century and then uses those concepts in criticizing current approaches and proposing alternatives. His essay continues the conversation on educational visions, goals, and missions explicitly begun in John Henry Newman's *The Idea of a University* (p. 49) and the college mission statements (p. 57). This text, with its lengthy historical survey of educational ideals, may prove difficult for students, so a preview of its sections may be helpful. You might point out that the historical ideas, presented in the first fourteen paragraphs, are important to understanding the rest of the argument, as Kagan continually refers to past examples. In paragraphs 15 through 21, Kagan argues that American liberal education most closely resembles that of eighteenth-century England—a claim that may surprise readers—and shows how this education fails students and society. Finally, from paragraph 22 to the end of the essay, Kagan offers a proposal of what liberal education today should entail. Such a preview may help students engage in **Questions 1** and **2**, which encourage discussion of how Kagan makes his argument and how students find themselves responding to it.

In paragraph 2, Kagan outlines four goals attributed to liberal education by past proponents, which still resonate in educational philosophies today. **Question 3** asks students to read or reread the college mission statements (p. 57) and to compare and contrast them with the traditional goals Kagan outlines. **Question 4** involves a comparison of Kagan's views with those of other authors, asking students to consider the potential relationship between each author's academic field and his or her views. Kagan is a Classics and history professor; Adrienne Rich is a writer and teacher of creative writing; Jennifer L. Croissant is an associate professor in a material science and engineering department; Shelby Steele is an English professor.

Questions 5–7 continue to place Kagan's comments in context with other authors' perspectives, adding a consideration of students' own college experience. **Question 6** suggests that students apply Kagan's ideas to an analysis of their own college curriculum, asking them to consider whether their college needs a common curriculum (whether or not it currently has one). This question also extends the discussion beyond Kagan's essay—and beyond the classroom—as it suggests how students might use the essays of Adrienne Rich (p. 71) or Mike Rose (p. 109) to support arguments addressed to college administrators advocating curricular change. **Question 5**, which places Kagan in conversation with Rich, would lend itself to a class activity in which students work in pairs or small groups to invent a short dialogue between the two authors and then present their dialogues to the class. **Questions 5** and **7** are good preparatory exercises for the writing assignment in **Question 6**. They help students to consider the sociopolitical ramifications of Kagan's proposal, as well as potential counterarguments offered by the class- and gender-oriented perspectives of Rose and Rich.

GWENDOLYN BROOKS We Real Cool (p. 154)

Gwendolyn Brooks's short and well-known poem describes the lives of a group of young men who "left school." As such, they are outsiders whose voices would not typically be heard in a conversation about the value of higher education. It is interesting, then, for students to consider what these young men, as speakers of the poem, might be saying about the relationship between education and "real life" (**Question 1**) and to imagine what the students described by Mike Rose, students who might also have been tempted to "leave school," might say to the speakers of the poem (**Question 2**). **Question 3** invites students to write a poem of their own, perhaps in rap or some other contemporary form. In their poem, they might express their own or a fictional character's feelings about what school means.

Texts in Context: Sequenced Writing Assignments about Education

Assignment 1

Mike Rose tells stories of moments in education that were particularly important to him. Spend some time thinking about the education you've received—the schools and classes you've attended, the teachers you've had, the books you've read, the projects you've worked on. Then write a brief essay for your class telling about a particularly important moment or event as concretely as possible and explaining why it was (or is) important to you.

Assignment 2

Several years ago, the NBA and its players mounted a large television campaign urging students everywhere to "Stay in School." The assumption of this ad campaign—and of a number of readings in this chapter (including those by Newman, Rich, Rose, Sokolove, and Brooks)—is that education provides a means to a better life. Reread several of these pieces, and then reread the essay you wrote for Assignment 1. Then draw up a list (of sentences or paragraphs) of the reasons for pursuing an education and staying in school.

Assignment 3

Spend some time gathering and considering the metaphors several authors in this chapter use (or might use) to represent school or education. Newman, for example, might think of education as a lamp that illuminates, or brings the light to us, while Spayde refers to education as "jazz." What metaphors for education do you find in the essay by Shelby Steele, Mike Rose, or Adrienne Rich? Choose two or three readings, and decide whether the metaphors associated with education or school are primarily positive or negative. Then spend some time brainstorming the metaphoric associations you have with education, noting whether they are primarily positive or negative. Finally, write a brief report for your class on "what a close look at metaphors reveals about attitudes toward education."

Assignment 4

Several writers in this chapter explore the ways in which educational institutions exert powerful pressures on students, pressures that are often oppressive or that favor conformity to certain ways of seeing the world and one's place in it. Look closely at one selection in this chapter and try your hand at summarizing its take on the power of educational institutions to shape us in harmful or counterproductive ways.

Assignment 5

Spend some time brainstorming about the ways in which educational institutions have shaped or influenced you, have "written" you into your role as a certain kind of student. Then consider which influences have helped to give you a sense of personal power and which have perhaps given you a sense of helplessness or lack of power. Make detailed notes, and be prepared to discuss your views in class.

Assignment 6

Read over your responses to and notes from Assignments 1–5. Then prepare an essay in which you present your position on the place of higher education in American society and in your life. Consider the aims of education and how those aims do or do not carry out the larger goals of the United States as well as your own goals.

Assignment 7

Write a memo to your instructor and classmates, explaining in detail why you take the stand you do in your essay for Assignment 6. Note what in your experience has led you to that stance, and close by reflecting on what you feel most confident about in that position and what you have some doubts about.

Part Two What We Believe

4 ■ Moralities: Most Sacred Values (p. 159)

The selections in Chapter 4 invite students to join a conversation about the importance of moralities—whether gained from traditional religions, culture, or stories—to individuals and to society. The introductory questions give students the opportunity to write about their own beliefs and values while also asking them to consider the relationship between moralities and American society. It may be useful to ask students (individually, in small groups, or as a class) to come up with working definitions of the key terms that recur in different contexts throughout the chapter: *morality*, *virtue*, *integrity*, and *ethics*. Students can also get a sense of the variety of approaches to morality that are represented in this chapter by asking them to eavesdrop on the conversation already in progress in the introductory quotations.

Some of the questions that recur throughout this chapter include the following:

- From where do (or should) people gain their moral sensibilities? (King, Norris, J. Carter, Wiesel)
- What is the relationship between religion and morality? (King, S. Carter, Vowell, Brandt, Gomes, Norris)
- What is the relationship between gender and morality? (Cohen, Shalit, Norris)
- What is moral (or immoral) behavior? (King, S. Carter, Clayton, Pollan, Gomes, Shalit, J. Carter, Wiesel)

MARTIN LUTHER KING JR. Letter from Birmingham Jail (p. 163)

If this is the first letter your students will read for the class, it might be useful to begin your discussion with an overview of the form and conventions of letter writing. You could ask about letters they've written or received that they found particularly effective or ineffective, and why. What are some different purposes for letter writing? Students should be encouraged to think about how a writer's purpose affects the writer's choice of technique or format. **Questions 7** and **8** are designed to introduce students to some of the rhetorical concerns of letter writing: audience, purpose, evidence, style, and language use. **Question 8** focuses particularly on the effects of pronoun usage.

In what ways does King's lettter fit with students' understanding of what a letter should be and should do? **Question 4** will help guide students in this discussion. Two important and related conventions of letter writing are (1) establishing ethos and (2) understanding your audience. King establishes ethos in his introduction by pointing to his audience as sincere "men of genuine good will" and by establishing himself as "patient" and "reasonable." Students should be encouraged to locate other places in the text where King's ethos is evident. Part of knowing one's audience is recognizing the kinds of sources and evidence that will be persuasive to that person or group (**Questions 1–3**). Some of King's sources include the Old and New Testaments, historical events, personal experience, philosophers, and theologians. While many students will be familiar with some of King's sources (Socrates, Saint Paul, and Saint Augustine, for instance), they might need some more information on theologians who may be less familiar to them (such as Paul Tillich and Martin Buber).

Question 5 continues to focus on King's rhetorical approach, asking students to compare it to that of Michael Pollan in "An Animal's Place" (p. 222), as both writers carefully position themselves between two extreme stances on the issues they address. **Question 6** places King in dialogue with Stephen L. Carter by asking students to imagine how King might respond to Carter's steps toward achieving integrity (p. 179).

STEPHEN L. CARTER The Rules about the Rules (p. 179)

Like King, Stephen L. Carter believes that morality and integrity require action, that they are not passive beliefs. As Carter states, and King would affirm, living with integrity may involve fighting "openly for what one believes to be true and right and good, even when there is risk to oneself." Risk is evident in King's letter as well as in Terry Tempest Williams's essay in **Chapter 8, At Home**. Based on their beliefs and commitments, King and Williams both participated in acts of civil disobedience. **Question 4** points to Williams's essay, asking students whether they believe Williams's civil disobedience meets Carter's qualifications for acting with integrity. This question also brings up the larger issue of what general conditions "make acts of civil disobedience defensible." Are certain acts never defensible? What situations warrant civil disobedience? Students should also consider the answers that other authors in this chapter might give in response to this question. For example, King argues that "one has the moral responsibility to disobey unjust laws." But how does one determine which laws are just and which are unjust?

Both Carter and Clayton deal with the issue of cheating. **Questions 3** and **6** give students the opportunity to reflect on whether any act of academic dishonesty could possibly meet Carter's qualifications for integrity and whether there are ever good reasons to cheat. Carter opens his essay with an anecdote about a time when he cheated. **Question 1** asks students to consider how this anecdote affects them as readers. Such a question can be used to discuss not only issues of integrity (for instance, whether Carter's admission is a sign of integrity) but also how personal narrative functions within a text.

Carter writes that "integrity is like *good* weather, because everybody is in favor of it." This quotation provides the basis for **Question 2**, which asks students to make a record of when and in what context they hear or see the word *integrity* over the course of several days. In preparation for this activity, you might dedicate some class time to discussing where the word might be written or spoken: newspapers, television, magazines, informal conversations, church sermons, and so on. Another way of responding to Carter's quotation and of having students think about their own attitudes toward integrity is to have them create similes, using Carter's "Integrity is like good weather" as an example. What do students think integrity is? Such an assignment helps students recognize the simile as a form of definition.

Definition is the concern of **Questions 5** and **7** as well, though these questions consider other ways of defining an abstract concept to make it more understandable and concrete. Before students can respond to these questions, they may need to review the section on defining in **Chapter 2, From Reading to Writing** (p. 16). **Question 5** asks students to define a moral abstraction "by enumerating its three necessary characteristics" and by providing examples of the concept. In contrast, **Question 7** calls for a more indirect form of definition, asking students to write a portrait of someone they recognize as a person of integrity. After students practice with these different modes of definition, you could ask them which option they find most effective for illuminating and understanding a concept.

JESSICA COHEN Grade A: The Market for a Yale Woman's Eggs (p. 191)

In this essay from the *Atlantic Monthly*, Yale student Jessica Cohen describes a modern moral dilemma she faced when she responded to an ad from a couple seeking an egg donor. At first attracted by the money and novelty of the prospect, Cohen writes that she grew uneasy with the couple's effort to buy the perfect child. Eventually she decided she "did not want to be part of [the process]" (paragraph 23), and shortly thereafter the couple informed her they did not want her egg. Students may readily relate to Cohen's dilemma, since, as she points out, ads for egg donors are fairly common, with young college women a prime target audience.

The narrative of Cohen's experience drives the essay, presenting occasions for the author to inform her audience about the donor process (paragraphs 4–6), infertility (paragraph 10), and the market for women's eggs (paragraphs 11–14), and to reflect on moral issues related to human reproduction (18–20). In both the narration and the commentary, Cohen's tone is rather dispassionate. **Questions 1–3** focus on this technique, asking students to examine their response to the essay and to Cohen's persona.

Wendy Shalit's "The Future of Modesty" (p. 251) also uses personal experience to comment on a broader moral issue. **Question 5** invites students to compare the two essays and to speculate on the courage involved in sharing publicly one's personal experiences with such issues as egg donation and coed dorm life. Cohen's essay foreshadows concerns about the human impacts of scientific innovation raised in **Chapter 5, Science and Technology**, beginning with the excerpt from Mary Shelley's *Frankenstein* (p. 276) (addressed in **Question 4**). Students who wish to write about the ethical use of surplus embryos produced in fertility treatments (paragraphs 18–20) should be directed to President George W. Bush's speech on stem cell research (p. 355), which Cohen mentions in paragraph 18, as well as Molly Ivins's commentary on the Bush administration's stem cell policy (p. 352). **Question 6** encourages students to try to empathize with Michelle and David, the couple whose ad drew Cohen into the egg donation process. The question is posed in an open way to allow discussion of diverse situations, including gay partnerships, that might lead people to consider alternative methods of conception. You might have students reflect on this question individually and then talk in small groups of their own choosing to encourage open, respectful discussion. **Questions 7** and **8** elicit empathy toward the role of the donor and specifically toward Cohen for other reasons—the physical difficulties, the moral issues at stake, and in Cohen's case, the role that money played in the situation. Asked to consider work they would do—or have done—for pay or for free, students will have the chance to reflect more broadly on ways in which money can affect moral decision-making.

SARAH VOWELL Democracy and Things Like That (p. 198)

While other selections in this chapter address moral choices, Sarah Vowell's essay examines the ethical dimensions of a professional mistake. When reporters misquoted Al Gore's remarks at a high school during his presidential campaign, the students protested and expressed dismay. Vowell investigates the incident from the perspectives of students, teachers, and reporters, illuminating the likely causes of the error as well as its potential effects on democratic processes. This essay, like that of Jessica Cohen (p. 191), is journalistic in its restraint; rather than arguing forcefully for one position (even though Vowell admits she identifies with the reporters), it presents each view in a favorable light, complicating the issues of media and citizen responsibility in a democracy. **Question 1** asks students how effective they find Vowell's style, a major feature of which is her frequent reliance on quotations. This technique is crucial to the impression Vowell gives of being fair to different viewpoints; by using direct quotations, Vowell avoids putting words in others' mouths. As **Questions 2** and **8** suggest, the essay can serve as a vehicle for discussing when and how to use quotations effectively, as well as a model of this writing technique.

Question 3 directs students' attention to a possible cause of the journalists' error in covering Gore's school visit, asking them to consider the extent to which reporters' preconceived notions about candidates resemble the racial prejudice Martin Luther King Jr. writes about (p. 163). You might ask students to consider the moral implications of their answers. Given their comparison of the two kinds of prejudging, do students find the journalists' actions more or less culpable than they did at first?

Vowell's essay, as well as Wendy Shalit's (p. 251), raises questions about the effectiveness of students' participation in public debate (**Question 4**). At Concord High School, where Gore spoke, the students found their participation in democracy—what they felt to be a genuine encounter with a political leader and candidate—downplayed in the press. Shalit describes a different situation, in which her public criticism of coed bathrooms elicited strong support—and strong evidence that the ostensibly democratic process of dorm voting may not have represented consensus as much as a skewed product of peer pressure. Stephen L. Carter (p. 179) also addresses the tension between speaking up for one's beliefs and going along with the crowd (paragraph 30). In suggesting that media can also divert or subvert people's efforts to act with integrity, Carter presents a view worth comparing to Vowell's somewhat more sympathetic treatment of the media (**Question 5**). The activity in **Question 6** gives students a chance to try on the role of reporter and to compare their results with those of their classmates, while **Question 7** asks them to consider whom they identify with in Vowell's essay—the journalists, as she does, or someone else? If students do the reporting exercise (**Question 6**), you might ask them to answer **Question 7** before and after their experience with reporting, to see if the experience changes their sympathies.

MARK CLAYTON A Whole Lot of Cheatin' Going On (p. 207)

With the growing availability of papers on the Internet and the relative ease of cheating in many other situations, Mark Clayton's essay brings up a timely and important issue for students to discuss. **Questions 1, 2, 4**, and **6** all deal with attitudes toward cheating. **Question 1** asks students how they would go about determining the validity of a claim by a Vanderbilt provost that nobody cheated in the 1960s. This question will help students consider research techniques involved in looking for information about past events. They could go to archives of school newspapers, interview parents or other relatives who might have been in college in the sixties, interview school administrators or teachers, or try to find records—if they are open to the public—that document disciplinary action taken against students. After going to these and other sources, they might find that people did, indeed, cheat in the sixties, but they may also find out something about attitudes toward cheating, and whether or not those have changed over time.

One student quoted in Clayton's article argues that cheating could be educationally valuable. Question 2 refers to this quotation and encourages further conversation concerning the implications of such a belief. This question will help students get at their own attitudes toward cheating and plagiarism, attitudes that may be changing over time due, in part, to changes in technology. It might also be valuable to ask students what constitutes cheating in their minds. Clayton refers on several occasions to collaboration as a form of cheating. In what instances is collaboration wrong? In what situations is it a good idea (without cheating)? Many of the questions and assignments in *The Presence of Others* encourage collaboration and working with others, though the editors do not advocate cheating. In addition to eliciting students' views of cheating, you might want to be explicit about your own beliefs and expectations. **Question 4** asks students to reflect on Sarah Vowell's account of journalists' error (p. 198) and to consider the similarities and differences between intentional wrongdoing by student writers and unintentional wrongdoing by professional writers. You may also ask whether the journalists in Vowell's essay committed a fault similar to that of unintentional plagiarism by students (e.g., a failure to quote or paraphrase correctly or a careless omission of attribution).

After discussing their own views on cheating, students will be more prepared to take on **Question 6**, which asks them to interview members of a small group on campus about cheating. Before doing so, however, they may need some guidance in class on choosing their group, coming up with appropriate interview questions, and summarizing their findings. In preparation for their interviews, they could answer **Question 7** by analyzing their own institution's policies on cheating, plagiarism, and collusion. While the question doesn't explicitly recommend group work, this might make a good in-class activity. It will make students aware of existing school policies and help them discuss and interpret those policies within a group context.

After assessing existing statements, students may be ready to create their own statement, one that adds to, reimagines, or significantly changes the policy already in place. **Question 5** invites students to imagine the statement they have come up with as a Web page, giving them practice in thinking about selection, layout, and visuals. (**Question 3** also helps students analyze visuals.)

ANTHONY BRANDT Do Kids Need Religion? (p. 213)

If you are regularly asking students to annotate or write responses to the reading they are doing, you may want to begin each chapter with its annotated reading and ask students to read and write about the annotations fairly early in your discussion of the reading. **Question 3** explicitly asks students to respond to the editors' commentary on this selection by Anthony Brandt. In addition to comparing the kinds of questions each editor asks in the annotations, students might reread the editors' profiles and their annotations on other readings in an effort to explain why the editors respond differently to Brandt's essay. Students might then be asked to reread their own annotations or their responses to Brandt and to reflect on why they respond in the way they do.

You might organize a discussion of this reading by asking students to respond in several different ways to Anthony Brandt's question, "Do kids need religion?" For example, students could write an informal response to this question before they read Brandt; they could then read and annotate Brandt with the purpose of answering **Question 2**, which asks them to describe how Brandt would answer this question. **Question 4** is a logical follow-up to **Question 2**, asking students to answer Brandt's question from the perspective of Martin Luther King Jr. or Stephen L. Carter. Finally, **Question 8** asks students to write a fully developed response to the question, one in which they draw on their own experience, on the experiences of their peers (as revealed through small group or class discussions), on the readings in this chapter, or on additional research.

The question "What is the relationship between religion and morality?" could also be used to guide discussion of Brandt's essay. (**Question 1** asks students to consider the effect of changing the essay's title to "Do Kids Need Morality?") Again, students could begin with their own definitions of terms, then move to an explicit comparison of Brandt and King, for example (**Question 6**), or Brandt and Kathleen Norris (**Question 5**). This preliminary writing could lead students to a more extended exploration of the relationship between religion and morality in which they draw on several other readings from this chapter (**Question 6**) or other chapters or sources and reflect on the different ways that religion, belief, and morality play roles in people's lives.

MICHAEL POLLAN An Animal's Place (p. 222)

In this essay, Michael Pollan considers the morality of killing animals for food and clothing. One by one, he presents the common objections to killing animals, arguing for and against each and arriving finally (in paragraph 69) at his position on the issue. The "principle" of killing animals is not immoral, he posits, but many "practices" of slaughter are. As J.R. suggests in his headnote, this piece can serve as a model for students' own arguments; though lengthy, the piece is included in its entirety mainly for this reason. **Question 1** asks students whether they agree with J.R.'s assessment of the argument as a particularly powerful and well-crafted one, while **Question 2** asks them to consider the effects of the delayed thesis.

In linking arguments about practice and principle, this essay offers several points of connection with other readings in the chapter. **Question 3** invites students to refer to Jessica Cohen's "Grade A: The Market for a Yale Woman's Eggs" (p. 191) to compare moral and ethical issues involved in practices of human reproduction and animal breeding, including economic influences on these issues. Because Pollan draws a comparison between speciesism and anti-Semitism, students may wish to judge this analogy by Martin Luther King Jr.'s arguments against racism (p. 163) (**Question 4**). They might compare Pollan's arguments from principle to those of Peter J. Gomes in "Civic Virtue and the Character of Followership" (p. 242) (**Question 5**). Students might also consider whether Pollan's argument is one of "integrity," judged by Stephen L. Carter's definition (p. 179).

Question 6 aims at eliciting students' empathy with those whose livelihood is connected to the killing of animals, asking them to respond to Pollan from this perspective. **Question 7** further encourages them to consider whether they feel strongly enough about animal welfare—or a similar issue—to get involved. In directing them to the Internet to research consumer boycotts or similar activist movements, you might discuss approaches to evaluating Internet sources.

PETER J. GOMES Civic Virtue and the Character of Followership: A New Take on an Old Hope (p. 242)

In this speech, Peter J. Gomes argues for what he calls "civic virtue"—the obligation of citizens to serve on behalf of the greater good—and for a focus on duties rather than rights. He urges listeners to stop looking for great leaders and, instead, to start being good followers. You might need to spend some time in class discussing what Gomes means by his term *followership* (**Question 4**). Some students might ask, for instance, "If we don't have leaders, who or what do we follow?" Gomes would answer, "Follow visions, ideas, ideals, passions." **Question 7** invites students to evaluate and test Gomes's answer on the basis of historical evidence and their own experiences. Students may find that many past leaders—such as Martin Luther King Jr.—were followers of ideals and passions, but that those ideals and passions were not always shared by the majority of the population at any given time. Does it take a leader like Gomes or King to persuade people to be followers? What is the relationship between leading and following? In what ways have the reception of ideals today (such as civil rights) been shaped by our leaders of the past (**Question 3**)?

Question 5 allows students to consider carefully the relationship between leading and following by comparing and contrasting how institutions shape people and how people can shape institutions. This assignment urges students to think in terms of particular actions and policies. If their focus is their own college or university, they might think of particular ways that students can work together for a common good. What "good" or "goals" do students have in mind? What changes would they like to effect? Can they find a common goal worth working toward?

To help students understand what he means by "followership," Gomes provides the analogy of people together at a football game, focusing on a common goal. **Question 6** asks students to evaluate the appropriateness of this analogy. The question might also be the basis for a class discussion of metaphor, analogy, and simile. What are the limits and functions of such tropes? If students do not find Gomes's analogy effective, ask them to think of other analogies that they think would work better.

This discussion of analogy could lead into a focus on several other features of Gomes's selection. **Question 1** asks students to point out the elements of a speech that they recognize in the reading. If they've read carefully, students will be sure to notice that Gomes addresses his University of Texas audience throughout the text, saying at one point, for example, "I was driven around your enormous campus today." In addition, he makes it clear that he is speaking to students when he says that his examples "may be strange to some of you but that's your problem, you haven't read widely or deeply enough." Do students feel that they are part of the audience Gomes addresses? They may notice still other features of a spoken text, such as repetition and the special use of quotations and examples.

Question 2 focuses more closely on the mechanics of Gomes's text as well as on his explanation of Willa Cather's use of the semicolon. Many students will take note that, according to most writing handbooks, neither Cather's use of the semicolon nor Gomes's explanation of it is technically correct. Which mark of punctuation would students find more effective—and why?

WENDY SHALIT The Future of Modesty (p. 251)

If the reviews of Wendy Shalit's work on Amazon.com are any indication, this essay will provoke much discussion in your class. Here are just a few excerpts from those reviews. One reader points to Shalit as "another smug and overprivileged young woman who thinks her shallow life experiences in elite schools qualifies her to make vast generalizations about American sexual culture." Yet another reader refers to Shalit as "my new role model. Her book gives new hope for a return to moral values." Others point to her argument as "a little of this and a little of that, an amateurish and undigested attempt at proving a thesis which is frankly untenable." But most of the reviews praise the author, as this one does: "Ms. Shalit lends flawless genius to the examination of the pressures, social structures, and true inner desires of the human female. Further, Shalit's logic, presentation, and productive attitude of discussion is the voice of discovery, not pedantic morality."

Question 1 invites students to read these and other reviews and to summarize readers' reactions. Once they do so, most students will be ready to share their own review of Shalit's essay. **Question 3** may help focus this discussion by pointing students to one of Shalit's main claims—that today's young people are rebelling against sexual permissiveness—and asking them to assess and evaluate her evidence for that claim.

A reader's response depends to some extent on his or her own position—age, sex, experiences, training, and many other factors. Do students see themselves as the audience for Shalit's text? Who is her intended audience? Does she connect with her audience (**Question 2**)? **Question 6** can also be used to get at the issue of audience. Many readers would likely define Shalit's audience as young women in their late teens to late twenties. **Question 6** asks students to write an imaginary dialogue between a *modestynik* and a fan of *Cosmo* or *GQ*, as they watch a contemporary television show marketed to people in the age group Shalit is addressing. Such dialogues have the potential to show how people who are similar in some ways (perhaps age and gender) can interpret things in very different ways. While such dialogues may become stereotypical, they can also be humorous and even enlightening. This dialogue may also lead students to consider some of the issues that **Question 7** raises: the assumptions behind the sexual behavior of one's generation and how one's surrounding culture influences one's choices. (**Question 4** also deals more generally with social pressures.)

Even those who disagree with Shalit's position can probably recall a time when they were hesitant about voicing their opinion on a policy or situation that they did not agree with. **Question 5** gives students the chance to speak up, asking them to write a narrative or a letter to the editor of a local newspaper about a policy they consider wrongheaded.

JIMMY CARTER Just War—or a Just War? (p. 259) and ELIE WIESEL Peace Isn't Possible in Evil's Face (p. 262)

These essays, by Jimmy Carter and Elie Wiesel, address the morality of war, arguing against and for, respectively, the U.S. invasion of Iraq in the spring of 2003. The essays lend themselves to comparison, because both are newspaper op-eds and both writers are recipients of the Nobel Peace Prize. Carter uses just-war theory, presenting four criteria for waging a just war and arguing that the situation in Iraq does not meet the criteria. Wiesel argues that in face of the danger Saddam Hussein poses to his own people and to other nations, war is the most conscionable response. Each argument, like many op-eds, makes implicit and explicit appeals from ethos, a point worth drawing to students' attention (**Carter, Questions 1** and **3; Wiesel, Question 1**). As a reference for considering ethos, students can consult the brief biographies offered in the headnotes, which relate well-known highlights of these leaders' efforts toward world peace. Implicit appeals from ethos occur when the writers make claims that depend upon knowledge of their experiences, or allude to them, for support. For example, Wiesel alludes to his survival of the Holocaust in paragraph 1 of his essay. In addition, the writers make explicit appeals from ethos when they mention their experiences, as Carter does in the opening of paragraph 2 of his essay.

Both writers also work under the space constraints of the op-ed, making their arguments within the seven hundred to eight hundred words typical of the genre. Students should consider this constraint and its potential impact on the authors, as they think about how well each author supports his claim and which argument is more convincing (**Carter, Questions 2** and **4; Wiesel, Questions 2** and **3**). Using these essays as examples, students may write their own op-eds on the question of whether the invasion of Iraq was justified (**Carter, Question 5**) or on another moral issue.

Each essay can also be related to others in the chapter by considering the way they are written (**Carter, Question 3**) or the moral questions they address (**Wiesel, Question 4**). Finally, in response to Wiesel's essay, students are invited (1) to think about what it is like to have to make a decision of life-or-death importance and (2) to freewrite on possible ways of making such a decision, drawing from their experience with these and other readings in the chapter (**Wiesel, Question 5**).

KATHLEEN NORRIS Little Girls in Church (p. 265)

The speaker in Kathleen Norris's poem is an adult woman who, through her observation of and interaction with others, reflects on the condition of her own faith and shows concern for other girls in church. While the first six stanzas relate a series of experiences and memories, the final stanza is a direct address to the little girls in church and a hope or prayer on their behalf. You may want to engage students in a class discussion of the tension between the spiritual imagery (the litany, icons, confession, prayer) and the mundane imagery (lace collars, church bulletins, sleeping, smoking) in this poem and of what these conflicting images say about the speaker's moral beliefs. In addition, you could ask how Kathy's drawing of "the moon, / grass, stars . . ." (lines 6–7) functions as a metaphor for the wish the speaker expresses in the final stanza: that the girls may "find great love / . . . starlike / and wild, as wide as grass, / solemn as the moon" (lines 51–54). Or you could focus your discussion on the accompanying study questions by (1) encouraging students to remember songs from their childhood (**Question 1**), or (2) asking them to share their beliefs about morality with the class in a poem of their own, one using metaphors grounded in concrete imagery (**Question 2**).

Texts in Context: Sequenced Writing Assignments about Moralities

Assignment 1

Reread Kathleen Norris's poem (p. 265), and consider the place of song in her expression of belief. Working with several classmates, brainstorm about songs you sang or prayers you said as a child. Try to remember the songs or prayers as exactly as possible and talk about each one in turn, noting what they imply is (or is not) moral, good, and right. Then try your hand at writing the lyrics of a song or a prayer you would like to teach your children or children close to you.

Assignment 2

Keeping in mind the prayer or song you wrote for Assignment 1, reread Martin Luther King Jr.'s letter (p. 163). List the things King's letter suggests we should do and believe. Then make a similar list for your song or prayer. Do the lists have anything in common? What differences are most striking to you? Write a couple of paragraphs about the similarities and differences you see in the two lists and bring them to class for discussion.

Assignment 3

The essays by Jessica Cohen (p. 191), Mark Clayton (p. 207), and Wendy Shalit (p. 251) describe situations in which college students faced moral decisions. Think about the moral choices presented in each of these essays (or others that you relate to) and how you might respond in similar situations, or how you have already done so. Choose a hypothetical or real situation that might (or did) present you with a difficult moral challenge. Briefly describe the situation and the decision you would make now. Make a list of the likely consequences of your decision, both for yourself and for others. Bring your description and list to class for discussion.

Assignment 4

Based on your thinking and discussions thus far, compose an extended definition of *morality*. Include examples of morality as well as the positive and negative consequences you associate with it. Make your definition at least one hefty paragraph in length. Then meet with several classmates to compare your definitions and talk about what they do and do not have in common. As a group, draw up a brief report for your class on "the current thinking on moralities in America," noting the points on which you and the others in your group agree and disagree.

Assignment 5

Using the lists you made for Assignments 2 and 3 and the definition you wrote for Assignment 4, find twelve words or phrases that describe your moral beliefs. List these words or phrases as quickly as you can. Then return to the readings in this chapter to choose the one writer whose moral beliefs most differ from your own. Make another list, this time brainstorming twelve words or phrases that characterize the moral beliefs of the writer you chose. Work with a group of classmates to compare your lists and your reasons for choosing the items in each list, considering what they reveal about your attitude toward the moralities of others. Finally, working independently, write a letter to the author you chose, detailing any points on which the two of you can agree and explaining why you hold the beliefs you do.

Assignment 6

With the letter you wrote in Assignment 5 in hand, reread that author's selection. Then think about how the author would likely "read" or respond to your letter. Write his or her brief response to you. Then record your answer to this question in your reading log: in what ways does the author's response help you think in new or different ways about what you said in your letter?

Assignment 7

Finally, write an essay for your class on "Do People Need Morality?" Be sure to define what you mean by *morality* and to offer as many good reasons as possible in support of your answer.

5 ■ Science and Technology: O Brave New World (p. 273)

The selections in Chapter 5 ask students to think about the nature and roles of science and technology in American culture and the world at large. In particular, the chapter explores Americans' seemingly contradictory attitude toward science and technology. On the one hand, Americans revere science and are in awe of its power to discover what was once thought to be unknowable and of technology's power to help people do what was once thought to be undoable. On the other hand, Americans fear the power of science and technology to escape the control of human beings. The chapter's introductory questions invite students to explore their own ideas about and attitudes toward science and technology as well as to consider the roles these two forces play in American culture. The readings present a number of different voices, both scientists and nonscientists, as illustrated by the chapter-opening quotations. Students should be encouraged to consider why people—themselves included—express such different attitudes toward something that is usually not thought of as controversial.

The questions that the selections in this chapter address include the following:

- Should the quest for (scientific) knowledge be boundless? (Shelley, Bishop, Rifkin)
- What drives human beings to seek scientific knowledge of the world? (Shelley, Bishop, Wilson)
- Whose interests should science and technology serve? (Shelley, Rifkin, Walton, Ivins, Bush)
- What is the relationship between science and reality, and what might be the real-world effects of particular scientific and technological changes? (Shelley, Rifkin, Oppenheimer, Turkle)

MARY SHELLEY Frankenstein (p. 276)

Most students will have some familiarity with Mary Shelley's *Frankenstein*, having read her novel or seen film versions or even cartoons based on the well-known story. **Questions 4** and **6** give them the opportunity to draw on the knowledge they already have about the Frankenstein tale and to consider the differences among the versions they've read or seen.

Some students may find it unusual that the initial reading for a chapter on science and technology is an excerpt from one of the earliest science fiction novels ever written. Although the term *science fiction* contains the word *science*, many students think of science fiction as escapist literature and of science as a dry litany of facts to be memorized. Perhaps only those students actively involved in science will have thought about the relationship between the imagination and scientific inquiry. Shelley's essay foregrounds this relationship; it also highlights the human origins and human consequences of science and technology. These topics are then taken up by several other authors represented in this chapter, including J. Michael Bishop, Jeremy Rifkin and Todd Oppenheimer.

Questions 1 and **2** draw attention to Victor Frankenstein's motivation and his single-minded pursuit of giving "life to an animal as complex and wonderful as man." As students respond to **Question 1** by annotating the text and considering what motivates Victor Frankenstein, they are likely to point to his imagination, past successes, hope for future improvement, desire to accomplish something great, and pursuit of knowledge as driving forces. As students consider the other part of **Question 1**—whether these motives account for modern scientific development and technology—you might ask them to make connections with other readings in this chapter, having them point to writers (**Question 5** points to J. Michael Bishop) who would most likely be motivated by similar forces. Are these motivations good ones? Do good motivations sometimes lead to negative consequences? If so, what should be the relationship between ambition and action?

Question 2 takes up the issues of ambition and behavior, asking students to consider what Victor Frankenstein has to do to himself and others in order to create the monster. This question thus invites students to write about the consequences—good or bad—of single-minded ambition. You might want to broaden the context of this question to include nonscientific pursuits by athletes, entertainers, scholars, businesspeople, and others driven by ambition. Does ambition always require sacrifice? How does the person decide what (or who) is worth sacrificing? And what happens when the person realizes his or her goal but is disappointed by it? **Question 3** takes up the issue of Victor Frankenstein's disappointment with his creation, asking students to explore the meanings and implications of his rejection of the monster.

Question 8 asks students to discuss the Frankenstein monster as being like and unlike a human being, and then to compare the monster with people in our society who are considered "different." Students may quickly link the Frankenstein monster with people who have visible physical handicaps, but you may want to lead them to think about such other differences as race, social class, and sexual orientation. Students who have read Shelley's novel will be aware that the monster is not responsible for his fate and that he uses his status as victim to defend his monstrous actions, including the murder of a child. To what extent are the people labeled "different" by society victims of stereotyping? **Question 7** invites students to define *monster* more broadly or metaphorically in order to write a parody of the Frankenstein tale.

The research project on the industrial revolution (**Question 9**) will require effort for students to complete. However, if you plan to teach library research skills and research writing, this question provides an opportunity to do so. If time or library resources are limited, students could work collaboratively in small groups to research issues related to the industrial revolution and then as a class to prepare a report of their research.

J. MICHAEL BISHOP Enemies of Promise (p. 282)

Question 1 offers students two choices for writing about the selection by J. Michael Bishop. The first is to write about the postmodern attitude toward science. To respond to this question, students will need to understand the term postmodern—both its conventional usage and Bishop's use of the term. Bishop claims that the postmodern school of thought considers "science to be wholly fraudulent as a way of knowing." It may be worth having your students consider whether those who believe science is socially constructed and that scientific principles are "useful myths" would truly believe science to be "wholly fraudulent." Before students begin writing, you could discuss as a class who would likely fit Bishop's definition of the postmodernist. Among the writers in this chapter, might Todd Oppenheimer fit Bishop's definition, given his description of "the computer delusion"?

The other option for **Question 1** is to write about science as "the best way to learn how the world works." Students are asked to work together to explore the differences between the two understandings of science. You might ask how scientific principles can be used in different ways, depending on how one views scientific knowledge. In addition to discussing differences between views of "science as a useful fiction and science as an ennobling fact," students could discuss the similarities between these views. Since some students will probably point to the obvious difference between fact and fiction, be sure to discuss the modifiers *useful* and *ennobling* and what they say about attitudes toward science.

Question 2 asks students to look for words, concepts, or examples in the selection that they do not understand, and then to consider Bishop's intended audience. What textual clues help readers identify his audience? You could have students work in small groups to examine such elements as evidence, direct address to the audience, diction, tone, and place of publication in order to best analyze Bishop's intended audience. You could also ask students which elements of the essay they find most or least convincing—and why. (For another take on Bishop's essay, have students read Jennifer E. Smith's critical response essay at the end of **Chapter 2, From Reading to Writing**, p. 16.)

Question 6 aims to focus students' attention on the most important points of Bishop's essay by asking them to write an abstract or summary of it. (In preparation for this assignment, students should review the section on summarizing in **Chapter 2, From Reading to Writing**, p. 16.) **Questions 4** and **7** ask students to carry out different types of research (**Question 4** requires Internet research, and **Question 7** requires library research). In either case, the research will likely be conducted outside of class, though most students will need suggestions and guidance before they can take on a research project. For **Question 4**, you could point students to the electronic resources listed at the end of Chapter 5 or ask if anyone in the class already follows a Usenet or Listserv discussion on scientific or technological issues. You may wish to prepare a handout for students that gives guidelines and suggestions on how to use such technologies. Since **Question 7** (which deals with an examination of technological change) requires library research, you could ask students to consider how the research methods they use have changed over the years due to technology. How do they feel about technological change, both in terms of how it affects research in general and how it affects their personal lives?

Students will probably be attentive to a discussion of the positive and negative aspects of certain technologies, and this discussion should prepare them for responding to **Question 8**. It asks students to examine a technology they believe has caused more problems than it has solved; it also pushes students to consider the cause of the problem and to propose a solution. This assignment might be attempted in small groups to encourage students to use and sharpen their problem-solving skills through collaboration on the assessment and proposal.

JEREMY RIFKIN Biotech Century: Playing Ecological Roulette with Mother Nature's Designs (p. 289)

Jeremy Rifkin warns against the dangers of genetic engineering, arguing that each "new synthetic introduction is tantamount to playing ecological roulette" and urging scientists to think hard about the potential effects of "bypassing natural species boundaries." It might be useful to begin your discussion of Rifkin's essay by ascertaining what students already know about biotechnology and where they learned what they know. What are their sources? Does the information they already have conflict with or support Rifkin's main points? How do they respond to Rifkin's essay? What questions remain unanswered for them (**Question 5**)? Whether students know a lot or a little about biotechnology, most will benefit from completing **Question 6**, a research project intended to give them a sense of the larger conversation surrounding Rifkin's ideas.

As students consider the information they've gathered from various sources, they can analyze their data by considering the metaphors and analogies used in reference to genetic engineering and its associated risks and benefits. Do the metaphors and analogies make the technology and its potential effects more or less understandable? In what ways do metaphors reveal attitudes and positions? **Questions 1** and **2** help students apply this same kind of analysis to Rifkin's essay. Such a study of metaphor will reveal that language—even language used to discuss science—is not objective.

Like metaphors, visuals can reveal and affect the ways in which people understand and relate to certain concepts or arguments. The editors of *The Presence of Others* have included at least one selection in each readings chapter with an accompanying image, so that students gain experience analyzing visual texts in relation to the printed text. **Question 3** asks students to consider the relationship between Rifkin's thesis and the illustration that accompanies his essay. In what instances do writers have some control over the illustrations that are published with their texts? Are there times when writers might not have any control over the selection of images? These questions bring up issues involving the relationships among editors, writers, and illustrators. Although it is not always possible to determine conclusive answers to these questions, it is useful for students to understand the many ways in which arguments are affected and made.

Question 4 asks students to imagine how the Frankenstein monster might have been depicted by Shelley if she had written her novel in the twenty-first century. What characteristics might the monster have, and what pitfalls might the doctor face? This question highlights the good intentions scientists have in seeking to develop new technologies and reminds students that there can be both pitfalls and serious negative effects. Some people are more sanguine than others about humans' ability to control such effects.

TODD OPPENHEIMER The Computer Delusion (p. 300)

Students should be encouraged to read the editors' annotations and Afterwords that accompany this selection; doing so will allow them to listen in on the conversation in response to

Todd Oppenheimer's ideas. **Question 5** invites students to join that conversation by reflecting on the technologies they've used in school and then using their own experience to support or challenge Oppenheimer's argument. In order to answer the second part of **Question 5**, students will need to look closely at Oppenheimer's argument, which **Question 1** asks them to do. Oppenheimer focuses his critique on five main arguments that he believes "underlie the campaign to computerize our nation's schools," and he uses evidence from academic literature and experience (his own experience and that of others) to test those arguments. As students outline this essay and consider which points Oppenheimer gives the most attention to (**Question 1**), encourage them to be aware of the sources he uses (**Questions 2** and **3**). What other sources are students aware of that support, contradict, or might help modify Oppenheimer's claims? How do students interpret Oppenheimer's solution (to ban federal spending on classroom computers) to the problems he sees? Would they—or J. Michael Bishop—label him an "enemy of promise" (**Question 4**), or do they see his caution as prudent?

Through the invention technique of looping, **Question 6** helps students see how their own thinking takes shape and becomes more focused. This question encourages them to respond to Oppenheimer's discussion of the real (physical) world and the virtual world of computers. After completing the discussion and looping exercises, students are asked to write a one-page response to Oppenheimer. **Question 6** asks students to start the discussion they base their response paper on in groups; it might be interesting to have them share their response papers in those same small groups, so they can discuss the differences and similarities in their positions on this topic.

ANTHONY WALTON Technology versus African Americans (p. 331)

Anthony Walton examines the historical relationship between African Americans and technology and finds in it unique consequences that have prevented African Americans from achieving parity with people of other races and ethnicities. In answering **Question 1**, students should keep in mind Walton's caution in paragraph 19 against reading his argument as simply blaming technology for keeping African Americans from progressing. Rather, his essay is more nuanced, drawing connections between the historical developments of technology and the historical oppression of African Americans. This essay may serve as inspiration for students to conduct historical research of their own, as suggested in **Questions 2** and **3**. With the larger project of examining the relationship between technology and another group (**Question 3**), students might find ways of challenging Walton's view.

Questions 4–6 continue to probe the relationships between people and technology raised here and in other selections in this chapter. Pursuing a common theme in this chapter, **Question 5** asks students to think and write about the unintended negative consequences of technological developments. Students are invited to think about the emphasis on antagonistic relationships in essays by Walton, J. Michael Bishop (p. 282), and James Q. Wilson (p. 340), as indicated in the essays' titles (**Question 4**). Todd Oppenheimer's essay presents a viewpoint that may be used to challenge Walton's suggestion that African

Americans could benefit from increased attention to technology education in schools (**Question 6**).

Walton assigns considerable importance to technology, a judgment that students are asked to interrogate in a short essay or letter to the editor (**Question 8**). **Questions 7** and **9** offer students a chance to consider how culture or individual preference might affect their own attitudes toward technology or other fields recommended to them as promising lucrative opportunities.

JAMES Q. WILSON Cars and Their Enemies (p. 340)

James Q. Wilson contends in this selection that "the automobile, the device on which most Americans rely for not only transportation but mobility, privacy, and fun would not exist if it had to be created today." This statement could very well be Wilson's thesis (**Question 2**). And he gives a whole list of (potential and actual) criticisms against automobiles to support his main point. While Wilson answers his critics, he still believes that "the campaign against them [cars] will not stop. It will not stop because so many of the critics dislike everything the car stands for and everything that society constructs to serve the needs of its occupants." Wilson, though, values the privacy, speed, and "joyous sensation" of the drive; and he wants to be able to get to Wal-Mart and Home Depot. Thus, his point is not only to prove that car critics remain but also to remind readers that cars are essential to the way of life that many Americans have grown accustomed to and deeply value.

Wilson's argument rests on his characterization of car critics (**Question 1**) and his defenses against their accusations. In addition, his argument is supported by his ethos, which is established by his tone and use of evidence. **Question 3** invites students to consider Wilson's use of statistics, his inclusion of personal experience, and his tone. How do students characterize his tone? Do they find it effective, given his argument and audience? Who is his audience? If students respond well to Wilson's use of evidence and his tone, they may wish to explore these elements in the writing they are asked to do in **Question 8** on "________ and Their Enemies." If they don't find Wilson's tone and use of evidence persuasive, students should be instructed to explain how they would construct their argument differently—and why. **Question 7** explicitly tells students to use the first several paragraphs of Wilson's essay for their own exploratory essay on a similar topic—whether some other existing technology might be built today if it had not been built in the past. As a class, you could brainstorm a list of such technologies and discuss the pros and cons associated with them from various perspectives.

Whether students agree or disagree with Wilson, they are likely to have strong feelings about cars and transportation—as well as about the environmental and social issues associated with the car culture in American society. While Wilson suggests that people choose transportation "based on individual, not social, preferences," there are clear social ramifications to what might seem to be individual choices. **Questions 4** and **5** ask students to think about future and past ramifications of the development of computers, much in the same way Wilson considers cars. Can they imagine future circumstances that might cause us to regret the development of computers and their role in our lives (**Question 4**)? Do they read history in the same way that Wilson does, or in the way that Walton does in "Technology versus African Americans" (p. 331) (**Question 5**)? Students' answers to these questions could inform essays or letters responding to the authors. **Question 6** provides students with an opportunity to consider further the place of the automobile in American culture by writing an editorial for the college newspaper.

MOLLY IVINS Bush's Brain Straddles the Fence Once Again (p. 352)

This essay is perhaps best read in conjunction with the next selection, George W. Bush's speech on stem cell research. Although Molly Ivins wrote this selection before Bush gave his speech (as the headnote points out), her anticipation of its gist suggests that the Bush administration may have informed the press of the upcoming speech and its likely contents (**Question 1**). The controversies over the use of stem cell research are rich with possibilities for students' exploration and writing. They are, as Jessica Cohen suggests in "Grade A: The Market for a Yale Woman's Eggs" (p. 191), related to moral questions about reproductive technologies, as well as to those issues raised by Ivins in this essay.

For students unfamiliar with Ivins, it might be helpful for the instructor to discuss her sarcastic wit and her liberal viewpoint or to have students find other columns by her to get a sense of her work. **Questions 1–5** focus on the argument she makes and the effectiveness of her stylistic choices, including tone and allusions. Her explicit reference to Frankenstein invites comparison to the excerpt from Mary Shelley's *Frankenstein* in this chapter (p. 276) (**Question 5**). Students can also check Ivins's use of the term *slippery slope* (paragraph 4) and discuss whether they find it effective (**Question 5**) and how they might apply a similar concept in their own writing (**Question 7**). In further considering this argument and coming up with their own position on the issue (**Question 6**), students should consult Bush's speech as well as other recent sources.

PRESIDENT GEORGE W. BUSH Speech to the Nation on Stem Cell Research (p. 355)

With this speech, President George W. Bush announced his policy on the controversial issue of stem cell research, a topic that leads almost inevitably to a discussion of the human effects of scientific advances. As mentioned in the notes to "Bush's Brain Straddles the Fence Once Again" by Molly Ivins (p. 356), students can gain insight into the issue and into a means of argument by reading Ivins's essay alongside Bush's speech. Bush's speech may be read as a response to some of Ivins's concerns, even though we can't know whether he crafted it with that purpose in mind (**Question 6**).

The stylistic differences between Bush's speech and Ivins's essay are worth noting as points of instruction for students' own writing. While Ivins uses irreverent sarcasm and wit to make her point, Bush's speech necessarily takes a more serious tone (**Question 3**), and it uses a cautious strategy of building audience support before presenting its main claim (**Question**

1). In identifying "fundamental questions" regarding stem cell research (paragraph 1), Bush defines the limits of debate on the issue (**Question 2**), creating another subtle means of support for his thesis. Students should also consider the characteristics of a speech, prepared for oral presentation, as distinct from a text meant to be read silently (**Questions 4** and **8**).

In forming their own opinions about the uses of stem cell research, students can consult other readings in the chapter, including the excerpt from Mary Shelley's *Frankenstein* (p. 276) and Jeremy Rifkin's "Biotech Century" (p. 289) (**Question 5**). One way to approach an essay on the issue would be to write in response to the president's policy as presented in this speech (**Question 7**).

SHERRY TURKLE Cuddling Up to Cyborg Babies (p. 361)

In this article, Sherry Turkle suggests that just as computers have changed people's conception of intelligence, computer toys seem to be changing children's understanding of emotions and relationships. Like other magazine articles presented so far—such as Michael Sokolove's "Football Is a Sucker's Game" (p. 124), Jessica Cohen's "Grade A: The Market for a Yale Woman's Eggs" (p. 191), and Anthony Walton's "Technology versus African Americans" (p. 331)—Turkle's argument proceeds largely inductively, with supporting claims implicit in examples (**Questions 1** and **2**).

Like many selections in this chapter, including those by Molly Ivins (p. 352) and George W. Bush (p. 355) on stem cell research, this one touches on moral questions, which are worth exploring in light of Turkle's insights into children's interaction with computer technology (**Questions 4** and **5**). **Questions 3** and **5** present opportunities for students to articulate their own opinions on the role computer technology ought to play in children's learning and development. If your class has a range of ages represented, **Question 5** might make for especially fruitful discussion, as it allows students to compare their experiences playing with various types of technology.

THE *ONION* New National Parks Web Site Makes National Parks Obsolete (p. 368)

This spoof pokes fun at Americans' newfound love of technology and the resulting tendency for people to substitute virtual experience for real experience. As J.R. mentions in his headnote, most students are probably familiar with the *Onion*, but for those who aren't, the opening questions make it clear that this piece is a parody. Students are invited to examine how the parody works and who might be behind it (**Questions 1–3**). **Question 6** offers students the chance to try their hand at writing parody, working in teams.

In considering potential issues raised by this selection, students can review Todd Oppenheimer's essay (p. 300) and compare his concerns with those expressed here about potential overreliance on technology (**Question 4**). Pursuing a different path of reasoning offered by this selection, they can also review James Q. Wilson's "Cars and Their Enemies" (p. 340), which argues that the technology of automobiles enabled more people to visit national parks (**Question 5**). Web sites can be seen, as the *Onion* suggests, as making parks even more widely accessible, at least online. Is this development good or bad, or something in between? Perhaps evaluating a park Web site or two can help students decide (**Question 7**).

Texts in Context: Sequenced Writing Assignments about Science and Technology

Assignment 1

Writing several decades ago, Professor Richard Weaver of the University of Chicago argued that we can learn a lot about people's values by looking closely at what he calls their "God terms"—that is, those words or terms that represent what people believe in almost implicitly. In the United States, Weaver suggested, *progress* and *science* were such terms. Indeed, in many ways, people see science and technology as things that bring about progress. Spend some time thinking about what associations you have with the terms *science* and *technology*, reflecting on what you know about science and technology that has changed, contributed to, or affected your experience. Then make a list of the words or phrases that immediately come to mind when you think of science and technology. Finally, write a one-page statement for your class in which you explain your major associations with science or technology. You might think of your statement as a way of saying "where I stand on science or technology as a 'God term' today."

Assignment 2

Choose the one reading in this chapter that most appeals to you. Reread the selection to see if you have the same response to it. Then decide where the author seems to stand on the question of science or technology as a strongly positive or "God term." Compare your findings against the statement you wrote for Assignment 1. In what ways does your statement agree with the position of the author you chose for Assignment 2? Do you note any differences? Write a brief memo for your class on "why writer X and I agree on the question of science or technology and its status in our society."

Assignment 3

Anthony Walton implicitly argues that technology is neither objective nor neutral, despite its attempt to present itself as such. Reread Walton's essay, paying special attention to this claim. Then look at the Rifkin selection to see what you can find to support or refute Walton's claim. Does what you find lead you to rethink the statement that you wrote for Assignment 1? Why, or why not? Record your response in your reading log.

Assignment 4

Now add Bishop to the conversation. How might he respond to Walton's claim? Write an imaginary dialogue between Walton and Bishop on this topic. Bring the dialogue to class, and be prepared to read it aloud.

Assignment 5

Reread or review this chapter's initial reading by Mary Shelley. Then reread either the Rifkin or Oppenheimer essay on contemporary technology. In what ways does Shelley anticipate some of the issues and ideas that Rifkin or Oppenheimer raises? Assume you are going to write a modern-day update of *Frankenstein*, probably for TV or video. Meet with several classmates to brainstorm about such an update. Then sketch out a plot line and one or two main characters. Finally, compare your story with the work you did for Assignments 1–3. Does the same picture or image of science or technology emerge in each case? Write a brief report for your class entitled "My Different Takes on Science or Technology."

Assignment 6

Spend some time thinking about how you may have arrived at your ideas about and attitudes toward science and technology. Consider how family, school, religion, politics, and the mass media may have influenced your views. Decide which of these or other possible influences have most strongly shaped your thinking about science and technology. Then write a page or two of notes on those influences, describing what they are and why you consider them significant.

Assignment 7

Look back at all of the work you did for Assignments 1–6, studying it to see what it reveals about your overall perspective on science and technology. Then write a four- to five-page essay for your class entitled "The Hazards—and Benefits—of Science and Technology: My Stand, Where My Position Comes From, and My Take on the Future."

Part Three Who We Are

6 ■ Identities: The One in Many / The Many in One (p. 377)

Chapter 6 invites students to participate in a conversation about identity and the many elements that contribute not only to who people are but also to how they define themselves and how they are defined by others. Some topics taken up in this chapter include the differences between men and women and between masculinity and femininity; the relationship between majority and minority cultures in the United States; and differences in the ways in which individuals and groups construct identities—or have those identities constructed for them by others. Although many people see the United States as a cultural melting pot, a place where people of many origins come together to become members of a new culture, this view has been challenged by many groups and individuals. They argue that assimilating to (majority) American culture can be difficult or impossible for many and that, instead, the country should work to be a multicultural society, one that values the differences (rather than the commonalties) among its members. Opponents argue that an emphasis on cultural difference can only result in political tension and hostility.

This chapter presents diverse perspectives on the subject of both individual and group identity and includes texts that discuss identity in various ways. The chapter introductory questions give students an opportunity to explore their own thoughts and feelings on identities—thoughts and feelings that they may not realize are part of a long-standing conversation. As students engage with the selections in this chapter, you might encourage them to explore not just their reactions to the readings but also their reasons for reacting as they do. What elements work together to help them define who they are, and in what ways do their own identities affect how they respond to others? How does their position—who they are as people who belong to differing communities—affect their responses and the responses of their classmates?

Some of the questions that recur throughout this chapter include the following:

- What is the relationship between majority and minority cultures in the United States? (Hurston, King, Nguyen, Allen, Patel, Hughes)
- What do Americans have in common? (Hurston, King, Etzioni, Hughes)
- In what ways is identity embedded in the stories people tell and listen to? (Kingston, King)
- How do differences between and among different men and women affect their ability to relate to one another? (Truth, Sullivan, Kingston, Barry, Bradsher)

SOJOURNER TRUTH Ain't I a Woman? (p. 380)

Question 1 turns students' attention to the oral nature of Sojourner Truth's speech. The repetition of rhetorical questions (in this case, "And ain't I a woman?") is a feature common to oral discourse, though students may think it sounds out of place in a written text. In order to better understand how such repetition can work, **Question 6** gives students the opportunity to write their own "manifesto of identity," structuring the piece with a recurring question. Students might also point out other elements of Truth's text that mark it as a speech. What differences do they see between a written text and a speech? In considering the effect of the recurring rhetorical question as well as other oral elements, students should consider both the effect of these elements in a written text and the effect in a spoken text. To illustrate, have one or several students read Truth's speech aloud to the class. Do students respond differently to the text when it is delivered orally than when they read it to themselves?

One especially important element of a speech is that it is meant to be spoken by a particular person, someone who, in most cases, can be both seen and heard by an audience. In what ways do a person's appearance, voice, and gesture affect how his or her words are received? If you had more than one student read Truth's text aloud, have all students consider whether they responded differently to the text depending on who delivered it. This consideration might also lead to a discussion of how identity is constructed in a text and how students' understanding of written and spoken texts is shaped by what they know of the author and even by how the author looks.

In addition, you could ask several students to read the pieces they wrote in response to **Question 6** aloud in class. Do students respond differently to a text delivered by someone other than the author of that text? What do they think of the profession of speech writing (writing speeches for someone else to deliver)? And what do their answers to these questions reveal about how they view identity—especially as it is constructed in or revealed by texts and performances? **Question 3** gives students the opportunity to write another speech, this one from Truth's perspective, using her humorous and conversational tone. Answering this question could also lead to a discussion of the ways that elements of style (word choice, tone, sentence rhythm, and so on) reveal or conceal identity.

Much of the power of Truth's speech comes from its oral qualities as well as from our knowledge that Truth was a former slave who couldn't read or write. In her introduction to Truth's speech, A.L. reveals her respect for Truth, but **Question 2** asks students to consider not only the power of Truth's speech but also the kinds of criticisms A.L. could have leveled against Truth's argument. As students come up with possible criticisms of Truth's speech (her lack of evidence beyond her own experience, her admission that she might have less intellect than a man, the absence of linear logic), be sure to have them make explicit their assumptions about what makes an argument effective. This discussion would be a good prelude to **Question 4**, which asks students to find similarities and differences among the argumentative strategies employed by Truth and other authors in the chapter.

In responding to **Question 5**, most students will take the position that men and women should have equal rights, and many believe that they already do, but others will recognize areas of life where there is still inequality. For example, why has the United States never had a woman president? Should men have equal responsibility for child rearing and care of the home? Again, students will benefit from having an opportunity to read and talk about their responses.

ANDREW SULLIVAN What Are Homosexuals For? (p. 382)

In his headnote, J.R. says Andrew Sullivan's essay "speaks quietly and eloquently to the entire political spectrum." **Question 3** asks students to assess whether "What Are Homosexuals For?" is, as J.R. claims, an example of "civil argument," balanced and reasonable. Whether or not students agree wholly with Sullivan's discussion of homosexuality, they are likely to affirm and understand some of his claims: that American culture at large tends to define "normal" sexuality as heterosexuality (**Question 1**) and that gay people often feel like outsiders (**Question 2**). **Question 1** encourages students to consider "how the cultural dominance of heterosexual marriage" affects society in general and people in particular. While Sullivan discusses how the ideal of heterosexual marriage affects young gay people, this question broadens the issue somewhat. How does the expectation of marriage—the power of heterosexual marriage as an institution—shape individuals and society? Some students will not be able to relate to Sullivan's feeling like an outsider because of sexuality, but **Question 2** invites them to describe a time when they have felt like an outsider because of gender, class, physical capabilities, or political preference.

Question 4 refers to Kingston's "No Name Woman" and brings up the issue of the constraints society puts on sexuality. Before asking students to respond to this question regarding the differences among constraints, taboos, and prejudices, you may want to ask them what particular constraints they think society does put on sexuality. Depending on their religious, political, and social beliefs and experiences, students are likely to answer this question differently. They can be encouraged to consider how religious, political, and societal forces have shaped their identities and behaviors, and how they respond to the identities and behaviors of others.

Question 6 invites students to explore the appropriateness of a writing assignment about a first date or first love. If you've already talked about sexual constraints and issues of people feeling like outsiders because of their sexuality, students may be particularly sensitive to how such an assignment might further alienate people. What if a person has never been on a date or been in love? What if a person prefers not to talk about his or her love life? What might be the advantages and disadvantages of such an assignment? In order to help students answer **Question 6**, you could have them think of times when they were given an assignment that made them uncomfortable. How did they respond to the assignment?

Some of the study questions accompanying Dave Barry's selection encourage students to think about stereotypes, how they're used in humorous writing like Barry's, and how they can be limiting and not entirely true. **Question 5** asks students to consider "Barry's world of guys" in light of Sullivan's piece and whether such a world has "room for homosexuals." While Barry doesn't explicitly talk about homosexual men, are there any ways in which his essay implicitly offers a space for them?

Question 7 helps students explore the issue of stereotyping further by asking them whether one can make assertions or generalizations about any group of people "without engaging in harmful stereotypes." What are some reasons for arguing that certain groups of people—women, guys, lesbians, poor people, people with learning disabilities, the elderly—share some similarities? Are there ways of talking about similarities without confining people or negatively stereotyping them? **Question 7** invites students to explore these issues in a written dialogue. They should think carefully about who they will represent in the dialogue and how the participants' identity and experiences might affect their positions on such issues.

MAXINE HONG KINGSTON No Name Woman (p. 393)

One interesting characteristic of Maxine Hong Kingston's story that students may overlook is its impact on the author/narrator. Students may become so engaged by No Name's story that they overlook the story's functions as a lesson against the consequences of sex outside of marriage and as an illustration of the ways in which stories can be appropriated by readers for their own purposes. **Question 1**, which asks students to consider the different versions of the story Kingston posits, can help students see that the story is open to interpretation: the narrator/author tells the story differently than her mother did; A.L. interprets the story differently than the villagers would (**Question 3**); and the father of No Name's child would likely tell yet another version of the story.

Question 6 invites students to rewrite one of Kingston's versions of the story from the point of view of a man and to consider this man's relationship to women, thereby emphasizing that a story changes depending on who tells it. Comparing these versions of No Name's story should help students arrive at their own interpretations of it. Through a discussion of the openness of the story of No Name Woman, students will be encouraged to consider how a reader's identity affects his or her interpretation of stories.

Kingston's text, like those of Sojourner Truth and Andrew Sullivan, considers the ways in which gender roles are influenced by society. **Question 2**, which asks students to explore the narrator's attitude and their own attitude toward the villagers who attack No Name Woman, provides the opportunity for students to think about society's power over the gender identity of individuals. Are people completely free to be the kind of men or women they want to be? Although to the present-day American reader the villagers might seem irrational, superstitious, and vengeful, the reader can also see that their actions are the product of cultural beliefs and values. Students might think about other situations in which American beliefs and values have produced seemingly irrational behavior (one obvious example is slavery).

Kingston's comparison of an old Chinese culture with a contemporary American one allows readers to consider the role of social forces in the construction of identity. As a first-generation Chinese American, Kingston is preoccupied with the differences between Chinese and American culture. For students, too, these differences may seem obvious: what happened to No Name Woman would not have taken place in the United States today. But does what happened to No Name Woman differ from the lynching of black men in the South who were accused of looking at white women?

Having students interview older friends or relatives about the sexual norms that they grew up with (**Question 5**) will give students insight into the social constraints on gender identity and sexuality that those born after the sexual revolution may not be aware of. Students who are reluctant to talk with their parents or others about sex could consult magazines and books that were popular during the 1940s and 1950s to get a sense of American society's views on men, women, and sex at that time.

Comparing Kingston's telling of No Name Woman's story with Andrew Sullivan's discussion of homosexuality (**Question 4**) will allow students to consider the extent to which society continues to write the rules that men and women are expected to follow. In addition to considering the kinds of secrets people are expected to keep, students might compare the speakers in these pieces—Kingston and Sullivan—and their motives for writing. What lessons are Kingston and Sullivan trying to teach?

DAVE BARRY Guys vs. Men (p. 404)

As the tone of J.R.'s headnote implies, Dave Barry's humorous piece is rather exaggerated and "plays off of gross stereotypes about men" (**Question 1**). Many of the study questions for "Guys vs. Men" aim to help students take a closer look at Barry's piece and to analyze the various techniques he uses for effect. If your students are unfamiliar with such terms as *analogy*, *parody*, and *irony*, you may find it helpful to assign other selections that make use of these conventions or to have students experiment with analogy, parody, irony, and the like in their own writing (**Question 3**). **Question 6** asks students to write an anecdote, using Barry's anecdote about the stereotypical competitiveness of guys as a model while choosing their own stereotype of guys or gals as their subject. This question also gives guidelines to help students tell their story in a funny way. Before students respond to this question in writing, however, you might focus a class discussion on Barry's use of understatement ("considerable pain"), exaggeration ("twenty-three Advil in my bloodstream"), irony (Barry knew his coworkers were being "ridiculous," but he joined them anyway and pulled a muscle while doing so), and self-deprecation (the quote from a typical fan letter: "Who cuts your hair? Beavers?").

Question 2 points to Barry's use of analogy and asks students to work in groups to discuss the features of Barry's extended comparison between his dog Zippy and the moral behavior of guys. How is Zippy's tendency to get into the garbage and, when scolded, to poop on the floor similar to the moral behavior of guys? Do students find the comparison effective—and why? Can they think of alternative analogies that might be more effective? As **Question 5** points out, Barry's entire piece is an extended definition; the question names many of the techniques Barry uses to make his definition clear, giving students helpful suggestions for writing their own extended definitions. As a class exercise, you might have students write a chart on the board that shows contrasts between two similar terms, such as *kids* versus *children*, *dads* versus *fathers*, and *maids* versus *housekeepers* (**Question 5** provides other examples), in order to highlight how similar words can carry very different connotations. This exercise implies that the words we choose to use have important effects on meaning, depending on our purpose, intended audience, and style. Students should be encouraged to consider these elements as they analyze the rhetorical situations in which the various terms are used.

Unlike many of the other study questions for Barry, **Question 4** focuses more on content than on style, asking students to examine the author's claim that science is "really a male obsession with how things work." In their response, students should consider Barry's use of the adjective *male* in light of women's interest in or even obsession with "how things work" as well as the notion that science is motivated by such an obsession. What other motivations might there be for scientific practice and inquiry? Do students see science as a primarily male interest? Why, or why not?

ZORA NEALE HURSTON How It Feels to Be Colored Me (p. 416)

In praising the commonalties that Americans share and acknowledging the racial and cultural differences among Americans, Zora Neale Hurston suggests that American society is partially responsible for overemphasizing difference. Hurston's references to color throughout her essay (**Question 1**) illustrate the ways in which a person's difference becomes apparent only when the person is measured against his or her surroundings. For example, Hurston is "colored" only when she finds herself in a predominantly white environment, and she suggests that she stops being "colored" when she is feeling self-confident.

Students will likely have different reactions to Hurston's essay, depending on their own attitudes toward racial difference and their experiences with people of different races. Some readers may feel comforted by Hurston's ability to ignore or rise above her racial difference; others may consider her statements unbelievable or escapist. Be sure students have the opportunity to explore why they respond to Hurston's essay as they do and to discuss why various classmates may respond differently. In addition, students might consider whether A.L.'s introduction to this selection "colored" their reading of it (**Question 2**). As students discuss their responses, you might ask them to sympathize with Hurston's point of view and to complicate it, perhaps by considering it in conjunction with Langston Hughes's poem, "Theme for English B" (**Question 4**). As students consider the similarities and differences in Hurston's and Hughes's attitudes toward racial difference, you might want to point out that both authors were writing at about the same time and were influential members of the Harlem Renaissance; in addition, Hughes openly criticized Hurston for what he believed was her failure to use her position to fight for the rights of African Americans.

Another way for students to complicate Hurston's seemingly idealistic view of racial difference is to consider the various labels that have been used to refer to African Americans. What connotations does the term *colored* have, especially in contrast to *white*? Why would the term *colored* be replaced by *black* or *African American*? Ask students to consider the power of words and the power of naming. Hurston was certainly aware of the power of the majority culture to shape the minority culture's attitude toward itself—Hurston would not have become "a little colored girl" in her own mind if she had not known that she was thought of in that way by the white people she lived with.

As students work to come up with their own explanation of the relationship between majority and minority cultures in the United States, they might begin by considering the ways in which they might be considered different from the "norms" of American culture (**Questions 3** and **5** provide ways to explore these differences). To what extent do students think people are expected to assimilate to the "norm"? Is the pressure to assimilate the same for all Americans? Are the benefits—and losses—the same for all people? Students can draw on their responses to these questions as they construct their own metaphorical descriptions of their racial or ethnic identities (**Question 6**) and compare them with those of their classmates (**Question 7**). It might be interesting to work as a class on a metaphorical description of an "American" that takes into account as many students' descriptions of themselves as possible.

ANDRE DUBUS Witness (p. 421)

This essay differs from most others in this chapter, in that it deals with a shift in identity encountered by the author during adulthood, when an accident left him disabled. Through vivid imagery (**Question 3**), Andre Dubus offers poignant insights into the pain and difficulty he lives with every day. His essay unfolds like a story or memoir, through narrative that presents information selectively and artfully; much of the meaning is revealed obliquely through the essay's use of narrative and its structure. Even the title can be read in more than one way (**Question 1**). **Questions 2** and **4** draw students' attention to Dubus's use of a story-within-a-story structure to reveal his struggles with the disability caused by the accident and his struggles with the writing of this essay.

Though the essay's topic, a life-changing event, is unique in this chapter, it resembles those by Zora Neale Hurston (p. 416) and Bich Minh Nguyen (p. 443), which describe the authors' experiences of being uprooted early in life and adapting to new cultures (**Question 5**). This comparison may help students answer **Question 8**, which asks them to think of ways in which they might relate to Dubus's essay and to write a reflection to share with the class. **Question 6** poses another possibility for helping students relate to this essay, suggesting that they reflect on the family relationships described by Maxine Hong Kingston (p. 393), Dubus, and Nguyen. While these questions encourage students to relate Dubus's narrative to their own experiences, **Question 7** offers a less personally revealing way of engaging with the essay—by writing reviews of it for an instructor and for a friend.

ROBERT D. KING Should English Be the Law? (p. 430)

Robert D. King's essay brings up an important strain in the conversation about identity: national identity and what constitutes it. According to King, "language is a symbol, an icon," akin to the American flag or a marriage license. It stands for something, but differences in language do not, according to King, "threaten American unity." Rather than resting only on a common language, the "unique otherness" of the United States depends more on a plethora of other things, big and small. King emphasizes national unity (as does Peter J. Gomes in **Chapter 4, Moralities**, as indicated by **Question 5**); he sees people united by everything from hot dogs and automobiles to respect for the individual. **Question 7** encourages students to define in their own terms what constitutes America's "unique otherness" or to question the notion altogether. Do students see the notion as idealistic or even oppressive, or as an enabling belief that helps establish community? King argues that there is something "different" about the United States and that difference is more than a legislated common language. He argues that Americans can "relax and luxuriate in our linguistic richness and . . .

traditional tolerance of language difference." **Question 1** asks students to consider some of King's other basic claims and the evidence he uses to support his argument.

Much of King's evidence is based on historical events and references, some of them more familiar than others. If students are not aware of certain major historical events, they may not fully understand how King supports his argument. **Question 2** refers to one allusion in particular, and asks students to undertake library research to discover its significance. (You might include the Internet as a resource.) The phrase "mystic chords of memory" (to which **Question 2** refers) comes from Lincoln's First Inaugural Address, given on March 4, 1861:

> We are not enemies, but friends. We must not be enemies. Though passion may have strained, it must not break our bonds of affection. The mystic chords of memory, stretching from every battle-field, and patriot grave, to every living heart and hearth-stone, all over this broad land, will yet swell the chorus of the Union, when again touched, as surely they will be, by the better angels of our nature.

In class discussion you might provide some context about the Civil War and Lincoln's reputation as the preserver of the Union, or you could have students provide such context by presenting the results of their research.

As students seek to answer King's central question—"Should English be the law?"—they should consider the relationship between language and identity. You might initiate the conversation by asking students to draw from their own experiences—to think about their own first language (whether it's English or another language) and how it relates to their identity, or to consider a time when they were in another culture or country where English was not the primary language. To help broaden this discussion of language and identity, **Question 4** refers students to Mike Rose's selection (in **Chapter 3, Education**), asking them to determine whether King's analysis supports Rose's observations. Students are also encouraged to offer their own analyses in class discussion.

The analysis called for in **Question 3** is not limited to the printed text; it also points students to the illustration that appeared on the cover of the *Atlantic Monthly* issue in which King's essay was published. This question invites a detailed analysis of the image and asks students whether they think the image fits King's article. As they consider this question, and perhaps offer ideas for alternative images that might better fit the article, students should be encouraged to think about the purpose of a magazine cover. Does its purpose differ from the purpose of images used alongside an article? Is it more important to catch readers' attention or to represent the argument of a printed text? Must the two be mutually exclusive? What is—or should be—the relationship between the image and the print blurb that accompanies it? These and other questions can be used to provoke discussion and help students focus their analyses.

BICH MINH NGUYEN The Good Immigrant Student (p. 443)

Like Andre Dubus's "Witness" (p. 421), this essay makes an implicit argument through narrative, as Bich Minh Nguyen reminisces about her experiences as an immigrant student

(**Questions 1–3**). While students may interpret her overall message in different ways, Nguyen's encounter with bilingual classes (paragraphs 3 and 4) offers a critique that can be compared to that of Robert D. King in "Should English Be the Law?" (p. 430) (**Question 4**). Whereas King criticizes the English-only movement, Nguyen's experience illustrates some potential problems with efforts to provide bilingual education for immigrant students. Students could use these two essays to analyze and critique the ways in which particular curricula systematically attempt to shape identities of nonimmigrant and immigrant students alike.

Nguyen's vivid descriptions of classroom scenes reveal her painful shyness, a characteristic that appears in Maxine Hong Kingston's essay as well (**Question 5**). Many students will relate to these and other evocative passages, perhaps enabling them to identify with Nguyen's experiences (**Question 6**). Through their engagement with this essay, students can begin to explore and write about how their personal experiences in school have influenced their own identities (**Question 7**).

KEITH BRADSHER *From* Reptile Dreams (p. 452)

This excerpt from Keith Bradsher's *Reptile Dreams* presents the psychological views of men's and women's identities advanced by Clotaire Rapaille and used in marketing American cars. Rapaille's theory, which Bradsher says is developed from Jungian psychology, posits that people are motivated by reptile-like instincts to preserve their species through survival and reproduction. According to Bradsher, Rapaille uses this theory to explain the appeal of sport-utility vehicles (SUVs) and to further develop and market the vehicles' instinctual appeal. This piece of writing is unusual among the selections in this chapter in its rhetorical approach; while other pieces present their author's opinions firsthand, this one presents Rapaille's ideas secondhand, through Bradsher's observations. Thus, the first three questions address Rapaille's credibility and how it is affected by Bradsher's writing (**Questions 1–3**). You may want to refer students to the description of reporting in Chapter 2 (p. 36) to gather some criteria for assessing Bradsher's handling of his subject.

This selection presents a serious treatment of gender differences (**Question 4**) like those satirized in Dave Barry's "Guys vs. Men" (p. 404). In comparing the two essays (**Question 5**), students can evaluate how well each essay persuades the reader of the existence of such innate differences in men's and women's thought and emotions. **Question 8** encourages students to do more research to test the validity of Rapaille's ideas. Despite the controversial nature of Rapaille's psychological theory, the marketing decisions based on it seem quite successful, as the increasingly aggressive-looking SUVs with luxurious interiors continue to sell in great numbers across the United States. **Question 6** suggests that perhaps Bradsher's essay captures an aspect of a distinctly American identity, pointing students toward other essays in the chapter that may help them explore this idea. **Question 7** provides an opportunity for students to think about what their tastes in cars may reveal about their own identities. It might be fun and illuminating to have them share their answers in class.

PAULA GUNN ALLEN Where I Come From Is Like This (p. 460)

Paula Gunn Allen's essay delves into aspects of women's identity from various Native American perspectives. For those who are used to the stereotype of women as the weaker sex, Allen's essay presents refreshingly powerful images of women, culled from tribal folklore. Like the selections by Maxine Hong Kingston (p. 393), Zora Neale Hurston (p. 416), Andre Dubus (p. 421), and Bich Minh Nguyen (p. 443), this essay makes extensive use of narrative in conveying its message. The essay is divided into three sections (**Question 1**). The first section introduces the differences between Native American and Anglo-European American images of women. The second explores in more depth some traditional Native American ideas of womanhood. And the third points to current Native American experience that demonstrates the need for these traditions to be kept alive as sources of inspiration and insight. Allen alludes throughout to Native American traditions, often presenting long lists of images and characters recalled from oral folklore (**Question 2**). This technique has the effect of accumulating support for her argument for alternative ways of viewing women, while reinforcing the importance of the oral tradition she advocates preserving.

Students are invited to contrast the images of femininity offered here with those presented by Clotaire Rapaille in Keith Bradsher's *Reptile Dreams* (**Question 4**) or with some of the selections in Chapter 7 on American cultural myths (**Question 5**). **Question 3** asks students to imagine what Allen might think of Amitai Etzioni's proposal for a multicultural category on the U.S. Census. Would she welcome such a change or not? Why? Finally, Allen's essay, like Hurston's, offers a model for students who wish to explore moments in which they became aware of conflicts in their own identities—conflicts arising, perhaps, from a clash of cultures like those described by these authors.

AMITAI ETZIONI The Monochrome Society (p. 469)

While many of the selections in this chapter address identity from a personal perspective, Amitai Etzioni takes a sociopolitical approach to the topic, arguing that race and ethnicity are less significant to the shared communal life of Americans than they are commonly perceived to be. The length and academic style of this essay may be intimidating to students, so discovering Etzioni's main claim may prove challenging (**Question 1**). A preview might be helpful; you could suggest that students read through the headings and first lines of the sections, which will give a general sense of how the argument is arranged. The structure is fairly conventional for social-scientific writing. After introducing the problem—how to view the shrinking of the white majority in the United States—Etzioni suggests a middle alternative to the celebratory/alarmist dichotomy, carefully debunking the major points of each extreme position. As a communitarian, Etzioni advocates a view of plurality that respects diverse cultures while placing a priority on the common values shared by the broader community of Americans. **Questions 2** and **6** encourage students to engage with the essay and form their own responses to its potentially controversial claims.

Whereas other chapter selections draw substantially from personal narrative, Etzioni amasses evidence from sociological research, citing many statistics that students can examine by conducting their own research (**Question 3**). Students can also interrogate the author's claims by consulting other readings in the chapter. For example, in the section of the essay entitled "The Lessons of 'Nonwhite' States and Cities" (paragraph 58), Etzioni addresses the political character of regions similar to the African American town of Eatonville described by Zora Neale Hurston (p. 416). Students might consider whether Eztioni's and Hurston's descriptions of homogeneous nonwhite culture seem to mesh (**Question 4**). They can also compare Etzioni's views of race as a social construct with those of other authors in this chapter, such as Sojourner Truth (p. 380), Hurston, or Robert J. King (p. 430).

In its discussion of race and ethnicity, Etzioni's essay may inspire students to research a related topic such as affirmative action. The essay serves as a potential source for supporting evidence or counterarguments, and it provides a good model of research-based argument (**Question 7**).

EBOO PATEL On Nurturing a Modern Muslim Identity (p. 503)

Eboo Patel adds an important perspective to this chapter by addressing the role of religion in identity formation. Patel informs his audience about varieties of Muslim culture, ultimately arguing against the fundamentalism espoused by the Taliban to advocate a "progressive Muslim identity" (paragraph 11) associated with the Islamic beliefs and practices of the Aga Khan Development Network (paragraph 10). He asserts that religious institutions, which he carefully defines (paragraph 8), "nurture identity." This claim provides a basis of comparison with several other readings in this chapter that discuss similar roles for other types of institutions (**Question 4**).

Before conducting such a comparison, students may first wish to examine the rhetorical situation that prompted Patel to write this text, including the events that inspired its content (**Question 2**) as well as the occasion (i.e., a conference) that may have influenced its style (**Question 1**). **Question 3** draws attention to another contextual aspect: the writers whom Patel joins in discussion on the issues of Muslim identity and the significance of religious education. Patel's claims may prompt students to write personal essays exploring the role of religion in forming their identities (**Question 5**). They may wish to consider more broadly how institutions can be encouraged to nurture identity in constructive ways, an issue that may be effectively addressed in an op-ed or a letter to community leaders (**Question 6**).

LANGSTON HUGHES Theme for English B (p. 509)

Langston Hughes's poem, written from the perspective of a college student trying to complete an assignment for a composition course, serves as a poignant closing to the conversation about identities in this chapter. For the speaker of the poem, what it means to be an "American" (**Question 1**) is complicated by the fact that, while he has many things in common with all Americans, he lives in a time when African Americans are not free to live where they wish or to eat in any restaurant or to sit in any seat on a bus. If students are reading this poem as the conclusion to this chapter, you might want them to consider the ways in which the speaker's definition of "American" would—or would not—be different now. Perhaps students could rewrite Hughes's poem from a contemporary perspective.

Question 2 asks students to think about a time when they had an experience similar to the one described in Hughes's poem, perhaps a time when they wrote something that, consciously or not, represented both their own thoughts or feelings and those of a teacher or someone else who influenced them. Although this activity gives students one way of understanding Hughes's poem—highlighting the common experience of college students regardless of their race or ethnicity (**Question 6**)—students should also consider the special difficulties faced by the student in Hughes's poem, a poor African American student attending an elite college at a time when segregation was legal (**Questions 3** and **4**). **Question 5** gives students the opportunity to reflect on how their own position—which is affected by gender, race, class, and family background—has influenced their success in school.

Texts in Context: Sequenced Writing Assignments about Identities

Assignment 1

Brainstorm a list of the various elements that make up your identity. (Some general elements might include gender, age, ability, class, sexuality, religion, race, ethnicity, appearance, and personality traits.) Bring your list to class in order to make a composite list of all the traits or markers of identity represented by the students in your class. What, if anything, about this list surprises you—and why?

Assignment 2

Imagine that you could change one major aspect of who you are for one week. Working with several classmates, discuss the effects that the change might create in your life and behavior. Then write something for your class exploring the advantages and disadvantages this change would mean for you. You may decide to compose an essay, a humorous sketch, or a play or short story about an imaginative experience entitled "A Day in My Life as a ___________."

Assignment 3

How would you characterize the man who impregnates No Name Woman in Kingston's story? Make a list of words that come to mind when you think of this character. Then make a similar list of words that characterize the guys and men Dave Barry talks about. What similarities and differences do you note in the two lists? Write a brief analysis of the man in "No Name Woman" from Barry's perspective.

Assignment 4

If the views of men presented by Kingston and Barry differ substantially, so do the views of other writers on what it is to be American. Look carefully at the words and phrases that each writer uses to describe and characterize Americans. The readings in this chapter all speak in one way or another to the title and subtitle, "Identities: The One in Many / The Many in One." Reread two or three selections, asking what motto each author might offer instead of or in addition to the subtitle of this chapter. Choose one author, and write a brief profile from that author's point of view, putting forth the new motto and explaining why it could serve as a motto for identity in the United States.

Assignment 5

You have noted the varying ways in which writers in this chapter represent themselves and others. Now, working with two classmates, take some time to examine how a particular group of people (such as men, women, or those with disabilities) is represented in some other arena you are interested in investigating (for example, soap operas, advertisements for cars, children's toys, or clothing; or a favorite book, movie, video, or song). Begin your analysis by asking this question: "If all we knew about __________ was what we could learn from looking closely at how __________ depicts them, what would we know?" Working independently, gather as much information as you can in response to this question, and bring it to the group. Then work together to draft a group report for your class. As a class, discuss the ways in which your own and others' attitudes may be influenced by such representations.

Assignment 6

Try your hand at describing the America or Americans you see reflected in or emerging from one of the following sources: MTV, the U.S. armed services, IBM, General Motors, rap music, Disney, a Woody Allen or Spike Lee film, or the film director of your choice. Imagining that all you know of America or Americans is gleaned from this source, write a page or so describing your findings. Work with several classmates to compare notes on what you have discovered. Do you agree or disagree with your classmates? Why? What might account for your opinion on how one of these sources represents America? Bring a report of your group's work to class for discussion.

Assignment 7

Working with two or three classmates, form an editorial group charged with assembling a chapter for a book like *The Presence of Others*. The title of the chapter will be "Identities: The One in Many / The Many in One," and it will include between eight and twelve selections. Suggest your nominees for the chapter, and explain and defend your choices. As a group, negotiate the final list of selections, and draft a one-page introduction to the chapter. Then choose one selection from the list, perhaps the one you like most, and write a headnote for it, using one or more headnotes in *The Presence of Others* as a model. Finally, write a reading-log entry in which you respond to the following questions about the headnote: Where do you see your own agenda or preferences at work in the headnote? What does it suggest about identity? In what ways does it favor the selection or writer that it introduces?

7 ■ American Cultural Myths: The Good, the Bad, and the Ugly (p. 513)

The readings in Chapter 7 present a lively and varied conversation about the power and effects of American cultural myths. Although we are surrounded by such myths and their symbols every day, how often do we step back and analyze them and the persuasive power they exert over us? The selections ask students to question what is "real" and to look more closely (and critically) at the myths that shape American experience. They also encourage students to contemplate nature and culture and the ways the two can often become inseparable in myths.

One good way to get students thinking about the power of myths is to have them write about those that have been powerful in their lives. They might peruse the list provided in the chapter introduction (pp. 515–516) for ideas. Which of these myths, or others that come to mind, help define who they are or how they perceive the world? For students who identify several examples of particularly powerful myths, it might be helpful for them to explore and write about how the myths relate to one another. Are the myths compatible, or are they in tension with one another?

Some of the questions taken up by the selections in this chapter include:

- What are some common American myths? And what is their relationship to reality? (Jefferson, Douglass, Churchill, Atwood, Shindle, Abbey, Lazarus)
- How are American cultural myths perpetuated? How well have they stood up over time? How have they changed? (Jefferson, Douglass, Churchill, Postman, Atwood, Kingsolver)
- Are American cultural myths equally accessible to all Americans? Do they usually unite or divide Americans? (Douglass, Churchill, Brooks, Kingsolver, Delgado)
- How do American cultural myths depict Americans to the rest of the world? (Jefferson, Atwood, Legrain, Lazarus, Delgado)

THOMAS JEFFERSON Declaration of Independence (p. 517)

As the founding document of the United States, the Declaration of Independence can be read as part of the nation's genesis myth. Certainly it reflects many of the values commonly shared by Americans as well as those who support our system of government. Many of the selections in this chapter, some critical of Americans' actions and attitudes, will refer to these values, often alluding implicitly or explicitly to the Declaration (**Questions 3** and **4**).

To review the Declaration's basic claims and ideas, it will be helpful for students to summarize the text in their own words (**Question 1**). Perhaps the main claim the signers present to justify their demand for political independence is that the king of Great Britain had overstepped the bounds of legitimate rule by failing to respect the colonists' basic human rights. In response to the assignment in **Question 5**, students can take this examination of content a step further, perhaps producing a more pointedly critical summary. In answering **Question 2** regarding the audience the signers may have envisioned for their text, students may examine stylistic features such as tone and the use of pronouns. In doing so, they should keep in mind the more formal conventions of the era; for example, it would have been improper to use the informal "you" in addressing the king. Students might ponder the ways in which the Declaration's language might have been considered bold and impudent, or deferent and decorous—and what these stylistic characteristics may indicate about the drafters' stance toward their audience.

As mentioned previously, several selections in this chapter will offer a chance to revisit the Declaration of Independence. For now, students might look ahead to Ward Churchill's essay (p. 536) to consider what the Declaration meant to Native Americans or to others present at the country's founding (**Question 3**). They might also consider what the Declaration means today, in light of Neil Postman's commentary (p. 545) on the loss of meaning in American symbols (**Question 4**). The answers to these questions may inform students' opinions in their writing on "What the Declaration of Independence Really Says" (**Question 5**). **Question 6** offers an opportunity for students to conduct research into other movements and declarations inspired by this seminal American text and to write a substantial argument based on their discoveries.

FREDERICK DOUGLASS What to the Slave Is the Fourth of July? (p. 522)

In this classic text of the abolition movement, Frederick Douglass delivers a powerful indictment of white Americans' failure to live up to the standards of just rule set forth in the Declaration of Independence (**Question 5**). This speech demonstrates Douglass's renowned oratorical skill, as he uses well-crafted emotional, ethical, and logical appeals to argue against the institution of slavery (**Questions 1–3**). **Question 4** focuses on the expression of anger in this speech, asking students to compare Douglass's expression of this emotion with two other, quite different, uses of anger presented in Edward Abbey's *Desert Solitaire* (p. 619) and Abelardo Delgado's "Stupid America" (p. 625).

Douglass's speech has endured to become a classic example of American oratory. In hindsight, his reference to a shrinking world (paragraph 74) even sounds prescient. **Question 6** asks students to imagine how Douglass might respond today to Philippe Legrain's comments on globalization (p. 570). They might have some fun trying to reproduce Douglass's tone and diction, or they might try to portray Douglass as if he were to reappear now as one of their contemporaries. **Questions 7** and **8** invite students to try composing two commemorative speeches or essays—one celebrating a holiday, another honoring Douglass's speech.

WARD CHURCHILL Crimes against Humanity (p. 536)

Ward Churchill delineates the blatant racism against American Indians expressed by a variety of images and demands the end to such "crimes against humanity." He supports his argument by detailing the many ways in which American Indians have been made to seem unreal

(**Question 2**), and he uses comparisons to show how outraged people might be if other groups were imaged in the same offensive ways. The tone of his essay is revealed in several ways—for example, through his use of quotation marks (**Question 1**), repetition (especially in the two final paragraphs), and direct address ("Okay, let's communicate"; "Now, don't go getting 'overly sensitive' out there"). Analyzing the tone of Churchill's essay is part of what is required by **Question 4**, which also asks students to compare Churchill's tone with Zora Neale Hurston's tone in "How It Feels to Be Colored Me" (p. 416). As they answer this question, students should be encouraged not only to characterize the tone taken by each author but also to list the ways and places in which tone is made clear to the reader.

Much of Churchill's essay is devoted to a discussion of the offensive use of American Indian names and images by sports teams and fans. **Questions 3** and **6** deal with this issue and can be assigned in conjunction with each other, guiding students by providing a grounding in the details of the text and then allowing them to find local examples in their school or community. (**Question 7** also encourages local research.) Do the examples students find support Churchill's argument? Do students have another interpretation of what they find?

Question 8 deals personally with labels and the effects they can have on people, by having students reflect on the labels that have been applied to them or that they've applied to themselves or others. Such questions help broaden the discussion of labels and their effects. For instance, what effect might the label *fat* or *ugly* have on a person? What expectations are implied by the terms *brilliant* or *stupid*? In addition to painful effects, can labels engender positive results or feelings?

Photo Essay: American Myths and Images—From the Covers of *Time*

Images are not mere decorations; they convey important messages that can shape values and actions. *The Presence of Others* encourages critical analysis of and response to not only printed texts but also images. This photo essay, composed of *Time* magazine covers from six decades, offers eight iconic images that suggest American cultural myths, or stories that define some common aspects of American identity. The values and beliefs reflected in these and other cultural myths passed on from one generation to the next are some of the most compelling—and provocative—notions in American culture. As the introduction to the photo essay notes, "To make the cover of *Time* magazine means something in American culture." The covers often reflect and sometimes also shape Americans' self-image. Accompanying each image are several questions that encourage reflection on American myths and values as a means of generating thoughtful discussion, research, and writing in class. While these images and questions are especially relevant to readings in **Chapter 7, American Cultural Myths**, they may also be useful in helping students respond to selections in other chapters. Additionally, the study questions suggest approaches to these messages that can be applied to others throughout the book.

The first image, of **Hollywood Dreams**, is a portrait of **Marilyn Monroe** (1926–1962), featured on a *Time* cover in 1956, about midway through Monroe's brief Hollywood career. As this is the first of two *Time* covers featuring Monroe, students might go to *Time*'s Web site at <www.time.com/time/magazine/archives> and look up the second image

(July 16, 1963) for comparison. The later cover, published on the occasion of Norman Mailer's 1963 study of Monroe, presents a very different image, with her hair bleached platinum and falling over one eye, her shoulders bare, and her hands atop a superimposed image of Mailer's head as if she were tousling his hair. This later image may accord more closely with some students' images of the star (**Question 1**), and comparing it to that of the earlier cover may help them consider ways in which films, magazines, and other media convey notions of gender and sexuality (**Question 3**). More broadly, students may discuss and write about the ways in which Hollywood films construct or portray American cultural myths (**Question 2**). In doing so, they might consider the images of **Rugged Individualism: John Wayne** and **Technology as Progress: Secrets of the Matrix** along with this one of Monroe.

The **Land of Equality** image of **Martin Luther King Jr.** (1929–1968) is also just one *Time* cover (February 18, 1957) featuring him as its subject. Another presents King as "Man of the Year" (January 3, 1964), and a third features a sketch of King (March 19, 1965). As with Monroe's image, the earlier image of King encourages thought about how this influential figure was portrayed and viewed earlier in his career, while the later covers offer images that students could compare or contrast with the earlier one. In the 1957 cover, King's image appears amid others that create a context for considering his role in events occurring at the time; these images, of African American children boarding a school bus and a robed African American man at a bar or pulpit, may also suggest different ways in which the United States may be understood as living up to—or falling short of—its ideal as the "land of equality" (**Question 1**). In considering the use of color in this image (**Question 2**), students should think about not only skin color, but also the use of grays to create the effect of a black-and-white photo for part of the image and the use of full color for other parts. How does the relative vividness of these different images influence the messages conveyed by the magazine cover? To help students reflect on and discuss positive and negative images of equality (**Question 3**), you might refer them to some of the readings in the book. Selections in **Chapter 7, American Cultural Myths**, by Frederick Douglass (p. 522) and Ward Churchill (p. 536) as well as those in **Chapter 6, Identities**, by Sojourner Truth (p. 380) and Maxine Hong Kingston (p. 393), challenge the image of the United States as a land of equality; other selections, such as the Declaration of Independence (p. 517), support the image. Students might also study this portrait of King alongside his "Letter from Birmingham Jail" (p. 163) in **Chapter 4, Moralities**. How does *Time*'s cover image of King compare to the persona that emerges in his writing?

The image of **Man on the Moon** (July 25, 1969) offers a chance for students to explore the myth of **American Frontiers**. This cover is one of many that *Time* has devoted to space exploration, which students might research for comparison. A particularly interesting image that may help students consider how this 1969 cover may have been perceived by people in other countries or cultures at that time (**Question 3**) is one that appeared just six months earlier. On this cover, two astronauts in different uniforms, one emblazoned with a red star, the other with a U.S. flag, run through the air toward the moon, above the caption "Race for the Moon" (December 6, 1968). Competition may thus be among the values represented by the 1969 cover (**Question 2**); others might be patriotism or courage. The image can also be read as a reflection of the **Technology as Progress** myth discussed hereafter. As students propose values they find portrayed in the image, they should be encouraged to think about what those values entail: for example, competition against whom, courage in the face of what dangers, patriotism as exemplified in what ways? **Question 1** asks students to come up with a list of films or songs that conjure images of American frontier-seeking. Westerns may be among the films that come to mind, especially since the next image is one of John Wayne.

The myth of **Rugged Individualism** is closely related to the myth of American frontiers, because the rugged individual embodies much of the pioneer character presumed necessary to successfully explore and tame wild, unknown frontiers. In this cover image (August 8, 1969), **John Wayne** (1907–1979) is depicted, appropriately enough, in a statue of his iconic character from the movie *True Grit*, released that year. The sculpture itself—an artist's rendering of a film portrayal of a fictional character (*True Grit* was based on a novel)—suggests the embellished, mythical quality of this character. The size of the statue, extending beyond the bounds of the image's red-framed border, also suggests its larger-than-life quality (**Questions 1** and **3**). Comparing this cover to the "Race to the Moon" cover mentioned previously provides one approach to considering how this mythic aspect of American character might be viewed in other countries (**Question 2**). In thinking about how people of different cultures may respond to this image of the mythical American cowboy, students might consult the essays by Paula Gunn Allen (p. 460) and Ward Churchill (p. 536), which present Native American perspectives on the history of European conquest in North America. How do these essays challenge the idea of the cowboy as an icon of the rugged individualism prized by many Americans? Could Native Americans, so often portrayed as the savage villains in Westerns, also be seen as rugged individuals in the American tradition? Why, or why not?

Rebels, portrayed in *Time*'s **Protest!** cover (May 18, 1970), are an integral part of the American mythos, as the country itself was founded in rebellion. For discussion of this seminal connection between the country's founding and the myth of the rebel, you might refer students to the Declaration of Independence (p. 517). The cover image presented here may evoke more recent images of student protests (**Question 1**). By doing some research on student antiwar protests of the 1970s (**Question 2**), students in your class may come up with some common themes or topics that may suggest the appeal of protest or rebellion to youth of different eras. Why were youth so prominent and influential in the Vietnam War protests and in more recent protests against the World Trade Organization? How do these protests compare to those associated with leaders such as Martin Luther King Jr., discussed previously, or Malcolm X? In comparing and contrasting the role of the rebel and the protester (**Question 3**), students might consult not only the Declaration of Independence but also some later documents patterned after it, such as the 1848 Seneca Falls Declaration of Women's Rights and the 1962 Port Huron Statement of the Students for a Democratic Society. Which of these documents represent *protest*, and which *rebellion*? Do some represent both? The students' answers will depend on how they define the terms—to include the connotations they impart to the terms. *Protester* may be more readily applied to advocates of even those causes we don't necessarily support, while *rebel* may imply a certain amount of admiration, perhaps accruing from the mythical status of the rebel in American culture. You may wish to discuss these possibilities with your class.

Lady Liberty represents the American value of liberty, as suggested by the welcoming words of Emma Lazarus's poem (p. 622), inscribed at the base of the statue, which depict the United States as a refuge for the oppressed. In researching the timing of *Time*'s cover (July 14, 1986), **Hail Liberty** (**Question 1**), students may discover that the Statue of Liberty, a gift the French originally planned to complete in time for the U.S. centennial in 1876, was not erected until ten years later. Constructed in France and finished in 1884, the statue arrived in the United States in June 1885. The pedestal, built in the United States, was ready in April 1886. The statue, once reassembled and placed on the pedestal, was dedicated on October 28, 1886, a date that corresponds neither to Independence Day (July 4) nor to Bastille Day (July 14). In listing other symbols of liberty (**Question 2**), students may find that this ideal is connected with other American values and myths, such as equality, discussed previously in the context of **Martin Luther King Jr.**, or opportunity, discussed in the questions following Emma Lazarus's poem. What do fireworks contribute to this symbol of American liberty (**Question 3**)? Fireworks, a staple of Independence Day celebrations, may allude to the Revolutionary War by which the country gained its independence. Barbara Kingsolver (p. 604) offers a thoughtful critique of the use of such violent imagery to evoke feelings of patriotism. You might refer students to her essay as they contemplate the images commonly associated with liberty and other American ideals.

If Lady Liberty welcomes "your tired, your poor . . ." to this country, it is in part because the United States, eschewing the tradition of royal bloodlines, established itself as the land of opportunity, where the **Rags to Riches** myth continues to offer a strong message of hope to many. Rags-to-riches stories, or those in which the "little guy makes good," are ubiquitous in American popular culture, in many variations (**Question 2**). This image of **Napster's Shawn Fanning** can be viewed as presenting a real-life version of the myth. In discussing how this cover presents Fanning as the "little guy" (**Question 1**), you might ask students to think about what it would be like to have one of their classmates featured on the cover of *Time* (October 2, 2000). Fanning was a first-year student at Northeastern University in Boston when he devised the Napster software. In addition to *Time*'s cover image of Fanning, students might look up some articles on him to find out whether they are consistent with the "little guy makes good" myth. To what extent do the articles focus on Fanning's age, background, and other features that seem to emphasize disadvantages he overcame to achieve success? The fact that Fanning dropped out of college to pursue the Napster project opens the possibility of addressing some of the selections in **Chapter 3, Education**, in discussions or writing assignments on this image and the myth it represents. With some research into Fanning's achievement and the legal controversy over Napster, students can begin to consider some of the ethical issues Fanning's success story may raise (**Question 3**). How often does the little guy make good at someone else's expense? Is the suggestion that someone else may suffer while another thrives necessarily part of this American myth, or is this kind of trade-off circumstantial? Students should refer back to the examples they identified in response to **Question 1** as they consider the ethical implications of this American myth. They might also consult Stephen L. Carter's "The Rules about the Rules" (p. 179) to discuss whether Fanning's invention or other instances of the "little guy makes good" myth meet Carter's definition of integrity.

Time's **Secrets of the New Matrix** cover (May 12, 2003) suggests the American myth of **Technology as Progress** in at least a couple of ways: the plot of *The Matrix* films addresses the myth of technology as progress, while the highly praised technology behind the film's special effects embodies this notion. The films challenge Americans' faith in technological progress by placing characters in conflict with technology as they seek ever more sophisticated knowledge in an effort to outsmart what amounts to an elaborate computer game (**Question 1**). Other myths suggested in this cover image (**Question 3**) might include the American frontier or the rugged individual, discussed previously. You might use this cover image and perhaps a video clip or two from the movies to open discussion of some of the issues addressed in **Chapter 5, Science and Technology**, as well as in **Chapter 7, American Cultural Myths**. Some films that deal with the myth of technological progress, presenting Americans' complex attitude toward science and technology (**Question 2**), include *2001: A Space Odyssey*, *A Clockwork Orange*, the *Star Trek* films and television series, the *Star Wars* films, the *Alien* films, *Blade Runner*, the *Terminator* films, and the *X-Men*. While all of these examples challenge the promises of technology to some extent, these and other science fiction films present a range of attitudes through their use—or avoidance—of humor. Students interested in pursuing the American love-hate relationship with technology and scientific innovation could come up with some interesting research projects by investigating ways in which technology as progress has been addressed in films or other media across different decades.

NEIL POSTMAN The Great Symbol Drain (p. 545)

Neil Postman argues that the "trivialization of significant cultural symbols" makes those images impotent, and that this "drain" has already happened to our most important cultural and religious symbols because of a deification of technology and an abuse of those symbols through overuse. **Question 1** asks students to list examples of the commercial misuse of symbols some consider sacred and to analyze their own reactions to such commercial practices. This question provides a specific means of gauging student reactions to Postman's argument and can be used to start a discussion of students' reactions to the selection as a whole. As students take their own positions on the issues Postman brings up, you might also ask them to consider how their positions compare with those taken by the editors in the Afterwords.

Like Postman, J.R. views faith in technology as "ultimately an empty narrative, vacuous, and morally bankrupt." J.R. refers to Postman as a prophet and suggests that "we're now living in the dark shadows of his prophecy," but J.R. also offers a bit of hope for some new story to come and the possibility of some other prophet to point the way. A.L. is more hopeful in her Afterword; instead of looking for a prophet, she holds out "some faith in our ability to resist these commercial images, to read them critically, and to analyze the motives that lie behind their use." Her faith rests more in education than in individual "prophets." And H.R. takes a middle ground, finding Postman's argument "too pessimistic," yet agreeing with him that educators cannot completely solve the problem of "technopoly." H.R. believes that certain symbols, despite overuse, "are still held sacred by many people," including herself. **Question 2** gives students the opportunity to test Postman's claim that words and symbols lose their power through overuse by conducting their own campus survey. In addition to other powerful symbols, they might include mascots, logos, and emblems in this survey. Which symbols, if any, retain—or even increase—their power no matter how often they're used?

According to Postman, the power of symbols comes from the ways in which they help structure narratives or stories that give meaning to a group of people. Postman suggests some symbols (the Constitution and the Statue of Liberty) that are part of America's shared narrative, and **Question 6** invites students to discuss other symbols they think should also be a part of the narrative. They might review the Declaration of Independence (p. 517) or look ahead to Emma Lazarus's poem (p. 622) to consider how the myths represented by these texts have withstood the test of time. In considering whether *Frankenstein* (p. 276) may be the great narrative for technopoly (**Question 4**), students might also ponder whether that text, by British author Mary Shelley, has become by now an American myth, with its many representations in American popular culture. Postman claims that "advertising is a symptom of a world-view that sees tradition as an obstacle to its claims." And in his argument it's the decline of tradition that causes the devaluation of symbols, which is followed by a loss of important narratives. Do students agree with the cause-effect argument Postman puts forward? Do they recognize differing relationships among narrative, myth, and symbol?

MARGARET ATWOOD Letter to America (p. 565)

In "A Letter to America," Margaret Atwood casts a critical eye toward her American neighbors from across the border in Canada. In fact, her tone in this essay might be described as that of a friendly but concerned neighbor (**Questions 2** and **3**). Drawing many allusions to American culture, she displays a fond familiarity with the narratives and symbols that represent American values (**Question 1**). Which of these narratives might be considered mythical? Whether she alludes to myth or tradition (**Question 7**)—or something else—Atwood's allusions use familiar cultural icons to steer America back to an ethical course from which she claims the country has strayed. Are there other allusions she could have made? As students consider how Atwood's argument could be revised to include other cultural references, they might consult the Declaration of Independence or other texts in this chapter (**Question 4**).

In trying to hold the United States responsible to its purported values, Atwood's essay resembles the selections by Frederick Douglass (p. 522), Ward Churchill (p. 536), and Abelardo Delgado (p. 625), which students may review for comparison in assessing the validity of Atwood's criticisms (**Question 5**). After composing letters in response to Atwood's claims (**Question 6**), students will have an opportunity to reconsider the limitations Atwood faced with this genre (**Question 2**), by reflecting on their own writing experience.

PHILIPPE LEGRAIN Cultural Globalization Is Not Americanization (p. 570)

As the title of his essay suggests, Philippe Legrain argues against the common complaint that globalization is synonymous with a commercial and cultural Americanization, a "Coca-colonization" of the world (paragraph 8). On the contrary, he claims, "American cultural products are not uniquely dominant" (paragraph 22), and foreign cultures exert considerable influence on Americans. His view of globalization is optimistic, as seen in his thesis: "Globalization not only increases individual freedom, but also revitalizes cultures and cultural artifacts through foreign influences, technologies, and markets" (paragraph 10). Throughout the essay, Legrain does acknowledge some concerns about globalization and the U.S. role in this process, which **Question 1** encourages students to search out and examine. In most cases, he dispenses with these counterarguments fairly quickly (for example, the case of cinema, paragraphs 23–25), and students may find that he overlooks or underestimates some problems. **Question 2** draws attention to Legrain's claim that common attitudes toward diversity and globalization are contradictory, a position he argues in paragraphs 31–38. His assertion that "cultural pessimists are typically not attached to diversity per se but to designated manifestations of diversity, determined by their preferences" (paragraph 36) is especially provocative and ripe for discussion. You may want to direct students to readings in this chapter or Chapter 6 to find examples that would support or refute Legrain's claims.

Legrain's views are somewhat similar to those expressed by Amitai Etzioni (p. 469) and David Brooks (p. 581), who also downplay the significance of cultural differences (**Question 3**). It may be useful for students to refer to two essays as they contemplate the existence of a national identity (**Question 6**). Legrain's comments on the spread of technology also invite comparison to Neil Postman's "The Great Symbol Drain" (p. 545) (**Question 4**). Legrain's observation that "many archetypal 'American' products are not as all-American as they seem" (paragraph 13) may inspire curiosity about the origins of other cultural features presumed to be quintessentially American (**Question 5**). Students can explore these mythical aspects of American culture through research and writing.

DAVID BROOKS One Nation, Slightly Divisible (p. 581)

David Brooks uses a map of the 2000 presidential election results to investigate the differences between the states shown in blue, signaling that their electoral votes went to Al Gore, and those shown in red, depicting their support of George W. Bush. The premise alone for such a study is intriguing: the voting differences among states might signify some meaningful regional differences among the general populations of those states, and among Americans as a whole. On one hand, this premise seems highly questionable; less than half of those eligible to vote typically do so, and the electoral vote is a generalization based on these low returns. So any messages gleaned from the redness or the blueness of a state would seem diluted at best. On the other hand, Brooks's premise seems to get at something so obvious as to hardly warrant further study: country folk and city folk are different. What else is new? Perhaps this very conundrum is one of the reasons that Brooks's essay seems intriguing. In any case, he wastes little time pondering the validity of his question. Instead he follows his hunch that Red America is somehow different from Blue America, where he lives, and he begins gathering evidence for his portraits of each. Students should consider Brooks's self-identification as a city person as they look for clues about the audience he envisions (**Question 1**) and begin to evaluate his characterizations of Red and Blue America (**Question 2**). Their trust in Brooks as a competent observer and interpreter of American culture may be an important factor in their response to his conclusions (**Question 3**).

Completing his study after the terrorist attacks of September 11, 2001, Brooks concludes that while the election map may suggest a divided nation, Americans are united by traditional values of freedom, opportunity, and equality (paragraph 90). **Questions 4** and **5** give students different ways of interrogating that claim. While Brooks's title alludes to the Pledge of Allegiance, students can refer to another definitive American document, the Declaration of Independence, to consider whether Brooks has identified any significant differences between the country's founding principles and the values that seem to unite Americans today (**Question 4**). Ward Churchill's essay (p. 536) provides another perspective on the extent of national unity (**Question 5**). Though Churchill seriously challenges America's commitment to its stated values, he does not question the values themselves. You might ask students to think about whether a country's failure to act on its values diminishes their unifying power.

Question 6 invites students to write an essay that explores an apparent cultural divide that is close to them, perhaps one between schools or neighborhoods. **Question 7** provides an opportunity for them to reflect on whether they identify with certain aspects of life in Red or Blue America described in Brooks's essay. Either of these topics could serve as the basis for an insightful personal essay, perhaps for publication as a guest column or op-ed.

BARBARA KINGSOLVER And Our Flag Was Still There (p. 604)

David Brooks's conclusions about the United States were based in part on his observations of the country's reactions to the September 11, 2001, attacks on the World Trade Center and the Pentagon. Barbara Kingsolver concentrates on the patriotism that emerged after those attacks and questions why patriotism is so often associated with violent solutions to conflicts, with the will to wage war. Defending her right to question the need for war—indeed to thoughtfully challenge any decisions the nation's leaders may make—Kingsolver argues that real patriotism lies in "lov[ing] the country enough to do the hard work of living up to its highest ideals" (paragraph 18). In her essay, Kingsolver draws upon an engaging combination of personal experience and more general observations based on knowledge of national and world affairs. After summarizing Kingsolver's argument and its supporting claims (**Question 1**), students should examine further the diverse anecdotes and illustrations she uses as evidence (**Question 2**). As a class, they can research some of the prominent dissidents she names and discuss whether they share her admiration for these individuals (**Question 3**).

Kingsolver notes that were it not for another group of dissidents—women's rights activists Ida B. Wells, Lucy Stone, Susan B. Anthony, and their compatriots—she would not be a "full citizen." She adds a point that resonates with Frederick Douglass's speech (p. 522): When the Declaration of Independence was written, she and other women, along with any non-property-owning and nonwhite people, "would have been guaranteed . . . the same voting rights as a horse" (paragraph 19). In fact her argument can be compared to Douglass's as a whole, because both writers seek to be allowed full patriotic participation. **Question 4** asks students to discuss the similarities and differences in the two writers' arguments.

Similarly, Kingsolver's argument for revising some of the symbolism associated with the American flag can be productively compared to Neil Postman's argument about the diluted meaning of such symbols (**Question 5**).

Questions 6 and **7** invite students to explore their own thoughts on *patriotism* by reflecting on the meaning of the word itself or by composing an essay that takes a well-known line from a patriotic text as its title. They may want to share their writing in class or in a broader public forum.

KATE SHINDLE Miss America: More Than a Beauty Queen? (p. 613)

Kate Shindle challenges the Miss America Organization to make a more concerted effort to represent publicly the values it supports through scholarships and contests that reward and encourage young women's intelligence, political vision, and leadership. As a former Miss America, Shindle has a certain degree of credibility on this topic. In analyzing the effectiveness of her argument (**Question 1**), students might consider how Shindle's experience contributes to the essay's persuasiveness. Students may approach the essay with different preconceptions about the Miss America pageant and its contestants, and Shindle's essay may offer some of them new insights on the topic (**Question 2**). A.L. suggests in her headnote that the essay challenges myths of American womanhood as well, a point that students are invited to debate among classmates (**Question 3**) and to explore through research (**Question 6**).

In identifying values that Shindle associates with the Miss America pageant, students may turn once again to the Declaration of Independence for reference, or to other texts in this chapter to see how Shindle may be drawing from common American ideals (**Question 4**). Like several of the selections in this chapter, this one criticizes some Americans (in this case, Miss America organizers) for not living up to certain ideals. Students might compare Shindle's approach with that of other critics in this chapter, including Frederick Douglass (p. 522), Ward Churchill (p. 536), Margaret Atwood (p. 565), or—as suggested in **Question 5**—Edward Abbey (p. 619).

Shindle's essay, originally published as a "My Turn" column in *Newsweek*, can serve as a model for students who may wish to pursue this venue for their own work (**Question 8**). An essay on myths of American womanhood (**Question 6**), or on the absence of a men's equivalent to the Miss America pageant (**Question 7**), could be potential "My Turn" topics, if the writer had a personal perspective or experience to offer.

EDWARD ABBEY *From* Desert Solitaire (p. 619)

In this reflection, Edward Abbey presents what he undoubtedly wished he could say to some of the visitors he encountered during his time as a ranger at Arches National Park in Utah. Though published in 1968, this passage captures sentiments that remain relevant today, as suggested by the more recent selection from the *Onion* in Chapter 5 (p. 368). As J.R. remarks in his headnote to Abbey's selection, the "sense of wilderness," long a strong mythic element of American culture, is lost to those who "don't know how to experience it."

Abbey begins by comparing Labor Day tourists to herds of buffalo, and his commentary on his subjects degenerates from there, winding up to a tirade, replete with obscenities, addressed directly to them. The passage gives the impression that Abbey's emotions finally get the better of him, after a season of dealing with visitors unwilling to leave their cars to experience even a small part of the beauty the park has to offer. It may be hard to separate his message from the style in which he delivers it, but **Question 1** asks students to try to do so as they consider how Abbey's tone affects his message. Students may have very different reactions to Abbey's language, and so their responses to **Questions 2** and **3** may vary quite a bit. Responses to the questions can help the class consider how this piece of writing might affect different audiences—and what kinds of risks Abbey takes in his stylistic approach. **Question 5** invites students to try expressing anger in a short piece of creative writing, using Abbey's excerpt and Abelardo Delgado's "Stupid America" (p. 625) as examples.

The frustration expressed in this selection may be related to American myths that Abbey sees thwarted or embodied in the tourists' behavior. For example, the chapter introduction describes the myths of the "American frontier" and of "the American as a rugged individual" (p. 515), neither of which the tourists seem to honor. The myth of "America as the land of opportunity" (p. 515) may be misconstrued as a myth of America as a land of incessant, easy opportunities—with national parks among a list of sights to be seen, or experiences to be had, quickly and effortlessly. In pondering how this passage may reflect frustrations and misconceptions like these (**Question 4**), students might also gain some ideas for writing an essay on their own experiences with frustration (**Question 6**). Those moved to write about how nature may best be preserved and experienced could do some research into the challenges of creating and maintaining spaces like the national park Abbey writes about here (**Question 7**).

EMMA LAZARUS The New Colossus (p. 622)

Beyond the lines of this poem that have been immortalized on the Statue of Liberty, the rest may be unfamiliar to many students. Yet it is powerfully evocative of America as a land of opportunity, an enduring cultural myth. **Question 1** draws students' attention to A.L.'s headnote to the poem, asking them to consider the tensions she finds in its images. Some examples to consider include the "imprisoned lightning" of the torch (line 5), the "mild eyes" that "command" (line 7), the "silent lips" through which the statue "cries" an exclamation (lines 9–10).

Students should think further about the poem's context, including the circumstances under which Lazarus composed the poem (**Question 2**). How does the context inform their reading of the poem? Research into Lazarus's life and writings and the Statue of Liberty's origins can provide material for an intriguing essay exploring the poem's meaning in American culture. Beyond its original context, Lazarus's poem, like any piece of writing, can take on new meanings when read in other times and places. How might today's audiences impart new and different meanings to the words she wrote so long ago? Students might reflect on this question in their reading journals or in essays to share with the class (**Question 4**). Finally, some selections in this chapter challenge the myth presented in this poem: America is the land of opportunity, welcoming all with open arms. **Question 5** invites students to examine and respond to those critiques in an essay written in the form of a letter to Lazarus.

ABELARDO DELGADO Stupid America (p. 625)

In this poem, Abelardo Delgado criticizes a cultural stereotype, which A.L. suggests in her headnote is also part of an American cultural mythos. You might invite several students to read this poem aloud in class, and to discuss how the different readers choose to interpret the poem in their oral presentations of it. In discussing its style on the printed page (**Questions 1** and **2**), students might address how the poet's choices of language and punctuation influenced their oral readings.

For further study of issues raised in the poem (**Question 3**), you might suggest that students review some of the selections on racial and ethnic identity in chapter 6. Examples include those by Zora Neale Hurston (p. 416), Bich Minh Nguyen (p. 443), Paula Gunn Allen (p. 460), or Michael Nava (p. 647). What do these readings suggest about the idea of a common American culture? What do they suggest about the power of American myths? **Questions 5** and **6** suggest ways of studying and responding to the argument Delgado advances with this poem.

Texts in Context: Sequenced Writing Assignments about American Cultural Myths

Assignment 1

Write up a description of your nomination for "The Most Powerful (or Memorable) Presentation of an American Myth." Choose a symbol, image, movie, song, story, poem, advertisement, or other representation of the myth. In a few paragraphs, explain why your nominee deserves "most powerful (or memorable)" status. Be prepared to argue for your nomination in class.

Assignment 2

A number of writers in this chapter deal explicitly or implicitly with the relationship between myth and reality. Reread the selections by two of the following authors: Frederick Douglass, Ward Churchill, Margaret Atwood, Barbara Kingsolver, and Abelardo Delgado. As you read, take notes on what each author sees as the reality behind the myth. Then write a statement that compares and contrasts the two authors' views on that relationship. Bring your statement to class, and working in a small group, discuss the different relationships between American myth and reality that the statements reveal.

Assignment 3

With your notes from Assignment 2 in mind, work with several classmates to study the images presented in this chapter. Examine each image for clues about its purpose and its relationship to American cultural myth. What does the image intend for you, the viewer, to believe or value? Make a list of these beliefs or values as part of your analysis, and bring it to your next group meeting. Together, write a description of your analysis entitled "American Myth in Images: Portrayals of Belief and Disbelief." Bring the description to class, and be prepared to defend your views as a group.

Assignment 4

What does your group's list and description (in Assignment 3) suggest about American society's views on the value and power of the country's cultural myths? What kinds of people, characters, events, or objects are represented positively? Negatively? Not at all? Make notes in response to these questions. On the basis of your notes and the list you drew up for Assignment 3, answer this question: how does the myth presented by the images compare with your own sense of the persuasive power of myth? Write a brief response, and bring it to class.

Assignment 5

Ask six to eight people to nominate their choice for "The Most Powerful (or Memorable) Presentation of an American Myth" and to give one or two reasons for their choice. As much as possible, try to survey people of different ages, cultures, backgrounds, personalities, and so on. Bring your findings to class, and list them on the chalkboard. Then, working in a group, spend 15 to 20 minutes discussing what may account for the differences of opinion among the respondents. Finally, draw up a group report of your findings and discussion to present to the class.

Assignment 6

Reread the description you wrote for Assignment 1 in light of the work you have since completed in Assignments 2–5. Revise or defend your nomination for "The Most Powerful (or Memorable) Presentation of an American Myth." Then write a memo to your instructor and classmates reflecting on what you have learned about your own values and preferences by examining the mythical image you chose. Consider what in your life influenced you to choose this particular representation of the myth.

Part Four How We Live

8 ▪ At Home: The Places I Come From (p. 631)

The readings in Chapter 8 invite students to join a conversation about home—an issue they have experience with but may never have analyzed in terms of what a home is or what it should be. Although this chapter's overt focus on personal experience makes it somewhat different from the other chapters in this book, the readings illustrate, as do many of the readings in other chapters, how personal experience is related to political position. The focus on the personal in this chapter also suggests in concrete ways how much is at stake in government and public debates on such issues as welfare reform, gay parenting, teenage pregnancy, abortion rights, and the nuclear family.

As students enter the conversation about home and family in this chapter, you might encourage them to think about the issues from several perspectives—from their own personal experience as well as from the perspective of American culture and values. Although some students will welcome the opportunity to write about their own family and home experiences, others will be reluctant to reveal such personal information. Helping students to see that notions of home and family are public as well as personal will allow them to engage with the readings in this chapter more comfortably.

Some of the questions raised by the selections in this chapter include the following:

- What constitutes a typical American home, and how has the typical home changed along with American culture? (Whitehead, Coontz, Frawley, Sedaris)
- How do the issues of race, gender, and social class affect one's home life? (Suskind, Walker, Nava, Williams, Kincaid)
- To what extent does the natural environment contribute to one's sense of home? (Walker, Williams, Kincaid, Madden)
- In what ways does the experience of loss affect one's relationship to and understanding of home? (Walker, Williams, Whitehead, Coontz, Madden)

RON SUSKIND A Hope in the Unseen (p. 634)

Ron Suskind's piece contains two juxtaposed narratives. In the first narrative, Suskind describes Cedric at home in Washington, D.C., where he shares a close relationship with his mother and where gunshots "are part of the background score." In the other narrative, Suskind describes Cedric at a college dorm with roommate Rob, who is unlike Cedric in nearly every way. While many of the selections in **Chapter 8, At Home**, are narratives, others are personal essays written from a first-person perspective. This selection, written in the third person, differs in that the narrator (Suskind) seems to know what is going on in both Cedric's and Rob's minds. This piece occupies a space between journalism and fiction. In class discussion, it might be illuminating to discuss the conventions of "literary" or "new" journalism and how students read and interpret this form. Do they question how

Suskind knows what he reveals, or do they take for granted that his interpretations and renderings are correct?

Several study questions point to issues or moments in Suskind's text and ask students to make connections with their own experiences. Some of these questions (such as **Question 2**, which asks students to consider the noises at the place they currently think of as home, and **Question 3**, which asks them to evaluate the role that television plays in their home life) will be relevant to all students. However, other questions (such as **Question 5**) deal with roommates, which may not apply to all students, since some may live alone and may never have shared a room. But most students will have lived in close spaces with others, and those who now live alone can think back to when they lived in close proximity with family or others in order to draw from personal experience. For those who do live in a dorm (or who have chosen not to live there for specific reasons), **Question 7** will be particularly interesting. When students think of "home," do they ever think of a dorm room? In what ways might a dorm room provide a sense of home that other places cannot?

In class, you could spend some time having students list elements that represent home for them (such as geography, a childhood house, a certain level of comfort, and family). **Questions 4** and **8** prompt students to think specifically about the ways in which family can represent home and influence one's ambitions and hopes. As you discuss this initial reading as a class, you might wish to ask students to write down provisional definitions of *home*, which they can revise as they read and discuss the other selections in this chapter.

ALICE WALKER The Place Where I Was Born (p. 642)

In this selection, Alice Walker employs both poetry and prose to demonstrate feelings of loss, longing, and love. A central figure in the piece is a tree with "tall, old-growth pine nobility," one that functions as a metaphor for Walker's heart, symbolizing not only the destruction of nature but also the loss of her childhood. **Question 1** points to the importance of the tree and asks students to consider what in the natural world they most love. Since intimacy with the natural world is a recurring theme in much of Walker's work, you might ask students to keep this in mind as they research Walker's life and work for **Question 6**. Before starting more in-depth research, students should reread A.L.'s introduction to Walker's piece (**Question 3**), which emphasizes Walker's education and work for civil rights.

Referring to the landscape of her birth in the first stanza, Walker writes, ". . . to save myself I pretended it was *you* / who died." Two couplets later, she says, ". . . now I can confess how I have lied." **Question 2** points to this passage, asking students to identify the lie Walker says she has told. Because of her separation from the landscape of her birth, Walker sees herself as a "displaced person." **Question 5** encourages students to consider what other writers or people in this chapter might be displaced. Surely the people in the nursing home Jill Frawley describes would be displaced. Could Cedric, in Suskind's narrative, also be described as displaced? What about the speaker in Barbara Smith's piece? In what ways might these people's displacement be similar or different?

Like Walker, Terry Tempest Williams feels a strong connection to the landscape of her birth—the deserts of Utah. And she, too, writes of loss. What descriptions of home are present in Suskind's narrative? **Question 4** asks students to make connections between the three pieces and then to write about which description of home is most compelling to them. The description students choose may be the one that reflects their own feelings about home—feelings of longing, peace, anger, ambivalence. These feelings might also be reflected in their response to **Question 7**, an essay or a poem entitled "The Place Where I Was Born."

MICHAEL NAVA Gardenland, Sacramento, California (p. 647)

As A.L. suggests in her headnote, Michael Nava's essay calls to mind the familiar saying, "Home is where the heart is." Nava uses detailed visual imagery to depict his home—including the neighborhood and its immediate environs, the houses of his parents and grandparents—but he also describes a home within this physical place and within himself. He describes a private place he conjured through books as a child, and it is this idea of home as a sheltering, nurturing space that remained a haven to him once he moved away from Gardenland. **Questions 1** and **2** ask students to examine these physical, mental, and emotional images of home and to contemplate their effects. **Questions 5** and **6** invite students to write reflective essays on home inspired by Nava's writing style, especially his use of description, as well as his ideas.

In sharing his experience of discovering the need to escape home, which he accomplished first figuratively and later literally, Nava writes lovingly of the home he left, even as he conveys his growing unease there. His complex relationship with a home he felt the need to escape is reminiscent to the situation Alice Walker describes in "The Place Where I Was Born" (p. 642). Comparing the two authors' reflections on home, students may gain insight into their relationships with homes they have left—in some cases perhaps recently, and for the first time, to attend college (**Question 3**). Barbara Dafoe Whitehead's essay (p. 667) offers a different opportunity for comparison, as Nava describes relationships between two couples—his parents and grandparents—that might be examined in terms of Dafoe's characterization of a current "divorce culture" (**Question 4**). As students consider whether the question of divorce would have arisen in Nava's family, they can also discuss the extent to which Dafoe's observations about ethical obligations to self and others seem applicable to the home life depicted in Nava's essay.

TERRY TEMPEST WILLIAMS The Clan of One-Breasted Women (p. 655)

Terry Tempest Williams doesn't explicitly define *home*, but elements of her home—family and the Utah landscape—are central to her essay. Williams discusses loss—the loss of her mother, aunts, and grandmother to cancer and the destruction of the land she loves. A.L. ties these two losses together by invoking the metaphor "Mother Earth" to show how the destruction of our environment also affects mothers and others who people the earth (**Question 4**). Williams links these two losses to nuclear fallout from bomb testing in the 1950s and 1960s.

She admits that she can't prove that the women in her family developed cancer because of nuclear fallout, but she provides evidence to show the connections between the two. As A.L. writes in her Afterwords, "Williams is not writing a traditional academic 'argument,' in which she sets up building blocks of 'proof' to support her." Rather, she weaves stories together to evoke a response in readers. **Question 1** asks students to identify the strategies and evidence Williams uses to support her belief. This essay isn't only about loss; it is also life-affirming, with death and birth images juxtaposed in evocative ways (**Question 2**). Despite death and destruction, the essay ends on a hopeful note, with a group of women "stranded" in the desert, knowing they are home. **Question 7** invites students to think about some environmental issue that affects their own home; such an assignment should help students relate Williams's essay concretely to their own lives and concerns.

Questions 3 and **8** both deal with dreams—the dreams Williams includes in her essay and the dreams students have themselves. Williams includes two dreams in her piece—a recurring dream of a flash of light in the desert night, which her father explains as the bomb they saw one night when Williams was a child; and the dream of women who trespass on contaminated land, the way Williams and others do later in the piece. The dreams seem to affirm and authorize Williams's beliefs and actions, emphasizing the importance of intuition. While **Question 3** asks students to consider why Williams includes her dream in the essay—what purpose the dream serves—**Question 8** asks them to further explore the relationships between dreams and reality by considering their own dreams.

It could be argued that Williams's dreams help give her the courage to cross the line at the Nevada test site, an act of civil disobedience. **Question 9** asks students to explain their position on civil disobedience. If you discuss this question in class, you could have students think about others who have committed such acts—from Thoreau refusing to pay taxes to Rosa Parks refusing to give up her seat on a bus. You could list other acts of civil disobedience (like blocking the entrance to an abortion clinic or freeing animals in laboratories), asking students when, if ever, such acts are justified. Students could also discuss times when they have participated in acts of civil disobedience—and their reasons for doing so. Or, as **Question 6** asks, what are a citizen's responsibilities in the face of social and environmental problems?

BARBARA DAFOE WHITEHEAD The Making of a Divorce Culture (p. 667)

As J.R. suggests in his headnote, given the high rate of divorce among American families, many students are likely to be interested in Barbara Dafoe Whitehead's essay. They are also likely to have very strong opinions about it, and your class discussions can draw on the thinking students have already done about divorce and its causes and effects. Whitehead points to several ideas that she claims have helped to shape a divorce culture. One of these ideas is a shift away from "an ethic of obligation to others and toward an obligation to self." **Question 2** points to Whitehead's claim and asks students to analyze how compatible these two views of family are. **Question** 3 offers an opportunity to examine her argument further by comparing her notions of parental commitment to those presented by Ron Suskind (p. 634) and David Sedaris (p. 697) in their characterizations of parents. **Question 4** points students to selection from **Chapter 4, Moralities**: Stephen L. Carter's "The Rules about the Rules," asking them to consider whether a divorce can ever fit Carter's three criteria for acting with integrity. What is the relationship in students' minds among morality, obligations to self and others, and divorce? Can a divorce be in the best interest of all parties involved? What is at stake when children are involved?

In contrast to those who believe that divorce, in making one or both adults happier, can also make children happier, Whitehead argues that divorce does hurt children—economically and otherwise. **Question 5** prompts students to research this issue, using library materials, personal experiences, and interviews to support their position. This research can be linked to **Question 6**, which encourages students to consider policies designed to make divorce less devastating and divorced families more stable. In their research, students might consult Stephanie Coontz's "The Way We Wish We Were," which argues that traditional family life was anything but ideal (for parents or children) even before divorce became so common. Like Coontz, Whitehead isn't interested in calling for a return to an earlier era of American family life, so while their arguments may seem very different, the two authors also share common ground. What common ground can students find, despite differing views on and experiences with divorce?

STEPHANIE COONTZ The Way We Wish We Were (p. 676)

Stephanie Coontz claims that "visions of past family life exert a powerful emotional pull on most Americans." The problem, she asserts, is that these visions are not based on real families but on idealized television representations of family life, representations that **Question 5** asks students to analyze by undertaking their own research. Coontz claims that these visions evaporate on closer examination, and closer examination is what the study questions encourage. **Questions 1** and **2** ask students to focus their own examination on Coontz's text, specifically her use of statistics (**Question 1**) and evidence relating to her assumptions about family (**Question 2**). As students consider Coontz's use of statistics, they might need some guidance in how to read and evaluate statistics. For instance, they should be reminded that numbers in and of themselves are not an argument; instead, numbers are interpreted within the context of an argument. Could the statistics Coontz uses be interpreted in other ways? Another important consideration is sources—whether they are named at all and whether those sources that are named are reliable.

As students seek to articulate Coontz's assumptions about and definition of family, they should look not only for clear definitions but also at how her treatment of the subject matter reveals her assumptions. By showing both the positive and negative aspects of family systems from different time periods, she assumes that no one "model" of family is ideal. And in various ways students' own family experiences will likely match up with and differ from the paradigms Coontz offers (**Question 6**), showing that no one paradigm fits all families and that simplified generalizations are not particularly helpful. As Coontz argues, family life, both past and present, is diverse. While Coontz warns against defining "a typical American family," this sort of definition is just what **Question 7** calls for. However, this question doesn't simply ask for definition; it also asks for analysis, prompting students to work together and to question their own generalizations.

JILL FRAWLEY Inside the Home (p. 693)

Jill Frawley's exposé of the nursing home in which she worked should prove thought-provoking to students whether or not they know people living in nursing homes. In addition to asking students to summarize Frawley's position on the degree to which nursing homes are what they claim to be (**Question 1**), invite them to bring their own experiences with and feelings about nursing homes to bear on their responses to Frawley, as A.L. has done in her introduction (**Question 3**). In addition, students can work in groups to do research on nursing homes, perhaps even researching such homes in the community in an effort to determine whether Frawley's generalizations about the inhospitable and even harmful environments of nursing homes are accurate (**Question 7**).

Before answering **Question 4**—which asks students to look at a number of selections in this chapter and to write a definition of "home" that accounts for all of them—students may wish to respond to **Question 5** by writing a dialogue among Suskind, Frawley, and Kincaid about the definition and importance of home. Writing such a dialogue will help students see the complicated ways that people conceive of and relate to home. Is it likely that Cedric, from Suskind's narrative, would put his mother in a nursing home? And if so, under what circumstances?

In addition to complicating the idea of what constitutes "home" in America, Frawley's essay raises the interesting issue of a person's relationship to work and employer (**Question 6**). Certainly, some of the power of Frawley's description of the nursing home comes from the fact that she was an employee of that home, one charged with caring for patients but unable to do so because of the workload (something she ascribes to the greed of her employers). **Question 2** asks students to consider Frawley's attitude not only toward her employer but also toward the patients and herself—and where (and how) these attitudes are revealed in her essay.

DAVID SEDARIS Cyclops (p. 697)

David Sedaris's poignant and funny recollections of home life convey the power of parents' words as heard and interpreted, sometimes for years to follow, by their children. Other family members or even teachers can have similar influences on children (**Question 6**). Students may respond in different ways to this essay, dwelling more or less on its poignancy or its humor. **Question 1** asks them to attend to their emotions as they read the essay the first time and a second time. In considering Sedaris's embellishment of fact in this essay (**Question 2**), students might also consider how omission may contribute to the exaggerated effects he achieves. For instance, might additional detail in some of the anecdotes reduce the shock and humor of his father's messages? What if he had waited just a moment longer, describing an aspect of his father's appearance or character, for example, before delivering what is effectively the punch line of one of his father's admonitions? In humorous writing, as in joke-telling, timing is crucial, a concept well illustrated by Sedaris's writing. This discussion of humor and exaggeration may help students address the aspect of tone as well (**Question 3**).

Sedaris depicts his father as someone who took his parental responsibilities quite seriously—absurdly seriously at times, if Sedaris's account is to be believed. Students may gain some understanding of Sedaris's view of parenthood by comparing his depiction of parent-child relationships with those presented by Ron Suskind (p. 634) and Michael Nava (p. 647), as suggested in **Question 4**. How nostalgic does Sedaris seem to be for home? And how much does he seem to value a traditional home life? By considering these questions from the point of view offered by Stephanie Coontz in "The Way We Wish We Were" (p. 676), students may gain further insight into Sedaris's views of home life (**Question 5**).

Students may be inspired by Sedaris's writing to reflect on parents' or other adults' influence on their lives, taking a humorous or serious approach (**Question 6**). Students can conduct research into their pasts by asking other family members how they remember shared events. This research can form the basis of a brief memoir that follows Sedaris's example in challenging the reliability of memory as a source (**Question 7**).

JAMAICA KINCAID Sowers and Reapers: The Unquiet World of a Flower Bed (p. 705)

Jamaica Kincaid argues in this essay that "[t]he garden is not a place to lose your cares; the garden is not a place of rest and repose" (paragraph 18). Instead she suggests, offering several illustrations, that gardens are places that present opportunities for learning and contemplation about our responsibilities as human beings (**Question 1**). This alternative view of gardens can be inferred from Kincaid's allusions to the Garden of Eden in paragraphs 5 and 18 (**Question 3**). The argument in this essay unfolds inductively, offering only a broad thesis at the end, in the final paragraph. This thesis tells us only how Kincaid does not view gardens, though, not how she does view them. The specifics omitted from the thesis are revealed in the process of the essay, as Kincaid accumulates examples of gardens, offering description, narrative, and interpretation to express her vision of gardens (**Question 2**).

Kincaid acknowledges the common association of gardens and memorials, but her focus in this essay is on gardens that are part of people's homes, as she spends the most time discussing Thomas Jefferson's gardens and her own. Reading Ed Madden's "Family Cemetery, near Hickory Ridge, Arkansas" (p. 711) along with Kincaid's piece can encourage students to think about the personal relationships people honor with gardens and memorials (**Question 4**). They might look ahead to selections in Chapter 9 to consider further Kincaid's comments on the labor relationships entailed in the making of gardens (**Question 5**). Discussions of these ideas, combined with additional research, can provide material for students' explorations of gardens familiar to them (**Question 6**).

ED MADDEN Family Cemetery, near Hickory Ridge, Arkansas (p. 711)

Ed Madden's poem provides a fitting close to this chapter, not only because it is about the end of life and the ways in which the deaths of family members bring an end to family life as it once was, but also because it addresses the complicated connections within families that manage to endure. Both "Family Cemetery" and Terry Tempest Williams's "The Clan of One-Breasted Women" are about the loss of family, and students may want to compare these two pieces for what they say about both physical and emotional losses—and connections. Both pieces also share an attention to nature, and students might benefit from considering the ways in which our relationship to the natural world is like or unlike our relationships to one another. To what extent is the natural world our home? To what extent is our extended family our home? In what ways do students respond to the sensory images Madden includes in this poem (**Question 2**)?

Question 3 asks students to write about an important moment in their own experience of family. You might have them compare the subjects of their descriptions or poems and discuss the range of topics they chose. Are there specific moments that several students chose to write about? Could those moments be considered archetypal or universal family experiences? What kinds of differences emerge in their choice of topics, and how might they account for those differences? Based on this activity, and on the other reading and writing students have done for this chapter, would they say that families are generally alike or generally different?

Texts in Context: Sequenced Writing Assignments about Home

Assignment 1

The selections in this chapter offer widely different definitions and representations of "home"—from the nursing home in Jill Frawley's essay to the sense of home evoked in Ed Madden's poem. Brainstorm a list of things you associate with "home"—feelings, sights, smells, sounds, tastes, objects, and anything else that comes to mind. What picture of "home" emerges from your list? Does that picture match memories of your home or what you wish for in a home—or perhaps some of both? Using your notes and responses to these questions, draft a statement for what might become a class report on the concept of home. You might begin by thinking about how you would complete this sentence: "For me, home means ___________."

Assignment 2

Some demographic studies suggest that the traditional American family—defined as a married heterosexual couple, one of whom is primarily at home to care for the children—is already a thing of the past. What evidence can you find in this chapter's readings to support or refute this claim? What evidence can you offer from your own experience and that of people you know to support or refute it? Bring your responses to these questions to class. Then work in a small group to compare and contrast your responses, noting in particular any differences of opinion among the members of your group. Finally, based on your reading, responses, and group discussion, write a brief essay, story, scene, or poem entitled "What the Typical American Family Will Look Like in the Year 2075."

Assignment 3

Choose the one selection in this chapter that you find most irritating, problematic, or unsettling. Then reread that selection, this time trying to figure out where the writer's views on home and family may have come from. To help you answer this question, think for a while about where your views on home and family come from. In addition to the most obvious influences—your personal experience with one or several homes and families—what other influences can you detect? For example, what do your favorite TV shows, books, magazines, movies, and songs say about home and family? Do they convey the same picture of home and family that you have? Make extensive notes on what you find out from investigating one or more sources of influence on your ideas about home. Then go back and review the selection you chose for this assignment. What does your investigation into the sources of your ideas about home and family suggest about why you dislike the selection? What external forces might have influenced the selection writer's views on home and family? Finally, write a three- to four-page essay for your class entitled "Alternative Representations of Home and Family in __________."

Assignment 4

In class, work in a group of three students to create a dialogue in which three writers from this chapter exchange their ideas about "home." For example, the conversational exchange might involve Alice Walker, Stephanie Coontz, and David Sedaris; Barbara Dafoe Whitehead, Jill Frawley, or Ed Madden; or any other grouping of three writers represented in this chapter. The dialogue—of two to three pages in length—should reflect what the writers would probably say about "home" based on your reading of their selections. Be prepared to role-play the dialogue for the class.

Assignment 5

Based on your review of the readings in this chapter and on the work you did for Assignments 1–4, revise the statement you wrote for Assignment 1 on what home means to you. Include with your revised statement your reasons for thinking about home as you do and how your thinking has developed or changed since you first wrote the statement. Gather this material together as your contribution to the "Class Report on Contemporary Perspectives about 'Home' "—and consider asking your instructor to write the preface for the report.

9 ■ Work: As Poor Richard Says . . . (p. 717)

Since many students view a college education as a means to more satisfying or better paying work, this final chapter's focus on economic problems and opportunities is likely to be of great interest to them. Chapter 9 also interacts with the chapters on education, science, identity, and home by showing students how these factors can affect one's work life. Although a few selections emphasize the individual worker's role in achieving success through work (for example, Benjamin Franklin), most other selections focus on the social forces that shape working conditions and the economy. The chapter introductory questions ask students to consider how Americans feel about work and the economy, how workers should be treated, and how technology affects work. The study questions for each reading invite students to consider their own experiences with and feelings about work in relation to the selection author's viewpoint.

Some of the questions raised by the selections in this chapter include the following:

- What makes work valuable or meaningful? (hooks, Piercy, Gilb)
- Do proper training and good work habits necessarily lead to success? (Franklin, Krystal, Schlosser)
- To what extent do factors beyond one's control affect the work one can do? (Franklin, LeSueur, Barko, Pinker, hooks)
- What kinds of jobs can (or should) college students hold while in school? And afterward? (Tenner, Gilb, Schlosser)

BENJAMIN FRANKLIN The Way to Wealth (p. 720)

As J.R. observes in his headnote, "common sense and thrift never go out of style," and these two qualities—along with hard work, little rest, and no debt—provide, according to Benjamin Franklin, "The Way to Wealth." In the voice of Poor Richard, Franklin implies that anyone who lives by his maxims is certain to earn wealth. Some of the other writers represented in this chapter would probably find Poor Richard's maxims timely and true, while others would likely question the simplicity of some of his claims based on their experiences with work. How would the United States be different today if people followed the advice given in "The Way to Wealth" (**Question 8**)? Would there still be a deficit? Would Americans own houses (without taking out loans)? Would people take vacations? What jobs would no longer be necessary? What would the economy be like if people really spent little and saved and worked a lot? Would shopping malls exist? Would people have the time to shop? **Question 1** asks students to identify any aphorisms they see as outdated, and **Question 9** gives them the opportunity to write a list of contemporary maxims. What advice would Poor Richard give to Americans of the twenty-first century?

Although students may find some of the specifics of Franklin's maxims outdated, they will probably consider many of the principles behind his maxims as sound advice. **Questions 2** and **7** point students to issues that are important to America's present-day economy—the role of government in the lives of citizens and the importance of staying out of debt. Students could be asked to consider which other writers in this chapter would be likely to agree with Franklin (or Poor Richard) on these issues and why. One way for students to compare and contrast the views Franklin presents with those held by other contemporary figures—many of whom are represented in *The Presence of Others*—is in an imaginative dialogue (**Question 6**). In this dialogue, for example, students might imagine Poor Richard as an employee of Bill Gates, construct a conversation between Poor Richard and Peter J. Gomes on politics or shopping for a suit, or place Jeremy Rifkin and Poor Richard together in a debate on the possibilities and perils of genetic engineering.

J.R.'s headnote points to Poor Richard's mistrust of leisure. What roles do work-related maxims play in students' lives? Do students feel guilty when they're not working? Do they work in order to finance their leisure time? What factors influence their attitudes toward work and rest? Should a healthy lifestyle combine the two?

MERIDEL LESUEUR Women and Work (p. 729)

The introduction to this chapter discusses some of the tensions between capitalism and communism, topics that will be most familiar to students who have studied American history. These tensions affected writers and actors, for example, whose work was public and, therefore, blacklisted at one time. Students should be encouraged to consider how social issues—such as political associations, gender, and sexual orientation—can affect not only what one is allowed to do for work but also how that work is received by others. With her emphasis on community and on being a voice for others, Meridel LeSueur's narrative offers implicit qualifications to some of Franklin's tidy aphorisms. **Question 4** invites students to write a few Poor Richard–like maxims in LeSueur's voice.

As a young girl in 1910, LeSueur knew that women had few career options and that those options were further limited for her because she was poor and could not afford an education. Of course, students are likely to argue that times have since changed and that there are many more options open to women today. But LeSueur's narrative shouldn't be dismissed on the basis of these points alone. You could ask students to discuss the changes that have taken place in LeSueur's lifetime and what things have not changed much. For instance, **Question 1** points students to LeSueur's discussion of female stereotypes. Are some of these stereotypes still expressed today? **Question 2** takes up LeSueur's assertion that the film industry was a "meat market," asking whether her analogy still holds true today. Certainly there have been changes in people's experiences with work since 1910. **Question 5** gives students an opportunity to interview people who are in their eighties or nineties about their work lives—recalling their earliest jobs and other memorable moments from work. One important assumption behind *The Presence of Others* is that the positions an individual takes can be illuminated and better understood when seen in the context of the positions others take. **Question 3** asks students to assess which writers in the chapter LeSueur would have the most and least in common with in terms of views on work—and why. Putting people in dialogue together (even imaginatively, as several study questions encourage) helps show the differences and similarities between the stances various writers take and clarifies students' understandings of the pieces.

In reading and discussing the selections in this chapter, students will have many opportunities to consider the work that others do—and the negative and positive aspects of that work. **Question 6** gives them an opportunity to consider the work they would most like to do and to explore their knowledge and feelings about that type of work. If you discuss this question in class, you could also ask students what they, as children, dreamed of doing for work—and whether as college students they are preparing to do that work. If not, why? What kinds of influences and pressures (finances, talent, parents, expectations, education) affect the work one ends up doing? What considerations do students take into account in preparing for a career?

NAOMI BARKO The Other Gender Gap: Why Women Still Fail to Receive Comparable Wages for Comparable Work (p. 733)

This essay can be read as an update to Meridel LeSueur's work (p. 729), showing that concerns for gender equity in wages are still being debated today (**Question 4**). As A.L. points out in her headnote, Naomi Barko argues for a controversial approach to the problem presented by women's lower earnings compared to men's—that of implementing laws that require compensation based on the principle of comparable worth. In the essay following Barko's, Steven Pinker (p. 740) challenges not only this solution but also the existence of the problem in the first place. The three essays can be used to generate discussion that will inform students' writing on issues related to gender's influence on the world of work. In summarizing and assessing Barko's argument, students should find it helpful to do some research into her use of sources (**Questions 1** and **2**). Through this research, students can begin to list some of the issues that arise in discussions of gender and wages, which will be useful in considering how Barko might respond to Pinker's essay (**Question 3**).

Question 5 encourages students to apply the research they have done in studying these texts to situations in their communities. Using public sources and interviews with community or campus leaders, they might investigate how well women are compensated, relative to men, and write an article on their findings. **Question 6** invites them to study a case of labor activism and to write an opinion article on what was or should be done about the situation.

STEVEN PINKER Gender (p. 740)

Steven Pinker argues that the disparity between men's and women's earnings may be caused more by biological differences between men and women than by discrimination or other social factors. To some extent this selection can be read as a counterargument to Naomi Barko's essay (p. 733), although the two writers may be read as agreeing, or at least not disagreeing, on some points (**Question 4**). Pinker's argument, although much longer than Barko's, is nevertheless straightforward. In previewing Pinker's essay, you might point out his use of transitional sentences, words, and phrases at the beginnings of paragraphs, which help guide readers. Some examples can be found in the first few pages: "The problem with this analysis is that . . . ," "Before presenting the new analysis, . . ." and "first," "second," and "third." Like Barko, Pinker draws from considerable research in making his argument. Once students have summarized the argument (**Question 1**), they should do some research to examine Pinker's use of sources (**Question 2**). The style of Pinker's writing conveys much meaning as well, as A.L. suggests in her Afterword to the essay. Students should consider his use of sentence structure and diction, and the ways such elements affect Pinker's tone and credibility (**Question 3**).

Students might consider how effective Pinker's arguments might be if applied to questions of pay equity among workers of various races or ethnicities (**Question 5**). Readings in other chapters could be of help in addressing this question. For example, Chapter 6 selections by Zora Neale Hurston, Paula Gunn Allen, and Langston Hughes and Chapter 7 selections by Frederick Douglass, Ward Churchill, and Abelardo Delgado can provide insights into various forms of discrimination. **Questions 6** and **7** give students an opportunity to explore their own experiences with gender expectations, in class discussion and in writing.

ARTHUR KRYSTAL Who Speaks for the Lazy? (p. 758)

Arthur Krystal observes that "[s]ome men are born lazy, some acquire laziness, some have laziness thrust upon them." Instead of offering a single definition of laziness that would apply to all who fit the criteria, Krystal argues that there are differences among the lazy: "Energetic people may all be alike, but the lazy cruise along at their own varying rates of speed." **Question 1** asks students to consider how Krystal defines laziness and whether, by his own definition, he is lazy. In answering this question, students should be encouraged to recognize the various modes of definition employed by Krystal. For example, he defines laziness by telling what it is not or what lazy people don't do ("Profound laziness is not so much about doing nothing as it is about the strain of doing practically *anything*"; "The lazy don't come to the table"); by using analogies, metaphors, or similes ("Laziness just is. It's like being freckled or color-blind"); and by telling what lazy people do (they refuse "to affix their signatures to the social contract"). Some of his definitions, as students will quickly learn, are not based on factual evidence; rather, they are implied through context and metaphor. Being aware of multiple ways of defining will also help students write their own extended definitions of laziness in answer to **Question 6**.

Throughout this essay, Krystal is interested in the work of the mind—the work that writers do, a kind of contemplative work that is sometimes seen as lazy. However, as **Question 3** asserts, Krystal reveals at the end of his essay how he has made laziness "work" for him by becoming a screenwriter. This question asks if Krystal is being ironic, prompting students to explain what his true meaning might be. Their explanations should take into account the ways in which Krystal characterizes writers and the work of writing throughout his essay. Is it ironic that he refers to himself as lazy even as he is writing an article and presumably doing research on laziness?

Questions 4 and **5** bring Krystal into dialogue with two other writers in this chapter, hooks and Franklin. **Question 4** asks students to compare and contrast Krystal's and hooks's attitudes toward success and money and to decide which view they find more persuasive and why. In **Question 5**, too, students are asked to consider which argument is more effective or persuasive—the one they think Krystal would make for laziness or the one Franklin would make for avoiding laziness. Students should be asked to consider how Krystal and Franklin would be likely to defend their particular stances. Would Franklin speak in aphorisms? Would Krystal use literary characters or historical understandings of laziness to support his points? What kinds of evidence do students find most convincing?

EDWARD TENNER Body Smarts (p. 767)

As J.R. remarks in his headnote, this selection could fit as easily among those in **Chapter 6, Technology**, as it does among those on work, and yet its inclusion here helps highlight some ways in which technology is changing the world of work. As Edward Tenner argues, technology has long influenced changes in work processes, in ways that are not always predictable. His essay gives students a chance to consider the ways in which technology is changing physical and mental processes we use in work (**Question 2**) and to form opinions about the possible effects of those changes (**Question 3**). Tenner's use of *technique* and *technology*, including his use of italics to suggest a relationship between the two words, enhances his argument about the two-way effects that occur between these elements of human work (**Question 1**).

As Tenner suggests, the costs of technology advancements are worth considering. Students could use Dagoberto Gilb's praise of physical labor (p. 783) as a way of thinking about the "body techniques" in work that may be lost with emerging technologies (**Question 3**). Does Gilb's essay suggest a clash of cultures is inevitable between those who embrace the new computer-driven technologies and those who value physical labor? Edwin Schlosser's selection may also provide insight into Tenner's argument, perhaps lending support or challenging some of his claims (**Question 4**). Should we lament the replacement of cooking techniques with more easily standardized technological processes in the fast food industry?

Tenner's argument offers a valuable corrective to alarmist assumptions about the dangers of technology. Students can have some fun looking for such assumptions, especially in popular culture, and then refuting them, using Tenner's claims or some of their own (**Question 5**). They might also try writing a satirical essay, perhaps in the style of an *Onion* article (p. 368), that predicts dire consequences from an actual technological development. Sharing the essays with others, they might see how many of their readers believe their exaggerated predictions (**Question 6**).

BELL HOOKS Work Makes Life Sweet (p. 774)

According to bell hooks, "To know the work we are 'called' to do in this world, we must know ourselves." Throughout this essay, hooks writes about herself and others and the relationships they have with their work. For work to be satisfying, hooks believes people should practice "right livelihood"; **Question 1** points to this term, asking students to define it from hooks's and Marsha Sinetar's perspectives. Hooks writes of right livelihood as "a concept initially coming from the teachings of Buddha which emphasized 'work consciously chosen, done with full awareness and care, and leading to enlightenment.' " According to Sinetar, right livelihood "embodies self-expression, commitment, mindfulness, and conscious choice . . . , high self-esteem and self-trust." One of the similarities between these definitions is an emphasis on personal choice, and as hooks makes clear in her essay, the people who are most satisfied with their work are those who have chosen their profession.

Question 2 asks students to consider the circumstances under which work can "make life sweet" in hooks's terms. Do students agree with the conditions she offers? What else would they add? In answering **Question 2**, students might wish to draw on their own work experiences, as **Question 5** also encourages. To what extent are emotional well-being and satisfying work related? For hooks, there is a strong connection between positive thinking about work and being able to do the work one has chosen. **Question 6** allows students to imagine the specific job that would be most satisfying to them and to write the job description for the work that would make their life sweet. Can they also imagine schoolwork that would make life sweet? **Question 7** gives students the opportunity to define the conditions that would be necessary for schoolwork to be satisfying.

Question 3 puts hooks in dialogue with Dagoberto Gilb. To focus this question and make the imagined dialogue manageable, students should find a particular topic or issue for the two writers to discuss. For instance, they could discuss the difference between a job and a fulfilling vocation, what it would take for one to practice right livelihood, or the ways in which work is—or should or should not be—related to self-esteem. Whatever issue they choose, students should also be encouraged to draw on the specifics hooks and Gilb use; such specifics will make the dialogue more interesting and more representative of the positions each author holds.

DAGOBERTO GILB Work Union (p. 783)

Dagoberto Gilb argues that the emphasis on computer-industry work is misplaced and misleading to young people. Moreover, he suggests that it contributes to a devaluation of continually important work of a more physical kind: the building of "offices, highways, bridges where those others do their business through modems and cell phones" (paragraph 2). Ultimately Gilb places a moral value on hard, physical work, concluding that "the very best people are those who work hard" (paragraph 6). In responding to this essay, some students may feel Gilb speaks directly to them, while others may not. Studying the text for clues about his intended audience may give them insight into their own responses (**Question 1**). **Question 2** asks students to examine Gilb's claim that overemphasis on the computer industry serves to perpetuate a power imbalance between high-tech and physical work. In doing so, they might reread Anthony Walton's "Technology versus African Americans" (p. 331), which finds the dearth of African Americans working in the high-tech industry troubling. Students might also think about whether the dot-com and high-tech crash that occurred on the cusp of the new millenium—and the resulting high unemployment rates in high-technology centers like Silicon Valley—has an effect on how they respond to Gilb's argument.

Selections in this chapter offer further opportunities for discussing the relative effectiveness of Gilb's argument. Students may consider Gilb's work ethic in comparison with that of Benjamin Franklin (p. 720), bell hooks (p. 774), and Marge Piercy (p. 793), for example (**Question 4**). Gilb remarks that the only aspects of work that merit complaint are work conditions and wages (paragraph 5), a claim that invites comparison with the discussions earlier in this chapter about gender equity in wages (**Question 5**).

Gilb's essay can inspire students to reconsider work they are doing now or have done in the past. You might invite them to discuss in class whether or not the jobs they have held seem to take on greater dignity in light of Gilb's comments (**Question 7**). His essay may also serve as a model for students who wish to write a short piece praising or criticizing a particular type of work. This topic could lend itself to a humorous approach as well as a more serious one like that taken by Gilb (**Question 6**).

ERIC SCHLOSSER From *Behind the Counter* (p. 787)

As the title of this excerpt suggests, Eric Schlosser provides a glimpse behind the counter of a fast food restaurant, illuminating the history of its factorylike production of food and the people who keep the production lines running (**Question 1**). Schlosser's movement among the diverse elements of this story about fast food production is worth studying to see how he achieves transitions (**Questions 2** and **3**). The fast food industry is dominated by teenage workers, Schlosser explains, practically by design. The production and service of food has become increasingly efficient through the introduction of mechanical and computer-ized technology, to keep the work simple and the wages low while standardizing the quality of products.

It may be enlightening for students to compare this selection to others in the chapter, especially if some of them have worked or are currently working in the fast food industry. They might discuss how they see the value of this work, perhaps in terms of the work ethic presented by Dagoberto Gilb or another writer, after reading Schlosser's excerpt (**Questions 4** and **5**). Whether students have worked in fast food positions or not, Schlosser's essay may change their thinking about the restaurants and their practices. **Question 6** invites students to explore and write about their own experiences behind—or in front of—the counter. Schlosser suggests that fast food jobs, like other jobs, can teach young or inexperienced workers some "basic job skills." Students might reflect in class or in writing on their own experiences in learning such skills. They could address what those skills entailed and share anecdotes that reveal how they learned those skills.

MARGE PIERCY To Be of Use (p. 793)

Marge Piercy's poem deals with two recurring themes in this chapter—the desire for work that is satisfying and the importance of working hard. In the first stanza, Piercy uses the metaphor of people jumping into water "head first" and becoming "natives of that element" to show the kind of worker she values. Another metaphor follows in the second stanza: people as hard-working as oxen who demonstrate "massive patience" and "do what has to be done, again and again." These are the kinds of people the speaker loves best. **Question 2** asks students to compose their own stanza, describing the people they love best. Perhaps they could follow Piercy's example and use a metaphor in their own stanza to create a vivid picture. In addition to pointing to the kind of people they admire, **Question 1** asks students to identify work that is worth doing, the kind that "has a shape that satisfies." What kinds of work would (or would not) fit this definition? If the "work of the world," as Piercy describes it, "is as common as mud," what kinds of work might Piercy define as "real"? **Question 3** poses this question and prompts students to give reasons for their answer. You could encourage students to use lines from the poem and background information on the poet from A.L.'s headnote to support their response.

Texts in Context: Sequenced Writing Assignments about Work

Assignment 1

The selections in this chapter offer various viewpoints on work—from Carlisle's desire for work that is meaningful and financially rewarding, to LeSueur's understanding of her work (writing) as a way of bearing witness, to Piercy's belief that the "work of the world is common as mud." Brainstorm a list of your associations with work. Are they primarily negative or positive associations—or a mix of both? What viewpoint can you offer on the subject of work? Is it similar to one of the points of view represented in this chapter? Drawing from your list of associations and your answers to the preceding questions, draft a two- to three-page statement about work for your class. It might begin, for example, "From where I stand, work is . . ."

Assignment 2

Choose the one selection in this chapter that most appeals to you. Then reread that selection, this time trying to figure out where that writer's views on work have come from. To help you answer this question, think for a while about where your views on work come from, such as from your own experience with different kinds of work as well as from the work you've seen your parents or other family members do. Does the position that the selection writer takes on work reflect some of your own hopes or fears? Is that writer in a situation you've been in or expect to be in in the future? What attitude toward work is expressed in the selection? Now imagine that you are a coworker of the writer you've selected. What would it be like to work with him or her? Write a story, poem, scene from a play, or narrative essay entitled "A Day on the Job with _________."

Assignment 3

Interview four people who each do a different type of work (for example, a homemaker, lawyer, garbage collector, and factory worker) and who vary as much as possible in terms of age, gender, and class. Talk with these people about the work they've done in the past and the work they do today. How do they feel about their work? Do they see the work that they do as, in Marge Piercy's words, "work that is real"? What are the similarities and differences among the people you've interviewed? Using the information you've gathered from your interviews, write a statement for your class entitled "The Kinds of Work That Are Real." (Remember to provide a provisional definition of what you mean by *real.*)

Assignment 4

Working in class in a small group, share the information you've gathered through interviews and the statement you wrote. Then focus a group discussion on the types of work you would not describe as "real" or "satisfying"—and why. Working together, prepare a brief (10-minute) report of your group's findings for the class. Be sure to report on areas of both disagreement and agreement.

Assignment 5

Review all of the work you've done for Assignments 1–4. Consider again the different perspectives on work that various people hold (you; your classmates; the writers, characters, and editors in this chapter) as well as the feelings associated with those views (excitement, fear, hope, anxiety, weariness, satisfaction, ambivalence, disgust). Think about how these multiple perspectives combine to create a complex view of work—one that reveals the positive and negative elements of work and of society's views on work. Brainstorm (alone or with several classmates) ideas about these issues. In what ways can work be advantageous and "real"? In what ways can it be disadvantageous or even harmful to the worker, society, or even the environment? Finally, using your brainstorming, your notes, your work for assignments 1–4, and selected readings from this chapter, write an essay of four to six pages in length in response to the following question: in what ways does work constrain and free, enslave and liberate, people today?

A Conversation on the Composition Classroom: Exploring the Personal and Political

The three essays reflect important conversations taking place among composition instructors and theorists about what it means to teach college-level reading and writing today. One issue in particular has provoked much debate: whether or how to bring into the classroom what advocates and critics call *politics*, a term that invites a wide range of definitions. Because this ongoing debate over the politics of writing instruction is one of many conversations that provide the background and contents of this edition of *The Presence of Others,* it will be useful for you to consider how this book fits into that conversation.

As you read the three essays in this section, we invite you to join the conversation represented by these texts, to engage with them in the same ways you ask your students to engage with the texts you assign. First, consider your initial response to the question they pose: what is the relationship between politics and writing instruction? Then read the texts critically, and analyze your responses to them. Enter into conversations with other teachers of writing about the issues raised in these texts. Articulate your position on the issue, one based on your experience as well as on your reading. And finally, take some time to reflect on why you hold the position you do.

GERALD GRAFF What Has Literary Theory Wrought?

Recent literary theory has had many harsh critics, and I was once one of the harshest. Perhaps in spite of myself, however, literary theory has profoundly changed the way I teach.

Since the mid-1960s, I have frequently taught Joseph Conrad's *Heart of Darkness*. When I first assigned the novella in 1966 or 1967, I taught it in much the way that it had been taught to me in college in the late 1950s, as a profound meditation on a universal moral theme. I presented Conrad's story of the destruction of the idealistic trader Mr. Kurtz as a universal parable of the precarious status of civilized reason in a world too confident it has outgrown the seductions of the primitive and the irrational.

Recent literary theory teaches us that what we don't see enables and limits what we do see. My reading of *Heart of Darkness* as a universal parable of reason and unreason allowed me to see certain things in the novel that I still think are important. But it also depended on my not seeing certain things or treating them as not worth thinking about.

Of little interest to me, for example, was the fact that Conrad sets the novella in the Congo in the high period of European colonialism or that he chooses subjugated black Africans to represent the primitive, irrational forces that are Kurtz's undoing. That Conrad chose black Africa to represent primitive impulse was, I thought, incidental to his main intention, which was to make a statement about the human condition that transcended mere matters of geography and race.

It did not occur to me that black readers of the work might not have the luxury of dismissing the question of race so easily, and the small number of black students in my classes at that time helped guarantee that the question never came up. Political issues like the subjugation of black Africans might interest historians, sociologists, and political scientists, but in teaching literature such issues were at best of ancillary interest.

Today I teach *Heart of Darkness* very differently. One critical work that caused me to change was an essay by the Nigerian novelist Chinua Achebe, "An Image of Africa: Racism in Conrad's *Heart of Darkness*." Mr. Achebe argues that Conrad's presentation of black Africa is thoroughly racist. And he is able to accumulate an uncomfortable number of quotations from the novel and from Conrad's letters and diaries that make it painfully clear how cruelly stereotyped Conrad's thinking about the black African is.

Mr. Achebe argues that Conrad reduces Africa to a mere "setting and backdrop which eliminates the African as human factor" and directs all our attention instead to the tragedy of the white imperialist Kurtz. As Mr. Achebe puts it, "Can no one see the preposterous and perverse arrogance in thus reducing Africa to the role of props for the breakup of one petty European mind?"

The real issue, Mr. Achebe says, "is the dehumanization of Africa and Africans. . . . And the question is whether a novel which celebrates that dehumanization, which depersonalizes a portion of the human race, can be called a great work of art." My answer is: No, it cannot.

After reading Mr. Achebe's essay, I could not teach *Heart of Darkness* as I did before. It was not that he convinced me that *Heart of Darkness* is totally racist—in fact, he didn't. What he did convince me of was that Conrad's assumptions about race are not simply an extraneous or nonliterary element of the novel but something that the novel's literary and aesthetic effect depends upon. In this sense, Conrad's novel is not a disinterested work of art but a text that has played an active role in constructing the Western image of black Africa and in justifying the West's political and economic treatment of black Africa.

In short, Mr. Achebe's essay forced me to rethink my theoretical assumptions about literature. First, I was forced to recognize that I had theoretical assumptions. I had previously thought I was simply teaching the truth about *Heart of Darkness*, "the text itself." I now had to recognize that I had been teaching an interpretation of the text, and one that was shaped by a certain theory that told me what was and wasn't worth noticing and emphasizing in my classroom. I had been unable to see this theory as a theory because I was living so comfortably inside it.

When I assign *Heart of Darkness* to undergraduates now, I also assign the Achebe essay. I don't, however, simply teach his interpretation as correct; I ask my students to weigh it against competing interpretations. Nor do I simply discard my former reading of the novel as a contemplation of universal truths about the human soul. I assign another critical essay that advances that interpretation. I also assign essays by critics who take issue with Mr. Achebe, conceding that he is right about Conrad's racism and colonialism but arguing—and I agree with them—that he overlooks the powerful critique of racism and colonialism that coexists in the novel with these more sinister attitudes.

After reading Conrad we read Mr. Achebe's novel, *Things Fall Apart*. When you come to this novel after reading his essay on Conrad, it is hard to avoid reading it—and the very different view of Africa it presents—as an answer to Conrad. It is as if the Nigerian writer were attempting to wrest the power to represent Africa away from the great European, testifying again to the way aesthetic representations are involved in struggles for power.

Finally, I supplement those materials with several short essays presenting opposing sides in the debate over the place or non-place of politics in art. I also invite conservative colleagues into my class to debate the issues with me and my students. To make sure that my students enter the debate rather than watch passively from the sidelines, I usually assign a paper or ask them to present their own positions in class.

In short, I now teach *Heart of Darkness* as part of a critical debate about how to read it, which in turn is part of a larger theoretical debate about how politics and power affect the way we read literature. With such an approach, I think I am following the dominant trend in contemporary theory, which is not to reduce literary works to transparent expressions of ideology. That is the impression that has been given by critics, whose hostility to current theory exceeds their willingness to read it.

The most influential recent theories say that literature is a scene of contradictions that cannot be subsumed under any "totalizing" system or ideology. The only critic of literary theory I know who gets this right is Frederick Crews, professor of English at the University of California at Berkeley. In an essay called "The Strange Fate of William Faulkner," in the March 7, 1991, issue of *The New York Review of Books*, Mr. Crews accurately summarizes recent theorists as saying "that literature is a site of struggle whose primary conflicts, both intrapsychic and social, deserve to be brought to light rather than homogenized into notions of fixed authorial 'values.' " Mr. Crews presents a model of what a scrupulous critique of current theory should look like: He shows how at its worst this kind of theory simply replaces the clichés and predictable readings of earlier critical schools with a new set of clichés and predictable readings, but how at its best it has revitalized fields such as the study of William Faulkner's work.

What, then, has theory wrought for my own teaching of literature? Teaching *Heart of Darkness* as I now do does constitute a "politicized" way of teaching, for it puts ideological conflicts at the center of literary works and of the conflicts over interpretation. Yet contrary to the charge that such an approach lowers academic standards, introducing ideological conflicts seems to me to have made my course more challenging, not less. Theory seems to have raised the academic standards of my course considerably; my students now have to be more reflective about their assumptions than before, and they must take part in a set of complex debates that I previously hadn't expected them to.

Students don't seem to feel that the interpretive and theoretical debate distracts them from close reading of literature itself. On the contrary, I believe that the debate over the critiques of Mr. Achebe and others forces them to pay closer attention to the verbal and stylistic texture of *Heart of Darkness* than they would otherwise. Theory is not something added on, to talk about if there's time left over after you've finished teaching the work itself; it is a reflection on what is being assumed while you teach the work.

Nor has any student complained that reading Conrad alongside a non-Western writer "dilutes" the Western tradition, as so many conservatives charge. On the contrary, students have told me they felt Mr. Achebe's novel gave them a better grasp of Conrad's "Westernness," since they had something to compare it with.

I believe that all sides are being political in the dispute over literature, theory, and other educational issues today; the neo-conservatives' pretense that it is only their opponents who are acting politically is pure hypocrisy. The real question we should be addressing is not who is being political but whose politics are *better*—better grounded in truth and justice.

For it does not follow that once you say that a statement is "political" or "ideological," you have undermined its truth. What I have been arguing here is deeply political but no less true for that fact. Nor does it follow that raising political issues and taking positions on them in class means forcing my students to conform.

I believe the way to turn what is now an ugly scene of anger and recrimination into a useful and productive debate is to bring out present disagreements into our classrooms. The way to protect students from intimidation by dogmatists of the left, the right, and the center is to expose them to the debates among these factions. We are already implicitly teaching these conflicts every time a student goes from one course or department to another; we should start doing it in a way that enables students to experience and enter the debate.

I recognize how difficult this can be when there is so much hatred and acrimony in the air, but the hatred and acrimony seem to me all the more reason for channeling the debate into the orderly forums of the classroom.

Gerald Graff is professor of English at the University of Chicago. This selection is adapted from a speech presented at a meeting of the National Association of Scholars.

MAXINE HAIRSTON Diversity, Ideology, and Teaching Writing

Where We Have Come From

In 1985, when I was chair of CCCC [Conference on College Composition and Communication], as my chair's address I gave what might be called my own State of the Profession Report. On the whole it was a positive report. I rejoiced in the progress we had made in the previous fifteen years in establishing our work as a discipline and I pointed out that we were creating a new paradigm for the teaching of writing, one that focused on process and on writing as a way of learning. I asserted that we teach writing for its own sake, as a primary intellectual activity that is at the heart of a college education. I insisted that writing courses must not be viewed as service courses. Writing courses, especially required freshman courses, should not be *for* anything or *about* anything other than writing itself, and how one uses it to learn and think and communicate.

I also warned in my chair's address that if we hoped to flourish as a profession, we would have to establish our psychological and intellectual independence from the literary critics who are at the center of power in most English departments; that we could not develop our potential and become fully autonomous scholars and teachers as long as we allowed our sense of self-worth to depend on the approval of those who define English departments as departments of literary criticism.

We've continued to make important strides since 1985. We have more graduate programs in rhetoric and composition, more tenure track positions in composition created each year, more and larger conferences, and so many new journals that one can scarcely keep up with them. In those years, I've stayed optimistic about the profession and gratified by the role I've played in its growth. Now, however, I see a new model emerging for freshman writing programs, a model that disturbs me greatly. It's a model that puts dogma before diversity, politics before craft, ideology before critical thinking, and the social goals of the teacher before the educational needs of the student. It's a regressive model that undermines the progress we've made in teaching writing, one that threatens to silence student voices and jeopardize the process-oriented, low-risk, student-centered classroom we've worked so hard to establish as the norm. It's a model that doesn't take freshman English seriously in its own right but conceives of it as a tool, something to be used. The new model envisions required writing courses as vehicles for social reform rather than as student-centered workshops designed to build students' confidence and competence as writers. It is a vision that echoes that old patronizing rationalization we've heard so many times before: students don't have anything to write about so we have to give them topics. Those topics used to be literary; now they're political.

I don't suggest that all or even most freshman writing courses are turning this way. I have to believe that most writing teachers have too much common sense and are too concerned with their students' growth as writers to buy into this new philosophy. Nevertheless, everywhere I turn I find composition faculty, both leaders in the profession and new voices, asserting that they have not only the right, but the duty, to put ideology and radical politics at the center of their teaching.

Here are four revealing quotations from recent publications. For instance, here is James Laditka in the *Journal of Advanced Composition*:

> All teaching supposes ideology; there simply is no value-free pedagogy. For these reasons, my paradigm of composition is changing to one of critical literacy, a literacy of political consciousness and social action. (361)

Here is Charles Paine in a lead article in *College English*:

> Teachers need to recognize that methodology alone will not ensure radical visions of the world. An appropriate course content is necessary as well. . . . [E]quality and democracy are not transcendent values that inevitably emerge when one learns to seek the truth through critical thinking. Rather, if those are the desired values, the teacher must recognize that he or she must influence (perhaps manipulate is the more accurate word) students' values through charisma or power—he or she must accept the role as manipulator. Therefore it is of course reasonable to try to inculcate into our students the conviction that the dominant order is repressive. (563–64)

Here is Patricia Bizzell:

> We must help our students . . . to engage in a rhetorical process that can collectively generate . . . knowledge and beliefs to displace the repressive ideologies an unjust social order would prescribe. . . . I suggest that we must be forthright in avowing the ideologies that motivate our teaching and research. For instance [in an experimental composition course he teaches at Purdue], James Berlin might stop trying to be value-neutral and anti-authoritarian in the classroom. Berlin tells his students he is a Marxist but disavows any intention of persuading them to his point of view. Instead, he might openly state that this course aims to promote values of sexual equality and left-oriented labor relations and that this course will challenge students' values insofar as they conflict with these aims. Berlin and his colleagues might openly exert their authority as teachers to try to persuade students to agree with their values instead of pretending that they are merely investigating the nature of sexism and capitalism and leaving students to draw their own conclusions. (670)

Here is C. H. Knoblauch:

> We are, ultimately, compelled to choose, to make, express, and act upon our commitments, to denounce the world, as Freire says, and above all oppression and whatever arguments have been called upon to validate it. Moreover, our speech may well have to be boldly denunciative at times if it is to affect its hearers in the midst of their intellectual and political comfort. . . . We are obliged to announce ourselves so that, through the very process of self-assertion, we grow more conscious of our axioms. . . . The quality of our lives as teachers depends on our willingness to discover through struggle ever more fruitful means of doing our work. The quality of our students' lives depends on [it]. ("Rhetorical" 139)

These quotations do not represent just a few instances that I ferreted out to suit my thesis; you will find similar sentiments if you leaf through only a few of the recent issues of *College English, Rhetoric Review, College Composition and Communication, Journal of Advanced Composition, Focuses*, and others. Some names that you might look for in addition to the ones I've quoted are James Berlin, John Trimbur, Lester Faigley, Richard Ohmann, and Linda Brodkey. At least 40 percent of the essays in *The Right to Literacy*, the proceedings of a 1988 conference sponsored by the Modern Language Association [MLA] in Columbus, Ohio, echo such sentiments, and a glance at the program for the 1991 CCCC convention would confirm how popular such ideas were among the speakers. For that same convention, the publisher HarperCollins sponsored a contest to award grants to graduate students to attend; the topic they were asked to write on was "Describe the kind of freshman writing course you would design." Nearly all of the contestants described a politically focused course. All ten essays in the 1991 MLA publication *Contending with Words* recommend turning writing courses in this direction.

Distressingly often, those who advocate such courses show open contempt for their students' values, preferences, or interests. For example, in an article in *College English*, Ronald Strickland says, "The teacher can best facilitate the production of knowledge by adopting a confrontational stance toward the student. . . . Above all, the teacher should avoid the pretense of detachment, objectivity, and autonomy." He admits that his position "conflicts with the expectations of some students [and] these students make it difficult for me to pursue my political/intellectual agenda."(295)

David Bleich dismisses his students' resistance with equal ease:

> There is reason to think that students want to write about what they say they don't want to write about. They want a chance to write about racism, classism, and homophobia even though it makes them uncomfortable. But what I think makes them most uncomfortable is to surrender the paradigm of individualism and to see that paradigm in its sexist dimensions.

He cites his students' religion as one of the chief obstacles to their enlightenment:

> Religious views collaborate with the ideology of individualism and with sexism to censor the full capability of what people can say and write. . . . By "religious values" I mean belief in the savability of the individual human soul. The ideal of the nuclear family, as opposed to the extended or communal family, permits the overvaluation of the individual child and the individual soul. (167)

And here is Dale Bauer in an article from *College English*:

> I would argue that political commitment—especially feminist commitment—is a legitimate classroom strategy and rhetorical imperative. The feminist agenda offers a goal toward our students' conversations to emancipatory critical action. . . . In teaching identification and teaching feminism, I overcome a vehement insistence on pluralistic relativism or on individualism.

Bauer acknowledges that her students resist her political agenda. She says,

> There is an often overwhelming insistence on individualism and isolation . . . [They] labor at developing a critical distance to avoid participating in "the dialectic of resistance and identification."

Bauer quotes one of her students as saying in an evaluation,

> "The teacher consistently channels class discussions around feminism and does not spend time discussing the comments that oppose her beliefs. In fact, she usually twists them around to support her beliefs."

Bauer dismisses such objections, however, claiming she has to accept her authority as rhetor because "anything less ends up being an expressivist model, one which reinforces . . . the dominant patriarchal culture."(389)

Often these advocates are contemptuous of other teachers' approaches to teaching or the goals those teachers set for their students. For example, Lester Faigley assails the advice given about writing a job application letter in a standard business writing text:

> In the terms of [the Marxist philosopher] Althusser, [the applicant who writes such a letter] has voluntarily assented his subjectivity within the dominant ideology and thus has reaffirmed relations of power. By presenting himself as a commodity rather than as a person, he has not only made an initial gesture of subservience like a dog presenting its neck, but he has also signaled his willingness to continue to be subservient. (251)

In discussing Linda Flower's cognitive, problem-solving approach to teaching writing, James Berlin calls it "the rationalization of economic activity. The pursuit of self-evident and unquestioned goals in the composing process parallels the pursuit of self-evident and unquestioned profit-making goals in the corporate market place." (What a facile non-logical leap!) He continues in the same article to deride Donald Murray's and Peter Elbow's approaches to writing because of their focus on the individual, saying

> Expressionist rhetoric is inherently and debilitatingly divisive of political protest. . . . Beyond that, expressionist rhetoric is easily co-opted by the very capitalist forces it opposes. After all, this rhetoric can be used to reinforce the entrepreneurial virtues capitalism values most: individualism, private initiative, the confidence for risk taking, the right to be contentious with authority (especially the state). (491)

How We Got Here

But how did all this happen? Why has the cultural left suddenly claimed writing courses as their political territory?

There's no simple answer, of course. Major issues about social change and national priorities are involved, and I cannot digress into those concerns in this essay. But my first response is, "You see what happens when we allow writing programs to be run by English departments?" I'm convinced that the push to change freshman composition into a political platform for the teacher has come about primarily because the course is housed in English departments.

As the linguistics scholar John Searle pointed out in a detailed and informative article in *The New York Review of Books*, the recent surge of the cultural [left] on major American campuses has centered almost entirely in English departments. He says,

> The most congenial home left for Marxism, now that it has been largely discredited as a theory of economics and politics, is in departments of literary criticism. And [because] many professors of literature no longer care about literature in ways that seemed satisfactory to earlier generations . . . they teach it as a means of achieving left-wing political goals or as an occasion for exercises in deconstruction, etc. (38)

I theorize that the critical literary theories of deconstruction, post-structuralism (both declining by now), and Marxist critical theory have trickled down to the lower floors of English departments where freshman English dwells. Just as they have been losing their impact with faculty above stairs, they have taken fresh root with those dwelling below.

Deconstructionists claim that the privileged texts of the canon are only reflections of power relations and the dominant class structures of their eras. Thus the job of the literary critic is to dissect Shakespeare or Milton or Eliot or Joyce to show how language reflects and supports the "cultural hegemony" of the time. They also claim that all meaning is indeterminate and socially constructed; there is no objective reality nor any truth that can be agreed on.

Marxist criticism echoes these sentiments. For example, Ronald Strickland writes in *College English*:

> Marxist critics have demonstrated that conventional literary studies have been more complicitous . . . than any other academic discipline in the reproduction of the dominant ideology. . . . Traditional English studies helps to maintain liberal humanism through its emphasis on authorial genius. . . . [Thus] there is a political imperative to resist the privileging of individualism in this practice, for, as Terry Eagleton has demonstrated, it amounts to a form of coercion in the interests of conservative, elitist politics. (293)

All these claims strike me as silly, simplistic, and quite undemonstrable. Nevertheless, if one endorses these intellectual positions—and sympathizes with the politics behind them—it's easy to go to the next step and equate conventional writing instruction with conventional literary studies. Then one can say that because standard English is the dialect of the dominant class, writing instruction that tries to help students master that dialect merely reinforces the status quo and serves the interest of the dominant class. An instructor who wants to teach students to write clearly becomes part of a capitalistic plot to control the workforce. What nonsense! It seems to me that one could argue with more force that the instructor who fails to help students master the standard dialect conspires against the working class.

How easy for theorists who, by the nature of the discipline they have chosen, already have a facile command of the prestige dialect to denigrate teaching that dialect to students. Have they asked those students what *they* want to learn? And how easy for these same theorists to set up straw men arguments that attack a mechanistic, structuralist, literature-based model of composition and call it conservative, regressive, deterministic, and elitist when they know such models have long been discredited in the professional literature.

But I think this is what happens when composition theorists remain psychologically tied to the English departments that are their base. Partly out of genuine interest, I'm sure, but also out of a need to belong to and be approved by the power structure, they immerse themselves in currently fashionable critical theories, read the authors that are chic—Foucault, Bakhtin, Giroux, Eagleton, and Cixous, for example—then look for ways those theories can be incorporated into their own specialty, teaching writing.

This, according to Searle's article, means that they subscribe to a view of the role of the humanities in universities that is

> . . . based on two primary assumptions. 1. They believe that Western civilization in general, and the United States in particular, are in large part oppressive, patriarchal, hegemonic, and in need of replacement or at least transformation. 2. The primary function of teaching the humanities is political; they [the cultural left] do not really believe the humanities are valuable in their own right except as a means of achieving social transformation. (38)

Searle goes on to point out that this debate about what is "hegemonic," "patriarchal," or "exclusionary" has been focused almost entirely in English departments.

I find it hard to believe that most English professors seriously hold these opinions or that they are ready to jettison their lifelong commitment to the humanities, but evidently significant numbers do. News releases and many professional articles suggest that these attitudes have permeated the Modern Language Association, and the associate chair of the English Department at the University of Texas recently said in a colloquium of the College of Liberal Arts that the "mission of English departments is always to oppose the dominant culture."

For those who agree, how natural to turn to the freshman writing courses. With a huge captive enrollment of largely unsophisticated students, what a fertile field to cultivate to bring about political and social change. Rhetoric scholars who go along will also get new respect now that they have joined the ideological fray and formed alliances with literature faculty who have been transforming their own courses.

Composition faculty who support such change can bring fresh respectability and attention to those often despised introductory English courses now that they can be used for "higher purposes." They may even find some regular faculty who will volunteer to teach freshman writing when they can use it for a political forum. Five years ago the regular faculty in our department at Texas tried to get rid of freshman English altogether by having it taught entirely in extension or at the local community college; this past year, many of those who had previously advocated abandoning the course were in the forefront of the battle to turn it into a course about racism and sexism. Now the course was suddenly worth their time.

The opportunity to make freshman English a vehicle for such social crusades is particularly rich: in many universities, graduate students in English teach virtually all of the sections, graduate students who are already steeped in post-structuralism and deconstruction theory, in the works of Foucault, Raymond Williams, Terry Eagleton, and Stanley Fish, and in feminist theory. Too often they haven't been well trained in how to teach writing and are at a loss about what they should be doing with their students. How easy then to focus the course on their own interests, which are often highly political. Unfortunately, when they try to teach an introductory composition course by concentrating on issues rather than on craft and critical thinking, large numbers of their students end up feeling confused, angry—and cheated.

I also believe that two major social forces outside the liberal arts are contributing to creating the environment that has given rise to this new model.

The first is the tremendous increase in diversity of our student population, especially in states like California and Texas and in all our major cities. With changing demographics, we face an ethnic and social mix of students in our classes that previews for us what our institutions are going to be like in the year 2000. These students bring with them a kaleidoscope of experiences, values, dialects, and cultural backgrounds that we want to respond to positively and productively, using every resource we can to help them adapt to the academic world and become active participants in it. The code words for our attempts to build the kind of inclusive curriculum that we need have become "multiculturalism" and "cultural diversity." They're good terms, of course. Any informed and concerned educator endorses them in the abstract. The crucial question, however, is how one finds concrete ways to put them into practice, and also how one guards against their becoming what Richard Weaver called "god terms" that can be twisted to mean anything an ideologue wants them to mean.

As writing teachers, I think all of us are looking for ways to promote genuine diversity in our classes and yet keep two elements that are essential for any state-of-the-art composition course.

First, students' own writing must be the center of the course. Students need to write to find out how much they know and to gain confidence in their ability to express themselves effectively. They do not need to be assigned essays to read so they will have something to write about—they bring their subjects with them: the writing of others, except for that of their fellow students, should be supplementary, used to illustrate or reinforce.

Second, as writing teachers we should stay within our area of professional expertise: helping students to learn to write in order to learn, to explore, to communicate, to gain control over their lives. That's a large responsibility, and all that most of us can manage. We have no business getting into areas where we may have passion and conviction but no scholarly base from which to operate. When classes focus on complex issues such as racial discrimination, economic injustices, and inequities of class and gender, they should be taught by qualified faculty who have the depth of information and historical competence that such critical social issues warrant. Our society's deep and tangled cultural conflicts can neither be explained nor resolved by simplistic ideological formulas.

But one can run a culturally diverse writing course without sacrificing any of its integrity as a writing course. Any writing course, required or not, can be wonderfully diverse, an exciting experience in which people of different cultures and experience learn about difference firsthand. More about that shortly.

Forces from Outside

The second major force I see at work is directly political. There's no question in my mind that this new radical stance of many composition faculty is in some ways a corollary of the angry response many intellectuals have to the excesses of right-wing, conservative forces that have dominated American politics for the past decade. Faculty in the liberal arts tend to be liberals who are concerned about social problems and dislike the trends we've seen in cutting funds for human services and for education. We're sick over the condition of our country: one child in five living in poverty; one person in eight hungry; 33 million people with no health insurance; a scandalous infant mortality rate; hundreds of thousands homeless. Yet we see our government spend billions on a dubious war. No need to go on—we all know the terrible inequities and contradictions of our society.

As educators of good will, we shouldn't even have to mention our anger about racism and sexism in our society—that's a given, as is our commitment to work to overcome it. I, for one, refuse to be put on the defensive on such matters of personal conscience or to be silenced by the fear that someone will pin a label on me if I don't share his or her vision of the world or agree on how to improve it. *Ad hominem* arguments don't impress me.

But it's entirely understandable that academics who are traditional liberals sympathize at first with those who preach reform, even when they sound more radical than we'd like. On the surface we share common ground; we'd all like to bring about a fairer, more compassionate society. But I fear that we are in real danger of being co-opted by the radical left, coerced into acquiescing to methods that we abhor because, in the abstract, we have some mutual goals. Some faculty may also fear being labeled "right-wing" if they oppose programs that are represented as being "liberating." But we shouldn't be duped. Authoritarian methods are still authoritarian methods, no matter in what cause they're invoked. And the current battle is *not* one between liberals and conservatives. Those who attempt to make it so—columnists like George Will—either do not understand the agenda of the cultural left, or they make the association in order to discredit liberal goals. Make no mistake—those on the cultural left are not in the least liberal; in fact, they despise liberals as compromising humanists. They're happy, however, to stir up traditional liberal guilt and use it for their purposes.

What's Wrong with Their Goals?

Why do I object so strongly to the agenda that these self-styled radical teachers want to establish for composition courses and freshman English in particular?

First, I vigorously object to the contention that they have a right—even a *duty*—to use their classrooms as platforms for their own political views. Such claims violate all academic traditions about the university being a forum for the free exchange of ideas, a place where students can examine different points of view in an atmosphere of honest and open discussion, and, in the process, learn to think critically. It is a teacher's obligation to encourage diversity and exploration, but diversity and ideology will not flourish together. By definition, they're incompatible.

By the logic of the cultural left, any teacher should be free to use his or her classroom to promote any ideology. Why not fascism? Racial superiority? Religious fundamentalism? Anti-abortion beliefs? Can't any professor claim the right to indoctrinate students simply because he or she is right? The argument is no different from that of any true believers who are convinced that they own the truth and thus have the right to force it on others. My colleague John Ruszkiewicz compares them to Milton's "the new forcers of conscience." We don't have to look far to see how frightening such arguments really are. They represent precisely the kind of thinking that leads to "reeducation camps" in totalitarian governments, to putting art in the service of propaganda, and to making education always the instrument of the state.

Those who want to bring their ideology into the classroom argue that since any classroom is necessarily political, the teacher might as well make it openly political and ideological. He or she should be direct and honest about his or her political beliefs; then the students will know where they stand and everyone can talk freely. Is any experienced teacher really so naive as to believe that? Such claims are no more than self-serving rationalizations that allow a professor total freedom to indulge personal prejudices and avoid any responsibility to be fair. By the same reasoning, couldn't one claim that since we know it is impossible to find absolute, objective truths, we might just as well abandon the search for truth and settle for opinion, superstition, and conjecture? Would that advance our students' education? Couldn't one also say that since one can never be completely fair with one's children, one might as well quit trying and freely indulge one's biases and favoritism? It's astonishing that people who purport to be scholars can make such specious arguments.

The real political truth about classrooms is that the teacher has all the power; she sets the agenda, she controls the discussion, and she gives the grades. She also knows more and can argue more skillfully. Such a situation is ripe for intellectual intimidation, especially in required freshman composition classes, and although I think it is unprofessional for teachers to bring their ideology into any classroom, it is those freshman courses that I am especially concerned about.

The Threat to Freshman Courses

I believe that the movement to make freshman English into courses in which students must write about specific social issues threatens all the gains we have made in teaching writing in the last fifteen years. I also think that rather than promoting diversity and a genuine multicultural environment, such courses actually work against those goals. Here are my reasons.

First, we know that students develop best as writers when they can write about something they care about and want to know more about. Only then will they be motivated to invest real effort in their work; only then can we hope they will avoid the canned, clichéd prose that neither they nor we take seriously. Few students, however, will do their best when they are compelled to write on a topic they perceive as politically charged and about which they feel uninformed, no matter how thought-provoking and important the instructor assumes that topic to be. If freshmen choose to write about issues involving race, class, and gender, that's fine. They should have every encouragement. I believe all topics in a writing class should be serious ones that push students to think and to say something substantial. But the topic should be their choice, a careful and thoughtful choice, to be sure, but not what someone else thinks is good for them.

Second, we know that young writers develop best as writers when teachers are able to create a low-risk environment that encourages students to take chances. We also know that novice writers can virtually freeze in the writing classroom when they see it as an extremely high-risk situation. Apprehensive about their grades in this new college situation, they nervously test their teachers to see what is expected of them, and they venture opinions only timidly. It is always hard to get students to write seriously and honestly, but when they find themselves in a classroom where they suspect there is a correct way to think, they are likely to take refuge in generalities and responses that please the teacher. Such fake discourse is a kind of silence, the silence we have so often deplored when it is forced on the disadvantaged. But when we stifle creative impulse and make students opt for survival over honesty, we have done the same thing. In too many instances, the first lesson they will learn as college students is that hypocrisy pays—so don't try to think for yourself.

My third objection to injecting prescribed political content into a required freshman course is that such action severely limits freedom of expression for both students and instructors. In my view, the freshman course on racism and sexism proposed at the University of Texas at Austin in the spring of 1990 would have enforced conformity in both directions. Students would have had no choice of what to write about, and the instructors who were graduate students would have had no choice about what to teach. Even if they felt unqualified to teach the material—and many did—or believed that the prescribed curriculum would work against their students' learning to write—and many did—they had to conform to a syllabus that contradicted their professional judgment and, often, their personal feelings. That course has since been revised and the freshman course in place since the fall of 1991 offers choices to both students and teachers.

New Possibilities for Freshman Courses

I believe we can make freshman English—or any other writing course—a truly multicultural course that gives students the opportunity to develop their critical and creative abilities and do it in an intellectually and ethically responsible context that preserves the heart of what we have learned about teaching writing in the past two decades.

First, I resist the effort to put any specific multicultural content at the center of a writing course, particularly a freshman course, and particularly a required course. Multicultural issues are too complex and diverse to be dealt with fully and responsibly in an English course, much less a course in which the focus should be on writing, not reading. Too often attempts to focus on such issues encourage stereotyping and superficial thinking. For instance, what English teacher wouldn't feel presumptuous and foolish trying to introduce Asian culture into a course when he or she can quickly think of at least ten different Asian cultures, all of which differ from each other drastically in important ways? What about

Hispanic culture? Can the teacher who knows something of Mexico generalize about traditions of other Hispanic cultures? Can anyone teach the "black experience"? Do black men and women whose forebears come from Haiti and Nigeria and Jamaica share the experiences and heritage of African Americans? Is Southern culture a valid topic for study? Many people think so. What about Jewish culture? But I don't need to labor the point. I only want to highlight the concerns any of us should have when the push for so-called multicultural courses threatens the integrity of our discipline and the quality of our teaching.

I believe, however, that we can create a culturally inclusive curriculum in our writing classes by focusing on the experiences of our students. *They* are our greatest multicultural resource, one that is authentic, rich, and truly diverse. Every student brings to class a picture of the world in his or her mind that is constructed out of his or her cultural background and unique and complex experience. As writing teachers, we can help students articulate and understand that experience, but we also have the important job of helping every writer to understand that each of us sees the world through our own particular lens, one shaped by unique experiences. In order to communicate with others, we must learn to see through their lenses as well as try to explain to them what we see through ours. In an interactive classroom where students collaborate with other writers, this process of decentering so one can understand the "other" can foster genuine multicultural growth.

Imagine, for example, the breadth of experience and range of difference students would be exposed to in a class made up of students I have had in recent years.

One student would be from Malawi. The ivory bracelet he wears was put on his arm at birth and cannot be removed; he writes about his tribal legends. Another student is a young Vietnamese man who came to America when he was eight; he writes about the fear he felt his first day in an American school because there were no walls to keep out bullets. Another is a young Greek woman whose parents brought her to America to escape poverty; she writes about her first conscious brush with sexism in the Greek Orthodox church. One student is the son of illegal aliens who followed the harvests in Texas; he writes with passion about the need for young Hispanics to get their education. A young black man writes about college basketball, a culture about which he is highly knowledgeable. A young man from the Texas panhandle writes about the traditions of cowboy boots and the ethical dimensions of barbed wire fences. Another young black man writes about the conflicts he feels between what he is learning in astronomy, a subject that fascinates him, and the teachings of his church.

It's worth noting here that religion plays an important role in the lives of many of our students—and many of us, I'm sure—but it's a dimension almost never mentioned by those who talk about cultural diversity and difference. In most classrooms in which there is an obvious political agenda, students—even graduate students—are very reluctant to reveal their religious beliefs, sensing they may get a hostile reception. And with reason—remember the quotation from David Bleich. But a teacher who believes in diversity must pay attention to and respect students with deep religious convictions, not force them too into silence.

Real diversity emerges from the students themselves and flourishes in a collaborative classroom in which they work together to develop their ideas and test them out on each other. They can discuss and examine their experiences, their assumptions, their values, and their questions. They can tell their stories to each other in a nurturant writing community. As they are increasingly exposed to the unique views and experiences of others, they will begin to appreciate differences and understand the rich tapestry of cultures that their individual stories make up. But they will also see unified motifs and common human concerns in that tapestry.

In this kind of classroom not all writing should be personal, expressive writing. Students need a broader range of discourse as their introduction to writing in college. The teacher can easily design the kinds of writing assignments that involve argument and exposition and suggest options that encourage cross-cultural awareness. For instance, some suggested themes for development might be these: family or community rituals; power relationships at all levels; the students' role in his or her family or group; their roles as men and women; the myths they live by; cultural tensions within groups. There are dozens more rich possibilities that could be worked out with the cooperation of colleagues in other departments and within the class itself.

The strength of all the themes I've mentioned is that they're both individual and communal, giving students the opportunity to write something unique to them as individuals yet something that will resonate with others in their writing community. The beauty of such an approach is that it's *organic*. It grows out of resources available in each classroom, and it allows students to make choices, then discover more about others and themselves through those choices. This approach makes the teacher a midwife, an agent for change rather than a transmitter of fixed knowledge. It promotes a student-centered classroom in which the teacher doesn't assume, as our would-be forcers of conscience do, that he or she owns the truth. Rather the students bring their own truths, and the teacher's role is to nurture change and growth as students encounter individual differences. Gradually their truths will change, but so will ours because in such a classroom one continually learns from one's students.

This is the kind of freshman English class from which students can emerge with confidence in their ability to think, to generate ideas, and to present themselves effectively to the university and the community. It is a class built on the scholarship, research, and experience that has enabled us to achieve so much growth in our profession in the last fifteen years. It is the kind of classroom we can be proud of as a discipline. I don't think we necessarily have to take freshman English out of English departments in order to establish this model, but we do have to assert our authority as writing professionals within our departments and fiercely resist letting freshman English be used for anyone else's goals. We must hold on to the gains we have made and teach writing in the ways we know best. Above all, we must teach it for the *students'* benefit, not in the service of politics or anything else.

Freshman English is a course particularly vulnerable to takeover because English departments in so many universities and colleges refuse to take it seriously and thus don't pay much attention to what happens in it. They can wake up, however, to find that some political zealots take the course very seriously indeed and will gladly put it to their own uses. The scores of us who have been studying, writing, speaking, and publishing for two decades to make freshman English the solid intellectual enterprise that it now is must speak out to protect it from this kind of exploitation. It is time to resist, time to speak up, time to reclaim freshman composition from those who want to politicize it.

What is at stake is control of a vital element in our students' education by a radical ... We can't afford to let that control stand.

Maxine Hairston has chaired the Conference on College Composition and Communication and taught English at the University of Texas.

Works Cited

Bauer, Dale. "The Other 'F' Word: Feminist in the Classroom." *College English* 52 (Apr. 1990): 835–96.

Berlin, James A. "Rhetoric and Ideology in the Writing Class." *College English* 50 (Sept. 1988): 477–94.

Bizzell, Patricia. "Beyond Anti-Foundationalism to Rhetorical Authority: Problems in Defining 'Cultural Literacy.' " *College English* 52 (Oct. 1990): 661–75.

Bleich, David. "Literacy and Citizenship: Resisting Social Issues." Lunsford, Moglen, and Slevin 163–69.

Faigley, Lester. "The Study of Writing and the Study of Language." *Rhetoric Review* 7 (Spring 1989): 240–56.

Harkin, Patricia, and John Schilb. *Contending with Words: Composition and Rhetoric in a Postmodern Age.* New York: MLA, 1991.

Knoblauch, C. H. "Literacy and the Politics of Education." Lunsford, Moglen, and Slevin 74–80.

———. "Rhetorical Constructions: Dialogue and Commitment." *College English* 50 (Feb. 1988): 125–40.

Laditka, James N. "Semiology, Ideology, Praxis: Responsible Authority in the Composition Classroom." *Journal of Advanced Composition* 10.2 (Fall 1990): 357–73.

Lunsford, Andrea A., Helen Moglen, and James Slevin, eds. *The Right to Literacy*. New York: MLA and NCTE, 1990.

Paine, Charles. "Relativism, Radical Pedagogy, and the Ideology of Paralysis." *College English* 51 (Oct. 1989): 557–70.

Searle, John. "The Storm over the University." Rev. of *Tenured Radicals*, by Roger Kimball; *The Politics of Liberal Education*, ed. by Darryl L. Gless and Barbara Hernstein Smith; and *The Voice of Liberal Learning: Michael Oakeshott on Education*, ed. by Timothy Fuller. *The New York Review of Books* 6 Dec. 1990: 34–42.

Strickland, Ronald. "Confrontational Pedagogy and Traditional Literary Studies." *College English* 52 (Mar. 1990): 291–300.

Weaver, Richard M. *The Ethics of Rhetoric*. Chicago: Henry Regnery, 1953.

SUSAN C. JARRATT Rhetorical Power: What Really Happens in Politicized Classrooms

The furor over educational change propelled by the new social movements arises from anxieties about power. Over the last two or three years, the popular press has been full of charges that teachers who call into question traditional knowledge and pedagogical methods are indoctrinating their students—using their authority as teachers irresponsibly. This same charge has been leveled against "rhetoric" in general over the centuries and against sophistic rhetoric in particular. One name for the accusation is *demagoguery*: the unethical manipulation of public opinion by a powerful speaker.

Along with the charge of demagoguery is a complaint that the so-called enforcers of political correctness limit free speech of others. Arguments over free speech always begin with rules passed by schools like Michigan, Wisconsin, and Brown restricting hate speech. But for the critics of curricular change, just about any successful challenge to the educational status quo counts as a threat to free speech. Articles in *Time, Newsweek, New Republic*, and elsewhere describe the failures of attempts to reverse educational decisions expanding the canon and building programs in minority studies as evidence of "intolerance," "intellectual intimidation," and "taboos" rather than as what they really are—outcomes of struggles for control over curriculum, programs, and hiring that go on all the time in the academy. The language used is an artful rhetorical maneuver of reversal: accusing your adversary of your own wrong. What's missing or seriously muted in this discussion of free speech is an acknowledgment that at the very heart of the new educational transformations is the *freeing* of speech—bringing to voice knowledges, experiences, and histories for whole bodies of people previously unheard. But, as Foucault teaches, the powerful mechanisms of disciplinary knowledge operate by hiding themselves within institutions. And so disruptions of stable, traditional disciplines and their objects of study are read as "a decline in tolerance," when the critics know well that such "disruptions" are linked to the larger project of making social and economic conditions more "tolerable" for many citizens. But these material considerations are artfully ignored by the neoconservative critics of educational change.

It's difficult to get even well-intentioned but hard-line civil libertarians to acknowledge the link between social injustice and the limits, exclusions, and silences pervading discourses of all types—unwritten rules that let some voices in and keep others out. William A. Henry III, author of a 1991 article, has it right when he finds things being turned upside down. We hear Henry reporting with something between outrage and astonishment that educational changes "amount to mirror-image reversal of basic assumptions held by the nation's majority" (66). Precisely the point. The "outlandish" courses Henry names represent the perspectives of outlanders—those whose standpoint offers versions of rationality, aesthetics, and even science outside the parameters of the Euramerican heritage. Decisions at many levels making possible the restructuring of higher education to allow for those viewpoints have emerged out of struggle; the traditionalists focus attention on the struggle itself as indecorous, avoiding the real issues.

Even George Bush, in his commencement address at the University of Michigan in May 1991, has entered the fray, expressing dismay that "neighbors who disagree no longer settle matters over a cup of coffee." In evoking this homey scene, Bush insulted those participants in the civil rights movement who, often denied the chance to live in neighborly proximity to their white oppressors, struggled courageously and at such great cost for the opportunity to sit down for a long-denied cup of coffee. But then Alexander Cockburn reminds us that "the will to retain a useful historical amnesia lies at the heart of the fury about PC [politicized classrooms]" (690). In another moment of amnesia, Bush forgot his own campaign strategy of racial hatred and admonished that those "creating" divisiveness in our harmonious social system by insisting on change haven't successfully conquered the temptation to assign bad motives to people who disagree with them. It's worth noting on this point that the same edition of the *New York Times* that reported these remarks included an article about black high school students who organized a separate prom because of the climate of racial tension in their southwest Chicago school. Bush must be perceptive indeed to have guessed the motives of those who participated in racial incidents on 115 campuses in 1989. He must know more than meets the eyes and ears about the three thousand white students at the University of Massachusetts who chased and beat blacks in a mob attack in 1986, about the football players at the University of Connecticut in 1987 who spat on Asian American women, shouting "Oriental faggots" (Cockburn 690). Perhaps I should ask him about the motives of my students (more than one) who believe that homosexuals deserve to die of AIDS, who have proposed transporting "them" all to an island to die together, and who are not in the least interested in discussing this "disagreement" over a cup of coffee, or even over a beer.

Rhetoric in the Classroom: Indoctrination or Rhetorical Authority?

While I have been engaging here in an eristic rhetoric, sparring rhetorically with George Bush and others who have passionately resisted attempts to open the gates of the academy a bit wider, I believe that the classroom often requires a different rhetoric. The instructor who offers counterhegemonic explanations of reading and writing practices—like the feminist who teaches students to recognize the way language constructs knowledge on the lines of a gender system or the Marxist who examines the historical connections between social class and reading habits—forces an epistemic break from the comfortable paradigms of liberal humanism, positivist science, and capitalist progress. But these fundamental differences in pedagogical and epistemological theory are often misread—either willfully or out of ignorance. Those who hold to a view of teaching as the value-neutral transmittal of a body of objective knowledge accuse teachers who raise questions about how their subject matter has evolved within historical circumstances determined in part by the dominance of specific social groups of having dropped any disinterested attempt to present "content" and giving over the class to an unethical effort to force students to accept a set of opinions about race and gender difference. The popular press contributes to the process of blurring any distinction between taking up the politics *of* the classroom and offering up politics—that is, partisan issues—*in* the classroom. The media create the general impression that so-called politicized teachers use classrooms as platforms. Of course, any full discussion of "politicized classrooms" would take in every class, for the teacher who offers a Great Books survey course is no less entailed in issues of institutional power and social difference than a teacher offering the courses with "obfuscatory titles and eccentric reading lists" (Henry 66) named triumphantly as evidence of the corruptions of "politically correct" thinking. But here I wish to focus on instructors who introduce questions of power and difference in discourse—to counter the charge that teachers who acknowledge the political nature of their profession necessarily exercise demagoguery.

When David Laurence organized the ADE session from which this paper comes, he suggested, as a historical point of orientation for this question, an essay by Max Weber called "Science as a Vocation." In this 1918 analysis of the institutionalization of science, Weber outlines a distinction like the one I make above: between an approach to the subject of study through methods of cultural critique and the teacher's use of the lecture halls to act as prophet or demagogue. Weber acknowledges that students want more from their educators than mere analyses and statements of fact; they crave leaders and not teachers, he says. His formulation of the goal of critical teaching as responsible self-clarification approximates closely the critical pedagogy of today, but Weber's sensitivity to the pedagogical setting leads him to warn professors against the temptation to use the classroom to air their opinions about specific political or social issues. In the lecture hall, he explains, students are a captive audience; there is no possibility for critique or even response.

Even though most of us in English departments teach at least some of our classes to small groups of students, in which discussion is an essential element of the pedagogy, we are mindful of the complaint that the power wielded by the teacher—specifically, the power of the grade, but also the power of age, knowledge, the institution, the emotional power of giving or withholding approval and professional guidance—may mute dissent or criticism from students even when the classroom structure in principle provides opportunity for it. For some critics of political correctness there is little question about the domination of teachers' voices when they present their subject through the lens of sociological critique, only a question of how that power is wielded. On this model, two things can happen, both bad. In the first case, the teacher is overt about the political agenda of the course. Dialogue is impossible, critics say, because students are so intimidated by the teacher and so determined to get good grades that they won't risk expressing an opinion contrary to the teacher's. In the case of teachers who are more covert, the argument is that simply raising social issues in the current climate tips off students that you're "one of them." They will then respond by parroting a generally left position out of fear and without thinking through the issues on their own.

Certainly those things can and do happen. All kinds of things happen with our students: alienation and tune-out, but also resistance and opposition; dutiful reproduction, interested experimentation, even conversion. I heard recently of a kind of student manipulation that was new to me. Instructions are given by one male student to another about how to succeed in a feminist classroom: pretend to be a male chauvinist, then have a conversion. You're bound to get an A. This strategy raises an issue that the critics of political correctness never consider because it doesn't fit within their monolithic phantasm of the teacher: the ways teachers are positioned differently along multiple power axes within classrooms. For example, I sometimes have an easier time convincing my students in a composition class to try out unfamiliar pedagogical methods than my graduate-student teachers do, because of their youth and lower status in the institution, but perhaps I have more trouble than my male colleagues. Class and race offer more complications. The point is that there are more kinds of power than simply the institutional status of the teacher at work in a classroom at every moment. Indeed, everyone in the room—even at a mostly white, middle-class school like

Miami—brings a rich history of diverse social relations. In my view, the aim of "politicized" teaching is to mobilize those histories into a complex interplay of authority and counter-authority in the classroom (see Graff). The pedagogy I advocate does not demand that students adopt a "politically correct" position; in fact, it argues against any fixed agenda in favor of a process of learning how technologies of discourse make possible the exploration of personally grounded and historically located knowledge. I'd like to offer two theoretical orientations for the exercise of rhetorical power in the classroom and then propose some suggestions for generating and sustaining dialogic classroom discourse.

Politics of Location and Dialogic Classrooms

In offering these ideas, I can't speak for everyone who claims to teach from liberatory or transformative pedagogical principles. The practices I describe have evolved out of my own experiences as a white, middle-class woman teaching first-year composition and graduate courses in rhetoric and social theory, from several years' work as a mentor and teacher of a pedagogy workshop for new graduate assistants, out of the feminist sophistics summer institute and seminar I co-directed in the summer of 1990 with Dale M. Bauer, and from ongoing collective work in feminist pedagogy at Miami. The pedagogy developed within these contexts advocates teachers' exercise of rhetorical authority toward ends of social transformation. In this pedagogy, English studies is defined along lines explored by Henry Giroux, Linda Brodkey, James Berlin, Patricia Bizzell, John Trimbur, Ira Shor, and many others as the development of critical literacies—one element in an education toward critical citizenship. While this goal may differ from the scientist's model of value-free knowledge transmission, or from the aesthete's aim of cultivating literary taste and sensibilities, I would argue that it shares with the humanism of William Bennett, Allan Bloom, and Lynne Cheney the goal of making students into certain kinds of human beings. I reject the charge that liberatory pedagogy is somehow more intrusive or manipulative than what it seeks to replace. When teachers make their own political and ethical commitments to social change a part of the course, students who have internalized a model of education as the transferral of "objective" knowledge may feel an uncomfortable dissonance. Speaking openly about ethics can create for students a painful awareness of the absence of a strong community consensus about right and wrong in our huge, diverse social system. But it can also provide a source of relief, pleasure, and challenge in confronting these anxieties.

Motivating students to locate themselves socially and historically in relation to the subject of the class can mediate institutional (teacher) authority and create the possibility for counterauthority to emerge within students' own discourses. This process takes place when students are led to describe their lives, especially their educational experiences, as socially and historically embedded—to articulate the self in history. It's a way to approach the understanding of differences without by exploring differences within. What's encouraged here is not political correctness but what I call a historical attitude. To have an attitude, one must have a position, a stance, instead of remaining undifferentiated. One must be situated not only in space but in time and social order, the last of these elements invoking "attitude" in its colloquial sense of "having an attitude" as an aggressive challenge to social hierarchies. I'm not suggesting we turn our students into little James Deans but rather that we teach them to see the act of speaking and writing as always relational. For writing classes, this view is a break out of the tyranny of the present; for literature classes, a break into tyrannically discrete historical pasts.

Having a personal investment or location in relation to class material protects students against indoctrination or coercion; further, it's the basis of any meaningful educational experience, as theorists from many camps would agree. But the process I'm describing needs to be attached to specific theoretical spheres; namely, cultural studies and feminist politics of location. It shouldn't be confused with self-satisfied psychologizing, with a purely confessional mode of consciousness-raising, or with a kind of composition teaching that uses narratives of student experience as a means of discovering the true self or unique voice. Nor does this approach represent a pluralistic embrace of all points of view as equally valuable and defensible. It's more aptly described in Nietzschean terms as a continual process of negating, consuming, and contradicting—enacted through the connection of singular with collective histories. Through this pedagogy students orient themselves as readers and writers within the asymmetrical power relations currently crisscrossing our society but also within their own specific histories as students, family members, and citizens. Further, this teaching method asks students to re-see those experiences in terms of social difference and power imbalance and within historically located disciplinary practices. It's not a demand that students express white or male guilt, nor does it participate in the race essentialism the critics of political correctness assume to be the theoretical basis of multicultural education. Rather, students identify their stances as provisional and dialogic and try on the role of transformative intellectual in their own historical moments and culture spheres.

The difference between classroom demagoguery and an alternative politics of the classroom depends on the theories of discourse underlying these competing accounts of language in the classroom. In a simple communication theory of language, one individual speaks to another, so that the speaker is an agent and the listener is characterized as a passive recipient of a reified message. This theory grounds narratives of indoctrination, coercion, or other manipulative rhetorical effects. But according to Marxist linguistic theorists like L. S. Vygotsky and M. M. Bakhtin, any discursive act involves a complex interplay of "voices," internal as well as external, present and past. When students use class materials to confront or re-create their own histories and present locations as social beings, they bring to voice internalized conflicts among authoritative voices as part of the dialogic classroom experience. Active engagement with language in the classroom shapes the consciousness of all the participants, teacher included. This shared linguistic experience is best described not in terms of communication—the delivery of the message from one, or even two, subjects to others—but rather in terms of a collective activity through which we are all constantly engaged in processes of semiotic transformation. Instead of conversion, the "politicized" teachers I know look for dialogic reflection in our students' writing and oral responses.

The practices of location and dialogism open a space for the teacher not as demagogue or prophet but as what Weber calls "leader" and Henry Giroux calls "public intellectual." The complex flow of language and interplay of power in the classroom calls for many different responses from the liberatory teacher; silent listener, supportive encourager, equal participant in debate, or, sometimes, advocate of a position that remains unrepresented or challenger of oppressive discourses generated by students. I think it's a mistake to advise teachers that they should never express opinions on vital public issues or to neutralize the composition teacher into the role of "facilitator." We should be able to demonstrate, when it is rhetorically appropriate, what our opinions are and, more important, how we derived them—how they may be connected to personal histories and social positions and how each of us will necessarily be limited in assessing those histories and views. These are delicate decisions, hard to generalize about. But that difficulty should not prevent us from taking seriously our role as public intellectuals to make the formation of political consciousness the subject of literacy education. Doing so within the theoretical parameters I've described is fundamentally different from using the lectern as a platform for partisan views on specific issues.

Classroom Practice

Moving from a descriptive to a prescriptive mode, I wish to suggest ways to foster a dialogic climate—to encourage the development of counterauthority—in English classrooms of all kinds: composition, literature, and theory. These are not all original ideas but draw on work—some of it unpublished, some in the form of lectures, discussions, and private conversations—by many colleagues, most significantly Patricia Bizzell, bell hooks, Steven Mailloux, and John Trimbur.

Mediating the conventional classroom dynamic. The most material way to affect counterauthority is to create an actual, physical intervention of another voice into the teacher-class dialogue (see Graff). Inviting former students or guest authorities to address the class members and team teaching in various forms (including simply trading off or combining classes for a day) are possible ways to accomplish this goal. The English department at Miami University allows advanced undergraduate majors to act as teaching fellows for faculty members, building in a triangulation of authority through the semester.

Foregrounding pedagogical decisions. Pointing out ways our teaching differs from traditional classes—making the educational institution itself the subject of the class—taps student resistance to authority but converts it into a collective critical inquiry. What does it mean to study writing, or literature, or rhetorical theory now, at this institution? What did it mean twenty years ago or two thousand? Such questions bring into focus issues of professionalization, disciplinary language, and paradigm change.

Making classroom discussion—how people talk—the subject of the course. Stepping out of the discussion from time to time to assess how language is working allows for reflection on power and difference in discourse. Rather than the "micro-management of everyday conversation" George Bush warns about, this practice encourages a microlevel attention to the way ideas are shaped. Readings on language and social difference—for example, Dale Spender on gender and Henry Louis Gates Jr. on Black English—build concrete knowledge about formerly unconscious practices. Audiotapes can help in this process in at least three contexts. In addition to bringing tapes into the classroom, teachers can use them to engage in self-critique or to work with other teachers interested in analyzing the complex play of power and difference in classroom discussion from day to day.

Using keywords. Each semester my students and I select and work closely with certain "keywords" (a concept created by Raymond Williams) that seem to emerge with some significance in public discourse from any of a number of spheres: within the class, on campus, in national or global news. We do a series of inquiries into each word, investigating its histories for us and the groups using it. For example, in work with sexist language in a composition class one semester, first-year students seemed really angry and resistant to a feminist critique of *lady*. While my analysis had emphasized economic dependence and class hierarchy, the students revealed, through discussions of how and where the word had entered into their experiences, the heavy weight of sexual socialization it had carried in high school and its use as a reward for "maturity." The point of these inquiries is not to resolve differences in liberal compromise but to gain a fuller understanding of the particular histories, differences, and powers language carries.

Taking advantage of the multiple sites for dialogue between teacher and student. While we may think of class discussion most immediately as the site of "politicized" teaching, a dialogic pedagogy exploits differences in rhetorical context provided by various opportunities for exchange between teacher and student and among students. Different kinds of exchange can occur in class (the most public context), in conference, on ungraded assignments, on graded papers. We should be aware of using different theoretical strategies for different occasions.

Reducing grade pressure where possible. Though students and teachers almost always work under the shadow of grades, doing a number of ungraded writing and speaking assignments allows students to perform the work of social and historical location in an exploratory mode without being measured and judged in the reductive terms of grades.

These suggestions concern the classroom instructor; on the departmental level, chairs can create a supportive climate for counterhegemonic teaching by looking carefully at student evaluations in dialogue with teachers' own accounts of their classes. This is not to imply that critical pedagogy always produces low student ratings, or that low student ratings can be explained simply by labeling the pedagogy "politicized." It is to point out that counterhegemonic teaching produces challenges to traditional ways of thinking and learning not often resolved within a quarter or even a semester. If the teacher's goal is to raise questions, to initiate new forms of reading and writing rather than to perfect old ones, and the effort is successful, the students' responses may be more tentative than effusive. In such cases, the best measure of success may not be high numerical ratings from students.

Another way to create a supportive climate is by organizing regular opportunities for faculty members to discuss the politics of the classroom. These discussions should not occur only when decisions have to be made about curriculum, program, or policies—situations in which various factions of the faculty have turf to guard or reputations to protect and when time constraints may create pressure to truncate discussion of complex questions. When teaching becomes an ongoing collective project, departmental practices reinforce the commitments of a critical pedagogy outlined above in terms of the single classroom.

Correctness Revisited

I'd like to end with a few more words about the phrase *political correctness*. My source is Geoffrey Nunberg, a linguist from Stanford, who in an editorial on National Public Radio's "All Things Considered" offered a historical perspective on the phrase. Nunberg sees the language of "correctness" today as a trivialization of political debate but reminds us of an earlier era when there was a more substantial connection between civility and civil liberties. As English teachers, we might be especially susceptible to the accusation of fussing over correctness and want to distance ourselves from that association. But it's the accusers themselves who frame the debate as one concerned with taste, manners, and propriety in the most reductive sense when it suits their purposes, though they sometimes turn the tables. For George Bush, manners become serious business when he depicts political debate in terms of lapses from neighborliness. Those of us invested in transformative pedagogy need to provide a vigorous counterdiscourse to the characterization of our teaching as a faddish fixation on political correctness. The same rhetorical tradition that gives us the concept of demagoguery (as well as its critique) offers a long and venerable tradition of rhetorical instruction as a practice of civic responsibility. When we ask students and the public as well to engage in collective inquiry into language in society, we improve the prospects for progressive social change within and outside the classroom.

Note

In preparing this article, I used some ideas from "Feminist Sophistics: Teaching with an Attitude," which I co-wrote with Dale M. Bauer. I'm also indebted to Patricia Bizzell's essay "Power, Authority, and Critical Pedagogy." Works by Paulo Freire, Henry Giroux, bell hooks, and Ira Shor are sources for my discussions of critical literacy, critical pedagogy, critical citizenship, and public intellectuals.

Susan C. Jarratt is director of the Women's Studies Program and associate professor of English at Miami University.

Works Cited

Bakhtin, M. M. *Speech Genres and Other Late Essays*. Trans. Vern W. McGee. Ed. Caryl Emerson and Michael Holquist. Austin: U of Texas P, 1986.

Bizzell, Patricia. "Power, Authority, and Critical Pedagogy." *Journal of Basic Writing* 10.2 (1991): 54–70.

Bush, George, Commencement address. U of Michigan. Ann Arbor, 4 May 1991. *New York Times* 5 May 1991: 1+.

Cockburn, Alexander. "Bush and PC—A Conspiracy So Immense. . . ." *Nation* 27 May 1991: 685+.

Downing, David, ed. *Changing Classroom Practices*. Urbana: National Council of Teachers of English, 1994.

Giroux, Henry A. *Schooling and the Struggle for Public Life*. Minneapolis: U of Minnesota P, 1988.

Graff, Gerald. "My Classroom Authority Problem." Downing.

Henry, William A., III. "Upside Down in the Groves of Academe." *Time* 1 Apr. 1991: 66–69.

Jarratt, Susan C., and Dale M. Bauer. "Feminist Sophistics: Teaching with an Attitude." Downing.

Nunberg, Geoffrey. Editorial. "All Things Considered." NPR. 15 May 1991.

Vygotsky, L. S. *Mind in Society*. Ed. Michael Cole, Vera John-Steiner, Sylvia Scribner, and Ellen Souberman. Cambridge: Harvard UP, 1978.

Weber, Max. "Science as a Vocation." From: *Max Weber: Essays in Sociology*. Trans. and ed. Hans Gerth and C. Wright Mills. New York: Oxford UP, 1946. 129–56.

Williams, Raymond. *Keywords: A Vocabulary of Culture and Society*. New York: Oxford UP, 1976.